This book is dedicated to Gabriella and Tony Grey

TRAVEL COMPANION

CHILE

AND EASTER ISLAND

Gerry Leitner was born in Vienna, Austria, in 1935 and became fluent in English, French and Spanish during his travels throughout Western Europe and North Africa. In 1958 he migrated to Australia, where he first worked in the outback before settling in Sydney in 1965. Gerry became fascinated by South America during his first trip there in 1976, and has returned numerous times since.

TRAVEL COMPANION

CHILE

AND EASTER ISLAND

GERRY LEITNER

© 1996 Gerry Leitner

First published in 1996 by Companion Travel Guide Books, PO Box 321, Miller NSW 2168, Australia.

ISBN 0-646-06042-2

The information in this book is as up-to-date as possible, but no responsibility for any loss, injury, or inconvenience sustained by the user of this book is accepted by the author or publisher.

Edited and laid out by Michael Wyatt, Keyword Editorial Services, 22 Kendall Street, Surry Hills NSW 2010, Australia.
Photographs by the author.
Maps drawn by Graham Keane, Cartodraft, PO Box 367, Carlingford NSW 2118, Australia.
Cover design by Kathleen Phelps.
Printed by Colorcraft Pty Ltd, Kodak House Phase II, Unit 8–9, 16th floor, 321 Java Road, North Point, Hong Kong.

ACKNOWLEDGMENTS

Y ou will appreciate that a book of this scope could not have been written without the assistance and expertise of others.

In the first instance I wish to express my appreciation for the assistance afforded to me by Sernatur, the state tourist office all over Chile, but in particular to Señor Eduardo Viveros Saavedra, Head of the Promotion Department, Sernatur Santiago; Señor Enzo Martínez Bustos, Director Regional de Turismo, Coihaique; Señor Jorge Carrasco Cornejo, Director Sernatur Región de O'Higgins; Señor Gonzalo Lagos Puccio, Director Regional de Turismo, Copiapó; Señor Gonzalo Sainz Olavarrieta, Director Regional de Turismo, Región de Magallanes y Antártida Chilena; Señor René Rojas Salinas, Director Regional de Turismo, Concepción; and Señor Luis Spoerer Herrera, Director Regional de Turismo, Región de Valparaíso.

On the home front in Australia, I am indebted to Graham Keane who produced the maps to this book. Again my special thanks go to Michael Wyatt who was saddled with the task of making a readable book out of my draft. Both Michael and Graham supported this project far beyond the call of duty. My thanks also go to Barbara Bessant who did the proofreading.

My family also deserves special thanks for patiently awaiting the completion of this compendium on Chile and Easter Island. Special thanks to my son Gerald who helped finance this book.

Gerry Leitner

CONTENTS

COLOR MAPS

SYMBOLS

☘	Festivals	▣	Sightseeing
ⓘ	Tourist information	◉	Excursions
⌷	Accommodation	(	Telephone number
Ⓐ	Camping	i	Single room
ⓤ	Eating out	ii	Double room
ⓧ	Entertainment	☞	Recommended
ⓒ	Post and telegraph		
✉	Post office		
ⓒ	Telephone service	**Keys to maps**	
Ⓢ	Financial	●	Accommodation, Camping
⌂	Services and facilities	○	Eating out, Clubs
▭	Visas, passports	⊙	Entertainmnent
✈	Air services	▲	Airline offices and railroad
⌷	Buses		stations
▦	Trains	△	Tour operators, Car rental
⚓	Water transport	□	Services
⛟	Motoring	■	Sights
⌘	Shopping	▪	Metro stations in Santiago
◉	Sport		

INTRODUCTION

With its back to the Andes, and extending its territory to the Pacific Ocean like a silent offering, Chile is immersed in isolation … its geography enclosing it within a natural prison… The country is bounded in the north by the salty expanse of the Atacama desert, and in the south by the floating cathedrals of polar ice.

*from "Beyond the Silver River" by Jimmy Burns,
published by Bloomsbury Publishing Ltd*

Chile is a fascinating country, with a more diverse landscape than any-where else in South America. Add to this, the history of its turbulent colonial past and the remains of pre-Columbian archeological sites, and you have the makings of an interesting and exciting holiday. There is something for everyone: extensive beaches, high mountains, active volcanoes, exotic food, lush southern valleys, and waterways with plenty of fishing. The growing sophistication of tourist facilities make you wonder why Chile has escaped mainstream tourism for so long.

Chile's almost complete isolation from neighboring countries has helped to forge an independent national character and culture. Chileans' ancestry is predominantly European, mixed with the original Indian inhabitants.

History

Before the Europeans

Chile's early history is shrouded in mist. The oldest human remains have been found in the north together with signs that sophisticated civilizations also started there. It seems reasonable to assume that the first hunter-gathering people came from the north and moved slowly down the country. By around 1200 AD, the Aymará tribes had founded small urban settlements in the northern valleys of the *altiplano* and built fortified villages at strategic points. They terraced the mountain slopes and introduced irrigation techniques. Their cultural center was on Lake Titicaca.

The Diaguitas settled the area around and to the south of present-day Copiapó. They immigrated from the Argentine side of the Andes, where they still live in large areas of Jujuy, Salta, and Catamarca provinces. The Diaguitas were probably the first Indian tribe to begin working with metal in Chile.

Around 1471 AD, the Incan king Topac led his people south from Cuzco through Bolivia into what is now Chile. The Incas subdued the local population, appointed Quechua-speaking chieftains, and exchanged some of the indigenous population for loyal subjects. Customs from central Peru influenced the locals; this is particularly noticeable in the weaving and pottery industries. It is thought that the resident tribes of Aymará and Diaguitas, as far south as Santiago, submitted to the Incas without too much resistance. The invaders connected existing roads to become the Royal Road of the Incas or *Capac Ñan*. But, south of the Río Maule, the Mapuches stopped the Incan advance. The southernmost outpost of the Inca Empire was on the Río Maule, and its boundaries followed the river eastward to Lagunas del Maule, and from there across the Paso del Maule into present-day Argentina.

The arrival of the Europeans

The first, but unsuccessful, Spanish invasion of Chile was led by Diego de Almagro in 1536. In 1540 Pedro de Valdivia arrived and founded Santiago. For the next three hundred years Chile was embroiled in the Araucanian Wars which drained money, materials, and human lives from Spain.

The Spanish *conquistadores* expected Chile to be El Dorado, but their hopes were soon dashed. Instead of handing out gold, Pedro de Valdivia rewarded his followers with huge grants of land. This was the start of the *encomendero* system. The politically powerful Spanish "landholders" virtually owned the Indians under their jurisdiction, and forced them to work in the mines and on the land. In time, the number of indigenous people dwindled through disease and exploitation. The new labour force came from the *mestizo* population who were excluded from land ownership. Landowners employed *mestizos* (as the people of mixed Indian and Spanish blood were called) on their *haciendas*,

giving them some land to use for themselves in exchange for their labor. They were free to move about, but while they occupied part of the land they were obliged to work on the large estates as farmhands. This *latifundio* system lasted in a modified and weakened form until 1960.

In retrospect, it appears that most of the Spanish governors were remarkably able, and many courageous and talented military leaders became governors. The Mapuches also produced outstanding leaders. They maintained their independence for 340 years, and their story is one of unbelievable heroism against the mighty Spanish empire.

Spanish domination began badly. Two Spanish governors lost their lives in battles with the Mapuches. Pedro de Valdivia, founder of Chile and the first governor, died at the Battle of Tucapel in 1549. Martín de Loyola was ambushed and killed by Mapuches under the command of Chief Pelantarú in 1598 at Sorpresa de Curalaba. In 1575 an earthquake levelled Santiago and destroyed Imperial, Osorno, Castro, Villarrica, and Valdivia. This natural disaster prompted the Huilliches and other tribes to rise against their Spanish masters. After the great Mapuche uprising in 1599, the Spanish abandoned their search for land south of the Río Bío Bío. Only Valdivia and Isla Grande de Chiloe were firmly in Spanish hands.

From 1586 onwards, English and Dutch pirates sailed the Pacific and harassed the coastal towns. Chilean governors had to defend the coast as well as attend to problems inland.

During the next 180 years the status quo remained. The Spanish authorities periodically met Mapuche chiefs to work out a peaceful co-existence. Although these *parlamentos* were usually held with great pomp, the Mapuches yielded little. They did, however, permit a Spanish trail between the cities of Concepción and Valdivia. Other concessions included handing over renegade Spaniards who had escaped from the authorities.

In 1776, the Bourbon Kings created the Virreinato de La Plata, which drew the dividing line between Chile and Argentina at the crest of the main chain of the Andes. Thus, the Cuyo provinces were separated from Chile and came under the jurisdiction of the Viceroy of La Plata.

Despite the troubles in southern Chile, the north was quickly Hispanicized, and local tribes became absorbed into Spanish culture. Toward the end of the 18th century, many towns were founded by viceroys. American-born *criollos* were excluded from certain privileges; the upper hierarchy, for example, was reserved for Spanish-born aristocrats. By the end of the 18th century, there was already some discontent among the Chilean upper class, and changes were mooted long before the Wars of Independence.

The first skirmishes between royalist armies and independent nationalist armies did not augur well for the Chilean patriots: they were defeated in 1814 at the Battle of Rancagua, and many Chileans fled across the border to Argentina to join the Army of San Martín who had already liberated Argentina. San Martín realized that the independence from Spain for all South America was only possible with the defeat of the royalist army in Chile.

In 1816 his liberation army, the Ejercito de los Andes, crossed into Chile and within two years had liberated all of Chile with the exception of Valdivia and Isla Grande de Chiloe. The Declaration of Chilean Independence was signed in 1818 by Don Bernardo O'Higgins (son of Viceroy Don Ambrosio O'Higgins), who became the first president of the Chilean republican government.

In the conflict for Independence, many native Chileans were sympathetic to the Spanish cause and fought in the Spanish army. After the Spanish army was defeated, marauding bands terrorized central Chile and the neighboring Cuyo provinces in Argentina for about 20 years.

Independence from Spain did not bring equal rights to Chilean society. The Spanish aristocracy was simply replaced by a Chilean aristocracy. Most political power was wielded by the rich landowners, and their ranks were joined later by the saltpeter and mining magnates of the north. Nevertheless, by 1830 Chile was one of the strongest and most economically stable countries in South America. With political and economic achievements came territorial expansions. The area to the north of Copiapó was annexed by Chile; Fuerte Bulnes was founded in Magallanes in 1843; and in 1883 the Mapuche territory was incorporated into Chile.

In 1879, Chile declared war on a Peruvian–Bolivian confederation over the possession of the rich nitrate fields in the north. The successful conclusion of the War of the Pacific in 1880 added the regions of Antofagasta and Tarapacá to Chile.

Chile entered the 20th century in good financial shape, with income from saltpeter exports to England and Germany, and grain exports to the west coast of America. In the 1930s, the government agency, CORFO, was set up to foster new industrial development. CORFO and North American mining interests became second to agriculture as the mainstay of the economy. However, labor-aligned, center-left governments took office without being able to improve the lot of the masses or gain the full approval of the middle and upper classes. Political frustration came to a head when, in 1970, a leftist coalition under Salvador Allende came to power.

Part of their platform was nationalization of the large mining enterprises, that is the North American copper agglomerates, and the dismantling of the large *latifundios*. With Cuba now communist, the USA did not want a second communist-dominated country in the western hemisphere. Western countries refused to help shore up Chile's struggling economy, which caused inflation and shortages of food. The Communists called for an armed class struggle. On September 11, 1973 a military coup brought down the Government, and Salvador Allende was killed in an aerial bombardment of the presidential palace. General Augusto Pinochet was installed as President, and reigned until October 1988. Ruling Chile by decree, he made a swift transition to a free market economy. This phase, achieved through the loss of some civil liberties, was completed by 1985. Once the economy was stabilised, Pinochet sought to improve his legitimate standing by inviting selected political parties to declare their agendas. An assassination attempt in 1985 by the Communist Patriotic Front made the fledgling Democratic parties wary of associating with the Communists.

Pinochet quit as head of state after a plebiscite which he advocated and lost. But when he left, Chile was in much better shape economically than during any period since the 1920s.

Chilean history would not be complete without mentioning the impact on the country's history and society of the religious orders, in particular the Compañía de Jesús (or Jesuits) and the Franciscan *padres*. There was keen competition among the various religious orders to secure the right to found churches and monasteries and to evangelize the native population. The Jesuits combined their evangelical work with teaching worldly skills to their flock: carpentry, farming, and later printing were high on their agenda. Some of their properties grew into immense landholdings and consequently flourishing enterprises. In the early 17th century they influenced the direction of the Araucanian Wars by advocating the "Guerra Defensiva". This doctrine was in direct contradiction to the thought of the day, and was based on securing the Río Bío Bío as a line of defense and leaving the Mapuche in peace, with the proviso that missionaries were allowed into their territory to evangelize them. Because they advocated a more humane treatment of natives, and possibly because their flourishing enterprises aroused the envy of the Spanish, they were expelled in 1767 from all Spanish and Portuguese territories. Their place was taken by the Franciscan order, which from the very begining was active in northern Chile.

The Indians today

Of the many tribes that lived in Chile at the time of the Spanish invasion, only two large groups remain: the Aymarás living in the northern *altiplano*, mainly in Región I de Tarapacá, Región II de Antofagasta, and Región III de Atacama; and the Araucanians, also known as Mapuche, living in Región VIII del Bío Bío, Región IX de La Araucania, and Región X de Los Lagos. A small scattering of Huilliche villages still survives on the coast of Región X de Los Lagos and on Isla Grande de Chiloe.

The Aymarás survived more or less by default because they inhabited areas which were of no commercial interest to the Spanish. Modern technology and the proliferation of administrative centers in native habitat areas pose a greater threat to the survival of Aymará culture than did armed conquest by the Europeans.

The Mapuches survived as a group because they were never conquered by the Spanish. Araucanians number about 250 000, and inhabit whole towns in and around Temuco. The Araucanians have a good chance of survival as a native unit, and Chileans are not only proud of their Spanish ancestry, but also of their Araucanian ancestors.

Famous men and women

Travelers in Chile will come across monuments and references to a long line of governors and viceroys and other people significant in Chile's history. The following list describes the most outstanding of them.

- Francisco de Villagra, Governor of Chile 1561–63. Villagra pacified Isla Grande de Chiloe in 1562, thus completing the task begun by Pedro de Valdivia in 1549.

- Alonso de Sotomayor, Governor of Chile 1583–92. The Royal Court in Madrid could not understand the dishonorable stalemate between the Araucanians and the "cream of the European Army". Sotomayor, a brilliant soldier, realized from the very beginning that he could not pacify Araucania with the scarce resources available to him. He tried to cut down the resistance of the Mapuche by wiping out their villages and exterminating the inhabitants. He refounded Purén and built new forts on both sides of the Río Bío Bío. These did not survive the great Mapuche uprising.

- Alonso de Ribera y Zambrano, Governor 1601–5. A military man of the highest caliber, Zambrano represented the best of Spanish military command. He expelled the Dutch from Chiloe. Villarrica had already been destroyed when he arrived there with a military force in 1602. The only cities south of the Bío Bío still defended by Spain were Arauco, Osorno, and Valdivia. Zambrano founded the permanent Chilean army, and started service industries to make the army independent of outside resources. He realized that he could not wage war on two fronts: from the north across the Río Bío Bío and from the south from Valdivia. Valdivia and Osorno were abandoned in 1603–4.

- General José de San Martín, 1777–1850, Liberator of half of

South America during the Wars of Independence.

- Libertador Bernardo O'Higgins, 1778–1842, son of an equally famous Viceroy of Chile of Irish descent.
- Almirante Manuel Blanco Encalada, 1790–1842, Chief of the Chilean Navy and President of Chile in 1826.
- Diego Portales, 1793–1837, lawyer and instigator of the political constitution of 1833.
- José Francisco Vergara, 1833–89, founder of Viña del Mar.
- Carlos Condell, 1843–87, hero of the naval battle of Iquique during the War of the Pacific.
- Juan José Latorre, 1846–1912, hero of the War of the Pacific.
- Arturo Prat Chocón, 1848–79, hero of the naval battle of Iquique during the War of the Pacific
- Gabriela Mistral, 1889–1957. Mistral was a poet, diplomat and teacher who was born in Vicuña. She taught at Columbia University, Vassar, and in Puerto Rico, and won the Nobel prize for literature in 1945.
- Pablo Neruda, 1904–73. Neruda was born in Parral, in southern Chile. He was a famous poet, and won the Nobel prize for literature in 1971.

Economy

Chile is one of the few countries in South America with a positive export balance and a stable currency, the Chilean *peso*.

Copper and agriculture are major industries. A large percentage of Chile's fruit and vegetables are exported to North American markets;

no doubt, the inverted seasons has helped this industry. The paper and pulp industry, based on efficient pinus radiata plantations south of the Bío Bío, also earns export income. Development of new ore deposits in Antofagasta and extraction of lithium from the *salares* in the north have added new momentum to the mining industry.

Administration and government

Chile is a republic consisting of 12 regions and the metropolitan area. Each region is subdivided into provinces. Santiago is the capital and seat of government, headed by the President. The national congress, however, has been transferred to Valparaíso. Since the defeat of Pinochet, Chile has had a democratically elected government, but it is not a two-party system because the strongest party is usually unable to govern without allying with another party.

The regions elect their own regional governments and raise their own revenue.

Religion

The Catholic church is the dominant faith for some 96 per cent of the people. But religious freedom exists for all. In some cities and towns, Anglicans (or Episcopalians) form quite large congregations; their churches were built in the 19th century when Englishmen played a dominant role in commerce and in the development of the saltpeter mining industry. There are Lutheran churches, particularly in the German settlements in the south and in Valparaíso. The Church of Latter Day Saints is also very active.

Climate

Chile stretches from the tropics to the Antarctic circle, but is without tropical rainforest. The cold Humboldt current prevents rain falling in the north which is, consequently, largely arid desert. Further south, a pleasant Mediterranean climate prevails from La Serena to San Antonio.

There are great extremes of temperature between the coastal areas and central valley and the *sierras*, where the higher you get, the colder it becomes. Some parts of the *altiplano* are definitely not very inviting places to live. Many peaks in the Andes are over 5000 m and snow-covered all year round. In Región I de Tarapacá there is precipitation in November and December, including snow which is known as *Invierno Boliviano* ("Bolivian Winter") — clouds formed over the Atlantic and the Chaco region are forced west over the Andes to create precipitations on the Pacific side.

South of Santiago as far as and including Coihaique in Región XI de Aisén, the climate is temperate with definite seasonal changes. Rainfall increases steadily, the further south you go, and reaches 4000 mm per annum on the Chiloe Archipelago, south of Puerto Montt. Rainfall diminishes toward the Argentine border where it becomes semi-dry *pampa*. This contrast is particularly pronounced in Región XI de Aisén — when it rains on the coast, Coihaique may not have a drop.

Further south still, in the Magellanic region, rainfall is high on the Pacific coast but the Atlantic coast is very dry. Strong winds from Antarctica blow across this area.

Most of Chile may be visited in any season. From Santiago north to the Peruvian border is accessible all year round. From Santiago south, tourism proper is restricted to spring, summer, and autumn. Winter, however, is the best time for skiing enthusiasts. Visits south of Puerto Montt are definitely restricted to the summer months.

Visa requirements

Visitors from countries belonging to the western European Union can get a 90-day tourist visa stamped into their passport at the point of entry into Chile.

Border crossings

At the time of writing there were 24 authorized Chilean border crossings, of which five were reserved for Chileans or Argentines in local transit. Most of the high-altitude passes into Bolivia or northern Argentina are subject to adverse weather conditions. The sea-level border crossing into Peru is always open.

Do not bring any fruit or vegetables into Chile. Fruitfly is a problem for the South American fruitgrowing industry, and border crossings often incorporate SAG checkpoints to prevent its spread.

Región I de Tarapacá

Crossing into Peru
• **Complejo Fronterizo Concordia**, also known as **Chacalluta**, altitude 96 m, located on the Peruvian border, 8 km north of Arica at the end of RN 5 or the Panamericana. Open all year round, 0800–2300. The road is sealed between Arica and Tacna in Peru, 48 km north.

Crossings into Bolivia
• **Portezuelo de Tambo Quemado**, also known as **Complejo Aduanero Lago Chungará**, altitude 4678 m, located 209 km east of Arica on RI 11, between Arica and La Paz in Bolivia. Open all year round, 0800–2000, subject to

weather conditions. Most of the road between Arica and the border is now sealed or being upgraded. The nearest Bolivian town is Oruro.

- **Cerrito Prieto**, located 250 km north east of Iquique at 3770 m on Ruta A-55 near **Colchané** on the Bolivian border. Open all year round in daylight only, subject to weather conditions. This border crossing is not recommended, because the road is in really bad condition from the **Pachica** turnoff onwards. The road is sealed from Iquique to 20 km past Huara, a distance of 90 km, the rest is gravel or worse. The nearest towns in Bolivia are Uyuni and Oruro. Chilean passport control is in Colchané.
- **Visviri**, a railroad crossing. There are bus services from Arica to Visiviri- which connect with bus services from Charaña in Bolivia to La Paz.

Región II de Antofagasta

Crossing into Bolivia
- **Ollagüe**, altitude 3696 m, a railroad border crossing into Bolivia, located 160 km north-east of Calama. RN 21 from Calama to Ollagüe is passable, but poor in Bolivia. Open all year round, subject to weather conditions. Chilean passport control is at the railroad station in Ollagüe.

Crossings into Argentina
- **Paso de Jama**. This is a new pass linking Antofagasta with Jujuy and Salta in neighboring Argentina. The road has been upgraded on both sides of the border and is the latest in Scenic Andean crossings. Buses Tramaca runs two bus services per week from Antofagasta via Calama and San Pedro de Atacama. See "Buses" from Antofagasta (page 87), Calama (page 96), and San Pedro de Atacama (page 108); "Trains" from Calama (page 95); and Ollagüe (page 98).
- **Paso de La Laguna Sico** replaces the **Paso de Huaitiquina** between Antofagasta and Salta in Argentina, altitude 4089 m. Located on RI 23, 175 km south-east of San Pedro de Atacama. The road is frequently cut in winter. RN 23 is intermittently sealed between Calama and San Pedro and is

good; there is a new dirt road from San Pedro to the border. The road on the Argentine side is also much improved as far as San Antonio de los Cobres, where Argentine passport control is located. Chilean passport control, open between sunrise and sunset, is in San Pedro de Atacama. If the bus from Argentina is delayed, *carabineros* are on duty late at night.

Región III de Atacama

- **Paso de San Francisco** on RN 31. Open from sunrise to sunset, but usually closed in winter as heavy snowfalls make the road impassable between June and September. The road passes along the eastern edge of the **Salar de Maricunga**, connecting Copiapó with Catamarca in Argentina, and is sealed only from Copiapó to Chulo. The distance from Copiapó to the border is 286 km; to La Rioja in Argentina is another grueling 490 km. Argentine passport control is at La Grotto. Note that the recently established **Parque Nacional Nevado Tres Cruces** can be reached from Complejo Fronterizo by taking the turnoff south.

Región IV de Coquimbo

- **Paso del Agua Negra**, altitude 4775 m, between La Serena and San Juan in Argentina, was reopened for tourist traffic in 1991. Passport control on the Chilean side is in **Juntas** and on the Argentine side in **Baño Centenario**.

Región V de Valparaíso

- **Paso del Bermejo**, known as Complejo Fronterizo Los Libertadores, altitude 3860 m, open 0830–2000 in summer. This important border crossing connects the cities of Santiago, 142 km south-west, and Mendoza in Argentina, 199 km east. The border post is 10 km east of Portillo. In winter, snow chains are compulsory and heavy snowfalls may close the pass temporarily. The pass is on RI 60, which starts in Valparaíso. Most traffic however comes from Santiago, where regular buses depart in the morning to cross the Andes. From Los Andes onwards, the road passes through beautiful scenery. Part of the road from La Juncal onwards is called Los Caracoles — an awe-inspiring scenic stretch where the road negotiates a height of 660 m in 10 km.

Región VII del Maule

- **Paso del Maule** or **Paso Pehuenche** between **Talca** and San Rafael in Argentina has been open to tourists since 1991. The distance from Talca on RI 115 to the border is 180 km and from the border to San Rafael 345 km.

Región IX de La Araucania

- **Paso de Pino Hachado**, altitude 1884 m, located on Ruta R-89 connects **Temuco** with **Zapala** in Argentina. It is closed in winter from the end of May to October. Border control is at **Liucura**, open from 0830–1630. The road from **Victoria** is sealed as far as **Manzanar** and good gravel from there onwards. It is 219 km from Temuco to the border via Victoria; from the border to Zapala in Argentina is a further 114 km. There are regular buses between Temuco and Zapala and Neuquén in Argentina.
- **Paso de Icalma** on Ruta S-61, altitude 1298 m, open from 0830–1630. This alternative route from Temuco to Zapala in Argentina may be closed in winter because of heavy snow. approximately 20 km of the 59 km from Temuco to Cunco are sealed. It is 66 km from **Cunco** to the border via **Melipeuco**; from the border to Zapala is a further 148 km. Passport control is in **Icalma** on the lake, about 2 km west of the border. On the Argentine side the road skirts Lago Aluminé and passes Primeros Pinos, a fledgling tourist resort — see the entry for Primeros Pinos in *Travel Companion Argentina*.
- **Paso Mamuil Mallal** on RI 119, altitude 1207 m, open from 0830–1830. This pass is closed in winter. Argentines call it Paso Tromen, and it connects Temuco with Junín de los Andes in Argentina. The road from Temuco to Pucón, 110 km, is sealed and then good gravel to the border. Border control is at **Puesco**. Regular buses run between Temuco and Junín in summer.

Región X de Los Lagos

- **Paso Huahum**, altitude 659 m, between Valdivia and San Martín de los Andes in Argentina on RN 203, open all year round 0800–1730. This border crossing is recommended to tourists because of its scenic beauty. This pass connects the port of **Valdivia** with San Martín de los Andes in Argentina. The gravel road from Puerto Pirehueico to Huahum is in good condition. Chilean border control is in Puerto Pirehueico at the boat ramp. There are regular buses from Huahum to San Martín. It is more interesting, however, to make the scenic trip by boat across the **Lago Lacar**, enclosed by steep mountains. See "Border crossings" in Panguipulli on page 697.
- **Portezuelo de Puyehué**, altitude 1308 m, connects **Osorno** on RN 215 with San Carlos de Bariloche in Argentina. The pass remains open all year round: in summer 0800–2400; in winter 0800–1700. This is another very scenic trip. The distance from Osorno to the pass is 121 km, and sealed for 95 km as far as Anticura. The distance from the border to San Carlos de Bariloche is 133 km. This is the second most important border crossing between the two countries, especially in the summer tourist season. On the Chilean side the road runs through the **Parque Nacional Puyehué**, and on the Argentine side through Parque Nacional Nahuel Huapi. There is regular public transport from Osorno to San Carlos de Bariloche.
- **Paso de Pérez Rosales**, altitude 1022 m, connects **Puerto Montt** on RI 225 with San Carlos de Bariloche. Although some snow falls in winter, the pass is open all year round from 0830–1830. This outstanding scenic expedition can be made only with a tour operator (Andina del Sud) which starts in Puerto Montt, but may also be joined in Puerto Varas. The trip, which takes 11 hours, alternates six times between road and lake transport.
- **Futaleufú**, altitude 515 m, connects the port of Chaitén with Esquel in Ar-

gentina. Chilean passport control is open 0830–1700. RI 231 branches off Carretera Austral at **Villa Santa Lucia**. The Argentine border control is a short distance before the bridge over the Río Futaleufú. The distance from Chaitén to the border is 176 km and from the border to Esquel is 61 km. See also Esquel in *Travel Companion Argentina*.

- **Palena**, altitude 1200 m, also known as Paso de Carrenleufú connects **Chaitén** with Esquel in Argentina. It is difficult for foreign passport holders to use this crossing, because the Argentines consider it an official pass only for Chilean and Argentine ID card holders living in the border area. This may have changed, but do not be surprised if you are stopped at the border. If crossing here, report to the authorities in Esquel to get an entry stamp. The route from Chaitén is the same as the one for the Futaleufú crossing as far as **Puerto Ramírez**. At Puerto Ramírez, continue on RN 235 to Palena. The 152 km gravel road to Palena lacks bridges, and is cut by snow occasionally in winter. Palena to the border is a further 8 km. The **Río Encuentro** forms the border between the two countries. There are regular public buses from Chaitén to Palena, weather permitting, and all river crossings are passable. From Palena, you have to find a lift to the border — the *carabineros* will usually help. Public transport runs three times a week directly from the Argentine border control post to Esquel, via Corcovado, a further 121 km. The border is open from sunrise to sunset all year round, weather permitting. The nearest accommodation is in Palena and Trevelín in Argentina.

Región XI de Aisén

There are numerous border crossings into neighboring Argentina. Since not all of them are accessible or even open to tourists, I have listed only those which are of interest to tourists.

- Complejo Fronterizo **Coihaique Alto**, altitude 795 m, open all year round 0800–2200, connecting **Coihaique** with Río Mayo and Comodoro Rivadavia in Argentina. It is not only a major connection between Chile and Argentina, but one of the major border crossings between the Pacific and the Atlantic. From Coihaique to passport control in Coihaique Alto is 43 km along RN 240. Coihaique Alto to the border is a further 6 km, and from the border to Río Mayo in Argentina another 114 km. The road on either side is gravel and passable all year round. Buses run regularly between Coihaique and Comodoro Rivadavia via Río Mayo. The nearest accommodation is in Coihaique and Río Mayo in Argentina.

- **Chile Chico**, altitude 200 m, open from 0800–2400 all year round, weather permitting. Chilean border control is located in Chile Chico, and Argentine border control in Los Antiguos. This is the second most important border crossing in the region. Chile Chico is now directly linked with the main Chilean road network; moreover, the Argentines have built a major road from Perito Moreno to Los Antiguos. There are now regular buses between Chile Chico and Los Antiguos (see Chile Chico and Los Antiguos in *Travel Companion Argentina*).

Región XII de Magallanes

- **Complejo Fronterizo Mina Uno**, altitude 761 m, open from sunrise to sunset all year round, connects **Puerto Natales** with Río Turbio in Argentina. Border control is in **Villa Dorotea**. Nine kilometers east of Puerto Natales is the junction with RI 250 which is a gravel road. The 11 km of road to the border is also gravel. There are regular bus services from Río Turbio with connections to Río Gallegos. In summer, tour buses run to El Calafate. The ski slopes of **Mina Uno** are almost next to the Argentine border post.

- **Complejo Fronterizo Laurita**, altitude 239 m, open 0800–2400 all year round. Connects **Puerto Natales** with Casas Viejas in Argentina. Passport control is at the border.

- **Complejo Fronterizo Monte Aymond**, altitude 180 m, open 0800–2400 all year round. Connects **Punta Arenas** with Río Gallegos in Argentina.

Located on RI 255, 201 km north-east of Punta Arenas. Take RN 9 55 km north to **Gobernador Phillipi** and at the intersection turn east into RI 255. The road between Punta Arenas and the border is being upgraded. There are regular buses between Punta Arenas and Río Gallegos. The nearest accommodation is at the turnoff to Punta Delgada and in Río Gallegos.

- **Control Fronterizo de San Sebastián**, altitude 296 m, open from sunrise to sunset all year round, with occasional interruptions due to bad weather. This pass is located on Isla Tierra del Fuego. Connects **Porvenir** with Río Grande. Ruta Y-71 to the border is 149 km and is mostly dirt road. From the border to Río Grande is a further 107 km. The road is being upgraded on the Argentine side and about 40 km north of Río Grande becomes sealed. There are regular bus service between Porvenir and Río Grande; indeed there are now bus connections between Punta Arenas and Río Grande. See also"Buses" from Punta Arenas on page 857.

Road services in Chile

The naming system

There are two sets of road systems: national and regional. *Rutas Nacionales* or national roads also incorporate Rutas Internacionales (international roads) wherever a *Ruta Nacional* crosses an international frontier. Regional roads are maintained by regions. National roads are indicated as "RN" followed by a number. International roads are indicated as "RI" also followed by a number. The maps in this guide use "RN" for both types of major road.

Ruta Nacional 5, the main arterial road usually referred to in this guide as the Panamericana, travels almost the full length of Chile, from Arica on the Peruvian border to Quellón on Isla Grande de Chiloe. The Panamericana Norte runs north from Santiago; the Panamericana Sur runs south from Santiago. This road is sealed throughout Chile, and is in perfect condition. Many sections have three lanes in both directions. There are numerous daily bus services north and south along the Panamericana. Buses traveling direct from Santiago to Arica take 28 hours; direct buses from Santiago to Puerto Montt take 18 hours.

Regional roads are indicated as "Rutas" followed by a letter and number. For example, "Ruta A-21" refers to a road inside Región I; "Ruta A-21-B" means the road is shared by both Región I and Región II. In Región II this road will be shown as B-21-A. Mostly these are lateral roads, leading from the Panamericana east into the *cordillera* or west to the Pacific.

Bus services on these lateral roads serve the needs of the villagers, leaving in the morning from the valleys in the high *sierra* for the nearest provincial town in the central valley, and returning in the evening to the Andean valleys. Tourists should note that these buses may be crowded. Some remote villages have no tourist facilities, but bus drivers are happy to direct you to families who rent beds. These tours are suitable for backpackers and mountain hikers who are interested in the beautiful areas of unknown Chile, away from the tourist mainstream. There are still many sequestered valleys where villagers are unused to seeing *gringo* tourists.

Rutas Nacionales are always well signposted. Regional roads are not well signposted. It is hoped, however, that regional roads crossing or starting from a national road will be signposted in the not-too-distant future.

✈ Flights to Chile

LAN Chile offers a special discount to overseas visitors. A 21-day complete Chile pass costs $550.00, and entitles you to visit Copiapó, Antofagasta, and Arica in the north, with a stopover in Concepción, Puerto Montt, Coihaique, or Punta Arenas. Alternatively, two 21-day passes, $300.00 each, can be bought for northern Chile and for southern Chile.

From	Airline	Services	Stopovers
Europe			
• Amsterdam	KLM	3 services per week	2
• Frankfurt	LAN Chile	4 services per week	2
	Lufthansa	3 services per week	1
• London	British Airways	3 services per week	1
• Madrid	Iberia	1 service per week	1
	LAN Chile	4 services per week	1
• Paris	Air France	3 services per week	1
• Rome	Alitalia	2 services per week	1
• Stockholm	Aeroflot	2 services per week	3
• Zurich	Swissair	3 services per week	2
North America			
• Los Angeles	Líneas Aereas Costarricenes		
		5 services per week	2-3
	LAN Chile	6 services per week	1
• Miami	American Airlines	7 services per week	direct flight
		7 services per week	1
	LADECO	1 service per week	2
		1 service per week	direct flight
	LAN Chile	7 services per week	direct flight
		2 services per week	1
	United Airlines	7 services per week	direct flight
• Montreal	Canadian Pacific	3 services per week	1
• New York	LADECO	7 services per week	1
	LAN Chile	7 services per week	1

Australasia

Via Papeete

Most flights from Sydney and Auckland have no direct connections in Papeete with LAN Chile, and involve a free stay at a LAN Chile hotel for one night plus all meals. A stopover in Easter Island is optional but recommended.

• Auckland–Papeete			
	Air New Zealand		1
• Papeete–Easter Island–Santiago			
	LAN Chile	2 services per week	
• Sydney–Papeete	Air Calédonie	1 service per week	2
	Qantas	2 services per week	1

Via Buenos Aires
• Sydney–Buenos Aires

	Aerolineas Argentinas		2 services per week
• Buenos Aires–Santiago	Aerolineas/LAN Chile		daily services

Falkland Islands/Malvinas
DAP has direct flights every Friday from Puntas Arenas; return ticket $800.00.

Carretera Austral General Pinochet, running from Puerto Montt south to Villa O'Higgins, is the latest in Chile's scenic roads, and is interrupted by ferry crossings of the fiords. The last major bridges over the Rí Palena and the Río Rosselot in Región XI de Aisén have been completed in 1991.

Chileans drive on the right-hand side, and wearing seat belts is compulsory. Hitchhiking is possible, but not encouraged by the authorities.

Bus services in the south

Bus services from Puerto Montt go as far as Hornopiren, with a few irregular services further south. There is no direct road service from Puerto Montt to Chaitén. From Chaitén there are buses south to Coihaique. This service is influenced by the weather — more buses run in summer than in winter. From Coihaique there are weekly services south to Cochrane. The road is pushing further south towards Villa O'Higgins, and is outstandingly scenic between Chaitén and Cochrane, but is only used by adventurous travelers. The main attraction are the many huge glaciers which give rise to many powerful streams and large lakes — Lago Cochrane, Lago General Carrera, Lago Yelcho, and many more. The water in these rivers and lakes is very cold.

Thermal resorts

Abundant thermal water surfaces in remote valleys as a result of Chile's highly volcanic topography. There are major resorts in Región I de Tarapacá, Región V de Valparaíso, Región VI del Libertador, Región VII del Maule, Región VIII del Bío Bío, Región IX de la Araucania, Región X de Los Lagos, and Región XI de Aisén. For details, refer to the introduction to each region.

Please write to us:

Companion Travel Guide Books
PO Box 321
Miller NSW 2168
Australia

19 Kilmorey Street
Busby NSW 2168
Australia

Telephone and fax: +61 2 9608 1169
E-mail: keyword@ozemail.com.au

HOW TO USE THE *TRAVEL* COMPANION

This book consists of chapters for each region, with the exception of Región X de Los Lagos and Región V de Valparaíso, where Isla Grande de Chiloe and Easter Island respectively are in separate chapters. The regions are arranged in numerical order, from north to south.

Regions

Each chapter provides first an overview of the region: a detailed contents list of the places described, together with symbols indicating the facilities and features to be found in each town, an introductory section describing its size, location, political division into provinces, population, history, topography, economy, climate, transport, national parks, thermal resorts, best tourist destinations, and a distance table.

This is followed by descriptions of cities or towns, and national parks or reserves in alphabetical order. In each entry, an opening section details the telephone area code, size of town, distance from nearest regional capital or provincial center, and in the case of regional capitals, distances from Santiago. This distance indicator is also a rough guide to where bus services originate for particular destinations in this region. Large cities, such as Santiago, Valparaíso, Puerto Montt, and Concepción, may be partially subdivided into *barrios* or geographical sections to make the entries, for example, "Accommodation" and "Eating out", easier to follow.

Cities and towns

Places are included if they fulfill one of the following criteria:

- there is something of interest there
- there are tourist facilities, in particular accommodation, eating places, and transport
- the place is en route to a place of interest and is suitable for a stopover.

In many cases I have included a small place within the text of a larger town in the vicinity, usually under "Accommodation", Eating out", or

"Camping", indicating the distance and providing a brief description. If there is a large entry or description of the route, you may find this under "Excursions" in the entry for the nearest town from which the itinerary starts — check the index.

Travel Companion Chile is designed to help travelers find eating places, accommodation, bus services, or gas stations wherever they may be in Chile. Some places may have these amenities only and little else of interest. The accommodation and restaurants in large towns are not fully covered, but all facilities are listed for small country towns. This book encourages people to venture beyond the "normal" tourist circuit. Travelers often avoid places because they think there is nowhere to stay, but locations off the beaten track may well reveal something of particular interest. If it is not already in this book, I should like to hear about it.

When I have stayed at a hotel, eaten at a restaurant, or used some facility, and particularly enjoyed it or found it of excellent value or the staff exceptionally helpful, I have marked the entry with a pointing hand ☞ to indicate a personal recommendation.

Index

At the end of the Travel Companion is an index to all the places mentioned in the Companion. Each name referred to appears in the text as bold type. To get the most out of the index read the Index's "Introduction" on page 875 carefully.

Sample entry

The following explains how to use the information provided in the listing for each town. It is laid out to resemble a typical entry. Entries may be for city or town, a national park or reserve, or even a "Cajón" — a river system in the high Andes including tributaries.

TOWN OR CITY

Area code: The telephone number prefix code
Population: Indicated for major towns when available
Altitude: Provided when available
Distances: For regional capital cities, the distances to Santiago and usually to the nearest regional capital north and south are given, together with highway numbers. For smaller towns, the distance and road number to the regional capital and/or the nearest provincial capital is given. Indication of the nearest provincial or regional capital also indicates the starting point of bus services to the town under review.

Introductory information, giving, where appropriate, the location, brief history and description, items of interest in the locality, and instructions on how to get there.

⊕ Festivals

Chilean *fiestas* usually honor the patron saint or foundation of a particular city. Festivals of particular note are listed, sometimes with a brief description of the festivities and historic origins. Some peo-ple may prefer to avoid *fiestas* because hotels may be booked out and banks closed. Sometimes festivals held in nearby villages are also included with distance.

ⓘ Tourist information

The main outlets for tourist information are Sernatur, municipal information offices and CONAF. In small towns there is usually a *Municipalidad* block which houses not only the town's administration but also tourist information, police, post office, and public telephones. A visit to the local Sernatur or CONAF office is always a good starting point in a particular area.

Sernatur is the regional arm of the state-sponsored Servicio Nacional de Turismo. The main office is in Santiago, but each regional capital and larger provincial capitals have a local office. Sernatur offices provide information on local accommodation and tourist destinations, but they do not make hotel bookings. Much of the practical information contained in this book is from information received from various regional Sernatur offices.

CONAF is the state-sponsored Corporación Nacional Forestal. Again, the main office is in Santiago, with regional offices in capital cities. CONAF regulates restricted logging in *reservas nacionales*, reafforestation, and the selection of suitable trees for planting. CONAF is in charge of all *parques nacionales* and *reservas nacionales*. On the whole, Chile is very conscious of its natural heritage, and protects it wherever possible. CONAF publishes pamphlets and excellent nature books on flora, fauna, scenery, and archeological sites in the areas under their jurisdiction, which are available from their information centers. CONAF have marked the trees on many tracks with their Latin and common names. CONAF *refugios* (mountain huts) and camping areas are open to travelers.

⊟ Accommodation

Accommodation is listed primarily in alphabetical order, but "star establishments" are placed first. Stars are assigned by Sernatur. For large towns the list starts with a fairly comprehensive but selective list of accommodation in the center; in very large towns accommodation is listed by suburbs or by location on the Panamericana. In smaller towns and villages, all accommodation is listed where known.

Accommodation listings are subdivided into *apart hotels*, hotels, *hosterías, hostales,*

residenciales, cabañas, departamentos, motels, and *pensiones*. These terms are all explained in the glossary beginning on page 867. *Hosterías* must be taken on their individual merits — some only provide meals. Private *hostales* and *residenciales* are the cheapest accommodation. *Residenciales* are licensed by the local government and have to conform to certain standards. *Pensiones*, sometimes just listed as private accommodation, are suitable for backpackers and/or budget travelers. *Hostales* are slightly better places to stay and consequently dearer. *Hospedajes* are private accommodations, usually only one room. *Pensiones* and *hospedajes* are interchangeable terms. *Apart hotel* is a term used when a complete flat or apartment is let; this is the latest trend in accommodation construction, especially in the ski resorts.

Codes are provided for facilities and for price ranges where these are known. Prices are indicated for double (🏠🏠) or single (🏠) rooms.

Ⓐ Camping

Camping is popular in Chile, and there are many camping sites, often on the outskirts of cities and usually with overnight vans for hire. Most camping places are being converted into *cabaña*-style accommodation. In many of the national parks and reserves, CONAF provides camping places for a nominal fee.

ⓘⓘ Eating out

This section lists restaurants, *pizzerias, cafeterías,* cafés, and tea rooms (*salones de té*). In larger centers eating places are shown under the various areas of the town. Wherever possible, cuisine (for example Chinese, Chilean, International, French, seafood, German, Italian) and sometimes price range codes are noted. Entertainment in restaurants is also indicated: *peñas*, dancing, music, nightclub, or disco. Restaurants in neighboring small towns are listed, with a short description and the distance to the town. The major hotels also have first-class restaurants but are not listed under "Eating out" unless they have a different name. Sometimes eating out in nearby villages or towns is given as a subheading; distances are always given.

◙ Accommodation — Sernatur symbols

Sernatur has established a set of symbols to denote services provided at places of accommodation. I have expanded those symbols further and these symbols have been used in the "Accommodation" section and to a lesser extent "Camping" sections throughout this book.

- A   Hot water
- B   Kitchenette
- C   Bar fridge
- D   TV in room
- E   *Cafetería*
- F   Restaurant
- G   Bar
- H   Parking
- I   Luggage stored
- J   Lounge
- K   Credit cards accepted
- L   Laundry - Service and facilities
- M   Conference room
- N   Children's games
- P   Private bathroom
- R   Swimming pool
- S   Breakfast included
- $ Money exchange for guests
- T   Telephone in room
- U   Room service
- V   Heating provided
- W   Open in season only
- X   Disco
- Y   Air-conditioning
- Z   Pickup service/tour buses/car rental

◙ Accommodation — Price range codes

Accommodation in apartments, *cabañas*, hotels, *hosterías*, motels, *residenciales, pensiones*, and private accommodation are indicated by means of price range codes, usually for doubles.

Note that the symbol **i** indicates that the price is for a single room; and the symbol **ii** indicates that the price is for a double room.

- $A   Over $250.00   ii
- $B $200.00–$249.00   ii
- $C $150.00–$199.00   ii
- $D $100.00–$149.00   ii
- $E $75.00–$99.00   ii
- $F $50.00–$74.00   ii
- $G $35.00–$49.00   ii
- $H $20.00–$34.00   ii
- $I $10.00–$19.00   ii
- $J $5.00–$10.00   ii

HOW TO USE

⑪ Eating out — price range codes

- $X   Over $20.00   Recommended for de luxe travelers
- $Y $11.00–$20.00   Recommended for intermediate travelers
- $Z   Under $10.00   Recommended for budget travelers

⚡ Entertainment

Entertainment includes lists of discos, restaurants with dancing, *cafés de concierto*, nightclubs, and casinos.

⛩ Post and telegraph

Post offices
The main post office of each town is generally found near the main plaza. In smaller towns, it is part of the *servicios municipales*, which incorporates administrative offices, telephones, postal services, *carabineros*, and, sometimes, the CONAF office. Correos de Chile has a monopoly on carrying letters and parcels, and usually provides a fax service at post offices. There are no postal codes in Chile. Some places have separate Telex Chile offices, which deal with telegrams and telexes.

Telephones
Chile is divided into telephone calling areas, each of which has a dialing code or prefix; these are indicated in the introductory information for each town. If there is a different area code within the text, this usually means that the particular hotel or service is located in an area where there is no direct area code, or that bookings have to be made in a different town. Very frequently hotel bookings in outlying areas have to made through an agency located in the regional capital or even in Santiago (02).
There are several telephone companies — the biggest one is Compañía de Teléfonos de Chile (CTC), a private company which operates in all regions except Región X de Los Lagos and Región XI de Aisén. This does not prevent calls between different telephone systems. In most regions, public telephones do not take coins; instead tokens or Tarjetas Telefónicas CTC are used which can be bought from newsstands or tobacco shops. Blue telephones are for long-distance calls; yellow telephones are for local calls. Overseas calls can be made from public telephones or a *centro de llamadas* or an Entel office. At present, Entel is a state-owned company which handles overseas calls only, but there is talk of privatization.
Telefónica del Sur operates only in Región X de Los Lagos for local and overseas calls. Coins are used instead of tokens, and you can make local or long-distance calls inside Chile from the same phone. Dial "142" for information in Spanish about accommodation and prices, restaurants, tours and activities in the region, and transport. Throughout their area of operation, Telefónica del Sur have installed public telephones (called the "Red Interlaken") where you can make and receive national and international phone calls.
In listings within Región X de Los Lagos and Región XI de Aisén, a three-digit telephone number preceded by the code "CRELL" indicates that it is an operator-connected call.
Compañía de Teléfonos de Coihaique SA operates only in Región IX de La Araucania for local and overseas calls. Coins are used instead of tokens. This company is linked with Telefónica del Sur.
VTR Telecomunicaciones specialize in data transmission, and have offices in all major towns with facilities for sending faxes, telexes, telegrams, and data transmissions.
The Chilean telephone system is no different from the system in any other country: for direct dialing, use the prefix indicated for the town (e.g. 080 Arica) displayed in each telephone booth. If the prefix is preceded by the letters "LD" for Larga Distancia ("Long Distance"), calls are operator connected — dial the prefix and ask the operator for the telephone number. Telephone opetrators usually have a good command of English. All telephone booths and directories have a list of all area codes which can be dialed directly.

$ Financial

Here are listed places whose sole function is to exchange money. Some hotels change money for their guests. Some tour operators also exchange money. Fincard, which has offices in all regional capitals and sometimes in provincial capitals as well, makes cash advances against Visa cards. American Express in Santiago changes travelers' checks into US dollars.

Services and facilities

Here are a listed of photographic shops, supermarkets, dry cleaners, sports equipment shops, and so on.

Visa, passports

Consulates are listed under this heading.

Air services

Lists airlines and internal services — destinations, fares, frequency, and duration of flight.

Buses

Under this heading are the addresses of the various bus terminals, and the addresses and telephone numbers of bus companies serving the town, followed by lists of destinations with fares, frequency, duration of trip, and bus companies providing each service. In larger towns to condense the tables codes have been used for the names of companies: those beginning with "A" represent companies operating north of Santiago, and those beginning with "B" represent companies operating south of Santiago. Some major companies operate both north and south; in these cases "A" is used for all operations, e.g. "A153" representing Tur–Bus Jedimar, a major bus company which runs bus services south of Santiago and north.

Motoring

Car rental
This section lists car rental companies. All major car rental agencies are represented in major regional centers.
- American Rent-a-Car
- Automóvil Club de Chile
- Avis Rent-a-Car
- Budget Rent-a-Car
- First Rent-a-Car
- Galerías Rent-a-Car

- Hertz Rent-a-Car
- Juncal Rent-a-Car
- Lider Rent-a-Car
- National Car Rental
- Rentaequipos Rent-a-Car SA
- Viva Rent-a-Car
- Western Rent-a-Car

Avis accepts Avis travel vouchers, American Express, Visa card, Diners Club, Mastercard. Sixteen per cent IVA (sales tax) and insurance are added to the weekly rates, but be sure to check this.
Weekly rates vary from US$350 (Supercuore) to US$900 (Toyota 4WD). Kilometer rates vary from $0.15 to $0.30.
Most car rental agencies employ English-speaking staff.

Gas stations
If there is a city map, gas stations are marked on the map. Otherwise, gas stations are listed here.
On the main highways gas stations are sometimes called *Rutacentro*: this is a gas station with a mechanic service and road diner attached. All major gas distribution companies are represented in Chile: Esso, Shell, and the state–owned company Copec. Shell and Copec have particularly good road maps on their sales outlets.

Trains

The only passenger trains operating in Chile are on the southern line from Santiago to Puerto Montt, on a spur line from Chillán to Concepción, and on the Valparaíso–Los Andes line. Trains no longer run from Santiago to Mendoza in Argentina, nor between Santiago and Valparaíso. Each station on the southern railroad line displays the frequency of services and fares.

Water transport

South of Puerto Montt, regular ferry services connect Isla Grande de Chiloe with the mainland and the islands. Eventually, the completion of the Carretera Austral from Puerto Montt to O'Higgins in Región XI de Aisén will make many ferry services redundant. Many of the lake services are being phased out as the road system is extended. The Lago General Carrera ferries have been greatly reduced, but services still operate between Chile Chico and Puerto Ingeniero Ibañez.

⊞ Shopping

This heading locates the major shopping street or commercial sector of a town. It also gives a list *artesanía* (handicraft) shops, and lists specialties of the region or town.

⊛ Sport

Here are listed the various sports that are available, and where applicable where the clubrooms, grounds, and so on are located.

Fishing
The Servicio Nacional de Pesca (SERNAP) is the controlling body for offshore and inland fishing, and issues fishing licenses and advice on conditions. No licenses are required for offshore fishing. The head office is in Santiago: SERNAP, San Antonio 427, upstairs ℂ 6980543, open Mon–Fri, 0900–1400. Fishing permits are also available from SERNAP regional offices and some municipal and CONAF offices. A SERNAP fishing permit is valid for the whole of Chile and cannot be transferred. Closed seasons must be strictly observed; they are listed for each species in the introduction to each region.
Trout fishing is permitted all year round in the following lakes shared with Argentina: Lagos General Carrera, Puelo, Palena, Cochrane, O'Higgins, and Fagnano.
Fishing in inland waters, particularly for trout and *pejerrey,* starts from Región V de Valparaíso and extends southward. There is very little inland fishing in the north.
Distribution of trout only is indicated through this guide, as it seems unlikely that anybody will come to Chile solely to fish for *pejerrey,* as the Chilean atherine is called here. As a general rule, trout occur in the streams coming down from the high *sierras,* but once those streams pass through the central valley they become too polluted to support delicate trout — their place is taken by *pejerrey*. The exceptions are the clear streams from the coastal *cordillera,* in particular from the Nahuel-buta Ranges southward.

▣ Sightseeing

This section highlights those places which can be visited in the particular town itself such as museums, churches, parks, and colonial houses, and indicates opening times and admission charges where relevant.

⬤ Excursions

Tour operators
The major tour operators are listed under this heading, together with examples of tours and details about duration and fares, if available. Tour operators sometimes also have car rental and money exchange.

Excursions
Here are listed the most interesting places that can be visited from the town, together with the distance and direction, a description of the interesting features both during the journey and at the desitnation, and, where approprirate, instructions on how to get there.
In this book I have differentiated between an "excursion", which I have used to mean a journey under 50 km which usually returns to its starting point; and a "trip", a journey of usually more than 50 km, which may finish in a different town, in another region, or even in Argentina.

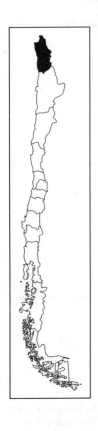

REGIÓN I
DE
TARAPACÁ

Size: 59 000 square km (22 774 square miles)
Population: 280 000
Regional capital: Iquique, on the Pacific coast
Provinces (and provincial capitals):
- Parinacota (Putre)
- Arica (Arica)
- Iquique (Iquique)

Large National Parks and Reserves have been created in Tarapacá's *altiplano* to preserve the flora and fauna. In particular, the fleet-footed *vicuña*, recently almost extinct, has been successfully re-established. The habitat of *vicuñas* can be easily reached from the coastal towns of Arica and Iquique. The Aymará people of the *altiplano* hold frequent colorful fiestas, mixing Catholic celebrations with elements of their ancestral religion. Of particular interest are also the many *altiplano* churches in their distinctive robust style with their belfries usually standing apart from the main body of the church.

The *pre-Cordillera* contains many hot springs with associated well-established hotels.

During the saltpeter boom, the English were very influential in this area. A number of them settled here and acquired great wealth, leaving many splendid mansions built in the Georgian, Victorian, and Edwardian styles.

Región I de Tarapacá, and in particular Arica, became the major battleground for fierce skirmishes at sea and on land fought during the War of the Pacific.

On the coast, marlin and other game fishing trips are organized by local fishermen and tour operators in Arica and Iquique.

It is located in the extreme north of the country, between 17° and 21° south. It borders Peru to the north, Bolivia to the east, and Región II de Antofagasta to the south.

The main urban centers are Arica, Iquique, Putre, Pica, Matilla and Pozo Almonte.

Road and air transport

Road

The Carretera Panamericana (RN 5) runs the full length of the region, linking **Arica** with Tacna in Peru. Most of the highway runs through desert, encountering vegetation only when it crosses valleys such as **Quebrada de Tana** (near the turnoff to Pisagua on the coast), **Quebrada de Camarones** (near the village of **Cuya**) and of course the **Azapa** and **Río Lluta** valleys. In the **Pampa de Tamarugal** between the northern and southern turnoff east to **Pica** are new plantings of the *tamarugal* trees native to this region, which were until recently almost extinct due to their use by the saltpeter mining operations. Side roads branch off the highway to the coast or into the mountains.

The main road to Bolivia is the Ruta Internacional (RI 11), which starts in Arica and reaches the Bolivian border at Tambo Quemado (204 km).

Air

There are two major airports:

- Aeropuerto Chacalluca, in Arica, used by LanChile, Ladeco, and Lloyd Aereo Boliviano
- Aeropuerto Diego Aracena, some 40 km south of Iquique, used only by Chilean aircraft

Topography

Geographically, this region like most of Chile falls longitudinally into four distinct sections: these are (from the west) the coastal strip, the coastal *cordillera*, the central valley or *pampa*, and the Andes. In the north, the central valley is a desert — rain has not been recorded there for several hundred years. Here the coastal *cordillera* averages 1400 m, with peaks reaching 1700 m. The mountains catch the passing clouds, so that tiny green patches stand out on the peaks against the barren mountainsides.

The coastal strip is very narrow, falling off sharply to the sea. Most of the few coastal towns are squeezed in between the sea and the wall of the Cordillera de la Costa.

To the east of the coastal *cordillera*, the desert valley rises gradually from west to east, dissected by deep canyons. Further east the Andes reach peaks over 6000 m, many of them volcanoes or of volcanic origin like **Volcán Isluga** (5551 m), **Volcán Guallatiri** (6063 m), and **Volcán Parinacota** (6342 m). The *altiplano* is a high-altitude *meseta* of great beauty. The government has created several national parks and reserves to protect this unique area and its distinct flora and fauna: **Parque Nacional Lauca**, **Reserva Nacional Las Vicuñas**, and **Parque Nacional Volcán Isluga**.

Climate

The coastal climate is mild and dry
all year round. Desert oases dot the
pampas; the climate is hot all year,
with temperatures averaging 23°C
(73°F).

The climates in the Cordillera
and the *altiplano* are dependent on
the altitude. At the higher altitudes
temperature differences between
day and night are great: at night it can
plummet to below freezing even in
summer. Between November and
March in the Cordillera, during what
is known as the *Invierno Boliviano* or
Bolivian winter, it rains and snows
heavily.

The indigenous inhabitants

Before the arrival of the Spaniards,
Tarapacá had been inhabited by different tribes since as long ago as 5000
BC. The change from nomadic to sed-
entary life is clearly visible from archeological finds. The settlements
were strongly influenced by the Tiahuanaco culture and later by the Incas — it even formed part of the Inca
empire for about 80 years. When the
Spanish *conquistadores* arrived in the
region in 1536, it was not densely
populated; most of the tribes lived in
the valleys of the *pre-Cordillera.*

These early indigenous peoples
have left a wealth of rock paintings of
a high artistic value. Most of them are
located in the **Valle de Azapa** and the
Valle de Río Lluta, both easily accessible from Arica. But the most spectacular ones are near Pintados in the
Salar de Pintados, in the Reserva Nacional Pampa del Tamarugal; they
are most easily reached from
Iquique.

European history

The first Spanish settlements were
founded in the more fertile valleys
and at the mouths of the rivers. The
first landholder was Lucas Martínez
de Vegazo in 1540, whose holdings
corresponded approximately to the
whole of the present-day region.

Economy

The mainstay of the region's economic activity is the trade generated
by the proximity of the two neighboring countries Bolivia and Peru —
with Bolivia virtually depending on
Arica as the sole outlet for its exports
and most of its imports. However in
1992 Peru ceded its port of Mollendo
for the next 50 years to provide Bolivia with its own access to the sea.
This will become the official seaport
of Bolivia, and, once connected by
rail to La Paz, will have a definite
impact on the economic future of
Arica.

Minerals

Up till the end of World War I, Tarapacá was the world's major exporter
of nitrate. The hinterland is full of
ghost towns which were flourishing
communities until Germany in-
vented artificial nitrogen. The area is
still rich in nitrate deposits, some of
them still being mined. Moreover,
there are proven deposits of copper,
silver, gold, potassium, sulfur and
other minerals, which are still awaiting commercial exploitation.

Fishing

The fishing industry is by far the
most important industry sector, the
region producing 66 per cent of the
national total. There are twelve fishmeal plants and about 200 fishing
vessels.

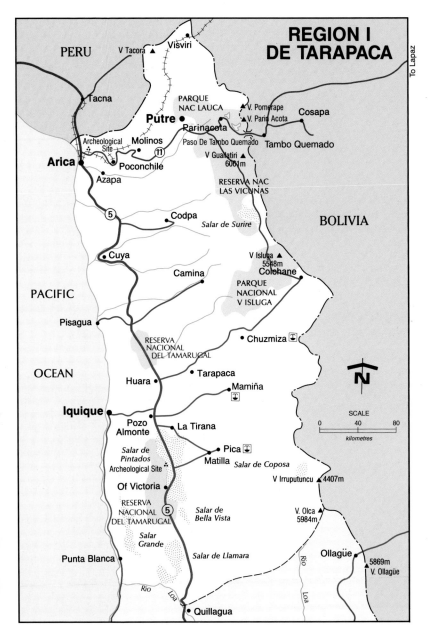

Plate 1
Map of Región I de Tarapacá

Plate 2   Región I de Tarapacá
Poconchile, church

Agriculture

Although arable land is scarce, some citrus orchards and olive groves have been established in the oases where irrigation is possible. On the outskirts of Arica I even saw a pilot plantation of *jojoba* beans. Besides citrus and olives, the area grows garlic, oregano, corn and green beans (*porotos*). In the *altiplano* an attempt is being made to revive the *vicuña* industry. The area also produces tropical fruits (mangos, guavas, bananas), as well as prickly pear, pawpaws, and temperate-zone fruits such as pears, grapes, watermelons, and apricots. Some cattle is raised.

Local cuisine

The cuisine of this region is strongly influenced by the two adjoining countries Peru and Bolivia.

- *Huatía*: A mixture of roast beef, lamb, *alpaca*, pork, and chicken, with a side dish of potatoes, sweet potatoes (*camote*), corn (*choclo*), *humitá* (maize cake), and beans. The authentic preparation incorporates cooking in a natural cavity lined with heated rocks. Dishes containing the meat are placed inside the cavity and more hot rocks placed on top. The last layer is made of *choclos, humitas,* potatoes, and other vegetables. Wet sacks and moist soil are placed over the lot. When the earth has been dried by the heat, the meal is ready — and it is considered a very delicious meal indeed.
- *Papas a la huancaina* (Potatoes à la *huancaina*): A Peruvian dish made of potatoes, with a sauce prepared from groundnuts, peanuts, mayonnaise, nutmeg, goat cheese and garlic, and garnished with lettuce leaves.
- *Conejo con papas y chuños* (Rabbit with potatoes): A dish made with rabbit meat, a special type of potato grown only in the *altiplano,* and chili peppers.
- *Cala purka*: A dish made of llama meat with a lot of garlic and potatoes.

For drinks try pisco sour, mango sour, mango cocktail, and *maracuya* juice.

Fishing

The best deep-sea fishing is in Arica and Iquique between April and September, but fishing is good all year round. The area abounds in marlin, albacore tuna, swordfish and tuna. Some world records have been broken in Iquique. Sport fishermen do not need a license to fish here.

National parks and reserves

The first four of these national parks, reserves and natural monuments form a continuous wildlife sanctuary in the *altiplano.*

- **Parque Nacional Lauca**: 137 883 ha (340 451 ac), 160 km east of Arica on RI 11 (road to La Paz, Bolivia). Marked educational and excursion paths, information center, picnic area, *refugios*, and shop nearby. Best reached from Arica. See the entry for the park on page 64.
- **Reserva Nacional Las Vicuñas**: 209 131 ha (516 373 acres), 190 km east of Arica on RI 11; turn off the main road south at the CONAF hut near **Chuyuncallani** on the banks of the **Salar de Surire**. Excursion paths. See the entry for the reserve on page 72.

- **Monumento Natural Salar de Surire**: 11 298 ha (27 896 acres), 220 km east of Arica on RI 11; turn off south at the CONAF Refugio Las Cuevas at KM 160. Near the Salar de Surire is a picnic area; excursion paths.
- **Parque Nacional Volcán Isluga**: 174 700 ha (431 350 acres), 210 km south-east of Iquique, turn off at **Huara** into Ruta A-55 and follow it until just before **Colchané** at the Bolivian border. Educational and excursion paths, picnic area, camping area. Best reached from Iquique but difficult; also possible with a tour operator from Arica. See the entry for the park on page 65.
- **Reserva Nacional Pampa del Tamarugal**: 108 266 ha (267 323 acres). Located in the central valley, it consists of two separate areas along the Panamericana: one south of **Pozo Almonte** (including the rock paintings in the Salar de Pintados), and the other north of **Huara** before the turnoff to Camiña and Pisagua. Best reached from Iquique. Formerly wide areas were covered with the *tamarugal* tree, which grows on saline soil, but during the saltpeter boom it was almost exterminated, used as firewood in the saltpeter works. CONAF has replanted it extensively. See the entry for the reserve on page 73.

Thermal resorts

In order of importance:
- **Mamiña**: Altitude 2700 m. There are three separate hot springs: Tambo 51°C (124°F), Ipla 37°C (99°F), and Barro 30°C (86°F). This resort town is open

all year round. The pure air and the clear skies are another great attraction. Many hotels of low to medium standard with regular daily buses to and from Iquique. The thermal waters are said to be therapeutic for respiratory problems, nerves, rheumatism, skin, arthritis, diabetes, mental fatigue/stress, sleeplessness, anemia, lumbosciaticas, sciatica, neuralgia, ulcers, and joint diseases. See the entry for Mamiña on page 59.
- **Pica**: Altitude 1350 m. Water temperature 32°C (90°F). Open all year round. Pica consists of two sectors: the town proper, and Sector Resbaladero with the hot springs, approximately 1 km up from the administration center. It consists of several "*cochas*", small ponds fed by hot underground springs. The largest is Cocha Resbaladero, which has picnic grounds and kiosks. It is very crowded at weekends. Accommodation in both sectors. Regular daily buses to and from Iquique. See the entry for Pica on page 67.
- **Chusmiza**: Altitude 3200 m. Water temperature 42°C (108°F). Open all year round. Therapeutic properties are said to include treatments for kidneys, rheumatism, skin, digestive organs, liver complaints, gastrointestinal problems, convalescence and asthma. Accommodation is in a basic *hostería*. Irregular public transport, usually only when the market is on in Colchané on the Bolivian border; otherwise private transport only from Iquique. See the entry for Chusmiza on page 45.

Shopping

The local craftsmen have retained many aspects of the pre-Colombian population, especially in the small *altiplano* villages which are still mostly inhabited by Aymará Indians. These weavers still use old looms and incorporate mythical themes into their fabrics

In the suburb of Zofri in **Iquique** is a duty-free zone where you can buy goods exempt from Chilean taxes. In crossing the border from Región I de Tarapacá into Región II de Antofagasta, luggage is checked for items bought in Zofri. Tourists are not normally subjected to a search.

Tourism

Tarapacá can be visited all year round, from the sophisticated town of Arica with its splendid southern and northern beaches, its casino and good hotels to Iquique with its historical city center steeped in the period of the saltpeter industry and the War of the Pacific. Iquique has received a new impetus with the creation of the free trade zone of Zofri. Large salt lakes abound in the desert, which occupies the central valley right through to the *altiplano*.

Indian culture

In the *altiplano* is some of the most striking Andean scenery: active volcanoes and herds of *vicuñas* and *llamas* can be seen. This is the home of the stoic but proud Aymará tribes who live in their adobe cottages in the same way as their forebears did during the time of the Inca reign. These mountain villages come to life during the celebration of the patron saints' *fiestas*, which draw large crowds. These religious festivals are a mixture of Christian and pagan beliefs.

Many of the picturesque *altiplano* churches are hundreds of years old, and have been declared *monumentos nacionales*; the best examples are at **Parinacota** (reached from Arica), **Isluga** (from Iquique, difficult), and **Matilla** (from Iquique).

The coastal valleys have a large number of rock paintings left behind by the early aboriginal settlers who lived here 7000 years ago. Many archeological artifacts are in the museums in Azapa and Iquique, but many smaller collections exist in remote villages, usually collected by the local priest.

National parks

To preserve the habitat of many endangered species and to protect the flora and scenic areas, several national parks and wildlife sanctuaries have been created — see page 27.

Sport

Fishing, sailing and skin-diving along the many beaches stretching between the **Río Loa** and the Peruvian border are possible all year round. The beaches are virtually unspoilt by mass tourism: the only drawback is the lack of drinking water.

Roads

The coastal towns such as Arica, Iquique and the central desert *pampas* are easily accessible, as they are linked by the excellent Panamericana. However, side roads branching into the Cordillera are mostly dirt. The only exception is RI 11 from Arica to Tambo Quemado on the Bolivian border which is being substantially upgraded.

There are reasonable roads to Pica via La Tirana, from Pozo Almonte to Mamiña and from Huara to the Huasquiña turnoff; the remaining roads leading into the *cordillera* are only passable by four-wheel drive vehicles.

Don't miss

☞ Parque Nacional Lauca
☞ Arica

Worth a visit

☞ Parque Nacional Volcán Isluga
☞ Reserva Nacional Pampa de Tamarugal witht he Petroglyphs
☞ Iquique

Worth a detour

☞ Putre
☞ The scenic route from Arica to Lago Chungará

Of interest

☞ Pica
☞ Mamiña
☞ The scenic route along the coast from Iquique to Antofagasta
☞ The rail journey from Arica to the Bolivian border at Visviri

Distances

From Arica

*   Belén: 143 km east
*   Codpa: 113 km south-east
*   Iquique: 312 km south
*   Lago Chungará: 205 km north-east
*   Parque Nacional Lauca: 155 km north-east
*   Parinacota: 185 km north-east
*   Putre: 145 km north-east
*   Socoroma: 125 km north east
*   Tacna: 58 km north
*   Tambo de Zapahuira: 110 km east
*   Visviri: 273 km north-east

From Iquique

*   Rock paintings of Pintado: 96 km south-east
*   Huara: 75 km north-east
*   Humberstone: 47 km east
*   Oases of Pica and Mantilla: 114 km south-east
*   Parque Nacional Volcán Isluga: 230 km north-east
*   Pozo Almonte: 52 km south-east
*   Termas de Mamiña: 125 km east

ARICA

Area code: 080
Population: 150 000
Altitude: Sea level
Distance from Santiago: 2050 km north on the Panamericana

Arica, Chile's northernmost city, is known as "the town of eternal spring", because it never rains and the temperature throughout the year is 25°C (77°F). The sea temperature averages 20°C (68°F) throughout the year.

Its natural harbor became the port of call for many ships bringing goods for Bolivia and shipping out the region's products. It was founded in 1565, when a *corregidor* was appointed. In 1570 it was named Villa San Marcos de Arica.

During the Spanish era Arica was raided by pirates and suffered many disasters. For many years it was the capital of this region. Frequent outbreaks of malaria and yellow fever made it a hell-hole until the nineteenth century, and eventually the capital was moved to Tarapacá.

However, thanks to modern medicine, Arica has rid itself of these scourges, and since 1950 the city has grown rapidly.

Arica and its better-class suburb of **Azapa** have been transformed into a modern city, with green parks and wide palm-lined avenues. It is an important port; goods into and out of Bolivia are shipped to Arica and from there to Bolivia or their final destination. The beaches extend north to the Peruvian border, and there are beaches near the southern part of town past the Morro Rock.

In the evening the modern casino invites you to a game of roulette, blackjack and the usual poker machines; it is open all year round. Besides, the town has a variety of historical places bearing witness to its often turbulent history.

In the city center is the Plaza de Armas, with its steel church built by Gustave Eiffel, consecrated in 1876, only a couple of years before the battle of the Morro de Arica.The most conspicuous landmark is the Morro, a 150 m rock dominating the town; it has been declared a *monumento nacional* because of the role it played in the Battle of the Pacific. Remains of the Peruvian fortifications still abound on the Morro, and on top is the Museo de Armas, containing memorabilia of the War of the Pacific.

Only a short distance east of the town center, at the beginning of the Azapa valley, is the plush suburb of

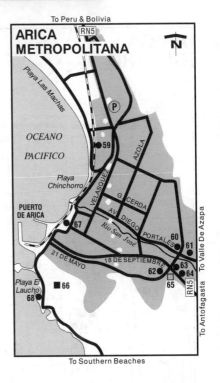

To Peru & Bolivia

ARICA METROPOLITANA

OCEANO PACIFICO

Playa Las Machas

Playa Chinchorro

PUERTO DE ARICA

Playa El Laucho

To Southern Beaches

To Antofagasta

To Valle De Azapa

Key to map

● **Accommodation**

59	Hotel Aldea Polinésica
60	Hostería Los Híbiscus
61	Hotel Saint Georgette
62	Motel Carlos III
63	Motel Saucache
64	Hostería Azapa Inn
68	Hostería Arica

⊙ **Entertainment**

67	Casino de Arica

■ **Sights**

65	Poblado Artesanal
66	Museo de Armas El Morro

Arica

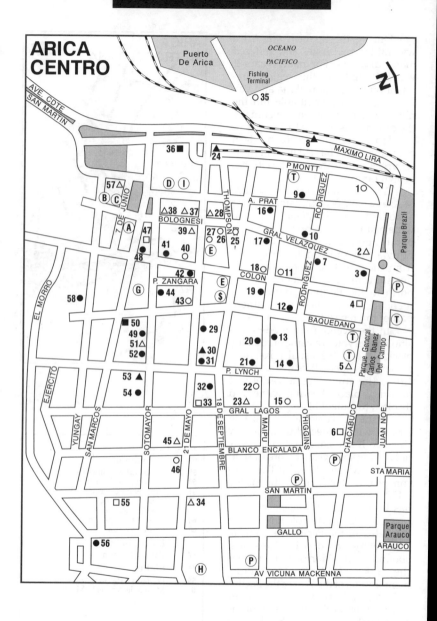

ARICA CENTRO

Puerto De Arica

OCEANO PACIFICO

Fishing Terminal

○ 35

AVE. CDTE SAN MARTIN

MAXIMO LIRA

▲ 8

36 ■

▲ 24

P MONTT

Ⓣ

9 ●

RODRIGUEZ

1 ○

57 △

Ⓑ Ⓒ

Ⓓ Ⓘ

A. PRAT

16 ●

10 ●

7 DE JUNIO

Ⓐ

47 □

48 ●

△ 38 △ 37

BOLOGNESI

39 △

41 ●   40 ○

THOMPSON

△ 28

27 ○ 26 ○

25

Ⓔ

GRAL VELAZQUEZ

17 ●

2 △

7 ●

3 ●

EL MORRO

58 ●

42 ●

P. ZANGARA

44 ●

43 ○

Ⓖ

Ⓔ

Ⓢ

COLON

18 ○

19 ●

12 ●

○ 11

RODRIGUEZ

4 □

Ⓟ

Ⓣ

BAQUEDANO

50 ■

49 ●

51 △

52 ●

29 ●

▲ 30

31 ●

20 ●

● 13

21 ●   14 ●

Ⓣ

5 △

Ⓣ

Parque General Carlos Ibañez Del Campo

EJERCITO

53 ▲

54 ●

P. LYNCH

32 ●

□ 33

22 ○

23 △   15 ○

GRAL LAGOS

YUNGAY

SAN MARCOS

SOTOMAYOR

2° DE MAYO

18 DE SEPTIEMBRE

MAIPU

O'HIGGINS

CHACABUCO

JUAN NOE

45 △

46 ○

BLANCO ENCALADA

6 □

Ⓟ

Ⓟ

STA MARIA

SAN MARTIN

□ 55

△ 34

GALLO

Parque Arauco

ARAUCO

56 ●

Ⓗ

Ⓟ

AV VICUNA MACKENNA

Parque Brazil

TARAPACÁ

Key to map

A	Iglesia San Marcos
B	Gobernación Provincial (Government)
C	Municipalidad (Town hall)
D	Post office and telex
E	Telephone
G	Mercado Municipal (Market)
H	Hospital
I	Tourist information
P	Gas stations
$	Money exchange
T	Bus terminals

● Accommodation

3	Hotel del Rey Robert
7	Residencial Chillán
9	Residencial Las Parinas
10	Residencial Velásquez
12	Residencial Madrid
13	Residencial Maipú
14	Residencial Chungará
16	Hotel Amadis
17	Hotel Concorde
19	Hotel Aragón
20	Residencial Blanquita
21	Hotel Lynch
29	Hotel Central
31	Residencial 21 de Mayo
32	Residencial El Hostal
41	Residencial Leiva
42	Hotel King
44	Hotel San Marcos
48	Hotel Plaza
49	Residencial Sotomayor
52	Hotel Diego de Almagro
54	Hotel Tacora
56	Residencial Los Portales
58	Hotel Savona

○ Eating out

1	Restaurant Caribe
11	Restaurant Bavaria
15	Restaurant Kong Chau
18	Restaurant El Rey del Marisco
22	Restaurant Shanghai
25	Restaurant Schop 18
26	Restaurant Centro Schop
27	Café Americano
35	Restaurant Acuario
40	Restaurant La Bomba
43	Restaurant Casanova
46	Restaurant Los Aleros de 21

△ Tour operators and car rental

2	Avis Rent a Car
5	Automóvil Club de Chile
23	American Rent a Car
28	Transtours
34	Viva Rent a Car
37	Kijo Tour
38	Turismo Payachatas
39	Jurasi Tour
45	Budget Rent a Car
51	Huasquitur

▲ Airline offices and trains

8	Trains to Tacna (Peru)
24	Trains to La Paz (Bolivia)
30	LADECO
53	Lloyd Aereo Boliviano
57	LAN Chile

■ Sights

36	Casa de la Cultura
50	Teatro Municipal

□ Services

4	Centro Comercial Colón
6	Supermercado La Sureña
33	Bolivian consulate
47	CONAF
55	Peruvian consulate

San Miguel de Azapa. Frequent public buses ply between San Miguel de Azapa and the city center, and many good hotels and motels are situated here. There is also the splendid Museo Arqueológico de San Miguel de Azapa, with a collection of archeological artifacts and mummies dating back thousands of years. Most of the pieces on exhibit were found in and around Arica, particularly in the

Valle de Río Lluta, about 5 km north of Arica.

For information on Azapa, see the separate entry beginning on page 41.

The main tourist season runs from December 1 to March 14, when prices tend to increase sharply.

The residents' favorite seafood consists of albacore tuna, sole and sea urchin. In general it is strongly influenced by its northern neighbor Peru, of which it was for centuries a part. ☞

To the north is the long beach of Las Machas (with *colectivos*, swimming, fishing, camping, kiosks, seabird-watching), which stretches to the mouth of the **Río Lluta**. Closer to town is Playa Chinchorro. Note that the northern beaches between the airport and the border are off limits. There is excellent fishing from the many beaches and the rocky outcrops that separate them.

⊞ Festivals
- January: Carnaval Ariqueño
- June 29: San Pedro
- July 27–28: La Tirana Chica
- October: Virgen de las Penas, **Livircar**

ⓘ Tourist information
- CONAF, Sotomayor 216, upstairs ☏ 231559
- Sernatur, Prat 375, upstairs ☏ 232101, ☞ fax 244506

⊞ Eating out
See also "Eating out" in Azapa on page 42.

Cafeterías
- Café Americano
- Di Mango, 21 de Mayo 425

Pizzerías
- Pizza Hut, Centro Comercial Colón, Chacabuco 300 $Z

Restaurants
- Acuario, Maximo Lira, in fishing terminal $Z. Seafood
- Aduana, Baquedano 373, in Edificio Alborada $Z. Seafood
- Bavaria, Colón 611 $Y. *Parillada*
- Cantaverdi, Diego Portales 840
- Caribe
☞ - Casanova, Baquedano 397, upstairs $Y. International cuisine
- Centro Schop
- Chifa Kau-Chea, Prat 466 $Z. Chinese cuisine
- Club de Yates, Isla Alacrán
☞ - Da Aurelio, Baquedano 369 $Y. Italian cuisine
☞ - El Arriero, 21 de Mayo 285 $Y. Seafood and *parillada*

- El Rey del Marisco
☞ - Exquisito, 21 de Mayo 170 $X
- Illimani, San Marcos 374
- Kon Chau, General Lagos 659 $Z. Chinese cuisine
- La Bomba
- Los Aleros de 21, 21 de Mayo 736 $Z. Chilean cuisine
- Natura, Bolognesi 367, upstairs $Z. Vegetarian
- Onda, Comandante San Martín 55 $Z. Chinese cuisine
- Primera Compañía de Bomberos, Colón 357 $Z
- Shanghai, Maipú 534 $Z. Chinese cuisine
- Suceso Inn, 18 de Septiembre 250

Salon de Té
- Amazonas, Bolognesi 341 $Z

Schoperías
☞ - Schop 18, 18 de Septiembre 240 $Z
☞ - Schop 21, 21 de Mayo 311 $Z

Eating out along the Costanera Sur
- Maracuya, Avenida Costanera Sur 0321. Seafood and steaks

ⓣ Entertainment

Night clubs
- Casino de Arica, Avenida General Velázquez 955 $X. Open all year round. Good dining-room, bars and disco with shows (roulette, baccarat, blackjack, poker machines). Admission. $3.00. Open 2100–0330

Discos
- El Fascinador, Avenida Comandante San Martín 1010
- El Tambo, Huaiies 2825 $Y. Chilean cuisine and show weekends
- Habana, Avenida Comandante San Martín 320

⊞ Post and telegraph

Post office
- Correos de Chile, Arturo Prat 305

Telephones
- Centro de Llamados CTC, Colón 211, fax 231702
- CTC, 21 de Mayo 217
- ENTEL Chile (international calls) Baquedano 388

⊟ Accommodation in Arica

See also "Accommodation" in Azapa on page 42.

Apart hotels
- Star Apart, Avenida Consistorial corner of R. Carnicer
  ℂ 214691
  Fax 211107

Hosterías
★★★★Arica, Comandante San Martín 599 ℂ 254540/231201 $E ⋮⋮

Hotels

★★★El Paso, Velásquez 1109	ACDEFGHIJKLMNPRS$TUZ			
		ℂ 231965	$E	⋮⋮
Car rental, tennis, 44 rooms				
★★★San Marcos, Rafael Sotomayor 367	ADEGHIJKLP$TU	ℂ 232149	$H	⋮⋮
34 rooms, fax 251815				
• Amadis, A. Prat 588		ℂ 232994	$G	⋮⋮
• Aragón, Maipú 344	ACDEHIJKPS$TU	ℂ 252088 fax	$G	⋮⋮
36 rooms				
• Central, 21 de Mayo 425	ACDEFGHIJKLMPS$TUXZ			
•		ℂ 252575	$F	⋮⋮
Car rental, fax 251168				
• Concorde, General Velásquez 580		ℂ 252000	$H	⋮⋮
• Del Rey Robert, Velásquez 792		ℂ 231327	$E	⋮⋮
• Diego de Almagro, Sotomayor 490	ADEFHIJKLP$TUZ	ℂ 224444	$H	⋮⋮
30 rooms				
• King, Colón 376	AEGIJKLPTU	ℂ 232094/5	$G	⋮⋮
Fax 251124				
• Lynch, Patricio Lynch 589	ADEHIJLP$TUZ	ℂ 231581	$H	⋮⋮
• Plaza Colón, San Marcos 261	APS	ℂ 231244	$H	⋮⋮
• Savona, Yungay 380	ADEFGHIJKLMP$TU	ℂ 231000	$H	⋮⋮
Fax 231606				
• Tacora, Sotomayor 540	ADEGHIJKLPU	ℂ 251240	$H	⋮⋮
Shared bathroom cheaper				

Residenciales

• Atenas, Colón 678	AEIJ	ℂ 251336	$I	⋮
• Blanquita, Maipú 472	AHIJU	ℂ 232064	$J	⋮⋮
• Cantón, Maipú 608	AEHIJU	ℂ 231379	$I	⋮
• Caracas, Sotomayor 867	APS	ℂ 253688	$H	⋮⋮
• Chillán, General Velásquez 719		ℂ 251677	$I	⋮⋮
• Chungará, Patricio Lynch 675	ADEGHIJLM$U	ℂ 231677	$H	⋮⋮
12 rooms				
• Concepción, O'Higgins 1069		ℂ 254815		
• Durán, Maipú 25	AP	ℂ 252975	$I	⋮⋮
• Ecuador, Juan Noe 989	AP	ℂ 251573	$H	⋮⋮
• El Hostal, 18 de Septiembre 524	AEJPS	ℂ 251727	$H	⋮⋮
• Las Condes, Vicuña Mackenna 628	APS	ℂ 251583	$I	⋮
• Las Parinas, Arturo Prat 541	AP	ℂ 231985	$I	⋮
• Leiva, Colón 347	ADFHIJU	ℂ 232008	$J	⋮⋮
• Los Portales, A. Gallo 228		ℂ 226816		
• Maipú, Maipú 443			$J	⋮⋮
Backpackers only				
• Madrid, Baquedano 685	AHIJ	ℂ 231479	$J	⋮⋮
• Patricia, Maipú 269	AEFGJ		$I	⋮

Accommodation in Arica — continued

• Sotomayor, Sotomayor 442	AHJU	(252336	$I	i	
• Stagnaro, Arturo Gallo 294 Shared bathroom cheaper	AJPS	(231254	$I	ii	
• Sur (formerly Nuñez), Maipú 516 Backpackers only	A	(252457	$I	i	
• Universo, Colón 662 Backpackers	AJP	(232652	$J	ii	
• Valencia, General Velásquez 719		(233479			
• 21 de Mayo, 21 de Mayo 487 Back packers	AEIJL		$I	ii	
• Velásquez, General Velásquez 669	AJL	(231989	$I	ii	
• Venecia, Baquedano 739 Backpackers	AI	(252877	$I	ii	

Accommodation in Balneario Chinchorro

Hotels
• Aldea Polinésica, Avenida Las Dunas   (211382

$ Financial
• Cambio Marta Daguer, 18 de Septiembre 330 (231373
• Cambio Yanulaque, 21 de Mayo 175 (232839 fax 2523956
• Fincard, 21 de Mayo 252 (252015. Cash advances against Visa and Mastercard

🚻 Services and facilities

Hospital
• Hospital Dr Juan Noe, 18 de Septiembre 1000 (229200

Laundry
• Lavandería La Moderna, 18 de Septiembre 457

Pharmacy
• Farmacia 18, 18 de Septiembre 225

Photographic supplies
• Kodak Express, 21 de Mayo 385

Supermarkets
• Supermercado La Sureña, Chacabuco 560

▣ Visas, passports
• Departamento Extranjería, 7 de Junio 188, upstairs (231397. Chilean visa extension
• Bolivia: Consulado General de Bolivia, 21 de Mayo 575 (231030
• Peru: Consulado del Perú, San Martín 220, (231020

⌧ Border crossings
Passport control when going into Peru is 6 km north of town at Chacalluta, just north of Chacalluta airport.
When traveling by train to Tacna, passport control is at the train station.

🚌 Motoring services
For gas stations, see city map.

Car rental
• American (Allen) RentaCar, General Lagos 559 (252334 fax 252600
• Automóvil Club de Chile, Chacabuco 460 (232780
• Avis Rent a Car, Chacabuco 180 (232210
• Budget Rent a Car, 21 de Mayo 650 (252978
• Hertz Rent a Car, Hotel El Paso, General Velázquez 1109 (231487
• Viva Rent a Car, 21 de Mayo 821 (251121, fax 251409

🚆 Trains

Tacna (Peru)
• Maximo Lira 889 (231115. Departs 1200 and 1800 Mon–Sat; duration1½ hrs

La Paz (Bolivia)
• 21 de Mayo 51 (224570/231786. Fares: Pullman $28.80, *Especial* $21.70; departs midnight, every 2nd and 4th

✈ Air services from Arica

Companies
* LADECO, 21 de Mayo 443 ☎ 252025
* LAN Chile, 7 de Junio 148, office 107 ☎ 214430 fax 252600
* Lloyd Aereo Boliviano (LAB), P.Lynch 298 near Sotomayor ☎ 251919, fax 251821
* National Airlines, 21 de Mayo 417 ☎250001 fax 250003

Flights

Destination	Fare	Services	Duration	Airlines
• Antofagasta	$71.00	1–2 services daily	1½ hrs	LAN Chile, LADECO
• El Salvador	$93.00			
• Iquique	$28.00	1–2 services daily	½ hr	LAN Chile, LADECO
• La Paz (Bolivia)	$89.00	Tues, Thur, Sat	1 hr	Lloyd Aereo Boliviano
• Santiago	$154.00	2–4 services daily	3½ hrs	LAN Chile, LADECO

Tues in the month. A cold and uncomfortable 20-hour journey — avoid it
* *Ferrobus* ☎ 232844. Fare $59.00 including meals; departs 0930 Tues and Sat; duration 10 hrs
* *Automotor* ☎ 231453. Fare $55.00; departs Tues, Thurs, and Sat at 10.30; duration 10 hrs. Tickets available from Agencia Payachatas

⊛ Sport
* Club Aéreo de Arica, Cancha El Buitre ☎ 241418

Beaches
Most of the beaches descend gradually into the water, although the beaches at the southern end have some rocky outcrops bordering the sea. You can enjoy a swim here at any time of the year. The beaches are clean and there is little pollution. The best beaches starting 2 km to the south are listed here from north to south. Access is by regular buses on a paved road. Swimming, fishing, showers. Along the beaches are restaurants discos and camping spots.
* Playa La Lisera: 2 km south of town on Avenida Costanera Sur Comandante San Martín, a good paved road. The beach is curved and good for swimming and diving; it is the best protected of all the beaches. The sand is pebbly and white. Changing cabins, showers, gardens and two restaurants. Half-day excursion
* Playa Brava: Reached by continuing further south on the Avenida

Costanera Sur, has fine white sand. Half-day excursion
* Playa Arenillas Negras: 3 km from town, directly beneath El Morro, reached on Avenida Costanera Sur. Not a really safe beach; half-day excursion
* Playa Corazones: 12 km south of town on the Costanera Sur. The beach is lined with large natural boulders. Camping, but bring your own water. Protected for swimming, fishing. Half-day excursion

📷 Sightseeing
To get to know the city, I suggest a two-hour tour, starting from the Plaza de Armas. On the Plaza is the Catedral San Marcos; nearby is Parque Baquedano with the old *Aduana* (Customs) building, now a *monumento nacional*. Quite interesting also is the fishing harbor. Further north is the Fería Maximo Lira with crowds of Peruvians selling their goods; on Sundays a *fería turístico* is held here. Passing Parque Brasil and continuing further north is the Casino de Arica, and further on the University's Campus Velázquez. It is worth making a visit to the top of El Morro. Below the Morro, the Avenida Comandante San Martín, also known as Avenida Costanera, follows the seaside south. At the far southern end (away from the beaches) are the fish-processing plants.
* Iglesia San Marcos: Designed by Gustave Eiffel and completed in 1875. It is

Arica

🚌 Buses from Arica

The central municipal bus terminal is in Parque Baquedano, on the corner of San Marcos and Maximo Lira.
Buses No. 5 and 7 go south to the Balneario Arenillas Negras (10 minutes) and to a few nightclubs built against the El Morro mountain.
Colectivos to Azapa leave from the corner of General Lagos and Maipú.

Companies operating from the interregional bus terminal
This terminal is on Diego Portales, near the corner of Avenida Santa María.
* A27   Buses Cuevas y González, office 3 (241090
* A35   Buses Geminis, office 25 (241647
* A42   Buses Carmelita, office 2 (241591
* A67   Buses Ramos Cholele, Local 5 (221029,
* A77   TAL-Los Diamantes de Elqui
* A78   Buses Tramaca, office 9 (241198 fax 222586
* A83   Buses Zambrano Hermanos, office 12 (241587
* A86   Chile Bus, Oficina 14 (222217 fax 221226
* A94   Cooperativa Perú
* A106 Buses Fenix Pullman Norte, office 15 (222457
* A110 Flecha Dorada, office 8 (241099
* A112 Flota Barrios
* A128 Pullman Bus Fichtur, office 11 (241972
* A147 Tepsa
* A156 Turis Auto
* A158 Turis Taxis

Companies with their own bus terminal
* A61   Empresa La Paloma (also called Francisco Paco), corner of G. Riesco and Tucapel
        Buses leave for Putre, Chapiquiña, and the *altiplano*
* A151 Empresa de Transportes Martínez, Pedro Montt 622
        Services to Visviri

Companies providing international services
* A13   Buses Adsublata, Terminal de Buses, Local 19 (241972
        Buses run daily every 2 hrs
* A49   Empresa de Transportes Litoral, Chacabuco 454
        Services to La Paz
* A143 Taxis Chile Lintur, Baquedano 789 corner of Chacabuco
        (232156/157/232048
        Buses leave daily every hour from 0800
* A144 Taxis Chasquitur, Juan Noe 321 (231376
        Buses leave daily every hour from 0800
* A145 Taxis San Remo, Chacabuco 320 (251925
        Buses leave daily every hour from 0800

Services

Destination	Fare	Services	Duration	Companies
• Antofagasta	$15.20	13 services daily		A27, A35, A78, A83, A86, A106, A110, A112
• Belén	$ 4.10			A61
• Calama	$11.40	7 services daily	10½ hrs	A27, A78, A112
Sleeper	$13.70	1 service daily	10½ hrs	A35
• Chañaral	$26.50	9 services daily		A83, A86, A106, A110, A112
• Chapiqueña	$ 3.60			A61
• Chuquicamata	$11.40	2 services daily		A78, A86

Buses from Arica — continued

Destination	Fare	Services	Duration	Companies
• Coquimbo	$36.00	5 services daily		A27, A86, A110
• Copiapó	$23.20	11 services daily		A42, A67, A78, A83, A86, A106, A110, A112
• Iquique	$9.50			A156, A158
	$5.70	15 services daily		A27, A42, A67, A83
• La Calera	$45.50	3 services daily		A83, A110, A112
• La Paz (Bolivia)	$27.40			A49
• La Serena	$36.00	21 services daily		A27, A42, A78, A83, A86, A106, A110, A112, A77
Sleeper	$60.70	1 service daily	24½ hrs	A128
• Los Vilos	$39.80			A110, A112
• María Elena	$11.50	2 services daily	7½ hrs	A78, A112
• Ovalle	$38.00	5 services daily		A27, A78, A83, A110
• Pedro de Valdivia	$11.50			A112
Sleeper	$45.50	13 services daily		A27, A67, A78, A83, A86, A106, A110, A147
• Putre	$ 2.70	Tues & Fri	5 hrs	A61
• Santiago	$68.30	2 services daily		A67, A128
• Socoroma	$ 2.80			A61
• Tacna (Peru)	$ 7.60	12 services daily	2 hrs	A13, A67, A94, A143, A144
	$19.00		2 hrs	A145
• Tocopilla	$17.00	3 services daily		A110, A112
• Vallenar	$33.40	9 services daily		A83, A86, A106, A110, A112
• Valparaíso	$45.50	services daily	30 hrs	A83, A86, A106, A112
• Viña del Mar	$45.50	8 services daily	29 hrs	A83, A86, A112, A106
• Visviri		3 services weekly		A151
• Zapahuira	$ 2.80	Tues & Fri	2 hrs	A61

made of iron, with an octagonal tower.

- Isla Alacrán: Now connected with the mainland. A short walk from Iglesia San Marcos. Site of Spanish fortifications. Here is also the Club de Deportes Náuticos (Water Sports Club).
- Morro de Arica: A mountain outcrop of some 150 m, the landmark of the city. On top is the Museo de Armas which commemorates the fierce fighting that took place here during the War of the Pacific in 1880. The museum exhibits weapons used by Chilean and Peruvian troops. From the top are sweeping views over the town, the sea, the Valle de Azapa, and right up to the Peruvian border. There is a footpath leading up from Calle Colón.

✦ Excursions

Tour operators
- Agencia de Viajes Globotour, 21 de Mayo 260 ☎ 232909, fax 231085
- Agencia de Viajes Huasquitur, Sotomayor 470 ☎ 223875
- Agencia de Viajes Jurasi, Bolognesi 360A ☎ 251696/251096
- Kijo Tour, Bolognesi 357 ☎ 232245. Ecotourism
- Agencia de Viajes Turismo Payachatas, Sotomayor 199 ☎ 251514. Organizes trips in conjunction with Azapa Inn. Also sells *automotor* tickets to La Paz
- Transtours, Bolognesi 421 ☎ 253927, fax 251675

Excursions from Arica
- **Valle de Azapa**: Regular municipal buses run as far as **Ausipar**. Visit the

archeological museum. The rim of the valley is studded with pre-Hispanic archeological sites. Half-day excursion.

- **Valle de Río Lluta**: Regular municipal buses run as far as **Poconchile**. A taxi costs $20. The rock carvings are right at the entrance to the valley. Visit also the colonial churches in Poconchile (KM 37) and Molinos (KM 57). The valley starts 10 km north of town and finishes in the *pre-Cordillera*. The drive is mostly through desert. It becomes somewhat greener once you turn into the valley, but the mountains on either side are bare of all vegetation. Half-day excursion.

Trips to the *altiplano*
These trips bring you from the hot coastal desert through the *pre-Cordillera* into the cold *altiplano*. On the way up you pass some pre-Colombian *pukarás* and quaint small Spanish towns with picturesque *altiplano* churches. Past Putre the Parque Nacional Lauca starts, with its breathtaking views of volcanoes and herds of *vicuñas* which have been re-established here. On the *salares* are huge flamingo colonies.

- **Putre** bus trip: Bus services run regularly to Putre. Bolivian buses going to La Paz via Putre often charge the full fare to La Paz even if you get off before the border. The mountains near the coast are covered with huge sand dunes, and the road has to be cleared after dust storms. The bus climbs up the Valle de Río Lluta — see above. Once the sand dunes in the coastal valley and the *pre-Cordillera* are left behind, sparse grass gradually appears as you climb higher. Near the **Pukará de Copaquilla**, the first terraces appear, going back to pre-Hispanic times. Visit the *pukará* at **Copaquilla**, at 2800 m, and the Inca *tambo* at **Zapahuira**. From the *pukará* there are sweeping views over the valley. The drive through the **Quebrada de Taichué**, where you may encounter the first *vicuñas* and *alpacas*, is very scenic. Between **Zapahuira** and Putre are terraces built on the mountain slopes in pre-Hispanic times and still in use. **Putre** has a colonial church

dating back to the 17th century. See entry for Putre on page 69.
- **Parque Nacional Lauca**: A 10-hour 400-km day trip, through a tour operator. See the entry for the park on page 64.
- Two-day trip into the *altiplano* with a tour operator: Includes **Parque Nacional Lauca** and **Lago Chungará**. 400 km, $180. First day: depart from the Azapa Inn for Parque Nacional Lauca and Lago Chungará, stay overnight in Hostería Las Vicuñas in **Putre**. Second day: short trip through the *altiplano* and return in the afternoon to Azapa.
- Three-day trip into the *altiplano* with a tour operator: 750 km, $210. The first day is the same as two-day trip. Second day: visit the **Reserva Nacional Las Vicuñas**, **Salar de Surire** and stay overnight in a CONAF shelter (bring your own sleeping bag). Third day: **Parque Nacional Volcán Isluga**, thermal spa at **Chusmiza** and return to Azapa. See also the entries for Reserva Nacional Las Vicuñas (page 72), Parque Nacional Volcán Isluga (page 65), and Chusmiza (page 45).
- **Iquique**, Five-day round trip through the *altiplano* in your own four-wheel drive vehicle. This will give you a chance to explore parts of the national parks and nature reserves at your leisure. Take gas for at least 500 km. You must bring your own sleeping bag, warm clothes (it gets bitterly cold at night), a tent and enough food for five days, as between Putre and Chusmiza there is no accommodation. Check with CONAF in Arica which *refugios* in the Parque Nacional Lauca are open for tourists. Stay the first night in Putre (see "Accommodation" in Putre on page 71), or the CONAF *refugio* in the **Parque Nacional Lauca**. The following day try to reach the small *altiplano* village of **Guallatiri**, in the shade of the **Volcán Guallatiri**, in the **Reserva Nacional Las Vicuñas**. On the third day reach **Chilcaya** on the **Salar de Surire**. From **Chilcaya** there is a track leading down from the *altiplano* to **Belén** via **Itisa** and **Timalacha**. If you feel that you cannot make it to **Colchané**, it is better to return to **Putre**.

From **Colchané** there are trucks going at least once a week down to **Huara** (on the Carretera Panamericana), or even to **Iquique**. Relax at Chusmiza at the hot bath before returning to the Panamericana. This trip is only for the hardy and intrepid outdoor enthusiast. See also the entries for Iquique (page 48), Parque Nacional Lauca (page 64), Reserva Nacional Las Vicuñas (page 72) Belén (page 43), Colchané (page 46), Putre (page 69), and Huara (under "Exursions" from Iquique on page 57).

- **Tambo Quemado** across the border in Bolivia: 206 km. Can be made as an excursion on a local bus.
- **La Paz** in Bolivia via Tambo Quemado: A grueling 30-hour bus trip. From Arica to La Paz it is better by train.
- **Chapiquiña**, **Belén** and **Tignamar**: This is a do-it-yourself trip into the *pre-Cordillera* to some pre-hispanic Aymará villages and archeological sites. Buses La Paloma (also known as Francisco Paco) run buses there twice weekly. Accommodation is not available, so take your sleeping bag. Approximately 10 km before **Zapahuira** is the turnoff from the carretera internacional south to Chapiquiña, off the highway. Nearby is a hydro-electric power station. Continuing south along the track you come to Belén, founded by the Spaniards in 1625 and located in the *pre-Cordillera* 148 km east from Arica. See also the entry for Belén on page 43.

- **Visviri**: 278 km north-east, at an altitude of 4030 m. It is the northernmost settlement in Chile, where the borders of Chile, Bolivia, and Peru meet. Only 3 km across the border in Bolivia is Charaña, where Bolivian customs officials approve entry visas. Its only importance is as a border crossing point to and from Bolivia for train and bus travelers. The population is completely Aymará, and many have kinsfolk in neighboring Peru and Bolivia. There are no hotels; the only accommodation is in private homes. When you are entering Chile at this point, I suggest you wait until Arica before changing money. In Visviri itself, people accept both Bolivian and Chilean *pesos*. This area is only for the seasoned mountain hiker who is prepared to rough it with tent and sleeping bag. You may cross just for the day to Charaña in Bolivia to visit the colorful Aymará market without going through the normal passport formalities. If you are arriving by bus from Arica and wish to continue to La Paz, there are buses from Charaña (in Bolivia) on Wed and Sat. Taking the bus from Arica to Visviri and then crossing the border and taking a bus from Charaña to La Paz is cheaper than the direct Arica–La Paz bus. However, be prepared for a cold wait. The buses leave Arica on Tues and Fri to connect with the bus across the border. There are also frequent *colectivo* services from Parinacota to Visivir. Trains to La Paz in Bolivia and Arica run twice a week; they are always late — take the *ferrobus* instead.

AZAPA

Distance from Arica: 6 km east

San Miguel de Azapa, its full name, is a better-class suburb of Arica, located in a rural setting. Because of its excellent facilities, some of the best hotels, eating places and discos are located here, so we have treated it separately.

The Valle de Azapa begins 2 km outside Arica. Regular *colectivo* services ply between Azapa and Arica. It is a fertile but narrow valley watered by the **Río San José**, which is usually dry near the coast. In the valley, irri-

TARAPACÁ

⊟ Accommodation in Azapa

See also "Accommodation" in Arica on page 35.

Hotels
- Azapa Inn, Guillermo Sánchez 660   ABCDEFGHIKLMPRS$TUXZ   ℂ 244537 $C-E⚋
  Tennis, car rental, golf. Special 3-day weekend rates
- Los Hibiscos, Capitán Avalos 2041   ABCDEFGHIJKLPRTUXZ   ℂ 222289 $F ⚋
  Tennis, car rental. 20 rooms
- Saint Georgette, Diego Portales 3221 KM 1   ADFMRUXZ   ℂ 221914/223513 $D ⚋
  Cabins $F ⚋. Piano bar, discos for teens and adults, self-serve dining room, squash court, travel agency, sauna, gymnasium
- Motel Saucache, Guillermo Sánchez 27   ABCHIKPT   ℂ 241458 $G ⚋
- Motel Carlos III, 18 de Septiembre 2463   ABP   ℂ 221149 $G ⚋

gation allows the growing of citrus and olives all year round. Further up the mountain the Azapa valley becomes a canyon. The Río San José has its source high up in the *sierra* in **Laguna Parinacota**; the road there is sealed as far as **Sobraya**.

Rock carvings from between 1000 and 1400 AD in the Azapa valley can be seen on Cerro Sombrero and Alto Ramírez. They are unique, and can only be compared with those in the south- western US and Nazca.

⚇ Festivals
- September 29: San Miguel

⚇ Eating out

Restaurants
- Arica de Antaño, KM 8 Alto Ramírez. Weekends only
- Club de Huasos, KM 3.5. Sunday only
- El Parrón, KM 1. *Parillada*
- Tourist Ranch, Pago de Gómez, KM 4

⚇ Entertainment

Discos
- Fejoteca Swing, Azapa KM 3.5
- Sun Set, Azapa KM 3.5

⚇ Buses
- Arica: Fare $0.40 on a *colectivo*

⚇ Shopping
- Poblado Artesanal, Hualles 2025, on the southern exit road in Calle Hualles on Río San José. This is a small tourist complex constructed in the style of the Chilean *altiplano* villages. Here the artisans live and work. There is a small church, restaurant and a school for artisans

⚇ Sightseeing
- Museo Arqueológico: Azapa KM 13 ℂ 224248. Open Tues–Sun 1000–1800. The archeological collection is most impressive, and the 20 000 artifacts include some dating back to 800 BC. It provides a good overview of the people who lived in the region in pre-Hispanic days. Admission: $1.00.

⚇ Excursions
The Valle de Azapa has been inhabited for thousands of years, and the early tribes have left many rock carvings and rock paintings in the valley. There are also a few pre-Colombian *pukarás* such as **Pukará San Lorenzo** overlooking San Miguel de Azapa. Most of them are situated along the rim of the *quebrada*.

BELÉN

Population: 120
Altitude: 3200 m
Distance from Arica: 143 km east on Ruta A-225 and RI 11

The picturesque little village of Belén in the *pre-Cordillera* is dominated by its ecclesiastical buildings. The mountains surrounding the town are completely bare. Very little rain falls, and the town depends on the water coming down from the *altiplano*. It is inhabited largely by people of Aymará descent, but was founded by the Spaniards early in the 17th century. The exceptional mildness of climate was the reason for its foundation, as the coast in colonial days was constantly afflicted by epidemics. The layout of the town betrays its hispanic origin: regular *manzanas* or street blocks and a central *plaza* built in tiers against the slope of the mountain. The small adobe houses look as if they are supporting each other.

In colonial days it was an important stop-over from Arica to the *altiplano*. The old Spanish trail via **Livircar** down through the **Valle de Azapa** to **Arica** is still used by the locals. Irrigation has brought fertility to the valley; an irrigation channel runs through the middle of the main street!

Nowadays Belén is off the beaten track, and very few tourists make it here. One reason is its lack of tourist facilities: for a start there is no accommodation, but the bus drivers can point you to a local family who will put you up for the night. In the river flats are plantings of eucalyptus trees. The road from the turnoff at **Zapahuira** runs for some time along the western limit of the **Parque Nacional Lauca**.

A visit to this area is ideal for those who are prepared to rough it and to visit an area outside the normal tourist circuit. The mountains to the east form a spectacular mountain barrier: **Cerro Chapiquiña**, **Cerro Belén**, and **Cerro de Anarabe** are all over 5000 m. The mountains to the west are not as high.

⚐ Festivals

Despite its small population, the town celebrates a large number of *fiestas* which attract many people from the *altiplano*. This is a very traditional place, and the *fiestas* mirror ancient pagan beliefs.
- February 2–3: Virgen de la Candelaria
- June 24: San Juan Bautista
- July 15–16: Virgen del Carmen
- July 25: San Santiago
- August 4: San Salvador
- October 1–7: Siembra de la Papa (potato planting festival)

🚌 Buses

If you are visiting the area, I suggest you take the Tuesday bus from Arica and return on Saturday. The road could be cut after sudden downpours in the *altiplano*, particularly in February.
- Arica: Fare $3.40; departs Wed, Sat; duration 5 hrs; Francisco Paco

📷 Sightseeing

- Iglesia Nuestra Señora de Belén: Built at the time the village was founded. Very small with thick walls and a belfry.
- Iglesia Nuestra Señora del Carmen: Built in the 18th century. The main entrance is in baroque style, otherwise the church is a typical *altiplano* church. Inside, an unusual feature is the spiral columns.

Belén

Excursions

- **Tignamar Viejo**: Old Tignamar, now abandoned. Situated 14 km south in the shade of **Cerro de Anarabe**. The attraction here is another *altiplano* church with a baroque portal and an altar made of rocks of various colors. Continuing further south, near the junction of **Río Tignamar** and **Río Saxamar**, you come upon **Pukará de Saxamar**, an archeological site with the remains of a fortified village and terraces built in the 12th century. Villagers gather here on August 30 to celebrate the fiesta of Santa Rosa.
- **Pachama**, 7 km north in the **Quebrada San Andrés** has a substantial 17th-century colonial church. It stands on a plaza encircled by adobe walls with an arched entrance; the belfry outside the enclosure is in the shape of a cupola. Pachama at first glance appears to be abandoned, as most of the houses are locked. But following *altiplano* custom, most of the villagers spend their time with the flocks in the pasture. Two *fiestas* are celebrated in Pachama which attract a large number of *altiplano* dwellers: June 29: San Pedro and November 30: San Andrés Trails lead north into the **Parque Nacional Lauca** and into the *altiplano* — be prepared for cold nights when camping out, and always carry water.

CAMIÑA

Population: 400
Altitude: 2400 m
Distances:
- From Arica: 272 km south on Ruta A-45 and Panamericana
- From Iquique: 204 km north-east on Ruta A-45, Panamericana and RN 16

Camiña was an important Indian settlement when the Spaniards arrived here. Located in the *pre-Cordillera* on Ruta A-45 (a dirt road), 67 km east of the Panamericana, Camiña is an oasis in the *pre-Cordillera* and very scenic. The turnoff is just before you descend into the **Quebrada de Tiviliche**.

The existence of a Catholic chapel was recorded as early as 1613. During colonial times it was the center of the *encomienda* of Camiña, which included the whole **Río Tana** valley right down to **Pisagua** on the coast and as far as **Isluga** on what is now the Bolivian border. It never acquired any importance, and remained an Aymará village throughout the colonial period as it never attracted sufficient Spanish settlers. The buildings are of adobe, and the present church was built in the 18th century — its doorway is most impressive.

For photographers, this is the best area to take photos of the contrast between the desert and the green belt running along the *quebrada*. There are tracks going further up the **Quebrada de Camiña** into the *altiplano* in the Parque Nacional Volcán Isluga, but you need a four-wheel drive vehicle.

Festivals

- July 3: Santo Tomás
- December 21: Santo Tomás, in the village of **Nama**

Accommodation

- Hospedaje with full board, but very basic. $J

Buses

Irregular bus services run to and from Iquique once a week in summer only.

Excursions

This is unknown Chile. Its main attractions are the rock paintings in the valleys, colonial churches in nearby village, the splendid pristine scenery, and the pre-Colombian irrigated terraced fields. Only for those who are not held back by a little discomfort.

CHUSMIZA

Altitude: 3500 m
Distance from Iquique: 167 km north-east

Chusmiza is an underdeveloped thermal resort in the *pre-Cordillera*, with a mineral water bottling plant. Access is difficult but possible. A spa hotel is located 5 km off the main track to Colchané down in the *quebrada*. It is a convenient stopover on the way to or from the national parks.

Accommodation

- Hostería Chusmiza. For reservations in Iquique: Patricio Lynch 1461 (22179 $G ⚇. Open in summer only

Buses

- Iquique: Fare $11.40; irregular services; Flonatur

Excursions

- **Sibaya**: Located in the **Quebrada de Tarapacá** south of Chusmiza. A colorful *altiplano fiesta* is held on September

4 in honor of San Nicolás; the church was founded in 1620 and financed by wealthy Indians who worked in nearby gold mines.
- **Huaviña**: Located in the Quebrada de Tarapacá. Turn off from Ruta A-55 30 km before Chusmiza; difficult access. An *altiplano fiesta* for San Juan Bautista is held on June 24. The 18th-century *altiplano* church is a *monumento nacional,* and contains paintings of the Cuzco School.

CODPA

Altitude: 1950 m
Distance from Arica: 113 km south on Ruta A-35 and Panamericana

Codpa's origins are pre-Hispanic. The Spanish proclaimed it a parish in 1670. Even during colonial days an Indian chief was installed here as *cacique* (local ruler).

Located in the valley of the **Río Vitor**, just where the *quebrada* comes out of the *pre-Cordillera*, Codpa is best reached from Arica. The turnoff from the Panamericana is just where the road comes out of the Cuesta de Chacas, 70 km south of Arica. The climate is enjoyable all year round. The water is of prime quality; the valley floor is very fertile and produces high-quality fruit. A particular brand of wine called "Pintatani" is made here.

There are interesting walks to nearby small Indian villages with a colonial past.

This is a quiet place to charge up your batteries again without the hustle and bustle of a modern town, and at the same time enjoy unpolluted air and water in a congenial environment where time has stood still.

🏃 Festivals
- June 29: San Pedro, in the nearby village of Guañacagua
- July 15–16: Virgen del Carmen
- November 22: San Martín de Tours

⊟ Accommodation
- Hostería Codpa, a modern hotel complex AFR ((58) 228703 $D for4

🚌 Buses
There is public transport once a week to and from Arica.

📷 Sightseeing
- Iglesia San Martín de Tours: This was a Franciscan mission center during the colonial period. Inside the church is a statue of San Martín de Tours riding a donkey. There are still some old adobe colonial houses left.

✦ Excursions
There are pleasant walks in the rich valley planted with fruit trees, particularly on the 5 km walk to **Ofrajia**. It is possible to visit **Guañacagua**, a small village with narrow streets and a 16th-century colonial church. Its 11 m stone baroque belfry is built in three tiers; on top of the cupola is another tier. On the stones you can see the traces of names from the Spanish era.

COLCHANÉ

Population: 200
Altitude: 3750 m
Distance from Iquique: 250 km east

Located in the *altiplano* right on the Bolivian border, Colchané is of some administrative importance as an official border crossing into Bolivia. Although it is a border crossing, I suggest you don't make the crossing here, but instead at Tambo Quemado on RI 11.

Twice each month a Saturday market is held to which *colectivos* and trucks come from Iquique and other *altiplano* villages. There are a few shops here, and the village has radio contact with the outside world; it also has electricity. Because it is in an open flat part of the *altiplano* unprotected by high mountains, the afternoon winds blow strongly through the only street.

This area is interesting from an archeological viewpoint. On many peaks, sanctuaries or sacrificial places have been found (possibly Inca). There are also some *chullpas* or burial places of chieftains in the form of small towers, which point to the Aymará culture, and some *pukarás* or fortifications. Along the old trails are *apachetas* or mountain pass markers. *Apachetas* also had a symbolic meaning: Indians used to pick up rocks some distance from an *apacheta* and lay them on the *apacheta* to express relief at having reached the highest point.

The mountain people enjoy expressing themselves in music. They are expert musicians on the *charango* (a string instrument made of armadillo shell), the *quena* (reed flute), and other native instruments. You can hear them practicing while tending their flocks.

Their *fiestas* revolve around sowing, harvesting, and taking the flocks to their pastures, and their customs are strongly influenced by ancestral paganism.

With a four-wheel drive vehicle the trip through **Parque Nacional Volcán Isluga** and further north to **Parque Nacional Lauca** is possible but difficult. Because of the harsh climatic conditions hiking is difficult: it is the domain of the seasoned outdoor enthusiast. I strongly recommend that tours in and around Colchané be made with a tour operator.

⊛ Festivals

Festivals in Cariquima
Cariquima is 28 km south.
* June 24: San Juan Bautista
* July 3: Asunción
* August 30: Santa Rosa

Festival in Chijo
Chijo is 21 km south.
* April 22: Nuestra Señora de los Dolores

🚍 Buses
You can get to and from Iquique by means of small private trucks and *colectivos* departing from the market in Iquique.

🛍 Shopping
The villagers are expert weavers, and you can buy of them fine ponchos, gloves, and carpets made either entirely of *alpaca* wool or mixed with sheep wool.

◉ Excursions
* **Cariquima**: 28 km south, at an altitude of 3850 m in the shade of **Cerro Cariquima** (5390 m), an extinct snow-covered volcano. This old Aymará village is a thriving pentecostal community; this has given them a progressive outlook, to the extent that they have electricity for part of the day and night, and the streets even have names! Between Colchané and Cariquima you go through flat *altiplano* country. From Cariquima there are views over the plain into the Salar de Coipasa in Bolivia where the **Río Isluga** ends, and of the **Volcán Isluga**. On this drive you will see Aymarás tending their flocks of *llamas*, and occasionally eagles, always in splendid mountain scenery, especially between Huaitani and Ancuaque. A trail goes around the base of Cerro Cariquima— only for the trail-blazer with tent, sleeping bag, and supplies for a two-day excursion. Cariquima is best visited with a tour operator from Iquique or with a four-wheel drive vehicle.
* **Parque Nacional Volcán Isluga**: There is a CONAF hut in **Enquelga**, near the thermal baths. See the entry for the park on page 65.
* **Chijo**: 21 km south. Colorful *altiplano fiesta*, Nuestra Señora de los Dolores, held April 22.
* **Mauque**: Located 30 km west in the Parque Nacional Volcán Isluga. See Parque Nacional Volcán Isluga on page 65.

IQUIQUE

Area code: 057
Population: 155 000
Altitude: Sea level
Distance from Santiago: 1844 km north on RN 16 and Panamericana

Iquique, capital of Región I de Tarapacá, is a picturesque city on the Pacific coast. It is wedged in on a narrow stretch of coastal strip between the sea and the coastal *cordillera*, which drops to the sea in sheer 800 m cliffs. You can reach it from the Panamericana Norte, through the coastal *cordillera*; and also via the coastal road from Antofagasta, which is far more scenic. The turnoff from the Panamericana is 5 km north of Pozo Almonte. It is the focal point for deep-sea fishing (particularly marlin), and the starting point for trips to the hot springs such as Mamiña, Pica and Chuzmisa in the *pre-Cordillera*.

Iquique is located in one of the few areas along the coast where the mountains recede slightly to make room for a small coastal plain. The mountains surrounding the town are completely barren. Where the road leads up to the plateau, you have a view over a huge dune at least 200 m high and covering the southern part of the coastal plain; it is known as Cerro El Dragón.

Iquique has one of the best harbors in northern Chile. The city is of historical interest, with many reminders of its saltpeter past.

The tourist facilities are adequate, and the climate is pleasant throughout the year.

The beaches in the vicinity slide gradually into the sea. The sand is white and fine, and the beaches are good for swimming and water sports. The nearest to the town are Playa Saint Tropez and Playa Cavancha; there are *colectivos* from downtown; beaches are suitable for swimming, fishing; kiosks and showers, with a paved promenade and seafood restaurants. Further south along Avenida 11 de Septiembre is Playa Brava; near Hotel Playa Brava are the tennis courts. Still further south, but within easy reach of Iquique by public transport, are Playa Primeras Piedras, Huaiquique, and Playa Blanca with a

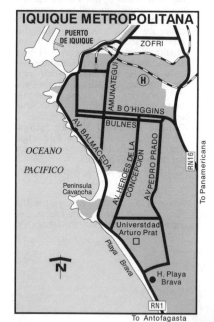

IQUIQUE METROPOLITANA

PUERTO DE IQUIQUE
ZOFRI
AMUNATEGUI
B O'HIGGINS
BULNES
AV BALMACEDA
OCEANO PACIFICO
Peninsula Cavancha
AV. HEROES DE LA CONCEPCION
AV PEDRO PRADO
RN16
To Panamericana
Universtdad Arturo Prat
Playa Brava
N
H. Playa Brava
RN1
To Antofagasta

nearby golf course. Between Iquique and the mouth of the **Río Loa** some 140 km south there are more than 30 beaches, few alas with drinking water. The 140 km of coast south of the town offers good fishing all year round.

This narrow platform with a few wells was populated in pre-Hispanic times by the Changos. Spanish settlement goes back to 1556. In those days it was nothing more than a forlorn outpost on the desert coast: its only importance was the water which surfaced on the rocks (*puquios*) and the collection of *guano*, the origin of the saltpeter industry. In the middle of the 18th century, the nearby silver mines of Huantajaya had some importance, which increased the population to around 2000. As a result, water had to be brought from as far away as Arica to sustain the growing population. As early as last century a sea-water distillation plant operated here to increase the drinking water supply. Nowadays water is brought from the aquifers near Pica and Matilla. This diversion of water from the aquifers has caused a downturn in agriculture in those places as less water became available for irrigation.

In 1878 under the Peruvian Government Iquique became a provincial capital. The modern city is of recent origin, dating from when it was the hub of the saltpeter export industry which ran from about the end of the War of the Pacific to World War I. With the downturn in the saltpeter mining industry, it became a fishing port, and a fish meal plant was built in the 1950s. It is now the first port of the region, and the creation of a free port ("Zona Franca de Zofri") has given some impetus to the economy.

The *Zona Franca* in the suburb of Zofri is a duty-free zone. This is fully explained on page 29.

The weather is warm all year round; the average temperature is 20°C (68°F). The water temperature is 19°C (66°F)in summer and drops to 16°C (61°F) in winter. It never rains.

The city has retained much of its 19th-century charm, echoing the time when it was a bustling saltpeter shipping port. The main street is Calle Baquedano, which runs between Plaza Prat and Avenida Balmaceda. It is the city's show-piece, with many neoclassical buildings dating to the turn of the century, most of them built from Oregon pine by saltpeter barons.

Plaza Prat is the hub of the city, and most things of interest are around the Plaza — at the Club de la Unión you can get a good meal for $10.00.

A good spot to take a scenic photo is the corner of Aníbal Pinto and Riquelme, at the COPEC gas station: here you can take a shot of the mountains dropping 800 m to the sea.

Along the beach is a wide palm-lined promenade, extending for several kilometers right up to Península Cavancha. Along the promenade are ice cream parlors and restaurants. The seaside is fairly rocky with a few exceptions, but it is a beautiful walk. One of the beaches — more a rocky inlet — has a shark net. The best restaurant on this seaside promenade is Los Quillos, a drive-in-cum-snack bar. A taxi between Cavancha and the city costs $1.00.

From Iquique it is possible to visit many of the abandoned saltpe-

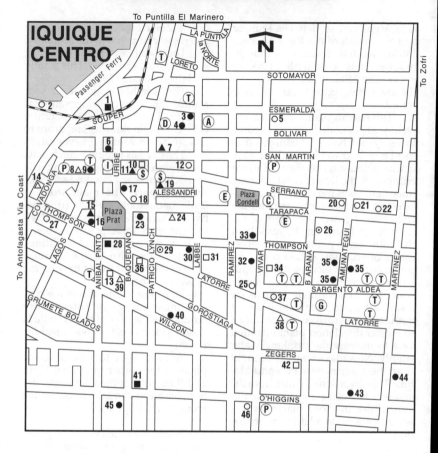

IQUIQUE CENTRO

To Puntilla El Marinero

To Zofri

To Antofagasta Via Coast

ter mines. Because of their historic importance, many of them have been declared *monumentos nacionales* (such as Humberstone and Santa Laura). **Pozo Almonte**, 4 km further south of Humberstone in the **Pampa de Tamarugal**, has a Museo Histórico del Salitre. You can reach the hot springs and oases of Pica and Matilla easily by bus from Iquique, passing through the **Salar de Pintados**, which has some of the most astonishing rock paintings in South America. A recommended two-day excursion is to **Mamiña** in the *pre-Cordillera*, with its hot thermal spas and mud baths.

⚅ Festivals

- June 29: San Pedro
- July 27–28: La Tirana Chica

Festivals in La Tirana
La Tirana is 71 km east.
- January 3– 6: Pascua de los Negros
- July 15–17: Virgen del Carmen

Key to map

A	Catedral de Iquique	22	Restaurant Chung Wah
C	Municipalidad (Town hall)	25	Pizzería d'Alfredo
D	Post office and telex	26	Restaurant Cheers
E	Telephone	27	Restaurant Misia Carmela
G	Mercado Municipal (Market)	29	Restaurant La Caleta
I	Tourist information	37	Pizzería La Tentazione
P	Gas stations	46	Restaurant Chifa Pekin
$	Money exchange		
T	Bus terminals	△	**Tour operators and car rental**
		8	Automóvil Club
●	**Accommodation**	14	Hertz Rent a Car
3	Residencial Catedral	24	Viajes Iquitur
4	Residencial Bolívar	38	Turismo Mamiña
6	Hotel Durana	39	Viajes Lirima
9	Hotel Phoenix		
16	Hotel Arturo Prat	▲	**Airline offices**
17	Hotel de la Plaza	7	LADECO
23	Hotel Tamarugal	11	Lloyd Aereo Boliviano
30	Hotel Inti Llanka	15	LAN Chile
33	Residencial Condell	19	National Airlines
35	Cheap accommodation		
40	Residencial Wilson	■	**Sights**
43	Hotel Corona	1	Museo Naval
44	Hotel Colonial	28	Teatro Municipal
45	Hostal Cuneo	41	Palacio Astoreca
○	**Eating out**	□	**Services**
2	Restaurant Club de Yates	10	Telex Chile
5	Restaurant Buenos Aires	13	ENTEL Chile
12	Restaurant José Luis	31	Artesanías Savuña Aymara
18	Restaurant Club Español	34	Supermercado Decer
20	Restaurant Chifa Nan King	36	Consulado de Bolivia
21	Restaurant Valentino	42	Feria Persa

Festivals in Tarapacá

Tarapacá is 110 km north-east, in the *quebrada* of the same name. ☞
- February 2–3: Virgen de la Candelaria ☞
- August 10: San Lorenzo, the village's patron saint ☞

ⓘ Tourist information ☞
- Sernatur, Aníbal Pinto 436 ℂ 461523

ⓨ Entertainment

⑪ Eating out

Here in the harbor area — mainly in Bolívar between A. Pinto and Souper — are many small eating places. This is the historical part of town.

Restaurants
- Buenos Aires, Vivar block 200 near Bolívar
- Canto del Agua, F. Valenzuela 230 $Z

- Cheers, Barros Arana 668A $Z
- Chifa Chung Chan, Serrano 756 $Z
- Chifa Chung Wha, Tarapacá 948 $Y
- Chifa Pekin, Vivar 1199 $X
- Circolo Italiano, Tarapacá 477 $X
- Club de la Unión, Tarapacá 278, on Plaza Prat, upstairs $Z
- Club Español, Plaza Prat 584 $Y
- Club de Yates, Recinto Portuario $Y
- Don Antonio, Filomena Valenzuela 295 $Z
- José Luis, Serrano 474 $Y
- La Caleta, P.Lynch near Thompson
- Misia Carmela, Thompson 123 $Y
- Nan-Kin, Amunátegui 533 $Z. Chinese cuisine
- Phoenix (Hotel), Avenida Aníbal Pinto 451 $Y
- Rincón de Amigos, Avenida Aníbal Pinto 404 $Z
- Sicoteca, Vivar 908 $Z. Asian meals

⊟ Accommodation in Iquique

Accommodation in the city center

Apart Hotels
- Consiglieri, Vivar 793   APST   ☎ 429189
  Fax 413981

Hotels

★★★ Arturo Prat, Aníbal Pinto 695	ACDEFGHIJKLMPSTUZ		
		☎ 411067	$D ♟
Car rental, fax 429088			
★★★ Barros Arana, Barros Arana 1330	ACDEFGHIJLPU	☎ 412840	$F ♟
Fax 42670			
★★ Inti-Llanca, Obispo Labbé 807	ADEGHIJLPU	☎ 412511	$F ♟
Fax 413858			
• Belén, Vivar 803	AEFGIKLS	☎ 413644	$H ♟
• Camino del Mar, Orella 340	AEIS	☎ 20465	$G ♟
• Camanchaca, Vivar 955	BCDEFGHSTU	☎ 412666 / 423727	$F ♟
Fax 421666			
• Carani, Latorre 426	AHKLT	☎ 413646	
Fax 425124			
• Colonial, J. Martínez 1020	APS	☎ 426097	$H ♟
• Corona, Libertador Bernardo O'Higgins		☎424593	$F ♟
• De la Plaza, Plaza Prat 302	ADILPS	☎ 414268	$H ♟
• Durana, San Martín 294	AFHIJLPSU	☎ 428085	$H ♟
10 rooms			
• Gavina, Avenida Balamaceda 1497		☎ 413030	
Fax 411111, directly on the beach			
• Icaisa, Orella 434	ABEFGHKPST	☎ 412324	$E ♟
Fax 428462			
• Phoenix, Aníbal Pinto 451	AFGIJKLPSU	☎ 411349	$G ♟
• Playas, Segunda Sur 981 near General Fuenzalida			
	ADFGHIJLPSU	☎ 423706	$F ♟
Fax 429111			
• Reginaldas, Bulnes 157	ADEFGHIJLPU	☎ 422997	$G ♟
• San Diego, Orella 1665	ADEGHIJKLM	☎ 413445	$G ♟
• San Martín, San Martín 823	ADEHILPS		
• Savina, Avenida Balmaceda 1497	APS		$F ♟
• Tamarugal, Tarapacá 369	ACDEFGIJLPU	☎ 413910	$E ♟
• Winnie, Orella 456	AFGP	☎ 426509	
Fax 422126			
• Yala-Yala, Libertad 1092	AEFGHKLMP	☎ 414906	
Fax 414915			

Hostales

• América, M. Rodríguez 550	APS	☎ 427524
60 beds		
• Arboleda, Juan Martínez 778		☎ 422502
16 rooms		
• Camino Real, Zegers 1611		☎ 412266
• Casa Blanca, Gorostiaga 127		☎ 420007
• Cuneo, Baquedano 1175	AJLPS	☎ 428654 $H ♟
• Errázuriz, Errázuriz 889	ALP	
• 21 De Mayo, 21 de Mayo 780	ALP	☎ 423282
Fax 421750		

Accommodation in Iquique — continued

Residenciales
- Baquedano, Baquedano 1315   AFIJP   (422990 $J ⅲ
  Shared bathroom cheaper
- Bolívar, Bolívar 478   AFIJU $H ⅲ
  Budget travelers
- Catedral, Obispo Labbé 253   AEIJLPSU   (412184 $G ⅲ
  Shared bathroom cheaper
- Condell, Thompson 684   AP   (413948 $H ⅲ
  Shared bathroom cheaper
- Danny, Vivar 1266   ADFHIJP   (414161 $H ⅲ
  15 rooms; shared bathroom cheaper
- Li-Ming, Barros Arana 705   AFHIJP   (421912 $H ⅲ
- Nan-King, Thompson 752   AFGHIJLP   (423311 $H ⅲ
  Shared bathroom cheaper
- Petersen, P. Lynch 1257   (428191 $J ⅲ
  Backpackers only
- Vivar, Vivar 1770   ADFIJPU   (422724 $H ⅲ
- Wilson, Wilson 422   AEIJLPU   (423789 $H ⅲ

Accommodation along the road to Zofri

Hotel
- Abraipa, Amunátegui 218   APS   (412078 $G ⅲ
  Fax 415178

Accommodation on Península Cavancha (or nearby)

Apart hotels

- ★★★★ Atenas, Los Rieles 738   ACDEFGHIJKLMNPRS$ (431100 $D ⅲ
  Car rental
- Ricuzzi, J. A. Ríos 2874   (431628
- Hotels
- Cavancha Marina, Los Rieles 250   ACDEFGHIJKLMNPRS$TUZ
     (434800 $C ⅲ
  Car rental, tennis, beach frontage, boat hire
- Charlie Inn, Tomas Bonilla 899   AEFGPST   (413835 $E ⅲ
  Fax 428438
- Chucumata, Balmaceda 850 near Avenida Cavancha
     ABCDEFIJKLMPRS$TUZ(411311 $D ⅲ
  Beach frontage, shows, tennis, car rental, 42 rooms, fax 429276
- Corona, Libertador B. O'Higgins 940   (424593 $F ⅲ

Motels
- Venecia, Primera Sur 1196 near Tomas Bonilla
     AEGHJL   (423779 $G for 3

Accommodation at Playa Brava

Hotels
- Playa Brava, Avenida Playa Brava 3118
     ACDEFGHIJKLMPRS$TYZ
     (441068 $E ⅲ
  Car rental, sauna, shows, fax 441284

Accommodation in Iquique — continued

Accommodation at Playa Huantajaya

Hotels
- Huantajaya, Avenida Costanera Sur 3607
  ACFGHLRU   (441015 $F ♀♂

Acommodation at Playa Primeras Piedras

Motels
- Primeras Piedras, Avenida Primeras Piedras, Camino Huaquique
  ACDEGHIJLMNS$UZ   (441023 $E for 4
  Car rental, 52 cabins all with views over the sea

- Splendid, Vivar 793 $Z
- Valentino, Amunátegui near Serrano
- ☞ Yugoslavenski Dom, Plaza Prat $Y

Cafeterías
- ☞ Ciocolatta, Aníbal Pinto 487 $X
- Sciaraffia, Barros Arana 803
- Dino's, Avenida 11 de Septiembre 1975 $X
- ☞ Tamarugal, Tarapacá 369 $X

Pizzerías
- ☞ D'Alfredo, Vivar 631 $X
- La Tentazione, S. Aldea 749
- L'Italianissima, Vivar 855

Salón de Té
- ☞ Pastelería Alemana, Barros Arana 750 $Z. Good cakes

Schoperías
- El 680, Ramírez 680$Z
- Pileta Alemana, Latorre 709 $Z

Eating out in Avenida Costanera, Balmaceda and Península Cavancha

Restaurants
- Casino de Iquique, Balmaceda 2755 $Y
- Club Náutico Camancha, Los Rieles 110 $Y
- Don Antonio, Península Cavancha $Y
- ☞ El Sombrero, Los Rieles 704, Cavancha $Y. Seafood
- ☞ Schopería Los Quillos House, Avenida Balmaceda 851 on the beach $Y
- YMCA, Península Cavancha $Z
- Yugoslava, Península Cavancha $Y

! Entertainment

Entertainment at Playa Cavancha
- Casino de Iquique, Avenida Balmaceda 2755(431391, fax 431383. Roulette, black jack
- The Pink Cadillac, Balmaceda 2751. Disco

Night clubs
- Bolero, Barros Arana 466
- Casino AGPIA, Vivar block 1000 near Zegers. *Peña*
- ☞ Valentino Valentino, Amunátegui 540A $X.Piano bar

Post and telegraph

Post Office
- Correos de Chile, Bolívar 458

Telephone
- CTC, Ramírez 587, fax 429058
- CTC, Vivar 923, fax 427561
- ENTEL Chile (international calls), Gorostiaga 289
- Telex Chile, San Martín 385

$ Financial
- Cambio's, P. Lynch 548, upstairs (411057
- Fincard, Serrano 392 (426990. Cash advances against Visa and Mastercard

Money exchange in Zofri
- Cambio Fide's Ltda, Plaza de Servicio local 11 (427794

Services and facilities
Zofri is the duty free zone of Iquique. Stock up here on duty-free items such as films, cameras, etc.

🚌 Buses from Iquique

Municipal bus no. 2 goes from the city center to Zofri; fare $0.15
The central bus terminal (Rodoviario) is in Patricio Lynch. Major bus companies hardly ever use it, as they have their own terminals; sometimes several bus companies pool their resources and share a common terminal. Most of the buses are located around the municipal market in Calles Latorre, B. Arana and Sargento Aldea

Bus companies
- A27 Buses Cuevas y González, Sargento Aldea 850 ☎ 412471
- A31 Buses Evans, Vivar 955 ☎ 413462
- A42 Buses Carmelita, Barros Arana 841 ☎ 412237
- A67 Buses Ramos Cholele, Barros Arana 851 ☎ 411650
- A71 Buses Santa Rosa, Avenida P. Prado 2382 ☎/fax 431729
- A78 Buses Tramaca, Sargento Aldea 988 ☎ 412323
- A82 Buses Waldorf Tour, Latorre 779 ☎ 420330
- A83 Buses Zambrano Hnos, Sargento Aldea 742 ☎ 413215
- A86 Chile Bus, Latorre 773 ☎ 428172
- A106 Buses Fénix Pullman Norte, A. Pinto 431 ☎ 412423
- A110 Buses Flecha Dorada, Barros Arana 825 ☎ 414305
- A111 Flonatur, Sargento Aldea 790 ☎ 428757
- A112 Flota Barrios, Sargento Aldea 987 ☎ 426941
- A117 Kenny Bus, Latorre 944 ☎ 414159
- A128 Buses Pullman Fichtur, A. Pinto 865 ☎ 414304
- A146 Taxis Tamarugal, Sargento Aldea 783 ☎ 424856
- A150 Via Géminis, Obispo Labbé 151 ☎ 422902 fax 429567
- A152 Transportes Rojas, Sargento Aldea 783
- A156 Turis Auto, Serrano 724 ☎ 413446
- A157 Turis Norte,from Mercado
- A158 Turis Taxis, Barros Arana 897B ☎ 424428
- A159 Turismo Mamiña, Latorre 779

Taxi *colectivos* make unscheduled departures from Mercado Iquique (central market) as the need arises, waiting until all seats are taken.

Destinations

Destination	Fare	Services	Duration	Companies
Antofagasta	$12.50	8 services daily	6 hrs	A42, A78, A110, A112, A117
Arica	$9.50	6 services daily		A146, A156, A158,
	$5.70	12 services daily		A27, A67, A42,
Calama	$12.50	7 services daily		A78, A110, A112, A117, A150
Caldera	$24.70	1 service daily		A110
Camiña		2 services per week in summer only		
Chañaral	$23.20	3 services daily		A42, A110, A112
Chusmiza	$11.40	irregular services		A111
Copiapó	$25.80	10 services daily		A31, A42, A67, A78, A83, A106, A110, A112, A128
Coquimbo	$26.60	2 services daily		A42, A110
La Calera	$34.20	1 service daily		A110
La Serena	$30.00	15 services daily	2½ hrs	A42, A106, A110, A112
Sleeper	$60.30		2½ hrs	A128
La Tirana	$ 2.60			A111
Los Vilos	$30.40	1 service daily		A110
Mamiña	$3.80	2–3 services daily	3 hrs	A111, A152, A159
Ovalle	$28.50	3 services daily		A42, A83, A110
Pedro de Valdivia	$9.50	1 service daily		A42
Pica	$3.00	2 services daily	2 hrs	A71, A111

Buses from Iquique — continued

Destination	Fare	Services	Duration	Companies
• Pozo Almonte				Taxi *colectivos*
• Santiago	$38.00	9 services daily		A31, A67, A78, A86, A106, A110, A112, A117
Sleeper	$48.50	1 service daily		A128
• Tocopilla				
Via coast road	$7.60	1 service daily	4½ hrs	A82
Via RN 5	$7.60	3 services daily	4 hrs	A117, A157
• Vallenar	$24.70	4 services daily		A42, A110
• Valparaiso	$39.80	6 services daily		A67, A83, A86, A106, A112
• Viña del Mar	$39.80	6 services daily		A67, A83, A86, A106, A112

Pharmacy
• Farmacia Victoria, Vivar 626

Photographic supplies
• Kodak Express, Tarapacá 453

Supermarkets
• Supermercado Decer, Vivar 786

Visas, passports

Consulates
• Bolivia: Latorre 399 (421777
• Peru: San Martín 385 (41466

Air services

Aeropuerto Diego Aracena is located 40 km south of the city center. A bus from the airline offices costs $2.00, a taxi costs $12.50.

Companies
• LAN Chile, Aníbal Pinto 641 (414378
• LADECO, San Martín 428 (413038
• Lloyd Aereo Boliviano, Serrano 430 (426780
• National Airlines, P. Lynch 548, office 1/2 (427816, fax 416082

Flights
• Antofagasta: fare $43.00; 2–3 services daily; duration 1 hr; LAN Chile, LADECO
• Arica: Fare $ 28.00; 2–3 services daily; duration ½ hr; LAN Chile, LADECO
• Calama: 1 service daily; duration ½ hr; LADECO
• Santiago: $150.00; 3–4 services daily; duration 2½ hrs; LAN Chile, LADECO

Motoring services

Car rental
• Automóvil Club de Chile, Serrano 154 (413206 fax 427333
• Budget Rent a Car, O'Higgins 1361 (429566
• Rent's Procar, Serrano 796 (413470
• Hertz, Souper 650 (426316, fax 420213

Shopping

The main shopping street is Tarapacá, between Plaza Prat and Plaza Condell.
Zofri is a free trade zone and all items are sold duty free. An air-conditioned three-storied building houses most of the shops. There are also money exchange facilities. There is an *artesanía* shop here.
• Municipal market, Barros Arana Block 800 near Latorre
• Casa Bolivia, Thompson 817. *Artesanía*
• CEMA Chile, Plaza Prat 570
• Savuña Aymará, Obispo Labbé 768. Sells articles made from *alpaca* and *vicuña* wool
• Fería Persa, Zegers corner of B. Arana.

Sport

South of the city there are more than 140 km of beaches and rocky outcrops You can fish along here all year round; there is no closed season.

Sightseeing

To get to know the city, I suggest a three-hour walking tour, starting from Plaza Prat. Inside the park is Torre Reloj, a clock tower made of steel. The Spanish and the Yugoslav clubs are nearby, and the houses now occupied by the clubs, dating from the time of the nitrate boom, have been declared *monumentos nacionales*. Continue your stroll through Calles Gorostiaga and Baquedano. Here the wealthy saltpeter barons of English descent and their imitators built their mansions between 1880 and 1930 in the English Georgian style.

- Commemorative Buoy of the Iquique Naval engagement during the War of the Pacific marks the spot where the Chilean vessel *Esmeralda* sank. Launch cruises.
- Museo Regional, Baquedano 951. Old court house has been transformed into museum specializing in exhibits on local indigenous population. On exhibit are archeological finds of the area. Open Mon–Sat 0830–1300 and 1500–1900. Admission $1.00.
- Museo Naval, Aníbal Pinto, next to the Aduana building. Exhibits of sea battles during the War of the Pacific. Open Tues–Sun 0930–1230 and 1430–1800.
- Aduana (Customs) building, Aníbal Pinto, next to the Museo Naval, near the wharves. Built in Peruvian times. The plaque in front of the building says: "The foundation stone to the Customs Building was laid by Nicolás de Pierola, President of Peru, on January 6, 1871."
- Teatro Municipal, Plaza Prat, south side, a *monumento histórico*.
- Palacio Astoreca, P. Lynch near Libertador Bernardo O'Higgins. On exhibit are furniture used by the well to do merchants during the saltpeter boom; also paintings.

⊕ Excursions

Tour operators
- Iquitur, Tarapacá 465B ℂ 412415
- Flonatur, Sargento Aldea 790 ℂ 428292 / 425227. Regular daily buses to Mamiña and Pica, less regular buses to Chusmiza
- Transportes Rojas, Sargento Aldea 783 ℂ 424856. Regular buses to Mamiña
- Turismo Santa Rosa, Latorre 973 ℂ 426368. Regular buses to Pica
- Turismo Mamiña, Latorre 779 ℂ 420330
- Turismo Isluga, Latorre 342 ℂ 421090

- Turismo Lirima, Avenida Baquedano 823 ℂ 413094

Organized tours
- **Pintados:** Visit the rock paintings in the **Reserva Nacional Pampa del Tamarugal**. Located 95 km south east of Iquique. The actual archeological zone is 7 km west of the Panamericana. Tour operators sometimes combine the trip to Pica with a visit to the rock drawings. See also Reserva Nacional Pampa del Tamarugal on page 73.
- Oficina Humberstone and Oficina Santa Laura, 52 km east near the junction of RN 16 with the Panamericana or 5 km north of Pozo Almonte. These abandoned saltpeter mines have been preserved as *monumentos nacionales*. If you are interested in mining activity these two sites can easily be reached from either Iquique or **Pozo Almonte**.
- **Huara:** 85 km north-east, in the central desert at an altitude of 1100 m. It was founded in 1885 during the saltpeter boom, and at its peak had 7000 inhabitants. When the district's saltpeter mines closed, the towns' economic base disappeared. It is still inhabited, but many houses are vacant and decaying. The main attractions are the Calle Comercial, the house with two balconies and the now-closed chemist shop with its collection of porcelain bottles; a large swimming pool is just outside the old railroad station. Huara is the junction of Panamericana Norte and Ruta A-55, where you turn east to Tarapacá, the former colonial administration center, and into the *pre-Cordillera* and the *altiplano* near the Bolivian border. At the junction there is a gas station-cum-road diner Hostería Flor de Huara and *carabineros* post. If you are going into the *altiplano*, Huara is the last major town where you can buy gas and get information from the *carabineros*. In the vicinity of Huara are some abandoned saltpeter mines and major battlefields of the War of the Pacific: Batalla de **Pampa Germania** (November 15, 1879), Batalla de Tarapacá (November 27, 1879), Batalla de Dolores (November 19, 1879) and the landing at **Pisagua** (November 2, 1879). At **Pampa Germania**, a mono-

lith has been erected to commemorate the battlefields of the War of the Pacific. The main attraction in the vicinity is the rock paintings of **Cerro Unitá** 10 km east of Huara, which feature the Giant of Atacama, an 80 m high figure engraved into the mountain. On August 4 the town celebrates San Salvador, the town's patron saint. This is a 210 km round trip up to Huara and back, and takes about 9 hours. On the way up from Iquique there are some rock paintings at KM 30. At KM 37, before turning onto the Carretera Panamericana, are the ghost towns of **Humberstone** and **Santa Laura**, both declared *monumentos nacionales* (Humberstone takes its un-Spanish name from a British saltpeter magnate). Although regular *colectivos* make the trip to Huara from the market, not much is gained, as from Huara there is no transport to the places of interest. I suggest you go with a tour operator, who may also include a trip to Tarapacá and/or Chusmiza. See also the entry for Reserva Nacional Pampa del Tamarugal on page 73.

- Twenty-three kilometers further east of Huara the **Quebrada de Tarapacá** begins; it has a long and varied historical and archeological past. At the beginning of the Quebrada is **Tarapacá**. Now a forgotten village, Tarapacá, located in the **Río Pedregoso** valley, altitude 1400 m, was in colonial days the provincial capital. Traces of this glorious past can still be seen on the treeless flagstone-paved plaza with its grand arcades on two sides. Its importance derived from the fact that it was on a direct route from Potosí, South America's biggest silver mine, to the coast. The first European "tourist" was Diego de Almagro, who, convinced Pizarro had cheated him, hurried along the Inca trail back into Peru in 1536. In 1540 Pedro de Valdivia passed through Tarapacá on his way south to take possession of Chile in the name of the Spanish kings. A chapel existed here as early as 1613, and in 1685 it became a parish. Tarapacá region was administered from Arica until 1768, when the capital was moved here to escape the then unhealthy climate of

Arica. It remained the provincial capital until 1855, when the seat of government was relocated to Iquique, which had sprung up as the most important town as a result of the growing saltpeter industry. There are several *monumentos nacionales,* such as Iglesia de San Lorenzo, built of adobe bricks with three aisles; built in the late 1600s, it was refurbished in the mid-1700s by an illustrious citizen, Basilio de La Fuente. Nowadays it is in ruins as the result of a fire. Other indications of the town's Spanish past are the remains of the once-sumptuous Palacio de Gobierno on a cobbled street. Many of the houses are in ruins, but some arched doorways remain, their wooden doors held together by copper nails. At **Pachica**: 5 km north in the **Quebrada de Tarapacá**, down in the valley on the old colonial road a colorful *altiplano* festival is held on March 19 to celebrate San José Obrero. At **Caserones** is an archeological site, as well as the remains of houses going back to the Spanish invasion. Many rock paintings are between Huarasiña and **Pachica**, a mere 8 km.

- **Laguna del Huasco**: 172 km east in the *altiplano*. This trip is best made with a tour operator who goes via Pica and returns via Mamiña. This is a gruelling three-day trip and only for the adventurous. The area is virtually untouched by tourism — you can see flamingoes and a rarely visited *salar!*
- **Aeropuerto Diego Aracena**: $12.50 each (minimum 4 persons).
- *Altiplano:* There are irregular *colectivo* services from Iquique to Chusmiza. Although there are trucks and *colectivos* which leave from the market in Iquique for the Saturday market in Colchané it is suggested you rent your own four-wheel-drive vehicle. Take the route via **Huara**, turning off east into the Chusmiza valley. From Huara it is a two-and-a-half-hour uninspiring trip to **Chusmiza** apart from the side trip to the archeological site at Cerro Unitá and Tarapacá. In Chusmiza (3000 m) you can stay at the hotel and enjoy the thermal baths. Continue the following day to **Colchané**, a three-and-a-half hour drive (123 km)

Plate 3   Región I de Tarapacá
Top: Arica, El Morro
Bottom: Río Lluta Valley, rock paintings

Plate 4   Región I de Tarapacá
Arica, Iglesia San Marcos, built by Eiffel

through varied, mostly dry *altiplano* scenery. This is a slow but interesting uphill drive over a bad road. In the *altiplano* you visit **Cariquima, Ancuaque, Isluga, Enquelga.** The turnoff to the **Parque Nacional Volcán Isluga** is a short distance before arriving in Colchané. This is Aymará country. Apart from Chusmiza there is no accommodation. Observing the customs of the Indian population is interesting. Remember that the closest non-Aymará Chilean Indian community, the Mapuche, is 2500 km further south — there is a difference between the two cultures.

• **Pisagua**: 104 km north on the Pacific coast in the **Quebrada de Tiviliche**. Founded in 1836, in its heyday it was the third largest saltpeter port in the Tarapacá province. In those days there was a rail link between the port and the major saltpeter fields. It is now almost deserted, as all the saltpeter mines on which its livelihood depended have closed down. The town is wedged in on a narrow ledge between sea and mountain. It was taken by Chile from Peru during the War of the Pacific on November 2, 1879. From its illustrious past a few testimonies remain, such as the wooden Torre Reloj (clock tower, built in 1887) which sits on a rock overlooking the harbor and the Teatro Municipal (built in 1892). The houses of the era were built of wood with small balconies, but few remain intact. Two small beaches to the north at the mouth of the Quebrada de Tiviliche also attract some visitors. At the turnoff from Panamericana inside the Quebrada are the rock

paintings of Tiviliche; up from the paintings is the old English cemetery. This is unknown Chile, bypassed by the main stream of tourists. On June 29 the Fiesta de San Pedro is held. It is interesting but difficult to reach as it is not included by tour operators on their guided tours.

• **Salar Grande**: A 200 km return trip south, mostly along the coast, to one of the driest areas in the world. The turnoff from RN 1 into the coastal *cordillera* is 1 km before Punta Patillos. The road is sealed and initially runs in a straight line until it hits the sheer cliff, and from here it climbs steeply uphill. As soon as you reach the **Pampa de las Zorras** ("Vixen Prairie") you have splendid views over the Pacific and the coastal plain which is fairly wide here. A further 26 km brings you to the northern end of the Salar Grande. Here is the entrance to Mina Punta de los Lobos which is still worked. You must get authorization from the guard at the entrance to visit the mine. It is a huge hole in the ground with stepped ledges over which the trucks circulate. At this mine the sealed road ends.

• **La Tirana**: 77 km east, a village just north of the **Salar de Pintados**. Its only fame is the Fiesta de la Virgen del Carmen, held in July, a very popular *altiplano* festival with Indian overtones. Some 2000 dancers take part, dressed in multicolored costumes. The *fiesta* lasts uninterrupted for three days. Flonatur has regular bus services and passes through Tirana on the way to Pica and Matilla.

MAMIÑA

Area code: 81
Population: 400
Altitude: 2700 m
Distance from Iquique: 125 km east on Ruta A-65

Built on a mountain spur between Bajo España and Quebrada El Tambo, Mamiña, meaning "Girl of my eyes", is named after the blind favorite daughter of an Inca chief who regained her sight here. The terraces on which most of the fruit and vegetables are grown were constructed in pre-Hispanic times. Many archeological sites in the valley and on the cliff overlooking the valley are testimony to the fact that the valley was already densely populated in pre-Inca times. There is no doubt that it was an Incan administration center.

The inhabitants are direct descendants of the Aymarás. This has helped to preserve many ancestral customs, which come to the fore when they are celebrating their *fiestas*.

The valley floor is irrigated, and is one sheet of green crops — maize and wheat. This is an interesting place not only because it is a thermal spa with reasonable facilities, but also because of its pre-Colombian past.

A side trail ascends to the *altiplano,* linking it with the *Capac Ñan* or Royal Road of the Incas. The present layout of the village dates from the Spanish occupation. It is built on a hill jutting out into the middle of the valley, giving it a dominant position and panoramic views. The green irrigated fields in the valley stand out in sharp contrast to the surrounding bare hill. The village's fame as a health spa came about during the saltpeter boom, when mine owners started to come here to rest and enjoy the hot springs. The Hotel Salitre was built during this time.

Nearly every property in the township has access to thermal water, and many of the larger hotels have their own thermal springs. The thermal water differs from one spring to another: some are slightly radioactive, some are richer in chloride, silicates or sulfurates. They all are beneficial, particularly for varicose veins, rheumatism, and respiratory ailments. The main thermal springs are:

- Baños Ipla: 45°C (113°F), slightly radioactive, 7 pH.

⊟ Accommodation in Mamiña

Hotels

• Colonial, El Tambo 4	AEFGHIJKLR	✆ 796298	$H	♙♙
Full board, all rooms hot thermal water, mud baths				
• La Niña de Mis Ojos, Ipla	AEFGHL	✆ (57) 420451	$H	♙♙
Full board, mud baths				
☞ • Refugio del Salitre, El Tambo 01	AFGHIJLRU	✆ 751203	$F	♙♙
Full board, thermal swimming pool				
• Tamarugal, Ipla	AFHIL	✆ (57)412833	$H	♙♙
Full board				

Hosterías

• Complejo Termal La Coruña, Santa Rosa 687	AEFGHNR	✆ 751298	$H	♙♙
Full board, mud baths, 25 rooms				
☞ • El Tambo de Mamiña, Avenida El Tambo 07	AFHIJL		$G	♙♙
Full board				
☞ • Sol de Ipla, Ipla	AFHJL			
Reservations in Iquique: Sargento Aldea 783 ✆ 424856				

- Vertiente El Tambo: 57°C (135°F), slightly radioactive, 8 pH. This is the major thermal spring.
- Vertiente de Radium: Recommended by the locals for the treatment of eye complaints.
- Vertiente La Magnesia emerges from a mine tunnel, and is cold delicious drinking water.
- Baños El Chino: These are radium mud-baths highly appreciated by visitors who cover their whole body with the mud. Located near the river bed, there are separate fenced-in sites for men and women. It is a bit primitive, as you wash the mud off in the nearby stream; bring your own towel. It is open in the morning from 0900 to 1300, and again in the afternoon. The morning is the best time to take a mud bath; in the afternoon strong winds coming up the valley from the coast hit this spot directly and make it uncomfortable. There is a small fee, payable to the attendant.

The area's climate is dry. Electricity is available only from 2000 to 2400. The only public telephone is at the Hotel del Salitre.

Festivals
- July 25: San Santiago, in the village of **Macaya**
- December 21: Santo Tomás
- December 13: Santa Lucia, in the village of **Parca**

Buses
- Iquique: $3.80; 2–3 services daily; 3 hrs; Flonatur, Turismo Mamiña, Transportes Rojas

Shopping
Weaving is a long-established handicraft and possibly goes back to pre-Hispanic times. There are particularly fine weavings by the Mamani family, with Andean motifs like pumas and serpents.

Sightseeing
The town was established on top of an existing pre-Hispanic village on an isolated easily defended hill in the middle of the valley. A few of the streets are paved. Most of the houses are thatched, and some have elaborate stone doorways. The church, a jewel of colonial architecture built in 1632, has two steeples and stone buttresses. The belfries are of stone for the bottom two-thirds, and the top consists of a blue wooden structure containing the bells. The doorway is made of cut pink stone, and the door is of solid wood. The altar has three levels, with a staircase leading up on either side.
- Cerro Ipla: A trail leads to the remains of a pre-Hispanic fortification, most likely built by the original Aymará population to fend off intruders (perhaps Incas). It is in a commanding position, with sweeping views over the valley and the "new" or Spanish village on the opposite hill.
- Pukará del Cerro Inca: This archeological site is some 3.5 km upriver in the **Quebrada de Mamiña**. The Universidad de Tarapacá intends to attempt a reconstruction of this Inca *tambo*, a very difficult task.
- Cemetery: High above the village, with sweeping views of the village below and the green valley. The entrance to the cemetery is through a cracked portal. The graves indicate the deep-seated affinity of the population with ancestral beliefs. The cemetery was originally outside the church on what is now the central Plaza, and was transferred to its present location in 1865.

Excursions
- **Parca**: A small village 8 km north of Mamiña. A very scenic Andean community with a lively *fiesta* held on December 13 in honor of Santa Lucia. It is a two-hour leisurely walk from Mamiña.

MATILLA

Altitude: 1200 m
Distance from Iquique: 115 km south east on Ruta A-75, Panamericana and RN 16

Matilla is located in the central desert valley, and like its twin town Pica 4 km away is an oasis made possible by the underground streams which find their way to the surface as thermal water, most of them hot.

It was founded by Spaniards from Pica around 1760, but most likely it is of pre-Hispanic origin. Early this century strong winds shifted the desert sands and destroyed a large area under cultivation. Many aquifers have been diverted into aqueducts to supply Iquique with drinking water; this has reduced the amount of water available for irrigation.

Matilla is best reached from Iquique, either on the regular daily buses or on a conducted tour.

⌧ Festivals

• June 13: San Antonio de Padua

▣ Sightseeing

• Iglesia de San Antonio: Built in the 17th century and partially destroyed by an earthquake. The new church was started in the 19th century and incorporates the original tower and altar, and has been declared a *monumento nacional*.

• Museo del Lagar de Matilla: A wine museum. Here the implements used in wine-making (including an old grape press and the clay wine vessels) are shown to visitors. The wine made in Pica and Matilla was famous during the Spanish era (and still is); the wine-making process is deeply rooted in the Spanish tradition, and wine-growing families and their vines go back for centuries.

• La Botijería: An old colonial hacienda outside Matilla in the **Quebrada de Quisma**. Of special interest are the tunnels and underground chambers, some of which are 30 m long to tap underground streams. In the **Quebrada de Quisma** is a mango plantation.

• Agricultural experimental station: 3 km outside Matilla. Run by CORFO, this farm is being converted to drip irrigation to increase the arable land. They are also experimenting with date palms. Here you can buy the most delicious fruit.

PARINACOTA

Altitude: 4400 m
Distance from Arica: 185 km east on RI 11

Parinacota is located inside the **Parque Nacional Lauca**. The whole village, only a small settlement of just under 50 houses, has been declared a *monumento nacional*. It looks deserted, but most of the people are out on the pastures tending their herds, and only return to the village at *fiesta* time — this is common practice throughout the *altiplano* where you travel through hamlets apparently deserted, or inhabited only by old people.

The village is a unique example of a curious blend of Spanish colonial and *altiplano* architecture, although the Spanish colonial style of house prevails. The homesteads are made of volcanic rocks, and are scattered irregularly, but there is a central plaza surrounded by benches, with a small structure known as a *glorieta* in the center.

The whitewashed church on the east side of the plaza is surrounded by a stone wall. The original church was built in the 17th century and re-built in 1789. It is a show-piece of colonial art. Don't miss the interior — there are old murals which appear to be of the Cuzco school of painters. The belfry has three tiers, and its roof is in the form of a cupola. The church is thatched and covered with clay. At *fiesta* time the procession winds through the village, stopping at little shrines dotted all over the village.

The village dates back to pre-Hispanic times. During the colonial period it was on the important road linking Potosí with its port in Arica.

The best view over the village and **Laguna Parinacota** can be obtained by climbing up the little hill on the south side of the village. To the west of the village the Bofedal de Parinacota begins; it can best be described as an *altiplano* swamp area, inside which are small patches of open water which attract a lot of bird life. These *bofedales* are nature's own device for storing glacier water, which seeps out at the lower end or forms springs well below the *bofedales*. To preserve this unique *al-tiplano* village no new buildings may be erected.

It is estimated that one third of all existing bird species in Chile is represented in the national park. The *vicuña*, under the auspices of CONAF, has made a remarkable comeback in the park from almost near extinction.

It is cold all year round. The landscape is bleak but superb.

⊞ Festivals
• September 5: San Domingo

ⓘ Tourist information
Here is the headquarters of the CONAF national park administration. CONAF has a visitors' information center and museum only 200 m from Laguna Parinacota — a trail leads down from here to the lake. In the main hall is a relief model of the national park.

⊟ Accommodation
There is a CONAF *refugio* just inside the national park near the entrance. Kitchen and water. Bring a sleeping bag and food. You must obtain prior permission from CONAF in Arica. In the main tourist season it is usually taken up by tour operators.

⊟ Buses
Buses Humire and Buses Martínez pass through the national park on Tues and Fri on their way to the border town of Visviri/Charaña, and return Wed and Sat. Fare $6.60. Be careful: buses are not reliable. They can be canceled without warning if the bus breaks down or there are insufficient passengers.

⊕ Excursions
• **Parque Nacional Volcán Isluga, Colchané** and Iquique: A difficult trip, best done through a tour operator in Arica. See the entries for Parque Nacional Volcán Isluga (page 65), Colchané (page 46), and Iquique (page 48).

PARQUE NACIONAL LAUCA

Distance from Arica: 155 km north-east on RI 11

The altitude of this *altiplano* park varies between 3200 and 4600 m, with various peaks rising to over 6000 m. It covers 138 000 ha (53 682 ac) and includes several *altiplano* villages such as **Caquena** and **Parinacota**. It is predominantly volcanic, with nearby volcanoes (**Volcán Parinacota** (6342 m), **Volcán Pomerape** (6282 m), active **Volcán Guallatiri** (6060 m) and **Acotongo** (6050 m); and **Crater Ajoya** and **Crater Teneje**. The lava fields of **Cotacotani** bear witness to an active volcanic past.

The park adjoins **Reserva Nacional Las Vicuñas** and **Monumento Natural Salar de Surire**.

The park's main attractions are its mountains of volcanic origin such as **Nevados de Payachatas**; **Lago Chungará** with its flamingo colony; **Lagunas de Cotacotani**; and **Salar de Surire**. You can see *llamas, alpacas,* mudhens, and *vicuñas.* Also interesting is the village of **Parinacota** (see page 62) and the remains of the Inca *tambo* of **Chungará**.

Lago Chungará, at an altitude of 4517 m, covers 21 square km (8 square miles) and has an average depth of 20 m. It is an intense blue and very calm. It is inhabited by giant mud hens, Andean gulls (*Gaviota andina*) and wild ducks. Behind the lake are the twin volcanoes of Parinacota (6342 m) and **Volcán Pomerape** (6282 m), more commonly known as **Nevados de Payachatas**; their peaks are reflected in the lake.

The national park is drained by two rivers: **Río Lauca**, which runs into Salar de Coipasa in Bolivia and **Río Lluta** which runs into the Pacific Ocean. There are many *lagunas* and lakes. The flora consists of cacti, *altiplano* grass (*ichu*) and a few areas with *quenuales* trees (such as southern end of **Lago Chungará**) and *llare-* *tas.* The fauna is represented by *vizcachas, guanaco,* Andean geese, *ñandues, vicuñas,* and *tarucas,* a kind of stag.

The park is located in the Parinacota province, 175 km east of Arica on RI 11. The starting point for a visit here is Arica. It takes 6 hours by local bus and 5 hours by tourist bus.

The average daytime temperature varies between 12° and 20°C (54°–68°F), but falls to between –2° and –10°C (24°–14°F) at night. Most rain falls during summer (December–January), and snow falls in winter (June–August).

If you are driving, bear in mind that you have to bring up all supplies including gas from Arica. There is no accommodation inside the park, except for a few CONAF mountain huts which are in various states of repair. Take warm gear, including a sleeping bag.

ℹ Tourist information

The CONAF national park headquarters is in Parinacota. If you intend scaling the mountains on the border, you must get permission from CONAF and from the Gobernación Provincial de Parinacota.

⊗ Border crossing

Passport control for the trip to La Paz in Bolivia is at Chungará, 3 km from the Bolivian border. Bolivian passport control is in Tambo Quemado in Bolivia.

◉ Excursions

All tours start from Arica and are in minibuses, which carry 8–11 people. Tours are operated by Huasquitur, Turismo Payachatas, and Jurasi Tours. Tours usually include a trip to the Reserva Nacional Las Vicuñas.

I suggest a visit to the village of **Churiguaya**, in the Reserva Nacional Las Vicuñas 20 km south. The main attraction here is the unserviced thermal baths. Leave the international road at the south-ernmost corner of Lago Chungará. A trail leads south-west and is easily recognized. Most of the time you will be within sight of **Volcán Guallatiri** (6028 m). It is estimated that *vicuñas* have now reached over 20 000 head, and are now well established. Don't be alarmed as you pass hamlets with many unoccupied houses; they are not abandoned, only temporarily vacated while their owners tend their flocks on the pastures or work in the mines. These people are still pure-bred Aymarás, and speak their local dialect of Aymará in preference to Spanish.

PARQUE NACIONAL
VOLCÁN ISLUGA

Altitude: 3500–3800 m
Distance from Iquique: 230 km north-east on Ruta A-55

The national park, covering 174 700 ha (431 500acres), was created because of its natural beauty and to preserve the lifestyle of the native population which have several large settlements in the national park: Enquelga, Isluga, and Mauque.

The park is rather isolated, and few tourists visit it. The flora consists of cacti, *llaretales*, and *quenuales*; and the fauna of *vizcachas, llamas*, and *alpacas*. The park is suitable for long hikes and walks and observing the local flora and fauna.

The best way to reach the park is from Iquique — see "*Altiplano* Excursions" from Iquique on page 58 — but tour operators in Arica also make the complete *altiplano* circuit from Arica to Iquique. The trip from Iquique takes 10–12 hours to reach the park entrance near the village of Isluga. There are sporadic bus services from Iquique to Colchané, but if you prefer a do-it-yourself trip, hire a four-wheel drive vehicle. If you are attempting this trip yourself, take all provisions including gas from Iquique; gas is also available in Huara at the intersection of Panamericana with Ruta A-55.

The average daytime temperatures oscillate between 10° and 5°C (50° and 41°F). This calls for warm clothing, as during the night temperatures more often than not are below freezing point.

▧ Festivals in Isluga
- February 2–3: Virgen de la Candelaria
- March 19: San José Obrero
- December 4: Fiesta de Santa Barbara
- December 12: Corpus Cristi
- December 21: Santo Tomás

ⓘ Tourist information.
Before attempting to drive this trip on your own, contact *carabineros* in Iquique

who are in radio contact with their counterparts in Colchané.

CONAF has an administrative ranger's hut at Enquelga. Near the ranger's hut are hot springs which flow into a natural basin.

🚌 Buses

There is irregular public transport from Iquique to Colchané, usually on market days. It is a 6 km walk from Colchané to the park entrance.

⚑ Excursions

For all hikes in the area take a tent and a sleeping bag. When you are hiking in the area, it is easy to cross the border inadvertently, as the trails link Aymará villages on either side of the border. Bring your own food. Water is available.

- **Isluga** is one of the most picturesque *altiplano* villages in the region, with its backdrop of **Volcán Isluga** and Cerro Cabarray in Bolivia. Some of the buildings are of pre-Hispanic origin. The only time it comes to life is during one of the 11 annual festivals. It is inhabited by Aymará Indians, most of whom live with their flocks of *alpacas* and *llamas* in the surrounding *altiplano*, returning to the village only for supplies and for the festivals. Living conditions are harsh, based on a subsistence economy. Of all Aymará villages it has best preserved its Indian character, as the other Aymará settlements have been turned into administrative centers with schools, first-aid posts and *carabineros*. The most striking feature in Isluga is the 16th-century church, surrounded by a low wall made of volcanic rock, with little arches on top. Through the wall are two arched entrances. The church roof is made of clay tiles, and its walls are reinforced by very thick buttresses.

The belfry, standing apart from the church, is of two sections and shaped rather like a pyramid. The space within the wall serves the villagers as the gathering place for their fiestas and for sporting events. It has no accommodation or restaurants so bring your own supplies, tent and sleeping bag — it is freezing at night.

- **Enquelga** at an altitude of 3800 m, is located inside the national park some 12 km west of the border town of Colchané. It consists of about a hundred dwellings, whose inhabitants are Aymará. Nearby, the **Río Isluga** runs into a swampy area. Enquelga has preserved a rich Andean tradition which finds its best expression in the weavings. The village is surrounded by fields of potato and *quinúa*, a type of cereal grain. The church has paintings inside. It is interesting to observe the communal spirit of the villagers — all tasks are performed on a communal basis.

- **Mauque** and **Géiser de Puchultisa**: Mauque is a 30 km hike west over fairly flat *altiplano*. It is a small Aymará village of 20 families. Nearby is **Laguna Vilacolla** and some terraced fields. The church is in the usual *altiplano* style and has two tiers. The geysers, with a temperature of 85°C (185°F), and hot springs are 28 km south, past the village of **Puchultisa**. There are abandoned sulfur mines in the area. This is the private property of Corfo, a company which investigated the possibility of using the heat generated by the geysers for commercial use. There is a caretaker in residence. A colorful *altiplano fiesta*, Nacimiento de María, is held on September 7.

PICA

Population: 1600
Altitude: 1300 m
Distance from Iquique: 108 km south
east on Ruta A-665 Panamericana and
RN 16

Pica is located in the central valley near the foothills of the Andes. It is a typical oasis town, depending on the subterranean water which surfaces as hot springs and accumulates in natural ponds (*cochas*). Pica has a fine climate: it is summer all year round, and from early in the Spanish occupation it has given rise to a large orchard industry: grapes, mangoes and citrus fruit. It is even claimed that the vineyards in the district were planted with vines brought by Pedro de Valdivia, but it is more likely the original vines were brought by the Franciscans who set out from Arequipa to convert the natives.

Key to map

A	Iglesia
C	Municipalidad (Town hall)
E	Telephone
H	Hospital
P	Gas stations
T	Bus terminals

● **Accommodation**

2	Camping Municipal Miraflores
3	Motel El Tambo
4	Motel Resbaladero
7	Hotel Camino del Inca
8	Hotel Nuevo O'Higgins
11	Hotel San Andrés

○ **Eating out**

9	Restaurant Los Naranjos
10	Restaurant El Palmar

■ **Sights**

1	Cocha Miraflores
5	Cocha Resbaladero
6	Cocha de Cancova

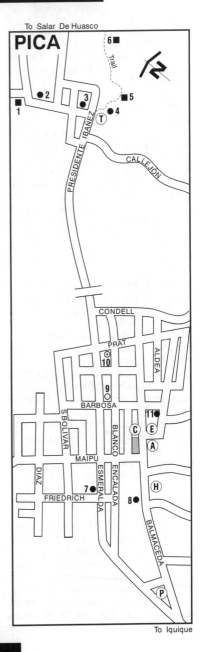

To Salar De Huasco

PICA

To Iquique

Pica

The area was settled by Indian tribes long before the arrival of the Spaniards, as far back as 6000 BC. The old Inca word "*puquío*" is used widely in the area to denote a water well, proving that Pica was on the coastal Inca trail running from Coquimbo through Pica and Tarapacá to Tacna.

Diego de Almagro (who recorded a skirmish with the local Indians) and Pedro de Valdivia passed through Pica with their troops. The Spanish *conquistadores* settled here as early as 1556, and in 1559 the first *encomendero* was rewarded with possession of the area. Until 1767 it was governed civilly from Arica and ecclesiastically from Arequipa. After that it belonged to the newly created province of Tarapacá. The Spaniards left a rich colonial heritage. The villagers formed a closely knit, prosperous Spanish society. They introduced wine and citrus fruit, built intensive irrigation systems, and even tapped the underground water by tunneling into the mountain slopes. The wine was famous and exported to Peru and Bolivia. One of the original wine presses is kept by an old Piqueña family.

The original church dedicated to San Andrés was built first in the early 1600s and again in 1768 after being destroyed by an earthquake. The present church was built towards the end of the 19th century. Inside is a life-sized scene of the Last Supper carved from wood.

The Spanish settlers were preoccupied from the beginning with the supply of enough water to maintain agriculture. They brought mining engineers from Potosí in Bolivia, who drove underground tunnels to tap the water from the underground water systems. The ventilation shafts can be seen in the desert; these kilometer-long tunnels are still in use. One of the largest underground streams descending from the Andes surfaces in the **Quebrada de Quisma** but disappears again in the desert. This is the area from which Iquique draws its main water supply.

Silver was found nearby in the 18th century and brought additional wealth to Pica. When the era of the saltpeter mines began around 1850, many of the vineyards were replaced with other fruits.

The main attraction nowadays is the hot thermal springs located in the upper part of the town. The water collects in rock pools which are called "*cochas*" and are used by the locals and tourists for swimming. The biggest thermal springs are Cocha Resbaladero, where the hot water emerges from a deep cave (located in a picnic area, small admission fee, kiosk); Cocha de Cancova is a few hundred meters further east; and Cocha Miraflores is up from the camping area. At weekends many buses from Iquique come here, and the area around Resbaladero is very crowded. For this reason it is advisable to come here on weekdays.

Festivals
- January 3–6: Pascua de los Negros
- November 29–30: Fiesta de San Andrés, the town's patron saint. A large festival

Tourist information
Municipalidad de Pica has information on travel into the *altiplano*, Laguna del Huasco, Lirima, etc.

Eating out

Restaurants
- El Palmar, Balmaceda near Condell $Z
- La Casona, Esmeralda between Presidente Ibañez and Condell $Z

⊟ Accommodation in Pica

Accommodation in the town center

Hotels
- Camino del Inca, Esmeralda corner of Friedrich
- Nuevo O'Higgins, Balmaceda 6   **AEHIJLU**   ℂ 741322 $G ♟
- San Andrés, Balmaceda 197   **AFGIJLS**   ℂ 741319 $G ♟

Accommodation in Sector Resbaladero
Buses from Iquique normally drive up to this thermal area. If you are lodging in the center of town it is a 10-minute walk uphill.

Motels
- El Resbaladero, General Ibañez 57   **ABIJL**   ℂ 741316 $H for 6
- El Tambo, General Ibañez 68, near hot thermal pools
                                               ABFGHIJL   ℂ 741322 $G for 4

  Shared bathroom cheaper

- El Tambo, near entrance to Cocha Resbaladero $Z
- Los Naranjos, Barbosa corner of Esmeralda

⌨ Post and telegraph

Telephone
- CTC, Balmaceda 141 (on the plaza)

🚌 Buses

Conducted tours take in Pintados with its many rock paintings.
- Iquique: Fare $3.00; 3–4 services daily; duration 3 hrs; Flonatur, Buses Santa Rosa y Julieta

⊞ Shopping

Being an orchard town, it is not surprising that the conserves and marmalades are of excellent quality. From the *altiplano* at Lirima, villagers bring down hand-woven ponchos, gloves, and carpets, mostly made from *alpaca* with an admixture of sheep's wool.

⚑ Excursions

- **Pintados**: 40 km west, 2 km on other side of the Panamericana. Rock paintings. See Reserva Nacional Pampa del Tamarugal on page 73; and "Excursions" from Iquique on page 57.
- **Matilla**: 4 km west. See the entry for Matilla on page 62.
- **Chacarilla**: 80 km south-east in the **Quebrada de Alona**, in the *pre-Cordillera*. Further up in the valley there are rocks with the imprints of prehistoric animals.

PUTRE

Population: 1000
Altitude: 3500 m
Distance from Arica: 45 km north-east on RI 11

A pre-Hispanic Aymará village, Putre is located within view of the **Nevados de Putre**, in superb mountain scenery. It has been capital of Parinacota province since 1982. During the colonial period it became important as a stopover for supplies from the coast on their way to Potosí, and for silver on its

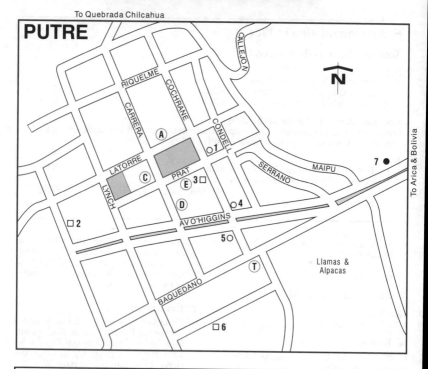

To Quebrada Chilcahua

PUTRE

To Arica & Bolivia

Llamas & Alpacas

Key to map

A	Iglesia
C	Municipalidad (Town hall)
D	Post office and telex
E	Telephone
T	Bus terminals

● **Accommodation**
7 Hostería las Vicuñas

○ **Eating out**
1 Restaurant Santiago
4 Restaurant El Oásis
5 Restaurant Nuevo Amanecer

□ **Services**
2 CONAF
3 Banco del Estado
6 Handicraft shop

way from Potosí to Arica. Through Avenida B. O'Higgins in the center of the town runs a canal of ice-cold water.

Because of its importance, in 1580 the Spanish rebuilt the original village in the Spanish *"manzana"* grid system to make it attractive to Spanish settlers. A new impetus was given to the town when the **Choquelimpie** gold mines were opened in 1643; they are still producing. When Bolivia gained its independence in 1825, the town lost its importance as Bolivia redirected its trade via Antofagasta. At that time, Arica was part of Peru and

Bolivia still controlled Antofagasta. In 1868 the town was destroyed by an earthquake.

The oldest Spanish part of the town is Avenida B. O'Higgins, with bridges crossing a canal carrying a mountain stream. Some houses of the last century have doorways and windows made of stone salvaged from houses built in the 17th century. Many old colonial houses still survive, the biggest concentration being in Baquedano (such as the office of Paloma transport), along the south side of Avenida B. O'Higgins, and around the Plaza (such as the Restaurant Santiago).

Because of its reasonably good facilities, Putre can be a good base for excursions into the **Parque Nacional Lauca**.

At the town's entrance on the lower slope to the left, is the town common, where the locals keep their *llamas* — a delightful picture with the mountainous background and vistas down the *quebrada*.

☒ Festivals
* May 15: San Isidro
* October 24–26: Fiesta

ⓘ Tourist information
* CONAF office

⊟ Accommodation in Putre

Hosterías
★★★ Las Vicuñas, San Martín AE-FGHIJLM $F ♁. Reservations in Arica: ☎ 224997. Reservations in Iquique: Azolas 2257 ☎251172/222377, fax 222166
* San Martín de Putre, Arturo Prat 399 AFHIJN ☎1 $I ♁. Cold, but there is electricity. Reservations in Arica: ☎224997
* Residencial El Oásis, Avenida O'Higgins near Arturo Pérez Canto $J ♁. Shared bathroom, cold water. For budget travelers

⑪ Eating out

Restaurants
* El Oasis, Avenida B. O'Higgins
* Nuevo Amanecer Andino, Arturo Pérez Canto
* Santiago, Arturo Pérez Canto (on the Plaza)

⑱ Post and telegraph

Post office
* Correo de Chile, Calle Carrera

Telephone
* CTC, Prat (on the Plaza)

🚍 Buses
The office of Empresa La Paloma is on Baquedano. near Arturo Pérez Canto.
* Arica: Fare $2.70; 2 buses per week; duration 5 hrs; Buses Paloma

⊞ Shopping
Talleres Artesanales, between the *pulpería* (general store) and the school (overlooking the wide valley with its corrals full of *llamas*) sells *alpaca* weavings of finest quality made by the local people, and alabaster reproductions of *altiplano* belfries. Open Mon–Sat 0900–1300 and 1500–1830.

▣ Sightseeing
The village church dates back to the 17th century, but the present structure was built after the 1868 earthquake. A major restoration took place in 1871. Remnants of the old arched portal which surrounded the Plaza prior to the earthquake are incorporated in the house next to the church.

⦿ Excursions
* **Termas de Jurasi**: Some 8 km on the road to Bolivia there are hot thermal springs at 3800 m. There are two hot fountains; the water is slightly arsenic; facilities are very primitive.
* **Parque Nacional Lauca**: The park entrance is 25 km east. See page 64.
* Through the **Quebrada de Tilivire** to **Socoroma** (7 km) and **Zapahuira** (a further 7 km): A downhill mountain hike through the Quebrada de Tilivire to Zapahuira via Socoroma, and a bus trip back to Arica. Make sure you do this trip on a day when there is a bus service back to Arica.

RESERVA NACIONAL LAS VICUÑAS

Distance from Iquique: 334 km north-east

Covering 210 000 ha (518 519 ac), this reserve located in the *altiplano* near the Bolivian border stretches south from the **Parque Nacional Lauca** which adjoins it, and at its southern boundary merges with the **Monumento Natural Salar de Surire**. The altitude ranges from from 4000 m to 6060 m — the highest point is **Volcán Guallatiri**.

The reserve was created to save *vicuñas* from extinction. Nowadays there are once more 20 000 of those fleet-footed animals roaming the reserve, and they are extending into the adjoining national parks and other areas. It also serves to preserve the flamingo nesting areas around the **Salar de Surire**. This lake, at 4150 m, is the nesting place and breeding ground of all three flamingo species native to Chile. Rising from the center of the lake is **Cerro Oquecollo** (4325 m); the highest mountain near the lake is **Cerro Lliscaya** (5616 m), which forms the border with Bolivia. The *salar* has a few open patches of water. Most of the peaks surrounding the *salar* on all sides reach 5500 m and over. This is a fantastically beautiful *altiplano* area, unfortunately (or fortunately) not easily accessible to large-scale tourism. You are surrounded by high snow-covered peaks, and the highest mountains to the east form the border with Bolivia. You can see flocks of the shy *vicuña*, mostly at dawn and dusk, as they graze in the drier areas of the *bofedales* or high-altitude swamp areas around the lakes. The mountain air is crisp, and free of all contamination; because of the thinness of the air all sound is very subdued. There are CONAF *guarderías* at Guallatiri and at the southern end of the Salar de Surire.

The climate is typical of the *altiplano:* warm during the day and below freezing at night, so be prepared.

This area is for hikers of the hardened outdoor type. Walking with a backpack is difficult at 4000 m. You need a tent and sleeping bag, and bring your own fuel plus a cooking utensil. Do not use the already rare *llareta* for firewood.

You can visit the Aymará villages of **Ancuta** and **Guallatiri** (where there is a CONAF hut). Most of the villagers, however, are absent tending their flocks on the *altiplano*.

The reserve is best visited from Arica with a tour operator. It is one of the highlights of a visit to the northern part of Chile.

You can reach Salar de Surire with a four-wheel drive vehicle, but it is best to do it with Payachata tours from Arica. The CONAF *guardería* and a *carabineros* outpost are at the northern approach to the *salar*. Before embarking on a hike or drive off the RI 11 inform the *carabineros* for your own protection.

Excursions

At the southern end of the *salar* in the shade of **Cerro Lliscaya**, near the Bolivian border is the small hamlet of **Polloquere**, with hot springs and sulfur geysers called *fumaroles*, which are stronger in the morning.

RESERVA NACIONAL
PAMPA DEL TAMARUGAL

Distance from Iquique: 63 km east

Located in the central valley, this reserve consists of two separate areas along the Panamericana: one south of **Pozo Almonte** (including the rock drawings known as **Geoglifos de Pintados**) and the other area situated roughly 17 km north of **Huara** and stretching for 23 km north as far as the turnoff to **Camiña** and **Pisagua**. The total area measures 108 266 ha (267 323 ac). It is best reached from Iquique.

For the rock drawings at **Pintados**, turn south at **Humberstone** into the Panamericana, and follow the road for 27 km. There is a combined picnic and camping area. These artistic expressions of pre-Hispanic tribesmen are located in the southern section of the reserve. Access is at the former saltpeter mine **Oficina Aurora** opposite the southern turnoff to Pica and Matilla; it is well sign-posted. Its only claim to fame is the extensive and well-preserved rock paintings. One large group shows *llama*-like animals (some of them running) and in their midst are *pumas*. The paintings stretch over a distance of 6 km, and if you are in the area try not to miss them. Transport by tour operators from Iquique — see "Excursions" from Iquique on page 57.

SOCOROMA

Altitude: 3100 m.
Distance from Arica: 125 km east on RI 11

Socoroma is located 5 km off RI 11, virtually on a ledge looking down into the **Quebrada de Tilivire**. The only access for cars is from the south. There is however a mountain trail going through the Quebrada de Tilivire to **Putre** (see page 69).

The origins of this village go back to pre-Colombian times. In the narrow streets the bus has hardly enough room to maneuver and has to reverse carefully so as to come out the same way.

The first Spaniards settled here around 1550, as it was an important stop-over on the *altiplano* trail to Potosí. The town is a time capsule from colonial days. Now it is inhabited mostly by Áymará Indians. Some of the houses have stone pillar portals, where possibly the owners of mule teams lived. There are no tourist facilities.

🕺 Festivals

• July 15–16: Virgen del Carmen
• October 1–7: Siembra de la Papa (potato planting)

🚌 Buses

• Arica: Fare $2.30; departs Wed, Sun; Francisco Paco (also known as La Paloma)

📷 Sightseeing

• Iglesia de San Francisco: Located on the north side of the plateau with spectacular vistas down the terraced mountain slope into the **Quebrada de Tilivire**. The altar is made from adobe. The old murals are possibly from the Cuzco school. Next to the church is the soccer ground, and one wonders if the soccer ball is shot beyond the field whose job it is to retrieve it.

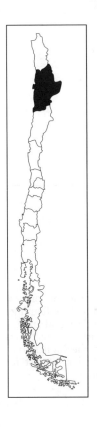

REGIÓN II
DE
ANTOFAGASTA

ANTOFAGASTA

Size: 126 000 square km (49 000 square miles)
Population: 350 000
Regional capital: Antofagasta
Provinces (and provincial capitals):
- Antofagasta (Antofagasta)
- El Loa (Calama)
- Tocopilla (Tocopilla)

Desert covers most of Región II de Antofagasta. Its major attractions are the indigenous Andean villages, and the *salares* with their flamingo colonies. The region was part of the Incan empire, and several archeological sites and pre-Incan *pukarás* can be visited. A further attraction is the geysers and hot springs which are very common in the high *sierras*, indicating strong volcanic activity in the region; of particular interest for geologists as much of the economic activity is based on mining.

Antofagasta shares borders with Región I de Tarapacá in the north, Bolivia in the east, Región III de Atacama in the south and the Pacific Ocean in the west.

As most of the region is desert, more than 80 per cent of the population lives on the coast. The largest inland population centers are around the copper mine at **Chuquicamata** and at its sister city **Calama**. Water has been a problem in this region ever since the saltpeter mines were opened.

Transport

Road

The major road is the Panamericana (or RN 5), which traverses the whole region. Side roads branch off into the mountains to the east and west to the sea. No roads cross into Bolivia, perhaps because of the region's barrenness or the lack of suitable mountain passes, or because it may be political/military strategy to isolate this part of Chile from Bolivia. There is, however, an important road connection between Antofagasta and Salta in Argentina, via the **Paso de La Laguna Sico** (at an altitude of 4079 m). This much improved road replaces the former road over the **Paso de Huaitiquina** which has fallen into disuse. This route is one of the best *altiplano* trips in South America. Note that buses from Salta to Calama run in the daytime only, whereas buses from Calama to Salta do most of the trip at night. Arrange your travel accordingly. There is also a new pass road connection between Antofagasta and Jujuy in Argentina via the Paso de Jama.

Sea

The main seaports are at **Antofagasta** and **Tocopilla**. **Taltal** and **Mejillones** are smaller fishing ports with fishmeal manufacturing facilities. Copper, brought from Chuquicamata by long freight trains, is exported from Antofagasta. A new port facility just south of Antofagasta has been built to ship the copper from **Mina La Escondida**.

Rail

Passenger trains to Uyuni in Bolivia start in **Calama**. Passenger trains do not run between Calama and Antofagasta any longer.

Air

The major airports are Aeropuerto Cerro Moreno for larger planes and La Chimba for smaller ones in Antofagasta, and El Loa in Calama. There are smaller aerodromes in Tocopilla (Barriles) and San Pedro de Atacama.

Topography

Geographically, Región II de Antofagasta is similar to Región I de Tarapacá. The coastal *cordillera* falls abruptly to sea level and in most parts the coastal plain is almost non existent. Towards the east, the coastal *cordillera* loses height gradually

across a plain and then rises to form the Andes. The widest point of Chile lies between **Península Angamos** and **Nevado de Poquis** (5745m). The interior is for the most part desert, with no trace of any vegetation. Here the Andes are made up of two ranges: **Cordillera de Domeyko** in the west with peaks over 4800 m, and the main mountain chain which forms the border with Argentina and Bolivia.

Most of Chile's major ore deposits are found between these two mountain ranges, and this basin is covered in *salares* or salt evaporation pans, the largest being **Salar de Atacama**.

In many places, the Andes rise to over 6000 m. Some peaks are volcanoes: **Volcán Llullaillaco** (6739 m), **Volcán Azufre** (5697 m), and **Volcán Licancábur** (5916 m), **Volcán San Pablo** (6116 m), and **Volcán Ollagüe** (5865 m).

The main river is the Río Loa. Thanks to its tributary, the Río Salado, it is the only waterway north of Santiago which reaches the sea.

Climate

The climate on the coast changes very little throughout the year. It is influenced by the Pacific anticyclone belt and the Humboldt current which brings cold water from the Antarctic. The annual mean temperature varies between 15°C and 24°C (59°F and 75°F).

The **Desierto de Atacama** is one of the most barren areas in the world. Its climate is extremely dry and the complete absence of moisture results in very clear skies. The temperature differences between day and night are considerable, especially above 1500 m. High altitude desert begins from 3000 m onwards. The higher you get, the colder it becomes, and at around 4500 m the cold combined with strong winds can be very unpleasant. The average annual day temperature is 10°C (50°F).

Snow storms are common in the *altiplano* even in summer.

The indigenous inhabitants

Traces of human habitation in this region go back 14 000 years. Most archeological sites are in the **Río Loa** and **Río Salado basins**, and prove that this area was settled at least 10 000 years ago. Before the Spaniards arrived, the Atacameño tribes lived here. Their culture was strongly influenced by the Tiahuanaco culture of Lake Titicaca. Around 1450, the Incas appeared on the scene. At first they did not dominate the indigenous tribes, but their influence gradually grew stronger.

European history

Pedro de Valdivia left the first Spanish settlement in **Chiu Chiu**. Later he also established settlements in **San Pedro de Atacama**, **Peine** and **Toconao**. These settlements lay along the Inca road which started in Cuzco in Peru and went all the way to the **Río Maule** in central Chile. This was the starting point of the conversion of the indigenous people to Christianity and the introduction of Spanish as the major language.

Nothing changed in these areas until Independence. Before the War of the Pacific, the whole region belonged to Bolivia, although Bolivia did not have much say in its affairs. After the War of the Pacific, Antofagasta became part of Chile because of the importance of the saltpeter fields.

Economy

Minerals

As in days gone by, the region's economic future still rests solidly on mineral wealth, although the establishment of a fishing industry has provided an additional source of income. Until the end of World War I, the nitrate fields near the coast were the backbone of the economy. Copper mining has now replaced them. Of the hundreds of saltpeter mines once worked, there are now only two in operation: **María Elena** and **Pedro de Valdivia**. The main power station in the region is in **Tocopilla**; it supplies electricity to the major copper mine in **Chuquicamata** near Calama, the site of one of the biggest open-cut mines in the world.

A similar huge copper mining complex, **Mina La Escondida**, has been opened up in the region Small silver mines also exist in the region worked by so- called *pirquineros* (dry stone miners). Lithium extraction has recently begun from the salts of the Salar de Atacama.

Agriculture

Agriculture, restricted by the availability of water, is located in the river valleys which depend on irrigation. The **Río Loa** forms the border between Región I de Tarapacá and Región II de Antofagasta, and agriculture is mostly centered in oases such as **Calama**, **San Pedro de Atacama**, **Chiu Chiu** and **Toconao**. The only other agricultural oasis outside this area is **Quillagua** on the Río Loa. Tomatoes, potatoes, maize and some fruit are grown; most of these crops are consumed in the region itself.

Beaches

The 320 km shoreline of Región II de Antofagasta has many delightful sandy beaches, but it is a very inhospitable coast with the Desierto de Atacama fringing the Pacific Ocean. Most of the beaches can be reached by an all-weather road, but lack of facilities, especially water, limits their tourist value. The only part of coastline south of Antofagasta between Caleta Coloso and Blanco Encalada has no coastal road. Likewise, there is no coastal road from Taltal to Parque Nacional Pan de Azúcar which straddles both Región II de Antofagasta and Región III de Atacama.

The beaches near the coastal cities are open all year round. The best beaches are in the vicinity of Antofagasta itself at two fledgling seaside resorts — **Mejillones** in the north and **Balneario Juan López** in the south — and near **Caleta Coloso**. The area north of Taltal also has some fine beaches and impressive views, with the coastal *cordillera* dropping abruptly over 1500 m with very few canyons opening onto the Pacific. North and south of Tocopilla, the coastal *cordillera* drops sharply 2000 m, but there are some attractive beaches nearby. The water temperature is between 17°C and 20°C (63°F and 68°F), and the air temperature between 18°C and 28°C (64°F and 82°F) over the whole region.

Thermal springs

* **Géisers de El Tatío**: Altitude 4500 m. By private transport from San Pedro de Atacama or Calama. No facilities. See the entry for the *géisers* on page 100.
* **Baños de Puritama**: No facilities. By private transport from San Pedro de Atacama or Calama.

National parks and reserves

* **Parque Nacional Flamenco**: See "Excursions" from San Pedro de Atacama on page 105.
* **Reserva Nacional La Chimba**, 2583 ha (6380 acres), 15 km north of Antofagasta on RN 1 to Tocopilla. Picnic area, walking trails, eating place, shop. A municipal bus runs from Antofagasta.

Tourism

The major tourist attractions are the beaches, the eternal summer and the archeological sites along the former Inca road near **Chiu Chiu**, **Lasana**, **Pukará de Turi** and **San Pedro de Atacama**. San Pedro de Atacama is the gateway to excursions around Salar de Atacama. The **Géisers de El Tatío** are also worth a visit, and can be reached by tourist bus either from Calama or from San Pedro de Atacama. The standard of hotel and restaurant services is good and transport reliable. There are daily flights connecting Antofagasta and Calama with the southern centers and Iquique and Arica in the north.

Don't miss

☞ Géisers de El Tatío
☞ Antofagasta
☞ Calama–Chuquicamata
☞ San Pedro de Atacama

Worth a detour

☞ Scenic route Calama–Salta (Argentina)

Of interest

☞ Toconao
☞ Chiu Chiu

- ☞ Lasana
- ☞ Paposo
- ☞ Balneario Juan López

Distances

From Antofagasta

South

- Caleta Coloso: 18 km south on RN 1
- Taltal: 303 km south on RN 28 and Panamericana

North

- Aeropuerto C. Moreno: 22 km north on RN 1
- Arica: 740 km north on RN 26 and Panamericana
- Balneario Juan López: 38 km north on RN 1 and Ruta B-446
- Hornitos: 93 km north on RN 1
- Iquique: 504 km north on RN 26 and Panamericana
- La Portada: 16 km north
- María Elena: 205 km north on RN 26 and Panamericana

- Mejillones: 65 km north
- Tocopilla: 188 km north on RN 1
- Tropic of Capricorn: 40 km north-east

From Tocopilla

- María Elena: 68 km south-east
- Pedro de Valdivia: 98km south-east

From Taltal

- Salitrera Alemania: 108 km north-east

From Calama

- Chiu Chiu: 33km east
- Chuquicamata: 16 km north
- Géisers de El Tatío: 125km east
- Salar de Atacama: 131 km south-east
- San Pedro de Atacama: 105 km south-east
- Valle de la Luna: 103 km south-east

ANTOFAGASTA

Area code: 055
Population: 240 000
Altitude: Sea level
Distances

- From Santiago: 1370 km north on RN 28 and Panamericana
- From Salta (Argentina): 790 km west on RN 26, Panamericana and RN 23 (via Paso Laguna Sico)

A ntofagasta, the regional capital, is situated on the Pacific Ocean just 20 km south of the Tropic of Capricorn. The climate is mild throughout the year and the tourist facilities are excellent. There are daily flights to and from Santiago, as well as daily bus services to Arica, Calama, Santiago and Valparaíso.

Antofagasta was founded in 1867 as an export harbor for the saltpeter mined in the region. At this time it was a forlorn outpost in the coastal desert. Many old buildings, declared *monumentos nacionales*, date from this period. An anchor painted on the mountains behind the town has guided ships into the harbor since 1860.

Water has been a problem ever since Antofagasta was founded. In the early days it was shipped from Arica by sea vessels. Late last century the first desalination plants making use of solar power were established to cope with the water shortage.

Antofagasta's economic activities center around shipping, fishing and mining. It is one of the fastest growing towns in the north. In 1995 it was the fifth largest city in Chile and the seaport for the copper produced in Chuquicamata. New port facilities are developing to cater for the extraction of the major copper ore deposits at Mina La Escondida, complete with its own railroad.

Antofagasta is a fairly clean city, at least in its center. It has two universities: Universidad del Norte and Universidad de Antofagasta. The shops are well stocked with a wide range of goods.

Beaches

There are many beaches to the north and south of town, and wonderful coastal walks — for example, along the Paseo del Mar, which is the continuation of Balmaceda and Grecia. The best sandy beaches near town are to the south; they slope gradually to the sea and are also suitable for fishing. The water temperature is between 17° and 20°C (63° and 68°F). The air temperature is between 17° and 28°C (63° and 82°F).

Beaches further north

- **Balneario Juan López**: 31 km north on RN 1 and Ruta B-446., on the southern tip of **Península Mejillones**. It is a small fishing village-cum-seaside resort in

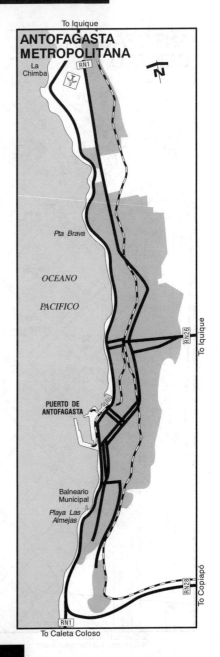

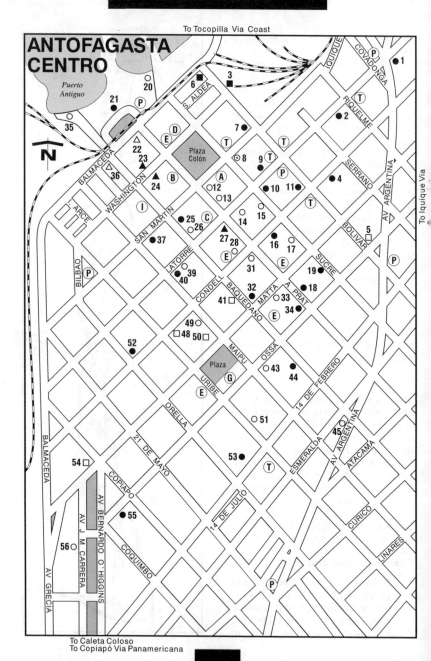

ANTOFAGASTA CENTRO

To Tocopilla Via Coast

Puerto Antiguo

To Iquique Via

Plaza Colón

Plaza

To Caleta Coloso
To Copiapó Via Panamericana

Key to map

A	Iglesia Catedral	15	Pizzería Venecia
B	Gobernación Provincial (Government)	17	Restaurant Pollos Mac
		20	Restaurant Club de Yates
C	Municipalidad (Town hall)	26	Pub Tradición
D	Post Office and Telex	28	Restaurant d'Alfredo
E	Telephone	31	Restaurant Apoquindo
G	Mercado Municipal (Market)	33	Restaurant Carrilón
I	Tourist information	35	Restaurant Playa Club
P	Gas stations	39	Restaurant Shanghai
T	Bus terminals	43	Restaurant Bavaria
		45	Restaurant La Casona de Cordillera

● **Accommodation**

		49	Restaurant Rincón de Don Quijote
1	Hotel Del Norte	51	Restaurant Los Huaquinos
2	Hotel San Marcos	56	Restaurant Pizzarante
4	Hotel Ciudad Avila		
7	Hotel San Martín	⊙	**Entertainment**
9	Hotel Mikysan	8	Teatro Municipal
10	Hotel Pieper		
11	Residencial Toconao	△	**Tour operators and car rental**
16	Apart Hotel Diego de Almagro	22	Budget Rent a Car
18	Residencial Paula	36	Hertz Rent a Car
19	Hotel Rawaye	48	Automóvil Club de Chile
21	Hotel Antofagasta		
25	Hotel Plaza	▲	**Airline offices**
32	Hotel Astore	23	LADECO
34	Residencial El Cobre	24	LAN Chile
37	Hotel Colón	27	National Airline
40	Hotel Latorre		
44	Hotel La Rinconada	■	**Sights**
52	Hotel San Antonio	3	FACB railroad station
53	Hotel Lyon	6	Old "Aduana" (Customs) building
55	Hotel Brasil		
		□	**Services**
○	**Eating out**	5	Goethe Institut
12	Restaurant Club de la Unión	41	Laundromat: Lavandería La Ideal
13	Café Caribe	50	Supermercado Maipú
14	Restaurant Chicken House	54	Medical center: Clínica Antofagasta

desert country. However, it is well frequented at weekends. Water is brought by trucks from Antofagasta. There is a small bay, and the sea water is warm all year round. Cerro Moreno behind the beach is 1150 m high. Across the bay you can see Antofagasta and La Portada. Swimming, fishing, water sports, kiosks, paved road, no drinking water. Public transport is irregular; *colectivos* run in summer only. For further information, see under "Excursions" below.

- **Playa de Mejillones**: 65 km north. *Colectivos*, swimming, fishing, water sports, kiosks, asphalted road.
- **Caleta Hornitos**: 80 km north. Swimming, fishing, water sports, partly asphalted and partly dirt road, no drinking water.

Beaches south

- **Balneario El Huáscar**: 12 km south. Best beach south of town. *Colectivos* run in summer only. Swimming, fishing, water

🛏 Accommodation in Antofagasta

Center of Antofagasta
★★★★ Apart Hotel Diego de Almagro, Condell 2624

	ABCDEFGHIJKLPSU	☎ 268331		$G 👥
Fax 251721				

Hotels

★★★★ Antofagasta Cristóbal Inn, Balmaceda 2575 ☎ 268259 $E 👥
ACDEFGHIJKLMNPRSTUXZ
Beach front with access to its own sheltered beach, shows, car rental, 168 rooms
★★★★ Plaza, Baquedano 461 ACDEFGHIJKLMNPR$TUYZ
☎ 269046 $F 👥
Snackbar, sauna.
★★ San Marcos, Latorre 2946 ADEFHIJP ☎ 251763 $H 👥
Fax 221492, 253 rooms
★★ San Martín, San Martín 2781 AEGHIJKLP$TU ☎ 263502 $H 👥
Fax 268159, 50 rooms
★ Hostal del Norte, Latorre 3162 ADIJLPUZ ☎ 251265 $H 👥
Car rental
• América, Copiapó 1208 ☎ 263703 $G 👥
• Astore, M.A.Matta 2537 ☎ 261203
Fax 267439
• Atenas, M.A.Matta 2317 AEPIJ ☎ 263323 $H 👥
• Brasil, Ossa 1978 A ☎ 267268 $I 👥
• Ciudad de Avila, Condell 2840 ☎ 221040 $H 👥
• Colón, San Martín 2434 APST ☎ 260872 $F 👥
• La Rinconada, Baquedano 810 ABDET ☎ 261139 $H 👥
Fax 268749
• Latorre, Latorre 2450 AP ☎ 221886
• Libertad, Latorre 3064 A ☎ 221509 $I 👥
Backpackers
• Loa, Bolívar 558 $J 👥
Backpackers
• Lyon, 14 de Febrero 2253
• Nadine, Baquedano 519 corner of Latorre
ABDEPT ☎ 227008
Fax 26522, sauna, 75 rooms
• Nikyasan, Latorre 2743 ADP ☎ 221297
• Pieper, Sucre 509 ACDIJKLPS ☎ 266448 $G 👥
Fax 266715
• Rawaye, Sucre 762 AHIJLU ☎ 225399 $I 👥
Budget travelers
• San Antonio, Condell 2235 AEFGHIJKLPTU ☎ 268857 $G 👥
fax264463, 20 rooms
• Stuttgart, Covadonga Vieja 410 ☎ 225266
• Tatío, Avenida Grecia 1000 ADFGHIJLPSTUZ ☎ 247561 $F 👥
24 rooms

Residenciales
• El Cobre, Arturo Prat 749 AIP ☎ 225162 $I 👥
Budget travelers, shared bathroom cheaper
• Gran Via, Avenida Angamos 250 AH ☎ 247480
• Lautaro, Latorre 3203 AP ☎ 221886 $H 👥
• O'Higgins, Sucre 665 $J 👥
Budget travelers

Accommodation in Antofagasta — continued

•	Paula, A. Prat 766 AHU	(222208	$J	ïï
	Budget travelers			
•	Richard, Ossa block 2300 near Maipú		$J	ïï
	Backpackers			
•	Riojanita, Baquedano 464	(268652	$H	ïï
	Budget travelers			
•	Rolando, Washington 2374		$J	ïï
	Backpackers			
•	Toconao, Bolívar 580	(263449		
•	Vargas, Carlos Condell 2342		$J	ïï
	Back packers			

Accommodation in Balneario Juan López
- Centro Turístico La Rinconada, Caleta La Rinconada KM 28 Norte
  Reservations in Antofagasta: Baquedano 800 (222907
- Hotel Sandokan, Caleta Abtao   AEFGHIJUX   (692031 $H ı
  Beach frontage

Accommodation at Playa Huáscar
Playa Huáscar is south of Antofagasta.
- Motel Siete Cabañas, Camino Coloso AHILNPS   (221988 $G for 4

sports, camping, kiosks, life-savers, sealed road. The beach is 300 m long.

⌘ Festivals
- February 14: Anniversary of the city
- May 23: Anniversary of Universidad del Norte
- June 29: San Pedro
- August 10: Fiesta del Minero

ⓘ Tourist information
- CONAF, Avenida Argentina 2510 (222250
- Sernatur, Maipú 240 (264044, fax 264044

⑪ Eating out in Antofagasta

Eating out in the town center
Antofagasta is well known for its seafood dishes. *Frutas del mar* consist of round clams, crabs, and sea urchins.

Restaurants
- Apoquindo, Prat 616
- Bavaria, Ossa 2424, upstairs $Y

- Carrillón, Matta 2540

- Casa Vecchia, Avenida Libertador B. O'Higgins 1456
- Casino Club de Yates Antofagasta, Balmaceda 2705 $Y
- Centro Español, A. Prat 430
- Chicken's House Center, Latorre 2660 $Z
- Club de la Unión, Prat 474
- Deutsches Haus, Antonio Toro 982 $Y
- El Arrayán, Díaz Gana 1314 $Z
- El Arriero, Condell 2644 $Z
- La Casona de Cordillera, Baquedano 1006
- La Selecta, Coquimbo 1102 $Z
- Los Huasquinos, Uribe 831
- Marina Club, Avenida Ejercito 0809 $X. Seafood
- Nuevo Flamingo, Condell 2505 $X
- Pollos Mac, Sucre 646 $Z
- Pub Tradición, Latorre 2509
- Rincón de Don Quijote, Maipú 620
- Shanghai, Latorre 2426
- Tabarín, Copiapó 999 $Z. Seafood; show weekends
- Toledo, in Mercado Central. Early breakfast
- Un Dragón, Copiapó 951 $Y

Cafeterías
- Bongo, Baquedano 743 $Z
- ☞ Café Caribe, A. Prat 482, Local 12 $Z
- ☞ Café Haiti, A. Prat 485 $Z

Pizzerías
- Al Modelo Mio, Sucre 889 $Y
- D'Alfredo, Condell 2539
- D'Angelo Pizza, Latorre 1893
- Pizzarante, Carera 1857
- Venecia, Sucre 540

Salón de Té
- ☞ Macry's, Libertador B. O'Higgins 1868

Eating out Balneario Juan López (north)

Restaurants
- La Portada, Balneario La Portada $Y

ⓣ Entertainment

Town center

Discos
- Topsy, Condell 2689

Night clubs
- ☞ Con Tutti, Avenida Grecia 421

Southern suburbs

Discos
- Cúpula de Cristal, Camino Coloso
- Fórmula 1, Playa El Huáscar

✉ Post and telegraph

Post office
- Correos de Chile, Washington 2613 (on the plaza)

Telephone
- CTC, M.A. Matta 2625, fax 223524
- ENTEL Chile, Condell 2142. Overseas calls
- Telex Chile, Washington 2602

$ Financial

- Cambio Inter Santiago, Latorre 2528, Local 12 ℂ 268802
- Cambio San Marcos, Latorre 2489 ℂ 224814
- Fincard, A. Prat 427 ℂ 222890

🚗 Services

Laundries
- Lavandería La Ideal, Baquedano 660
- Laverap, 14 de Febrero 1812. Self service

Medical services
- Centro Odontológico (Dental Hospital), San Martín 2531
- Clínica Antofagasta, M.A. Matta 1945 ℂ 208102
- Farmacia Chile, M.A. Matta 2483

Photographic supplies
- Foto Quick (Agfa), M.A. Matta 2556

Sport and camping equipment
- Nortesport, M.A. Matta 2383 ℂ 251578

Supermarkets
- ☞ Supermercado Maipú, Maipú block 600 near M.A. Matta

⚑ Visa, passports

- Argentine consulate, Manuel Verbal 1640 ℂ 222854
- Bolivian consulate, Grecia 563 ℂ 221403

✈ Air services

Cerro Moreno International Airport is located 25 km north of town. The airport bus leaves town half an hour before the plane. Taxi $15.00

Airlines
- American Airlines, Washington 2507 ℂ 221730
- Iberia, Latorre 2580 ℂ 268994, fax 268996
- LAN Chile, Washington 2552 ℂ 265151, fax222526
- LADECO, Washington 2589 ℂ 269170
- Línea Aérea National Airlines, Latorre 2572 ℂ 224418, fax 268994
- Lloyd Aéreo Boliviano, Latorre 2528 ℂ 227986
- Lufthansa, Copiapó 574 ℂ 224476/223975

Flights
- Arica: Fare $71.00; 1–3 services daily; duration 1½ hrs; LADECO, LAN Chile
- Calama: Fare $28.00; 1–2 services daily; ½ hr; LADECO, LAN Chile
- El Salvador: Fare $52.00; Sun only; duratonly; duration 1 hr; LAN Chile
- Iquique: Fare $43.00; 2–3 services daily; duration 1 hr; LADECO, LAN Chile
- Santiago: Fare $132.00; 3–4 services daily; 2 hrs; LADECO, LAN Chile

🚙 Motoring

For gas stations, see city map.

🚌 Buses from Antofagasta

The municipal interstate bus terminal is on Avenida Argentina 1155 corner of Diaz Gana (225109, but beware as many bus companies have their own terminals and some do not call at the central bus terminal. From town center municipal buses nos 2, 7, 10, and 11 go to the central bus terminal.

Companies operating from the interstate terminal
- A18   Buses Camus (267424
- A31   Buses Evans
- A42   Buses Carmelita
- A45   Buses Libac (247569
- A49   Buses Litoral (224550
- A59   Buses Pacífico Norte
- A67   Buses Ramos Cholele (226452
- A83   Buses Zambrano Hnos
- A131   Pullman Norte
- A157   Turis Norte (247564

Companies operating from local bus terminal Riquelme 513
- A73   Buses Shadday (266724
- A86   Chile Bus (223326/251741
- A107   Fepstur (281627
- A117   Kenny Bus (251741
- A124   Maravilla Bus (251741

Companies operating from their own terminals
- A8   Atahualpa, Uribe 936 (223624
- A9   Buses Blizzard, Latorre 2751 (
- A35   Buses Géminis, Latorre 3099 (263968
- A78   Buses Tramaca, Uribe 936 (251770, fax 226203
- A106   Fenix Pullman Norte, San Martín 2717 (268896, fax 221014)
- A110   Flecha Dorada, Latorre 2751 (264487
- A112   Flota Barrios, Condell 2764 (268559 fax 268986
- A116   Incatur, Maipú 554 (247566
- A127   Buses Pullman Bus, Latorre 2805 (262591
- A141   Taxi Colectivos Mejillones, Latorre between Sucre and Bolívar

Services

Destination	Fare	Services	Duration	Companies
Arica	$15.20	10 services daily		A35, A78, A110, A112, A117
Calama	$4.60	19 services daily		A35, A45, A78, A110, A112
Caldera	$11.40	7 services daily		A45, A110
Chañaral	$10.60	11 services daily		A35, A45, A78, A110, A112
Chuquicamata	$4.60	16 services daily		A45, A78, A110, A112
Copiapó	$13.30	15 services daily		A31, A35, A42, A45, A67, A78, A83, A106, A110, A112
Coquimbo	$17.50	10 services daily		A35, A45, A78, A110
Illapel	$22.40	Tues, Thurs		A35
Iquique Via RN 5	$12.50	7 services daily	6 hrs	A42, A78, A110, A112, A117
Jujuy (Argentina) Via Paso de Jama	$52.00	Tues, Wed	22 hrs	A78
La Calera	$25.80	10 services daily		A110, A112
La Portada	$7.60			Taxi

Buses from Antofagasta — Continued

Destination	Fare	Services	Duration	Companies
• La Serena	$17.50	20 services daily	14 hrs	A35, A42, A45, A78, A86, A110, A112
Direct	$22.80	1 service daily	14 ½ hrs	A106
Sleeper	$41.00	3 services daily		A112
• Los Vilos	$24.70	10 services daily		A35, A110, A112
• María Elena	$4.00	7 services daily		A78, A112
• Mejillones	$1.40	21 services daily	1 hr	A59, A73, A107, A117, A124, A141
• Ovalle	$19.00	11 services daily		A35, A42, A78, A83, A110, A112
• Pedro de Valdivia	$4.00	7 services daily		A112
• Salamanca	$23.90	Tues, Fri		A35
• Salta (Argentina)				
Via Paso de Jama	$52.00	Tues, Wed	23 hrs	A78
Via Paso de La Laguna Sico				
	$48.00	Wed, Sat	15 hrs	A8, A35
• Santiago	$27.50	18 services daily	20 hrs	A42, A78, A106, A110, A112, A117
Sleeper	$38.00	2 services daily		A112, A127
• Taltal	$5.70	3 services daily	3 hrs	A49, A67, A78
• Tocopilla				
Via coastal road	$3.40			A78, A157
Via inland road	$3.50	16 services daily	2 ½ hrs	A9, A18, A110, A112, A157
• Vallenar	$15.20	11 services daily		A35, A45, A78, A110, A112
• Valparaíso	$28.50	7 services daily		A78, A83, A112, A131
• Viña del Mar	$28.50	7 services daily		A78, A83, A112, A131

Car rentals
- Automóvil Club de Chile, Condell 2330 (225332
- Avis Rent-a-Car, Balmaceda 2499 (221073
- Budget Rent-a-Car, A. Prat 206, Local 5 (251745
- Bulnes Rent-a-Car, Sucre 220, office 407 (224103
- Hertz Rent-a-Car, Balmaceda 2492 (269043
- Rentaequipos Rent-a-Car, Baquedano 300 ((083)269223, fax 226403

Shopping

The main shopping street is Arturo Prat, a pedestrian mall between San Martín and M.A. Matta.

Sport

- Tennis Digeder, Parque Yugoslavia, Avenida Ejercito
- Club Aéreo de Antofagasta, Aeródromo La Chimba (237837
- Club de Golf, north of town at the intersection of Avenida Edmundo Pérez Zujovic with Avenida Pedro Aguirre Cerda, might be of interest to keen golfers. Don't expect too much green in this desert environment.
- Club de Tennis de Antofagasta, Angamos 906 (247756

Sightseeing

The center of town is the Plaza Colón, with a clock tower in the middle, presented by the British community. The most important public buildings such as the cathedral, town hall, regional seat of government, and post office surround this plaza. On Avenida Balmaceda between Maipú and Bolívar some of the buildings are over one hundred years old, and the historical part of the town includes the dock area. The Museo Regional occupies one of these preserved buildings and nearby are monuments commemorating the War of the Pacific. The largest shops and the Museo Antropológico are on A. Prat.

The town has wide streets and many parks and *avenidas* which are masterpieces of town planning. Examples are the broad Avenida J.M. Carrera, separated by a wide palm-tree studded park from the Avenida Bernardo O'Higgins; and the Avenida Grecia, which continues southwards as Avenida del Ejercito but is better known as Paseo del Mar.

Parks, beaches, eating places and recreational facilities line the Paseo del Mar. This road, with its tree-lined center strip, leads to the Parque Yugoslavia. Immediately after the turnoff to the Panamericana, Disco Popo's is on the left-hand side, then Plaza Francisco Vergara, the relocated remains of an authentic *oficina salitrera* (a saltpeter mine lease), an open-air museum, and the Universidad de Antofagasta.

The last suburb is Barrio Jardín del Sur, where the Automóvil Club's tennis courts lie opposite the Universidad de Antofagasta. Beyond this elegant suburb, there are many beaches where camping is possible: Playa Poza de los Gringos (swimming and rock-fishing), Playa Poza Llacolen, Balneario El Huáscar (Motel Siete Cabañas, Disco Cúpula de Cristal, swimming) and Playa Amarilla. The Paseo del Mar finishes at **Caleta Coloso**, a fishing village 18 km south of town that offers swimming, fishing, a hotel and discos. The road continues south but becomes a dirt track and is not suitable for ordinary cars.

From Plaza Colón, the Avenida A. Pinto heads north past the harbor and the fish market where fishing vessels unload their catch. Either turn right into P. Aguirre Cerda or continue along the coast. The coastal road passes Playa del Galeón where there is a floating restaurant with dancing at weekends. The Chimba sector is located where the road turns inland; it has been declared an *Area de Protección Natural* to preserve the rich bird life and the rock outcrops along the coast. At the intersection with RN 1, turn off north to **La Portada** and **Balneario Juan López**. Further on, turn left for Aeropuerto Cerro Moreno.

- Museo Regional de Antofagasta, Bolívar 188. From the early inhabitants to the development of modern settlements. A large section is dedicated to the War of the Pacific and the development of the salpeter mining industry. Open Tues–Sun, 1000–1300. Admission $0.50.

- Ruinas de Huanchaca: These are the remains of an old silver foundry just outside the southern city limits, known as Fundición Playa Blanca and run by the Compañía Huanchaca. Take local buses either along Avenida Argentina or along Paseo del Mar and get off at Universidad Católica del Norte.

- Universidad Católica del Norte: Visit the Museo Geológico, which displays fossils found in the region that are 250 million years old.

⬥ Excursions

Tour operators
- Corssa Turismo, San Martín 2769 ℡ 251190/221668. Also car rental
- North Gate Tour, Baquedano 498, Local 14/15 ℡ 281803, fax 2515868
- Nortour, Baquedano 461 ℡ 227171
- Parina Tour, Washington 2675 Edificio Centenario ℡ 260497
- Tatío Travel Service, Latorre 2579 ℡ 263532

Excursions
- **Tocopilla**: The road leading north (RN 1) along the seaside is sealed all the way; there are regular daily bus services. See the entry for Tocopilla on page 117.
- **Caleta Coloso**: A picturesque small fishing hamlet 12 km south of town. Can be reached by public transport.
- **La Portada**: This short trip 16 km north on RN 1 along the Costanera Norte, takes about half an hour by taxi and costs $8.00 return. The same turnoff leads to Balneario Juan López. At La Portada there is a restaurant and a lookout across the Bahía Moreno to Balneario Juan López and south to Antofagasta. The main attraction is La Portada, a huge rock arch near the shoreline, shaped by wind and water erosion, which now looks like a forlorn copy of the Arc de Triomphe. A narrow fringe of beach is visible from the viewing platform, and the surrounding rocks contain fossilized crustaceans. The bay is edged with huge rocks pounded by the sea and is not good for swimming. Buses from Antofagasta leave every two hours

from 0730 onwards from the Terminal Pesquero.

- **Balneario Juan López**: The trip to La Portada can be combined with a visit to Balneario Juan López, 18 km further round the bay, opposite La Portada. Balneario Juan López is a growing seaside resort frequented by the rich from Antofagasta. The sheltered beach has grey sand and the warm and tranquil waters invite swimming and diving. **Cerro Moreno** (1148 m), the highest point on Península Mejillones, towers behind the beach. Once only fishermen inhabited this shore, but there is now a hotel and dancing at weekends. Some holiday cabins have been built, and there is free camping along the beach. Drinking water is brought from Antofagasta and sold to the houses.

- **Mejillones**: A seaside resort and fishing port. This 64 km trip north on a sealed road takes about an hour, passing Aeropuerto Cerro Moreno and heading through desert country with the Cordillera de la Costa on the right. Frequent buses leave the Maravilla depot. See the entry for Mejillones on page 103.

- **Caleta Hornitos**: 80 km north on RN 1. This is a large unspoilt beach of white sand with high temperatures all year round. Take one of the regular buses to Tocopilla.

- Archeological tour into the *pre-Cordillera*: This three-day conducted tour includes visits to an abandoned saltpeter mine and to the open-cut copper mine at **Chuquicamata**. The first overnight stay is in **San Pedro de Atacama**. On the second day the tour visits **Quebrada de Jeria** near **Toconao**. On the return to San Pedro, stops are made at the archeological museum and the so-called Casa de Pedro de Valdivia. A trip to **Valle de La Luna** in the late afternoon for the optimal effect of the setting sun on the rock formations is an optional extra. On the third day, the tour visits **Pukará de Quitor** and **Pozo Tres**, a natural water source in the *pre-Cordillera*.

- **Calama**: A four-day version of the previous tour includes an overnight stay in Calama. Next morning it visits **Chiu Chiu** and **Lasana** and returns to Antofagasta. See the entry for Calama below.

- **Géisers de El Tatío**: The independent-minded traveler might like to take a regular bus to Calama or even to San Pedro de Atacama and join a conducted tour there. Tours to the geysers and other places of interest inland are also possible. A three to four day tour starts in Antofagasta. The first two days same as the archeological excursion. On the third day, the tour leaves early in the morning for the Géisers de El Tatío when they are the most active: 0600–0700. The tour continues to **Toconce**, **Baños de Turi**, **Pukará de Turi**, **Lasana**, **Caspana**, and **Laguna Chiu Chiu** and returns the same evening to Antofagasta. See the entry for Géisers de El Tatío on page 100.

- **Taltal**: Tramaca line buses make the trip in three hours along the Panamericana, an excellent sealed road. The more interesting tourist option is via the old colonial interior road which turns off the Panamericana 75 km south of Antofagasta (at KM 1337) to **Blanco Encalada** on the coast, and then proceeds along the coast to Taltal via **Paposo**. This is said to be a fabulous trip, but it is very difficult to do as there are only irregular bus services going this way. On the way visit the abandoned saltpeter mines at Alemania. The beaches in the vicinity of Taltal are within easy reach. Visit the town itself and one of the many restaurants to sample the specialty eel dish: *congrio colorado*. See the entry for Taltal on page 111.

- **European Southern Observatory**, located on Cerro Paranal. For visits contact Balmaceda 2536 office 504 (260032 fax 260081.

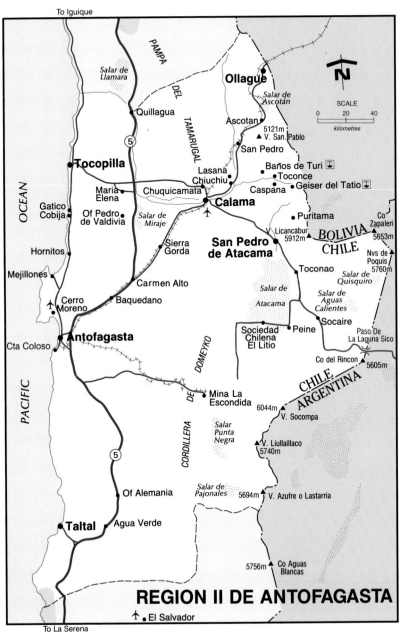

Plate 5
Map of Región II de Antofagasta

Plate 6   Región II de Antofagasta
Top: Geisers de El Tatío
Bottom: Río San Pedro Valley, near San Pedro de Atacama

CALAMA

Area code: 056
Population: 88 000
Altitude: 2250 m
Distance from Antofagasta: 215 km north-east on RN 25 and Panamericana

Calama is situated on the **Río Loa** in the copper belt, and is surrounded by desert. Here the north–south (Copiapó–Arequipa) and the east–west Inca roads met, and later Diego de Almagro passed this point. From 1833, Calama became a staging post on the road from Potosí to Cobija on the Pacific coast, Bolivia's main administrative center before the War of the Pacific. The town was officially proclaimed in 1870. However, Calama's past has been completely blotted out by the new township established to service the nearby mine of Chuquicamata.

Lately the town has grown popular with tourists because of its good facilities and its closeness to many places of interest in the *pre-Cordillera* and *altiplano*. The passenger railroad to Bolivia, built in 1867, starts here and there are also buses to Salta and Jujuy in Argentina. However, the main attraction is the Chuquicamata mine located 16 km north. Calama is the supply base for many smaller mines operating in the area as well as for many prospectors.

The town is a good starting point for visits to the **Géisers de El Tatío**, **Baños de Turi** and the many villages in the *pre-Cordillera* — time capsules with their still largely Aymará and Atacameño Indian population and their Andean-style agriculture of irrigated terraces on the slopes.

By using the waters of the Río Loa for irrigation, Calama has become the biggest oasis in the *pre-Cordillera,* and is set in a green belt of *chacras.* Diverting the sulfuric waters of the Río Salado for use in mineral processing in Chuquicamata has improved the water quality of the Río Loa.

The main commercial activity is on Calle Ramírez. The town comes to life after sunset because many people working in Chuquicamata return home in the evening.

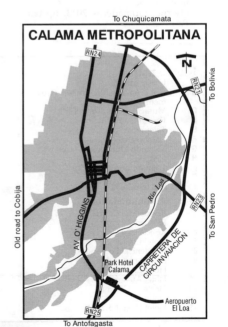

To Chuquicamata

CALAMA METROPOLITANA

RN24

To Bolivia

Old road to Cobija

Río Loa

AV. O'HIGGINS

RN23

To San Pedro

CARRETERA DE CIRCUNVALACION

Park Hotel Calama

Aeropuerto El Loa

RN25

To Antofagasta

Calama

⌘ Festivals

- March 23: Anniversary of city
- June 24: San Juan
- August 10: Miners' celebration

ⓘ Tourist information

- Oficina Municipal de Información Turística, Latorre 1689

⅋ Eating out

Eating out in the town center
- Gelatería Fiori di Gelatto, Ramírez 2099

Restaurants
- Bacio Freddo, Vivar 2002
☞ - Bavaria, Sotomayor 2095. Also *cafetería*
- Chifa Cantón, Vargas 1925 $Z. Chinese cuisine
- Los Adobes de Balmaceda, Sotomayor 1504 $Y
- Los Braseros de Hanstur, Sotomayor 2402 $Y
- Mariscal JP, Félix Hoyos 2127 $Y
- Nueva Chong Hua, Abaroa 2006. Chinese cuisine
- Osorno, Granaderos 2013, upstairs. *Parrillada, peña*

Pizzería
- D'Angelo, Latorre 1983 $Z

Eating out outside town
- Quinta America, Avenida La Paz $X
- Quinta El Bosque, Avenida La Paz 1615 $X

☂ Entertainment

Restaurants
- Hotel Alfa, Sotomayor 2016 $Y. Dancing weekends
- Las Llaves del Rey, Abaroa 2258 $Y. International cuisine, dancing

✉ Post and telegraph

Post office
- Correos de Chile, Vicuña Mackenna 2197

Telephone
- CTC, Abaroa 1978, fax 342180
- CTC, Abaroa 1756, fax 342860
- ENTEL Chile, Hurtado de Mendoza 2139. International calls
- Telex Chile, Abaroa 1926

$ Financial

- Burdiles María, Sotomayor 1826 ℂ 341595

Key to map

A	Iglesia Matriz
B	Gobernación Provincial (Government)
C	Municipalidad (Town Hall)
D	Post office and Telex
E	Telephone
F	Carabineros (Police)
G	Mercado Municipal (Market)
H	Hospital
I	Tourist information
P	Gas stations
T	Bus terminals

● Accommodation

3	Residencial Capri II
5	Residencial Palermo
6	Residencial Capri I
7	Hotel El Cid
8	Residencial Los Andes
9	Hotel Splendid
11	Hotel Lican Antai
12	Hotel Atenas
13	Hostería Calama
14	Hotel Alfa
15	Hotel Hostal del Sol
16	Residencial Casa de Huéspedes
18	Hotel El Loa
19	Hotel Quitor
20	Hotel Casablanca
21	Hotel Claris Loa
22	Hotel Génesis
23	Hotel Olimpo
26	Residencial Internacional

○ Eating out

1	Restaurant Los Adobes de Balmaceda
10	Restaurant Bavaria
17	Cafetería Bavaria
24	Restaurant Mariscal

▲ Airline offices

2	LADECO
27	LAN Chile
28	Railroad station

□

Services

25	Bolivian consulate

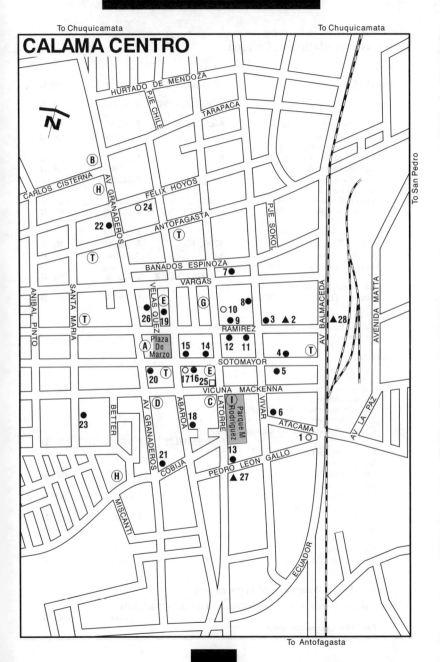

CALAMA CENTRO

To Chuquicamata

To Chuquicamata

To San Pedro

HURTADO DE MENDOZA

PJE CHILE

TARAPACA

CARLOS CISTERNA

AV. GRANADEROS

FELIX HOYOS

PJE SOKOL

O 24

ANTOFAGASTA

22

SANTA MARIA

BANADOS ESPINOZA

VARGAS

7

ANIBAL PINTO

VELASQUEZ

E

G

8

O 10

9

3 ▲ 2

▲ 28

AVENIDA MATTA

AV. BALMACEDA

26 19

RAMIREZ

Plaza De Marzo

A

15 14

12 11

4

SOTOMAYOR

5

20

17 16 25

E

VICUNA MACKENNA

AV. GRANADEROS

D

BETTER

ABAROA

C

LATORRE

VIVAR

I

Parque M Rodriguez

6

23

18

ATACAMA

1 O

21

COBIJA

13

PEDRO LEON GALLO

H

MISCANTI

▲ 27

AV. LA PAZ

ECUADOR

To Antofagasta

ANTOFAGASTA

☒ Accommodation in Calama

Hotels

★★★ Hostería de Calama, J.J.Latorre 1521	ACEFGHJLMPS$TU	☎ 341511	$F/G ♙♙
★★ Alfa, Sotomayor 2016	ACDEFGHIJKLPS$TUX	☎ 342496	$G ♙♙
★★ Olimpo, Santa María 1673	ADEFGHIJLMS	☎ 342367	$G/H♙♙

* Atenas, Ramírez 1961 — AIJ — ☎ 342666 — $I ♙♙
  Shared bathroom, fax 315399
* Claris Loa, Granaderos 1631 — AEI — ☎ 311939 — $I ♙♙
* El Loa, Abaroa 1617 — ☎ 341963 — $H ♙♙
* Génesis, Granaderos 2148 corner of Antofagasta — ☎ 342841 — $J ♙♙
  Budget travelers
* Hostal El Sol, Sotomayor 2064 — ADIJLS — ☎ 341235 — $I ♙♙
* Lican Antai, Ramírez 1937 — AEFGIJLS — ☎ 341621 — $F ♙♙
  Fax 341308
* Palermo, Sotomayor 1889 — ☎ 341283
* Quitor, Ramírez 2116 — ACDEIJLPS — ☎ 341716 — $G ♙♙
* Splendid, Ramírez 1960 — AJP — ☎ 341841 — $I ♙♙
* Turismo Casablanca, Sotomayor 2160 — ACDEFHIJKLPS$UZ — ☎ 312966 — $G ♙♙
  Car rental, fax 341938
* Turismo El Cid, Vargas 1947 — ☎ 319075 — $F ♙♙

Motels
* Kalu, Avenida Ecuador 1697 — AGH — ☎ 342902
  14 cabins

Residenciales
* Bello Kin's, Balmaceda 2040
  Budget travelers
* Capri, Vivar 1639 — ☎ 342870 — $J ♙♙
  Budget travelers
* Casa de Huespedes, Sotomayor 2073
  Budget travelers
* Casa de Huéspedes King's, Balmaceda 2040 — ABCDEFGHIKLPS — ☎ 341868/342179 — $H ♙♙
* El Tatío, Pedro Leon Gallo 1987 — AIJ — ☎ 342284 — $J ♙♙
  Backpackers
* Internacional, G. Velazquez 197 — A — ☎ 341553 — $J ♙♙
* Janett, Sotomayor 2424 — ☎ 342966
* John Kenny, Avenida Ecuador 1991 — AHIP — ☎ 341430 — $H ♙♙
  Shared bathroom $I ♙♙
* Los Andes, Vivar 1920 — ☎ 341073 — $J ♙♙
  Budget travelers
* Tacora, Sotomayor 1982
  Backpackers
* Toño, Vivar 1970 — ☎ 341185 — $J ♙♙
  Backpackers

Accommodation along the road to the airport

★★★ **Hotel Park,** Camino Aeropuerto 1392 ACDEFGHJKLMPRS$TUXYZM
☎ 319900 — $D ♙♙
Fax 319901, sauna, car rental

- Fincard, Latorre 1763, Edificio Hernani, office 207, 2nd floor ℂ 341666
- Flota Barrios
- International Exchange, Sotomayor 1818 ℂ 312063

🖳 Services and facilities

Pharmacy
- Farmacia Cotoras, Sotomayor 1898

Laundries and dry cleaners
- Laverap, Abaroa 2204. Self serve
- Lavaseco Express, Sotomayor 1984

Photographis supplies
- Foto Quick, Latorre 1899

Supermarket
- Supermercado El Cobre, Vargas 2148

▣ Visas, passports

- Bolivian Consulate, V. Mackenna 2020 ℂ 341976

✈ Air services

Airlines
- LADECO, Ramírez 1858 office 1 ℂ 312626
- LAN Chile, Latorre 1499 ℂ 211394

Flights
- Antofagasta: Fare $28.00; 2 services daily; ½ hr; LAN Chile, LADECO
- El Salvador: Sun only; duration 2 hrs; LAN Chile
- Iquique: 1 service daily; LADECO
- Santiago: Fare $145.00; 2 services daily; duration 2½; LANChile, LADECO

🚆 Trains

- Ferrocarriles, Balmaceda 1777 ℂ 342004. Book well in advance. Bookings also at Tramaca bus
- Calama–Ollagüe every Wednesday
- Connections with Bolivian train to Uyuni ($18.50) and Oruro ($23.00) in Bolivia. An uncomfortable journey, bring blankets

🚗 Motoring

Car rental
- Automóvil Club de Chile, Ecuador 1901 ℂ 342770
- Avis Rent-a-Car, Latorre 1492 ℂ 315881
- Budget Rent-a-Car, Comercial Ipanema, Punta de Diamantes ℂ 341076

- Hertz Rent-a-Car, Latorre 1510 ℂ 341380

Gas station
- Esso Servicenter, Avenida Granaderos 3657

🛍 Shopping

The main shopping street is Calle Ramírez.

📷 Sightseeing

- Parque El Loa, a tourist complex with an archeological museum and handicrafts exhibition and sale. Replica of the church in Chiu Chiu. Open every day, 1000–1800.

🕭 Excursions

Tour operators
- Atacama Desert Expeditions, Avenida Libertador Bernardo O'Higgins 415 ℂ 312019 fax 312064
- Nativa Expediciones, Abaroa 1796 ℂ 319834
- Tokori Tour, Sotomayor 2016, Galería Hotel Alfa, Local 18 ℂ 342415, fax 340196. Tours to Géisers de El Tatío, Valle de la Luna, Salar de Atacama
- Turismo Hector Ochoa Olivares, Brasilia 1102 ℂ 212479. Also has an office in San Pedro de Atacama. Runs tours to San Pedro and Géisers de El Tatío

Excursions
- **Ayquina**: 75 km east, at 2950 m. This picturesque Andean village is located in the **Río Salado** valley just where it leaves the *pre-Cordillera* and enters the **Pampa Borax**. The village overlooks the three tiers or terraces of the valley with a trail connecting them; the terraced fields are artificially irrigated. The area was uninterruptedly settled by the Atacameño tribes for many thousands of years, and they have left many rock paintings in the surrounding *quebradas*. There is evidence that prehistoric stone tools were manufactured here: knives, hammers, chisels, and spear tips. And fragments of potsherds show the influence of the Tiahuanaco and Inca empires after the initial period. Nowadays, Ayquina is a small village inhabited by the descendants of the Atacameño tribes

🚌 Buses from Calama

There is no central bus terminal in Calama.
For excursions to San Pedro de Atacama, Tocanao (on the Salar de Atacama),
Chiu-Chiu, Pucará de Lasana, Géisers de El Tatío, see "Tours" below.
Colectivos run to Chuquicamata from Plaza 23 de Marzo.

Companies
- A8   Atahualpa, Granaderos 3048
- A18   Buses Camus, Balamceda 2044 (342800
- A35   Buses Géminis, Antofagasta 2239 (341993
- A45   Buses Libac, B. Espinoza 2098 (342156
- A78   Buses Tramaca, Granaderos 3048 (342587
- A110 Flecha Dorada, Ramírez 1802 (341472
- A112 Flota Barrios, Ramírez 2298 near Santa Maria (341497
- A117 Kenny Bus, Vivar 1854 (212514
- A127 Buses Pullman Bus, Sotomayor 1808 (311410
- A166 Empresa de buses Morales Moralito, Sotomayor 1802 (342671

Services

Destination	Fare	Services	Duration	Company
Antofagasta	$4.60	23 services daily		A35, A45, A78, A110, A112, A127
Arica	$11.40	6 services daily	10½ hrs	A35, A78, A112, A127
Chañaral	$15.20	8 services daily		A110, A112
Sleeper	$18.60	1 service daily		A35
Copiapó	$17.00	11 services daily		A45, A78, A110, A112
	$20.90	1 service daily		A35
Coquimbo	$18.20	8 services daily		A45, A78, A110
Sleeper	$23.90	1 service daily		A35
Illapel				
Sleeper	$24.70	1 service daily		A35
Iquique	$12.50	7 services daily		A78, A110, A112, A117, A127
Jujuy (Argentina)				
Via Paso de Jama	$45.00	Tues, Wed	18 hrs	A78
La Calera	$30.00	9 services daily		A78, A110, A112
La Serena	$21.50	17 services daily	17 hrs	A45, A78, A110, A112, A117
Sleeper	$23.90	1 service daily		A35
Los Vilos	$24.70	10 services daily		A78, A110, A112
Ovalle	$22.80	10 services daily		A35, A45, A78, A112, A110
Salamanca	$25.90	Sun		A35
Salta (Argentina)				
Via Paso de Jama	$45.00	Tues, Wed	19 hrs	A78
Via Paso de la Laguna Sico				
	$40.00	Wed, Fri	16 hrs	A8, A35
San Pedro de Atacama				
	$3.80	2 services daily	2 hrs	A78, A166
Santiago	$30.00	10 services daily		A78, A110, A112, A117
Sleeper	$44.80	1 service daily		A35
Toconao	$5.30	Tues, Thurs, Sat	3 hrs	Rural bus
Tocopilla	$4.20	2 services daily		A18
Vallenar	$22.40	10 services daily		A35, A45, A110, A112
Valparaíso	$30.00	1 service daily		A78
Viña del Mar	$30.00	1 service daily		A78

Buses from Calama — continued

Buses from Chuquicamata
Chuquicamata is a mining town 16 km north — see "Excursions" below.

Companies
- A18   Buses Camus
- A35   Buses Géminis
- A45   Buses Libac
- A78   Buses Tramaca, O'Higgins 81 ℂ 326340
- A110   Flecha Dorada, O'Higgins 479 ℂ 326334
- A112   Flota Barrios, O'Higgins 966 ℂ 326349

Services

Destination	Fare	Services	Duration	Companies
Antofagasta	$4.60	17 services daily		A45, A78, A110, A112
Chañaral	$14.40	4 services daily		A110
Copiapó	$17.00	11 services daily		A45, A78, A110, A112
Coquimbo	$18.20	1 service daily		A45
Illapel	$25.00	1 service Tues, Fri		A35
La Serena	$21.30	11 services daily	17½ hrs	A45, A110, A112
Ovalle	$19.60			A35, A45, A112
Salamanca	$25.80	Tues, Fri		A35
Santiago	$30.00			A78, A112
Tocopilla	$4.20	2 services daily		A18
Vallenar	$22.40			A45, A112
Valparaíso	$29.60	3 services daily		A78, A112
Viña del Mar	$29.60	3 services daily		A78

who, under the mantle of Christianity, still cling to their ancestral customs. This is best observed when they celebrate their colorful *fiestas*. The village attracts thousands of faithful *altiplano* Indians on September 8 to celebrate the Fiesta Nuestra Señora de Guadalupe de Ayquina. Their houses, which seem to be hanging in the walls of the canyon, are made from cactus wood. Don't forget your camera as this scene is very photogenic. Ayquina has one of the most impressive *altiplano* churches of the region, dedicated to Nuestra Señora de Guadalupe. The tall belfry has five tiers ending in a cupola with a cross. Just 2 km from the village there are rock paintings depicting *llama* and *guanaco* hunting in pre-Colombian times. **Baños de Turi** and the **Pukará de Turi**: are some 8 km north of Ayquina. The *pukará*, a formidable fortification in its time, stands on a platform. The town surrounding it was

very regularly laid out and the houses built of volcanic rock. Although Ayquina was founded long before the Incan invasion, it is believed the Incas took over the existing settlement and established a *tambo* from the late 15th century onwards. Potsherds of Incan origin are found in the vicinity. Worth a visit, especially for those interested in archeology. Modern day Ayquina is scattered over an irregular 1 km stretch, with houses clustering around Calle A. Prat and Diego Portales. Many homes were abandoned when villagers found employment in the mines and moved their families to join them. Rural buses run to Calama, but the service is irregular. I suggest you visit Ayquina with a tour operator.

- **Caspana**: A small Atacameño village of about 500 inhabitants at an altitude of 2900 m, reached by RN 21 and Ruta B-159. It is 80 km north-east of Calama in the *pre-Cordillera* and 50 km west of the Géisers de El Tatío. The river irri-

Calama

gates the green and well-kept fields on the valley floor and pre-Colombian terraces. The villagers live off agriculture and raising *llamas* and sheep, selling their produce in the market at Calama. Most of the houses are built of liparit, a white volcanic rock. The main attraction of this picturesque *altiplano* village is Iglesia San Lucas, a *monumento nacional*, founded in 1641. The church's roof is made of cactus wood, and it has a small sacristy attached. A staircase leads up to the three-tiered belfry; you can visit the church for a small donation. The church precinct is surrounded by a wall. The small museum exhibits archeological artifacts found in and around Caspana, and gives an overview over the development of people in this area. There are some impressive silver pieces on show. The villagers celebrate a number of festivals which attract many *altiplano* inhabitants. Local artesans make replicas of the belfry of red volcanic rock. Although rural buses go from Calama to this village, those buses are geared towards the need of the villagers. Tour operators include Caspana in their tours.

- **Chiu Chiu** and **Lasana**: Chiu Chiu is 33 km north-east on RN 21 at 2550 m, Lasana 41 km on the same road. This 90 km round trip can be made by public transport or with a tour operator. Both villages are supplied by a small stream which enables the population to grow some agricultural products, and are high enough for *llamas, alpacas* and *guanacos* to live here. Chiu Chiu has one of the oldest churches in Chile. The 10 km unsealed road from Chiu Chiu to Lasana leads through a steep canyon whose walls are covered in rock paintings. In pre-Colombian days, Lasana was a fortified place on the Inca road. The *pukará* has been restored to some extent. For further information on both Chiu Chiu and Lasana, see the entry for Chiu Chiu below.

- **Chuquicamata**: A mining town 16 km north, at an altitude of 2400 m. It is the biggest and most important mining town in Chile, producing half the country's copper and silver and the biggest single export earner in Chile. Guided tours of the mine are conducted free of charge on weekdays at 1000 at gate no. 1 from the mine office marked "Relaciones Públicas". The tour is conducted by bus and takes about 2½ hours; guides usually speak English, German, and French. There are two open-cut mines: Mina Chuqui, the larger and older one (4800 m long, 2500 m wide and 600 m deep), is located north of town; and Mina Sur is located beyond the slag heap to the east of the town. Regular *colectivo* services ply between the two towns.

- **Géisers de El Tatío**: Located at 5000 m 129 km east on Ruta RN 21 or Ruta B-159. The hot water regularly shoots 10 m and forms a series of small *lagunas*. The water emerges at 35°C (95°F) and as it trickles downhill turns into ice — the temperature of the place ranges between +15°C and –5°C (59°F and 41°F). A poorly maintained dirt road leads to the geysers. This 250 km round trip, which can include other *altiplano* villages, is best made with a tour operator. See also "Excursions" from San Pedro de Atacama on page 109; and the entry for Géisers de El Tatío on page 100.

- **Ollagüe**, 187 km north east of Calama at an altitude of 3600 m is nothing more than a forlorn *altiplano* village halt for Chilean border formalities for the train passengers coming from or going into Bolivia. Border formalities for train travelers usually occur in the middle of the night in bitterly cold conditions, an uncomfortable process to say the least. It lies in the shade of **Volcán Ollagüe** (5865m). The road and railroad from Calama run parallel for many kilometers. The nearest town in Bolivia is Uyuni.

- **San Pedro de Atacama**: 92 km southeast on RN 23. See the entry for San Pedro on page 105.

CHIU CHIU

Altitude: 2535 m
Distance from Calama: 33 km east on RN 21

Chiu Chiu is located on the **Río Loa** just above the junction with the **Río Salado**. From afar it looks like an oasis in the dry desert.

Chiu Chiu goes back to pre-Colombian times, and it became a major administration center on the Inca trail. Ruins of the old pre-Colombian fortified town are about 1 km north of the present village. The conquering Spaniards, including Pedro de Valdivia, frequently passed through the village without bothering to make it a Spanish town. Despite the comparatively late Spanish occupation, the church is one of the oldest in the region and contains some paintings that are jewels of colonial art: *El Cristo de la Agonia* and *Nuestra Señora de los Dolores*. The tower has inscriptions in Dutch. There is also a small archeological museum. Holy Week celebrations are reminiscent of the festivities held in Seville in Spain.

The rebellion of Tupac Amaru in 1780, which swept Alto Peru, was felt here, and Pedro de Panire led the local Indians to join the uprising in 1781. Later, the town was laid out in Spanish style in east–west–north–south rectangular form and was called Atacama la Chica.

Chiu Chiu's population is shrinking. The villagers are mostly subsistence farmers and produce very little in excess of their own needs.

This village is usually visited as part of a conducted tour which includes Lasana, Ayquina, and Géisers de El Tatío — see "Excursions" from Calama on page 98.

⚡ Festivals

Good Friday is a particular colorful festival when Indian and Christian beliefs mix.
- February 11: Virgen de Lourdes
- October 4: San Francisco
- December 8: Purísima

⊞ Eating out

- Restaurant Comercial de Chiu Chiu, Calle Esmeralda

▣ Sightseeing

- Iglesia de San Francisco, built in the 17th century, is an outstanding example of colonial art, with the added distinction of two belfries, a rare feature. The walls of the church are 1.5 m adobe; a staircase on the outside leads up to the towers. An old cemetery lies within the church precinct.
- **Lasana:** 8 km north. This pre-Colombian Pukará de Lasana was built by the Atacameños in the 12th century. The earliest construction dates from 400 AD, and its zenith was about 1300. It was taken over by the Incas and most likely was destroyed by the advancing Spaniards. The *pukará* has been restored to some extent. The streets are laid out in a zigzag pattern. The road from Chiu Chiu goes through a narrow canyon where the vertical walls are covered in part by rock paintings dating back to the early inhabitants of this part of Chile. It is best reached from Calama with a tour operator.

COBIJA

Altitude: Sea level
Distance from Antofagasta: 150 km north on RN 1

Cobija is located on the Pacific coast in arid country. It is now an abandoned ghost town, and there are few signs that before the War of the Pacific this was the Bolivian administration center on the Pacific coast.

A pre-Colombian trail went from here into the *altiplano* via **Chacance** on the **Río Loa**, and from there followed the Río Loa Valley to its source near the Bolivian border and beyond.

Before the arrival of the Spaniards, Cobija was permanently settled by the Chango Indians taking advantage of a fresh water spring nearby. They traded dried fish with the valleys of the interior. In the 1800s Cobija became an important port for an *altiplano* route going into Bolivia. Simón Bolívar changed its name in 1825 to Lamar and founded the harbor, an important port for inland cities such as Potosí in Bolivia, Charcas (now Sucre in Bolivia), and even Jujuy and Salta in Argentina. Shortage of water restricted the town's growth until in 1857 José Santos Ossa established the first desalination plant to supplement the dwindling supply of natural water. It became a seaside resort for rich *altiplano* families in the last century. In 1855 a yellow fever epidemic broke out; and the town had scarcely recovered from this disaster when in 1877 an earthquake followed by a tidal wave destroyed it completely. By 1907 Cobija was a ghost town. The ruins hardly reveal its 19th-century importance.

GÉISERS DE EL TATÍO

Altitude: 4320m
Distances
* From Calama: 125 km east
* From San Pedro de Atacama: 98 km north-east

The Tatío area has 40 geysers forming little cones of water and steam, 60 thermal wells, and 79 fumaroles emitting sulfuric gases. The geysers are formed by an underground stream coming into contact with the hot magma inside the mountain; the resulting steam and hot water escapes through the rock fissures. The water may reach 85°C (195°F), but the temperature differs from geyser to geyser, as do their colors and chemical composition. A change in the early morning atmospheric pressure at about 0700 causes the geysers to emit water and/or steam, some spurts reaching 10 m. The hot water forms little streams and lakes, all of which sustain some form of microbes. The air temperatures range from +10°C to -15°C (50°F to -5°F). In the cold air the little streams soon freeze over even, during the day.

The ever-present moisture in the air stimulates the growth of *altiplano* plants such as *yaretas*, *tola* or *ichu* grass, and some small bushes which support *llamas* and *guanacos*. Condors can also be seen.

The highest mounds around the fissures are made by the geysers. This is the source of the **Río Salado**, the largest tributary (80 km long) of the Río Loa. The flow of 2400 litres of water per second gives the river impetus to reach the Pacific Ocean, despite the demands made on it for irrigation and to sustain large human settlements: Calama and Chuquicamata.

The junction of the Río Salado with the Río Loa is just east of Chiu Chiu, at an altitude of 2500 m. A hot spring at the southern end of the geyser field fills a natural rock pool which has been cement-rendered, but very few people swim there as it is bitterly cold out of the water; on leaving the pool, the warm water freezes a short distance away. CORFO has established a geothermal camp there to investigate commercial use of the steam and hot water.

Located close to the Bolivian border, the Géisers de El Tatío can be reached from either San Pedro de Atacama or Calama by means of organized tours. It takes about three hours from San Pedro de Atacama. The roads are deplorable but the trip is worthwhile. Coming from San Pedro just before passing through the Campamento Geotérmico CORFO, the high peaks of **Cerro Tatío** (5215 m), **Cerro La Torta** (5018 m) and **Cerros de Torcorpuri** (5808 m) are on the right. The latter form the border with Bolivia. The biggest concentration of geysers are located in a basin approximately 3 km long and 700 m wide, surrounded by Cerro Tatío Norte (4375 m), Cerro Tatío Oeste (4463 m) and Cerro Tatío Sur (4322 m). Tours leave from San Pedro de Atacama at 0400; see "Excursions" from San Pedro on page 109.

⊛ Sport
The surrounding mountains are inviting for *andinismo* and mountain hikes; not for the novice.

⊕ Excursions
See "Excursions" from San Pedro de Atacama (page 109) and Calama (page 98).

MARÍA ELENA

Area code: 055
Population: 7800
Altitude: 1250 m
- DistancesFrom Tocopilla: 68 km east on RN 24
- From Chuquicamata: 85 km west on RN 24'

María Elena is located in the central valley on a rather flat plain surrounded by a few low hills. Founded in 1926, together with Pedro de Valdivia it is one of the few saltpeter mining towns still operating. At one stage there were more than one hundred saltpeter mines in the desert, with a network of railroad lines going to the port at Tocopilla.

The clmate is dry with no extreme fluctuations in temperatures between day and night. The sun shines intensely from a radiant blue sky.

María Elena only exists because of the mine. It is run by the Soquimich company which also owns Pedro de Valdivia. The town is well separated from the industrial area. All buildings are owned by the mining company.

María Elena is a model mining town with well defined suburbs and a sprinkling of trees on the plaza and in the hospital grounds. The green of the trees is a welcome sight in the otherwise treeless desert. Sporting amenities include tennis courts, a baseball field and several soccer fields. There are restaurants and good transport to Antofagasta and Iquique in the north and La Serena and Santiago in the south. Regular buses run to Tocopilla.

The pre-Colombian trail from the coast to the *sierra* passed nearby, and was also used in colonial times to link Potosí in Bolivia with its port Cobija on the Pacific. Traces of the old colonial traffic remain near **Coya Sur**.

ⓘ Tourist information
* Ignacio Carrera Pinto

⊟ Accommodation
* Residencial Chacance, Claudia Vicuña 437 ℂ 632749

⑪ Eating out

Restaurants
* Casino Soquimich, Balmaceda 173
* Club Social María Elena, Rancho 4
* Santiago, Guacolda 1001
* Yerco, Avenida Latorre 110

▦ Post and telegraph
* Correos de Chile, San Martín

* Telephone CTC, Latorre 112
* Telex Chile, B. O'Higgins 50
* Entel, Radio Estación Entel

▦ Services and facilities
* Large supermarket, Avenida Balmaceda on the plaza

▣ Buses
The bus terminal is at the town entrance. There are 3 services daily to Antofagasta, La Serena, and Santiago; 2 services daily to Arica; and 1 service daily to Calama, Iquique, and Viña del Mar

Companies
* Buses Camus, O'Higgins 268 ℂ 632902
* Buses La Carmelita, Latorre 118 ℂ 632901
* Buses Tramaca, O'Higgins 274 ℂ 632903
* Flota Barrios, O'Higgins 279 ℂ 632900
* Kenny Bus, Latorre 118 ℂ 632901
* Transportes Géminis

▤ Motoring
* Esso Servicentro, Alonso Russel

▦ Sightseeing
* Museo Antropológico Municipal: Corner of Ignacio Carrera Pinto and Avenida A. Prat. Many artifacts from the archeological site of Chacance are on show. Open Mon–Sat 0800–1300.

✢ Excursions
* **María Elena**: 10 km east on the Río Loa, with picnic grounds, barbecue places, and camping.
* **Chacance**: 18 km south-east in the **Río Loa valley**. It is a remarkable spot in the otherwise arid area. Good camping facilities. Good drinking water. Pre-Colombian archeological site nearby.
* **Oficina Vergara**: An abandoned saltpeter mine situated halfway between Pedro de Valdivia and María Elena 13 km south. There is a 44 m deep well with good drinking water.
* **Puente La Posada**: Bridge over the Río Loa (generally referred to by the locals as "Crucero" or "Crossroads").

MEJILLONES

Area code: 055
Population: 5000
Altitude: Sea level
Distance from Antofagasta: 65 km north on RN 1 and Ruta B-272

Mejillones is located on a wide coastal plain at the northern end of **Península Mejillones**, on the bay of the same name. It is a fairly extensive town, but was more important last century as a saltpeter port. Before the War of the Pacific, Mejillones was part of Bolivia. There was even a large railroad workshop here. The main street is called Almirante Latorre.

Mejillones has a very beautiful beach with tranquil waters, but it seems its days as a quiet retreat are numbered as the area is marked for industrial development. Already some explosives factories and fishmeal plants operate there.

In the middle of town is the recently opened Museo del Mar de Mejillones, on the corner of Francisco A. Pinto and Avenida A. Latorre, which gives a good overview of the area's flora and fauna.

⌘ Festivals
* June 29: San Pedro
* August 8: Anniversary of the Battle of Angamos (War of the Pacific)

⌘ Accommodation

Hostería
* Luz de Luna, Almirante Goña 99 ADE-FGHIJLP (621582 $l ⁂

Residenciales
* Don Viti, Borgoña 855
* Elizabeth, Almirante Latorre 440 (621568 $l ⁂
* Marcella, General Borgoño 150 AJP $l ⁂. Shared bathrrom cheaper
* Marco, Riquelme 160 AFGHI $H ⁂

⌘ Post and telegraph

Post office
* Correos de Chile, Las Heras 205

Telephone
* CTC, Almirante Latorre 748

⌘ Buses
On Sunday nights buses returning to Antofagasta are crowded.

Bus companies
* Buses El Shadday, Latorre 691
* Buses Fepstur, Latore corner of Goñi

Services
* Antofagasta $1.40, 21 services daily 1hr Fepstur, El Shadday

PEDRO DE VALDIVIA

Population: 6000
Altitude: 1476 m
Distance from Tocopilla: 98 km south-east

Pedro de Valdivia, founded in 1931, is one of the few saltpeter mining towns still operating. It belongs to the mining company Soquimich which also operates the María Elena mining complex further north.

There are good bus connections to the north and south and major bus companies call.

⑪ Eating out

Restaurants
- Chacabuco, Portales 28
- Club Social Pedro de Valdivia
- Gran Palace, Francisco Pizrro corner of San Martín

⑱ Post and telegraph

Post office
- Correos de Chile, Balmaceda 375

Telephone
- Telex Chile, Lib. B. O'Higgins 50

- CTC, Concepción 2, corner of Washington

🚌 Buses

There are three services daily to Antofagasta, Copiapó, La Serena and Santiago; and two services daily to Arica and Iquique.

Companies
- Buses La Carmelita, O'Higgins 42 (634686
- Buses Tramaca, San Martín 49 (634228
- Flota Barrios, O"Higgins 9 (634625
- Kenny Bus
- Transportes Geminis

PEINE

Altitude: 2420 m
Distance from San Pedro de Atacama: 104 km south on Ruta B-335 and RN 23

This oasis village is a pre-Colombian Atacameño settlement which came early under Incan domination. A spur of the Inca road passing through was used by the early *conquistadores* and by explorers in the middle of last century. There are abandoned silver mines in the area. Thermal water enables the villagers to grow crops in the *quebrada*.

The village has gained a new lease of life since the establishment of a mining settlement at the western end of the village to extract lithium from the Salar de Atacama.The present-day settlement dates from the 17th century, when it was decided to abandon Peine Viejo, probably to be closer to the water. The old site of Peine Viejo together with the old chapel is a *monumento nacional*.

The new church in the modern village is an imitation of the old colonial church. The plaza has a few huge trees and many of the houses appear to be abandoned. From the plaza a track goes to the water reservoir which comes from the nearby thermal springs and *cochas*, and continues to Peine Viejo with views over the green oasis. Public transport to Peine from San Pedro de Atacama is a problem. A tour is recommended. As far as I could ascertain, a rural bus from San Pedro runs once or twice a week. You may also get a lift with vehicles of Sociedad Chilena del Litio.

⑳ Festivals
- August 16: San Roque

QUILLAGUA

Altitude: 1000 m
Distance from Antofagasta: 248 km north on Panamericana

Quillagua is situated in the **Río Loa valley**, just south of the Pampa de Tamarugal, at a very pretty spot in the middle of the desert. This is the northernmost town in Región II de Antofagasta, and one of the most fertile spots in the Río Loa valley. In pre-Colombian times it was inhabited by the Kunza tribe. Pedro de Valdivia passed through in 1540.

Nowadays Quillagua is a small village with barely more than 250 inhabitants. The climate is very enjoyable, and it is a good spot to break the tiresome, monotonous journey through the desert. There are picnic spots, camping and swimming opportunities on the nearby Río Loa.

Quillagua is a police checkpoint and also a SAG checkpoint to prevent carrying diseased fruit and vegetables into central Chile.

There is a COPEC gas station nearby.

⊠ **Festivals**
- May 2, 3: Fiesta de la Cruz
- September 29: San Miguel del Angel

⑪ **Eating out**
COPEC has a *rutacentro* with restaurant on the Panamericana.

▨ **Post and telegraph**

Post office
- Correos de Chile, Ferrocarril

Telephone
- CTC, Comercio

▣ **Buses**
Regular buses run to Iquique, Tocopilla and Antofagasta.

SAN PEDRO DE ATACAMA

Area code: 056
Population: 1250
Altitude: 2240 m
Distances
- From Antofagasta: 314 km north-east on RN 23 and RN 25
- From Calama: 105 km south east on RN 23
- From Salta (Argentina): 494 km west on RN 23

San Pedro de Atacama is located at the northern end of the **Salar de Atacama** near the mouth of the Río San Pedro in the Salar de Atacama.

In pre-Colombian times, Atacameño tribes lived in San Pedro, and it is here that Atacameño folklore has retained its purest expression. The Incas conquered the area around 1460 and built an administration center in the **Río San Pedro valley**, at **Catarpe**.

In the early days of colonial rule, San Pedro was the major entry port for the Spanish *conquistadores*. In 1540

San Pedro de Atacama

SAN PEDRO DE ATACAMA

Key to map

A	Iglesia San Pedro
C	Municipalidad (Town Hall)
E	Telephone
F	Carabineros (Police)
I	Tourist information
P	Gas stations
T	Bus terminals

● Acommodation

1	Residencial Chiloe
2	Residencial La Florida
3	Residencial Pukará
5	Residencial Porvenir
6	Hostal/Camping Puri
7	Hotel Kimal
10	Hotel/Camping Tulor
11	Cabañas/Camping Thaka Thaka

12	Hostería San Pedro de Atacama

○ Eating out

4	Restaurant Juanita
8	Café Chañas Club
9	Restaurant Tambo Cañaveral
17	Restaurant La Estanca

▲ Tour operators

16	Turismo Hector
18	Atacama Inca Tours

□ Sights

13	Casa de Pedro de Valdivia
14	Museo Arqueológico Padro La Paige

□ Services

15	Supermarket

⊟ Accommodation in San Pedro de Atacama

Hotels
- Kimal, Domingo Atienza   ☏ 530

Hostales
- Puri, Caracoles   ☏ 549 $H ♙♙
- Supai, Magallanes 635   ☏ 576
- Tulor, Domingo Atienza

Hosterías
- San Pedro de Atacama, Solcor   AEFGHILPR$Z   ☏ 511 $H ♙♙
  $E cabins for 6
- Takha Takha, Calle Tocopilla next to passport contr ol   ☏ 538 $I ♙♙
  Back packers, large camping area in the backyard, caretaker/owner, hot showers, toilets, benches and tables, camping $J per person

Residenciales
- Andacollo, Andacollo 11   ☏ 511 $I ♙♙
- Calama   ☏ (55) 340 107
- Chiloe, Domingo Atienza   AEFGHIL   ☏ 517 $I ♙♙
- La Florida, Tocopilla   AEFGHU   ☏ 521 $I ♙♙
  Budget travelers
- Porvenir, Pedro de Valdivia corner of O'Higgins   ☏ 58
- Pukará, Tocopilla 28 $I ♙♙
  Budget travelers
- Solcor, Domingo Atienza   AEFGHI

Don Pedro de Valdivia came through and designed the outline of the town which is preserved to this day. The present-day church was built in 1730, fronting the main plaza; it is one of the oldest churches in Chile. The town has retained its colonial character and attracts many tourists. The plaza is surrounded by the civic buildings, and it is said that the construction of the *cabildo* (or town council) precinct was by order of Pedro de Valdivia himself. Calama and San Pedro are linked by a 100 km sealed road (RN 25).

From here the road continues to Salta in Argentina over the **Paso de la Laguna Sico** (4089 m). This new road is a lot better than the former road over the **Paso de Huaitiquina**. During adverse weather conditions, the pass may be closed after heavy snowfalls. However, in the summer months a weekly bus service runs between the two towns. Furthermore, a new pass road has been built to connect San Pedro with Jujuy and Salta in Argentina via the **Paso de Jama.**

☼ Festivals
- June 29: Major celebrations for the patron saint, San Pedro
- August 15: Virgen de la Asunción

ⓘ Tourist information
- Hostal San Pedro de Atacama, Solcor,☏ 11

⑪ Eating out

Restaurants
- Chañar Club, Caracoles near Toconao
- Hostería San Pedro, Calle Solcor $X
- Porvenir, O'Higgins corner of Caracoles
- Juanita, main plaza $Z

🚌 Buses from San Pedro de Atacama

Companies
- A8   Atahualpa; wait at passport control
- A35   Transportes Geminis; wait at passport control
- A78   Buses Tramaca

Services

Destination	Fare	Services	Duration	Companies
Antofagasta Change in Calama				
Calama	$3.80	2 services daily	2 hrs	A78
Jujuy (Argentina)		Tues, Wed		A78
Peine Irregular rural buses				
Salta (Argentina)		Wed, Sun	12 hrs	A8, A35
Toconao Irregular rural buses				

- La Estanca, Caravoles. Vegetarian
- Takha Thaka, Calle Toconao
- Tambo Cañaveral, Caracoles corner of Toconao

🏤 Post and telegraph

Post office
- Correos de Chile, Calle Gustavo Le Paige

Telephone
- CTC, Caracoles 43

🏨 Services and facilities

Supermarket
- Supermercado San Pedro, Calle Solcor

🛂 Visas, passports

- Exit passport control, Calle Tocopilla next to Cabañas Takha Takha

🚗 Motoring

- COPEC gas station, near Hostería de San Pedro

🏬 Shopping

- Centro Artesanal, Pedro de Valdivia
- Fería de Artesanía, Gustavo Le Paige

📷 Sightseeing

- Museo Arqueológico Padre Gustavo Le Paige is an internationally renowned museum with a splendid collection of archeological artifacts. It houses nearly 300 000 anthropological and archeological artifacts of the Atacameño culture. Most of the pieces were collected and classified by Padre Le Paige, a Belgian priest. Open daily 0800–1200 and 1400–1800; small admission fee.
- Casa Colonial: The oldest house in town, it is said to have belonged to Pedro de Valdivia. This building was definitely constructed by the first Spanish settlers, although it is not so certain that de Valdivia lived there. The trapezoid windows suggest Inca-trained stonemasons. The keys to the house are kept next door; small admission fee.
- Iglesia de San Pedro: On the west side of the Plaza de Armas. One of the best preserved *altiplano* churches. The original church was built in 1640, but not on the same spot. The present-day church dates from the mid-18th century. The belfry was added in the late 19th century. The altar is chiseled out of rock.

✈ Excursions

Tour operators
- Andino Expediciones, Caracoles ☎ (56) 313037 fax (56) 310203. English and German spoken
- Atacama Inca Tours, Toconao

☞ • Turismo Hector Ochoa Olivares, Toconao (22

Tours
- Géisers de El Tatío, cheapest $25.00
- Lasana and Chiu Chiu
- Géisers de El Tatío and Termas de Puritama, $30.00, leaving at 0415, 10 hrs
- Toconao and Salar de Atacama, $18.00, leaving 0630
- Valle de la Luna, $7.50, leaving 1745
- Lagos del *altiplano*, $30.00, leaving 0600
- Salar de Atacama plus Laguna Legia, $25.00
- Socaire–Laguna Miñiques–Laguna Miscanti. Views over Salar de Atacama

Excursions
- **Géisers de El Tatío**: 91 km north, near the Bolivian border at an altitude of 4200m. Organized tours leave at 0400 and arrive at the site just in time for the geysers to start spouting at 0700. See the entry for Géisers de El Tatío on page 100.
- **Peine**: A small village at an altitude of 2421 m, 105 km south on the eastern side of Salar de Atacama. Its foundation goes back approximately 1000 years when the Incas advanced south and it became one of their outposts. The outlines of the old Inca trail are still discernible in some places to the north. The *algarrobo* trees are 400 years old. See the entry for Peine on page 104.
- **Pukará de Quitor**: Located upstream 5 km north-east in the Río San Pedro valley. This pre-Colombian defensive fortification built of rocks is situated on a hill and dominates the **Río San Pedro** valley just where it opens up into the plain of the Salar de Atacama and the surrounding area. It was built about 700 years ago, and again demonstrates the advanced culture of the Atacameños. Quitor dominates the valley and is inaccessible on the north side. The chief lived in a tower-like building at the very top of the hill. It appears that the site was inhabited concurrently with the Inca settlement further up the valley. In 1540 Pedro de Aguirre attacked the fort and destroyed it. Some attempt has been made to restore this *monumento nacional* of the first order. It can be reached on foot in 30 minutes. On the same trip a visit to **Catarpe** a few kilometers past can be made. This was the Incan administration center. Little survives and the ruins are certainly not as spectacular as the ones in Peru.
- **Reserva Nacional Los Flamencos:** This national reserve has been created recently and does not constitute one continuous area: altogether there are six separate areas scattered south and east of San Pedro de Atacama. Three areas are in the Salar de Atacama and three areas are in the *altiplano*. As the name implies it was created to protect the habitat of the flamingos which live around the various salares. Altogether the national reserve comprises 74 000 ha (182 780 acres). The largest area in the *altiplano* is around **Salar de Tara** and includes **Cerro Negro**, 5157 m. The new **Paso de Jama** road to Jujuy passes the park's southern fringe. Also accesible via the new Paso de Jama road is the national park area around **Salar de Pujsa**. The furthest reserve area is located 100 km south of San Pedro; this area includes **Laguna Miscanti, Laguna Miñiques**, and also **Cerro Miñiques** 5910 m. The turnoff to this sector is 20 km south of Socaire. There is a CONAF information center in San Pedro which is open daily 1000–1300 and 1400–1630. Admission costs $1.50, and entitles you to visit all six reserve areas. It is best visited with a tour operator.
- **Río Grande** is a tiny *altiplano* village situated in a narrow canyon. It is best reached by turning off RN 23 between Calama and San Pedro at **Barros Arana**. The 45 km track from the turn-off onwards is bad. There is no public transport except when the villagers gather to hold their colorful *altiplano fiestas* — a mixture of Catholic and pre-Columbian beliefs. This is unknown Chile. The intrepid might like to hike up the Río Grande valley from San Pedro de Atacama. I only went as far as the junction of **Río Licán** with the Río San Pedro, but locals tell me the trail continues — I suspect this is the pre-hispanic trail. There is no

shortage of water. A bit further up you pass the **Pukará de Quitor** and **Catarpe**, an Inca *tambo*.

- **Salar de Atacama**: San Pedro is located on the northern edge of this great salt lake, but there are other interesting areas to the south. However, they are difficult to reach because there are no regular bus services. The sparkling light on the lake's surface is spectacular. Lithium is now being extracted.

- **Socaire:** 102 km south. Socaire is an *Atacameño* village in the *pre-Cordillera* at an altitude of 3218 m, with a colonial church. Spread out along irrigated terraces and fields, it was founded in pre-Colombian times. It owes its existence to thermal springs which emerge from the mountain nearby. The water is used for irrigation in a wide *quebrada* leading up to **Cerro Leña**. The villagers grow fruit and vegetables and grind their corn using old water mills. Skilled craftsmen make all sorts of handicrafts from cactus wood. The best views over **Salar de Atacama** are from the road leading up the mountains just 8 km from the village. About 30 km further up are **Laguna Miscanti** and **Laguna Miñiques** in very scenic surroundings, now part of **Reserva Nacional Los Flamencos**. The new international highway through **Paso de la Laguna Sico** skirts the town. You can visit Socaire as part of an *altiplano* tour with a tour operator.

- **Talabre**: On the old Huaitiquina pass road to Argentina, 63 km south-east, at an altitude of 3500 m. It is a small settlement, which only comes to life when the villagers return to their homesteads to celebrate their colorful

altiplano fiestas — the most colorful is Virgen del Rosario, celebrated on July 16. Tour operators pass through this village on the way to **Salar de Aguas Calientes**. The road skirts the southern flank of **Volcán Lascar** (5154m) and offers views of **Volcán Aguas Calientes** (5924 m) and **Cerro de Pili** (6046 m), and spectacular altiplano scenery. There are flamingos on Salar de Aguas Calientes. Contact tour operators listed above.

- **Toconao**: 37 km south on the eastern side of the **Salar de Atacama**, at an altitude of 2400 m. Frequent rural buses run from San Pedro. There are many conducted tours to Toconao and the adjacent **Quebrada de Jeria**. See the entry for Toconao on page 115.

- **Tulor**: 9 km south. About 2500 years ago this prehistoric village was a flourishing community of about 500 inhabitants. Sand covered it, and thus preserved much of it as a time capsule. It was discovered by the eminent Belgian archeologist Padre Gustavo Le Paige. The igloo-shaped buildings are inside a compound surrounded by a wall to protect against aggression.

- **Valle de la Luna**. About 12 km north, in the **Cordillera de la Sal**, a small mountain range west of San Pedro, extending west of the Salar de Atacama. Wind erosion has shaped these rocks in the middle of the desert. This area is a major tourist attraction with its multicolored rocks and in the background the majestic cone of Volcán Licancábur. Excursions leave San Pedro at about 1700 to get the best effect for sunset photographs with **Volcán Licancábur** in the background.

TALTAL

Area code: 055
Population: 7500
Altitude: Sea level
Distance from Antofagasta: 303 km south on Panamericana

Taltal lies on the Pacific coast in the desert *pampas*. The area was settled in pre-Colombian days by the Changos, who obtained sufficient fresh water from coastal springs. The modern town, which was founded in 1858 when José Antonio Moreno opened up his first saltpeter mine, was obliged to tap aquifers in the vicinity of Agua Verde.

Taltal reached its zenith with a population of 20 000 in 1876, when more than twenty saltpeter mines opeated in the hinterland and shipped their products through this port. In those days it had an opera theatre, bullfights, and a race course. From Cerro la Virgen in the town center there are splendid views over the town and bay.

Swimming at the beaches is possible all year round. The average annual temperature is 18°C (64°F), with generally high humidity in the morning owing to the cold Humboldt current. A cool breeze always blows from the sea.

Taltal is now virtually reduced to a fishing port, because most of the major saltpeter mines on which it depended have closed down. It is famous for its fish, and main meals usually feature *fruta del mar* — "fruit of the sea". Lately exploration for gold, silver, and copper has begun again. Taltal has some very colorful *fiestas*.

If you have your own four-wheel-drive transport, you can travel north via the coastal gravel road to Antofagasta. The coastal *cordillera* is a formidable mountain barrier, rising abruptly from the sea and in some places reaching over 2600 m — **Cerro Ventarrones** (2622 m), **Cerro Cometa** (2374 m), and **Cerro de la Colorada** (2027 m) — and there are many dry ravines. In the Sierra Vicuña Mackenna further east there are peaks over 3000 m. Buses take the Carretera Panamericana inland (RN 5) and turn off to the coast 24 km before Taltal.

⚅ Festivals
- February 1: Virgen de Lourdes
- July 12: Anniversary of the town
- August 10: Fiesta del Minero

⊟ Accommodation in Taltal

Hotels
- San Martín, Juan Martinez 279, opposite lane

	AFGL	((55) 263503	$I	♙♙
Budget travelers				
Verdi, Ramírez 345	AFGJP	(105	$H	♙♙
Budget travellers				

Hostería
Taltal, Esmeralda 671	AFGHJLPU	(173/101	$G	♙♙

Residenciales
Plaza, Esmeralda 450			$H	♙♙
Ramírez, Ramírez 519 corner of Sargento Aldea			$I	♙♙
Backpackers				
Taltal City, Ramírez block 300 opposite Verdi			$I	♙♙
Backpackers				
Viña del Mar, Serrano 762	FJL	(96	$I	♙♙
Budget travelers				

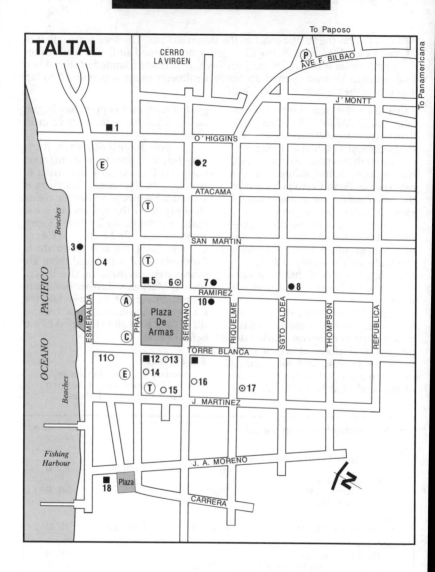

TALTAL

To Paposo

CERRO LA VIRGEN

AVE F. BILBAO

J'MONTT

O'HIGGINS

ATACAMA

SAN MARTIN

RAMIREZ

TORRE BLANCA

J MARTINEZ

J. A. MORENO

CARRERA

OCEANO PACIFICO

Beaches

Beaches

Fishing Harbour

Plaza De Armas

Plaza

ESMERALDA

PRAT

SERRANO

RIQUELME

SGTO ALDEA

THOMPSON

REPUBLICA

To Panamericana

ANTOFAGASTA

Key to map

A	Iglesia	**11**	Restaurant Club Taltal
C	Municipalidad (Town Hall)	**13**	Restaurant Don Pedro
E	Telephone	**14**	Restaurant Toosy
P	Gas stations	**15**	Restaurant Caverna
T	Bus terminals	**16**	Café El Andino

● **Accommodation**

2	Residencial Viña del Mar
3	Hostería Taltal
7	Residencial Verdi
8	Residencial Ramírez
10	Residencial Taltal City

⊙ **Entertainment**

17 Disco Keops

○ **Eating out**

4 Restaurant Souvenir
6 Restaurant Capri

□ **Sights**

1	Railway Museum
5	Museo de Taltal
9	Plaza Riquelme
12	Teatro Municipal
18	Caleta Pesquera

ⓘ Tourist information

- Oficina de Información Turística, in the Casa de la Cultura, A. Prat 642

🍽 Eating out

Restaurants
- Al Passo, Terminal Pesquero. Seafood
- Casona Shop, Ramírez near Serrano
- Caverna, Juan Martínez 247
- Club Social Protectora, Serrano 580
- Club Social Taltal, Torreblanca 162
- Don Pedro, Torreblanca 280
- El Andino, Serrano 428
- Hostería Taltal, Esmeralda 671
- Las Brisas, Terminal Pesquero. Seafood
- Oásis, Riquelme 896
- San Remo, Juan Martínez 398 near the corner of a lane
- Souvenir, Esmeralda 646
- Toosy, A. Prat 453

Salón de Té
- Capri, Ramírez 32
- Jugo's A. Prat 637

ⓣ Entertainment

Disco
- Keops, Riquelme block 400 between Martínez and Torreblanca
- Tiburón, Riquelme 656

Night clubs
- Boite Blue Moon, Atacama 398
- Boite Nuria, J.Martínez corner of Riquelme

Restaurants
- Eden, Bilbao 271, Sector Quintas. Shows and dancing weekends
- Lucerito, San Martín corner of Sargento Aldea. Shows and dancing weekends

📮 Post and telegraph

Post office
- A. Prat 515

Telephone
- CTC, Esmeralda 836
- Telex Chile, A. Prat 525

Services and facilities

Medical center
- Centro Médico, J.Antonio Moreno ℄ 83

Pharmacy
- Farmacia Tal Tal, Juan Martínez 285 ℄ 111

🚗 Motoring

Gas station
- Servicentro Bilbao 101

🛍 Shopping

- CEMA Chile, A. Prat 555. *Altiplano* handicraft

📷 Sightseeing

The town's main attraction is Plaza Prat with its central fountain, the town hall, and the Iglesia San Francisco Javier built in 1897. Most of the old wooden pioneer

🚌 Buses from Taltal

There is no central bus terminal; each bus company has its own terminal.

Companies
- A49   Buses Litoral, Prat 644 @115
- A67   Buses Ramos Cholele, Prat 766
- A78   Buses Tramaca, A. Prat 428 (134
- A110 Flecha Dorada

Services

Destination	Fare	Services	Duration	Companies
Antofagasta	$5.70	3 services daily	3 hrs	A67, A78
Chañaral	$5.00	6 services daily	2 hrs	A49, A78, A110
Copiapó	$8.40	1 service daily		A78
Santiago	$21.00	2 services daily		A78
Valparaíso	$21.00	1 service daily		A78
Viña del Mar	$21.00	1 service daily		A78

houses are around this plaza and in streets nearby. There is a fine sandy beach in the middle of town between Plaza Riquelme which displays two old cannons from the War of the Pacific, and Muelle Fiscal with its old clock tower. Street vendors with small carts roam the town selling seafood. The disused railroad workshop houses a steam locomotive and is now a museum and *monumento nacional*, as is the Muelle Salitrero a few hundred meters north of it. A picturesque little fishing community nestles in the shelter of the hill at the south end of the town.

- Museo Augusto Capdeville displays archeological pieces found in the area.

⊕ Excursions

La Puntilla lies south of the town. It commands panoramic views over the sea and the bare mountains surrounding Taltal.
Excursions further north lead to **Paposo**. The best beaches start 3 km north of Taltal on the road to Paposo. Follow Avenida M.A. Matta for Playa Muelle de Piedra, Playa Poza La Tortuga, and Playa Tierra del Morro. The beaches at the northern end towards Paposo are unspoilt by mass tourism.
To the south of town are many good beaches such as Las Tórtolas. They are only accessible by four-wheel drive vehicles.
Abandoned saltpeter mines are concentrated in the east, around the small village of **Agua Verde** at the upper end of **Quebrada Taltal**. Oficina Flor de Chile, Oficina Alemania, Oficina Chile, and Oficina Britania once employed thousands of people. The railroad line and the secondary road Ruta B-902 follow the Quebrada Taltal down to the port. This is dry desert country.
To the north, 38 km from town, on the road to Paposo near **Punta Cachinalito**, is a pleasant beach area with some vegetation and grey sand. Camping is possible between huge boulders. It is a very picturesque spot with the mountains rising steeply in a 600m backdrop. There are no facilities — you are on your own. There is water in Paposo and some supplies. Good fishing and skin diving are available 20 km further north.

- **Caleta Cifuncho**: A small fishing village on **Bahía Lavata**, about 43 km south. It has good fishing and spear fishing, and it is possible to camp on a very picturesque beach nearby. Caleta Cifuncho is at the mouth of **Quebrada La Cachina**. This area abounds in cacti and shrubs, and the spring growth is profuse. It is a beautiful place unspoilt by mass tourism, but unfortunately you have to bring your own water supplies. The camping ground has no facilities and very little water. The sea is crystal clear, but the currents can be treacherous.

- **Paposo**: 56 km north of Taltal on RN 1, on the Pacific coast where the coastal strip widens and where the **Quebrada de Paposo** descends from the *sierra*. Chango Indians lived here long before the arrival of the Spaniards. Its importance has declined ever since the mines in the coastal *cordillera* closed. The weather is warm all year round with an average of 18°C (64°F), tempered by a mild breeze. Sector La Rinconada lies 15 km north of Paposo. The thick vegetation, composed of cacti and shrubs, is somewhat of a surprise in the middle of such arid country. It is intended to create a national park here to safeguard the rich flora and fauna created by the moist fogs. This is home to the *yara* or long-eared desert rat. There are also a few condors around. An archeological site lies in the **Quebrada El Médano**, 30 km north of Paposo approximately 5 km inside the *quebrada*. Long ago a river ran through this canyon which sustained a large pre-Colombian settlement. More than 500 rock paintings, painted mostly in an ochre/reddish color and estimated to be 1000 years old, are difficult to reach at an altitude of 1500 m. There is a small restaurant, Posada Paposo. Irregular rural buses run from Taltal.

TOCONAO

Population: 500
Altitude: 2400 m
Distance from San Pedro de Atacama: 37 km south on RN 23

Toconao is an oasis on the eastern side of the **Salar de Atacama**. It originated in pre-Colombian times; the villagers still till their plots in the way their Indian ancestors did. Each family has a little *chacra* where they plant fruit and vegetables. Most fruit is sold in Calama and Chuquicamata.

Water from the **Quebrada de Jeria** is the little town's lifeline. The stream does not quite make it to the *salar* as all its water is used for irrigation, distributed to the little plots according to an age-old system.

White volcanic rock, *liparit*, quarried and sold as building material, is another source of income — *toco* is an indigenous word meaning "rock". Many houses in the village are built from *liparit*, and the town's narrow streets are interesting.

The new international road going up to Paso de la Laguna Sico bypasses the town.

⚐ Festivals
- June 13: San Antonio, held in Camar in the Quebrada de Camar
- October 18: San Lucas

ⓘ Tourist information
- CONAF, Calle Huaytiquina

⊟ Accommodation
There is one *residencial* in Calle Huaytiquina; and several *pensiones* in 21 de Mayo, Calle Huaytiquina, and O'Higgins

ⓘ! Eating out
There is a restaurant in Calle Esmeralda; *residenciales* and *pensiones* also serve meals.

⊠ Post and telegraph

Telephone
- CTC, Atacama

⊟ Buses
- Calama: Fare $5.30, services Wed, Fri, Sun; duration 3 hrs; rural bus

To Calama

TOCONAO

Jeria

To Argentina

Key to map

A	Iglesia
E	Telephone
F	Carabineros (Police)
G	Money exchange
T	Bus terminals
1	Residencial
2	Restaurant/accommmodation
3	Restaurant/accommodation
4	Artesanías
5	Artesanías

◙ Sightseeing

- Iglesia San Lucas, a typical *altiplano* church built of white stone early in the 18th century. The belfry has three tiers and stands some distance away from the church in the middle of the village; this was typical of churches built around 1750. The whole complex is a *monumento nacional*.
- *Liparit* quarry, where the white masonry stone is mined, is 2 km east of town near Quebrada de Jeria. A road leads into the canyon covered by irrigated fields. The river forms little pools and invites bathing.

⊡ Shopping

The villagers are skilled in making small replicas of *altiplano* churches out of the white *liparit*. Most shops are concentrated in Calle 18 de Octobre.

◉ Excursions

Although San Pedro de Atacama has better tourist facilities, Toconao is a good base for backpackers and budget travelers.

TOCONCE

Altitude: 3200 m
Distance from Calama: 88 km east

Toconce is a pre-Colombian Atacameño village built along the main irrigation canal which contours the mountain. From the village you have splendid views over the terraced fields; the most spectacular is looking down from the plaza to the river.

The church, which has no tower, is not in the plaza but at the far eastern end near a crevice. The untilled fields and the locked houses indicate that

Toconce is also a dying village. Many of the villagers work in the mines and take their families with them. However, they return to their villages for the big religious *fiestas*.

There are no tourist facilities. Irregular rural buses run to and from Calama, but it is best to go by tourist bus as you can visit other interesting areas at the same time.

⌧ Festivals

- February 24: Fiesta del Enfloramiento del Ganado—adorning cattle with flowers
- March 19: San José
- June 13: San Antonio
- July 25: San Santiago

TOCOPILLA

Area code: 055
Population: 23 000
Altitude: Sea level
Distances
- From Antofagasta: 188 km north on RN 1
- From Iquique: 380 km south on RN 1

Tocopilla is on the Pacific coast, 90 km south of the mouth of the Río Loa. Founded in 1843 by the Frenchman Domingo Latrille, it grew from a small fishing village into an important seaport for the export of the saltpeter and copper mined in the hinterland. The first saltpeter deposits were mined at **Punta Paquica**. A French town planner laid out the town in 1877.

Since 1915, the thermo-electrical plant, generating 400 megawatts, has supplied electricity for the copper refinery at **Chuquicamata**. This and the still operating saltpeter mines of **María Elena**, 69 km east on RN 24, and **Pedro de Valdivia** are the mainstay of Tocopilla, which provides an important highly mechanized harbor for the fishing fleet and saltpeter export. Power generation causes some air and sea pollution.

Many of the buildings in the historical center round Calle A. Prat and Avenida 21 de Mayo date from the last century and gives the town old-time charm. Entertainment is lively after sunset.

Tocopilla's location is superb. It is hemmed in by the sea, and the high mountains falling abruptly to the Pacific Ocean left barely enough space for a town. The coastal plain here forms a triangle pointing north. Smaller streets climb the hills forming almost vertical cliffs.

The climate is coastal desert, enjoyable all year round. The mountain tops ringing the city are covered in vegetation watered by fog condensation, called *camanchacas*, caused by the cold Humboldt current; cacti grow on the slopes. The average summer temperature is 19°C (66°F); in winter it averages 13°C (55°F). Animal life is represented by pelicans, sea swallows and seals on rocks to the north and south. The sea is rich in fish and all the restaurants serve fish.

Tocopilla has direct road links with Antofagasta, either via the scenic coastal road or the more monotonous but faster Panamericana, and with Chuquicamata.

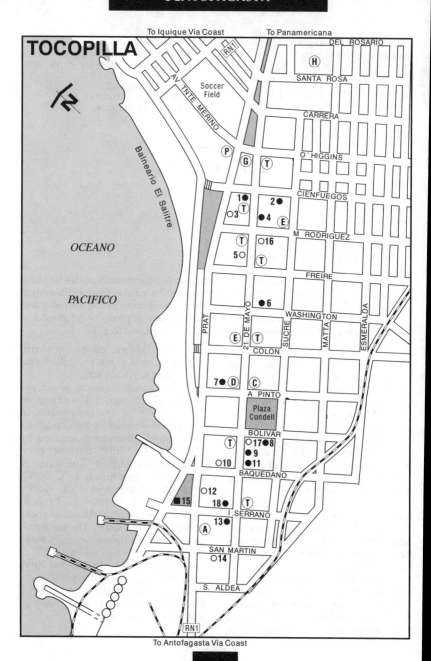

Key to map

A	Iglesia
C	Municipalidad (Town Hall)
D	Post office and Telex
E	Telephone
G	Mercado Municipal (Market)
P	Gas stations
T	Bus terminals
●	**Accommodation**
1	Hotel/Restaurant Vucina
2	Residencial La Españolita
4	Hotel Casablanca
6	Residencial Sonia
7	Hostal Central
8	Hostería Bolívar
9	Gran Hotel
11	Hotel Chungará
13	Residencial Alvarez
18	Hotel América
○	**Eating out**
3	Restaurant Internacional
5	Luciano's Pizza
10	Restaurant Club Chilex
12	Restaurant Club de la Unión
14	Restaurant Chifa Hongkong
16	Restaurant Royal
17	Restaurant La Naranja
■	**Sights**
15	Clock tower

There are adequate facilities at Tocopilla to make a stay in one of the lesser frequented regions of Chile enjoyable. Most hotels, restaurants and shops are on Avenida 21 de Mayo in the center of town. Fishing records have been established in Tocopilla by sports fishermen from all over the world.

Accommodation in Tocopilla

Hotels				
★ Casablanca, 21 de Mayo 2054	ADFMPS	☎ 5813104	$H	👥
• América, Serrano 1243 Budget travelers		☎ 813068	$I	👥
• Chungará, 21 de Mayo 1440	AEKPS	☎ 811036	$H	👥
• Gran Hotel, 21 de Mayo 1460 Budget travelers		☎ 811791	$H	👥
• Vucina, 21 de Mayo 2069	AFGHIJLPU	☎ 813088	$H	👥
Residenciales				
• Alvarez, Serrano 1234	AJL	☎ 811578	$I	👥
• Esmeralda, Esmeralda 2059 Backpackers		☎ 813200		
• Españolita, Cienfuegos 1380 Backpackers		☎ 811226	$J	👥
• Royal, 21 de Mayo 1988		☎ 81188	$J	👥
• Sonia, Washington 1329 Budget travelers		☎ 813086	$I	👥
Hostería				
• Bolívar, Bolívar 1332	AIJL	☎ 812783	$I	👥
Hostales				
• Central, A.Pinto 1241 Backpackers	ADFIJ	☎ 811890	$J	👥

Coming down from the Panamericana, the road passes for the first 15 km through a narrow *quebrada*. Tocopilla is one of the few places along this coast where the coastal *cordillera* permits good access to the Pacific Ocean. Mountains rise to 1900 m north of town and 1200 m eastwards. The coastal *cordillera* north and south of Tocopilla reaches 2000 m.

⊠ Festivals
- August 10: Miners' Celebration Day
- September 29: Anniversary of Tocopilla and Fiesta de San Miguel del Angel

ⓘ Tourist information
- 21 de Mayo 1377, Local 4

⑪ Eating out in Tocopilla

Restaurants
- American Bar, 21 de Mayo 1485 $Z
- Aquí Está la Papa, 21 de Mayo 1993 $Z
- ☞ Chifa Hong Kong, 21 de Mayo 1301 $Y. Chinese cuisine; open only at night
- Club de la Unión , A. Prat 1354 $Y
- Club Social Chilex, Baquedano 1225 $Z
- D'Ismael, 21 de Mayo 1377 $Z
- Drive Way Inn, Bolívar 1326 $Z
- El Arriero, Cienfuegos 1220 near A. Prat $Z
- Gastronómica, Bolívar 1348 $Z
- ☞ Hotel Vucina $Y
- ☞ Internacional, A. Prat 2040 $Z. Views over the bay
- La Naranja, 21 de Mayo 1496
- Luciano's Pizza, 21 de Mayo 1963
- Jok San, 21 de Mayo $Z. Chinese cuisine
- Royal, 21 de Mayo 1980
- Scorpio's, Avenida Leopoldo Guzmán
- Tong Fong, 21 de Mayo 1995 $Z. Chinese cuisine

Salón de Té
- Spejo's, 21 de Mayo 1589

Eating out at Caleta Boy
- Casino Caleta Boy, Balneario Covadonga $Y

⊤ Entertainment
Entertainment is geared towards the mining community who work in remote areas.
- Bar Grill La Naranja, 21 de Mayo 1472
- Boite Brasil, 21 de Mayo 1995
- Disco La Cabaña, Avenida Sloman
- Foxi Topless, Baquedano 1259
- Night Club Sara'o, 21 de Mayo 1377
- Restaurant Taberna El Pirata, 21 de Mayo 1999 $Y. Shows and dancing at weekends
- Topless Sensación, 21 de Mayo 1248

⊠ Post and telegraph

Post office
- Correos de Chile, 21 de Mayo 1686, Edificios Públicos

Telephone
- CTC, Avenida 21 de Mayo 1721, fax 812947
- ENTEL Chile, Overseas Telephone, Manuel Rodríguez 1212
- Telex Chile, 21 de Mayo 1686

⊟ Services and facilities

Camping equipment
- Sport Brazil, Avenida 21 de Mayo block 1900 near M.Rodríguez

Pharmacy
- Farmacia Moderna, 21 de Mayo 1401 ℂ 813103

Photographic supplies
- Full Color, 21 de Mayo 1753; films

⊟ Motoring
For gas stations, see city map.

Car rental
- Automóvil Club de Chile, 21 de Mayo 1377, Local 4 ℂ 811059

Gas stations
- Servicentro COPEC, 11 de Septiembre
- Servicentro Shell, Costanera
- Shell, A. Prat near Cienfuegos

⊠ Sightseeing
- Museo Arqueológico Municipal, 21 de Mayo 1653, second floor
- Old wooden church, A. Prat block 1200, near Serrano
- Old clock tower, A. Prat block 1300 near Baquedano

🚌 Buses from Tocopilla

Companies
- A9   Buses Blizzard, 21 de Mayo 1495 ℂ 813095
- A18   Buses Camus, 21 de Mayo 1940 ℂ 813102
- A78   Buses Tramaca, 21 de Mayo 2196 ℂ 813195
- A82   Buses Waldorf Tours, Heidi Bazar, 11 de Septiembre 01 ℂ 811703
- A110 Flecha Dorada, 21 de Mayo 1495 ℂ 813095
- A112 Flota Barrios, 21 de Mayo 1720 ℂ 813224
- A117 Kenny Bus, 21 de Mayo 1997 ℂ 811653
- A157 Turis Norte, 21 de Mayo 1348 ℂ 811390

Minibuses to Iquique depart from 21 de Mayo 1536 ℂ 811832

Services

Destination	Fare	Services	Duration	Companies
• Antofagasta				
Via RN 5	$3.50	9 services daily		A9, A18, A78, A110, A112, A157
Via the coastal road				
	$3.00	2 services Mon–Sat	2½hrs	A157
• Arica	$13.70	2 services daily		A112
• Calama	$4.20	2 services daily		A18
• Chañaral	$14.50	4 services daily		A110, A112[1]
• Chuquicamata	$4.20	2 services daily		A18
• Copiapó	$17.10	4 services daily		A110, A112[1]
• Coquimbo	$21.30	4 services daily		A110, A112[1]
• Iquique				
Via RN 5	$8.60	3 services daily		A18, A117, A157
Via the coastal road				
	$ 7.60	1 service daily	4½ hrs	A82
• La Calera	$29.60	4 services daily		A112[1]
• La Serena	$21.30	4 services daily		A110, A112[1]
• Ovalle	$22.80	5 services daily		A110, A112[1]
• Santiago	$29.60	6 services daily		A112[1], A117
• Vallenar	$19.00	4 services daily		A110, A112[1]
• Valparaíso	$29.60	1 service daily		A112[1]
• Viña del Mar	$29.60	1 service daily		A112[1]

[1]A112 only: Change in Antofagasta

🔎 Excursions

- **Cobija** and **Gatico**: Ghost towns 76 km south on RN 1 which is completely sealed. They were important shipping places during the nitrate boom. Now they are just silent reminders of a more ebullient past. See the entry for Cobija on page 100.
- **María Elena** and **Pedro de Valdivia**: Mining towns in the nitrate belt 72 km east on RN 24. The nitrate belt is about 700 km long, north to south, and between 15 km and 75 km wide. The mines are 1200 m above sea level and some of them are still worked. These operations can be visited by regular bus services. See also the entries for María Elena on page 101 and Pedro de Valdivia on page 103.

Beaches
The best beaches are south of town. The road is wedged between the sea and steep mountains and is partly asphalted.
- **Balneario Caleta Boy**: 3 km. Take a *colectivo*. Swimming, fishing water sports, kiosks, showers, toilets, sealed road.
- **Playa Punta Blanca**: 20 km south along an intermittently sealed road. Although the conditions are not really

suitable for bathing, this beach attracts many people to its scenic views and good restaurants which serve shellfish and fish fresh from the sea.

- **Playa Punta Atala**: The road to this small protected beach, 25 km south, is intermittently sealed. The water is safe for swimming and rock fishing, and seals and pelicans gather in nearby colonies. Restaurants serve mostly seafood and discos operate at weekends.

Plate 7   Región II de Antofagasta
Top: San Pedro de Atacama with Volcán Licancabur
Bottom: Altiplano near border with Bolivia

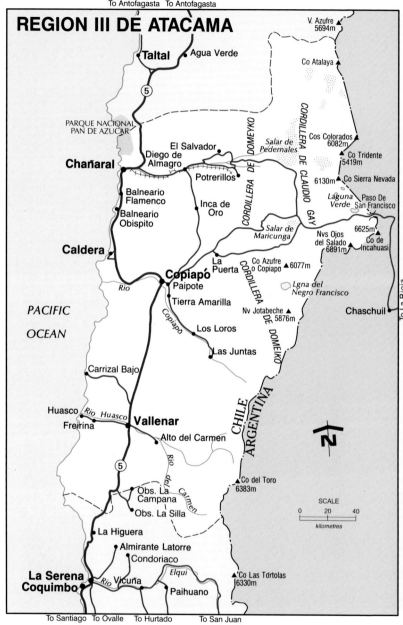

Plate 8
Map of Región III de Atacama

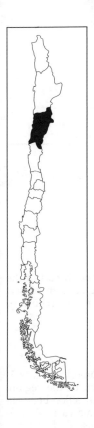

REGIÓN III
DE
ATACAMA

Size: 76 000 square km (29 340 square miles)
Population: 200 000
Regional capital: Copiapó
Provinces (and provincial capitals):
- Chañaral (Chañaral)
- Copiapó (Copiapó)
- Huasco (Vallenar)

The desert blooms! Occasionally this part of Chile, although part of the Atacama desert, receives a little rain (usually in spring), and the desert awakens to new life: shrubs sprout and flowers bloom. The rebirth of nature attracts many tourists to the region.

In 1994 a new national park was created in the *altiplano* — Parque Nacional Nevado Tres Cruces. Although the park is difficult to reach, it is worth making the effort from Copiapó.

The beaches of this region are splendid and unpolluted, but alas (or fortunately!) most of them are not within easy reach of the average tourist.

The Inca trail is still visible in some parts of the region, and some remains of the culture can be seen.

Chile's third region lies between 26° and 29° south, and between 69° and 71° east, bordering Región II de Antofagasta in the north, the Andes and Argentina in the east, and Región IV de Coquimbo in the south. The biggest population centers are **Copiapó** and **Vallenar**.

Transport

Road

The Carretera Panamericana (RN 5) runs the full length of the region. There is a road connection between Copiapó and Catamarca in Argentina through the Paso de San Francisco (4726 m).

Rail

The rail network is only used for transporting bulk ore from the mines to the shipping centers.

Air

There are six flights a week from Copiapó to Santiago and Antofagasta. There is also a twice-weekly plane service to El Salvador.

Topography

Physically, Región III de Atacama is very like Región II de Antofagasta, but the coastal plain widens from **Chañaral** onwards, replacing the coastal *cordillera*. The 450 km long coastline has many beautiful beaches with fine, white sand and clear warm water. The **Desierto de Atacama** finishes at **Copiapó**, and is replaced by a series of small mountain chains spreading out from the Andes with valleys between them. The chain of the Andes is a real barrier between Chile and Argentina at this point. Most passes are over 4500 m high; the highest mountains are **Ojos del Salado** (6885 m), **Incahuasi** (6618 m), and **Nevado de San Francisco** (6018 m). The main rivers, **Río Huasco** and **Río Copiapó**, are icy at their sources in the high *sierra* in altitudes above 5500 m.

Climate

From the northern border to Caldera, the climate resembles that of the other northern regions — dry desert conditions with almost no rain. From Caldera southward, the annual rainfall increases gradually and it becomes cooler. On the coast, the mornings are foggy with mild temperatures which remain unchanged at night. Caldera has a mean annual temperature of 16°C (61°F). Towards the interior, where the rainfall is only 64 mm per year, the fog disappears and the sky is always blue. In the *pre-Cordillera*, the mean annual temperature is 11.5°C (54°F). The valleys above 700 m have a pleasant climate and produce many crops.

The indigenous inhabitants

The first inhabitants settled in the fertile valleys of the interior and on the coast wherever there was water. The Diaguitas lived from Copiapó in the south to La Ligua. Their ancestral homes were in Argentina, and they crossed the Andes to form their own culture. They were makers of fine pottery. Around 1470, during the rule of Topac Inca, these people were absorbed into the Cuzcan Empire.

The Incas established *mitimaes*, settled by loyal highlanders brought from the Inca homelands. An efficient communications network was installed and administrative centers were created. There is no doubt that **Copiapó** was a *tambo* on the Inca road. These very roads later became the access trail for the invading Spanish army. The Incas mined gold — a former mining site lies in the upper **Río Copiapó** valley near Viña del Cerro.

The semi-nomadic coastal tribe known as Changos was absorbed into the mainstream of Chilean life towards the end of the nineteenth century. They were expert swimmers, divers, and navigators, and went fishing in inflatable rafts made from seal skin.

European history

In 1536 Diego de Almagro entered Chile through the **Paso de San Francisco** on the *Capac Ñan* or royal road of the Incas. He arrived in **Copiapó** in March 1536 and took possession of land in the name of the King of Spain. The Spaniards, however, were only interested in gold and silver and not in the fertile river valleys.

The Franciscan order established a church and convent in **Copiapó** in 1662 and a church in **Huasco Bajo** in 1667. In 1700 silver was found in **Capote** near **Freirina**, and Reales Minas de Santa Rosa was opened. **Copiapó** was officially founded in 1744 and **Vallenar** in 1789 by Don Ambrosio O'Higgins. Until the early 1800s, there was a stable Spanish population in the region dedicated to agriculture and some gold mining. In 1823 Diego de Almeyda discovered copper in **Las Animas**.

In 1853 the Chilean government decided to explore the Atacama region systematically. The most famous explorers of the day were Diego de Almeyda, born in Copiapó; Rudolf Philippi, a German naturalist, who later took charge of the German immigration in southern Chile; Francisco San Roman, from Copiapó; and Friedrich Philippi, son of the famous naturalist. These men traversed the region from north to south and found the area rich in minerals. Diego de Almeyda made his last exploration journey into the desert at the age of 73!

The new-found mineral wealth made **Copiapó** a very cosmopolitan place. The mines and ore crushing plants were owned by several rich families: Carvallo, Subercaseaux, Matta, Cousiño, Gallo, Montt, Ossa, and Goyenechea, who between 1840 and 1870 dominated the social and intellectual life of the region. The mining enterprises attracted skilled workers, especially from the USA and England. Many wealthy families held shares in the Caldera railway line established by August Edwards in 1849. Ships coming from the north to pick up copper ingots brought building materials, such as Oregon pine and bamboo, to be used in new mansions, some of which still grace the towns of the region, especially at **Copiapó**.

Economy

Minerals

Present day economic activity is still predominantly based on mineral extraction. About 65 per cent of Chile's iron and 10 per cent of its copper are mined in the Atacama region and there are considerable deposits of silver and gold as well. The largest iron ore mines are in **El Carmen**, **La Suerte**, **Hermanita**, **Los Cristales**, **Cerro Negro**, **Huantame**, and **Bandurrias**. The most important iron mine is **El Algarrobo** south-west of **Vallenar**. Copper is mined at **El Salvador**, 61 km east of **Chañaral**. **Huantame** and **Bandurrias** have the biggest iron ore processing plants, and there are pelletizing plants at **Huasco**, copper lixiviation plants at **Potrerillos** and copper smelters at **Paipote**. Highly sought-after barite is mined on a small scale in the **Domeyko** and **Chañarcillo** area.

Agriculture

Agriculture is concentrated in the irrigated areas beside the two main rivers: **Río Copiapó** and **Río Huasco**. The region also produces *Vino Añejo*, a fine liqueur. and *pisco*, a type of brandy. Olive oil is made from olives harvested in the irrigated areas of the Río Copiapó and Huasco valleys.

Fishing

Fishing in the region is mostly concentrated around **Caldera**, which is also a seaside resort.

National parks

Parque Nacional Pan de Azúcar, 30 km north of Chañaral on the coastal road, is 43 769 ha (106 400 acres) and has a picnic area, camping area, a lookout, and walking paths.

Parque Nacional Tres Cruces, approximately 180 km east of Copiapó, comprises two sections: the northern part around Salar de Maricunga and Laguna Santa Rosa, and the southern section around Laguna del Negro Francisco. The landscape dotted with *salares* and *lagunas* is of a strange brownish colour which contrasts starkly with the bright blue sky. Lakes abound with several varieties of flamingos and Andean geese and ducks. Herds of *guanacos* and *vicuñas* can be seen. The best access is from Copiapó — see "Excursions" from Copiapó on page 147.

Beaches

This region is blessed with 450 km of excellent beaches in isolated desert surroundings, which means that you have to carry fresh water for camping. Behind extensive sand dunes, the coastal *cordillera* dwindles to about 1000 m. The Panamericana runs along the coast only between Chañaral and Caldera. Most of the beaches between Caldera and the border with Región IV de Coquimbo almost at La Serena are inaccessible other than by four-wheel drive vehicles. The average summer temperature along these beaches is 26°C (79°F); in winter it is 14°C (57°F).

Local dishes

Excellent seafood dishes retaining a faint Peruvian influence, such as *ceviche de corvina* (pickled fish), are prepared along the coast. Try freshwater shrimps and *anguillas* (young eels). **Alto del Carmen** produces fine table grapes which are also exported.

Tierra Amarilla produces *Pajarete* and *Guagero*, both fine sweet wines.

Tourism

The coastal and *pre-Cordillera* areas of Región III de Atacama are accessible all year round. Snow in the high *sierra* is not uncommon even in summertime.

The main places of interest are **Copiapó** and **Caldera**, but the more adventurous may like to go to **Salar de Pedernales** and **El Salvador** mine. Nature lovers will enjoy the **Parque Nacional Pan de Azúcar**. The quiet valleys of the headwaters of the **Río Huasco** await the intrepid mountain hiker. During the short rainy period, desert flowers bloom. The region is still a little-known tourist destination. Following in the footsteps of the first Spanish *conquistadores* up the **Quebrada Paipote** towards the **Paso de San Francisco** — or even crossing into Argentina — is another challenging trip, but prepare yourself for the cold and sometimes snow even in summer.

The churches in these parts have a curious style quite distinct from the square fortress-like churches encountered in the Antofagasta and Tarapacá regions. Here, the church steeple is set atop the main building. Examples are the cathedral in **Copiapó** and the church of **Nantoco** 7 km south of **Tierra Amarilla**.

The Inca trail

A major branch of the royal road of the Incas (*Capac Ñan*) came down to the Pacific through Región III de Atacama. It is clearly recognizable and visible in one particular part descending in zigzags from the *pampa* into the **Quebrada del Río Salado** near **El Jardín**. It is only about a meter wide, but rocks are placed on either side to mark the road through flat terrain. Some *topos* (distance markers) have been identified, and there is no doubt that the road was built by the Incas to reach the **Río Maule** through the central valley. This was only one of many trails coming down from the *sierra*. The Inca trail comes across from Argentina near **Volcán Llullaillaco**, passes along **Sierra de Domeyko**, crosses **Pampa del Indio Muerto**, passes to the east of Mina De El Salvador, descends **Quebrada El Jardín** into the **Quebrada del Río de la Sal**, rises again, and crosses the *pampa* towards **Finca de El Chañaral** where it peters out. Most likely the Incas exploited gold mines (*yapu*) in the area around **Inca de Oro**, which is still dotted with abandoned mines from the colonial period. The **Finca de Chañaral**, 19 km north-east of Inca de Oro, has many relics of the pre-Colombian past, including rock paintings and remains of buildings, pointing to the existence of an Inca *tambo*. The Inca trail vanishes here, but reappears further south in the upper Río Copiapó valley where the Incas had a metallurgical center near **Valle Hermoso**.

Festivals

The towns in which events are held are listed here by month. For details, see under "Festivals" in the entries for individual towns.

- January: Alto del Carmen, Vallenar
- February: Caldera, Copiapó, Tierra Amarilla

Distances

From Alto del Carmen

- Caldera: 258 km north

- Diego de Almagro: 335 km north (via Inca de Oro)
- Tierra Amarilla: 199 km north

From Caldera

- Bahía Inglesa: 7 km south
- Diego de Almagro: 150 km east

From Chañaral

- Alto del Carmen: 348 km south
- Caldera: 90 km south
- Copiapó: 165 km south-east
- Diego de Almagro: 60 km east
- Freirina: 352 km south
- Huasco: 370 km south
- Parque Nacional Pan de Azúcar: 20 km north
- Tierra Amarilla: 181 km
- Vallenar: 310 km south

From Copiapó

- Alto del Carmen: 183 km south
- Bahía Inglesa: 72 km north-west
- Caldera: 75 km north-west
- Chañaral: 164 km north-west
- Diego de Almagro: 152 km north (via Inca de Oro)
- Freirina: 175 km south -west
- Huasco: 200 km south -west
- Tierra Amarilla: 16 km south-east
- Vallenar: 145 km south

From Freirina

- Alto del Carmen: 70 km east
- Caldera: 250 km north
- Diego de Almagro: 330 km north
- Tierra Amarilla: 191 km north

From Huasco

- Alto del Carmen: 86 km
- Caldera: 268 km north
- Chañaral: 358 km north

- Diego de Almagro: 360 km north
- Freirina: 21 km east
- Tierra Amarilla: 209 km north

From Tierra Amarilla

- Caldera: 91 km north-west
- Diego de Almagro: 176 km north

From Vallenar

- Alto del Carmen: 38 km south-west
- Caldera 220 km north
- Chañaral: 310 km north
- Copiapó: 145 km north
- Diego de Almagro: 300 km north
- Freirina: 32 km west
- Huasco: 57 km west
- Tierra Amarilla: 161 km north

BAHÍA INGLESA

Area code: 052
Altitude: Sea level
Distance from Copiapó: 72 km north-west on Panamericana

Bahía Inglesa, 6 km west of Caldera, has clean beaches and unpolluted water. The beach front is on Avenida El Morro around a wide protected bay. Playa Blanca runs from north to south, where rocks separate it from Playa El Chuncho, and more rocks separate Playa El Chuncho from Playa Las Piscinas. After still more rocks, Playa La Macha extends for many kilometers around the bay to **Punta Morro**. This is one of the best spots for swimming and skin diving — the water is unbelievably clear.

Playa La Piscina is the main beach in Bahía Inglesa, directly on the Costanera. This is a place for swimming in unpolluted waters and for camping; there are kiosks, showers, and toilets.

◻ Accommodation

Motels
★★★★ Apart Hotel Rocas de Bahía Inglesa, Avenida El Morro (316005 $D ♪♪. Fax 316032
★★★ El Umbral de Bahía Inglesa, Camino Bahía Inglesa **AB-CHIKLPR** (315000 $E ♪♪. Tennis
- Cabañas Los Jardines de Bahía Inglesa, Copiapó 100 **ABCE-**

HIJKLR (315359 $F for 5. Fax 315752, 35 cabins
- El Coral, Avenida El Morro 564 **ABCDFHIJP** (315331 $F ♪♪
- Villa Alegre, El Morro 578 **ABDHIP** (315074 $E for 4

◻ Buses
Regular municipal buses run between the plaza in Caldera and the beach in Bahía Inglesa. The trip takes 15 minutes.

◉ Sport
Swimming, fishing, and diving are all popular here.

◉ Excursions
- **Playa Caleta El Cisne**: 15 km south on a small protected bay. The track is bad and you have to bring drinking water.

BAHIA INGLESA

Key to map

A   Capilla

●   **Accommodation**

1   Cabañas Los Jardines de Bahía Inglesa
2   Apart Hotel Rocas de Bahía

3   Motel Villa Alegre
4   Hotel/restaurant El Coral
5   Cabañas y Camping de Bahía Inglesa

CALDERA

Area code: 052
Population: 4400
Altitude: Sea level
Distance from Copiapó: 75 km north-west on Panamericana (RN 5)

Although founded during colonial times, Caldera did not become a town until 1850. In the 19th century it was the port for exporting minerals from the rich Chañarcillo mine. Now only the rail station (*Estación de Ferrocarriles*), a *monumento nacional*, is left from its former glory.

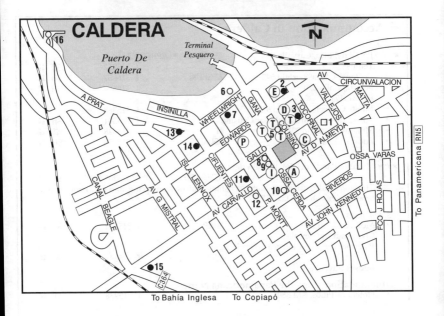

Key to map

A	Iglesia
C	Municipalidad (Town hall)
D	Post office and telex
E	Telephone
I	Tourist information
P	Gas stations
$	Money exchange
T	Bus terminals

● **Accommodation**

2	Hotel Los Andes
3	Hotel Fénicia
7	Hotel Costanera
10	Hotel Pucará
11	Residencial Molina
13	Hostería Puerta del Sol
14	Residencial Palermo
15	Hotel Portal del Inca

○ **Eating out**

5	Restaurant Il Pirón d'Oro
6	Restaurant Nuevo Miramar
8	Restaurant Le Galeón
9	Restaurant New Charles
12	Mistic Pizza
16	Restaurant Club de Yates

□ **Services**

1	ENTEL

There are some good beaches near the harbor. Not far offshore is one of the deepest depressions in the Pacific Ocean. Caldera (and its offshoot **Bahía Inglesa**) are seaside resorts with good tourist facilities. It is also a fishing port.

The beaches in and around Caldera are accessible throughout the year. Playa Mansa is in town; Playa

⊟ Accommodation in Caldera

Hotels

★★★★Portal del Inca, Carvallo 945	ABCDEFGHIJKLMPR$TUXZ			
Tennis		ℂ 315252	$D	⚌
• Costanera, Wheelwright 543	AEGHIJKL	ℂ 316007	$H	⚌
• Fénicia, Gallo 370		ℂ 315594	$H	⚌
Fax 315171				
• Monte Carmelo, Carvallo 627		ℂ 315388		
• Los Andes, Edwards 360 near Cousiño		ℂ 315301	$H	⚌
• Millaray, Cousiño 331	AI	ℂ 315528	$I	⚌
• Pucará, Ossa Cerda 460	AEIJKLPS	ℂ 315258	$H	⚌

Hostería

★★★ Hostería Puerta del Sol, Wheelwright 750

	AEFGHLPU	ℂ 315205	$F	⚌

The *hostería* also organizes high sea fishing cruises, skin diving, and excursions in four-wheel drive vehicles; fax 315507

Residenciales

• Molina, Montt 346	AHILP	ℂ 315941	$I	⚌
Cook your own meals				
• Palermo, Cifuentes 150 near Wheelwright				
	ADHI	ℂ 315847	$H	⚌
Budget travelers				

Accommodation along the Panamericana Norte

• Hotel Los Pinos, KM 880		ℂ 315238	$D	⚌

Loreto is to the south-west. See the entry for Bahía Inglesa on page 129. ☞ Playa Brava and Playa Blanca are north of town, separated by a rock outcrop called Punta Peligrosa.

⊠ Festivals
• February 15-17: Festival de Caldera

ⓘ Tourist information
Hotel prices are at a premium during the main holiday season from December to the end of February. During the rest of the year, the better hotels are considerably cheaper.
• Sernatur, Ossa Cerda 350, open Mon–Sun 1000–1400 and 1700–2100 in the tourist season

ⓘ Eating out

Bar
• Bar Clips, Ossa Cerda corner of Wheelwright 497

Restaurants
• Il Pirón d'Oro, Cousiño 218
• La Mistic Pizza, Carvallo 607
• Le Galeón, Ossa Cerda 330 $Y. Best meeting place in town
• New Charles, Ossa Cerda 350
• Nuevo Miramar, Gana 090

ⓨ Entertainment
• Disco Dixcine, Ossa Cerda opposite plaza
• Bartholomeo Pub, Wheelwright 742

Post and telegraph

Post office
• Correo, Edwards 325 near Cousiño

Telephone
• CTC, Edwards 360, fax 315373
• ENTEL, Tocornal 393
• Telex Chile, Ossa Cerda 370

🚌 Buses from Caldera

There is no central bus terminal, but most buses depart from streets west of Plaza de Armas.

Companies
- A10   Buses Casther
- A54   Buses Muñoz, Ossa Cerda 215
- A68   Buses Recabarren, Cousiño 260
- A78   Buses Tramaca, Edwards 415 ℂ 316235
- A115 Incabus/Lasval, Gallo 560 ℂ 315261
- A128 Pullman Bus Fichtur, Cousiño corner of Gallo ℂ 315227

Services

Destination	Fare	Services	Duration	Companis
Antofagasta	$12.40	6 services daily		A78
Chañaral	$2.70	10 services daily		A115, A128
Copiapó	$1.60	50 services daily	2¼ hrs	A10, A54, A68, A115, A128
Coquimbo	$7.20	3 services daily		A128
Diego de Almagro	$2.50	8 services daily		A115, A128
El Salvador	$5.70	8 services daily		A115, A128
Iquique	$24.70	1 service daily		A78
La Calera	$15.20	1 service daily		A128
La Serena	$9.50	12 services daily	6 hrs	A115, A128
Los Vilos	$11.40	5 services daily		A115
Ovalle	$9.50	8 services daily		A115, A128
Potrerillos	$5.30	5 services daily		A115, A128
Santiago	$17.00	4 services daily		A115, A128
Change in La Serena				
Vallenar	$4.60	5 services daily		A128
Valparaíso	$16.00	4 services daily		A128
Viña del Mar	$16.00	4 services daily		A128

🏧 Services and facilities

Supermarket
- Carvallo, in lane between Montt and Ossa Cerda

🚗 Motoring

- COPEC gas station, Montt corner of Edwards

🔹 Excursions

Beaches north
- Playa Ramada and Playa Rodillo: Approximately 11 km north stretching for several kilometers. Both are easily accessible from the Panamericana. There are no facilities whatsoever, and you may find yourself bathing alone on the fine white sand.
- Four kilometers further north on the Panamericana is a *Santuario de la Natu-raleza* ("Nature Sanctuary") where some unusual circular rocks are located. This is possibly the only place on earth where a freak of nature has produced spherical granite rocks of this kind. They are black and gray in color and impossible to miss. Still further north you pass the small beaches of Playa Zentena, Playa Zapatilla and then reach **Balneario Obispillo**, 36 km north, where a small restaurant serves excellent seafood. This is not, however, the end of the beaches; the Panamericana runs very close to the seashore most of the time and passes many more beaches and coves en route to Chañaral.

Beaches south
- Bahía Calderilla: About 5 km south of the main plaza. It has many calm coves and beaches. Playa Calderilla and

Caldera

Playa Loreto are the most frequented. Vacation homes and condominiums have been established in this area, but there are still no facilities for tourists. There are fish meal plants and fish canneries at Playa Blanca on the north side of the bay and mechanized port facilities at Punta Ester on the south side.

- Playa Bahía Inglesa: About 7 km south. An extensive beach where a small natural enclosure in the water is called "La Piscina". The good facilities here attract visitors. The mean annual water temperature is 17.5°C (64°F). Municipal buses from the main plaza to the beach take 15 minutes and leave every 15 minutes; fares $0.50. The road is sealed between Caldera and Bahía Inglesa.

CHAÑARAL

Area code: 052
Population: 12 000
Altitude: Sea level
Distance from Copiapó: 164 km north-west on Panamericana

Chañaral is the provincial capital and the main port for the copper mine of **El Salvador**. The modern port has been relocated 2 km south to **Barquito**.

Chañaral is located on the **Bahía Chañaral de Las Animas** where the **Quebrada de Las Animas** and the **Quebrada del Salado** reach the Pacific Ocean.

Before the arrival of the Spaniards, the Chango people lived here. They were fishermen and foragers who lived along the coast. The first Spanish *encomendero* was Juan Cisternas in 1678.

The initial economic rise of the town occurred in the 19th century after Diego de Almeyda discovered the copper deposits at **Las Animas** in 1824. Chañaral was officially founded in 1833 by Diego de Almeyda to serve as a port for the rich copper mine. In 1860 the first smelters opened; they closed in the 1930s. A railroad line was built from the major mines to Chañaral in 1872. In those days there was a large English

Key to map

A	Iglesia	7	Hotel La Marina
B	Gobernación Provincial (Government)	○	**Eating out**
C	Municipalidad (Town hall)	5	Restaurant Rincón Porteño
D	Post office and telex		
E	Telephone	◉	**Entertainment**
T	Bus terminals	3	Disco Octopus
●	**Accommodation**	■	**Sights**
1	Hotel Mini	4	Iglesia Anglicana (Episcopalian Church)
2	Hostería Chañaral		
6	Hotel Jiménez		

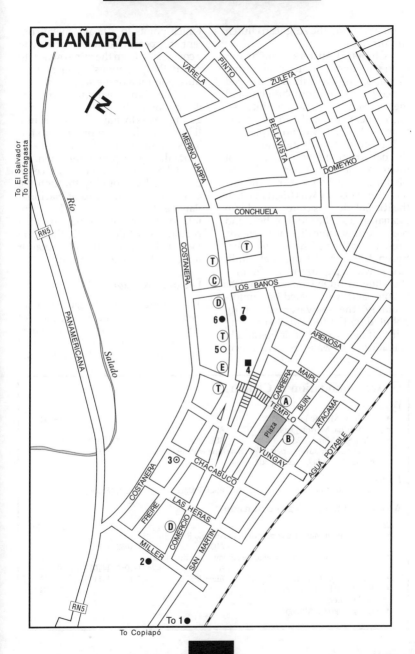

CHAÑARAL

To El Salvador
To Antofagasta

Río

RN5

PANAMERICANA

Salado

VARELA

PINTO

ZULETA

BELLAVISTA

DOMEYKO

MERINO JARPA

CONCHUELA

COSTANERA

T

T

C

LOS BANOS

D

6

7

ARENOSA

T

5

E

4

CARRERA

MAIPU

T

TEMPLO

A

BUIN

ATACAMA

Plaza

B

YUNGAY

AGUA POTABLE

COSTANERA

3

CHACABUCO

FREIRE

LAS HERAS

D

COMERCIO

MILLER

SAN MARTIN

2

RN5

To 1

To Copiapó

population, and the Anglican church still survives.

Chañaral suffers from water shortages, and its water comes from Copiapó. The town itself is wedged in between the narrow shoreline and the sea, and has some very interesting corners. Walk down the stairs from the Plaza to Merino Jarpa.

There is a beautiful view over the bay from the southern end of town. A *cafetería* sits on a viewing platform over the rocks and the former pier. This bay was filled in when the Río Salado was transformed into a canal, and so the old foreshore and piers are now some distance from the present seashore. The *costanera* between Miller and Conchuela indicates the approximate former shoreline. A huge beach of whitish-yellow sand was created but, unfortunately, the seawater is heavily polluted by the Río Salado carrying mine effluent from Potrerillos and El Salvador. The water is dark green,

which points to a heavy metal content. It appears that the town has won a concession from the mine owners to divert the poisonous water and reduce pollution of the sea.

The Panamericana runs for 90 km south along the Pacific coast, giving access to many sandy beaches. It bypasses the town proper and follows the shoreline. The railroad also skirts the upper part of the town.

Chañaral is a good place to break the long journey through the desert, to visit the **Parque Nacional Pan de Azúcar** and to make a trip inland to some of the most isolated regions in Chile around **Salar de Pedernales**. The huge El Salvador mine can be visited en route.

Diego de Almagro

The mining town of Diego de Almagro, 64 km east at an altitude of 500 m, with a population of 7000, is an important crossroads, connected by a sealed road to Chañaral on the

---

🛏 Accommodation in Chañaral

Hotels
- Jiménez, Merino Jarpa 551   ADEFH $H ‖
- La Marina, Merino Jarpa 572   AF $I ‖
- Mini, San Martín 528   ADEHIJKP   ((052) 480079 $G ‖
  Shared bathroom cheaper; built on a slope with sweeping views over the sea
- Nuria, Avenida Costanera 302

Hostería
- Chañaral, Miller 268   ADEFGHIJKLP   ((052) 480050/55 $G ‖

Accommodation in Diego de Almagro

Hotels
- Crillón, Juan Martínez corner of Juan Antonio Rios
                                 AHJP   ((052) 441011 $I   ‖
- Crillón Annex, Avenida Diego de Almagro (on the plaza)
                                 A   ((052) 441011 $H   ‖
- Emelin, Colo Colo 12   AEFHIJPS   ((052) 441159 $H ‖
- Residencial Paris, J.Martínez $J ‖
  Backpackers
- CTC, Diego de Almagro

---

coast and a good gravel road south to Copiapó via **Inca de Oro**. It was founded towards the end of the 19th century when the Mina Tres Gracias was opened 1 km outside town. There is an Esso Servicentro in town.

⑪ **Eating out**

Restaurants
- Hostería Chañaral, Miller 268
- Pizzería Long Beach, Merino Jarpa 546

🚌 **Buses from Chañaral**
The central bus terminal is at Merino Jarpa 858. Clean rest rooms and *cafetería.*

Companies departing from the central terminal
- A106 Fénix Pullman Norte
- A150 Transportes Geminis
- A153 Tur-Bus Jedimar
- A164 SITACO

Companies departing from their own terminals
- A78   Buses Tramaca, Merino Jarpa 867 ☎ 480838
- A112 Flota Barrios, Merino Jarpa 567 ☎ 480071
- A128 Pullman Bus Fichtur, Freire 493 ☎ 480153

Services

Destination	Fare	Services	Duration	Companies
Antofagasta	$10.60	10 services daily		A78, A112, A150
Arica	$25.80	1 service daily		A112
Calama	$15.20	13 services daily		A112
Sleeper	$18.60	1 service daily		A150
Caldera	$3.50	5 services daily		A106, A128
Chuquicamata	$15.20	4 services daily		A78
Copiapó	$3.80	16 services daily	2½ hrs	A106, A112, A128
Coquimbo	$11.40	8 services daily		A106
Diego de Almagro	$1.90	4 services daily		A106, A164
El Salvador	$3.00	5 services daily		A106, A128
Illapel		Tues Fri 1545		A106, A150
Iquique	$23.20	5 services daily		A42, A112
La Calera	$17.10	6 services daily		A112
La Serena	$11.40	20 services daily	7 hrs	A42, A106, A112, A128
Los Vilos	$15.20	6 services daily		A106
Ovalle	$11.40	10 services daily		A42, A106, A112
Potrerillos	$4.60	2 services daily	2½ hrs	A106, A128
Salamanca	$16.00	2 services Tue and Fri		A106, A150
Santiago	$15.20	11 services daily		A78, A106, A112, A128
Taltal	$5.00	6 services daily	2 hrs	A78
Tocopilla	$14.50	5 services daily		A112
Vallenar	$7.60	9 services		A106, A112, A128
Valparaíso	$22.80	8 services daily		A112, A128, A131
Viña del Mar	$22.80	8 services daily		A112, A128, A131

Buses from Diego de Almagro
Incabus, Pullman Bus Fichtur and SITACO run 10 services daily to Chañaral; 3 services daily to Copiapó, 5 services daily to El Salvador, and 3 services daily to Potrerillos.

Eating out along the Panamericana

Restaurants
* La Querencia, Panamericana Norte/Merino Jarpa

🅈 **Entertainment**
* Disco Octopus, Freire 405
* Night Club Mini Bar, San Martín 528

🏛 **Post and telegraph**
Post office
* Correos de Chile, Comercio 172

Telephone
* Telex Chile, Los Baños 200
* CTC, Merino Jarpa 506
* ENTEL Chile, Avenida Aeropuerto ☎ 480555

🗟 **Services**

Supermarket
* Supermercado El Vergel, Rancagua 0244

🚘 **Motoring**

Gas station
* COPEC gas station, Merino Jarpa corner of Panamericana

Car rental
* Car rental in Hostería Chañaral

⚑ **Excursions**

Chañaral is the starting point for excursions further up the *sierra* to the mining towns of **El Salvador**, **Potrerillos** and

Salar de Pedernales. The town stretches for 5 km around the bay. The white sandy beach slopes gently to the sea and the water is shallow for some way out. However, because of its openness, the bay is sometimes subject to strong winds and high waves. The water has a mean annual temperature of 17°C (62°F). Bathing is not advised as the outlet of the El Salvador mine discharges directly into this bay and the water is contaminated! Use the beaches further south instead.

* **Parque Nacional Pan de Azúcar**: 29 km north. See the entry for the park on page 154.
* **Playa Obispito**: Approximately 53 km south. This is a quiet and isolated beach with shallow water, where the average annual temperature is 17°C (63°F). There is good fishing from some of the rocky sections, and opportunites to eat local seafood.
* **El Salvador**: A mining town located in a circular valley basin surrounded by high mountains. The modern township is a complete surprise — an oasis in the middle of the desert offering every conceivable comfort for the mining community. See the entry for El Salvador on page 148.
* **Salar de Pedernales**: 164 km east or 60 km east of El Salvador. This salt, almost dry, 20 square km *laguna* still has a few green patches of water where pink flamingos (*parinas*) gather.

COPIAPÓ

Area code: 052
Population: 70 000
Altitude: sea level
Distances
* From Antofagasta: 565 km south on RN 5 (Panamericana)
* From La Serena: 333 km north on RN 5 (Panamericana)
* From Santiago: 804 km north on RN 5 (Panamericana)

Copiapó, the capital of Region III de Atacama, lies in the **Río Copiapó valley** surrounded by low bare hills. It is a large city with a well-known mining university.

Originally, this place was called by the native inhabitants "Copayapu" an Indian name meaning "gold cup", and pointed to the fact that gold was being mined in the area in pre-Hispanic times. The valley was intensively cultivated by the native Indian population. In 1540 Don Pedro de Valdivia conquered the indigenous people and established a Spanish garrison. The first mass in Chile was read in Copiapó. The Franciscan order founded their monastery and church in 1662.

Officially the town was founded in 1744 and named Villa de San Francisco de la Selva de Copiapó by the *corregidor* Don Francisco Cortés y Cartabio acting on orders from the then Viceroy José Manso de Velazco. The town has developed around three nuclei: the Franciscan convent in the west near Cerro La Cruz, the "modern" foundation in 1774, and the indigenous Diaguita settlement to the east further up along the river.

In 1832 Juan Godoy discovered the rich silver vein of Chañarcillo, 60 km south of Copiapó, giving the region economic impetus. The most impressive buildings date from this era onwards; among them are the Museo Mineralógico y Regional and Iglesia San Francisco. The first railroad line in South America, between Copiapó and Caldera, opened in 1851. The journey took three hours.

The hinterland is rich in archeology and history. Many interesting items linked with past settlement and mining exploitation are exhibited in the two museums in Copiapó. Archeological sites, such as **Viña del Cerro** and **Pucará de Punta Brava** are found in the vicinity. The beach resort of Caldera is only an hour's drive by bus. The Río Copiapó is used in-

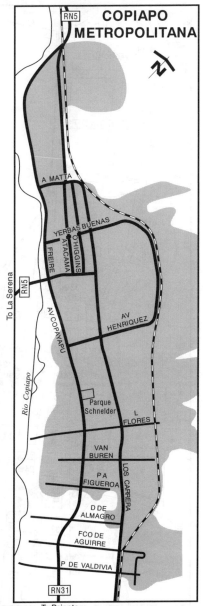

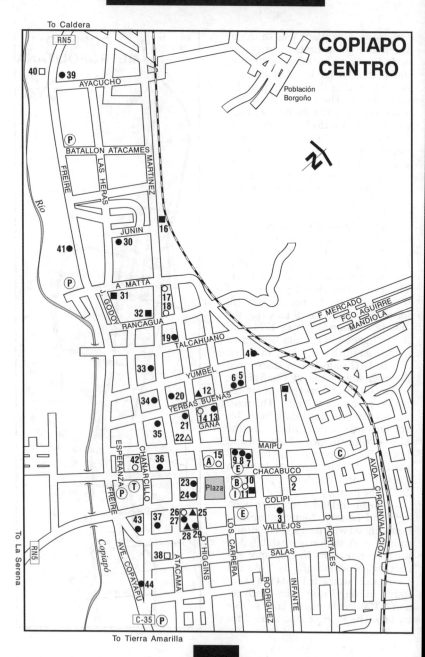

COPIAPO CENTRO

To Caldera

RN5

Población
Borgoño

40 □   ● 39
AYACUCHO

Río

FREIRE

BATALLON ATACAMES

LAS HERAS

MARTINEZ

(P)

JUNIN   ■ 16

41 ●   ● 30

(P)

A MATTA
GODOY
■ 31   ○ 17
              ○ 18
■ 32
RANCAGUA

● 19
TALCAHUANO

● 33   ▲ 4

F MERCADO
FCO AGUIRRE
MANDIOLA

YUMBEL
                ● 6 5
● 34 ● 20 ▲ 12   ■ 1
         YERBAS BUENAS
         ○ 14 13
● 35   ● 21   GANA
       △ 22

ESPERANZA

CHAÑARCILLO

FREIRE

42 ○   ● 36   MAIPU
                (A) ○ 15   (C)
                    ● 9 ○ 8
                    (E) ● 7
(P)(T)   CHACABUCO
         ● 23 Plaza (B) ○ 10
         ● 24   (I) ○ 11 ■
                    COLIPI   ○ 2
         ● 26 ▲ 25 (E)   ● 3
● 43 ● 37 ● 27   VALLEJOS
       ○   ▲
         ● 28 29
                              SALAS

AVE. COPAYAPU

Copiapó

38 □

ATACAMA

O HIGGINS

LOS CARRERA

■ 44

C-35 (P)

RODRIGUEZ

INFANTE

D PORTALES

AVDA CIRCUNVALACION

To La Serena

RN5

To Tierra Amarilla

tensively for irrigation, and the green fields contrast sharply with the Atacama Desert which borders them.

Those wanting to combine mountaineering with archeology may climb to the top of **Volcán Copiapó**, where there are remnants of an Incan shrine — see under "Excursions" below. This climb is not for beginners!

A short walk through the center of Copiapó is rewarding — see under "Sightseeing" below.

The town has retained Don Francisco Cortés's original layout from 1744. The Museo Mineralógico is in the same block as the Intendencia Regional on the corner of Rodríguez and Colipi streets. This is one of the most interesting mineral museums in Chile and should not be missed. It has ore samples and semiprecious stones from all over the region, as well pieces of meteorites. Near the corner of Yerbas Buenas on Infante is an old private chapel (Iglesia de Belén) built by the Fraga family in 1858. It is a jewel of neoclassical style. Follow Yerbas Buenas from the corner with Infante two blocks down to Los Carrera, then walk three blocks north-west down Los Carrera, turning right into Calle Rancagua for a small road leading up to Cerro la Cruz, topped by a huge cross and commanding sweeping views east and south over the city down below in the valley. To the west you can see

Key to map

A	Iglesia	37	Residencial Chañarcillo
B	Gobernación Regional (Government)	39	Hotel Pán de Azúcar
C	Municipalidad (Town hall)	41	Hosterí Las Pircas
D	Post office and telex	43	Hotel Archi
E	Telephone	44	Hotel Del Rey
H	Hospital		
I	Tourist information	○	**Eating out**
P	Gas stations	2	La Pizza de Tito
$	Money exchange	14	Restaurant Spiedo
T	Bus terminals	15	Bavaria
		17	Restaurant Il Pirón d'Oro
●	**Accommodation**	18	Restaurant Puerto Viejo
3	Hotel Montecatini I	26	Restaurant Hao Hwa
4	Apart Hotel Camasquil	42	Small restaurants
5	Hotel Edy-Maryros		
6	Hotel España	△	**Car rental**
7	Residencial Rodríguez	22	Avis Rent a Car
8	Hotel Rocca D'Argento		
9	Hotel San Francisco de la Selva	▲	**Airline offices**
13	Residencial Cristi	12	LADECO
19	Hotel La Casona	25	National Airline
20	Hotel Inglés	28	LAN Chile
21	Hotel Derby		
23	Hotel Diego de Almeida	■	**Sights**
24	Residencial Plaza	1	Iglesia Belén
27	Hotel Palace	10	Museo Mineralogíco de Copiapó
29	Hotel Chagall	16	Museo de Sitio Estación Ferrocarril
30	Hostería Corona del Inca	31	Iglesia San Francisco
33	Residencial Torres	32	Museo Regional de Copiapó
34	Hotel Montecatini II		
35	Hotel Flamenco	□	**Services**
36	Residencial Chacabuco	38	CONAF
		40	Universidad de Atacama

Copiapó

the irrigated fields in the riverflats which are petering out in the distance as the desert takes over. Return the same way (although there are a few alternative descending trails), and follow Rancagua/Los Carrera for another block to Alameda Matta, a wide avenue of two lanes separated by a tree- studded park. On the right-hand side are the Casas de los Empleados Ferrocarril (the former railroad employees' living quarters), built in 1860, in neoclassical style with Doric columns, which have been declared a *monumento nacional*. In the center strip which separates the lanes of Alameda Matta there is a bust of Manuel Matta, an illustrious citizen of the last century, and another statue of Juan Godoy. Round the corner in Martínez is the old railroad station, which has been turned into a *monumento nacional*. Return to Alameda Matta and follow it almost to the intersection with Avenida Copayapu, until you reach the old Franciscan convent and Iglesia de San Francisco on the left-hand side, built by the brothers of the order in 1800. This is the oldest part of town. Continue one block east to Rancagua and turn north into Calle Rancagua. On the left-hand side at the corner with ☞ Calle Atacama Casa Hermanos Matta is the home of Guillermo and José Matta, well-known 19th century poets and politicians. The facade of the building with its columns is very imposing. Nowadays it is the Museo Regional. Historical memorabilia re- ☞ lating to the beginnings of the town shows the living style of the rich in the last century.

The main shopping streets are Libertador B. O'Higgins between Vallejos and Yerbas Buenas, and Calle Chacabuco between Chañar-cillo and Rodríguez.

☒ Festivals
* February, first Sunday: La Candelaria. Celebrated every year in a chapel just 3 km outside the town center. Pilgrims from afar arrive in multicolored old-fashioned garments. The dancers belong to different brotherhoods and compete against each other. The Santuario de la Candelaria is located on Los Carrera. The shrine has been venerated since 1780 when a statue was brought by a mule driver but the first church was not built until 1800. There are some fine murals inside the church.
* December 8: Foundation day of Copiapó

Festivals in Tierra Amarilla
* February 17 and 18: Festival Vid (Wine Festival)
* Februrary 24: Carnival Pullay

☒ Tourist information
* Sernatur, Los Carrera 691 ℓ 212838, fax 217248; in a small building in front of Intendencia Regional
* CONAF, Atacama 898 ℓ 213404/212571. Information about Parque Nacional Pan de Azúcar

⑪ Eating out
Restaurant
* A. Chau, Rodríguez 775. Chinese cuisine
* Bavaria, Chacabuco 497. International cuisine
* Carpaccio, Salas 463
* Club Libanés, Los Carrera 350
* Don Elias, Chacabuco 101 corner of Panamericana. Seafood
* El Corsario, Atacama 245
* El Quincho, Atacama 109
* Hotel Diego de Almeyda, Plaza Prat
* Hao-Hwa, Colipi 340. Chinese cuisine
* Il Pirón d'Oro, Atacama 1
* La Pizza de Tito, Infante 603 corner of Chacabuco
* Pub La Puerta del Norte, Avenida Henriquez 365
* Puerto Viejo, Atacama 95 corner of Rancagua
* Spiedo, Libertador B. O'Higgins 440

🛏 Accommodation in Copiapó

Apart Hotel
- Camasquil, Avenida Circunvalación   ABCDEGH   ☎ 212579 $G ♙♙

Hotels
★★★★Diego de Almeyda, Libertador B. O'Higgins 656
                                       ACDEFGHIJKLMPRSTUZ
                                                          ☎ 212075/76 $E ♙♙
- ★★★ La Casona, Libertador B. O'Higgins 150   ☎ 217278 $F ♙♙
- ★★★ San Francisco de la Selva, Los Carrera 525
                                       ADEHP   ☎ 213255 $F ♙♙
    Fax 213255
- ★★ Montecatini II, Atacama 374   AEGHILPS   ☎ 211516 $F ♙♙
    Fax 214773
- ★★ Pan de Azúcar, Avenida Ramón Freire 430
                                       ACDEFGHIKLPRSUY   ☎ 214399 $G ♙♙
    Fax 217052
- Archi, Vallejos 111   ADEHIJ   ☎ 212983 $H ♙♙
- Chagall, Libertador B. O'Higgins 760   ☎ 213775 $E ♙♙
    Fax 211527
- Copa de Oro, Infante 530   ☎ 216309 $G ♙♙
    Fax 217604
- Del Rey, Avenida Copayapu 935   ☎ 218836 $G ♙♙
- Derby, Yerbas Buenas 396   AEGHIJLP$U   ☎ 212447 $G ♙♙
- Edy-Maryros, Yerbas Buenas 593   ☎ 211408 $H ♙♙
- El Sol, Rodríguez 550   ACDHIJKL $H ♙♙
- España, Yerbas Buenas 571   ☎ 217197 $G ♙♙
- Flamenco, Atacama 456   ☎ 212729 $G ♙♙
    Fax 218004
- Inglés, Atacama 337   AEFGIJLPU   ☎ 212797 $H ♙♙
    Large patio onto which all rooms emerge, budget travelers
- Montecatini I, Infante 766   AEGHILPS   ☎ 211363 $G ♙♙
- Palace, Atacama 741   AEFGIJLPU   ☎ 212852 $G ♙♙
    $H ♙♙ shared bathroom
- Rocca d'Argento, Maipú 580   ☎ 211191 $F ♙♙

Hostals
- Hastol, Chacabuco 230   ☎ 216615

Hosterías
- Corona del Inca, Las Heras 54   ☎ 213851 $G ♙♙
- Las Pircas, Ave. Copayapu 95   AFGHLPRS$ ☎ 213220 $F ♙♙
    Fax 211633

Residenciales
- Ben Bow, Rodríguez 541   ADIJLP   ☎ 217634 $I ♙♙
- Chacabuco, Chacabuco 271   ☎ 213428 $H ♙♙
- Chañarcillo, Chañarcillo 741   AEFJ   ☎ 213281 $H ♙♙
- Cristi, Los Carrera 440   ADHIJP   ☎ 218132 $I ♙♙
- Nueva Chañarcillo, Rodríguez 540   ☎ 212368 $H ♙♙
- Plaza, O'Higgins 670   AEIJLU   ☎ 212671 $I ♙♙
- Rodríguez, Rodríguez 528   AEFGMPU   ☎ 212861 $I ♙♙
- Torres, Atacama 230   AEI   ☎ 219600 $I ♙♙

Accommodation along the Panamericana Norte
- Hostal Maray, KM 812   ☎ 212560/219076 $F ♙♙

- Tijuana, Infante 656
- Tong Fan, O'Higgins 398. Chinese cuisine
- Villa Rapallo, Atacama 1080
- Pub La Puerta del Norte, Avenida Henriquez 365
- Puerto Viejo, Atacama 99. Chilean cuisine
- Spiedo, O'Higgins 440. Chilean cuisine
- Tijuana, Infante 656

Cafés
- Haiti, Atacama block 600, corner of Chacabuco
- Willy, Maipú 386

Eating out along the Panamericana
- Criollisimo, Panamericana Sur 261. *Show folklórico*

Eating out in Tierra Amarilla
- Restorant, Miguel Lemeur 328

⊤ Entertainment
- Discotheque Alai, Maipú 279
- Disco Splash, Juan Martínez 46
- Sala de Baile Top-Top, Romulos Peña 215

Entertainment along the road to Tierra Amarilla
- Sala de Baile El Jardín
- Sala de Baile El Cortijo, Los Carrera 2483

✆ Post and telegraph

Post office
- Correos and telex, Los Carrera 691

Telephone
- ENTEL Chile, Infante 684. Overseas phone calls
- CTC Los Carrera 599, Fax 212056

$ Financial
- Banco de Chile, Libertador B. O'Higgins 694, on the plaza
- Fincard, Chacabuco 389 ℂ 213983. Cash advances against Visa and Mastercard

▣ Services and facilities

Dry cleaner
- Lavaseco Atacama, Maipú 370

Laundromat
- Lavasuper, Mackenna 430 self service

Photographic equipment
- Fotocolor, Maipú 285. Agfa, Fuji
- Nortsur Color, Chacabuco 310. Agfa

Supermarket
- Supermercado Las Brisas, Los Carrera 530

✈ Air services

Airlines
- LAN Chile, Hotel Diego de Almeyda, Libertador B.O'Higgins 640 ℂ 213512
- LADECO, Yerbas Buenas 431 ℂ 219135
- National Airlines, Colipi 340

Flights
- Calama: Fare $100; LAN Chile
- El Salvador: Fare $47.00; 1 service daily except daily except Thurs and Sun ; duration ½ hr; LAN Chile
- La Serena: 1–2 services daily; duration 1 hr; LADECO
- Santiago: Fare $154.00; 1–2 services daily; duration 1½ hrs; LAN Chile, LADECO

▦ Motoring
For gas stations, see city map

Car rental
- Automóvil Club de Chile, Libertador B. O'Higgins 676 ℂ 213180
- Avis Rent-a-Car, Autocentro Elias Nicolás E., Libertador B. O'Higgins 480 ℂ 217047, fax 212827. Also at the Chamonate airport
- Budget Rent-a-Car, Libertador B. O'Higgins 640 ℂ fax 217355
- First Rent-a-Car, Avenida Copayapu 923 ℂ 212369, fax 211633
- Galerias Rent-a-Car, Panamericana Sur 260 ℂ 212147
- Hertz Rent-a-Car, Copayapu 173 ℂ 213522/211333
- Rent-a-Car Rodaggi, Colipi 121 ℂ 212153 fax 212003

▣ Sightseeing
A short walk through the city center is rewarding. Start on Plaza Prat (formerly Plaza de Armas). The marble statue in the center of Juan Godoy, discoverer of the rich Chañarcillo silver mine in 1832, was sculpted in Paris from Carrara marble and installed in 1872, replacing the original statue. The plaza was planted with nearly a hundred *pimiento* trees in 1880; shoe-

🚌 Buses from Copiapó

The bus terminal is located on Chacabuco block 100.

Companies departing from the terminal
- A10   Buses Casther, Officina 4 ☎ 218889
- A45   Buses Libac, office 1 ☎ 2122237
- A54   Buses Muñoz, office 9 ☎ 2132059
- A68   Buses Recabarren, office 11 ☎ 216991
- A78   Buses Tramaca, office 15 ☎ 213979
- A106 Fénix/Tal, ☎ 214929
- A112 Flota Barrios, office 5 ☎ 213645
- A115 Incabus/Lasval, office 3 ☎ 213488
- A150 Transportes Geminis

Companies departing from their own terminals
- A42   Buses Carmelita, Chacabuco 176 ☎ 213113
- A128 Pullman Bus Fichtur, Colipi 109 ☎ 212629
- A137 Tas Choapa, Chañarcillo 432

Companies departing from the corner of Rodríguez and Chacabuco
- A162 Taxi colectivo No Urbano
- A163 Colectivo Intercomunal

Services

Destination	Fare	Services	Duration	Companies
• Antofagasta	$20.00	18 services daily		A42, A45, A78, A106, A112, A150
Sleeper	$30.00	2 services daily		A78, A112
• Arica	$28.50	12 services		A42, A78, A106, A112, A128
Sleeper	$45.00	3 services daily		A78, A106, A128
• Calama	$21.00	13 services daily		A45, A78, A112, A150
• Caldera	$1.60	39 services daily	2¼ hrs	A54, A68, A115, A128
• Chañaral	$5.00	17 services daily	2½ hrs	A112, A115, A128
• Chuquicamata	$21.00	4 services daily		A45, A78, A112
• Combarbalá	$8.00	1 service daily		A115
• Coquimbo	$11.50	12 services daily		A42, A45, A112, A115, A128, A137
• El Salvador	$7.00	7 services daily		A78, A115, A128
• Illapel	$14.00	2 services daily		A128
• Iquique	$25.80	11 services daily		A42, A78, A106, A112
	$55.00	1 service daily		A128
• La Calera	$12.00	7 services daily		A78, A112, A115
• La Serena	$ 8.70	26 services daily		A42, A45, A78, A112, A115, A128, A137
• Los Loros	$ 1.30	1 service daily		A10, A98
• Los Vilos	$18.60	3 services daily		A115, A137
• Nantoco	$1.40			A98, A162
• Ovalle	$10.60	18 services daily		A42, A78, A83, A104, A112, A115, A128
• Pabellón	$1.20	6 services daily		A10, A98
• Paipote	$0.60	every 15 minutes		A163,
• Potrerillos	$9.50	4 services daily	5 hrs	A78, A128
• Salamanca	$15.00	2 services daily		A128
• Santiago	$20.00	27 services daily	12 hrs	A42, A78, A106, A115, A128, A137, A166
Sleeper	$30.00	3 services daily		A45, A112, A137
• Taltal	$8.40	1 service daily		A78
• Tierra Amarilla	$0.60	every 15 minutes		A98, A162, A163

Buses from Copiapó — continued

Destination	Fare	Services	Duration	Companies
• Tocopilla	$17.50	5 services daily		A112
• Vallenar	$5.00	13 services	2 hrs	A45, A54, A112, A115, A128, A137
• Valparaíso	$22.00	13 services daily		A78, A112, A115, A128
• Viña del Cerro	$1.50	6 services daily		A10, A98
• Viña del Mar	$22.00	13 services daily		A78, A112, A115, A128

shine boys and girls now work in their shade. The buildings of the Intendencia Regional (regional seat of government) take up the complete north-east side of the plaza. The former town hall is on the south side next to the Hotel Diego de Almeida. The cathedral is on the western side of the plaza — see below.

You can make a longer tour of the city on foot in four hours, with brief visits to most of the places mentioned below.

*   Iglesia Catedral Nuestra Señora del Rosario, on the western side of Plaza Prat, is a *monumento nacional*; it was built in 1851 in neoclassical style with a strong English influence. In contrast to the *altiplano* churches further north, the belfry is the centerpiece and an integral part of the building. It has three sections. The portico roof is supported by eight columns. The end ones are square shaped; the four pillars in the center are round. On the main altar there is an image of the Virgen del Rosario which was brought from France. Famous citizens of the town are buried inside.
*   Iglesia Belén, Infante 17, was built in the middle of last century for a rich Copiapó family as a private chapel. It is located in a picturesque setting, with a small plaza in front.
*   Museo Mineralógico de Copiapó, corner of Colipi and Rodríguez. There are 14 000 mineral examples on show, making this one of the most complete collections of minerals in South America. Among other exhibits are a meteorite piece weighing 80 kg, and a piece of ruby silver ore. This is an interesting museum, open Mon–Fri 1000–1300 and 1500–1900.
*   Museo de Sitio Estación de Ferrocarril de Copiapó (Railroad Station Museum). This *monumento histórico* was

built in 1851 when the first rail line was inaugurated in South America. Inside the building there is an interesting overview of the development of the rail system in the middle of the 19th century.
*   Museo Regional de Copiapó, Atacama 98. Exhibits from pre-Hispanic times to the present day. This former residence of the Matta brothers is now a *monumento nacional.*
*   Iglesia de San Francisco de Copiapó, corner of Alameda and Chañarcillo. This is the oldest church in town. Its present form dates from 1872. The religious images are Flemish.

⊕ Excursions

Tour operators
*   Turismo Atacama, Los Carrera 716 ℂ 212712 fax 217357

Excursions
*   **Caldera** and **Bahía Inglesa** and its many beaches are only 75 km northwest, and can be reached by frequent buses. The best beaches are near Bahía Inglesa, which is a small beach resort in its own right. Caldera and nearby Bahía Inglesa are the foremost seaside resorts in Región III de Atacama. There are good facilities and swimming is possible all year round. See the entries for Caldera (page 130) and Bahía Inglesa (page 129). This is a day excursion from Copiapó. Between Copiapó and Caldera, the Panamericana goes through desert-like *pampa.* However, when it rains, flowers bloom here for a couple of months. The drier *pampa*, with very little vegetation for most of the year, lies to the north of Caldera. South is semi-desert, with shrubs and cacti.

- **El Salvador** via **Inca de Oro**: This inland route is the original pre-Hispanic route taken by the Incas into Chile. Part of the original Inca trail is still visible on some private landholdings, especially around Inca de Oro. The first section of this trip from Copiapó to Diego de Almagro can be made by rural buses. At Diego de Almagro change onto a long-distance bus. See also the entry for El Salvador on page 148.

- **La Serena**: A five-hour trip of 333 km. Numerous buses service this stretch. The landscape is not as barren and hostile as it is further north, and thorny shrubs and cacti grow. There are long straight stretches through fairly flat country with low hills between Copiapó and Vallenar. From **Incahuasi** onwards the landscape becomes more varied. The most scenic part is the descent through the **Cuesta Buenos Aires** just before reaching the coast at **Los Hornos** 57 km north of La Serena. The only gas stations between Copiapó and La Serena are in Vallenar and Incahuasi.

- **Los Loros**: 71 km south on Ruta C-35, in the upper **Río Copiapó** valley. The road from Copiapó passes through fertile irrigated vineyards and orchards. Los Loros is a good base for walks in the upper tributaries of the Río Copiapó. The Inca remains of **Pucará de Punta Brava** are nearby, as are those of the **Palacio Incaico de la Puerta** some 5 km south of the village. The Incan metallurgical center of **Viña del Cerro** is 20 km further south. The remains of a *"huaycra"*, an Incan furnace, are here. Accommodation is available in Cabañas y Restaurant Los Loros on Walker Martínez. Buses Casther and Abarcia run daily buses there.

- **Parque Nacional Nevado Tres Cruces**: 180 km north-east. This park was created in 1994 to preserve the *altiplano* flora and fauna around **Laguna Santa Rosa** and incorporates **Salar de Maricunga** and **Laguna del Negro Francisco**. Altogether it covers 60 000 ha (148 000 acres). The national park consists of two sections: the northern part includes Laguna Santa

Rosa and Salar de Maricunga, which is the southernmost *salar* in Chile. On the west side of Laguna Santa Rosa there is a CONAF *refugio*. The southern section is around Laguna del Negro Francisco some 80 km further south, on the southern shore of which is another CONAF *refugio*. Access is rather difficult through some of this remote and strikingly beautiful part of the Andes. The turnoff is 10 km from the SAG (fruitfly) and Carabinero checkpoint on **Salar de Maricunga**. Check with the staff of the meteorological station or with the *carabineros*. From the northern section it is approximately 90 km to the Laguna del Negro Francisco. You may find field geologists at Campo Anglo-América who know the area pretty well. Use only four-wheel drive vehicles for this trip, or better still make it with a tour operator from Copiapó or from the mining town of El Salvador. Alternatively you could approach CONAF in Copiapó, as they have regular staff trips to the park — you will have to pay. The mountain scenery includes **Volcán Copiapó** (6052m) which rises abruptly from the north shore of the *laguna;* and **Nevados Jotabeche** (5880m) south of the *laguna*. It is bitterly cold, so take adequate clothing. This area is the breeding ground for native falmingos — *flamenco de James, flamenco Andino* and *flamenco chileno*. Other birdlife includes condors and the Andean bullfinch, *gaviota andina*. *Vicuñas* and *guanacos* graze in the *bofedales* (a type of highland swamp) around the *lagunas*. The altitude ranges from 3700 m to 4500 m. The temperature may rise to 20°C (68°F) during the day, and in summer the "Bolivian winter" may bring some snow.

- Ruins of **Chañarcillo**: 70 km south. This is the site of Juan Godoy's legendary silver find of 1832. In its heyday it was probably the wealthiest town in northern Chile. Mansions from those days still survive. This side trip can be made on the way south to Vallenar by making a 10 km detour east of the Panamericana.

- **Tierra Amarilla**: 15 km south, at an altitude of 600 m. Tierra Amarilla stretches along the road for 1 km, and has a population of 2000. There are small mines in the district and a very fine type of grape is grown, mostly for export. The contrast of green vineyards against bare mountains and blue sky is striking. The main attractions are **Nantoco** at KM 24 with its church, a *monumento nacional*, and Ha-

cienda Jotabeche at KM 31. This building is near the old railroad station on the line to the Chañarcillo silver mine. It was the home of the famous writer José Joaquín Vallejos and is now a *monumento nacional* to him. There is a COPEC service station. Frequent taxi *colectivos* ply between Tierra Amarilla and Copiapó

EL SALVADOR

Area code: 052
Population: 20 000
Altitude: 2300 m
Distance from Copiapó: 200 km north on Ruta C-13 and C-17

El Salvador is an oasis on a high altitude desert plain cut off to the east by high mountains, the first spurs of the Andes. Around the township it is bleak barren country. Nearby, the remains of the pre-Colombian coast-to-*sierra* track (an Inca trail) can still be seen.

The El Salvador mine, opened in 1959, is one of the biggest copper mines in Chile, and a modern town has been built to accommodate the workforce. The ore concentrate is sent 41 km inland to the smelters at the abandoned copper mine at Potrerillos, and copper ingots are shipped to Chañaral for export.

The mine itself is at 2600 m in the vicinity of **Cerro Indio Muerto**. The presence of copper was already known to the early explorers in the 19th century. The mine now produces more than 100 000 tonnes of copper annually.

El Salvador can be used as a base for excursions to Salar de Pedernales and Potrerillos, and into the *altiplano* region further east towards the Argentine border. Portions of the nearby Inca trail can also be explored on foot — take a compass and maps. There are regular flights to El Salvador from the main population centers.

ⓘ Tourist information

Club Exploradores del Desierto have their meetings in the Hotel Camino del Inca. They have the best knowledge of the *altiplano* and make excursions with four-wheel drive vehicles right up to **Volcán Ojos del Salado** on the Argentine border. Contact them if you intend to go on such a trip.

If you intend to "do your own thing", especially when you have your own transport, check with the *carabineros* and let them know where you are going and when you expect to return. Always carry plenty of water and petrol on your trips.

⊟ Accommodation

Hotels
★★★ Camino del Inca, Avenida El Tofo 330 ACDEFGHIJKLMPS$UV (475223 $E ⚹. Fax 475207
• Pukará, Avenida 18 de Septiembre 2308 AFJ (475558 $G ⚹

Hostería
• El Salvador, Avenida Potrerillos 003 AEFGHIJPU (475749 $H ⚹

Accommodation in Potrerillos
Potrerillos is 41 km south of El Salvador.

✈ Air services from El Salvador

Destination	Fare	Depart	Services	Duration	Airlines
Antofagasta		1 service per week	1 hr		
Arica	$153.00				LAN Chile
Calama	$ 71.00	1 service daily	1½ hrs		LAN Chile
Copiapó	$ 47.00	1 service daily	except Thurs, Sun	½ hr	LAN Chile
Iquique	$116.00				
Santiago	$198.00	1 service daily except Thurs, Sun		2¼ hrs	LAN Chile

There is a Residencial/Restaurant in A. Prat near the Inca bus terminal.

⏷ Eating out

Restaurants
- Bavaria, Avenida Los Andes
- Casablanca
- Club Pampa, Ricketts
- Club Social Esmeralda, Avenida 4 de Julio
- Hostería El Salvador, Avenida Potrerillos 003

▦ Post and telegraph

Post office
- Avenida Libertador B. O'Higgins, opposite the plaza

Telephone
- CTC, Potrerillos Norte 701
- ENTEL Chile ☏ 472274
- Telex Chile, 4 de Julio 692 ☏ 475115

🚗 Motoring
- Rent a Car Rodaggi, Hotel Camino del Inca ☏ 472314

⚅ Sport
- Golf course at the end of Ave. Los Andes

🚌 Buses from El Salvador

Companies
- A115 Incabus/Lasval, Avenida 4 de Julio 810 ☏ 475251
- A128 Pullman Bus Fichtur, Avenida Potrerillos 719 ☏ 472812
- A131 Pullman Norte
- A164 SITACO

Services

Destination	Fare	Services	Hour	Company
Caldera	$5.70	6 services daily		A115, A128
Chañaral	$3.00	6 services daily		A115, A128
Combarbalá	$11.40	1 service daily		A115
Copiapó	$7.00	11 services daily		A115, A128
Diego de Almagro	$1.90	5 services daily		A164
La Serena	$11.40	5 services daily		A115, A128
Ovalle	$12.20	5 services daily		A115
Potrerillos				Taxibuses
Santiago	$19.00	4 services daily		A115
Valparaíso	$19.00	4 services daily		A131
Viña del Mar	$19.00	2 services daily		A131

⦿ Excursions

Tour operators

Taxis Azules make trips to Salar de Pedernales and Salar Maricunga and other *salares*. They may be contacted through hotels.

- Señor Baeza, Avenida 4 de Julio 514 ☏ 475083

Excursions

- **Potrerillos**: 41 km south. This is a scenic high-altitude drive reaching 2800 m. The mine in in the *pre-Cordillera* was closed in 1959. Now only the foundry is used for the copper ore extracted from the El Salvador mine. Near Portal del Inca there are traces of the Inca trail which led into central Chile. Once past **Cerro Barrancas**, the road descends into the **Río de la Sal** valley. The trickle of water in the river is enough for some grass patches to sprout on which goats feed. The water is soon contaminated once it joins with the effluent coming down from Potrerillos. The last 11 km up to Potrerillos go through the scenically striking **Cuesta Los Patos**. The chimney stack is a landmark that can be seen looming against the sky from the valley below.
- **Salar de Pedernales**: 70 km east and beyond. With a four-wheel drive vehicle you can make an *altiplano* trip on a dirt road to Salar de Pedernales and beyond to Argentina or down to

Copiapó. Phone Rent-a-car Rodaggi beforehand to secure a vehicle, and if there is no vehicle available, hire one in Copiapó. This trip to Salar de Pedernales is 82 km one way at altitudes of mostly 3000 m and above. Check with the locals about the state of the road and accept their advice; it is best to talk to field geologists at El Salvador or Potrerillos. Take enough petrol and provisions for your visit to these uninhabited *altiplano* areas. The few remaining *lagunas* inside the *salar* are a dark-blue color. The *salar* has a radius of 30 km, but it is obvious that the area covered by water was once much bigger. Although there are abandoned mines in the area there are still a few prospectors around. Once you reach the Salar de Pedernales, the road turns south into the **Río La Ola** valley which is flat *altiplano* country at around 3500 m. Halfway between Salar de Pedernales and **Salar de Maricunga** there is a small dam across the Río La Ola which forms a small lake with slightly briny water. The bushes and other vegetation around this waterhole attract *llamas* and *guanacos*. The **Ojos de Agua La Ola**, the source of the Río La Ola, are a few kilometers further south. The road continues south and joins the main road linking Copiapó with Catamarca in Argentina.

FREIRINA

Area code: 051
Population: 3000
Altitude: 100m
Distance from Vallenar: 32 km west on Ruta C–46

Freirina, once a mining settlement, is a delightful little town with roots far back in colonial times. During the colonial period it was the most important Spanish settlement in the valley. Officially founded in 1752 as Santa Rosa de Huasco, it was renamed after the War of Independence in honour of Freire, one of the independence heroes who defeated the last Spanish stronghold on Isla Chiloe. Gold has been mined in the **Quebrada Capote** since 1700, and another gold mine was reopened nearby early this century. Although it is clear

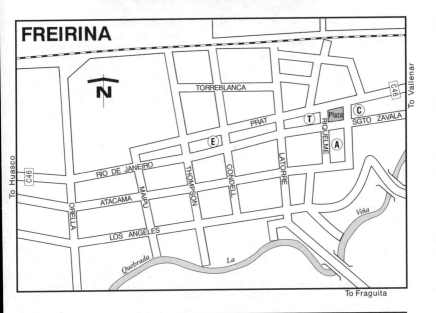

FREIRINA

Key to map
A   Iglesia
C   Municipalidad (Town hall)

E   Telephone

that the glorious days of the last century are gone, the town is holding its own as an olive packaging and olive oil production center and is still the center of a mining area.

Freirina has an enchanting and photogenic Plaza de Armas with two buildings listed as *monumentos nacionales*: the former Casa de Gobierno on the east side of the plaza (now the Municipalidad) and the Iglesia de Santa Rosa at the southern end. Some houses bear the inscription of the former mine owners on the porch.

🍴 Eating out
- Restaurant El Uranio, Río de Janeiro near Plaza. Specialty freshwater crayfish if available.

- Restaurant Haiti, Plaza
- Restaurant George, Rio de Janeiro 305

🚌 Buses from Freirina

Companies
- A52 Taxis Colectivos Los Huasquinos, Brasil ℂ 611127
- A128 Pullman Bus Fichtur, Río de Janeiro 116 ℂ 518771

Services
- Vallenar: Fare $1.20; A52, A128

📷 Sightseeing
A visit to an olive oil producing plant, such as Casa Rearte, is interesting.

- Iglesia de Santa Rosa, corner of Riquelme and Sargento Zavala.
- Municipalidad. The town hall building was the former regional government building and has a colonnade supported by carved wooden columns, built around 1870. It is a remarkable building preserved as a *monumento nacional*.

⊕ Excursions

- **Torres de Labrar**: 40 km south on a four-wheel drive road. Only the chimney stacks of a copper foundry remain. This smelter worked the ores extracted at nearby **La Cobaltera** and **Fraguita**, which are now ghost towns, but until the end of the 19th century were flourishing communities.

HUASCO

Area code: 051
Population: 6500
Altitude: Sea level
Distance from Vallenar: 57 km west on Ruta C-46

Huasco is a picturesque little coastal town, near the mouth of the **Río Huasco** on a bay ringed with excellent beaches. The valley is intensively used for agricultural production. Huasco was officially founded in 1850, but the Dutch pirate Van Noort occupied the site in 1600, and in 1681 it was taken over by the English sea captain Bartholomew Sharp. Huasco is the birthplace of the intrepid Atacama explorer José Santos Ossa who acquired his survival skills from the local Changos, who had not yet disappeared.

In 1922 an earthquake partially destroyed the town. However a few old colonial homesteads are left — Casa Santana in Craig, another in Sargento Aldea, and the old railroad station.

Huasco has had a new lease of life with the installation of an iron ore pelletizing plant and excellent port facilities geared towards the exportation of iron and copper. The new ore export harbor and industrial complex is situated at **Puerto Guacolda**, at the extreme end of the peninsula next to the thermoelectric plant. The port area is covered with fine iron ore dust. The end of the peninsula is also a fishermen's wharf.

There are good views over the town and its extensive beaches from a vantage point above the fishing harbor near the old customs building. Playa de Huasco and Playa Los Toyos have fine sand and small waves. Behind Playa Larga stretches a huge dune for several kilometers north.

Ruta C-46 from Vallenar is sealed all the way to Huasco, with the occasional pothole.

⊟ Accommodation

- Cabañas Skitniza, Prat 840 ℓ 531343 $G for 4
- Hostería de Huasco, Ignacio Carrera Pinto 110 near Avenida Pajaritos **ADEFGHIJKLP$** ℓ 531469 $H ⋮⋮
- Residencial Campos Saguez, Serrano 165 ℓ 531415
- Residencial San Fernando, Pedro de Valdivia 176 **ADEIJL** ℓ 531726 $I ⋮

⑪ Eating out

Restaurants
- El Escorial, on Playa Chica near Cantera $Z

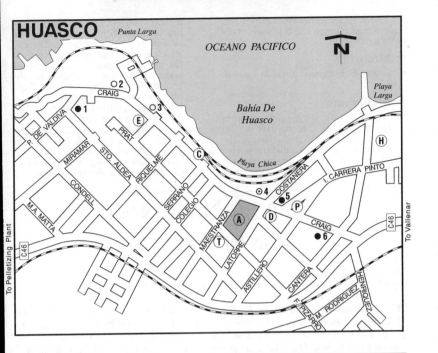

Key to map

A	Iglesia
C	Municipalidad (Town hall)
D	Post office and telex
E	Telephone
H	Hospital
P	Gas stations
T	Bus terminals

● **Accommodation**

1 Residencial San Fernando
5 Hostería de Huasco
6 Cabañas Skitniza

○ **Eating out**

2 Restaurant Las Delicias del Mar
3 Restaurant Don Baucha
4 Restaurant Paulina Pub

- El Rincón del Marino, Craig 134 $Z. Seafood
- Hostería de Huasco, Craig corner of Carrera $Y
- Las Delicias del Mar, Bajada al Muelle
- Marín Pizarro, Bajada al Muelle $Z. Chilean cuisine
- Thiele, Craig 199

Eating out in Huasco Bajo
- Restaurant Don Baucha, on the main street $Z

🚌 **Buses**
- Hidalgo, Serrano 120 ℂ 531762
- Pullman Bus Fichtur, Craig 326 ℂ 531023

Vía Transvall, Buses Los Huasquinos, and Buses Línea Huasco run 5 services daily to Vallenar

Motoring

- Garaje El Esfuerzo, Avenida Lautaro 87

Excursions

- **Tres Playitas**: Best reached from Huasco Bajo by crossing over the Río Huasco bridge. After crossing the bridge this becomes a dirt track. This beach is located 12 km north near Cabo Norte on the road to the small fishing village of **El Boratillo** in **Quebrada Carrizalillo**. Free camping is available on an almost isolated beach, which is small but very protected. A few local fishermen live nearby. Fresh water is scarce and you should supply your own. No public transport. Supplies in Huasco. Good fishing. It is a wide beach with calm waters, undisturbed by passing tourists.
- **Playa Larga:** The beach starts from the Restaurant El Escorial, just outside town. Take a *colectivo* from the town center. Swimming, water sports, camping, kiosks, showers, toilets.

PARQUE NACIONAL PAN DE AZÚCAR

Altitude: Sea level–774 m
Distance from Chañaral: 20 km north on Ruta C-30, a dirt track

The coastal zone of **Pan de Azúcar** is a stretch of the utmost scenic beauty and has been declared a *parque nacional*, administered by CONAF. It covers 43 769 ha (108 100 acres), and incorporates **Isla Pan de Azúcar**, a short distance out to sea. The island is approximately 2 km long and 1 km wide and is occupied by many birds: seagulls, pelicans, boobies, and rare auks, and a colony of Humboldt penguins. This park is ideal for those who like camping in isolation, but water is scarce. The average temperature is 16°C (61°F), and it is always very humid.

The Changos, the indigenous tribe who once lived here, left many marks of their existence in cemeteries and in rock paintings in caves. This site was formerly a port with a copper foundry, but the buildings are now in ruins.

All along the coast you can observe dolphins and seals. The moisture-laden *camanchacas neblinas* produce fog in the higher parts, which has encouraged the growth of vegetation: cacti, succulents and bushes. These sustain animal life, such as *llamas, guanacos,* foxes and sea otters (*chugungos*). The facilities include picnic and camping grounds, walking paths and safe places to swim.

Transport from Chañaral is erratic. The best bet is a taxi, but fares are rather expensive because of the bad road conditions. When hiking in the national park, bring supplies from Chañaral. There is a dirt access road from the Panamericana at KM 1015 through the **Quebrada Salitrosa**, which becomes the **Quebrada Pan de Azúcar** — bus drivers will drop you there on request. This is the suggested start for hikers who want to walk through the national

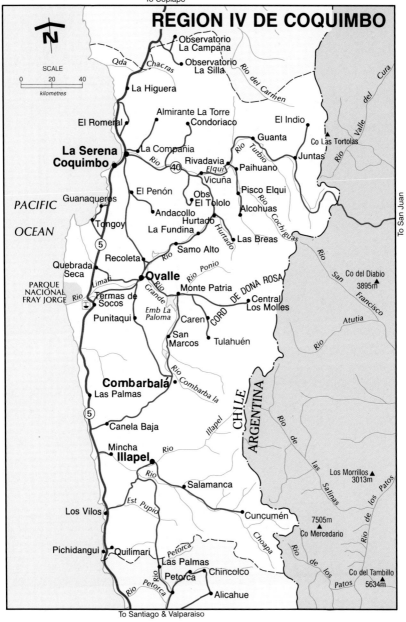

Plate 9
Map of Región IV de Coquimbo

Plate 10   Región IV de Coquimbo
Combarbalá Central Plaza with church

park and back along the coast via **Caleta Pan de Azúcar** to Chañaral. Water is available in Caleta Pan de Azúcar, but bring your own when you start the walk on the Panamericana, which is mostly downhill. Although the northern part of this national park lies in Región II de Antofagasta, note that the main access is from Región III de Atacama: Chañaral and KM 1015 on the Panamericana. The northern access from Caleta Esmeralda is not recommended.

ℹ️ **Tourist information**

CONAF has a ranger's hut in Caleta Pan de Azúcar.

🚌 **Buses**

There is no direct public transport from Chañaral to the national park. On request, buses going along the Panamericana will drop hikers off at Las Bombas at KM 1015 on the Panamericana. Taxis charge $20.00 for the six-hour trip, including a short stay at the park.

VALLENAR

Area code: 054
Population: 39 000
Altitude: 370 m
Distance from Copiapó: 145 km south on RN 5 (Panamericana)

Vallenar lies in a valley where the Carretera Panamericana intersects with the **Río Huasco** valley. This valley was settled by Spanish *conquistadores* in the early days of conquest. The town was founded in 1789 by the then Governor of Chile, Don Ambrosio O'Higgins, the father of the independence hero.

Vallenar is the capital of Huasco province and the hub of its mining and agricultural activities. The town looks very green because of its many trees, and it retains an air of colonialism from the colonial buildings with large patios that survived a severe earthquake in 1922.

Vallenar was very important in the early 19th century after the discovery of the Agua Amarga silver mines. It boasts the first bank of Chile and the first bank notes were issued here. Irrigation began in 1820. A rail line was built in 1892 between Vallenar and its port of Huasco. The city received a new lease of life when iron ore was discovered and conse-

quently mined near Santa Fé and Los Colorados.

The **Río Huasco** is the lifeline of the Huasco province. The valley is famous for its olive groves and viticulture. From Vallenar with its good tourist facilities, you can make excursions into the inland valleys and to the beaches on the coast near the port of **Huasco**.

The town's major attractions are located around the plaza. There are good views over the town from Calle Lourdes near the cemetery.

🎭 **Festivals**
• January 5: Foundation day

ℹ️ **Tourist information**
• Información Turística, Caseta de Informaciones, Carretera Panamericana

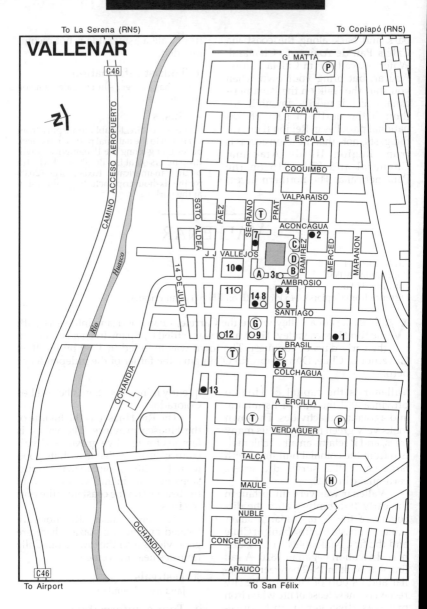

VALLENAR

To La Serena (RN5)

To Copiapó (RN5)

To Airport

To San Félix

Key to map

A	Iglesia	4	Hotel Real de turismo
B	Gobernación Provincial (Government)	6	Hotel Cecil
		7	Hostal Viña del Mar
C	Municipalidad (Town hall)	10	Residencial Oriental
D	Post office and telex	13	Hostería de Vallenar
E	Telephone	14	Hotel Atacama
G	Mercado Municipal (Market)	○	**Eating out**
H	Hospital		
I	Tourist information	3	Restaurant Capri
P	Gas stations	5	Restaurant Club Social
T	Bus terminals	8	Restaurant Venecia
●	**Accommodation**	9	Cafetería Bavaria
1	Residencial Camino del Rey	11	Restaurant Bavaria
2	Hostal Vall	12	Restaurant La Picá

⑪ Eating out

Cafetería
- Bavaria, Santiago 678

Restaurants
- Bavaria, Serrano 802. International cuisine
- Capri, Prat 761
- Club Social, Prat 899
- Hostería de Vallenar, Alonso de Ercilla 848
- La Picá, Faez 950
- Venecia, Santiago 654

Eating out outside the town centre

Restaurants
- COPEC Rutacentro, Panamericana Norte
- Esso, Panamericana Norte Cruce Huasco
- Galo de Raucourt, on acceso Sur to Panamericana

① Entertainment

- Disco El Castillo, southern exit to Panamericana
- Disco Joe, Calle Serrano
- Pub Dream, Hotel Cecil
- Salón de Baile Billboard, Prat 362,

⑱ Post and telegraph

Post office
- Correos de Chile, José Joaquín Vallejos (on the Plaza de Armas)

Telephone
- ENTEL Chile, Serrano 676
- CTC, Arturo Prat 1035, fax 612005
- Telex Chile, Plaza O'Higgins 85

🛏 Motoring

Car rental
- Hertz Rent-a-Car, Hostería Vallenar, Alonso de Ercilla 848

📷 Sightseeing

- Museo del Huasco: Located in Sargento Aldea opposite Hostería de Vallenar. Open Tues–Sat 1000–1300 and 1500–1800. Mineralogical exhibits and historical memorabilia. Admission $0.50.
- Iron building of Compañia Minera del Pacífico: Avenida Brasil near Ochandia

⊕ Excursions

- **Alto del Carmen**: 38 km south-east, at an altitude of 700 m in the *pre-Cordillera* where the **Río del Tránsito** joins the **Río del Carmen** to form the **Río Huasco**. The villagers have a long tradition of making woolen materials. This home of sweet wine is an agricultural area dotted with small settlements and villages with irrigated fields. From Alto del Carmen the excursion can be extended to include **Albaricoque**, where very palatable apricot and other fruit liqueurs are made. Near **Cerro Blanco** there is a

☕ Accommodation in Vallenar

Hotels

★★★ Hostería de Vallenar, Alonso de Ercilla 848

	ACDEFGHIJKLMPRS$TU			
		☎ 614379	$E	♟♟
Fax 614538				
★★ Real de Turismo, Prat 881	AEFGHIJKLPU	☎ 613963	$G	♟♟
• Atacama, Serrano 873	ADHIJ	☎ 611426	$G	♟♟
• Cécil, Prat 1059	ABDEGHIJO	☎ 614071	$F	♟♟
Fax 614400				
• Ro-del, Prat 1190-A	AEIJKL	☎ 611257/440	$H	♟♟
Shared bathroom cheaper				
• San Martín, Merced 950		☎ 611937		
• Viña del Mar, Serrano 611	ADEHILP	☎ 611478	$H	♟♟

Hostal

• Vall, Aconcagua 455	AP	☎ 613380	$H	♟♟

Residenciales

• Camino del Rey, Merced 943	AP	☎ 613184	$H	♟♟
• Garrote Valdés, Sargento Aldea 945		☎ 613056		
• Matty, Arturo Prat 1193		☎ 614301		
• Oriental, Serrano 720	AJ	☎ 613889	$H	♟♟

Cabañas

• Centro Galo, Carretera Huasco	ABCDHJP	☎ 613989	$G for 4

Accommodation in San Félix
San Félix is 22 km south of Vallenar
• Small *pension* on the plaza
• *Refugio* in Pueblo Albaricoque

Acccommodation in Albaricoque
• Refugio

Accommodation in El Tránsito
El Tránsito is in the Río Conay valley some 80 km south.
• Pensión Santa Anita

huge wall of rock paintings dating back to 1000 BC. The road goes as far as **La Arena** (50 km south) in the Río del Carmen Valley. Alternatively, you can go up to **Conay** in the **Río del Tránsito Valley**. Eighteen kilometers past Alto del Carmen in the Río del Tránsito valley, there is a quarry for white marble. It is more picturesque towards **Junta Valeriano** in the **Río Conay** valley with the high *sierras* in the background. The mountain streams flowing down from the high

sierra are crystal clear. This is unknown Chile, and very few tourists ever venture here. Buses Aurelio Pallauta Trigorun regular daily services from Vallenar.

• **Huasco**: A 47 km trip west to the coast on the sealed Ruta C-46 through the fertile Río Huasco valley which makes extensive use of irrigation to sustain agriculture. Passing through **Freirina**, there is an old church and the Los Portales building, both of which are *monumentos nacionales.* Huasco and its

🚌 Buses from Vallenar

The bus terminal is on the corner of Serrano and Aconcagua.

Companies departing from the central terminal
- A3   Andes Mar-Bus Calama
- A31 Buses Evans
- A42 Buses Carmelita (613037
- A54 Buses Muñoz
- A77 Buses TAL (214929
- A78 Buses Tramaca office 8 (612075
- A83 Buses Zambrano Hnos
- A112 Flota Barrios, office 1 (614295
- A115 Incabus/Lasval (613827
- A122 Los Corsarios, Serrano 551 (613851
- A128 Pullman Bus Fichtur, Serrano 551 (613851
- A137 TAS Choapa, Serrano 581 (613822
- A150 Transportes Geminis

Companies departing from their own terminals
- A15 Buses Aurelio Pallauta Trigo, Juan Verdaguer 670 (614263
- A30 Buses Espinoza Orellana, Juan Verdaguer 670
- A38 Buses Hidalgo, Sargento Aldea 687 (614665
- A45 Buses Libac, Brasil 715 (613755
- A52 Buses Los Huasquinos, Brasil
- A79 Buses Transvall, Talca (614231
- A120 Linea Via Huasco
- A121 Los Conquistadores Serrano 873-B (613895
- A153 Tur-bus Jedimar, Merced

Services

Destination	Fare	Services	Duration	Companies
Alto Del Carmen	$1.20	5 services daily		A15
Antofagasta	$15.20	10 services daily		A45, A78, A112, A150
Calama	$22.40	10 services daily		A45, A112, A150
Caldera	$5.00	2 services daily		A128
Chañaral	$8.00	9 services daily		A112, A115, A128
Combarbalá	$ 6.50	1 service daily		A115
Conay	$ 2.80	2 services daily		A30
Copiapó	$5.00	14 services daily	2 hrs	A45, A54, A112, A115, A121, A128, A137
Coquimbo	$ 4.00	1 service daily		A45
Chuquicamata	$19.50	2 services daily		A45, A112
El Tránsito	$ 2.00	4 services daily		A30
Freirina	$ 1.50	2 services daily		A52, A120
Huasco	$ 1.80	2 services daily		A52, A79, A120
Iquique	$24.70	1 service daily		A42
La Serena	$ 5.00	28 services daily	$3\frac{1}{2}$ hrs	A42, A45, A112, A115, A128, A137
Los Vilos	$ 8.40	4 services daily		A115, A137
Ovalle	$ 5.70	5 services daily		A42, A83
Salamanca	$13.30	1 service Tue and Fri		A150
San Félix	$ 1.80	4 services daily		A15
Santiago	$15.00	15 services daily		A3, A31, A42, A45, A77, A115, A112, A121, A122, A128, A137
Tocopilla	$19.00	1 service daily		A112
Valparaíso	$18.20	10 services daily		A83, A115, A128
Viña del Mar	$18.20	10 services daily		A83, A115, A128

beaches are 15 km further west. See also the entries for Huasco (page 152) and Freirina (page 150).

- **Carrizal Bajo**: 82 km north-west. Extensive beaches. Excursion buses at weekends. No facilities.
- Up the **Río Vallenar** to **Conay**.

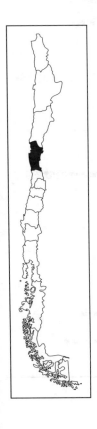

REGIÓN IV

DE

COQUIMBO

Area: 41 000 square km (15 826 square miles)
Population: 440 000
Regional capital: La Serena
Provinces (and provincial capitals):
- Elqui (Coquimbo)
- Limari (Ovalle)
- Choapa (Illapel)

En el valle de Elqui, ceñido
de cien montañas o de más
que como ofrendas o tributos
arden en rojo y azafrán …

In the valley of Elqui, girt
by a hundred mountains or more
that like offerings or tributes
burn in red and saffron …

Thus Gabriela Mistral, the first Nobel Laureate for Literature in the Americas, described her home town in the province of Elqui.

Región IV de Coquimbo has many lovely beaches lying within sheltered bays. There are beautiful mountain- ous areas, and in the valleys grapes and apricots are cultivated exten- sively, with crops irrigated by several dams in the region. It also has an exceptional climate with clear skies, which has led to the setting up of several observatories in the region and also to the creation of a number of national parks. The many thermal springs in the region attract tourists and people seeking remedies for various conditions. There is also much of archeological interest in the region.

Chile's fourth region lies between 29° and 32° south, and 69° and 71° west. It borders Región III de Atacama in the north; the Andes form the border with Argentina in the east; and Región V de Valparaíso lies in the south.

Transport

Road

The Pan-American highway was built in the 1940s and at first closely followed the original Inca trail through the center. The Carretera Panamericana (RN 5) runs the full length of the region, with side roads branching off to the mountains in the east and westwards to the sea. RN 41 links La Serena over the **Paso del Agua Negra** (4766 m) with San Juan in Argentina.

Air

There are three major airports: La Florida (La Serena), Tuqui (Ovalle), and Auco (Illapel).

Rail

The first railroads were built from 1860 onwards. Nowadays the railroads are only used to bring the ores from the mines inland to the coastal cities. The north south rail line has fallen into disuse.

Topography

The region is made up of little valleys originating in the Andean *cordillera*. The rivers running through the valleys are fed by the melting snow in the high *sierras*. The main river is the Río Elqui whose water is used for irrigation and therefor does not bring much water into the sea. Many rivers north of La Serena run underground. The coastal *cordillera* which reaches 1500 m acts like a barrier and forces the clouds to rise. The effect is that clouds bring enough moisture to isolated barren mountaintops to allow grass and shrubs grow. This is called the *Camanchaca* effect. There are some places where the coastal mountains end abruptly in the sea without any foreshore, and from the air they look like huge stepping stones. In the most southern part, the central valley between the central *cordillera* and the coastal *cordillera* starts, and goes as far as **Puerto Montt**. The fertile zones are named after the rivers that formed them, such as **Valle del Choapa**, the **Valle de Limari**, and the **Valle de Elqui** made famous by the writings of Gabriela Mistral. Because these rivers are used for irrigation, their valleys have become the population centers of the region.

Climate

The sea has a strong influence on the coastal climate, and there are morning fogs, dispersing towards midday. This often occurs even in valleys as far as 50 km from the sea. The mean annual temperature is 14°C (57°F) in the coastal areas. In the interior the climate is a mild "steppe" climate and depends on the altitude. Clear skies, low humidity and high temperatures during the day are characteristic of areas above 800 m.

The temperatures on the coast are pleasant all year round; in winter they hardly ever drop below a mean temperature of 7°C (45°F), and in summer rarely exceed 22°C (72°F). Most of the rain falls in winter. This special climate with clear skies has led many scientific organizations to set up observatories in this region. Because of prolonged dry periods, the region is partly desert, yet whenever rain falls the desert blooms. This dry climate means that cacti, thorn bushes, and drought-resistant trees are the predominant vegetation. Areas with special climatic conditions have been declared national parks, such as **Parque Nacional Fray Jorge** where the height of the coastal *cordillera* is enough to produce condensation from the clouds coming from the Pacific, so that the vegetation grows densely on top of the mountains. Many tropical fruits grow in the valleys where there is plenty of water.

In summer the water temperature is 19°C (66°F).

The indigenous inhabitants

There has been human habitation in the semi-arid north since about 12 000 BC. Traces of this oldest human settlement have been found at **El Quereo** near Los Vilos. They apparently were contemporaries of now extinct animals such as giant sloths, which also points to a drastic change in the climate. Between 10 000 and 2000 years ago, it was a hunter and collector society, archeological evidence of which has been found on the coast and in the valleys. The coastal tribes of the Changos were fishermen and collectors and became extinct as a social unit towards the end of the 19th century. Two thousand years ago, the agricultural–pottery culture

began, the semi-nomadic people producing a sophisticated form of pottery, with red and black the dominant colors in the highly stylized decoration. Metal objects at this period were made from copper. Major archeological sites are at **El Molle** in the Valle de Río Elqui. Because of the importance of the archeological finds this entire era is called the "El Molle period".

Around the ninth century the Diaguitas appeared on the scene. Their civilization is recognizable by the excellent artistic expression of their ceramics and pottery. In their turn, they came under the Incan sphere of influence around 1470. The Incan domination was carried out by the forced displacement of local people, replacing them with loyal Incan subjects. Major Incan settlements, the so-called *mitimaes* settlements, were founded in all the main valleys.

European history

In 1536 and 1540 the Spanish invasion under Diego de Almagro and Pedro de Valdivia began. La Serena was founded in 1544 by Juan Bohón, but was destroyed shortly after by the Diaguitas and then re-established in 1549 by Francisco de Aguirre. The Diaguita people living in the valleys were conquered and gradually absorbed into the dominant European culture, becoming extinct as a separate culture around 1850.

From the very early days, **La Serena** was a center of Catholicism, and the Franciscan monks founded many churches and monasteries. In the early colonial period and during the next 200 years **La Serena** and **Coquimbo** were frequently raided by English, Dutch and French pirates. Usually the land and the Indians living in a certain area were given to deserving Spanish conquistadors as *encomiendas*. Until 1790 La Serena was the only major urban settlement in Coquimbo, with isolated estates (*estancias*) in the fertile valleys in the rest of the country. The only other towns founded during the colonial era were **Illapel** and **Combarbalá** in 1788, by the remarkable viceroy Don Ambrosio O'Higgins.

When the Spaniards arrived they used the existing indigenous trails, in particular the Inca trail to penetrate into what is now Chile. This Inca trail (the *Capac Ñan* or Royal Road of the Incas) came down from **Copiapó** through the center of the region. Nowadays all that remains of the *tambos* that the *Capac Ñan* passed through is a few non-Spanish names. This trail probably passed through the **Quebrada Marquesa**, **Andacollo**, **Ovalle**, **Punitaqui**, **Combarbalá**, **Illapel**, and **La Ligua**. These Inca trails were also used during the Spanish colonial rule, when they were known as the *Caminos Interiores* ("Interior Trails"). There is also believed to have been a rudimentary pre-Hispanic coastal trail, which later became the major Spanish road link between La Serena and Catapilco south of La Ligua in today's Región V de Valparaíso. As a seafaring nation, the Spanish also needed roads to connect the valleys of the interior with the coastal towns.

Economy

The economic activity in this region centers around mining and agriculture, with some manufacturing.

Minerals

Copper is still mined in the Limarí valley, iron is mined at **Romeral**, and gold near **Andacollo**. There are also semi-precious stones such as lapis lazuli and turquoise in the area.

Gold has been mined at **Andacollo** since the days of the Incas and this continued under the Spaniards. During the colonial period the Spanish worked gold mines in Illapel and Combarbalá until they were exhausted in around 1700.

From the middle of the 18th century copper came into demand and the abandoned gold mines were reopened, this time to produce copper. Many new mines were discovered in the 19th century, and with new technology brought from Europe allowed a very enterprising business to be created. Some of the wealthiest present-day Chilean families are descended from the pioneers who founded the big mining companies, created railroad lines and also used their newfound wealth to set up banks and agricultural enterprises, with some diversifying into coal mining (such as José Tomás Urmeneta and Ramón Subercaseaux to name two).

Fishing

The fishing industry is also quite significant, producing fishmeal, sardines, oysters and fish oil.

Agriculture

Winegrowing is the most important agricultural crop, with approximately 9000 ha (22 230 acres) planted out to vines. The most famous vineyards are in the **Río Elqui** valley and tributaries east of La Serena, where the famous *Pisco Elqui* is produced.

Other important crops are potatoes, garlic, tomatoes and peppers. The most important agricultural region is the **Río Limari** valley with **Ovalle** as its center. Irrigation from the many dams in this area (such as **Embalse Recoleta** and **Embalse La Paloma**, all east of Ovalle) has transformed large semi-arid areas into productive land. Goats and sheep are kept in the semi-arid areas but are not of great economic significance.

Tourism

The main tourist attractions are the many sheltered beaches with their warm water, fishing on the seaside and rivers, national parks (such as **Parque Nacional Fray Jorge** and **Monumento Natural Pichasca**), thermal springs (such as **Termas de Socos** and **Baños del Toro**), archeological sites (such as **Monumento Nacional Valle del Encanto**), and also the local wine products, such as *pisco*.

Observatories

Also of interest are the many astronomical observatories (such as **Observatorio Astronómico Cerro Tololo, Observatorio Astronómico Cerro La Silla** and **Observatorio Astronómico Cerro Las Campanas**) built in the region because of the particularly clear skies.

The *pisco*

Long adaptation of muscatel grapes in a micro-climate — the *Zona Pisquera* — has perfected the production of the local liquor known as *El Pisco*. It is distilled from muscatel wine in small kettles holding a maximum of 1500 liters. They are heated by steam, a slow process which preserves the brandy's distinctive flavor. Then it is stored in wooden casks until state authorities have tested it, after which it is kept for anything from two to 12

months. The brandy that has been stored for 12 months is called *Gran Piscos* and is the most sought after. The name *pisco* is reserved for several selected areas in the region, the best known being the **Río Elqui** valley.

Thermal resorts

Termas de Socos is in the **Río Punitaqui** valley where the river meets the **Río Limari** at an altitude 80 m, at the junction of Panamericana with RN 45 leading to Ovalle 38 km east. The thermal water's temperature is 28°C (82°F); there is an excellent thermal hotel with camping attached. Regular buses run to Ovalle and La Serena. See the entry for Ovalle on page 207.

There are many other thermal springs in the region, but either they have no facilities or they not accessible to the average tourist. Two such are Termas El Toro and Termas de Pangue.

National Parks and Reserves

*   **Parque Nacional Fray Jorge**: 100 km south of La Serena on Panamericana. Take the turnoff to the coast near the *carabineros* outpost at **Cerillos Pobres**. Walking trails, information center, picnic area, camping area. See the entry for the park on page 214.

*   **Monumento Natural Pichasca**: 53 km east of Ovalle on road to Hurtado on the left shortly after Pinar and just before village of Pichasca. Walking trails, picnic area.

*   **Reserva Nacional Las Chinchillas**: 20 km north of Illapel on Ruta O-55 (the road to Combarbalá). Information center, excursion paths.

Beaches and seaside resorts

The coastline of Región IV de Coquimbo extends for about 350 km
and has many good beaches and
some major seaside resorts. The high
sierras and beaches virtually meet at
La Serena.

The major resorts are **La Serena**,
Peñuelas, **La Herradura**,
Guanaqueros, **Tongoy**, **Los Vilos**,
and **Pichidangui**. There are other
good beaches, but some excellent
beaches have not been developed because of lack of water — a perennial
problem right down to the Región V
de Valparaíso. In the Coquimbo–La
Serena region alone there are 12 km
of excellent beaches, all with tourist
facilities of international standard.

In addition to the major seaside
resorts, beaches with some tourist facilities are Playa Totoralillo, Playa
Las Tacas, Playa Lagunillas, Playa
Morillos, and Playa Blanca. Most of
them are a few kilometers off the
Panamericana and are accessible via
dirt roads.

Festivals

The towns in or near which events
are held are listed here by month. For
details, see under "Festivals" in the
entries for individual towns.

- January: Coquimbo, La Serena,
  Ovalle, Vicuña
- February: Coquimbo, Guana-
  queros, La Herradura, Vicuña
- April: Ovalle
- May: Combarbalá, Coquimbo,
  Illapel, La Serena, Vicuña
- June: La Serena, Los Vilos,
  Vicuña
- July: Illapel, La Serena, Ovalle,
  Vicuña
- August: Andacollo, Coquimbo,
  La Serena, Ovalle, Salamanca

1: The beginning of Mes de la
Montaña ("Mountain Month"),
held throughout the entire re-
gion
20: O'Higgins' birthday, held
throughout the entire region
- September: Coquimbo, La Her-
  radura, La Serena, Vicuña 18:
  Día de la Independencia Na-
  cional ("National Independence
  Day"), celebrated thoughout
  Chile
- October: Andacollo
- December: Andacollo

Distances

From La Serena
- Andacollo: 54 km south
- Coquimbo: 13 km south
- Illapel: 316 km south
- Los Vilos: 254 km south
- Ovalle: 88 km south
- Pichidangui: 284 km
- Tongoy: 57 km south
- Vicuña: 66 km east

From Coquimbo
- Andacollo: 50 km south-west
- Illapel: 307 km south
- Los Vilos: 245 km south
- Ovalle: 84 km south
- Pichidangui: 275 km south
- Tongoy: 48 km south
- Vicuña: 75 km east

From Ovalle
- Andacollo: 87 km north
- Combarbalá: 99 km south
- Illapel: 255 km south
- Los Vilos: 193 km south
- Pichidangui: 223 km south
- Punitaqui: 32 km south
- Tongoy: 97 km north west

ANDACOLLO

Area code: 051
Population: 10 000
Altitude: 1040 m
Distance from La Serena: 54 km south-east on Ruta D-51 and RN 43

A ndacollo is in the **Quebrada de Andacollo**, a basin formed by the erosive forces of the river. It is surrounded by low bare hills which contrast sharply with the town.

The most surprising sight is the huge basilica which is quite unexpected in such a place and which dominates the skyline.

Huge mounds of mine workings surround the town and are in the town itself, because besides being a religious center it is also a mining town. Gold was mined by the Diaguitas and later by the Incas (*andacollo* is a Quechua word indicating that gold is found here), and of course the Spaniards expanded the mining activity. Gold is still mined nowadays and Andacollo has remained a center of this activity, but the emphasis has shifted from actual mining to mineral processing. There are crushing mills (*trapiches*) in and around town, where the small mine owners of the district bring their ore to be extracted. There are about ten crushing mills in this town, and their activity, as well as the abandoned mines of the past, accounts for most of the mining debris scattered in the surrounding district. The district still has over 1500 prospectors working their own small mines. If you are interested, you can visit a crushing mill and a small gold-mine in the vicinity.

⍾ Festivals

Most of the year this is a quiet town but on two occasions the town comes to life, with dances going back to pre-Columbian times and the participants wearing very colorful garments.

- October, first Sunday: Religious festival
- December 23–26: Fiesta de la Virgen de Andacollo. The statue of the Virgin was brought here from Peru in 1676, and this area has become an important religious center. As many as 30 000 pilgrims congregate here from all over the country for this occasion. Many pilgrims come on foot over the arid valleys and mountains, usually choosing to walk at night when it is cooler and rest during the day

Festivals in El Manzano
- August 10: San Lorenzo

⌨ Accommodation

There are no hotels here. Pilgrims sleep in private houses or with relations; some just pitch a tent or stay in their cars or buses.The town suffers from water shortages. Private accommodation is charged per bed and is usually communal.

⍾ Eating out

Most food is sold from stalls which spring up at weekends and for big events. These stalls and restaurants are in Calle Urmeneta.
- Restaurant Edo, Urmeneta between Colón and Rodríguez
- Restaurant Tirado, Urmeneta between Colón and Condell

⌨ Post and telegraph

Post office
- Correo de Chile, on the south side of the plaza

Telephone
- CTC, Alfonso between Rodríguez and Colón

🚌 Buses

Companies
- Taxi colectivos Anserco, Urmeneta 697

Services
- Coquimbo: Fare $3.00; 4 services daily; duration 2 hrs; Araya Bus, Sol y Mar, Taxi Colectivos Anserco
- Hurtado: Fare $3.40. Only runs on special occasions
- La Serena: Fare $2.80; 6 services daily; duration 1 hr; Anserco, Postal Bus, Arayabus
- Ovalle: Fare $3.00; 3 services daily; duration 1½ hrs; Buses Canela

🚗 Motoring

There is an excellent dirt road to La Serena, beginning with a steep descent through a canyon to Ovalle.
There are two gas station at the northern exit to La Serena, near the parking lots.

🏪 Shopping

Because this is a religious center, all souvenirs are on a religious theme, with figurines and so on. The main streets are lined with souvenir stalls.

📷 Sightseeing

- Iglesia Colonial, Plaza Videla. The original temple (Templo Antiguo) is also a *monumento nacional*. Building started in 1772 and was completed in 1789. Altars are made from embossed silver, with fine detail. This is the usual home of the Virgen Morena de Andacollo. Two masses are held daily.
- Museo de la Virgen, Plaza Videla. Visiting hours daily 0900–1200 and 1500–1800.
- Basilica Mayor, Plaza Videla. Built in 1892 in neoclassical style by an Italian architect, the Basilica holds 10 000 people, is 50 m high and is the main religious center. It has been declared a *monumento nacional*. The poor and dilapidated houses in the town are in sharp contrast with this magnificent building.

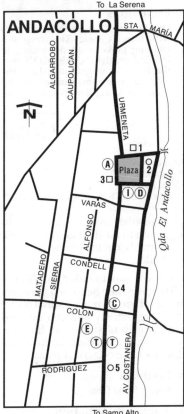

To La Serena

ANDACOLLO

To Samo Alto

Key to map

A	Iglesia Parroquial
C	Municipalidad (Town hall)
D	Post office and telex
E	Telephone
I	Tourist information
T	Bus terminals

	Eating out
2	Cafetería
4	Rest. Edo
5	Rest. Tirado

	Sights
1	Basilica
3	Museo

⊕ Excursions

- **Ovalle**: This trip takes about 1½ hours with Buses Canela. The steep and winding gravel road descending to Ovalle through the **Quebrada Higuer-illa** is being upgraded. Along the roadside many small mines are still being worked. Many pilgrims make their way on foot up to the sanctuary. After about half an hour you will reach the flat part near **El Crucero**. Near Higuerillas is the intersection with RN 43 which links La Serena with Ovalle through the interior. From here on the road is sealed. See the entry for Ovalle on page 207.

COMBARBALÁ

Area code: 053
Population: 5000
Altitude: 800 m
Distance from Ovalle: 99 km south via Punitaquí

Combarbalá is in a wide basin through which the **Río Combarbalá** runs from south to north. It is surrounded by mountains which can make it uncomfortably hot in summer, as the cooling winds from the coast cannot reach this valley.

The town was founded by Viceroy O'Higgins when he toured the north in 1789. Then, as now, it was a center of mining activity and you can find semi-precious stones in the surrounding hills. There is an adobe church on the octagonal plaza.

⊛ Festivals

- May 7: Santa Cruz

ⓘ Tourist information

Roberto, a young local, is the unofficial tour guide in this town. He is usually at the bus stop when buses arrive. He has a pleasant unobtrusive personality and will help you find suitable accommodation, knows all the precious stone cutters and best semi-precious stone buys, and will also act as a guide on excursions for a very reasonable fee.

⊟ Accommodation

- Hotel Chile, Chacabuco 391 ☏ 741008 $J ♒
- Residencial La Canelina, San Carlos 467 $J ♒. Backpackers
- Residencial Combarbalina, Libertad 542 $J ♒

- Motel La Piscina, J. I. Flores 334 between San Carlos and Unión **AFP** ☏ 741024 $H ♒. Share cabins $J ♒

⑪ Eating out

- Club Social, Chacabuco corner of Unión
- El Parrón, San Carlos 467
- Imbiss, San Carlos opposite Residencial Canelina

⊠ Post and telegraph

Post office
- Correos de Chile, Avenida Oriente 673

Telephone
- CTC, Flores between San Carlos and Unión
- Telex Chile, next to Incabus

⊟ Services and facilities

- Hospital, J.I. Flores near Antonio Aguirre

⊟ Motoring

For gas stations, see city map.

⊞ Shopping

Combarbalá is the center for precious stone polishing, with most gem polishers on Calle Flores.

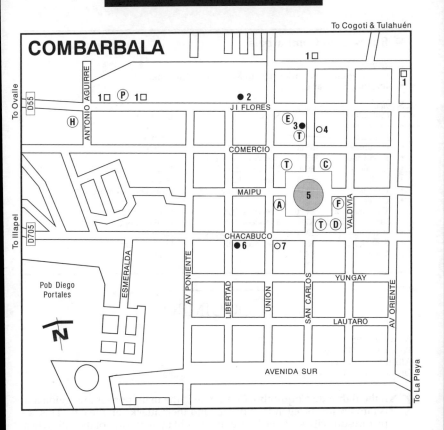

Key to map

A	Iglesia
C	Municipalidad (Town hall)
D	Post office and telex
E	Telephone
F	Carabineros (Police)
H	Hospital
P	Gas stations
T	Bus terminals

● **Accommodation**

2	Motel La Piscina
3	Residencial La Canelina

6	Hotel Chile
○	**Eating out**
4	Restaurant Imbiss
7	Restaurant Club Social
□	**Services**
1	Semi-precious stones
■	**Sights**
5	Plaza de Armas

🚌 Buses from Combarbalá

Companies
- Buses Dhino, San Carlos next to Residencial Canelina
- Incabus, San Carlos

Services

	Destination	Fares	Services	Companies
•	Chañaral	$11.00		Incabus
•	Copiapó	$9.70		Incabus
•	Coquimbo	$5.00		Incabus
•	El Salvador	$13.70	2 services per week	Incabus
•	La Calera	$6.40	2 services daily	Empresa Rima
•	La Serena	$5.00	1 service daily	Incabus
•	Los Vilos	$4.00	3 services daily	Buses Dhino, Empresa Rima
•	Ovalle			
	Via Punitaqui	$4.20	2 services daily	Empresa López
	Via Monte Patria	$3.30	3 services daily	Incabus, López
•	Potrerillos	$13.70	2 services per week	Incabus
•	Santiago	$8.30	2 services daily	Empresa Rima
•	Vallenar	$7.40		Incabus

COQUIMBO

Area code: 051
Population: 115 000
Altitude: Sea level
Distance from La Serena: 13 km south on Panamericana

On the **Bahía de Coquimbo**, Coquimbo is the main port of the region and is famous for its legends of pirates and their attacks on the city. This is a picturesque city with the houses built right up to the top of the hills which make up the town. The streets are usually stairs leading uphill — when you get to the top of the hill, you're in a good spot for taking photographs over the city and the Bahía de Coquimbo to the north or the **Bahía Herradura de Guayacán** to the south. There are many good beaches nearby, such as the northern suburb of Peñuelas and the southern suburb of La Herradura.

Travel south along Bahía Guanaqueros to get to several beaches — Playas Totoralillo (10 km south), Playa Lagunillas, Playa Morillos, Playa Mostazas, and the little seaside resort of **Guanaqueros** (33 km south), all with ample tourist facilities.

🎇 Festivals
- January 15: Nuestra Señora del Rosario de Guayacán
- February 8–22: Summer regatta
- May 5: Foundation day celebrations
- August 6: Virgen del Carmen y San Pedro
- September 18–20: Fiesta de la Pampilla

ⓘ Eating out

Restaurants
- Bassaure, Henriquez 239
- Baviera, Henriquez corner of Melgarejo
- Don Tito, Melgarejo 1189. Chilean cuisine
- El Callejón, Pasaje Los Artesanos (in the Market). Seafood
- El Treból, Aldunate 1169
- Mai Lan Fan, Avenida Ossandon 1 $Y. Chinese cuisine
- Popular, Henriquez 234
- Silvia, Melgarejo (in the Market)
- Tierra Nueva, Aldunate 1522. Seafood

Pizzerías
- Pizzería Pastissima, Aldunate 927
- Sal y Pimiento, A Pinto corner of Portales

Schopería
- Baviera, Aldunate 1598

Eating out on the Avenida Costanera de Coquimbo
- La Picada $Y. International cuisine

Eating out on the Panamericana Norte
- Chiringuito, KM 445
- Los Arcos de Panul, KM 455. International cuisine; two orchestras

ⓘ Entertainment
- Discotheque Gin's, La Higuera

ⓘ Post and telegraph

Post office
- Correo, Aldunate block 900 corner of Borgoño

Telephone
- CTC, Henriquez 457, fax 313025
- Telex Chile, Aldunate corner of Lastra

ⓘ Services and facilities

Laundry
- Lavachic, Aldunate 852 A. Self-service

Supermarket
- Supermercado Multimarket, Juan Antonio Ríos 1165

ⓘ Air services
See "Air services" in La Serena on page 198.

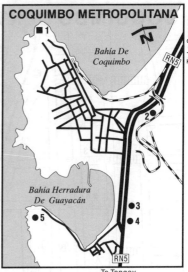

COQUIMBO METROPOLITANA

Bahía De Coquimbo

Bahía Herradura De Guayacán

To La Serena

To Tongoy

Key to map
- ● **Accommodation**
- 2   Hotel Garza
- 3   Motel Travelers
- 4   Cabañas Antares
- 5   Complejo Turístico Las Gaviotas
- 6   Suite Vista Al Mar
- ■ **Sights**
- 1   Fuerte de Coquimbo

ⓘ Motoring

Car rental
- Pacífico Rent a Car ☏ 312894

Gas stations
For gas stations, see city map.

ⓘ Sport
- The golf club (Club de Campo Pan de Azúcar de Coquimbo) is 6 km west of town

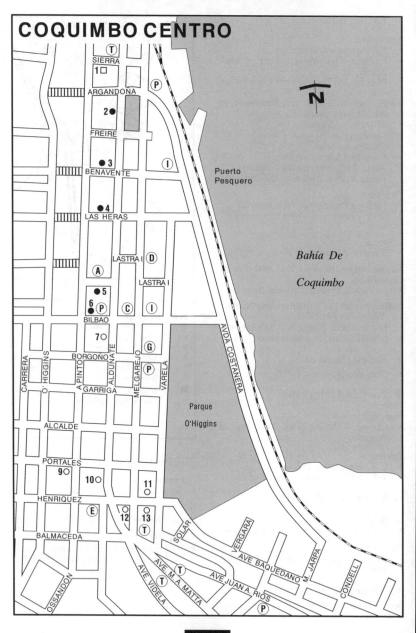

Key to map

A	Iglesia	**6**	Hotel Prat
C	Municipalidad (Town hall)	**10**	Hotel Lig
D	Post office and telex	○	**Eating out**
E	Telephone		
G	Mercado Municipal (Market)	**7**	Cafetería El Trébol
I	Tourist information	**8**	Restaurant La Bahía
P	Gas stations	**9**	Restaurant Sal y Pimiento
T	Bus terminals	**11**	Restaurant Popular
		12	Restaurant Baviera
●	**Accommodation**	**13**	Restaurant Bassaure
2	Hotel Claris	■	**Sights**
3	Hotel Inglés	**1**	Casa Pablo Garriga
4	Hotel Vegamar		
5	Hotel Iberia		

⊟ Accommodation in Coquimbo

Between March and November it is possible to bargain. For accommodation on the Panamericana between Coquimbo and La Serena see "Accommodation" in La Serena (page 192), Peñuelas (page 216), and La Herradura (page 185).

Accommodation in the city center
- Complejo Turístico Tiki Tano, Aldunate 1022   ℂ 313331
  Fax 322652

Hotels
- Claris, Aldunate 669   AF $H ♊
- Costanera, Baquedano 419 near Condell
  Clean, backpackers
- Iberia, Lastra 400   AEHIJKLMP$UZ   ℂ 312141 $I ♊
  Shared bathroom $I ♊
- Inglés, Aldunate 669   P $J ♊
  Budget travelers
- Lig, Aldunate 1577   ACEHIJKLP   ℂ 311171 $H ♊
  26 rooms
- Prat, Bilbao corner of Aldunate   AEIJLP   ℂ 311845 $H ♊
- Punta del Este, Avenida Videla 170   AIJKLP   ℂ 312768 $H ♊
  Shared bathroom $I ♊
- Vegamar, Aldunate 897 corner of Las Heras 403
    AEIJLP   ℂ 313 $I/J ♊

Accommodation outside town
See also "Accommodation" in La Herradura (page 185) and Peñuelas (page 216).

Hotels
- La Garza, Miraflores 695 corner of Santa Elena, suburb of San Juan on Panamericana
  near Universidad del Norte   ℂ 322819

🚌 Buses from Coquimbo

Every company has its own terminal, mostly located at the intersection of Avenida Videla and Avenida Juan A. Ríos where they merge with Melgarejo.

Companies
- A12   Bus Ruta Costera
- A17   Buses Bugueño, Avenida Videla 125 ☎ 312086 (Tongoy)
- A20   Buses Carlos Araya
- A31   Buses Evans
- A35   Buses Géminis, J.A. Ríos near Videla/Henriquez ☎ 246724
- A38   Buses Hidalgo, J.A. Ríos near Videla/Henriquez
- A42   Buses Carmelita, Avenida Videla 131 ☎ 324675
- A45   Buses Libac, J.A. Ríos 8 ☎ 321607
- A47   Buses Liserco, Aldunate Block 400
      Here all buses to and from La Serena stop
- A48   Buses Lit, Avenida Videla 180 ☎ 321192
- A60   Buses Palacios, J.A. Ríos 292 ☎ 322548
- A77   Buses TAL/Fénix, Avenida Videla 129 ☎ 321111
- A78   Buses Tramaca
- A83   Buses Zambrano
- A110 Flecha Dorada, J.A. Ríos 306-A ☎ 321639
- A112 Flota Barrios
- A115 Lasval, Baquedano 825 ☎ 314871
- A121 Los Conquistadores, Avenida Videla 168 ☎ 321227
- A122 Los Corsarios, J.A. Ríos 05, ☎ 321071
- A77   Los Diamantes de Elqui, Avenida Videla 129 ☎ 321111, fax 322131
- A126 Postal Bus, Baquedano 793 ☎ 323988
- A128 Pullman Bus Fichtur, J.A. Ríos 05-A ☎ 321231
- A135 Sol y Mar, Avenida Videla 109 ☎ 313492
- A137 Buses TAS Choapa, Avenida Videla 055 ☎ 321671
- A138 Taxi Colectivo Anserco
- A142 Los Tongoyinos, Avenida Videla 36 ☎ 36

Services

Destination	Fare	Services	Companies
Andacollo	$3.10		A20, A135, A138
Antofagasta	$19.25	10 services daily	A35, A45, A78, A110,
Calama	$23.40	10 services daily	A45, A78, A110
Sleeper	$26.30	1 service daily	A35
Caldera	$7.90	3 services daily	A128
Chañaral	$12.50	11 services daily	A45, A110, A115
Chuquicamata	$18.20	1 service daily	A45
Combarbalá	$4.60		A110
Copiapó	$7.20	12 services daily	A42, A45, A110, A115, A128
Guanaqueros	$1.40	6 services daily	A12, A17, A135, A142
Iquique	$29.30	3 services daily	A42, A110
La Serena	$0.40		Municipal bus
Los Andes	$13.00		A137
Los Vilos	$8.50	8 services daily	A45, A115, A137
Ovalle	$1.70	8 services daily	A42, A110, A115
Salamanca	$9.60	2 services Mon–Wed, Fri	A35, A110
Santiago	$15.40	18 services daily	A42, A45, A48, A77, A78, A110, A115, A121, A122, A128
Tocopilla	$23.40		A112
Tongoy	$1.70	8 services daily	A12, A17, A135

Buses from Coquimbo — continued

Destination	Fare	Services	Companies
• Vallenar	$4.00	1 service daily	A45
• Valparaíso	$12.50	9 services daily	A83, A115, A128
• Viña del Mar	$12.50	9 services daily	A83, A115, A128

▣ Sightseeing

• Iglesia de Guayacán, Los Rieles. Built by a Belgian engineer in 1889 to the design of Gustav Eiffel. The electronic carillon was installed by Padre Jan Van Hecke.

✦ Excursions

Tour operators
• Turismo Seguros Levar, Aldunate 1029 ☏ 322344

Excursions
• **La Serena:** See the entry for La Serena on page 187.
• **Peñuelas:** 6 km north-east. Well-known large beach resort with some of the best motels: Club Hípico, the Exposition complex, and the Casino — see the entry for Peñuelas on page 215.
• **La Herradura:** Beach resort 13.5 km south of town. Famous for its tranquil and warm waters. Yachting club and accommodation. See the entry for La Herradura on page 185.
• **Totoralillo**: 27 km south, in an attractive small peninsula, warm water and gentle waves.
• **Las Tacas**: 28 km south. A small beach with camping all year round.
• **Guanaqueros**: 42 km south. A small fishing village on a beautiful beach with calm waters sheltered in a bay. Camping available all year round. See the entry for Guanaqueros below.
• **Tongoy**: 57 km south of Coquimbo. See the entry for Tongoy on page 223.

GUANAQUEROS

Area code: 51
Altitude: Sea level
Distance from Coquimbo: 33 km south on Panamericana

This picturesque little beach resort is situated on the southern rocky end of the **Bahía de Guanaqueros**, 3 km off the Panamericana. It is 14 km north of **Tongoy**, another fashionable seaside resort. There are regular buses from Coquimbo, with increased services during holiday season.

The beach extends north along the bay for 17 km right up to **Punta Lagunillas**, and is dotted with camping grounds. There are plenty of hotels and restaurants, and during summer discos are open. Despite the large influx of summer tourists, the beach is so extensive that you can always find a quiet spot. It has fine white sand and slopes gradually into the sea.

Fishing is also an attraction here and you can buy directly from the fishermen when they return with their boats. This resort offers swimming, fishing, water sports, camping, kiosks, life savers, showers, toilets

Key to map

A	Iglesia
E	Telephone
T	Bus terminals
●	**Accommodation**
9	Cabañas Guanaqueros
○	**Eating out**
1	Restaurant La Picada
2	Restaurant La Nave

3	Restaurant La Bahía
5	Restaurant Miramar
7	Restaurant El Suizo
8	Restaurant La Ruca
⊙	**Entertainment**
4	Disco La Coca Loca
6	Disco El Pequeño

(there is a small fee for the use of toilets and showers).

Guanaqueros comes to life only in summer. Many holiday cabins have sprung up in the area.

⚐ Festivals
• February 8–22: Summer regatta

✉ Accommodation

Hotels
• La Bahía, Arturo Prat 058 ℂ 391107. Restaurant
• El Pequeño, María Ibsen 1130 ℂ 391149, fax 391341

Cabañas
★★ Guanaqueros, at town entrance ℂ 391288. 4 km off Panamericana, opposite intersection to Tongoy. One of the best camping grounds here, a flat area with plenty of shade provided by eucalyptus trees, 140 camping sites. $H per site up to 6 persons. 11 cabins for 5 with kitchenette $E/F. Open all year round, electricity, separate toilet blocks for men and women, cold water showers, laundry, shop
★★ Las Dunas de Guanaqueros, 1 km north of town and 3 km off Panamericana, indicated on Panamericana ℂ 391135, fax 391282. About 200 m from the beach, flat area partly shaded, 50 camping sites, $I per campsite for 6. Eight cabins for 6 with kitchenette $E. Open all year round, electricity, water, toilet block, cold showers, laundry, shop

Complejo turístico
• Andalué, on the access road to Guanaqueros from Panamericana ABCHILNPR ℂ 391296 $G ♙♙. Cabins for 6 with kitchen $E

⚏ Eating out
There is a lively fishing port, and fresh seafood is one of the attractions of Guanaqueros. There are many good restaurants and people from La Serena come here on weekends for a drive and to enjoy the delicious food.

Restaurants
• El Pequeño, Avenida Costanera 306. Views from the terrace over the bay, dancing
• El Suizo, Avenida Costanera
• La Coca Loca, 21 de Mayo off Avenida Costanera. Dancing
• La Nave, Avenida Costanera, near fishing harbor
• La Picada, Avenida Costanera
• La Ruca, on Playa Grande just down from Camping Guanaqueros
• Miramar, 21 de Mayo 302

⚎ Post and telegraph

Telephone
• CTC, Avenida Costanera

⚌ Buses
The bus terminal is on Avenida Costanera opposite Restaurant El Suizo.
• Coquimbo: Fare $1.50; 8 services daily; Los Tongoyinos, Ruta Costera, Buses Bugueño, Sol y Mar
• Ovalle: 2 services daily; Empresa Ossandon
• Santiago: Fare $13.75; Los Diamantes de Elqui

HURTADO

Population: 800
Altitude: 1250 m
Distance from Ovalle: 74 km east on Ruta D-595

The settlement of Hurtado is in the upper reaches of the **Río Hurtado valley** where it meets Ruta D-445 leading over the **Paso Tres Cruces** to Vicuña.

High on a cliff overlooking the river, Hurtado is a long extended village, probably because of the Andean custom of not building a house on land that could be used for growing crops. The people are very friendly, which is a sign they have not been exposed to too many tourists.

Mountain peaks ranging from 3500 to 4000 m make up the valley, with **Altos del Pangue** to the east the highest at 4365 m. The valley floor is at an altitude of 1500 m. Even on sunny days the air is cool, as it blows from the many snow-capped peaks to the east which form the border with Argentina. Warm clothing is essential in these altitudes as the weather can change rapidly.

The Río Hurtado carries a lot of water, although much of it is used for irrigation. The valley floor is green and the houses are perched on rocks high above the river so all arable land can be used for cropping. Grapes and apricots are the main crops. but maize, potatoes and wheat are also grown here.

Report to the *carabineros* outpost here before setting out on a mountain hike; they know the area and are quite helpful and it is for your own protection.

Accommodation

There are very few tourist facilities, as the only *pensión* has three rooms which are usually full of boarders. However the innkeeper will always find you a place in a private home.
Private accommodation costs $J **i**, including breakfast.

Buses

There is a rural bus service from Hurtado to Ovalle for the country people to bring their produce to the market and do some shopping and return home again in the evening.

The 48 km bus ride from Hurtado to Vicuña is very spectacular, especially the first part up the mountain pass road.
- Andacollo: Fare $3.75; irregular services; duration 4 hrs
- Ovalle: Fare $2.30; 1 service daily except Sun; duration 2½ hrs
- Vicuña: Fare $3.60; Sat only; duration 3 hrs; Frontera Elqui

Excursions

- **Las Breas:** The 14 km to Las Breas is a 3½ hour gentle uphill walk. The road going up the Río Hurtado valley follows the contours of the mountains, climbing imperceptibly. You can get as far as **Pabellón** in the upper Río Hurtado valley which is a further 14 km. The fresh water from the streams that tumble down from the mountains everywhere means you need not go thirsty. Walnut trees are planted in groves along the roadsides, and sometimes you feel as if you are going through a tunnel. The first settlement after Hurtado is **Chañar,** where the **Quebrada El Chañar** starts. The valley is wider here as several quebradas and valleys converge. If you visit in December you can enjoy the delicious ripe apricots, which you can pick everywhere along the road. Las Breas is a little village where the dirt road ends; from here onwards only mountain tracks go higher up in the high *sierra.* There are bus services from Las Breas to Ovalle on Sun, Tues, and Thurs at 1100. Further up the mountain a house offers private accommodation for hikers. Stock up at the kiosk here (this is your last chance) which sells cookies and other goodies. The woman who runs it is very informative and lives in the house behind it, so knock there if the kiosk is closed. A few kilometers past the village up the valley, you will reach the property of Sociedad El Bosque, where deer are kept. The road ends right outside their gate, by a sign that says no trespassing. However if you ask permission, they will allow you to go through. The valley is wider here and less spectacular than near Hurtado. Past the Sociedad El Bosque the climb starts; you will come across some marshy sections — and it is also puma country.

ILLAPEL

Area code: (053)
Population: 16 000
Altitude: 400 m
Distance from Los Vilos: 66 km north-east on Ruta D-85

The capital of Choapa province, Illapel is situated in a wide basin on the north side of the **Río Illapel**; it is built against the northern slopes, wedged in between the river and the mountains. The cooling winds of the coast cannot reach the town because of the barrier formed by the *Cordillera de la Costa*. The surrounding barren mountains reflect the heat, so this can be an uncomfortably hot place at times. Nearly all the streets crossing Avenida Recabarren link the upper section of town with stairs — there are seven sets of stairs. From the top there are sweeping views over the Río Choapa valley and the surrounding mountains.

The city was founded in 1754, but relocated in 1788 by Viceroy Ambrosio O'Higgins. This has been a mining town since colonial times, and in the 19th century it was the center of a busy mining region. Mining still continues, though on a reduced scale, and it is a now a sleepy town. The landscape is scarred with abandoned mines and slag heaps lie on many mountain slopes. Its port of Los Vilos was connected with a railway line. There is a good sealed road all the way to the coast (with a few bad sections), and to Salamanca 31 km east.

The town's main attractions are the colonial church, a quite interesting Museo de Arqueología and the Plaza de Armas. Some of the streets have retained their colonial charm with 19th century houses, easily recognized by their adobe walls and interior patios. Very few tourists find their way here, although there are some good hotels. The hub of the town is Avenida Silva climbing from the now unused train station. The main shopping street is Constitución.

The water coming down from the mountains is used to irrigate the river flats and produces an illusion of lushness, but cannot conceal the fact that this is a dry place. The mountains around town have few shrubs and less cacti than might be expected.

In pre-Hispanic times the Río Choapa valley was densely settled by Diaguita tribes. However, when the Incas penetrated the region without fully conquering the area they founded *mitimaes* settlements which served as Incan outposts. One such *tambo* was in the modern-day village of **Cuz-Cuz**, 9 km west of Illapel.

According to a plaque in the main plaza, Lieutenant-General Don Domingo Ortiz de Rozas, who lived from 1683 to 1756, was Governor-General of the Vice-regency of Chile. He founded Illapel on November 12, 1754 with the name Villa de San Rafael de Rozas.

⊠ Festivals
- May 7: Santa Cruz
- July 16: Virgen del Carmen

ⓘ Tourist information
- CONAF, Vicuña Mackenna 93 ☏ 522331.

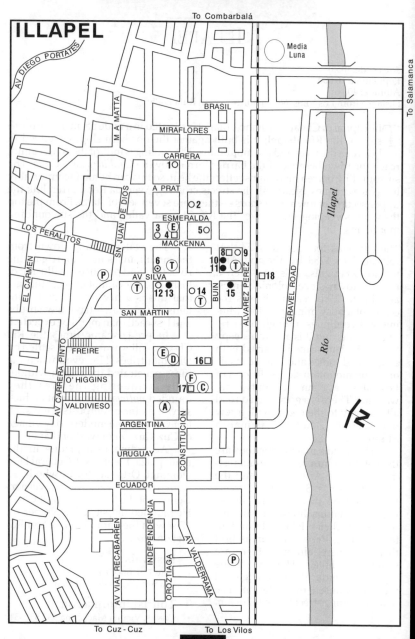

ILLAPEL

To Combarbalá

AV DIEGO PORTALES

Media
Luna

To Salamanca

M A MATTA

BRASIL

MIRAFLORES

CARRERA
1○

SN JUAN DE DIOS

A PRAT

○2

ESMERALDA

LOS PERALITOS

3 ○ (E)
○ 4□   5○

Illapel

MACKENNA

EL CARMEN

8□ ○9
6   10 ●
○ (T)   11 ● (T)

(P)

□18

AV SILVA

(T)   ○ ●
12 13

○ 14 ●
(T) 15

GRAVEL ROAD

Río

SAN MARTIN

AV CARRERA PINTO

FREIRE

(E)
(D)

16□

O'HIGGINS

(F)
17□ (C)

/N

VALDIVIESO

(A)

CONSTITUCION

ARGENTINA

URUGUAY

ECUADOR

AV VIAL RECABARREN

INDEPENDENCIA

OROZTIAGA

AV VALDERRAMA

(P)

To Cuz - Cuz   To Los Vilos

☒ Accommodation in Illapel

Hotels

★★★ Domingo Ortiz de Rozas, Avenida Ignacio Silva 241

		ADEHIJLP	(522127	$G	⁛
•	Alameda, Avenida Ignacio Silva 20	ADEFGIJ	(522355	$I	⁛
•	Alemán, Avenida Ignacio Silva 45	AEHIJL	(522511		
•	Londres, Vicuña Mackenna 21 near Pérez				
		P	(521350/211906	$J	⁛
	Shared bathroom, backpackers				

Hostería

•	Illapel, Buin 452	F	(521877	$J	⁛
	Budget travelers				
•	Hotel Roxi, Buin 587			$H	⁛

⊞ Eating out

The hotels have good dining rooms; see "Accommodation" above.

Restaurants
- Guerra Santos, Constitución 799
- Nicco, Avenida Ignacio Silva 279
- Turismo TAP, Constitución 382

Cafés
- *Cafetería* in disused railroad station, Alvarez Pérez
- La Pergola, V. Mackenna
- Leity Mac, Constitución 642

⊤ Entertainment

- Disco Fama, Independencia near Vicuña Mackenna

- Disco La Naranja, Avenida Silva block 200 near Independencia

⊞ Post and telegraph

Post office
O'Higgins near Constitución

Telephone
- CTC, Freire near Independencia
- CTC, Constitución 523
- ENTEL Chile, Alvarez Pérez 45 (521093
- Telex Chile, Constitución 279

⊟ Services and facilities

Supermarket
- Supermercado Los Naranjos, Constitución near Vicuña Mackenna

Key to map

A	Iglesia
B	Gobernación Provincial (Government)
C	Municipalidad (Town hall)
D	Post office and telex
E	Telephone
F	Carabineros (Police)
P	Gas stations
T	Bus terminals
●	**Accommodation**
5	Hotel Roxi
9	Hotel Londres
10	Hostería Illapel
11	Hotel Alemán
13	Hotel Domingo Ortiz de Roza
15	Hotel Alameda

○	**Eating out**
1	Restaurant Guerra Santos
2	Restaurant Leity Mac
3	Café La Pergola
12	Restaurant Nicco
14	Restaurant TAP
⊙	**Entertainment**
6	Disco La Naranja
■	**Sights**
17	Casa de la Cultura
18	Old railroad station, now a *cafetería*
□	**Services**
4	Supermercado Los Naranjos
8	CONAF
16	ENTEL

🚌 Buses from Illapel

There is no central bus terminal.
Rural buses to Cárcamo and Río Carén valley leave from Avenida Silva near Independencia.

Companies
- A5   Asociación de Buses Intercomunales, Avenida Silva block 100 near Constitución
- A35   Buses Géminis, San Martín 180
- A41   Buses La Canela
- A76   Tacc Via Choapa, Avenida Silva 94, opposite Hotel Alemán ☎ 522651
- A115 Incabus, Avenida Ignacio Silva 2 ☎ 522159
- A128 Pullman Bus, Buin 424 ☎ 521734

Services

Destinations	Fares	Services	Duration	Companies
Antofagasta	$24.60	1 service Tues, Thurs		A35
Calama	$27.20	1 service daily		A35
Carén	$1.30	1 service Mon, Thurs, Fri		
			2 hrs	Buses Carén
Chañaral		1 service Tues, Fri		A115
Chuquicamata	$27.20	1 service daily		A35
Copiapó		1 service daily		A35
Coquimbo		1 service Tues, Fri		A35
La Calera		4 services daily		A5
La Serena	$6.30	4 services daily		A35, A76, A115
Limache	$5.00	3 services daily		A5
Los Vilos	$2.10	5 services daily	1hr	A5, A41, A115
Ovalle	$5.00	1 service Mon, Wed, Fri		A35, A115
Pichidangui	$2.30			A76
Salamanca	$0.90		1 hr	A5, A76
Santiago	$6.90	8 services daily		A76, A115
Valparaíso	$6.40	4 services daily		A5
Viña del Mar	$6.40	4 services daily		A5

🚗 Motoring
- Esso gas station on top of Avenida Silva intersection with Recabarren

📷 Sightseeing

There are several houses still standing that date back to the relocation to the present site in 1788 by Viceroy Ambrosio O'Higgins.
- Hacienda La Puntilla: Follow Avenida Irarrazabal for about 1 km. This old *hacienda* with its thick reinforced adobe walls dates back 200 years.
- Casa de la Cultura: Avenida Valderrama corner of Valdivieso opposite Plaza de Armas. A small museum with archeological artifacts found in the district.

- Cerro Quillaicillo: A path starting off Avenida Diego Portales leads up to the mountain top with panoramic views over the town and the Río Choapa valley.

⊕ Excursions
- **Reserva Nacional Las Chinchillas** (4229ha, 10 445 ac): 20 km north of Illapel on Ruta O-55 (the road to Combarbalá). Information center, excursion paths.
- **Carén**: On Ruta D-805, at the junction of **Río Illapel** and **Río Carén**. This is hiking country, and from here you can go into the *pre-Cordillera* up the Río Illapel valley. You can hike up the **Río Cenicero** towards the high *sierra*. There are rural buses to Carén (45 km)

and the trip takes 1½ hours. The Río Illapel valley narrows considerably, with mountains rising either side to over 4000 m.

LA HERRADURA

Area code: 051
Distance from Coquimbo: 6 km north

A small horseshoe (*"herradura"*) shaped bay, **Bahía Herradura de Guayacán** protects a 2 km beach just south-east of Coquimbo; the waters are calm and very warm. Local buses operate a shuttle service.

The tourist facilities include motels, camping grounds, seafood restaurants and a yacht club. You can enjoy swimming, water sports, sailing, water skiing, and camping. There are kiosks, life savers, showers, and toilets.

La Herradura is a well-frequented seaside resort with excellent tourist facilities.

⚐ Festivals
• February 8–22: Summer regatta

• September, first and second weeks: Regattas

⚐ Eating out

Restaurants
The hotels have good dining rooms; see also the box marked "Accommodation in La Herradura" below.
• Club de Yates, on the beach
• El Cocodrilo, Avenida La Marina corner of Caprí
• Mario, Niza 40, sector Capri

⚐ Buses
Regular municipal buses run to and from Coquimbo.

⚐ Accommodation in La Herradura
In the prime holiday season (December to the end of February) all accommodation is at a premium. Outside the main season prices are moderate and bargaining is possible.

Apart hotels
• Brisas del Mar, Los Pastores 90   **ABCDHILP**   ☎ 312641 $F for 4
  200m from beach, fax 315962
• Villa Náutica, Avenida Costanera 1223   ☎ 314677 $D ⚏
  Fax 324619

Cabañas
  ★★★ Cabinas Antares, Sector El Mirador, O'Higgins 1250 (Panamericana Norte KM 459)
                                        ABCDHLP   ☎ 312998 $G for 6

Accommodation in La Herradura — continued

- Cocodrilo's, Avenida La Marina corner of Capri   (324435
  Fax 324427

Complejos Turísticos
- Las Gaviotas, Avenida Costanera 1755, past the marina   (324718 $C for 4
  ABCDEGHIKLMPRTUZ
  Fax 314262, car rental, beach frontage, radio
- Las Golondrinas, Calle del Rancho 190   (313745 $F ⚥
  Fax 314426
- Las Terrazas de la Herradura, Avenida Costanera 1275   (313377
- Mistral, Avenida Costanera 1284   ABCDEFGHJKLNPR   (314198
  $F cabins for five, fax 313538
- Remanso de la Herradura, Panamericana KM 459   (314206 $D for 4
  Fax 322395

Hotels
- Bucanero, Avenida Costanera   ACDEFGHIJKLPS$TUXZ
     (312231 $F ⚥
  Magnificent views over the bay, beach frontage
- Cabañas de Turismo Terranova, Los Loros 1094   (324348
  Fax 321792
- La Herradura, Avenida Costanera 200
     AEFGHIJKLMPS$UZ   (321320 $H ⚥
  Car rental, boat hire, beach frontage, fax 314414
- El Portal de Los Alamos, El Cerrito 10   (313088 $F ⚥
  Fax 313088
- Cabañas de Turismo San Juan, Caprí Sur 151   (311110 $H ⚥
  ACDEFGHIJLPU
  On the beach front
- Traveler's Motel, Panamericana KM 460 (6 km south of Coquimbo)
     ADEIKLMP$U   (312045 $G ⚥
  On the beach front, 12 rooms

Motels
- Camping La Herradura, Antigua corner Escuela
     ABCDHIKLP   (312084 $H for 4
  30 units, 40 camp sites mostly on flat ground, open all year, electricity, trees giving
  shade, toilets, hot showers, short walk to beach, 10 cabins for 6 persons, tent site $l

Key to map
● **Accommodation**
1 Camping Los Olivos
2 Cabañas Cocodrilo
5 Hotel San Juan
6 Hotel la Herradura
7 Hotel las Golondrinas
8 Hotel Bucaneros
9 Motel Brisas del Mar
11 Cabañas La Herradura

12 Motel la Herradura
13 Complejo Turístico Mistral
14 Complejo Turístico Las Terrazas
15 Apart Hotel Villa Náutica
○ **Eating out**
3 Restaurant Cocodrilo
4 Restaurant Mario
10 Restaurant Club de Yates

Plate 11   Región IV de Coquimbo
Top: Pichidangui, coastal resort
Bottom: Tulahuén, Río Torca Valley

Plate 12   Región IV de Coquimbo
Top: Los Vilos, coastal resort
Bottom: Tongoy, fishing fleet

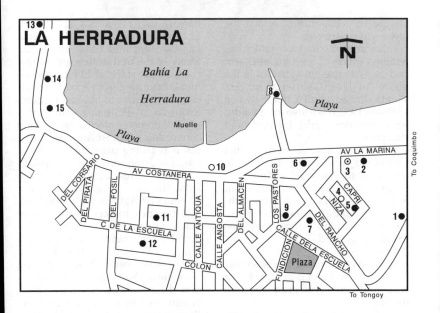

LA SERENA

Area code: 51
Population: 115 000
Altitude: Sea level
Distances:

- From Copiapó: 334 km south on Panamericana
- From Santiago: 470 km north on Panamericana

La Serena is in the fertile **Valle de Río Elqui** close to the sea front, near the mouth of the river on a beautiful bay just 13 km north of Coquimbo. It stands above the magnificent beaches in the low hills overlooking the bay.

As one of the first towns established by the Spanish *conquistadores* in Chile, its colonial character has been well preserved with many parks, churches, and colonial houses. Indeed, La Serena may be called a city of churches, as most religious orders built their monasteries and churches here from the early days of the colony. Founded in 1544 by Juan Bohón, its original name was Villanueva de la Serena, in honor of the birthplace of *conquistador* Pedro de Valdivia. It was founded again in 1549 by Francisco de Aguirre, after the first foundation was destroyed. During the 17th and 18th centuries La Serena was frequently raided by English, Dutch and French pirates. One of the worst assaults was by English pirate

Sharpe in 1680, during which the town was destroyed.

It is an attractive town which has retained much of its colonial charm and owes its present splendor to the vision of Don Gabriel González Videla, President of Chile between 1946 and 1952. It is a town of splendid wide avenidas, parks, convents and churches.

The beach extends around Bahía Coquimbo from Punta Teatinos in the north to Peñuelas, a suburb of Coquimbo in the south, about 12 km in total. Along the beach is the fashionable Avenida del Mar with a number of resort hotels, restaurants, camping grounds, caravan parks, discos, as well as a growing number of seafood restaurants. The beach has fine white sand and is at least 400 m wide and converges gradually into the sea.

The average summer temperatures are around 15°C (59°F), and the lowest winter temperature is 8°C (46°F); the highest temperatures are in February with a median of 18.4°C (65°F). In summer the water temperature is 19°C (66°F). June and July are the coldest months, but you can swim during the rest of the year. It is becoming increasingly popular with sailing enthusiasts.

The area is famous for its papaya fruits which are used in fruit salads, in preserves, and in juices. The hinterland is famous for the well known *pisco,* a type of brandy used to make the fashionable pisco sour. The region is also known for its delightful seafood dishes.

The most "showy" road is Avenida del Mar, which links all the major beaches west of La Serena such as (from north to south) Playas El Faro, Los Fuertes, Mansa, Blanca, La

Barca, Cuatro Esquinas, La Marina, El Pescador, El Corsario, La Sirena, Las Gaviotas and Canto del Agua. Many of the best motels are on this road, which starts at El Faro Monumental, running from Avenida Francisco de Aguirre to Avenida Cuatro Esquinas in Peñuelas. Along this seven kilometer stretch an exciting conversion into a world-class tourist resort is taking place: first-class hotels, condominiums, and restaurants.

You can reach the nearest beach from the city center by following Avenida de Aguirre for about 2 km. The beaches further south can be reached using *colectivos* going to Coquimbo and alighting at Cuatro Esquinas or Peñuelas. During the main tourist season public buses run along Avenida del Mar. Life-guards are stationed at some beaches. The area between Avenida del Mar and the Panamericana, called "Las Vegas de La Serena", has some tourist facilities as well: trailer parks, camping grounds, motels, and high-rise condominiums.

Named in honor of the city's second founder, Avenida Francisco de Aguirre is the main artery. It is broad with a center park which starts at the beach at Faro Monumental and passes through the whole town. Its huge trees provide shade so that it is a cool place even on the hottest day, and there are benches and statues throughout the park.

From Colina del Pino (the western campus of the Universidad de La Serena), there are sweeping views over the town and the Bahía de Coquimbo. With its splendid tourist facilities, this city of churches makes a good base to explore the interior valleys, relax on the beaches, or visit its many old colonial churches and interesting museums. Because of the clear air, many astronomical observatories have been built in the surrounding districts which tourists can also visit.

Another showpiece is the Parque Pedro de Valdivia, between Avenida Juan de Bohón (the Panamericana) and Avenida P. Pablo Muñoz. Gently rising from the Panamericana to P. Pablo Muñoz, it has large green spaces, clusters of trees, and also the soccer stadium. It offers excellent views down to the beaches.

History

The hinterland of La Serena was settled by Diaguitas, and later the Incans came and founded *mitimaes* settlements. There are villages dating from Incan *mitimaes* settlements in the Valle de Río Elqui: **Altovalsol**, 15 km upriver on the north bank of ☞ the Río Elqui, and **La Marquesa**, 30 km upriver at the junction of the Quebrada Marquesa with the Valle de Río Elqui.

In 1991 the **Paso Del Agua Negra** was reopened. There are bus services between La Serena and San Juan in Argentina in summer. This is a beautiful (and wild) scenic area, with great tourist potential on both sides of the border, which outdoor enthusiasts are sure to appreciate.

⊛ Festivals

As may be expected, the strong activity of the religious orders which made La Serena a city of churches has also bequeathed a legacy of many religious festivals. Many of the festivals celebrated in La Serena are also celebrated on the same dates in other villages and towns of the region.

- January, second week: Encuentro Musical de La Serena
- May 21: San Isidro Labrador

- July 16: Virgen del Carmen
- August 23: Foundation day celebrations
- September 18–20: Fiesta de la Pampilla

Festivals in La Higuera
- June 29: San Pedro
- September 24: Nuestra Señora de la Merced
- September 26: Patron saint's celebration

ⓘ Tourist information

- Sernatur, Casa González Videla, Plaza de Armas, Prat corner of Matta, upstairs ☎ 213134
- Oficina de Información Turísticas, Kiosko de Información Plazuela San Francisco, corner of Balmaceda and Eduardo de la Barra
- CONAF, Cordovez 281 ☎ 215073. Señor Carlos J. Noton Ramírez is the tourist liaison officer

⑪ Eating out

Eating out in the city center

Cafeterías
- Gelatería Bocaccio, Prat 498 corner of Balmaceda. Good spot, good snacks

To Copiapó

LA SERENA METROPOLITANA

To Vicuña

N

AV DE AGUIRRE

AVE. DEL MAR

CARRETERA PANAMERICANA

AV BALMACEDA

4 ESQUINAS Ⓟ

To Coquimbo   To Ovalle

Key to map

A	Iglesia
B	Gobernación Provincial (Government)
C	Municipalidad (Town hall)
D	Post office and telex
E	Telephone
I	Tourist information
P	Gas stations
$	Money exchange
T	Bus terminals

● **Accommodation**

2 Residencial El Cobre
3 Residencial Casa del Turista
5 Hotel del Cid
7 Hotel Viña del Mar
8 Hotel El Escorial
9 Hotel Los Balcones de Aragón
10 Hotel Pukará
15 Hotel Brasilia
16 Residencial El Loa
18 Hostería Montegrande
20 Hotel Francisco de Aguirre
22 Hotel Londres
25 Gran Hotel La Serena
27 Hotel Casablanca
29 Residencial Chile
30 Hotel Pacífico
33 Hotel Berlín
34 Residencial Petit
35 Hotel Mediterráneo
42 Hotel Alameda
47 Residencial Norte Verde
50 Hotel Los Balcones de Alcalá
51 Residencial Americana

○ **Eating out**

6 Restaurant Le Clarousset
11 Café Rapsodia
12 Café Bocaccio

14 Restaurant Domingo Domínguez
21 Restaurant Patio Andaluz
24 Restaurant La Mia Pizza
32 Club Social La Serena
36 Restaurant Quick Biss
39 Restaurant Mai Lan Fan
44 Restaurant Milán
46 Café La Creperie
49 Restaurant Ciro's
52 Restaurant Las Palmeras
53 Restaurant Croata

◉ **Entertainment**

40 Teatro Municipal

△ **Tour operators and car rental**

23 Gira Tour
41 First Rent a Car
43 Automóvil Club de Chile
48 Dollar Rent a Car

▲ **Airline offices**

55 LADECO
56 LAN Chile

■ **Sights**

1 Iglesia Santa Inés
4 Iglesia Sagrado Corazón
13 Iglesia La Merced
19 Casa González Videla
26 Iglesia San Agustín
28 Iglesia Santo Domingo
38 Museo Arqueológico
45 Iglesia San Francisco
54 Museo Mineralógico

□ **Services**

17 Mercado La Recova
31 Fería Artesanal
37 Supermercado Brisahorro

Restaurants

- Club Social, Cordovez 516
- Croata, Balmaceda 871 $Y
- Domingo Domínguez, Arturo Prat 572 $Y
- Estercita, Cienfuegos
- Las Palmeras, Balmaceda 842
- La Vie Claire, Cantournet 880. Vegetarian
- Le Clarousset, Colón 255. French cuisine
- Mai Lan Fan, Cordovez 740 $Y. Chinese cuisine

- O'Higgins, Libertador B. O'Higgins 646 $Y
- Patio Andaluz, Balmaceda 432 $Y. Spanish cuisine
- Pollo en Canasta, Cienfuegos 680. Specialty chicken-in-a-basket
- Pub C-E, Colín 251
- Pub Mr Ed, Colón 360
- Quick Biss, Cienfuegos 545, upstairs. Self-serve
- Schopería El Cliché, Cantournet 840
- Taiwan, Cantournet 844. Chinese cuisine

LA SERENA CENTRO

Parrilladas and pizzerías
- Ciro's, Avenida Francisco de Aguirre 431. Seafood and grills
- Hotel Francisco de Aguirre 210
- La Creperie, O'Higgins 601
- La Mia Pizza, Libertador B. O'Higgins 460 $Y. International cuisine
- Pizzería Pastisseria, Libertador B. O'Higgins 663

Salón de Té
- Milán, Balmaceda 661
- Rapsodia, Prat 470, in back garden of old colonial house

Schoperías
- El Carmen, Vicente Zorilla 766

Eating out at Mercado La Recova
Mercado La Recova is in Los Arrayanes 0777.
- Do Brasil. Seafood
- Don Fierro. International cuisine
- El Castillo Suizo,
- Il Bavaglino. Italian cuisine

Eating out in Sector Avenida del Mar

Restaurants
- Don Fierro, Avenida del Mar. International cuisine

🛏 Accommodation in La Serena

Prices indicated are for the main holiday season from mid-December to mid-March.

Apart hotels

- Aníbal Pinto, Aníbal Pinto 2502   ✆ 222585 $F 👥
  Fax 227057

Hotels

★★★ Alameda, Avenida Francisco de Aguirre 452

       AFGIJLPS   ✆ 213052 $G 👥

★★★ Casablanca, Vicuña 414   ADEFHIJLPS   ✆ 226869 $F 👥
   Fax 212062

- Berlín, Cordovez 535   ADEFGHIJKLP   ✆ 222927 / 211323 $F 👥
  Shared bathroom $G 👥, fax 223575
- Brasilia, Brasil 555   ADEFGHIJLPUYZ   ✆ 225248 $G 👥
  Fax 211883
- Del Cid, Libertador B. O'Higgins 138   ✆ 212692 $F 👥
  Fax 212692
- El Escorial I, Colón 617   ADEHIJKLP$T   ✆ 224793 $F 👥
  Fax 221433. Car rental,
- El Escorial II, Brasil 476   PS   ✆ 215193 $F 👥
  Fax 221433
- Francisco de Aguirre, Cordovez 210   ACDEFGHIJKLMNPRS$TUXZ

     ✆ 212351 $E 👥
   Fax 222991. Car rental, sauna, 90 rooms
- Gran Hotel La Serena, Cordovez 610   AEFGHIJKLPST   ✆ 211145 / 222975 $H 👥
- Hostal Santo Domingo, Andrés Bello 1067   ✆ 212718
- Hostal de Colón, Colón 371   ✆ 223979
  Fax 221433
- Londres, Cordovez 550   AEFGILPS$U   ✆ 214673 $H 👥
  20 rooms
- Los Balcones de Alcalá, Avenida Francisco de Aguirre 781

     ACDEHIJKLP   ✆ 212169 / 214722 $E 👥
   Fax 211800
- Los Balcones de Aragón, Cienfuegos 289

     ACDEHIJKL   ✆ 211982 $E 👥
   Fax 211800
- Mediterraneo, Cienfuegos 509 corner of Cordovez PS

     ✆ 225837 $G 👥
   Fax 225837
- Pacífico, Eduardo de La Barra 252   AEFIJKLP$U

     ✆ 225674 $H/I 👥
   Shared bathroom
- Pucará, Balmaceda 319   ADEFGHIKLPS   ✆ 211966 $H 👥
  Fax 211933
- Viña del Mar, Brasil 308   AILP   ✆ 212349 $H 👥

Hosterías

- La Serena, Avenida Francisco de Aguirre 0660

     ACDEFGHIJKLMNPRS   ✆ 225745 $F 👥
   Fax 222459
- Montegrande, Avenida Juan Bohón 403

     PS   ✆ 223256 $E 👥
   Fax 227075

Accommodation in La Serena — continued

Residenciales
- Central, Lautauro 864   ℂ 225191
- Americana, A. Bello 869
  Backpackers
- Carrera, Los Carrera 682
  Backpackers
- Casa del Turista, Colón 318
  Backpackers
- Chile, M.A. Matta 561   AFIJL   ℂ 211694 $H ♦♦
  Shared bathroom
- Colo Colo, Juan de Dios Pení 626
  Backpackers
- El Cobre, Colón 290   ℂ 214673
  Backpackers
- El Loa, O'Higgins 362   AFIJL $I ♦♦
  Shared bathroom
- El Silo, Larrain Alcalde 1550   AFHIJLP   ℂ 213944 $I ♦♦
- Lido, M.A. Matta 547   AFIJLS   ℂ 213073 $I ♦♦
  Shared bathroom
- Norte Verde, Cienfuegos 672   AFGIJKLP   ℂ 213646 $J ♦♦
  Budget travelers
- Petit, Eduardo de la Barra 586   AFIJ   ℂ 212536 $I ♦♦
  Shared bathroom
- Hospedaje, Avenida Francisco de Aguirre 411
  Backpackers
- Hospedaje, Avenida Francisco de Aguirre 159
  Backpackers
- Hospedaje, Isabel Riquelme 860 near Avenida F. de Aguirre
  Backpackers
- Hospedaje, Los Carrera 880, near Avenida Francisco de Aguirre
  Backpackers

Motels
- Claro de Luna, Almagro 529   ℂ 222891
- Tourist House, Avenida Francisco de Aguirre 411   ℂ 222845

Accommodation along Avenida del Mar
The best approach to hotels along Avenida del Mar is by La Serena–Coquimbo bus. Alight at Cuatro Esquinas. Between Cuatro Esquinas and Peñuelas (3km) is the biggest concentration of hotels and motels.

Apart hotels
- La Fuente, Avenida Del Mar 5665   ℂ 245755
  Fax 241259
- Les Mouettes, Avenida Del mar 2500, opposite La Barca Beach
  ABCDEGHIKLNP$ ℂ 225665 $F ♦♦
  Fax 226278
- Mar Serena, Avenida Del Mar 4900   ℂ 241863
  Fax 241855. Swimming pool, tennis, sauna, grill bar

Accommodation in La Serena — continued

Hotels

★★★★Canto del Agua, Avenida Del Mar 5700   ☏ 242203 $E ♦♦
ABCDEFGHIJKLMNP$TUXZ

      Fax (051) 222027. Beach, tennis, boat hire, sauna, car rental. $F cabins for six

 ★★★ Hostal del Mar, Cuatro Esquinas 0680 corner of Avenida Del Mar
                    ABCDFHIKLP$UZ   ☏ 225559 $E ♦♦
     Fax 225816. Beach frontage, car rental. $F cabin for 6, 8 cabins

Cabañas
- Bahía Drake, Avenida del Mar 1300   ☏ 223367 $H for 4
  Fax 223367.
- Cabañas de Turismo Tramonte di Sole, Avenida Del Mar 990
                                 ☏ 223536
  Fax 221226. $F cabins for four
- Don Carlos, Avenida Del Mar Parcela 39   ☏ 212453
  Fax 212453
- Hipocampo, Avenida Del Mar, opposite Playa El Corsario
                 ABCDFGHIJKLNPRT   ☏ 214316 $E ♦♦
  Beach frontage, $E cabins for 4, 60 camping sites, open all year round; electricity, water, toilets, hot showers, laundry, restaurant
- Mar Pacífico, Los Copaos off Avenida Del Mar, Playa La Barca
                                 ☏ 213202 $F ♦♦

Hostals
- Campanario del Mar, Ave Del Mar 4600   ☏ 245516 $D ♦♦
  Fax 245531

Hotel cabañas
- Las Añañucas, Avenida Del Mar 4100   ☏ 221996
  Fax 215881, luxury bungalows
- Mar de Ensueño, Avenida Del Mar 900
                        CDERU   ☏ 222381
  Fax 222083

Complejo turístico
- Jardín del Mar 2, Avenida del Mar 2900   ☏ 222223
  Fax 221827
- Vega Sur, Los Arrayanes Poniente 0200 off Avenida Del Mar
                                 ☏ 226629 $E for 4
  Fax 227734

Accommodation south on RN 43 to Ovalle
- Motel Quilacán, Balmaceda 2271   ABCDHIKLNPR$ ☏ 225668 $H ♦♦
  Tennis court, $F cabins for 6
- Residencial Casa de Huéspedes, Balmaceda 4455   ☏ 241748

Accommodation in La Serena — continued

Accommodation north of La Serena
- Cabañas and Camping Maki Payi, Vegas Norte, Parcela 153
                       AEFGHINP   ☏ 214276 $G for 4
  Beach frontage

Accommodation in La Serena — continued

Accommodation at Cuatro Esquinas

Cabañas
- Hotel Motel Villa Los Plátanos, Panamericana near Cuatro Esquinas, Vegas Sur, Parcela 10   **ABCDHIJNP$**   (213494 $G ♟♟
Tennis, also cabins for four
- Parador El Frutillar, José Joaquín Pérez   (243785 $H ♟♟
Fax 222853

- La Mia Pizza Avenida del Mar 2100 $Y. International cuisine
- Piano Bar Le Croq'Monsieur, Avenida del Mar 2500
- Pub El Papayo, Avenida del Mar 4600. International cuisine
- Saint Laurent, Avenida del Mar

Eating out along the Panamericana

Restaurants
- Ristorante Amici Miei, KM 470 $Y. Italian cuisine
- Don Oscar, Shell gas station, Carretera Panamericana near Juan de Dios Peñí

Eating out Sector La Pampa, on the road to Ovalle

Restaurants
- El Alero de Don Chuma, Balmaceda 2455 $Y. Chilean cuisine
- Isidoro, Balmaceda 3812 $X. International cuisine; two dance orchestras
- Mesón Matías, Balmaceda 1940 (at bus stop 3)
- Mi Familia y Yo, Balmaceda 2687 $Y. International cuisine

ⓨ Entertainment
- Restaurant Vadihno, Balmaceda 545. Piano bar

🕮 Post and telegraph

Post office
- Arturo Prat, Casa González Videla, Plaza de Armas

Telephone
- CTC, Cordovez 446, Edificio La Recova, fax 212273
- CTC, Cordovez near Los Carrera
- ENTEL Chile, A. Prat block 500 near O'Higgins. Overseas calls

- Telex Chile, Casa González Videla, Plaza de Armas

$ Financial
The banking sector is in Balmaceda between Cordovez and A. Prat.
- Intercam Turismo, Balmaceda 431 (224673
- Cambios Fides, Balmaceda 460, Edificio Caracol, Local 10 (214554
- Fincard, Balmaceda 383, Edificio Italia (214931. Cash advances against Visa and Mastercard

🖷 Services and facilities

Dry cleaners
- Lavaseco Silvana, Eduardo de la Barra 495 behind stalls

Photographic supplies
- Fotocolor Braun, Cordovez block 646. Agfa film

Supermarket
- Supermercado Brisahorro, Cienfuegos near Eduardo de la Barra

✈ Air services

Airlines
- LAN Chile, Cienfuegos 463 (221531
- LADECO, Cordovez 484 (225753

Services
- Santiago: Fare $60.00; departs 1800–1900; 1–2 services daily; duration 1 hr LADECO
- Copiapó: Departs 1550–1650; 1–2 services daily; duration 1 hr; LADECO

🚍 Motoring

Car rental
- Automóvil Club de Chile, Eduardo de la Barra 435 (225279

🚌 Buses from La Serena

Long-distance bus companies
The long-distance bus terminal is on the corner of El Santo and Amunátegui ☎ 212351.
A few regional buses leave from here also.

- A3   Buses Andes Mar–Bus Calama
- A31   Buses Evans
- A35   Buses Géminis
- A42   Buses Carmelita
- A45   Buses Libac
- A67   Ramos Cholele
- A76   Buses Tacc Via Choapa
- A77   Buses TAL/ LosDiamantes de Elqui
- A78   Buses Tramaca
- A83   Buses Zambrano
- A86   Chile Bus
- A106 Fénix Pullman Norte
- A110 Flecha Dorada / Flecha Norte
- A112 Flota Barrios
- A115 Lasval
- A121 Los Conquistadores
- A122 Los Corsarios
- A128 Pullman Bus Fichtur
- A137 TAS Choapa
- A149 Transporte Algarrobo

Rural bus companies and municipal bus companies
Each rural bus company has its own terminal.
Municipal buses to Coquimbo leave from Avenida Francisco de Aguirre corner Balmaceda. Bus no. 8; fare $0.50; duration 20 minutes.
Colectivos leave from Avenida Francisco de Aguirre block 400 just outside Hotel Alameda for Ovalle and Paihuano, and for Tongoy, Valle Río Elqui, and Valle Río Marquesa.
Colectivos leave from O'Higgins corner of Francisco de la Barra for Vicuña.

- A17   Buses Bugueño, Juan Dios Pení 401 corner of Regimiento Coquimbo
- A20   Buses Carlos Araya, Juan Dios Pení 401, corner of Regimiento Coquimbo ☎ 221664
       Services to Andacollo
- A55   Nevada, Domeyko 524 ☎ 211071
       Services to Tongoy and Vicuña
- A81   Buses Via Elqui, San Juan Dios Pení corner of Benavente
       Services to Andacollo
- A114 Frontera Elqui, Juan Dios Pení 401 corner of Regimiento Coquimbo ☎ 221664
       Services to Huanta, Ovalle, Paihuano, Pisco Elqui, Tongoy, and Vicuña
- A119 Linea 41 Ruta Elqui, Avenida Francisco de Aguirre 460 ☎ 213364
       Services to Tongoy and Vicuña
- A126 Postal Bus, Juan Dios Pení 401 corner of Regimiento Coquimbo ☎ 221664
       Services to Andacollo
- A133 Secovalle, Balmaceda 825 ☎ 222419
       Services to Ovalle
- A134 Sol de Elqui, Domeyko 524 corner Francisco de Aguirre ☎ 211071
       Services to Tongoy and Vicuña
- A136 Tacso, Domeyko 524 ☎ 211071
       Services to Ovalle

Buses from La Serena — continued

- A138 Taxi Colectivos Anserco, Domeyko 524 (211071
       Services to Andacollo
- A195 Buses Covalle, Infante 538 (213127, fax 221751
       Services to San Juan in Argentina via Paso del Agua Negra

Services

Destination	Fare	Services	Duration	Companies
Andacollo	$2.50	10 services daily	1 hr	A20, A126, A138
Antofagasta	$19.25	33 services daily	14hrs	A35, A42, A45, A78, A86, A106, A110, A112
Sleeper	$45.10	5 services daily		A112
Arica	$35.90	21 services daily	24 hrs	A42, A86, A106, A110, A112
Sleeper	$66.70	5 services daily	24 hrs	A128
Calama	$23.50	11 services daily		A45, A78, A110, A112
Sleeper	$26.30	1 service daily		A35
Caldera	$10.50	12 services daily	6 hrs	A45, A115, A128
Chañaral	$12.60	24 services daily		A42, A45, A110, A112, A115, A128
Chapilca	$3.10			A119
Chuquicamata	$23.50	11 services daily	17 hrs	A45, A110, A112
Combarbalá	$4.60			A115
Copiapó	$9.60	33 services daily	5 hrs	A42, A45, A78, A110, A112, A115, A128, A137
Coquimbo	$0.40		½ hr	Municipal buses
Diaguita	$1.40	6 services daily	2 hrs	A81
El Salvador	$12.20			A115, A128
Horcón	$2.50	3 services daily		A114
Huanta	$2.50	2 services daily Mon, Fri		A114
			2 hrs	A114
Hurtado	$3.30	2 services per week		A114
Change in Vicuña				
Illapel	$6.30	3 services daily		A35, A76, A115
Iquique	$33.00	16 services daily	21 hrs	A42, A106, A110, A112
Sleeper	$66.30	7 services daily	21 hrs	A128
La Calera	$9.20	3 services daily		A115, A128
La Higuera	$1.70	8 services daily		A119
Las Breas	$4.60	2 services per week	7 hrs	A114
Los Vilos	$6.30	7 services daily	4 hrs	A115, A137
Montegrande	$2.30	3 services daily	2 hrs	A114
Ovalle	$2.80	28 services daily	1 hr	A42, A77, A110, A112, A115, A128, A133, A136
Paihuano	$2.50	9 services daily	1 hr	A81, A114, A119
Peralillo	$1.30	6 services daily	2 hrs	A81
Pisco Elqui	$2.30	3 services daily	2 hrs	A114
Potrerillos	$14.60	10 services daily	10 hrs	A115, A128
Quebrada de Paihuano				
	$2.10	3 services per week		A114
Rivadavia	$1.70	2 services daily	1 hrs	A114
Salamanca	$9.60	2 services daily		A35, A76, A115
San Juan (Argentina)			12 hrs	A137, A195
	$29.20	2 services per week		

Via Paso Los Libertadores in winter, Tues only

Buses from La Serena — continued

Destination	Fare	Services	Duration	Companies
• Santiago	$10.50	48 services daily	7 hrs	A31, A42, A45, A67, A77, A78, A106, A110, A112, A115, A128, A149, A121, A122, A137
• Tocopilla	$23.70			A112
• Vallenar	$4.20	29 services daily	3 hrs	A42, A45, A112, A115, A128, A137
• Valparaíso	$12.50	14 services daily	7 hrs	A83, A112, A115, A128
• Vicuña	$1.20	14 services daily	1 hr	A55, A81, A114, , A119, A134
• Viña del Mar	$12.50	14 services daily	6 hrs	A83, A112, A115, A128

- Avis Rent a Car, Avenida Francisco de Aguirre 068 ☎ 227171
- Budget Rent a Car, Avenida Francisco de Aguirre 0240 ☎ 225057
- Dollar Rent a Car, Avenida Francisco de Aguirre 335 ☎ 224726
- First Rent a Car, Matta 670 ☎ 222323
- Hertz Rent a Car, Francisco de Aguirre 0225 ☎ 225471
- Tracker Cienfuegos 700 ☎ 226820. Four-wheel drive rentals

Gas stations
For gas stations, see city map.

Shopping
On the corner of Eduardo de la Barra and Balmaceda is a small plaza with stands selling all kinds of *artesanias*, jewelry and souvenirs.
- Viña Santa Carolina, Libertad 871. *Pisco* and liqueurs.
- Mercado La Recova. Located at Los Arrayanes 0777 corner of Cienfuegos. A very comprehensive *artesania* and souvenir area with restaurants. There are shops selling beautiful souvenir items (weavings, carvings, and semi-precious stones), and upstairs is a *salón de té*. From the balcony you can see the activities on the plaza and enjoy the music of traditional Andean musicians. It aslo has a CTC telephone. A picturesque area
- CEMA Chile, Los Carrera 570. *Artesanias*

Sport
- Hang gliding: Cerro Mirador hang glider meeting
- Tennis: Club de Tenís de La Serena, Juan de Dios Pení near Panamericana

Sightseeing
Take a Coquimbo bus from the center and get off at Peñuelas. Walk down towards the beach past the casino and back towards La Serena on Avenida del Mar, and you will get an idea of the size and beauty of this beach. In summer there are bus services along Avenida del Mar. At the northern end is the huge lighthouse and the beginning of the wide tree-studded Avenida Francisco de Aguirre which leads up into town. Hotels are also being built in the lower part of town, known as Avenida Juan Bohón, before it crosses the Panamericana.

Museums
- Museo Arqueológico, the corner of Cordovez and Cienfuegos. A good collection of Diaguita artifacts and pottery and also items from the El Molle period. The library has 15 000 books on archeology and history, and extensive collections on the Huen-telauquen and the primitive hunting and gathering Anzuelo de Concha cultures. Open Tues–Sat 0900–1300 and 1600–1900. Small admission charge. Interesting.
- Museo Mineralógico "Ignacio Domeyko", Anfión Muñoz. There are over 2000 mineral samples on display. Open Mon–Fri 0930–1230.
- Museo Colonial de Arte Religioso, Balmaceda 640. Many pictures from the Cuzco and Quito School of the 17th century.
- Museo Histórico y Pinacoteca, Matta 495. This was the home of Gabriel González Videla, one of the most outstanding Presidents of Chile from 1946 to 1952. The exhibition includes docu-

ments relating to the city's history. Open Tues– Sat 0900–1300 and 1600–1900; Sun from 0900–1300.

Churches

- Iglesia Catedral, a *monumento nacional*, Los Carrera opposite Plaza de Armas. Built in 1844 by Frenchman Jean Herbage.
- Iglesia San Francisco, Balmaceda 640, a *monumento nacional*. The sacristy of this church was built in 1627. There is also a Museo de Arte Colonial with a collection of ecclesiastical art.
- Iglesia San Agustín, corner of Cienfuegos and Cantournet. The sacristy has a barrel vault made of stone, the only one in Chile.
- Iglesia Santo Domingo, Cordovez 235. This mid-18th century church has sculptures at the front representing the seasons.
- Iglesia Nuestra Señora María Magdalena de La Merced, Balmaceda. This church was burnt by the English pirate Sharpe in 1680 when he sacked the town; rebuilding commenced in 1683 and was completed in 1709.
- Iglesia Santa Inez, corner of Matta with Almagro, a *monumento nacional*. Made of adobe, this is possibly the oldest church in La Serena, going back to the foundation of the town. In its present form it dates back to 1819.
- Iglesia de San Juan de Dios, on the corner of Balmaceda and San Juan de Dios Pení, was formerly the chapel of the hospital. It was built in 1842.

⊕ Excursions

Tour operators
- **Viajes Val**, A. Prat 540 ℂ 226404, fax 224927. Car rental, money exchange
- **Giratour**, Arturo Prat 689 ℂ 223535, fax 225742

Tours
- **Parque Nacional Fray Jorge** and **Termas de Socos**: Day trip, leaving at 0800 and returning 1800, lunch at Hotel Termas de Socos included. Fare $12.50 per person; minimum four. See the entry for Parque Nacional Fray Jorge on page 214.
- **Valle de Limari** including the town of **Ovalle**. Day trip leaving at 0800 and returning 1800. Visit the Monumento Nacional Valle del Encanto where there are rock paintings and archeological sites. Continue up the **Río Grande** valley past **Embalse La Paloma** and **Monte Patria**. Lunch at **Palqui** (included in price) on the shores of the lake. Return via **Sotaqui**, with short visit to an old church. Fare $12.50 per person; minimum four. See also the entry for Ovalle on page 207.

Excursions
The beaches north of the mouth of the Río Elqui are Cruz Grande, Temblador, Totoralillo Norte, **Caleta Hornos**, Punta Teatino and **Caleta San Pedro**. The easiest way to reach them is from Calle Los Choros. These beaches are good for rock fishing and spear-fishing. There is Camping Aky-Payi in the suburb of Los Pescadores.

West of the town, beaches extend for 7 km along the Avenida del Mar. Go 6 km south and halfway to Coquimbo to get to the seaside resort of **Peñuelas**, where there are drive-in movies, casino-hotels, restaurants and the racecourse Club Hípico. See the entry for Peñuelas on page 215.

- **Mirador Cerro Grande**: 13 km east. From the summit (520 m) there are views over the Bahía de Coquimbo and the Valle de Río Elqui. The best access is from the Panamericana, by taking the eastern turnoff at Cuatro Esquinas. You can go hang gliding from its slopes.
- **Valle de Elqui**: Starting in La Serena in Calle Colo-Colo, which becomes Ruta 45, you pass La Florida Aerodrome. At KM 34 you pass through **El Molle**, a typical picturesque north Chilean village. At KM 49 the turnoff to **Observatorio Astronómico Cerro Tololo**, a fully functional observatory. **Vicuña** is at KM 62, the birthplace of Gabriella Mistral — see the entry for Vicuña on page 227. At KM 69, just outside Vicuña, is **Peralillo** the home of the Industria Pisco Capel, a famous *bodega* or winery, open for *pisco* tasting. At KM 83 you can turn off south to **Paihuano** on a dirt road, which leads further south to Pisco Elqui another famous *bodega*. At

KM 96 is **Chapilca**, known for its traditional weaving industry.

- **Coquimbo** and **La Herradura**: Regular municipal buses go from Avenida Francisco de Aguirre in La Serena to Aldunate in Coquimbo. Buses go along Panamericana and on the outskirts of Coquimbo, and turn into Avenida Juan Ríos. The seaside resort of La Herradura which also has hotels and restaurants is 2 km south of Coquimbo on the Panamericana and it has a 2 km long beach with calm, warm water all year round. This is also a retreat for the rich as you will see by the many private villas. See the entries for Coquimbo (page 172) and La Herradura (page 185).

- **Playa Chungungo:** Located on a small bay 73 km north. The nearest town is La Higuera, 19 km east. This is for campers who want to enjoy an unspoilt beach without the usual noise of a large beach resort. There are no facilities, but water is available. To reach it you need your own transport. At La Higuera there are shops and a small restaurant. Linea 41 and Ruta Elqui run buses from La Serena daily; fare $1.90.

Day trips

- **Pisco Elqui**: If you want to stay longer in this beautiful, mountainous area, accommodation is available in Vicuña and Pisco Elqui. All the water coming down from the high *sierra* is used to irrigate the vineyards. There are daily buses from La Serena to Pisco Elqui. See the entry for Pisco Elqui on page 220.

- **Tongoy**: 58 km south: Buses Liserco run buses to Tongoy; the trip to Tongoy takes about 1½ hours, including waiting time for connection in Coquimbo. Taxi Colectivos Sol y Mar departing from Coquimbo takes 1 hour. This trip takes you to some major seaside resorts south of La Serena. There are many regular bus services between Tongoy, Guanaqueros, and Coquimbo, and also to Ovalle. See the entry for Tongoy on page 223.

Observatories

From La Serena you can reach three observatories, but you must obtain permission in La Serena and you will need your own transport to reach them.

- **Observatorio Astronómico Cerro Tololo**: The closest to La Serena, 95 km — see the trip to Valle Elqui above. You can get information from Colina El Pino in La Serena (225415. Visiting hours are Saturdays 0900–1600.

- **Observatorio Astronómico Cerro La Silla**: 150 km north-east at an altitude of 2440 m. It belongs to the European Union. The turnoff from the Panamericana is 18 km south of **Domeyko** in Región III de Atacama, although the observatory itself is in Región IV de Coquimbo. The turnoff is clearly signposted. For information and permission to visit call (224527 in La Serena. For transport, inquire at the bus terminal (225387. The observatory is only open for visits on the first Saturday of each month.

- **Observatorio Astronómico Cerro Las Campanas**: 145 km north-east of la Serena at an altitude of 2510 m. This is geographically the least accessible observatory. Information and permission to visit may be obtained at Colina El Pino, La Serna (224680, fax 227817. Office hours are Mon–Fri 0830–1730.

Los Vilos

Area code: 053
Population: 10 000
Altitude: Sea level
Distances

- From Santiago: 229 km north on Panamericana
- From La Serena: 250 km south on Panamericana

Los Vilos is a small seaside resort and fishing village situated on the **Bahía de Conchalí** which became a port for shipping minerals and agricultural products to and from the inland in 1855.

The town is 2 km off the Panamericana, and it retains its character with the local fishermen continuing their traditional lifestyle. There are several hotels of all grades, many good restaurants and a couple of well-frequented discos.

Los Vilos is one of the most attractive seaside resorts in Región IV de Coquimbo. It is easy to reach from Santiago via the Panamericana and along the coast linking La Serena with Valparaíso with excellent roads. The beaches in and around Los Vilos are the reason for its popularity. The major beaches, with fine white sand, are just north of town and extend to the mouth of the Río Conchalí.

The main beaches are:

- Playa Principal: Adjacent to the town. Swimming, fishing, water sports, camping, kiosks, life-savers.
- Playa Amarilla: 4 km north of Los Vilos merging with Playa Principal. Swimming, water sports.
- Playa Conchalí: 6 km north east of Los Vilos. Swimming, fishing, water sports.

Six kilometers north on the beach near **Caleta Nagué** is a camping ground. There are also lagoons near the mouth of the Río Conchalí.

There is a picturesque fishing wharf, with an excellent seafood restaurant. Seafood is ample and excellent. West of the fishing pier a rocky area starts. The many small rocky islands offshore are inhabited by birds and seals. The rocks surround the promontory and continue south.

Tourists can hire boats and visit nearby little islands such as **Isla de los Lobos** with its large seal colony and **Isla de Huevos** (this means "Island of Eggs" and is so named because of the many birds nesting there) to go rock fishing or fishing from the beach.

Here at Los Vilos the coastal *cordillera* reaches right down to the sea. The Panamericana cuts across the small peninsula on which Los Vilos stands. Because of the moisture, the high mountain slopes have some vegetation and to a lesser extent there are also shrubs and cacti; CONAF has an experimental tree plantation here, and can point to its success in greening the slopes and foreshores.

According to legend, the English pirate "Lord Willow" was shipwrecked on this coast. He liked the place and decided to stay. In time more people settled and "Willow" became "Los Vilos".

In colonial times bands of highway robbers used to hold up the horse-drawn coaches and buggies passing between La Serena and Santiago. Their hideaway was a cave called Cueva del Negro, situated 7 km south of town in the rocks coming down to the sea. They used to rob and kill the passengers and attendants, and according to legend, most of the booty is still hidden around Los Vilos.

Los Vilos comes to life from the end of December to the end of February. Using Los Vilos as a base, you can make excursions inland to **Illapel** and **Salamanca**. There are regular buses to the interior and the road is sealed as far as Salamanca. A

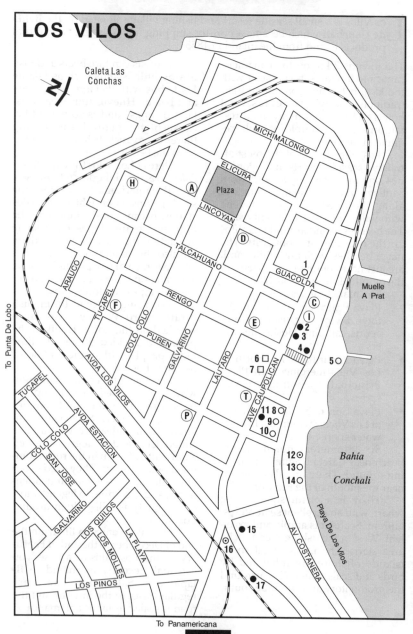

Coquimbo

Key to map

A	Iglesia parroquial
C	Municipalidad (Town hall)
D	Post office and telex
E	Telephone
F	Carabineros (Police)
H	Hospital
I	Tourist information
P	Gas stations
T	Bus terminals

● Accommodation

2	Motel El Pelusa
3	Residencial Turismo Drake
4	Hotel Bellavista
11	Residencial Angelica
15	Residencial La Escala
17	Hostería Lord Willow

○ Eating out

1	Salón de Té Di Carloti
5	Restaurant La Caleta
8	Restaurant Rincón Marino
9	Restaurant Internacional
10	Restaurant Costanera
13	Restaurant Millahué
14	Restaurant Carmencita

◉ Entertainment

12	Disco Las Brisas
16	Disco La Terraza

□ Services

6	Supermercado El Pelusa
7	Telex Chile

further 30 km south is the new high-class beach resort of **Pichidangui**, which has many private weekend homes and a few fairly expensive hotels.

The mean annual temperature is 19°C (66°F), and the water is 18°C (64°F) in summer.

Festivals
• June 29: San Pedro

Tourist information
There is a tourist information kiosk on the Panamericana on the triangle at the entrance to town.
• Municipal tourist information, Avenida Caupolicán, next to the *Municipalidad*

Eating out

Restaurants
• Bellavista, up the stairs from Avenida Costanera $Y. Excellent views over the bay
• La Caleta, opposite fish market near fishing harbor $Y. Seafood
• El Faro I, Colipi 242
• El Faro II, Tegualda 111
• Terraza II, Caupolicán 768

Salón de Té
• Di Carloti, Guacolda 110

Eating out on Panamericana Norte

Restaurants
• Casapiedra, KM 224
• De Turismo Los Vilos Ltda, KM 224 (in the COPEC gas station). Seafood. Long-distance buses from Santiago to Antofagasta and Arica make a meal break here, and you may be able to buy a seat here by talking to the drivers
• Hostería Shell, KM 224
• Los Arbolitos, KM 224
• Sajonia, KM 215 $Y. International cuisine

Entertainment

Discos
• Costanera, Purén 80 corner of Avenida Costanera, Bajada Playa los Vilos. Seafood. Dining room upstairs with vistas over the sea; disco floor above
• Las Brisas, Avenida Costanera East. Seafood and grill; dancing weekends
• Terraza I, Avenida Los Vilos 020, upstairs. Seafood and grill; dancing weekends

Post and telegraph

Post office
• Correo, Lincoyán near Galvarino

Telephone
• CTC, Caupolicán 498
• Telex Chile, Caupolicán 686

🛏 Accommodation in Los Vilos

Hotel
- Bellavista, Rengo 020   AFJLPS   ☎ 541196/541073 $I 👥
  Views over the bay

Hostería
- Lord Willow, Hostería Lor 1444   AEFGHIJLP$UX   ☎ 541037 $H 👥

Motels
- Corsario Drake, Avenida. Los Vilos 1665
     AHS $I 👥
- El Conquistador, Avenida Caupolicán 210
     AEHLPS   ☎ 541040 $I 👥
- El Pelusa, Caupolicán 411, opposite calle Talcahuano
     ABCDEHIKLPS   ☎ 541041 $G 👥
- Hardy's, Avenida Uno Norte 248   ADEHIJKLNPTU   ☎ 541098 $G 👥
  Beach frontage,
- New Pacific, Tres Oriente   AHILP   ☎ 541077 $I 👥

Residenciales
- Angelica, Caupolicán 627
- La Escalera, Los Vilos near Caupolicán $J 👥
  Vistas over beach and bay, budget travelers
- Lemus, Caupolicán 333   AFIJL
- Las Rejas, Caupolicán 1331
- Turismo formerly Drake, Caupolicán 437 $I 👥

Accommodation on the Panamericana

Motels
- American, KM 224   ADFHIKLPU   ☎ 541020 $G 👥
- Choapa, Avenida Caupolicán near Panamericana
     ADEHILP$U   ☎ 541093 $H 👥
- El Arrayán, Caupolicán 1 near Panamericana
     ADEFGHILP$U   ☎ 541005 $H 👥
- Santa Emilia, Caupolicán 1877 on Panamericana
     ADFHLP   ☎ 541036
- Residencial Calamiña, next to Motel Santa Emilia on Panamericana
  Backpackers

🗒 Services and facilities

Supermarket
- Supermercado El Pelusa, Caupolicán 578

🚌 Motoring
For gas stations, see city map.

🛍 Shopping
Carvings made from *guayacán* wood (a very hard timber) are available in souvenir shops.

⛹ Sport
Wind surfing, fishing, and scuba diving.

📍 Excursions
A short distance south is the Quebrada and Cueva del Negro, and Cueva del Quintrala and Piedra del Indio.
Near **Las Vacas** further inland on a dirt road there is a goldmine.
- **Quebrada de Querero**: 3 km south. In prehistoric times, this was a lagoon, and remains of prehistoric animals and some archeological finds have been found here. There is a small iso-

🚌 Buses from Los Vilos

Bus companies
Most long-distance buses do not enter Los Vilos. All buses entering town have their own offices on Caupolicán.
* A25   Buses Combarbalá-Rima, Caupolicán
* A28   Buses Dhino
* A35   Buses Géminis
* A37   Buses Golondrina II
* A41   Buses La Canela
* A44   Buses La Porteña, Caupolicán block 700
* A45   Buses Libac
* A77   Buses TAL/Los Diamantes de Elqui, Caupolicán block 700
* A78   Buses Tramaca
* A110 Flecha Norte/Flecha Dorada
* A112 Flota Barrios
* A115 Buses Lasval, Caupolicán 766
* A137 TAS Choapa, Caupolicán 712 ℡ 541032
* A163 Buses Intercomunal, Caupolicán Block 700

Services

Destination	Fare	Services	Duration	Companies
Antofagasta	$27.20	4 services daily	14 hrs	A35, A110, A112
Calama	$32.60	8 services daily		A78, A110, A112
Caldera	$12.50	5 services daily		A115, A137
Chañaral	$16.70	6 services daily		A110, A115
Combarbalá	$3.60	3 services daily		A25, A28, A115
Concón				A44
Copiapó	$11.60	4 services daily		A115, A137
Coquimbo	$8.40	12 services daily	3 hrs	A45, A115, A137
Diego de Almagro	$13.70	2 services Mon, Wed–Fri, Sun		A115
Illapel		5 services daily	1 hr	A41, A115, A163
Iquique	$33.40	1 service daily		A110
La Serena	$6.30	14 services daily	4 hrs	A45, A115, A137
Los Andes	$6.30			A137
Ovalle	$7.50	7 services daily		A110, A115, A137
Pichidangui		1 service daily		A37
Potrerillos	$15.80	2 services daily		A115
Quilimarí		1 service daily		A37
Salamanca	$2.80	6 services daily	2 hrs	A115, A163
San Felipe		4 services daily		A44
Santiago	$5.80	8 services daily		A25, A77, A115, A137
Tongoy		3 services daily		A137
Vallenar	$9.20	4 services daily		A115, A137
Valparaíso	$3.70	9 services daily		A28, A44, A163
Viña del Mar	$3.70	4 services daily		A44, A163

lated beach (Playa de Quereo) here, but without any facilities. The road continues further south to a vantage point for Isla de los Lobos, where there is a substantial seal colony.

- **Mincha**: 49 km north in a very fertile part of the **Río Choapa** valley. The village dates back to pre-Hispanic times. The turnoff east from the Panamericana is 1 km north of Hacienda Huentelauquen, and from here it is 12 km to the village. Most of the river's water is used to irrigate the vineyards which line the road. Mincha Norte is located on the north bank of the river, overlooking the wide valley below. This part of the valley was settled very early by Spaniards, the first church being built in 1668 and rebuilt in 1763, and now declared a monumento nacional. The green valley contrasts sharply with the bare mountains. Rural buses run regularly from Los Vilos.

MONTEGRANDE

Altitude: 1000 m
Distance from La Serena: 102 km east on Ruta D-485 and RN 41

Montegrande is located in the upper **Río Elqui** valley at the junction with the **Río Cochiguas** valley. Nobel laureate Gabriela Mistral grew up in Montegrande, and she is buried here.

Accommodation
- Posada del Peregrino **FHP**
- Cabañas El Albaricoque

Buses from Montegrande
- La Serena: Fare $2.30; 3 services daily; duration 2 hrs; Frontera Elqui
- Vicuña: $1.50; 3 services daily; duration ³⁄₄ hr; Frontera Elqui

Sightseeing
- Museo Casa Escuela. Formerly a post office and school and now a monumento nacional. Gabriela Mistral spent part of her childhood here, and memorabilia are on exhibit. Mistral's tomb is nearby. There is more information on Mistral in the introduction to this Travel Comapnion. Open Tues–Sun from 0930–1300 and from 1500–1900. Admission free.

Excursions
- **Río Cochiguas** valley: At El Colorado, further up this valley, there is a camping spot, and also a Buddhist colony. For mountain hikes in the area use Instituto Geográfico Militar maps 1:50 000 "Pisco Elqui" and "Sierra Cochiguas".

OVALLE

Area code: 53
Population: 55 000
Altitude: 200 m
Distance from La Serena: 88 km south on RN 43

Ovalle, founded in 1831, is the capital of the province of Limari. It is the center of an agricultural and wine-growing district. The extensive irrigation has made it a green oasis at the expense of the water which reaches the sea. This is olive grove country.

Part of Ovalle is on a low plateau, and the rest is in the alluvial plain inside the wide **Río Limari** valley, just 5 km west of the junction of **Río Grande** and **Río Hurtado** where they become the Río Limari. The junction is at a narrow gorge.

The Río Limari valley is crossed by two rivers: Río Ingenio and Río Limari. Until the two rivers meet west of Ovalle, they are separated by a low mountain ridge. To the north, the terrain is quite steep on the Río El Ingenio side, but on the southern side of the valley the mountain slopes are more gradual, reaching 1000 m. A long irrigation canal starts at Embalse La Paloma and runs along the southern slopes.

For those wishing to explore untouched Chile, especially mountain hikers, Ovalle makes an excellent base — see "Excursions" below.

The main points of interest for tourists are the Plaza de Armas, the wide boulevard formed by Aristía Oriente and Aristía Poniente separated by a wide park between them, the Museo Arqueológico, and views from Avenida Errázuriz over the town, the valley and the nearby mountains.

With its good tourist facilities and good public transport into the surrounding district, the town makes a good base for visiting the upper Río Hurtado valley, the Valle Encantado with its archeological sites, the Catholic shrine at **Andacollo**, and of course the huge Embalse La Paloma.

The Río El Ingenio (on the inland route north to La Serena) is heavily polluted by a mine which spills its effluent into the river a couple of kilometers north of the town, virtually dyeing the water green.

Most rivers to the east and south of the region have been dammed in their upper reaches for electricity generation and irrigation. As well as Embalse La Paloma (with 750 million cubic meters of water), there are two other dams: **Embalse Recoleta** and **Embalse Cogoti**. Even though tourist facilities have not yet been established, these lakes attract many tourists.

The small township of **Monte Patria** has some interesting old colonial homesteads and some restaurants.

The hinterland and river valleys were settled by Diaguitas long before the arrival of the Spaniards, but there are several modern townships such as **La Chimba** (5 km south), **Sotaqui** (9 km east n the Río Grande valley), and **Guamalata** (5 km north in the Río Hurtado valley) which were originally Incan *mitimaes* settlements.

Termas de Socos

Termas de Socos, 24 km east on RN 45, has a thermal spa and an excellent hotel. There is also a camping ground with cabins, which has a separate thermal swimming pool. The spa is located 2 km east of the Panamerican near the junction with RN 45; the turnoff is well signposted.

The area is very flat and like an oasis. You can see the Andes in the east, and the coastal *cordillera*, here called **Altos de Talinay**, to the west. It is a relaxing place, and a good spot to spend a day or two to use as a base for excursions to the nearby Parque Nacional Fray Jorge or to the Monumento Nacional Valle del Encanto with its prehistoric rock paintings.

The thermal water is 28°C (82°F), and is open all year round. Its

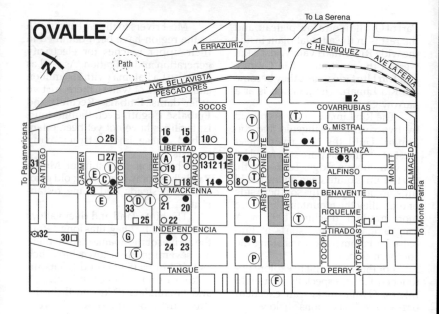

OVALLE

To La Serena

To Panamericana

To Monte Patria

Key to map

A	Iglesia parroquial (Parish church)
C	Municipalidad (Town hall)
D	Post office and telex
E	Telephone
F	Carabineros (Police)
G	Mercado Municipal (Market)
I	Tourist information
P	Gas stations
T	Bus terminals

● Accommodation

3	Hotel Quisco
4	Hotel Castillo Azul
5	Hotel Pucará
6	Residencial Benavente
7	Hotel Piamonte
9	Residencial. Londres
10	Hotel Roxi
11	Hotel Buenos Aires
14	Hotel American
15	Hotel Francesa
16	Hotel Venecia
20	Hotel Gran Ovalle
24	Residencial. Lolita

28	Hotel Turismo

○ Eating out

8	Restaurant Yum-Yum
13	Restaurant Rancho Criollo
17	Club Arabe
19	Restaurant Comercial
21	Cafetería Oásis
22	Restaurant El Encuentro
29	Club Social
31	Restaurant Alamar
32	Restaurant Palmeiras
33	Restaurant Toupet

■ Sights

2	Old railroad station
25	Museo Arqueológico
30	Iglesia

□ Services

1	Supermercado 2001
12	Automóvil Club
18	Foto Ichmann
23	Lavaseco
27	Precious stones

properties are said to help many conditions including respiratory disorders, nervous conditions, rheumatism, skin problems, heart disease, digestive disorders, arthritis, diabetes, neuralgia, asthma, neuritis, and obesity, and to assist in convalescence.

🕮 Festivals
• April 22: Foundation day celebrations

Festivals in Monte Patria
Monte Patria is 38 km east.
• July 16: Virgen del Carmen

Festivals in Palqui
Palqui is 47 km east.
• August 15: El Tránsito

🛏 Accommodation in Ovalle

Hotels

★Gran Hotel Ovalle, Vicuña Mackenna 210, upstairs	AEILPS	☎ 621084	$H	♨♨
Shared bathroom $I ♨♨				
• American, Vicuña Mackenna 169	AFGHIJLPU	☎ 620722	$H	♨♨
Fax 670722				
• Buenos Aires, Libertad 136, upstairs	AFGIJL		$J	♨♨
Shared bathroom; backpackers				
• El Castillo Azul, Maestranza 66				
• Francia, Libertad 231	AFIJL	☎ 620828	$J	♨♨
Shared bathroom; backpackers				
• Piamonte, Libertad 60				
• Pukará, Benavente 50				
• Roxy, Libertad 155	AFGIJKLPS	☎ 620080	$H/I	♨♨
• Turismo Ovalle, Victoria 295	ADFGIJKLPS	☎ 620159	$G	♨♨
• Quisco, Maestranza 161	ADFGILP	☎ 620351	$I	♨♨
Shared bathroom $J ♨♨				
• Venecia, Libertad 261	AEIJLP	☎ 620968	$I	♨♨
Shared bathroom $J ♨♨				

Residenciales
• Alfaro Hidalgo, Independencia 274 ☎ 622477
  Restaurant, budget travelers
• Benavente, Benavente 32
  Small restaurant, backpackers
• Días Cortés, Socos 22 ☎ 624157
• Lolita, Independencia 274
• Londres, Independencia 60

Accommodation in Termas de Socos

★★ Hotel Termas de Socos, 2 km off Panamerica at KM 368
AFGHIJKLPR
$E ♨♨ full board, $F ♨♨ full board in lower section. Five cabins $G ♨♨. Meal $X. Reservations in Ovalle: ☎ 621 373. Attached to the hotel are 40 camp sites with electricity, water, toilets, hot showers, laundry, tent hire, thermal swimming pool; those staying at the camping ground may use the facilities at the hotel (restaurant, hydro-massage, etc.). Camping is open all year round; fees per tent $H for up to 5 persons

Festivals in Rapel
Rapel is 64 km east.
• August 1: Virgen del Carmen

Festivals in Sotaqui
Sotaqui is a village 9 km south-east.
• January 6: El Niño Diós, a religious festival with colorful groups of dancers, attracts a large crowd. Pilgrims start to arrive from the first Sunday in January

ⓘ Tourist information

• Sernatur information kiosk, Miguel Aguirre on the main Plaza
• CONAF, Vicuña Mackenna 627

ⓘ Eating out

Restaurants
• A La Mar, Santiago 259
☞ • Casa Grande VIP, Avenida Romeral 285. International cuisine
• Club Social Arabe, Arauco 261
☞ • Club Social Ovalle, V. Mackenna 498
• Comercial, Aguirre next to church opposite plaza
• El Encuentro, Miguel Aguirre 155. *Parrillada*
• Nuevo Rancho Criollo, Libertad 116. *Parrillada*
• Oásis, V. Mackenna 290
☞ • Palmeiras, Independencia 606. Dancing weekends
• Toupet, V.Mackenna 382
☞ • Yum Yum, V. Mackenna 21

ⓨ Entertainment

Discos
• Vip, Avenida Romeral

🕮 Post and telegraph

Post office
• Correos de Chile, Vicuña Mackenna 350 on main Plaza

Telephone
• CTC, Miguel Aguirre 256, fax 621658
• ENTEL Chile, Vicuña Mackenna 210
• Telex Chile, Vicuña Mackenna 283

🖳 Services and facilities

Dry cleaners
• El Palacio del Limpiado, Arauco 318

Pharmacy
• Farmacia Peñaflor, Vicuña Mackenna block 0 near Coquimbo

Photographic supplies
• Foto Ichmann, Vicuña Mackenna, AGFA fast film development

Supermarket
• Supermercado 2001, Antofagasta block 400 near Riquelme

🚗 Motoring

• Automóvil Club de Chile, Libertad 144 ℂ 620011
• Ovalle Rent a Car, Victoria 362, oficina 3, ℂ 624192
• Shell Service Station, Aristía Poniente corner of Tangue

🏦 Shopping

The main shopping street is V. Mackenna, between Aristía Poniente and Carmen.
• Central market, Independencia block 400 corner of Victoria
• Fería Modelo, Benavente block 400 near Caupolicán

🖾 Sightseeing

The best views over the town are from Avenida Bellavista, climbing a path from Avenida Errízuriz.
• Museo del Limari, Independencia 339. Admission $0.50. Within its three rooms, it displays a very comprehensive exhibit on the Diaguita period and an excellent overview of other pre-Hispanic cultures which flourished in the Ovalle region. Its director, Don Rodrigo Irribaren, is an authority on the history and archeology of the region, so be sure to visit this museum if you are interested in history and archeology.
• Old railroad station, Covarrubias opposite Maestranza, a *monumento nacional*.

⊕ Excursions

Excursions west towards the Panamericana
• **Monumento Nacional Valle del Encanto**: 21 km west on the Panamericana to Termas de Socos. Take an early bus and ask the driver to let you off at the turnoff to the archeological site. Valle del Encanto is a semi-arid area strewn with boulders on which suc-

🚌 Buses from Ovalle

There is no central bus terminal. Most long-distance bus companies are located on either side of Aristía (Aristía Poniente and Aristía Oriente).
Rural buses leave from the following locations:
* Some have joint offices with long distance companies on both sides of Aristía (Aristía Poniente and Aristía Oriente)
* Buses to the coast (Tongoy, Panamericana, Cerillos de Tamaya, Termas de Socos) leave from Tangue corner Victoria (behind the market)
* Some rural buses depart from Coquimbo corner of Tangue
* Rural buses into the *cordillera* (Hurtado, Samo Alto) leave from Benavente outside the former rail yard
* The following bus companies are located on Aristía Oriente: Incabus, San Carlos, Empresa Rima, Empresa López (**A50**)

Companies
* A17 Buses Bugueño
* A35 Buses Géminis, Aristía Poniente 245 ☎ 620430
* A39 Buses Juan Flores
* A42 Buses Carmelita, Aristía Poniente block 300 near Vicuña Mackenna
* A45 Buses Libac, Aristía Poniente 217 ☎ 620570
* A56 Buses Norte
* A77 Buses TAL/Diamantes de Elqui, Aristía Oriente 324 ☎ 621371
* A78 Tramaca, Aristía Poniente 351 ☎ 620656
* A83 Buses Zambrano, Aristía Poniente 245 ☎ 620430
* A89 Colectivos El Palqui, Ovalle–Monte Patria, Antofagasta 319
* A91 Colectivos Ovalle–Monte Patria, Benavente 102
* A101 Empresa Ossandón, Aristía Poniente 245 ☎ 620430
* A110 Flecha Dorada, Aristía Poniente 143 ☎ 62115
* A112 Flota Barrios, Aristía Poniente 217 ☎ 620578
* A115 Buses Lasval, Aristía Oriente 398 ☎ 620886
* A121 Los Conquistadores, Aristía Poniente 141 ☎ 620040
* A133 Secovalle
* A136 Colectivos TACSO, Ovalle–La Serena, Aristía Poniente 245 ☎ 620430
* A137 TAS Choapa, Aristía Poniente 371 ☎ 620500
* A149 Transporte Algarrobo, Aristía Oriente 324 ☎ 621371

Services

Destination	Fare	Services	Duration	Companies
Andacollo	$3.00	4 services daily	2 hrs	
Antofagasta	$20.90	10 services daily		A35, A42, A78, A83, A110, A112
Arica	$37.60	1 service daily		A83
Calama	$25.00	12 services daily		A35, A45, A78, A110 A112
Caldera	$10.50	8 services daily		A110, A115, A128
Carén	$1.80	3 services daily		A56
Chañaral	$12.50	10 services daily		A42, A83, A110, A112, A115
Chuquicamata	$18.00	2 services daily		A35, A45, A112
Combarbalá	$3.00	4 services daily		A50, A115,
Via Punitaqui	$3.70	2 services daily		A50
Copiapó	$11.60	17 services daily		A42, A83, A78, A110, A112, A128, A137
Coquimbo	$1.80	8 services daily		A42, A110, A115,
El Salvador	$13.40	5 services daily		A110, A115
Guanaqueros		2 services daily		A101
Hurtado	$2.10	1 service daily		

Buses from Ovalle — continued

Destination	Fare	Services	Duration	Companies
• Illapel	$5.00	2 services daily		A35, A115
• Iquique	$31.40	3 services daily		A42, A83, A110
• La Calera	$9.60	3 services daily		A110, A115
• Las Breas	$3.30	1 service daily		
• La Serena	$2.10	26 services daily	1 hr	A42, A77, A110, A112, A115, A128, A133, A136,
• Los Vilos	$7.50	7 services daily		A110, A115, A137
• Monte Patria	$1.80			A56, A89, A137
• Potrerillos	$15.10	3 services daily		A110, A115
• Quilpué		2 services daily		A110
• Salamanca		1 service Mon, Wed, Fri		A115
• Santiago	$10.50	12 services daily		A77, A78, A110, A115, A121, A128, A137, A149
• Tocopilla	$25.00	6 services daily		A110, A112
• Tongoy	$2.30	4 services daily		A17, A101
• Tulahuén		4 services daily		A39, A56
• Vallenar	$6.00	5 services daily		A42, A83, A110
• Valparaíso	$10.50	9 services daily		A83, A110, A115
• Viña del Mar	$10.50	9 services daily		A83, A110, A115

Buses from Termas de Socos

Regular public buses run along the Panamericana and to Ovalle. Ask the driver to set you down at the turnoff to the the Termas. The bus stop for Santiago and La Serena is near KM 368.

cessive pre-Hispanic cultures have left rock paintings. The older ones, dating from about 2000 BC, are almost obliterated. The most recognizable ones are from the El Molle to Diaguita period. The Punitaqui valley was settled by early aboriginal tribes, and the many rock paintings encountered there make it an area of archeological interest. There is a camping spot but no shade. The area is administered by CONAF, and there is a small admission fee.

• **Termas de Socos**: 15 km further on from Monumento Nacional Valle del Encanto. There is an excellent hotel and thermal spas here. Situated 2 km off Panamericana, it makes a useful stopover for excursions to Parque Nacional Fray Jorge.

• **Parque Nacional Fray Jorge**: The entrance is 47 km west of Ovalle. Its main attraction is the unusual (for this latitude) dense growth of bushes and trees due to the *camanchaca* effect of the rising moisture-laden clouds from the

Pacific. There is public transport (most of it in the morning) north to Tongoy. Ask the driver to let you off at the turnoff to the national park 2 km north of the *carabineros* check point. From there it is a 20 km hike to the sea shore. Best reached with a tour operator, or arrange transport with CONAF personnel. See the entry for the park on page 214 .

Excursion north-east

• **Río Hurtado valley**: This is a 150 km return trip with the option to return to La Serena via Vicuña. This is rural Chile at its best, with views of the snow-capped Andean *cordillera* the further up you go in the valley. From Ovalle a road leads up the Río Hurtado valley. Regular rural buses ply between Ovalle right up to **Las Breas** where the road ends. On the way you pass **Embalse Recoleta**, altitude 400 m, which is only 15 km east on Ruta D-595, and was created by damming the Río Hurtado. There are two camping spots on this lake and it is popular as a weekend water sports destination. Beneath the waters of the lake is the site of one of the oldest Franciscan monasteries in Región IV de Coquimbo. The road continues uphill, going east. If you would like to visit **Monumento Natural Pichasca**, 1370 m, ask the driver to set you down at the turnoff to San Pedro (between the villages of Pinar and Pichasca). The villagers will direct you to the site. The large pieces of petrified wood are the main attraction at the Monumento Natural Pichasca. Many of the paleontologic objects found here are in the Museo Arqueológico in Ovalle. **Hurtado**, with a small *pensión*, is in the *pre-Cordillera*; it is the starting point for many excursions into the high *sierra*. Experienced mountain hikers would be able to climb across the **Altos del Pangue**, first into the upper **Valle Alcohuas**, and continue into the Valle de Río Elqui. The mountain trails start from **El Bosque** and **Chañar**. Check with locals if you decide to hike. Once a week a bus goes across **Portezuelo Tres Cruces** to Vicuña — it's a splendid but rough trip, passing crystal-clear mountain streams and a hot spring. This is a mountain pass, and the climb starts almost as soon as you leave Hurtado. Once you have reached the pass near **Alto Tres Cruces**, there are splendid views down into the Río Hurtado valley and the Andean peaks.

Excursion north to La Serena via Andacollo

• **La Serena** via **Andacollo**: There is a fast 86 km road link to La Serena on RN 43 with regular public buses. Instead of going directly to La Serena you can make a detour to visit the major Catholic shrine at Andacollo, 87 km northeast. The turnoff from RN 43 is at Higueritas 22 km north of town. From here the road climbs a sheer seemingly endless mountain road full of hairpin bends. The road is being upgraded. Along the roadside you can see mines still being worked. Andacollo is on a small plateau at about 1200 m. There is no accommodation in Andacollo. There is a regular bus service from Ovalle. See also the entries for La Serena (page 187) and Andacollo (page 168).

Excursion south-east up the Río Grande valley

• **Sotaqui**: 10 km east on Ruta D-55. There are daily regular buses to and from Ovalle. The road continues up the Río Grande valley passing Embalse La Paloma to **Tulahuén**, **Los Molles** and **Las Ramadas**. At **Monte Patria** the road forks: east to **Carén** and Central Los Molles **and south to** Chañar Alto **and** Combarbalá.

Excursion south along the former Inca trail

• **Punitaqui**: 32 km south on Ruta D-605 at an altitude of 700 m. During the colonial period Punitaqui was first an important gold mining center, and at the end of the 18th century mercury was mined here — one mine still produces quicksilver. It is in a narrow valley dominated by a pointed mountain peak to the south. Because it is still an important mining center, the road north to Ovalle is sealed. In pre-Hispanic times a branch of the Inca trail came through this settlement. Interesting for those who wish to see a rarely visited part of Chile. The valleys to the south are very dry. Empresa López runs regular bus services from Ovalle and Combarbalá.

PARQUE NACIONAL
FRAY JORGE

Altitude: Sea level to 710 m
Distances:
• From Ovalle: 72 km west on Panamericana and RN 45.

- From La Serena: 98 km south on Panamericana;
Admission: $2.00

The national park covers 10 000 ha (24 000 acres). This national park is interesting because the coastal *sierra* — here called Altos de Talinay — is high enough to condense the water from the clouds, so that here you will find dense vegetation of the type generally only encountered in the south near Valdivia. Here in the *camanchaca* conditions even ferns grow profusely in the moist air. On fine days you can see beyond the park and you will notice the contrast with the semi-arid savannah around it. The Río Limari has wedged its way through the Altos de Talinay creating a deep gorge.

Set in the **Altos de Talinay** with the **Río Limari** forming its southern border, the park is best reached from Ovalle. The best time to visit is between August and October when the winter rains have finished and the park is in full bloom.

From the turnoff on the Panamericana, you travel through open savannah with isolated shrubs and cacti, and the vegetation becomes denser as you get closer to the coastal range. There is no public transport from Ovalle to the park. The CONAF administration center is on a side road. Although there is no accommodation inside the park, camping is possible in the picnic area with water, toilets and barbecue area. A walking track and a small bridge over a little gorge has been constructed by CONAF, which takes about an hour to walk. Along this track are signs naming and describing all the tree and shrub species represented; some of them are in danger of extinction outside the park. The wildlife consists mostly of birds but also of foxes and the odd wild cat. With your own transport, you can reach Fray Jorge from Ovalle in two hours; from the turnoff at the Panamericana it is a 20 km dirt track which peters out near the picnic area but a path continues to the beach.

There is also a spot with pre-Columbian rock paintings.

The first owners of the area were the Franciscan monks, who used the timber for their convents. The wood was used to build part of the belfry of the San Francisco church in La Serena. The national park was closed for 20 years to give nature a chance to recuperate from the damage that had been done before it was declared a national park, and to give scientists a chance to measure the damaging effects of human occupation.

ⓘ Tourist information
- CONAF in La Serena — see "Tourist information" in La Serena on page 190.

⊟ Accommodation
The nearest accommodation is at Termas de Socos, 17 km south-east of the turnoff to the park. A short stay there in the thermal spa is time well spent. See under "Accommodation" in Ovalle on page 209.

⊟ Buses
Buses from La Serena or Coquimbo south to Santiago pass the turnoff to Parque Nacional Fray Jorge. Ask the bus conductor to set you down at the intersection. Public transport runs from Ovalle to Tongoy, the best time being early in the morning. From the turnoff it is an 18 km hike to Punta Talinay — a four-hour walk. Bring your own supply of water, sunglasses and sun cream. CONAF in La Serena will arrange transport for paying visitors in their own four-wheel drive vehicles.

PEÑUELAS

Altitude: Sea level
Distance from La Serena: 8 km south on Avenida del Mar.

Peñuelas is 6 km north of Coquimbo on the south side of the bay and is one of the most popular seaside resorts in Región IV de Coquimbo. It has many high-class hotels and good restaurants and there are also discos and a casino. The main beach is 300 m wide with fine sand and stretches for several kilometers right up to La Serena; it is well protected and the water is warm, with no rough seas. There are life-guards on all beaches.

⊗ Festivals

- Fería Internacional del Norte, January

⑪ Eating out

Restaurants

- El Bosque (in the Shell service station), Panamericana Norte. Seafood

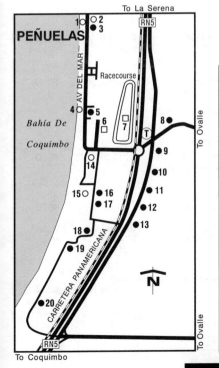

Key to map

● **Accommodation**

3	Motel Canto del Agua
5	Complejo Turístico Jardín del Mar I.
8	Cabañas Maroal
9	Motel Niko's
10	Motel Capilla del Mar
11	Hostal Casa de Piedra
12	Cabañas El Frutillar
13	Cabañas Lonquimay
16	Motel Los Refugios
17	Cabañas Antares
18	Complejo Turístico Peñuelas
20	Hotel Tahiti Beach

○ **Eating out**

1	Restaurant Vakulic
2	Restaurant Velamar
4	Restaurant Paladino
14	Restaurant Los Pescadores
15	Restaurant Kamanga

⊙ **Entertainment**

6	Casino de Peñulas
7	Club Hípico de Peñuelas

⊟ Accommodation in Peñuelas
The main season is from middle of December to the end of February. After February prices fall considerably and you can bargain.

Apart hotels
- Los Jardines de Peñuelas, Avenida Los Jardines 300   ℂ 242935
  Fax 244843
- Peñuelas, Avenida Los Pescadores 5050   ℂ 244237 $H ⁚⁚
  Fax 244237

Cabañas
- Agua Dulce, Panamericana KM 467   BTU   ℂ 245212
- Lonquimay, Panamericana KM 467   ℂ 244295
  Fax 244295
- Montemar, Cruce Peñuelas a las Parcelas   ℂ 245684

Complejos turísticos
- Antares, Avenida Los Pescadores 4655   ℂ 243753
  Fax 245207
- Jardín del Mar I, Avenida Costanera 5425
     ABCDFGHIJKLMNPR   ℂ 242835 $F ⁚⁚
  Fax 242991. Pool room, sauna, squash, 35 cabins for 4 $C
- Tahiti Beach, Avenida Costanera 2501   ℂ 314421 $D for 4
  Fax 315221

Motels
- Cabinas de Peñuelas, directly on beach
     ABCDHIKLP$ ℂ 313860 $H ⁚⁚
- Los Refugios, Avenida Los Pescadores 4727   ℂ 242771 $E for 4
  Fax 245691
- Playa Casino, Peñuelas Norte 118, near Casino
     ABCDH   ℂ 242967 $G ⁚⁚
  $F cabins 4–6 persons. Reservations in Coquimbo

Accommodation along the Panamericana

Motels
- ★★★ Niko's Motel, KM 466   ABCDHIJKLP   ℂ 242912 $H ⁚⁚
- Capilla del Mar, KM 466, Vegas Sur   ABCDEHIKLNP$TUZ   ℂ 242820 $G ⁚⁚
  Radio, beach, car rental, cabins for 4 $G, weekends dearer

Hostal
- Cabañas de Turismo El Frutillar, Avenida Miramar, KM 465
     ABCDHIKLPS $G ⁚⁚
  Reservations in Coquimbo: ℂ 312369/315335
- Cabañas de Turismo Maroal, corner of Panamericana and Peñuelas, Parcela 24 Vegas
  Sur   ABCDHNP   ℂ 243083 $G for 4
- Casa de Piedra, KM 466   ℂ 241893
  Club house

Accommodation on the Panamericana south of La Herradura
- Apart Hotel Las Tacas, KM 445   ℂ 399100 $C ⁚⁚
  Fax 399133
- Cabañas de Panul, KM 455   ℂ 326051
- Cabañas Morrillos, KM 432   ℂ 397132
  Fax 397140

- Grill Pub Kon Tiki, Avenida Costanera 5685
- Los Pescadores, near Avenida Costanera
- Paladino, Avenida del Mar. International cuisine
- Vakulic, Avenida Costanera, Chicken
- Velamar, Avenida del Mar $Y. International cuisine
- Il Passo, Panamericana Norte. Chicken

Ⓨ **Entertainment**
- Casino Municipal de Coquimbo 〖 212003. International cuisine

🚌 **Buses**

Colectivos operating all day long between Coquimbo and La Serena will set you down at the intersection of the Panamericana and the Calle Peñuelas. From there it is a short walk to the beach, passing on the right the casino and the racecourse.

🏊 **Sport**

Swimming, sunbathing, surfing and sailing. The racecourse is on the Panamericana.

PICHIDANGUI

Altitude: Sea level
Distances
- From La Serena: 284 km south on Panamericana
- From Santiago: 200 km north on Panamericana

Built on a rocky promontory 30 km south of Los Vilos, Pichidangui is an exclusive seaside resort where many wealthy people have their summer residences. It is about 4 km off the Panamericana, with two access roads into the small township; one is just south of the Río Quilimarí bridge. There are plenty of hotels, restaurants and entertainment, and the yacht club has a marina and restaurant. But the main attraction is the fine white sandy beach which stretches northwards for 7 km — Playa Principal. The mountains come close to the shore, but they are no higher than 1500 m near the town.

The mean summer temperature is 19°C (66°F), and the water is 18°C (64°F) in summer. The bay is very attractive, with a few islands just across from the fishing harbor, of which the largest is Isla Locos.

Inland from Pichidangui is the **Valle de Quilimarí**, where you will pass numerous picturesque little villages as you go along the road which meanders gently uphill. Local fruit and weaving are the main produce in this area.

🍴 **Eating out**

There are good seafood restaurants offering generous helpings of *paila marina,* a sort of bouillabaisse.
- Fogón de Don Luis, 2 Poniente
- El Buzo, 2 Poniente 17
- La Curva, Avenida Costanera

Eating out along the Panamericana Norte
- Servicio Pichidangui, Panamericana Norte KM 195

Ⓨ **Entertainment**
- Disco Carolina, on the beach
- Disco L Red, Esquife

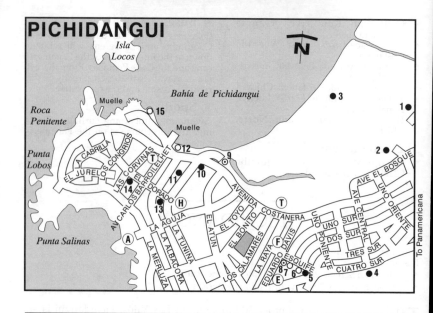

PICHIDANGUI

Isla Locos

Bahía de Pichidangui

Roca Penitente

Punta Lobos

Punta Salinas

To Panamericana

Key to map

A	Iglesia
C	Municipalidad (Town hall)
D	Post office and telex
E	Telephone
H	Hospital
T	Bus terminals

● Accommodation

1	Cabañas del Bosque
2	Cabañas Bahía Marina
3	Camping El Bosque
4	Motel Pichidangui
5	Hostería Puquén
10	Motel Antulauquen
11	Cabañas La Tunina
13	Hotel Lucero
14	Hotel La Rosa Náutica

○ Eating out

6	Restaurant El Buzo
7	Restaurant El Rincón
12	Restaurant (seafood)
15	Club de Yates

◉ Entertainment

8	Disco La Red
9	Disco Carolina

Post and telegraph

Post office
• Correo, Los Calamares

Motoring
• COPEC gas station at the entrance to town on Panamericana intersection

Sightseeing
Visit the church built overlooking the rocky seaside on the south side of town. The beach extends north towards the mouth of the Río Quilimari; marine erosion has caused the huge grotto you can see at the northern end.

Excursions
About 5 km south over a rough stretch of sea you can see **Isla de los Lobos**, so called

Plate 13 Región V de Valparaíso
Top: Paso de Bermejo, mountain pass over the Andes to Argentina
Bottom: Portillo, ski resort

Plate 14
Map of Región V de Valparaíso & Región Metropolitana

⊟ Accommodation in Pichidangui

Hosterías
- Puquén, Dos Poniente   **AFHL**   ☎ (09)33113830

Hotels
- La Rosa Náutica, El Dorado   ☎ 541182
- Lucero, Albacora   **AFGHIJLNPS** $G/H▮▮
  Full board included

Motels
- Antulauquen, Avenida Costanera   **ABCDEFGHIJLMNPU** $F ▮▮
  View over bay,
- Cabañas del Bosque, off Avenida El Bosque near beginning of town
      AFGHIJKLNP   ☎ 541182
- Cabañas y Camping Bahía Marina, located directly on beach
      ABCHILN   ☎ 541006 $F for 4
  60 camping sites $I for 3. Open all year round, hot and cold showers, electricity, laundry, toilet block, kiosk, tennis court, camping sites are in eucalyptus forest
- Cabañas del Sol, Avenida Santa Inés, entrance to Pichidangui
      ABHIJKLNPS   ☎ 541182 $F ▮▮
  Tennis courts. $E cabins for 4
- Pichidangui, Francis Drake   **ACDEFGHIJKLMNPRTU** ☎ 541006 $E ▮▮
  Radio, 20 cabins. Sea water is pumped up 700 m from the sea into the swimming pool
- Tunina, La Tunina 4   ☎ 541661

⊟ Buses from Pichidangui

There is a *colectivo* bus service between Pichidangui and Quilimari. Long-distance services stop on highway, from there by taxi into town.

Bus companies
Not all buses make the detour into town, but usually there are taxis waiting just near the gas station at the entrance to town. The following buses come into the village:
- A5   Intercomunal
- A44   La Porteña
- A76   Bus TACC Via Choapa Avenida Costanera opposite Los Calamares
- A77   Buses Los Diamantes de Elqui, Avenida Costanera
- A118   La Golondrina II
- A137   TAS Choapa

Services

Destination	Fare	Services	Companies
Illapel	$2.30		A76
La Calera	$1.90		A44
Los Vilos		1 service daily Mon–Sat	A118
Santiago	$4.60	5 services daily	A77, A137
Valparaíso	$2.80		A5, A44

because of its colony of about 1400 seals. The island is separated by a 200 m channel, but you can see the animals from a rock protruding into the sea.

With your own transport you can make a trip 103 km inland up the Río Quilimari valley to **Tilama**; and from there north to **Caimanes** and the Estero Cavilolén valley back to the coast to Los Vilos (Rutas D-875, D-37-E, and D-865), or continue further north on Ruta D-37-E to **Salamanca** and **Illapel**, to return to the coast via **Mincha**. This adds a further 114 km to the trip. This trip gives you an opportunity to travel over part of the old colonial (and pre-Hispanic) inland route and see unspoilt places like Angostura, Marmalican and **Embalse Culimo** (where there is a camping ground) and Tilama. This valley is intensively used for agriculture and there is also some mining activity.

The village of **Quilimarí**, just off the Panamericana, has a long weaving tradition that reaches back to pre-Hispanic times.

At **Guangali**, 12 km up the Quilimari valley, is an established pottery industry. At **Los Condores** there is a small private museum with ceramics and pieces of rocks with rock drawings from the **Quebrada Infiernillos**, an archeological site near El Sifón. A further 28 km up the valley, the Río Quilimari has been dammed to form the Embalse Culimo. You can camp on its banks and also fish for *pejerreyes* and trout. There is a large quartz mine at Tilama, at the junction of Ruta D-875 with the north–south Ruta D-37-E. Tilama is on the old pre-Hispanic inland route which the Incas used to penetrate the inland, as did the Spaniards later during their conquest.

PISCO ELQUI

Area code: LD 108
Altitude: 1200 m
Distance from La Serena: 104 km west on Ruta D-485 and RN 41

In the upper Valle de Río Elqui, Pisco Elqui is the center of *pisco* production around La Serena. It has a pleasant climate, and is the starting point for excursions into the high *sierra*.

◩ Accommodation

- Hostería Don Juan, Arturo Prat AHIP
  Hotel Carillón Elqui, Arturo Prat
- Hotel Elqui, O'Higgins

◩ Buses

- La Serena: Fare $2.30; 3 services; duration 2½ hrs; Frontera Elqui

◉ Excursions

Pisco Elqui is a good starting point for hikes further up in the **Río Claro** valley, where you will find picturesque villages such as **Horcón**. Mountain hikers can hike from **Alcohuas** into the **Río Hurtado** valley, and return via Ovalle to the coast. If you are doing this trip, use Instituto Geográfico Militar 1:50000 map "Sierra Cochiguas". Stay overnight at Refugio El Chañar, and follow the trail up **Quebrada El Chañar**, which brings you through Quebrada Elqui into the Río Hurtado valley. Only for experienced mountain hikers, this trip is very rewarding with its many mountain streams and high altitude *lagunas*.

SALAMANCA

Area code: 053
Population: 10 000
Altitude: 450 m
Distance from Illapel: 32 km south east on Ruta D-81

At the junction of **Río Chalinga** with **Río Choapa** is Salamanca, founded in 1843. As well as being steeped in the *huaso* ("cowboy") tradition, this town is also renowned for producing high quality fruit, much of which is exported. Witchcraft was still practised in this part of Chile until the early part of this century — the Cueva de Manquehua in the nearby Río Chalinga valley was a meeting point for the local witches and warlocks (*curanderos*). Chalinga itself was a former Incan *mitimaes* settlement.

⊗ Festivals

Festivals in El Tambo
El Tambo is 5 km downriver. Do not confuse it with El Tambo in the Río Elqui valley.
- February, second or third Sunday: La Inmaculata. Six dancers participate
- August 15: El Tránsito

⊟ Accommodation

- Hostería Galvez, Pérez 540 **AFHJP** ℂ 551017 $H ♈
- Hotel Choapa, Bruno Larrain 311 $J ♈. Shared bathroom, hot water when requested, backpackers
- Hotel Bogorin, Etcheverría 440 **P** ℂ 551016 $I ♈. Shared bathroom $J ♈
- Residencial O'Higgins, O'Higgins 430 ℂ 108 $J ♈. Backpackers

⒯ Eating out

Restaurants
- D'Carlo, Monte Pío on Plaza
- Choapa, Bruno Larrain 311
- El Tropezón, Bulnes 540
- Hostería Galvez, Pérez 540 $Y
- Malacún, Monte Pío 241
- Salamanca, Etcheverría 340 corner of O'Higgins. Here rural bus drivers congregate; the bus stop is just outside

⒯ Entertainment

- Disco Embrujo Inn, corner of Ruiz Valledor and Bulnes

⒤ Post and telegraph

Post office
- Correos de Chile, Bulnes on Plaza

Telephone
- CTC, Pérez 598
- Telex Chile, Matilde Salamanca 320

⊜ Motoring

Gas stations
- COPEC, Monte Pio near plaza
- COPEC, Etcheverría on plaza
- Sunoco, O'Higgins block 300 corner of Bruno Larrain

⚑ Excursions

- **Chalinga:** 5 km north. Originally an Incan *mitimaes* settlement, it was mainly inhabited by an Indian population until the late 18th century. The church dates from the middle of the 18th century. Further up the valley, near **San Agustín**, are some very old *estancias*. This is a very fertile valley in the *pre-Cordillera*. There are many clear mountain streams coming down from the high *sierra*, full of trout for fishing enthusiasts. Rural buses run from Salamanca to San Agustín in the upper Río Chalinga valley each evening. There is no accommodation, so bring your tent if you intend to hike or fish further upstream.
- **Cuncumen:** This is a trip east into the upper Río Choapa valley. Roads follow the **Río Choapa** on either side of the river: Ruta D-835 on the north

🚌 Buses from Salamanca

There is no central bus terminal. Most interregional bus companies have their office on the Plaza. Rural buses leave from Etcheverria corner of O'Higgins at 1700.

The buses on the southern side of Río Choapa go to Tranquila via Queñe, Panguecillo, Quelén and Coirón.

All rural buses leave for the interior valleys at 1700 from their depots, and make a stop on the main plaza to pick up more passengers. By this time the bus is often already full, and you may have to stand.

Companies

Taxis to El Tambo (where there is a camping ground) depart from Bulnes block 500 near Etcheverria

- A5   Bus Intercomunal, Central Plaza near O'Higgins block 500
- A34 Buses Galvez, Etcheverria 440
- A35 Géminis, Monte Pío 421C ℂ 551278
- A69 Buses Rodríguez, Central Plaza near O'Higgins block 500
- A76 Buses Tacc Vía Choapa, Monte Pio on Central plaza
- A115 Lasval, M. Salamanca 9 ℂ 551063
- Rural bus to Quelén–Coirón, Etcheverria corner of O'Higgins
- Rural bus to Panguecillo, Etcheverria corner of O'Higgins

Services

Destination	Fare	Services	Duration	Companies
Antofagasta	$26.30	1 service Tues, Fri		A35
Calama	$28.40	1 service Tues, Fri, Sun		A35
Chañaral	$17.60	2 services per week		A35, A115
Chuquicamata	$28.40	3 services per week		A35
Copiapó	$15.40			A35
Coquimbo	$9.60	1 service daily		A35, A115
Cuncumen		1 service daily		A69
El Salvador	$13.90			A115
Illapel	$0.90		1 hr	A5, A76
La Calera		3 services daily		A5, A76
La Serena	$9.60	3 services daily		A35, A76, A115
Los Vilos	$2.80	6 services daily	2 hrs	A5, A76, A115
Maria Elena	$28.40			A35
Ovalle		1 service Mon, Wed, Fri		A115
Pedro de Valdivia	$28.40	1 service per week		A35
Quillota		3 services daily		A5
Quilpué		3 services daily		A5
Santiago	$9.60	8 services daily		A76, A115
Vallenar	$14.60	2 services per week		A35
Valparaíso	$9.60	4 services daily		A5
Villa Alemania		3 services daily		A5
Viña del Mar	$9.60	4 services daily		A5

bank and Ruta D-863 on the south bank. There are separate rural bus routes on both sides of the river, as once you pass Salamanca the bridges across the Río Choapa are not suitable for vehicular traffic. This is vineyard country, and grapes are grown far up into the **Río Cuncumen valley** (also known as **Río de los Pelambres valley**). Most of the water coming down from the mountains finds its way into irrigation channels. This 44 km trip takes two hours on daily rural buses. The Cuncumen area is the domain of the sport fisherman and mountain hiker. Cuncumen (altitude 1000 m) is in a valley where the Río Cuncumen meets the Río Choapa. The mountains around Cuncumen are between 2600 m on the north side (**Monte Colorado**) 3173 m (**Cerro Los Mineros**) on the south side and 3600 m (**Cerro Cebollar**) to the east. The Andes near **Laguna del Pelado** (on the Argentine border) reach an average height of 4400 m.

- **Río Choapa valley:** You can take an interesting trip up the valley by bus, going to the hanging bridge at KM 39 (7 km past **Llimpo** and crossing to the village of Coirón and returning to Salamanca via **Quelén** and **Panguecillo**. Rural buses further up the Río Choapa valley go along both sides of the river to Cuncumen on the one hand and Tranquila on the other,

because the hanging bridges upriver are not suitable for cars or buses. A very interesting trip would be from Salamanca to **Santa Rosa**, **Chellepin**, and Cuncumen in the shade of **Cerro Tencadan** (3530 m). The upper Río Choapa valley is densely populated, and with the irrigation channels through the hills even the slopes are used for agriculture — rather like the terraced fields in Peru where rock walls support the soil. Another 25 km further on, there is an impressive hanging bridge to **Coirón**. From Coirón it is a further 24 km to the source of the Río Choapa near **Tranquila**. Regular rural buses only as far as Coirón and once a week to Tranquila. Fishing and hiking are the main attractions here. The area around **Cerro Jorquera** (3743 m) could be an interesting hiking area.

TONGOY

Area code: 051
Altitude: Sea level
Distance from La Serena: 57 km south on Panamericana Norte

Just 14 km south of Guanaqueros, Tongoy is a tourist center built on a small peninsula jutting out from the mainland. Tongoy extends from the **Cordón Lengua de Vaca** to the Bahía de Tongoy, dividng the beach into two sections — the 4 km long Playa Socos and the 14 km long Playa Grande.

From a hill on the peninsula there are impressive views of the extensive beaches, particularly to the south along **Bahía Tongoy** and west to **Punta Lengua de Vaca** ("Cow Tongue Point").

With an average temperature of 18°C (64°F) almost throughout the year, the local climate attracts a great many tourists. Both the beaches have fine white sand leading gradually into the water, which is fairly calm and warm. Local tourist facilities include hotels, motels, restaurants and discos, and the main recreational activities are sailing, swimming, fish-

ing, and diving. Daily regular buses go there from Coquimbo and Ovalle running more frequently in summer.

The excellent seafood restaurants here have oysters as a main dish, with crabs and prawns of all sizes on the daily menu. There is camping, kiosks, and life-guards.

About 14 km south of the Playa Grande, are the little fishing villages of **Tangue** and **Puerto Aldea**. The water there is warm and most of time there is a breeze coming in from the sea. At Tangue there are some small *algorrobo* forests. There are exceptionally large sand dunes, often formed in unusual shapes because of the strong waves and the wide open arc of the bay.

Playa Socos comes to an abrupt end where the rocky coastline starts ☞ called **Cerro Guanaqueros**. In the middle of the hills is a small and sheltered beach called Playa Blanca with a camping ground which is open most of the year. This beach is accessible from the Panamericana on a 15 km dirt road.

There are many tours you can take from Tongoy; there are plenty of bus services to and from Coquimbo, as well as buses going south to Ovalle and Santiago. The most popular tourist destinations to the south are **Parque Nacional Fray Jorge**, **Termas de Socos**, and Ovalle, while Coquimbo and La Serena to the north are suitable for excursions.

⚑ Eating out

Tongoy is famous for its seafood (lobster, prawns, and oysters), and there are many fine seafood restaurants in Calle La Serena at the northern end of Playa Grande. On Playa Socos there are a few bar restaurants, access by a bridge near the mouth of Estero Tongoy.

Restaurants
- Costa Azul, Fundición Sur 072
- El Buque, Playa Grande 17. Seafood
- Hostería Tongoy, Avenida Costanera Humberto Galvez 10 $X
- Hotel Yachting Club, Avenida Costanera Humberto Galvez 20 $X
- Mercado de Marisco, Playa Grande. Seafood
- Playa Blanca, Playa Blanca

▣ Entertainment
- Disco Donde Horacio, Esmeralda
- Disco CAP

▦ Post and telegraph

Telephone
- CTC, Fundición Sur 046 ☏ 391949

▤ Bus services from Tongoy

Most bus companies have their offices on Fundición Sur near corner of La Serena (next to CTC telephones).

Services
- Coquimbo: Fare $1.70; 6 services daily; Costera, Bugueño, Taxi Colectivos Los Tongoyinos, Sol y Mar
- La Serena: Fare $2.10; irregular services; Taxi Colectivos, Buses Bugueño
- Los Vilos: 3 services daily; Tas Choapa
- Ovalle: Fare $2.30; 3 services daily; Ossandon, Bugueño
- Santiago: Fare $13.40; Diamantes de Elqui

Key to map

A	Iglesia		**9**	Cabañas Tongoy
D	Post office and telex		**11**	Hotel Yatching Club
E	Telephone		**12**	Hostería Tongoy
F	Carabineros (Police)		**13**	Hotel Plaza
H	Hospital		**16**	Residencial Prat
I	Tourist information		**18**	Hotel Arrocet
P	Gas stations		**19**	Hostería La Villa
T	Bus Terminals		**20**	Cabañas Villa Estero
●	**Accommodation**		○	**Eating out**
2	Hostería Talinay		**14**	Seafood Restaurants
3	Hotel Panorámico			
4	Residencial La Bahía		◉	**Entertainment**
5	Hostería Las Pasmanias		**1**	Tennis Courts
6	Apart Hotel El Tambo		**10**	Disco Abracevistux
7	Hotel Alamar		**15**	Disco Cap
8	Hotel Samay		**17**	Disco Donde Horacio

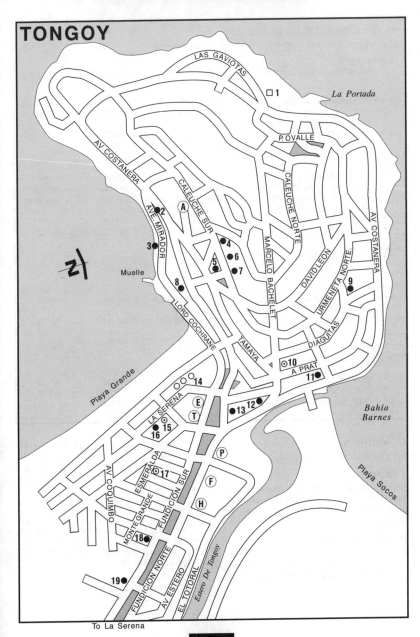

TONGOY

La Portada

P. OVALLE

AV COSTANERA

CALEUCHE SUR

AVE. MIRADOR

CALEUCHE NORTE

MARCELO BACHELET

DAVID LEON

URMENETA NORTE

AV COSTANERA

Muelle

LORD COCHRANE

TAMAYA

DIAGUITAS

Playa Grande

LA SERENA

ESMERALDA

AV COQUIMBO

MONTEGRANDE

FUNDICION SUR

FUNDICION NORTE

AV ESTERO

EL TOTORAL

Estero De Tongoy

Bahía Barnes

Playa Socos

A PRAT

To La Serena

🛌 Accommodation in Tongoy

During January and February bookings are advisable.

Apart hotels
- El Tambo, Urmeneta Sur 55 — ABCHIP$U — ℂ 391202/391132 — $F for 4

Hotels

★★★ Yachting Club de Tongoy, Avenida Costanera 20
  AEFGHIJKLPS — ℂ 391154/391259 — $F 👥
  Located directly on beach
- Agua Marina, Fundición Sur 092 — ℂ 391870
- Alamar, Urmeneta Sur 99 — AEFGHIJLP — ℂ 373444
- Arrocet (formerly R y R Inn), Fundición Sur 160
  AIJP — ℂ 391969
- Cabañas Anakena, Avenida El Totoral 1 — ℂ 391126
- Panorámico, Ave Mirador 455 — AEGIJLPS — ℂ 391944 — $F 👥
  Plaza, Fundición Norte 29 — AEFGHIPS — ℂ 391184 — $H/I 👥
  Shared bathroom
- Samay, Fundicion Norte — AHI — ℂ 391355
- Talinay, Costanera Sur 74 — AEFGHJLPS — ℂ 391122/391253 — $G 👥

Cabañas
- Playa Blanca, Playa de Tongoy — ℂ 391373
- Tongoy, Urmeneta Norte — BCH — ℂ 391902

Hosterías

★★★ La Villa, Fundición Sur 230 — ADEFGHIJLMNP$UX — ℂ 391204 — $F 👥
  Fax 391956. Full board, tennis, sauna, beach, shows
- Las Pasmanias, Urmeneta Sur 94 — AEFGHIJKLMPSU — ℂ 391437 — $H 👥
- Tongoy, Avenida Humberto Galvez 10
  AEFGHIJLPS — ℂ 391203 — $E 👥

Residenciales
- D'Pardo, Fundición Sur 068 — ℂ 391903
- La Bahía, Urmeneta Sur 95 — AFILPS — ℂ 391244 — $I 👥
- Prat, La Serena 573 — AEFILPS — $H 👥
- Punta Arenas, La Serena 455 — ℂ 391214

🚗 Motoring

For gas stations see city map.

⛵ Sport

Besides swimming, fishing and skin diving, there is an active yacht club and also tennis courts. You can hire boats in the harbor.

📷 Sightseeing

- The Costanera Humberto Galvez runs around the whole peninsula, with excellent views across the bay, particularly from the tennis club at the far western end. Many streets around the hill continue up the hill as stairs. Take a stroll up to Parque Silva on the hill, where you can see as far south as Punta Lengua de Vaca, the most southerly point of Bahía Tongoy. Tongoy has many weekend homes built on little streets around the center hill, all with a perfect view over the bay. Once summer ends, most of them are shut down.

VICUÑA

Area code: 051
Population: 8000
Altitude: 600 m
Distance from La Serena: 66 km east on RN 41

Vicuña in the Valle de Río Elqui was founded in 1821, its main claim to fame being that it is the birthplace of Gabriela Mistral, Nobel prize winner in 1945 (see the introduction to this *Travel Companion*). It is a traditional Chilean town, and is a good starting point for excursions in the surrounding district and to the center of *pisco* production. Further up the valley you will find **Chapilca**, known for its good quality tapestries and blankets, and very colorful *artesanías*. Tourist facilities are good. Visit the Museo Gabriela Mistral; also one of the oldest *pisco* plants (Pisco Capel) in Peralillo.

The Valle de Río Elqui has been almost completely cleared of native vegetation to make way for vineyards.

☒ Festivals
- February 22: Anniversary of Vicuña
- April: Birthday of Gabriela Mistral
- May 14: Santa Cruz
- July 30: Virgen del Carmen
- September 3: Virgen del Carmen

Festivals in Chapilco
- May 7: Santa Cruz

Festivals in El Molle
- September 24: Nuestra Señora de la Merced

Festivals in Paihuano
- July 30: Virgen del Carmen

Festivals in Rivadavia
Rivadavia is 18km east, at the junction of Río Elqui and Río Turbio.
- June 13: San Antonio

Festivals in Varillar
- July 23: Virgen del Carmen

ⓘ Tourist information
- Torre Bauer, San Martín on Plaza de Armas, part of the town hall

‼ Eating out

Restaurants
- Club Social Elqui, Gabriela Mistral 404 $Z

- Continental, Gabriella Mistral 516
- Halley, Gabriella Mistral 404 $Z. Garden restaurant
- Hostería de Vicuña, Sargento Aldea 101 $X
- Yo y Soledad, Prat 364
- Pizzería Virgos, Prat corner of chacabuco
- Portal del Sol, Avenida Las Delicias

ⓒ Post and telegraph

Telephone
- CTC, Arturo Prat 378

🚍 Buses
All buses depart from the main Plaza, opposite restaurant Halley.

Bus companies
- A81   Via Elqui
- A114 Frontera Elqui
- A119 Linea 41 Ruta Elqui
- A134 Sol de Elqui

Services
- Hurtado: Fare $3.30; duration 3 hrs; A114
- La Serena: Fare $1.80; 14 services daily; duration 1 hr; A81, A114, A119, A134
- Montegrande: Fare $1.50; duration ¾ hr; A114

🚗 Motoring
- COPEC, Avenida Las Delicias

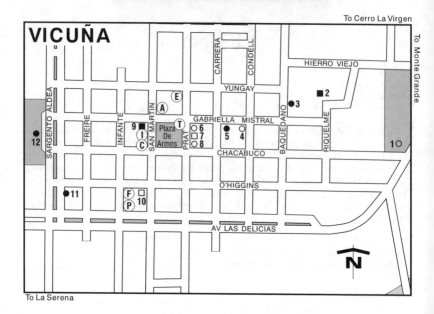

Key to map

A   Iglesia
C   Municipalidad (Town hall)
D   Post office and telex
E   Telephone
F   Carabineros (Police)
I   Tourist information
P   Gas stations
T   Bus terminals

●   **Accommodation**

3   Motel Américo
5   Hotel Yasna
11   Complejo Turístico Yunkay
12   Hostería Vicuña

○   **Eating out**

1   Restaurant Portal del Sol
4   Restaurant Continental
6   Restaurant Halley
8   Pizzería Virgos

■   **Sights**

2   Museo Gabriela Mistral
9   Torre Bauer

□   **Services**

7   Telex Chile
10   CEMA Chile

📷 Sightseeing

- Museo Gabriela Mistral, Calle Gabriela Mistral 749. This museum with photos, manuscripts, and books of the famous writer is built on the site of the house where she was born. She won the Nobel prize for literature in 1945 — see the introduction to this *Travel Companion*.

- Torre Bauer, an oddly shaped tower on one side of the plaza was built in the early 1900 with wood brought from Ulm in Germany.
- Cerro de la Virgen. From the top of the mountain there are panoramic views over the vineyards and the town.

⊟ Accommodation in Vicuña

Hostales
- Michel, Gabriela Mistral 573   AP   ☎ 411060
  Trail bike hire.
- Valle Hermoso, Gabriela Mistral 706

Hosterías
★★★ Hostería De Vicuña, Sargento Aldea 101
         ACDEFGHIJKLNPRS$TUZ $E ♀♂

   Tennis, gaming room, 15 rooms

Hotels
- Yasna, Gabriela Mistral 542   AEFGIJLP   ☎ 411266 $H ♀♂
  $J ♀♂ shared bathroom

Motels
- Américo (formerly Sol del Valle), Gabriela Mistral 741   ☎ 411078

Residenciales
- La Moderna, Gabriela Mistral 718   AFLP $J ♀♂
- Elquina, O'Higgins 65   AS $J   ♀
  Shared bathroom, budget travelers

Complejo Turístico
- Yunkay, Libertador B. O'Higgins 72   AGHM   ☎ 411195 $F ♀♂
  Fax 411593

Accommodation in Rivadavia
Rivadavia is 18km west at the junction of Río Elqui and Río Turbio.
- Hotel Diaz, Libertador B. O'Higgins 48

⊕ Excursions

- **Iglesia de San Isidro**: 2 km north-east. The actual date of construction is unknown, but it must have been early in the colonial period. The floor is made of squares of oak which look like parquetry.
- **Iglesia El Tambo:** 9 km west. One of the oldest churches in the valley and its bells have an unusual chime. As the word "*tambo*" suggests, it was originally a pre-Hispanic settlement. The Fiesta de la Inmaculada is held on the second or third Sunday in February, attracting many of the faithful.
- **Paihuano**: 26 km east, in the Río Cochiguas valley, center of a rich wine-growing area.
- **Cochiguas**: Still further up the valley of the same name — this drive takes you through some beautiful mountain scenery.
- **Pisco Elqui**: 43 km south-east. Center of a famous wine-growing area. There are many well known *bodegas* in and around town such as Pisco Iglesia, Pisco Peralta, Tres RRR and many more. See the entry for Pisco Elqui on page 220.
- **Chapilca**: 32 km east, at the end of the sealed road in the **Río Turbio** valley at 500 m on the road to **Paso del Agua Negra**. The road between Rivadavia and Chapilca passes through some very steep parts of the mountain and the valley is very narrow. At Chapilca the road widens again at the meeting point of the two valleys. From Varillar onwards there is a good dirt road; beyond Chapilca it is mostly mine traffic. The area is known for its rustic weavings and the fabrics are made by traditional methods; everything from spinning and weaving to dyeing is done by the villagers.

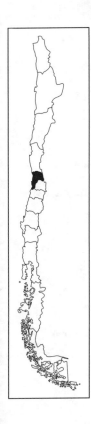

REGIÓN V
DE
VALPARAÍSO

VALPARAÍSO

Size: 16 400 square km (6330 square miles)
Population: 1 250 000
Regional capital: Valparaíso
Provinces and provincial capitals:

- Valparaíso (Valparaíso)
- San Antonio (San Antonio)
- Quillota (Quillota)
- San Felipe de Aconcagua (San Felipe)
- Petorca (La Ligua)

This region has the largest harbors in Chile and great numbers of people live in Valparaíso, Viña del Mar, and San Antonio. Easter Island, situated 3700 km west of the mainland, and the Juan Fernández Archipelago are administered by Valparaíso. Easter Island is famous for its enormous stone figures — it is dealt with in a separate chapter, beginning on page 357. The Juan Fernández Archipelago contains Isla Robinson Crusoe, named for and immortalized in Daniel Defoe's novel of 1719 about a shipwrecked mariner.

Región V de Valparaíso lies between parallels 32° and 34°. It shares its northern border with Región IV de Coquimbo, and its southern border with Región VI del Libertador General Bernardo O'Higgins. Like the rest of Chile, natural borders mark the east and west — the Andes and the Pacific Ocean.

Topography

The Andes reach altitudes of over 5500 m in the region, and the north is traversed by valleys — in particular, those shaped by the **Río Aconcagua**, the **Río Petorca** valley, and the **Río La Ligua**, which run from the high *sierra* to the coast. Some peaks of the coastal *cordillera*, such as **Cerro del**

Región V de Valparaíso

Roble and **Cerro Las Viscachas**, are over 2200 m.

Climate

The climate is generally hot with a dry spell between October and March that affects the whole region. The average annual temperature is 14.6°C (58°F); the average annual rainfall is 350 mm. The northern part, around **Petorca**, is a fairly dry area reminiscent of the areas further north. The coast between Valparaíso and Zapallar is very reminiscent of the French Riviera: a Mediteranean climate, over 20 high-class seaside resorts with casinos and beautiful beaches, scenic roads which run along the coast and over the crests of mountains with views over the sea and the towns along the coast, and an interior road just like the *"corniche"* roads in southern France between Mentone and Toulon — hence my preferred name for this stretch "The Chilean Riviera". It is colder in the high Andean *cordillera*. Parts of the central valley behind the coastal *cordillera* are afflicted by low rainfall.

The indigenous inhabitants

When the Spanish arrived in 1536, they found the indigenous people firmly integrated into the Incan empire. Known pre-Columbian settlements were Catapilco, Puchuncaví, and many more.

European history

One of Valdivia's lieutenants, Capitán Juan de Saavedra, was the first European to set foot in this part of Chile. Valparaíso was founded as the port of Santiago in 1544.

The coastal area was settled very early after Spanish conquest. Many coastal towns and beach resorts originated with *encomiendas* given to the Spanish who arrived with Pedro de Valdivia.

These grew into larger *haciendas* which shipped wheat directly to Peru. During the colonial period, Chile exported huge amounts of grain, and many of the *haciendas* had their own shipyards. From 1820 onwards, Valparaíso, which had attracted a large number of European immigrants, became the dominant port of call and most of the smaller ports fell into disuse.

Economy

A well-balanced climate and effective irrigation, especially in the Río Aconcagua valley, made this region a granary for the newly founded colony. Other crops now harvested include grapes and apricots around Los Andes and San Felipe, and *chirimoyas* (custard-apples) and avocados around **Quillota**. Large areas are devoted to citrus, walnuts, apples, and cherries. In the 19th century, fishing and maritime services were concentrated in Valparaíso. Industry, especially textile and food processing factories, soon developed around Valparaíso because of the density of population and the availability of finance, energy, and natural resources. **Concón**, with its oil refineries, is a minor industrial area. Mining in the region is restricted to copper and kaolin.

Transport

Road

The region is traversed from north to south by the Panamericana (RN 5), and from east to west by the Ruta Internacional (RN 60) which links Valparaíso with Mendoza in Argentina. There is also a well-defined road system along the coast.

Rail

Passenger services run between Valparaíso and Los Andes in the Aconcagua valley. The rail service between Valparaíso and Santiago does not exist any more.

Air

The region has 15 airports. The airport of Torquemada near Concón is earmarked for upgrading to an international airport.

National parks and reserves

- **Reserva Nacional Río Blanco**: 10 175 ha (25 132 acres), a small native forest 32 km east of Los Andes on RN 60 to Mendoza (in Argentina), near the village of Río Blanco, at an altitude of 1350 m. CONAF has logging trails. This reserve is not much visited.
- **Parque Nacional La Campana**: 8000 ha (19 760 acres), the altitude ranges from 200 m to 1800 m. The entrance to the park is east of Olmué — see "Excursions" from Olmué on page 287. Camping sites and trails have been installed by CONAF in many parts. The park can also be reached from both Valparaíso/Viña del Mar and Santiago. The Sector Palmar de Ocoa is located 100 km northwest of Santiago on RN 5 (Panamericana Norte); it contains many palm groves, hence its name "Palmar". See the entry for the park on page 292.
- **Reserva Nacional Lago Peñuelas**: 9094 ha (22 343 acres), on RN 68. The reserve was created to protect the water supply for Valparaíso. The western entrance is 30 km east of Valparaíso and the eastern entrance is 91 km from Santiago. It has a picnic area, excursion paths and a lookout. See "Excursions" from Valparaíso on page 336.
- **Parque Nacional Archipiélago de Juan Fernández**: This island group covers 9290 ha (22 946 acres), and is 650 km west of the mainland. It takes 60 hours by boat and 2 hours by plane from Santiago. It has a picnic area, excursion paths, accommodation nearby, eating places, shops, and a lookout.
- **Monumento Natural Isla de Cachagua**: 4.5 ha (11 acres), an island off the coast of Cachagua, 66 km north of Viña del Mar. This bird sanctuary can be visited in a fisherman's boat from Cachagua.
- **Jardín Botánico Nacional**: 404.5 ha (999 acres), on Ruta F-66, 9 km from Viña del Mar at El Salto. Picnic area, excursion paths, eating places, and shops nearby.
- **Santuario de la Naturaleza Laguna El Peral**: 5 km north of Cartagena on Ruta G-98-F, in the estuary of a small stream, with nesting places of seabirds. It is a very small reserve; the coastal road passes close by.

Beach resorts

Chile's most beautiful beaches are located in Región V de Valparaíso. Many become very crowded in summer, but there are still a few lesser-known ones for those who want peace and quiet. Viña del Mar is the most popular resort, closely followed by Reñaca and Algarrobo. Other well-patronized northern beaches are Concón, Quintero, Maitencillo, Cachagua, Zapallar, Papudo, and Los Molles; favorite southern beaches include Laguna Verde, Algarrobo, El Quisco, El Tabo, Balneario Las Cruces, San Sebastián, and Cartagena.

Trout fishing

The trout fishing season starts on the second Friday in November and ends on the first Sunday in May. Streams and rivers near Los Andes, Portillo, Río Blanco, San Felipe, Limache, and Quilpué may be fished.

Thermal resorts

The thermal resorts of this region are located in the *pre-Cordillera*.

- **Termas de Jahuel**: Altitude 1190 m, water temperature is 22°C (72°F), open all year round. This resort is located about 20 km north of San Felipe in the Río Aconcagua–Santa María valley. See under "Excursions" from San Felipe on page 322.
- **Baños del Corazón**: Altitude 995 m, 21°C (70°F), open all year round. This resort is approximately 10 km north of Los Andes in the Río Aconcagua valley. The peaks of the Andes, rising to 6000 m, loom to the east. There is an excellent thermal hotel with a good restaurant accessible by buses and taxis from Los Andes. See under "Excursions" from Los Andes on page 279.

Distances

From Valparaíso

- Antofagasta: 1320 km north
- Arica: 2016 km north
- Calama: 1528 km north
- Castro: 1335 km south
- Chañaral: 930 km north
- Chillán: 525 km south
- Concepción: 633 km south
- Copiapó: 766 km north
- Coquimbo: 423 km north
- Coihaique: 2320 km south
- Iquique: 1815 km north
- La Serena: 437 km north
- Ovalle: 372 km north
- Puerto Montt: 1167 km
- Punta Arenas: 3345 km south
- Puerto Natales: 3595 km south
- Rancagua: 206 km south
- Santiago: 131 km east
- Talca: 377 km south
- Temuco: 794 km south
- Valdivia: 958 km south
- Vallenar: 622 km north

Festivals and sporting events

The towns in which events are held are listed here by month. For details, see under "Festivals" in the entries for individual towns.

- January: Olmué, Quillota, Reñaca, Rinconada, Santo Domingo, Valparaíso, Viña del Mar
- February: Algarrobo, Cabildo, Cartagena, El Quisco, Laguna Verde, Limache, Llay-Llay, Los Andes, Maitencillo, Papudo, Quillota, Quintero, Santo Domingo, Valparaíso, Viña del Mar
- March: Cabildo, La Ligua, Llay-Llay, Los Andes, Nogales, Putaendo, San Estebán, Viña del Mar
- April: Limache, Llay-Llay, Quilpué, Valparaíso
- May: Isla Robinson Crusoe, La Calera, Limache, Olmué, San Antonio, San Felipe, Valparaíso, Villa Alemana, Viña del Mar

1: Día del Trabajo (Labor Day)
25: Corpus Christi
- June: La Ligua, Petorca
29: San Pedro
- July: Cabildo, Concepción, Hijuelas, La Cruz, La Laguna, Los Andes, Petorca, Puchuncaví
- August: Cabildo, Cartagena, La Cruz, San Felipe
- September: El Quisco, Los Andes
10: San Nicolás de Tolentino
11: Día de la Liberación Nacional
17–19: Rodeo Oficial (or Fiesta Huasa) in Catemu, La Calera, Los Andes, Olmué, Puchuncaví, Putaendo, Quebrada Alvarado, Quillota, Quilpué, San Felipe, and Valparaíso
- October: Calle Larga, Cartagena, Curimón, La Cruz, La Ligua, Llay-Llay, Los Andes, Olmué, Papudo, Petorca, Puchuncaví, Quilpué, Rinconada
12: Día de la Raza, held throughout Chile (and all former Spanish and Portuguese colonies), celebrating a common bond with the Iberian peninsula
- November: El Quisco, Isla Robinson Crusoe, Limache, Papudo, Quillota, Quintero, Santa María, Villa Alemana
1: All Saints' Day
- December: Casablanca, Los Andes, Santa María

Tourism

The region has a summer and a winter season.

Don't miss

☞ Viña del Mar
☞ Portillo
☞ Río Aconcagua valley, between Los Andes and Portillo

Worth a visit

☞ Valparaíso
☞ Chilean Riviera between Valparaíso and Papudo
☞ Parque Nacional La Campana
☞ Baños El Corazón
☞ Termas de Jahuel
☞ Parque Nacional Archipiélago de Juan Fernández

Of interest

☞ Algarrobo
☞ Papudo
☞ Los Andes
☞ Rocas de Santo Domingo

ALGARROBO

Area code: 035
Population: 3200
Altitude: Sea level
Distances
- From Santiago: 141 km west on Ruta F-960-G and RN 68 (via Casablanca)
- From Valparaíso: 80 km south on Ruta F-960-G and RN 68 (via Casablanca)

Algarrobo, where the average summer temperature is 20°C (68°F) and the water 15°C (59°F), is the most attractive and best developed beach resort on the coast south of Valparaíso. It began in the 19th century as a private port for a large *hacienda* nearby. The approach roads are lined with huge eucalyptus trees. The beach slopes gently into calm waters. Houses, built on low hills, blend with the beach scenery. The hinterland is partly forested.

Tourist facilities include many hotels, *residenciales*, and a good selection of seafood restaurants. During the summer holidays, many larger hotels are booked out. All southern beach resorts from Algarrobo to San Antonio are served by regular daily shuttle buses, and there are regular buses to Santiago and Valparaíso.

Aquatic events, including regattas, are organized by the very active Club de Yates ("Yacht Club"). Most of the beaches are within walking distance of the town. Small rocks litter Playa San Pedro. The aptly named Isla Pajaro ("Bird Island") lies south along Avenida Marina, and is connected to the mainland by a short pier; nesting here are flocks of seagulls, comorants, and pelicans.

The best beaches in Algarrobo are:

- Playa Pejerrey: Center of town. Swimming, water sports, kiosks, life-guards.
- Playa Las Cadenas: Within town limits. Swimming, water sports, kiosks, life-guards.
- Playa Los Palos: Northern continuation of Playa Las Cadenas. Swimming, water sports, kiosks, life-guards.
- Playa Laguna: Northern continuation of Playa Los Palos near the estuary of Estero San Jerónimo (which finishes up in a coastal lagoon, hence the name). Swimming, water sports, kiosks, life-guards.
- Playa Grande: Northern continuation of Playa Laguna for 3 km, merging with Playa Mirasol. Swimming, water sports, kiosks, life-guards, showers, toilets.

Festivals
- February, third week: Semana Algarrobina

Tourist information
- Municipalidad, Avenida Peñablanca 250
- COPEC gas station, Avenida Peñablanca corner of Santa Teresita. Sells maps

Camping
There are camping sites on Playa Tunquén and Playa Los Clarines.

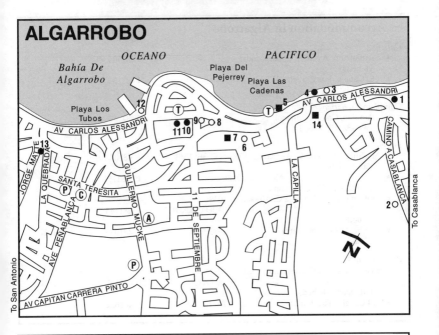

ALGARROBO

Key to map

A	Iglesia
C	Municipalidad (Town hall)
P	Gas stations
T	Bus terminals

● Accommodation
1   Hotel Internacional
4   Residencial Vera
7   Hotel de Pacífico
10 Hotel Uribe
11 Hotel Costa Sur
13 Cabañas El Canelo

○ Eating out
2   Restaurant El Rancho
3   Restaurant Las Tinajas
6   Restaurant Cecconi
8   Restaurant Aberdeen Angus
9   Pizzería La Regata
12 Club de Yates

⊙ Entertainment
5   Centro Cultural

■ Sights
14 Iglesia La Candela

ⅱ Eating out

Restaurants
See also hotels.
- Aberdeen, Avenida C. Alessandri 1955
- Bauhaus Pub, Avenida C. Alessandri
- Cecconi, Avenida C. Alessandri 1870. International cuisine
- El Hoyo, Avenida C. Alessandri 2195
- La Regata, Avenida C. Alessandri 2092. Pizzas
- Los Patitos, Avenida C. Alessandri 278
- Las Tinajas, Avenida C. Alessandri 1345
- Mi Rancho, Road to Casablanca 676
- Pacífico, Avenida C. Alessandri 1930. International cuisine
- Rockola, Avenida C. Alessandri 1915. Jazz sessions in summer

🛏 Accommodation in Algarrobo

Cabañas
- Aquarium, Avenida C. Alessandri   ☏ 481905
  20 beds
- El Canelo, Los Claveles 3535   ☏ 482139
  42 beds

Complejo Turísticos
- Pao Pao, Camino Mirasol,   ☏ 482145
  Fax 482145, 30 beds

Hotels
- Pacífico, Avenida C. Alessandri 1930   AEFGHIJKMR   ☏ 481040
  Fax 481779 sauna
- Costa Sur, Avenida C. Alessandri 2156   ☏ 481151
  Fax (02) 2115294, 45 rooms
- Internacional, Avenida C. Alessandri 1038
       ADEFGHIJKLN   ☏ 481145
  47 beds
- Uribe, Pasaje del Teatro   ADGHILP   ☏ 481035 $H ♟
  27 beds

Residenciales
- ★ Vera, Avenida C. Alessandri 1521
       AEFHJLP   ☏ 481131 $H ♟
  Full board; 46 beds
- El Canelo, Yucatan 11   AEFHLP   ☏ 481622

▣ Entertainment
- Disco Pao-Pao, Camino Mirasol. *Salón de té*

📧 Post and telegraph

Post office
- Correos Avenida Peñablanca 250, inside town hall building

Telephone
- CTC, Edificio Madrid
- Telex, Avenida C. Alessandri 1967

🚌 Buses

Companies
- A103 Empresa Robles, Avenida C. Alessandri 1497
- A127 Pullman Bus, Edificio Madrid, Local 3 ☏ 81105
- B98   Buses Longisur

Services
The local bus companies Asociación de Dueños de Taxibuses San Antonio and Asociación Gremial de Dueños de Buses Litoral Central run services at 20 minutes interval to Cartagena, El Quisco, El Tabo, and San Antonio, with intermediate stops.
- Santiago: Fare $3.30; 18 services daily; duration $2\frac{1}{2}$ hrs; A103, A127, B98
- Valparaíso: Fare $1.50; 14 services daily; A127

🚘 Motoring
For gas stations, see city map.

⚽ Sport

Yacht clubs
- Club de Yates, Avenida C. Alessandri 2447 ☏ 81055
- Club de Yates Cofradía Náutica del Pacífico, Avenida La Marina ☏ 81180

Tennis
- Cancha de Ténis Santa Inez, km 3 Ruta F-960-G
- Cancha de Ténis Torrealba, km 3 Ruta F-960-G

CABILDO

Area code: 33
Population: 10 000
Altitude: 400 m
Distance from Valparaíso: 135 km north-east on Ruta E-35 to Panamericana RN 60

Originally, Incan settlers from Alto Perú were brought to Cabildo to instruct the local population in Incan ways and to establish a garrison and trading post (or *tambo*). The Inca trail through central Chile branched into three here. One track followed the **Río La Ligua** and then wound over the **Cuesta de Melón** to Catapilco on the coast. The second went over the **Portezuelo del Portillo** into the Calingasta valley in San Juan Province in Argentina. The third continued south toward Santiago via the **Cuesta de Chacabuco** and beyond to the Río Maule.

The skyline is dominated by a hill on which the inhabitants built a huge cross.

⊠ Festivals
- February: Semana Cabildana
- March: Aniversary of Cabildo
- July 16: Virgen del Carmen
- August 10: Virgen de San Lorenzo

⊟ Accommodation

Residenciales
- Brimar, Avenida Humeres 940
- Domeyko, Domeyko 106 ℂ 761218
- Santa Teresita, Avenida Humeres 948A, outside town

⊞ Eating out
- Restaurant El Mono, Aníbal Pinto 21

- Restaurant La Rueda, Avenida Humeres 155

⊜ Motoring
There is a COPEC gas station.

⊟ Buses

Companies
- Buses Ligua runs 3 services daily to Santiago; fares $3.00
- Buses la Porteña runs 5 services daily to Cabildo, Chincolco, La Calera, La Cruz, La Ligua, Limache, Los Andes ($2.80), Petorca, Quillota, San Felipe ($2.50), Valparaíso ($2.90), Villa Alemana, and Viña del Mar ($2.80)

⊛ Excursions
- **Alicahué** 30 km east and further up to **Laguna Chepical**. Fishing and hiking.

CACHAGUA

Altitude: Sea level
Distances:
- From Santiago: 183 km north-west
- From Valparaíso: 76 km north on Ruta F-30

Summer homes are tucked into the low hills surrounding Cachagua, an exclusive beach resort with mostly private accommodation and a few restaurants. The average summer temperature is 17°C (63°F) and the water is 14°C (57°F).

The southern end of the beach near the rocky outcrops is used by hang-gliding enthusiasts. This is one of the region's longest northern beaches. **Monumento Natural Isla de Cachagua**, off the foreshore, is a *sanctuario de la naturaleza* for a species of penguin known here as *pájaro niño*. There is a regular bus service to Cachagua from Valparaíso. Swimming, fishing and water sports are all available and the beach has kiosks and life-guards. The main attractions are the beach and the golf club.

Accommodation
- Motel Aguas Claras, Ave. Zapallar 125, Reservation Santiago ((02) 696136; 36 beds

Camping
There is a camping site 2 km south on the coastal road.

Eating out

Restaurants
- Club de Golf Cachagua. Seafood
- Los Coirones, Playa Cachagua. Seafood
- Nato, Avenida Cachagua 296

Post and telegraph

Post office
- Avenida Cachagua near Avenida Del Mar

Telephone
- CTC, Avenida Cachagua near Vicuña

Buses
Sol del Pacífico runs daily services to Papudo and Viña del Mar.

Sport

Golf
- Club de Golf de Cachagua, opposite Fundo Cachagua just outside town

Beach
- Playa Larga extends for 2 km south and joins with Playa Las Agatas

Excursions
- **Quebrada de Aguas Claras**: Take a *colectivo* from Cachagua and alight at Quebrada Claras. The trail starts 3 km south of Cachagua opposite the trail leading down to Camping Bosque de Cachagua. This small coastal canyon is still covered in the dense vegetation that grew in these parts before Europeans arrived. The native trees are very old. The natural scenery is enhanced by a little river which runs through the *quebrada* with clear water for most of the year. The slopes offer splendid views over the coast. This was the main 19th-century route from the coast to **Catapilco** in the central valley, when the area was heavily mined for gold. The once dense forests were cut down to provide timber and firewood for the mines. It is not advisable to enter the old horizontal mine shafts, as they are unsafe.
- **Monumento Natural Isla de Cachagua**: 4.5 ha (11 acres), off the coast of Cachagua. See "National parks and reserves" on page 235.

CAJÓN DEL RÍO ACONCAGUA

Altitude
- Guardia Vieja 1800 m
- Río Blanco 1400 m
- Río Colorado 1200 m

Distances from Los Andes
- Guardia Vieja: 40 km east on RN 60
- Río Blanco: 36 km east on RN 60
- Riecillos: 33 km east on RN 60
- Río Colorado: 19 km east on RN 60

Cajón del Río Aconcagua is the collective name for the upper part of the **Río Aconcagua** and its tributaries from Los Andes right up to the **Complejo Fronterizo Los Libertadores** at the **Paso del Bermejo**. This 69 km-section incorporates the spectacular serpentine windings leading up the pass between **Juncalillo** and Portillo known as **Los Caracoles**. The road over Caracoles rises 660 m over a distance of 10 km. This entry incorporates Guardia Vieja, Riecillo, Río Blanco; and Río Colorado; the skiing resort of **Portillo** is described separately, beginning on page 295.

Guardia Vieja and Riecillos

A *carabineros* post in the narrow upper Río Aconcagua valley, Guardia Vieja is frequented by anglers in summer and skiers in winter. Ski accommodation is much cheaper here than in Portillo, but skiers have to commute to Portillo. The mountains on either side reach a height of over 4000 m.

Río Blanco

The village of Río Blanco is located in the Río Aconcagua valley where the **Río Blanco** descending over 5000 m from the **Sierra Morada** joins the Río Aconcagua.

Río Colorado

A little village, Río Colorado is at the point where the **Río Colorado** and Río Aconcagua meet in the *pre-Cordillera*. This is the gateway to some exciting mountain hikes up the Río Colorado valley into the **Cordón de Tordillo**, following the many mountain trails up the valleys and *quebradas* from Río Colorado.

Ⓐ Camping

There is a camping site in Guardia Vieja.

⊟ Accommodation in Cajón del Río Aconcagua

Accommodation in Guardia Vieja

Hosterías
- Alborada (formerly Cordillera), RN 60, 26 km west of Portillo near Río Blanco
  AEF
- Donde El Guatón, RN 60, KM 38   ADEFGHIKLN
  Reservations in Los Andes: Restaurant Donde El Guatón, Avenida Sarmiento 240 ℂ (34) 423596

Accommodation in Río Blanco and Riecillos
- Hostería Alborada, RN 60 km 180   AEFGHKLPUV
- Hostería La Gringa, KM 18   AFGHIJKLP $H ♗
  14 beds. Reservations in Los Andes: ℂ 421464
- Hostería La Luna, RN 60, 8 km west of Río Blanco, 28 km east of Los Andes
  AEFGHLPRV
  From the hotel it is a short walk to Salto del Soldado, where the Río Aconcagua has cut through a huge rock.
- Hotel Refugio Río Colorado, KM 18   AEFGHIJKPRU $I ♗
  13 rooms. Reservations in Los Andes: ℂ (09) 3316609; 60 beds

Accommodation in Río Colorado
- Hotel Nobile   ADHPR
  45 beds

⟨!⟩ Eating out

Eating out in Guardia Vieja

Restaurants
• Hostería Guardia Vieja

Eating out in Río Blanco
• Restaurant Club de Campo. Swimming pool and golf course open to the public

🚌 Buses

Buses run regularly but infrequently from Los Andes to Guardia Vieja.

🚗 Motoring

There is a COPEC gas station in Río Blanco.

⊛ Sport

Trout fishing in Río Aconcagua, Río Riecillo, and Estero Saladillo.

⚑ Excursions

Excursions from Río Blanco
There is a trout hatchery up the *quebrada* del **Río Blanco**. Further up is **Saladillo**, a mining town belonging to the Sociedad Minera Andina, a subsidiary of CODELCO, the state-owned mining company. If you want to go into the mining compound, you will have to get permission. Beyond the mine, there are thermal waters at **Baños Aguas Saladas**.
• **Reserva Nacional Río Blanco** (10 175 ha (25 132 acres): 32 km east of Los Andes on RN 60 to Mendoza (Argentina), near the village of Río Blanco.

Excursions from Río Colorado
• **Los Chacayes**: 5 km north in the high mountains of the *pre-Cordillera*. You can go on many mountain hikes in the canyons.
• **Los Maitenes**:. Climatic conditions here in this mountainous region have created a forest of the native trees called *maitenes*.
• **Cajón del Río Colorado**: The Río Colorado and its tributary **Río Riecillo** provide a superb area for mountain hikes. The mountains reach 4800 m, and there are many trails leading up into the *sierra*.
• It is possible to scale **Cerro Piedras Negras** (3770 m). A mountain trail leads up the **Río Riecillo** valley toward **Nevado de Leiva** (4680 m) near the Argentine border.

Excursions from Guardia Vieja
• **Salto de La Mona:** Access from El Juncal just before the start of **Los Caracoles.**

Excursions from Riecillo
• **Salto del Soldado:** A remarkable scenic spot where the Río Aconcagua plunges in a waterfall. During the Wars of Independence, a Chilean pursued by a royalist preferred to kill himself by jumping his horse over the cliff rather than being captured.

CARTAGENA

Area code: 035
Population: 9000
Altitude: Sea level
Distances
• From Santiago: 108 km west on RN 78 (sealed)
• From Valparaíso: 103 km south on Ruta F-98-G (sealed), F-90 (gravel), RN 68 (sealed)

Cartagena lies just south of the **Estero Cartagena** where the coastal *cordillera* falls abruptly to the sea. The town, founded early in the 17th century by a Spanish nobleman, is built around the plaza on a fairly steep hill. At first, it served the agricultural hinterland, shipping mostly wheat to Peru.

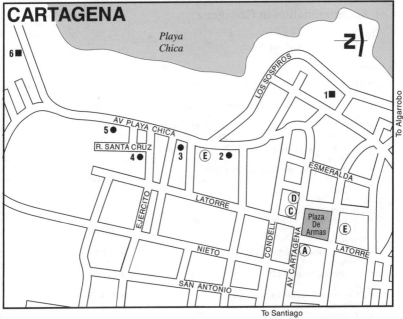

Key to map

A	Iglesia
C	Municipalidad (Town hall)
D	Post office and telex
E	Telephone
●	**Accommodation**
2	Hotel Biarritz
3	Hotel la Bahía
4	Hotel Bellavista
5	Hotel Playa
■	**Sights**
1	Castillo Foster
6	Iglesia Berguesío

Cartagena has retained its 19th-century charm. Some very fancy buildings adorn the coastline; one looks like a castle.

This highly developed seaside resort south of Valparaíso is well frequented in summer and at weekends when the large influx of tourists strains the facilities. These include hotels, restaurants, and a golf course on the outskirts of town. The average summer temperature is 20°C (68°F) and the water is 15°C (59°F).

Playa Grande merges with Playa San Sebastián, within walking distance north of the town center. Cartagena and San Sebastián are only 5 km distant. The beaches offer swimming, fishing, water sports, camping, kiosks, life-guards, showers, and toilets.

⊟ Accommodation in Cartagena

Cabañas
- Julio César, San Martín 58   ℂ 450668

Hotels

★★ Playa, Avenida Playa Chica 98 48 beds	AEFGIJP	ℂ 450370	$G	ⅈⅈ
• Bellavista, Ricardo Santa Cruz 216 68 beds	AEFGJ	ℂ 450369		
• Biarritz, Avenida Playa Chica 196 52 beds	ADEFGHKMP	ℂ 450476		
• La Bahía, Avenida Playa Chica 190 199 beds	ADEFGHIJKMP$T	ℂ 450534/211246	$G	ⅈⅈ
• Reina del Mar, Subida Playa Chica 360 69 beds	AEFGJP	ℂ 450487		

Residenciales

• Aguas Azules, Estado 92	AFGIJP			
• Anita, Tarapacá 219 18 beds		ℂ 450554		
• Aysha, Alcalde Cartagena 11 30 beds		ℂ 211022		
• Carmelita, Serrano 125 27 beds		ℂ 231809		
• Carmona, Avenida La Marina 5 55 beds		ℂ 450485		
• Cartagena, Chacabuco 223 41 beds	AEFGJP			
• Casa Rosada, Chacabuco 340 90 beds	AEFGHJP			
• Condell, Condell 176 20 beds	AEFGJP			
• El Castillo, Chacabuco 82 Beach frontage, 19 rooms	AEFGHIJLP$UV	ℂ 450241	$I	ⅈⅈ
• Europa, Suspiros 147	AEFGHIJ	ℂ 450015		
• La Casa Blanca, Los Suspiros 172 27 beds	AP		$I	ⅈ
• Paty's, Avenida Cartagena 295	P		$H	ⅈ

Accommodation in Lo Abarca
- Complejo Turístico Lo Abarca, on the road to Cartagena
     AEFGHIJLMNPR   ℂ 231475
Also camping; 70 beds
- Ecoturismo Familiar Lo Abarca, Camino Parroquial
30 beds

Accommodation in San Sebastián

Hotels

• La Marina, Uno Oriente On beach		ℂ 231514		
• Riviera, Avenida El Peral 0294 46 beds	AEFGHIJKLM	ℂ 212443	$H	ⅈⅈ

Accommodation in Cartagena — continued

Hosterías
- San Sebastián, Primera Oriente 390   ABCEFGHJLMP   ℓ 233748
  Near beach, open all year

🏃 Festivals
- February, second week: Semana de Cartagena
- August 2: Foundation day
- October: Rodeo Oficial (or Fiesta Huasa)

ℹ️ Tourist information
- Municipalidad, Casanova 268 ℓ 31156
- In summer there is a kiosk on Terraza Playa Chica

⛺ Camping
There are camping sites on Playa Grande and in Lo Abarca, 5 km inland.

🍴 Eating out

Restaurants
- Cholita, Garland 10
- Don Nano, Los Suspiros 570
- El Estribo, Covadonga 137
- La Casona, Avenida Cartagena 502. Chilean cuisine
- Los Copihues, Los Suspiros 600
- San Luis, Los Suspiros 548

Eating out at Playa Grande

Restaurants
- El Tiburón, overlooking the beach

Eating out at Playa Chica
- Morocco, Playa Chica 82
- San Sebastián, Calle Sur Terraza, Local 2-3
- Sol Rojo, Playa Chica 136

Eating out in Lo Abarca
- Quinta de Recreo Colo-Colo. Seafood
- Quinta de Recreo El Sauce, Luis Palomino. Pork dishes

Eating out in San Sebastián

Restaurants
- El Esfuerzo, 1A Oriente 183
- La Piedra, 1A Oriente 205, on the beach
- La Posada, 1A Oriente 147, on the beach

🎭 Entertainment
- Disco Iskra, Avenida El Peral

🚌 Buses
Regular municipal buses run every 20 minutes to Algarrobo and San Antonio.
- Santiago: Fare: $2.50; Buses Longuisur, Empresa Robles, Pullman Bus

🚗 Motoring
- COPEC gas station

Sport
Swimming and surfing.

Excursions
- **Lo Abarca** is a small village about 5 km inland from the coast on the **Estero Cartagena,** which usually only flows in springtime. There is a picturesque plaza surrounded with adobe buildings and an old church. Lo Abarca is best known for its *quintas* or country-style eating places, usually with country dancing, and also for the many old *haciendas* which dot the countryside. The Museo Lo Abarca exhibits implements and ornaments found on a pre-Columbian archeological site and artifacts from the colonial period.
- **Santuario de la Naturaleza Laguna El Peral**: 5 km north on Ruta G-98-F. See "National parks and reserves" on page 235.
- **San Sebastián** is virtually a northern suburb of **Cartagena**, separated from Cartagena by the **Estero Cartagena**, which forms a *laguna*. This picturesque little resort, just 2 km north of Cartagena, is served by shuttle buses from San Antonio. It has an excellent beach which is suitable for swimming and water sports, and there are lifeguards. The mean summer temperature is 18°C (64°F), and the water temperature is 15°C (59°F).

CASABLANCA

Population: 9000
Distances:
- From Santiago: 78 km west on RN 68 (sealed)
- From Valparaíso: 42 km south on RN 68 (sealed)

Casablanca is the center of a rural community with some industry as well. The Santa Bárbara church in the main plaza was built in 1680. The present lay-out of the Plaza de Armas dates from 1753.

⌘ Festivals
- December 8: Pilgrimage to Lo Vazquez sanctuary

ⓘ Tourist information
- Municipalidad, Portales 60 ℄ 341, ext. 9

✉ Accommodation
- Hotel Continental, Portales 672 ℄ 11
- Residencial Casablanca, Chacabuco 315. 12 beds

⛺ Camping
There is a camping site at Tranque Lo Ovalle, 10 km north.

🍴 Eating out

Restaurants
- Club Social Casablanca, Portales 114. Specialty turkey
- Don Pepe, Constitución 243. Chilean cuisine
- La Carreta, Maipú 39

Eating out at Lo Vazquez
Lo Vazquez is a Catholic shrine 8km west of Casablanca on RN68.
- Restaurant La Carreta

✉ Post and telegraph

Post office
- Correos, Diego Portales 60

Telephone
- CTC, Constitución 325

🚌 Buses from Casablanca
All buses pass through the town center. Buses Carrera Hnos, Buses Mirasol and Buses Pullman Bus run regular daily services to Algarrobo, Cartagena, El Quisco,

El Tabo, San Antonio and Valparaíso; fares $0.90

🚗 Motoring

Gas stations
- COPEC, Constitución
- Sunoco, Avenida Portales

📷 Sightseeing
- Iglesia San Jerónimo, 9 km south of town in the tiny settlement of the same name. **San Jerónimo** lies on a small plain formed by the headwaters of **Estero El Membrillo** falling from the slopes of **Cerro Pan de Azúcar** ("Sugarloaf Mountain") (562 m), and is reached by dirt roads F-830 and F-930. Artificial lakes have formed below the village. The church, once part of the *hacienda*, is a small jewel of colonial art.
- Santuario de Lo Vázquez, a Catholic shrine venerating La Virgen Purísima de Lo Vázquez on the main highway (RN 68), 11 km west of town. This shrine attracts pilgrims all year round, but especially on December 8 when the main pilgrimage takes place. It has been a shrine since 1864.

☞ Excursions
- **Embalse de Pitama**: A small lake set in eucalyptus and pine trees, 1 km west of the main highway. The lake covers 400 000 square meters and is greenish in color, and offers fishing and windsurfing. There is an adjacent picnic area.
- **Embalse Lo Ovalle**: This lake is situated 9 km north of town on Ruta F-850, a dirt road. The surrounding area is fairly heavily forested, mostly with eucalyptus and thorn bushes. This is a

good spot for picnics and for fishing and sailing.

- **Embalse Lo Orozco**: This lake is located 12 km north-east. The turnoff is 3 km past Santuario Lo Vázquez onto Ruta F-50, a dirt road which links up with Quilpué. The surrounding area is forested, mostly with native plants which include lots of thorn bushes. There is a picnic area with toilets and opportunities for water sports.
- **Fundo Orrega Arriba**: *Hacienda* 5 km south on Ruta F-90, the road to Algarrobo. It was built around 1860 and retains the Spanish colonial style of the

period. It is private property, and permission to visit must be obtained from the owners. Some tour operators include this *hacienda* on their itinerary.

- **Tunquén**: An isolated beach, reached from the turnoff on RN 68 at Las Taguas (passing Embalse Pitama) onto a 38 km dirt track. Very few tourists go to this picturesque beach. The area is partly forested with native trees and pines. It is possible to reach **Playa Quintay** over a mountain trail. Direct buses run from Valparaíso, operated by Buses Vía Quintay ((032) 663615.

CATEMU

Area code: 34
Population: 5500
Distances
- From Santiago: 95 km north on Ruta E-65, RN 60 and RN 5 (sealed)
- From Valparaíso: 98 km north-east on Ruta E-65 RN 60 (sealed)

Catemu lies 8 km north of Llay-Llay in a rich agricultural valley. The two ranges which form this valley reach 2200 m and 2300 m respectively. The main crop is tobacco.

During the colonial period, the town was a copper mining center with many foundries. At **La Varilla**, 6 km north is the Escuela Agrícula Salesiana, an agricultural high school in a former *hacienda*.

🎭 Festivals
- September 17–19: Fiesta Huasa, which lasts two days

ℹ️ Tourist information
- Municipalidad, Las Máquinas

🛏 Accommodation
- Residencial Capri, Calle Dr Eduardo Raggio 27 AFHJN (631319. 40 beds

🍴 Eating out

Restaurants
- Chilla, Borjas García Huidobro. Seafood
- El Parrón, A. Prat 204. Chilean cuisine
- Galaxia, Borjas García Huidobro. Seafood
- La Catita, Ignacio Carrera Pinto. Chilean cuisine
- Los Chinos, Borjas García Huidobro. Seafood
- Manolo, A. Prat. Chilean cuisine
- Tricolor, Dr. Eduardo Raggio 090. Seafood

🚌 Buses
- Buses Dhino's, Calle El Cobre
  Services to El Cobre
- Buses Golondrina, Calle García Huidobro
  Services to Santiago
- Buses Puma, Calle García Huidobro
  Services to Valparaíso
- Buses Provincial, Calle García Huidobro
  Services to Llay-Llay and San Felipe
- Colectivos Ruta 60, Calle Arturo Prat
  Services to Llay-Llay

- Colectivos El Cobre, Calle García Huidobro
  Services to El Cobre
- Colectivos Cerillos, Calle García Huidobro
  Services to Cerillos

🚌 Motoring

- COPEC gas station

⭐ Excursions

- **Pura Sangre** Horse stud and training school near Santa Isabel, 10 km east on

the Río Aconcagua between small hills and native forests. For horse lovers.

- **Refugio Casa de Piedra**: North of Catemu on top of **Cerro Caqui** (2196 m) with magnificent views over the Aconcagua valley. The building is of concrete with a slate roof. People ski here in winter, although there are no facilities. There is also a rich flora and fauna — condors can be seen in the nearby area.

CONCÓN

Area code: 32
Altitude: Sea level
Distances

- From Santiago: 151 km west on RN 60 and RN 68 (via Viña del Mar)
- From Valparaíso: 20 km north on Ruta F-30

Concón is an established beach resort, lying at the mouth of the **Río Aconcagua**. It is well-endowed with tourist facilities. Although not as fashionable as Viña del Mar or Reñaca, Concón has many attractions, including slightly cheaper accommodation. The southern suburb of Higuerillas is a particularly picturesque spot. The beaches are open to the sea and swimming is not recommended, except in marked places attended by life-guards. The average summer temperature is 18°C (64°F), and the water is 15°C (59°F).

Key to map

A	Iglesia	10	Restaurant El Coral
E	Telephone	11	Restaurant La Perla del Pacífico
T	Bus stop	12	Restaurant Roca Snak
		13	Restaurant Las Brisas
●	**Accommodation**	15	Restaurant La Carla
4	Hotel Casa Rosada	16	Restaurant La Sirena
14	Motel Las Gaviotas	17	Restaurant Central
19	Hotel Internacional	21	Restaurant Dinson
20	Hotel Concón	22	Restaurant Alicia
○	**Eating out**	⊙	**Entertainment**
1	Restaurant Caletilla	2	Disco Happy Hours
3	Restaurant Tirol	18	Disco César
5	Restaurant Bella Rosa		
6	Restaurant Trocadero	□	**Services**
7	Restaurant La Picada de Emerito	23	Lavaseco Reñaca
8	Restaurant El Rincón de Charlie		
9	Restaurant Donde Jacobo		

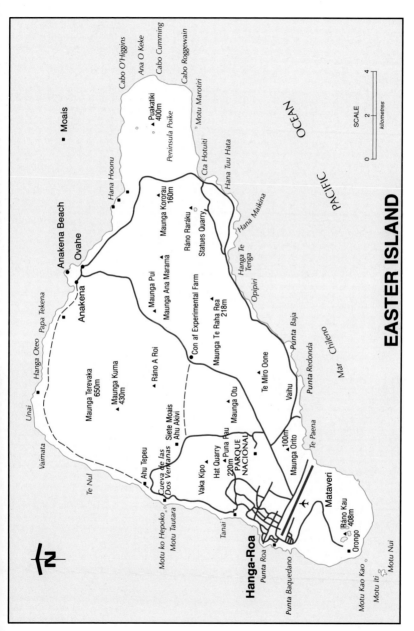

Plate 15
Map of Easter Island

Plate 16   Región V de Valparaíso
Top: Portillo, ski lifts
Bottom: Laguna del Inca

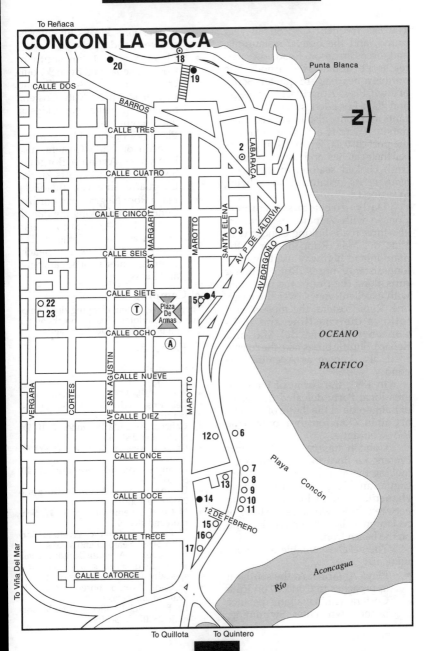

CONCON LA BOCA

To Reñaca

Punta Blanca

CALLE DOS
BARROS
CALLE TRES
CALLE CUATRO
CALLE CINCO
CALLE SEIS
CALLE SIETE
CALLE OCHO
CALLE NUEVE
CALLE DIEZ
CALLE ONCE
CALLE DOCE
CALLE TRECE
CALLE CATORCE

STA MARGARITA
MAROTTO
SANTA ELENA
AV P DE VALDIVIA
AV BORGONO
LABARACA

VERGARA
CORTES
AVE SAN AGUSTIN
MAROTTO

Plaza De Armas

OCEANO
PACIFICO

Playa Concón

1 DE FEBRERO

Río Aconcagua

To Viña Del Mar

To Quillota   To Quintero

Concón

Tourists frequent Concón all year round, and the hotels, restaurants, and discos are good. Roadside eateries serve delicious seafood. The northern beaches are quieter. South of town, Playa Amarilla, Playa Negra and Playa Los Lilenes all have restaurants and some also have accommodation. There is a fishing village in the port district, where fishing boats sell their catches, and you can sample fresh cooked seafood at the many *marisquerías*, restaurants specializing in seafood.

Daily direct buses connect Concón with Valparaíso. There are also three roads linking Concón with Viña del Mar. Ruta Interior is the main inland highway used by most long-distance buses. Ruta Superior runs along the rim of the mountain with excellent views over the coastline. Ruta Costera, the most scenic, follows the coastline and links Concón with Viña del Mar and Reñaca. Shuttle buses take the coastal road, also known as Avenida Borgoño.

In 1891, the Army of the Congressional Party defeated the forces of Balmaceda at the Battle of Concón at **Colmo**, 7 km from the mouth of the Río Aconcagua.

Concón has two gastronomic centers: La Boca to the north, overlooking the mouth of the Río Aconcagua; and Higuerilla, from Playa Higuerilla to the Club de Yates. In between these two areas, a string of restaurants lines Avenida Borgoño on the beach front.

The beaches suitable for swimming are:

- Playa Amarilla: At the southern approaches to Concón, on Ruta Costera within walking distance of the town center. Swimming,

water sports, kiosks, life-guards, showers, and toilets.
- Playa Negra: 1 km south of Concón, separated by rocky outcrops from Playa Amarilla and further south on Ruta Costera. Swimming, water sports, kiosks, and life-guards.
- Playa Los Lilenes: 4 km south of Concón on Ruta Costera, also known as Avenida Borgoño. Swimming, water sports, kiosks, life-guards, showers, and toilets.
- Playa Roca Negra: 7 km north of Concón, overlooking the mouth of the Río Aconcagua, also known as Playa Matagua. The main road passes the beach. Fishing, water sports, camping, and kiosk.

▲ Camping

There is an excellent camping site, Camping Las Gaviotas, 300 m north of the Concón bridge over Río Aconcagua.

⑪ Eating out

Eating out in La Boca

Restaurants
- Alicia, Calle 7 791. Chilean cuisine
- Bella Rosa, Pedro de Valdivia 514. Italian cuisine
- Caliche, Avenida Borgoño 25010 $Y. Seafood and steaks
- Central, Avenida Borgoño 25300 $Y. Seafood
- Denny's, Avenida Borgoño 25140. Seafood
- Donde Jacobo, Avenida Borgoño 25120. Seafood
- El Coral, Avenida Borgoño $Y. Seafood and steaks
- El Rincón de Charlie, Avenida Borgoño 24985. Seafood and steaks
- El Trocadero, Avenida Borgoño 24965 $Y. Seafood; *Arroz a la Valenciana* a specialty. Credit cards accepted
- La Carla, Avenida Borgoño 25260 $Y. Seafood and steaks
- La Perla del Pacífico, Avenida Borgoño 25007 $Y. Seafood

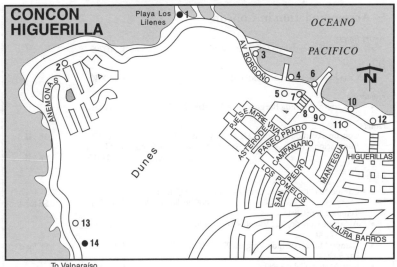

CONCON HIGUERILLA

Playa Los Lilenes

OCEANO PACIFICO

To Valparaíso

Key to map

● Accommodation

1 Cabañas Los Lilenes
14 Cabañas Edelweiss

○ Eating out

2 Restaurant Reinaldo
3 Club de Yates
4 Restaurant Albatros
5 Restaurant Chila

6 Restaurant Vista Al Mar
7 Restaurant Aqui Jaime
8 Restaurant El Tiburó
9 Restaurant Don Chapo
10 Restaurant Mar Azul
11 Restaurant La Higuera
12 Restaurant Bello Mar
13 Restaurant A La Bordero

- La Picada de Emeterio, Avenida Borgoño 25069 $Y. Seafood
- La Sirena, Avenida Borgoño 25290 $Y. Seafood
- Las Brisas, Avenida Borgoño 25070 corner of La Boca $Y. Seafood
- Las Deliciosas, Avenida Borgoño 25370 $Z. Seafood
- Roca Snak, Avenida Borgoño 24930 $Z. Seafood and steaks
- Tirol, Pedro de Valdivia 350 $Y. Seafood and steaks; views over the bay, *salón de té*

Eating out in central Concón, along the beach front

Restaurants
- Dinson, Avenida Borgoño 22902 overlooking Playa Amarilla. Seafood and steaks
- Grandiella, Avenida Borgoño 22100. Italian cuisine

Eating out in Higuerilla

Restaurants
- Albatros, Avenida Borgoño 21295 $Y. Seafood
- Aquí Jaime, Avenida Borgoño 21303. Seafood and steaks

Concón

🛏 Accommodation in Concón

Apart hotels
- Temaukel, Magdalena Paz near Las Elenas   ☏ 903799

Hostales
- Casa Rosada, Pedro de Valdia 514   ☏ 813040

Hosterías
- Trocadero, Avenida Borgoño 24965   ADEFGHLR   ☏ 811359

Hotels
- Concón, Avenida Borgoño 23100, Playa Amarilla   ☏ 813955 $F 🛏
- Internacional Playa Amarilla, Avenida Borgoño 23280 corner of Lo Abarca
     ACDEFGHIJKLT   ☏ 811915 $F 🛏

Motels

- ★★★Campo Mar 1, Avenida Cortés 440 corner of Calle Tres
     ABCDHIJKLNPTUVY   ☏ 811971 $E for 4
Tennis, fax 680294
- Al Sur de Concón, Las Violetas 21   ABD   ☏ 814213
Fax 812230
- Campo Mar 2, Avenida Vergara 977   ABCDHIJKLNPTUVY   ☏ 811971 $F for 6
Fax 903606
- Inter Motels, Calle 3 680   ☏ 812101
- Las Gaviotas, Avenida Marotto 1409   ABCHIKL   ☏ 812274

Accommodation in Mauco
Mauco is 11 km upstream, on the north bank of the Río Aconcagua.

Complejo Turístico
- Las Vertientes del Mauco   ☏ 811282
Open all year, 8 cabins; 40 beds

Accommodation along the road to Quintero

Cabañas
- Sol y Mar, KM 5   ☏ (09) 3313907

Motels
- Mantagua Playa, 3 km north from Puente Concón across Río Aconcagua, on Ruta F-30-E
     ABEFGHKLRV $G for 5
Fax (32) 811415, beach frontage, 70 camping sites, 27 cabins, open all year round electricity, water, toilets, boat hire, horse-riding, bicycle and tent hire

Accommodation in Sector Los Romeros

Cabañas
- Do Brasil, Los Quillayes 1155   ABCEGHP   ☏ 811631 $G for 5
- Los Romeros, Los Coigües 578   ☏ 903937

Accommodation at Playa Los Lilenes

Cabañas
- Los Lilenes, Avenida Borgoño   ☏ 811581
Directly on the beach

Accommodation in Concón — continued

Accommodation south of town
Along the coastal road to Viña del Mar (Avenida Borgoño).

Hosterías
☞ • Cabañas Edelweiss, Avenida Borgoño 19200
　　　　　　　　　　　　　ADEFGH$　　　　(814044

　　German spoken, sea views; fax 903666

Accommodation along RN 60

Motels
• Hostería La Cascada KM 20, Reñaca Alto

• Bella Mar, Avenida Borgoño 21550 $Y. Seafood
☞ • Chila, Avenida Borgoño 21220 $Y. Seafood. Credit cards accepted
• Don Chicho, Avenida Borgoño 21410. Seafood
• El Tiburón, Avenida Borgoño 21440 $Y. Seafood
☞ • La Higuera, Avenida Borgoño 21450 $Y. Seafood. Credit cards accepted
• Los Lilenes, Avenida Borgoño $Y. Seafood. Downstairs and upstairs; overlooking Playa Los Lilenes; credit cards accepted
• Mar Azul, Avenida Borgoño 21069$Y. Seafood. Credit cards accepted
• Vista Al Mar, Avenida Borgoño 21270 $Y. Seafood

Eating out south
Along the seaside, starting from Costa Brava.

Restaurants
☞ • Reinaldo's, Las Catalpas 99. International cuisine. *Salón de té*. Credit cards accepted. Built on top of cliff, with magnificent views over the sea
☞ • Edelweiss, Avenida Borgoño 19200 $X. International cuisine. Credit cards accepted

Eating out along RN 60
• Restaurant Donde La Cuca, near turn-off into Ruta Interior to Concón

ⓣ Entertainment
• Disco Happy Hour, Barros corner of Abarca
• Disco César, Playa Amarilla. Also a restaurant $Y

⊞ Post and telegraph

Post office
• Correos, Calle 8 corner of Santa Laura

Telephone
• CTC, Avenida Marotto 833

▤ Services

Dry cleaner
• Lavaseco Reñaca, Vergara corner of Calle 7

▣ Buses
Regular municipal buses run at 20 minutes interval between Viña del Mar and Concón.

Companies
• A2 Alfa Tres
• A44 La Porteña
• A125 Nueva Transmar, Calle 7
　　　corner of Santa Margarita
　　(812252

Services
• Los Andes: Fare $1.90; 13 services daily; A2
• Los Vilos: A44
• San Felipe: Fare $1.90; 10 services daily; A2
• Santiago: Fare $2.80; A125

▦ Motoring
• COPEC gas station

⊛ Sport

Yachting
• Club de Yates, Avenida Borgoño near Puente Higuerillas

EL QUISCO

Area code: 035
Population: 4100
Altitude: Sea level
Distances
- From Santiago: 136 km west on Ruta F-98-G, Ruta F-90 RN 68 (via Casablanca)
- From Valparaíso: 81 km south on Ruta F-98-G, Ruta F- 960-G and RN 68 (via Casablanca)

El Quisco is a major seaside resort. It is built around a quiet bay on the Pacific coast. The calm waters are ideal for swimming, skin diving, water skiing and sailing, and the hinterland offers scenic excursions. The town has good hotels, *residenciales*, motels, and restaurants, as well as a yacht club. There is daily public transport to Santiago and Valparaíso, and buses link all the resorts south of Valparaíso to San Antonio.

The average summer temperature is 20°C (68°F) and the water is 15°C (59°F). The best beaches within easy reach of town are Playa Los Clarines, Playa Diamantes Azul, Playa La Poza, Playa Grande, Playa Los Ahogados, and Playa Los Caracoles. They all offer swimming, water sports, kiosks, and life-guards, and some are also suitable for fishing.

Festivals
- February, second week: Semana Quisqueña
- September 24: Nuestra Señora de la Merced, at El Totoral, a small village 12km inland on the Estero Carvajal
- November: Spring festival

Tourist information
- Municipalidad, Avenida Italia y Francia ℂ 81101

Eating out

Restaurants
- Casino Social La Caleta Miramar, Costanera
- El Cordovés, Avenida I. Dubournais 296.Seafood
- El Mastique, Avenida I. Dubournais 190.Seafood
- El Sabao, El Leoncillo 525. International cuisine
- La Caleta del Quisco, Avenida I. Dubournais 166. Seafood
- Münchnerhof, Avenida Costanera Norte 111. German cuisine
- Yolita, Avenida I Dubournais 1020. Seafood

Café
- Toroko, Avenida I. Dubournais 121

Entertainment
- Cabaret Chez Camilo, Avenida Isidora Dubournais 05. International cuisine, dancing, shows

Post and telegraph

Telephone
There is a public telephone on Los Boldos.
- Telex Chile, Avenida Isadora Dubournais 187

Buses

Companies
Asociación de Dueños de Taxibuses San Antonio runs bus services at 30-minute interval between San Antonio in the south and Algarrobo in the north.
- A51 Buses Los Héroes
- A103 Buses Empresa Robles
- A127 Buses Pullman Bus

Services
- Santiago: Fare $1.90; departs every 30 minutes; A103, A127
- Valparaíso: Fare $1.90; departs every 30 minutes; A51, A127

📧 Accommodation in El Quisco

Apart hotels
- El Alfil, Laberinto 60 — ☎ 481804
- Victoria, Victoria 129 — ☎ 481938/483313

Cabañas
- El Peñn, Ana Luis 240; — ☎ 472069
  14 beds
- Hanga-Roa, De Las Estrellas 710 — ☎ 472300
  35 beds
- Pinomar, Avenida Pinomar 0350 — ☎ 482058
  60 beds
- Cabañas Quisco Centro, Avenida Francia 0315 — ☎ 481740
  20 beds

Complejos Turísticos
- Paraíso del Mar, Avenida I. Dubournais 0402 — ☎ 472846
  185 beds

Hotels
- ★★ Gran Italia, Avenida Isidora Dubournais 413 — AEFGHIJKLMNP — ☎ 481090/481631
  110 beds
- Chelita, Avenida Isidora Dubournais 115 — AFGHPV — ☎ 481015
  Sea views; 35 beds
- El Quisco, Avenida Isidora Dubournais 166 — AFGJ — ☎ 481092/481923
  28 beds
- La Playa, Avenida Isidora Dubournais 102 — AEFGP — ☎ 481651
  35 beds
- Las Gaviotas, Santa Juana 154 — AFGHJP — ☎ 481521
  40 beds

Motels
- ★★★ Barlovento , El Quisco 0520 — ABCDEGHILMP — ☎ 471030 — $H for 5
  25 beds
- Costanera, Avenida Costanera Sur 278 — ABCF — ☎ 482204
  24 beds

Hostales
- Del Angel, Laberintos 290 — ☎ 481271
  12 beds

Residenciales
- Aurora, Del Medio Dia 790 — AFGJP
  31 beds
- Julia, José Narciso Aguirre 0210 — ☎ 471546
  15 beds
- La Flor, José Narciso Aguirre 0249 — ☎ 481554
  32 beds
- La Posada, Avenida Francia 0236 14 beds
- Oriental, San Pedro 110 — AEFGP — ☎ 471662 — $I 🛈
  46 beds

VALPARAÍSO

Accommodation in El Quisco — continued

- Saint Michel, José Narciso Aguirre 0250   (481156
  20 beds
- San Pedro, San Pedro 094   (482158
  13 beds

Accommodation in El Quisco Sur

Motel
- Cabañas Pozo Azul, Capricornio 234 ABCFGHLM   (481401
  22 beds

Accommodation in El Quisco Norte

Motel
- Rocas de Algarrobo, Rocas de Algarrobo 190, near the bridge to Isla Negra
                              ABCF   (481366 $F for 6
  Views over the sea and the rocky shoreline

🚌 Motoring
- COPEC gas station, Avenida I. Dubournais 725

Sport

Tennis
There are tennis courts at Motel Barlovento, El Quisco 0520

Yachting
- Club de Yates El Quisco, Avenida
  Costanera

🌴 Excursions
- **Isla Negra**: 5 km south. This picturesque village is famous for embroidery. Here is the former home of
  Nobel prize-winner Pablo Neruda,
  now a museum. See "Excursions"
  from El Tabo on page 259.
- **El Totoral**: A small village 20 km east
  in the **Quebrada Carvajal**. The colonial church and houses, built from
  adobe bricks, remain just as they were
  a hundred years ago. Small restaurant.
  Pure air and walks.

EL TABO

Area code: 035
Population: 3000
Altitude: Sea level
Distances:
- From Santiago: 133 km west on Ruta G-98-F (sealed) RN 78 (sealed, via San Antonio)
- From Valparaíso: 85 km south on Ruta G-98-F (sealed), Ruta F-90 (gravel) and RN 68
  (sealed, via Algarrobo)

El Tabo is situated on a rocky promontory, backed by eucalyptus and pine
forests. This resort town, which draws crowds of summer visitors, has good
tourist facilities with hotels, motels, seafood restaurants, and discos. The
average summer temperature is 20°C (68°F) and the water is 15°C (59°F).
Beaches within easy reach merge into one another and shelve abruptly into
deep water.

Playa Puente de Córdova offers swimming, water sports, camping, kiosks, and life-guards. Playa Castilla, Playa El Caleuche and Playa Chepica have similar facilities without the camping. Playa El Caleuche to the north has rock pools. Playa Chepica is a wide open beach with shallow water.

ℹ Tourist information
- Municipalidad El Tabo, Carretera F-98-G ℓ 231441

Ⓐ Camping
There are excellent camping sites on the beaches north of town.

🍴 Eating out

Restaurants
- La Posada, Errázuriz 719
- La Puerta de Alcalá, Josefina Nieto 197. $Y
- Rengo, Avenida San Marcos 823
- San Pedro, Avenida Baquedano 1164 $Y. Seafood

Eating out in Isla Negra
- El Rincón del Poeta, Pablo Neruda. Seafood
- El Cielo, Avenida Isadora Dubournais. Seafood and steaks
- Hostería Santa Elena, Avenida Isidora Dubournais
- Papi's Pizza, Avenida Isadora Dubournais

▼ Entertainment
- Tabo's Discotheque

📧 Post and telegraph

Post office
- Correos, Riquelme 88

Telephone
- Operator connected phone calls, Residencial Victoria, San Marcos 857

🚌 Buses
- Asociación de Dueños de Taxibuses San Antonio serves the coast between San Antonio and Algarrobo. Buses run every 20 minutes

- Pullman Bus runs services to Valparaíso (fare $1.80) and Santiago (fare $2.20). During summer they run every 20 minutes, and in winter every hour

🚗 Motoring
- COPEC gas station, Avenida San Marcos

⊛ Sport

Fishing
Fishing is good on Playas Las Salinas and Playas Blancas.

Tennis
- Club de Ténis Rocas de Córdova, on the northern exit
- Club de Ténis Las Gaviotas, at the southern end of the town

♠ Excursions
- **Isla Negra**: 2 km north. Agates are found in the area and can be bought locally. Embroidery is a home industry. The newly established seaside resort has good beaches. Playa Isla Negra, within easy reach of the town, offers swimming, water sports, kiosks, and life-guards. Playa Las Agatas, further south near the mouth of the Estero Carvajal, has similar facilities. The main attraction is Casa de Pablo Neruda (Pablo Neruda Museum). Pablo Neruda, one of Chile's two Nobel prize-winner poets, lived here for a time, and the beauty of the central coast inspired much of his poetry. On exhibit are his collections of nautical figureheads and other memorabilia. His burial place is in the garden. In the house next to it is a library containing his complete works. The museum is open daily. Admission $2.00.
- **Caleta Las Cruces**: Fishing village, 7 km south of town. Good beaches, several hotels and restaurants specializing in seafood.
- **Laguna** and **Quebrada de Córdova**: Laguna de Córdova is not suitable for swimming, but you can look for agate in the river bed. The Quebrada de Córdova is formed by Estero Carbajal. It runs dry in summer, but the abundant winter and spring flow sustains a dense native bush cover throughout the year.

🛏 Accommodation in El Tabo

Hotels
- Bilbao, Avenida San Marcos 802 near Riquelme
  ADFGHIJL   ✆ 461271
  39 beds
- El Tabo, José Francisco 037   AFGHIJLMNPU   ✆ 212719 / 233719
  $G ⅱ
  39 rooms, overlooking the beach
- Victoria, Avenida San Marcos 857   ✆ 212932
  28 beds

Cabañas
- El Bosque, Avenida El Peral, parcela 3   ✆ 234654
  23 beds
- Las Gaviotas, Estero de Chépica, parcela 43   ✆ (09)32311364
  42 beds

Hostería
- Montemar, Carlos Monckeberg 406   AEFGHLRPU   ✆ 213204
  19 beds

Residencial
- El Mar, Avenida Del Mar 1111   ✆ 461232
  35 beds

Accommodation in Isla Negra
- Hostería Santa Elena, Calle de la Hostería 67 near Avenida Isidoro Dubournais
  AEFGHIMP$UVZ   ✆ 461139 $H ⅰ
  TV, beach frontage, tennis

ISLA ROBINSON CRUSOE

Population: 600
Distance from mainland: 670 km west

Archipiélago de Juan Fernández was discovered in 1574 by the Spanish navigator Juan Fernández. For the next 150 years it was used by many European freebooters and pirates as a hideout and supply base.

This widely scattered archipelago consists of three islands: Isla Robinson Crusoe, 21 km long, **Isla Alejandro Selkirk**, and **Isla Santa Clara**. Isla Alejandro Selkirk is 180 km west of Isla Robinson Crusoe, and features the highest point of the archipelago. Isla Robinson Crusoe's highest elevation is **Cerro Yunque** at 915 m.

In 1977 the 9313 ha (23 000 acre) archipelago was declared a World Reserve, and became part of the Parque Nacional Archipiélago de Juan Fernández. The park has picnic areas, excursion paths and a lookout.

The islands have a rugged volcanic topography with deep canyons and mountain chains, narrow at the top, with abruptly rising pinnacles.

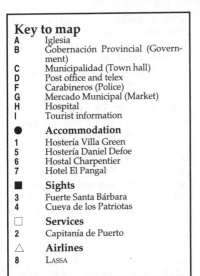

Key to map

A Iglesia
B Gobernación Provincial (Government)
C Municipalidad (Town hall)
D Post office and telex
F Carabineros (Police)
G Mercado Municipal (Market)
H Hospital
I Tourist information

● **Accommodation**
1 Hostería Villa Green
5 Hostería Daniel Defoe
6 Hostal Charpentier
7 Hotel El Pangal

■ **Sights**
3 Fuerte Santa Bárbara
4 Cueva de los Patriotas

□ **Services**
2 Capitanía de Puerto

△ **Airlines**
8 Lassa

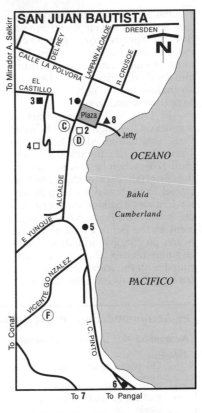

Brooks flow through the valleys to the sea without forming any main river systems. There are few signs of wind and water erosion because, geologically speaking, these land masses have been created relatively recently. The sea is warm and clear, and multicolored fish species may be observed to a great depth. Seals abound. Lobsters are the islanders' main source of income.

The climate is Mediterranean, with 75 per cent humidity all year round and an average annual rainfall of 1800 mm. The average annual temperature is 16°C (61°F); the lowest average monthly temperature is 6°C (43°F). The most appropriate time to visit when the rainfall is lowest is between December and March. The islands are outside the cold Humboldt current, and are considerably warmer than the sea in the same latitude on the mainland.

The lush subtropical rainforest has a variety of plant life, most of it peculiar to the islands. The sandalwood tree is now apparently extinct as a result of ruthless overlogging. The humid, rainy climate encourages thick forest cover of palm-like ferns, known as *palmillos*. Ferns are extraordinarily large and there are many climbing species. Ñalcas (*Gunnera masafuera*), small palm-like trees with large umbrella-like leaves, are encountered in the ravines. Many introduced mammals, such as goats, cats, and rats, have proliferated and pose a potential threat to the native species. Seals and sea elephants are native to the region, and favor inaccessible rocky outcrops. The most obvious birds are red hummingbirds and fieldfares. There are no snakes, and the only frog species have been introduced.

In 1704, Alexander Selkirk, a seaman on the English vessel *Cinque Ports*, was marooned on Isla Mas a Tierra (now Isla Robinson Crusoe) until 1709, when he was rescued by the English pirate ship *Duchess*. Daniel Defoe based his hero Robinson Crusoe on Selkirk's four years on the island. In 1915, a naval engagement in the Bahía Cumberland between an English squadron and a German man-o'-war, the *Dresden*, ended with the scuttling of the *Dresden* by Admiral Graf Spee. One of the German sailors escaped and survived for 12 years in the interior of the island, avoiding contact with the native population.

San Juan Bautista, the main settlement, is located on the Bahía Cumberland. About 4000 tourists go to the island annually. The best time to visit is between October and February. Access to the archipelago from the mainland is by sea from Valparaíso or by air from Santiago — see "Air services" and "Water transport" below. Most tourists only stay on Isla Robinson Crusoe for a few days. Very few tourists take the opportunity to visit Isla Alejandro Selkirk with a lobster fishing boat.

Note that from time to time certain areas may be closed to the public, to allow regeneration or for controlled scientific studies.

⊟ Accommodation on Isla Robinson Crusoe

Accommodation in San Juan Bautista

Cabañas
- Charpentier, Ignacio Carrera Pinto 256   ℓ (32)751020
  8 beds
- Dafne, Ignacio Carrera Pinto 198   ℓ (32) 751025
- Paulentz, Ignacio Carrera Pinto 120   ℓ (32) 751055
  8 beds
- Robinson Crusoe, Larrin Alcalde 380   ℓ (32)751107
  4 beds

Hosterías
- Daniel Defoe, Dresden 98, Bahía Cumberland
                           ACEFGIJLUZ $F ⚄
  Sauna, boat hire,TV, beach front, 10 cabins. Reservations in Santiago: Monumento 2570, Maipú ℓ 557364
- Hostería El Pangal, Sector El Pangal   AEFGIJLPU
  Reservations in Santiago: Lineas Aeras LASSA, Avenida Larrain 7941, La Reina
  ℓ 2734309/354
- Villa Green, Larrain Alcalde 246   AEFGIJLP
  12 beds. Reservations in Santiago: Viajes Marbella, Guardia Vieja 50, office 50 ℓ (02) 5313772

Residenciales
- Martínez-Green, El Castillo 118   ℓ (032) 751039
  8 beds

VALPARAÍSO

⚥ Festivals
- May: Fiesta de la Langosta ("Lobster Festival")
- June 29: Fiesta de San Pedro
- November 4: The discovery of the island is celebrated

ⓘ Tourist information

On the mainland
- Sernatur, Viña del Mar

On the island
- CONAF, Castillo, Edificio Servicios Públicos. Their administration office on the island also acts as a tourist information office

⚠ Camping
There is a picnic area at Plazoleta El Yunque but no official camping spots. There are some camping sites near the village and there is also camping at Puerto Inglés near Cueva Robinson Crusoe.

⑪ Eating out
The island is a major exporter of lobsters and other crustaceans, and there is no shortage of fine seafood. Try *perol*, lobster marinated in *escabeche* sauce. Most accommodation includes meals, and there are a few small local restaurants.
- Restaurant Club Deportivo Nocturno, Larrain Alcalde. Lobsters a specialty
- Comedores Bahía, Larraín Alcalde

▣ Post and telegraph

Post office
- Correo, Calle Castillo, in the Edificios Servicios Públicos

Telephone
The only telecomunication is by radio, but in an emergency FACH (the Chilean airforce) will receive and send messages.

✈ Air services
The airport is situated at the extreme western side of the island, and consists of a landing strip suitable for small aircraft only. There is no road connecting the airstrip with Juan Bautista yet — only a 15 km CONAF trail through the rugged interior which finishes across the ridge on the Cordón Escarpado. At present, there is a two-hour launch service from the pas-

senger embarkation point to San Juan Bautista.

LASSA has twin-engined plane flights to the islands leaving from Aerodromo Eulogio Sanchez in Santiago (also known as Aerodromo Tobalaba). These planes carry 6–8 passengers, and take 3 hours. LASSA also makes reservations for accommodation in Hostería El Pangal in San Juan Bautista. For inquiries and bookings contact Línea de Aeroservicios S.A. ("LASSA"), Avenida Larrain 7941, La Reina, Santiago ☎ (2)2734309, fax (2) 2735209 Also, Transportes Aereos Isla Robinson Crusoe has flights from Santiago and arranges bookings for accommodation on Isla Juan Fernández ☎ and fax (2) 5313772/ 4343.

⚓ Water transport
Empremar provides services from Valparaíso once a month between November and March, taking 60 hours. Occasionally, the Chilean navy makes a trip to the island, and it is possible to travel with them. However, the islanders have first preference, and navy cruises are not advertised. Check with the Armada de Chile or the Capitanía (harbormaster) in the port of Valparaíso.

▦ Shopping
Kiosko de Artesanía in Larraín Alcalde sells seashells and wood carvings made from Juan Fernández palm ("*chonta*").

◎ Sport
There is water skiing, scuba diving, fishing, and yachting.

▣ Sightseeing
- Fuerte Santa Barbara, in Juan Bautista, built in 1749 to prevent pirates using the island as a hideout. The fort is located on a hill behind Hotel Green. This historical monument was reconstructed in 1974.
- Cueva de los Patriotas, near Fuerte Santa Barbara. The Spanish imprisoned 42 Chilean patriots here in the early days of the Chilean independence movement.

◉ Excursions
- Mirador Selkirk ("Selkirk's Lookout"): On **Cerro Portezuelo**, at 565 m,

with sweeping views over both the sea and the island, obstructed only by **Cerro El Yunque** (915 m) to the south. The trail starts from Fuerte Santa Bárbara.

- **Puerto Inglés**: A half hour's walk from the settlement. Robinson Crusoe's cave is about 50 m from the beach.
- **Puerto Francés**: Near the island's eastern extreme and accessible only by boat. It is supposed to have been used as a hideout by French pirates. The guns were placed there by the Spaniards in 1779.
- **Playa Arenal**: The only sandy beach on the island. Accessible by a three-hour boat ride past cliffs and rocky outcrops where you can see seals. The water is warm and transparent to a great depth.
- **Isla Alejandro Selkirk**: 180 km west of the main archipelago and only accessible by lobster boat.

LA CALERA

Area code: 033
Population: 39 000
Altitude: 200 m
Distances
- From Santiago: 132 km north on Panamericana
- From Valparaíso: 65 km north on RN 62 (sealed)

La Calera is situated on a sharp bend of the **Río Aconcagua**. The coastal *cordillera* rises on both sides of the river to approximately 1000 m, and is clothed in dense mountain shrubs. La Calera is also an important road junction where the international road to Argentina (RN 60) joins the Panamericana (RN 5).

Although still largely a rural center, it is becoming an industrial center as well. Río Aconcagua already shows signs of pollution. Most industry is linked with the agricultural products harvested here — fruit and vegetables for export and the markets in Santiago and Valparaíso.

Three smaller towns near La Calera have some excellent restaurants:

- **Nogales,** located in a wide basin on the **Río Melón**, 16 km north. It has a population of 12 500. Here a road turns west to the coast to Puchuncaví.
- **El Melón**, 14 km north, on the Panamericana.
- **Hijuelas** is a small town of 5500 in the Aconcagua valley 6 km east. It is an important agricultural center, and exports carnations internationally.

⚙ Festivals
- March, second half: Fiesta de Nogales
- May 21: Combate Naval de Iquique (commemorates the naval battle of Iquique)
- August 20: Birthday of the Liberator Bernardo O'Higgins
- September 18–19: Independence day and Rodeo Oficial (or Fiesta Huasa)
- October 12: Día de la Raza. Observed in all Latin American countries, Spain, and Portugal to commemmorate the common bond which unites them: language, history, and religion
- November 1: All Saints
- December 8: Inmaculada Concepción

ℹ Tourist information
- Municipalidad, J.J.Pérez 65 (154

⊟ Accommodation in La Calera

Hotels
- Los Leones, Prat 703   ADEFGHIKPTV   ☏ 221927
  Fax 221479, 30 rooms
- Maracaibo, Aldunate 235   ☏ 221940 / 222543
  38 beds
- Oásis, Caupolicán 722   ☏ 222158
  25 beds
- Rex, Latorre 537   AFGIJ   ☏ 221238
  23 beds
- Turismo, Cochrane 420   ☏ 221223
  25 beds

Residenciales
- Cochrane, Cochrane 345   ☏ 222508
  10 beds
- La Parada, Caupolicán 725   ☏ 221612
  22 beds
- Mesias, Cochrane 357   A   ☏ 222457
  9 beds

- Esso gas station, Panamericana Norte km 1

⏸ Eating out

Restaurants
- El Canario, J. Cortés 205
- Club de Campo Melón, Avenida Marathon 312. International cuisine. Dancing weekends
- Chaulin, J.J. Pérez 23
- La Bodega Calerana, Pedro de Valdivia 453
- Oásis, Caupolicán 722. *Parrilladas*
- Pan-Bun, Aldunate 239. *Parrilladas*
- Quik Lunch, Aldunate 196
- Tutto Pollo, Manuel Rodríguez 221

Café Bar
- Willy's, A. Prat 596. Pizzas

Eating out in El Melón
El Melón is 12 km north on Panamericana
- La Parada del Melón. Chilean cuisine

Eating out in Hijuelas
Hijuelas is 8 km east on Panamericana

Restaurants
- Bahamondes, Manuel Rodríguez 1470
- Bambinas, Panamericana
- Hanga Roa, Panamericana
- Las Rucas, Panamericana
- Los Paltos, La Sombra Romeral
- Samoa, Manuel Rodríguez 1582
- San Pablo, Panamericana KM 107

⏹ Entertainment

- Bodega Calerana, Pedro de Valdivia 451. Piano bar open daily from 2100 onwards; Fri and Sat dancing with orchestra. *Parrilladas*

Entertainment in Nogales
- Disco Spider, Pedro F. Vicuña

⊞ Post and telegraph

Post office
- Correos, Zenteno 134

Telephone
- CTC, Prat 560
- Telex Chile, A. Prat 593

⊟ Motoring

Gas stations
- COPEC gas station, J.J.Pérez 401
- Esso, Caupolicán corner of M.Rodríguez
- Shell, Carrera 1240

⊟ Trains

Trains run regularly to Quillota, Limache, Peña Blanca, Villa Alemana, Quilpué, Viña del Mar, and Valparaíso; and to San

🚌 Buses from La Calera

There is no central bus terminal. Many companies have their own terminal, but all buses pass through the center of town.

Companies
- A2   Buses Alfa Tres, Rodríguez 485
- A5   Asociación Gremial de Buses Intercomunales, Prat 783 ℂ 588
  Services to Illapel, Los Vilos, and Salamanca
- A21   Buses Carolina, Caupolicán 709 ℂ 55
  Services toNogales, Ocoa (Parque Nacional La Campana), and El Melón
- A25   Buses Combarbalá-Rima
- A28   Buses Dhino's, Avenida Oriente 431 ℂ 221298
- A37   Buses Golondrina, Carrera 767 ℂ 221833
- A42   Buses Carmelita, Prat 783 ℂ 222588
- A44   Buses La Porteña
- A45   Buses Libac, Prat 783 ℂ 588
- A75   Buses TAC, Prat 743 ℂ 222439
  Services to Mendoza in Argentina
- A78   Buses Tramaca, Prat 783 ℂ 222588
  Services to Chuquicamata, María Elena, Pedro de Valdivia, and Taltal
- A83   Buses Zambrano Hnos, Prat 743 ℂ 222439
- A106 Buses Fénix Pullman Norte, Prat 793 ℂ 222683
- A112 Flota Barrios, Caupolicán 722 ℂ 222158
- A115 Incabus-Laval, Prat 743 ℂ 222439
- A127 Buses Pullman Bus, Prat 798 ℂ 222392
  Services to Diego de Almagro, El Salvador, and Potrerillos
- A137 Buses TAS Choapa, A. Prat 783 ℂ 222588
  Services to Mendoza in Argentina
- B58   Buses Dima, Caupolicán 730 ℂ 222136
  Rural services to Canela, Huentelauquen, and Los Vilos

Services

	Destination	Fare	Services	Duration	Companies
•	Arica				A42, A83, A112
•	Antofagasta	$28.40	4 services daily		A78, A110, A112
•	Calama	$33.00	10 services daily		A78, A110, A112
•	Chañaral	$18.80	4 services daily		A110, A112, A127
•	Combarbalá	$6.40	2–3 services daily		A25, B58
•	Copiapó	$14.60	7 services daily		A45, A78, A110, A112, A127
•	Iquique	$37.60	1 service daily		A42, A106, A110
•	La Ligua	$1.10		1 hr	A44
•	La Serena	$9.20	2 services daily		A115, A127
•	Los Andes	$1.70	13 services daily		A2
•	Ovalle	$9.50	3 services daily		A110, A115
•	Pichidangui	$1.90			A44
•	San Felipe	$1.50			A2
•	Santiago	$1.90			A2, A37
•	Tocopilla	$32.50			A78, A112
	Change in Antofagasta				
•	Valparaíso	$1.10	10 services daily	1¼ hrs	A2, A5, A28, A44
•	Viña del Mar	$1.10		1 hr	A2, A5, A28, A44

Felipe and Los Andes. In both directions 4 services daily.

⊕ Excursions

- **Parque Nacional La Campana:** Buses Carolina run a service to Ocoa at the northern entrance to this national park, and from there you can walk 10 km up the Estero Rabuco. See the entry for the park on page 292.

LA CRUZ

Area code: 033
Population: 7100
Altitude: 500 m
Distances:

- From Santiago: 119 km north-west on RN 62 and Panamericana
- From Valparaíso: 64 km north-east on RN 62 (sealed)

La Cruz lies between Quillota and La Calera, just south of La Calera in the lower **Río Aconcagua** valley. Because it is the center of an important fruit and vegetable growing area, it is the site of Chile's chief plant health and experimental station. Every house offers fruit for sale. The houses fronting on the road have adobe walls.

⚡ Festivals

- July 9: Battle of Concepción
- August 20: Birthday of the Liberator Bernardo O'Higgins
- September 18 or 19: Independence day
- October 12: Foundation day
- December 8: Inmaculada Concepción

ⓘ Tourist information

- Municipalidad, Gabriela Mistral 03 ℂ 312484

⊟ Accommodation

★★ Hotel Villa Capri, 21 de Mayo 3799 ADFGHJKM ℂ 310624 $l 🛈. 34 beds

🍴 Eating out

- Restaurant Club Social, Avenida 21 de Mayo. Chilean cuisine
- Restaurant El Chaparral, Pasaje Galvarino

📧 Post and telegraph

Post office
- Correos, Avenida 21 de Mayo 4296

🚗 Motoring

- COPEC gas station, Camino Troncal

🚆 Trains

The railroad station (Estación La Cruz) is at the corner of Simpson and Avenida Santa Cruz. Trains go to Valparaíso and Los Andes; 3–4 services daily.

🚌 Buses

There is no bus terminal. All buses pass through the town's main street.

- Buses Alfa Tres Ltda runs daily services to Los Andes, Valparaíso and intermediate towns
- Bus Rural Línea Quillota runs daily services to Pocochay
- Buses Dhino's runs daily services to La Calera, Limache, Peña Blanca, Quillota, Quilpué, Valparaíso, Villa Alemana, Viña del Mar @LIST = Buses Golondrina runs regular daily services to Santiago
- *Colectivos* run to Balneario Poza Cristalina

⊕ Excursions

- **Balneario Poza Cristalina:** 2 km from town center, regular *colectivos*. Three natural springs where crystalline waters surge from the ground. Swimming pools, camping grounds, restaurant. Very relaxing atmosphere.

LA LIGUA

Area code: 035
Population: 17 000
Altitude: 100 m
Distances
- From Santiago: 154 km north-west on Ruta E-35 and Panamericana
- From Valparaíso: 110 km north on Ruta E-30-F

La Ligua is located in the lower **Río La Ligua** valley where it forms a wide valley on its way out of the coastal *cordillera*. Large crops of oranges, walnuts, avocados, papaws, and *chirimoyas* are grown in this area.

La Ligua was originally founded in 1754 by Governor Don Domingo Ortiz de Rozas. At first it was nothing more than a miners' settlement, but in 1789 the town was planned along the Spanish grid pattern. It retains much of its colonial charm, with most houses built from adobe. Virtually every house produces homemade woven woolens. La Ligua is a convenient stopover for trips to Petorca and Chincolco.

⚡ Festivals
- June 21: Foundation of La Ligua
- October 12: Virgen del Carmen — religious procession

ⓘ Tourist information
- Municipalidad, Avenida Diego Portales (711036

✉ Accommodation

Hotels
★★★ Anchimallén, Ortiz de Rosas 694 PS (711696 fax $F ⚏ 33 beds
- Chile, Polanco 7 near Papudo AEG (712000/711344. 11 beds

Residenciales
- Aconcagua, Esmeralda (711103. 25 beds
- Esmeralda, Esmeralda 72 ADEPV (711103; 9 beds
- Regine I, Esmeralda 27 AEPV (711192; 15 beds
- Regine II, Condell 360 (711916. ⚏. 5 beds

▲ Camping
There is a camping in Pichicuy, 22 km north.

⑪ Eating out

Restaurants
A specialty of this district is *cazuelas* — meat or chicken stewed in earthenware pots.
- Antares, Portales 404. Chilean cuisine; *cazuela*
- Don Blas, Goyenechea 110 near Avenida Portales. Seafood, *parilladas*
- Illalolen, Polanco 299 near Esmeralda
- La Polloteca, Serrano 354. Chicken and chips
- Montemar, Portales 699. Chilean cuisine
- Pizzería El Mago, Luis E. Laulie 010. Pizzas. Artistic atmosphere
- Plaza, Ortíz de Rozas 598. *Cazuelas*

Eating out in Pichicuy
- Restaurant Posada El Bosque, Panamericana KM 181. Seafood

ⓣ Entertainment
- Disco Jaito, Ortiz de Rozas
- Disco Lua, Esmeralda

▨ Post and telegraph

Post office
- Correo, Serrano, Local 8

Telephone
- CTC, Portales 636 (711620

🚗 Motoring

Gas stations
- COPEC, Portales
- Esso, Quinquimo, intersection of Panamericana with Ruta E-30-F

🏬 Shopping

The town is famous for homemade woolen weavings. Most shops are located in Ortíz de Rozas. The best known is Casa Baltrain Goyenechea, Ortíz de Rozas 1000, a colonial mansion worth visiting.

⊙ Sport

There are tennis courts near the airstrip.

⊕ Excursions

- **Caleta Los Molles:** 43 km north, 2 km off Panamericana. This is the north-ernmost beach in the region. It has camping grounds and overlooks seal colonies.
- **Casa Patronal de la Quintrala:** Hacienda El Ingenio, 13 km west on road to Cabildo. An old colonial *hacienda* which belonged once to members of the Lisperguer family.
- **Chincolco**: It is possible to continue on Ruta E-35 via Cabildo and Petorca to Chincolco in the *pre- Cordillera*. This is a 52 km trip to **Petorca** and a further 11 km to Chincolco. The most scenic route — and the one taken by buses — is via **Cabildo**. At Cabildo you leave the Río La Ligua valley and turn north. Here begins a scenic ascent over the **Cuesta La Grupa**, with the road passing through a tunnel halfway up the mountain. Emerging from the tunnel, you are in the **Río Petorca** valley. This is a wide valley at first, at its widest where the Estero Las Palmas joins the

🚌 Buses from La Ligua

The bus terminal is on Papudo corner of Polanco.
Colectivos leave from the Polanco bus stop (*paradero*) on the corner of Papudo and Polanco for the suburb of Valle Hermoso and for Pullally beach.

Companies
- A43   Buses Ligua, Polanco *paradero*
- A44   Buses La Porteña' ,Departs from its own bus terminal in Esmeralda
- A105 Buses Sol del Pacífico, Polanco *paradero*
- A153 Tur-Bus Jedimar, Polanco *paradero* ℂ 711101

Services

Destination	Fare	Services	Duration	Companies
• Cabildo		3 services daily		A44
• Chincolco	$2.30	4 services daily		A44
• La Calera	$1.10	6 services daily	1 hr	A43, A44
• La Cruz				A44
• Limache		10 services daily		A44
• Los Andes	$2.30	4 services daily		A44
• Los Vilos	$6.30	4 services daily	2 hrs	A44
• Papudo	$2.30			A153
• Petorca	$2.00	3 services daily		A44
• Quillota				A44
• Quilpué				A44
• San Felipe	$2.10	4 services daily		A44
• Santiago	$2.70	6 services daily		A43, A153
• Valparaíso				
via La Calera	$1.90	2 services daily		A44
via Puchuncaví	$1.90	1 service daily		A44, A105
• Villa Alemana				A44
• Viña del Mar	$1.90			A44

Río Petorca. Shortly after Hacienda Pedegua, there is a road junction: Ruta E-35-D continues north — it is the former colonial road to La Serena and possibly the pre-Hispanic trail. Take the north-easterly road which follows the Río Petorca. At Hacienda Hierro Viejo the valley narrows again: the mountains on either side reach 2000 m and are covered with shrub-like vegetation; the rivers and little mountain streams are unpolluted. There are a few bad stretches from Petorca to Chincolco, and some sections are subject to flooding. If you have a four-wheel-drive vehicle it is possible to return to Santiago via **Putaendo** and **San Felipe**, but the stretch between Chincolco and Putaendo is very rough. This is not an altogether spectacular trip, but it brings you into an area which is off the beaten track and still can be reached with public transport. Simple accommodation is available at Cabildo, Petorca and

Chincolco. This trip is for those who enjoy the outdoors. See the entry for Petorca on page 294.

- **Pichicuy:** A small fishing village, 1.5 km off the Panamericana some 31 km north-west of La Ligua. The beach is very popular in summer, but the facilities are basic. The average annual temperature is 17°C (63°F). There are a few kiosks, holiday cabins, and summer villas, and in summer there is also a disco in the village. The fine white sandy beaches are the main attraction, extending 7 km south to **Caleta La Ligua**. There is no accommodation. Outside the tourist season it is quiet. During the holiday season, cars visiting the village have to pay a toll. The beach is suitable for windsurfing, yachting, rowing, and skin-diving. La Porteña runs 12 services daily south to Viña del Mar/Valparaíso; buses stop on the Panamericana.

LAS CRUCES

Area code: 35
Altitude: Sea level
Distances
- From Santiago: 126 km west on Ruta G-98-F and RN 78 (via Melipilla)
- From Valparaíso: 97 km south via Casablanca.

L as Cruces is a small beach resort on the coastal plain, halfway between El Tabo and Cartagena. It is built on two hills, Vaticano and Quirinal, which are part of the county of Comuna El Tabo. The foreshores are rocky, and the main activity centers around Playa Blanca, a small beach wedged between the two hills. In the early part of this century, Las Cruces was a fashionable resort for the wealthy, and it has recently become popular again in summer and at weekends. Tourist facilities include hotels and restaurants. A few buildings survive from the early days, such as Casa Smith, Casa Pacheco, and a house built like an English castle in the Vaticano district. Splendid sunsets can be observed from the lookout at Punta El Lacho, accessible from Avenida Osvaldo Marín.

The average summer temperature is 18°C (64°F) and the water is 15°C (59°F). Playa Blanca is in town and Playa Larga which becomes Playa

Costa Azul is further south. The beach facilities include swimming, fishing, water sports, and kiosks. In summer, life-guards patrol Playa Las

Salinas, Playa Chica, and Playa Blanca.

From the lookout located in the promontory called Punta El Lacho, there are magnificent views north over Playa las Salinas and south across the Bay to Cartagena. Pleasant walks may be taken in the eucalyptus forests to the north.

Ⓐ Camping

There are a camping sites on the southern and northern outskirts of Las Cruces.

⑪ Eating out

Restaurants
- Bellavista, Avenida La Playa, overlooking Playa Blanca
- Casino Club Deportivo El Tabo, San Martín corner of Serrano. Seafood
- La Cabaña, Avenida Las Salinas

- Puesta del Sol, Avenida la Playa 852. Seafood

🚌 Buses

Note that most buses do not enter the town but pass on the outskirts.
Buses Via Mar run daily regular services Santiago; fare $2.50.

⊛ Sport

Playa Las Salinas, north of Las Cruces, is an extensive beach.

● Excursions

- **Laguna El Peral**: A large sandbank stops the **Estero de los Helechos** flowing into the sea and creates a large *laguna*. It is home to ducks, black-necked swans, and other seabirds. The area has been declared a *Sancturio de la Naturaleza* to preserve the wildlife. The *quebrada* has enough water throughout the year to sustain many tree-ferns (or *helechos*).

⊟ Accommodation in Las Cruces

Cabañas
- La Coruña, Avenida Las Salinas — (212210

Complejo Turístico
- Quirinal, Avenida las Salinas 747 — (212476
  36 beds

Hotels

La Posada, Avenida Errázuriz 719 20 rooms	AFGHPU	(233520	$I 👫
Las Cruces, Avenida Errázuriz 783 43 beds	ADEFGHK	(212898	$G 👫
Puesta de Sol, Avenida La Playa 855	AEFGIJP	(233520/212679	$H 👫
Villa Trouville, Santo Domingo near Lincoln	AEFGHIJK	(212558	
99 beds			

Residenciales

Alvarez, Avenida Errázuriz 804 21 beds	PS	(212729	$I 👤
Mario, Mercedes 473 23 beds		(212519	
Villa Luisen, Avenida Las Salinas 729 24 beds			

LIMACHE

Area code: 033
Population: 26 000
Distances
- From Santiago: 101 km north-west on RN 57 and Ruta G-16, F-10-G
- From Valparaíso: 44 km east on RN 62

Limache is a medium-sized town on the **Estero Limache**, which rises in the **Parque Nacional La Campana**.

The hub of the town spreads for nearly two kilometers along Avenida Urmeneta, which is lined with large century-old trees which form a shady archway over the street. At weekends, a band plays in the Parque Brazil and there is dancing in the open.

Limache is a good base for excursions into the nearby valleys of the *coastal cordillera* and to places such as **Embalse Lliu-Lliu** in the picturesque upper **Valle Lliu-Lliu** beneath **Cerro La Chapa** (1740 m), or **Embalse Los Aromos de Michimalonco**, west of town on the Estero Limache.

The area around Limache is known for growing fine tomatoes.

⊠ Festivals
- February 28: Virgen de las 40 Horas. The statue of the virgin, salvaged from a shipwreck by fishermen in Concón some 200 years ago, is an object of veneration. Festivities are held outside Iglesia de la Cruz on Plaza de Armas
- April 23: San Jorge
- May 3: Santa Cruz de Mayo
- November: Fiesta de la Cerveza (Beer Festival)

ⓘ Tourist information
- Municipalidad, República 371

ⓐ Camping
There is a camping site in Parque La Victoria RN 62, near Puente Colmo.

⑪ Eating out

Restaurants
- Club Arabe, Condell 173. Lebanese cuisine
- Club Social Italo Chileno, Avenida República 35. Italian cuisine
- Jockey Club, Avenida Urmeneta 22
- Scorpio Bar, Avenida Urmeneta 92. Cocktail bar

Eating out along the road to Olmué

Restaurants
- Rancho Carolina, Avenida Eastman 840 (alight at bus stop no. 2). Chilean cuisine. Swimming pool
- Rancho Portus, Avenida Eastman 616 (alight at bus stop 2.5). Grill

ⓨ Entertainment
- Disco Punto, Avenida Granizo
- Pergola Gabriela Mistral, Parque Brazil. On Sundays, there is dancing from 2100 onwards

ⓚ Post and telegraph

Post office
- Correos, Serrano

Telephone
- CTC, Plaza de las 40 Horas on Avenida República 38
- Telex Chile, Serrano 131-B

🚍 Buses from Limache
- Agdabus, Estación Limache ℓ 495 Runs *colectivo* services to Granizo, Limachito, Olmué, and San Francisco de Limache every 10 minutes
- Alfa Tres Ltda
- Asociación Gremial de Buses Intercomunales

🛏 Accommodation in Limache

Hotels
- Deutsches Ferienheim, Caupolicán 286
  A   ☎ 412374 $G ⚎
  Fax 412780, German spoken
- Mónaco, Ramón de la Cerda 14   AGHIJV   ☎ 411441 $H ⚎
  15 rooms

Residenciales
- Fernández, 5 de Abril corner of Independencia   ☎ 412341
  8 beds
- Los Troncos II, Balmaceda 31   ☎ 412304
  8 beds
- Prat, Arturo Prat 446

Accommodation outside Limache
- Hotel Fundo las Tórtolas, at the Quillota–Olmué crossroads
  AF   ☎ 412780

Runs 3 services daily to Illapel and Salamanca
- Buses Dhino
- Buses Golondrina, Echaurren ☎ 411530
  Runs daily buses to Santiago;
- Buses La Porteña
- Ciferal Express
  Runs services to Cuesta La Dormida and Olmué every 15 minutes

There are 5 services daily to La Calera, Peña Blanca, Quillota, Quilpué, Valparaíso, Villa Alemana, Viña del Mar.

🚗 Motoring

Gas stations
- COPEC, Troncal corner of Echaurren
- Esso, Urmeneta
- Shell, Urmeneta 119

🚆 Trains

The railroad stations is on Avenida Urmeneta.

There are four services daily to Limache, Quillota, La Calera, Llay-Llay, San Felipe, and Los Andes; and to Peña Blanca, Villa Alemana, Quilpué, Viña del Mar, and Valparaíso.

🎾 Sport
- Club de Ténis, Avenida Urmeneta, opposite Parque Brazil
- Trout fishing in Estero Limache

📷 Sightseeing
- Iglesia Santa Cruz, Plaza de Armas (also known as Plaza de las 40 Horas)

🏕 Excursions
- **Complejo Turístico Los Aromos de Michilongo**: 5 km before the junction of Estero Limache with the Río Aconcagua, where the valley narrows to form a canyon. This is a favorite picnic and camping spot.
- **Tranque Lliu-Lliu**: An artificial lake 11 km south-east at the headwaters of the Estero Lliu-Lliu offering water skiing, windsurfing, fishing, and camping. The mountains of **Alto del Totoral** form a backdrop — the highest peak, **Cerro La Chapa** rises to 1744 m. The nearby monastery Convento San Benito belongs to the Benedictine monks.

LLAY-LLAY

Area code: 034
Population: 15 000
Altitude: 365 m
Distances:
- From Santiago: 86 km north on Panamericana
- From Valparaíso: 99 km east on RN 60

Llay-Llay is an important road junction where the Panamericana (RN 5) intersects with the RN 60 to Mendoza in Argentina. Since trains stopped running between Santiago and Mendoza, it has lost much of its importance as a railroad junction. The only train that still stops here runs between Valparaíso and Los Andes.

Nowadays it is the center of a grape and fruit producing area. Descending the Panamericana from Cuesta Las Chilcas the Valle de Llay Llay presents itself at its best: well-laid-out vineyards and orchards as far as the eye can see. Odd-shaped huge boulders are strewn around everywhere in the valley.

⚒ Festivals
- February, first week: Fiesta Provincial del Cantar — singing competition
- March: Rodeo Oficial (Fiesta Huasa)
- April 6: Foundation of Llay-Llay
- October: Rodeo (Fiesta Huasa)

ⓘ Tourist information
- Municipalidad, Balmaceda 98

⊟ Accommodation

Residenciales
- Meléndez, Balmaceda 18 (611541. 12 beds
- Rex, Enrique Meiggs 58 (611108

⑪ Eating out
- Club Social Llay-Llay, Balmaceda 85
- Patti Buch, Edwards 33
- Central, Edwards 75

Eating out Panamericana
- Restaurant Toro Frut, KM 80
- Restaurant Alamo Huacho, KM 83

- Hostería Los Hornitos de Llay-Llay, KM 85
- Hostería Shell, KM 85

▨ Post and telegraph

Telephone
- CTC, Balmaceda 179

⊟ Buses
The Rodoviario or bus terminal is on Avenida Yungay.

Companies
- Buses Puma run regular buses every half an hour to San Felipe and Los Andes
- Expreso Sol del Pacífico runs buses every half hour to La Calera, Limache, Quilpué, San Felipe, Valparaso, Villa Alemana, and Viña del Mar

▤ Motoring
There is a COPEC gas station on the Panamericana.

▤ Trains
- Los Andes: Fare $0.80; 4 services daily
- Valparaíso: Fare $0.75; 4 services daily

◉ Excursions
- **Las Chilcas:** 8 km east. This is a scenic drive through the *quebrada*. At **Quebrada Las Chilcas** is a pre-Columbian cemetery.
- **Catemu:** 8 km east. See the entry for Catemu on page 249.

LOS ANDES

Area code: 034
Population: 47 000
Altitude: 800 m
Distances:
- From Santiago: 80 km north on RN 57
- From Valparaíso: 139 km east on RN 60
- From Mendoza in Argentina: 225 km west on RN 60

L os Andes, sited in the fertile **Río Aconcagua** valley, was founded in 1791 as Santa Rosa de Los Andes. Los Andes is in the *pre-Cordillera*, but the ascent to the pass starts a few kilometers east of town. This is the center of an important fruit- and-grape growing area and the gateway to some exciting excursions into the *pre-Cordillera* and high *sierra*. For further information see Cajón del Río Aconcagua which deals with tourist information east of Los Andes on page 242.

The area has been densely populated since pre-Hispanic times, and this was the first area to feel the full impact of the Spanish *encomienda* system. The indigenous peoples were gradually absorbed into the mainstream of Spanish life and eventually disappeared. In line with a numerous pre-Colombian population there are many archeological sites. These are mostly rock paintings, such as those at El Guapi and Cerro Mecachas, also known as Cerro La Mesa ("Table Mountain") because of its flat top. Most of the sites consist of rock drawings, some of which have yet to be properly investigated by archeologists.

Los Andes and the surrounding villages have retained many colonial features — houses of adobe, vineyards, and some monasteries.

There are many thermal springs in the area, most of them in their natural state, such as **Baños el Lobo** near Cariño Botado. **Baños del Corazón** has a fully fledged thermal resort hotel.

⚐ Festivals
- February, third week: Fiesta de la Chaya
- March/April: Feria Internacional de Los Andes — agricultural show
- July 26–31: Foundation day
- September: Canoeing championships
- September 18–19: Rodeo Oficial (or Fiesta Huasa)
- October: Fiesta de la Primavera (Spring Festival)
- December: Boat regatta held on the Río Aconcagua

Festivals in Rinconada
- January, second week: Aniversario Rinconada
- October 12: Rodeo Oficial (or Fiesta Huasa) — cowboy festival

Festivals in San Estebán
- December 26th: San Estebán

ⓘ Tourist information
- Municipalidad, Avenida San Martín 607 ℂ 420029
- Oficina Central de Informaciones Turísticas, at the entrance to Los Andes. Open Mon–Sun, 0900–2100, during summer holidays only

ⓘ Eating out
Los Andes is famous for its *cazuela de ave*, a casserole of chicken or turkey with walnuts and avocados.

Restaurants
- Casino Comercial, Maipú 144. *Parrilladas*
- Centro Español, General Freire 332. Spanish cuisine
- Círculo Italiano, Esmeralda 246 $X. *Parrilladas*
- Cristo Redentor, Sarmiento 197
- Dónde El Guatón, Sarmiento 240. Pizzas and grills
- Don Pascual Baburizza 421. Chilean cuisine
- Guatón Loyola, Santa Rosa 279. Pizzas
- Hotel Continental, Esmeralda 221. Italian cuisine
- Hotel Plaza, Esmeralda 367. International cuisine
- Los Olmos, Los Olmos 1002
- ☞ Mi Reina, Esmeralda 333, inside Galería Comercial $Y. Chilean cuisine
- The Rainbow, Sarmiento 194. Pizzas
- Willy, Maipú 57

Eating out on RN 60
- ☞ El Sauce, 4 km. *Parrilladas*

Eating out in Rinconada
Rinconada is a small rural community 8 km west.

Restaurants
- La Estrella, Avenida San Martín 2700. Chilean cuisine

- Sao Paolo, Avenida San Martín. Chilean cuisine

Eating out in San Esteban
San Esteban is a small rural community 4 km north of Los Andes.
- Restaurant El Kaki Tour Resort, Foncea 819. International cuisine
- Restaurant El Rancho, 26 de Diciembre 164. Chilean cuisine

Entertainment
- Cabaret Domino, Esmeralda 277. Open daily from 2200 onwards
- Disco El Flamingo, El Bolsón road to Rinconada

Entertainment in Bucalemu
Bucalemu is a small rural community 3 km south of Curimón on the road to Rinconada.
- Restaurant La Ruca. Chilean cuisine, Huaso shows daily

Post and telegraph

Post office
- Correos, Libertador Bernardo O'Higgins 387

Telephone
- CTC, Libertador Bernardo O'Higgins 405, fax 423500
- Telex Chile, Esmeralda 387

Key to map
A	Iglesia
B	Gobernación Provincial (Government)
C	Municipalidad (Town hall)
D	Post office and telex
E	Telephone
H	Hospital
P	Gas stations
$	Money exchange
T	Bus terminals

● **Accommodation**
2 Residencial Serena
5 Hotel Valparaíso
8 Hotel Estación
13 Hotel Plaza
16 Hotel Continental
21 Hotel Central

○ **Eating out**
3 Restaurant Peces Marina
4 Restaurant Willy
6 Restaurant Club Social
7 Restaurant Casino Social
9 Restaurant Donde El Guatón
12 Restaurant Guatón Loyola
14 Restaurant Mi Reina
20 Restaurant Círcolo Italiano
22 Restaurant Maznic

△ **Tour operators and car rental**
19 Turismo Teocan

■ **Sights**
17 Convento Carmelita
18 Museo Arqueológico

□ **Services**
1 Railroad station
10 Supermercado La Granja
11 Automóvil Club de Chile
15 Agfa - Nort Sur
23 Fería Artesanal
24 Cerámicas Artisticas de los Andes

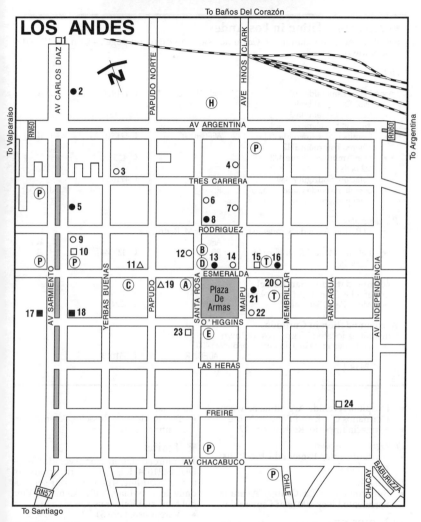

LOS ANDES

$ Financial

- Cambio Hotel Plaza, Esmeralda 367 (421979
- Cambios Inta, Esmeralda block 300 near Maipú

🖳 Services and facilities

Dry cleaner
- Lavaseco Trelli, M. Rodríguez 196

Medical services
- Centro Médico Los Andes, Yerbas Buenas 310 (421704

▣ Accommodation in Los Andes

See also "Accommodation" in Cajón del Río Aconcagua on page 243, on the RN 60 east of town.

Hotels

★★★ Plaza, Esmeralda 367	AEFGHIJLP$	(421929	$G ♙
Fax 426029; 61 beds			
• Central, Esmeralda 278		(421275	
Budget travelers			
• Continental, Esmeralda 211	AEFGHIJLP	(421510	$H ♙
Shared bathroom $l ♙			
• Don Ambrosio, Freire 472		(425496	
22 beds			
• Estación, Rodríguez 389	AFGLPV	(421026	
• Serena, Avenida Carlos Díaz 57	F		$J ♙
Backpackers			

Residenciales

• El Portón, Avenida Sarmiento block 200 near M. Rodríguez			
	AF		$l ♙
• Italiana, Manuel Rodríguez 76	PS	(423544	$H ♙
15 beds			

Accommodation in San Rafael
San Rafael is 5 km west on RN 60.

• Motel Zava, San Rafael	AEPV	(422419	

Accommodation in Curimón
Curimón is located 18 km west of town

• Hotel San Francisco de Curimón, Bueras 400			
	ADEGJLR	(531013	
24 beds			

- Hospital, Avenida Argentina between Hermanos Clark and Papudo Norte
- Farmacia Imperio, Rodríguez 317

Photographic supplies
- NortSur Agfa, Esmeralda block 200 near Maipú

Supermarket
- Supermercado La Granja, Avenida Sarmiento block 200 near Esmeralda

▣ Motoring

For gas stations, see city map.
- Automóvil Club de Chile, Esmeralda 536 (21939. Information about road conditions over pass to Mendoza in Argentina in winter

Car rental
- Bert Rent-a-Car Rosselot, Avenida Argentina 1130 (421761

▣ Trains

The railroad station is on Avenida Carlos Díaz (421054. It is the eastern terminal of the railroad line. There are four services daily to Llay-Llay, Villa Alemana, Viña del Mar, and Valparaíso.
- Valparaíso: Fare $1.50

▣ Shopping

Los Andes is known for its porcelain figurines and chinaware.
- Cerámica Manque, Avenida Carlos Díaz
- Fábrica de Cerámicas Artísticas de los Andes, Rancagua 594

⊛ Sport

Los Andes is the gateway to the high sierra. Fishing in the mountain streams such as Estero San Francisco and its tributary Estero El Maitén the Río Aconcagua attracts many *aficionados*. A growing number of hikers explore the valleys and peaks of the nearby cordillera. And of course skiing at Portillo and other localities. For further information, see Cajón del Río Aconcagua on page 243 and Portillo on page 295.

▦ Sightseeing

- Museo Arqueológico, Avenida Sarmiento 392. This museum has a very extensive collection of pre-Columbian artifacts found in the region. The oldest samples go back to 800 BC. Inca, Diaguita, Atacameño, Mapuche, and Los Molle cultures are well represented. Open Tues–Fri, 1000–1300.
- Parque Yerbas Buenas, corner of Avenida Chacabuco and Avenida Sarmiento. Inside this park is a small hill, on whose summit is a plaque with an inscription that can be translated as: "Ambrosio O'Higgins, Governor, Founder 31/7/1791: I came to found a town with the title Villa Santa Rosa de los Andes".

✦ Excursions

Tour operators
- Turismo Teocolan, Esmeralda 500

Excursions
- **Portillo** skiing region: 59 km east on RN 60. See the entry for Portillo on page 295.
- **Baños del Corazón:** Also known as Termas de Corazón, it is an excellent thermal spa in the *pre-Cordillera* with a good restaurant. The road to Baños del Corazón crosses a long bridge over the **Río Aconcagua** with the snow-covered peaks of the high *sierras* to the east. After the bridge, there is a turnoff to the left to San Felipe (Ruta E-85); continue straight on past the turnoff and turn east at the village of San Esteban, and drive for a further 20 minutes to the thermal resort. Buses San Esteban run regular *colectivo* services from the *colectivo* terminal to Termas del Corazón; fares are $0.80.

- **Campo de Ahumada Alto**: 30 km north at 1700 m in the **Quebrada El Arpa,** has been earmarked as a ski center. At the moment it is an almost forgotten colonial village, and is a good starting point for mountain walks into the high *sierra*. Nearby **Cerro Alto del Cobre** reaches over 3600 m.
- **Cerro Paidahuen** (915 m): 3 km north on the road to La Florida. The rock paintings on top of the hill, made in prehistoric times, represent human beings as well as geometrical and abstract figures.
- **Curimón**: 18 km west in the **Río Aconcagua** valley, altitude 650 m. This village was founded by the Franciscan order, and the monastery and church go back to 1583. On October 4 is the *fiesta* of St Francis of Assisi — with a blessing of the animals which attracts a large crowd. The main attraction however is the Museo y Convento Franciscano de Curimón, one of the earliest Franciscan missions in Chile. The exhibits include objects of the colonial period and some priceless paintings of the Cuzco School. Open Mon–Sun 1000–1300 and 1500–2000; small admission fee. From Curimón there are frequent daily buses to San Felipe and Los Andes.
- **Rinconada** (not to be confused with Rinconada de Silva or Rinconada de Guzman further north in the Río Putaendo valley): In the **Río Aconcagua** valley some 8 km west, famous for its country-style taverns. A farming community with 3600 inhabitants, it is chiefly engaged in wine-making and horticulture, with apricots and peaches being grown extensively. This is a typical central Chilean village with adobe houses serving as a reminder of its colonial past. The Ruta de San Martín is one of the oldest roads in Chile — notice the ancient trees lining it between Rinconada and the Chacabuco tunnel. There are also many smaller colonial villages with a picture-book appearance, such as **San Miguel** and **San Regis** and also **Casuto**, 1 km off Carretera San Martín. At **Auco** 4 km south is the Convento de las Carmelitas Descalzas

🚌 Buses from Los Andes

The taxi *colectivos* terminal is at Esmeralda block 200 near Membrillar to San Felipe. All fares are $0.50.

The bus terminal is on the Membrillar corner of Esmeralda. Left luggage room and a cafetería. Local buses to Curimón ($0.35) and San Estebán depart from here every hour.

Companies
- A2   Buses Alfa Tres Ltda ☎ 421262
- A14   Buses Ahumada ☎ 422401
- A22   CATA, office 9 ☎ 422514
- A32   Flota Imperial ☎ 422514
- A40   Buses JM, office 5 ☎ 422009
- A70   Buses Ruta 57 ☎ 422092
- A75   Buses TAC, Sarmiento near Avenida Argentina ☎ 422651
- A106   Fénix Pullman Norte, office 8 ☎ 421231
- A137   TAS Choapa, ☎ 421232

Services

Destination	Fare	Services	Company
• Antofagasta	$31.50	1 service daily	A106
• Arica	$46.00	1 service daily	A106
• Cabildo	$2.50	13 services daily	A44
• Concón	$2.10	13 services daily	A2
• Copiapó	$17.20	1 service daily	A137
• Coquimbo	$13.00	2 services daily	A137
• Horcón	$3.40	13 services daily	A2
• Iquique	$37.60	1 service daily	A106
• La Calera	$1.70	13 services daily	A2
• La Ligua	$2.30	13 services daily	A44
• La Serena	$13.00	2 services daily	A106, A137
• Los Vilos	$6.20	2 services daily	A137
• Mendoza (Argentina)	$20.00	8 services daily	A22, A75, A106, A137
• Ovalle	$10.50		A137
• Papudo	$2.70		A44
• Portillo	$2.70	Irregular services, usually one service early in the morning	
• Quillota	$2.10	13 services daily	A2
• Quintero	$3.30	13 services daily	A2
• San Felipe	$0.50	12 services daily	A44
• San Juan (Argentina)	$23.00	Thurs	A137
• Santiago	$2.10	38 services daily	A14, A32, A70
• Termas del Corazón	$1.50		Taxi
• Vallenar	$14.60	1 service daily	A137
• Valparaíso	$2.90	12 services daily	A2, A40, A106
• Viña del Mar	$2.90	12 services daily	A2, A40

with the remains of Chile's first Saint — Sor Beata Teresa de los Andes, which is visited by many pilgrims all year round. The typical Chilean cuisine of this area is based to a large extent on pork and beef. Try *chicha* and *mistela* drinks made from grapes Buses Imperial runs regular buses to San Felipe and Los Andes.

- **San Esteban**: In the **Río Aconcagua** valley, 5 km north. It is the starting point for mountain hikes into the Andean *cordillera*, such as up the San Francisco valley. Many of the houses in San Esteban feature the triangular double-entry building style of the late 1800s, which is bound to disappear soon as the old houses make room for more modern buildings. A feature of this style is that the ornate column on the corner supports the roof. Buses Rurales Linea 8 run regular daily services to Los Andes and further up the valley to Lo Calvo.

LOS MOLLES

Altitude: Sea level
Distance from Valparaíso: 155 km north on RN 5 and Ruta F-30

Los Molles is a picturesque fishing village at the mouth of **Estero Los Molles**. There is a beach and the local fishermen are friendly. There are caves and rocky outcrops with plenty of wildlife, in particular many kinds of birds.

The beach, approximately three kilometers long, is the northernmost beach in Región V de Valparaíso. The rocks form a natural swimming pool, but there are no facilities.

⊟ Accommodation

There are two *hospedajes*, usually booked out in January and February.
- Cabañas Lourdes, Vicente Huidobro

ⒶCamping

There is a good camping site with facilities on the beach.

⑪ Eating out

Restaurants
- Armandita, Avenida Los Molles. Seafood

- El Churro, Vicente Huidobro. Seafood
- El Pirata Suizo, Los Pescadores. International cuisine

⛌ Buses

- Valparaíso: Fare $2.50; Intercomunal. Stops on the Panamericana

⊛ Sport

Playa los Molles is suitable for windsurfing and skin-diving.

⊡ Sightseeing

To the north of the village, the peninsula has been sculpted by the sea into interesting rock formations and partly submerged caves.
- **Isla de los Lobos**: An island with a seal colony opposite rocky outcrops, clearly visible from the coast.

MAITENCILLO

Altitude: Sea level
Distances:
- From Santiago: 178 km north-west on Ruta F-30-E and RN 68
- From Valparaíso: 65 km north on Ruta F-30-E

Maitencillo is a small beach resort on the Chilean Riviera with good tourist facilities, two kilometers off the main road. The township stretches beside the sea for five kilometers, and its rural aspect is enhanced by the surrounding eucalyptus and pine tree forest.

The resort has ample tourist facilities, and is visited by regular buses from Valparaíso. Discos, however, operate only in summer. Seafood dishes predominate in the restaurants. The jewel in the crown is Centro Recreativo Marbella club, with its own golf course and polo facilities.

The average summer temperature is 18°C (64°F) and the water is 15°C (59°F). The beaches consist of white sand and slope gently toward the water. Most of them are within easy walking distance of Maitencillo:

- Playa Aguas Blancas: South of town, beginning just past Restaurant La Pajera. The white sand of this beach extends from the southern exit for five kilometers. Good swimming, fishing, water sports, camping, kiosks, and life-guards.

To Papudo

MAITENCILLO

AV DEL MAR

OCEANO PACIFICO

MAITENCILLO (F)

To Valparaíso

Key to map

P   Service stations

●   **Accommodation**
1   Hotel Villa Regina
2   Centro Turístico Delfín
3   Hotel Las Rocas
4   Motel Fundo Cerro Colorado
6   Motel Centro Recreativo Marbella Club

○   **Eating out**
7   Restaurant La Pajarera

⊙   **Entertainment**
5   Cancha de Polo (Polo field)

Plate 17   Easter Island
Top: Parque Nacional Isla Pascuas, Siete Moais
Bottom: Parque Nacional Isla Pascuas, rock paintings

Plate 18   Easter Island
Top: Puna Pau, 'hat factory'
Bottom: Rano Kau, crater

⊟ Accommodation in Maitencillo

Cabañas
- Hermansen, Avenida del Mar 0592   ☏ 771028
  50 beds

Hotels
  ★★★ Villa Regina, Avenida Del Mar 100 corner of San Miguel
                                  ABHPU   ☏ 771030
         30 beds
- Las Rocas, Avenida Del Mar 1685   AEFGHIJMP$V   ☏771008
  Located on a rocky promontory, open only during summer holidays; 51 beds

Motels
  ★★★★★Centro Recreativo Marbella Club, Ruta F30 KM 35   ☏ 931155 $C 👫
     Not directly on the beach. It consists of 100 ha (246 acres) of parkland setting on a hill
     overlooking Playa Aguas Blancas. Access is from the southern entrance to Maitencillo
     on the main highway. There is a *residencial* area with furnished houses which can be
     rented all year round. The club has three swimming pools, restaurant, tennis court, golf
     course, sauna and horse riding. 46 rooms, 22 apartments, polo; 267 beds
- Centro Recreativo Javier Carrera, Avenida Del Mar 2538
                               ABCFGHIJPRV   ☏ 771051
  258 beds
- Centro Turístico Delfín, Avenida Del Mar 180
                               ABCHU   ☏ 771025
  55 beds
☞ - Fundo Cerro Colorado, Camino Antiguo, part of Copec gas station
                            ABCEFGHIJLNPR$V $G 👫
  Tennis courts, 11 rooms, fax (32) (9) 2231299; 50 beds

Accommodation beside Laguna de Zapallar
This small laguna is located on the road to Catapilco (Ruta E-46).
- Cabañas Bio Fitness Farm, Fundo Santa Bertina
                           ABCEFGHJNR
  Open all year. Surrounded by small hills in a forested area. German spoken. Every Sunday from 1100 onwards a German "Fruehschoppen" is held — brunch with beer and music.

- Playa Los Pocitos: A smaller beach, more like a sheltered pool, within the town limits. Swimming, fishing, kiosks, and life-guards.
- Playa El Abanico: Six kilometers north of Maitencillo and reached on a dirt road. Buses will set you down at the turnoff. Swimming, fishing, water sport, kiosks, and life-guards.

⌘ Festivals
- February, second week: Semana Maitencillena

Ⓐ Camping
There are good serviced camping sites north and south of town.

⑪ Eating out

Restaurants
- El Pacífico, Avenida del Mar 1029. Seafood
- La Caracola, Playa El Abanico, Avenida del Mar 1078. Seafood. Open summer and weekends only
- La Caleta, Avenida del Mar. Seafood

- Unicorno Azul, Avenida del Mar 895. Seafood

Post and telegraph

Post office
- Correos, Avenida del Mar 2538

Telephone
- Public telephone, Avenida del Mar in Hotel Las Rocas

Buses

Nueva Transmar Bus, opposite Playa El Abanico, runs buses to Puchuncaví, Las Ventanas, Quintero, Viña del Mar, and Santiago.

Excursions

- **La Laguna**: A small beach resort located a few kilometers north, excellent for scuba diving. The seaside between La Laguna and Horcón is undergoing a fairly intensive tourist development because of the attractive beaches and scenic drive north along the coastal road to Cachagua and beyond. On July 16 the *fiesta* of the Virgen del Carmen is celebrated. The best beaches are Playa Las Agatas, 3.5 km north, reached by means of a trail; and Playa Las Frutillas, 400 m outside La Laguna. Regular daily bus services are provided by Buses La Porteña south to Viña del Mar and north to Papudo; and to Santiago by Buses La Ligua, fare $3.10.

For trips into the interior, see "Excursions" from Puchuncaví on page 298.

OLMUÉ

Area code: 033
Population: 6600
Altitude: 200 m
Distance from Valparaíso: 50 km east on RN 62 and Ruta 550 (sealed)

Olmué is a small town located in the coastal *cordillera*. It was founded as an Indian community in 1612 during the second governorship of Don Alonso de Ribera. The decision was probably influenced by the very vocal Jesuit Padre Luis de Valdivia, who advocated a more lenient treatment of the native population. Olmué was visited by Charles Darwin in 1835, who commented on its beautiful location.

The air here is supposed to be very rich in ozone, which makes it ideal for people suffering from lung complaints. **Cerro La Campana** (1828 m) rises behind the town, one of the highest peaks in the coastal *cordillera* and the center of the Parque Nacional La Campana. It is known for its colorful *huaso* fiestas. The amphitheater in Parque El Patagal is the site of the annual *huaso* musical festival.

Olmué has good tourist facilities, and during the summer holidays it attracts a large number of Chilean tourists, but so far few foreign tourists have found their way to this attractive little town at the gateway to **Parque Nacional La Campana's**.

Olmué, together with its "suburbs" of Granizo, Cajón Grande, and Lo Narvaez, stretches for several kilometers east toward the national park. In the listings for this town, I have indicated the location of facilities within the town perimeter by providing the closest *paradero* or bus stop.

The road leading east toward the national park is called Avenida Granizo, and the road leading west

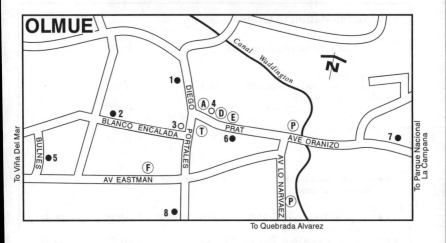

Key to map

A	Iglesia	**2**	Complejo Turístico La Campana
C	Municipalidad (Town hall)	**5**	Cabañas Don Matías
D	Post office and telex	**6**	Hotel Scala de Milán
E	Telephone	**7**	Condominio Don Pepe
F	Carabineros (Police)	**8**	Hostería Llacolen
P	Gas stations		
T	Bus terminals	⊙	**Entertainment**
		3	Disco Estación 23
●	**Accommodation**	**4**	Peña Huaso Calderón
1	Hostería El Copihué		

toward the coast is called Avenida Eastman. If you prefer to be closer to the national park, choose accommodation near or on Avenida Granizo.

⊠ Festivals

- January 23–25: Festival del Huaso, held in Parque El Patagual — country festival and display of horsemanship
- May: Procesión Cristo Padre — street procession
- October: Rodeo Oficial (or Fiesta Huasa)

Festivals in Quebrada Alvarado
- September 17–19: Rodeo Oficial (or Fiesta Huasa)

ⓘ Tourist information

- Municipalidad, Arturo Prat 12 ☎ 9063

Ⓐ Camping

The nearest camping areas are inside Parque Nacional La Campana.

⊞ Eating out

Most hotels also have good restaurants.

Restaurants
- El Latigazo, Colegio 5210
- Parador de Betty, Eastman 4801 near Diego Portales. Grill, international cuisine
- Sarmiento, Blanco Encalada 4689

Cafetería
- Turismo, Prat 4937, next to town hall

◧ Accommodation in Olmué

Cabañas
- Don Matías, Bulnes 1800, Paradero 18 ☏ 441933
  16 beds

Complejos Turísticos
- La Campana, Avenida Blanco Encalada 4651 ☏ 441051
  Fax 441983; 100 beds
- La Siesta, Sector Las Cruces   R ☏ 412697
  50 beds
- Paraíso, Avenida Eastman 2761. *paradero* 13
           AFR ☏ 441643
  Tennis

Hotels
- ★★Scala de Milán, Prat 5058   ADEFGHJMNPR$V ☏ 441414 $H ∎
  Fax 411028; 29 beds

Hosterías
- ★★★El Copihué, Diego Portales 2203   ADEFHKLMPRSTUVZ ☏ 441544 $F ∎∎
  Tennis, sauna, 20 rooms
- ★★★Llacolén, Avenida Diego Portales 1879, *paradero* 22 ☏ 441978 $G ∎∎
  AEFGHIJKLMNPR$TUVZ
- Ibiza, Portales corner of Blanco ☏ 441938
  20 beds
- Los Portones de Olmué, Portales 2099 ADEFGHMPRV
- Los Acacios, Avenida Eastman 2784 near Cock 2950 ☏ 441652 $F ∎∎
  ADEFGHIJLMNPR$TUVZ

Motels
- El Arrayán, Mariana de Osorio 5855 ☏ 441626
  30 beds

Residenciales
- Sarmiento, Blanco Encalada 4647   AF ☏ 441263

Accommodation Sector Granizo

Condominios
- Don Pepe, Avenida Granizo 5933, *paradero* 29½ ☏ 441477
  35 beds

Complejo Turístico
- Las Montañas de Olmué, Granizo Alto, *paradero* 43
           ABCDEFGHIJLMNPRS ☏ 441253 $G ∎∎
  Shared bathroom cheaper
- Los Vikingos, Caupolicán 2371 ☏ 441494

Hosterías
- Aire Puro, Avenida Granizo 7672, *paradero* 30 ☏ 441381
- Las Hamacas, Avenida Granizo, *paradero* 34
           FGHRUV ☏ 441916
  12 beds

Residenciales
- Alondra, Avenida Granizo, *paradero* 40 ☏ 441163

Accommodation in Quebrada Alvarado
- Residencial El Almendral ☏ (02)2192870

Eating out in Granizo

Granizo is a suburb starting 2.5 km east of Olmué and stretching for 3 km east right up to the national park.

Restaurants
- El Limonar, Paradero 40
- La Violeta, Avenida Granizo 8375, *paradero* 41. Chilean cuisine
- Los Aromos, *paradero* 34. *Parrilladas*

Eating out in Quebrada Alvarado
- Restaurant No me Olvides, Andrés Toledo. Chilean cuisine
- Restaurant Pasar a Verme, Andrés Toledo. Chilean cuisine

Entertainment
- Disco Estación 23, Avenida Diego Portales on Plaza de Armas
- Peña Folklórico Huaso Calderón, Parque El Patagual next to Municipalidad

Entertainment in Sector Granizo
- Quinta de Recreo La Campana, on road to Granizo Paradero 27 (bus stop), shows and dancing
- **Disco Punto 33**, Avenida Granizo

Post and telegraph

Post office
- Correos, Arturo Prat

Telephone
- CTC, Arturo Prat 4871 (on the plaza)

Buses
- Ciferal Express runs 6 services daily to Valparaíso and Viña del Mar
- Buses Golondrina, Arturo Prat 4863 (in the Minimercado Escorial) runs 3 services daily to Santiago
- Taxi Colectivo Independiente, Taxi Colectivo Villa Alegre, and Agdabus, depart from main plaza for Granizo, La Dormida, La Vega, Lo Narvaez, and Quebrada Alvarado every 15 minutes

Motoring
- COPEC gas station, El Colegio 1986

Shopping
- Antiguedades Olmué, Avenida Eastman 2862. Antique shop

Sightseeing
- Parque Patagual. Site of the annual *huaso* festival; very colorful.

Excursions
- **Parque Nacional La Campana**: 9 km east, along a gravel road which finishes at Mina La Merecita. From the mine, a trail leads north into the Rabuco valley. A plaque near the park entrance records the visit of Charles Darwin. See the entry for the park on page 292.
- **Las Palmas**: Catholic shrine, 15 km south-east. Here, the faithful venerate the image of Niño Jesús de Las Palmas. This trip can be combined with the excursion to Cuesta La Dormida: turn off north from Ruta F-10-G at Quebrada Alvarado.
- **Quebrada Alvarado**, a colonial village, is on the western approach to Cuesta La Dormida, 13 km east of Olmué. The area used to be covered with Chilean palm forests, but now only a few palms remain. Despite the loss of most of its native tree cover, this mountainous area is still very picturesque. This is winegrowing country, and the village is well known for its *chicha de uva*, an unfermented sweet grape juice. Try to be here at carnival time in January — it is a very colorful event. From here you get splendid views over the most attractive part of the coastal *cordillera*. Agdabus runs regular services from Olmué. Quebrada Alvarado is at the beginning of the **Cuesta La Dormida**, which was one of the roads connecting Santiago and the Pacific coast in colonial times. The 13 km section of winding road toward and over the pass is very scenic. The road over the pass is gravel. You can go hiking into the southern slopes of the **Parque Nacional La Campana** — see the entry for the park on page 292 — and south into the **Cerro Chapo** massif.

Olmué

PAPUDO

Area code: 033
Population: 3000
Altitude: Sea level
Distances
- From Santiago: 172 km north-west on Ruta E-30-F and Panamericana (via La Ligua)
- From Valparaíso: 85 km north on Ruta F-30-E

Papudo is the northernmost seaside resort of the Chilean Riviera, with beaches suitable for wind surfing. Further north are more beaches but these cannot be classified as seaside resorts such as Pichicuy and Los Molles. Papudo is located on a little bay surrounded by wide beaches, well protected from southerly winds. At the southern end, near the yacht club, the rocks come down to the sea, and rocky outcrops separate Playa Chica from Playa Grande. The average summer temperature is 18°C (64°F) and the water is 15°C (59°F).

Papudo has an excellent beach promenade, where the main tourist activities are concentrated. There are attractive beach resort homes on the hillside above the promenade with views over the bay and the beach.

This developing beach resort goes to sleep once the main tourist season is over. Most of the hotels and *residenciales* shut in early May, although the weather may still be beautiful with clear skies.

The highest mountain in this part of the coastal *cordillera* is **Cerro Cenizas** (770 m).

Access to Papudo is from the Panamericana (15 km east) or via the coastal road from Viña del Mar. If you have to get off the bus at the Panamericana intersection, there are usually taxis waiting.

The best beaches are Playa Larga, 1.5 km north of town, suitable for sailing and windsurfing; and Playa Chica, suitable for sailing, windsurfing, and yachting. At Caleta Papudo you can hire pedal-driven boats.

⊞ Festivals
- February: Tennis championships
- February: Windsurfing championship
- February, last week: Semana Papudana — a celebration with a fireworks display
- October: Open golf championships
- November 26: Naval Battle of Papudo. Celebrating the capture of a Spanish man-o'-war in 1865 when Spain tried to regain control of the former colonies

ⓘ Tourist information
- Municipalidad, Plaza de Armas ℂ 711412

Ⓐ Camping
Camping sites on Playa Grande 3 km north.

⑪ Eating out

Restaurants
- El Casino, Irarrázaval 205. Seafood
- La Cabaña, Avenida Costanera 539 $X. Seafood. Overlooks Playa Larga, access from Irarrázabal corner of Cochrane and walk 200 m
- Lilén, Avenida Costanera, directly on Playa Papudo beach
- Moderno, Fernández Concha 150. Steaks and seafood

Ⓣ Entertainment
- Disco Vivo, Avenida Irarrázaval

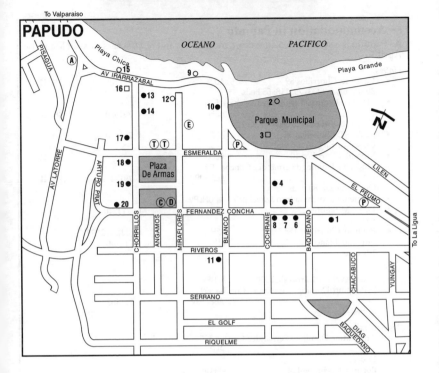

Key to map

A	Iglesia	**13**	Hotel Mocelli
C	Municipalidad (Town hall)	**14**	Hotel La Abeja
D	Post office and telex	**17**	Hotel Carandé
E	Telephone	**18**	Residencial Valencia
P	Gas stations	**19**	Hotel Papudo
T	Bus terminals	**20**	Hotel Moderno

●	**Accommodation**	○	**Eating out**
1	Hotel D'Peppino	**2**	Restaurant La Cabaña
4	Residencial Bogarín	**9**	Restaurant Lilen
5	Residencial Donde Tito	**12**	Restaurant El Casino
6	Residencial Armandini	**15**	Restaurant El Huiro
7	Residencial Papudo		
8	Hotel El Golf	⊙	**Entertainment**
10	Hotel Turismo	**3**	Tennis courts
11	Residencial Silva	**16**	Casa de la Cultura

◙ Accommodation in Papudo

As Papudo is a summer seaside resort, most hotels and *residenciales* close in March or April.

Hotels

- Carandé, Chorrillos 89   ADJKLPSV   ☎ 791105 $G ♙♙
  30 rooms, fax (33) 791118; 55 beds
- El Golf, Domingo Fernández Concha 415
     AEFHV   ☎ 791370 $H ♙♙
  Shared bathroom; 22 beds
- La Abeja, Chorrillos 36   AFJL   ☎ 711450
  Closed during off season
- Mocelli, Chorrillos 10   AEFGHIPV $H ♙♙
- Moderno, Domingo Fernández Concha 150
     AEFGIJPV   ☎ 79114 $G ♙♙
  Open all year; 80 beds
- Montemar, Avenida Irarrázaval 253   AFGHLPV
- Plaza, Miraflores 176   AFH   ☎ 711240
  93 beds
- Papudo, Chorrillos 153   AFH   ☎ (02)2272199
- Turismo, Blanco 19   AH   ☎ 711240
  101 beds

Motels

- Lilén, Avenida Irarrázabal 300   AFHPV
- D'Peppino, Domingo Fernández Concha 609
     ABHLP$V   ☎ 711482
  64 beds

Residenciales

- Armandini, Domingo Fernández Concha 525
     ALP
  17 beds
- Bogarín, Cochrane 184   AEFGP
  27 beds
- Donde Tito, Domingo Fernández Concha 550
     AEFGHILPV   ☎ 791096
  30 beds
- La Plaza, Esmeralda 119   AHPV
  23 beds
- Mary, Domingo Fernández Concha 535
     AHPV
  18 beds
- Papudo, Domingo Fernández Concha 512
     AEFGHIPSV   ☎ 711482 $I ♙♙
  40 beds
- Silva, Rivero 309 near Blanco   AEHIJP
  Closed in off season; 29 beds
- Valencia, Chorrillos 107   AEFGIJPV $I ♙♙
  47 beds

- Disco Yachting Club, Avenida Irarrázaval

🏣 Post and telegraph

Post office
- Correos, Miraflores, in the town hall building on the plaza

Telephone
- CTC, Fernández Concha 609 (inside Motel D'Peppino)

🚌 Buses

There is no central bus terminal. All buses pass through the town center.

Companies
- A62   Buses Papudo
- A105 Buses Sol del Pacífico
        6 services daily to Concón, La Calera, La Ligua, Las Ventanas, Limache, Maitencillo, Quillota, Quilpué, Quintero, Valparaíso, Villa Alemana, Viña del Mar, and Zapallar
- A153 Tur-Bus Jedimar, Plaza de Armas

Services
- La Ligua: Fare $5.70; 2 services daily; A62, A105 . You can also take a taxi
- Los Andes: Fare $2.50; 6 services daily; A44, A62, A105
- San Felipe: Fare $2.50; 6 services daily; A44
- Santiago: Fare $4.00; 5 services daily; A153
- Valparaíso: Fare $1.90; 6 services daily; A105

🚗 Motoring

- COPEC gas station, Irarrázabal corner of Blanco

⛹ Sport

- Tennis courts, Esmeralda next to Parque Municipal
- Club de Golf Papudo
- Club de Yates de Papudo (Papudo Yacht Club), Avenida Irarrázabal

📷 Sightseeing

On the stairs leading down from Calle Miraflores to the beach there is a memorial plaque whose inscription can be translated thus: "In colonial times the Spanish *conquistadores* called Papudo 'Carandé' after the residing *cacique* [chief]. In 1561 Don Garcia Hurtado de Mendoza sailed from here for Spain after he was recalled from his Chilean vice-royalty. The Spanish battleship *Virgen de Covadonga* also surrendered in these waters after a naval battle with the Chilean frigate *Esmeralda* in 1865."

- Las Dunas de Lilén, 3 km north on the gravel road to Quinquimo at the extreme northern end of Playa Larga.

🏵 Excursions

- **Maitencillo**: 28 km south. The coastal road from Papudo is particularly scenic. See the entry for Maitencillo on page 282.
- **Los Molles** and **Pichicuy** are fishing villages further north, with beaches offering spear fishing, skin diving, and visits to the caves at **Puquén,** which are blowholes excavated by the sea. For a description of Los Molles see the entry on page 281; and for Pichicuy see "Excursions" from La Ligua on page 270.

Papudo

PARQUE NACIONAL LA CAMPANA

Distances
- From Olmué: 8 km east (Sector Granizo)
- From La Calera: 24 km east (Sector Ocoa)

This national park lies in the coastal *cordillera*. It covers 10 984 ha (27 130 acres) and ranges in altitude from 200 m to 1800 m. The highest peak inside the park is **Cerro La Campana** at 1828 m. **Cerro del Roble**, outside the national park boundaries, is 2220 m high. From Cerro La Campana you have views west over the coastal *cordillera* and sweeping views to the Andes. On top of Cerro La Campana is a meteorological station which can be visited with prior permission from CONAF.

Large areas are forested with native trees up to about 1500 m. Enough rain falls in this area to produce natural springs, which run through the valleys as crystal-clear brooks. While the high *sierra* of the Andes may not be suitable for some people, this national park with its clean air can safely be visited by people who are not conditioned for high altitudes.

The average annual rainfall is 800 mm, mostly falling in winter (July–August), which makes the summers rather hot. The average annual temperature is 14°C (57°F), and the best time to visit is between September and May. Nights can get chilly and campers should bring warm gear. This is a perfect hiking area all year round. The main rivers are **Estero Rabuco**, **Agua del Manzano** and **Río Opositora** which usually flow only in winter and spring. But there are little streams higher up.

The flora includes oaks growing at their northernmost limit. Other tree species are the *lingue* (whose bark is used for tanning), *lignum vitae*, and a Chilean shrub called *maqui*. This is one of the few areas where the

Palma chilensis — Chile's native palm — can still be seen, particularly in the Rabuco valley. Some of the palms are 300 years old. Foxes, *viscachas*, weasels, and many species of reptiles are common in the park. Eagles, giant humming birds, and white owls are among the more spectacular birds.

There are also archeological and historical sites inside the park. The pre-Hispanic tribes used to crush the rocks to get copper. They also cooked the sap of the palm trees to obtain sweet molasses — the remains of one of their stoves is still visible at La Bodega.

The park contains excursion paths, a CONAF information center, picnic and camping areas, and kiosks.

The main administration building and information center is at Granizo. It displays information about flora, fauna, geology, and archeology. CONAF has made nature trails along which some of the trees and plants are labeled. The 11 km hiking trail starts from the main building. There are rangers' huts at the other sections. At La Mina there is an unattended campsite; at the Ocoa ranger hut there is also a picnic area and the start of a 3 km excursion trail to Salto de la Cortadera.

Because the park is so close to the two largest population centers in Chile, Santiago and Valparaíso/Viña del Mar, it attracts 30 000 visitors annually. At weekends the more accessible picnic and camping areas are often full.

The most scenic areas are **Valle de las Palmas de Ocoa** (best reached from RN 60 turning south at Rabuco into the Estero Rabuco) and **Paso Ocoa,** which gives splendid views of **Cerro Robles** (2222 m) to the east.

The park is in three *sectores*: Granizo and El Cajón (both best reached from Olmué), and Palmas de Ocoa (best reached via La Calera or Llay-Llay). The main access to the national park is from Olmué (see the entry for Olmué on page 284). Sector Palmar de Ocoa is 100 km north-west of Santiago on RN 5 (Panamericana Norte). Turn off south 12 km past Llay-Llay onto a dirt road just before crossing the Río Aconcagua. Sector Granizo and Sector El Cajón are 57 km east of Viña del Mar and Valparaíso on RN 62, turning onto the Olmué road.

If you are using public transport, the best access to Sector Granizo and Sector Cajón Grande is by bus from Viña del Mar, leaving every 30 minutes to Olmué. Buses on weekends usually drive up to the national park entrance. The best access to the Ocoa or northern sector is from La Calera (Buses Carolina, Caupolicán 709). It

is also possible to take the train from Valparaíso or Viña del Mar to Pachacama railroad station and walk from there — from the station it is 12 km south to the Sector Ocoa entrance. Admission is $1.50.

ⅈ Tourist information
- CONAF, Viña del Mar, 3 Norte 541 ℂ 976189/970108

⊟ Accommodation
Olmué and La Calera have small hotels — see "Accommodation" in Olmué (page 286) and La Calera (page 265).

Ⓐ Camping
All camping grounds inside the park are administered and maintained by CONAF. There are camping sites in Sector El Granizo, Sector Cajón Grande, and Sector Las Palmas de Ocoa.t

🚘 Motoring
You can drive to Sector El Granizo and Sector Cajón Grande from Santiago via Til Til, Lampa, and Cuesta La Dormida. This is a very scenic drive but the road is not sealed. Access to Sector Ocoa is via Llay-Llay or La Calera.

🏵 Sport
Scaling of Cerro La Campana should only be attempted by experienced mountaineers, and you should tell the CONAF administration in the park if you intend to do so.

⊕ Excursions
The most worthwhile trips are into the **Río Ocoa** valley with the palms and the three-kilometer hike to Salto de la Cortadera; and a hike up the **Quebrada Agua del Manzano** past **Poza El Coipo** in Sector Cajón Grande, the Cajón Grande trail, and a climb up **Cerro La Campana**.

PETORCA

Area code: 033
Population: 2500
Altitude: 500 m
Distances
- From Santiago: 206 km north on Ruta E-35 and Panamericana (via La Ligua)
- From Valparaíso: 157 km north-east on Ruta E-35, Panamericana and RN 60 (sealed)

Petorca is the birthplace of Don Manuel Montt (1809) who was President of Chile for a term in the 19th century. The facade of the building where he was born is all that is left and is now a *monumento nacional*. Some houses with old colonial doors made of *algarrobo* wood are also preserved in Calles Manuel Montt and Siena.

Iglesia Nuestra Señora de las Mercedes in the Plaza de Armas was originally built in 1640. The altar is made of silver. The image of Cristo de la Cruz was brought to this church by the Jesuits in 1660.

☒ Festivals
- June 9: Sagrada Corazón
- July 16: Virgen del Carmen (also known as Virgen de Petorquita)
- September, last week: La Merced
- October 5: Nuestra Señora del Rosario

ⓘ Tourist information
- Municipalidad, corner of Cuartel and Silva

◱ Accommodation
- Hotel Valsof, Silva 248 AFIJP ℂ 781007
- Residencial Gallardo, Matriz A

Accommodation in Chincolco
Chincolco is 11 km away.
- Hotel Restaurant Rincón Criollo, Pedro Montt AEFGHJLPV ℂ 298130

⑪ Eating out
- Restaurant Donde Manuel, Silva 335. *Parrillada*
- Restaurant El Yugo, Covadonga 260. *Parrillada*
- Restaurant Tammy's Club, Silva 360. Chilean cuisine, dancing

▦ Post office and telegraph

Post office
- Correos, Silva 625

Telephone
- CTC, Silva 248

▤ Buses
There is no central bus terminal. All buses pass through the town center and pick up passengers from the plaza.
Colectivos depart from Silva opposite the *Carabineros* for Cabildo every half hour.

Companies
- Buses Ligua runs 4 services daily to Santiago
- Buses La Porteña, Avenida Silva near Cuartel runs 4 services daily to Cabildo, La Calera, La Ligua, Valparaíso, and Viña del Mar
- Tur-Bus Jedimar runs services to Cabildo, La Calera, and La Ligua

▨ Motoring

Gas stations
- COPEC, Colombo Cade near Silva
- COPEC, Silva near Covadonga

⊛ Sport
Trout fishing, hiking.

◉ Excursions
- **Chincolco**: 11 km further up in a wide section of the upper **Río Petorca** valley. The mountains surrounding it are nearly 2400 m in the north, over 3000 m in the east, and 1700 m in the

south. Rock paintings, believed to date from the Inca period, may be seen in the **Río de Pedernal** valley (at **Chaloco** and **El Pedernal**) and in the **Río del Sobrante** valley. The trout fishing is good in both rivers. For the mountain hiker it is possible to hike to **Laguna Conchuca** which is the source of the **Río Choapa**. Maps and camping gear required as you pass over **Paso El**

Gallo (2900 m). Buses La Porteña runs 5 services daily to Petorca and direct buses to Valparaíso, fare $3.30; Buses La Ligua runs direct daily buses to Santiago, fare $3.50.
- Other old and picturesque villages or *haciendas* in the area are **Pedegua**, **Manuel Montt**, and **Hierro Viejo**.

PORTILLO

Altitude: 2860 m
Distances
- From Santiago: 145 km north-east on RN 60 and RN 57
- From Viña del Mar: 190 km east on RN 60

Portillo ski village lies in a high Andean valley nestling among the peaks of **Ojos de Agua** (4239 m) and **La Parva** (4852 m) to the west. **Cerro Aconcagua** (6956 m), although very close as the crow flies, is obscured. The views from Portillo and the ski slopes are magnificent. The **Laguna del Inca** lies behind the main hotel with **Cerro Tres Hermanas** 4760m dominating in the distance.

This superb mountain setting is near the Argentine border on the international highway between Valparaíso and Mendoza in Argentina; the road between Santiago and the border remains open throughout the year.

The skiing season runs from June to October. You can hire skiing equipment at the hotel, and there is also ice skating on the frozen lake. A bit further down is the mountain-rescue school (*Escuela de Montaña*) run by the army. The ski school with international skiing instructors is part of Hotel Portillo.

⊟ Accommodation
See also Guardia Vieja under "Accommodation" in Cajón del Río Aconcagua on page 243.
★★★★ Hotel Portillo, RN 60 ABCDEFGHIJKLMNPR$TUVXZ ℂ 2433007. Ski rental, car rental, gaming room, tour buses, heated outside swimming pool, sauna, 177 rooms. Note: strict dress rules apply when eating in the dining room. A la carte meals cost $X. Weekly prices for double rooms range from $650.00 to $1350.00, and include all meals and lift tickets. Daily prices for bunks range from $53.00 to $106.00, including meals. Reservations in Santiago: Roger de Flor 2911 ℂ 2313411, fax 2317164
- Hostería Cristo Redentor. Open all year. Reservations in Santiago ℂ 383810

⑪ Eating out
- Restaurant Tío Bob at the end of Plateau chair lift at an altitude of 3100 m. Full meals served

⑳ Entertainment
- Disco in Hotel Portillo

⑤ Financial
There are exchange facilities at the border checkpoint (see below) and in the hotel.

⊠ Border crossing

Complejo Fronterizo Los Libertadores (also known as **Paso de Bermejo**) is 8 km east of Portillo on RN 60. It is 145km north east of Santiago and 200 km west of Mendoza in Argentina. In the complex there is a telephone, money exchange, and a *cafetería*.

▤ Services and facilities

There is a ski hire outlet, a ski school, and an ice-skating rink. Ski hire is $15.00 per day.
There are 12 ski lifts, one of them (Juncalillo) 1414 m long, with a lift of 340 m. A daily lift ticket costs $25.00. The ski runs range from easy ("fácil") to very difficult ("muy difícil")

✈ Air services

Helicopters
- Helicopteres Andes, Avenida Larrain 7941, Santiago (2276854
- Alfa, Bilbao 3771, Santiago (2746905/2274717

▤ Buses

Buses to Mendoza (in Argentina) will drop you off at Portillo. Esportur buses leave during the skiing season from Hotel Carrera in Santiago; return fare $20.00. Buses to Santiago leave at 0800.
- Los Andes: Fare $2.30

⊟ Motoring

Heavy snow falls are not uncommon at Portillo. The road is a major international arterial road, and is kept open even in winter.

⊛ Sport

- Skiing and mountain hiking

- Trout fishing in Río Juncal and Laguna del Inca

⊕ Excursions

Tour operators
- American Bus, Agustinas 1173, Santiago (6960518/6983341
- Tour service, Teatinos 333, 10th floor, Santiago (6960415/727166

Excursions
You can also start many mountain hikes and climbs from here, such as an ascent of **Cerro La Parva** (4856 m).

- Cristo Redentor: A huge bronze statue erected at the crest of the mountain to celebrate peace between Chile and Argentina. The old road connnecting Santiago with Mendoza used to negotiate the pass nearby. In 1980 the 4 km tunnel traversing the main chain of the Andes at 3185 m was opened. Mountaineers who wish to climb to Cristo Redentor should start their climb from Las Cuevas in Argentina — see the entry for Las Cuevas in *Travel Companion Argentina*.

- **La Juncal**: If you are a keen mountain walker, try the walk down **Los Caracoles** for splendid views in exhilarating mountain scenery. This is a 10 km walk all the way downhill and takes about 2½ hours. Instead of following the highway, you can stay on a mountain trail who cuts off the lengthy U-turns of the Los Caracoles road and takes you past springs and cascades. *Colectivos* run from Juncal down to Los Andes, but try to be in Juncal not later than 1500 as there is no accommodation there and you need to catch the last bus to Los Andes.

PUCHUNCAVÍ

Population: 7000
Altitude: Sea level
Distance from Valparaíso: 53 km south on Ruta F- 30-E

Puchuncaví is about 6 km inland from the Pacific coast, and was an Incan *mitimaes* settlement when the Spaniards arrived.

Horcón

Seven km west of Puchuncaví, is a small fishing village on the Pacific coast which becomes a beach resort for the summer tourist season. The protected bay is surrounded by steep hills. This is an idyllic place, where you can buy a local painting for a bargain price from the street sellers. Many young *gringos* find their way to this beautiful isolated place. Playa Cau Cau, 200 m south of Horcón, is suitable for windsurfing; Playa Las Agatas has good fishing near the rocky outcrops at the northern end of the beach. The bus terminal is on Avenida Costanera in the fishing village.

Las Ventanas

Located 6 km south-east of Puchuncaví, Las Ventanas is a small fishing village and beach resort at the northern end of **Bahía Quintero**, almost opposite Quintero, 1 km from the intersection with Ruta F-30-E. Nearby are rock cliffs where the sea has made a window-like opening — hence the name Las Ventanas. Vacation homes dot the coastline. The water is calm and shallow, and the beach is sheltered and suitable for water-skiing. In the summer it becomes a tent city. Many small fish restaurants along the waterfront serve excellent meals at very competitive prices.

Festivals

- July 16: Virgen del Carmen
- July 21: Corpus Christi
- September 17–19: Rodeo Oficial (or Fiesta Huasa)
- October 5: Nuestra Señora del Rosario

Festivals in Horcón

- June 29: San Pedro, patron saint of the fishermen; a colorful *fiesta*

Tourist information

- Municipalidad, Avenida B. O'Higgins ☎ 250097

Accommodation

Accommodation in Horcón

- Cabañas La Brasileira, Ruta F-50 ☎ (09)2344604. 12 beds
- Residencial Arancibia, Avenida Costanera A ☎ (09)3241985

Accommodation in Las Ventanas

- Motel Los Leones, Pedro Aldunate Solar ABCEFGHIJLPV. Safe-keeping of luggage, TV room. Reservations in La Calera: ☎ 221479

Camping

There are good camping sites north and south of Horcón.

Eating out

- Restaurant Campo Alegre

Eating out in Horcón

Restaurants

- El Ancla, Costanera. Seafood
- El Faro, Juana Veas. Seafood
- Santa Clara, La Playa

Eating out in Las Ventanas

Restaurants

- El Central, Pedro Aldunate
- El Progreso, Costanera

- Miramar, Costanera
- San Felipeño, Pedro Aldunate
- Schopería Cocodrilo, Pedro Aldunate corner of Daniel de la Vega

🍸 **Entertainment**

Entertainment in Horcón
- Disco Gloria, Avenida Costanera

🚌 **Buses**

All bus companies have their offices on the plaza.
- Taximar Taxi Colectivos, on the plaza near Velázquez runs daily *colectivo* services to Horcón, Las Ventanas, Maitencillo, Quintero, and Papudo
- Expreso Sol del Pacífico runs daily services to Concón, La Ligua, Papudo, Valparaíso, Viña del Mar, and Zapallar

Buses from Las Ventanas
- Buses Sol del Pacífico runs two services daily to Viña del Mar and Papudo,

and also two services daily to Santiago; fare $3.20

🌂 **Excursions**
- **La Quebrada**: A small village with many adobe houses on the **Estero La Canela**. The highest mountain is **Cerro Las Terneras** (760 m), and the river has cut a gorge through here. Time has stood still here despite the hustle and bustle of the nearby beach resorts. This is a 12 km hike one way, or you could take a *colectivo* part of the way.
- **La Canela**: There are three picturesque little villages off the beaten track within the coastal *cordillera*, located in the upper Estero La Canela valley: Baja (lower), Media (middle), and Alta (upper) Canela. From Canela Media you can hike to **Cerro Alto de Yerbas Buenas**, the highest mountain in this section of the coastal *cordillera*. There are irregular taxi *colectivos* along dirt roads.

PUTAENDO

Population: 9000
Altitude: 800 m
Distances
- From Santiago: 97 km north on Ruta E-71, E-89 and RN 57
- From Valparaíso: 125 km north-east on Ruta E-71, RN 60 (sealed)

Putaendo has been settled since pre-Hispanic times. When the Incas arrived, it became an Incan *mitimaes* settlement and from 1485 a regional administration center. The first Spanish invasion under Diego de Almagro also passed through this village. The last invasion came through this town in 1817 during the Wars of Independence, when San Martín crossed the Andes with the Ejercito de Los Andes or Liberation Army.

Putaendo is 15 km north of San Felipe in the Río Putaendo valley. The big commercial upswing came in the 18th century with the discovery of gold nearby: the new Spanish town was founded around Iglesia San Antonio.

The town has all the characteristics of a Spanish colonial foundation with a main *plaza* where the important ecclesiastical and administrative buildings are located. The houses are built of adobe and are at least a hundred years old.

Although the tourist facilities are not yet fully developed, Putaendo makes a good starting point for exciting mountain walks into high *sierra* country and for fishing in the brooks for trout. You might like to retrace the trail taken by the Liberation Army on the Chilean side through the Valle **Río Rocín** to **Paso de los Patos**.

⊛ Festivals

- February: Fiesta de la Chaya
- February 7: Anniversary of the Battle of Coima
- March, third week: Festival Putaenda
- March 20: Foundation day
- July 16: Virgen del Carmen; the procession goes from Rinconada de Silva to Baños del Parrón
- September 18–19: Rodeo Oficial (or Fiesta Huasa) — display of horsemanship, dancing, and celebrations in cowboy style

ⓘ Tourist information

- Municipalidad, Prat 1 ℂ 501004. Open Mon–Fri 0830–1300 and 1400–1800

⊟ Accommodation

Hosterías
- La Carreta, Alameda 72 AF ℂ 41
- La Estancia, La Cruz 1 ADIJ ℂ 501074; 22 beds

Accommodation in Rinconada de Silva
Rinconada de Silva is 6 km south-east of Putaendo. Its beginnings were as a monastery of the order of San Agustín. The turnoff east to Rinconada de Silva and Baños del Parrón is 3 km south of Putaendo.
- El Parrón, Centenario 1000 AFR ℂ 501109

Ⓐ Camping

There is a camping site in Baños del Parrón, 16 km east.

ⓘ Eating out

Restaurants
- Club Deportivo y Social Putaendo, Camus 178
- Ermita, Brasil 476. Chilean cuisine
- La Palmera, Sarmiento 604. Chilean cuisine. Dancing weekends

- La Rosa Chilena, Bulnes 35. Chilean cuisine
- La Tinaja, Brasil 1653. Chilean cuisine
- Las Camelias, Comercio 448. Chilean cuisine
- Pensión Andacollo, Eduardo Weggener 174. Chilean cuisine

Cafeterías
- Lilianette, Camus 100. Hot dogs
- "Fatto's Inn", on the main plaza. Bar and grill

Eating out in Rinconada de Guzman
Rinconada de Guzman is 9 km north of Putaendo.
- Restaurant Los Tres Aromos, La Cancha. Chilean cuisine. Dancing weekends

Eating out in Rinconada de Silva
Rinconada de Silva is 8 km south-east of Putaendo.
- Restaurant El Negro Bueno, Centenario. Chilean cuisine. Dancing weekends
- El Parrón, Centenario 1000
- La Estancia, La Cruz 1

ⓨ Entertainment

- Restaurant Tatio's Inn. Dancing weekends

📧 Post and telegraph

Post office
- Correo, Prat 1

Telephone
- CTC, Bulnes 140
- Telex Chile Bulnes 91

🚌 Bus services

All Buses to San Felipe and rural buses to destinations in the high *sierra* depart from Plaza de Armas, near the church.
The following bus companies operate from Putaendo:
- Buses Puma, Alameda Alessandri corner of San Martín. Runs three services daily to San José de Piguchén, fares $0.50; the same bus goes further up the valley to Rinconada de los Guzmanes. To San Felipe there are six services daily, fares $0.50
- Buses Ruta 57, Bulnes 91 ℂ 501040. Two services daily to Santiago, fares $1.30; two services daily to Resguardo de los Patos, a two- hour bus trip, fares $0.90

🚌 Motoring

- Esso gas station, Bulnes corner of Cura Montes

🏛 Shopping

Crocheted items are available in Bulnes 55 (on the plaza).

🎯 Sport

Río Putaendo flows down from the high *sierras* into a wide valley. The riverbed is also very wide, and full of large rocks; the water is very cold and clean. There are good fishing spots at Tártaro de La Vicuña (6 km upstream) and still better fishing spots in the Río Rocín (40 km north-east of town), Río Chalaco, and Río Hidalgo, all of them headwaters of the Río Putaendo. The scenery is rugged and mountain hikers can follow the trails leading up to the high *sierras*. The *carabineros* at **Resguardo de los Patos** can give you more information. If you decide on a mountain hike, let them know which route you are taking and how long you expect to be.

🏞 Sightseeing

Enjoy the views over the town from Cerro El Llano, almost in the center of town.

- Casa José Antonio Salinas, the birthplace of this independence hero. Not much of the house is left, but what remains is now a *monumento nacional*.
- Casa de Juan Rozas, an art gallery in an old colonial house.

◆ Excursions

- To **Rinconada de Silva** and **Baños del Parrón**: Rinconada de Silva, 8 km east, is an old colonial village. The San Felipe–Putaendo area is full of "Rinconadas" (or "corners"), and Rinconada de Silva is just one of them. On a hill overlooking the village is a huge statue of Christ on the cross; it is almost 4 m high. This is the site of a colorful "Via Crucis" procession at Easter. From the top scenic views. Baños del Parrón, a further 8 km east of Rinconada da Silva, is famous for its thermal springs.
- **Monumento Batalla de las Coimas**: This monument is halfway between Putaendo and San Felipe, and is dedicated to the *Ejercito de los Andes*, the Liberation Army. The main body of 1700 men under General San Martín crossed the Andes at the **Paso de los Patos** into Chile. Where the monument stands was the scene of the first skirmishes with the Royalist Army which took place on February 6, 1817.
- **Quebrada de las Minillas**: 18 km north. You might like to try your luck at gold fossicking here, because there are still a few finds made here from time to time.
- **Salto de Agua El Chorro** : A 20 m waterfall near Resguardo de Los Patos 19 km north where three rivers join to form the **Río Putaendo**.

QUILLOTA

Area code: 033
Population: 50 000
Altitude: 125 m
Distances

- From Santiago: 125 km north-west on RN 60 and Panamericana
- From Valparaíso: 58 km north-east on RN 60

Quillota is in the lower **Río Aconcagua** valley, on the east bank of the river, some 25 km before it reaches the Pacific Ocean. Quillota is the capital of Quillota province and center of an agricultural area, producing mostly fruit and vegetables. It is particularly well known for the fine avocados and *chirimoyas* or custard-apples produced locally.

Wealthy merchants of Valparaíso bought large tracts of land during the 19th century and put in irrigation canals which have led to the productivity of this rich agricultural zone.

When the Spaniards arrived, the region was densely populated and firmly under the rule of the Incas. Their administrative center was in San Isidro, 3 km south of Quillota. The first foundation of Iglesia de San Francisco goes back to 1609. During the colonial period it was an important religious center, with all major religious orders maintaining a church in Quillota. San Martín de Quillota was officially declared a town by Don Bernardo O'Higgins in 1822.

With its Mediterranean climate, this town can be quite hot in summer. As it is an important provincial center, it has all services and good tourist facilities, with many bus services to Valparaíso and Santiago and also to northern Chile.

The main highway from Valparaíso to Mendoza in Argentina (RN 60) skirts the town on its southeastern side. A lot of tourists give this township a miss, but it is worth making a short visit to see some of the reminders of its colonial past.

⚀ Festivals
- January, second week: Festival Folklórico de la Uva y El Durazno — grape and apricot festival
- February, first week: Fiesta de la Canción Comunal — song festival
- September 17–19: Rodeo Oficial (or Fiesta Huasa)
- November 11: Foundation day

ⓘ Tourist information
- Oficina de Informaciones Turísticas, Municipalidad de Quillota, San Martín 290. Open Mon–Fri 0900–1300 and 1500–1830

⊞ Eating out
Restaurants
- Café Joao, O'Higgins 175
- Chau San, Maipú 132. Chinese cuisine
- Da Carlo, O'Higgins 215. International cuisine
- Juanita, Maipú 237. Grill
- La Casa degli Italiani, Blanco 315. Italian cuisine
- O'Higgins, O'Higgins 85. Grill

ⓨ Entertainment
- Club de Campo Las Palmas, road to La Palma. International cuisine, dancing Saturdays from 2100 onwards

---

⊟ Accommodation in Quillota

Hotels
- Caprí, 21 de Mayo 3799 — ☎ 310624
- Turismo, Prat 14 — AHFGPV — ☎ 310898

Motel
- Berlín, Camino Troncal, at *paradero* 3 — AH — ☎ 352306

Residenciales
- Osorno, 21 de Mayo 109
- San Martín, San Martín 115 — APV

Accommodation in Sector Boco
Sector Boco is 3 km north of town center on the Río Aconcagua.
- Complejo Turístico El Edén, Balmaceda 385 — ABP — ☎ 312342 — $G for 5

- Disco Silo, road to La Palma, dancing Saturdays
- Hostería El Eden, Balmaceda, Sector El Boco. Dancing Saturdays

☏ Post and telegraph

Post office
- Correo, O'Higgins corner of Concepción

Telephone
- CTC, Blanco 160, fax 313351
- Telex Chile, Concepción 399

$ Finance

- Fincard, Freire 78 ☏ 312892. Cash advances against Visa and Mastercard

🚗 Motoring

- Automóvil Club de Chile, San Martín 355, office B-1 ☏ 311201

Gas satations
- COPEC, Freire corner of Echeverría
- Esso gas station, Maipú corner of Pinto

🚆 Trains

The railroad station is on 21 de Mayo 118

Trains run from Quillota to Valparaíso via Limache, Peña Blanca, Villa Alemana, Quilpué, and Viña del Mar; and to Los Andes via La Calera, Llay-Llay, and San Felipe.
- Valparaíso: Fare $0.60; 3-4 services daily

🏬 Shopping

The hub of town and commercial center is B. O'Higgins, Concepción, and Prat.

📷 Sightseeing

- Iglesia San Martín de Tours, San Martín near the Plaza de Armas, was built in 1642.
- Iglesia Santo Domingo, O'Higgins near the Plaza de Armas. There has been a church on this site since 1767.
- Convento San Francisco, Chacabuco 184 corner of San Francisco. One of the oldest ecclesiastical buildings in town, it is surrounded by gardens. The early missionary work in the Santiago–Valparaíso region was entrusted to the Franciscan monks.
- Casa Colorada, San Martín 366, on the Plaza de Armas. Built in 1722, this is one of the town's oldest colonial build-

🚌 Buses from Quillota

The bus terminal is on the Plaza de Armas.

Companies
- A2   Alfa Tres Ltda
- A5   Asociación Gremiales de Buses Intercomunales
  Runs 1 service daily to Illapel and Salamanca.
- A28 Buses Dhino
- A37 Buses Golondrina, Concepción 495 ☏ 310338
- A44 Buses La Porteña
- A78 Buses Tramaca, Portales 745

Services

Destination	Fare	Services	Duration	Company
• Limache		10 services daily		A2, A28, A44
• Los Andes	$1.90	13 services daily		A2
• Peña Blanca		10 services daily		A2, A28, A44
• Quilpué		10 services daily		A2, A28, A44
• San Felipe	$1.70	10 services daily		A2
• Santiago	$2.10	6 services daily		A2, A37
• Valparaíso	$1.00	10 services daily		A2, A28, A44
• Villa Alemania		10 services daily		A2, A28, A44
• Viña del Mar		10 services daily		A2, A28, A44

ings. The Libertador Bernardo O'Higgins stayed here in 1822 when he officially proclaimed Quillota a town. These days it is a private house, so only the outside can be inspected.

- Museo Municipal, Merced 145. Open Mon–Fri 0900–1230 and 1500–1800. On exhibit are samples of the 15th- and 16th-century colonial life, colonial newspapers, and old maps.
- Centro Turístico El Edén. This park is in Barrio El Boco, behind Cerro Mayoca, and has century-old trees and well- kept lawns in a picturesque setting. Its attractions include a small lake, mini-golf grounds, tennis courts, swimming pools, small restaurants, and picnic areas. It is also the venue for the official rodeos. Frequent *colectivos* run from the city center.

- Plaza de Armas. On the Plaza is the Monumento al Arból. Into a huge tree trunk an allegory of planting and harvesting has been carved.

⊕ Excursions

- **Rautén**: 7 km west. Has a small lake, and the area is dotted with colonial-style picturesque farm houses made from adobe. Dairy products, in particular the local cheeses, are sold here.
- **Pocochay**: Fruit-growing area on the outskirts of town well known for its avocados and *chirimoyas*.

QUILPUÉ

Population: 85 000
Distances:
- From Santiago: 144 km north-west on RN 68 and RN 62 (via Viña del Mar)
- From Valparaíso: 20 km east on RN 62

Lying between **Estero Quilpué** and the **Río Marga Marga**, Quilpué and **Villa Alemana** have already become almost a single population center.

Near **Los Quillayes**, in the middle Marga Marga valley, you can see signs of the pre-Columbian tribes who made cup-like cavities into the rocks, presumably used to grind corn. Most of the archeological sites are in Sector Paso Hondo. You might also like to visit the Convento Los

---

⊟ Accommodation in Quilpué

Motels
- 2000, La Paz 452 — ADFGHKLPV
- Los Jardines, Calle 6 corner of 7 Paso Hondo — DEFGHKLP — ☎ 905536 — $H ♁♁

Residenciales
- Blanco, Avenida Blanco 1046 — AFGKLPV — ☎ 911732 — $I ♁♁
  18 beds
- Buon Viaggio, Portales 782 — ADEFGIJP — ☎ 910592 — $I ♁♁
- Quilpué, Cumming 976 — ☎ 911092
  21 beds
- San Antonio, Camilo Henriquez 345 — AEFGHIJLPRUV — ☎ 910760 — $I ♁♁
  Also full board; open all year; 20 beds
- Complejo Turístico Los Almendros, Chacabuco 150 — ☎ 910673

Perales which has a famous *bodega* or wine cellar.

Quilpué has good tourist facilities.

⚐ Festivals
- April 25: Foundation day
- September 17–19: Rodeo Oficial (or Fiesta Huasa)
- October 14: Foundation day

ⓘ Tourist information
- Municipalidad, Vicuña Mackenna 684 ☎ 910710

Ⓜ Eating out

Restaurants
- Círcolo Italiano Chileno, Los Carrera 712. International cuisine
- La Primavera, Claudio Vicuña 791. Grill
- La Nueva Casona, San Martín 644. Chilean cuisine
- Centro Turístico Los Almendros, Chacabuco 150, El Retiro
- Pau San, Blanco 1002. Chinese cuisine

Cafetería
- La Bombonera, Claudio Vicuña 847. Cakes and ice-cream

✉ Post and telegraph

Telephone
- CTC, Los Carrera 722, fax 915332

⛟ Motoring
- COPEC gas station

⚙ Sport
Trout fishing in Estero Colliguay.

⛟ Buses from Quilpué
The bus terminal is at the railroad station, Garita Estación de Ferrocarriles Quilpué, on Baquedano near Claudio Vicuña.

Companies departing from the bus terminal
- A5   Asociación Gremial de Buses Intercomunales
- A16   Buses Biotal
- A28   Buses Dhino
       Services to La Calera, Limache, and Quillota
- A44   Buses La Porteña
- A48   Buses Lit
- A88   Ciferal Express
       Five services daily to Granizo, Limache, Olmué, and Quebrada Alvarado
- A93   Buses Cóndor
- A105 Buses Sol del Pacífico

Companies departing from their own terminals
- A48   Buses Lit, Vicuña Mackenna 621 ☎ 912969
- A93   Cóndor Bus, Carrera 673 ☎ 911057
- A127 Buses Pullman Bus, Diego Portales 791 ☎ 9 10233

Services

Destination	Fare	Services	Duration	Company
Ovalle		2 services daily		A110
Santiago	$2.70	5 services daily		A48, A93, A127
Salamanca		1 service daily		A5
Villa Alemana		10 services daily		A5, A28, A88, A105
Valparaíso		10 services daily		A5, A28, A88, A105
Viña del Mar		10 services daily		A5, A28, A48, A88, A93, A105, A127

QUINTAY

Altitude: Sea level
Distance from Valparaíso: 47 km south on RN 68 and Ruta F-800

Although it is so close to one of Chile's major population centers, this is a fairly quiet and isolated spot. There are two parts to Quintay: the *caleta* or fishing village and the beach area north. There is a lighthouse south of the fishing village; in days gone by this was a whaling station and the remains of it can still be seen. Nowadays the whales are coming back and you will probably see some in the bay. Many of the houses are owned by descendants of whalers — the houses are adorned with huge whale bones.

The beach, which is just north of the Caleta, has fine white sand and slopes gradually into the sea. This is a good spot for swimming and camping and does not get too crowded in summer.

Traveling here from Valparaíso, you pass through **Peñuelas** among huge pine plantations, interspersed with eucalyptus. At Peñuelas take the turnoff to **Las Tablas** — this is a gravel road from there on. Pine plantations continue for most of the way and the road passes through small hills and valleys. As you leave the little village of **San Juan**, you can see the cliffs and the sea in the distance, quite spectacular views.

Accommodation
- Hostería Quintay, La Playa 449, Playa Grande AF ((02) 2717317. 36 beds
- Hostería Bosquemar, Jorge Montt (241763 $H ▮▮. 42 beds
- Residencial Mónica, Caleta de Pescadores AF. 12 beds

Camping
- Quintay. Good fishing, no facilities, beautiful spot, small fee for camping, no shade, huge beach. You can get water at the caretaker's house

Eating out
Quintay's eateries are quite modest establishments, mostly serving freshly caught seafood.

Restaurants
- Rancho de Doña Tatito. Open only during summer holidays
- El Rey del Congrio, Ave. Jorge Montt
- Hostería Karla, Camino El Jote. Seafood
- Miramar, Caleta Quintay. Seafood
- Posada Mónica, Avenida Teniente Merino (on the beach). Seafood

Buses
- Valparaíso: departs Mon–Sat; Buses Quintay

QUINTERO

Area code: 032
Population: 14 000
Altitude: Sea level
Distances
- From Santiago: 159 km north-west on Ruta F-30-E and RN 68
- From Valparaíso: 43 km north on Ruta F-30-E

Quintero is a beach resort on **Bahía Quintero**, named after Almagro's navigator who discovered the bay in 1536. During the colonial period, the bay was frequented by pirates, hence the name Cueva del Pirata ("Pirate Cave") on the promontory.

The town's commercial existence came about through Luis Cousiño, who invested his money in port facilities and railroads. Today it is a fairly large town with good facilities for the growing numbers of tourists attracted by the extensive beaches to the east and south. A very active yacht club organizes many events in summer and is one of the best on the Chilean Riviera. The mean summer

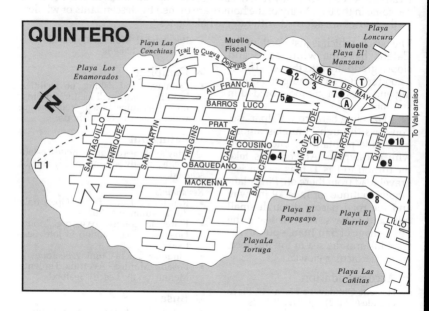

Key to map

A	Iglesia
H	Hospital
T	Bus terminals
●	**Accommodation**
2	Residencial Panamericano
4	Residencial Ferry Boat
5	Hotel El Refugio
6	Hotel Isla Capri

7	Hotel Monaco
8	Hotel Yachting Club
9	Hotel California
10	Residencial La Moderna
○	**Eating out**
3	Restaurant La Nave
■	**Sights**
1	Cueva del Pirata

🛏 Accommodation in Quintero

Hotels
- California, Alonso de Quintero 463   AEFGHIPV   ℓ 930176
  43 beds
- Capri, Avenida 21 de Mayo 1299   AEFGHJKLPV   ℓ 930939
  44 rooms
- Mónaco, Avenida 21 de Mayo 1530   AEFGJKLMP$UVXZ   ℓ 930939 $H 👥
  Car rental, beach frontage; 63 rooms
- Refugio, Avenida Francia 1130   ℓ 930146
  56 beds
- Yachting Club, Luis Acevedo 1736

       ACEFGHIJLPRV   ℓ 930061 $G 👥
  18 rooms

Hosterías
- María Isabel, General Baquedano 1642

       AHPS   ℓ 931679 $H 👥
  80 beds

Residenciales
- Brasilia, Avenida 21 de Mayo 1336   ℓ 930590 $H 👥
  20 beds
- Casa de Piedra, Luis Cousiño 2076   AEGHIJPV   ℓ 930196
  36 beds
- El Arriero, Normandie 1799   AEFGPV   ℓ 930323
  4 beds
- Ferry Boat, Luis Cousiño 1264   AFGHLPV   ℓ 930305
- La Moderna, Luis Cousiño 1781   AEFGHIJPV   ℓ 930110 $H 👥
  65 beds
- María Alejandra, Lord Cochrane 157   AHIJLPV   ℓ 930266 $I 👥
- Nueva, Arlegui 250   APV   ℓ 882263 $H 👥
  12 beds
- Panamericano, Avenida 21 de Mayo 1020

       AIJPV   ℓ 930261
  25 beds
- Quillota, Alonso de Quintero 446   AFHKV
- Santa Elena, Federico Albert 89   AEGJLPV   ℓ 930170
- San Victor, Luis Cousiño 1929   AEIJPV
- Victoria, Vicuña Mackenna 1460   AEFGHJPV   ℓ 930208
  16 beds

Accommodation on Playa Ritoque
Playa Ritoque is 6km south of town.
- Hotel Las Vegas de Ritoque   ACDEFGHMRV $G 👥
  Boat hire, beach frontage, 10 rooms

temperature is 18°C (64°F) and water is 13°C (55°F).

Most of the beaches are very sheltered, making them particularly suitable for swimming — but take care as the seafloor descends abruptly. Some of the beaches are good for water skiing.

- Playa Los Enamorados, the closest beach to town. Good for swimming and wind surfing.

- Playa Las Conchitas, separated from Playa Los Enamorados by rocky outcrops. It is within walking distance from the town center. Swimming, wind surfing, kiosks, and life-guards.
- Playa El Durazno is within walking distance from town. It is separated from Playa Las Conchitas by rocky outcrops. Swimming, sailing, windsurfing, kiosks, and life-guards.
- Playa El Manzano is near the Club de Yates and continues for several kilometers north as Playa Loncura around the Bahí de Quintero.
- Playa El Papagayo is two blocks south of the plaza in a small horseshoe-shaped bay. Swimming, surfing, wind surfing, kiosks, life-guards.
- Playa Ritoque is 4 km south of town and continues for several kilometers right down to the mouth of the **Río Aconcagua**. Fishing, water sports, camping, kiosk.

Festivals
- February: Semana Quinterana
- February, first week: Carnaval del Mar
- Easter week: Regatta
- June 29: San Pedro
- November 24: Foundation day

Tourist information
- Oficina de Información Turística, Plaza José Ignacio Pinto. Open Mon–Fri 1000–1400

Camping
There is a camping site 3 km north of Concón.

Eating out
Restaurants
- El Arriero, Avenida Normandie, on the central plaza
- Isla Capri, 21 de Mayo 1299. Seafood, panoramic views
- Naldo's, 21 de Mayo 1485. Seafood. Views over the sea
- La Nave, 21 de Mayo 1200. Seafood

Entertainment
Discos
- 21 (in the Hotel Monaco), 21 de Mayo 1530
- Casino El Durazno, Avenida Bulnes
- Waikiki, Playa Los Rieles

Buses from Quintero
Companies
- A58 Nueva Transmar, 21 de Mayo 1561 (930046
- A66 Buses Quintero, 21 de Mayo 1590 (930045
- A105 Buses Sol del Pacífico, in the center of town
  Runs 5 services daily to Concón, Horcón, La Ligua, Las Ventanas, Maitencillo, Papudo, Puchuncaví, Valparaíso, Viña del Mar, and Zapallar.

Services

Destination	Fare	Services	Companies
Concón		every ½ hour	A58, A105
Los Andes	$3.30	6 services daily	A2
Maitencillo		5 services daily	A58, A105
Santiago	$3.80		A58 A66
Valparaíso		every ½ hour	A58, A105
Viña del Mar		every ½ hour	A58, A105

🏤 Post and telegraph

Post office
- Correos, Piloto Alcayaga 1935

Telephone
- CTC, Piloto Alcayaga near Federico Albert

🚗 Motoring

Gas stations
- COPEC, Avenida Normandie near Ernesto Riquelme
- Sunoco, Avenida Normandie 2077

⚓ Water transport

During summer boat cruises leave from Embarcaderos, Avenida 21 de Mayo.

⛵ Sport

Yachting
- Club de Yates (Yacht Club) Avenida 21 de Mayo

Fishing
The best beaches for fishing are Playa Ritoque and Playa Loncura. At Playa Loncura there is a small fishing village which is gradually becoming a vacation home suburb.

REÑACA

Area code: 032
Altitude: Sea level
Distances
- From Santiago: 128 km north east on Ruta F-30-E and RN 68
- From Valparaíso: 17 km north on Ruta F-30-E

Reñaca is on a wide beach 6 km north of Viña del Mar. The main part of the town is built on the rocks that line the beach. Along the beach there are condominiums built in terraces up the slopes with their own elevators. The town is popular all year round — if you are lucky enough to be there at carnival time, you will enjoy it as it is particularly colorful.

Regular municipal buses travel between Reñaca and Viña del Mar. This is a town for the young, with plenty of entertainment and activity along Avenida Borgoño lining the beach on one side. There are small bars, cafeterias, and discos interspersed with the condominiums.

The most popular beaches are Playa Cochoa on a sheltered bay in the northern suburb of the same name and Playa Reñaca at the northern outskirts of town. Playa Las Cañitas is located south of town. The sand is fine and white, but the beaches fall off abruptly into the sea. The sea is a bit rough and is not particularly suited to swimming; however this should not detract from a very attractive beach resort. The mean summer temperature is 18°C (64°F) and water is 15°C (59°F). Many of the beaches have life-guards.

🎭 Festivals
- January, fourth week: Night fishing championships

ℹ️ Tourist information
- Central de Informaciones Turísticas, Avenida Borgoño near Puente Reñaca ℡ 902787. Open only in summer

⛺ Camping
There is a nice camping site at Santa Luisa 401, Subida Los Ositos, four blocks from beach.

Key to map

A Iglesia
C Municipalidad (Town hall)
D Post office and telex
E Telephone

● **Accommodation**
2 Apart Hotel Brisas del Mar
4 Hotel Nilahué
10 Motel Los Ositos
11 Motel Presidente
12 Cabañas Reñaca
14 Motel Iguazú
16 Cabañas de Reñaca
18 Apart Hotel Isla Verde
19 Motel Holiday
24 Motel Manquehué
25 Hotel Natania
27 Motel Amancay
28 Hotel Montecarlo

○ **Eating out**
3 Restaurant Afrika
5 Restaurant Bruno Tavelli
6 Restaurant Los Pomairinos
7 Restaurant Crepesucetix
8 Restaurant Long Beach
9 Osito Pizza
15 Restaurant Mangiare
20 Restaurant Mastrantonio
23 Restaurant Facundo

⊙ **Entertainment**
1 Disco Topsy Topsy
13 Claudio Disco
17 Delta Bowling
22 Disco Casados
26 Tennis courts

□ **Services**
21 Supermercado

⊞ Eating out

Restaurants
☞ • Africa 3, Avenida Borgoño 15000. German cuisine. Cocktail bar, views over the bay, credit cards accepted
• Adriatico, Las Olas 16 corner of La Playa. *Parrillada*. Credit cards accepted
• Long Beach, I. Carrera Pinto 176. Seafood and steaks. Self-serve, credit cards accepted
• Los Pomairinos, Avenida Borgoño 14890 near intersection with Pinto
• Mac Crocket, Avenida Borgoño 14797. Hamburgers, quick snacks
• Mangiare Trattoria, Segunda 95. Italian cuisine
• Mastrantonio, Avenida Central 17. Italian cuisine. Credit cards accepted

Pizzerías
• Ositos Pizza, corner of Borgoño and Santa Luisa

Eating out in Balneario Cochoa
Balneario Cochoa is 5 km north.

Restaurants
• Andrés, Avenida Borgoño 17140. International cuisine

• El Poncho, Avenida Borgoño 16180. International cuisine. Credit cards accepted
• La Pica de Mi Compadre, Avenida Borgoño 16182. International cuisine. Credit cards accepted, English spoken
• Mirador Cochoa, Avenida Borgoño 16805. International cuisine, bar
☞ • Pacífico, Avenida Borgoño 17120. International cuisine. Credit cards accepted
• Playa Cochoa, Avenida Borgoño. International cuisine. *Salón de té*, views over the bay, credit cards accepted
• Rincón Marino, Avenida Borgoño 17130 $X. International cuisine. Credit cards accepted
• Stella Maris, Avenida Borgoño 17205. International cuisine
• Toconao, Avenida Borgoño 16660. International cuisine. Credit cards accepted

⊞ Entertainment

Nightclub
• La Taquilla, Avenida Borgoño near Rafael Sotomayor

Discos
• Casados, Avenida Borgoño near Angamos

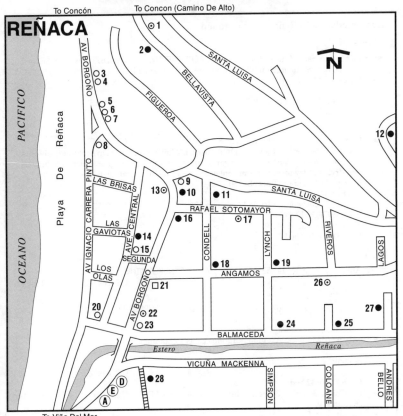

⊟ Accommodation in Reñaca

Apart hotels

★★★★Presidente, Sotomayor 215   ABCDEFGHIKPRV

                                                     ☏ 832958 $F ♁♁

      Fax 902307; 64 beds
- Brisas del Mar I, Bellavista 14850   ☏ 902716
      Fax 902651; 28 beds
- Brisas del Mar II, Las Olas 48   ☏902716
      Fax 902651; 26 beds
- Dei Templi, Camino del Alto 1475   AHR   ☏ 902228
      Fax 834362; 34 beds

★★★★Isla Verde, Angamos 207   ABDEFGHIJKLPR$UV   ☏ 834486 $D for 4
     34 cabins; fax 833334

Accommodation in Reñaca — continued

Cabañas

★★★ La Muerte, Santa Luisa 1371   ABCDEHIKPRUVZ   ☎ 902619 $F for 2
      Sauna, car rental, high on hill overlooking the bay; 38 beds
- Brisas del Mar, Las Brisas 50   ☎ 902651
   40 beds
- Costa Verde, Torreblanca 125   ☎ 834615
   Fax 902527; 18 beds

Hotels

- Conference Town, Dublé Almeyda 80   ☎ 830394
   Located in Sector Los Canelos, a hilly district, 2 km east of the town center. Eucalyptus
   trees, 90 camping sites. Open all year round, electricity, town water, toilet, hot showers,
   laundry, laundry service, restaurant, shop, tent hire, horse riding; 63 beds.
- La Fayette, Subida El Encanto 280   ☎ 832313
   Fax 822316
- Montecarlo, Avenida Vicuña Mackenna 136   ☎ 830397
   Fax 833971; 75 beds
- Natania, Balmaceda 429   ☎ 833181
   Fax 831285; 100 beds

Motels

★★★★ Amancay, Balmaceda 455   ABCDEFGHIJKLPR$TUV
                                                ☎ 902643 $C for 4
   102 beds

★★★★ Holiday, Angamos 367   ABCDEFGHIJKLMPRS$TUZ
                                                ☎ 830005 $C for 4
   Car rental, fax 832822; 42 cabins
- Cabañas de Reñaca, Avenida Borgoño corner of Sotomayor
                          ABCDGHT   ☎ 833729
- Iguazú, Segunda 95 corner of Avenida Central
                          ABCHL   ☎ 830280
   Fax 830900; 42 bed
- Los Ositos, Avenida Borgoño 14650   ABCDEFGHIKLPR   ☎ 831549 $F   ♟♟
   26 rooms
- Manquehué, Balmaceda 325   ABCHKLPV   ☎ 833374
   45 beds
- Nilahué, Avenida Borgoño 14920   ABCDEFGHIKLPR$UV   ☎ 831677 $F   ♟♟
   30 rooms; fax 830141
- Safari, Barros Arana 154   ABCDEFGHIKLPR$V   ☎ 833460 $E for 4
   35 cabins

Accommodation in Sector Los Pinos
Sector Los Pinos is 3 km north of the town center.

Cabañas

- Los Pinos de Reñaca, Ranco Parcela 36, on street to Santa Luisa
                          ABCH   ☎ 902137
- Rancho Ad Hoc, Ranco Parcela 30   ☎ 833328
   17 beds

Hotels

- Camino del Alto, Santa Luis 699   ☎ 833100
   18 beds

- Parilla Facundo, Balmaceda corner of Avenida Borgoño
- Topsy Topsy
- Yo Claudio, Avenida Borgoño near Rafael Sotomayor

⊞ Post and telegraph

Post office
- Correos de Chile (Central Post Office), Avenida Borgoño 14196, Local 2

Telephone
- CTC (central telephone office), Avenida Borgoño (next to church)

⊟ Buses

Municipal buses run to Viña del Mar every 20 minutes.

⊛ Sport

- Delta Bowling, Condell 150. Open Mon–Thur from 1500, Fri–Sun from 1000. Reservations: ℂ 902731 / 970475
- Squash courts in Motel Los Ositos, Rafael Sotomayor. Reservations ℂ 970915
- Tennis courts in Angamos

ROCAS DE SANTO DOMINGO

Area code: 035
Population: 1300
Altitude: sea level
Distances
- From Santiago: 110 km west on RN 78
- From Valparaíso: 106 km south on Ruta F-98-G (sealed), F-960-G (gravel), RN 68 (sealed)

Rocas de Santo Domingo (or just Santo Domingo) is a high-class seaside resort, just south of the mouth of the **Río Maipo**. It is situated on an elevation — *rocas* — in an otherwise flat area. It is susceptible to winds coming from the sea. In contrast to other seaside resorts, this town was created on the drawing board in the 1940s.

The coastal road goes inland from Santo Domingo, and there are several large *haciendas* en route. The coastal *cordillera* has disappeared here — only a few isolated hills venture above the rolling dunes.

This is a vacation home town, with villas surrounded by beautiful gardens. It has good tourist facilities. The extensive beaches have grayish colored sand, and the hills are covered with eucalyptus and pine trees.

However, being located on an elevated outcrop in a wide plain and open to the south-west makes it susceptible to gusty winds; the average summer temperature is 20°C (68°F),

and the water is 15°C 58°F). Playa Santo Domingo is within the town precinct and continues as Playa Sur for 15 km. The hub of beach activity is along Avenida del Mar. There is fishing, water sports, kiosks, changing cabins, and toilets; life-guards are only in the section close to town.

To the south there is the longest beach coast in Central Chile — 20 km — with dunes and *lagunas* that several streams and rivers drain into. Many parts of the cliffs along the coast are covered with seashells, indicating that this part was once under water. It is a lonely and

Key to map

C	Municipalidad (Town hall)
D	Post office and telex
E	Telephone
●	**Accommodation**
2	Hotel Rocas de Santo Domingo
3	Apart Hotel Inti Huasi
4	Apart Hotel Piedra del Sol
○	**Entertainment**
1	Club de Golf
■	**Sights**
5	Piedra del Sol

windswept area and the best way to get there is on horseback.

Festivals

- January, third week: Festival Rocas de Santo Domingo — music festival
- January or February: Semana de Santo Domingo
- February: Golf championships

Tourist information

- Municipalidad, Plaza del Cabildo ☎ 31479

Accommodation

★★★★ Apart Hotel Inti Huasi, Avenida El Litoral 54 ABCGHPV ☎ 443104 $F cabins for 6

- Apart Hotel Piedra del Sol, Avenida Pacífico 010 ABCHIJK ☎ and fax 283011. 18 beds
- Hotel Rocas de Santo Domingo, La Ronda 130 ABCDE-FGHIJKLPRVZ ☎ 444356 $G 👥. Fax 284494; 55 beds

Eating out

Restaurant

- Club de Golf de Santo Domingo, Avenida El Litoral 130

Entertainment

- Nightclub Drive in Cañaveral, Sector Huaso Uno

Post and telegraph

Post Office

- Correos, Arturo Phillips

Telephone

- Operator connected, La Ronda 130

Buses

Taxibuses Litoral Central runs regular services to all seaside resorts between San Antonio and Algarrobo, departing every 20 minutes.

Buses Pullman Bus run regular buses to Santiago and Valparaíso; fares to both destinations $2.60.

Motoring

- Copec gas station, Avenida El Golf corner of Litoral

Sport

- Club de Golf Rocas de Santo Domingo, Avenida El Golf 133. This is a huge complex with a first-class golf course where the South American Golf Championships are held. There are also tennis courts with full-time instructors, and there is a casino and an excellent restaurant

Plate 19   Región Metropolitana
Santiago, entrance to Cerro Santa Lucia

Plate 20 Región Metropolitana
Top: Santiago, Avenida del Libertador B. O'Higgins ('Alameda')
Bottom: Iglesia on top of Cerro Santa Lucia

📷 Sightseeing

- Mirador del Gringo, Neptuno 5. Lookout with sweeping views over the Pacific and the mouth of the Río Maipo.
- Piedra de Sol Intihuatana. This archeological site on Playa Norte is believed to be 4500 years old; its full story is not yet known. It is widely believed to have been a place for sun worship.

🍃 Excursions

Fifteen kilometers south of Rocas de Santo Domino, off the main road leading to Navidad and Lago Rapel, is Fundo Santa Helena. On this property one *laguna* is exploited for its salt. It is possible to observe the salt extraction process.

SAN ANTONIO

Area code: 035
Population: 65 000
Altitude: Sea level
Distances
- From Santiago: 109 km west on RN 78
- From Valparaíso: 100 km south on Ruta F-98-G, F- 90 and RN 68

San Antonio is an important port and industrial city. Although the city as such is only 150 years old, it has developed as a major port due to its sheltered position. In earlier times farmers from the hinterland used the port to ship their products to Peru.

Llo-Lleo virtually forms a twin city with San Antonio, separated from it by by **Estero Llo-Lleo**. You will find the best hotels in Llo-Lleo, as this is also a resort with a beach that extends south for several kilometers.

The beaches continue south as far as the mouth of the **Río Maipo** and are best explored using Llo-Lleo as a base. Because it it the hub of the coast south of Valparaíso and less dependent on tourism, there is an active night life all year round.

⚂ Festivals

- January or February: Carnival
- May 3: Santa Cruz de Mayo
- May 21: Naval Battle of Iquique
- June 29: San Pedro
- August 20: Bernardo O'Higgin's birthday
- September 18 or 19: Día de la Independencia Nacional (National Independence Day)
- October 12: Día de la Raza

- November 1: All Saints' Day
- December 8: Inmaculada Concepción

ℹ Tourist information

In the tourist season the *municipalidad* provides an information service at the now defunct railroad station.

🍽 Eating out

Restaurants
- El Porteñito Uno, Pedro Montt 28. Seafood
- Hotel de Turismo Jockey Club, 21 de Mayo 202. International cuisine
- Juanita, Antofagasta 157. Seafood
- Millaray, Avenida Pedro Montt 48 near Centenario 34
- Mónaco, Antofagasta 170. International cuisine
- Navoli, Pedro Montt 4. Seafood
- Norte Verde, Pedro Montt 185. Seafood
- Pancho Lucero, José Miguel Carrera 321.Seafood
- Pullman, Barros Luco corner of Centenario. Seafood

⊟ Accommodation in San Antonio

Hotels
- Central, Bombero Molina 162 — (231026
- Imperial, Avenida Centenario 330 — ADEFGHIJKP — (211676
- Jockey Club, 21 de Mayo 202 — ADEGHIJKLMNP$Z — (211777 — $H ⁇
  Fax 212922; 37 beds
- Terraza Inn, 21 de Mayo 280 — (212290
  Fax 212283; 15 beds

Cabañas
- Undumar, 21 de Mayo 550 — ABDEGHILPTUVZ — (211908 — $H ⁇
  Car rental; 15 beds

Complejo Turístico
- Casablanca, Leoncio Tagle 58 — ACDEFGHIJKLMNPRS — (212434 — $F ⁇
  Ocean views, fax 234217; 20 beds

Residenciales
- Carlos Witting, A. Valdivieso 655 — (231431

Accommodation in Llo-Lleo

Hotels
- Alhambra, Avenida Providencia 095 — (231935
- El Castillo, Avenida Providencia 253 — AIJP — (373821
- La Paloma, Avenida Chile 538 AFP — (232975
- Oriente, Imaculata Concepción 50 — AFGHIJNP — (282188
- Tropicana, Avenida Providencia 201 — AEFGIP — (232673/450248
  40 beds

Accommodation in San Juan de Llo-LLeo
Located off Ruta 79 on the way to Leyda.
- Centro Turístico La Patagüílla, Parcela 26
  EFGHP
  2 camping sites, 20 cabins, open all year round; electricity, water, toilets, hot showers, restaurant, shop, boat hire, horse-riding

Cafés
- Lucerna, Centenario 193

Eating out in Llo-Lleo

Restaurants
- Club de Tenis Llo-Lleo, Providencia 699. Seafood and *parrillada*
- D'*Borquez*, Avenida Chile 129. Seafood
- El Jardín, Del Canelo 380. Seafood and *parrillada*
- Establecimientos Providencia, Providencia 195
- Yangtse, Inmaculada Concepción 302. Chinese cuisine

Pizzería
- Dino's, Inmaculada Concepción 195 corner of Del Canelo

⊺ Entertainment

Entertainment in Llo-Lleo
- Bar Restaurant Bym's, Providencia 196. Dancing

⌨ Post and telegraph

Post office
- Correos, Avenida Centenario 296

Telephone
- CTC, Avenida Centenario 323, fax 232003
- Telex Chile Avenida Centenario 283

🚌 Buses from San Antonio

The bus terminal is on Angamos 1476 ☎ 31361.

Companies
- A33   Buses GGO Blanco, suburb of Barrancas ☎ 31473
- A51   Buses Los Héroes, Plaza 11 de Septiembre ☎ 33401
- A57   Buses Nueva Horizonte
         Three services daily south to Litueche, Navidad, Pupuye, and Rapel
- A90   Colectivos Alfa 21, 3 Norte corner of Sanfuentes ☎ 34102
- A99   Empresa Capricornio
- A127 Buses Pullman, at the terminal ☎32571

Asociación Taxi Buses San Antonio and Asociación Gremial de Dueños de Buses Litoral Central leave from Plaza de Antonio. Departing every ½ hour, they serve the towns along the seaside: Cartagena, San Sebastián, La Cruces, El Tabo, Isla Negra, El Quisco, and Algarrobo.

Asociación Taxi Buses San Antonio also runs services south to Rocas de Santo Domingo and LLo-Lleo; and on Thurs to Cajón de la Magdalena.

Services

Destination	Fare	Services	Duration	Company
Cuncumén		Mon–Wed		A99
Melipilla		6 services daily		A33
Santiago	$2.30	30 services daily	1½ hrs	A51, A127
Valparaíso	$2.30	24 services daily		A51, A90, A127

Colectivos leave when the taxi is full

💲 Financial

- Banco de Chile, Arturo Prat 03 ☎ 31377. Money exchange
- Banco de Credito e Inversiones, Centenario 145 ☎ 31868. Money exchange

🏨 Services and facilities

Medical services
- Clínica San Juan, Avenida 21 de Mayo 480
- Farmacia Manzur, Centenario 286

✈ Air services

- LADECO, Avenida Barros Luco 1475 ☎ 32519, in Barrio Barrancas

🚗 Motoring

- Automóvil Club de Chile, Barros Luco 1415 ☎ 32843
- Bert Rent A Car Rosselot, Avenida Barros Luco 2550 ☎ 233700

📷 Sightseeing

- Museo Municipal de Ciencias Naturales y Arqueología de San Antonio, in the Municipalidad building, Avenida Barros Luco. Small but interesting collection of artefacts of the pre-Columbian population, and also of the marine life found in this area. Open Mon–Fri 1900–1300 and 1500–1800. Admission free.

SAN FELIPE

Area code: 034
Population: 47 000
Altitude: 600 m
Distances
- From Santiago: 84 km north on Ruta E-89 and RN 57
- From Valparaíso: 120 km north east on RN 60

Founded in 1740 by Manso de Velasco, this central valley township on the banks of the **Río Aconcagua** is a well-preserved example of Spanish colonial town planning. It has many old buildings, and the Plaza de Armas with its old shady trees is a very attractive town center. An unusual architectural feature is found in many corner houses — they have a triangular porch with a pillar as corner post. This porch is open on both sides and from the porch the door goes into the house: you knock on the door under cover. The corner column is sometimes very ornate and supports the roof. There are some very good examples in Avenida Chacabuco. A large number of this peculiar house style are also found in San Esteban (see "Excursions" from Los Andes on page 281) and Rancagua (in Región VI del Libertador).

The historical center of the town is formed by Avenida Bernardo O'Higgins to the south, Avenida Yungay to the east, Avenida Chacabuco to the north, and Avenida Maipú to the west — all these *avenidas* have splendid center parks with century-old trees. An irrigation channel runs through Avenida Yungay.

The Río Aconcagua valley is very beautiful; it widens after Los Andes, and from San Felipe onwards there is intensive cultivation in the river flats. San Felipe is the center of a horticultural area specializing in olives and avocados.

The area around San Felipe is densely populated and villages and towns virtually merge into each other. Some excellent facilities are in neighboring communities such as:
- Curimón, 6 km east (page 279)
- Panquehué, 10 km west (page 321)
- Termas de Jahuel, 20 km north (page 322)
- Los Andes, 22 km east (page 275)

All these communities are linked by regular bus services.

⚐ Festivals
- February: Anniversary of the Battle of Las Coimas
- February, 2nd half: Fiesta de la Chaya
- May 1: Fiesta de la Chicha — wine harvest festival
- August 2: Foundation day
- September: *Cueca* competition on the Plaza de Armas
- September: Fiesta Nuestra Señora de la Merced
- September 18–19: Rodeo Oficial (or Fiesta Huasa)
- October: Novena de Andacollo — This is a religious festival with cowboy overtones; hundreds of mounted *huasos* take part, with folk dancing and music in the streets

ⓘ Tourist information
- Municipalidad, Salinas 203 (510043/77

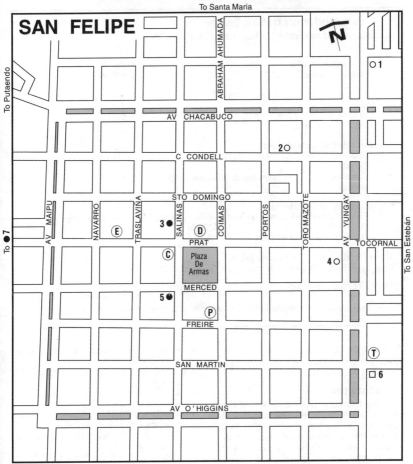

SAN FELIPE

To Santa Maria

To Putaendo

To ●7

To Valparaíso

To San Estebán

ABRAHAM AHUMADA

AV CHACABUCO

C CONDELL

STO DOMINGO

PRAT

MERCED

FREIRE

SAN MARTIN

AV O'HIGGINS

AV MAIPU

NAVARRO

TRASLAVINA

SALINAS

COIMAS

PORTOS

TORO MAZOTE

AV YUNGAY

TOCORNAL

Plaza De Armas

○1

2○

3●

Ⓔ

Ⓓ

Ⓒ

4○

5●

Ⓟ

Ⓣ

□6

Key to map

C	Municipalidad (Town hall)
D	Post office and telex
E	Telephone
P	Gas stations
T	Bus terminals

● Accommodation

2	Hotel Reinares
3	Hotel Europa

5	Hostería San Felipe
7	Complejo Turístico La Torre

○ Eating out

1	Restaurant Club Social
4	Restaurant Isla de Pascua

■ Sights

6	Convento Buen Pastor

⊟ Accommodation in San Felipe

See also "Accommodation" in Los Andes on page 278.

Hotels
- Europa, Salinas 175   ℂ 514134
- Reinares, Carlos Condell 75   AEFGIJPV   ℂ 510359
  26 beds

Hostería
- San Felipe, Merced 204   ADEFGHIJKLPV   ℂ 510508
  Fax 513356; 35 beds

Accommodation outside town
- Balneario Andacollo, Costanera Poniente   ℂ 511605
  19 beds
- Complejo Turístico la Torre, Benigno Caldera Lot 3   ℂ 511605
  16 beds

Accommodation in Palomar
- Centro Campestre Palomar Encon (horse-riding farm), 5 km west of San Felipe
    ACDHJM   ℂ 591004
  Open all year round; 27 beds

Accommodation in Termas de Jahuel
Termas de Jahuel is 16 km north — see "Excursions" below.

★★★★Hotel Termas de Jahuel   ACDEFGHIJKLMNPR$UZ
  ℂ 511240/412 $C ⚄
Full board, sauna, thermal water, tennis, mini golf, thermal swimming pool

Ⓐ Camping

There is a good camping sites in Panque-hué 4 km west of Panquehué.

⊞ Eating out

The most famous local dish is *codorniz asada a la parilla* (barbecued quail) with olives and avocados, accompanied by a glass of *chicha* (grape juice). You should also try *asado de vacuño* (roast beef) with *puré de papa picante* (spiced puréed potatoes) and lettuce salad.
- Centro Arabe, Arturo Prat 124. Mediterranean cuisine
- Club Social San Felipe, Yungay 10. International cuisine. Colonial house with a patio
- Cristal, Ave Maipú corner of Avenida O'Higgins. Chilean cuisine
- El Farolito, Arturo Prat 240. Hot dogs
- Flamingo II, Salinas 195. Italian cuisine
- Flamingo IV, Punta El Olivo. *Parrillada*

- Hostería San Felipe, Merced 204. International cuisine
- Hotel Reinares, Carlos Condell 75. *Parrillada*
- La Casona, Abraham Ahumada 91. Chilean cuisine
- Las Brisas Marinas, Combate de las Coimas 126. Lebanese cuisine
- Monserrat, Merced 154. Attraction: Historical mural
- Pizzería, Avenida Bernardo O'Higgins 199
- Sociedad de Artesanos La Unión, Combate de las Coimas 332. Chilean cuisine
- Yungay, Avenida Yungay 121. *Parrillada*

Eating out Sector Almendral
Almendral is a small rural community 3 km west of town on the road to Termas de Jahuel. The road passes through vineyards and orchards.
- Restaurant Piedras del Molino, Almendral 610. *Cazuela nogada* a beef or

chicken stew with walnuts; *huaso* shows

☞ • Viña Demetrio Mendoza, Almendral 613. This is a *bodega*, selling excellent vintage wine

Eating out in Panquehué
• Restaurant Casablanca, main road

Eating out in Santa María
Santa María is 8 km east.
• Restaurant Baños la Higuera

ⓣ Entertainment

See also "Entertainment" in Los Andes on page 276.
• Disco Flamingo, Carretera General San Martín, 3 km outside town
• Centro Español. Café concert from 2100 onward

🏛 Post and telegraph

Post office
• Correos, Combate de las Coimas 288

Telephone
• CTC, Arturo Prat 274
• CTC, Combate de las Coimas 214, fax 510969
• Telex Chile, Arturo Prat 740, office 11

💲 Financial

• Casa de Cambio Los Libertadores, Salinas 256 ℂ 510117
• Fincard, Salinas 251 ℂ 510863. Cash advances against Visa and Mastercard

▤ Services and facilities

Pharmacy
• Farmacia Alemana, Combate de las Coimas 206

⏺ Motoring

For gas stations, see city map.
• Automóvil Club de Chile, Santo Domingo 99 ℂ 51377. Open Mon–Sat 0900–1300 and 1400–1900

Car rental
• Bert Rent a Car Rosselot, Merced 130 ℂ 511269

▦ Trains

The railroad station is on Las Heras ℂ 510420.

Trains run to Llay-Llay, Viña del Mar, and Valparaíso; and to Los Andes; 3–4 services daily.

⌂ Shopping

• Viña Mendoza, Almendral 613. Chilean vintage wines

⚅ Sport

• Tennis, Avenida Yungay corner of Chacabuco
• Trout fishing in the Río Putaendo and Río Rocín

📷 Sightseeing

Go along to the Plaza de Armas on Sundays between 1200 and 1300 and you can hear a concert performed by a local band.
• Convento Buen Pastor, a *monumento nacional* built in the 19th century.

⦿ Excursions

• **Baños del Parrón**: 23 km north-east. These thermal waters are diverted into a swimming pool; otherwise they are in a natural state with no facilities. The turnoff is 12 km north on Ruta E-71, and signposted. From the turnoff to Baños del Parrón this becomes a one-lane sealed road to Putaendo.
• **Curimón**: 6 km east. It has an interesting Franciscan monastery and Museum. See Curimón under "Excursions" from Los Andes on page 279.
• **El Almendral**: 11 km north. In the Iglesia de San Francisco you can see furniture and paintings from the colonial period. Its tower was built in the middle of the 17th century.
• **Laguna del Copin** (2400 m): A hike further up the Estero Las Lajas valley.
• **Panquehué** is situated in an extremely wide part of the **Río Aconcagua** valley, halfway between Llay-Llay and San Felipe and has a population of 2200. In 1870 a northern mineral magnate acquired Hacienda Panquehué and built the irrigation canals which still bring water to the vineyards he established here. The area has many *bodegas* which continue to produce excellent wines. **Bodega Errázuriz-Panquehué** is located 4 km south-east of Panquehué. Watch wine-making in season, and take part in wine tasting.

San Felipe

🚌 Buses from San Felipe

The bus terminal is at Avenida Yungay 300. Local buses to Putaendo and Los Andes leave from the terminal as well.

Companies
- A2   Buses alfa Tres Ltda ℂ 510512
- A14   Buses Ahumada ℂ 510171
- A32   Buses Flota Imperial Ltda, office 8 ℂ 510244
- A40   Buses JMLtda, office 6 ℂ 510495
- A44   Buses La Porteña
- A65   Buses Puma ℂ 510039
   Buses depart outside terminal gate; runs daily services to Bellavista, El Asiento, Las Cabras, and Putaendo
- A70   Buses Ruta 57 ℂ 510742

Services

Destination	Fare	Services	Companies
Cabildo	$2.30	10 services daily	A44
Concón	$2.10	10 services daily	A2
La Calera	$1.50	10 services daily	A2
La Ligua	$2.10	10 services daily	A44
Los Andes	$0.50	12 services daily	A44
Papudo	$2.50	10 services daily	A44
Quillota	$1.70	10 services daily	A2
Santiago	$2.10	15 services daily	A14, A32, A70
Valparaíso	$2.70	13 services daily	A2, A40
Viña del Mar	$2.70	13 services daily	A2, A40

Buses Puma, Taxi Colectivos Los Conquistadores and Taxi Colectivos Ruta 60 run regular daily services from here to San Felipe, Los Andes, Llay-Llay, and Catemu; Buses Alfa Tres and Buses JM run regular services to Valparaíso and Viña del Mar.

- **Putaendo:** 15 km north, a ½-hour trip up the **Río Putaendo** valley on Ruta E-71. Buses leave from the central bus terminal. At first it is flat country, but as you head north toward the high sierras, the terrain becomes hilly. There are vineyards along the road and you have beautiful views of the snow-capped Andes through the wide valley of the Río Putaendo. The road follows the east side of the Río Putaendo, which has a fairly low water level in summer as much of it is used for irrigation. But the huge boulders in the riverbed are an indication that in spring water from flash floods can arrive with a vengeance. The riverbed is nearly 500 m wide, exending to almost the complete width of the valley. See the entry for Putaendo on page 298.

- **Termas de Jahuel:** A thermal spa located in the *pre-Cordillera*, in the **Río Aconcagua** valley 16 km north, at an altitude of 1190 m. The thermal water reaches a temperature of 22°C (72°F). It is open all year round. The waters are said to be beneficial for heart conditions, rheumatism, respiratory complaints, nervous disorders, digestive system, arthritis, mental fatigue and stress, sciatica, sleeplessness, convalescing, asthma, ulcers, and aching joints.

VALPARAÍSO

Area code: 032
Population: 310 000
Altitude: Sea level
Distance from Santiago: 107 km west on RN 68

Valparaíso, on the Pacific coast, is the oldest and most important port in Chile. Designated as port for Santiago and for the benefit of the surrounding area by Pedro de Valdivia, it certainly had a trying history: pirates and earthquakes were always a threat to its existence. Valparaíso rose to prominence through mining, with many mining barons settling there and establishing it as a commercial center in the 19th century.

In 1989, the National Congress was transferred to Valparaíso from Santiago, and occupies a recently built Congress building. But Santiago is still the nation's capital, with the executive powers there. The capital of Región V de Valparaíso, its houses are built in tiers up the hill and on the plateau surrounding the lower part of town.

The oldest parts of Valparaíso are around a small section of foreshore near Muelle Prat, and up on the plateau on Cerro Santo Domingo. The Spanish picked a perfect harbor for their ships, but were saddled with a very difficult topography to build a city: the small foreshore is ringed by small mountains which form a natural barrier preventing easy access to the plateau. There are streets leading up, but most of them finish up as a set of stairs, a dead end, or an elevator to the top.

Early in the 18th century, Fuerte Castillo San José was founded to guard against attack from pirates. At the time of the disastrous earthquake in 1822 which destroyed the city and the Fuerte San José, there were 16 000 inhabitants. It has retained its colonial flavour with its plazas, narrow streets, and the central section near the harbor.

Although not many buildings remain from the colonial period, Valparaíso has much to offer for sightseeing visitors: the difficult topography has forced the inhabitants to build their houses to follow the contours of the hills. Because many streets have sets of stairs in them, they are accessible to pedestrians only. To negotiate the hills, 15 coin-operated elevators (all named) have been built. From the plateau the views over Valparaíso and its harbor are superb.

You can go on numerous walks in and around the city, with views from the lookouts. The downtown area has inspired many artists.

Along the coast to the north, Valparaíso almost merges with Viña del Mar — the central districts are only 8 km apart. Valparaíso is an industrial city, but has many charming areas.

Although a large town, it does not offer much in the way of accommodation, but being so close to Viña del Mar there has been no necessity to build more hotels.

A launch trip in the bay gives plenty of opportunities to take won-

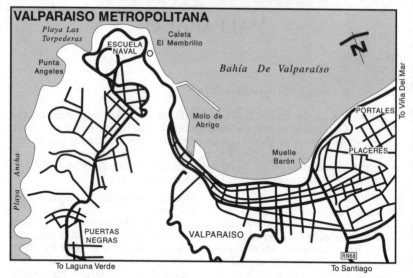

VALPARAISO METROPOLITANA

KEY TO MAPS

derful photographs. The best known beaches within the city are:

- Playa Caleta Portales. East of town center on the way to Viña del Mar; access from Avenida España. Fishing, water sports, kiosks, showers, toilets. Public buses go past.

- Playa Las Torpederas, 3 km west of the city center, enclosed by rocky outcrops. You can get there by public bus via the Costanera which changes its name along its course to Avenida Errázuriz, Avenida Antonio Varas, and Avenida Altamirano. There is swimming,

fishing, water sports, kiosks, and toilets.

In the hotels and restaurants the main dishes are seafood, as you would expect from the location. The center of town is Plaza Sotomayor in the port quarter.

The water is 15°C (59°F) in summer. The mean temperature is 17°C (63°F).

🎎 Festivals

- January 1: New Year celebrations are very colorful: boats are lit and there are fireworks
- January, third week: Festival Regional de Clubes de Cueca — *cueca* dancing competitions
- January, fourth week: Night fishing championships
- February, first week: International tennis tournament, Club de Ténis Unión (68105
- April 17: Foundation day
- May 21: Commemoration of the Naval Battle of Iquique

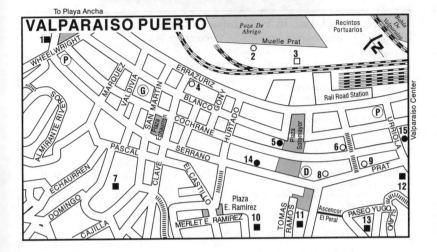

Key to map

A	Iglesia Matriz
D	Post office and telex
E	Telephone
G	Mercado Municipal (Market)
I	Tourist information
P	Gas stations

● Accommodation

5	Hotel Reina Victoria
14	Hotel Garden
15	Residencial Lily

○ Eating out

2	Restaurant Bote Salvavidas
4	Restaurant Proa Al Cañaveral

6	Restaurant Valparaíso Eterno
8	Restaurant Del Monico
9	Restaurant La Rotonda

■ Sights

1	Edificio de la Aduana
7	Iglesia Matriz
10	Museo Lord Cochrane
11	Palacio de la Justicia
12	Bolsa de Valores
13	Palacio Baburizza

□ Services

3	Fería de Artesanías

• September 17–19: Rode Oficial (or Fiesta Huasa)

ⓘ Tourist information

• Oficina Informaciones Turísticas, Municipalidad, Condell 1490 ℓ 251071, ext. 311. Open Mon–Fri 0830–1400 and 1500–1730
• Sernatur kiosk, Muelle Prat. Open September–March Tues–Sun 0900–1900

• Bus terminal, Pedro Montt near Rawson. Open 0930–1300 and 1600–2000

Ⓐ Camping

The nearest camping sites are 12 km east of town, and at Laguna Verde 20 km south of town.

⊟ Accommodation in Valparaíso

See also "Accommodation" in Viña del Mar on page 346.

Hotels

★★ Lancaster, Chacabuco 2362 46 beds	AEHILPTV	(217391	$G ♟
• Austral, Las Heras 622		(257034	
• Casa Baska, Victoria 2449 Fax 219915; 48 beds	AEFGPT	(234036	
• Condell, Pirámide 557 Fax 253083; 38 beds	ACDEGIJKLPTV (212788		
• Garden, Serrano 501 25 rooms	ADEFGHIJPV	(252776	$H ♟
• Pacariña, Avenida Elias 112		(256343	
• Prat, Condell 1443 60 rooms	ADEFGIJLP$TV	(253081/2/3	$G ♟
• Reina Victoria, Plaza Sotomayor 190 27 beds	AF (	212203	

Hostales

• Casa Kolping Valparaíso, Francisco Valdés Vergara 622			
	APS	(216306	$H ♟
Fax 230352, German spoken; 20 beds			

Residenciales

• Eliana, Avenida Brasil 2164 34 beds		(250964	
• Florencia, Victoria 2578		(257839	
• Geminis 1, Avenida Pedro Montt 2062			
	AJ	(255537	
20 beds			
• Geminis 2, Condell 1386	AJ	(215544	
• Lily, Blanco 866 25 beds	AFIJPV	(255995	
• Mi Casa, Rawson 310	AF	(210101	
• Valparaíso, Pedro Montt 2360	AEHIJPV	(257788	
• Vera Cruz, Avenida Pedro Montt 2879 next to bus terminal Shared bathroom, budget travelers			$I ♟

Accommodation in Laguna Verde
Laguna Verde is 20 km south.

Complejo Turístico

• Las Docas, Fundo El Chaparral, 8 km south			
	ABEFGJN		
Cabins for 2–8 persons			

Hosterías

• Laguna Verde, Parcela (Lot) 4	ADEFGHIJKLNP$V	((09)3319426	$H ♟
• El Tilo, Oteagui	AEFGJLNV	(2211177	$H ♟
• 9 rooms			

Accommodation in Placilla
Placilla is a small town 9 km south of Valparaíso nearest to the Reserva Nacional Lago Peñuelas, about 2 km south of the western entrance and the RN 68.

• Canelo's Motel, El Sauce 101	ADF	(291034	
• Motel El Bosque, Camino Real	ADF	(291075	

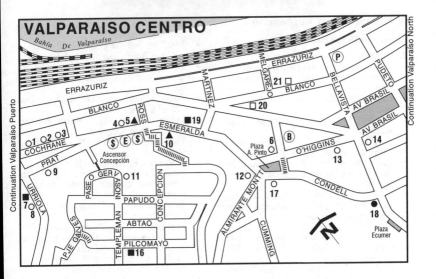

Key to map

B Gobernación Provincial (Government)
D Post office and telex
E Telephone
P Gas stations
$ Money exchange

● **Accommodation**
18 Hotel Condell

○ **Eating out**
1 Restaurant Westphalia
2 Restaurant Bar Inglés
3 Restaurant Mesón del Lord
4 Restaurant Plato Listo
6 Café Riquet
8 Restaurant La Nouvelle Cuisine
9 Restaurant Trolley
11 Restaurant Turri

12 Restaurant Cinzano
13 Restaurant Juan Cruz Martínez
14 Club Alemán
17 Restaurant Club Valparaíso

△ **Airline offices**
5 LADECO
10 LAN Chile

■ **Sights**
7 Bolsa de Valores
15 Iglesia Luterana
16 Iglesia Anglicana
19 Centro Cultural Valparaíso

□ **Services**
20 Peruvian Consulate
21 Argentine Consulate

VALPARAÍSO

ⓘ Eating out in Valparaíso

Eating out in the city center

Restaurants
- Ave César, Avenida Pedro Montt
- Bambú, Pudeto 450. Vegetarian cuisine
- Bar Inglés, Cochrane 551. International cuisine
- Bogarín, Independencia corner of Edwards ☞
- Bote Salvavidas, Muelle Prat $X. International cuisine, seafood
- Café Riquet, Plaza Aníbal Pinto 1199. International cuisine. Credit cards accepted
- ☞ Café Turri, Paseo Gervasoni near Tempelmann 147 Cerro Concepción. International cuisine
- ☞ Casados, Avenida Brasil 1580 corner of Huito 301. Spanish cuisine and bar
- Club Alemán, Salvador Donoso 1337. German cuisine
- Club Español, Avenida Brasil 1589. Spanish cuisine. Credit cards accepted
- Club Valparaíso, Condell 1190, edificio Plaza Aníbal Pinto. International cuisine ☞
- Del Monico, Prat 669. International cuisine
- Donato, Rodríguez 473. Chilean cuisine
- Don Willie, Retamo 544. Chilean cuisine
- El Castillo, Waddington 714. International cuisine. Views over the bay, credit cards accepted
- ☞ El Molinon, Freire 583. Chilean cuisine
- Galeone D'Oro, Independencia 1760
- Hamburg, Lib. B. O'Higgins 1274. German cuisine
- Juan Cruz Martínez, Pasaje Condell 1466 (in the Municipalidad building)
- La Folia, Avenida Pedro Montt 2382. International cuisine
- ☞ La Parilla de Pepe, Ave Pedro Montt 1872, upstairs. Steaks
- La Nouvelle Cuisine, Urriola 342. French cuisine. Bar, credit cards accepted
- La Rotonda, Prat 701. International cuisine. Credit cards accepted
- L'O Devi, Subida Ecuador 34. French cuisine
- Marco Polo, Avenida Pedro Montt 2199. Italian cuisine

- Mezón de Lord, Cochrane 859. International cuisine
- Mr. Egg, Subida Ecuador 50. Chilean cuisine. Bohemian atmosphere
- O'Higgins, Almirante Barroso 506. International cuisine. Background music
- Pagoda Hai-Nan, Avenida Argentina 825 $Z Chinese cuisine
- Pekin, Pudeto 422. Chinese cuisine. Credit cards accepted
- Plaza, Condell 1599. International cuisine
- Platolisto, Esmeralda 945. Self-serve
- Proa Al Cañaveral, Errázuriz 304. International cuisine. Credit cards accepted
- Taberna Pancho Pirata, Pudeto 489. Café bar, grill
- Trattoria Italiana, Plaza Victoria 1698. Italian cuisine. Credit cards accepted, bar and background music
- Trolley Club, Prat 836. International cuisine. Businessmen's club
- Tun San, Victoria 2361. Chinese cuisine
- Valparaíso Eterno, Blanco 698 corner of Almirante Segnoret 150. International cuisine. Background music, dancing ☞
- Valparaíso Liverpool, Subida Ecuador 130. Chilean cuisine. Bohemian atmosphere, background music
- Vitamin Service, Avenida Pedro Montt 1746
- Westfalia, Cochrane 847. International cuisine. Credit cards accepted

Eating out in Caleta Membrillo
- El Membrillo, Avenida Altamirano 1569. Seafood
- El Pescador, Avenida Altamirano 1581. Seafood
- San Pedro, Avenida Altamirano. Seafood

Eating out in Caleta Portales
Located north of the city center.
- Marisquería Caleta Portales, Avenida España. Seafood
- Marisquería El Timón, Pelle Local C-58. Seafood

ⓣ Entertainment
- Cinzano, Plaza Aníbal Pinto 1182. International cuisine, dance hall attached with Latin American music

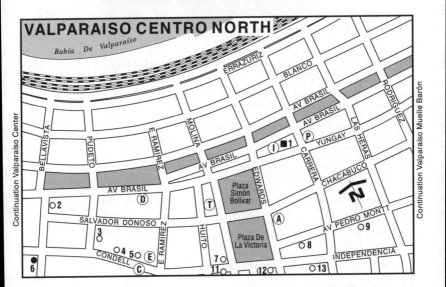

Key to map

A	Iglesia Catedral de Valparaíso	7	Restaurant Plaza
C	Municipalidad (Town hall)	8	Restaurant Ave César
D	Post office and telex	9	Restaurant La Parrilla de Pepe
E	Telephone	11	Club Naval
P	Gas stations	12	Restaurant Bogarín
T	Bus terminals	13	Restaurant Galeone d'Oro
●	**Accommodation**	⦿	**Entertainment**
4	Hotel Prat	5	Tanguería Imperio
6	Hotel Condell	■	**Sights**
○	**Eating out**	1	Biblioteca Santiago Severín
2	Club Alemán		
3	Restaurant La Cueva Pancho Pirata		

- Disco Gioka, Yungay corner of Las Heras
- El Castillo, Altamirano 1419. Tango nights on Friday
- Restaurant La Hacienda, Avenida Pedro Montt 2157. Dancing 2 orchestras weekdays
- Restaurant Nahuel, Donoso 1498. Dancing
- Restaurant Popeye's Club, Errázuriz 687, in the railroad station. International cuisine, dancing weekends

- Tanguería Imperio, Condell
- Tanguería Puerta del Sol, Avenida Pedro Montt 2033. Chilean cuisine

🏣 Post and telegraph

Post office
- Correos de Chile (central post office), Plaza Sotomayor near Cochrane

Telephone
- CTC, Avenida Pedro Montt 2023, fax 212765

🚌 Buses from Valparaíso

Companies operating from Terminal Rodoviario
Terminal Rodoviario is at 913 Pedro Montt near Rawson ℂ 213246.
* A2   Alfa Tres Ltda ℂ 252173)
* A16   Buses Bio Tal
* A40   Buses JM, local 21 ℂ 256581
* A48   Buses LIT, local 8 ℂ 253948
* A65   Buses Puma
* A74   Buses Sol Del Sur, local 3 ℂ 252211
* A75   Buses T.A.C., local 15 ℂ 685767
* A78   Buses Tramaca ℂ 250811
* A83   Buses Zambrano, local 21 ℂ 258986
* A86   Chile Bus, local 18 ℂ 258247
* A93   Cóndor Bus, local 4 ℂ 214637
* A97   Buses El Rápido, office 19
* A105 Buses Sol del Pacífico, local B-11 ℂ 213776
* A106 Fénix Pullman Norte ℂ 257993
* A112 Flota Barrios, local 20 ℂ 253674
* A115 Inca Bus-Lasval, local 17 ℂ 214915
* A127 Buses Pullman Bus, local 5 ℂ 256898
* A137 TAS Choapa, local 17 ℂ 252921
* A153 Tur-Bus Jedimar, local 4 ℂ 212028

Companies with private bus terminals
* A5   Asociación Gremial de Buses Intercomunales, Molina 372 ℂ 217436
* A6   Asociación Gremial de Dueños de Buses Litoral Central
* A7   Asociación Gremial de Dueños de Taxibuses San Antonio
* A23   Buses Carrera Hermanos
* A28   Buses Dhinos, Estadio Playa Ancha
* A29   Buses El Quisco
* A44   La Porteña, Molina 366 (on the Plaza Simón Bolívar) ℂ 216568
* A51   Buses Los Héroes
* A53   Buses Mirasol
* A64   Buses Quintay, Avenida Brasil corner of Yungay or Colón corner of
        Avenida Argentina ℂ 663615
* A84   Central Bus Placeres No 3, Avenida Argentina corner of Quito or Juana
        Ross and Victoria ℂ 217704
* A88   Ciferal Express, Terminal Playa Ancha or Blanco 1890 ℂ 252691
* A105 Buses Sol del Pacífico, Terminal Playa Ancha, Galvarino 110 ℂ 254462

Destinations

Destination	Fare	Services	Duration	Companies
Alicahué		daily		A44
Algarrobo	$1.70	14 services daily		A6, A51, A127
Antofagasta	$31.50	9 services daily		A78, A83, A86, A106, A112
Arica	$46.50	6 services daily	30 hrs	A78, A83, A106, A112
Buenos Aires (Argentina)				
	$55.00	3 services daily		A75, A86, A106
Cabildo	$2.10	1 service daily		A44
Calama	$33.00	2 services daily		A78, A112
Caldera	$17.60	4 services daily		A115, A127
Cartagena				A6, A7, A127
Casablanca	$0.85	14 services daily		A23, A51, A64, A127
Catemu		6 services daily		A2, A40, A65, A106

Buses from Valparaíso — continued

Destination	Fare	Services	Duration	Companies
• Chañaral	$25.00	8 services daily		A106, A112, A127
• Chillán	$11.60	17 services daily		A16, A40, A48, A74, A105, A137, A153
• Chincolco	$3.30			A44
• Chuquicamata	$33.00	2 services daily		A112
• Colliguay		Mon–Sat		A44
• Concón		daily		A28
• Concepción	$14.60	12 services daily		A40, A48, A74, A105, A106, A137, A153
• Copiapó	$18.80	11 services daily		A83, A86, A106, A112, A127, A128
• Coquimbo	$12.50	4 services daily		A78, A127
• Curacautín	$15.80	3 services daily		A106
• El Salvador		1 service daily		A115, A127
• El Quisco		14 services daily		A6, A29, A127
• El Tabo		14 services daily		A6, A51, A127
• Granizo		5 services daily		A88
• Horcón		5 services daily		A105
• Illapel	$4.60	3 services daily		A5
• Iquique	$43.80	6 services daily		A83, A106, A112
• La Calera	$1.10	10 services daily		A2, A5, A28, A37, A40, A44
• Laguna Verde		5 services daily		A84
• Lagunillas	$1.40	14 services daily		A127
• La Ligua				
via La Calera	$1.70	2 services daily		A44
via Puchuncaví	$1.70	1 service daily		A44, A105, A153
• La Serena	$12.50	13 services daily	7 hrs	A83, A86, A106, A112, A115, A127
• Las Ventanas		5 services daily		A105
• Limache		10 services daily		A28, A88
• Linares	$10.00	5 services daily		A105
• Llay-Llay		10 services daily		A65
• Los Andes	$2.90	12 services daily		A2, A40, A65, A106
• Los Angeles	$13.40	8 services daily		A105, A106
• Los Molles	$2.70			A5, A105
• Los Vilos	$3.10	9 services daily		A5, A28, A44, A105
• Maitencillo		daily		A105
• Mendoza (Argentina)				
	$20.00	5 services daily		A75, A86, A97, A106, A137
• Nacimiento		daily		A105
• Olmué				A88
• Osorno				A153
• Ovalle	$10.50	6 services daily		A110, A115, A127
• Panquehué				A65
• Papudo	$1.90			A105
• Peña Blanca		daily		A5, A28
• Petorca	$2.70			A44, A105
• Pichicuy		daily		A105
• Pichidangui	$2.70			A5, A44
• Potrerillos	$21.00	4 services daily		A127
Change in La Serena				
• Puchuncaví				A36, A58,
A105 via the coast road or the interior road				
• Pucón	$17.10	3 services daily		A106

Buses from Valparaíso — continued

Destination	Fare	Services	Duration	Companies
• Puerto Montt	$18.70	3 services daily		A48, A137, A153
• Putaendo				A65
• Quebrada Alvarado		6 services daily		A88
• Quilimari	$3.10			A5, A44
• Quillota	$1.00	10 services daily		A2, A28,
• Quilpué				A5, A44, A88, A105
• Quintay		Mon–Sat		A64
• Quintero				A105, A58
• Rancagua	$5.00	1 service daily		A153
• Salamanca	$5.10			A5
• San Antonio	$2.50	14 services daily		A6, A7, A51, A127
• San Carlos	$11.30	5 services daily		A105
• San Felipe	$2.70	10 services daily		A2, A40, A65, A153
• San Fernando	$7.20	5 services daily		A105
• San Salvador	$20.90	4 services daily		A127
Change in La Serena				
• Santiago	$3.30	8 services daily	2 hrs	A48, A74, A93, A105, A115, A127
• Tabolango		daily		A28
• Talca	$9.20	3 services daily		A74, A105, A153
• Talcahuano	$12.80	7 services daily		A40, A48, A74, A105, A106, A153
• Temuco	$15.80	4 services daily		A48, A106
• Tomé		daily		A105
• Valdivia	$17.60	4 services daily		A48, A106, A153
• Vallenar	$16.70	7 services daily		A106, A48
• Victoria	$14.60	3 services daily		A106
• Villa Alemana				A5, A28, A88, A105
• Villarrica	$17.20	4 services daily		A106, A137
• Viña del Mar	$0.50	every 10 minutes		A5, A28, A44, A88, A105
• Zapallar				A105

Key to map
G Mercado Municipal (Market)
P Gas stations

● **Accommodation**
3 Residencial Geminis I
5 Hotel Casa Baska
8 Hotel Lancaster

○ **Eating out**
2 Restaurant Marco Polo

4 Restaurant La Folia
7 Restaurant Don Willie

◉ **Entertainment**
1 Tanguería Puerta del Sol

■ **Sights**
6 Iglesia de los Padres Franceses

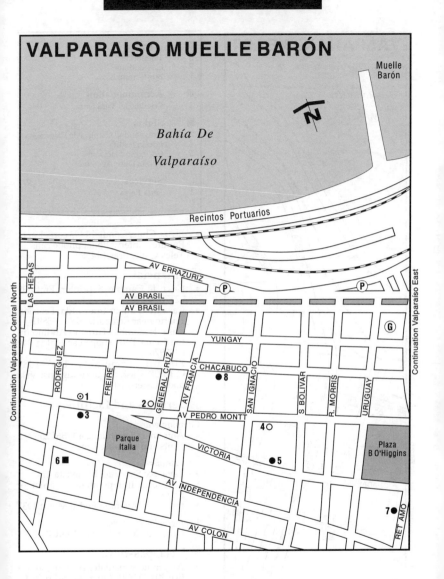

VALPARAISO MUELLE BARÓN

Muelle
Barón

Bahía De

Valparaíso

Recintos Portuarios

AV ERRAZURIZ

AV BRASIL

AV BRASIL

YUNGAY

CHACABUCO

●8

⊙1

2○

●3

AV PEDRO MONTT

4○

Parque
Italia

VICTORIA

●5

6■

AV INDEPENDENCIA

Plaza
B O'Higgins

7●

AV COLON

LAS HERAS

RODRIGUEZ

FREIRE

GENERAL CRUZ

AV FRANCIA

SAN IGNACIO

S BOLIVAR

R. MORRIS

URUGUAY

RET AMO

Continuation Valparaiso Central North

Continuation Valparaíso East

Ⓟ

Ⓟ

Ⓖ

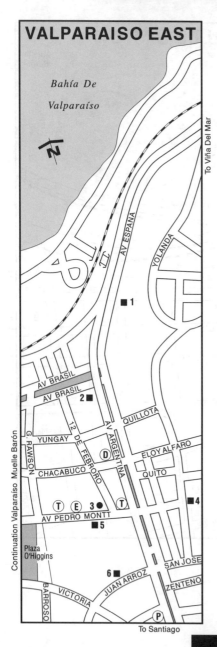

VALPARAISO EAST

Bahía De
Valparaíso

To Viña Del Mar

AV ESPANA
YOLANDA
■ 1
QUILLOTA
AV BRASIL
AV BRASIL
2 ■
12 DE FEBRERO
G. RAWSON
YUNGAY
D
AV ARGENTINA
ELOY ALFARO
CHACABUCO
QUITO
Continuation Valparaíso Muelle Barón
T E 3 ● T
AV PEDRO MONTT ■ 4
■ 5
Plaza
O'Higgins
6 ■ JUAN ARROZ
VICTORIA
SAN JOSE
ZENTENO
BARROSO
P

To Santiago

Key to map
E   Telephone
P   Gas stations
T   Bus terminals

●   **Accommodation**
3   Residencial Vera Cruz

■   **Sights**
2   Universidad Católica de Valparaíso
4   Iglesia Jesuita
5   Congreso Nacional
6   Iglesia Doce Apóstoles

□   **Services**
1   Fería Persa

- ENTEL Chile, Condell 1495 corner of E. Ramírez. International phone calls
- Telex Chile, Brasil 1458

$ Financial
- Casa de Cambio Exprinter, Prat 895 ℂ 217010
- Casa de Cambio Inter Ltda, Estación Puerto near Errázuriz 627 ℂ 255892
- Casa de Cambio Turismo Andino (in the Gema Tour shop) Esmeralda 940 ℂ 250976
- Fincard, Esmeralda 1087–1089 ℂ 210938. Cash advances against Visa and Mastercard

⊟ Services and facilities

Camping gear
- Antuan, Independencia 1736 ℂ 255992. Tents and sleeping bags

Dry cleaners
- Lavaseco Sandrilo, Bellavista 414
- Lavaseco, Independencia corner of Francia
- Lavaseco, Avenida Pedro Montt 1937

Photographic equipment
- Nort Sur Color, Pedro Montt 1922

▣ Visa, passports
- Argentine consulate, Blanco 890, office 20 ℂ 213691. Open Mon–Fri 0900–1300
- Belgian consulate, Prat 827, 12th floor ℂ 213494. Open Mon–Fri 0930–1230
- British consulate, Errázuriz 730 ℂ 256117. Open Mon–Fri 0900–1230

- Danish consulate, Avenida Errázuriz 940, 2nd floor (213942. Open Mon–Fri 0900–1230
- Dutch consulate, Prat 827, office 301 (259096
- Spanish consulate, Avenida Brasil 1589 (214466. Open Mon–Fri 0900–1300
- German consulate, Blanco 1215, 11th floor, office 1102 (256749. Open Mon–Fri 1000–1200
- Japanese consulate, Blanco 997 (250195. Open Mon–Fri 0900–1300
- Peruvian consulate, Blanco 1215, upstairs, office 1202 (253403. Open Mon–Fri 0930–1430
- Swedish consulate, Blanco 1215, office 1002 (256507. Open Mon–Fri 0900–1300

Air services

- LADECO, Esmeralda 973 (216355
- LAN Chile, Esmeralda 1048 upstairs (256443

Motoring services

For gas stations, see city map.

Car rental
- Western Rent A Car, Blanco 951 (253400
- Mach Viña Rent a Car, Las Heras 428 ((32) 259429

Trains

The railroad station is at Sotomayor 7 (212453.

Trains run to Viña del Mar, Quilpué, Villa Alemana, Peña Blanca, Limache, La Calera, Llay-Llay, and Los Andes. there are 4 trains daily.

On Sundays a tourist train goes to Los Andes. It is a 2½ hour trip, and the train stops in Los Andes for 4¼ hours before returning to Valparaíso.
- Llay-Llay: Fare $0.75
- Los Andes: Fare $1.50
- Quillota: Fare $0.60

Water transport

Harbor cruises leave from Muelle Prat in the Bahía de Valparaíso daily. Fare $1.00 per person.

Shopping

Avenida Pedro Montt is one of the town's major shopping streets. It starts on Avenida Argentina, ending on Plaza de la Victoria.

There is a large center strip with market stalls in Avenida Argentina.
- Fería de Anteguedades "La Merced", Avenida Pedro Montt, Plaza O'Higgins. Held Sat and Sun. This is a public market, where dealers and private persons sell anything from kitchen utensils to pictures. You may pick up some unusual items here

Sport

- Club Aereo de Valparaíso, Aerodromo Rodelillo (660817. Operates joyflights over the city
- Club de Regatas, Avenida Errázuriz

Sightseeing

Take a bus up to Barrio Santo Domingo on the plateau. This area, which is believed to be the original Valparaíso, is particularly attractive, being built on low hills with its views over the sea. The winding streets are lined with houses going back to last century. Take a walk down Calle Carampangue to the Plaza Aduana, and from there you can take an elevator ("Ascensor Artillería") up to Calle Artillería. Once you reach the top you will have panoramic views over the Bahía de Valparaíso. There is also a very good restaurant, Del Monico, here.
- Iglesia San Francisco. Access from the corner of Avenida Argentina and Quillota, near Ascensor Lecheros.
- Iglesia Jesuita. Access from the corner of Avenida Argentina and Pedro Montt, leading up to Cero Larrain.
- Monument to Juan Bautista Alberdí, noted Argentine author. Born in Tucumán in 1810, he came to Valparaíso in 1844 and died in 1884. He wrote some of his best books here in Valparaíso.
- Museo Naval, Paseo 21 de Mayo. The museum is in the building of the old navy school. Open 0930–1230 and 1430–1630.
- Museo de Historia Natural, Palacio Lyon, Condell 1546. Open 1000–1300 and 1400–1800; small admission charge.

- Museo Palacio Baburizza, Paseo Yugoslavo, Cerro Alegre. Built in 1910 by a rich saltpeter enterpreneur. It is now the home of the Museo de Bellas Artes de Valparaíso, mainly displaying art works. Open Tues–Sun 1000–1300 and 1500–1800. Admission free.
- Museo Lord Cochrane, Michelet 195, Cerro Cordillera, reached by Ascensor Cordillera. Built in 1842 by a rich Englishman. it was formerly known as Casa Mouat. Now it houses a naval museum. Open Tues–Sun 1000–1300 and 1500–1800. Admission free.

⊕ Excursions

With Valparaíso as a base, there are many excursions you can make into the interior, as well as visiting the beaches south of town. See also "Excursions" from Viña del Mar on page 354.

- **Parque Nacional La Campana**: Near Olmué, 50 km north east. Take Ciferal Express (leaving daily) from Terminal Playa Ancha or Blanco 1890, going directly to Sector Granizo inside the park. See the entry for the park on page 292.
- **Los Andes**: Day excursion by train through the **Río Aconcagua** valley. See the entry for Los Andes on page 275.
- **Reserva Nacional Lago Peñuelas**: 15 km east of Valparaíso on RN 68. Covering 9200 ha (22 724 acres), the reserve centers on a huge lake which was created in 1895 to supply Valparaíso and Viña del Mar with drinking water. The flora consists of *peumos* and *quillayes*, which form mixed forests around the lake and along the streams. Further away from the lake it becomes dry savannah with rosemary, white roses, and brambles, and also some eucalyptys and pine trees. In the still drier parts, *algarrobos* and thorn bushes predominate. Here you will find a variety of bird life, including *tenca, huiravo* eagles, and lots of ducks. Mammals are represented by grey foxes, skunks, otters, mountain cats; rabbits and hares have been introduced and are causing some damage to the ecosystem. The climate is dry in the summer months (which can last for as long as six months), and the average annual rainfall is 500 mm. The mean annual temperature is 16°C (61°F). You can visit the park throughout the year. This is a favorite weekend retreat with people from the coastal cities. CONAF has installed picnic areas with barbecue facilities, walking paths, and a lookout from which you can look over the lake and the low hills surrounding the lake. There are an eating place and a shop nearby. You can reach the reserve by public buses from Valparaíso and Santiago.

- **Laguna Verde**: 20 km south, on **Bahía Laguna Verde.** This small beach resort has attractive beaches which slope sharply toward the sea. Take Central Bus Placeres no. 3 from Avenida Argentina at the corner of Quito or from the corner of Juana Ross and Victoria. Access is through the Camino de Quebrada Verde. The best beaches in the vicinity are Playa Grande, Playa Chica (with fishing, water sports, camping, and kiosks), and Playa Doca, 10 km south. The restaurants serve mostly seafood. The average summer temperature is 17°C (63°F) and the water is 15°C (59°F). A cool southerly wind usually blows on summer afternoons. In the second week in February, Semana Lagunina is celebrated.
- **Caleta Quintay** and **Punta Loros**: 44 km south on a bay which was formerly used as a whaling base. These days the whales are returning, and sightings are not unusual.
- **Playa Caleta Portales:** Access from Avenida España. Fishing, water sports, kiosks, showers, toilets. Public buses go past.
- **Playa Las Docas:** 30 km south. Fishing, water sports. There are regular buses from Valparaíso.

VILLA ALEMANA

Area Code: 032
Population: 57 000
Distances:
- From Valparaíso: 29 km east on RN 62
- From Santiago: 160 km north-west on RN 62 (sealed) F-50 (gravel) RN 68 (sealed)

Villa Alemana is the center of a winegrowing area and is famous for its vintage wines. Further out there are still some charming hidden valleys which you can easily get to from here, such as the upper **Río Marga Marga** valley near **Los Yuyos**, a small village behind it, and **Cerro Roble Alto** (2185 m), which can be scaled from Los Yuyos.

The town has good tourist facilities and regular bus connections to Viña del Mar and Santiago. Keen shoppers should not miss the main street, Paseo de los Héroes, which is a shopping mall. New and old buildings blend together well here, with one of the older-style buildings being El Portal de Pompeya. There are discos, night clubs, and some excellent restaurants, particularly in the northern suburb of Lo Hidalgo in the Quebrada Escobares, 7 km north of town. Another find here is an old *bodega*, El Sauce, who are long-established makers of fine wine. The Quebrada is an attractive area with many vineyards and many native animals still to be found. While you are there you should also take the opportunity to see the colonial chapel built in 1817. In the nearby Quinta Quetrala, you can see a meteorite which fell on the property.

🎭 Festivals
- May: Fiesta de la Vendimia — Grape harvest festival
- November 8: Foundation day

ℹ️ Tourist information
- Coordinación Turística Municipalidad de Villa Alemana, Avenida Sexta 285[951520. Open Mon–Fri 0800–1400

🍽️ Eating out
See also "Entertainment" below.

Restaurants
- Anilio Ristorante, Avenida Valparaíso 1190. Italian cuisine
- Círcolo Italiano, Avenida Valparaíso 498. Italian cuisine
- El Corredor Del Baqueano Manuel, Buenos Aires 661. Chilean cuisine
- Sin Rival, Santiago 715. Chilean cuisine

Pizzería
- Chico, Avenida Valparaíso 677. Italian cuisine, dancing

Eating out in Quebrada Escobares and Lo Hidalgo

Restaurants
- El Quincho, Bellavista 2729. Spanish cuisine
- Mesón y Taberna Molino de Oro, Camino Troncal. Italian cuisine
- Rancho Los Aromos, Bellavista. Chilean cuisine
- Rancho Santana, El Patagual 26. Grill

🎭 Entertainment

Bars
- Charlie Shop, Paseo Los Héroes 33, in the Edificio Puerta del Sol
- La Alhambra, Avenida Valparaíso 659

Discos
- Drake, Avenida Valparaíso 1182, bus stop ("*paradero*") 11
- Kakey, Paseo Los Héroes 80, in the Edificio Nuevo Centro. Bar

---

☐ Accommodation in Villa Alemana

Hotels

• Central, Avenida Valparaíso 791	ACDRFGHIJKLMP$TUVY			
		ℂ 951114	$I	♙
Car rental, 12 rooms				
• Fersen, Avenida Latorre 192	AEFGHPV	ℂ 950200	$H	♙
• Villa Alemana, Avenida Latorre 76		ℂ 950197	$H	♙
30 beds				

Residenciales

• Mesias, Buenos Aires 731	AFJV	ℂ 950222	
• Punta Arenas, Carrera 455	AJPV	ℂ 950448	

Accommodation in Peñablanca
Peñablanca is 4 km east of Villa Alemana.
• Motel Los Acuarios, Los Aromos 268 AHPV

Accommodation in Quebrada Escobar
Quebrada Escobar is a suburb of Villa Alemana.
• Motel Los Patios, Lo Hildalgo AHPV

• Panorama, Lo Hidalgo, El Sauce 0207, on road to Limache
• Zíngaro, Paseo Los Héroes 91, in the Edificio Caracol. Bar

Dine and dance
• Donde Gilio, Avenida Valparaíso 1982. Fri–Sat dancing from 2100 onwards. Grill
• El Ensueño, Santiago 718. Fri–Sat tango dancing from 2100 onwards
• La Cabaña del Comendador, San Martín corner of Avenida Valparaíso. Shows Fri–Sat from 2300 onwards

☐ Post and telegraph

Post office
• Correo, Avenida Valparaíso 1015

Telephone
• CTC, Avenida Valparaíso 602
• Telex Chile, Santiago 655, local 4

☐ Motoring

Gas stations
• COPEC gas station, Avenida Valparaíso 1215
• Esso, Avenida Valparaíso 1164
• Shell, Santa Rosa 46

☐ Trains
The railroad station is on the corner of Buenos Aires and Latorre ℂ 950931
Trains run to Quilpué, Viña del Mar, and Valparaíso; and to Limache, Quillota, La Calera, Llay-Llay, San Felipe, and Los Andes.

☐ Shopping
• Artesanía en Cobres, Paseo Los Héroes. Copper artworks

☐ Sport
If you are keen on fishing, there are many artificial lakes or "tranques", although most of them are on private property, so you must get permission from the owners, Tranque El Sauce and Tranque Los Leones.

☐ Excursions
• **El Patagual**: A small village 6 km north, on RN 62 to Limache. It is famous for its vineyards, with Viña Santa Magdalena and Viña Santa Juana the best known.

🚌 Buses from Villa Alemana

Companies
- A2   Buses Alfa Tres Ltda, passing through Sector Céntrico
- A5   Asociación Gremial de Buses Intercomunales, Población Moraleda ☎ 950977
         Daily services to Pichidangui, Los Vilos, Illapel. and Salamanca
- A28   Buses Dhino, passing through Sector Céntrico
- A44   La Porteña, passing through Sector Céntrico
         Services to Cabildo, Chincolco, La Calera, La Cruz, La Ligua, Limache,
         Nogales, Petorca, Quillota, Quilpué, Valparaíso, and Viña del Mar
- A48   Buses LIT, Avenida Maturana 22 ☎ 950175
- A83   Buses Zambrano Hnos, Avenida Valparaíso 612-A
         Daily services to Antofagasta, Arica, Copiapó, and La Serena
- A88   Ciferal Express, Hipódromo 20 corner of Camino Troncal
         Daily services to Granizo, Limache, Olmué, and Quilpué
- A105 Sol del Pacífico, Población Moraleda ☎ 950977
- A108 Fhama Bus, Independencia corner of Riquelme
- A115 Incabus-Lasval Avenida Valparaíso 908 ☎ 950905
- A127 Buses Pullman Bus, Avenida Valparaíso 426 ☎ 951997

Services

Destination	Fare	Services	Companies
La Calera		10 services daily	A2, A28, A83
La Cruz		10 services daily	A2, A28
Limache		10 services daily	A2, A28, A88
Los Andes		6 services daily	A2
Quillota		10 services daily	A2, A28, A88
Quilpué		10 services daily	A2, A5, A28, A48, A88, A108,
San Felipe		6 services daily	A2, A105
Santiago	$2.70	4 services daily	A48, A127
Valparaíso		10 services daily	A2, A5, A28, A48, A88, A105, A108, A127
Viña del Mar		10 services daily	A2, A5, A28, A48, A88, A105, A108, A127

VIÑA DEL MAR

Area code: 032
Population: 270 000
Altitude: Sea level
Distances
- From Valparaíso: 7 km north on Ruta F-30-E
- From Santiago: 112 km west on RN 68 and F-66

The city is at the mouth of the **Río Marga Marga** which brings the water from the coastal *cordillera* in spring. In the early days of the Spanish occupation, gold was found here, and after the rains you can still find a few specks of gold. Nowadays only a trickle of water comes down during the rest of the year and the open space formed by the dry riverbed is used for *ferias*, parking and motorcross races.

Wine has been grown here since 1585. The town was officially founded in 1874 and is the number one seaside resort in Chile, attracting many foreign tourists. Nowadays it is also known as *Ciudad Jardín* (Garden City) because of its many open spaces and parks, but many Chileans refer to it simply as "Viña". The largest and most attractive park is the Parque Quinta Vergara, with an am-

phitheater and the Museo de Bellas Artes. Each February the Festival Internacional de la Canción de Viña del Mar ("International Song Festival") is held here.

The city's facilities include first-class accommodation, restaurants, a casino, and discos. On the east side of the plaza is the Teatro Municipal, built in the 1930s. Plays and concerts are held here.

The area around Viña is blessed with attractive and popular beaches, though from the middle of December to the end of February the place is full of tourists and you will need to book or you could well be disappointed. The major shopping street in the center is Calle Valparaíso which is full of cafeterias, restaurants, and boutiques selling leather goods, antiques, and jewelry.

The casino is in a wide park on the beach, north of the Estero Marga Marga. There is a large flower clock at Caleta Abarca, the entrance to Viña del Mar coming from Valparaíso. From Viña del Mar it is quite easy to get to Valparaíso, Concón, Reñaca, and many other seaside resorts just by hopping on one of the local buses which operate along the various coastal roads.

At the Valparaíso Sporting Club there is a race course where the annual Derby is held. The Jardín Botánico (Botanic Garden) is another attraction, with more than 3000 plants and trees from all parts of Chile (including a tree which was native to Easter Island but has since become extinct there). The Sporting Club hosts many cultural and sporting events, in particular yachting, sailing, tennis, and horse racing. Most of the sporting events are held in the Sausalito sports complex.

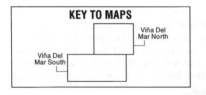

KEY TO MAPS

Viña Del Mar North

Viña Del Mar South

As development continues, Valparaíso, Viña del Mar, Quilpué, and Villa Alemana are gradually becoming one large urban area: the central districts of Viña del Mar and Quilpué are only 16 km apart, and Quilpué and Villa Alemana is already one built-up area.

The city is divided by the Río Marga Marga, the older part of town being on the south bank, and the new part with the casino complex on the north bank. The beach north of the Río Marga Marga is lined with modern high-rise hotels and condominiums.

Playa Las Cañitas is about 6 km north of Viña del Mar and only 2 km south of Reñaca, and you can get to it through Avenida Borgoño. It is one of the longest beaches, extending north and south of the city with hills and trees forming a backdrop. It is Chile's principal beach resort and attracts many sun (and fun) seekers every year during the summer holidays. It offers water sports and life-guards.

Around the clock bus services link Viña del Mar with its twin city Valparaíso and there are plenty of buses going to Santiago. The tourist facilities are excellent, with first-class hotels and restaurants.

The average summer temperature is 15°C (59°F), with the water reaching 14.7°C (58°F). Viña del Mar is a good base for visiting neighboring beach resorts, Valparaíso, and the hinterland.

Beaches around Viña del Mar

The best beaches are to the north of the estuary of the Río Marga Marga, such as Playa Acapulco, El Sol, Los Marineros, Playa Larga, Las Salinas, and Las Cañitas. South of town toward Valparaíso is Playa Caleta Abarca.

- Playa Acapulco: Within walking distance from the town center. Swimming, fishing, water sports, kiosks, and life-guards.
- Playa El Sol: Also within walking distance of town, and merging with Playa Acapulco. Fishing, water sports, kiosks, and life-guards.
- Playa Los Marineros: Merges with Playa El Sol, access from Avenida Jorge Montt. There are local buses. Fishing, kiosks, and life-guards.
- Playa Larga: Continuation of Playa los Marineros. Some distance from town, so use local buses to get there. Fishing, water sports, kiosks, and life-guards.
- Playa Las Salinas: 5 km north of town in Sector Las Salinas. Separated from Playa Larga by rocky outcrops. Access is from Avenida Borgoño. Use municipal bus to get there.
- Playa Las Cañitas: About 6 km north of Viña and only 2 km south of Reñaca. Access is from Avenida Borgoño. Water sports and life-guards.

⌘ Festivals

- January: Formula 3 boat race in Laguna Sausalito; Triatlon in Estadio Sausalito; International tennis competitions and international polo competitions, both in the Complejo Turístico Sausalito
- February: Tennis championships and Viceroy Tennis Cup, both held in the Complejo Turístico Sausalito; national regatta championships, Club de Yates (Yacht Club); national motorcross championships
- February, second week: Derby Day (horse races), at the Complejo Turístico Sausalito

VIÑA DEL
MAR SOUTH

OCEANO
PACIFICO

Plaza
Colombia

Estero Puente
Casino

Puente
Ecuador

Marga

Puente
Villanelo Marga

Puente
Quinta

Puente
Libertad

AV MARINA

IBERIA

LIBERTAD

BALMACEDA

ALAMOS

AV ESPAÑA

To Valparaíso

To Quilpué

To Viña Del Mar North

PORTALES

AGUA SANTA

SCHROEDERS

NIETO

BERGER

VON SCHROEDERS

ECUADOR

TRASLAVIÑA

VILLANELO

ETCHEVERS

QUINTA

COUSIÑO

GROVE

TOFFE

ERRAZURIZ

MONTAÑA

BOHN

AV VALPARAÍSO

ARLEGUI

VIANA

ALVAREZ

6 NORTE
5 NORTE
4 NORTE
3 NORTE
2 NORTE
1 NORTE

AV LIBERTAD

Plaza José
Fco Vergara

- February 11: Virgen de Lourdes, Gruta de Lourdes, Calle Agua Santa
- February, third week: Open international golf championships, at the Club de Golf de Granadilla ☎ 971590
- February 21–26: Festival Internacional de la Canción de Viña del Mar (International Song Festival). This is one of the biggest festivals in South America, and attracts tourists from all over the world ☞
- March: Ocean-going yacht regatta, Club de Yates Recreo (Recreo Yacht Club) ☎ 660802
- May 30: Foundation day

ⓘ Tourist information

- Sernatur, Avenida Valparaíso 507, Edificio Portal Alamos office 303/304, upstairs ☎ 684117/882285
- Municipalidad de Viña del Mar, Puente Libertad next to Telex Chile ☎ 883154
- CONAF, 3 Norte 541, ☎ 976189

⑪ Eating out

Eating out in the city center

Restaurants

- Africa I, Avenida Valparaíso 324. International cuisine
- Amadeus, Traslaviña 166. Grill, "pub"
- Anayak, Quinta 134. International cuisine. *Salón de té,* credit cards accepted
- Cabeza de Buey, Plaza José Francisco Vergara 191. *Parrillada.* Credit cards accepted
- Cap Ducal, Avenida Marina 51. International cuisine. Credit cards accepted
- Casa d'Italia, Alvarez 398. Italian cuisine, bar
- Casino Chico, Avenida Valparaíso 99. Seafood; open 24 hours
- Centro Español, Alvarez 580. Spanish cuisine
- Chaplin's Place, Pasaje Cousiño 16. Seafood and steak
- Chau San, Valparaíso 577. Chinese cuisine. Dancing, credit cards accepted
- Club Arabe, Avenida Marina 50. Libanese cuisine; bar

Key to map

A	Iglesia	54	Hotel Castelar
B	Gobernación Provincial (Government)	55	Hotel Alcantará
		56	Hotel de Viña
C	Municipalidad (Town hall)	65	Hotel Von Schröders
D	Post office and telex	66	Residencial Casino
E	Telephone	67	Hotel José Francisco Vergara
F	Carabineros (Police)	68	Hotel Casablanca
G	Mercado Municipal (Market)	69	Hotel Alcázar
H	Hospital	70	Hotel Quinta Vergara
I	Tourist information	71	Hotel Hispano
P	Gas stations		
$	Money exchange	○	**Eating out**
T	Bus terminals	1	Restaurant Delicias del Mar
		2	Restaurant Mamma Mia
●	**Accommodation**	3	Restaurant Chez Gerald
4	Hotel Vistazul	6	Restaurant Mastantonio
5	Hotel Alborada del Mar	12	Restaurant Lomito'n
7	Hotel Borrico	15	Restaurant Max und Moritz
8	Hotel Torres del Mar	21	Restaurant Public Pub
9	Residencial 555	25	Restaurant Flavia
10	Hostal del Mar	40	Café Alster
11	Hotel Rapa Nui	42	Café El Samoiedo
13	Hotel de Sathya	45	Restaurant La Cuisine
14	Hotel Cantamar	47	Restaurant Casino Chico
16	Residencial Misch	57	Restaurant El Mezón con Zeta
22	Hotel Las Americas	58	Restaurant Madroño Naturista
23	Hotel Monterilla	59	Restaurant Anayak
24	Hotel Andalué	60	Club de Viña
26	Hotel El Tepual	64	Restaurant Squadritto
27	Hotel Mount Royal		
29	Hotel Madrigal	◉	**Entertainment**
31	Hotel Cap Ducal	20	Casino Municipal
34	Hotel Bahia	62	Disco Scratch
35	Hotel Caprice		
36	Hotel O'Higgins	■	**Sights**
37	Hotel Miramar	17	Centro Cultural
38	Hotel Jardín del Mar	18	Museo Fonck
39	Hotel Kumey	19	Quinta Rioja
41	Hotel El Hostal	28	Iglesia de los Padres Franceses
44	Hotel Español	30	Castilo Wolff
46	Residencial Offenbacher Hof	32	Palacio Presidencial
48	Hotel Marbella	33	Castilo Brunet
49	Residencial Blanchard	43	Teatro Municipal
50	Hotel Las Palmas	63	Union Church
51	Hotel Andino		
52	Hotel Castellón	□	**Services**
53	Hotel Marina del Rey	61	Railroad station

- Die Promenade, Pasaje Cousiño 11-B, Barrio Bohemio. German cuisine
- Don Ambrosio in Hotel O'Higgins, Plaza Vergara. International cuisine. Credit cards accepted
- Don Tito, Arlegui 857 $X. Chilean cuisine

- El Mezón con Zeta, Pasaje Cousiño 9. Spanish cuisine. Credit cards accepted, cocktail bar and *peña española*
- El Ostral in the Hotel Miramar, Avenida Marina. International cuisine. Credit cards accepted
- Giacomo, Villanelo 137, upstairs. Italian cuisine
- Kumei, Avenida Valparaíso 121

Key to map

● **Accommodation**

4	Hotel Siglo Veinte
5	Hostal La Siesta
7	Hotel San Martín
12	Residencial Antojitos
13	Hotel Calabrés
14	Hostal Chacras de Coria

○ **Eating out**

1	Pub El Faro
3	Restaurant La Mia Papa
6	Restaurant Gipsy
8	Restaurant Donde El Guatón
9	Pizza Olé

10	Restaurant Gigi
11	Pizza Hut
15	Restaurant El Viejo Poncho
16	Restaurant San Marco
17	Restaurant Antonio Fornino
18	Restaurant Armandita
19	Restaurant La Vieja Armandita
20	Restaurant Han's Dragón
21	Restaurant HongKong

⊙ **Entertainment**

2	Disco La Grúa

- La Cuisine, Pasaje San Luis 1001. French cuisine, bar. Credit cards accepted
- Madroño Naturista, Paseo Cousiño 16 near Viana 645. Vegetarian cuisine
- Panzoni Ristorante, Pasaje Cousiño 12A. Italian cuisine
- Pau San, Quinta 122. Chinese cuisine
- Puerto Montt, Avenida Valparaíso 158-A, in Pasaje Amunátegui. Seafood
- Samoiedo, Avenida Valparaíso 637. International cuisine. Credit cards accepted
- Squadritto Ristorante, Von Schroeders 392. Italian cuisine. Credit cards accepted
- Supermercado Santa Isabel, Villanelo 236. Fast food. Upstairs and downstairs, bar, credit cards accepted
- Tasca Caballo de Fierro, Plaza Sucre at the railroad station. Chilean cuisine
- Unión club, Sucre near Valparaíso (in Plaza Sucre)
- Zum Kochloeffel, Avenida Valparaíso 1101. German cuisine

Cafeterías
- Café Tauros, Avenida Valparaíso 421
- Cerro Castillo, Balmaceda 102 (with panoramic views)
- Bruno Tavelli, Avenida Valparaíso 676
- Big Ben, Avenida Valparaíso 469 Galería Cristal. German cuisine. Credit cards accepted
- Salon de Té Alster, Avenida Valparaíso 225. German cakes. Credit cards accepted

Fast food
- Mcdonald's, Avenida Valparaíso 716
- El Guatón, Quinta 232 near Valparaíso

Pizzerías
- Il Successo, Avenida Valparaíso 263 $X. Credit cards accepted
- Pizza-Pizza, Arlegui 242. Bar, "pub"

Eating out north of Estero Marga Marga

Restaurants
- Antonio Fornino, Avenida San Martín 529. Italian cuisine
- Armandita, Avenida San Martín 501. *Parrillada*. Credit cards accepted
- Bravissimo, San Martín 302. Pastelería
- Chef Aldo Bagnara, 14 Norte 541. International cuisine

- Chez Gerald, Avenida Perú 496 corner of 6 Norte
- Flavia, 6 Poniente 121. Italian cuisine
- Gigi Ristorante, Avenida San Martín 611 in Pasaje Lima 5. Italian cuisine
- Gipsy, 8 Norte 323. French cuisine. Credit cards accepted
- Green Pub, 8 Norte 88. International cuisine. Credit cards accepted, piano bar
- Guris Brasileiros, Ave San Martín 304 near 4 Norte. Brasilian cuisine
- Han's Dragon, Avenida Libertad 705 corner 8 Norte. Chinese cuisine. Credit cards accepted
- La Fontana in Casino Municipal, Avenida San Martín 199. International cuisine. Credit cards accepted
- La Grúa, Avenida San Martín (in Muelle Vergara at the end). Fast food
- La Mia Pappa, Avenida San Martín (in Muelle Vergara). Italian cuisine. Eat as much as you like, views over the bay
- Las Gaviotas, 14 Norte 1248. Chilean cuisine
- Lomito's, 5 Norte 132. Hamburger chain
- Los Compadres, Calera 1445. International cuisine
- Las Delicias del Mar, Avenida San Martín 459. Seafood
- La Vieja Armendita, 7 Norte 620 corner Libertad. Parrillada
- Mascarade, 4 Norte 535. International cuisine. Credit cards accepted, bar
- Mastrantonio, San Martín 410. Italian cuisine, bar
- Max und Moritz, 2 Poniente 377. German cuisine
- Pollos Stop, Avenida Perú 100. Drive in chain
- San Marco, Avenida San Martín 597. Italian cuisine. Credit cards accepted

Pizzerías
- Diego's Pizza, San Martín 636
- Mamma Mia Pizza, San Martín 435
- Pizza Hut, Avenida San Martín 604
- Pizza Olé, San Martín 611 in Pasaje Lima 7
- Telepizza, San Martín 350

Eating out at Playa Las Salinas
Playa Las Salinas is between Viña and Reñaca.

▣ Accommodation in Viña del Mar

See also "Accommodation" in Reñaca (page 311) and Valparaíso (page 326).

Accommodation in Caleta Abarca
Caleta Abarca is located on Avenida España, just before the intersection with Viana.
★★★★★Hotel Miramar, Avenida Marina, overlooking the sea

	ACDEFGHIJKLMPR$TUVXY		
		ℂ 626677	$B ▪▪

- Car rental, beach frontage, sauna, fax (032) 665220
- Residencial Cristina, Chaienaux 155   ℂ 626888

Accommodation in the city center

Apart Hotels
- Sahara, Alberto Blest Gana 397   ABCDGHIPV   ℂ 685161
  $H per flat
- Villalpando, Prat 68 Cerro Castillo   AFHPS   ℂ 661671
  $F apartments for 6. Fax 660510

Hostales
- Mar, Alvarez 868   AHP   ℂ 884775
  Fax 624071; 26 beds

Hotels

★★★★Alcázar, Alvarez 646	ACDEFGHIJKLMPTUVZ		
		ℂ 685112	$D ▪▪
Fax 884245			
★★★★Casablanca, Alvarez 282	ACDEHMPT	ℂ 663243	$F ▪▪
Fax 664161			
★★★★Marina del Rey, Ecuador 299		ℂ883505	
Fax 978571			
★★★★★O'Higgins, Plaza Vergara	ACDEFGHIJKLMPR$TUVXYZ		
		ℂ 882016	$D ▪▪
Fax 883537, car rental			
★★★De Viña, Viana 619	ADEGHIKL	ℂ 685546	$E ▪▪
Fax 882953			
★★★Von Schroeders, Von Schroeders 392	ADEGHIJKLMP$UVZ	ℂ 626022	$D ▪▪
Fax 660474, car rental			
★★Castellón, Viana 135	AEIJKP	ℂ 687688	
$E apartments for 6; fax 977019			
★★El Hostal, Valparaíso 299	ADEHIJKLP$TUVZ	ℂ 882124	$G ▪▪
35 rooms, boat hire, car rental			
• Alcántara, Viana 575		ℂ 688986	$G ▪▪
Fax 680202			
• Balia, Von Schroeders 36		ℂ 978310	
Fax 680724			
• Cap Ducal, Avenida Marina 51	ACDEFGHJKLPTUV	ℂ (32) 626655	$E ▪▪
Fax 665478			
• Castelar, Traslaviña 253	ABCHJPV	ℂ 684368	
Fax 685478			
• Español, Plaza J.F.Vergara 191	ADEFGIJKLPS$V	ℂ 685145	$F ▪▪
• Gala, Arlegui 273	APS	ℂ 686688	$D ▪▪
• Hispano, Plaza Parroquia 391	AFIJKLPTV	ℂ 685860	
Fax 680981			
• Hostal Andino, Viana 31		ℂ 690817	
Fax 971996			
• Jardín del Mar, Avenida Valparaíso 107			
	AEGJKLP$V	ℂ 976771	$H ▪▪

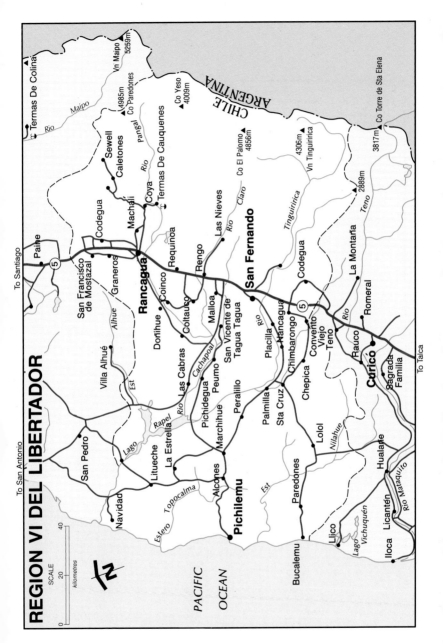

Plate 21
Map of Región VI del Libertador

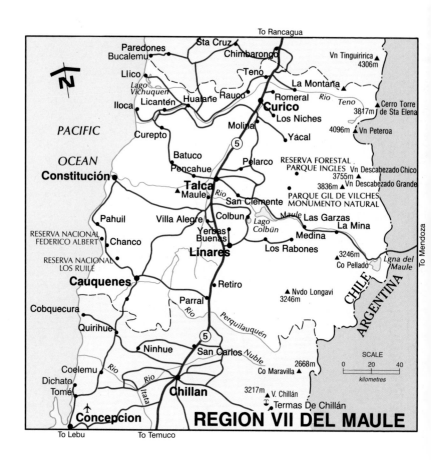

Plate 22
Map of Región VII del Maule

Accommodation in Viña del Mar — continued

- José Francisco Vergara, Von Schroeders 367
  ADFGHIJKLMPS$TUVZ (626023 $E ♔
  Car rental, fax 660474
- Kumei, Avenida Valparaíso 121   AEFGIJKL   (681296
- Las Palmas, Avenida Valparaíso 12   (688456
- Quinta Vergara, Errázuriz 690   ADEFGHIJKLPSUV   (685073 $G ♔
  English spoken, shared bathroom cheaper, fax 691978; 12 rooms
- Viana, Viana 645   (684877
  Fax 882953

Motels
- Diplomate, Calle del Agua 555   AEHKPV   (661647 $I ♔

Residenciales
- Agua Santa, Agua Santa 36   ADIJLPV   (901531 $I ♔
  Shared bathroom
- Angelina, Von Schroeders 167   (976520 $H ♔
  Budget travelers
- Blanchait, Avenida Valparaíso 82-F   AFGHIJKLP$V   (974949 $H ♔
  Budget travelers
- Caprice, Von Schroeders 35   AF   (978295 $H ♚
  Budget travelers
- Caribe, Von Schroeders 46   AHJLPV   (976191 $I ♔
- Casino, Alvarez 110   AHIPV   (662753
- El Carmen, Avenida Valparaíso 30   AHIJLPV   (977310
- Magallanes, Arlegui 555   AEFGHIJKPS   (685101 $J ♚
  Budget travelers
- Marbella, Valparaíso 78   ADEFGHIJPS   (978770 $G ♔
- Megros, Traslaviña 417   AEGIJLPS$UV   (625535 $I ♚
  10 rooms
- Miramar, Agua Santa 80   AFGHILPU   (625608
- Montaña, Agua Santa 153   AFILPV   (662751 $J ♔
- Offenbacher Hof, Balmaceda 102   PS   (621483 $F ♔
  Fax 662432
- Ona Berri, Avenida Valparaíso 618, upstairs
  ADIJLPV   (688187 $H ♔
  18 rooms
- Oxaran, Villanelo 136   AIJPV   (882360 $H ♔
  Shared bathroom cheaper
- Palace, Paseo Valle 387   ALPV   (663134 $G ♔
- Patricia, Agua Santa 48   AEFHIJLP$UV   (663825 $H ♔
- Puente Casino, Von Schroeders 13   (978037
  Budget travelers
- Punta Arenas, Alcalde Prieto Nieto 0332
  ADHJLPV   (681944 $I ♔
  $J with shared bathroom
- Victoria, Avenida Valparaíso 38   AFJPSV   (977370 $H ♔
- Villarrica, Arlegui 172   AJPV   (942807

Accommodation in Viña del Mar — continued

Accommodation north of Estero Marga Marga

Hostales
- Calabrés, 7 Norte 625   (973215
  36 beds
- Del Mar, 5 Norte 883   AEIJK   (974195 $H ▪▪;
  Fax 690694; 24 beds
- El Borrico, 3 Poniente 579   ADEIJK   (970617
  Near Acapulco beach; 20 beds
- Lady Kinnaird, 1 Oriente 1096   (975413
  11 beds
- Pucará, 5 Norte 739, Pasaje Pretot   AHLPV   (972101
- Villamar, 2 Poniente 440   AFTV   (974404 $H ▪▪
  Fax 970202

Hotels
★★★★San Martín, Avenida San Martín 667   ACDEFGHIJKLMP$TVYZ
         (689191
$D apartments for 7. Fax (32) 689195, sauna, piano bar, night club, 170 rooms directly overlooking the beach
- Alborada del Mar, San Martín 419 corner of 5 Norte
       ADEFGHIJKL   (975274
  Fax 970720; 43 beds
- Andalué, 6 Poniente 124   (684147
  Fax 684148
- Cantamar, 5 Norte 230   APS   (681364 $E ▪▪
  Fax 681364; 105 beds
- Chacras de Coria, 7 Norte 669   ADEFGHIJKLMPS   (901419 $G ▪▪
  Fax 884450; 46 beds
- De Sathya, 5 Norte 170   (975005
- Las Américas, 6 Poniente 131   ADFHPTV   (976708 $G ▪▪
  56 beds
- La Siesta de los Poetas, 9 Norte 843   (973028
- Madrigal, 1 Norte 1257   (977500
- Monterilla, 2 Norte 65   ABCDHPV   (976950 $F ▪▪
  Fax 683576; 22 beds
- Mount Royal, 1 Norte 449   (681255
  Fax 681145
- Rapa Nui, 4 Oriente 490
- Siglo Veinte, Libertad 859   (901446
- Tepual, 3 Norte 220   ADHPST   (682504 $E ▪▪
- Torres del Mar, 2 Poniente 439   (970202
- Vista Azul, 5 Norte 39 near Avenida Perú
       ACDFGHIJKLPUZ   (979755 $G ▪▪

Residenciales
- ★555, 5 Norte 555   ACDEFGHIJKLPSUVZ   (972240 $G ▪▪
- Anteojitos, 7 Norte 613
- El Escorial, 5 Poniente 441   AEIJPSV   (975266 $G ▪▪
  Near beach and casino
- Helen Misch, 1 Poniente 239   ADEFHIKPUSV   (971565 $G ▪▪
  16 rooms
- La Frontera, Avenida Libertad 342   APV   (9712050

Accommodation in Viña del Mar — continued

- Porto Bello, San Martín 611, Pasaje Lima
  | | PUV | (978395 | $G ⅱ |
- Pudahuel, 1 Poniente 661   AEJLPV   (979398 $H ⅱ
- San Martín, San Martín 304   ADHIJLPV   (975440
- Toconao, 6 Poniente 235   AEFHPUV   (978395 $H ⅱ

Accommodation at Playa Las Salinas
Playa Las Salinas is on Ruta Costera Norte, 7 km north of the city center.

Hotels

★★★★

Océanic, Avenida Borgoño 12925   ADEFGHIKLMPRS$TUVY
   (830006 $C ⅱ

Sauna, beach frontage, fax 830390, restaurant $X; 38 beds

Restaurants
- Rendez-vous in the Hotel Oceánico, Avenida Borgoño 12925. French cuisine. Views over the bay, bar, credit cards accepted ☞

ⓨ Entertainment

Entertainment in Caleta Abarca
Caleta Abarca is at the southern entrance to Viña del Mar.
- Disco Scala, directly on beach just before the intersection of Avenida España/Avenida de La Marina and Viana

Entertainment in the city center
During the holiday season symphony concerts and rock concerts are held in various places in the city.
- Disco Scratch, Bohn next to railroad station
- El Viejo Almacén, Avenida Valparaíso 131. *Parilla*, show daily from 2100
- Hotel Alcázar, Alvarez 646. Fri "Romantic dinners", Sat tango dance orchestra from 2100 onwards
- Hotel Miramar, Avenida Marina. Fri and Sat dancing from 2100 onwards
- Hotel O'Higgins, Plaza Latorre, Fri and Sat dancing
- La Nueva Frontera, Arlegui 847. $X, dancing nightly after 2100
- Peña, Avenida Valparaíso 1121. $Y, Mexican music
- Piano Bar El Barbero, Avenida Valparaíso block 100 corner of Von Schroeders

- Centro Español, Alvarez 580, Fri and Sat dancing from 2100 onwards
- Night Club Playboys, Avenida Valparaíso 117
- Restaurant Internacional, Arlegui block 200 near Traslaviña, upstairs. Tijuana brass band every day
- Teatro Municipal, Plaza Vergara

Entertainment north of Estero Marga Marga
- Casino Municipal and gardens, Avenida San Martín corner of Uno Norte. Bingo, roulette, poker machines, Salon Picadilly. Cabaret with shows from 1800. Reservations 973565
- Chez Gerald, Avenida Perú 496 corner of 6 Norte. Views over the bay, French cuisine, dance floor, credit cards accepted
- Disco Salsa, Avenida San Martín 431
- Pub El Faro, at the end of Muelle Vergara. Piano bar
- Restaurant Hotel San Martín, Avenida San Martín 667. Dancing at weekends
- Restaurant Pub Cuckoo, San Martín 467. Fri and Sat entertainment — higher prices

▣ Post and telegraph

Post office
- Correos de Chile (central post office), Avenida Valparaíso 846
- Post office and Telex, in lane off Sucre near Puente Libertad

Telephone
- CTC, Villanelo 190 corner of Avenida Valparaíso, fax 881219. Central office
- CTC, Avenida Valparaíso 618, fax 883985
- Telex Chile, Plaza Latorre 32

⑤ Financial
- Casa de Cambio Apex Cambio, Arlegui 641 ℓ 683543
- Casa de Cambio Inter Ltda, 1 Norte 655-B ℓ 977189
- Casa de Cambio Inter Ltda, next to Puente Libertad ℓ 883154. Open Sat
- Casa de Cambio Turismo Andino, Arlegui 646 ℓ 882675
- Cambios Norte, Quinta block 100, Galeria Masino
- Fincard Bancard, Ecuador 259 ℓ 901795. Cash advances against Visa and Mastercard

🖫 Services and facilities

Camping gear
- Antuan, San Antonio 1116-B ℓ 881717. Tents and sleeping bags

Dry cleaners
- Lavaseco Drymon, Viana 433. Self service
- Lavaseco Pony, Avenida San Martín 458

Laundries
- Laverap, Avenida Libertad 841. Washing and drying $5.00
- La Espuma, Traslaviña 148
- Lavablanco Alpino, Arlegui 389

Pharmacies
- Farmacia Bedoya, Avenida Valparaíso 367, in Galeria Fontana
- Farmacia Bedoya, Avenida San Martín 605

Photographic supplies
- Foto Cristal, Avenida Valparaíso 469
- Foto Nort Sur, Sucre near Arlegui Plaza Vergara

Supermarket
- Supermercado Santa Isabel, Arlegui block 1000 between Nuevo Central and Quillota

⊟ Visas, passports
- Austrian consulate, 7 Norte 1107 ℓ 971200
- French consulate Errázuriz 522 ℓ 680349
- Italian consulate, Alvarez 398 ℓ 664364

🚌 Motoring services
For gas stations, see city map.
- Automóvil Club de Chile, 1 Norte 901 ℓ 71815

Car rental
- Bert Rent a Car, Alvarez 762 ℓ 685515, fax 686134
- Cars, Bohn 837
- Euro Rent a Car, Hotel O'Higgins ℓ 882016
- Hertz Rent a Car, 1 Norte 499 ℓ 71085
- Lider Rent A Car, Hotel San Martín, Avenida San Martín 667 ℓ 032-972548
- Mach Viña Rent a Car, Libertad 1080 ℓ 972526 / 680362
- Western Rent-a_Car, Plaza Latorre (in the Hotel O'Higgins) ℓ 882016 / 685552

🏛 Shopping
In the dry season there are market stands in the dry bed of the Río Marga Marga near Arlegui.
- Lapis Lazuli Maldon, Avenida Libertad 1045. Semi-precious stones
- Mercado Municipal (Public Market), Arlegui block 1100 between Batuco and Quilpué

🚃 Trains
The railroad station is on the corner of Bohn and Sucre; it houses a restaurant. There are four services daily
- Llay-Llay: Fare $0.75
- Los Andes: Fare $1.50
- Quillota: Fare $0.60

⊛ Sport
Viña del Mar has been blessed with a string of beaches which are a major attraction. Although these beaches too suffer from the worldwide problem of seaside pollution, it is still fairly safe to indulge in beach activities.
- Club de Golf, Granadilla Country Club, Laguna Sausalito
- Horse races: Since 1885 a typical English "Derby Day" has been held at the racecourse. The biggest racing events are held in February
- In February several ocean races are held between Algarrobo and Quintero

🚌 Buses from Viña del Mar

Local buses
Bus No. 1 (marked "Centro Placeres") to Concón and Reñaca departs from Plaza Vergara.
Bus No .10 to Concón and Reñaca departs from the corner of Valparaíso and Quillota.
Both buses go to the same destinations.

Companies operating from the bus terminal
The bus terminal (Terminal Rodoviario) is at Avenida Valparaíso block 1000, corner of Quilpué (883404.

- A2   Buses Alfa Tres Ltda
- A5   Asociación Gremial de Buses Intercomunal
         Daily services to Pichidangui, Los Vilos, Illapel, and Salamanca
- A16   Buses Biotal
- A22   Buses CATA (882809
         Services to Argentina
- A23   Buses Carrera Hnos
- A28   Buses Dhino
- A40   Buses JM, office 6-A (883184
          Services to Chillán, Concepción, and Talcahuano
- A44   Buses La Porteña
         Services to Pichidangui, Los Vilos,
- A48   Buses LIT (882348
         Services to Temuco, Valdivia, Osorno, and Pueto Montt
- A51   Buses Los Héroes
- A55   Buses Nevada
         Services to Argentina
- A64   Buses Quintay
- A65   Buses Puma
- A74   Sol del Sur
         Services to Rancagua, San Fernando, Curicó, Talca, Linares,
         Concepción, and Talcahuano
- A78   Buses Tramaca, office 1-A (881324
- A83   Buses Buses Zambrano Hnos., office 5 (883942
- A86   Chile Bus, local 2 (881187
- A93   Buses Cóndor (882345
- A100   Buses Empresa O'Higgins
         Services to Argentina
- A105   Expreso Sol del Pacífico (883156
         Services To Chillán, Los angeles, Concepción, and Talcahuano
- A112   Flota Barrios (882725
- A115   Incabus-Lasval, office 3 (684121
- A125   Buses Nueva Transmar, office 3 (881082
- A127   Pullman Bus, office 1 (882901
- A137   Buses TAS Choapa, office 4 (882258
- A153   Tur-Bus Jedimar, office 1 (882661
         Services to Temuco, Valdivia, Osorno, Puerto Montt, Villarrica,
         and Victoria
- B81   Buses Igi Llaima
         Services to Temuco

Buses from Viña de Mar — continued

Interregional services
Fares to interregional destinations are the same as for Valparaíso; see to "Buses" from Valparaíso on page 330 for frequency and fares.

Local services

Destination	Fare	Services	Duration	Companies
• Alicahué	$3.20			A44
• Cabildo	$2.10	1 service daily		A44
• Casablanca	$0.85	14 services daily		A23, A51, A53, A64, A127
• Catemu		6 services daily		A28, A65
• Chincolco	$3.30			A44
• Combarbalá		daily		A28
• Concón	$0.45		½ hr	A28, A44, A105, A125
• Horcón				A105
• La Calera	$1.10	10 services daily		A2, A5, A28, A37, A40, A44
• La Ligua				
via La Calera	$1.70	2 services daily	A44	
via Puchuncaví	$1.70	1 service daily		A44, A105, A153
• Limache				A28, A88
• Llay-Llay		6 services daily		A28, A65
• Los Andes	$3.00	12 services daily		A2, A40, A65, A127
• Los Molles	$2.70			A5, A105
• Maitencillo				A105
• Olmué				A88
• Papudo	$1.90			A105
• Petorca	$2.70			A44, A105
• Pichicuy		daily		A105
• Pichidangui	$2.70			A5, A44
• Puchuncaví				A105, A125
• Putaendo				A65
• Quilimari	$3.10			A5
• Quillota	$1.00	10 services daily		A2, A28, A44
• Quilpué				A5, A44, A88, A105
• Quintero				A105, A125
• Reñaca	$0.45			Colectivos
• San Felipe	$2.70	23 services daily		A2, A40, A65, A153,
• Santiago	$3.30	60 services daily	2 hrs	A16, A48, A74, A93, A105, A115, A125, A127, A153
• Tabolango		daily		A28
• Valparaíso	$0.45			A16
• Las Ventanas				A105
• Villa Alemana				A5, A28, A44, A88, A105
• Zapallar				A105

• A giant chess tournament is held in the court of the Centro Cultural annually. Sometimes the chess pieces are humans clad in medieval costumes

📷 Sightseeing

On Plaza Vergara (corner of Avenida Valparaíso and Sucre) there is a horse and buggy stand (*fiacres*).
You can take an interesting stroll by starting at the flower clock at the intersection of Avenida España and Avenida Marina. Follow Avenida Marina north, skirting

the base of Cerro Castillo. You pass the impressive Hotel Miramar, and a bit further on on the right is the Club Arabe. Behind the Club Arabe is a road leading up to the Presidential Palace. Cerro Castillo was fortified during colonial days — two old cannon still point down from the presidential gardens. Continuing on Avenida Marina, on your left you come to Castillo Wulff, which was formerly the home of an illustrious citizen of this town who built a remarkable building across the rocks (see Museo Naval below). A few yards further on is Hotel Cap Ducal, built in the shape of a ship overlooking the sand-barred mouth of the Río Marga Marga and with views over the casino complex and gardens just across the river. Hotel Cap Ducal is also a Tourism Academy where young cooks, waiters, and hotel managers are trained. Follow Avenida Marina along Río Marga Marga to Puente Casino (the very first one) and cross over. To the right is Plaza Mejico with a fountain which is floodlit at night time. Instead of continuing straight north on Avenida San Martín, turn after the bridge and take a left turn into Calle Uno Norte. Overlooking the mouth of Río Marga Marga is Pollo Stop — a sort of a Kentucky Fried Chicken place — and on your right is the casino complex which in itself is worth strolling through and paying a visit to the gambling rooms. However the casino also has a nice restaurant-cum-cafeteria.

Needless to say, during the main tourist season there are scores of people milling around here, especially when the Song Festival is being held in February. On reaching the sea, Calle Uno Norte turns right along the beach and becomes Avenida Perú. This road continues along the seashore, which is rocky here until Avenida Peru merges with Calle Ocho Norte.

From here onwards, the world-famous beach starts; on the right it is lined with modern apartment buildings, condominiums, and hotels. Turn left here into Avenida San Martín to continue along this beach which extends beyond the city limits further north for several kilometers.

Parks

- Jardín Botánico (also called Parque Salitre), on Camino El Olivar (Ruta F-66), 8 km from the town center in the suburb of El Salto, on the main road linking Viña del Mar with Quilpué. Take public bus Linea 20 which runs along Calle 1 Norte to El Olivar. The area used to belong to Pascual Baburizza, owner of a saltpeter empire. It covers 405 ha (1122 acres) and has 3000 different plant species, not only native plants but also from Europe, Asia, and South America. From the moment you enter, you are in a world of lush green splendor leading to a little *laguna*, the Laguna de Linneo. Take special note of a tree near the entrance — this is the *tormiro* tree which is now extinct on Easter Island (the famous Easter Island tablets were made from the wood of these trees). This botanic garden is now administered by CONAF, and is open Wed, Sun, and holidays 0900–1800. There is a small admission charge.

- Laguna Sausalito. This attractive area at the end of Avenida Los Castaños used to be a weir used to irrigate the vineyards (*viñas*). Now it has become a reserve planted with pine and eucalyptus trees, used for sports and recreation. There is a stadium here which will seat 30 000 spectators, and there is also a velodrome. On the lake you can water ski and hire boats, and there is also a floating disco on the lake, the *SS Louisiana*. Tennis courts and the stylish Restaurant Las Terrazas overlooking the lake and the town complete the picture.

- Parque de Fauna Nativa, adjoining Jardín Botánico and also administered by CONAF. This 240 ha (593 ac) park is used to study species in danger of extinction.

- Quinta Vergara. Right in the center of town, this was formerly the property of the founders of Viña del Mar, the Vergara-Alvarez family. It is now a park full of exotic trees and flowers, and you can walk through following little paths overgrown by lush trees. It houses the Museo Municipal de Bellas Artes in the former Palacio Vergara, Errázuriz 596. On show are the works of Chilean painters, and the museum also houses the Escuela de Bellas Artes (School of Fine Arts). In the open air theater (called the Anfiteatro) the annual Festival Internacional del Canción (Song Festival) is held in February.

Museums

- Museo Arqueología Sociedad Francisco Fonck, 4 Norte 784 corner of 1 Oriente. Specialises in local pre-Columbian history. It has Araucanian silver artifacts and also a very comprehensive section on Easter Island. Open daily 1000–1800, Sat, Sun, and holidays 1000–1400. Small admission charge.
- Museo de Cañones, Avenida Jorge Montt, Sector Las Salinas. Outside you can see cannons which were used in the War of the Pacific.
- Museo de Historia Natural, Avenida Valparaíso 155. The name "Historia Natural" is a bit misleading, as it also exhibits archeological artifacts from the Mapuche culture, the pre-Columbian tribes on the central coast, and the Incan period. The fauna of Chile is well represented, and there are also botanical and mineralogical sections.
- Museo Naval, also known as Castillo Wulff, Avenida Marina 37. This museum lies between the mouth of Río Marga-Marga and Caleta Abarca on the rocks below Cerro El Castillo. As a matter of fact it is built over a small crevice in the rocks and you can look through a glass floor and see the sea breaking against the rocks right beneath your feet. It was the home of German immigrant Gustav Wulff, who was particularly interested in researching the history of the Chilean Navy from its early days to the present. The result of his labours is a complete documentation of famous ships, naval battles, and illustrious leaders of the Chilean Navy. There are several rooms in the museum with pictures and models of Chilean Naval ships, memorabilia, and paintings of famous Chilean Naval commanders, and of whaling fleets, which operated in these waters last century. Another interesting feature is the tree which stands forlorn on an isolated rock on the property. The entire museum is well worth a visit.

- Museo Palacio Rioja, Quillota 214. This was formerly the home of Don Fernando Rioja Medel, a Spanish industrialist. The exhibition includes antique furniture from the baroque and rococo periods, and there are also sculptures by famous Chilean artists. Open Tues, Sun, and holidays 1000–1400 and 1500–1800. Small admission charge.

⊕ Excursions

Tour operators

- Aguitur, Avenida Marina corner of Puente Libertad (681882
- Anditour, Viana 31 (690817, fax 971996. Adventure tours, car rental
- Alegrias Viajes, Arlegui 441, office 3 and Kiosk Calle Quinta (on Puente Quinta) (882023 / 688768, fax 560032 / 680294
- Turismo Cocha, Arlegui block 600 corner of Sucre

The following tours are run by various tour operators for a minimum of four persons:

- City tour: Casino, Quinta Vergara, Museos, and Playa Reñaca; duration 3 hrs; cost $12.00
- Northern beaches: Zapallar and Cachagua; duration 8 hrs; cost $20.00
- Southern beaches: Algarrobo, El Quisco, and Isla Negra; duration 8 hrs; cost $20.00
- Santiago: Museums, Palacio de Gobierno, Catedral, and Cerro San Cristobal or Cerro Santa Lucia; duration 10 hrs; cost $30.00

Excursions

From Viña del Mar you can take trips to the northern beaches, known as the Chilean Riviera, and to some towns in the interior. Many day trips can be made using the frequent local buses.

- **Río Aconcagua** valley: You can go on a day excursion by train to the central Aconcagua valley, either to San Felipe or Los Andes. You could combine this trip with a visit to the Termas de Jahuel (near San Felipe) or to Baños del Corazón (descending at Los Andes). This is vineyard country, with many *bodegas*, and it is also very picturesque *pre-Cordillera* with the high Andes in the background on your right.

ZAPALLAR

Area code: 033
Population: 3000
Altitude: Sea level
Distances
- From Santiago: 182 km north-west on Ruta F-30-E and Panamericana (sealed)
- From Valparaíso: 82 km north on Ruta F-30-E (sealed)

Zapallar is on a small inlet at the northern end of the Chilean Riviera. It has a very protected white sandy beach, and the local council has ensured that the buildings blend with the natural beauty of this spot. This area was owned by Don Olegario Ovalle, who donated building lots around the bay to his friends. Thus Zapallar came into being. The new owners surrounded their homes with gardens which flourished in the excellent climate. In its short history Zapallar has experienced two major earthquakes — one in 1906, which virtually flattened the town, and another in 1965.

The main attraction is the beach, which has a walking path around it (*rambla*) and finishes up in the rocky area further north opposite Isla Seca. You will enjoy excursions along the seashore which is very beautiful, especially around **Cachagua** about 7 km south, and you can also visit the coastal canyons. There are many sporting facilities — tennis in Zapallar and golf in nearby Cachagua — making this a very attractive summer vacation destination. See also the entry for Cachagua on page 241.

You can get to Zapallar by regular buses from Santiago and Valparaíso. The mean summer temperature is 17.5°C (64°F), and the water temperature is 12°C (53°F). The tourist facilities consist of hotels and restaurants, and in summer there are discos. There are swimming, fishing, water sports, kiosks, and life-guards.

Festivals
- February 11: Virgen de Lourdes, Gruta de Lourdes on Cerro de la Cruz. On top is a statue of Christ.
- June 29: San Pedro

Tourist information
- Municipalidad, Germán Riesco 399 (711413

Accommodation
- Motel Aguas Claras, Avenida Zapallar 125 ABCHLP$V (Reservation Santiago: (02) 6966136 $D cabins for 6
- Hotel César, Olegario Ovalle 345 AEFGHIJPSV (711313 $F ⚑
- Hotel Isla Seca, Camino Costero (711508, fax 711502
- Residencial La Terraza, Del Alcalde 142 AEFGIPV (711409; 14 beds
- Residencial Villa Alicia, Moisés Chacón 280

Eating out

Restaurants
- César, Rambla, overlooking beach
- El Chiringuito, Rambla
- La Terraza, Del Alcalde 142. Seafood
- Morea, Rambla, overlooking beach

Post and telegraph

Post office
- Correo, Germán Riesco near Avenida Zapallar

Telephone
- CTC, Olegario Ovalle 337 near Prat

🚌 Buses

There is no central bus terminal; all buses pass through the town center.
Taxi *colectivos* run to Papudo as required and when the *coletivo* is full.

Companies
- Buses Sol del Pacifíco runs daily services to Concón, Maitencillo, Papudo, Quintero, Valparaíso, Las Ventanas, and Viña del Mar
- Tur-Bus Jedi Mar runs daily services to Papudo, Santiago

🚗 Motoring

- COPEC gas station, Olegario Ovalle

🎾 Sport

- Playa Chica: Suitable for surfing and sailing
- Tennis courts, Diego Sutil

📷 Sightseeing

Some of the old mansions built by the original owners still exist.

📍 Excursions

The coastal road between Zapallar and Maitencillo is particularly attractive.
- **Quebrada del Tigre**: If you enjoy walking, try the interesting five-hour walk to this *quebrada*, starting from Zapallar and returning via Cachagua. The Quebrada del Tigre is one of the few coastal valleys where the original native tree cover has survived the onslaught of the Europeans. Its lush green forests, with ferns of all sizes and subtropical climbing plants, make this a unique and memorable experience. It is a fairly steep climb from the coastal road to the rim of mountains which surround the coastal area, and then it is a steep descent into the Río Tigre valley. The vegetation is so dense and lush here because of the humidity when the clouds meet the barrier of the coastal *cordillera* (known as the *camanchaca* effect). This area has not yet been officially declared a nature reserve.

EASTER ISLAND

Area code: 039
Population: 2800
Altitude: Sea level–650 m
Distances
- From Santiago: 3700 km east (as the crow flies), 5 hours by plane
- Tahiti: 4050 km west, 6 hours by plane

E aster Island — Isla Pascua is its official name in Spanish, or Rapa Nui in the native language — lies 3700 km west of the mainland (27° south and 109° west) at the latitude of Caldera. Most of the population lives in the capital, **Hanga Roa**.

It is assumed that the first Polynesian settlers arrived around 500 AD from the Marquesas Islands. The Dutch navigator Jakob Roggeveen was the first European to see this volcanic land mass on Easter Sunday April 6, 1722, hence his name for it, "Ooster Eylandt". It was annexed by Chile in 1888.

Parque Nacional Rapa Nui was created in 1935 to protect the archeological sites which so far have yielded no explanation for how such an isolated people could produce a culture of such magnitude. The park takes up most of the island — 6666 ha (16 465 acres) rising in altitude from sea level to the 509 m of Maunga Terevaka, an extinct volcano. The giant statues, called *moais*, are the park's outstanding feature. There are about 700 of them scattered over the island in various shapes and sizes.

They were erected between 1000 and 1650 AD, and most of them stare inland from deep, empty eye sockets. It is believed that some of them once had inlaid eyes — the whites made from white coral and the irises from red scoria or obsidian, two volcanic stones readily available on the island. Besides the *moais*, there are caves showing traces of the first people on the island, rock paintings, terraced places of worship, and a trench on the north-eastern side which looks like some form of defense system. Two small islands — Ra Minenhaha and Sala y Gomez — lie to the east of the main island.

The average annual temperature is 20°C (68°F), with a short rainy season in April–May and a longer one in July–September. The average annual rainfall is 1150 mm — May's average is 140 mm. September is the driest month with an average of 70 mm and October–November are also fairly dry months. The summer rains, called *chubascos*, are usually short in duration and fairly heavy. In winter, continuous light rain may last for a week.

Most of Easter Island is covered with fairly thick grass savanna where pineapples grow wild. The *toromiron*, the island's only unique tree species, is now extinct on the island. It has been replaced by eucalyptus forest in large areas of the interior. The ancient population inscribed tablets of *toromiron* — very few remain. A single specimen of this original Easter Island tree is now kept in the Jardin Botanico Nacional near Viña del Mar on the mainland. There are no mammals native to the island; only rodents introduced by Europeans. However, the reptile population is plentiful. Birdlife consists of land species introduced from Chile and migratory sea birds. There are many species of fish, and lobsters are a large export income earner, although they are being overfished and returns are diminishing. There are opportunities for amateur anglers — no permit is required.

The island is part of a huge volcanic mountain in the eastern Pacific Ocean. It formed around the three major volcanic areas: **Volcán Maunga Terevaka**, **Volcán Puakatiki**, and **Volcán Rano Kau** which help to form the triangular shape of Rapa Nui. There are no surface rivers and most of the underground water is deep down and saline. Some springs surface near Volcán Rano Raraku and Volcán Rano Kau, which supplies water to Hanga Roa. The most abundant source of water near

Rano Aroi feeds a CONAF experimental citrus farm.

The pre-European monuments dominating the landscape attract a constant flow of tourists. The archeological site at Orongo, just west of the Rano Kau, is within easy walking distance of Hanga Roa. The island is perfect for hiking. There are tracks leading to Rano Raraku, where the *moais* were sculpted from volcanic rock, and a path leading through the center of the island to the two beaches — Anakena and Ovahue. A *moai* platform at Anakena overlooks the beach. It is also possible to walk round the western coast of the island to Anakena and return to Hanga Roa through the center. This is a full day's outing with an hour on the beach at Anakena. Take plenty of water. On the way back, you can stop at the CONAF experimental farm for water refills and to sample oranges if in season. I did this 45 km-walk myself in one day with a side excursion up Rano Aroi, through the "highland" and past the "hat factory". There are camping sites at Anakena, but you can camp virtually anywhere provided you can carry enough water.

The islanders are very friendly. All *residenciales* are spotlessly clean, and the food is delicious. Easter Island's nightlife can be experienced in two discos and at the Hotel Hanga Roa when there are enough guests.

The recommended visiting time is from September to March. December to February is popular with Chileans, and July to September with North Americans and Europeans. The rest of the year is fairly quiet.

Administratively, Easter Island is part of Región V de Valparaíso, and is governed from Valparaíso. However, Hanga Roa does have a

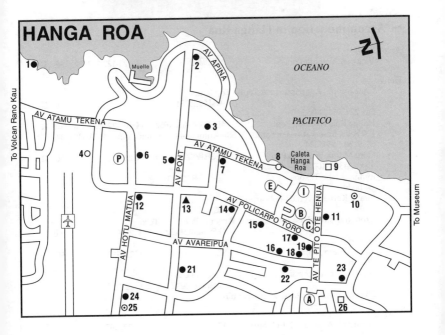

Key to map

A   Iglesia
B   Gobernación Provincial (Government)
C   Municipalidad (Town hall)
D   Post office and telex
E   Telephone
P   Gas stations

● **Accommodation**

1   Hotel Iorana
2   Hotel Hanga Roa
3   Hotel Topa Ra'a Inn
5   Apart Hotel Victoria
6   Residencial Aloha Nui
7   Residencial Apina Nui
11   Hostería Otai
12   Residencial Rapa Nui Inn
14   Residencial Pedro Atan
15   Hotel Orongo Easter Island International
16   Residencial Sofia Gomero
17   Residencial Tekena

18   Residencial Vaika Pua
19   Residencial El Tauke
21   Residencial Villa Tiki
22   Hotel Chez Joseph
23   Hotel Poike
24   Hostería Manutara

○ **Eating out**

8   Restaurant Mai Tai

⊙ **Entertainment**

10   Disco Toroko
25   Disco Piriti

▲ **Airline offices**

13   LAN Chile

□ **Services**

4   Aeropuerto Mataveri
9   Boat hire
26   Mercado Artesanal (Craft market)

🛏 Accommodation in Hanga Roa

Apart hotels
- Victoria, Avenida Pont   AGHJMPZ   ☎ 123-122 223272 $E   ♟

Hotels
- Chez Joseph, Avareipua near Tepito Te Menua
  AHJ ☎ 223281 $D   ♟
  Fax 224305, 22 beds
- Hanga Roa, Avenida Pont   ADEFGHIJKLMNR$Z   ☎ 105-223299 $C   ♟
  120 beds. Reservations in Santiago: San Antonio 486, upstairs, office 182 ☎ 6396834/ 6339130/ 6395334
- Hotu Matua, Avenida Pont   AEGHJMPZ   ☎ 223242 $C   ♟
  Fax 224305, 100 beds
- Iorana, Ataho Tekona   AEFGHJR ☎ 223312 $D   ♟
  64 beds
- Iorana Korua, Avenida Policarpo Toro
  AGHJM
- Orongo Easter Island International, Avenida Policarpo Toro
  AEFGHIJKLMNRZ   ☎ 223294 $E   ♟
  20 beds
- Poike, Petero Atamu   PS   ☎ 223283 $E   ♟
  16 beds
- Topa Ra'a Inn, Sebastián Engel near Atamu Tekena
  AFGHJLMPUXZ   ☎ 223225 $E   ♟
  33 beds, beach frontage, tennis, car hire

Hosterías
- Manutara, Avenida Hotu Matua   AZ   ☎ 223297 $F   ♟
  40 beds
- Otai, Tepito Te Henua   AEFGHIJLPS   ☎ 223250 $E   ♟
  44 beds, runs a tour bus for guests

Residenciales

- ★ Tahai, Sector Tahai Pasaje Reimiro   AIJP   ☎ 223395 $F   ♟
  14 beds
- Aloha Nui, Avenida Policarpo Toro   AJP   ☎ 223274 $F   ♟
  12 beds
- Apina Nui, Hetereki   AFJPZ   ☎ 223292
  22 beds
- Chez Cecilia, Avenida Policarpo Toro PS   ☎ 223499 $F   ♟
  12 beds
- Chez Erika, Tuki Haka Hevari $F   ♟
  24 beds
- El Tauke, Te Pito Te Henua   AJP   ☎ 223253
  8 beds
- Hanga Roa Reka, Tu'uko Ihu   AJP   ☎ 223433
  4 beds
- Mahina, Avenida Policarpo Toro   AJP   ☎ 223282
- Paperati, Tepito Te Henua   AJP ☎ 223288
- Pedro Atan, Avenida Policarpo Toro   AHJPRZ   ☎ 223329 $G   ♟
  15 beds
- Rapa Nui Inn, Avenida Policarpo Toro   ☎ 223228 $F   ♟
  12 beds

☞

Accommodation in Hanga Roa— continued

• Sofia Gomero, Tu'u Koiho 13 beds, full board	APZ	ℂ 223313	$G	♟♟
• Taheta One One, Tu'u Koiho 8 beds	AP	ℂ 223257	$F	♟♟
• Tekena Inn, Avenida Policarpo Toro 12 beds	AJP	ℂ 223289	$F	♟♟
• Vai Ka Pua, Te Pito Te Henua 10 beds	AJP	ℂ 223377	$G	♟♟
• Villa Tiki, Avenida Pont 11 beds	P	ℂ 223327	$E	♟♟
• Vinapu Tu'u Ko Ihu 6 beds	AJP	ℂ 223393		

local town council (*Gobernación*) like any other Chilean town.

⊠ Festivals

- January–February: Tapiti Rapa Nui (Islander Week)
- February, first week: Semana de Rapa Nui
- March: Hanga Roa foundation day

ⓘ Tourist information

- Sernatur, Tu'u Maheke corner of Apina ℂ 255
- CONAF, Atamu Tekena ℂ 236, runs an experimental station for citrus and eucalyptus trees in the center of the island

Ⓐ Camping

There are two suitable beaches for camping, both at the northern end of the island. There are five camping areas and seven picnic areas altogether. However, water has to be carried.

⑪ Eating out

Full board is normally included in your accommodation.

Ⓨ Entertainment

- Disco Piriti, Hotu Matua
- Disco Toroko, Hanga Roa
- Night club Hotel Hanga Roa, Avenida Pont

⊞ Post and telegraph

Post office
- Correos de Chile, Te Pito o Te Henua

Ⓢ Financial

- Banco del Estado de Chile, Tuú Maheke ℂ 223 221

⊕ Air services

LAN Chile provides one or two weekly services from Santiago and one from Papeete. Airport tax is $5.00.
- LAN Chile, Avenida Policarpo Toro, corner of Avenida Pont

Services
- Papeete (in Tahiti): Leaves Hanga Roa 1600 and arrives Papeete 2200 (1800 Papeete time); duration 6 hrs; LAN Chile
- Santiago: Fare $198.00; departs 0940 Mon, Thurs, Sat; duration 6 hrs; LAN Chile

⚓ Water transport

Twice-yearly supply ships visit Easter Island from Valparaíso, usually in March and December. There is no fixed schedule, but these vessels take some passengers. The trip takes six days.

⊟ Motoring

It is possible to hire motor cyclces from the islanders or from tour operators.
- Hertz Rent-a-Car, Hotel Hanga Roa. Four-wheel drives

⊞ Shopping

Hanga Roa is the only place on the island where you can buy provisions.

⊛ Sport

Sailing, fishing, swimming, horse-riding.

📷 Sightseeing

- Museo Antropológico R.P. Sebastián Englert, 2 km north on the road leading to Sector Tahai. Open Tues–Fri 0900–1300 and 1400–1800, Sat 0930–1730; admission $1.00. There is a tablet of *tomiron* wood in the museum which is inscribed with some form of writing. The writing has never been deciphered, but is it believed that every clan on the island had one such tablet. Outside the museum stands a *moai* which seeems to be an early attempt to make a statue or by an apprentice stone mason.

⊕ Excursions

- **Parque Nacional Rapa Nui**, 6666 ha (16 465 acres) takes up most of the island outside Hanga Roa. It has educational and excursion paths, an information center nearby, picnic and camping area; and accommodation, eating places, and shops and and information center in nearby **Mataveri**. Admission $9.00.

Hikes from Hanga Roa

- **Rano Raraku**, **Vaitea**, and back to Hanga Roa: 46 km, 2 hours by car. I have walked this myself in one day. **Volcán Rano Raraku** is the site where *moais* were carved out of the rock. Some half-finished statues still await completion. The largest is nearly 22 m tall and weighs 250 tonnes.

- **Ahu Te Peu**, **Ahu Akivi**, **Puna Pau**, and back to Hanga Roa: 22 km, 6 hours' walk. Akivi is also known as Siete Moais — "seven statues on a pedestal". Puna Pau is the location of a reddish rock formation where the *moais'* stone hats were manufactured.

- **Rano Kau**, **Orongo**, and back to Hanga Roa. **Volcán Rano Kau** is the main water supply for Hanga Roa. A variety of flora, ranging from grapes to bananas, grows inside the crater.

This vegetation prevents water from evaporating too quickly.

- **Vinapu** and **Tahiri**: Two temples with *moais* located at the end of the airport runway. Tahiri Temple is very similar to Macchu Picchu in the Andes.

- **Anakena beach**: A 50 km walk around west side of the island, returning through the center in one day. The beach can be reached in a brisk five-hour walk. Starting out from Hanga Roa, I made a two-hour detour to include the seven *moais*, and continued on the western coast of the island. This is dry country, though rainwater sometimes collects at the foot of the mountains. After the seven *moais*, the trail to the northernmost part of the island is not marked on maps. It goes along sheer cliffs round the base of two extinct volcanoes, **Maunga Kuma** and **Maunga Terevaka**, and is about 100 m above sea level. Anakena beach is a beautiful beach with palm trees and a group of shrines called "*ahus*". The western shore approach is a 25 km walk, and you must carry plenty of water. The island center approach is a 16 km walk. Motorcycles and vehicles use this track, and it is possible to get a lift. CONAF administers an ongoing reforestation program in the center of the island, and have planted orange and eucalyptus trees on the slopes of Rano A Roi. They are watered by springs in the area. From the CONAF experimental station, I went uphill again to return via Puna Pau. It was dark when I arrived in Hanga Roa.

- **Cerro Puna Pau** (220 m): The direct trip from Hanga Roa is an easy half-day excursion. It is best to start early in the morning to allow for a few detours. From here, you can take a mountain trail north-east to the CONAF experimental station.

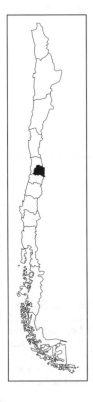

REGIÓN

METROPOLITANA

Size: 15 400 square km (5946 square miles)
Population: 4.5 million
Regional capital: Santiago
Provinces (and provincial capitals):
- Área Metropolitana (Santiago)
- Chacabuco (Colina)
- Cordillera (Puente Alto)
- Maipo (San Bernardo)
- Melipilla (Melipilla)
- Talagante (Talagante)

When Pedro de Valdivia founded the city of Santiago and thus Chile, he wrote in great excitement to Emperor Charles V: "All merchants and people who wish to come to this part let them come because in our time there is no better place to settle." The central valley, which has abundant rainfall and plenty of water, quickly attracted a large number of settlers. The indigenous inhabitants initially resisted the Spanish, but soon became their most trusted allies. Intermarriage between them and the Europeans has produced the Chilean nation.

Región Metropolitana is dominated by one city: Santiago. With Santiago as a base, virtually all parts of this region (and to some extent the neighboring Región V de Valparaíso and Región VI del Libertador) can be visited as day excursions from this main population center. For this reason, I have not covered in great detail accommodation in satellite towns. Instead, the eating places and tourist attractions of suburbs and satellite towns have been incorporated into the entry for the city of Santiago. Furthermore, towns in the vicinity of Santiago with tourist attractions and/or accommodation and restaurants have been included in the respective Santiago sections.

This region shares boundaries with Región V de Valparaíso in the north and west and with Región VI del Libertador Bernardo O'Higgins in the south. The Andes form the border with Argentina in the east.

Topography
Geographically, Región Metropolitana is enclosed by mountains on all sides — the **Cordón de Chacabuco** in

the north, the coastal *sierra* which reaches over 2000 m (**Cerro del Roble** 2222 m and **Cerro Chache** 2338 m) in the west, the slightly elevated **Cerros del Paine** in the south, and the mighty Andes which reach 6000 m (**Cerro Tupungato** 6570 m, and **Nevado de Los Piuquenes** 6019 m, **Nevado Los Leones** 5930 m) in the east. Santiago's outer suburbs almost touch the Andes, and some of the best hiking and skiing areas, such as La Parva and Farellones, are within easy reach.

Climate

There are four distinct seasons. Summer is very dry. The hottest months are between December and March when the temperature reaches 35°C (95°F). The coolest, wettest months are June, July, and August. Temperatures rarely drop below freezing point.

Economy

This is Chile's most important economic region. Most manufacturing industries are concentrated here and, unfortunately, Santiago has some of the highest air pollution in South America. Agriculture, cattle raising, vineyards, and horticulture are mostly confined to the provinces of Melipilla, Maipo, and Talagante. Some mining is done in the *cordillera*, for example, copper at the La Diputada mine.

Transport

Road

Región Metropolitana is almost exactly in the center of Chile. It is connected by the Panamericana (RN 5) with all regions except Región XII de Magallanes which can only be reached by bus via Argentina or by boat from Puerto Montt.

Rail

The railroad carries passengers as far as Puerto Montt. The northern line does not exist any more. The line over the Andes to Mendoza in Argentina has been closed for several years, and it does not look as if it is to be reopened in the foreseeable future.

Between Temuco and Valdivia, passenger rail services have been suspended and replaced by a bus service coordinated with the arrival and departure times of trains.

Air

Most international visitors to Chile arrive at the Aeropuerto Internacional Comodoro Arturo Merino Benítez. The smaller airports at Tobalaba and Las Condes are used for private and national flights.

National parks

- **Santuario de la Naturaleza Yerba Loca:** Area 11 575 ha (28 580 acres), 38 km east of Santiago on Ruta G-21 on the road to Farellones, turning into the Río Yerba Loca just before El Manzano. The park contains an information center, picnic and camping areas, and walking trails. See the entry for the sanctuary on page 418.

- **Reserva Nacional Río Clarillo:** Area 10 185 ha (25 148 acres). Located 45 km south-east of Santiago on Ruta 73 past Puente Alto. See the entry for the reserve on page 377.

- **Parque Nacional El Morado:** Area 3000 ha (7407 acres). Located 95 km south-east of Santiago in the upper Río Maipo valley on Ruta G-25. See "Excursions" from Cajón del Maipo on page 370.

Thermal resorts and thermal springs

- **Termas de Colina:** 43 km north of Santiago. Altitude 909 m, 25°C (77°F). Open from September to March.
- There are natural thermal springs near **El Volcán** in the upper Río Maipo valley.

Trout fishing

The trout fishing season starts on the second Friday in November and ends on the first Sunday in May.

- Colina: Río Colina, Embalse Huechún
- El Volcán: Río Yeso, Río Claro, Río Volcán
- Las Condes: Estero Covarrubia, Estero Arrayán, Río Molina
- Melipilla: Río Maipo, Embalse Rapel, Estero Puangue, Estero Cocalán

- Melocotón: Estero El Ingenio, Río Pollanco
- San José de Maipo: Estero San José

Tourism

Although the region has a summer and winter season, it can be visited all year round.

Don't miss

☞ Santiago

Worth a visit

☞ Ski resorts at Farellones, La Parva, and Valle Nevado

Worth a detour

☞ "Cajón del Maipo", a side excursion from the San José–El Volcán trip

Of interest

☞ Laguna Aculeo
☞ Termas de Colina
☞ Pukará de Chena

CAJÓN DEL MAIPO

Cajón del Maipo is the name given to the valley of the **Río Maipo** and its tributaries. It begins in the Cordón de San José near the Argentine border and finishes at Puente Alto. The Cajón is a favorite weekend destination for *Santiagueños*. The Río Maipo is also suitable for rafting.

The various townships located in the Cajón del Maipo are briefly described under the headings for facilities encountered in a particular village or town.

The 90 km trip from Santiago by car to the end of the road at Lo Valdés takes about three hours. The road is open all year round. From the center of Santiago take Avenida Vicuña Mackenna which becomes Avenida Concha y Toro. Follow it south as far as Puente Viejo, and then follow Ruta G-25 east up the Río Maipo valley. From El Volcán, the road is dirt to Lo Valdés.

The townships, their facilities, and possible excursions are described in this entry, in the order of their distance from Santiago. The following towns or villages are described briefly.

La Obra

La Obra is located at KM 26, just where the Río Maipo emerges from the *pre-Cordillera* into the central valley.

Las Vertientes

Located at KM 29.

El Canelo

El Canelo is located at KM 33, near the junction of Estero El Canelo with Río Maipo. The mountains on both sides of the river reach nearly 2000 m. There are many picnic areas near the junction of the Estero del Canelo and Río Maipo, such as Los Peumos del Canelo, which has large trees and a swimming pool.

El Manzano

El Manzano is a small village at KM 37. This is orchard country.

Guayacán

Located at KM 41.

San José de Maipo

San José de Maipo is located at KM 48, at an altitude of 1000 m, in a beautiful part of the Río Maipo valley, where the mountains rise fairly steeply over 2200 m. This is the main town in the Cajón del Maipo, with a population of 9000; the climate is excellent.

Settlement began in response to silver mining in the district, and Gobernador Ambrosio O'Higgins formally founded the town in 1791. It is laid out in the usual chessboard pattern, with the Plaza de Armas in the center and adobe houses giving it a colonial air.

The turnoff to the ski resort Lagunillas, one of the earliest established in the region, is two kilometers past the village opposite Restaurant El Campito.

El Melocotón

Located at KM 52 at an altitude of 1000 m. *Melocotón* means peach, and there are still many almond and peach trees in the area.

San Alfonso

San Alfonso, at KM 62, at an altitude of 1110 m, in the upper Río Maipo valley near the junction of the Río San Alfonso with the Río Maipo is in a beautiful location, with mountains in the north reaching over 3000 m and in the south 2400 m.

Lagunillas

The small ski resort of Lagunillas is at KM 66, 19 km north of San José de Maipo, at an altitude of 2130 m. Its facilities consist mostly of ski lodges owned by ski clubs. The road is sealed as far as San José. The 16 km gravel road from the turnoff to Lagunillas is edged with low adobe walls. On weekends and holidays *carabineros* regulate the traffic flow. Snow chains are required in winter. The ski season lasts from the middle of June to the middle of October. There are four ski lifts going up to 2580 m. You can hire ski equipment and there are also ski classes.

San Gabriel

At an altitude of 1260 m, San Gabriel is located at KM 70, in the upper Río Maipo valley at the junction of **Río Yeso** with Río Maipo. The air becomes thinner the valley narrows and the vegetation looks drier and not so lush. It used to be a copper mining town. The houses lose their *hacienda*-like appearance and are built more solidly.

⊟ Accommodation in Cajón del Maipo

Accommodation in La Obra
- Hostería El Tucán, Camino El Volcán 675
  AFPRV   (8711044 $H ⁇

Accommodation in Las Vertientes

Hosterías
- ★★★ San José, Vista Hermosa corner of Los Almendros
  AEFGHIJKLMPR$TUV (8502842 $F ⁇
  Tennis

Accommodation in El Canelo
- Posada El Canelo, Camino El Volcán 5472
  AFGHJLPSV $I ⁇
  Reservations in Santiago: (8899002

Accommodation in El Manzano
- Cabañas Rancho El Añil, Camino El Volcán 9716
  AHPS   ((2) 8711113 $E for 6
  Fax (2) 8711109. 22 cabins and camping

Accommodation in San José de Maipo
- Cabañas Pollanco, across the river over the El Toyo bridge
  ABCHLNPR
  Open all year, sandy and rocky ground, just adequate facilities, boil water from stream

Accommodation in San Alfonso

Hotels
- ★★ Hostería Los Ciervos, Avenida Argentina 711
  AEFGHJLPRSUV $G ⁇
  9 rooms. Reservations in Santiago: (2790128/2276156

Hosterías
- Carrio, Avenida Argentina   AEFGHLNPR   (8899012 $F ⁇
  Reservations in Santiago: (2210756
- Café Cordillera, Avenida Argentina 740
  AEFHIPUV $H ⁇
  10 rooms. Reservations in Santiago: (2276156

Cabañas
- Cascada de Las Animas, Ruta G-21   ABCEFHLR   ((2) 2327214
  Located on the banks of the Río Maipo, one block off main road. 13 tent sites, 5 cabins. Open all year round, electricity, water, toilets, hot showers, sauna, horse-riding, fax 2339768

Residenciales
- El Cóndor, Avenida Argentina 775   AFI
- España, Avenida Argentina 731   AFHIV $G ⁇
  Reservations in Santiago: Sr. Arenas, Monjas Alferes 3621, San Miguel (5561791

Accommodation in Lagunillas

Refugios
- Club Andino de Chile   AEFGHJKR
  Ski hire, ski schools. Reservations in Santiago: Sierra Bella 1231 (2337608
- Suizo, 18 km from San José de Maipo   AEFGHN
  Reservations in Santiago: Colegio Suizo (2055423/465423/ 2745915

Accommodation in Cajón del Maipo — continued

Accommodation in El Melocotón
- Casa Pensión Ulloa $J ♙
- Cabañas La Paz, Camino El Volcán 29618, 10 km past San José
  ABCEFGHIJPR $F ♙
- Hotel Millahué, Camino El Volcán 17724
  ACEFGHLMNPRZ   ((2) 8899006 $F ♙
  English and German spoken
- Posada El Montanés, Camino El Volcán 27130
  PS $H ♙
  Reservations in Santiago: (8611575
- Hostería Posada Roma, Camino El Volcán
  ADEFGHJKLNPU $G ♙

Accommodation in San Gabriel
- Casa Pensión Los Rodados, road to Los Rodados

Accommodation in El Volcán
- Baños Colina   FHR
  Reservations in Santiago: (5516299 for information only

Accommodation in Lo Valdés
- Refugio Andino Alemán Lo Valdés   ACEFGHIKLNRUV   ((2) 8501773 $F ♙
  Breakfast and dinner included, ski hire, sauna, open all year round, with splendid views of the mountains from the terrace

Accommodation in Baños Morales
- Hostería Baños Morales, Villa del Valle $G ♙
  Shared bathroom, full board. Reservations in Santiago: (2251495/2269826
- Residencial Díaz, Río Maipo $H ♙
  Shared bathroom, full board
- Refugio Los Chicos Malos, Manzana 1 $H ♙
  Reservations in Santiago: (2885380

El Volcán

The old mining settlement of El Volcán lies at KM 77, at an altitude of 1420 m, where the **Estero Colina** and **Quebrada El Morado** join to form the **Río Maipo**. The narrow valley is wedged between mountains of more than 4000 m on either side, such as **Cerro San Francisco** (4345 m) and **Cerro Los Amarillos** (4000 m).
El Volcán's main attractions are the thermal bath and the majestic mountain country suitable for long hikes.

Lo Valdés

Lo Valdés is located at KM 92, at an altitude of 1800 m. There are hot thermal springs and a national park nearby. Fossils found in the vicinity indicate that this area was once below sea level.

Baños Morales

Baños Morales, located at KM 95, is at an altitude of 2700 m. The peaks surrounding Baños Morales are all over 4000 m. The highest peaks are Cerro Marmolejo (6100 m) and Volcán San José. The water from the glaciers form the source of the Río

Maipo. It has hot springs, but facilities are a bit primitive. Some travel agencies in Santiago organize weekend excursions to this destination. Recommended for the outdoor enthusiast.

ⓘ Tourist information

The *carabineros* in Santiago (133 supply information about road conditions.

⑪ Eating out

Eating out in La Obra
• Hostería España, Camino El Volcán 275

Eating out in El Canelo
• Restaurant El Castillo del Canelo, Camino El Bajo 223 Chilean cuisine
• Posada El Canelo. Open Sat–Sun and public holidays

Eating out in El Manzano
• Restaurant y Salón de Té Cordillera, Camino El Volcán 1156
• Parrillada Guayacán, Camino El Volcán
• La Cochera, Camino El Volcán

Eating out in San José de Maipo
• Restaurant Cordillera de Guayacán, Camino El Volcán 1156
• Restaurant El Campito, Camino El Volcán 1841 (KM 27)
• Restaurant El Toyo, KM 51. Also camping, horse riding

Eating out in San Alfonso
• Restaurant Cóndor
• Restaurant Cordillera

🚌 Buses
• Buses Cajón del Maipo leave Santiago from Terminal de Buses, Pueblito del Parque O'Higgins
• Manzur Expediciones, Sotero del Río 475, 5th floor, Santiago (7774284/ 7723273. Services to Santiago and to Lagunillas ski resort

🐾 Excursions

Excursions from El Melocotón
El Melocotón is the starting point for rafting down the Río Maipo, organized by Expediciones Altué, Encomenderos 83 ((02)2321103, fax 2336799.

Excursions from El Volcán
• **Volcán Maipo** (5856 m) and **Cerro Marmolejo** (6108 m), and the Marmolejo glacier north-west of El Volcán. This is the domain of seasoned mountaineers, with magnificent views over the snowy peaks of the *cordillera* which forms the border with Argentina.

Excursions from San Gabriel
• To **Embalse El Yeso, Laguna Negra,** and **Laguna del Encañado:** The mountain hike up the **Río Yeso valley** towards **Cerro La Campana** (4430 m) is in a northerly direction. The Embalse El Yeso is 23 km further up. Along the road you have vistas of **Cerro Punta Negra** (4650 m) and the glacier which dominates the landscape. Those with enough breath left can hike a further 12 km to the hot springs. The difference in altitude from San Gabriel to the hot springs is about 1500 m

Excursions from Lo Valdés
• **Baños Colina:** 11 km up the Río Volcán valley from Lo Valdés. It offers splendid views to **Volcán San José** (5860 m) and to the glaciers along the border with Argentina. Experienced and well-prepared walkers only should hike at this altitude.
• To **Parque Nacional El Morado**, 3000 ha (7407 acres). Altitude: 2500–5200 m. The **Cerro Morado**, at an altitude of 4490 m, forms the center of the park, but this mountain is surrounded by even taller glaciated peaks rising more than 5000 m. This is a favorite area for summer hiking near **Lo Valdés**. The average temperature in summer is 10°C (50°F). The park's flora consists mostly of mock privet, *llaretas*, and *maticos;* the fauna is represented by foxes, condors, *vizcachas,* and partridges. It is administered by CONAF and has walking trails.

CENTRO CORDILLERA
LAS CONDES

Area code: 02
Altitude
* El Colorado 2500 m
* Farellones 2300 m
* La Parva 2700 m
* Valle Nevado 3000 m
Distances from Santiago
* El Colorado 38 km
* Farellones 32 km
* La Parva 36 km
* Valle Nevado 56 km

Centro Cordillera de Las Condes is the name given to the whole of the skiing area to the east of Santiago. It includes the ski resorts of **Farellones**, **La Parva**, **El Colorado**, and **Valle Nevado**. The ski slopes are visited by a growing number of foreign tourists. This is one of the best ski areas in Chile and is also a summer resort. Ruta G-21 starting from El Arrayán is sealed as far as Farellones and El Colorado. The road follows the **Río Mapocho**, and in winter *carabineros* regulate the traffic at El Arrayán. Snow chains, which are compulsory, can be hired near the *carabinero* control post. During weekends and holidays, vehicles are allowed up the road until 1200. From 1400, the traffic flow is downhill.

In summer, many splendid hikes and mountain climbs can be made in this area where the mountain peaks are over 6500 m, such as **Cerro Tupungato** on the Argentine border.

El Colorado

This ski resort is on a sealed road some six kilometers from Farellones. It has good tourist facilities with a hotel, restaurants, and cafeterias. The Edificio Monteblanco and Edificio El Parador offer indoor swimming pools, child care centers, sauna and ski lift ticket offices, a supermarket, and ski hire. The ski season is from June to October when the slopes are covered in powder snow.

Farellones

This was the first ski center to open in this region. Together with El Colorado only 6 km further up, it is the largest ski resort in Región Metropolitana. In Farellones proper there are five ski lifts which bring you up to El Colorado. The ski runs are suitable for both experts and beginners, and range from easy to difficult; none are classified as very difficult.

La Parva

La Parva is located 14 km east of Farellones on a sealed road. The turn-off is 2km before Farellones. It is supposed to have the best powder snow in the upper **Río Mapocho valley**. It commands splendid views over the

Mapocho valley, with the haze over Santiago in the distance. The ski season is from June to October. The backdrop to La Parva is **Cerro La Parva** (3890 m), with ski lifts. La Parva's tourist facilities are excellent and include many hotels, cafeterias, restaurants, supermarkets, ski hire outlets, and discos. The difficulty of the ski runs ranges from easy to difficult. Suitable for both experts and beginners.

Valle Nevado

Twelve km up from Farellones, Valle Nevado is the latest addition to the ski resort near Santiago. The turnoff is 3 km before arriving at Farellones. This is the resort with the most difficult ski runs suitable for expert skiers. It is also the area where heli-skiing is possible: helicopters fly skiers to an altitude of 4000 m. Enjoy the vistas over the high *sierra* with peaks in the 6000 m ranges.

The area is surrounded by mountains more than 5000 m high. At the moment there are two luxury hotels in Valle Nevado, but the breathtaking mountain scenery is sure to make this resort an international tourist attraction before long. There are restaurants, cafeterias, a child-minding center, a shopping center, and a discotheque. The ski season lasts from June 16 to October 15.

ⓘ Tourist information

Snow and road reports may be obtained from the *carabineros* in Santiago (133 or 2209501.

$ Financial services

- Money exchange in Hotel Tupungato, Farellones
- Money exchange in the hotel complex in Valle Nevado

⌨ Services and facilities

Services and facilities in Farellones and El Colorado

The 17 ski lifts of El Colorado and Farellones are run in conjunction. The combined area has three triple chair lifts, one double chair lift, and 13 T-bars. Four ski lifts go to or near the top of Cerro Colorado 3330 m. Ski hire $30.00 per day. Ski repair shops.

Services and facilities in La Parva

La Parva has altogether 13 ski lifts, 10 T-bars, one double chair lift, and one quadruple chair lift. Lifts go up to 3600 m, giving a vertical drop of 1000 m. There are ski schools.

Services and facilities in Valle Nevado

There are two chair lifts, eight T-bars, and one T-bar for beginners. Ski school. Skiing equipment hire and repair. Ski lifts reach 3700 m.

🚌 Buses

Buses run to Farellones, La Parva, El Colorado, and Valle Nevado.

Companies
- Centro de Esquí "El Colorado", Avenida Apoquindo 4900, Local 48 (2463344, Santiago
- Sportstour, Teatinos 333, upstairs (6960415, Santiago. They also arrange private excursions
- Manzur Expediciones, Sotero del Río 475, upstairs (7774284
- Turismo Cocha, Avenida El Bosque Norte 0430, Las Condes (2301000

✈ Air services

Air services fly to El Colorado, Farellones, La Parva, and Valle Nevado.
- Helicópteres Alfa, Aerodromo Tobalaba, Avenida Larrain 7941 (2734359, Santiago

🚗 Motoring

- COPEC gas station in Farellones

☒ Accommodation in Centro Cordillera La Condes

Accommodation in Farellones

Hotels
- Farellones   **AEFGHIJKLRVX**
  Ski hire, ski school. Reservations in Santiago: Las Bandurrias 1998 ℂ 7221493/72112725; and Fanor Velasco 70 ℂ 6962225
- Tupungato, Cancha El Embudo, Avenida Guayacán 141
  AEFHIKL$VZ
  Ski hire, ski school. Reservations in Santiago: Candelaria Goyenechea 4750 ℂ 2182216/2117341

Hostería
- La Posada de Farellones, Avenida Los Condores
  AEFGHJLPUVXZ $C ⚄
  Ski hire. Reservations in Santiago: Camino Piedraroja 1190, Avenida Apoquindo 4900, office 43, Edificio Omnium ℂ 2460660/2293948

Refugios
- Club Andino Gaston Saavedra, Los Condores 1142
  AEFGHJLPV
  Reservations in Santiago: ℂ 398182/332993/2220888
- Manquimávida, Area Cancha El Embudo, Los Chirigues 138
  AEFGHV
  35 beds, ski hire, ski school. Reservations in Santiago: ℂ 2286804/2206879, fax 2463535
- Club Alemán Andino, Avenida Los Condores
  AEFGHJLMPV $F ⚄
  Includes breakfast and dinner, ski hire, ski school. Reservations in Santiago: ℂ 2324338 El Arrayán 2735 Tues, Thurs, 1800–2000; and El Trueno 13858 ℂ 2425453
- Farellones
  Reservations in Santiago: ℂ 2425453

Accommodation in El Colorado

Departamentos
- Edificio Los Ciervos, La Paloma 146 opposite Edificio Monteblanco
  AEFGHRX
  Ski hire, ski school. Reservations in Santiago: San Antonio 486, office 152 ℂ 6393908/6398142
- Edificio Monteblanco, Sector La Paloma 145
  AEFGHLPRTUX $C for 4
  Ski hire, ski school. Reservations in Santiago: San Antonio 486, office 152 ℂ 6393908/6396142; also Pueblo del Inglés, local 122 ℂ 2110663/2111837
- Edificio Villa Palomar, Camino Casa de Piedra
  Reservations in Santiago: ℂ 2323407

Apart hotels
- Colorado, next to the Rotonda, a large round building
  ABCDEFGHIJKLPV $C for 4
  Ski hire, ski school. Reservations in Santiago: Turismo Blanco, Edificio Omnium, Avenida Apoquindo 4900, office 43 ℂ2463344/2324022/2460660, fax 2207738

Accommodation in La Parva
- Condominio Nueva La Parva, Nueva La Parva 77
  ADEFGHKPR$UVZ   ℂ 2208510
  $450.00 for 4 per week. Ski hire, ski school. Reservations in Santiago: Roger de Flor 2911 ℂ 2065068/2313411, fax 2317164

Accommodation in Centro Cordillera Las Condes — continued

Accommodation in Valle Nevado

Hotels

★★★★★Puerta del Sol   (6980103

★★★★★Valle Nevado, next to ski-lifts   ACEFGHJKLMNP$TUVXZ
(2128730/6980103
High season $2200.00 ♦♦ per week; low season $1200.00 ♦♦ per week. Ski hire, ski school, sauna. Reservations in Santiago: Gertrudis Echeñique 441 (2060027, fax 2115255/487525

Apart hotel
• Mirador del Inca   ACDEFGHKLMP$TVX   (6980103
Apartments for five $710.00 per week in low season; $1250 per week in high season. Ski hire, ski schools. Reservations in Santiago: (6980103/6480839, fax 6983618/ 6487525

COLINA

Area code: 02
Population: 22 000
Altitude: 930 m
Distance from Santiago: 46 km north on RN 57

Colina is situated in the central valley. The origins of the town are pre-Colombian, and it seems to have been an Incan outpost before the arrival of the Spaniards. Nowadays, it is an agricultural community.

To reach the thermal complex turn off from RN 57 near Peldehué. It has a hotel, swimming pool, and picnic areas. The water ranges from 18 to 33°C (64–91°F), and supposedly has therapeutic properties for respiratory and nervous ailments, rheumatism, arthritis, neuralgia, obesity, and skin complaints.

⊟ Accommodation
• Hotel Termas de Colina, Esmeralda AEFGHIKNR (8441502 $G ♦♦. The complex is open from the end of September until the end of April
• Motel La Ponderosa, Carretera General San Martín 068 ACDEFGHKLMPRTUVX (8441502 $H ♦♦

⑪ Eating
• Restaurant Piscina La Ponderosa, Carretera General San Martín 068

⊟ Buses
• Santiago: Fare $0.60; Taxibuses Sedan, depart from Terminal de Buses Estación Cal y Canto. More frequent services September–April

⊟ Motoring
• COPEC gas station on RN 57

⊕ Excursions
• **Hacienda Peldehué:** 4 km north. This property was established as a Dominican convent and *hacienda* (called Santa Catalina de Peldehué) in the middle of the 18th century. The gold mine nearby is now abandoned. Turn off east from here to Termas de Colina (7 km) in the *pre-Cordillera*. Peldehué

was destroyed last century by an earthquake, and a new church has since been built.

- **NASA tracking station:** Can be seen from afar and is open to visitors. The turnoff west is at KM 53.
- **Hacienda de Chacabuco:** Open daily. This was a Jesuit *hacienda* which was acquired in 1696 just 70 years before the order was expelled from Spanish and Portuguese colonies. In this short period of time, the Jesuits combined a

successful agricultural enterprise with their religious life. The church was built around 1732, and the basic building plan of the Jesuit settlement is still clearly distinguishable. The *hacienda* is also of historic value, because San Martín and Bernardo O'Higgins stayed here after the battle of Chacabuco. Nowadays, it is a *monumento histórico nacional* and is worth visiting, despite its rather poor state of repair.

LAGUNA ACULEO

Distance from Santiago: 73 km south on Panamericana Sur

Laguna Aculeo is situated 15 km west of the Panamericana Sur. Turn off at the tiny settlement at **Champa**.

The lake is a favorite tourist destination for *Santiagueños*, despite the fact that long stretches of the shore are muddy because the lake contracts in the dry season and fills when the snow melts in the hills. The lake is surrounded to the north, west and south by the low Cordón Yerbas Buenas which reaches 1300 m. In the east, it drains towards **Río Angostura**, a tributary of the Río Maipo. There are many camping areas and weekenders around the lake. The best boat ramps and the largest concentration of tourist facilities are on the north shore near Playa La Lagartija only a short distance from the village of Pintué.

A gravel road circles the lake, following the contours of the mountains. It skirts the swampy areas on the southern and western sides. Part of the road from Pintué to Rangue goes through old forests. The mountains to the south reach 2200 m and the peaks harbor small residual oak forests. It is not advisable to return to Santiago via Melipilla as the road

from Rangue to Melipilla is in bad condition.

▲ Camping

The best camping is on the northern rim of the *laguna*.

▣ Buses

In summer, buses also call on the tourist facilities located on the north shore. There is public transport to Santiago on the Pintue–Rangue road every two hours.

- Santiago: Fare $0.90; services Mon–Sat; Buses Paine

⊛ Sport

Swimming, wind surfing, fishing for *pejerrey*. Sailing is best in the afternoon; water-skiing is best in the morning.

◉ Excursions

- **Casas de Pintué:** A small settlement on the south side of the laguna, formerly a large *hacienda* The old *hacienda* complex still exists, surrounded by a large, green park. Parts of this *hacienda* were constructed towards the end of the 18th century, in particular the wine cellars and stables. The little chapel and the mansion were built towards the end of the 19th century.

MELIPILLA

Population: 43 000
Altitude: 180 m
Distance from Santiago: 85 km west on RN 78

There was already a large Indian settlement here before the Spanish arrived. In 1603, Alonso de Ribera set up a factory to supply the army with clothing. Melipilla was officially founded in 1743 by Viceroy Manso de Velasco at the crossroads to Lago Rapel. A recent earthquake has destroyed many of the former colonial buildings. An important livestock fair is held in Melipilla every Wednesday.

Accommodation

Hotels
- De Turismo, Ortúzar 538 ADEFGHIJKLM (8323345 $G ::
- Melipilla, Avenida Vicuña Mackenna

Hostería
- Los Troncos, Riquelme 561 AFHIKLM (8323200/4134

Residencial
- Santa Ana, Ortúzar 1022 FP (8323505 $H ::

Accommodation along RN 78
- Hotel El Castillo, Los Jazmines 3592 ADH (8323512

Eating out
- Restaurant Centro Arabe, Avenida Santiago
- Restaurant El Comendador

Eating out along RN 78, east of town
- Restaurant Parrilladas Argentinas. Well frequented weekends. Steaks

Eating out along RN 78, west of town
- Restaurant El Descanso. Chilean cuisine

Buses

Rural buses continue from here south to Navidad, Pichilemu, and Lago Rapel via **San Pedro** on Ruta G-60. Although this goes mostly through flat farming land, it is nevertheless an alternative to see this part of Chile. The return trip can be made from Pichilemu or Lago Rapel via Rancagua in the central valley.

- Santiago: Fare $1.30; departs daily; duration 1 hr; Jimenez, Ruta 78, Buses Melipilla
- Pichilemu: Buses Ruta Mar
- San Antonio: Duration ¾ hr

Motoring

Gas stations
- Mobil, Avenida Vicuña Mackenna
- Shell, Avenida Vicuña Mackenna
- Esso, Avenida Vicuña Mackenna
- COPEC, Avenida Vicuña Mackenna

Sightseeing
- Convento y Iglesia San Agustín, a *monumento nacional.*

Excursions

An interesting trip north into the **Río Puangue** valley and returning via **Cuesta Barriga** to RN 78 near **Padre Hurtado** takes you into the **Valle de Mallarauco**, which was settled by warlike Indians at the time of the arrival of the Spanish. There are many *haciendas* in this area, a charming and traditional part of Chile that is rarely visited by foreign tourists. In the 19th century one of the landowners built a huge irrigation canal which transformed this formerly arid valley into a rich agricultural region. The region produces dairy products and wine. Continue to **María Pinto**, where there is another old *hacienda*. At **Santa Inés**, turn south into Ruta G-68 which takes you over the **Cuesta Barriga** to **Padre Hurtado** and back to Santiago on RN 78. Cuesta Barriga is a long winding mountain pass only 800 m high but with excellent views over the central valley to the Andes. It is 104 km back to Santiago. Rural buses run north from Melipilla to **Maria Pinto**. The trip, however, is best made with your own vehicle or with a tour operator.

RESERVA NACIONAL RÍO CLARILLO

Distance from Santiago: 45 km south on Ruta 73

Reserva Nacional Río Clarillo covers 10 185 ha (25 148 acres), located in the *pre-Cordillera*. The best approach is to take the road south from Puente Alto. It is administered by CONAF, which also organizes weekend trips.

The area is a sanctuary for many tree and flower species such as *peumo, litre, arrayán*, and *boldo*. The fauna is represented by foxes, *chingues* (skunks), wild pigeons, and the occasional condor.

CONAF has installed walking trails, a visitors' information center, and picnic grounds near some water pools. The camping ground has 60 spots and is dispersed over a wide area; it is open from December to April, costs $J per tent site up to 8 persons, and makes a good base for day trips into the surrounding Reserva Nacional. The best area is El Peumo, among the shady native trees, with a toilet block that includes cold showers. Remoter areas have latrines only. All areas have benches and tables and laundry facilities. The river is usually crystal clear, and forms little rock pools where you can swim. However after heavy rain or when the snow melts the river becomes rather wild and the water turns brown. The area is high enough for snow in winter, but is open all year round. Some of the highest peaks of the Andes form a backdrop to this idyllic location.

Bus no. 32 from Plaza Gandarilla in Puente Alto stops within easy walking distance of the park entrance; the fare for taxi *colectivos* is $1.50. Admission to the reserve costs $3.50.

SANTIAGO

Area code: 02
Population: 4.5 million
Altitude: 528 m

Santiago, the capital of Chile, consists of 32 counties which constitute greater Santiago. It is located in the central valley with the Andes forming a formidable background in the east. Gran Santiago covers an area of 2360 square km (911 square miles), and its population represents a third of Chile's people. Santiago is the center of commercial activities, industry, and tourism.

Pedro de Valdivia founded the original city on February 12, 1541, near Cerro Huelen, now Cerro Santa Lucia. Although Santiago was the official capital of the Reino de Chile (Kingdom of Chile), Concepción was the de facto capital until the 17th century because most governors spent their time fighting the Mapuche Indians just south of Concepción. In fact, many governors could not even present themselves to the *Cabildo* (Town Council) of Santiago to be confirmed, as they had to hurry down to defend the southern frontier.

Santiago was destroyed in 1541 by Chief Michimalonco, who gathered the western tribes of the Río Pangue and lower Río Maipo valleys against it. When the Spanish settlements south of the Río Bío Bío were lost in 1599, many refugees settled in Santiago. The town has suffered many earthquakes such as the one which destroyed it in 1647 during the reign of Governor Martín de Mujica. Another large earthquake occurred in 1730. In 1606 the *Real Audiencia* (Royal High Court) was set up in Santiago.

Santiago's climate is very mild with short winters from June to August, occasional rain and moderate temperatures. Pollution, however, is a problem as the coastal winds cannot penetrate the central valley to clear the accumulated smog in the basin. The highest average annual temperature is 16°C (61°F); the lowest is 8°C (46°F).

For the tourist, Santiago is an excellent base for excursions into the *sierra* which contains some of the highest peaks in the Andes (**Cerro Tupungato** is 6570 m). There are excellent summer mountain hikes and world class skiing resorts just a few hours away from the city.

Santiago is a very cultural city, a city with large parks, museums, churches, and theaters. Under "Sightseeing" beginning on page 402 I have listed the most important tourist attractions. To list all the cultural venues of Santiago would go far beyond the scope of this book. For an excellent detailed guide to the parks, museums, and stately houses of Santiago, I recommend *Guía de Santiago* by Carlos Ossandon Guzman and Dominga Ossandon Vicuña.

Tourism

The areas of greatest interest for the tourist are (spiralling out from the center):

- The city of Santiago itself

East of the city centre

- Barrio Bellavista, just east of the center
- Barrio Providencia, east of Barrio Bellavista
- Barrio Las Condes, east of Providencia
- Barrio El Arrayán

West of the city centre

- Barrio Estación Central, with the major bus and train terminals and some hotels
- Barrio Quinta Normal, featuring "Quinta Normal de Agricultura", a 40-ha (99-acre) park with museums

South and south-west of the city centre

- Barrio Ñuñoa and Barrio La Reina, with some good restaurants

Plate 23   Región VIII del Bio Bio
Parque Nacional Laguna del Laja, waterfall

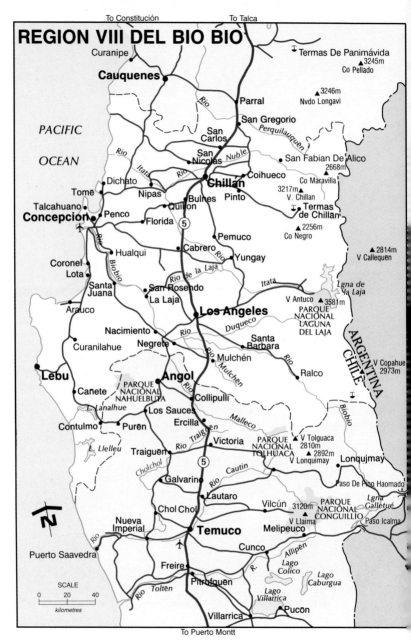

Plate 24
Map of Región VIII del Bio Bio

Key to map
☐ **Services**

1. Aeropuerto Comodoro Arturo Merino Benitez (International Airport)
2. Aerodromo de los Cerillos
3. Aerodromo Eulogio Sanchez

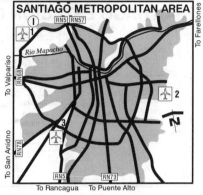

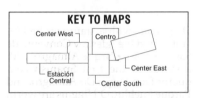

- Barrio Lo Prado, west of the center near Pudahuel airport has some good restaurants

North of the city center

- Independencia, just north of the center across Río Mapocho, also has a few good restaurants

Southern suburbs

- Puente Alto, in the extreme south at the beginning of the Cajón del Maipo, has restaurants, picnic areas, and the Autodromo Las Vizcachas where car races are held

Eastern suburbs

The better-class areas are from Las Condes east towards the high Andes. As the terrain becomes higher, much of the smog which is ever-present in downtown Santiago is left behind; the air becomes clearer and the houses show that this is a wealthier suburb. In El Arrayán you are already in the foothills of the Andes, and snow in winter is not uncommon.

Center north

The center north covers the area between Río Mapocho to the north, Plaza Baquedano to the east, the north side of Avenida Bernardo O'Higgins (also called Alameda) and Avenida Norte Sur (which becomes

the Panamericana) to the west. This area has the biggest concentration of cultural treasures such as museums, parks, and plazas, Chile's financial center, and large shopping centers. The majority of hotels in Santiago are located here, as well as some of the best restaurants.

Center south

This area covers south of Avenida Libertador Bernardo O'Higgins (also called or Alameda) between Avenida Vicuña Mackenna in the east and Avenida Exposición in the west, and south to Avenida Carlos Valdivinos. Last century this area was the preferred location where rich mining magnates and industrialists built their mansions: Palacio Cousiño, Palacio Errázuriz, Palacio Ariztia, and Palacio Irrarázabal. Here is also Plaza del Libertador Bernardo

O'Higgins, with a statue of the Liberator, and the Iglesia y Convento de San Francisco. Parque Almagro, with a statue to the first Spanish conqueror Don Diego De Almagro, and Parque Pueblito O'Higgins are worth a visit. At the Club Hípico de Santiago, Chile's most prestigious horse races take place.

The *barrios* of Santiago

Barrio Bellavista

Barrio Bellavista, wedged in between Cerro San Cristóbal and the north side of Río Mapocho (roughly between Loreto in the west and Arzobispo in the east) is the Bohemian quarter of Santiago, containing the artists' colony and nightlife venues. There are good restaurants, art galleries and museums, burlesque theaters, shows, and dance halls concentrated in a small area. Barrio Bellavista is best reached from Metro Baquedano and Metro Salvador.

Providencia

This covers the area from Cerro Santa Lucia and Río Mapocho in the north, Avenida Vicuña, Mackenna to the west, Avenida Tobalaba to the east, and Avenida Francisco Bilbao to the south.

Providencia is a better-class suburb. This is reflected in the many shopping centers such as Centro Comercial Plaza Lyon, Mall Panorámico, Centro Comercial Unicentro. There are good restaurants, pubs, and discos, as well as three-star hotels. For ease of reference, under "Acccommodation" hotels and restaurants are listed under Providencia south of Río Mapocho and Providencia north of Río Mapocho.

Las Condes

Las Condes covers the area from Avenida Tobalaba in the west, Avenida Presidente Kennedy to the north, Avenida Francisco Bilbao to the south, and the foothills of the An-

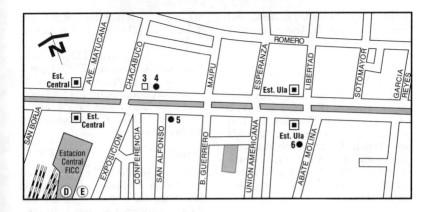

Key to map

D	Post office and telex	**5**	Hotel Imperio
E	Telephone	**6**	Hotel Turismo
P	Gas stations	■	**Sights**
T	Bus terminals	**1**	Universidad de Santiago
■	Metro stations	**2**	Planetario
●	**Accommodation**	**3**	Iglesia Sagrada Corazón de Jesús
4	Hotel Alameda		

des making a natural border in the east. This is a very exclusive suburb with villas, golf clubs, and polo clubs, and for some reason many sports clubs have their facilities here. On top of Cerro Calán is the Observatorio of the Universidad de Chile. On Avenida Presidente Kennedy is the prestigious Centro Comercial Parque Araucano, which covers a huge area with plenty of car parking space. To the south of the Centro Comercial is Parque Araucano. The district also has exclusive restaurants and excellent hotels. Estación Escuela Militar on Avenida Apoquindo is the eastern terminal of the Metro — only 20 minutes from downtown Santiago.

Vitacura

Vitacura straddles the Río Mapocho. A small mountain range limits the expansion to the north and west, Avenida Presidente Kennedy to the south, and Avenida Tabancura to the east. It is a better-class suburb with many villas and much open country. Museo Ralli in Alonso Sotomayor 4110 has exhibitions of paintings of local contemporary painters, and is open Tues–Fri 1000–1330 and 1430–1800.

El Arrayán

East of Avenida Tabancura, this suburb is in the *pre-Cordillera*. El Arrayán is the starting point for trips to the Centro Cordillera Las Condes. Here the Río Mapocho valley narrows and becomes a *quebrada*. There are some good restaurants here. The air is clear.

La Reina

La Reina is situated east of Providencia. It covers the area between Avenida Amerigo Vespucio Sur and Avenida Ossa in the east, Avenida José Arrieta in the south near Tobalaba airport, and in the east the foothills of the *pre-Cordillera*. It is a better-class suburb with some nice restaurants.

Ñuñoa

Ñuñoa covers the area between Avenida Vicuña Mackenna to the west, Rodrígo Arraya to the south, Avenida Amerigo Vespucio east and and Diagonal Oriente to the north.

Towns on the outer fringe

Buin

Buin, in the central valley with 31 000 inhabitants, altitude 300 m, lies 40 km south of Santiago on the Panamericana. It was originally founded in 1844 as a large *hacienda*. Fruit is the main export industry, and packing factories line the Panamericana. Its main attraction is a string of good restaurants on the Panamericana and motel-type accommodation. Buin is serviced by Buses Paine from Terminal de Buses San Borja in Santiago; fare $0.70.

Curacaví

Curacaví is situated in a large basin 48 km west on RN 68 in the coastal *cordillera*. Its altitude is 200 m and it has 8800 inhabitants. Access to the village lies a short distance off the highway. A 36 km track leads north to Carén which is at the foot of Cerro Roble Alto (2185 m) which can be scaled.

Pullman Curacaví (7760062 and Ruta Bus Curacaví (7760112 run regular buses from Terminal de Buses San Borja, Borja 184 Santiago. There are also buses to Valparaíso and Viña del Mar. A gas station is on the highway.

Maipú

Maipú (altitude 507 m) is located only 16 km south-west of Santiago on RN 78 and forms part of greater Santiago. Although it is a city in its own right with 110 000 inhabitants, it is only half an hour by taxi from downtown Santiago. Although this is a working-class suburb, it attracts visitors to see the Templo Votivo de Maipú, and it also has some colorful *fiestas*. Tourists tend to stay in nearby Santiago and visit the sights of Maipú as part of a tour. Local buses run from Santiago from the corner of Teatinos and Avenida Bernardo O'Higgins marked "Templo" (for "Templo Votivo de Maipú"). Taxi *colectivos* depart from Amunátegui.

Paine

Paine is situated 48 km south of Santiago off the Panamericana. Its main attraction is the string of good restaurants along the Panamericana from Buin to Paine. It has a population of 12 000, altitude 200 m. Buses Paine run regular services to and from Santiago: fare $0.70. There is an Esso gas station at Puente Paine.

The Metro

The Santiago Metro is the fastest means of transport around Santiago. At this stage it consists of two lines which intersect at Los Heroes on

Avenida Bernardo O'Higgins, and serves the inner suburbs of Santiago only. Línea 1 (with 24 stations) runs east–west, starting in Estación Militar in the east and terminating in San Pablo in the west. Línea 2 (with 13 stations) runs north–south, starting at Puente Cal y Canto on the south side of the Río Mapocho in the north and terminating at Lo Ovalle in the south. At the Metro terminals are bus terminals for commuters living further out of town.

Trains operate Monday to Saturday from 0630 to 2230, and on Sundays and holidays from 0800 to 2230. Subway stations are locked during the night. Tokens cost $0.30 for all trips regardless of destination.

Whenever a place listed in the *Travel Companion* is within walking distance of a Metro station, we have given the name of the line and the station, preceded by the symbol ▪.

⚹ Festivals

- January: Festival Folklórico San Bernardo, Estadio Municipal
- January: Festival del Barrio Bellavista
- February 12: Foundation Day
- November: Fería Chilena del Libro, Parque Forestal
- December: Fería Artesanal Tradicional, Parque Manuel Rodríguez

Festivals in Maipú
- First week after Easter: Cuasimodo. This festival attracts a large number of pilgrims. Horse and bicycle riders form a colorful procession through the streets of Maipú

Continued on page 389

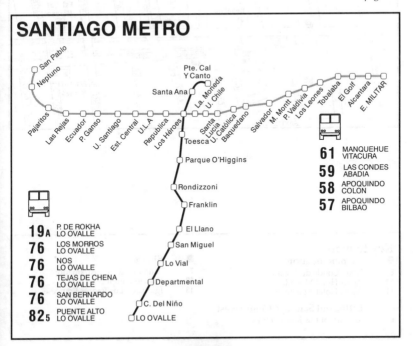

SANTIAGO METRO

SANTIAGO CENTRO WEST

Key to map

●	**Accommodation**
8	Hotel Conde de Ansurez
10	Apart Hotel Moneda
11	Apart Hotel Agustinas

○	**Eating out Santiago Centro west**
9	Restaurant Los Ricos Pobres

■	**Sights**
7	Santuario María Auxiliadora
12	Palacio Elguin
13	Iglesia de Los Padres Franceses

⊟ Accommodation in Santiago

Santiago is an expensive town to stay in.

Accommodation near Estación Central

Apart hotels
★★★Conde Ansurez, Avenida República 31 (■1 República) $F   ♟
AEHKLPS$TUVZ   ☎ 6960807 / 6983779

    Car hire, fax 6996368, 42 rooms
  ★★ Alameda, Avenida Bernardo O'Higgins 3117, opposite central train station
                                     ☎ 6814336 $G ♟

    Fax 6816015, 21 rooms
  ★★ Imperio, Avenida B. O'Higgins 2876 (■1 Unitad Latino Americana)
          ADEFGHIJKLMPTUVZ   ☎ 6897774 / 6892950 $G ♟

    Sauna, fax 6892916, 70 rooms

Accommodation in city center

Between Avenida B. O'Higgins (also called Alameda) in the south, Ismael Valdés Vergara in the north, Plaza Baquedano in the east, and Avenida Brasil in the west.

Apart hotels
★★★★Carlton House, Maximo Humbser 574 (■1 Santa Lucia)
         ABCDHIJKLPTVZ   ☎ 6383130 $E ♟

    Car rental, 331 rooms, fax 331844
  ★★★ Agustinas, Agustinas 1990   ABCDEHIJKLPZ   ☎ 6951271 / 6711002 / 6726739
                                                      $G ♟

    Fax 6951271, 46 rooms
  ★★★ Turismo Moneda, Avenida Brasil 102 ABDEGHIJK   ☎ 6961940 / 8 / 6710477 $G ♟
  • El Marqués del Forestal, Ismael Valdés Vergara 740   ☎ 6333462 $F ♟
    Fax 6394157

Hotels
★★★★★Carrera, Teatinos 180   ACDEFGHIJKLMPR$TUVXYZ
                                         ☎ 6982011 / 6961414 $B ♟

    Sauna, car rental, fax 6721083
★★★★★Galerías, San Antonio 65 (■1 Santa Lucia)   ☎ 6384011 $C ♟
         ACDEFGHIJKLMPR$UTVYZ

    14 conference rooms for 10–450 persons, sauna, gym, 162 rooms, fax 6395240
★★★★El Conquistador, Miguel Cruchaga 920 (■1 Universidad de Chile)
         ABCDEFGHIJKLMPS$UVYZ $C ♟
                                       ☎ 6965599 / 6966826 / 713165

    Fax 6965599, 112 rooms
★★★★Tupahué, San Antonio 477   ACDEFGHIJKLMNPRS$VYZ
                                         ☎ 6383810 / 6393861 $D ♟

    garden restaurant, Cafetería Hangaroa, garden piano bar, 10 conference rooms for up to 500 persons, heliport, fax 6395240, 209 rooms
  ★★★ Majestic, Santo Domingo 1526 (■2 Santa Ana)
         AEFGHKPS   ☎ 6958366 $F ♟

    Fax 6974051
  ★★★ City, Compañía 1063   ACDEFGHIJLMPTUVZ
                             ☎ 6954526 $F ♟

    Fax 6956775, 72 rooms
  ★★★ Calicanto, Santo Domingo 444   ACDEFGHIJKLPTVZ $F ♟
                                   ☎ 6333001 / 6330913
  ★★★ El Libertador, Avenida B. O'Higgins 853 (■1 Santa Lucia) ☎ 6394211 / 2 / 3 / 4 / 5 / 6 / 7
         ABCDEFGHIJKLMPR$UVZ $F ♟

    Fax 6337128, 123 rooms

Accommodation in Santiago — continued

★★★ Foresta, Avenida Victoria Subercaseaux 353   (6396261 $F ⁀
    ACDEFGHIJKLMPRTVZ
   Fax 6394071, 35 rooms

★★★ Gran Palace, Huérfanos 1178, upstairs (6712551/6712795 $F ⁀
    ACDEFGHIJKLMPR$TUVXYZ
   Sauna, tennis, car rental, fax 6951095, 88 rooms

★★★ Metrópoli, Sotero del Río 465, near Monjitas block 1000
    ACDEFGHIJKLP$STVZ (6723987/6713112 $F ⁀
   Fax 6952196, 37 rooms

★★★ Panamericano, Teatinos 20   ACDEFGHIJKLMNPTVZ (6723060 $F ⁀
   Fax 6964992, 102 rooms

★★★ Ritz, Estado 248 (▣1 Universidad de Chile)
    ACDEFGHIJKLPS$TUVZ(6393401/2 $F ⁀
   Car rental, fax 6393403, 65 rooms

★★★ Riviera, Miraflores 106 (▣1 Santa Lucia)
    ADEFGHIJKLPTUVZ   (6331176/6392945 $F ⁀
   Fax 6335988, 41 rooms

★★★ Santa Lucia, Huérfanos 779, upstairs 4ABCDEFGHIJKLMP$TUVZ $F ⁀
    (6398201/2/3/4/5/6
   Fax 6331844, 79 rooms

★★★ Turismo Montecarlo, Victoria Subercaseaux 209
    ADEGHIJKLMPRVZ   (6392945/6391569 $F ⁀
   Fax 6335577, 56 rooms

★★ España, Morandé 510   ADEFGHIJLMP$UVZ   (6985245 $H ⁀
   Car rental, fax 6966066, 59 rooms

• Cervantes, Morandé 31   ADEFGIJKLPTVZ   (6965318/7966 $G ⁀
• De Don Tito, Huérfanos 578   ADEFGHIJKLPSTVZ   (6398175 $E ⁀
   Car hire
• Hostal del Parque, Merced 294   ABCDEFGHIJKLMP$UVYZ
    (6392694/6392712 $C ⁀
   Car hire, 29 rooms, fax 6392754
• Isla de Pascua, Rosa Eguigurén 831   (6381041 $G ⁀
• Japón, Almirante Barroso 60   ADEHIJL   (6984500 $G ⁀
• Nuevo Valparaíso, Morandé 791   (6715698
• Sao Paolo, San Antonio 359   AEFGIKLPTUVZ   (6398031/32 $G ⁀
   Car rental, 75 rooms

Residenciales
• Santo Domingo, Santo Domingo 735 AF   (6396733
  Backpackers

Accommodation in center south
This area covers Alemada between Avenida República in the west to Avenida Vicuña Mackenna in the east.

Hotels
★★★★★ Crowne Plaza Holiday Inn, B. O'Higgins 136 (▣1 Baquedano)
    ABCDEFGHIJKLMNPR$TUVXYZ
    (6381042 $B ⁀
   Tennis, car rental, sauna, 296 rooms, fax 6336015

★★★★★ Plaza San Francisco Kempinski, Avenida B. O'Higgins 816 (▣1 Santa Lucia)
    ACDEFGHIJKLMPR$TUVYZ $B ⁀
    (6393832/6394413
   Sauna, car rental, fax 6397826

Accommodation in Santiago — continued

- Opera, Paris 898 (■1 Santa Lucia)   ☎ 6382726 $I   ♟
  Shared bathroom budget travelers
- El Fundador, Paseo Serrano 34   ☎ 6322566 $C   ♟
  Fax 6322566
- Maury, Tarapacá 1112   ☎ 6725859
  Fax 6970786, English and French spoken
- Santa Victoria, Santa Victoria 6 corner of Vicuña Mackenna (■1 Baquedano)
            AGHIJKLM   ☎ 2220031
- Vegas, Londres 49 (near San Francisco Church) (■1 Santa Lucia)
            DKP   ☎ 6383225 $F   ♟
  Large comfortable rooms, fans

Residenciales
- Alemana, Avenida República 220   ☎ 6712388 $I   ♟
- Londres, Londres 54 (■1 Universidad de Chile) $J   ♟
- Mery, Avenida República 36 (■1 República)   ☎ 6968883 $I   ♟
- Paris, Paris 613 (■1 Universidad de Chile) $I   ♟

Accommodation in Providencia, south of Río Mapocho
Between Avenida Circunvalación Américo Vespucio in the east, Avenida Vicuña Mackenna in the west, and Avenida Eliodoro Yañez south.

Apart Hotels
- Ibiza, Joaquín Díaz Garcés 012   ADEFGIKL   ☎ 6343548
                                                  $H   ♟
- Victoria, Lota 2325, Oficina 11   ☎ 2330458

Departamentos
- Tempo Rent (furnished flats), Nueva de Lyon 97 (■1 Los Leones)
                      ☎ 2320013
  Fax 2519124
- Hotelera Alicante, Avenida 11 de Septiembre 2155, office 901-B (■1 Los Leones)
                      ☎ 2318989
  Apartments for 1–7 persons

Hotels
★★★★★Santiago Park Plaza, Avenida Ricardo Lyon 207
         ABDEFGHIJKLPTUVZ   ☎ 2336363 $A   ♟
   Fax 2336668
★★★★ Aloha, Francisco Noguera 146 (■1 Pedro de Valdivia)   ☎ 2332230/237 $C   ♟
   Fax 2332494/2332838
★★★★Leonardo Da Vinci, Málaga 194   ADEFGHIJKLPS$TUVZ   ☎ 2060591 $B   ♟
   Fax 2341729
 ★★★Bonaparte, Avenida Ricardo Lyon 129
         ADEFGHIJKLPS$TUVZ   ☎ 2259081 $C   ♟
 ★★★Hostal Reina Sofia, Luis Thayer Ojeda 1250 (■1 Tobalaba)
         ADEFGHIJKLMS   ☎ 2514349 $E   ♟
   Fax 2333181, 10 rooms
★★★Lyon, Ricardo Lyon 1525   ADEFGHIJKLPS$TUVZ $E   ♟
                                ☎ 2267732/2741777
   Fax 2258697, 11 rooms
★★★María Angola, Avenida José Miguel Claro   ☎ 2351280 $D   ♟
   Fax 2355914
★★★ Orly, Pedro de Valdivia 027 (■1 Tobalaba]) $F   ♟
         ADEHIJKLPTV   ☎ 2328225/742063/745455
   15 rooms

Accommodation in Santiago — continued

★★★ Posada del Salvador, Eleodoro Yañez 893 (T1 El Salvador) $F ♔♔
AEFIJLPTUVZ   (2359450 / 2516197

Fax 2518697, 32 rooms
★★★ Principado, Arturo Burhle 015 corner of Avenida Vicuña Mackenna (■1 Baquedano)
(2228142 $F ♔♔
Fax 2226065
• Gala, J. Diaz Garcés 049, Vicuña Mackenna Block 274   (2225508
• Presidente, Eleodoro Yañez 867 (■El Salvador)
ABDEFGHIJKLPTUVZ   (2358015 $D ♔♔
Fax 491393

Accommodation in Providencia, north of Río Mapocho
★★★★★ Sheraton San Cristóbal, Avenida Santa María 1742
ABCDEFGHIJKLMNPR$TUVXYZ
(2335000 / 2745000 $A ♔♔
Sauna, car rental, golf, tennis, fax 2341729, 339 rooms
★★★ Los Españoles, Los Españoles 2539   ABCDEFGHIJKLP$TUVZ (2321824 / 2254009 $E ♔♔
Car rental, fax 2331048, 40 rooms
★★★ Santa María, Avenida Santa María 2050 $E ♔♔
ACDEFGHIJKLPTVYZ   (2326614 / 2230568 / 2323276
Car rental, fax 2316287, 100 rooms

Hostales
• Diego de Almagro, Diego de Almagro 3170
AEHIJL   (2275792

Accommodation in Las Condes

Apart hotel
• Alessandria, Avenida El Bosque Norte 033 (■1 Tobalaba)
(2332079 $D for 4
Fax 2332086

Hotels
★★★★★ Hyatt Regency, Avenida Presidente Kennedy 4601   (2181234 $B ♔♔
★★★★ Manquehué, Esteban dell'Orto 6615   ACDEFGHIJKLMNPR$UVYZ $D ♔♔
(2128862 / 2121159 / 2209269
Tennis, car rental, sauna, fax 2207929 / 2207055, 40 rooms
★★★ Irazú, Noruega 6340   ABCDEFGHIJKLPS$TUVZ $E ♔♔
(2206123 / 2205941
Car rental, fax 2124359, 20 rooms
★★★ Montebianco, Isidora Goyenechea 2911
ADEGHIJKL   (2330427 $D ♔♔
Fax 2330420

Accommodation in Vitacura

Hotels
★★★★ Acacias de Vitacura, El Manantial 1781 (block 10000 Avenida Las Condes
ACDEFGHIJKLMNPR$VY
(2290575 $D ♔♔
Fax 2127858, 35 rooms
★★★★ Río Bidasoa, Avenida Vitacura 4873   ACDEGHIJKLMPRSTUVYZ
(2421525 $D ♔♔
Fax 2289798, 30 rooms

Accommodation in Santiago — continued

★★★★

Rothenburg, Avenida Las Condes 13343
FHMR $D ♒

Fax 2151535

Hostería
- Las Delicias, Raúl Labbé 340   (471386

Motel
- Los Refugios del Arrayán, El Refugio 15051   (472690 $G ♒

Cabañas
- Cuatro Pinos, Rojas Magallanes 2243, Avenida La Florida block 8500, on road to Las Vizcachas   (2811870
- Hotel Ipanema, Geronimo de Alderete 970, Americo Vespucio block 8000
(2217321

Accommodation on the outskirts of Santiago

Accommodation in Curacaví
- Hotel Inglés, Bernardo O'Higgins   **AF**

Accommodation in Peñaflor
- Hostería Villa Los Rosales, Pajarito Paradero 99
AFR
- Motel Las Paneras, RN 78 near the turnoff to San Nicolás and Peñaflor

Accommodation in Talagante
- Complejo Recreativo Valle Verde, Parcela 35-B, Esmeralda 917, on road to Santa Adriana   **HNR**
- Parque Balneario Tegualda, KM 2 km **HR**

- July 16: Fiesta de la Virgen del Carmen, the patron saint of Chile and of Maipú
- September, first Sunday: Fiesta del Huaso. This is a very colorful cowboy festival which attracts a huge crowd.
- Horsemanship and *cueca* dancing.

ⓘ Tourist information

If you plan to go south into the Magellanic regions of Aisén and Magallanes, see "Water transport" on page 401 and "Tour operators" on page 414. Services and travel south of Puerto Montt are severely restricted outside the main tourist season.
- Sernatur, Avenida Providencia 1550 (6982151/69604741, Manuel Montt)
- Sernatur, Aeropuerto C. Arturo Merino Benítez (6019320
- CONAF, Eliodoro Yañez 1810 (462372
- Municipalidad de Santiago Oficina de ☞ Turismo Cultural (33573. Open Mon–Fri from 0830–1715

- Instituto Geográfico Militar, Dieciocho 369, four blocks south of Avenida Libertador Bernardo O'Higgins (■1 La Moneda). Hiking maps and regional maps are available here

Ⓐ Camping

There are camping sites in Buin and in Paine on the Panamericana Sur

!! Eating out

See also "Dine and dance" and "Dinner and show" under "Entertainment" beginning on page 397.

Eating out in the city center

American restaurant
- Gatsby, Ahumada 340 corner of Pasaje Edwards, downstairs $Y

Brazilian restaurant
- La Brasileña, San Diego 265 $Y

Chilean restaurants
☞ • Círculo de Periodistas, Amunátegui 31 $Z
• Las Delicias de Quinhué, Domeyko 2059 $Z

Chinese restaurants
• Kam Thu., Santo Domingo 769 $Z
☞ • Lung Fung, Agustinas 715, downstairs $Z
☞ • Sing Hwa, Merced 627 $Y

French restaurant
• Maistral, Mosqueto 485 $Y

International restaurants
☞ • Hotel Plaza San Francisco Kempinski Santiago, Avenida Bernardo O'Higgins 816 $X
• Jockey Club, Bombero Salas 1369 $Y
• La Cumbre, Hotel Galerias, San Antonio 65 $X

Italian restaurants
☞ • Da Carla, MacIver 577 $Y
• Le Due Torri, San Antonio 258 $Y
• San Marco, Huérfanos 618 $Y
☞ • Trattoria Italiana, Lira 485 $X

Parrilladas
☞ • El Cordobés, Miraflores 461 $Y. Dancing
• El Lagar de Don Quijote, Catedral 1203 $Y
☞ • El Novillero, Moneda 1145 $Y
• Hereford Grill, Tenderini 171 $Y. Open for lunch only

Peruvian restaurant
• Club Peruano, Miraflores 443 $Y

Seafood restaurants
• El 27 de Nueva York, Nueva York 27 $Z. Seafood
• Ostras Squella, Avenida Ricardo Cumming 94 $Y

Vegetarian restaurants
☞ • El Naturista, Moneda 846 $Z
• El Vegetariano, Huérfanos 827, Galería Victoria, Local18 $Z
• Vegetariano, San Martín 457 $Z

Fast food
• Snackbar Hotel Cervantes, Morandé 631 $Z
• Steak House, Huérfanos 713, downstairs in arcade $Z
☞ • Burger Inn, Ahumada 167 $Z

• Steak House, Huérfanos 1046 $Z

Eating out center south

Restaurants
• La Jaula Dorada, Pueblito Parque O'Higgins, Local 15 $Y. *Parrillada.* Dancing Fri, Sat, Sun
• Sabor Limeño, Lira 933 $Z $Z. Peruvian cuisine
☞ • Círculo Español, Avenida Libertador Bernardo O'Higgins 1550 $Y. Spanish cuisine

Eating out in Barrio Bellavista

Chilean restaurants
• El Caramaño, Purísima 257 $Y
• El Fierrito, Mallinckrodt 98 $Y

International restaurants
• Café de La Dulcería Las Palmas, Antonia Lope de Bello 0190 $Z
☞ • El Retablo, Constitución 270, upstairs $Y
• Mesón del Arzobispo, Calle del Arzobispo 0601 $Y

Parrillada
• Eladio, Pio Nono 241

Other restaurants
• El Otro Sitio, A. Lope de Bello 53 $Y
• La Brújula, Constitución corner of A. Lope de Vega $Z
• La Divina Comedia, Purísima 215 $Z

Eating out in Providencia

American restaurants
☞ • A Pinch of Pancho, General del Canto 45 (◼1 Manuel Montt) $Y. Clam chowder, cheesecakes
• Gatsby, Avenida Providencia 1984 (◼ 1 Pedro de Valdivia)

Argentine restaurants
☞ • Cambalache, Bravo 911 near J.M.Infante (◼1 Salvador) $X
☞ • La Leña Asados, Augusto Leguía Sur 60 (◼1 El Golf) $Y

Chilean restaurants
• Casa de Cena, Almirante Simpson 20 near Vicuña Mackenna block 100 $Z
• Lutecia, Mardoqueo Fernández 105 between Suecia and Avenida Los Leones $Z

Continued on page 396

Key to map

E Telephone
P Gas stations
T Bus terminals

◼ **Sights**

14 Palacio Errázuriz
15 Palacio Ariztia (*Monumento Nacional*)
16 Palacio Irarrazabal (*Monumento Nacional*)

17 Iglesia San Ignacio
18 Universidad de Chile
20 Palacio Cousiño (*Monumento Nacional*)

☐ **Services**

19 Instituto Geográfico Militar

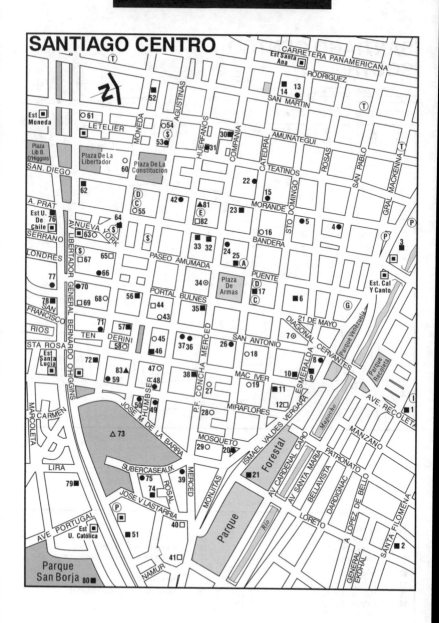

SANTIAGO CENTRO

Key to map

A	Catedral
B	Gobernación Provincial (Government)
C	Municipalidad (Town hall)
D	Post office and telex
E	Telephone
G	Mercado Municipal (Market)
H	Hospital
P	Gas stations
$	Money exchange
T	Bus terminals

● **Accommodation**

4	Hotel Nuevo Valparaíso
5	Hotel Cervantes
8	Apart Hotel El Marqués del Forestal
13	Hotel Majestic
15	Hotel España
20	Hotel Calicanto
22	Hotel Metropolí
24	Hotel City
26	Hotel Tupahué
31	Hotel Panamericano
36	Hotel Sao Paolo
37	Hotel Santa Lucia
39	Hotel Foresta
42	Hotel Gran Palace
48	Departamentos San Rafael
49	Hotel de Don Tito
50	Apart Hotel Carlton House
53	Hotel Carrera
59	Hotel Riviera
66	Hotel El Conquistador
70	Hotel El Libertador
71	Hotel Galerias
75	Hotel Turismo Monte Carlo
77	Hotel Plaza San Francisco

○ **Eating out**

16	Restaurant El Lagar de Don Quijote
18	Restaurant Kam Thu
19	Restaurant Da Carla
27	Restaurant Singh Hwa
28	Restaurant El Cordobés
29	Restaurant Maistral
43	Restaurant Le Due Torri
45	Restaurant Lung Fung
47	Restaurant San Marco
54	Restaurant Jockey Club
55	Restaurant El Novillero
58	Restaurant Hereford Grill
61	Restaurant Circolo de Periodistas
62	Restaurant Club de la Unión

63	Restaurant El 27 de Nueva York
68	Restaurant El Naturista

⊙ **Entertainment**

7	Restaurant El Villorio
34	Restaurant Chez Henry

▲ **Airline offices**

81	LADECO
83	LAN Chile

■ **Sights**

1	Iglesia y Convento Recoleta Franciscano
2	Iglesia Santa Filomena
3	Estación Mapocho
6	Iglesia y Convento de Santo Domingo
9	Posada del Corregidor
10	Iglesia San Pedro
11	Casa Velasco
14	Iglesia Santa Ana
17	Palacio de la Real Audiencia
21	Museo de Bellas Artes
23	Ex Congreso Nacional
25	Palacio Arzobispal
30	Palacio de La Alhambra
32	Real Casa de la Aduana
33	Museo Precolombino
35	Casa Colorada
38	Basilica y Museo de la Merced
46	Palacio Subercaseaux
51	Edificio Portales
56	Iglesia San Agustín
57	Teatro Municipal
60	Palacio de la Moneda
64	Iglesia de las Agustinas
72	Biblioteca Nacional
73	Cerro Santa Lucia
74	Iglesia de la Vera Cruz
76	Universidad de Chile
78	Iglesia y Convento de San Francisco
79	Universidad Católica
80	Iglesia San Borja

□ **Services**

12	Goethe Institute
40	Alliance Français
41	US Consulate
44	Galeria Imperio
52	Instituto Chileno Norteamericano
65	Eurocentro
67	Santiago Centro
69	Almacenes Paris
82	ENTEL

Key to map

T   Bus terminals

● **Accommodation**

23   Hostal del Parque
27   Hotel Crowne Plaza
31   Hotel Principado
36   Hotel Presidente
37   Hotel Posada del Salvador

● **Eating out**

2   Restaurant El Retablo
3   Restaurant Eladio
7   Café de la Dulcería

9   Café del Cerro
10   Restaurant El Caramaño
11   Restaurant La Divina Comedia
12   Restaurant el Otro Sitio
13   Restaurant Sibaritas
15   Restaurant Esquina Al Jerez
17   Restaurant La Zingarilla
18   Restaurant El Fierrito
21   Restaurant El Mesón del Arzobispo
28   Restaurant Casablanca
32   Restaurant Japón
33   Restaurant Sir Francis Drake

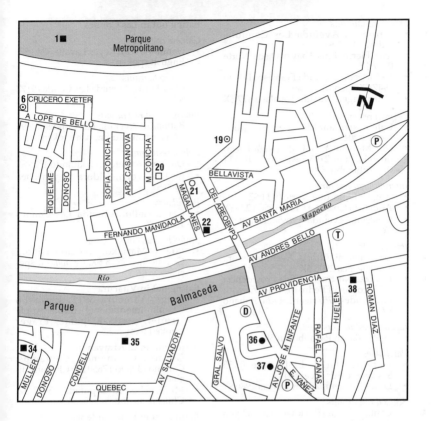

French restaurants

☞ • Carousel, Avenida Los Conquistadores 1972 $X
• Jean Pierre, Luis Thayer Ojeda Norte 0127 $Y
☞ • La Cascade, Avenida Francisco Bilbao 1947 $XOpen Mon–Sat
☞ • L'Ermitage, Avenida Tobalaba 477 $X

German restaurants

☞ • Café Restaurant München, El Bosque Norte 0204
☞ • Der Münchner Hof, Plazoleta Diego de Velázquez 2105, near block 2000 11 de Septiembre $Y

International restaurants

• Angus, El Bosque Norte 0111 $Z
☞ • Aquí Está Coco, La Concepción 236 $Y
• Lancelot, Avenida Providencia 1130 $Y

Italian restaurants

☞ • Da Renato di Vittoria, Avenida Isidora Goyenechea 2908 $X
☞ • La Pizza Nostra, Avenida Providencia 1975, corner of Pedro de Valdivia with Las Condes 6757 near Estadio Italiano $Y

Japanese restaurants

• Japón, Barón P Coubertin 39

Parrilladas

• Hereford Grill, El Bosque 0355 $YCredit cards accepted
• Lomit's, Avenida Providencia 1980 $Y

Seafood restaurants

☞ • Canto del Agua Pavlovic, Nueva Lyon 0129 $Z. Lobsters a specialty

Spanish restaurants

☞ • Catala, San Sebastián 2868, corner of El Bosque Norte $Y
☞ • Centro Vasco, Avenida Vicuña Mackenna 547 $Y
☞ • Centro Catala, Suecia 428 $Y
☞ • El Caserio, Avenida Manuel Montt 126 $Y

Pizzería

• La Vera Pizza, Avenida Providencia 2630 (■1 Tobalaba) $Y

Snack bar

• Red Pub, Suecia 029 $Z

Eating out in Las Condes

Chinese restaurants

☞ • Danubio Azul, Reyes Lavalle 3240 $Z. English spoken

French restaurants

☞ • Chez Louis, Avenida Las Condes 9177 $Y

International restaurants

☞ • Balthasar, Avenida Las Condes 10690 $X. German and English spoken

Italian restaurants

☞ • Da Dino, Avenida Apoquindo 4228 $X
☞ • Le Due Torri, Isidora Goyenechea 2908 $Y

Parrilladas

☞ • Canta Gallo, Avenida Las Condes 12345 $Y

Seafood restaurants

☞ • Puerto Marisko, Avenida Isidora Goyenechea 2918 $X. *Centollas* a specialty

Eating out in Vitacura

• Praga, Vitacura 3917, Plaza Lo Castillo. International cuisine. Apple strudel, goulash, game, Prager smoked ham

Eating out in El Arrayán

• Gordos, Cocinamos, Cantamos, Camino El Bajo 17650 $Y. Chilean cuisine
• Mi Rancho, La Diputada 15457 $Z. Chilean cuisine

Eating out in Independencia

☞ • Círculo Libanés, Avenida Domingo Santa María 1880 $Z. Lebanese cuisine

Eating out in Recoleta

☞ • Omar Khayyam, Avenida Perú 570 (■ 1 Pajaritos) $Y. Lebanese cuisine

Eating out in Ñuñoa

• La Casa Vieja, Avenida Chile España 249 $Y. Chilean cuisine. Credit cards accepted
• De Peyo, Lo Encalada 465 $Z. International cuisine
• Satiricón, Monseñor Eyzaguirre 246 $X. International cuisine
• Las Conchitas, Avenida Los Leones 2500 $Y. Seafood

Eating out in Buin
*   Restaurant La Casona de Don Toto, Balmaceda 604 ☞

Eating out on Panamericana
*   Café de Los Alpes, Panamericana KM 33
*   Restaurant Pollo Palta, Panamericana KM 38 just after Carabineros (going south)
*   Restaurant Overo Negro, Panamericana KM 34
*   Restaurant Dario, Panamericana KM 39, Linderos

Eating out in Maipú
*   Restaurant Chancho con Chaleco, Ramón Freire 99 Chilean cuisineDance orchestra Fri and Sat

Eating out in Paine
Between Buin and Paine along the Panamericana is a stretch of high quality restaurants, well frequented at weekends by motorists from Santiago.

Restaurants
*   Bavaria, Panamericana Sur KM 48. *Picada*
*   Las Tranqueras de Paine, Panamericana Sur KM 46. *Parrillada* ☞
*   La Peña del Paine, Panamericana Sur KM 45. *Parrillada*, music
*   Donde Marco Antonio, Panamericana Sur KM 40 near Linderos. *Parrillada*
*   Los Buenos Aires de Paine, Panamericana Sur KM 47 $Y. *Parrillada*
*   Pavoteca, Panamericana Sur KM 47

Eating out inPeñaflor
*   Restaurant Der Münchner Hof, Colonia Alemana KM 36 on old road to the coast 4 km east of Peñaflor

Eating out in Puente Alto–Pirque
*   Restaurant Katmandu, Ramón Subercaseaux, 2km south of Puente Alto ☞
*   Restaurant La Vaquita que Echa, Ramón Subercaseaux, in a rural setting. *Parrillada*

Eating out in Talagante
*   Restaurant Nuria, on the main plaza

ⓨ Entertainment

Entertainment center north

Dine and dance
*   Casablanca, Hotel Holiday Inn Crowne Plaza, Avenida Bernardo O'Higgins 136 $X. Dancing, show. International cuisine
*   Chez Henry, Portal Fernández Concha 962, Plaza de Armas $X. Two dance orchestras. International cuisine
*   El Carillón, Huérfanos 757 $X. International cuisine
*   Le Trianon, Santo Domingo 2096. Orchestra. French cuisine
*   La Ermita, Catedral 1143. International cuisine

Dinner and show
*   El Villorrio, San Antonio 676 in Pasaje Lidice $X. Music every night, dancing Sat–Sun dancing. *Parrillada*
*   Ostras Viuda de Azocar, Bulnes 37 $X. Piano bar. Seafood, lobster from the fish tank a specialty

Theaters
*   Teatro Municipal, Agustinas 794, Plaza Mekis ℂ 331407/332804. The opera and ballet season is from April to December

Entertainment in the center south

Dinner and show
*   Los Adobes de Argomedo, Argomedo 411 near Lira $X. International and *Huaso* shows Cueca performances, two dance orchestras. Chilean cuisine
*   Los Buenos Muchachos, Avenida Ricardo Cumming 1031. *Peña*, Sun dancing, cabaret, *cueca*. International cuisine

Entertainment in Barrio Bellavista

Dinner and show
*   La Esquina al Jérez, Dardignac 199 $X. Flamenco dancing
*   La Zingarella, Pio Nono 185 $Y. Tango shows Fri and Sat. Italian cuisine
*   El Mar de Bellavista, Antonia López de Bello 62 $Y. Piano bar. Seafood

Entertainment in Providencia
*   El Huerto, Orrego Luco 054 $Y. Gentle jazz Fri and Sat. Vegetarian cuisine
*   El Parrón, Avenida Providencia 1188 $X. *Peña* Sat. *Parrillada*
*   Giratorio, Avenida 11 de Septiembre 2250, upstairs $Y. International cuisine, dinner and dance
*   Las Brujas, Avenida Principe de Galés 9040 $Y. Disco. International cuisine

- New Orleans, General Holley 2308 $X. Jazz Fri. International cuisine

Entertainment in Las Condes
- Mexicano, Avenida Vitacura 2916, Fri–Sat guitar player $Y. Mexican cuisine
☞ - Bali Hai, Avenida Cristóbal Colón 5146 $Y. Show Mon–Sun, dancing. Polynesian cuisine

Entertainment in El Arrayán
- La Querencia, Avenida Las Condes 14980 $X. Terrace overlooking the river, dance orchestra, *peña* show Thurs–Sat. Chilean cuisine
- Las Delicias, Raúl Labbé 340 $X. Dancing and shows Fri–Sun. Chilean cuisine
☞ - La Estancia, Avenida, Las Condes 13810 $X. *Peña* orchestra Tues–Sun. Chilean cuisine, *parrillada*

Entertainment in Macul
☞ - La Paila, Avenida José Pedro Alessandri 1550 $Y. *Parrillada*. Dance orchestra, *peña* show

Entertainment in La Reina
- El Refrán, Avenida Larrain 5961 $Z. Piano bar; folk songs, guitar players and piano Wed and Thurs. Chilean cuisine

📞 Post and telegraph

Post office
Most districts and larger shopping centers have a post office.
- Central post office (*Correo Central*) Monjitas, Plaza de Armas (In Palacio de la Real Aduana)

Telephones
- ENTEL Chile, Huérfanos block 1100 near Bandera, in the city center. Overseas calls
- CTC Moneda 1151, in the city center. fax 6965006
- CTC, Avenida 11 de Septiembre 2165, Providencia. fax 2319108
- CTC Apoquindo 7071, Las Condes. fax 2115314

💲 Financial

Visa and Mastercard are accepted for cash advances at the following banks: Banco de Chile, Banco de Concepción, Banco de Inversiones, Banco del Pacífico, Banco de Osorno y de la Unión, Banco de Trabajo, Banco Español Chile, Banco Hipotecario y Fomento, Banco Internacional, Banco Sudamericano, Centrobanco, and Fincard.

Fincard offices in Santiago
Fincard makes cash advances against Visa and Mastercard, and all subsidiary branches have automatic telling machines.
- Fincard, Casa Matriz, Alameda 1427 ☏ 724533
- Fincard, Morandé 315 ☏ 728518
- Fincard, Huérfanos 679 ☏ 395367
- Fincard, Providencia 1973 ☏ 2517272
- Fincard, Pedro de Valdivia 3412 ☏ 728518

Money exchanges
- American Express, Agustinas 1360 ☏ 6993919/6982164/6983341. Changes American Express checks into US dollars without any commission. This is a unique service and only available in Santiago
- Cambio Alfa Ltda, Agustinas 1052 ☏ 710653
- Cambios America Ltda, Ahumada 59 ☏ 6727785
- Cambio Andes Ltda, Agustinas 1036 ☏ 6960686
- Cambios Inter, Andrés de Fuenzalida 47 ☏ 6965426
- Exprinter Ltda, Agustinas 1074 ☏ 6982604
- Larrain Vial Ltda, Bandera 81 ☏ 721695
- Monex, Ahumada 370, office 519 ☏ 6712066
- Thomas Cook, Agustinas 1058
- Yanulaque Ltda, La Bolsa 81, upstairs ☏ 6982557

🏢 Services and facilities

Book store
- Fería Chilena del Libro, Huérfanos 623 corner of Plaza de Armas in the city center ☏ 6396758, fax 6339374.

Camping and sports equipment
- Sparta Deportes, Estado 107 ☏ 6964235. Camping and skiing equipment
- Ski Total Apoquindo 4900 ☏ 2465847. Hire of skis and skiing equipment
- Skiwind, Avenida Holanda 55 Providencia. Surfing equipment

Clubs
These are cultural centers with access to library and overseas magazine reading rooms.
- British: Instituto Chileno Británico, Santa Lucia 124 (■1 Santa Lucia) (382156
- German: Instituto Chileno Alemán, Goethe Institute, Esmeralda 650 (383185
- French: Instituto Chileno Francés, Merced 298 (332306
- Japanese: Instituto Chileno Japonés, Avenida Providencia 2653 (231406
- North American: Instituto Chileno Norte Americano, Moneda 1467 (363215

Laundromats
- Laverap, Manuel Montt 067. Washing and drying $3.50
- Laverap, Monjitas 507, washing and drying $3.50

Mobile homes
- Conbel, Santa Rosa 1757(5553268. hire of trailers

Photographic equipment
- CM Ingenieros, Alameda 723 Local 21 (393077. Camera repairs
- Nortsur, Huérfanos 947 Agfacolor

Visas, passports
- Argentine consulate, Vicuña Mackenna 41 (■1 Baquedano) (2228977. Open 0900–1200
- Australian embassy, Gertrudis Echeñique 420, Las Condes (2285065. Open 0900–1230
- Austrian embassy, Avenida Presidente Barros Errázuriz 1968, upstairs, Las Condes(2330557. Open 1000–1200
- Bolivian consulate, Avenida Santa María 2796 (2328180. Open 0930–1400
- British embassy, Avenida El Bosque Norte 0125 (■ 1 Tobalaba (2313737. Open 0900–1300
- Canadian embassy, Ahumada 11, upstairs (■1 Universidad de Chile) (6962256. Open 0830–1100
- Croatian embassy, Cruz del Sur 133 (2282775
- Danish embassy, Avenida Santa María 0182, upstairs (376056. Open 0900–1300
- French embassy, Condell 65 (■1 El Salvador) (2251030. Open 0930–1200

- German consulate, Agustinas 785, upstairs (6335785. Open 0900–1200
- Israeli embassy, San Sebastián 2812, upstairs (2461570. Open 1000–1200
- Italian embassy, Clemente Fabres 1050 near José Miguel Infante (2259439. Open 0830–1230
- Japanese embassy, Avenida Providencia 2653, upstairs (■1 Los Leones (2321807. Open 0900–1230
- Peruvian embassy, Andrés Bello 1751 (2352356. Open 0930–1400
- Swedish embassy, 11 Septiembre 2353, upstairs (■1 Los Leones) (2312733. Open 1000–1200
- Swiss embassy, Avenida Providencia 2653, office 1602 ((■1, Los Leones) (2322693. Open 1000–1200
- Spanish consulate, Avenida Providencia 1979 (2041791. Open 0900–1400
- United States embassy, Andrés Bello 2800 (2322600. Open 0830–1050

Motoring

Car rental
- Atal Rent-a-Car, Avenida Costanera 1051, Torres de Tajamar (2359222, fax 2360686
- Automóvil Club de Chile, Avenida Vitacura 8620 (2125702, fax 2119208
- Avis Rent-a-Car, Hotel Sheraton, Avenida Santa María 1742 (2747621; Hotel Crowne Plaza, Alameda 136 (6392268; Aeropuerto Comodoro A.M. Benítez (6019050
- Bert Rent-a-Car, Avenida Francisco Bilbao 2032 (2516477. Hire of four-wheel-drive vehicles
- Budget Rent-a-Car, Bilbao 3028 (2049091, fax 2041725; Airport (6019421
- Chilean Rent-a-Car, Bellavista 0183 (7376902
- Classic Rent-a-Car, Huérfanos 635, Local 22 (6383035
- Dollar Rent-a-Car, Santa Magdalena 163 (2332945, fax 2520253
- First Rent-a-Car, Rancagua 0514 (2256328
- Hertz Rent-a-Car, Avenida Costanera 1469 (2359666 fax, 2360252; Aeropuerto Internacional (6019262
- Las Palmas Rent-a-Car, La Concepción 334, Providencia (2351181, fax 2332493. English spoken

METROPOLITANA

✈ Air services from Santiago

Aeropuerto Comodoro Arturo Merino Benítez, located in Pudahuel, is the international airport (6019709. Airport departure tax is $15.00.

Aerodromo Eulogio Sánchez (also known as Aerodromo Tobalaba) is located in La Reina. It is the base for commercial aircraft, such as helicopter services to ski resorts and flights to Isla Robinson Crusoe.

Aerodromo de Los Cerillos is located in the suburb of Los Cerillos. Some commercial flights start at this small airport, in particular private aircraft and planes specializing in aerial photos.

Airport information (6010709/6019654.

Bus services to Aeropuerto Comodoro Arturo Merino Benítez
There are 32 services every half hour between airport and and downtown from 0630 to 2130. The later services are at 45-minute intervals.
*   Tours Express, Moneda 1523 (717380/719573 runs regular bus services from their terminal to airport and back every half hour, fare $2.00
*   Various other companies have bus services departing from center strip in Alameda between ◼1 Los Heroes and ◼1 Moneda
*   ETC bus No 54 also serves the airport
*   Airport taxis (719116/719333

All major car rental firms have an office at the airport — see "Car rental" on the previous page.

International airlines
*   Aerolineas Argentinas, Moneda 756 (6394121; and Tenderini 82, upstairs. Airport (6019305
*   Aeroperu, Fidel Oteíza 1955 (2743434. Airport (6019000
*   Alitalia, Avenida Bernardo O'Higgins 949, office 1003 (6983336. Airport (6901150
*   American Airlines, Huérfanos 1199 (6716266. Airport (6019218
*   Avianca, Moneda 1118 (6954105. Airport (6901051
*   British Airways, Isidora Goyenechea 2934 (2329560
*   Canadian Airlines, Huérfanos 669, Local 9 (6393058. Airport (6019669
*   Faucett, Avenida Bernardo O'Higgins 949, office 1002 (6993373
*   Iberia, Bandera 206 (6981716. Airport (6019132
*   LADECO, Huérfanos 1157 (6395053, fax 6321061
*   LAN Chile, Agustinas 640 (6323442. Lan Chile sells "Chilepass" for US$300.00. This is a cheap way to fly around in Chile. Normally this ticket is bought abroad but is also available for foreign passport holders in Chile.
*   Lloyd Aereo Boliviano (LAB), Moneda 1170 (6712334, fax 6711421. Airport (6019633
*   Lufthansa, Moneda 970, upstairs (6301000. Airport (6901111
*   National Airlines, Huérfanos 1160 (6958418, fax 6322698
*   Qantas, Avenida Isidora Goyenechea 2934 (2329562
*   Swissair, Estado 10, upstairs (6337014. Airport (6019580
*   TAN (Transportes Aereos Neuquinos), Bombero Ossa 1010 oficina 301 (6394422. Flights to San Carlos de Bariloche and Neuquén in Argentina
*   United Airlines, Avenida B. O'Higgins 949 (6990055, fax 6018830
*   Varig, Miraflores 156 (6395261. Airport (6901342

Domestic airlines
*   Aerocentro, Avenida Providencia 2653 (2328843, fax 2512853. Organizes short joy rides over Santiago and other parts of the country. Hires small planes for aerial photographers

Air services from Santiago — continued

- Linea de Aeroservicios S.A. (LASSA), Avenida Larrain 7941, La Reina ℂ 2734354, fax 2734309. Flights to Isla Juan Fernández and reservations for Hostería Robinson Crusoe in San Juan on Isla Juan Fernández
- Transportes Aéreos Robinson Crusoe, Monumento 2570 Maipú ℂ 5313772

Helicopter service
- Heli Alfa, operating from Aerodromo Tobalaba Avenida Larrain 7941 ℂ 2734359, fax 2731937. To Portillo, Farellones, Valle Nevado
- Helicop Services Chile S.A., Aerodromo Tobalaba ℂ 2260042. Trips to Portillo and Farellones
- Helicopteros 248, Pérez Valenzuela 1225 ℂ 2746383
- Heliflot S.A. Dieciocho 193 ℂ 499341

Services

Destination	Fare	Services	Duration	Airlines
Antofagasta	$205.00	3–5 services daily	2 hrs	LAN Chile, LADECO
Arica	$245.00	2–4 services daily	3½ hrs	LAN Chile, LADECO
Calama	$230.00	2 services daily	2½ hrs	LAN Chile, LADECO
Chaitén		1 service Mon, Wed, Thurs, Sat	4½ hrs	LAN Chile
Coihaique	$220.00	1–2 services daily	3½ hrs	LAN Chile, LADECO
Concepción	$97.00	2–6 services daily	1 hr	LAN Chile, LADECO
Copiapó	$154.00	1–2 services daily	1½ hrs	LAN Chile, LADECO
El Salvador	$198.00	1–2 services daily	2½ hrs	LAN Chile
Iquique	$234.00	3–4 services daily	2½ hrs	LAN Chile, LADECO
Isla Pascua (Easter Island)	$440.00	Tues, Thurs, Sun	5 hrs	LAN Chile
La Serena	$60.00	1–2 services daily		LADECO
La Paz		1 service daily except Sun	4½ hrs	
Osorno	$163.00	1–2 services daily	2½ hrs	LAN Chile, LADECO
Papeete		Tues, Thurs, Sun		LAN Chile
Puerto Montt	$163.00	3–4 services daily	1½ hrs	LAN Chile, LADECO
Punta Arenas	$312.00	2–4 services daily	4 hrs	LAN Chile, LADECO
Temuco	$137.00	1–3 services daily	1¼ hrs	LAN Chile, LADECO
Valdivia	$102.00	1–2 services daily	2 hrs	LADECO

- Lider Rent-a-Car, Avenida Vitacura 2941 ℂ 2465030, fax 2336595; Aeropuerto Comodoro Arturo Merino Benítez ℂ 2343490
- National Car Rental, La Concepción 212, Providencia ℂ 2517552; Aeropuerto Comodoro Arturo Merino Benítez ℂ 6019691
- New Rent-a-Car, Avenida Ossa 2123 ℂ 2776726, fax 2772378
- Rentaequipos Rent-a-Car S.A., Avenida Libertador B. O'Higgins 2558 ℂ 6894851, fax 6897270

⤵ Water transport

Most of the shipping companies with their head offices down in the southern part of the country are represented in Santiago by tour operators who act as booking agents and information offices. Visitors who want to go on boat trips are advised to find out all they need from these offices.
- Compañía Naviera Puerto Montt S.A., Avenida Providencia 199 ℂ 2748150 fax 2052197. Cruises from Puerto Montt to Laguna San Rafael
- Cruceros Australis S.A., Avenida El Bosque 0440 ℂ 2035030

- Navimag, Avenida El Bosque 0440 (2035030, fax 2035025. Information about trips from Puerto Montt to Puerto Natales and trips to Laguna San Rafael from Puerto Chacabuco. Operates the roll-on roll-off vessel *Evangelistas* from Puerto Chacabuco to Laguna San Rafael (from December 31 to the middle of March), a 36-hour trip, costing $115.00
- Turismo Mar del Sur, Matías Cousiño 82, office 1106 (6985100/6984784. Operators of the launch *Patagonia* from Puerto Chacabuco to Laguna San Rafael
- Transmarchilay S.A., Agustinas 715, office 403 (335959. This company runs ferry services south of Puerto Montt whenever the Carretera Austral is interrupted by a fjord. These services on the Carretera Austral run only during the tourist season from the end of December to the end of February. When intending to travel the Carretera Austral, inquire about these services or you may find yourself stranded north of Chaitén. Transmarchilay also runs year-round ferry services between the mainland and Isla Grande de Chiloe between Pargua and Chacao. There is a ferry service to Puerto Chacabuco from Puerto Montt. A ferry service between Puerto Ibañez and Chile Chico crosses Lago General Carrera

⊞ Shopping

Shopping in the city center

The main shopping streets in the center of Santiago are Avenida Bernardo O'Higgins (also known as Alameda), Paseo Ahumada, Estado, Agustinas, and Paseo Huérfanos. The shops are usually open in the downtown area from 1000 to 1800.

Shopping centers in other suburbs are listed in the city's introduction under each *barrio*, starting on page 380.

There are two pedestrian malls with shops and boutiques: Huérfanos between MacIver and Bandera; and Paseo Ahumada, between Alameda and Río Mapocho (■2 Cal y Canto).

- CEMA Chile, Avenida Portugal 351. Located in "Claustro del 900" which was constructed in 1854, a two-storey adobe building with a surrounding patio, so typical of Chilean architecture. The roof is made of Spanish tiles. This is a *centro artesanal* where you can examine and buy *artesanía* from all parts of Chile. It gives you a good idea of the location of Chile's artistic centers. The stalls exhibit ceramics, woolen materials, silverware, and cut and uncut semi-precious stones. Open Mon–Fri 0930–1830, Sat 0930–1300
- Gundert Artesanía, Estado 337, Local 16 (in Galeria España). Handicrafts
- Soproart Ltda, Huérfanos 1162. Handicrafts lapis lazuli, ponchos, wood carvings, silver and copper art, jewelry, rugs, pottery
- The Barrio Bellavista (■1 Baquedano or Salvador) across Río Mapocho, contains a large number of lapis lazuli gem shops that are well worth a visit
- Artesanía Chungará, Bellavista 0299. Lapis lazuli
- Artesanía Aquis Granx, Calle Del Arzobispo corner of Avenida Santa Maria
- Artesanía Lapis Lázuli, Bellavista 0430

⊛ Sport

- Club Hípico, Avenida Blanco Encalada 2540, established in 1869, is one of the best horse tracks in South America. Races are held on Sundays and every second Wednesday. There are about 15 races per race meeting. The Ensayo race, held on the first Sunday in November, and Copa de Oro in the third week in March are sought-after trophies
- Las Vizcachas (car racing track), at Puente Alto on the road to El Volcán, 23 km south-east of Santiago. The track is 3 km long and the stand holds 7500 spectators

▣ Sightseeing

Parks

- Cerro Santa Lucia, in the center of town, Alameda block 600 near Bernardo O'Higgins (■1 Santa Lucia). At the foot of the hill is a stone inscription of Pedro de Valdivia's letter to the King of Spain praising the beauty of the newly conquered lands. Stairs lead up from the Alameda to the fort erected by the early Spanish. In 1872

Continued on page 410

🚍 Buses from Santiago

Santiago has now five long-distance bus terminals, four regional bus terminals, and one bus terminal with both regional and long-distance bus services, and these bus terminals are strewn all over the metropolitan area.

Terminal de Buses Alameda
The Terminal de Buses Alameda is at Avenida Libertador Bernardo O'Higgins (also called "Alameda") 3724, one block east of the Terminal de Buses Sur.
• A153 Tur-Bus Jedimar (7763690

Terminal de Buses Torres de Tajamar
This terminal is at Avenida Providencia 1072.
For the services provided by these companies, see Terminal de Buses Norte and Terminal de Buses Santiago below.
• A45   Buses Libac (2352520
        Services along the Panamericana Norte as far as Copiapó
• A77   Buses Diamantes de Elquí (2359707
        Services along the Panamericana Norte as far as Antofagasta
• A106 Buses Fénix Pullman Norte (2359707
        Services along the Panamericana Norte as far as Arica, and
        along the Panamericana Sur as far as Pucón, Valdivia and Puerto Montt
• A122 Buses Los Corsarios (2354810
        Services along the Panamericana Norte as far as Antofagasta
• A128 Pullman Bus (2358142
        Services along the Panamericana Norte as far as Arica and Valparaíso
• A137 Buses Tas Chopa (2352405
• B83   Buses JAC (2352484
        Services along the Panmericana Sur as far as Valdivia and Pucón
• B179 Buses Varmontt (2313505
        Services along the Panamericana Sur to Puerto Montt

Terminal de Buses Santiago (or Sur)
The Terminal de Buses Santiago is at Avenida Libertador Bernardo O'Higgins (also called "Alameda") 3848 (🔲1 Universidad de Santiago) (7791385.
This is the main terminal for buses going south of Santiago, and for international buses to other South American countries (in particular Peru and Argentina), and some buses to the coast.

Companies serving the center and south
• A2   Alfa Tres
• A14   Buses Ahumada, Oficina 61 (7795243
• A16   Buses Pullman Biotal
• A46   Buses Línea Azul (7795234
• A48   Buses Lit, office 35 (7795710
• A74   Buses Sol del Sur, office 43 (7764095
• A75   Buses TAC, office 54 (7796920
• A78   Buses Tramaca, office 75 (7763849, fax 7763684
• A86   Chile Bus, office 55 (7765557
• A93   Buses Cóndor Bus, office 1 (7793721
• A103 Empresa Robles, office 2 (7791526
• A105 Buses Sol del Pacífico
• A106 Buses Fénix Pullman Norte, office 67 (7763253, fax 6814737
• A112 Flota Barrios, office 75 (7760665
• A125 Nueva Transmar
• A127 Buses Pullman Bus, office 39 (7792026

Buses from Santiago — continued

- A128 Pullman Fichtur, office 51 ℂ 7799285
- A137 TAS Choapa, office 52 ℂ 7794925 fax
- A153 Buses Tur-Bus Jedimar, office 30 ℂ 7780808
- A155 Buses Turibus, office69 ℂ 7791377
- A160 Viamar
- B23 Buses Andimar, office 13 ℂ 7793810
- B39 Buses Chi-Ar, ℂ 6951508, fax 6713204
- B46 Buses Colchagua, office 37 ℂ **7793852**
- B48 Buses Cordillera
- B81 Buses Igi Llaima, office 18 ℂ **7791751**
- B83 Buses JAC, office 68 ℂ 7761582, fax 5514941
- B117 Buses Nueva Longitudinal Sur, office 46 ℂ 7795856, fax 2515616
- B128 Buses Panguisur, office 76 ℂ 7796282
- B137 Buses Power, office 73 ℂ **7762812**
- B154 Buses Ruta Sur, office 20 ℂ 7764111
- B195 Buses al Sur, office 10 ℂ 7761205
- B217 Flota L
- B220 Interregional Abbeysur, office 82 ℂ 7760667
- B231 Pullman Bus Tacoha, office 12 ℂ 7799412, fax 7799622
- B237 Pullman Sur
- B244 Ruta H
- B250 Buses Transbus ℂ 7798649
- B260 Transportes Cruz del Sur, office 45 ℂ 7790607, fax 6816778
- B261 Transportes Lagos del Sur
- B269 Via Ruc
- B271 Buses Via Tur, office 29 ℂ 7793839
- B272 Unión del Sur, office 20 ℂ **7764111**

International buses
- A22 Buses CATA, office 77 ℂ 7793660
- A55 Buses Nevada, office 79 ℂ 6984716, fax 6965832
- B118 Buses Nueva O'Higgins, office 53 ℂ 7795727
- B124 Buses Ormeño, office 83 ℂ 6337150
- B193 El Rápido Argentina, office 77 ℂ 7790316
- B273 Unión del Sur

Services to the central and south coast of Región V de Valparaíso, southern part of Chile and to Argentina

	Destination	Fares	Services	Duration	Companies
•	Algarrobo	$3.30	15 services daily	2½ hrs	A103, A127, B117
•	Ancud	$23.20	5 services daily		A155, B260 (*Ejecutivo*)
	Sleeper	$30.50	1 service daily		B260
•	Angol	$11.40	9 services daily	8½ hrs	A48, A106, A127, A137, A153, B81,B179
•	Cañete	$14.60	2 services daily		A153
•	Cartagena	$2.50			A103, A127, B117
•	Castro	$20.50	3 services daily		A155, B260 (Pullman)
	Sleeper	$31.50	2 services daily		B179, B260
	Cauquenes	$6.80	4 services daily		A48
•	Chillán	$8.40	39 services daily	6½ hrs	A16, A48, A74, A75, A137, A153, B81, B250, B271
•	Codegua	$1.10	10 services daily		B154
•	Collipulli	$11.60	8 services daily		A106, A153, B272

Buses from Santiago — continued

Destination	Fare	Services	Duration	Companies
• Coltauco	$1.90	2 services daily		B217
• Concepción	$10.60	50 services daily	8½ hrs	A46, A48, A74, A75, A105, A137, A153, B179, B250, B271
• Constitución	$5.80	3 services daily		B237
• Curacautín	$10.50	3 services daily		A106, A153
• Curicó	$3.60	10 services daily	3½ hrs	A48, A127, B23, B117
• El Quisco	$1.70			B117, A127
• El Tabo	$2.10			B117
• Las Cruces	$2.50			A160
• La Unión	$15.20	4 services daily		A48, A153,
• Lebu	$14.60	2 services daily		A153
• Linares	$5.30	20 services daily	5 hrs	A48, A127
• Llanquihué	$17.20	5 services daily		A137
• Llolleo	$2.10		2 hrs	A127
• Lonquimay	$11.70	1 service daily		B83, B137
• Los Angeles	$18.40			B179
	$11.40	27 services daily	8 hrs	A48, A86, A105, A106, A127, A137, A153, B81, B220, B271, B272
• Los Lagos	$13.40			A153
• Mendoza (Argentina)				
	$22.50		7½ hrs	A22, A55, A75, A86, A106, A137, B39, B118, B193,

Arrives 1630. Note the 2-hr time difference

Destination	Fare	Services	Duration	Companies
• Osorno	$15.20	12 services daily	15½ hrs	A48, A137, A153, A155, B81, B250, B260, B271
Sleeper	$32.80			B179
• Panguipulli	$14.50	4 services daily		A154, B128,
• Parral	$5.90	5 services daily	5½ hrs	A48, B237
• Pichilemu	$4.20	19 services daily	5 hrs	B23
• Pucón	$16.70	9 services daily	13 hrs	A48, A86, A106, A153, B81, B83, B137
• Puerto Montt	$38.00	3 services daily		B179 express
	$19.00	31 services daily	17 hrs	A48, A137, A153, A155, B81, B250, B260, B261, B271
• Puerto Varas	$19.00	12 services daily	17 hrs	A48, A137, A153, A155, B81, B250, B260, B261, B271
Express	$38.00			B179
• Quilpué	$2.50			A127
• Quinta de Tilcoco	$1.90			B154
• Rancagua	$1.90	65 services daily	1½ hrs	A48, A153, B23, B154, B195, B250
• Rengo	$1.70			B195, B217
• Río Bueno	$15.20	4 services daily		A48, A153, B117
• Rocas de San Domingo				
	$2.50			A127
• San Antonio	$2.30			A127
• San Carlos	$7.50			A48, B269
• San Fernando	$2.70		2½ hrs	A48, A127, B23, B237
• San Francisco de Mostazal				
	$0.90			B154
• San Javier	$5.30			B237
• San Juan	$25.00			A137

Buses from Santiago — continued

Destination	Fare	Services	Duration	Companies
• San Vicente de Tagua				
	$2.90			B244, B269
• Santa Cruz	$2.90			B23, B237
• Talca	$5.00	27 services daily	4 hrs	A48, A74, A105, A127,A137, A153, B81, B117
• Talcahuano	$11.60	5 services daily		A48, A74, A105, A137, A153
• Temuco	$12.50	44 services daily	11 hrs	A48, A86, A106, A137, A153, B81, B83, B117, B128, B137, B220, B250, B260, B271, B272
Salón expreso	$15.20			A154
Ejecutivo	$19.00	1 service daily		A154, B83
Sleeper	$27.00			B179
• Termas del Flaco	$8.40	3 services daily		B23 (summer only), B48, B217
• Valdivia	$13.50	20 services daily	14 hrs	A48, A106, A155, A153, A137, B81, B83, B117 B250, B260, B271
Sleeper	$29.80	1 service daily	10½ hrs	B179
• Victoria	$9.90	6 services daily		A48, A106, A153, B137, B272,
• Villarrica	$16.30	1 service daily	11 hrs	A154 (express)
	$13.10	11 services daily	12½ hrs	A48, A86, A106, A137, B81, B83, B137
• Valparaíso	$3.00	30 services daily	2 hrs	A48, A93, A127, A153
• Villa Alemana	$2.80			A127
• Viña del Mar	$2.90	50 services daily	2 hrs	A48, A93, A115, A127, A153

Terminal de Buses Norte
Terminal de Buses Norte is on Amunátegui (◼2 Mapocho).

Companies
- A14 Buses Ahumada, office 3 (6717310
- A25 Buses Combarbalá-Rima
- A31 Buses Evans, office 27 (6985953
- A35 Buses Géminis, office 33 (6972132
- A37 Buses Golondrina, office 5 (6962306
- A42 Buses Carmelita, office 12 (6955230
- A43 Buses Ligua, office 32 (6987339
- A48 Buses Lit, office 23 (6992263
- A66 Buses Quintero, office 16 (6989659
- A67 Buses Ramos Cholele (6717388
- A70 Buses Ruta 57
- A76 Buses Tacc Via Choapa, office 9 (6980922
- A77 Buses TAL-Los Diamantes de Elqui, office 13 (6724415
- A78 Tramaca, office 20 (6726840
- A86 Chilebus, office 8 (6956898
- A93 Buses Cóndor Bus, office 1 (7793721
- A106 Fénix Pullman Norte, office (6952010
- A110 Flecha Dorada
- A112 Flota Barrios, office 1 (6981494
- A115 Incabus-Lasval, office 7 (6721817
- A117 Kenny Bus
- A121 Los Conquistadores (5555254
- A122 Los Corsarios, office 32-A (6963912
- A125 Nueva Transmar (6965551
- A127 Pullman Bus, office 29 (6985559

Buses from Santiago — continued

- A128 Pullman Bus Fichtur (6985559
- A137 TAS Choapa, office 11 (6954962
- A149 Transportes Algarrobo
- A154 Turbus Jedimar, office 18 (6987339

Services to the north and to the coast and northern part of Región de Valparaíso

Destination	Fares	Services	Duration	Companies
• Antofagasta	$27.30	20 services daily		A42, A67, A78, A106, A110, A112, A117
Sleeper	$38.00	3 services daily		A112, A128
• Arica	$39.30	8 services daily	30 hrs	A78, A117, A128
Sleeper	$49.30	1 service daily	28 hrs	A128
• Cabildo	$2.60			A43
• Calama	$30.00	10 services daily		A78, A110, A112, A117
Sleeper	$44.80	1 service daily		A35
• Caldera	$17.00	2 services daily		A127, A115
Change in La Serena				
• Casablanca				A127, A132
• Chañaral	$16.70	10 services daily		A67, A78, A110, A112, A115, A117, A127
• Chincolco	$3.20			A43
• Chuquicamata	$28.40	4 services daily		A78, A112
• Combarbalá	$6.80	2–3 services daily		A25
• Concón	$2.50			A66, A125
• Copiapó	$14.50	27 services daily	12 hrs	A31, A42, A67, A77, A78, A106, A110, A115, A117, A121, A122, A127, A137
• Copiapó Sleeper	$20.50	3 services daily		A45, A112, A128
• Coquimbo	$14.00	20 services daily		A31, A42, A45, A48, A77, A78, A110, A115, A117, A121, A122, A127, A137
• El Salvador	$15.40	1 service daily		A115
• Guanaqueros	$11.20	3 services daily		A77
• Illapel	$6.30	8 services daily		A76, A115
• Iquique	$38.00	9 services daily		A42, A67, A106, A110, A112, A117,
Sleeper	$47.50	1 service daily		A128
• La Calera	$1.70			A37, A66
• La Laguna	$3.20			A43
• La Ligua	$2.50	6 services daily		A43, A154
• La Serena	$14.00	52 services daily	7 hrs	A31, A42, A45, A48, A67, A77, A78, A106, A110, A112, A115, A117, A121, A122, A127, A137, A149
• Los Vilos	$5.30	9 services daily		A31, A35, A76, A77, A110, A115, A137
• Las Ventanas	$3.10			A125
• Los Andes	$1.90	30 services daily		A14, A70
• María Elena	$27.00	2 services daily		A42, A112, A117, A127
• Ovalle	$9.50	10 services daily		A42, A76, A77, A78, A110, A112, A115, A121, A127, A137, A149
• Papudo	$3.50	5 services daily	3 hrs	A154
• Pedegua	$2.80			A43
• Pedro de Valdivia	$27.00	3 services daily		A42, A112, A117, A127
• Petorca	$2.90	2 services daily		A43, A154
• Pichidangui	$4.20	4 services daily		A77, A137
• Quillota	$1.90	4 services daily		A37, A70

Buses from Santiago — continued

Destination	Fare	Services	Companies
• Quintero	$3.10	3 services daily	A66, A125, A161
• Salamanca	$7.00	7 services daily	A76, A115
• San Felipe	$1.90	15 services daily	A14
• Tal Tal	$19.00	2 services daily	A78
• Tocopilla	$29.60	5 services daily	A78, A110, A112, A117, A127
• Tongoy	$11.20		A77
• Vallenar	$13.80		A31, A42, A45, A67, A77, A78, A110, A112, A115, A117, A121, A122, A127, A137

Terminal Los Heroés
This terminal is at 21 Tucapel Jímenez, one block up from Alameda (■1 Los Heroes).

Companies serving the north
- A14   Buses Ahumada (6969798
- A45   Buses Libac, office 2 (6985974
- A78   Buses Tramaca, office 1 (6969839
- A106 Fénix Pullman Norte (6969089
- A112 Flota Barrios, office 3 (6969311
- A115 Incabus-Lasval (6724904
- A137 TAS Choapa, office 6 (6969326
- A161 Buses Via Transmar
- B260 Transportes Cruz del Sur, office 9 (6969324
- B265 Buses Trans-Tur, office 25 (7760977

Regional bus terminals
Transporte Santiago is the regional transport organisation which has regional bus terminals located all over Santiago. From these regional bus terminals, rural bus companies serve the Región Metropolitana and in some cases beyond. The major Regional Bus terminals are as follows also indicating name of bus company and the district they serve
For bus services to the airport, see "Air services" on page 400.

Terminal de Buses Tarapacá
This terminal is on the corner of Tarapacá and San Francisco.
- Taxibuses Puente Alto-Pirque
  Colectivos to Puente Alto and Pirque
- Empresa Asociación de San Bernardo, four blocks south of Alameda (■1 Santa Lucia)
  Service to San Bernardino. Their first bus leaves at 0700; fare $0.80

Terminal de Buses La Paz
This terminal is at Juarez Larga 878 on the corner of La Paz (one block from Dávila).
- Buses Noviciado (777787
  Services to Noviciado; fare $0.60
- Buses Tiltil (771430
  Services to Polpaico (fare $0.60) and Tiltil (fare $0.60)

Terminal de Buses Estación Metro Cal y Canto
■2 Mapocho.
- Buses Sedan (374572
  Services to Colina and Termas de Colina; fare $0.60
- Taxibuses Sapeca (361932/362796
  Services to Colina; fare $0.60

Buses from Santiago — continued

- Buses Lampa ℓ 375982
  Services to Batuco and Lampa; fare $0.60

Terminal de Buses Pueblito Parque O'Higgins
⊡2 Parque O'Higgins.
- Buses Cajón del Maipo
  Services to San José de Maipo, Melocotón, San Alfonso, El Volcán, and Baños Morales

Terminal de Buses Borja
This terminal is at Avenida Libertador Bernardo O'Higgins (also called "Alameda") 3250, corner of Borja (⊡1 Central) ℓ 7660645. This is next to Estación Central (where trains to the south leave from), and only four blocks east of the Terminal de Buses Sur.

Companies
- Buses Ruta Curacaví ℓ 7760112
  Services to Curacaví
- Buses Peñaflor ℓ 761025
  Services to Santa Rosa de Chena, Peñaflor, and Calera de Tango
- Buses Talagante
  Services to Malloco, Peñaflor, Talagante (fare $0.60), El Monte (fare $0.70), and Isla de Maipo
- Buses Melipilla ℓ 7762060
  Services to Padre Hurtado (fare $0.60), Malloco (fare $0.60), Talagante (fare $0.60), El Monte (fare $0.70), Pomaire, and Melipilla (fare $1.30)
- Buses J.A. ℓ 762230
  Services to Santa Inés and Maria Pinto
- Buses Isla de Maipo
  Services to Padre Hurtado (fare $0.60), Malloco ($0.60), Talagante, Isla de Maipo
- Buses Ruta 78 ℓ 763881 to Melipilla ($1.30)
- Buses Jimenez, to Melipilla ($1.30), Cruce Las Arañas, El Manzano, Llallauquen, El Carmen, Las Cabras (fare $3.30), and Lago Rapel (fare $2.50)
- Buses Navidad
  Services to Rapel (fare $2.50), Licancheu, La Boca, Navidad (fare $2.50), Matanzas (fare $2.80), San Vicente, and Litueche
- Buses Paine ℓ 7763134
  Services to Buin, Paine (fare $0.70), and Laguna de Aculeo (fare $0.90)
- Rul Bus
  Services to María Pinto

Buses to nearby ski resorts
- Tour Service, Teatinos 333, upstairs ℓ 6960415/727166
  Services to El Colorado, Farellones, La Parva, and Portillo
- American Bus, Agustinas 1173 ℓ 6960518/6983341
  Services to El Colorado, Farellones, La Parva, and Portillo
- Centro de Esquí "El Colorado", Avenida Apoquindo 4900, Local 47/48 ℓ 2463344
  Service to El Colorado
- Manzur Expediciones, Sotero del Río 475, upstairs ℓ 774284/723273
  Services to El Colorado, Farellones, La Parva, Lagunillas, Lo Valdés, and Valle Nevado

🖳 Trains from Santiago

Passenger rail services to the north of Santiago (and to Mendoza in Argentina) have been suspended.

There are no more train services from Mapocho station to Valparaíso. Trains to the southern region (Rancagua, Talca, Los Angeles, Temuco, Puerto Montt) leave from Estación Central, Avenida Bernardo O'Higgins. Trains depart from 0700–2200.

Destination	Salón	Económico		Duration
• Chillán			5	5 hrs
• Concepción	$13.00	$9.40	4	8–10 hrs
• Linares	$5.30	$3.80	5	4 hrs
• Osorno	$19.00	$14.00	2	16–24 hrs
• Parral	$6.25	$4.50	4	
• Puerto Montt	$19.00	$14.00	2	19–24 hrs
• Talca	$8.00	$5.75	6	3 hrs
• Temuco	$16.00	$11.40	2	11 hrs

the Intendente ("Mayor") of Santiago, Don Vicuña Mackenna converted the hill into a public garden. Footpaths, fountains, and *plazoletas* (small plazas) were installed to improve the hill. A cannon is fired from here daily at noon. There are kiosks and toilets.

• Parque Forestal runs along the south bank of the Mapocho river from the old Mapocho railroad station to Plaza Baquedano (🖳1 Baquedano). It was designed by the French architect George Dubois in 1901. There are many statues scattered throughout this green reserve, and most of the trees are Chilean. The fountain near Plaza Baquedano was donated by the German colony on the occasion of the hundredth anniversary of Chile's Independence Day.

• Parque Metropolitano (🖳1 Baquedano). This is a spur of the high Andes reaching into the heart of Santiago, incorporating Cerro San Cristóbal and Cerro Blanco Pirámide. The highest point is 860 m. The park covers 712 ha (1760 acres), and is a favorite picnic ground with the *Santiagueños*. The main access for cars is from Calle Pio Nono between 0830 and 2200, and from Pedro de Valdivia Norte between 0830 and 0200. There is a small admission charge. Public buses depart from Pio Nono 468 for the top at weekends from 1100 to 1830. A cable car (fare $4.00) and a *teleférico* both go to the top — one on tracks and

the other hanging in the air. The cable car station is at the end of Pedro de Valdivia Norte (🖳1 Pedro de Valdivia). At the summit is a giant statue of the Virgin Mary. Tree planting began in 1921. It contains a zoo, a botanical garden (Jardín Botánico Mapulemu), picnic grounds, swimming pools, restaurants, and a wine museum (Enoteca) where you can sample wines from every Chilean region. The cafeteria on top of the hill has sweeping views over the city and the Andes. Pedestrian access is from Pio Nono(🖳1 Baquedano).

• Quinta Normal de Agricultura. This 40 ha (99 acre) open space in the center of the city is bounded by Avenida Matucana in the east and Avenida Diego Portales in the south. Founded in 1830 it was used to propagate foreign plants. Nowadays it is a botanical garden. There are several museums inside the Quinta Normal de Agricultura. It is best reached by (🖳1 Central).

Plazas

• Plaza de la Constitución, Moneda between Teatinos and Morandé, in front of the Palacio de la Moneda. Public buildings surround the plaza. A statue in honor of President Diego Portales stands in the park.

• Plaza de Armas, bounded by Paseo Ahumada and Puente to the west, Catedral and Monjitas to the north, Com-

Plate 25 Región VIII del Bio Bio
Top: Parque Nacional Laguna del Laja
Bottom: Volcán Antuco

Plate 26
Map of Región IX de La Araucania

pañía and Merced to the south, and Estado and 21 de Mayo to the east. The plaza was designed by Pedro de Valdivia in 1541. This space was first used for military exercises, and a gunpowder storage tower once stood in the middle. It is considered the geographical center of the country and all distances are measured from this point. Important buildings surround this plaza, such as the Catedral Metropolitana, the Real Audiencia (Royal High Court), the main post office and the town hall. The Portal Bulnes on the eastern side and the Portal Fernández Concha on the southern side are both archways where stalls sell refreshments, flowers, and other merchandise. An equestrian statue of Pedro de Valdivia stands in the north-eastern corner of the plaza. Opposite the cathedral is the statue of Cardinal Caro, famous church leader and a marble monument inscribed "A la Libertad de América".

Buildings

- Casa de Velasco (a *monumento nacional*), Santo Domingo 899. Built around 1730 with thick adobe walls of reddish appearance. In the front is the coat of arms of Manso de Velasco which the original owner received from King Philip V. Upstairs was added by Rodríguez Aldea, one of Bernardo O'Higgins' ministers. It has a balcony around the whole house. Now the building is owned by CORFO who use it for functions.
- Edificio Bolsa de Comercio (Stock Exchange Building, a *monumento nacional*), La Bolsa 64 (■1 Universidad de Chile). Built in 1917 to house the stock exchange, which was founded in 1893. The stock market transactions take place in the *Sala de Rueda* Mon–Fri 1030–1230. The big mural inside the building is by the Chilean painter Pedro Subercaseaux.
- Edificio Club de la Unión, (a *monumento nacional*) Avenida Bernardo O'Higgins (also known as Alameda 1091. This building, erected in 1925, contains many paintings by Pedro Subercaseaux, Pedro Lira, and Alvaro Casanova.

- Edificio del Congreso Nacional (National Congress Building, a *monumento nacional*) takes up a complete block between Compañía, Bandera, Morandé, and Catedral. It was opened in 1876, but the Congress was transferred to Valparaíso in 1989, possibly because of Santiago's traffic congestion and heavy smog.
- Edificio del Correo Central (Central Post Office Building), north side of Plaza de Armas, corner of Puente. Until 1846, this was the residence of the governors and presidents of Chile. The present building, constructed by Richard Brown, dates from 1885 with a new facade from 1902. Stalls outside the building sell postcards of Chile.
- Mercado Central (Central Market), Ismael Valdés Vergara. Made of prefabricated steel in England and opened on the occasion of the *Exposición Nacional* in 1872. Open daily. There are small stalls where you can buy *artesanías* and good seafood restaurants.
- Palacio de Gobierno La Moneda (a *monumento nacional*), Moneda between Teatinos and Morandé (■1 Moneda). As the name suggests, this austere, classical-style building, dating from 1784, was originally intended as the mint. It was restored and refurbished in 1981. Since 1848, it has been the residence of Chilean presidents. The changing of the guard takes place at 1000 every second day.
- Palacio Cousiño, Dieciocho 438. A 19th-century neoclassic building erected by a coal baron. Open Tues–Sun 1000–1300.
- Palacio de los Tribunales de Justicia (Court of Justice Building), separated from the Edificio del Congreso by Compañía. The original building was the site of the 1810 agreement to make Chile an independent country, and of Bernardo O'Higgins' resignation in 1823.
- Municipalidad de Santiago (Town Hall, a *monumento nacional*), Plaza de Armas corner of 21 de Mayo. This is the original site of the Cabildo building, now the town hall of Santiago. It became the local jail in 1790 and was rebuilt in 1891 by Eugen Joannon.

- ENTEL tower, Avenida Bernardo O'Higgins near Amunátegui. The telecommunications tower, 128 m tall, is a landmark in the city.
- Casa Colorada ("Red House", a *monumento nacional*), Merced 860. Built in 1769 of red ashlars. Casa Colorada was formerly the home of Don Mateo de Toro y Zambrano, Conde de la Conquista who in 1810 became the president of the First General Assembly of the newly independent country. It functions now as the official museum of Santiago, showing objects dating back to Santiago's foundation and audio-visual programs of the early days. Open Tues–Sat 1000–1800; Sun and holidays 1000–1300.
- Biblioteca Nacional (National Library, a *monumento nacional*), corner of Avenida Libertador Bernardo O'Higgins 651 (also known as Alameda) and Mac-Iver (■1 Santa Lucia). The library was built between 1913 and 1924, and the inside walls are painted by Arthur Gordon and Alfred Helsby. This is one of the largest libraries in South America, and contains over six million documents and books. Open in summer Mon–Fri 0900–1800 and in winter 0900–2000 and 0900–1500.
- Palacio La Alhambra, Compañía 1340 (a *monumento nacional*) Constructed in 1862 by the Chilean architect Manuel Aldunate for a rich mining magnate. The masons, trades people, and much of the material used to build the palace were imported from Spain. La Alhambra contains an exhibition of paintings. Open Mon–Fri 1100–1300 and 1730–2000.
- Posada del Corregidor, Emeralda 732 (a *monumento nacional*). Completed in 1765 for the Corregidor Manuel de Zañartu who never occupied it, Posada del Corregidor is a splendid example of a colonial mansion. The front facade incorporates the coat of arms of the Zañartu family. The large front door is made of wood, and the second floor has a balcony with stone pillars at the corners. The building is beautifully restored and is used as a cultural center and to house exhibitions. Open Tues–Fri 1100–1330 and 1430–1800.

- Teatro Municipal (Municipal Theatre, a *monumento nacional*), Agustinas 794, corner of San Antonio ℂ 332804. The theatre was constructed by architect Claude François Brunet de Baines in 1853 and rebuilt by Lucien Hénault after a fire in 1870. It was heavily damaged again by the 1906 earthquake. The chandelier hanging from the cupola has 68 lights. The main hall is used for opera performances and the Salón Filarmonico for chamber music and exhibitions. (■1 Santa Lucia)

Museums
- Palacio de Bellas Artes (*monumento nacional*), Parque Forestal near José Miguel de la Barra and Puente Loreto. This fine arts museum was opened in 1880, and has more than 2700 paintings and drawings of local and international artists. Open Tues–Sat 1000–1800; Sun and holidays 1000–1330.
- Museo de Arte Contemporáneo (Museum of Contemporary Art), Parque Forestal in the Palacio de Bellas Artes. Contains more than 900 paintings of mostly south American painters. Open Tues–Sat 1000–1300 and 1400–1700.
- Museo de Santiago — see Casa Colorada above.
- Museo Histórico Nacional (*monumento nacional*), Monjitas 951 Plaza de Armas on the north side ℂ 381411/330462. Located in the former Real Audiencia (the Royal High Court). The present building dates from 1806, and was built by Juan José de Goycolea. The National History Museum contains portraits of historical personalities such as Juan Bautista Pasteni, Spanish sea captain (1507–1576), the first European to sail below the 40th parallel south; portraits of Spanish governors; pictures of battles during the War of Independence, dates of Spanish forts and town foundations; medieval firearms; and colonial furniture. Allow at least two hours for this museum, as there are many interesting exhibits and the collection is one of the best in South America. Open Tues–Sat 1000–1730; Sun and holidays 1000–1345.

- Museo de Arte Colonial (Colonial Art Museum) (monumento nacional), in the Convent of San Francisco, Londres 4 ℓ 398737 (■1 Universidad de Chile). Among the many paintings, there is a series of 54 paintings of the Cuzco School executed in the 17th and 18th centuries by indigenous painters taught by missionaries. They depict the life of San Francisco and are generally 180 cm high and between 260 cm and 400 cm wide. They are in the Gran Sala and should not be missed. Also noteworthy is the wooden door to the entry of the sacristy made in 1608. Open daily (except Mon) 1000–1300 and 1500–1800.

- Museo Tajamares (Dyke Museum), Avenida Providencia 222 Parque Balmaceda (■1 Salvador). In colonial times the Río Mapocho was dammed above and within the City limits to prevent periodical flooding in spring. Until the river was regulated in its present bed, Avenida Libertador Bernardo O'Higgins (also known as Alameda), now the main thoroughfare of Santiago, was once the main arm of the Mapocho river. In the 17th century, a brick wall was built to regulate this river; the mixture for the mortar included eggs. Part of this retaining wall has been incorporated into the Museo de Tajamares. On display are pictures and plans of how the city tried to tame the wild river. Open Tues–Sat 1000–1800, Sun and holidays 1000–1300.

- Museo del Huaso (Cowboy Museum), Pueblito del Parque O'Higgins (■2 Parque O'Higgins). This museum displays *huaso* traditions — implements and pictures of Chilean cowboys. Open Tues–Fri 1000–1300 and 1430–1700; Sat, Sun and holidays 1000–1800.

- Museo Nacional de Historia Natural (National Natural History Museum), Quinta Normal, entrance in Catedral corner of Matucana. This museum contains botanical and zoological collections and exhibits on Easter Island. Open Tues–Sat 1000–1300 and 1400–1800; Sun and holidays 1430–1800.

- Museo Ferroviario (Railroad Museum), Quinta Normal, entrance from Avenida Portales. Open Tues–Fri 1000–1215 and 1400–1700; Sat, Sun and holidays 1100–1315 and 1500–1800.

- Museo de la Catedral, also known as Museo de Arte Sagrado (Museum of Sacred Art), Bandera corner of Catedral ℓ 6962777. Access is through the Cathedral from Plaza de Armas. This museum houses a collection of religious items from the colonial period such as garments worn by former bishops. Open only on Mon 1030–1300 and 1530–1900.

- Museo de la Merced (Museum of the order of Merced), Mac Ivar 341, upstairs ℓ 336633. This museum contains religious paintings of the Quito and Cuzco schools, which flourished in the 17th and 18th centuries, and some Easter Island archeology. Open Tues–Fri 1000–1300 and 1500–1800; Sat 1000–1300.

- Museo de Arte Precolombino (Museum of Pre-Columbian Art), Bandera 361, corner of Compañía ℓ 717284. Located in the former Palacio de la Real Aduana (Royal Customs Building), this museum displays more than 4500 years of indigenous art, focusing on ceramics, paintings, and textiles. It also exhibits recently discovered archeological items. Open Tues–Sat 1000–1800 and Sun 1000–1400. Admission $1.00.

Churches

- Cathedral (a *monumento nacional*), on the west side of Plaza de Armas on the corner of Catedral. This is the site chosen by Pedro de Valdivia in 1541 for the original church. It was destroyed several times and rebuilt. The present church dates from 1745, and the baroque facade was designed by Joaquín Toesca. The two towers were added at the end of the 19th century.

- Iglesia San Francisco (a *monumento nacional*), Avenida Bernardo O'Higgins 834 (also known as Alameda) (■1 Santa Lucia). The site was acquired by the Franciscan monks in 1553 but their first church was destroyed by earthquake in 1583. It was rebuilt with a single nave in 1683. The present structure, incorporating the old church, has three naves. It is the oldest church of Santiago. The Virgen del Socorro on the main altar was brought by Pedro de Valdivia when he came to Chile. The church is also the resting place of Maria Ortiz de Gaete, wife of Pedro de Valdivia, and of the illustrious architect Joaquín Toesca.

- Iglesia de las Agustinas (a *monumento nacional*), Moneda 1060. Built in 1857 in Renaissance style with two octagonal towers. The pulpit is 18th century baroque.

- Iglesia San Agustín (a *monumento nacional*), Estado 185. Rebuilt several times after earthquake damage in the 18th and 19th centuries. El Señor de Mayo, an image of Christ, has worn the crown of thorns around his neck since the 1643 earthquake.

- Iglesia Santo Domingo (a *monumento nacional*), Santo Domingo 961. Built by Joaquín Toesca in 1747 in neoclassic style with Creole influence. The two towers are baroque. Inside, the life of St. Dominic is depicted in paintings.

- Iglesia de la Merced (a *monumento nacional*), Merced 628. The first church was started in 1549 and took 16 years to complete. Earthquakes and other disasters have destroyed the church buildings several times. The present structure dates from 1760. The pulpit is 18th century baroque and the main altar features a picture of the Virgen de las Mercedes. The picture *Cristo de la Agonia* was donated by Philip II of Spain. This is the resting place of Gobernador Rodrígo de Quiroga, who died in 1580, and his wife Inés de Suárez (see the history of Concepción in Región VIII del Bío Bío).

Sightseeing in Maipú
- **Templo Votivo de Maipú:** The church, which is unfinished, was started in 1944 and partly completed in 1974. It was built to honor a promise made by Bernardo O'Higgins during the battle of Maipú against the royalists on April 5, 1818.

- **Museo del Carmen de Maipú:** Located next to the main church. This museum houses a collection of colonial carriages, paintings, furniture, historical documents and memorabilia of later periods. Open Sat, Sun and public holidays from 1600–1900.

⊕ Excursions

Santiago city tours last about three hours. Tours to northern Chile last from 5–8 days.
Tours to southern Chile last from 8–13 days.

Tour operators
- Turismo Cocha, Agustinas 1173 ℂ 6983341. They are agents for Pehuen Expediciones, Castro, which specializes in excursions to Isla Chiloe and the Archipelago in the Canal Aplao

- Altué Expediciones, Encomenderos 88, Providencia ℂ 2321103, fax 2336799. Organizes rafting trips for the adventurous on Río Bío Bío, Río Maipo, Río Maule, Río Teno, Río Liucura, and Río Trancura. Rafting on Río Mapocho starts from El Melocotón. Rafters gather in Parque Los Heroes and are taken by jeep to El Melocotón where the rafting adventure starts. Altué Expediciones also organize hiking trips in Parque Nacional La Campana and trips to Radal and Siete Tazas

- Andina del Sud, Bombero Ossa 1010, office 301 ℂ 6971010, fax 6965121. Andina del Sud organizes fantastic tours from Puerto Montt via Lago Todos Los Santos and Paso Pérez Rosales and Lago Nahuel Huapí to San Carlos de Bariloche in Argentina. When going south, do not miss this trip

- Cascada, Orrego Luco 054, upstairs ℂ 2342274, fax 2327214. Rafting on the Río Bío Bío (3–5 days), and on the lower Río Maipo (for beginners) and upper Río Maipo (for the advanced).

- Empresa Sol y Nieve, Enrique Foster Sur 29 ℂ 2212728/2313573. Provides transport in the skiing season to Lo Valdés and Lagunillas

- Pared Sur Expediciones. Toro Zambrano 1453, La Reina ℂ 2770872, fax 2268736. Mountain bikes, rafting, ecotourism

- Turismo Cabo de Hornos, Agustinas 814, office 706 ℂ 6338481, fax 6338480. Excursions to King George Island in the Antarctic in October and March. For further details see "Excursions" from Punta Arenas in Región XII de Magallanes. Flights begin and end in Punta Arenas. Bookings can be made in Santiago

- Turismo Tajamar, Orrego Luco 023 (2329595, fax 2314332. Thomas Cook representative

Tours

The following day tours depart from Plaza de Armas at 0900:

- Santiago city tour: Plaza de Armas, civic district, Club Hípico, Palacio Cousiño, Santa Carolina vineyard

North

- Baños del Corazón tour: Panamericana Norte, Colina, Peldehué, Chacabuco tunnel, museum in Curimón, Los Andes, Baños del Corazón

South-west

- Cajón del Maipo tour: Plaza de Armas, Calle Merced, Plaza Baquedano, Macul, Las Vizcachas, La Obra, Las Vertientes, lunch in Complejo Turístico San José

South

- Termas de Cauquenes tour: Panamericana Sur, San Bernardo, Buin, Rancagua, Museum, Coya, lunch in Cauquenes

West

- Olmué tour: Panamericana Norte, Tiltil, Cuesta Dormida, Parque Nacional La Campana, lunch at Hostería El Copihué, Pomaire
- Algarrobo tour: Ruta 78, Talagante, Pomaire, Melipilla, San Antonio, Isla Negra, Algarrobo, coast
- Viña del Mar and Valparaíso tour: Ruta 68, Mapocho valley, Los Hornitos, Casablanca valley, Peñuelas, Viña del Mar, Valparaíso

North-east

- Portillo tour: Panamericana Norte, Monumento a la Batalla de Chacabuco, Curimón, Los Andes, Portillo

East

- Farellones tour: Providencia, Las Condes, Farellones, La Parva, El Colorado

Excursions

Many mountain and coastal resorts are within easy reach of Santiago.

- Ski resorts: Portillo, Farellones, La Parva, El Colorado, Valle Nevado, Lo Valdés, and Lagunillas. For transport to these places, see "Buses to ski resorts" on page 409.
- Seaside resorts: **Viña del Mar** and the Chilean Riviera north to Papudo, Algarrobo, El Quisco and south to Santo

Domingo near the mouth of the Río Maipo.

- **Embalse del Yeso**, in the upper Cajón del Maipo 85 km south-east of Santiago. This artificial lake is situated at 2500 m in a fabulous mountain region, 100 km south-east of Santiago.
- **Pukará de Chena** (Chena Inca Fortress): 25 km south of Santiago, 4 km west of the Panamericana near San Bernardo. This site is the mountaintop ruin of the southernmost Inca administrative outpost as well as the site of a former Jesuit mission monastery. It was discovered by archeologists in 1925. The site museum that used to be here has been shifted to Santiago, but Pukará de Chena is worth a visit for those interested in archeology. More information is available from Ruben Stehberg, Museo Nacional de Historia Natural, Casilla 787, Santiago (2263571. This is an easy half-day trip. Take the Metro line 2 to the terminal at Lo Ovalle. Outside the Metro station is a commuter bus terminal. A number 76 bus brings you to San Bernardo where the buses terminate on the central plaza. From here you take a taxi to Cerro Chena ($8.00 return). The taxi crosses the Panamericana and goes into Camino Catemito (where there is a sign saying "HUEVOS" —the site caretaker has a chicken farm). It is a 15-minute drive from San Bernardo to the Inca fortress. Spend about an hour there. Taxis have to park in the shade of some eucalyptus trees near the caretaker's house, and it is a ten-minute climb to the top of a small hill. This was a large Incan administrative center possibly built in the late 1400s. The *pukará* stood on a small plateau in a dominant position on top of Cerro Chena overlooking the valleys on either side. Vestiges of the old Inca trail are visible, coming up from the caretaker's house to the main entrance from the west through two tiers of fortified gates. The northern approach is on a ridge leading up to the fortress, and ancient terraces lay to left and right of that ridge. Modern irrigation has replaced the Incan terraced fields, though some are still visible on the slopes of the hill. Although this citadel

does not compare with the huge Incan cities like Sacsahuaman and Huanuco Viejo, it is a remarkable outpost, 2500 km from its home base in Cuzco in Peru. It was certainly an unimpregnable fortress in its time. Water was brought up from a river on the south side; but there is also water on the north side. From the top, you have sweeping views of the Andes to the east and the central valley to the south and west. Still further south-west, the coastal *cordillera* is fairly high. Look out for the millions of wasps that nest in the ruins and the shrubs — guardians of the Incas! Alternatively, there are direct buses from the Terminal de Buses Tarapacá, on the corner of Tarmacá and San Francisco, run by Empresa Asociación de San Bernardo, four blocks south of Alameda (■1 Santa Lucia). The first Empresa Asociación de San Bernardo bus leaves Santiago at 0700; fare $0.80. These buses take the Panamericana Sur and travel almost non-stop for 45 minutes. This route also stops on the main plaza in San Bernardo near the taxi stands. The trip to Pukará de Chena can be combined with a trip to Laguna Aculeo (described in the next entry). If you have your own transport, this can be done in a day. If using public transport, stay overnight in Laguna Aculeo and return to Santiago (or continue south to Rancagua) the following day.

- **Laguna Aculeo**: 65 km south, a 140 km return trip to one of Santiago's favorite weekend destinations. Buses Paine run daily buses from Terminal de Buses Borja, Alameda 3250. The route follows the six-lane Panamericana Sur (RN 5) until Champa where you turn west. There are several camping grounds and hotels scattered around the lake, which offers swimming and sailing. On the east side, the high chain of the Andes is visible all the way to **Paine**. Many peaks are snow-covered all year round. If you have your own transport, begin at the intersection of Avenida Bernardo O'Higgins and Avenida General Velázquez which becomes the Panamericana Sur from Aerodromo Cerillos (on your right) onwards. Past

Cerillos, the built-up area consists mostly of ugly factory sites. From San Bernardo onwards, the scenery improves. You pass Cerro La Chena which has a Catholic shrine on top of a hill. Catholic shrines, especially on mountains, often indicate an archeological site. In this case, an Incan road passed nearby leading to a fairly extensive Incan *tambo*, which must have been one of the largest in Chile. This trip can be combined with one to Pukará de Chena, described in the previous entry.

- To **Santuario de la Naturaleza Yerba Loca**: See the entry for the reserve on page 418.
- **Lampa** is a small village, 32 km north, at an altitude of 600. It is in a fertile and irrigated part of the central valley. The irregular design of the village indicates its pre-Colombian origins. In colonial times, gold was mined in the nearby mountains. The mountains in the background rise abruptly to 1200 m and **Cerro Roble Alto** to the north reaches 2100 m. Buses Lampa run regular services Mon–Sat from Terminal de Buses Estación Cal y Canto; fare $0.60.
- **Termas de Colina:** 50 km north. The bus leaves from Independencia 215 ℂ 374572 (see the entry for Colina on page 374). Not to be confused with Baños de Colina, high up in the Cajón del Maipo, which is an adventure excursion.
- **Termas de Jahuel**: 135 km north. Buses go to **San Felipe** from Bus Terminal Norte in General Mackenna and Amunátegui. From San Felipe, there are regular buses to Termas de Jahuel.
- **Baños del Corazón:** 90 km near Los Andes. Buses leave Santiago from Bus Terminal Norte in General Mackenna and Amunátegui. There are regular buses from Los Andes to the thermal resort.
- **Farellones:** Ski resort, 50 km east of Santiago at 2300 m. See also under Centro Cordillera Las Condes on page 371.
- **Lagunillas:** Ski resort 60 km east in the Cajón del Maipo. Transport is arranged by Organización Grez (a ski

club), Ahumada 312, office 315. See under Cajón del Maipo on page 367.

- **Parque Nacional La Campana:** See the entry for the park in Region V de Valparaíso on page 292.
- **Reserva Nacional Río Clarillo:** (10 185 ha or 25 148 ac): Located 42km south of Santiago. The reserve is in the *pre-Cordillera,* but nearby mountain peaks reach over 3000 m. This is a favorite weekend trip for *Santiagueños.* Taxibuses to Puente Alto and Pirque leave from the Terminal de Buses Tarapacá, Tarapacá corner of San Francisco. There are regular bus services from Puente Alto to the Reserva Nacional Río Clarillo every three hours. See the entry for the reserve on page 377.
- **Lo Arcaya**: In the Río Clarillo valley 32 km south. This is an old colonial *hacienda* built around 1800. It is a subdivision of the Hacienda El Principal which lies further up the Río Clarillo. Hacienda Lo Arcaya and Hacienda El Principal were established as model farms last century. Permission to visit the chapel at Lo Arcaya may be obtained from the caretaker in the school house. Hacienda El Principal may be visited on a conducted tour. This is an excellent example of colonial architecture, and gives a good insight into the lifestyle of wealthy landowners last century.
- **Peñaflor**, with a population of 56 000, altititude 400 m is 30 km west on RN 78. The oldest part of Peñaflor is located on the colonial road to the coast near the banks of the **Río Mapocho**. Nowadays, the modern highway bypasses the town. It is still an agricultural town. Buses Peñaflor and Buses Talagante run regular daily services from Santiago. There is a COPEC gas station on exit to RN 78. The main attraction is **Viña Undurraga:** one of the best-known wineries in Chile located at KM 40 on the old colonial road to the coast.
- **Puente Alto,** altitude 200 m   22 km south on Ruta G-31, was founded in 1898. Altough a provincial capital in its own right, it forms part of greater Santiago. It is the gateway to the **Reserva Nacional Río Clarillo** and to the Cajón del Maipó. The main attractions are the restaurants in nearby Pirque (see "Eating out in Puente Alto–Pirque" on page 397) and Autodromo Las Vizcachas, a major car-racing circuit where races held between November and March. Taxibuses Puente Alto, and Buses Pirque run regular daily services from Santiago.
- **Talagante** is the capital of the province of the same name. It is a rural town of 26 000 inhabitants situated 41 km west on Ruta G-78 in a wide section of the Río Maipo valley at the junction with Río Mapocho. Three kilometers south of town is Hacienda Santa Ana de Las Palmas, founded as a Franciscan monastery in 1579. It is now a private property, but a visit to Santa Ana de las Palmas is sometimes included in itineraries by tour operators in Santiago. It is interesting to note that at some time this property was owned by the illustrious Lisperguer family, who can trace their roots back to the early settlement of Chile: Juan and Pedro Lisperguer were captains in the Spanish Army under Pedro de Villagra in 1563. For accommodation and eating out see "Accommodation in Talagante" (page 389) and "Eating out in Talagants" (page 397). Buses Talagante and Buses Melipilla and Buses Isla del Maipo run daily direct services from Santiago; fare \$0.60. There is a COPEC gas station here.
- **Tiltil** lies on the slopes of a small hill in the Estero Tiltil valley, 73 km northwest. It has around 8000 inhabitants, and an altitude of 500 m. It was originally a gold-mining town, and around 1712 had five ore-crushing mills, but it has now become a quiet agricultural community. This is the starting point of the scenic road to the coast over the **Cuesta de la Dormida**. There is a beautiful colonial plaza flanked by the old colonial church built in the 17th century. Buses Tiltil run regular services from Santiago: fare \$0.60.

SANTUARIO DE LA
NATURALEZA YERBA LOCA

Altitude: 2000 m
Distance from Santiago: 38 km east on Ruta G-21

Santuario de la Naturaleza Yerba Loca was declared a nature sanctuary mainly because of its scenic beauty. It covers 1575 ha (3889 acres).

The reserve is administered by CONAF and has an information center, picnic area, camping area, and walking trails. There are small areas planted with conifers. The Estero Yerba Loca comes from the glaciers in the Cerro El Plomo massif.The turnoff into the Yerba Loca valley is near the sharp bend 8 km before arriving in Farellones. When taking the Farellones bus ask the driver to set you down there, near the CONAF camping ground. The nearest accommodation and restaurants are in Farellones or El Arrayán.

⦿ **Excursions**

• **Villa Paulina** at the end of the road is 46 km east of Santiago. It is the starting point for hikes further up the valley to the glaciers around **Cerro del Plomo** (5424 m) and **Cerro Altar** (5180 m). This is high alpine country, and temperatures are freezing at night, but the reward is seeing this magnificent wild area so close to Santiago. **Ventisquero Olivares** and **Glaciar Olivares Beta** are accessible glaciers. Beyond Villa Paulina it is the domain of the seasoned mountain hiker. Buy Instituto Geográfico Militar 1:50000 series maps for mountain hiking in this area: "La Disputada" (5-04- 05-052-00); "Cordillera de los Piuquenes" (5-04-05-053-00); "Farellones" (5-04-05-059-00); and "Río Olivares" (5-04-05-060-00). Information is also available from CONAF in Santiago (see "Tourist information" on page 389).

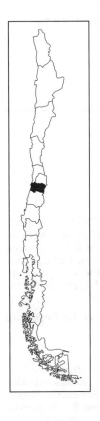

REGIÓN VI DEL LIBERTADOR GENERAL BERNARDO O'HIGGINS

Size: 17 000 square km (6562 square miles)
Population: 620 000
Regional capital: Rancagua
Provinces and provincial capitals:
- Cachapoal (Rancagua)
- Colchagua (San Fernando)
- Cardinal Caro (Pichilemu)

El Libertador General Bernardo O'Higgins is part of the Chilean heartland, which was overrun and colonized fairly early by the Spanish. Agricultural activities bear witness to the civilizing influence of the Jesuits who established a rural enterprise near Graneros. They founded a large *hacienda* where, besides teaching Christianity, they instructed the local people in land management skills. The region retains its rural charm. It is also one of the most traditional regions in Chile, home of the Chilean cowboy or *huaso*.

This region is located between latitude 33° and 35° south and on longitude 70°, and covers 2.2 per cent of Chile. It shares borders in the north with Región Metropolitana and Región VI de Valparaíso; in the east the Andes form the border with Argentina; and in the south is Región VII del Maule.

Some of the old *haciendas* are open to visitors; others have been converted into world-class hotels. There is a small ski resort at Chapa Verde, and a developing seaside resort at Pichilemu. Local buses run from Rancagua to the colonial villages of the fertile Cachapoal valley.

Transport

Road

The two-lane Panamericana highway runs through the whole region.

There is a tollgate at the Angostura tunnel.

Rail

The main rail line (from north to south) stops in San Francisco de Mostazal, Graneros, Rancagua, Requinoa, Rengo, Pelequén, San Fernando, and Chimbarongo. Train services are more frequent in summer.

Air

There are airfields at Rancagua, San Fernando, Santa Cruz, Pichilemu, Lago Rapel, Paredones, Peralillo, Peumo and La Estrella. Most of them are only suitable for small aircraft.

Topography

Most of the region lies in the coastal *cordillera*, which reaches 1400 m at its highest point, loses altitude southward, and peters out in the coastal plain to the west. The highest mountains in the Andean *cordillera* are **Cerro El Portillo** at 4980 m with a glacier, and **Volcán Tinguiririca** at 4300 m. The northern Andes reach almost 5000 m and gradually decrease in height to the south. The central valley is a fertile alluvial plain. The main rivers are **Río Cachapoal**, which flows from the **Cerro El Palomo** massif and **Río Tinguiririca**, which flows from the **volcano** of the same name.

Climate

The Mediterranean climate has eight fairly dry months and four wet ones; rain is more usual in fall and winter. Summer temperatures average around 32°C (90°F); winter temperatures can drop to 2°C (36°F), although this would be most unusual. It is generally mild all year round, becoming colder in the Andes as the altitude rises.

The indigenous inhabitants

Copequén, near the present regional capital Rancagua, was the Incan seat of government. The Incan influence stretched into the Cachapoal valley between Doñihué and Lo Miranda where they made a "population exchange" — loyal Indians from another Inca-dominated region were exchanged for the rebellious Indians of the area. The major work of the Incan "*mitimaes*" (forced settlers) was the construction and maintenance of a hanging bridge over the **Río Cachapoal**. The Spanish used this bridge to extend their influence when they came to Chile.

The local *caciques* did not lose their authority under Inca control as they did under the Spanish. The Incas left the tribal structure of the Piunches intact, superimposing an Incan leader only. The Incan *mitimaes* brought new skills from the *altiplano* to the area; traces of their techniques are still recognizable in the weaving, wood carving and pottery of local *artesanía*.

European history

Región VI del Libertador General Bernardo O'Higgins is named after the great Chilean patriot, who fought often in this territory; you will find more information about him in the introduction to this *Travel Companion*. Many battles took place here during the Wars of Liberation from 1810 to 1814.

Economy

The economy depends almost completely on mining and agriculture. Copper, gold and silver are the main minerals found, and **Mina El Teniente** is one of the largest mines in Chile. The chief agricultural products are fruit, wine, vegetables, maize, cereals, and a small amount of timber. Mineral water from the region's thermal springs is bottled commercially. Industrial output centers on electrical appliances.

Tourism

Interesting excursions may be made to Rancagua, San Fernando, and up the Río Cachapoal valley to **Reserva Nacional Río de los Cipreses**. This region has many thermal spas, some with good facilities such as Termas de Cauquenes and Termas del Flaco, which is open from January to April.

Unspoilt beaches may be found at **Pichilemu** or **Bucalemu**. There are also fairly good beaches north and south of Pichilemu and opportunities for water sports on Lago Rapel. The

Lago Rapel area is an up-and-coming tourist resort.

Local cuisine

Typical regional dishes include *cazuela de pavo* (turkey cooked in earthenware dishes) and *pastel de choclo* (sweets made from corn). *Chacolí* (made with orange juice), *chicha de uva* (made from grapes), and *el pihuelo* (toasted flour with red wine) are all worth trying. Doñihué is famous for its *aguardiente* ("fire water").

Trout fishing

The trout fishing season begins on the second Friday in November and lasts until the first Sunday in May. There is good fishing near the following towns; refer to "Sport" in the relevant town:

- Rancagua
- Termas de Cauquenes
- Rengo
- San Fernando

National parks and reserves

- Parque Nacional Las Palmas de Cocalán: 119 km south- west of Rancagua — see "Excursions" from Rancagua on page 440.
- Reserva Nacional Río de los Cipreses: 50 km east of Rancagua — see the entry for the park on page 443.

Thermal resorts

- La Leonera: 16 km north of Rancagua or 6 km south-east of Codegua — see Cadegua in "Excursions" from Rancagua on page 439.
- Termas de Cauquenes: 310 km east of Rancagua — see "Excursions" from Rancagua on page 441.
- Termas del Flaco, in the Valle Río Las Damas: 75 km east of San Fernando — see the "Excursions" from San Fernando on page 451.

Distances

From Rancagua

- Chimbarongo: 68 km south
- Curicó: 108 km south
- Doñihué: 23 km south-west
- Lago Rapel via Las Cabras: 80 km west
- La Leonera: 28 km north-east
- Linares: 220 km south
- Mina El Teniente: 53 km east
- Pichilemu: 148 km south-west
- Rengo: 30 km south
- Reserva Nacional Río de los Cipreses: 45 km south-east
- San Fernando: 54 km south
- Santiago: 86 km north
- Sewell: 53 km east
- Talca: 171 km south
- Termas de Cauquenes: 31 km south-east

From San Fernando

- Bucalemu: 119 km west
- Chimbarongo: 18 km south
- Curicó: 57 km south
- Hacienda Los Lingues: 20 km north-east
- Linares: 169 km south
- Lolol: 46 km south-east
- Marchigué: 71 km north-west
- Pichilemu: 124 km south-west
- Santa Cruz: 36 km west
- San Vicente de Tagua Tagua: 32 km north-west
- Talca: 120 km south
- Termas del Flaco: 77 km east

Major tourist attractions

Don't miss

☞ Rancagua

Worth a visit

☞ Termas de Cauquenes
☞ Termas del Flaco

Worth a detour

☞ Water mills in lower Río Cachapoal valley
☞ Lago Rapel

Of interest

☞ La Leonera
☞ Pichilemu

BUCALEMU

Area code: LD 108
Altitude: Sea level
Distance from San Fernando: 119 km west on Ruta I-72 and I-50

Bucalemu is a small seaside resort, 37 km south of Pichilemu on the Pacific coast. The trip from Pichilemu via Cahuil includes a ferry crossing. It is also possible to get there from San Fernando via Santa Cruz, Lolol, and Paredones on Rutas I-50 and 72. The road is sealed as far as Santa Cruz and dirt for 81 km after that.

▱ Accommodation
- Hotel Casablanca, Avenida Celedonio Pastene $H ⅈ. Shared bath, full board. Reservations in Santa Cruz: ℓ (72) 821620
- Hotel Rocha, Avenida Celedonio Pastene AEFGHIJLMPV $H ⅈ. English spoken, full board. Reservations in San Fernando: Negrete 315 ℓ (72) 712023
- Residencial Santa Cecilia, Avenida Celedonio Pastene 18 AEFGHIJLMNPT ℓ 881942 $I ⅈ. Full board, English spoken

▱ Buses
- Rancagua: Fare $3.90; Buses Rutamar runs 1 service daily
- Santiago: Fare $5.60; Buses Nilahué runs 1 service daily

LAGO RAPEL

Altitude: 100 m
Distances
- From Melipilla via Cruce de Araña: 74 km south on Ruta H-66-G and H-60
- From Rancagua via Pelequén: 92 km west on Ruta H-66-G and Panamericana

The **Río Cachapoal** and the **Río Tinguiririca** flowing from the Andes, and many little brooks starting in the coastal *cordillera*, feed an artificial lake in the northern part of the region. A dam, 115 m high and 360 m wide, forms the lake, which is 40 km long and covers 8000 ha (19 760 acres). The water is used for irrigation and to generate electricity.

The many bays and the favorable wind conditions make the lake suitable for water sports — yachting, water skiing and wind-surfing — although many parts cannot be accessed yet. Towards the Central Hidroeléctrica Rapel, the lake narrows.

Most of the tourist facilities — motels, camping places and summer houses — are located in the triangle formed by El Carmen, El Manzano and Punta Verde. If you have a permit, you can visit the **Parque Nacional Las Palmas de Cocalán** from El Manzano. This is one of the few places where you can still see large tracts of Chile's only native palm, *Jubaea chilensis*.

Access to Lago Rapel from Santiago is via Melipilla. Between Melipilla and El Manzano there is a 30 km stretch of dirt road. From Rancagua to Las Cabras via Doñihué, there is 42 km of dirt road.

Ⓐ Camping

Sector El Estero
There are camping sites in Sector El Estero, in Sector El Manzano and Sector El Durazno

🍽 Eating out
- Hostería Centur Rapel, Bahía Skorpio

🚌 Buses
Buses collect passengers from Las Cabras, El Manzano, and Llallauquen.

Services
- Rancagua: Fare $1.60; departs 0730–1800; 3 services daily; Buses Galgo, Sextur
- Santiago: Fare $3.50; departs Mon–Sat; Buses Jiménez via Melipilla

Ⓢ Sport
Fishing and sailing are good here.

🛏 Accommodation in Lago Rapel
The best tourist facilities are concentrated near Punta Verde. The west side of the lake near the Quebrada del Peral is gradually being opened up for tourism.

Accommodation at Bahía Skorpio

Hosterías
- ★★★ Centur Rapel   ABCEFGHIJLMNPUVX $F for 4
  Boat hire, tennis, beach frontage. Reservations in Santiago: Los Tres Antonios 2787, Macul ((02) 2086045
- Las Tinajas, Sector El Carmen de Peumo
  AEFGHPZ

Accommodation at Sector El Estero

Hosterías
- Marina Rapel   ADEFGHJLMNPTUZ   ((72) 890120 $F 👥
  English spoken. Reservations in Santiago ((02)6971288
- Hotel La Finca, Sector Llallauquen   ADEFGHPRV $H 👥
  Reservations in Santiago: ((02)2886309, fax (02)2882854
- Hotel Punta Verde Bahía Skorpios   ((09) 7516502
- Hotel Río Alhué   AEFGHIJNPV
  31 tent sites, open all year round. Electricity, water, toilets, hot showers
- Hostería y Camping Playa de Llallauquen
  AEGHIJLMNU   ((72) 343385 $G 👥
  35 tent sites, open all year round. Electricity, water, toilets, hot showers, shop, horse riding, English spoken

Excursions

- **Central Rapel**: The power generation plant, at the extreme western end of the lake, is the third largest power station in Chile. It is best reached from El Manzano via Cruce de Arañas on Ruta H-66-G and H-60.

NAVIDAD

Population: 1300
Altitude: Sea level
Distance from Rocas de Santo Domingo: 58 km south on Ruta G-80

Navidad lies to the south of the mouth of the **Río Rapel**. The best access is from Santo Domingo in the north or Melipilla in the north-east via Ruta G-60 and G-80. To get there from Santo Domingo, you cross the wide, seemingly endless, plain south of the **Río Maipo**, which contains many dunes and small *lagunas*. This is one of the least traveled parts of Chile.

Between La Boca and Caleta Matanza is a 5 km windswept stretch of beach with black sand. A "cabin" colony has been established near **Boca de Rapel** (mouth of the Río Rapel), and some of the cabins can be rented in summer.

The best beach is at **Las Brisas**, fringing a 300 m horseshoe-shaped bay. The water is very shallow and safe for swimming.

Accommodation

Accommodation in Matanzas
Matanzas is 4 km west of Navidad.
- Hotel La Bahía AEFGHIJMUVY $I ♙♙. Shared bath, full board, bilingual staff
- Hotel Pacífico AEFHPV $G ♙♙. Reservations in Santiago ((02)681639
- Residencial Don Luchito, Avenida Los Pescadores 0105 AEFGHPV

Camping

There is a municipal camping ground at Playa Mantanzas, and you can camp for free beside the Río Rapel near the river's mouth.

Buses
- Santiago: Fare $4.10; services Mon–Sat; Buses Navidad
- Rancagua: Fare $4.00; 1 service daily, leaving at 0645; Buses Sextur

Excursions
- **Lago Rapel:** 50 km east on Ruta G-80 — see the entry for Lago Rapel on page 423.
- **Hacienda Bucalemu**: On the road to Rocas de Santo Domingo. This was one of the finest foundations of the Jesuit order until their expulsion in 1767. Although it has been subdivided several times in its long history, it is still a huge *hacienda*. Now the property belongs to the Chilean Army and you can only glimpse the formidable old colonial buildings as you pass.
- **Matanzas:** 4 km south-west. This is a small but growing resort with a beach of gray sand. During the colonial period it was part of a Jesuit agricultural complex.

PICHILEMU

Area code: 072
Population: 7000
Altitude: Sea level
Distance from San Fernando: 124 km east on Ruta I-50

Pichilemu is the region's principal Pacific coast beach resort, and capital of Cardinal Caro province. The neighboring gray sand beaches are popular with tourists in the summer, and surfing championships are held at beaches in the south. Horses and buggies (*cabritas*) are used to pick up tourists from the bus terminals and to drive them around the town and beaches; there are no cabs in this town. The best conditions for surfing are at Punta de Lobos, 6 km south of town. As the name suggests, seals and sea lions gather on the rocks near the beach and can be easily observed. Playa Principal to the north extends for several kilometers and Playa Infiernillo extends south of town.

The town has good tourist facilities, although the setting is a bit rustic. Pichilemu's first hotel was estab- lished by Agustín Ross in 1885. The first casino in Chile was installed in the Hotel Ross in 1908. During the

---

Key to map

A	Iglesia (Church)	29	Residencial Victoria
C	Municipalidad (Town hall)	32	Hotel España
D	Post office and telex	33	Cabañas Hecmar
E	Telephone	34	Residencial Mi Rancho
H	Hospital	35	Residencial Diego Portales
I	Tourist information	36	Residencial Tajamar
P	Gas stations	37	Residencial Lucia
T	Bus terminals	39	Residencial Oróstica
		40	Residencial Belmar
●	**Accommodation**	41	Hotel Central
1	Hostería Paldoa	42	Hotel San Fernando
3	Cabañas El Mirador	43	Hotel Asthur
4	Hotel Terraza	44	Residencial Los Elena
5	Motel Terraza	45	Hotel O'Higgins
7	Hotel Ross		
8	Cabañas El Bosquecito	○	**Eating out**
9	Hostería Kitt	2	Restaurant Paldoa
10	Motel Lircan Ray	15	Restaurant Dónde Pin Pon
12	Hotel Pacífico	16	Restaurant The Fox and Vivian
13	Residencial Quenita	22	Restaurant La Ventana
14	Residencial Cecilia	27	Restaurant Los Colchaguinos
17	Hotel Rex	30	Restaurant Gigi
18	Hotel Nuevo Savoy	31	Restaurant Bristol
19	Residencial Las Salinas	46	Restaurant La Gloria
20	Hotel Pintana		
21	Hotel Chile España	◉	**Entertainment**
23	Motel Las Cabañas	6	Disco Sana
24	Camping Infiernillo		
25	Cabañas Santa Irene	■	**Sights**
26	Residencial Galaz	11	Palacio Ross
28	Hotel Rothwald	38	Iglesia

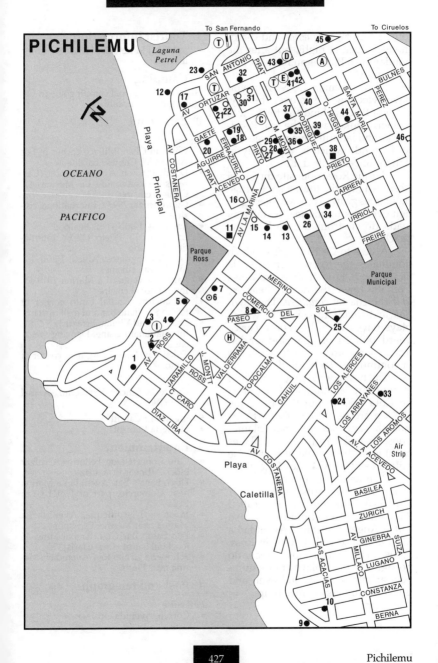

PICHILEMU

To San Fernando

To Ciruelos

Laguna Petrel

OCEANO

PACIFICO

Playa Principal

Parque Ross

Parque Municipal

Air Strip

Playa

Caletilla

Pichilemu

tourist season, *tanguerías* and disco-theques open at night, but after the holiday rush Pichilemu relapses into tranquility.

From Avenida La Marina you have sweeping views over the bay. Laguna Bajel, behind the town, was formerly linked with the sea. Road-works and landfill have reduced this to a "pond" which is apparently in danger of being filled in.

Parque Ross, opposite the Hotel Ross, is a favorite tourist spot. Huge palm trees grow in this well-kept garden overlooking the sea. A stairway leads down from the park to the beach.

Access to Cerro la Cruz, which ☞ dominates the town, is from Calle Santa María. From it, there are views ☞ over the town, the nearby beaches, and the coastal *cordillera*. The town has a difficult topography which plays havoc with the typical chess-board pattern of Spanish-founded towns: some streets finish in hollows or continue as stairs uphill.

The best approach to Pichilemu is from San Fernando via Marchihué on Ruta I-50. About 93 km of the 124 km are sealed and the last part runs through extensive pine planta-tions. The airstrip (for small planes only) is in the middle of town. The railroad station is a relic of the past.

Pichilemu's street names and ☞ numbers are confusing. For your guidance: Chacabuco is also called Acevedo; Independencia is also called Angel Gaete; and Avenida La Marina is also called Agustín Ross. House numbers in most streets do not agree with displayed block num-bers at intersections, and even and uneven numbers are mixed up.

ⓘ Tourist information
• SERNAP, J.J.Prieto 404 ℂ 681088. Fishing licenses

Ⓐ Camping
There is a municipal camping site in Ca-huil about 13 km south.

ⓝ Eating out

Restaurants
• Chilolan Chen, Millaco corner of Los Alerces $Y. Chinese cuisine
• Dónde Pin Pon, Agustín Ross 96 (Car-reras near Avenida La Marina) $Z. Chilean cuisine
• Gigi, Ortúzar 289 $X. International cui-sine
• Las Tejas, Pinto 41 $Z. Seafood
• La Gloria, J.J. Prieto 432 $Y. Interna-tional cuisine
• Los Colchaguinos, Aníbal Pinto 130 $Y. Chilean cuisine
• Paldoa, Avenida La Marina 1019 $Y. International cuisine
• Tabancura, Aníbal Pinto corner of Prieto $Y. Piano bar and grill upstairs
• The Fox and Vivian, Errázuriz 397 $Y. International cuisine. Dancing week-ends
• Tukai Bar, Joaquín Aguirre corner of Pinto $Z

Cafetería
• Cafetería Rincón Pichilemu, Aníbal Pinto Block 200

Eating out in Cahuil
• Hostería Marisol

ⓣ Entertainment
• Café Concert Don Federico, Ortúzar block 201 near Errázuriz
• Disco Sana's Bar, Avenida La Marina near Comercio, part of Hotel Gran Ross
• Master's Discotheque, Avenida La Marina near Merino. Old house
• Pub Salón Bar Gigi, Aníbal Pinto 45 (cocktail bar of Hotel Claris)
• Schopería La Naranja, Avenida la Ma-rina near Pinto

ⓔ Post and telegraph

Post office
• Correo, Avenida Ortúzar

✉ Accommodation in Pichilemu

Cabañas
- Ayún, Avenida Concepción   ☏ 841515 $G for 4
  Fax 841298
- Hecmar, Comercio 614 $G for 4
- El Mirador, Ave. Costanera 778   ☏ 81113 $F for 6
- El Bosquecito, Jaramillo 675   APS   ☏ 841075 $I   ⚏
- Santa Irene, Paseo del Sol 415   ☏ 841039 $F for 4
  Fax 841044
- Waitara, Cardenal Caro 1039   ABP $H for 4

Complejo turístico
★★★ Las Terrazas, Avenida La Marina 201, Población Ross
ADEGHIJKLMNPRUX   ☏ 841049 / 841588 $G for 4
Full board, central heating, beach frontage, medicinal baths, English spoken, heated swimming pool with sea water (small admission)

Hotels
☞ ★★ Asthur, Avenida Ortúzar 540   AEFGHIJKLMNPSTUV   ☏ 841072 $H ⚏⚏
  English spoken
- Central, Avenida Ortúzar 448   AEFGHJPSV   ☏ 841066
  English spoken
- Chile España, Ortúzar 255   PS   ☏ 841270 $H   ⚏
  Fax 841298, budget travelers
- City, Avenida Ortúzar 125   AEFGHLPV   ☏ 681031 $G ⚏⚏
- España, Avenida Ortúzar 138   ADEFGHIJKLMPTUV $H   ⚏
  English spoken
- O'Higgins, Ortúzar 210   AEFGHIJLMPTUV   ☏ 841099 $H ⚏⚏
- Pintana, Angel Gaete 15   AFGHJPV   ☏ 681000 $H ⚏⚏
- Rex, Avenida Ortúzar 124   AEFGHIJLMPT   ☏ 841003 $H   ⚏
  Central heating, English spoken
- Ross, Agustín Ross 130   ADEFGHIJKLMNP$TUV   ☏ 841038 $H   ⚏
  English spoken, fax 841010
- Rothwald, Dionisio Acevedo 124   ☏ 841057 $H   ⚏
- Terraza, Playa Principal   AGHJPU $H   ⚏
  Shared bathoom cheaper

Hosterías
- Kitt, Avenida Costanera 878

Motels
★★★ Las Cabañas, San Antonio 48   ADEGHIJKLMPRSUX   ☏ 841068 $F ⚏⚏
22 cabins, central heating, English spoken, overlooks Laguna Petrel
- Lircan Ray, Avenida Costanera1190   APS $G for 4

Residenciales
★ San Luis, Angel Gaete 237   AEFGHJLPSV   ☏ 841040 $H   ⚏
- Antumalal, Joaquín Aguirre 64   AEFGHIJKLMPUV   ☏ 841004 $H   ⚏
- Claris, Aníbal Pinto 47   AFGHLPV   ☏ 81050
- Comercio, Primer Centenario 31   AEFGHIJKLMPUZ   ☏841606 $I   ⚏
  14 rooms
- Diego Portales, D. Acevedo 188   AFGJLPV   ☏ 681089 $H ⚏⚏
- Galaz, Carrera 319 between M. Montt and Pinto
  AEGHJLP   ☏ 841025 $H   ⚏
  Full board, English spoken
- González, Aníbal Pinto 96   AEGHIJLMUV   ☏ 841087 / 841675 $I   ⚏

Accommodation in Pichilemu — continued

- Las Salinas, Avenida Aníbal Pinto 51   AFGHIJLMPUV   (841071 $H i
  Full board
- María Rosa, Avenida Aníbal Pinto 139
                                          AEPV   (841086 $H ii
- Mi Rancho, Los Carrera 177 between Rodríguez and M. Montt
- Montecarlo, Avenida Aníbal Pinto 234
                                          AEGHIJLMPSV   (841027 $H ii
- Oróstica, Dionisio Acevedo 520 corner of Rodríguez
                                          AEGJPV   (841337 $I i
  Full board, shared bathroom
- Quinteros, Avenida Ortúzar 673 corner Manuel Montt 27
                                          AEGJLPV   (841027/841338 $H i
  Full board, shared bathroom
- Tajamar, M. Montt 250 corner of J. Aguirre
                                          AFGHLMUVZ   (841063 $H ii
  Beach frontage
- Victoria, J. Aguirre 139   AFGHL   (841021 $H ii
  Shared bathroom, full board

Accommodation in Cahuil

Cahuil is 13 km south of Pichilemu — see under "Excursions" below.
- Pensión Santa Raquel
- Residencial El Sol $H i
  Shared bathroom, full board

🚌 Buses from Pichilemu

There is a central bus terminal in the lower section of town next to the old rail station, but all buses depart from the company offices on Ortúzar, calling at the terminal on the way out. So board and buy your ticket in Ortúzar if you want a seat.

Companies
- B23   Buses Andimar
- B46   Buses Colchagua, Avenida Ortúzar near Montt
- B72   Buses Galgo
- B116 Buses Nilahué, Avenida Ortúzar near Montt
- B153 Buses Ruta Mar, Avenida Ortúzar 147
- B157 Buses Sextur, Avenida Ortúzar near A. Prat

Services

Destination	Fare	Services	Duration	Companies
Lago Rapel	$2.80	1 service daily		B72, B153, B157
Marchihué		4 services daily		B157
Melipilla	$4.00	1 service daily		B153
Rancagua	$4.00	15 services daily		B23, B46, B72, B116, B157
San Fernando	$2.60	18 services daily	2½ hrs	B23, B116
Santa Cruz	$1.50	19 services daily		B23, B116
Santiago	$5.00	1 services daily	5 hrs	B23, B153, B116
San Vicente de Tagua Tagua				B72

Telephone
- CTC, Avenida Ortúzar 187
- Telex Chile, Avenida Ortúzar near O'Higgins

🖂 Services and facilities
- Gringo's International Surfboards, Avenida Ortúzar block 201 near Pinto

⊛ Sport

In recent years, the beaches of Pichilemu have attracted a growing number of surfers. Surrounded by rocks, they are small and very secluded. Playa Hermosa and Playa Infiernillo, to the south of town, are good for swimming and fishing. Surfing championships are held there.

📷 Sightseeing
- Parque Ross, with its century-old palm trees, overlooks the waterfront. It belonged to one of the founding families. The architecture of many older houses resembles Mediterranean styles, adopted by the founders of this seaside resort in the 19th century.

⊕ Excursions
- **Punta Lobos**: 6 km south. The waves are suitable for surfing and there is a good restaurant, open in summer.

- **Cahuil**: 13 km south at the mouth of **Estero Nilahué**. On the way you pass the freshwater **Laguna del Perro**, offering good *pejerrey* fishing and wind surfing. The free ferry across Estero Nilahué operates between 0830 and 2030. The villagers fish and work the salt flats along the coast. Cahuil is a small, picturesque fishing village, which attracts many tourists in summer. This is the site of a pre-Colombian Indian settlement, and the extraction of salt from **Laguna Cahuil** was already well developed then. Seawater is let into dykes and left to evaporate, which takes about four months, and the salt crystals are harvested at the end of January. The beaches, which are completely unspoilt and not overrun by tourists, are very attractive for a quiet rest. The low hills are mostly covered by pine trees. The surf is good enough for the national surf championships. There is a disco at weekends in summer. The village of **Ciruelos** further inland has an old church. Buses Nilahué runs 1 service daily to Rancagua (fare $3.60), and 1 service daily to Santiago.
- **Bucalemu:** 37 km south. See the entry for Bucalemu on page 423.

RANCAGUA

Area code: 072
Population: 180 000
Altitude: 200 m
Distance from Santiago: 86 km south on Panamericana

This historic center is laid out in the familiar Spanish colonial eight-by-eight *manzanas* (block) pattern. Located in the fertile central valley, where there is barely 30 km between the coastal *cordillera* and the Andes, Rancagua is the capital of Region VI del Libertador General Bernardo O'Higgins. The last known Picunche Chief Guaglen "voluntarily" surrendered his authority to the Spanish in 1743 to permit the foundation of Rancagua. Its first name was Villa Santa Cruz de Triana, during the reign of Viceroy José Antonio Manso de Velasco.

The town was repeatedly subjected to heavy fighting between the Chilean Independence Army and the Spanish Royalist Army. At the battle of Rancagua on October 1–2, 1814, the Spanish troops defeated the Chilean Liberation Army. The Iglesia de la Merced was the headquarters of General Bernardo O'Higgins, and the present-day Casa de la Cultura was the headquarters of the Spanish forces under the command of Don Mariano Osorio. Most of the townspeople who fought against the Spaniards were killed. Many houses survive from the colonial era or are built in the same style.

Rancagua is full of history. Germán Riesco, who was Chilean President from 1901 to 1906 came from Rancagua. A plaque identifies the house where he was born on Calle Presidente Germán Riesco. Padre Camillo Henriquez, the founder of Chile's oldest newspaper *La Aurora* in 1812, has a plaza named in his honor. The monument in the Plaza de los Héroes depicts the War of Independence in 1814. Number 498 Estado has a historical plaque commemorating the "Southern Trench" used during the trench warfare.

Some houses have triangular corner entrances with a wooden or stone column at the corner, forming a little porch, features peculiar to colonial houses. They are found especially in Calle Mujica, and on Estado corner of Ibieta. A colonaded house, worthy of note, stands in Estado block 700, between Ibieta and Alcázar. Avenida Independencia is a pedestrian mall between San Martín and Bueras.

The central valley around Rancagua is a rich farming area and has been tilled by Spanish landholders since the conquest: vineyards, avocado, and citrus plantations alternate with corn and wheat fields. Some of the old estates go back to the foundation of the colony.

Although steeped in tradition and the center of a rich agricultural area, Rancagua also serves the nearby mining industry at **Sewell** and **Coya** — both are described under "Excursions" below.

Local cuisine is a strong point — *cazuelas de ave* (poultry), *cerdo* (pork), and *pato* (duck) is a sort of stew, where you eat the soup first and then the pieces of meat with the potatoes. Also try *chacolí*, a local liqueur made from orange juice, grape juice, wine, and brandy.

Snow-capped mountains are clearly visible from town. Here, the Andes, to the east, form one of the highest sections of the whole range and are fairly close to the town.

Rancagua is the ideal starting point to explore the countryside towards the Pacific Ocean, as well as the nearby valleys of the *cordillera*. The thermal resorts of **La Leonera** and **Termas de Cauquenes** are also very close. Pre-Hispanic tribes knew about the medicinal properties of thermal water and used them as health spas — they called them "miracle waters".

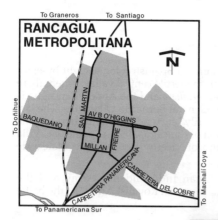

❄ Festivals

- March: Annual horse riding championship in the showground. This is a typical Chilean *fiesta* with dancing and singing and should not be missed

ℹ Tourist information

- Sernatur, Germán Riesco 277, office 11/12 (225777)
- CONAF, Cuevas 480 (222272

‼ Eating out

Restaurants
- Bavaria, San Martín 255 $Y. International cuisine
- Casas Viejas, Rubio 216$Y. Chilean cuisine
- Chimenea, O'Carrol corner of San Martín
- El Churrasco, San Martín block 400
- Electra, Alcázar 324 $Y
- El Solar de Don Pancho, Sargento Cuevas 649 $Y. Chilean cuisine
- Geo Algas, Independencia 677. Vegetarian cuisine
- Giovanni, Membrillar 230 $Y. Seafood and Italian cuisine
  Dancing weekends
- Guy, Astorga 319 $Y. French cuisine
- La Caleta del Rey, Estado 285 $Y
- La Cocina Artesanal, O'Carrol 60
- La Tavola, Sargento Cuevas 621 $Y
- McDonalds, Independencia 477 $Z. Hamburgers
- Perla Oriental, Sargento Cuevas 740 $Y. Chinese cuisine
- Rancho Chileno, Astorga 166 $Z
- Reina Victoria, Independencia 665 near Astorga $Y
- Roger's Place, G. Riesco 326. International cuisine; dancing
- San Javier, Calvo 493
- Sciro Bar, Edificio Plaza Oriente local 309 $Y. International cuisine

Cafeterías
- Astorga, Libertador Bernardo O'Higgins block 500
- Haití, Independencia 690, upstairs
- Serena, Independencia near Plaza Los Héroes

Pizzerías
- Non Troppo, Bueras 364 $Y
- Don Ostión, O'Carroll 582 $Y
- Rex, Astorga 352 $Z

Salón de Té
- Mini-Max, Independencia 483

Takeaways
- Fuente Alemana, Germán Riesco 2

Eating out along the Panamericana

Restaurants
- El Rancho, Longitudinal Sur 2615 $Y
- Kim Lung, Longitudinal Sur 146 (KM84) $Y. Chinese cuisine
- Munich, Longitudinal Sur 2855 $Y. German cuisine
- Pierot, Longitudinal Sur 2489

Parrilladas
- Lizana, Longitudinal 0585 $Y

Eating out in Doñihué
Doñihué is 23 km south-west of Rancagua on Ruta H-30.
- Restaurant Río Loco, California 56

⊤ Entertainment

Discos
- Chimenea, San Martín 489, Fri and Sat dancing
- Parilla Broadway, Longitudinal Sur 2499
- Disco Le Club, Longitudinal Sur 2499

▦ Post and telegraph

Post office
- Correos de Chile, Manuel Campos 322

Telephone
- CTC, San Martín 440, fax 233557
- ENTEL Chile, O'Carrol 1030
- Telex Chile, Bueras 323-A

$ Finance

- Fincard, Campos 376 (223321

▤ Services and facilities

Fishing and camping gear
- Caza y Pesca Colonial, O'Carrol 821

Laundromats and drycleaners
- Lavandería Status, Avenida Brazil 1030-B
- Lavaseco Moderno, O'Carrol 528

Photographic supplies
- Nort Sur Agfacolor, Avenida Independencia block 500 near Astorga

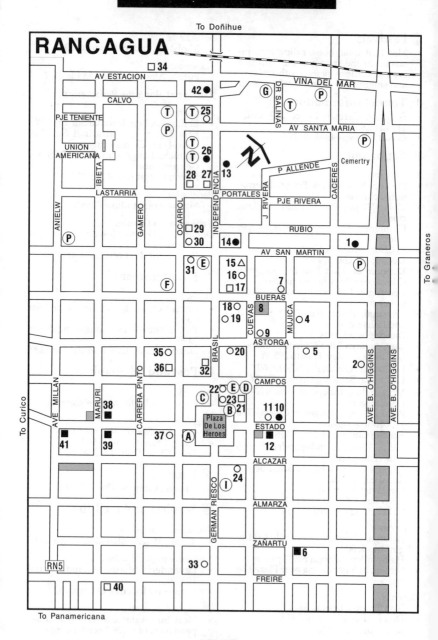

Key to map

A	Catedral	22	Restaurant Mini
B	Gobernación Provincial (Government)	23	Cafetería Serena
		24	Restaurant Electra
C	Municipalidad (Town hall)	25	Salón de Té
D	Post office and telex	30	Restaurant Chimenea
E	Telephone	31	Restaurant El Churrasco
F	Carabineros (Police)	33	Fuente Alemana
G	Mercado Municipal (Market)	35	Pizzería Don Ostión
H	Hospital	37	Club Rancagua
I	Tourist information	△	**Airline offices**
P	Gas stations	15	LAN Chile
T	Bus terminals		
●	**Accommodation**	■	**Sights**
1	Hotel Rancagua	6	Old house
10	Hotel Camino del Rey	8	Plaza Camillo Henriquez
13	Hotel Aguila Real	12	Iglesia and Convento La Merced
14	Hotel España	38	Museo Histórico
26	Hotel Turismo Santiago	39	Casa Del Pilar
42	Residencial Colón	41	Iglesia (Church)
○	**Eating out**	□	**Services**
2	Cafetería Astorga	17	Telex Chile
4	Restaurant El Solar de Don Pancho	21	CONAF
5	Restaurant Rancho Chileno	27	Lavandería Status
7	Restaurant Bavaria	28	Supermercado Las Palmas
9	Restaurant La Tavola	29	Caza y Pesca Colonial
11	Restaurant La Caleta	32	Fotos Nort-Sur
16	Restaurant Perla Oriental	34	Railroad station
18	Pizzería Non Troppo	36	Lavaseco Moderno
19	Restaurant Reina Victoria	40	Automóvil Club
20	Pizzería Rex		

Supermarket
• Supermercado Las Palmas, O'Carrol block 900. Big

© Clubs

• Club Rancagua, O'Carroll 334

✈ Air services

• LAN Chile, Sargento Cuevas 780 ℂ22641

🚗 Motoring

• Automóvil Club de Chile, Cuevas 776, offices B and F ℂ24192

🏬 Shopping

The main shopping street is Independencia. Most of the *artesanías* sold are made in the Camarico section of the town.

Shopping in Doñihué

Scarves and other woven items, and semi-precious stones are for sale at Rinconada de Doñihué, on the banks of the Río Cachapoal, just before arriving at Doñihué.

⚽ Sport

There is trout fishing in Río Cachapoal, Río Coya, and Río Pangal.

📷 Sightseeing

The Plaza de los Héroes is the best starting point for a stroll through the town center. It contains the Intendencia Regional (government house) built in 1930, the post office separated from the town hall by Calle Independencia, and the cathedral. Iglesia La Merced is one block north of the plaza on the corner of Cuevas and Estado Streets. The Museo de Rancagua is three blocks south of the Plaza on the corner of Estado and Ibieta Streets. Casa del Pilar de Esquina lies opposite it.
• Casa de la Cultura, Avenida Cachapoal, corner of Millán. This

▣ Accommodation in Rancagua

Hotels

★★★★Camino del Rey, Estado 275   ACDEFGHIJKLM   ☎ 239765 $F ⚌
    Fax 232314

★★★★Turismo Santiago, Avenida Brasil 1036
                       ADEFGHIJLP$ ☎ 230855 $F ⚌
    Central heating, fax 230822

★★★Aguila Real, Avenida Brasil 1045
                       ADEFHIJKLP   ☎ 230815 $G ⚌
    Central heating, fax 223002

  ★★Rancagua, Avenida San Martín 85   ADEFGHIJKLPU   ☎ 232663 $F ⚊
    Central heating
  ● España, Avenida San Martín 367   AEFGHIJLTV   ☎ 230141 $H ⚌
    Shared bathroom, budget travelers, 23 rooms

Residenciales
  ● Colón, Avenida Brasil 1214 $J ⚌
    Shared bathroom, backpackers

Accommodation along the Panamericana
  ● Moteles Carezu, KM 88   ☎ 254022

Accommodation on the road to La Cruz

Motels
  ● Cabañas Izcaragua, Camino La Cruz 1170   ☎ 252223
  ● Nevada, Camino La Cruz 1691   ☎ 233509
  ● Reno, Camino La Cruz 1645   ☎ 252587

Accommodation in Graneros
Graneros is located 10 km north of Rancagua on Ruta H-10.
  ● Motel Kilometer 75, on the Panamericana east

Accommodation in Coya
Coya is located 25 km east of Rancagua.
  ● Club de Campo Coya, Carretera Presidente Frei   ☎ 297837 $F ⚌
    Fax 297233

Accommodation at La Leonera
La Leonera is located 18 km north east of Rancagua.
  ● Hotel La Leonera   ADEFGHIJKLMNPR$TUZ $D ⚌
    Full board, central heating, bilingual staff, tennis, thermal pool, sauna. Reservations in
    Santiago: Huerfanos 1055, office 509 ☎ (02) 6958209

Accommodation in San Francisco de Mostazal
San Francisco de Mostazal is located 21 km north of Rancagua, on the Panamericana.
  ● Cabañas Turismo La Chimenea, Panamericana KM 57
                    AFRUX.

Accommodation in Termas de Cauquenes
Termas de Cauquenes is located 26 km east of Rancagua.
  ● Hotel Termas de Cauquenes, Hacienda Cauquenes
               ADEFGHIJKLMNPR$TUVX
                             ☎ 297226 $D ⚌
    Full board, golf course, sauna, thermal pool, English spoken. Reservations in Rancagua:
    ☎ 297226

🚌 Buses from Rancagua

Companies departing from the rural bus terminal
Rural buses run from Mercado Municipal Rancagua, on the corner of Avenida Viña del Mar and Avenida Brazil.
- B9   Bus Oriente Norte Andén 5
- B23   Buses Andimar, Dr Salinas near rural bus terminal ℂ 237818
- B44   Buses Coinco, Andén 8 & 11 ℂ 232905
- B46   Buses Colchagua
- B72   Buses Galgo, Andén 3/4 ℂ 223283
- B93   Buses Red Norte, Andén 4
- B102 Buses Machalí–Rancagua, Andén 12
- B116 Buses Nilahué, Andén 22 ℂ 642762
- B153 Buses Rutamar, Andén 22 ℂ 222566
- B157 Buses Sextur, Andén 7 ℂ 231342
- B221 Buses KMG, Andén 13
- B222 Microbus Termas de Cauquenes, Andén 8
- B271 Buses Viatur, Andén 23 ℂ 642763

Companies departing from Terminal de Buses Sur
The Terminal de Buses Sur for long-distance buses is on O'Carrol block 900.
- A48   Buses Lit
- B81   Buses Igi Llaima
- B237 Buses Pullman Sur
- B250 Buses Transbus
- B271 Buses Viatur

Companies with own terminals
- A153 Tur-Bus Jedimar, O'Carrol Block 900 corner of Calvo (same block as bus terminal) ℂ 241117
- B195 Buses Al Sur, O'Carrol 1039 (opposite the Sur bus terminal) ℂ 230340
- B250 Buses Transbus, O'Carrol 1034 (opposite the Sur bus terminal) ℂ 230826

Services
Services coded ^R depart from the rural terminal.

Destination	Fare	Services	Duration	Companies
Bucalemu^R	$3.90	2 services daily		B153
Cauquenes	$7.20			A48, A153
Chapa Verde^R		daily		Servicentro Gazpal
Runs during the skiing season only				
Chillán	$8.25	10 services daily	5½ hrs	A48, A153
Concepción	$12.50	2 services daily		B250, B271
Codegua^R	$0.50	12 services daily		B93
Coltauco^R	$1.20	every 10 minutes		B157
Coya^R	$0.70	13 services daily		B102, B221
Curicó	$3.10	8 services daily	2½ hrs	A153
Doñihué^R	$1.00	every 10 minutes		B157
Graneros^R	$0.50	12 services daily		B93
Lago Rapel^R	$1.60	5–6 services daily		B72, B157
La Leonera^R	$0.60	6 services daily		B9
Las Cabras^R	$1.70	8 services daily		B72, B157
Los Angeles	$12.00	10 services daily	7 hrs	A153, B271
Machalí^R	$0.50	10 services daily		B102
Osorno	$18.40	2 services daily		A48, A153, B81, B271
Peumo^R	$1.10	4 services daily		B72

Rancagua

Buses from Rancagua — continued

Destination	Fare	Services	Duration	Companies
• Pichilemu[R]	$3.30	15 services daily		B23, B46, B72, B157
• Pucón	$15.00	2 services daily		A48, A153,
• Puerto Montt	$21.00	2 services daily		A153, B81
• Puerto Varas	$21.00	2 services daily		B81, A153
• Quinta de Tilcoco	$1.30	every ½ hour		B72
• Rengo[R]	$1.00	every 20 minutes		B72
• San Fernando	$1.10	every 20 minutes	1½ hrs	B72
• Santa Inés (via Rapel)[R]	$2.10	5–6 services daily		B72, B157
• Santiago	$2.30	40 services daily	1½ hrs	A48, A153, B23, B195, B250
• San Vicente de Tagua Tagua[R]	$1.00	every 20 minutes		B72
• Talca	$4.00	10 services daily	3 hrs	A48, A153, B250
• Talcahuano	$12.50	2 services daily		A48, A153, B271
• Temuco	$14.30	5 services daily		A48, B271
• Termas de Cauquenes	$0.90	3 services daily		B122
• Valdivia	$16.30	5 services daily		A48, A153, B271
• Valparaíso	$5.00	2 services daily		A48, A153, B237
• Villarrica	$15.00	2 services daily		A48, A153
• Viña del Mar	$5.00	2 services daily		A48, A153

house was the headquarters of the Royalist General Don Mariano Osorio in 1814. It is now used for exhibitions of paintings and photographs.

- Casa del Pilar de Piedra, Estado corner of Ibieta. This house was built towards the end of the 18th century. One of the owners was Don Fernando Errázuriz Aldunate, who was deputy for the Rancagua region at the first national congress in 1811.
- Iglesia Catedral, on the Plaza de los Héroes. This was the site of a bloody battle in 1814. The original church was built in 1775 but it was rebuilt in 1861 by the Italian architect Eusebio Celli according to plans drawn up by the architect Herbage, who also built churches in La Serena and Concepción.
- Iglesia La Merced, on the corner of Estados and Sargento Cuevas. This building was completed in 1758 and forms part of the Convento de Mercedario de San Ramón Nonato de Santa Cruz de Triana. It was used in 1814 during the War of Independence as the headquarters of the Inde-

pendence Army. Now a national monument, a plaque tells how on October 1 and 2, 1814, the *Trinchera Norte* (northern trenches) were commanded on the patriots' side by Don Santiago Sánchez. The Chilean patriot, Coronel Cuevas, commander of the defence forces of Rancagua, was shot by Royalist forces in front of the Iglesia de la Merced.

- Museo Histórico Regional, corner of Estado and Ibieta. One room is furnished in the same style as a Rancaguan house during the 19th century and contains memorabilia belonging to General Bernardo O'Higgins. In another room are religious objects. The house itself is a typical Chilean adobe house, a style adopted by the Spanish from the earliest times of the colonization and still the predominant architectural style found in Chile. Open Tues–Fri 0900–1230 and 1430–1830; Sat, Sun and holidays 0900–1300.
- Plaza de los Heroes. This remains the same as it was when the town was founded in 1743. It was here that in 1814 the defenders of the town made

Trains from Rancagua

The station is on Avenida Estación near O'Carrol.

Destination	Salón	Económico	Services
• Concepción	$13.75	$9.70	3 services daily
• Chillán		$8.00	3 service daily
• Puerto Montt		$14.00	2 services daily
• Santiago			5 services daily
• Talca	$7.20	$5.00	4 services daily
• Temuco	$16.70	$12.10	2 services daily

their last stand against the troops of the Royalist commander, General Don Mariano Osorio.

Excursions

There are day excursions west into the densely populated **Río Cachapoal valley** passing through small settlements. Viña Santa Monica, a famous vineyard producing a well-established brand name, 6 km west, can be visited Mon–Fri. Day trips usually include Doñihué — see the trip to Doñihué below.

• **Chapa Verde** is a newly developed ski resort some 60 km east at 2060 m. At the moment it is just a mountain chalet with a *cafetería*, skiing equipment hire, and one ski lift. The slopes are suitable for both beginners and advanced skiers. For information in Rancagua contact the caretaker at Mujica (212603 between 1900 and 2100, fax (72) 294255. They will advise you of the bus schedules and where the buses depart from. Access by private vehicles is restricted, as the road belongs to CODELCO.

• **Coya**: 19 km east, in the **Río Cachapoal valley** in the *pre-Cordillera*, not far from Termas de Cauquenes.

• **Codegua:** A pretty spot in the *pre-Cordillera*, 18 km north-west on Ruta H-15 at 530 m, with 5200 inhabitants. Its name, derived from the Indian language, combined with the irregular layout of the village, suggests pre-Colombian settlement. Codegua belonged to the Jesuits until they were expelled in 1767. The first secular owner was Doña Catalina de los Rios y Lisperguer, known as *La Quintrala* — *quintrala* is Chilean mistletoe, and alludes to the fact that the lady be-

stowed her considerable favors rather freely on several of the Spanish Viceroys. The main attraction is **La Leonera**, 10 km east of Codegua; a thermal complex (the Hotel La Leonera) has been built on the site of the old Jesuit mission. It has saunas, a thermal swimming pool, tennis courts, and a mini-golf course, and the water temperature is 25–30°C (77–86°F). Open all year round, the water is reputed to benefit the respiratory, cardiovascular, arterial, nervous, and digestive systems; as well as being helpful during convalescence; and in the treatment of skin complaints, diabetes, sleeplessness, mental fatigue and stress, anaemia, allergies, neuralgia, neuritis, and obesity. Horses can be hired from the locals by arrangement. The hotel, located on property that was formerly part of a copper and silver mine, is 9 km east of the Panamericana, opposite the turnoff to Graneros, or along the Spanish colonial highway. At **Las Marcas**, 7 km from Codegua, the hot springs are in their natural state. Buses Oriente Norte run regular buses to Codegua and La Leonera from the Mercado Municipal in Rancagua.

• **Coinco**: 25 km west. This settlement of approximately 2700 inhabitants lies in the Río Cachapoal valley. It has retained a perfect colonial character. Buses Sextur runs regular daily services.

• **Doñihué**: 23 km south-west on Ruta H-30. A small village of pre-Hispanic origin, at an altitude of 340 m and with a population of 6700, it clings to the slopes of the **Río Cachapoal** valley. The houses are set widely apart between cultivated fields. Doñihué is famous for colorful scarves and blankets produced by weavers known as *chamanteras*. This weaving tradition is closely linked with the *huaso* tradition — a *chamanta* is a garment worn by *huasos*. The area between Rancagua and Coltauco, which includes Doñihué, is known for its colorful *huaso* traditions and festivals. The garden of the Escuela Agrícola (an Agricultural College in an old *hacienda*) at Quimávida, 4 km north, may be of interest to botanists. Buses Sextur and Taxi-Tur run regular daily services between Rancagua and Doñihué.

- **Graneros**: A small town 11 km north, with 15 000 inhabitants, at an altitude of 300 m. It was originally a country estate established after the Spanish conquest. From 1595 until their expulsion in 1767 the Jesuits owned it, and eventually held 120 000 ha (296 400 acres) of land. It was one of the major Jesuit religious-cum-agricultural enterprises and a success story in its own right. The name "*graneros*" dates from the times when wheat was stored in huge granaries. The town center is near the railroad station, and the streets are laid out round it in the usual chess-board pattern. The chapel was built in 1858. A large paper factory and a chocolate factory are the town's principal industry. The coastal *cordillera* and the Andes are very close here and enclose a narrow central valley. The Jesuits started a large canal and irrigation system, which made this part of the valley extremely fertile. In November the annual *cueca* competition is held here (the *cueca* is a traditional Chilean national dance). The main reason for coming to Graneros is **Parque de la Hacienda Callejones,** located a short distance off the Panamericana at KM 64, 12 km north of Rancagua. This old *hacienda* has an enormous landscaped garden which may be visited. During colonial times and in the early years of the Chilean republic, landholders lived a life of splendor on their estates. They converted large areas around their *haciendas* into beautiful gardens, sparing no expense in pursuit of this goal. Many 19th-century European landscape gardeners and architects had a guiding hand in designing the gardens, and Parque de La Hacienda Callejones is one such example. Buses Red Norte run frequent daily buses to Graneros and Parque de la Hacienda Callejones.

- **Machalí**: 7 km east, in a very fertile area in the first spurs of the *pre-Cordillera* with **Cerro Machalí** (1536 m) to the north. It is at an altitude of 550 m, and has 17 000 inhabitants. The fact that the town is not laid out in the usual Spanish chess-board pattern suggests pre-Hispanic origin. The usual plaza with huge trees forms the center and focal point of the town. Some historical buildings have been declared *monumentos nacionales*. The best views over the town are from Cerro San Juan — take the Calle Tarapacá. Much of its wealth comes from **Mina El Teniente**, where many of the townsfolk are employed. The scenic road with lookouts over the valley leading to the Mina El Teniente is known as La Carretera del Cobre (Copper Highway). Near Coya, the **Río Cachapoal** runs through a fairly narrow, deep gorge. The main attraction, however, is *hacienda* La Sanchina, complete with chapel, at the entrance to the town on the approach from Rancagua, which is open to the public. Buses KMG run regular daily services departing from Mercado Central.

- **Parque Nacional Las Palmas de Cocalán**, 3709 ha (9161 acres): 119 km south-west. Although classified as a *parque nacional*, this large area covered with the native Chilean palm (*Jubaea chilensis*) forms part of a private estate, which is only open to people interested in this plant species. Take RN 5 (Panamericana south) until Pelequén, turning west into Ruta H-66-G until you reach **Las Cabras**. A 10-kilometer dirt road leads from Las Cabras north over the **Cuesta Quilicura** with picturesque views down to Las Cabras. At the "Y" intersection at Casas de Lata turn east. From Casas de Lata onwards you see the first Chilean palms. The further east you go, the more palms appear on the hills. If you have permission to enter the Escuela Agrícola Las Palmas, continue further east.

- **Peumo:** 60 km south-west on Ruta H-30. It is another small, irregularly planned village, founded in pre-Hispanic days, but the indigenous population disappeared in the 17th century. The large trees in the plaza give ample shade on hot days. The belfry stands apart from the church building. The streets are picturesquely curved, and have retained their colonial charm. Window boxes full of flowers are an unusual feature of this village. Some 5 km west on the road to Las Cabras and Lago Rapel is Viña Concha y Toro, one of Chile's largest vineyards. It produces a well-respected wine, and the cellars and the sales room can be visited daily; appointments must be made on Sundays. Buses Galgo runs regular daily buses from Mercado Central in Rancagua.

- **Quinta de Tilcoco:** 43 km south-west. It is a small village with origins in pre-Hispanic times. Last century the owner of Hacienda Cailloma gave part of the estate to an eager priest full of missionary zeal. The priest set up a *hacienda,* and his parrish along Jesuit lines where he indoctrinated the native villagers in the Christian faith and taught them skills. This grew into a large religious complex. The *Casa de Ejercicios* ("Excercise House"), where the natives were taught Christianity, can be visited. When going to Tilcoco you may include a visit to **Guacarhué**, 5 km west — a village of colonial adobe buildings. Its plaza has a few palm trees separated from a small field by a creek. The church complex, a *monumento nacional*, was restored in interesting colonial style after an earthquake destroyed the 18th-century building. Originally, the faithful were seated separately: Spanish on one side and natives on the other side. Buses Galgo run several services daily from Rancagua

- **Reserva Nacional Río de los Cipreses,** 38 582 ha (95 300 acres): 50 km east on Ruta G-33 past **Coya**. The flora and fauna are typical of the high *cordillera.* This is a good spot for picnics.

You can watch colorful *loros* and walk to the cascades and rock drawings, or to a small lake of green water (its color indicates a high mineral content). Cypresses grow further up the mountains, where you may encounter the occasional group of *guanacos.* The reserve is administered by CONAF and there are few visitors. It has picnic and camping areas, and walking tracks. See the entry for the reserve on page 443.

- **Sewell** a mining town only 65 km east and 3000 m above sea level, is in the Andes. In July and August it receives a light covering of snow. You can reach it from Rancagua via the Carretera del Cobre. Miners' living quarters, built on terraces excavated from the mountain side, earned it the nickname "stairway town". Most miners now commute from Rancagua. The Mina El Teniente was formerly owned by Anaconda of the USA. If you wish to visit this town, you need a special permit from the Departamento de Relaciones Publicas CODELCO-Chile, Division El Teniente, Millán 1040, Rancagua.

- **Termas de Cauquenes**: 26 km east on Ruta H-255. Altitude 760 m, water temperature 48°C (118°F). It occupies a beautiful spot in the *pre-Cordillera* with views of the high *sierra.* The hot springs are located five kilometres further along a dirt road on the Hacienda Cauquenes near the Río Cachapoal, in an area which shows signs of strong volcanic activity with lava flows nearby. Open all year round. The indigenous people used the thermal waters for their healing properties long before Europeans began to seek cures for respiratory, nervous, rheumatic, skin and heart diseases; assistance with digestive, gastrointestinal, and arterial systems; and remedies for diabetes, sciatica, neuralgia, neuritis, mental fatigue and stress, sleeplessness, anaemia, allergies, and obesity. The property on which these thermal springs are situated, was part of a Jesuit monastery until 1767. The hotel has a thermal swimming pool, tubs, and conference rooms, and is known for its excellent cuisine. The spa was visited by many famous people in the 18th century including José de San Martín, Don Bernardo O'Higgins, and Charles Darwin. Some of the 19th-century buildings are still in use. Micro Termas de Cauquenes runs four services daily, departing from Mercado Municipal in Rancagua.

RENGO

Population: 22 000
Distance from Rancagua: 30 km south on Panamericana

Rengo lies in the central valley at the turnoff into the Río Claro valley. It was founded in 1692. It is the starting point for trips to Bollenar de las Nieves in the Río Claro valley.

🖂 Accommodation in Rengo
- Olimpo, Plaza de Armas 47 ACDE-FGIJKLMPSTUX (511981 $G ⚌. English spoken, fax 511424
- Turismo Rengo, Plaza de Armas AF (511281. Central heating

🕮 Post and telegraph

Post office
- Correo, Urriola 17

Telephone
- CTC, San Martín 123, fax 511484

🚍 Buses
- Rancagua: Fare $0.70; Buses Galgo

🚘 Motoring

There is a gas station on the Panamericana at the turnoff into Rengo.

⊛ Sport

There is trout fishing in the Río Claro.

⊕ Excursions
- **Bollenar de las Nieves**: 17 km east on a dirt road. This 8000 ha (19760 acres) protected area under the jurisdiction of CONAF has narrow valleys and steep slopes surrounding the **Laguna Los Cristales**. It is flanked by mountains reaching 3000 m which are snow-covered from June to September.
- **Malloa**: 12 km south-west. Malloa is a pre-Hispanic settlement, situated in a very fertile area. The town is laid out in an irregular pattern and has a picturesque plaza with a beautiful church. The houses, made of adobe and mostly still straw thatched, line the one main street even where the road curves. In colonial times, Malloa was a center of gold mining activity. Now its economic mainstay is growing fruit and vegetables, which are processed in the nearby factory. The village has approximately 4000 inhabitants. *Colectivo* services run from the main plaza in Rengo.

Plate 27   Región X de Los Lagos
Near Termas de Ralún

Plate 28   Región X de Los Lagos
Top: Estero Reloncaví
Bottom: Puerto Octay on Lago Llanquihué

RESERVA NACIONAL RÍO DE LOS CIPRESES

Distance from Rancagua: 45 km south-east on Ruta H-255

The Reserva Nacional Río de los Cipreses encompasses the **Río de los Cipreses valley** from its source to the junction with **Río Cachapoal** and the surrounding peaks partly in the *pre-Cordillera* and high *sierras*.

The park covers 38 000 ha (93 860 acres), varying in altitude between 900 and 4990 m. The climate is subject to altitude. The summer months (December–February) are usually dry, but sudden downpours can occur. Most precipitation is in winter in the form of snow, especially in the high *sierras*. Temperatures also fluctuate greatly between day and night. The best time to visit the reserve is from September to March.

The mountains are of volcanic rock, mostly andesite and basalt, and many of the peaks are volcanic in origin such as **Volcán Palomo** (4860m). Glaciers include Palomo and Ventisquero de los Cipreses.

The area has signs of pre-Hispanic occupation near Rincón de los Guanacos, Piedra del Indio, Cajón del Arriero, and Cajón del Baúl, and around **Laguna Piuquenes**.

Hares, foxes, *viscachas*, *guanacos*, *loro tricahués*, condors, and eagles are among the fauna in the park. The flora includes mock privet, *quillay*, *coironal*, and mountain cypresses.

Reserva Nacional Río de los Cipreses is an excellent hiking area. Favorite spots include **Laguna de los Piuquenes** with pre-Colombian rock paintings nearby. The mineral springs of Agua de la Vida and Agua de la Muerte are also worth visiting. The best hikes are from Camping los

Maitenes, where mountain climbers congregate. Mountain peaks within the reserve over 4000 m include **Cerro Cisne** (4578 m), **Cerro Hernán Cruz** (4565 m), and **Cerro Coton** (4295 m).

The most scenic spots are near Cerro Coton, and the waterfalls on Río El Relvo, Río El Indio and El Piuquenes, and Agua de la Vida. **Portezuelo de los Punzones**, a 3200 meter-high mountain pass, forms the watershed between **Río Tinguiririca** and Río Cachapoal. You can hike across this pass to the **Río del Portillo** valley. This is an exciting three- to four-day expedition for experienced hikers only. At the junction of **Río Azufre** with Río Tinguiririca, you can catch buses to **Termas del Flaco** or **San Fernando** in the central valley on the Panamericana Sur.

To reach the park, take the Carretera del Cobre from Rancagua 28 km east until Coya and turn off onto the dirt road to the Hotel Termas de Cauquenes. The park administration is at the end of a further 14 km. A dirt road leads further up the valley. The Reserva Nacional Río de los Cipreses displays the ecosystem of the *cordillera* and many of its trees and shrubs are characteristic of the Andean region. For further information, contact CONAF, Cuevas 480, Rancagua ℂ 22272.

Suggested Geográfico Militar area maps are "Río Cortadera" 5-04-06-0017-00, "Cerro Alto de los Arrieros" 5-04-06-0027-00, and "Termas del Flaco" 5-04-06-0036-00.

Ⓐ Camping

CONAF has built tourist facilities in Ranchillo 6 km up from the administration center with 23 barbecues, benches, and tables. This is where most visitors go because it is accessible by car. Nearby, rock pools invite a swim in the icy waters. The

Maitenes camping area is 17 kilometers further up, and also has barbecue facilities, tables, benches, and toilets.

🚌 Buses

There are regular daily buses from Rancagua to Termas de Cauquenes. Your best travel bet from Termas to Cauquenes to the park entrance is a lift from the CONAF office in Rancagua. A small fee is charged for this service.

⊛ Sport

Fishing, hiking, and mountain climbing are all available in the park.

SAN FERNANDO

Area code: 074
Population: 42 000
Altitude: 450 m
Distance from Rancagua: 54 km south on Panamericana

San Fernando, in the central valley on the **Río Tinguiririca**, is the capital of Colchagua province. It was founded in 1742 by Don José Antonio de Velazco and named Villa San Fernando de Tinguiririca. The center of town lies off the Panamericana. The main access, coming from Santiago, is along Avenida Bernardo O'Higgins.

Key to map

A	Iglesia (Church)	4	Restaurant Club Social
B	Gobernación Provincial (Government)	7	Restaurant Cinco Amigos
		8	Restaurant Olimpia 2
C	Municipalidad (Town hall)	9	Restaurant La Posada
D	Post office and telex	12	Restaurant Bristol
E	Telephone	13	Restaurant Lido I
G	Mercado Municipal (Market)	14	Restaurant Centro Español
H	Hospital	15	Restaurant Nuevo Rincón
P	Gas stations	20	Restaurant En Familia
T	Bus terminals	■	**Sights**
●	**Accommodation**	1	Casa Nincunlauta
5	Hotel Imperio	2	Capilla San Juan
10	Hotel Diego Portales	□	**Services**
16	Hotel Español	6	Supermercado Las Brisas
17	Gran Hotel Marcano	11	Lavaseco Damalo
18	Residencial Pupin	19	Railroad station
○	**Eating out**		
3	Restaurant La Casona		

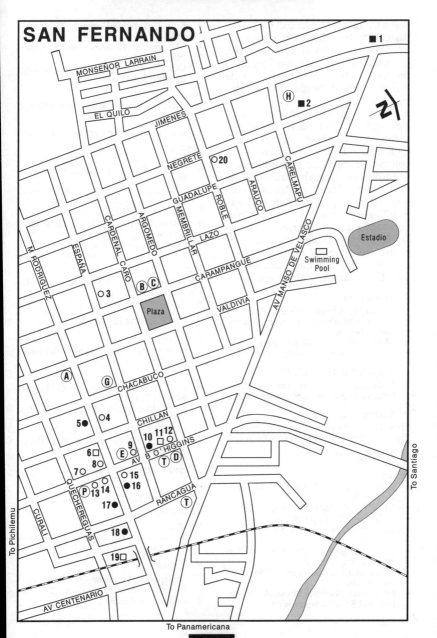

SAN FERNANDO

MONSEÑOR LARRAIN
EL QUILO
JIMENES
NEGRETE
GUADALUPE
MEMBRILLAR
ROBLE
LAZO
ARAUCO
CARELMAPU
CARAMPANGUE
VALDIVIA
AV MANSO DE VELASCO
M RODRIGUEZ
ESPAÑA
CARDENAL CARO
ARGOMEDO
CHACABUCO
CHILLAN
AV B O'HIGGINS
RANCAGUA
QUECHEREGUAS
CURALI
AV CENTENARIO

Plaza
Estadio
Swimming Pool

○ 20
○ 3
(B) (C)
(A)
(G)
5● ○ 4
6□ (E) 9 ○
8○
7○
(P) 13 14 ○ 15
17● ● 16
18●
19□
10● 11□ 12 ○
(T) (D)
(T)

■ 1
(H) ■ 2

To Pichilemu
To Santiago
To Panamericana

It is a traditional town and the buildings in the tree-shaded plaza are examples of colonial architecture, especially the Iglesia San Francisco on the south side. The Pedro de Valdivia side of the plaza has a shopping arcade.

San Fernando is the center of a rich agricultural area. Rice was first commercially grown on Hacienda Quilapán in 1932. Those interested in colonial architecture will find many examples in the nearby small villages and towns. Many traditional customs from the past still flourish here. In villages such as Lolol, Santa Cruz, and Marchihué, the farmers are also skilful artisans. Stands of wicker furniture are exhibited for several kilometers on the Panamericana as you pass Chimbarongo, 20 km south.

Festivals

- January 11: Chépica's Foundation Day — see Chimbarongo under "Excursions" below
- March 31: Chimbarongo's Foundation Day — see under "Excursions" below

Tourist information

- Municipal tourist information, Carampangue block 801 on the plaza

Camping

There is a good camping site at Termas del Flaco on your right as you enter the town.

Eating out

Restaurants
- Centro Español, Avenida Manuel Rodríguez 938 $Y
- Club Social, Manuel Rodríguez 789 $Y
- El Gato, Guadalupe 107 $Z
- En Familia, Negrete 1118 $Y. Chilean cuisine
- Hotel Diego Portales, Avenida Bernardo O'Higgins 703 $Y
- La Casona, M. Rodríguez 451 $Y. Chilean cuisine
- La Posada, Avenida Bernardo O'Higgins 651 $Y. Chilean cuisine

- Lido 1, Avenida Bernardo O'Higgins 590 $Y
- Marcano, M. Rodríguez 968 $Y. International cuisine
- Olimpia 2, Avenida Bernardo O'Higgins block 500, upstairs $Y

Salón de Té
- Bristol, Avenida Bernardo O'Higgins 775-A

Eating out along the Panamericana Sur

Restaurants
- Ronconi $Y
- El Trapiche, Longitudinal Sur KM 140 $Y
- Hostería El Yugo, KM 144 $Y. International and typical Chilean dishes in a rustic atmosphere; steaks
- Hostería Tyrol, KM 144. International cuisine
- Quilapán, Longitudinal Sur
- Talinay Club Aereo de San Fernando

Eating out in Chimbarongo
Chimbarongo is 18 km south on the Panamericana.
- Sandy, Miraflores 112

Post and telegraph

Post office
- Correos de Chile, Avenida Bernardo O'Higgins 768

Telephone
- CTC, Avenida Bernardo O'Higgins 645, fax 711145
- CTC, Manuel Rodríguez 791, fax 712198
- ENTEL Chile, Chacabuco 676
- Telex Chile, Avenida Bernardo O'Higgins Block 601

Services and facilities

Dry cleaner
- Lavaseco Damalo, Avenida Bernardo O'Higgins 735

Supermarket
- Supermercado Las Brisas, Avenida Rodríguez Block 800

Trains

The railroad station is on Quechereguas.
- Puerto Montt: Salón $13.00; Económico $11.50

⊟ Accommodation in San Fernando

Cabañas
- ★★★ Español, Manuel Rodríguez 959   AEFGHJMP   ℂ 711098 $G ⚏
  Central heating
- Los Troncos, Panamericana KM 145   ℂ 713748

Hotels
- Diego Portales, Avenida Bernardo O'Higgins 701
  AEFGIKLMP$U   ℂ 714696 $F ⚏
  Central heating
- Imperio, Manuel Rodríguez 770   ADHIJKLU   ℂ 714595 $G ⚏
  Shared bathroom, central heating
- Marcano, Manuel Rodríguez 968   AEFGILMPU   ℂ 712917 / 714759 $H ⚏
  Shared bathroom, 15 rooms. Central heating $I ⚏

Residenciales
- Pupin, M. Rodríguez near Rancagua $J ⚏
  Shared bathroom, budget travelers

Accommodation along the Panamericana
- Hotel Cabañas Los Troncos, KM 144   ℂ 713748
- Hotel Motel La Cantera, KM 144   ℂ 713491

Accommodation on the road to Puente Negro

Motels
- Las Arboledas, Paradero 22   ℂ 712012

Accommodation in Los Lingues
Hacienda Los Lingues is located 22 km north east of San Fernando.
★★★★★Hostería Los Lingues: 6 km south-east of Pelequén
ADEFGHIJKLMPR$TUVYZ $D ⚎
The *hostería* is part of an international hotel chain. Reservations in Santiago ℂ (02)2355446

Accommodation in Marchihué
Marchihué is 74 km west, on the road to the beach resort of Pichilemu.
- Hostería Las Cabañas
- Hostería Los Molinos

Accommodation in Termas del Flaco
Termas del Flaco is 77 km east. The hotels and *residenciales* at Termas del Flaco are only open for the summer season. This list is not exhaustive: there are plenty more *residenciales*. Accommodation is still somewhat basic, but there are a couple of hotels with up-market accommodation.

Hotels
- ★ Cabañas Las Vegas del Flaco   AEFGHIJKLPTUV   ℂ 222478 $G ⚏
  English spoken, full board. Reservations in Rancagua: O'Carroll 757 ℂ 223532
- Termas del Flaco,   AEFGHIJKLMPRTUV $G ⚏
  Full board, sauna, English spoken, 80 rooms. Reservations in San Fernando: España 949
  ℂ 711832. A plane service or helicopter service runs from San Fernando

Hosterías
- ★El Rancho, as you enter the village   AEFGHIJLMPRUV $F ⚎
  Full board, thermal pool, English spoken. Reservations in Santiago: Tenderini 26, upstairs, office 52 ℂ (02) 6382257

Accommodation in San Fernando — continued

Residenciales in Termas del Flaco

☞ ★ Posada Amistad, Leonardo Bassano
  AP $H i
  Full board, shared bathroom cheaper, 15 rooms. Reservations in Santiago: Ahumada 370, office 575 ((02) 6724082
• Posada La Ponderosa $G ii
  Reservation Rancagua: Obispo Larrain 0350 ((72) 262232
• Alero P $H ii
  Shared bathroom cheaper, all meals included, hot water all the time, 30 rooms (10 with private bathroom, 20 shared bathroom)
• Chépica, Leonardo Bassano $H i
  14 rooms
• Colo Colo $H ii
  Shared bathroom, 18 rooms
• Cordillera, Leonardo Bassano AP $H i
  Shared bathroom, 15 rooms, full board
• El Descanso $H ii
  Full board, cold water only
• La Gloria, Leonardo Bassano P $H i
  All meals, hot water all the time, 35 rooms (25 with private bathroom, 10 shared bathroom)
• Las Vegas $G ii
  Hot water, shared bathroom, 25 rooms
• Montanares $H ii
  Shared bathroom, cold water only, all meals included
• Roma P $H ii
  Full board, shared bathroom cheaper, 28 rooms
• Rancho Grande $H ii
  Cold water only, all shared bathrooms, all meals included, 20 rooms
• Valle Nevado, Leonardo Bassano P $H i
  Reservations in San Fernando: Acevedo 1146, Población San Martín, San Fernando ((72) 714596
• Victoria P $F ii
  Cabins vary between 2 to 4 beds, all meals included, shared bathroom cheaper, 20 rooms with private bathroom, 30 rooms shared bathroom
• Yolita, Camino a Las Pozas $H i
  Reservations in San Fernando: ((72) 711430

• Talca: Salón $4.10; Económico $3.30; 1st class $2.50. 7 services daily

⑥ Sport

There is trout fishing in Río Claro, Río Tinguiririca, and Estero Antivero.

🖻 Sightseeing

A brief stroll through the town center on Manuel Rodríguez takes you to the church with its large cupola. A right turn at Valdivia leads to the plaza and the Casa de Cultura, which serves as a tourist in-

formation office. Ask for permission to visit Casa de Nincunlauta, one of the oldest colonial buildings in this part of Chile. To get there, walk to the end of Valdivia (or Carampangue), and turn left into Avenida Manso de Velasco. Pass the swimming pool on the right, and continue for one block past the service station on the right, then turn left into J. Jímenez and proceed until you reach Casa de Nincunlauta.

• Casa de Nincunlauta: Avenida Manso de Velazco and J. Jímenez. This building, which is an outstanding example of early Chilean rural architecture, was probably constructed in the early 18th century. These early buildings served also as defense posts in case of attacks by the Indians. A chapel was usually part of the complex. The house belonged to an early Spanish settler who donated a large tract of land for the town site. The caretaker is a fine saddler — he is proud to show and to sell his products. Visits are organized through Casa de Cultura, Carampangue (750 anexo 450.

- Iglesia de San Francisco, a *monumento nacional* on the corner of Rodríguez and Valdivia. The outline of the church with its cupola can be seen as you approach the town.

⊕ Excursions

- **Casa Pintada de Tinguiririca**: 50 km east on the road to **Bellavista** off Ruta I-45. This site can be visited en route to Termas del Flaco. Detour at KM 28 south, past the camping spot. The partially destroyed, small cave was discovered in 1861. Its rock paintings are probably the work of indigenous people towards the end of the pre-Hispanic era or possibly during colonial times.

- **Chimbarongo:** 18 km south, in the central valley. This village is well known for its wicker ware, which is sold from stalls lining the main highway for several kilometers on both sides of town. It has a population of about 10 000 inhabitants. There is a remarkable colonial church in the village, which has a large arched main entrance made of *ladrillo* bricks. On the Panamericana at the turnoff into the village is a COPEC gas station.

- **Chépica**: 24 km further west of Chimbarongo (population 5600). A settlement founded in pre-Colombian times, with a main street called 18 de Septiembre and some interesting old colonial houses near the plaza. Tourist information is located in the town hall. The thick-walled colonial church, Iglesia San Antonio de Padua, has three naves. Rural buses depart from the main plaza next to this church. From San Fernando *colectivos* run frequent

daily services to Chimbarongo and Chépica.

- **Marchihué** : 73 km west on Ruta I-50, on a plain surrounded by low mountains on all sides. It reached its peak with the building of the railroad line to Pichilemu. It is a center for handicrafts from the nearby villages of **Alcones, Trinidad,** and **La Quebrada**, which you pass through on the way to Pichilemu. Wooden looms are still used to weave sisal carpets and woolen blankets and bedspreads. Buses Andimar and Buses Nilahué run 11 daily services from San Fernando.

- **Hacienda El Huique**: 56 km southwest. This was one of the large estates that was carved up into smaller land holdings during the agrarian reform. Its real name was Hacienda San José del Carmen. The *hacienda*, a *monumento histórico nacional*, remained in the same family from 1627 until 1966 and is representative of typical early Chilean architecture. Since 1976, the *hacienda* has been the property of the Chilean army and is not open to the public.

- **Hacienda Los Lingues**: 22 km northeast, in the central valley; the turnoff from the Panamericana is 14 km north at Pelequen. The *hacienda* covers 500 cultivated hectares (1235 acres) and another 3500 ha (8645 acres) of rolling hills, and is to this day worked as an agricultural enterprise. Its origins go back to 1545 when Emperor Charles V gave this land to the first mayor of Santiago — it remains the property of the same family to this day. Since 1760, this *hacienda* has been one of Chile's foremost horse-breeding studs of the so-called "Aculeo thoroughbreds". The oldest part of the *hacienda* complex was begun in the 17th century. The houses have thick adobe walls, which keep them many degrees cooler than the outside temperature. Many of the doors were made by German Jesuits. Additions to the original buildings over the past two centuries have not spoilt the well-presented and integrated Chilean colonial architecture. The *hacienda* contains a small museum with antique furniture and memora-

🚌 Buses from San Fernando

The bus terminal is located on Manso de Velasco 1009.

Companies
- A48   Buses Lit
- A74   Buses Sol del Sur
- A105 Sol del Pacífico
- A128 Pullman Bus
- A137 TAS Choapa
- A153 Tur-Bus Jedimar
- B8   Bus Araya
- B23   Buses Andimar Andén 21 ☎ 237818
- B46   Buses Colchagua ☎ 712712
- B48   Buses Cordillera
- B57   Buses Díaz–Ilomar
- B72   Buses Galgo, Rancagua ☎ 711779
- B116 Buses Nilahué
- B121 Buses Ocvall
- B159 Buses Tagua Sur
- B162 Buses Tepual
- B217 Buses Flota L
- B224 Minibus La Paloma, Avenida B. O'Higgins 751
        Services to Termas del Flaco
- B237 Pullman Sur
- B275 Buses Expreso Santa Cruz ☎ 713687

Services

Destination	Fare	Services	Duration	Companies
Chillán	$8.10	6 services daily	4 hrs	A48, A153
Chimbarongo	$0.50	every 15 minutes		B8
Concepción	$12.50	2 services daily		A137
Curicó	$1.70	5 services daily	1 hr	A48, A153, B23, B46
Los Angeles	$12.50	2 services daily	5½ hrs	A137
Osorno	$19.50	2 services daily		A48, A153
Pichilemu	$2.80	17 services daily	3½ hrs	B23, B46, B116
Puerto Montt	$21.00	2 services daily		A137
Puerto Varas	$21.00	2 services daily		A48, A153
Rancagua	$1.10	every 20 minutes	½ hrs	B72
Santa Cruz	$0.40	6 services daily		B275
Santiago	$3.30	8 services daily	2½ hrs	A48, A128, B23, B46, B57, B116, B121, B162, B217, B237
Talca	$3.20	3 services daily	1½ hrs	B237
Talcahuano	$12.50			A48, A153
Temuco	$14.30			A48, A153
Termas del Flaco	$7.50	8 services daily		B23, B224, B48
Runs during the summer season only				
Valparaíso	$7.80	5 services daily		A74, A105
Valdivia	$16.30	1 service daily		A137
Viña del Mar	$7.80	3 services daily		A74

bilia. Visit the chapel to see a marble crucifix which belonged to Pope Pius IX. Visiting this old *hacienda* is like a trip back into the past. The main building has been converted into a hotel of world-class standard. The gardens are kept in immaculate order for the enjoyment of guests, and there is a small *laguna* for swimming and boating. The food in the restaurant is of the highest international standard and incorporates many special Chilean dishes. For day-time visitors and guests, the hotel provides transport from either San Fernando or Rancagua — see Los Lingues under "Accommodation" above.

- **Laguna La Misurina**: 26 km southeast. A small holiday colony has been established around the lake in the middle of a fir tree forest.

- **Sierras de Bellavista**: 36 km southeast on an unsealed road. Take Ruta I-45 as far as El Encanche and turn off here to the right. The road starts to climb immediately. This area offers walks in the *pre-Cordillera*.

- **Termas del Flaco**: 77 km in the valley of the **Río Las Damas**, which is the upper Tinguiririca valley. The dirt road to the spa, though very picturesque, is narrow and winding. For this reason, between November and April, one-way traffic only is possible: from Termas del Flaco to San Fernando (downhill) from 0600 to 1200, and from San Fernando to Termas del Flaco (uphill) from 1500. For information on road conditions, ring the *carabineros* in San Fernando or *vialidad* (road services). The road is closed between May and November. The village is at an altitude of 1720 m and within striking distance of **Volcán Tinguiririca** (4300 m). The tourist season is from January–April. Nearly all the places shut down when the summer season is over. In winter, the climate is harsh, and Termas del Flaco may be inaccessible for weeks. There are three large open-air thermal bathing pools in the lower part of the village near the river. There is an entrance fee for the change room; lockers have to be paid for separately. Most people take their clothes with them to the pools' edges because the air is cool after leaving the warm water. Every house has thermal water piped to tubs. The village is quite large and consists almost entirely of hotels and *residenciales*. It is surprising to find such a large settlement up here in the high *sierra* so close to the Argentine border. A waterfall descends from the high mountains at the rear of the village and the views are breathtaking. There are two main streets, with the biggest concentration of rented accommodation in the one running down to the hot pools. The thermal water emerges from the ground at 55°C (131°F) making the water a bit murky. The healing properties of the thermal spring are supposed to benefit much the same list of complaints as Termas de Cauquenes (see "Excursions" from Rancaqua on page 441). In addition, they are recommended for arthritic and rheumatic disorders. The water temperature of the *fumaroles* rises to 96°C (205°F). The electricity supply in Termas del Flaco runs from 2000 to 2400 only. Many *residenciales* have their own generators and the noise is rather disturbing. There are walks to Volcán Tinguiririca and also to **Paso Las Damas** 15 km further up the valley. Five hundred meters above the military outpost are the **Huellas de Dinosaurios** ("Dinosaur Footprints"). The footprints were made by a pair of dinosaurs about 120 million years ago; they were a plant-eating species, 10 m long and 5 m high. It has been established that these animals lived by a shallow lake at sea level. Nowadays, the site is nearly 4000 m up. Marine fossils are also found in this area. Buses Andimar and Buses Colchagua run 8 services daily from San Fernando and 1 service daily from Santiago. All buses operate in summer only.

SANTA CRUZ

Population: 15 000
Altitude: 160 m
Distance from San Fernando: 36 km west on Ruta I- 50

Santa Cruz, located on a tributary of the lower **Río Tinguiririca** in the valley of the same name, was founded in 1850. An excellent road connects it to San Fernando. There is a carillon on the Plaza de Armas. Santa Cruz is the center of a rich agricultural area.

⊠ Festivals

• First week in March: *Cueca* competition

ⓘ Tourist information

• Kiosk on Palacios (Plaza de Armas), open only in summer

⊟ Accommodation

• Hotel Alcázar, Díaz Besoain 285 (822465 $H ⠸⠸
• Hotel Plaza, Plaza de Armas 286 AE-FGIMPT. Central heating, bilingual staff

Accommodation in Lihuelmo
Lihuelmo is 21 km west on Ruta I-50.
• Hostería Lihuelmo

⊞ Eating out

• Restaurant Casa Grande, Avenida Errázuriz 901
• Club Social, Plaza de Armas 178

⊞ Post and telegraph

Post
• Correo de Chile, Díaz Besoaín 96

Telephone
• CTC, Plaza de Armas 286, fax 821003

⊟ Buses

The bus terminal is on Rafael Casanova.

Bus companies
• Buses Andimar (822225
• Buses Colchagua (822011
• Buses Nilahué
• Tur Costa
• Pullman Sur
• Buses Santa Cruz (822058

Services
• Santiago: Fare $4.40; Andimar, Nilahué, Pullman Sur, Flota L, Diaz-Ilomar
• Pichilemu: 19 services daily; Colchagua, Andimar, Tur Costa, Diaz-Ilomar

⊞ Motoring

• COPEC service station, Avenida Errázuriz

⊞ Shopping

At **La Lajuela**, 8 km west, the villagers make straw hats from a local fiber called *teatina*. The leaves are cut and dried, then plaited into strands, from which hats are made and sold on the coastal road to Bucalemu.

⊡ Sightseeing

• Museo Histórico de Colchagua: In an old colonial building on Avenida Errázuriz.

⊡ Excursions

• **San Pedro de Alcántara**: 55 km west. The modern road follows the old Inca road to the coast passing through Lolol and on to Lago Vichuquén. The village grew around an early Franciscan monastery, which was destroyed by an earthquake. The church, which is surrounded by native Chilean palm trees, has been declared a *monumento nacional*. A colorful fiesta is held annually on the plaza in front of the church. A rock drawing, a few kilometers past the village on the track to Lago Vichuquén, was supposedly made by Incas.

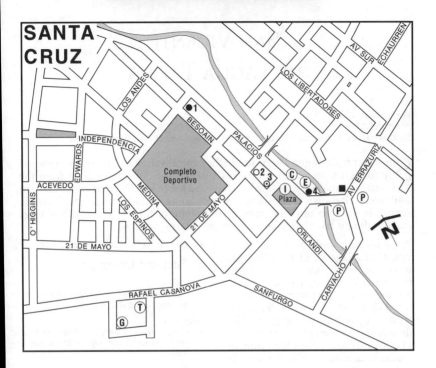

Key to map

C	Municipalidad (Town hall)	1	Hotel Alcázar
E	Telephone	2	Café de la Cuca
G	Mercado Municipal (Market)	3	Restaurant Club Social
P	Gas stations	4	Hotel Plaza
T	Bus terminals		

SAN VICENTE
DE TAGUA TAGUA

Area code: 072
Population: 14 300
Altitude: 200 m
Distance from Rancagua: 53 km south-west on Ruta H-56 and Panamericana

San Vicente de Tagua Tagua lies in the central valley and is not often visited by foreign tourists. To get to San Vicente, turn off at Pelequén from the Panamericana and follow the sealed road for 16 km. Once an ancient Indian settlement, the town is now the center of an agricultural area. The Plaza de Armas is the hub of social activity and some of the old colonial buildings surrounding it have balconies, which are very picturesque.

A prehistoric settlement was excavated in the lagoon, 8 km south of the township, which was drained dry in the 19th century. Its occupants hunted now extinct animals, such as mastodons, which roamed the country during the Pleistocene epoch. The date of the settlement has been set at 11 000 years ago —the oldest human presence detected in Chile so far. At the same site, there is a younger settlement of hunters dating back to 4200 BC.

⊟ Accommodation

★★★ Hostería San Vicente de Tagua Tagua, Diego Portales 222 ACDE-FGHIJLPUR ℂ 571336 $F ⅱ. Central heating, 16 rooms, fax 572062

⫟ Eating out

• Restaurant Requehua, Walker Martínez

• Confitería Portalón, Plaza de Armas

🕮 Post and telegraph

Post office
• Corner of Calle Prat and Calle Gallegos (opposite the plaza)

Telephone
• CTC, Carlos Walker 274 corner of Prat on Plaza de Armas opposite the town hall

🚌 Buses

Buses depart from bus terminal Avenida España corner of González.
• Pichilemu: Buses Tagua Sur
• Rancagua: Fare $1.00; services every 20 minutes; Buses Galgo

🚗 Motoring

• COPEC gas station, corner of Riesco and Portales

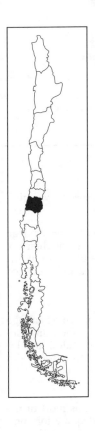

REGIÓN VII
DEL
MAULE

Population: 800 000
Area: 30 500 square km (11 773 square miles)
Regional capital: Talca
Provinces and provincial capitals: Curicó, Talca, Linares, and Cauquenes. Provincial capitals bear the same names as the provinces.

The region has great natural beauty, but many areas in the Andean *cordillera* can only be reached via dirt roads. There is a great choice of thermal resorts with good facilities, and the region is a producer of fine table wines. In the *pre-Cordillera* are some scenic reserves and protected areas.

Región VII del Maule lies between 35° and 36° south in central Chile, bordering Región VI del Libertador General Bernardo O'Higgins in the north; in the east the Andes form the border with Argentina; while to the south is Región VIII del Bío Bío. In the west is the Pacific Ocean.

The main population centers are concentrated around Talca in the central valley.

Transport

Road

The Panamericana crosses the region through the central valley, with side roads leading to the coast or into the mountains. Traffic from Talca via the Paso del Maule (or Paso Pehuenche) to Malargüe in Argentina in Mendoza province has been reopened after being closed for several years.

Rail

The railroad line runs from Santiago to Puerto Montt, and the train usually stops in Curicó, Talca, and Linares. A branch line goes from Talca to Constitución on the coast.

Air

Air traffic is limited as most of the airstrips are not adequate for commercial airlines; they are mostly used by private aircraft.

Topography

The region can be divided into three geographical areas: a narrow coastal plain to the west separated by the coastal *cordillera* from the central valley, the central valley proper, and the Andean *cordillera*. The coastal *cordillera* is not very high (700 m), and it is widest near Curicó in the north. Near Talca it narrows, but gains in altitude near Cauquenes in the south. Most of the central valley is about 40 km wide, but at Talca it is 80 km wide.

Within the valleys, there are little hills of volcanic origin such as the **Cerillos de Teno**. The valleys themselves are filled with volcanic ash, and because of the absence of hard rock, the rivers have formed deep "cuts" *within* the valleys, more like deep grooves below the normal valley floor. The main rivers rising in this region are **Río Mataquito** and **Río Maule**.

In the east, the Andes reach an average height of 3000 m, but there are a few peaks (usually volcanoes) that are more than 4000 m high: **Cerro Torre Santa Elena** (3820 m), **Volcán Peteroa** (4090 m), **Volcán Descabezado Grande** — its name means "Great Beheaded Volcano" because it looks as if its top has been blown off (3830 m) — and **Cerro Campanario** (4020 m). In Linares province the peaks are lower: **Cerro Toro** (3081 m) and **Nevado de Longaví** (3242 m). Ice and volcanic action have formed the mountains: through the erosion caused by ice, large valleys have been formed in the upper reaches which are taken up by lakes, in particular the upper **Río Maule**. The most important river is the Río Maule which rises in **Laguna del Maule** near the Paso del Maule (or Paso Pehuenche) and flows into the Pacific Ocean near Constitución.

Climate

The climate is Mediterranean, except that in the Andes the mountains affect the climate. In the central valley most of the rain occurs within about six months, but less rain falls in the central valley than on the coast and the Andes. In the Andes to the east of Talca and Linares, annual rainfall can

be as much as 3000 mm. Summers in the central valley are usually dry, with the average annual rainfall being 800 mm. The temperature is more uniform on the coast than it is in the interior, with a mean average annual temperature of 14°C (57°F).

The indigenous inhabitants

The Río Maule was as far south as the Incas got. Further south it was Mapuche country and remained so until the Spaniards arrived. The tribes lived in small villages and the central valley was not densely populated.

European history

This was one of the earliest parts of Chile to be divided among the Spanish *conquistadores*. Many of the local population were uprooted and sent by the Spaniards to the north to work in the silver and gold mines. Soon after their arrival, the Spanish started the large irrigation works which to this day are in use.

This region is important in Chilean history — in 1818 in Talca the Declaration of Independence was signed by Bernardo O'Higgins. Many of the battles of the Wars of Independence were fought in Talca province, such as Combate de Quechereguas, Batalla de Lircay, and Sorpresa de Cancha Rayada.

Economy

The region's economy is based on agriculture and cattle-raising. Pine trees (*Pinus radiata*) plantations have been established to feed a large pulp and wood factory in Constitución.

Maule produces about 45 per cent of the total Chilean wine production, the center of production being Cauquenes and Molina. Wheat and

MAULE

maize are grown in the central valley, mostly between Talca and the Río Longaví. The region is also an important producer of hydro-electricity from the power stations of Cipreses (101 000 kW), Isla (68 000 kW), Colbún (400 000 kW), and Machicura. Most of those energy centers are in the Río Maule basin, and the dams also store water for irrigation.

Cultural life

Famous citizens

Región VII del Maule is known for a number of important people, such as writers Pablo Neruda and Max Jara, and Abate Molina, a famous naturalist.

Customs

Customs in the Regón VII del Maule are distinctly rural or *huaso*. From September to February is rodeo time. The most famous rodeos are those held in Talca, Curicó, Linares, San Clemente, and Pencahué.

Religious festivals

The religious festivals have more local character, and the most colorful are held in smaller communities. The best known are:

* Fiesta de San Francisco is held in **Huerta del Maule**, 62 km south west of Talca, on October 4 in honor of St Francis of Asissi, the local patron saint.
* Fiesta de la Virgen del Rosario, held in **Lora**, 96 km west of Curicó — see "Excursions" from Iloca on page 480.
* Fiesta de Nuestra Señora del Rosario, held in **Sauzal**, 43 km north of Cauquenes on the first Sunday in October. It attracts a large crowd from the surrounding district.
* Festividad de la Virgen de las Mercedes is held in **Lipimávida** near **Curepto** on the first Sunday in September. This festival, full of religious fervor, attracts many people from the surrounding districts.
* Festividad Religiosa de San Pedro is celebrated annually in **Iloca** and **Constitución** (on the coast) on June 29 in honor of the patron saint of fishermen. For this occasion the fishing vessels are adorned with flowers and garlands, and it is a memorable sight.
* Festividad de la Inmaculada Concepción, also known as Fiesta la Purísima, held on December 8 each year in honor of the Virgin in **Corinto** (26 km southwest of Talca), **Pocillas** (near Cauquenes), and on Cerro de la Virgen in **San Javier**.
* Fiesta de la Candelaria, celebrated in **Chanco**, 43 km northwest of Cauquenes on February 2.

Handicrafts

The region also produces a variety of handicrafts. **Pencahué** (16 km west of Talca) is famous for its woolen fabrics, and for riding gear such as saddles and lassos for the local *huasos*. **Curepto** is another place known for its woolen fabrics, producing mainly blankets, bedspreads, and carpets. The finest woolen bed-coverings and blankets come from **Lipimávida** and **Rapilermo**. **San Clemente**, 22 km east of Talca, is well known for leather products and riding gear. Near **Termas de Quinamávida**, 16 km east of Linares, entire families, working on home-made looms, produce woolen fabrics, such as blankets and rugs.

In **Vara Gruesa** a small village 12 km north-east of Linares, the villagers make carvings from pear-tree wood.

The village of **Pilén**, 13 km south-west of Cauquenes, is the center of the pottery industry in the region. They make both practical and ornamental items, using traditional designs and working with simple tools. Their products have great artistic merit, and most are sold in the market in Cauquenes.

In **Rari**, 23 km east of Linares, the local inhabitants use horse hair and vegetable fibers to decorate their figurines. Curepto and Pencahué are famous for woolen fabrics coloured with natural vegetable dyes.

Cuisine

Local dishes in and around Talca include tasty *empanadas* (a type of pastry filled with spiced meat), *pejerreyes,* and also fried frogs. Frogs are considered a delicacy in this region — while I was on a trip in an outlying area the bus driver stopped in the middle of nowhere to allow his passengers to collect frogs in a nearby stream. The wine is excellent; a particular variety of vines is grown near Cauquenes, where the vines are left to creep along the ground.

Thermal resorts and beaches

Thermal resorts

The province of Linares has important thermal spas. The best known are **Termas de Panimávida** and **Termas de Quinamávida** near the city of Linares (see "Excursions" from Linares on page 482), and **Termas de Catillo** near Parral (see "Excursions" from Parral on page 488). Those three thermal resorts are fairly close to one another in the first spurs of the *pre-Cordillera,* all enjoying a temperate climate. The waters of all three are claimed to have curative powers for a number of complaints, among them rheumatism, arthritis, neuralgia, renal disorders, liver diseases, gastrointestinal problems, cardiovascular disease, diabetes, obesity, respiratory ailments, skin disorders, mental fatigue, stress, neurosis, insomnia, and nervous diseases.

There are many thermal springs in the Andean *cordillera,* such as **Baños de Mondaca** in the **Río Colorado** valley up from Molina, but they are inaccessible and lack facilities. There are also thermal springs at **Los Cipreses** on the road to **Paso del Maule** (or Paso de Pehuenche, 2553 m, on RN 115), but the *hostería* offering accommodation is not open all year round. The **Baños de Longaví** on the upper **Río Achibueno** are only accessible to mountain hikers.

Beaches

The best beaches to be found in the region are in Cauquenes province. The most popular are **Pelluhue** and **Curanipe**. Both have adequate tourist facilities, but only come to life during the summer season. Other extensive beaches with good facilities are **Llico**, **Duao**, **Lipimávida**, and **Constitución**.

Fishing

The trout fishing season runs from the second Friday in November until the first Sunday in May.

The best trout fishing is in the clear waters of the Andes. In the *pre-Cordillera* the waters get warmer and

Chilean atherine (or *pejerrey*) appears. The main rivers (**Río Teno**, **Río Maule**, and **Río Mataquito**) which pass through dense population centers are quite heavily polluted so they are no good for fishing. However, fishing in little coastal streams is still good in the less populated areas. Note that there are three rivers with the name **Río Claro** in this region, two of them in Curicó province: one is a tributary of Río Teno, and the other joins the Río Maule west of Talca; and Río Claro in Talca province joins the Río Maule near Armerillo.

- **Embalse Machicura**: Trout
- **Estero Potrero Grande** (from the junction with Río Lontué upriver): Trout. The best spots are near Quebrada Honda
- **Lago Colbún**: Trout and Chilean atherine
- **Lago Vichuquén**: *pejerrey, roncador* fish
- **Laguna del Maule**: Trout
- **Laguna de Teno**, also called Laguna El Planchón: Trout. Laguna de Teno is the source of Río Teno, near the Argentinian border; it is accessible only with your own transportation
- **Río Achibueno**: Trout
- **Río Ancoa**: Trout
- **Río Blanco**: Trout. Río Blanco is in a very scenic area east of Linares; only rural buses run there
- **Río Claro** (in Talca province, from Armerillo upstream towards Decabezado Grande): Trout, carp, and Chilean atherine
- **Río Lircay** (upstream from Alto Vilches): Trout
- **Río Longaví** (in the upper reaches, east of Parral): Trout

- **Río Lontué** (upstream from Culenar and all streams coming down from the *sierra*): Trout
- **Río Mataquito** (upstream from Curicó): Trout
- **Río Maule** (upstream from Armerillo): Trout
- **Río Maule** (near Maquehua): Some rainbow trout and Chilean atherine
- **Río Melado**: Trout
- **Río Perquilauquén**: Trout, Chilean and Argentinian atherine
- **Río Santa Ana**: Trout
- **Río Teno** (upstream from Río Los Queñes): Trout

National reserves and protected areas

There are no national parks in this region, but CONAF administers the following *reservas nacionales* and *areas de protección*:

- **Reserva Nacional Federico Albert**. Located on the coast near Chanco. Access from Panamericana via Parral. In 1898 the German scientist Dr Friedrich Albert planted pine trees along the extensive dunes on the Pacific coast in an attempt to stop the drift of the sand dunes and subsequent beach erosion. After many setbacks he managed to find a type of pinus radiata that was successful in the area, and now there are extensive pine forests along this coast under the control of CONAF. The most remarkable reforested area is near **Chanco** (in Cauquenes province). About 80 different varieties of trees have been planted within its 145 ha (358 acres). You can get there on foot from the village of Chanco. CONAF has upgraded the pine plantations and also planted several types of eucalyptus trees, with the result that the drift of the dune sands has been stopped. Lately native plants have begun to appear naturally in these forests, showing that it is possible for human beings to help nature instead of being destructive. There are pathways and picnic areas, and you can visit all year round. At the CONAF information center you can see photographs of how the area looked before this huge enterprise began. Accommodation, an eating place, and a shop are all nearby.

• **Reserva Nacional Los Ruiles**. This reserve consists of two separate areas, covering altogether 45 ha (111 acres): the most accessible part is between Chanco and Cauquenes — the main road Ruta M-50 passes directly through the reserve and the other area is near Empedrado. This reserve was created to protect the *ruiles* trees that grow profusely here. Although the Cauquenes–Chanco section has been intensively planted with pine trees, a large part has been left intact with original tree cover. CONAF has designated walking trails and fireplaces for picnics, blending them perfectly with the surroundings. Regular buses ply between Cauquenes and Chanco. The section near **Empedrado** is a bit isolated and not easily accessible, though there are rural buses from Constitución to Empedrado. While some areas are completely covered by *ruiles* trees, there are also large-leaved *maño*, *fuinque*, *taique*, *tineos*, *pitao*, *pelu*, *coigües*, *copihue* flowers, and wild filberts in other parts of the park.

• **Reserva Nacional Laguna Torca**. There are three separate sectors in this wildlife sanctuary, covering 600 ha (1482 acres): Bosque de Llico, Isla Cerillo, and Laguna Torca proper. The reserve, administered by CONAF, is particularly rich in birdlife; there are approximately eighty different species, with Chile's largest population of black-necked swan, as well as *taguas* (a type of mudhen unique to Chile), and purple herons. **Isla Cerillo** in **Lago Vichuquén** (in the southern part called Sector Paula) is the home of some rare native plants such as the *huillipatagua*. The best way to get to this protected area is from either Vichuquén or the village of Llico. There are daily buses from Curicó. The reserve, which can be visited all year round, is 105 km west of Curicó on Rutas I-60 and J-80. It is just before Retén Llico, near the Pacific coast: it has a picnic area, excursion paths, and a lookout.

• **Área de Protección Radal**. This lush and green area covering 7680 ha (18 970 acres) in the *pre-Cordillera*, on the **Río Claro** has been set up to protect native flora and fauna, such as the *coihué* and native oak, condors, *vizcachas*, and foxes. An area of great natural beauty with many forests and thick vegetation, it has an information center, picnic area, camping area, excursion paths and a lookout. Where the Río Claro passes throught the reserve it has carved narrow gorges through the rock — in some areas the water channel is more like a tunnel than a river bed. The river forms seven successive falls cascading into little rockpools that look like saucers, hence the name *Siete Tazas* ("Seven Cups"). The best-known cascades are **Salto La Leona** and **Salto Vela de la Novia** ("Bridal Veil Fall"), which has a free fall of 50 m. Access to the falls is along a rough track. The flora includes *cipres de la cordillera*, oaks, filberts, *coihué*, and *rauli*. This is also the northern limit of the large-leaved *mañio* which is represented by a few (protected!) examples. Wildlife in the park includes dwarf deer *(pudu)*, pumas, eagles, mountain cats *(gato montanés Andino* — already very rare), and condors. The best trout fishing is near Puente Frutillar y Costillar and also in a small tributary called El Toro. This whole reserve is a hiker's, angler's, and photographer's paradise, and you should not miss it when you are in the area. It is located 70 km south-east of Curicó, first on the Panamericana and Ruta K-15 as far as Molina and from there on Ruta K-25, a dirt road. Check in Curicó with CONAF in Edificio Gobernación (310321, as sometimes they have trucks or cars going there. The section called **Parque Inglés** is suitable for short walks in an undisturbed area of natural beauty. Fishing is permitted during the season. You can hike south through this reserve to the adjoining Parque

Gil de Vilches and return from there by bus to Talca. In summer Buses Hernández run regular services from Curicó via Molina to Radal near the protected area; fare $1.50.

- **Parque Gil de Vilches** is located 63 km east of Talca in the beautiful *pre-Cordillera* in the upper **Río Lircay** valley near the **Río Claro**. It includes the **Altos de Vilches** which dominate the scenery; those small mountains are snow-covered for part of the year. This reserve, administered by CONAF, extends for 16 884 ha (41 703 ac). Altitude ranges from 700 m to 2400 m. It is in a high rainfall area, and much of the native flora remains intact. It contains dense forests of oak, *coihué*, and *rauli*, with *lengas* and *ñires* in the higher parts; and the moist atmosphere also suits Chile's national flower, the *copihue*. These forests are the home of many kinds of wildlife, including pumas, foxes, eagles, condors, and mountain cats. The plentiful birdlife includes one particularly colorful species — the *loro* (parrot), which is in danger of extinction. There are trout in the river. You can easily get here from **Talca** by taking one of the frequent buses to **Alto Vilches**. From where the bus stops, it is a 500 m walk uphill to the entrance to the national park. Inside the park are many walking trails through the native forests, and there is also a ranger's headquarters with a visual display room of flora, fauna, and archeological finds. The main trail passes the park ranger's headquarters and leads up to a rocky area overlooking a small creek with clear drinkable water. The main points of interest are **Lagunas de los Patos**, **La Encantada**, and **El Toro**, and **Quebrada Los Coigues** (a canyon). The Pehuenches have also left their marks in the area. In Parque Gil de Vilches there are large rocks with grooves clearly made by humans. They are known as *tácitas*, their purpose is still not clear — perhaps they were used for mixing paints or grinding maize. Other archeological finds include spear tips and pieces of crockery. CONAF has marked out walking trails through some sections of the area, a few picnic areas and a lookout. From the CONAF information center the trail leads to a small clearing with a little pond on the right. This is also a picnic area, and you can swim in the pond. Many trees in the reserve have a plaque with their botanical and common names, and information about them. You can also hire horses from the locals. It is possible to hike across the park to the Área de Protección Radal. This interesting area can be visited almost all year round. See also "Accommodation" and "Camping" in Talca on pages 494 and 495. Asociación de Buses Rurales runs 3 services daily from Talca to Vilches Alto; fare: $1.90. See "Excursions" from Talca on page 495.

Distances

From Cauquenes

- Curanipe: 49 km west
- Pelluhue: 42 km west

From Curicó

- Área de Protección Radal: 70 km south-east
- Cauquenes: 206 km south
- Iloca: 127 km west
- Lago Vichuquén: 130 km west
- Linares: 114 km south
- Llico: 144 km west
- Los Queñes: 48 km east
- Santiago: 193 km north
- Talca: 68 km south
- Vichuquén: 118 km west

From Linares

- Cauquenes: 96 km west
- Lago Colbún and Lago Machicura: 32 km north-east
- Rari: 23 km north-east
- Parral: 41 km south
- Termas de Catillo: 60 km south-east
- Termas de Panimávida: 21 km east
- Termas de Quinamávida: 18 km east

From Molina

- Area de Protección Radal: 45 km east

From Parral

- Termas de Catillo: 23 km east

From Talca

- Armerillo: 75 km east
- Cauquenes: 143 km south-west
- Constitución: 109 km south-west
- Laguna del Maule: 152 km south-east
- Linares: 50 km south
- Maule: 11 km south
- San Clemente: 22 km east
- Vilches: 63 km east

Tourist attractions

Don't miss

☞ Talca

Worth a visit

☞ Área de Protección Radal–Siete Tazas
☞ Lago Vichuquén

☞ Termas de Panimávida and Lago Colbún

Worth a detour

☞ Los Queñes
☞ Vilches

Of interest

☞ Constitución

CAUQUENES

Area code: 073
Population: 28 000
Distance from Parral: 54 km west on RN 128

Cauquenes is in the coastal *cordillera* on the **Río Cauquenes**. It was founded in 1742 by Don José Antonio Manso de Velasco. He named the town Villa de Nuestra Señora de las Mercedes de Manso de Tutuvén, but fortunately for all, the town later became known as Cauquenes, in honor of the Cauquenes tribe who used to live here.

The center of a wine-growing area, it is a provincial capital and still has a very colonial atmosphere with many old buildings. In the usual colonial style, the focal point is the plaza where all the major civic buildings are, such as the town hall, church, and post office, as well as the bus companies. There is a plaque in the plaza commemorating the founder. There are reasonable tourist and transport facilities.

ℹ Tourist information

• Victoria 841 ℂ 294

⊟ Accommodation

Hotels
• Coppelia, Victoria 495 (on the plaza) ℂ 511092 $J ♙♙
• Gran Maule, Antonio Varas 545 AFGHIJKLPUV ℂ 512637 $H ♙♙
• Los Conquistadores, Victoria 640 AE-FGHLPUV ℂ 511202 $I ♙. 20 rooms

• Manso de Velasco, Victoria 453 (on the plaza) ℂ 511100 $J ♙. Shared bathroom, budget travelers

⑪ Eating out

• Restaurant Chez Moi, C. Urrutia 321B. Disco
• Café Oriente, Victoria 501
• La Fuente Alemana, Catedral near Victoria. Hamburgers, pizzas

▦ Post and telegraph

Post office
• Correos, Estado

Telephone
• CTC, Claudina Urrutia 504, fax 511025
• Telex Chile, Victoria 499

⊟ Motoring

• COPEC gas station, Maipú

◉ Excursions

• **Reserva Nacional Los Ruiles**: 28 km west. It is an area of native forest extending for 45 ha (111 acres). You can find *ruil, coihué, hualo,* and *canelo* trees here, and also the national flower, *copihué*. CONAF has established a pathway

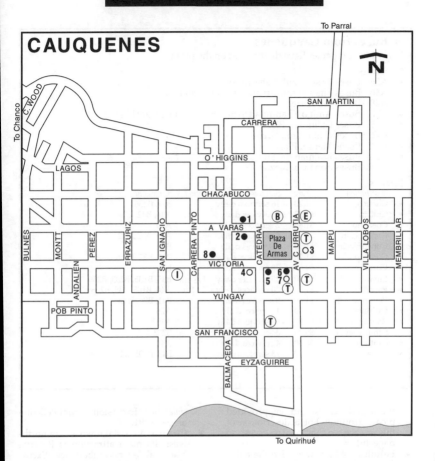

CAUQUENES

Key to map

A Iglesia
B Gobernación Provincial (Government)
E Telephone
I Tourist information
T Bus terminals

● **Accommodation**
1 Residencial

2 Hotel Gran Maule
5 Hotel Coppelia
6 Hotel Manso de Velasco
8 Hotel Los Conquistadores

○ **Eating out**
3 Café El Greco
4 Café Oriente
7 Restaurant Chez Moi

🚌 Buses from Cauquenes

Many bus companies have their offices on the plaza.

Companies
- A26 Buses Costa Azul, Catedral 298
- A46 Buses Linea Azul, Urrutia just off main Plaza
- A48 Buses Lit, Plaza
- B21 Buses Amigo, Claudina Urrutia 500 (on the plaza) ☎ 511992
- B35 Buses Calimpar, Plaza
- B42 Buses Cinta Azul, Urrutia
- B105 Buses Mansa, Plaza
- B233 Buses Pullman del Sur
- B256 Buses Bonanza, Plaza

Services

Destination	Fare	Services	Duration	Company
Chanco	$1.20	16 services daily		B21, B256
Chillán	$1.70	6 services daily	2 hrs	A46, B42
Coelemu	$1.80	2 services daily		A26
Concepción		6 services daily		A26, A46, B42
Constitución	$1.90	2 services daily		B21
Curanipe	$1.20	19 services daily		B21, B35, B256
Curicó	$4.60	20 services daily		B21
Linares	$2.10	25 services daily	1½ hrs	B35, B105, B233, B256
Parral	$1.20	20 services daily	1 hr	A48, B105, B35, B256
Pelluhue	$1.00	9 services daily		B21, B35, B256
Quirihué	$1.40	1 service daily		A26
Rancagua	$5.90	10 services daily		A153
San Fernando	$5.20	3 services daily		B233
Santiago	$6.80	4 services daily		A48
Talca	$3.10	23 services daily		B43, B105, B233, B256

through the forest and has provided picnic grounds. For a description of this reserve see "National reserves" on page 461.
- **Pelluhue**: 42 km west. See the entry for Pelluhue on page 489.
- **Curanipe**: 49 km west. A small seaside resort on the Pacific Ocean It has good beaches suitable for swimming and fishing. The beaches are skirted by shrubs and trees and there are *residen-ciales*. See "Excursions" from Pellehue on page 491.
- **Chanco**: A coastal town 49 km northwest. Its main attraction is Reserva Nacional Federico Albert. See "Excursions" from Pellehue on page 490.
- **Pilén**: A village 13 km south-west known for its pottery, with some of the best potters in the province working from here.

COLBÚN

Population: 5000
Distance from Linares: 32 km east on Ruta L-35

Colbún is a small town in the *pre-Cordillera* near **Lago Colbún** and **Lago Machicura**. These artificial lakes were created by damming the Río Maule for the hydro-electric scheme known as the Colbún–Machicura complex.

The lakes have encouraged the development of a local tourist industry for water sports like swimming and water-skiing, and for fishing.

⊟ Accommodation
- Residencial Colbún in main street
- Residencial El Parrón in main street

Accommodation on Lago Machicura
- Cabañas La Marina del Lago, Lago Machicura

Accommodation on the north side of Lago Colbún, along RN 115
- Casas El Colorado KM 46 ADEFGHKLMP ((71) 221750 or (09) 7427220. Tennis, golf

Accommodation on south side of Lago Colbún.
- Residencial El Mirador de Colbún, 9 km east of Colbún (near Colbún Alto) $H ⋮. 15 camping spots, near the lake edge. Level ground; trees have been planted but not much shade. Facilities are still a bit basic but are improving, electricity, kiosk, toilet block, cold showers, water from central container, laundry, boat hire, good spot for water sport; camping site for 6 $I. Open in January and February
- Motel Marina del Lago, 2 km east of Colbún on a nice beach and surrounded by pine trees. Facilities include a restaurant, boat ramp, electricity, 15 camp sites, toilets, hot showers, laundry, disco weekends. $J per camp site. Attached are also 12

cabins $H for 6. Excellent spot for sailing and fishing

▲ Camping
There is a camping site on Lago Machicura. Only sailing boats are permitted on this lake.

⑪ Eating out
- Restaurant Plaza, on the main plaza. Also has rooms to let

▨ Post and telegraph
The post office is on the main plaza.

▥ Buses

Services
- Linares: Fare $1.30; 10 services daily; Buses Interbus
- Talca: Fare $2.10; 3 services daily; Buses Colbún, Buses Pullman del Sur
- Termas de Panimávida: Fare $0.80; 10 services daily; Buses Interbus

▤ Motoring
- COPEC gas station

⦿ Excursions
- **Lago Colbún**: Near Alto Colbún there are some beaches with some tourist facilities such as camping places, boat hire, and sailing. See also "Camping" above.
- **Lago Machicura**: 3 km east, with an excellent camping ground. Fishing and sailing; motor boats are not allowed.

CONSTITUCIÓN

Area code: 071
Population: 32 000
Altitude: Sea level
Distance from Talca: 100 km south-west on Ruta M- 30-L and Panamericana

At the mouth of the **Río Maule** is Constitución, a charming seaside resort with wide and long beaches of black sand. It was founded by Don Ambrosio O'Higgins in 1794 who called it Nueva Bilbao because it reminded him of this northern Spanish city. Along the sandy beach there are some enormous and curiously shaped boulders — such as Las Termopilas, Piedra de la Iglesia, Calabocillos, and a natural arch called Arco de los Enamorados ("Lovers' Arch").

In colonial days this was an important port for wheat being shipped to Peru. The grain was carried in wooden sailing vessels made from the native oak. They were over 25 m long and were manufactured in Constitución at the local dockyards. Today there is a large pulp and paper plant here processing the pine timber from the plantations.

Key to map

A	Iglesia	**29**	Residencial Fabiani
C	Municipalidad (Town hall)	**30**	Residencial Los Mauchos
D	Post office and telex	**32**	Residencial Garrido
E	Telephone	**34**	Hotel Blanco Encalada
G	Mercado Municipal (Market)		
H	Hospital	○	**Eating out**
P	Gas stations	**2**	Restaurant Los Portales
T	Bus terminals	**17**	Restaurant El Nuevo Escorial
		18	Club de La Unión
●	**Accommodation**	**20**	Restaurant Lomits
3	Hostería de Constitución	**27**	Café Rapa Nui
5	Hotel Posada Colonial	**28**	Café Plaza
8	Residencial Florita	**31**	Restaurant Otto Schop
10	Hotel Santa Ana	**33**	Restaurant Stop 78
12	Residencial Bulnes		
13	Residencial Yolanda	■	**Sights**
14	Residencial Chepita	**7**	Astilleros Maulinos
15	Residencial Urrutia	**9**	Iglesia
16	Residencial Anita 2	**11**	Capilla Buen Pastor
19	Hotel Praderas		
21	Hotel Avendaño	□	**Services**
23	Residencial Plaza	**1**	Cruise boats
24	Residencial López	**4**	Boat hire
25	Residencial Ahumada	**6**	Ferry to Quivolgo
26	Residencial Ramírez	**22**	Supermercado Loyola

MAULE

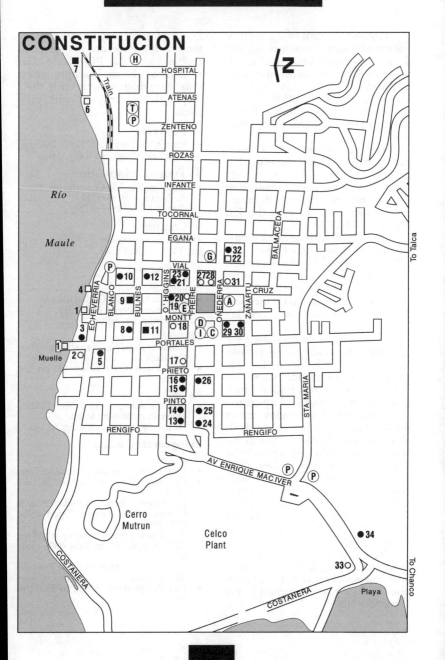

Around the turn of the century the town became a seaside resort, but despite its beautiful surroundings, it is somewhat restricted because of the pollution from the CELCO plant. However, a vigorous attempt is being made by Chilean authorities to make pollution control more effective.

The best views over Constitución are from **Cerro Mutrún**, a hill on the southern edge of the city above the CELCO plant, dominating the skyline. From the top there are good views over the city, the Río Maule, and Isla Orrego.

The city is surrounded by pine forests and is open only to the sea. It is linked with the Panamericana and Talca by a sealed road winding through the pine-covered hills. There is a gravel road south to **Chanco** and **Pelluhue**, and there are regular buses.

Calle Blanco continues along the Río Maule from Calle Vial as a gravel road. From the banks of the Río Maule there are splendid views upstream to the railroad bridge which spans the river about 5 km upstream.

Take some time to relax and sit on one of the benches on the path along the river bank and watch the fishing boats as they return from the sea and unload their catches. Then wander along to the interesting little church on Plaza de Armas, which dates from 1860. If you want to buy a souvenir of your trip, the local people make some interesting handicrafts from sea shells.

You can get to the southern beaches, camping spots and also seaside hotels and restaurants via Enrique MacIver past the turnoff to the Panamericana.

A pleasant way to spend an afternoon is to go on one of the launch cruises along the Río Maule. The river runs between low hills, which look very picturesque with their slopes thickly covered with pine trees.

Festivals

- March, second half: Fería Internacional de la Región VII del Maule

Tourist information

- Municipalidad de Constitución, Plaza A. Prat ☎ 671320 / 671317
- CONAF, Montt 156 ☎ 671249

Camping

There is a camping site on Playa Potrerillos, 5 km south of town.

Eating out

Restaurants

- Club de la Unión, O'Higgins 497
- El Nuevo Escorial, Freire 319
- Fandango, Rengifo

Cafeterías

- Cafetería Rapa Nui, Cruz Block 400 on the plaza
- Café Plaza, Cruz block 400 on the plaza

Fast food

- Lomit's Schop, Freire 586. Pizzas. Open daily 0900–midnight
- ☞ Parrillada Los Gomeros, Egaña 140

Eating out at the beaches

Restaurants

- Blue Moon, Avenida Enrique McIver
- Da Paula, Avenida Enrique McIver 1420
- De Turismo Jofre, Avenida Enrique McIver 1316. Seafood. Open daily 0900–0100
- El Caleuche, Avenida Enrique McIver 1434. Seafood. Open daily 0800–midnight
- Hostería Villa Mar, Avenida Enrique McIver 1300
- Los Picapiedras, Avenida Enrique McIver

⊟ Accommodation in Constitución

Hotels
- Avendaño, O'Higgins 681
- Gran Hotel, Freire 315   AEFKLPSV
- Praderas, Cruz 353   AFHIJKMPSV   (671213 $H ⚥
- Santa Ana, Blanco 666   AEHIJKLMPSVZ   (671344 $H ⚥
  Open during the season only
- Posada Colonial, Blanco 390   (671215 $E for 4
  Visa card accepted

Hosterías
- De Constitución, Echeverria 460   ADEFGHIJKLMPRVT   (671450 $F ⚥
  Fax 671480, sauna, overlooks Río Maule

Residenciales for budget travelers
- Chepita, Freire 160
- Florita, Bulnes 442   AS $J ⚹
- Garri-More, Enrique MacIver 679 near gas station
- Los Mauchos, Zañartu 448   AS   (671159 $J ⚹
- Ramírez, Freire 292   (671233
- Vilches, Rengifo 345   AS   (671309 $J ⚹

Residenciales for backpackers
- Ahumada, Freire 189

Accommodation on or near the southern beaches
- Hotel Blanco Encalada, Avenida Enrique McIver
      AFHIJKSV   (671222 $H ⚹
- Hostería Villa Mar, Avenida Enrique McIver 1300   (671104

Accommodation across Río Maule
- Moteles Quivolgo, Fundo Quivolgo   ABCDEFGHIJLMNPRTV
      (671209 $F for 4

  Sauna, overlooks river

⊤ Entertainment
- Disco Barbilla, Montt block 300 near O'Higgins

⊞ Post and telegraph

Post office
The post office is on Montt.

Telephone
- CTC, Freire 526, fax (71) 671037
- Telex Chile, Freire 522

⑤ Financial
- Banco del Estado, Freire 576 (671318

⊟ Services and facilities

Hospital
- Bulnes (671305

Supermarket
- Supermercado Loyola, Oñederra 781

⊟ Buses
The bus terminal is on Plaza Señoret, corner of Blanco and Zenteno.

Services
- Cauquenes: 2 services daily; Buses Amigo
- Chanco: Fare $1.80; 5 services daily; Buses Amigo
- Pelluhue: Fare $1.90; 3 services daily; Buses Amigo
- Santiago: Fare $5.80; 1 service daily; Buses Pullman del Sur (671254
- Talca: Fare $2.30; 20 services daily; Expreso O'Higgins, Buses Pullman del Sur

🚌 Motoring

For gas stations, see city map.

⚓ Water transport

- Ferry to Quivolgo leaves from Matadero corner of Blanco (near the shipyards); fare $0.75. At Quivolgo is a *hostería*
- River cruises leave from Muelle Fiscal on Portales near Blanco; fare $3.00
- A cruise around Isla Orrego takes 20 minutes; fare $0.50. Boat hire on the corner of Cruz and Blanco

📷 Sightseeing

- Asterillos Maulinos, Echeverria, past the railroad station just where the ferry leaves for Quivolgo. In the 19th century the vessels carrying grain to Peru were built in these shipyards. Open for inspection.

📍 Excursions

- **Calabocillo beach**: 4 km south; there is an irregular bus service. Near the beach there are some huge rocks and boulders, and there are caves in some of them.
- **Las Cañas beach:** 18 km south on Ruta K-24-M. A large beach with no tourist facilities.
- **Empedrado** is a small township 43 km south east of Constitución. It is in the western part of the coastal *cordillera* facing towards the Pacific ocean. The town, which is in hilly country, was founded in 1835. The town's 1600 population are largely working in the nearby pine plantations as loggers. Today the main attraction is the local museum and the vicinity to the northern sector of **Reserva Nacional Los Ruiles** which starts on the outskirts of town. For a description of this reserve see "National reserves" on page 461. Museo Arellano has memorabilia of the town's first settlers and some archeological finds. Open daily during January and February and on Sundays during the rest of the year. Rural buses run to and from Constitución. Also logging workers with trucks give lifts.

CURICÓ

Area code: 075
Population: 105 000
Distance from Talca: 66 km north on Panamericana

Curicó, founded in 1743 by Don José Antonio de Velasco, is in the northern part of the central valley on the Río Lontué, and is the capital of the province of the same name. It was initially called San José de Buena Vista, but its name was later changed to Curicó.

There is no doubt that the showpiece in this town is the Plaza de Armas which is really a botanical garden: most Chilean native species are represented and tagged. The sides of the plaza are lined with 64 palm trees which were brought from the Canary Islands. Complementing the natural beauty of the plants are the many ponds, fountains, and statues in the plaza. The particularly beautiful fountain in the center of the plaza is called Las Tres Gracias ("The Three Graces"), and was brought from France in 1865. Look for the tree trunk in which an artist has carved a monument in honor of the great Mapuche warrior Chief Lautaro. On the west side of the plaza there is a curious two-story metal kiosk which is a *monumento histórico*.

It is as if time had stood still here — horsedrawn carts and horses and buggies throng the streets, just as

✉ Accommodation in Curicó

Hotels
★★★Comercio, Yungay 730	ADEFGHIJKLMPSTUV			
		(310014/311516	$G	♁
German and English spoken				
• Luis Cruz Martínez, Arturo Prat 301	ADEFIJKLMPUV	(310552	$G	♁
☞ • Prat, Peña 427		(311069	$H	♁
☞ • Rahue, Peña 410		(312194		
• Savoy, Avenida Prat 726			$J	♁
Backpackers				
• Turismo, Carmen corner of Prat		(310552		

Residenciales
• Central, Avenida Prat 669			$J	♁
Budget travelers				
• Colonial, Rodríguez 461			$J	♁
Budget travelers				
• Francy's, Maipú 570			$J	♁
Backpackers				

Accommodation along the Panamericana Sur
• Hostal Villa El Descanso, KM 186		(312199		
Fax 312231				
• Cabañas La Laguna, KM 203 at the intersection with road leading into Lontué				
	APS	((09) 7513285	$F	♁

Accommodation in Área de Protección Radal
Located 79 km south-east of Curicó. For a description see "National reserves" on page 461.
• Hostería La Flor de La Canela, in Parque Inglés				
	APS	((75) 491613	$H	♀
Full boad				

Accommodation in Los Queñes
• Hostería Los Queñes, Avenida Freire	AEFGHIJLNPRUV	(1	$H	♁
Outdoor area				
• Residencial Garrido, Avenida Freire		(893121		

Accommodation in Hualañé
Hualañé, with a population of 3200, is a bustling agricultural town in the lower Mataquito valley 74 km west of Curicó. Two kilometres west of town is a Y- intersection: the road north leads to Vichuquén and the road west leads to Iloca. There are two gas stations in town. Restaurant Donde Jorge is in the main street. Buses Bravo, Buses Díaz, and Buses Ilomar run regular services to Curicó.

Hosterías
• Hualañé, Prat 421 next to gas station	(481069	$H	♁
Quite nice and quite big. Drivers usually make a stop here for a lunch break			
• Shell, Libertad 42			
Quite big, with a restaurant with saloon-type bar area			

Accommodation in Romeral
Romeral, 9 km east of Curicó, is a small rural community in a wine-growing district.
• Alemana, Yungay 98	AS	(311763	$F	♁
Shared bathroom				

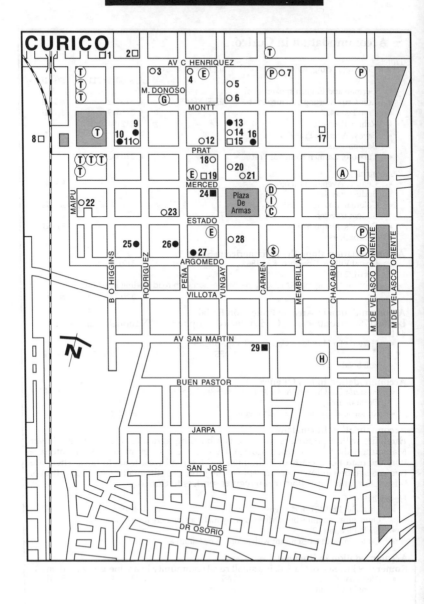

CURICO

AV C HENRIQUEZ

M. DONOSO

MONTT

PRAT

MERCED

Plaza De Armas

ESTADO

ARGOMEDO

VILLOTA

AV SAN MARTIN

BUEN PASTOR

JARPA

SAN JOSE

DR OSORIO

B O HIGGINS

RODRIGUEZ

PEÑA

YUNGAY

CARMEN

MEMBRILLAR

CHACABUCO

M DE VELASCO PONIENTE

M DE VELASCO ORIENTE

MAIPU

Key to map

A	Iglesia	7	Restaurant Germania
C	Municipalidad (Town hall)	9	Restaurant Vegas de Rodríguez
D	Post office and telex	11	Café Maxim
E	Telephone	12	Pizzería MazaPán
G	Mercado Municipal (Market)	14	Restaurant Luzzi
H	Hospital	18	Café American
I	Tourist information	20	Café Nápoli
P	Gas stations	21	Club de la Unión
$	Money exchange	22	Restaurant Donde Nino
T	Bus terminals	23	Club Italiano

●	**Accommodation**	■	**Sights**
10	Residencial Central	24	Ruinas Antigua Iglesia La Merced
13	Hotel Comercio	29	Iglesia del Carmen
16	Hotel Luis Cruz Martínez	□	**Services**
25	Residencial Colonial		
26	Hotel Prat	1	Horse and buggy stand
27	Residencial Rahue	2	Supermercado las Brisas
○	**Eating out**	8	Railroad station
3	Restaurant Vista Hermosa	15	Flash photographic eequipment
4	Restaurant Polo	17	Automóvil Club de Chile
5	Restaurant Apiac	19	Centro Cultural
6	Restaurant El Fogón Chileno	28	Telex Chile

they would have done a century ago. The main church on Plaza de Armas is in ruins — destroyed by the last earthquake — but it dates back to the town's foundation.

Not far from the town center is Cerro Condell, within easy walking distance. It is certainly worth taking a stroll there for the classic view of the city and the surrounding valley. The slopes have been planted with trees, and Avenida Manso de Velasco which passes along the hill is also tree-lined. At the foot of the hill is Iglesia San Francisco built towards the end of the 19th century and a *monumento histórico nacional*. You will also see monuments to the founder of the city and one of the heroes of the Independence wars, Luis Cruz Martínez, who fought in the battle of Concepción. The Club de Tenis de Curicó and an ice skating strip are also here.

Curicó is one of the major fruit export centers of Chile, exporting table grapes, apples, apricots, pears, and kiwifruit.

For those interested in river rafting, the upper **Río Teno** is suitable for rafting or boating. The most beautiful parts of the river are higher up from Los Queñes.

Curicó is the starting point for excursions to the **Laguna de Teno** and **Volcán Planchón** (3920 m) on Ruta J-55 into the Andes. It is also convenient if you want to get to the beachside resorts such as **Llico** and **Iloca**, and to **Lago Vichuquén** using Ruta J-60.

ⓘ Tourist information

- Municipalidad de Curicó, Plaza de Armas ℂ 310002
- CONAF, Edificio Gobernación ℂ 310321
- Turismo Bucalemu, Yungay 621 ℂ 312089. Information about Vichuquén

Ⓐ Camping

Camping in Área de Protección Radal
Área de Protección Radal is located 79 km
south-east of Curicó. For a description,
see "National reserves"on page 461.
CONAF maintains a camping ground inside the Área de Protección Radal, just
after crossing the Río Claro bridge. There
is also a camping site in Los Queñes,
46 km east of Curicó.

⑪ Eating out

Restaurants
- Apiac, Yungay 840
- Establecimiento Luzzi, Yungay 720.
  International cuisine. Self-service
- Centro Español, Avenida España 802
- Centro Italiano, Estado 531
- Club de la Unión, Merced 341. Chil-
  ean, international cuisine. Open Mon–
  Sun 0900–midnight
☞ • Colo Colo, Peña 898
- Deportivo, Manuel Montt 446
- Hostería Donde Nino, Maipú 550. Sea-
  food. Open Mon–Sat 1130–midnight
- El Fogón Chileno, Yungay 802
- La Guindalera, Avenida Prat 599
- Mazapan, Avenida Prat block 400 be-
  tween Peña and Yungay
- Savoy, Prat 726
- Villota, Merced 487. Chilean cuisine

Cafés
- Maxim, Avenida Prat 679
- Nápoli, Yungay 698
- Polo, Avenida Camilo Henriquez 498
☞ • Cafetería Vista Hermosa, Avenida
  Camilo Henriquez 598

Eating out along the Panamericana

Restaurants
- Hostería Aguas Negras, Longitudinal
  Sur KM 190 corner of Avenida Ales-
  sandri (northern entrance). Open
  0800–midnight. Chilean and interna-
  tional cuisine
- Hostería Shell, Longitudinal Sur
  KM 193 just past Río Guaiquillo
  bridge near turnoff to Los Nichos
  (southern entrance). Open 24 hours.
  Chilean nad international cuisine
- Da Orestino, Longitudinal Sur
  KM 191 between Avenida España and
  Avenida Velasco

Fast food
- Snackbar Cecinas Soler, KM 189
  (northern entrance). Open 24 hours

Ⓨ Entertainment
- American Bar, Yungay 647. Cocktail
  lounge and meals, with light background music by a small band

▦ Post and telegraph

Post office
- Correo Central, Carmen corner of
  Estado opposite plaza inside the Mu-
  nicipalidad building

Telephone
- CTC, Peña 650-A, fax 314719
- Telex Chile, Constitución

Ⓢ Financial
- Fincard, Carmen 598 ℂ 311792. Cash
  advances against Visa and Mastercard

▤ Services and facilities

Camping and fishing equipment
- Casa de Deportes, Avenida Arturo
  Prat 537

Dry cleaner
- Lavaseco Italia, M. Montt 323

Laundry
- Lavandería Aval, Merced 471

Medical services
- Hospital, Chacabuco 121

Photographic supplies
- Flash, Yungay 714

Supermarket
- Supermercado Las Brisas, Camilo
  Henriquez 619

▦ Trains
The railroad station is on Maipú opposite
Prat.
- Puerto Montt: *Económico* $11.20; 1st
  class $9.80
- Temuco: *Económico* $14.00: 1st class
  $10.00

▦ Motoring
For gas stations, see city map. There is also
a Shell station on the Panamericana outside town.
- COPEC, Carmen 890 corner of C. Hen-
  .riquez. Sells road maps

🚌 Buses from Curicó

The long-distance bus terminal is on Prat between O'Higgins and Rodríguez.
* B21   Buses Amigo
* B78   Buses Hernández
* B101 Buses Los Queñes
* B111 Buses Moraga
* B117 Buses Longitudinal Sur
* B227 Molibus ℂ 311065
* B233 Pullman del Sur

Rural buses depart from Maipú between Henriquez and Merced, near the railroad station.

Companies with own terminal
* A48   Buses Lit, Las Heras 0915 ℂ 310554
* A127 Pullman Bus, Avenida C. Henriquez block 200 near Membrillar
* A153 Tur-Bus Jedimar, M. de Velasco near Castellón ℂ 312115
* B23   Buses Andimar, Yungay 926 ℂ 31200
* B33   Buses Bravo, Prat 766 ℂ 312193
* B57   Buses Díaz, Prat 766 ℂ 311905
* B59   Buses Duarte, 5 Oriente 1078 ℂ 224866
* B274 Buses Ilomar, Prat 780 ℂ 310358

Services

Destination	Fare	Services	Duration	Companies
• Área de Protección Radal				
	$1.80			B78
• Aquelarre	$2.90			B33, B57, B274
• Cauquenes	$4.60			B21
• Chillán	$4.20		3 hrs	A153
• Concepción	$7.60			A153
• Curepto	$2.50			B57, B274
• Duao	$2.90			B274
• Hualañe	$1.70	5 services daily		B33, B57, B274
• Iloca	$3.10	3 services daily		B33, B274
• Linares	$2.30			A153
• Lipimávida	$3.30			B57, B274
• Llico	$2.90	1 service daily		B33
• Los Angeles	$7.60	5 services daily	$4\frac{1}{2}$ hrs	A153
• Los Queñes	$1.30	2 services daily		B101, B111
• Molina				B227
• Osorno	$14.40			A153
• Parral	$2.90		2 hrs	A153
• Pichilemu		1 service daily		B57
• Puerto Montt	$16.70			A153
• Puerto Varas	$16.70			A153
• Rancagua	$2.50	5services daily	$2\frac{1}{2}$ hrs	A153
• San Fernando	$1.40		1 hr	A153
• Santiago	$3.60	12 services daily	$3\frac{1}{2}$ hrs	A48, A127, B23, B57, B117, B233, B274
• Talca	$1.70	16 services daily	$\frac{1}{2}$ hr	A127, B119, B233
• Talcahuano	$8.00			A153
• Temuco	$11.80			A48
• Valdivia	$13.10			A153
• Vichuquén	$1.20	2 services daily		B57
• Viña del Mar	$7.60	3 services daily		A74

- Automóvil Club de Chile, Chacabuco 759

Shopping

Curicó is famous for its marzipan cakes.

Sport

- Trout fishing in Río Mataquito, Río Lontué, Río Upeo, upper Río Teno, Estero Potrero Grande, Río Guaiquillo, and Río Palos de San Pedro

Sightseeing

In Estado between Avenida Manso de Velasco and Carmen, the town still retains some of its original character and looks something like it must have done during the colonial period. Old colonial buildings flank the northern side of Estado.

- Casa de la Cultura, Merced 437. This belongs to the Universidad Católica de Chile and has a large library, theater, and *cafetería*. Exhibitions are often held here.
- Iglesia San Francisco on Plaza San Francisco is a *monumento nacional*. The original town was founded around this church and convent. Inside the church is a copy of the statue of the Virgen de la Velilla in Spain which was brought to Chile in 1734.
- Iglesia del Carmen, Avenida San Martín corner of Carmen. A large construction with three naves; spires and apses of elaborate stone masonry.
- Iglesia de la Merced, Chacabuco.

Excursions

- **Área de Protección Radal**. 48 km east. This trip is highly recommended, and there are rural buses leaving daily for Radal, the starting point for walks into the reserve. Check with Hostería Flor de la Canela at Parque Inglés (10 km east of Radal) whether accommodation is available (491367 Molina. The trip is on a rather bumpy dirt road which may be cut in sudden downpours. For a description of this reserve, see "National Reserves" on page 461.
- **Los Queñes**: A summer resort in the *pre-Cordillera*, 48 km east at an altitude of 600 m, where the Río Claro meets with the Río Teno. The original village

consists of old adobe houses, and a number of holiday homes have been built along the river. Buses Moraga and Buses Los Queñes run two services from the rural terminal in Curicó; fare $1.50. There is good fishing here, in the Río Teno; with its swiftly running water it is suitable for canoeing and rafting. In the vicinity of Los Queñes there are hot springs but no facilities. The road from Curicó is sealed for 20 km, and then is a good dirt road. On the way up, you pass through **Romeral**, a fruit-growing area — see below. The higher you get, the greener the countryside becomes. There is a small mountain pass (Cuesta Los Maquis) from which you have sweeping views over the Río Teno. And all the time in the background there are the high *sierras* looking down on you. Los Queñes is the starting point for mountain hikes further up the Río Teno valley, in particular the area around **Volcán Planchón** (3900 m) on the Argentine border, 96 km east, near **Paso de Vergara**. The huge crater has steep cliffs covered by snow; inside the crater there is a small lake. It snows here frequently. This area has wild and rugged scenery with the **Volcán Peteroa** and **Volcán Planchón** as a backdrop to the **Laguna de Teno**. To explore this area use the following Instituto Geográfico Militar 1:50 000 maps: "Lagunas de Teno" (5-04-86-044-00) and "Volcán Peteroa" (5-04-86-053-00). This is a tent and sleeping bag excursion for experienced mountain hikers. A trail branches off from the main track to Laguna de Teno. To get there you need your own four-wheel-drive transport. The road peters out towards the pass, and there is no road on the Argentine side to Las Leñas, the skiing resort. The *hostería* in Los Queñes has horses for trekking and is a good base for outings or fishing trips further up the mountains.

- **Molina**: 20 km south, in the heart of Chile's wine-growing country. It is easily accessible by bus from the rural bus terminal in Calle Prat. See the entry for Molina on page 486.

- **Reserva Nacional Laguna Torca**: 115 km west, near Lago Vichuquén. For a description of this wildlife sanctuary see "National reserves" on page 461.
- **Romeral:** A farming community 9 km east. Cherries, sour cherries, and apples are the major crops grown here, and the area is also known for vintage wines.
- **Vichuquén** and **Lago Vichuquén**: 100 km west, near the *lago* of the same name. See the entry for Vichuquén on page 500. There are regular daily buses run by the coastal bus companies in Calle Prat opposite the rural bus terminal and near the railroad station.

ILOCA

Distance: Curicó 127 km west on Ruta J-60-I

Iloca is a small seaside resort on the Pacific coast some 15 km west of Vichuquén. There are extensive beaches north and south of town of black volcanic sand. The main influx of tourists is between December and the end of February, but many hotels are open all year round. The fact that one beach is called La Pesca is an indication of the good fishing here. The area around Iloca is known for its homespun woolen clothes.

Ⓐ Camping

There is a camping site on the banks of Estero Iloca 800 m south of town, and also a serviced camping site between Pichibudi and Lipimávida.

Ⅲ Eating out

Eating out in Duao
Located 8 km north of Iloca.
- Restaurant Donde Gilberto. Seafood, open Mon–Sun 0800–midnight
- Restaurant Donde Nino. Seafood, open Mon–Sun 0800–midnight

🚌 Buses

Services
- Curicó: Fare $3.10; 3 services daily; 3½ hrs; Buses Amigo, Buses Díaz, Buses Ilomar
- Talca: Fare $2.90; Buses Ilomar

⊙ Excursions

- **Curepto:** 31 km south, with a population of 3000. It is an old colonial town. To get there turn off past the village of Lora and cross the Río Mataquito via Puente Lautaro. Its main attraction is the Iglesia Nuestra Señora del Rosario de Curepto on the Plaza de Armas and the many picturesque adobe buildings with verandahs which grace the town. Buses Díaz and Buses Ilomar have regular daily buses to Iloca and Curicó. For accommodation, see the box on the next page.
- **Duao**: A small seaside resort with good tourist facilities and nice beaches 8 km north. It is famous for its excellent seafood. Buses Díaz and Buses Ilomar run regular daily services to Iloca and Curicó; Buses Italmar run one service daily to Talca.
- **Lipimávida**: A small beach resort 12 km north. The local people make garments and other handicrafts from wool. On the first Sunday in September a colorful *fiesta* is held in honor of the Virgen de las Mercedes. The celebrations are held in a small chapel, but they attract many of the faithful from the surrounding area. Buses Díaz and Buses Ilomar run regular daily services to Curicó via Iloca.
- **Lago Vichuquén** and **Reserva Nacional Laguna Torca**: 14 km east. Inland lake resorts and nature reserves. For Lago Vichuquén see "Excursions" from Vichuquén on page 502; and for

Iloca

⊟ Accommodation in Iloca

Hotels

★★ Iloca, Agustín Besoain 221	AEFGHIJKLPSVZ	☎ 887998	$H ⚊
• Curicó, Agustín Besoain 264 Full board	AEFGHIJKLNPV	☎ (2) 5550023	$F ⚌

Hosterías

• De Iloca, Agustín Besoain 260	AEFGHIJLN		$F ⚌

Residenciales

• Las Camelias Full board	AP		$H ⚌
• La Bahía Full board	AP		$H ⚌

Accommodation along the road to Duao
• Cabañas La Puntilla, 1.5 km north   ☎ (75) 314745

Accommodation in Curepto
Curepto is 31 km south of Iloca.
• Hotel Curepto, basic

Accommodation in Duao

Hosterías

• Donde Gilberto	AEFGHIKLPSV		$F ⚌
Full board, overlooking beach. Reservations in Curicó: ☎ 312752
• Donde Nino	AEFGHIJKPS	☎ (75)311182	$G ⚊
Full board, terraces overlooking the beach

Residenciales

• El Alero de Clavito	S		$H ⚌

Reserva Laguna Torca see "National reserves" on page 461.

• **Lora:** In the Río Mataquito valley 23 km south-east, just before the turn-off to Puente Lautaro. Its church was built in the 16th century. During the third week in October, the village celebrates the Fiesta de la Virgen del Rosario. Its main event is the traditional *Baile de los Negros* ("Dance of the Negroes"), in which the participants (*compadritos*) cover themselves with hides and wear masks. As the dance progresses, one dancer with a whip and a pointed stick urges the onlookers to participate in the dance. Dozens of flutes are played, creating a magical sound. Buses Amigo Buses Díaz and Buses Ilomar run regular daily buses to Curicó and Iloca.

LINARES

Area code: 073
Population: 61 000
Distances
- From Talca: 50 km south on Panamericana
- From Santiago: 315 km south on the Panamericana Sur

Linares is a provincial capital in the southern part of the central valley. It was founded in 1794 by Don Ambrosio O'Higgins, father of the Liberator, and named in honor of the then Intendente of Concepción.

The focal point of the city is the Plaza de Armas, around which all important official buildings are grouped. Inside the park are statues, including one of Ambrosio O'Higgins. The cathedral, Iglesia de San Antonio, stands on the western side of the plaza and is built in Roman-Byzantine style. Do not miss the mosaic made by Giulio di Girolamo, and the mural paintings by Fray Pedro Subercaseaux in the chapel downstairs.

Nowadays Linares is an important industrial town known particularly for its sugar mills.

Tourist information
- CONAF, Salida Palmilla
- Información Turística Municipal, K.Moller corner of Quilo, opposite the plaza

Eating out
The specialty here is a long pork sausage called *longanizas*.

Restaurants
- Centro Español, Sotomayor 476
- Club de la Unión, corner of Maipú and Rodríguez, in an old colonial house
- El Golfo, Chacabuco 379. Seafood
- Hostería Colonial, Maipú 290
- La Rueda, Valentín Letelier 491
- Las Camelias, San Antonio 188
- Londres Chico, Manuel Rodríguez 394
- Manhattan, Independencia 470 $Y

Cafetería
- Santa Ana, Independencia block 500 between Lautaro and Chacabuco

Pizzería
- Capri, Independencia 483

Eating out outside town
- Hostería Esso, Panamericana KM 300. Chilean, international cuisine. Open 24 hours daily
- Hostería Malaga, KM 300. Chilean, international cuisine. Open Mon–Sun 0800–midnight

Post and telegraph

Post office
- Correos and Telex Chile, K. Moller 401

Telephone
- CTC, Independencia 488, fax(73) 213060
- Telex Chile, Constitución

Services and facilities

Dry cleaner
- Lavaseco Linares block 100 corner of Freire

Hospital
- Avenida Brasil 753

Motoring
For gas stations, see city map.

Sport
Trout fishing in Río Loncomilla, Río Achibueno, and Río Ancoa.

Sightseeing
- Iglesia Catedral, a fairly modern building on the west side of Plaza de

Linares

Arms. Its interior is of real architectural interest: the apse, pulpit, and bishop's throne are made of Carrara marble. Walls in the underground chapel, called the "Capilla de los Recuerdos", were painted by Fray Pedro Subercaseaux, and there is also a huge (100 square meter) mosaic showing religious themes created by Giulio di Girolamo.

- Museo de Arte y Artesanía, Avenida Valentín Letelier 580. This is an old manorial building housing a picture gallery of famous Chilean and foreign painters and a history room. At the entrance is a statue called "Militza" by Rebeca Matte, a famous Chilean sculptor. Open Tues–Sat 1000–1730 and Sun 1000–1300. Admission $1.00.

Excursions

- **Lago Colbún** and **Lago Machicura**: 32 km north-east. These artificial lakes are excellent for water sports and fishing. See the entry for Colbún on page 467.
- **Longaví:** A small rural town of about 4700 inhabitants 17 km south on the Panamericana in the central valley. In February, a Festival de la Canción Longaví Canta ("Longaví Sings" Song Festival) is held. On this occasion the town becomes very crowded. Buses Comunal Longaví runs regular daily buses from Linares.

- **Termas de Panimávida:** 21 km north-east, at an altitude of 174 m in the *pre-Cordillera*; the climate is temperate and enjoyable. The best time to visit is from the beginning of September onwards. The thermal water reaches a temperature of 33°C (91°F). The spa has been used by Chileans since 1820. The entrance to the thermal complex is on the main plaza, and is open all year round. The hotel is pleasant and has a complete medical clinic with a resident doctor. Termas de Panimávida has many different thermal springs, each enclosed by a stone wall, with a little statue on top, and each with its own name, such as Fuente Santa Luisa, or Fuente Dionisio. They are in a spacious garden with meandering pathways. Visitors may use the indoor pool, admission $8.00, or take a mud bath. The access road to the springs is completely sealed. Taxi *colectivos* and Buses Interbus run 13 services daily from Linares. From **Rari**, a small village 2 km east, you get wonderful views of the *cordillera*. The main attraction of this village is the local handicrafts: dolls and witches dressed in colonial garments made of horsehair and vegetable fibers. There are also old established country estates, making this a very interesting Chilean time capsule.
- **Termas de Quinamávida:** 17 km east, in the lowest spurs of the *pre-Cordillera*

Key to map

A	Iglesia Catedral de San Antonio	6	Hotel Real
B	Gobernación Provincial (Government)	7	Hotel Curapalihue
		9	Hotel Londres
C	Municipalidad (Town hall)		
D	Post office and telex	○	**Eating out**
E	Telephone	8	Club de la Unión
G	Mercado Municipal (Market)	11	Café Manhattan
I	Tourist information	13	Restaurant Londres Chico
P	Gas stations	14	Restaurant El Golf
T	Bus terminals		
		■	**Sights**
●	**Accommodation**	12	Iglesia Corazón de María
1	Residencial Madrid	15	Museo de Linares
2	Hotel Anggus Manor		
3	Hotel Turismo	□	**Services**
4	Hotel Comendador del Maule	10	Galería Chacabuco
5	Hotel Asthur	16	Railroad station

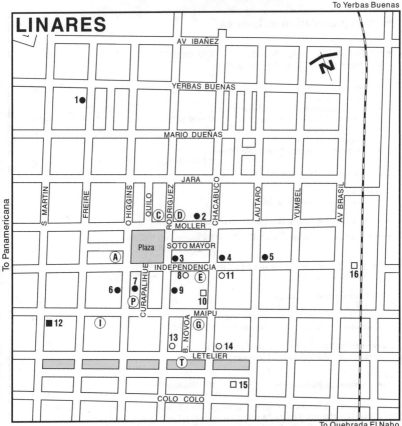

To Yerbas Buenas

LINARES

AV IBAÑEZ

YERBAS BUENAS

MARIO DUEÑAS

JARA

1●

To Panamericana

S MARTIN · FREIRE · O'HIGGINS · QUILO · RODRIGUEZ · CHACABUCO · LAUTARO · YUMBEL · AV BRASIL · CURAPALIHUE · B. NOVOA

© © © ● 2
MOLLER

Plaza · SOTO MAYOR
(A) · ● 3 · ● 4 · ● 5
INDEPENDENCIA
8○ (E) · ○11
6● · 7● · ● 9 · □ 10
(P)
MAIPU
■ 12 · (I) · (G)
13○ · ○ 14
(T) LETELIER

□ 15

COLO COLO

To Quebrada El Nabo
To El Salto

at an altitude of 180 m. The access road is sealed almost all the way. The thermal water is slightly radioactive and reaches a temperature of 21.5°C (71°F). There are extensive gardens around the complex. The hotel is adequate and has an indoor refurbished thermal pool; it is open from December to April. Taxi *colectivos* and Empresa Interbus run frequent daily services from the bus terminal in Linares.

- **Yerbas Buenas**: 12 km north; population 1500. It has strong associations with Chilean history. In 1813 one of the first battles took place here be-

tween Chilean patriots and the Spanish. The village itself is a relic from the past: old colonial houses made of adobe with large verandahs are the norm rather than the exception. Inside the parish church, Santa Cruz, is one of the oldest paintings in Chile, *Nuestra Señora del Rosario*, brought from Spain in 1585. The church was destroyed in the 1928 earthquake and rebuilt. The whole area around the plaza has been declared a *monumento nacional*, and must be preserved in its state as a cultural heritage — time has stood still in Yerbas Buenas. Another

⊟ Accommodation in Linares

Hotels
★★★ Curapalihue, Curapalihue 411   ADEFGHKMPTV   ℂ 212526 $G �
- Angus Manor House, Kurt Moller 467

    AP   ℂ 214159 $H ♀♀
- Asthur, Independencia 693 $J ♀♀
  Backpackers
- Comendador del Maule, Chacabuco 512   ℂ 210379/213727
- Londres, Manuel Rodríguez 456   AEHIJKPSUV   ℂ 210177 $H ♀♀
- Real, Freire 482   AS   ℂ 212896 $I ♀♀
  Shared bathroom
- Turismo de Linares, Manuel Rodríguez 522

    ADEFGHIJKL$UV   ℂ 210636 $H ♀♀
  Cheaper in the courtyard, fax 210636

Residencial
- Madrid, Freire 867 ℂ 211108

Accommodation along the Panamericana Sur

★★★★ Hostería y Moteles Málaga, KM 301 at the crossroads into town
    ABDEFGHIJKLMUZ   ℂ 211129 $H ♀♀

Accommodation along the road to Colbún
- Cabañas El Bosque, KM 4   ℂ 210359

Accommodation in Longaví
Longaví is 17 km south of Linares.
- Residencial Las Malvinas, 2 Norte 20   ℂ 411076 $I ♀
- Hotel Rancho Río Sol, Fundo Malcho   AEFGHLPRV

Accommodation in Termas de Panimávida
Termas de Panimávida is 21 km east of Linares.

Hotels
- Termas de Panimávida   ADEFGHIJKLMNPR$UVXZ

    ℂ 211743 $D ♀♀
  Full board, sauna, thermal spa, tennis, mini golf, horse-riding, and social events. The hotel is surrounded by parks with an open-air and indoor swimming pools. During summer vacation (January and February) booking is advisable. American Express, Mastercard, and Visa accepted
- Central, Capitán Rebolledo 158   AEFHIJKLPUV $H ♀
  Shared bathroom, full board

Accommodation in Termas de Quinamávida
Termas de Quinamávida is 17 km east of Linares.
- Hotel Termas de Quinamávida   AEFGHIJKLMNPRTUVZ ℂ 213887 $D ♀♀
  Full board, tennis, sauna, thermal indoor swimming pool, thermal spa, mini golf. The interior swimming pool is very attractive and spic and span; the water is 24°C (75°F) and is slightly radioactive. Facilities for 210 guests. The hotel is a bit isolated.

🚌 Buses from Linares

The Terminal de Buses Linares is on Valentin Letelier between Rodríguez and Chacabuco.

Companies leaving from the bus terminal
- A16   Buses Pullman Biotal, office 9 ☎ 212521
- A105 Buses Sol del Pacifíco
- B35   Buses Calimpar
- B42   Buses Cinta Azul ☎ 210816
- B97   Buses Linatal, office 8 ☎ 241949
- B105 Buses Mansa
- B233 Buses Pullman del Sur
- B256 Buses Bonanza, office 5 ☎ 214176

Companies with their own terminals
- A48   Buses Lit, M. Rodríguez corner of Delicias ☎ 210219
- B200 Buses Interbus, Delicias ☎ 210933

Services

Destination	Fare	Services	Duration	Company
Cauquenes	$2.10	23 services daily	1½ hrs	B35, B105, B233, B256
Chillán	$2.70	23 services daily		A16, A48, B42, B256
Colbún	$1.00	13 services daily		B200
Concepción	$4.60	5 services daily		A16, A48
Curanipe	$2.30	2 services daily		B35
Los Angeles	$4.60	4 services daily		A16, B256
Osorno	$11.40	4 services daily		A153
Parral	$1.30	14 services daily	1 hr	B35, B256
Pelluhue	$2.70	9 services daily		B35, B256
Puerto Montt	$13.70	4 services daily		A48
Rancagua	$3.80	4 services daily		A153
San Fernando	$3.20	3 services daily		B233
Santiago	$5.30	20 services daily	5 hrs	A48, A127, B217, B233
Talca	$1.40	30 services daily	1 hr	A16, B97, B200, B233, B256
Temuco	$8.50	2 services daily		A48, B256
Termas de Panimávida				
	$0.60	13 services daily	½ hr	B200
Termas de Quinamávida				
	$0.70	2 services daily	½ hr	B200
Valdivia	$10.10	2 services daily	8 hrs	B256
Valparaíso	$9.50	5 services daily		A105
Viña del Mar	$9.50	3 services daily		A74

remainder of the past is Museo Casa de Pareja, named in honor of the Spanish general who spent the night here on the eve of the battle at Yerbas Buenas, called the *Sorpresa de Yerbas Buenas* — a small army of Chileans attacked a much superior force of Spanish royalists and defeated them. The museum is housed in a Spanish colonial building over 200 years old. The memorabilia include armaments of the 18th century and historical documents, and it also exhibits traditional handicrafts made in the region. La Casa de Pareja has been declared a *monumento histórico nacional*. Plaza La Recova, opposite Casa de Pareja, is another relic of the colonial past. On the plaza is a memorial stone in honor of the Chilean novelist Max Jara who was born here in Yerbas Buenas. On December 22 the town celebrates its

🚆 Trains from Linares

The railroad station is on Avenida Brasil opposite Independencia.

Destination	Salón	Económico	Services	Duration
• Chillán			4 services daily	1½ hrs
• Concepción	$4.20	$3.30	3 services daily	5 hrs
• La Laja	$3.30	$2.30		
	Note: There are no train services to Los Angeles: trains stop at La Laja, and from there it is a bus ride to Los Angeles.			
• Osorno	$8.20	$5.70	1 service daily	9 hrs
• Puerto Montt	$9.50	$6.70	1 service daily	23 hrs
• Santiago	$5.30	$3.80	5 services daily	4 hrs
• Talca	$2.70	$1.50	4 services daily	
• Temuco	$5.30	$3.80	1 service daily	8 hrs

foundation. Rural buses leave daily from the center park in Letelier near Chacabuco. Yerbas Buenas has a tourist information office; post office and telephone are on Avenida Centenario; Central Telefónica is on Avenida España.

MOLINA

Population: 13 000
Altitude: 240 m
Distance from Talca: 51 km north on Panamericana

Founded in 1834, Molina is known as the heart of Chile's wine-growing country. Some of the best-known wine-producing estates in Chile are here, such as Viña Santa Catalina, Viña San Pedro, and Viña Cancha y Toro. The Fundo San Pedro with its century-old wine cellars situated on the Panamericana 4 km west of Molina is included by some tour operators in their itinerary. However, any house in the district with vineyards will sell wine.

Molina is about 4 km off the Panamericana and it is easy to get to as there are frequent rural buses from Talca and Curicó.

From Molina, excursions go up the **Río Claro**.

ℹ️ Tourist information

- Municipalidad de Molina, Yerbas Buenas 1389 (491994. They have information on which vineyards are open for inspection, but no maps of the *bodega* areas

🍽️ Eating out

- Restaurant Germania 2, Quechereguas 1936
- Restaurant Veas, Quechereguas 1897

📠 Post and telegraph

Telephone
- CTC, Maipú 1794, fax (75) 491036

🚌 Buses

The bus terminal is at Mercado de Molina, on the corner of Maipú and Membrillar.

Services
- Curicó: Buses Molibus and Buses Nueva Talcomur, office 3 (491436
- El Radal: Fare $1.40; Buses Hernández

- Santiago: fare $3.60; Buses Pullman del Sur
- Talca: fare $1.40 Asociación de Buses Rurales

Motoring

- Copec gas station, Avenida Luis Cruz Martínez corner of Independencia

Excursions

- Hacienda Quechereguas: 7 km west. This *hacienda* was founded about 1770 and includes an old chapel. During the Wars of Independence, it was often the scene of heavy artillery shelling by Spanish troops, and it changed hands frequently. This is called the Combate de Quechereguas.
- Viña San Pedro: 13 km south near the turnoff to Lontué. One of the oldest wineries in Chile, dating back to 1702, it may be visited during working hours. Throughout its history, it has continued to improve the quality of its wines and introduced some carefuly selected French vines during the 19th century.

Parral

Area code: 073
Population: 25 000
Distance from Talca: 89 km south on Panamericana

Parral is an agricultural center situated in the central valley. Since its foundation in 1795 by Don Ambrosio O'Higgins, it has experienced a number of earthquakes, the last one in 1960, so it is small wonder that very little remains from its colonial past. Today it is the center of an important agricultural area, in particular rice.

Parral is an important crossroads to the coast — RN 128, which runs via Cauquenes to Pelluhue and on to Curanipe, intersects here with the Panamericana.

Festivals

- February 27: Foundation day of Parral

Accommodation

Hotels

- Brescia, Igualdad 195 AFGHIJKLPSUV ☎ 462675 $G 👥. Shared bathroom cheaper
- Encina Bustamente Zoila, A. Pinto 125 near railroad station ☎ 462107 $J 👥. Basic, backpackers
- Santiago, A. Pinto 15 near railroad station AP $I 👤. Shared bathroom cheaper

Residencial

- Do Brazil, Dieziocho 140 ☎ 462555

Accommodation in Termas de Catillo

- Hotel Termas de Catillo AEFGHIJKLNPRTVXZ ☎ (73) 461420 $E 👥. Full board, thermal spa, tennis

Eating out

Restaurants

- Generación 2000, Dieciocho 630
- Las Terrazas, A. Pinto 715 (on plaza, upstairs) $Y
- Samoa, A. Pinto 411

Cafeterías

- Fancy, A. Pinto 787. Ice-cream parlor
- Morales, A. Pinto 211
- Plaza Schop, A. Pinto 787 (on plaza) $Y

Post and telegraph

Telephone

- CTC, A. Pinto 715, fax 461036

Services and facilities

Dry-cleaner

- Lavaseco Alemán, A. Pinto 423

🚌 Buses from Parral

Not all buses go into Parral, but there is a setdown point at the intersection with the Panamericana. Taxis from here to the town center cost $2.00.
The bus terminal is in center strip of Alameda, on the corner Ignacio Carrera.

Companies
All these companies operate from the bus terminal.
- A16   Buses Pullman Biotal
- A48   Buses Lit
- A153 Buses Tur-Bus Jedimar
- B35   Buses Calimpar
- B42   Buses Cinta Azul, office 14 ☎ 462234
- B105 Buses Mansa
- B233 Pullman del Sur ☎ 462196
- B256 Buses Bonanza

Services

Destination	Fare	Services	Duration	Companies
Cauquenes	$1.20	20 services daily	1 hr	A48, B35, B105, B256
Chillán	$1.90	10 services daily	1 hr	A16, B42
Concepción	$4.60	6 services daily		A16, A46, B42
Curanipe	$2.30	4 services daily		B35, B256
Curicó	$2.90	13 services daily	2 hrs	A153
Linares	$1.20	13 services daily	1 hr	B35, B256
Los Angeles	$4.60	4 services daily	1½ hrs	A16
Pelluhue	$1.90	4 services daily	2 hrs	B35, B256
Rancagua	$4.60	20 services daily	4½ hrs	A153
San Carlos	$1.20	10 services daily		A153
San Fernando	$3.60	13 services daily	3 hrs	B35
Santiago	$5.90	5 services daily	5½ hrs	A48, B233
Talca	$1.90	10 services daily	1½ hrs	B256

Supermarket
- Supermercado Italia, A. Pinto 502

🚆 Trains

- Chillán: 1 service daily
- Concepción: *Salón* $1.90; 3 services daily
- Osorno: 1 service daily
- Santiago: *Salón* $6.25, *Económico* $4.50, 1st class $3.80, 2nd class $3.30; 4 services daily

🚙 Motoring

- COPEC gas station at the crossroads with Panamericana

🏅 Sport

Trout fishing in Río Longaví, Río Perquilauquén, and Río Cauquenes.

📷 Excursions

- **Termas de Catillo**: 23 km east, a thermal resort in the central valley, at an altitude of 330 m, open from December to April. The thermal water has a temperature of 36°C (97°F). The water is claimed to be beneficial for arthritis, rheumatism, neuralgia, renal disorders, intestinal problems, cardiovascular disease, diabetes, respiratory ailments, mental fatigue, stress, and nervous diseases. The hotel in the thermal complex is adequate and is in a hilly area offering inviting short walks and fishing. Access is via a sealed road; you can get here by taxi from Parral railroad station. Empresa Chermocuya runs two services daily to Termas de Catillo; fare $1.10.

- **Embalse Digua**: 34 km east of Parral and 11 km east of Termas de Catillo. Camping spot at the exit of Río Catillo on the west side of lake. Free camping, directly on the lake shore, no facilities, fishing in lake.

PELLUHUE

Population: 1900
Altitude: Sea level
Distance from Parral: 90 km west on Ruta M-50 and RN 128

This small and relatively unknown seaside resort is 42 km west of Cauquenes on the Pacific coast. The nearby **Río Chovellen** is good for *pejerrey*, mullet, and salmon fishing.

Although the facilities are not yet quite of the highest standard, there are some good hotels and restaurants and good public transport. Pelluhue only comes to life for two months during the summer vacation; the rest of the year it is a quiet fishing village, with some of the local people working in the timber mills.

The very attractive beaches extend for several kilometers north, skirted by low hills and forests. There are some rocky outcrops, but it is mostly beach with black, volcanic sand. Many people from the central valley have holiday homes here as it is much cooler here due to the constant sea breezes. In Pelluhue itself, virtually every second house is either a hotel or *residencial* or a restaurant.

Ⓐ Camping

There are camping sites on the banks of Río El Manzano (3 km outside town). There is also a camping site south of Curanipe.

⑪ Eating out

Restaurant
- Ricco, Plaza
- Imalas, Avenida Prat 569
- La Terraza, Avenida Prat
- Rock and Roll, Avenida Prat near Condell

- El Caliche, Avenida Prat. Seafood

Eating out in Curanipe
Curanipe is 8 km south — see "Excursions" below.
- Hostería Pacífico, Comercio 509.
- Restaurant Varsovia

ⓨ Entertainment

Discos
- Concierto, Avenida Prat 631
- El Brujo, Avenida Prat
- Jim's Discotheque, Condell corner of Serrano
- Plaus's, Avenida Prat block 300
- Oddie, on road to Curanipe, on a hill looking down on the road

⌨ Post and telegraph

Post office
- Correo, on road to Cauquenes

ⓑ Buses

Most buses pick up passengers from Plaza de Armas.
Buses Amigo provides 4 services daily between Pelluhue, Chanco and Curanipe.

Companies
- B21   Buses Amigo, Plaza de Armas
- B35   Buses Calimpar
- B256 Buses Bonanza, on road to Curanipe

Services
- Cauquenes: Fare $1.20; 19 services daily; B21, B35, B256
- Constitución: Fare $1.90; 5 services daily; B21

▣ Accommodation in Pelluhue

This seaside resort is heavily booked in January and February. In the off season you can bargain. It is very popular with young people.

Cabañas
- Soledad Renovada, Caleta Blanca

Hosterías
- Caleta Blanca   AEFGHIJKPRV $E ♥♥
  Full board

Accommodation in the town center

Cabañas
- El Sol, Sargento Aldea 135   ℓ (73) 51196

Residenciales
- Blanca Reyes, Arturo Prat 915   AH $I ♥
  This has a commanding position on the clifftop, with views over the kilometer-long beach with black sand and the sea. Seafood restaurant $Y

Hostales
- Casablanca, Condell 1019   AS   ℓ 4591902 $H ♥
- Chillán, A. Prat
- La Playa, Prat 510   ℓ 591902 $H ♥♥
  Shared bathroom, backpackers only
- Pelluhué, A.Prat 570
- Trinidad, Plaza 270 near Condell
- Vista Hermosa, Condell 819   ℓ 495902 $I ♥

Accommodation along the road to Curanipe

Residenciale
- Longavi, Condell 816 $G ♥♥
  Overlooks the beach

Accommodation along the road to Cauquenes
- Hostería Residencial El Carmen

- Linares: Fare $2.70; 4 services daily; B35, B256
- Parral: Fare $2.30; 4 services daily; duration 2 hrs; B35, B256
- Talca: Fare $3.80; 4 services daily; B256

▣ Motoring

There is a gas station in Chanco and Pelluhue.

⊕ Excursions

- **Chanco:** 17 km north and about 4 km inland. It is a small town of 3500 inhabitants with plenty of colonial character in its quaint plaza and the colonial adobe buildings. Iglesia de San Ambrosio has remarkable paintings of saints. On February 2, the town celebrates Fiesta de La Candelaria, of which the highlight is a procession through the main street. Most of the local people work in the timber industry, either planting pine trees or cutting them down. The village is known for its pottery, with many of the villagers very skilful at their craft. In the streets you will still encounter old oxdrawn carts with large wheels. There are two attractive beaches with fine black sand nearby — Los Quinchos and Monolito. From Chanco north to **Faro Carranza**, the coast is a long dune landscape, with many extensive beaches. In recent years these dunes have been extensively planted with eucalyptus and radiata pines to control the advance of the sand dunes; this is how the **Reserva Nacional Federico Albert** was created. The reserve is 0.5 km from the town center, on the coast. For a description of the reserve see "National reserves" on page 460.

- **Reserva Nacional Los Ruiles**: 15 km east on Ruta M-50. For a description see "National reserves" on page 461.
- **Curanipe**: 8 km south in a beautiful setting on the Pacific Ocean. It is still more or less a rural community, although it is slowly developing as an attractive southern beach resort. There are adequate facilities, even though it may still be a bit rustic. It is still a very quiet resort, with a horseshoe-shaped beach which makes it ideal for swimmers. The local residents take a great deal of care with their gardens with very pleasing results. The road between Pelluhue and Curanipe runs mostly along the beach, and is lined with houses and small landholdings. The beach is strewn with huge boulders, sometimes half in the water and half on the beach — some of them are 15 m high. Near Puente Aiva you come to a picturesque little cove that is good for camping. The road continues south along isolated windswept beaches down to **Cobquecura** in Región VIII del Bio Bio, but a lack of public transport from Región VII del Maule makes this part of Chile practically inaccessible from Curanipe. Like so many of these small coastal towns, Curanipe comes alive for only two months of the year, although some hotels are open all year round — they offer a 50 per cent reduction during the off season. During the tourist season the local council runs an information kiosk at the entrance to the town. Past the small stream on the south side of town (Río Parrón), there is a camping zone near the beach. Between Pelluhue, Chanco and, Curanipe are regular daily *colectivo* services.

TALCA

Area code: 071
Population: 162 000
Altitude: 87 m
Distance from Santiago: 258 km south on Panamericana

Talca is the capital of Región VII del Maule. Founded in 1690 by Don Tomás Marín de Poveda, it was later abandoned due to the frontier wars with the Mapuche. It was refounded in 1742 by Don José Antonio Manso de Velasco.

The town was severely damaged during the Wars of Independence. In 1814 Coronel Carlos Spano died here defending the town against the guerrilla Ildefonso Elorreaga y Yarza. On February 2, 1818 the Chilean Declaration of Independence was signed by the Junta de Gobierno in the building that is the present-day

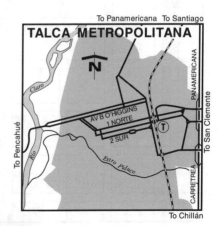

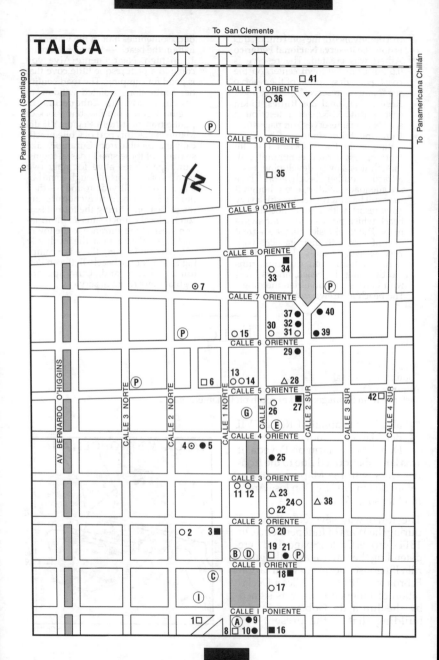

Museo O'Higginiano y de Bellas Artes. Just outside Talca is Rayada, where the Chilean forces fought in March 1818 with the Royal troops who were inside Talca.

The town's focal point is the Plaza de Armas with its palms, bougainvilleas, cedars, magnolias, and fountains. The town is laid out like a chess-board, with streets starting from the plaza and numbered. The names of most streets consist of a number followed by Sur (south), Norte (north), Poniente (west), or Oriente (east); the numbers progress numerically from the center.

The main street and hub of town is the beautiful Alameda Bernardo O'Higgins, running from Calle 11 Oriente to the banks of the Río Claro. A big open-air space called Parque San Agustín de Talca contains monuments to Bernardo O'Higgins, and gives the inhabitants an opportunity for walks and recreation right in the center of the city. From Cerro de La Virgen across the Río Claro to the west there are panoramic views over the city: directly onto Avenida Bernardo O'Higgins.

The main shopping street is Avenida 1 Sur. You can buy locally made handicrafts in the market on 1 Norte. The area around the market has many adobe houses, giving the town a distinctive colonial aspect.

Key to map

A	Iglesia Catedral	17	Cafetería Gobelino
B	Gobernación Provincial (Government)	20	Salón de Té Palet
		22	Restaurant Mykonos
C	Municipalidad (Town hall)	24	Restaurant Shangay
D	Post office and telex	26	Restaurant Ibiza
E	Telephone	30	Dino's Parrillada
G	Mercado Municipal (Market)	31	Restaurant Casino
H	Hospital	33	Cafetería Mallorca
I	Tourist information	36	Restaurant Don Willy
P	Gas stations		
$	Money exchange	⊙	**Entertainment**
T	Bus terminals	4	Sports Bowling
●	**Accommodation**	7	Disco Uni's
5	Hotel Angelmo 3	△	**Tour operators and car rental**
9	Hotel Plaza	1	Automóvil Club de Chile
10	Hotel Terrabella	23	Agencia de Viaje Onuba
16	Hotel Casagrande	28	Agencia de Viaje Bontour
21	Hotel Marcos Gamero	38	American Rent a Car
25	Hotel Claris	■	**Sights**
29	Hotel Amalfi	3	Museo O'Higginiano
32	Hotel Alcázar	18	Pinacoteca Talca
37	Residencial Maule	27	Iglesia
39	Hotel Nápoli	34	Iglesia Corazón de María
40	Hotel Cordillera	□	**Services**
○	**Eating out**	6	Supermercado Las Brisas
2	Restaurant El Alero de Gaston	8	CONAF
11	Varoli Pizza	19	Telex Chile
12	Centro Español	35	Nort Sur Color
13	Restaurant Matto Grosso	41	Railroad station
14	Schopería Don Otto	42	Entel Chile
15	Club Social Comercial		

🛏 Accommodation in Talca

Hotels

★★★★Marcos Gamero, 1 Oriente 1070 ACDEFGHIJKLMP$TUVZ
　　　　　　　　　　　　　　　　　　(223388　$F ♙

★★★★Plaza, 1 Poniente 1141 ACDEFGHIJKLMPR$TUVZ
　　　　　　　　　　　　　　　　　　(226150　$E ♙
　Sauna, fax 231515, 60 rooms

★★★Nápoli, 2 Sur 1314 ADEFGHIKLPTUVZ　(226010　$G ♙
　German and English spoken, 15 rooms

★★Amalfi, 2 Sur 1265 AEHIJKLMPUV　(233389　$G ♙
　Shared bathroom cheaper, fax 234019

★Cordillera, 2 Sur 1360 AHIJMV　(221817　$H ♙
　Budget travelers

• Alcázar, 2 Sur 1359　(233587　$I ♙
　Shared bathroom, budget travelers

• Casagrande, 1 Sur 642 AEGHIJLMP　(221977　$H ♙
　Shared bathroom cheaper

• Claris, 1 Sur 1026 AEFGHIJKLMPUVZ　(226207　$H ♙
　Shared bathroom cheaper

• Paris, 10 Oriente corner 2 Sur
　Budget travelers

• Pehuenche, Uno Poniente 1339　$H ♙
• Terrabella, 1 Sur 641 AEGHIJKLPTV　(226555　$H ♙

Residenciales

• Maule, 2 Sur 1381　(220995　$I ♙

Accommodation along the Panamericana Sur
• Cabañas de Turismo Entre Ríos, KM 250, 7 km north　((71) 220477
• Motel Sol de Alicante, KM 262, 5 km south
　ABEFGHJLPV　((71) 631033　$F ♙
• Hostería Villa San Agustín　(242641

Accommodation in Maule
Maule is a small rural community in wine country 11 km south.
• Hostería Las Vertientes del Maule, Las Vertientes　(631022

Accomodation in San Clemente
San Clemente is a rural community 20 km east on RN 115.
• Hotel Danubio, Huamachuco 881　(621240

Accommodation in San Javier
San Javier is 21 km south.
• Hostería, Panamericana KM 275　(321603
　Incorporates a restaurant

Accommodation in Villa Alegre
Villa Alegre is 24 km south.
★★★★Motel Alondra, KM 285, at the intersection with the road to Villa Alegre
　ABDEFGHIJLNKLPRUVZ
　　　　　((73) 211118　$G ♙
• Hostería y Moteles Villa Alegre, KM 285　(211719

Accommodation in Talca — continued

Accommodation in Vilches Alto
Vilches Alto is near the entrance to Parque Gil de Vilches, some 63 km east — see "Excursions" below.
- Hostería Rancho Los Canales   ABEFGHIJLPTV   ((71) 225055 $G i
  $F cabins for 4. Full board
- Cabañas Vilches Alto, near the bus terminal
  Cabins for 4. It is rather primitive; bring your own sheets and towels. There is electricity and water

---

From the start Talca was an industrial center: flour mills were the ☞ first industry. Nowadays Talca is still an important industrial town and ☞ also a university town. The tourist facilities are adequate, and it is a good base for excursions into the ☞ mountains and to the coast.

Despite the industry, Talca remains a typical rural town, with horses and carts still a familiar sight ☞ in the streets. Most of the houses are single-storied adobe, dating from colonial times. Time has stood still here. ☞

🎎 Festivals
- March, second half: Fería Internacional de la Región VII del Maule

ℹ️ Tourist information
- Sernatur, 1 Poniente 1234 (233669
- CONAF, 2 Poniente 1180 (232162/254358/234023

🅰️ Camping
There are several camping sites in Vilches Alto near the entrance to Parque Gil de Vilches, some 63 km east — see "Excursions" on page 499.

🍴 Eating out

Restaurants
- Angelmó, 4 Oriente 1265 $Y
- Casino 18 de Septiembre 2 Sur near 6 Oriente
- Centro Español, 3 Oriente 1109 $Y
- Club Social Comercial, 6 Oriente 1158
- Club Talca, 1 Oriente 1033
- Club Unión Social, 3 Oriente 1040
- Dino's Parrillada, 1 Sur 1302
- Don Willy, 1 Sur 1082
- El Alero de Gaston, 2 Norte 858 $X. International, Chilean cuisine. Open 1200–midnight Mon–Sun
- El Buen Socio, 2 Oriente 1135 near 1 Norte
- El Establo, Avenida Colin
- Flamingo's, 5 Oriente 1120
- Ibiza, 1 Sur 168. International cuisine. *Salón de té,* two stories
- La Casa Vieja, 5 Oriente 931
- Las Brasas, 1 Norte 1235
- Los Hornitos, Avenida San Miguel 2943
- Mallorca, 1 Sur 1472. Chilean, international cuisine
- Matto Grosso, 5 Oriente 1198
- Mikonos, 1 Sur 942. International cuisine. Open 1200–midnight Mon–Sun, Visa card accepted
- Papagayo, 1 Oriente 1426
- Rubén Bar, 1 Oriente 1074
- Shangay, 2 Sur 931

Schoperías
- Don Otto, 5 Oriente 1186. Pizzas. Open daily 1000–0200
- Hellas, 2 Oriente Block 1100 near 1 Sur
- Palet, 1 Sur corner 2 Oriente. *Salón de té*

Cafeterías
- Palestina, 1 Oriente 1052. Lebanese cuisine
- Cafetería Gobelino, 1 Sur near 1 Oriente, on the Plaza de Armas

Confitería
- Torre Lavega, at the bus terminal

Pizzería
- Varoli Pizza, 3 Oriente 1189 $Y. Open 0930–0100 Mon–Sat

Eating out outside the town center

Restaurants
- Cabaña El Bosque, Balneario Guillermo Urzua on east bank of Río Claro just before crossing the bridge. Open 1200–midnight Mon–Sun
- ☞ El Solar de Campito, on the southwest bank of Río Claro. Specialty frogs which are served whole; open 1000–0200 Mon–Sun
- Rancho Folklórico, B.O'Higgins corner of 3 Poniente

Eating out across the Río Claro bridge
- ☞ Restaurant Donde Gaete. Chilean cuisine

Eating out in San Javier
- Restaurant Curitambo, Panamericana

▼ Entertainment
- Bar Don Nicolás, 1 Oriente 1070, open 1800–0400
- Discoteca Uni's, 7 Oriente 1244
- Restaurant El Fogón del Maule. Dancing
- Restaurant Sport Bowling, 4 Oriente 1281. Pizzas, open 1600–0200 Tues–Sun

▦ Post and telegraph

Post office
- Correo Central, 1 Oriente 1150

Telephone
- CTC, 1 Sur 1156, fax 224611
- Entel, 6 Oriente 1080
- Telex Chile, 1 Sur 770, Local 4

$ Financial
- Casa de Cambio Barrientos Bravo, 1 Norte 999 (226674
- Fincard, 1 Sur 826 (236059. Cash advances against Visa and Mastercard

▦ Services and facilities

Medical services
- Farmacia Oriente #4, 1 Sur 1064
- Hospital Regional de Talca, 1 Norte 1990 (242406

Photographic supplies
- Reifschneider, 1 Sur corner of 4 Oriente
- Nort Sur Color, 1 Sur near 9 Oriente

Supermarket
- Supermercado Las Brisas, 1 Norte 1215

▣ Motoring
For gas stations, see the city map.

Car rental
- American Rent a Car, 2 Sur 971 (235611/221474/221425
- Automóvil Club de Chile, 1 Poniente 1267 (32774/34413

▣ Sport
Trout fishing in Laguna del Maule, upper Río Maule, Río Claro, Río Lircay, and Estero de Vilches.

▣ Sightseeing
Throughout the streets and parks of Talca you come across sculptures, such as *"La Quimera"* ("The Pipe Dream" in Calle 1 Oriente near 1 Sur, *"El Esclavo"* ("The Slave") in Calle 2 Norte near 1 Oriente, *"Loba Capitolina"* ("Capitoline Wolf") in Plaza Italia opposite the railroad station, and an equestrian statue of Bernardo O'Higgins in Alameda near 6 Oriente.
- Iglesia Catedral on the northern side of the Plaza de Armas. Under the main altar lie the remains of bishops Manuel Larrain and Carlos Silva Cotapos. The stained-glass windows were imported from Belgium. The paintings are by Fray Pedro Subercaseaux a famous Chilean painter, descendant of an equally illustrious Chilean entrepreneurial family.
- Museo O'Higginiano y Bellas Artes, corner of Calle 1 Norte and Calle 2 Oriente. This colonial house built in 1762 belonged to one of the teachers of Bernardo O'Higgins, and this is where O'Higgins signed the Independence Act in 1818 for the second time. For some years after independence, the house was used as the seat of government for the whole of Chile. On display here are works by famous Chilean painters such as Pedro Lira, Juan Francisco González, Rafael Correa, and Arturo Gordon. The archeological section includes exhibits such as some pre-Columbian arrow tips and other artifacts found in the *pre-Cordillera* near Vilches. Other rooms have collections on religious themes,

🚌 Buses from Talca

Buses leaving from the central bus terminal
The bus terminal (called "Rodoviario") is on 12 Oriente near 2 Sur 1920 ☎ 35699.
- A16   Buses Pullman Biotal, office 9 ☎ 243142
- A48   Buses Lit, office 11 ☎ 242048
- A74   Buses Sol del Sur, office 3 ☎ 241190
- A105 Buses Sol del Pacífico
- A137 Buses TAS Choapa, office 21 ☎ 24334
- A153 Tur-Bus Jedimar ☎ 241748
- B5   Asociación de Buses Rurales
- B43   Buses Los Cipreses
- B81   Buses Igi llaima, office 5 ☎ 241481
- B82   Buses Intersur
- B96   Linea Verde
- B97   Buses Linatal, office 16 ☎ 242759
- B105 Buses Mansa
- B119 Buses Nueva Talmocur, office 3 ☎ 243467
- B173 Buses Trans Sur
- B179 Buses Varmontt, 2 Sur 2213 ☎ 242631
- B183 Buses Vilches
- B199 Buses Estrella del Sur
- B200 Buses Interbus, office 10 ☎ 241919
- B212 Buses Expreso O'Higgins
- B219 Buses Italmar
- B233 Buses Pullman del Sur, office 8 ☎ 244039
- B250 Buses Transbus
- B256 Buses Bonanza, office 19 ☎ 242498
- B265 Buses Transtur

Companies with their own terminal
- B43   Buses Los Cipreses, 14 Oriente 297 corner of 9 Sur ☎ 244262
         Runs bus services on the following route: Talca, San Clemente, Lago
         Colbún Norte, Armerillo, Los Cipreses, La Mina.

Services

Destination	Fare	Services	Duration	Companies
Angol	$6.60	3 services daily		A153, B265
Armerillo	$1.90			B43, B183
Cauquenes	$3.10	21 services daily		B43, B105, B233, B256
Chanco	$3.30	5 services daily		B256
Chillán	$3.00	27 services daily	2½ hrs	A16, A137, A153, B82, B199
Colbún	$1.90	2 services daily		B233, Buses Colbún
Concepción	$5.90	19 services daily		A16, A48, A137, A153, B82, B96, B250
Constitución	$2.30	20 services daily		B212, B233
Curanipe	$3.30	2 services daily		B256
Curepto	$1.90	2 services daily		B219
Curicó	$1.70	18 services daily	½ hr	A127, B119, B233
Duao	$3.00			B219
Iloca	$2.90			B219
La Mina	$2.50	Fri		B43
Linares	$1.40	29 services daily	1 hr	A16, B97, B200, B233, B256
Los Angeles	$5.90	3 services daily	4 hrs	A16, A137, A153, B233
Los Cipreses		3 services daily		B5
Maule	$0.50	15 services daily		B200

Buses from Talca — continued

• Molina	$1.60	10 services daily		B5
• Osorno	$12.70	6 services daily		A137, B256
• Parral	$1.90	14 services daily	1½ hrs	B233, B256
• Pelluhue	$3.80	7 services daily		B256
• Pencahué	$1.10	5 services daily		B219
• Puerto Montt	$15.00	5 services daily		A137, A153, B82
• Rancagua	$3.20	10 services daily	3 hrs	A153
• San Clemente	$0.75	12 services daily		B200, B233
• San Fernando	$2.70	3 services daily	1½ hrs	B233
• San Javier	$1.20	15 services daily		B200, B233
• Santiago	$5.00	27 services daily	4 hrs	A48, A74, A105, A127, A137, A153, B81, B82, B117, B173, B199, B217, B233
• Temuco	$9.10	10 services daily		A48, A137, A153, B82, B256
• Valdivia	$11.40	5 services daily		A137, B82, B256
• Valparaíso	$8.40	4 services daily		A74, A105, A153
• Villa Alegre	$0.90	15 services daily		B200
• Vilches	$1.90	4 services daily		B43, B183
• Viña del Mar	$8.40	4 services daily		A74, A105, A153

colonial furniture, and military objects including some memorabilia from the War of the Pacific; and there is a very interesting old coin collection. Open Tues–Sat 0900–1300 and 1430–1900, Sun 1000–1300. Admission $0.50.

• Casa de Cuadrado, corner of 1 Norte and 3 Oriente, an old colonial house.

• Balneario Río Claro and Cerro de la Virgen. Following Avenida B. O'Higgins (also known as Alameda) down to the river you arrive at the banks of the Río Claro, where there are a few restaurants overlooking the river. Crossing the Puente Río Claro, the road goes uphill and leads to a lookout where you can enjoy some wonderful views over the town. On top of the hill there is a small chapel.

• Club Talca, containing Pinacoteca Ralca, 1 Oriente block 1000 near 2 Sur. Paintings on exhibit.

⊕ Excursions

Tour operators
• Agencia Ikarus, 1 Poniente 1141 (231515. Organizes tours to Vilches and Radal
• Onuba Tours, 1 Sur 975

▦ Trains from Talca

The railroad station is at 11 Oriente (32288.

Destination	Salón	Económico	Services
• Concepción	$9.90	$7.00	3 services daily
• Linares	$2.70	$1.50	5 services daily
• Los Lagos	$13.90	$10.25	2 services daily
• Osorno	$16.50	$12.35	2 services daily
• Puerto Montt	$16.50	$12.35	2 services daily
• Rancagua	$6.50	$4.50	5 services daily
• San Fernando	$3.80	$3.00	4 services daily
• Santiago	$8.00	$5.75	6 services daily
Timetables list the destination as "Alameda"			
• Temuco	$12.50	$9.10	2 services daily

Excursions

- **Constitución**: 107 km west. This is a coastal resort and industrial town of considerable size near the mouth of the Río Maule, which flows between wooded mountain slopes. You can get there from Talca on Ruta M-30-L which is sealed all the way. The turn-off from Panamericana is at San Javier de Loncomila. If you don't mind putting up with some dust for the sake of some splendid scenery, another route to take is Rutas K-60/K-68-M/M-20-K via **Pencahué** and **Carrizal**, arriving at **Quivolgo** on the Río Maule opposite Constitución (102 km). Cross the river by ferry to Constitución. See the entry for Constitución on page 468.
- **Corinto**: 26 km west, near the meeting point of the Estero de los Puercos and Río Lircay with the Río Maule. The Fiesta de la Virgen is held here on December 8.
- **Laguna del Maule**: 151 km east on RN 115, at an altitude of 2223 m, not far from the Paso de Maule (or Paso Pehuenche). The *laguna* is an ideal site for camping, fishing, and hikes in the area. The road you take to get to this beautiful area is only sealed for 27 km; after that it is a gravel road which after rain is usually in a bad state.
- **Maule**: A small rural community 17 km south. You can reach it via the Panamericana or via Ruta K-620. The main event is the *fiesta*, which is held on the anniversary of Maule, December 30. Taxibuses Turistal run frequent bus services; fare $0.50.
- **Nirivilo**: 64 km south-west, 3 km north of the main road connecting Constitución with the Panamericana Sur. The local church of thick adobe walls painted white, built in 1834, is the last resting place of the O'Higgins family, who served both the royalists and the republic. The church has been declared a *monumento histórico nacional*. Expreso O'Higgins runs regular daily buses to Constitución and Talca.
- **Parque Gil de Vilches**: An area of dense forest 67 km east in the beautiful *pre-Cordillera*. Asociación de Buses Rurales runs three services daily from Talca. See "National reserves and protected areas" on page 462.
- **Pelarco**: 26 km north-east. It is a small rural community which comes to life during the celebration of the anniversary of Pelarco on December 22.
- **San Javier de Loncomila** (generally known simply as San Javier): A major wine-producing area in the central valley, 21 km south, 1 km west of the Panamericana. There are frequent rural buses going there, and the trip will give you an insight into traditional rural life in central Chile. Rural buses continue south to Villa Alegre on a road lined with bodegas and country estates surrounded by leafy, flower-filled gardens. In the *bodegas* you can buy wines. Regular bus services to Talca are run by Buses Lit, departing form Avenida Presidente Balmaceda 371 ℓ 322267; and Buses Pullman del Sur, departing from Avenida Presidente Balmaceda 2271 ℓ 322385.
- **Villa Alegre**: 34 km south-west. It is the center of a wine-growing district, and *bodegas* where you can taste and buy the local wine abound in the area. On the corner of Avenida Abate Molina and Artesanos a tourist information bureau can direct you to the best *bodegas*. Villa Alegre is the resting place of one of Chile's famous sons, Abate Juan Molina González. Born in the nearby village of Huaraculen, he became famous as a naturalist and writer in the 19th century. The houses along the main street — Avenida Abate Molina — have been declared a *monumento nacional* as a typical colonial street. Little Chilean *picadas* (as they call their local restaurants) attract many visitors on weekends. The main street is planted with orange trees, and there are vineyards all around town. Although the town is 5 km west of the Panamericana, it is worth while taking a little detour to visit it. On December 22 the town celebrates its foundation. Regular daily buses run from Linares and Talca vía San Javier. For accommodation, see "Accommodation" in Talca on page 494.
- **Villa Cultural Huilquilemu:** 10 km east on the road to Vilches. This is an old Chilean homestead with adobe

walls and large verandahs, which was converted into a cultural center by the Pontificada Universidad Católica in Talca. The buildings, dating from 1850, are an excellent example of Chilean colonial architecture, set in a magnificent garden full of native and introduced plants. Within the building the rooms have been converted into little museums, such as the Sala de Arte Religioso Obispo Manuel Larrain with many religious artifacts from the Carmelite Convent and from the Iglesia San Agustín. There are also handicrafts and artifacts from the neighboring area on exhibit. Wine fanciers will have an opportunity to try out the local wines as there is also a wine-tasting section. The homestead's park is called Patio de América and contains many century-old trees. Open Tues–Saturday 1530–1830, Sun and holidays 1100–1400; admission $0.50.

VICHUQUÉN

Population: 900
Altitude: Sea level
Distance from Curicó: 118 km west on Ruta J-80 and Ruta I-60

Just 9 km east of **Lago Vichuquén** not far from the Pacific coast, lies the peaceful little village of Vichuquén, which dates back to the 16th century. It is a pre-Hispanic foundation as the indigenous name (*Huichai Quenco*) suggests. The Incas established a *tambo* here and brought settlers (*mitimaes*) from Peru.

While it still has a colonial flavor with its Spanish colonial buildings, it is not laid out in the usual Spanish town plan, with a central plaza. The colonial *adobe* buildings with big verandahs and thick walls are particularly noticeable on Calle del Comercio, but there are also some in other streets. There is a small but interesting museum with old documents relating to the history of Vichuquén. Vichuquén is visited in summer by tourists who enjoy a quiet vacation in unspoilt surroundings. The facilities are adequate, but the main attraction of course is the nearby lake, where you can swim and fish for *pejerrey*.

During the colonial era wheat was shipped to Peru, and one of the old wheat silos can still be seen here.

The listings below include various localities around Lago Vichuquén and the town of Vichuquén itself.

⍟ Festivals
• February 18: Aniversario de Vichuquén

ⓘ Tourist information
• Municipalidad de Vichuquén, Rodríguez

Ⓐ Camping

Camping on Lago Vichuquén
There are serviced camping sites on Lago Vichuquén in Sector Ensenada El Durazno, Sector Culenmapu and Sector Bahía Mansa.

ⓘⓘ Eating out
• Los Copihues

⊞ Post and telegraph

Post office
• Correo, Arturo Prat

Telephone
There is a public telephone on Comercio.

◳ Accommodation in Vichuquén

Accommodation in Vichuquén
- Residencial Pucará, Calle del Comercio near Balmaceda

Accommodation on Lago Vichuquén

Hosterías
- Aquelarre, Sector Aquelarre   ADEFGHLMNSUVZ
  English spoken, tennis court, boat hire, open December–February
- Brujas del Lago, Sector Punta de Barco
  AEFGHIJKLMNPSUV ☏ (75) 311244 $C ♟
  Beach frontage, tennis, boat hire; open December–February

Cabañas
- Rincón Suizo, Sector Paula   ABCDEFGHIJLNPRV ☏ (75) 400042 $F for 3
  Boat hire, tennis, mini golf, beach frontage, English spoken
- Tío Omar, Sector Culenmapu   AS   ☏ (75) 400198 $D for 4

Accommodation in Llico
Llico is 24 km west.
- Hostería Atlántida   ☏ (75) 400015
  Open December–February
- Hostería Llico, Avenida Ignacio Carrera Pinto
- Residencial Miramar, Avenida Ignacio Carrera Pinto
  Also seafood restaurant.

◳ Facilities

Facilities on Lago Vichuquén

Boat hire
- Hotel Suiza, Sector Paula

◳ Buses
- Curicó: 3 services daily; Buses Díaz, Buses Ilomar, Buses Amigo

◳ Motoring
- COPEC gas station, Sector Aquelarre

◳ Water transport

Boat trips on Lago Vichuquén
- Capitanía de Puerto, Bahía Paula on Lago Vichuquén

◳ Shopping
- Artesanía Arturo Prat, Sector Aquellarre

◳ Sport

Sport on Lago Vichuquén
Sailing, fishing and swimming in the lake. Boat hire at Aquellarre and at hotels around the lake.

◳ Sightseeing
- Museo Histórico de Vichuquén is in Rodríguez opposite the town hall. Old historical documents are exhibited, as well as pre-Columbian artifacts. The mummy of a women who perished in a nearby lake 3000 years ago is on exhibit. Although small, this museum is well organized in small rooms which cover pre-history, times of the Incas, and the colonial period. Interesting is the collection of pierced stones on exhibition as well as religious objects and some fossils. Open Tues–Sun 1030–1330 and 1600–1800; admission $1.00.

☞ Excursions

- **Lago Vichuquén**: Only 7 km west of the village is a beautiful lake ideal for water sports such as sailing and waterskiing. Lago Vichuquén is rather shallow, but measures more than 40 square km (15 square miles), and is a fairly warm freshwater lake. A road goes right around the lake, with hotels, motels, and camping grounds distributed around the shores. The main resort is **Aquelarre**, which resembles a Swiss resort with the holiday homes built in alpine style. Nearby are the **Reserva Nacional Laguna Torca** and **Lago Tilicura** which are both popular tourist destinations in summer because of the wildlife sanctuaries. Buses Bravo runs regular daily services to Curicó which calls on the resorts and camping sites along the west coast of the lake on the way to Llico.

- **Llico**: A small coastal beach resort situated in beautiful unspoilt surroundings just where **Lago Vichuquén** meets the Pacific Ocean. For most of the year, it is a quiet sleepy place, coming to life only for a short period in summer. In 1893 President Balmaceda intended to make it the main naval base of Chile, and the rusting docks remaining from his vision are still there. More inspiring are the large dunes along the seashore!

- **Reserva Nacional Laguna Torca**: Separated from Lago Vichuquén by a 2 km land strip. The reserve is a wildlife sanctuary with a huge colony of black-necked swans. See "National reserves" on page 461.

- **San Pedro de Alcántara**: 36 km north, in Región VI del Libertador. This little village has sprung up around a Franciscan convent. The monastery is a *monumento nacional*, and you can get to it through a road lined with a double row of Chilean palms. *Colectivos* run from Vichuquén.

REGIÓN VIII
DEL
Bío Bío

Size: 36 000 square km (13 896 square miles)
Population: 1.7 million
Regional capital: Concepción
Provinces (and provincial capitals) from north to south:
- Ñuble (Chillán)
- Concepción (Concepción)
- Bío Bío (Los Angeles)
- Arauco (Lebu)

Región VIII del Bío Bío was the theater for the most turbulent period of Chile's history. Because of the ongoing battle between two warrior nations — the Spanish on one side and the Mapuche on the other — the area is dotted with forts along Chile's "river of destiny" — the Río Bío Bío. Most of these forts are described in this chapter, together with their history.

This region has magnificent areas for the adventure-minded tourist, particularly in the Alto Bío Bío valley boasting river rafting for the intrepid. For the tourist seeking leisure and pleasure, Concepción is a fantastic travel destination, with excellent tourist facilities and some of the best shopping south of Santiago. Two ski areas have been developed: Centro de Esquí Las Lajas on Volcán Antuco and the plush ski and thermal resort of Termas de Chillán. Both are worth-while destinations, summer or winter.

South of the town of Arauco, you will encounter the first Mapuche villages, where the descendants of the once fierce warriors have settled, still building their *rucas* (Mapuche huts) and making the silver jewelry proudly worn by the women.

Finally, the beaches north and south of Concepción are worth mentioning. Most of them have adequate tourist facilities.

Región VIII del Bío Bío lies between 36° and 38° south and 71° and 73° west. Its northern border is Región VII del Maule and in the east it meets the *cordillera* of the Andes, that forms the border with Argentina. Its southern border is with Región IX de La Araucania, and the Pacific Ocean forms a natural border in the west.

Transport

Road

The Panamericana crosses the region's full length, linking the major cities; **Concepción**, the regional capital on the Pacific coast, is linked to the Panamericana by RN 148.

From Concepción roads go north and south, and the whole region has a good road system. Some sections of the roads have been classified as "tourist roads" by the Regional Tourist office either because of their importance in colonial times or because of their current economic importance.

The Ruta del Carbón ("Coal Road") leads south from Concepción as far as Curanilahué.

The **Ruta de la Colonia,** the colonial road which starts in Talca in

Región VII del Maule, passes through Quirihué and finishes in Concepción. In Concepción the so-called **Ruta de los Conquistadores** starts running through the heartland of Mapuche country to Lumaco. There are many areas along this road which are the sites of famous battles, skirmishes, and destroyed fortresses. On this road is **Cañete**, with the nearby battlefields of **Antihuala** and **Tucapel** and many others.

Rail

There are about 2000 km of railroad tracks in the region, with the first railroad built between Talcahuano and Chillán in 1873. Today most railroads are used for goods trains, although there is a major line from Santiago to Concepción for passenger trains.

Air

The region's major airport is Carriel del Sur, serving Talcahuano and Concepción; it is the second most important airport in Chile. Other airports are in Chillán (General Bernardo O'Higgins) and Los Angeles (María Dolores).

Ports

Talcahuano is the major port for this and neighboring regions, with the smaller fishing ports of **Tomé**, **Coronel**, **Lirquén**, and **Lota** also used for coal and timber exports.

Topography

The geology of this region is interesting, with the central valley becoming gradually wider and breaking up into undulating countryside. The rivers too increase in size, notably the **Río Bío Bío**, **Río Lajas**, and **Río Ñuble**. Above all, the country gets greener, particularly on the coast and in the central areas — zones where reforestation is taking place. In the east the Andes, still largely forested with native trees, reach an average height of 2500 m, but there are the towering peaks of **Volcán Antuco** (3585 m), **Volcán Chillán** (3212 m), and **Volcán Callaqui** (3164 m). Although the central valley between the Andes and the coastal *cordillera* is fairly flat in the north, it starts to become undulating at **Los Angeles** and beyond. The coastal *cordillera* is lower in the north (300 m) and rises to 1500 m in the **Cordillera de Nahuelbuta**.

Climate

The climate is moderate to hot, with the rainy season from April to September and fairly dry weather from December to March. Concepción has an average annual rainfall of 1200 mm; an average minimum winter temperature of 5°C (37°F) and an average maximum summer temperature of 24°C (75°F). The central valley becomes fairly hot in summer and some areas can look very dry.

European history

The Spanish *conquistador* Don Pedro de Valdivia arrived in the coastal area in 1550 and officially founded Concepción del Nuevo Extremo on October 5 at a place the indigenous people called Peguco. This soon became the area of bitter fighting between the Spanish invaders and the Mapuche (as the Araucanian people are known). There were continuing skirmishes between Spaniards and Mapuche for the next 250 years, and in order to retain command of the area, the Spanish invaders made Concepción the unofficial residence of the Governors of the Reino de Chile. It was for many years the seat of the Real Audiencia (Royal High Court). Some of the appointed governors went straight to Concepción, making only a token appearance in Santiago to present themselves to the *cabildo* (the town government in colonial times). The Mapuche certainly did not welcome these events, and two forts founded in 1553, Arauco and Tucapel, were destroyed during the great Mapuche uprising of 1599 — this is described in the Introduction to this *Travel Companion*. Nature also took a hand in things, with a strong earthquake, followed by a seismic tidal wave, destroying the first foundation of Concepción in 1751. In what was probably a well-advised move, it was transferred in 1764 to the Valle de Mocha, where it has remained.

Administration

In 1786 the Reino de Chile was reorganized into three administrative centers: La Serena, Santiago, and Concepción. The first chief administrator of the Intendencia de Concepción was Don Ambrosio O'Higgins, father of the future hero of the independence movement.

Independence

The Chilean independence movement began in Concepción in the early 19th century, through the energies of such leading local figures as Don Juan Martínez de Rozas, General Ramón Freire, Joaquín Prieto, Manuel Bulnes, and General Bernardo O'Higgins, Liberator of Chile and son of the Viceroy Don Ambrosio O'Higgins. Chile's inde-

Plate 29   Región X de Los Lagos
Top: Lago Todos Los Santos, Hotel Peulla
Bottom: Lago Todos Los Santos, Volcán Osorno

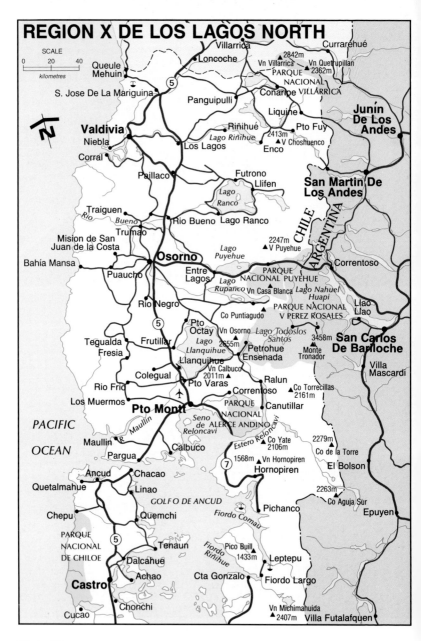

REGION X DE LOS LAGOS NORTH

SCALE
0   20   40
kilometres

Queule
Mehuin
S. Jose De La Mariguina

Villarrica
Loncoche
Currarehué
▲ 2842m
Vn Villarrica Vn Quetrupillan
PARQUE   2362m
NACIONAL
Conaripe VILLÁRRICA
Panguipulli
Liquine
Junín
De Los
Andes

Valdivia
Niebla
Corral
Paillaco

Riñihué
Lago Riñihue
Enco
2413m
▲ V Choshuenco
Pto Fuy
Los Lagos
Futrono
Llifen
San Martin De
Los Andes

Traiguen
Rio Bueno
Trumao
Rio Bueno
Lago
Ranco
Lago Ranco

Mision de San
Juan de la Costa
Bahía Mansa
Osorno
Lago
Puyehue
2247m
▲ V Puyehue
CHILE
ARGENTINA
Correntoso

Puaucho
Entre
Lagos
Lago
Rupanco Vn Casa Blanca
PARQUE
NACIONAL PUYEHUE
Lago Nahuel
Huapi
Llao
Llao

Rio Negro
Co Puntiagudo
PARQUE NACIONAL
V PEREZ ROSALES
San Carlos
De Bariloche

Pto
Octay
Vn Osorno
2655m
Lago Todoslos
Santos
3458m
Monte
Tronador
Tegualda
Fresia
Frutillar
Lago
Llanquihue
Petrohue
Ensenada
Villa
Mascardí

Colegual
Llanquihue
Vn Calbuco
2011m ▲
Pto Varas
Ralun
Co Torrecillas
2161m

Rio Frio
Los Muermos
Correntoso
Canutillar

Pto Montt
Maullín
Seno
de
Reloncavi
PARQUE
NACIONAL
ALERCE ANDINO

PACIFIC

Maullin
R Maullín
Calbuco
Estero Reloncavi
Co Yate
2106m
2279m
Co de la Torre
▲

OCEAN

Pargua
Ancud
Chacao
7
1568m ▲ Vn Hornopiren
Hornopiren
El Bolson

Quetalmahue
Linao
GOLFO DE ANCUD
2263m
Co Aguja Sur

Chepu
Quemchi
Fiordo Comau
Pichanco
Epuyen

PARQUE
NACIONAL
DE CHILOE
5
Tenaun
Fiordo Riñihue
Pico Buill
1433m
Leptepu

Castro
Dalcahue
Achao
Cta Gonzalo
Fiordo Largo

Cucao
Chonchi
Vn Michimahuida
▲ 2407m
Villa Futalafquen

Plate 30
Map of Región X de Los Lagos – North

pendence was proclaimed at Concepción on January 10, 1818 on the Plaza de la Independencia.

Economy

The demographic and economic upswing came towards the end of the 19th century, when intense agricultural development began. Today the economy is built on agriculture, commerce, industry, and services. The main agricultural products are wine, sugar beet (there are two sugar factories, Los Angeles and Cocharcas), and beef. Bío Bío is also home of Chile's biggest pine plantations, with 55 per cent of the country's paper and cellulose manufactured in the region. The coast provides another resource: fishing accounts for 32 per cent of the national fish catch. The largest coal reserves are concentrated around **Lota** and **Coronel**, with the large coal-mining industry started by the Cousiño family in the 19th century. Substantial ore resources are yet to be exploited in the Andean *cordillera,* and a further natural bonus for the region is its water power. There are hydroelectric power stations such as El Toro which generate 985 megawatts per year, using the water of the Río Polcura, Río Abanico, Río Las Lajas, and Río Antuco. There is a coal-fired power station at Bocamina. Much of the petrochemical and steel industry is located in and around Concepción, as well as wood-pulp and paper mills. A new power station has been built at **El Pangue** on the Río Bío Bío.

Regional dishes

The regional food is quite distinctive. One of the special dishes is called *sustancia de Chillán,* which is made from sweetened bone jelly.

The coal-mining towns of Lota and Coronel are famous for their *pan de mina* (mine bread), made from flour, yeast, pickles, and plenty of butter, and then baked in a clay oven. The miners would take this bread to work for their meals underground.

The *mariscal* is a special seafood dish made of shellfish, minced onions, and lemons, and can be eaten hot or cold. Try *apiado,* a liqueur with a brandy base and celery.

National parks and reserves

• **Monumento Natural Contulmo** lies 9 km east of Contulmo, just at the border with Región IX de Araucania in the Nahuelbuta range. Although the park is only small — 82 ha (202 acres) — there is a great variety of native flora and fauna. The road between Cañete and Purén crosses the reserve and forms its southern border. The climate ranges from 9°C (48°F) in July to 17°C (63°F) in January, and the rainfall is high — 1939 mm per year, with most of it falling between April and September. Much of the native forest which used to cover the whole area remains: mostly *coihues,* oaks, elm trees, and red-trunked *arrayanes.* Because of the humidity there are many ferns here, a number of them quite large trees. Some of the paths laid out by CONAF personnel become tunnels making their way through arches of large fern trees with huge leaves. It is an impressive sight. The CONAF trail starts near the caretaker's hut. Humming birds and dwarf deer or *pudus* are common in the area.

- **Reserva Nacional Ñuble**, 56 948 ha (140 612 acres), 78 km east of Chillán near Termas de Chillán on Ruta N-55. You can only get there on foot or horseback from Fundo Los Cipreses. This reserve was specially created to preserve the habitat of the South American deer (*huemul*), which once roamed from Magallanes to Santiago and are now only to be found in the northernmost pocket in the **Nevado de Chillán**, between San Fabián de Alico and Laguna del Laja. At the moment there are only about a hundred *huemules* left.
- **Parque Nacional Laguna del Laja**, 11 600 ha (28 642 acres), 93 km east of Los Angeles on Ruta Q-45 28 km past Antuco. It has an information center, picnic area, camping area, excursion paths, accommodation, restaurant, shop nearby, ski lifts, and a ski resort. See the entry for the park on page 563.
- **Reserva Nacional Ralco**, 12 425 ha (30 679 acres), 70 km south-east of Los Angeles on Ruta Q-61-R past Santa Bárbara on the upper Río Bío Bío in the *pre-Cordillera.*
- **Reserva Nacional Isla Mocha**, 2368 ha (5847 acres), 33 km off the coast from Tirúa and 80 km south of Cañete on Ruta P-70; accessible only by air or by boat.

Thermal resorts

- **Termas de Chillán** (1800 m), a spa 82 km south-east of Chillán on Ruta N-55 in the *cordillera,* with three separate springs at 43.8°C (111°F), 61.7°C (143°F), and 76.4°C (170°F). Open all year round. This is also a very good ski area. There is accommodation in an excellent thermal hotel, and daily transport to and from Chillán. It is said to have curative properties for gynecological and respiratory problems, rheumatism, skin disorders, arthritis, asthma, diabetes, anaemia, aching joints, and sciatica as well as being good for convalescents. See "Excursions" from Chillán on page 526.

Trout fishing

The trout fishing season is from the second Friday in November until the first Sunday in May. The season for Chilean trout (*percatrucha*) is from January 1 to April 15. There are restrictions on both types of fishing, the allowance being 3 per person per day. The best fishing is near the following towns — see the entries for the individual towns.

- Arauco
- Cañete
- Chillán
- Concepción
- Lago Lanalhué
- Curanilahué
- Los Angeles

Distances

From Concepción

- Arauco: 75 km south
- Cañete: 140 km south
- Chillán: 110 km north east
- Contulmo: 180 km south
- Coronel: 35 km south
- Dichato: 43 km north
- Laguna del Laja: 221 km southeast
- Lebu: 146 km south
- Los Angeles: 128 km south-east

- Lota: 42 km south
- Nacimiento: 105 km south-east
- Penco: 14 km north
- Tomé: 28 km north

From Chillán

- Cobquecura: 103 km north west
- Los Angeles: 105 km south
- San Fabián de Alico: 68 km north-east
- Yungay: 66 km south

Distances from Los Angeles

- Laguna del Laja: 93 km east
- Nacimiento: 36 km west
- Santa Bárbara: 66 km south-east
- Termas de Chillán: 82 km east
- Tomé: 94 km west

Distances from Lebu

- Arauco: 90 km north
- Cañete: 55 km south-east
- Contulmo: 90 km south- east

- Tirúa: 132 km south

Tourism

Don't miss

☞ Concepción

Worth a visit

☞ Salto del Laja
☞ Termas de Chillán

Worth a detour

☞ Chillán
☞ Salto del Itata
☞ Parque Nacional Laguna del Laja
☞ Los Angeles
☞ Lago Lanalhué and Contulmo

Of interest

☞ Cañete
☞ Lota
☞ Lebu

ARAUCO

Area code: 041
Population: 18 000
Altitude: Sea level
Distance from Concepción: 75 km south on Ruta P-20, RN 160

Arauco is on the Bahía de Arauco, 7 km west of RN 160. Fuerte de Arauco was founded in 1555 by Pedro de Valdivia, and later transferred to the present site. It fell in the great Mapuche uprising in 1599, to be re-founded in 1886. There are scant remains of the fort on forest-covered Cerro Colo Colo not far from the town center. This was the scene of many bitter battles between the Spaniards and the Mapuche. From the lookout there is a good view over the city and the **Golfo de Arauco**.

As well as mining and fishing, Arauco is a center for intensive pine forest plantations. The township is within striking distance of the **Cordillera de Nahuelbuta**, a coastal range of outstanding beauty, part of which is in the national park of the same name.

Not all bus services stop at the town, stopping instead in Carampangue, which villagers reach by taxi.

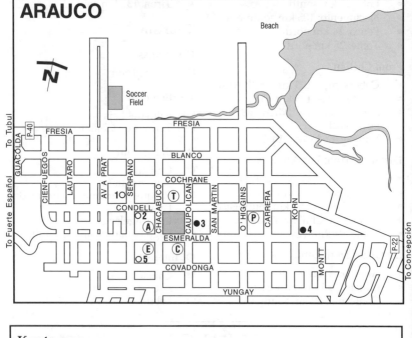

ARAUCO

Key to map

A	Iglesia	4	Hostería Arauco
C	Municipalidad (Town hall)	○	**Eating out**
E	Telephone	1	Restaurant El Colonial
P	Gas stations	2	Restaurant Serrano
T	Taxi to Carampangue	5	Restaurant El Apolo
●	**Accommodation**		
3	Hotel Plaza		

⚹ Festivals

• February 6–7: Rodeo

⌂ Accommodation

★★★ Hostería Arauco, Esmeralda 80
ACEFGHIJKLMNPU (551131 $F ⅲ.
38 rooms, fax 551100

• Hotel Alondra, Chacabuco 389
(551236

• Hotel Plaza, Chacabuco 347
AEIPS$UV (551265 $F ⅲ. Sauna

Accommodation in Ramadillas

Ramadillas is 13 km south-east of Arauco
on RN 160.

• Hostería Ramadillas, 13 km south-
east of town on Río Ramadillas ((108)
895950 San Miguel. Open December-
March. Electricity, toilet, laundry,
shop, also 60 tent spots

Accommodation in Curanilahué

Curanilahué is a substantial coal-mining
town of 23 000 inhabitants located 33 km

south of Arauco and about 2 km east of the main road. On the main road near the entrance to town is a gas station. Buses Los Alces, Buses Jota Ewert, Buses Tliver run regular services to Concepción, Arauco, Lebu, and Cañete. Change here for buses to Lebu.

- Hostería Johnny, Caupolicán

🍴 Eating out

- Club Social, Chacabuco 339 on the plaza. Chilean cuisine
- El Colonial, Serrano 239. Chilean cuisine
- El Apolo, Covadonga corner of Serrano
- El Pitufo, Condell 98. Chilean cuisine
- Jano, Caupolicán 498. Chilean cuisine
- Serrano, Serrano corner of Condell

Eating out in Carampangue
Carampangue is 7 km east of Arauco. It is a large coal-mining town.
- Restaurant El Rancho de Julio, intersection of RN 160

Eating out in Ramadillas
Ramadillas is 13 km south.
- Restaurant La Posada, L. Cruz Martínez. Chilean cuisine

📮 Post and telegraph
Telephone

- CTC Condell corner of A. Prat

🚗 Motoring
For gas stations, see city map.

⚽ Sport
Trout fishing in Río Carampangue, Río Lias, Río Llico, Río Ramadillas, Río Curanilahué and Río Lebu.

📷 Sightseeing

- Cerro Colo Colo, with the remains of Fuerte Español. Following Calle Esmeralda west from town leads you directly to the viewing platform, with vistas over the town.
- Church on the west side of plaza. A point of interest is the church steeple which is separate from the main body of the church and is made of concrete. The church was destroyed by an earthquake in 1960. The steeple was patched up with reinforced concrete to withstand future earthquakes.
- The extensive beach with its grayish sand is about 500 m down from the center. It is a very clean beach, with parts of it covered in small white seashells.

🚌 Buses from Arauco

Most buses bypass Arauco, and you may have to board the bus in Carampangue. The pick-up point is at the main plaza. Fares to all destinations are the same whether you board in Carampangue or Arauco. Locals and cab drivers will tell you when the bus is due.

It is a 15-minute taxi trip to Carampangue, and costs 50 cents.

Rural buses to Lebu via Millonhué leave from Avenida Prat near Cochrane at 0830 and 1500.

Bus companies
- A153 Buses Tur-bus Jedimar
- B88 Buses Jota Ewert
- B99 Buses Los Alces

Services

Destination	Fare	Services	Companies
• Concepción	$1.40	10 services daily	B88, B99
• Curanilahué	$1.00	10 services daily	B99
• Lebu	$1.60	10 services daily	B99
• Lota	$1.10	10 services daily	B99
• Santiago	$14.60	1 service daily	A153, B99

Arauco

⊕ Excursions

- **Carampangue:** 7 km east of Arauco. It was here that (according to Alonso de Ercilla in his *Cantos de la Araucania*) Caupolicán was elected leader of the united Mapuche tribes which led to the great Mapuche uprising in 1599.
- **Caleta** and **Punta Lavapié:** 42 km west on Ruta P-22. The first 10 km until **Tubul** is a flat stretch with a sandy beach. **Caleta Llico** and **Caleta Lavapié** at the extreme western side of the bay are small fishing villages.

There is a protected beach with white sand at Caleta Llico, which is suitable for camping and swimming but has no services. Between Caleta Llico and Punta Lavapié the road passes through rocky outcrops. Near Túbul are some small islands, nesting places for sea birds. Caleta Lavapié is a picturesque village built on the headland with the rocks behind it rising steeply from the sea to nearly 400 m and a small seafood restaurant.

CAÑETE

Area code: 041
Population: 16 000
Distance from Concepción: 140 km south on RN 160

Cañete stands on the **Río Leiva**, west of the **Cordillera de Nahuelbuta**. It was first founded in 1552 as San Diego de Tucapel by Don Pedro de Valdivia, then re-founded in 1558 by Don Hurtado de Mendoza. Officially it became Cañete in honor of Mendoza's father, the Marqués de Cañete. It was abandoned in 1602 during the Mapuche uprising and not resettled again until 1868. It is full of historic significance: both Pedro de Valdivia and his Mapuche adversary Chief Caupolicán met their deaths here.

Modern Cañete is the center of a pine plantation industry grown for cellulose production; there is also a coal-mining industry here.

⌦ Festivals in Cañete
- March 12–13: Rodeo

Festivals in Tirúa
- February 20–21: Rodeo

ⓘ Tourist information
- CONAF, Avenida General Bonilla 288 ☏ 611241. Information about Monumento Natural Contulmo and the western part of Parque Nacional Nahuelbuta

⌂ Camping in Cañete
There is a serviced camping site 4 km south of town on the banks of Río Leiva near the Mapuche Museum.

⑪ Eating out
- El Ronce, Segunda de Línea 901. Chilean cuisine
- La Casona, Saavedra 874. Chilean cuisine
- Nahuel, Saavedra 894. Chilean cuisine

⛟ Motoring
Ruta P-60-R to Contulmo follows the northern edge of Lago Lanalhué, and the scenery is particularly appealing from Peleco onwards.
- COPEC gas station at the northern exit of town near intersection with Avenida Bonilla

⊛ Sport
Trout fishing in Río Tirúa, Río Los Maquis, Río Matraquén, and Lago Quidico.

▣ Sightseeing
- Fuerte Tucapel: Situated a few kilometers north, this fort was the first casu-

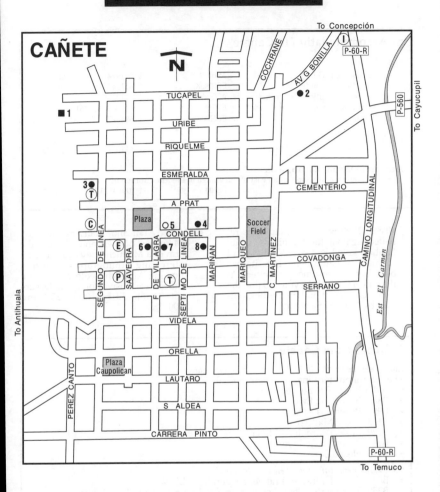

Key to map

C	Municipalidad (Town hall)
E	Telephone
I	Tourist information
P	Gas stations
T	Bus terminals

● Accommodation

2	Hostería VIPS
3	Hotel Gajardo
4	Hotel Central
6	Hotel Alonso de Ercilla
7	Hotel Nahuelbuta
8	Hotel Derby

○ Eating out

5 Restaurant Club Social

■ Sights

1 Fuerte Tucapel

⊟ Accommodation in Cañete

Hotels
- Alonso de Ercilla, Villagrán 641   AEHIPV   ☎ 611974 $H ♁
- Club Social, Condell 283   EFGHIJK   ☎ 611244
- Comercio, Septimo de Línea 817   AEGIPV   ☎ 611218
- Derby, Mariñan 693 near Condell   EFGHI   ☎ 611960/611261
- Nahuelbuta, Villagrán 644   EGHIJ   ☎ 611073 $H ♁

Hosterías
- VIPS, Avenida General Bonilla   ☎ 611012 $G ♁

Accommodation in Antihuala
- Hostería Caramávida, 5 km east of the village in the Río Caramávida valley
     FGHIJ   ☎ (09) 4521781 $H ♁

alty in 1599 when the Mapuches rebelled against the Spaniards. Chief Lautaro killed Pedro de Valdivia and his men in battle here. The site has been built three times altogether. At the end of Calle Uribe you will find the remains of a fort built in the 19th century by Coronel Saavedra.

- Museo Araucano "Juan Antonio Ríos" is 4 km east of town, and is built in the form of a Mapuche *ruca* (hut). It is an interesting ethnographic museum showing Mapuche culture, and includes an extensive library on the subject. Open daily 1000–1230 and 1400–1800.

⊟ Buses from Cañete

Companies departing from the central bus terminal
The central bus terminal is on Serrano 200.
- A153 Buses Tur-Bus Jedimar
- B88 Buses Jota Ewert
- B99 Buses Los Alces
- B103 Buses Malleco
- B129 Buses Pedro de Valdivia,
- B164 Buses Thiele-Ewert
- B215 Flecha Sur

Companies departing from their own terminals
- B84 Buses Jeldres, A. Prat near Segunda de Línea
- B259 Transportes Chevalier, corner of A. Prat and Segunda de Línea

Services

Destination	Fare	Services	Companies
Angol	$2.90	24 services daily	B164
Concepción	$2.90	14 services daily	B88, B99, B164
Contulmo	$1.00	7 services daily	B88
Lebu	$1.40	24 services daily	B129, B164
Purén	$2.20	3 services daily	B88
Santiago	$15.20	2 services daily	A153, B215
Temuco	$4.60	3 services daily	B88, B103, B164
Tirúa	$1.70	7 services daily	B84, B88

⊕ Excursions

- **Antihuala:** A small agricultural village 18 km north. In 1558 it was the scene of a battle between the Spanish and the Mapuche, whose leader, Chief Caupolicán, was captured and subsequently executed in Cañete. Buses Los Alces, Buses Pedro de Valdivia, and Buses Thiele-Ewert run regular buses and *colectivo* services to and from Concepción and Angol. It is possible to hike to Parque Nacional Nahuelbuta following the Río Caramávida valley.

- **Parque Nacional Nahuelbuta:** You can reach the western part of this park by following the **Río Caramávida** valley past **San Alfonso**. The main access however is from Angol. See "Excursions" from Angol in Región IX de la Araucania.

- **Lago Lanalhué:** 10 km south-west of Cordillera de Nahuelbuta. See the entry for Lago Lanalhué on page 546.

- **Peleco:** 11 km south on Lago Lanalhué. This is the home of the descendants of Chief Colipi, who led the final Mapuche uprising — this time against the Chileans.

- **Lago Lleu Lleu:** 43 km south on Ruta P-70. It is not very well known, but offers clean water for swimming and fishing, and it is also rich in birdlife. The turnoff to the lake is at **Peleco** — take Ruta P-70 heading straight south. At **Puerto Lleu Lleu** you can take a motor boat which serves the little homesteads around the lake. This is a serene countryside, much of it covered with native trees between the several arms which form the outlet of Lago Lleu Lleu to the sea. The road continues south to **Quidico** and **Tirúa**, with regular rural bus services from Cañete. This part of Región VIII del Bío Bío is inhabited mostly by Mapuche. The villagers are friendly and welcome tourists.

- **Tirúa:** 76 km south. Tirúa is virtually at the end of the coastal road south; further on there is only a trail to Carahué. During the later stages of the colonial period the Spaniards obtained permission from the local tribes to use this trail to link up Concepción with Valdivia via Carahué. This small village of 1200 inhabitants was once part of the Mapuche heartland, and it is still steeped in Mapuche tradition. South of Tirúa on the Río Paicaví an unsuccessful meeting took place between the Spaniards and the Mapuche to resolve their differences in 1610; this became known as the **Parlamento de Paicaví**. The locals are friendly, but be careful to respect their traditions. For the trail-blazer it is possible to retrace a section of the old colonial road further south to Carahué. There are still large forests of *araucanias* here. Buses Jota Ewert and Buses Jeldres run regular daily services to Cañete and Concepción; change in Cañete for Buses Thiele Ewert to Temuco.

CHILLÁN

Area code: 042
Population: 148 000
Altitude: 100 m
Distance from Concepción: 110 km north-east on Panamericana and RN 148

Chillán is in the northern part of the region in the fertile central valley, about 400 km south of Santiago. It developed as a town around Fuerte San Bartolomé, which was founded by Martín Ruiz de Gamboa in 1580. The area has had a chequered history, but has survived through the Mapuche uprising and an earthquake in 1835.

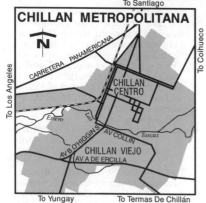

CHILLAN METROPOLITANA

To Santiago
To Coihueco
To Los Angeles
CARRETERA PANAMERICANA
CHILLAN CENTRO
Estero
Las
AV B.O'HIGGINS S
AV COLLIN
Toscas
CHILLAN VIEJO
AV A DE ERCILLA
To Yungay
To Termas De Chillán

It is also historically significant as the birthplace of Chile's own independence hero, Bernardo O'Higgins, son of a prominent Spanish Viceroy of Irish origin. He was born in Chillán in 1778.

The modern cathedral in the plaza was built on the site of an earlier building destroyed in the earthquake in 1939, in which thousands of *Chillanos* perished.

Chillán is the center of an agricultural area; it is a fairly modern town with wide avenues and many plazas.

Chillán Viejo is the old colonial part of the city. It is located 3 km

Key to map

A	Iglesia
C	Municipalidad (Town hall)
D	Post office and telex
E	Telephone
G	Mercado Municipal (Market)
H	Hospital
I	Tourist information
P	Gas stations
$	Money exchange
T	Bus terminals

● Accommodation

6	Hotel Floresta
11	Hotel Claris
13	Hotel Regional
14	Hotel Los Cardenales
15	Hotel Santiago
16	Hotel Chillán
17	Hotel Libertador
18	Hotel Nevado de Chillán
19	Hotel Réal
22	Hotel Javier Carrera (Americano)
25	Residencial El Valdiviano
28	Hotel Rucamanqui
31	Residencial Barcelona
34	Hotel Gran Isabel Riquelme
36	Hotel San Bartolomé
37	Hotel Cordillera
38	Hotel Las Terrazas
43	Hotel Quinchamalí
48	Residencial Las Delicias

○ Eating out

3	Restaurant Planka
5	Club Ñuble
12	Restaurant Centro Arabe
20	Restaurant Taipeh
21	Restaurant Zur Fliegerklause
23	Pizzería Scrón
26	Restaurant Jay Yang
29	Cafetería La Capucha
30	Centro Español
40	Café Paris
42	Restaurant Quick Lunch
44	Club Comercial

△ Tour operators and car rental

10	First Rent a Car
32	Automóvil Club de Chile
33	Centrotur
39	Alto Nivel Tours

■ Sights

4	Murales Escuela Mexico
7	Museo Y Iglesia Franciscano
8	Iglesia Santo Domingo
24	Iglesia Padres Carmelita
47	Iglesia La Merced
49	Iglesia San Vicente
50	Museo Naval A. Prat

□ Services

2	CEMA Chile
9	Clínica Chillán
35	Kodak Express
41	Carpas Catan
46	Supermercado Multimarket

south-east of the new town and is connected via the wide Avenida B. O'Higgins. It is now simply a suburb of Chillán.

Don't miss the market and Fería de Chillán, where the region's agricultural products are displayed and sold, as well as the crafts made by local people. Besides articles of a utilitarian nature you will see ceramics from Quinchamalí and wood carvings from Coihueco.

It is also the gateway to the high *sierras* and of course to **Termas de Chillán**, a splendid thermal resort and ski resort.

⚅ Festivals

- October 23–24: Festival Canta Chillán — a song festival
- November 20–24: Fería Exposición Ñuble — a rural regional trade fair

Festivals in Pinto

- February, second week: Semana de Pinto

Festivals in Quillón
- February, second week: Semana de Quillón

Festivals in San Carlos
- February, third week: Agro-Expo
- March 4–5: Rodeo

ⓘ Tourist information
- Sernatur, Centro Histórico Cultural, Chillán Viejo ℂ 223272. Fishing licenses.
- Sernatur, Libertad block 500, Plaza de Armas

Ⓐ Camping
There are camping sites at San Fabián de Alico, 68 km north-east, Pinto 23 km east, Yungay 66 km south, and in Quillón.

⑪ Eating out

Restaurants
- Café Paris, Arauco 666
- ☞ Centro Arabe, Bulnes 399
- Centro Español, Arauco 555. International cuisine
- Club Ñuble, 18 de Septiembre 224. International cuisine
- Club Comercial, Arauco 745 $Y. Chilean cuisine
- El Valdiviano, Libertad 240
- Fuente Alemana, Arauco 661. Light meals
- Juanito, Avenida B. O'Higgins 1215. *Parrillada*
- Planka, Arauco 103. International cuisine
- Hostería Terbuchi, Constitución 63 near small lane
- Hostería Turisur, Constitución block 1 near Rosas
- Jai Yang, Libertad 260 $X. Chinese cuisine
- ☞ Taipeh, Libertad 299 $X. Chinese cuisine
- Terminal, Avenida Brazil block 500 next to terminal
- Zur Fliegerklause, Libertad 398. German cuisine

Cafeterías
- El Cafetín, Constitución 568
- La Capucha, 18 de Septiembre 430

Fast food
- Quick Lunch, El Roble 610. $Y

Pizzerías
- Scron, Sargento Aldea block 400 between Libertad and Bulnes. Rugby players congregate here

Eating out along the Panamericana, near northern exit

Restaurants
- Kuranepe, Avenida B. O'Higgins 0420. Seafood
- La Estancia, KM4
- Las Encinas (at the hotel), KM 400

Eating out along the Panamericana, near southern exit
- Paja Brava (road diner in the Shell gas station), KM 410

Eating out in Chillán Viejo

Restaurants
- El Huaso Monroy, Avenida O'Higgins
- ☞ Los Adobes, Avenida Bernardo O'Higgins, opposite Parque O'Higgins $X

Eating out in Bulnes
Bulnes is 26 km south on the Panamericana.
- Hostería, right across from intersection with RN 148
- Hostería Cruz
- Hostería Las Brisas, at the intersection leading into Bulnes

Eating out in Quillón
Quillón is 44 km west.
- Hostería La Rueda
- Hostería Quillón, Avenida O'Higgins
- Hostería San Carlos, after turnoff to Nueva Aldea east of town. Specialty roast duck
- Salsoteca La Picada, Sedctor Coyanco. Chilean cuisine

Eating out in San Carlos
- San Carlos is 25 km north, on the Panamericana.
- Restaurant Navarrete, Maipú 670 $Z
- Restaurant Palacios, Balmaceda 467 $Z
- Hostería COPEC (also gas station), on the Panamericana

Eating out in Recinto
Recinto is 53 km east, near the snow fields.
- Restaurant El Rosedal
- Restaurant Los Pinos

🛏 Accommodation in Chillán

Hotels

• Javiera Carrera (formerly Americano), Carrera 481				
	AHIJLV	ℓ 221175	$H	ⅈⅈ
• Chillán, Avenida Libertad 65	AEGIJLPUV	ℓ 222481		
• Claris, 18 de Septiembre 357	AEHLPV	ℓ 221980	$H	ⅈⅈ
19 rooms				
• Cordillera, Arauco 619	ADEFGHIJKLPSUV	ℓ 215211	$F	ⅈⅈ
Fax 211198				
• Floresta, 18 de Septiembre 278	AEGHLPV	ℓ 222253	$G	ⅈⅈ
• Gran Isabel Riquelme, Arauco 600	ACDEFGHIJKLMPSTUV	ℓ 213663	$E	ⅈⅈ
90 rooms, fax 2223576				
• Las Terazas, Constitución 664		ℓ 227000	$E	ⅈⅈ
Fax 227001				
• Libertador, Avenida Libertad 85	AHIJLPUV	ℓ 223255	$G	ⅈⅈ
20 rooms				
• Los Cardenales, Bulnes 34	AEGHPT	ℓ 224251		
• Nevado de Chillán, Avenida B. O'Higgins 497				
	AEHIJV	ℓ 221013	$H	ⅈⅈ
• Quinchamalí, El Roble 634	ADEGHIJKLPUV	ℓ 223381	$G	ⅈⅈ
• Real, Avenida Libertad 219	AIJL	ℓ 221827	$H,I	ⅈⅈ
• Regional, Avenida Brasil 451	AEFHPV	ℓ 222414		
• Rucamanqui, Herminda Martín 590	ADEFGHIJKLMP$TUVZ			
		ℓ 222704	$F	ⅈⅈ
Fax 217072				
• San Bartolomé, El Roble 585		ℓ223748	$H	ⅈⅈ
• Santiago, Avenida Libertad 61	AEHILPV	ℓ 222068		

Residenciales

• Barcelona, Constitución 26 opposite bus terminal			$J	ⅈ
Shared bathroom, budget travelers				
• El Valdiviano, Libertad 240	F	ℓ 221263	$I	ⅈⅈ
Budget travelers				
• Las Delicias, Yerbas Buenas 860		ℓ 221872		
• Su Casa, Cocharcas 555		ℓ 223931		

Accommodation along the Panamericana near northern exit

Motels

• Bermudas Inn, KM 400	AHTV	ℓ 210866		
Fax 210869				
• Hotelera Alicante, KM 400		ℓ 221431		
Fax (42) 215685				
• Las Encinas, northern access KM 400	ACDEFGHIJKLPRYUVXZ			
		ℓ 223283	$G	ⅈⅈ
• Príncipe de Galés, Chillán Viejo		ℓ 221095	$G	ⅈⅈ

Accommodation along the Panamericana near southern exit

• Hotel Los Presidentes, by-pass 3.5 km south		ℓ 221095

Accommodation in Bulnes

Bulnes, with a population of 1000, is located on the Panamericana, 26 km south of Chillán at the junction with RN 148 leading to Concepción; it was founded in 1839. It is a convenient place to stop for a meal, or to refuel on your way to Concepción. Buses Chevalier and Buses Línea Azul run regular services to Chillán.

• Motel Lomas del Larqui, Panamericana		ℓ 631030

Chillán

Accommodation in Chillán — continued

Accommodation in Pinto
Pinto is 25 km east.
- Hostería and Cabañas, Parque Los Heroes, 800 m from the plaza
- Cabañas Las Vertientes, KM 20

Accommodation in Quillón
Quillon is l44 km south-west on RN 148. Accommodation in Coyanco, 2 km west of Quillon, is also included here.

Hotels
- Belvedere, Carrera 212   (581191 $G ♙♙
- Claris, 18 de Septiembre 357   AHIJL   (221980
- Floresta, 18 de Septiembre 278   AGHIJL   (222253

Cabañas
- La Playa, Coyanco   ABEFGHKIJKLNPRV   (581064 $H for 5
  River frontage, caretaker lives on property, many chestnut trees giving ample shade, level grassy ground, 18 tent sites, camping $I, open December to March, electricity, water, toilets, hot shower, shop, 11 cabins
- Lo Poquito, Coyanco   ABDEFGHILNR   (81077 $F for 6
  15 tent sites, campsite $J, river frontage, sandy soil but little shade, open November to February; electricity, water, toilets, heating, hot showers, six cabins
- Península de Quillón, Libertad 279   ((09) 7520556 $F for 6

Complejo Turístico
- Cayumanqui, Coyanco   ((42) 581077 $F ♙♙
  Restaurant

Accommodation in Las Trancas
Las Trancas is 73 km east.

Hotels
- Los Pirineos, KM 69   AEFGHLMPTUV   ((42) 293839 $D ♙♙
  Tennis court, horses, fax (41) 233297
- Parador Jamón, Pan y Vino, KM 72   ABCEFGHIJKLNPR$UVZ((42) 222682 $D ♙♙
  Full board, car rental, sauna, tennis, ski hire, ski schools
- Refugio El Aserradero Club Andino de Concepción. Ski lodge before Puente Aserradero

Cabañas
- Pacha Pulay, KM 70   ABCEHILNPV   ((41) 224560 $D for 6
- Taitalle, KM 70   P   ((41) 280228 $E for 6

Accommodation in Recinto
Recinto is 53 km east.
- Hotel El Nevado, Los Olmos   AEFHILPV   ((108) 492183
  10 rooms
- Cabañas Recinto, Javier Jarpa ABCEFHIJLNPRV   (221306 $F ♙♙
- Hostería Turismo Cordillera, on the road to Termas de Chillán
                                                  ((42) 221306
- Hotel Los Lleuques, KM 56
- Hostería Villa Laja, Avenida Javier Jarpa KM 61
                                 ABCEFGHIJLPRV   ((43) 461382 $F for 6
  Employees of Empresa Papelera Laja have priority

Accommodation in Chillán — continued

Accommodation in San Carlos
San Carlos is 25 km north.
- Hotel City, Serrano 583   (411908 $H ♀♀
- Hotel Paris, O'Higgins 465   AEGHLPV
- Hotel Portal de Itihué, Serrano 545   AEFGHIKP   (411654 $G ♀♀

Accommodation in Termas de Chillán
Termas de Chillán is 82 km east, on Ruta N-55.
There are some cheaper hotels about 9 km before you get to the ski lifts, but you need your own transport.
★★★ Hotel Pirigallo, KM 83   AEFGHIJKLMNPRVXZ (223404 / 232234 / 223987
                                                                              $A

Full board, room, sauna, hydro-massage, tennis, ski hire, ski school, two outside thermal heated swimming pools. Reservations in Chillán: Arauco 600 (223664, fax (42) 223576

Eating out in Yungay
Yungay is located 66 km south of Chillán
- El Co-Co,Angamos 72. Chilean cuisine
- San Marco, Chorrilos 235. Chilean cuisine

Ⓣ Entertainment
- Night Club Music Hall, Constitución 688
- Night Club People's Bar, 18 de Septiembre 342

Entertainment in Chillán Viejo
- Disco Fandango, Carretera Panamericana Sur. Open daily, dancing Fri–Sun
- La Tranquera, Avenida B. O'Higgins 3001. *Peña* and *parillada*

Ⓟ Post and telegraph

Post office
- Correo, Libertad 501 Plaza de Armas

Telephone
- CTC Arauco 625 fax 221742
- Telex Chile, 18 de Septiembre 498
- ENTEL Chile, 18 de Septiembre 746

Ⓢ Financial
- Cambio Biotur Ltda, Constitución 550 (inside Galería) (225580. Open Mon–Fri 1000–1400
- Fincard, Constitución 550 (225920

Ⓢ Services and facilities

Camping and sports equipment
- Carpas Catan, O'Higgins 701. Sleeping bags, repairs to tents
- El Vencedor, Maipón 631. Fishing and camping equipment
- Ski Center, Barros Arana 261 (215495. skiing equipment

Medical center
- Clínica Chillán, 18 de Septiembre 320 (215625

Laundry
- Lavandería Sandra, Libertad 379

Pharmacy
- Farmacia España, Constitución 623

Photographic supplies
- Kodak Express, Arauco 620

Supermarket
- Supermercado Multimarket, 5 de Abril 864

Ⓜ Motoring
For gas stations, see city map.

Car rental
- Automóvil Club de Chile, O'Higgins 677 (216410
- First Rent a Car, 18 de Septiembre 380 (221218

Motoring to Termas de Chillán
The road is sealed for 55 km to the bridge over the Río Renegado at Los Lleuques,

the rest is a good gravel road. It is kept open all year round. Vehicular traffic between Chillán and Termas de Chillán is organized as follows: traffic from Chillán to Termas runs between 0800 and 1400 and between 1900 and 2100; traffic from Termas to Chillán runs from 1400 to 1800. Many skiers stay in Chillán and shuttle daily to the snow fields. The road's final stretch is very narrow. You can hire snow chains at Las Trancas next to the *carabineros*.

⊞ Shopping

Fería de Chillán is the main shopping center and market for the local people. It is quite colorful and fairly clean, with plenty of practical items for sale made by local crafts people.

Shopping in Quillón
Viña Quillón, a winery 4 km north of Quillón towards Nueva Aldea, is famous for its excellent white wines.

Shopping in San Fabián de Alico
Local craftsmen carve wooden figurines and lamp bases.

⊛ Sport

Trout fishing in upper Río Chillán, Río Cholguan, Río Diguillín, upper Río Itata, upper Río Ñuble, Río Renegado, and near Salto de Itata.
In Río Diguillin you can also fish for *percatrucha* or Chilean trout.

▣ Sightseeing

- The huge mural in the railroad station is by the two artists David Siqueiros and Xavier Guerero, painted in 1939 after the earthquake which destroyed most of the town. The mural shows historic events of Mexico and Chile. Interesting.
- Parque Monumental Bernardo O'Higgins, Chillán Viejo. You can't fail to notice the mural 60 m long and 6 m high which was painted by Carlos and Maria Martner. It represents the life of the great Bernardo O'Higgins, the Liberator who was born in this town. In the midst of splendid gardens is a new Centro Histórico Cultural.
- Catedral de Chillán. A building in the modern style made of 13 parabolic arches, which makes the interior very

light. Alongside the cathedral is a 39 m high cross. It took nearly 20 years to build, and was completed in 1961.
- Museo Franciscano, Sargento Aldea block 200 on Plaza Franciscano corner of Vega. The historical and ecclesiastic artifacts shown here give a good overview of the turbulent history of the region. It is part of the Convento Franciscano which was relocated here in 1835 from Chillán Viejo after the disastrous earthquake which completely destroyed the town. The church dates from 1906. The original Franciscan mission, San Ildefonso, was founded in Chillán Viejo in 1590 to train missionaries in converting the Mapuches to Christianity.
- Museo Naval A. Prat, Isabel Riquelme 1173. Includes a restaurant.
- Fería de Chillán, Maipón corner of Isabel Riquelme (see "Shopping" above).

⊕ Excursions

Tour operators
- Alto Nivel Ltda., Arauco 683 ℂ 225267
- Centrotour, 18 de Septiembre 656 ℂ 221306
- South Pacific Cross, Carrera 2 ℂ 231592. Hires motorbikes, and organizes cross-country motoring

Excursions
- **Quinchamalí**: 32 km west on Ruta N-60-O. Famous for its fine pottery and black earthenware, such as little money boxes and figurines. Regular buses.
- **Las Trancas**: A fledgling ski resort 73 km east, at an altitude of 1100 m. It consists of a *carabineros* station, and well before you reach this station you will notice that the road is lined with holiday homes, hotels, and ski lodges. Around here are some really old native trees, real great-grandfathers of huge dimensions (3 m circumference), almost forming a forest. They give you some idea of what it was like before the arrival of the European woodcutter. The ski lifts are 7 km further up the hill; in winter there is a shuttle service to the ski lifts. There are daily regular services from Chillán.

🚌 Buses from Chillán

Companies operating from the rural terminal
The rural bus terminal is on Sargento Aldea between Maipón and A. Prat.
- B34   Buses Buchupureo
- B53   Buses Tacoha
- B67   Buses Flash
- B132 Buses Petorca
- B156 Buses San Sebastián
- B240 Buses Rembus

Companies operating from the long-distance terminal
The long-distance bus terminal is on Constitución 1 corner of Brasil. Some bus companies have their own offices nearby.
- A46   Buses Línea Azul, office 2 ℂ 211192
- A106 Fénix Pullman Norte
- A137 Buses TAS Choapa, Constitución 1, office 4 ℂ 223062
- B96   Buses Línea Verde
- B217 Buses Flota L
- B220 Buses Interregional Abbeysur
- B235 Buses JM
- B236 Buses Pullman JR
- B237 Buses Pullman del Sur
- B250 Buses Transbus
- B259 Buses Chevallier
- B271 Buses Galaxia Sur

Companies operating from their own terminal
- A16   Buses Biotal, Avenida Brazil corner of Constitución
- A153 Buses Tur-Bus Jedimar, Constitución 1, office 1 ℂ 212502
- B42   Buses Cinta Azul, Constitución 83 corner of Rosas
- B63   Buses EXPA, Avenida Schleyer 130 ℂ 211904
- B81   Buses Igi Llaima, Brasil 611 ℂ 222991
- B82   Intersur, Constitución 24
- B87   Buses Jota Be, Constitución 55 ℂ 215862
- B150 Buses Rometur, Independencia block 900 corner of A. Prat ℂ 22480
         Minibuses to Termas de Chillán
- B199 Buses Estrella del Sur, Avenida Brazil corner of Constitución
- B209 Buses Expresos Las Trancas, Sargento Aldea 921
- B246 Buses Somon Tur, Constitución 1042
         Minibuses to Termas de Chillán
- B256 Buses Bonanza, Constitución 34
- Minibus to San Carlos, Constitución block 600 near Arauco
- Pullman Bus–Taco, B O'Higgins block 500 near Avenida Libertad

Services

	Destination	Fare	Services	Duration	Companies
•	Angol	$3.40	4 services daily		A48, A153, B265
•	Bulnes	$0.50			A46, B259
•	Cauquenes	$1.70	7 services daily	2 hrs	A46, B42
•	Cobquecura	$1.70	10 services daily		B34, B132, B199
•	Concepción	$2.50	46 services daily		A16, A46, A48, A137, A153, B42, B82, B96, B236, B250, B259
•	Curacautín	$5.00	1 service daily		A106
•	Curicó	$4.20		3 hrs	A153

Bío Bío

Buses from Chillán — continued

Destination	Fare	Services	Duration	Companies
Dichato				B67
Runs only in summer				
Florida	$1.10			A46, B259
Huepil	$1.50	3 services daily	3 hrs	B156, B236
Las Trancas	$1.50	1 service Mon–Sat		B199
La Unión	$10.10	1 service daily		A153
Lebu	$5.70	1 service daily		B165
Linares	$2.70	21 services daily		A16, A48, B42, B256
Los Angeles	$2.50	18 services daily	1½ hrs	A16, A48, A137, A153, B81, B87, B237
Lota		2 services daily		A153, B96
Mulchén	$3.40	2 services daily		A153
Osorno	$10.10	6 services daily		A48, A137, A153
Parral	$1.90	7 services daily	1 hr	A16, B42, A137
Pemuco		3 services daily		B156
Polcura	$1.60	1 service Mon–Sat		B199
Pucón	$7.60	1 service daily		A48
Puerto Montt	$12.50	7 services daily		A48, A137, A153
Puerto Varas	$11.80	1 service daily		B81
Purén		1 service daily		B53
Quillón	$0.70			A46, B259
Quilpué		4 services daily		A16, A48
Quirihué	$1.20	2 services daily	1 hr	B199
Rancagua	$6.80	5 services daily	5½ hrs	A153
Recinto	$0.90	11 services daily		B240
San Fabián de Alico				
	$1.40	2 services daily		B156
Santiago	$8.40	60 services daily	6½ hrs	A16, A46, A48, A105, A137, A153, B81, B137, B165, B199, B217, B220, B236, B237, B250, B259, B265, B271
Talca	$3.00	27 services daily	2½ hrs	A16, A137, A153, B82, B199
Talcahuano	$2.50	4 services daily		A48, A137, A153
Temuco	$6.70	12 services daily		A48, A137, A153,
Termas de Chillán	$1.90	4 services daily		B199
Tomé	$2.30	3 services daily		A153
Traiguén	$4.80	1 service daily		A48
Tucapel	$1.70	1 service Mon–Sat		B199
Valdivia	$8.40	10 services daily		A48, A137, A153, B81
Valparaíso	$10.60	17 services daily		A16, A48, A74, A105, A137, A153, B235
Victoria	$4.60	2 services daily		A153
Villa Alemana	$7.60	4 services daily		A16, A48
Villarrica	$6.80	2 services daily		A137, B82
Viña del Mar	$10.60	14 services daily		A16, A48, A74, A137, A153, B235
Yumbel	$1.50	14 services daily	2 hrs	B67, B156
Yungay	$1.70	4 services daily		B156, B199, B236

🚆 Trains from Chillán

The railroad booking office is at the Ferrocarriles del Estado, 18 de Septiembre 656.

Destination	Salón	Económico	Services	Duration
• Concepción	$6.50	$4.60	3 services daily	4 hrs
• Puerto Montt	$15.20	$11.50	2 services daily	14 hrs
• Rancagua			4 services daily	
• Santiago	$9.00	$7.00	4 services daily	6 hrs
• Talca			3 services daily	2 hrs
• Temuco		$7.00	1 services daily	6 hrs

- **Ninhué:** 48 km west, on a good road. Here is the *hacienda* San Agustín de Puñual, birthplace of Arturo Prat who was a sea hero of the War of the Pacific; it is now a *monumento nacional*. On exhibit are memorabilia from the period and biographical information about the hero.

- **Pinto:** 25 km east, in the central valley just before the *pre-Cordillera* starts. With a population of 2000, it has accommodation and restaurants, and takes the overflow of skiers who cannot find accommodation closer to the ski fields near Termas de Chillán. On the plaza is a bar and restaurant with a disco at weekends. Regular daily buses run to Chillán. Buses coming from Chillán on their way to Termas de Chillán may be full during the skiing season.

- **Quillón:** 44 km south-west. It is the center of a wine-growing area, vineyards alternating with small forests and *araucania* trees. The main attraction is **Laguna Avendaño**, 2 km south of town at **Coyanco**, where you will find most of the tourist facilities. Its population is 4000. Buses Chevalier run frequent daily buses to Chillán and Concepción at 45-minute intervals.

- **Recinto:** 53 km east at an altitude of 700 m in the upper **Río Renegado** valley, at the end of the sealed road from Chillán. This is still a reasonably cheap area as far as accommodation is concerned for prospective skiers or hikers to use as a base for excursions in this wonderful area. The ski fields and Termas de Chillán are 30 km further up in the valley; there is a shuttle bus service from Recinto to the snowfields in win-

ter. A few kilometers past the Río Renegado bridge, there is a turnoff to the right leading to the Cueva de los Pincheira, which was used as a hideout by the Pincheira brothers in 1819 — see the entry for Malargüe in *Travel Companion Argentina*. After the defeat of the royalist troops they became outlaws; it is well sign-posted and only 500 m from main road. There is also a rock-pool there. REM Bus runs 11 services daily from Chillán.

- **San Carlos:** 25 km north, in the northern part of the region in the central valley. It was founded in 1723 by Gobernador Gabriel Aponte y Cano as part of his defense strategy. This old Spanish fort was restored some time ago, but looks rather neglected again. There are splendid views over the river. It has 27 500 inhabitants, a hotel, restaurants, and gas stations. Buses Lit and Buses Tur-Bus Jedimar run regular services to Santiago and Puerto Montt; Buses San Sebastián run regular daily services to Chillán and San Fabián de Alico.

- **San Fabián de Alico:** 68 km north-east in the *pre-Cordillera* in the **Río Ñuble valley**, at an altitude of 500 m. It is a small, traditional village in the shade of a 2000 m-high mountain range separating the Río Perquilauquen valley from the Río Ñuble catchment area. It is the starting point for hikers wishing to explore the northern part of the Volcán Chillán massif. From the turnoff at **San Carlos** the road goes at first through some rich farming land. Once you have passed the *carabineros* checkpoint near the turnoff to the ferry over the Río Ñuble, the road starts to climb. The low hills around Cachapoal are used for farming right up to the top. As the valley narrows the landscape changes: the river forms cascades and the mountains along the road are covered with dense native forests. The road continues for another 24 km east from San Fabián to **La Punilla**. From there onwards you are on mountain trails leading into the Volcán Chillán massif or further east to Paso Chureco on the Argentine border. As you leave San Fabián the valley narrows considerably, becoming a gorge, through which the river flows in torrents. This is quite spectacular country with glimpses of snow-covered **Volcán Chillán** to the south. You can hire horses in San Fabián for excursions into the *cordillera*. Buses San Sebastián run two services daily from Chillán.

- **Termas de Chillán**: 82 km east, at an altitude of 1723 m. This huge thermal complex with two outside thermal pools on the slopes of Volcán Chillán (3200 m) is open all year round. It is also an excellent ski resort in its own right; you have the best of two worlds. The hotel has first-class service of world standard with views down the valley and the **Volcán Chillán** within walking distance. A little way up the slopes you can visit geysers and *fumaroles* (jets of steam). Use the path leading up to the radio antenna; the biggest *fumaroles* are near the pylon about 800 m uphill. The ski season lasts from May to October, on powder snow. In contrast with the ski slopes around Santiago (which are bare), this area is forested up the slopes with na-

tive trees. This mountainous border region is almost the last domain of a group of *huemules* (South American deer). *Huemules* in larger quantities are only found in the Región XI de Aisén, 1300 km south — **Reserva Nacional Ñuble** was set up to preserve them. At present the total lift capacity is 8000 skiers per hour. Lift tickets cost $30.00 per day. Public transport goes only as far as the Río Renegado bridge, but tour operators run buses as and when required right up to the thermal and skiing complex — $30.00 return fare; duration 1½ hrs. Termas de Chillán is a good starting point for hikes in the nearby Volcán Chillán area. The hotel itself organizes five- and eight-day outdoor equestrian hikes on narrow mountain trails to **Cordilleras Las Bravas**, Valle Río Polcura, Valle Casa de Lata, and Valle Aguas Calientes. You get wonderful views of the glaciated Volcán Chillán and go through high alpine meadows with crystal-clear water running through them. When you get to the valley of the hot springs, the tour operators provide a day spent trout fishing and bathing in the hot thermal waters. Five days and four nights cost $350; eight days and seven nights cost $570.00; you can book at the thermal complex. These excursions only take place in summer, from December to March.

- **Yungay**: 66 km south on the **Río Itata,** surrounded by large forests. Yungay has approximately 9000 inhabitants and has some tourist facilities. The plaza surrounded by colonial-style houses is quite picturesque. But the

---

Ski lifts in Termas de Chillán

Lift	Length	Descent	Capacity/hour
• La Peta (Platter)	475 m	90 m	700 persons
• Beginners (Platter)	400 m	30 m	500 persons
• Don Otto (Double chair)			
	2500 m	700 m	450 persons
• Don Penno (T-Bar)	900 m	350 m	900 persons
• El Chuelo (Platter)	1305 m	275 m	1100 persons
• La Coto (T-Bar)	400 m	400 m	
• Las Tres Marías			
• New double chair lift			

main reason to visit is the **Salto del Itata** about 11 km west of Yungay: this magnificent horseshoe-shaped waterfall falls 70 m into a basin. The best way to get to the falls is to hire a taxi in Yungay on the plaza. There is trout fishing in Río Cholguan, and near Salto de Itata. Buses Flash and Buses San Sebastián run 14 services daily from Chillán.

COBQUECURA

Area code: LD 108
Population: 1500
Distance from Chillán: 103 km west on Ruta N-50 and Panamericana

Nestled on the Pacific Coast, this town with its long beach of gray sand dates back to the pre-Colombian tribes. In the 19th century it was an important wheat-growing area, but now it is becoming increasingly popular as a seaside resort. The beach extends south almost to the estuary of the **Río Itata**. The best beaches, with unserviced camping grounds, are south near the mouth of the **Río Taucu** and **Colmuyao**. Hundreds of seals make their homes in the rocky outcrops near the beach, which are exposed to strong westerly winds.

The streets of the town are lined with old stone houses, many with straw-thatched roofs. The local people are known for some interesting crafts, such as earthenware and woolen fabrics with traditional designs. There are some tourist facilities.

Cobquecura is an isolated beach resort, far away from the tourist hot spots. It is quiet, with long, wide expanses of clean unpolluted beaches. Tourist facilities are still developing — this is ideal for people looking for a quiet stay. The main road from town center to the beach has an elevated footpath over a low-lying area, as this spot gets easily inundated at high tide. One other interesting feature is the paving of sidewalks with slate.

⊟ Accommodation

For all accommodation in this town there is a common answering service: ☏ 492230.
- Hotel La Lobería, Independencia
- Cabañas Rucamar, Chacabuco 1000 AEFGHIL $H ⋮⋮

- Residencial El Atardecer, Independencia 834 $H ⋮⋮
- Residencial Rodríguez, Carrera 530 AEHIJL $H ⋮⋮. Shared bathroom cheaper

ⒶCampingCamping

There is an unserviced camping site on Playa Buchupureo, 10 km north of Cobquecura on a *laguna*.

⑪ Eating out

Restaurants
- Central, Independencia 421 near Balmaceda
- El Café, Independencia 521 near Isabel Riquelme
- El Barjón, Independencia 642 near Isabel Riquelme
- Los Copihues, Independencia 635 near Serrano

▦ Post and telegraph

Post office
- Correo, Chacabuco near Libertador O'Higgins

🚌 Buses

Companies
- Buses Petorca, Chacabuco near Arturo Prat
- Buses Costa Azul, Arturo Prat

- Buses Buchupureo, Arturo Prat

Services

If you are going to Cauquenes over part of the Camino de los Conquistadores, you will need to change in Quirihué and take a bus to Cauquenes.

- Chillán: Fare $1.70; 7 services daily; Buses Petorca, Buses Buchupureo

- Concepción: Fare $2.50; 2 services daily; Buses Costa Azul
- Quirihué: Fare $0.60; 7 services daily; Buses Petorca

🚗 **Motoring services**

- COPEC gas station on the road to Quirihué

CONCEPCIÓN

Area code: 41
Population: 330 000
Distance from Santiago: 500 km south on RN 148 and Panamericana

Concepción, near the mouth of the **Río Bío Bío,** is the capital of the Región VIII del Bío Bío. It is promoted by the local tourist board as "La Perla del Bío Bío" — the Pearl of the Bío Bío.

Although founded in the 16th century, nowadays it is a modern city, and together with the port of **Talcahuano** one of the most important industrialized centers of Chile. It is the third largest city in Chile. Talcahuano, the port of Concepción, is only 16 km west on the Bahía de Concepción; it has virtually become part of greater Concepción.

History

On February 22, 1550, on the outskirts of what are now the city limits, was the first great battle between Pedro de Valdivia and the Mapuche, known as Battle of Andalien. After this battle, Pedro de Valdivia proceeded to make the official (or first) foundation of Concepción, 14 km north of present-day Concepción at Penco (then Peguco). In 1751 Concepción was completely destroyed by an earthquake followed by a seismic tidal wave. In 1764 the town was re-founded on its present site in the Valle de la Mocha, and during the whole Spanish colonial era it was the

southern outpost of the Reino de Chile. In its early days it came under frequent attack by Mapuche in a series of battles called La Guerra de Arauco. In 1776 Don Ambrosio O'Higgins became chief administrator (or "Intendente") of the Intendencia de Concepción and later Viceroy of Chile.

The Chilean independence movement began here, and independence was proclaimed at Concepción on January 10, 1818 on the Plaza de la Independencia.

Industry

In the early days of the republic, Concepción was the focal point of an extensive agricultural region. Now it is the center of heavy industry based largely on the logging industry, as well as steel works and petrochemical plants.

Places of interest

Concepción is a town with magnificent public buildings, many dating from the 19th century.

There is a market two blocks west of the plaza, where you can buy locally made handicrafts; upstairs is a good seafood restaurant.

In the railroad station the painter Gregorio de la Fuente has painted a huge mural depicting important moments in the history of the city.

Other items of tourist interest include the cathedral, with a rather eclectic architectural style, and the Barrio Universitario (University District); and from top of the Cerro Caracol you get panoramic views over the city and the river.

Concepción has two important universities: Universidad del Bío Bío and Universidad de Concepción.

Road transport

Going south from Concepción as far as Curanilahué is the Camino del Carbón, which is the route taken by Pedro de Valdivia on his campaign to subdue the Mapuche. Nowadays this is a well-built highway with important towns along the way, such as **Coronel** and **Lota**, and further south **Arauco**, **Cañete**, and **Lebu**. Public transport runs frequently.

North of Concepción you can take a scenic drive through **Penco**, **Tomé**, and **Dichato**, with fine beaches and good restaurants. There is frequent public transport.

There are two large road bridges crossing the Río Bío Bío at Concepción: Puente Viejo (1800 m long) from Esmeralda, and Puente Nuevo (2000 m long) 2 km downstream to San Pedro. Between them is the railroad bridge.

Dichato

Dichato is a small and rather beautiful resort on the **Bahía Coliumo**,

38 km north, with a fine white sandy beach extending for more than 2 km. It is a quiet place, but in summer booking is advisable. Restaurants specialize in seafood, brought in daily by the fishing fleet. It is still unspoilt by mass tourism. The pine forests extend from the hills to the seashore at the northern and southern ends of the bay. The street names can be confusing: C. Vera and Avenida Daniel Vera are different streets; and Pedro Aguirre Cerda is also known as Costanera.

Florida

Florida, 45 km east on RN 148, is a convenient place to stop on your way to the Panamericana.

Nacimiento

Nacimiento is 105 km south-east, on top of a steep hill overlooking the **Río Vergara** just before it joins the Río Bío Bío. With a population of 20 000, the town is a time capsule — streets and houses in the town center have remained unchanged since the colonial period. The major tourist attraction however is the Fuerte de Nacimiento in General Freire, overlooking the

Bío Bío

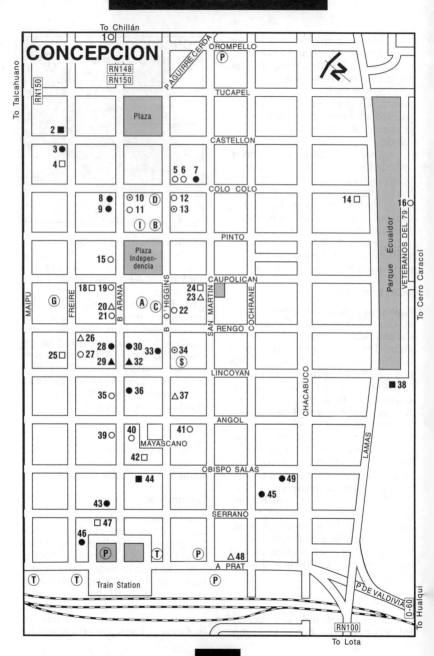

Río Vergara, but the view is marred by the huge stockpile of timber on the other side of the river, belonging to Celulosa Inforsa.

Nacimiento was founded by Governor Alonso de Ribera y Zambrano on December 24, 1603. This was a substantial fortress to secure the Bío Bío line and protect the areas to the north already firmly in Spanish hands from incursions by marauding Mapuche warriors, who destroyed the fort three times. The present fort was constructed in 1749 and re-mained part of Spanish Chile until independence.

These days the *carabineros* have their office in the old fortress complex, but the area can be freely inspected, and visitors can marvel over the work the Spaniards invested here in building this fort. The fortress is approximately 120 m above the Río Vergara, and it is almost a sheer drop to the riverbed. A stairway leads down from the fort to the river bank, and there is a wooden bridge across the river. The town center is still very

Key to map

A	Iglesia Catedral	21	Restaurant Dino's
B	Gobernación Provincial (Government)	22	Restaurant Club Concepción
		27	Restaurant Oba Oba
C	Municipalidad (Town hall)	35	Restaurant El Rancho de Julio
D	Post office and telex	39	Restaurant Viet Xiu
E	Telephone	40	Restaurant Chung Hwa
G	Mercado Municipal (Market)	41	Restaurant Sardana
I	Tourist information		
P	Gas stations	⊙	**Entertainment**
$	Money exchange	13	Disco Cosas Buenas
T	Bus terminals	34	Piano Bar Cat's

●	**Accommodation**	△	**Tour operators and car rental**
3	Hotel Cruz del Sur	20	Viajes Conceción
7	Hotel Alonso de Ercilla	23	Automóvil Club de Chile
8	Residencial San Sebastián	26	Avis Rent a Car
9	Hotel Ritz	37	Larma Turismo
10	Hotel Tabancura	48	Hertz Rent a Car
19	Hotel El Araucano		
28	Hotel Alborada	▲	**Airline offices**
30	Hotel San Sebastian	29	LAN Chile
31	Residencial Metropol	32	LADECO
33	Residencial O'Higgins		
36	Hotel El Dorado	■	**Sights**
43	Apart Hotel Concepción	2	Iglesia
45	Hospedaje Los Pirámides	38	Museo de Historia
46	Hotel Cecil	44	Iglesia Franciscana
49	Apart Hotel Don Aurelio, Salas 135		

○	**Eating out**	□	**Services**
1	Restaurant Chinatown	4	Laundromat
5	Restaurant Big Joe	14	Alliance Francaise
6	Restaurant Chateau	18	ENTEL
11	Restaurant Nuria	24	Instituto Chileno Norteamericano
12	Royal Pub	25	Supermercado Hiperbrisas
15	Restaurant Centro Español	42	Outdoor equipment
16	Restaurant El Parque	47	CONAF

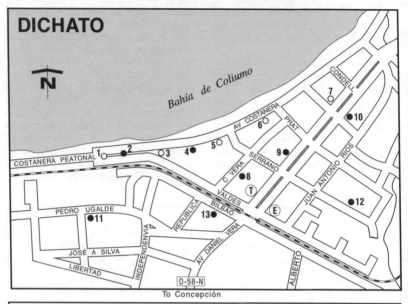

Key to map

E	Telephone	13	Residencial Santa Inés
T	Bus terminals	○	**Eating out**
●	**Accommodation**	1	Restaurant Santa Elena
2	Hotel/Restaurant Costanera	3	Restaurant Vicarack
8	Motel El Kalifa I	4	Schopería Asturias
9	Motel El Kalifa II	5	Restaurant Tío Agustín
10	Hotel Chamaruck	6	Restaurant Costa Bella
11	Hotel Chiki	7	Restaurant Chillán
12	Cabañas Sol y Mar		

much the same as when it was founded — the only high-rise buildings are the chimney stacks of the factories. Most of the houses are very old and made of wood.

With the conquest of the Mapuche heartland south of the Río Bío Bío, the fortress town lost its strategic importance. From the early days of the republic it became a wine-growing district. Since the introduc-

tion of the radiata pine plantations in the district, the town's economic fortunes are linked to the huge paper and pulp manufacturing plant across the Río Vergara, belonging to Cellulosa Inforsa. Postal services and telephone services are located in the Municipalidad building.

NACIMIENTO

Key to map

A	Iglesia
C	Municipalidad (Town hall)
D	Post office and telex
E	Telephone
F	Carabineros (Police)
G	Mercado Municipal (Market)
P	Gas stations
T	Bus terminals

Services

□	
1	Residencial
2	Lavandería La Esburna
3	Restaurant American Bar
4	Restaurant Jommsoll
5	Fuerte Nacimiento
6	Residencial

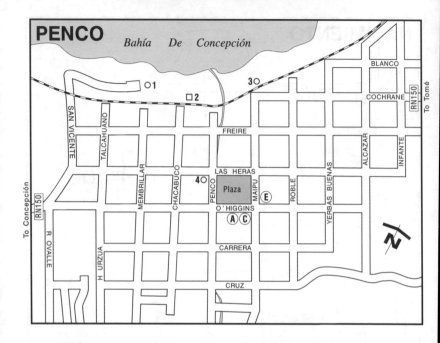

PENCO
Bahía De Concepción

Key to map

A	Iglesia	**3**	Seafood restaurants
C	Municipalidad (Town hall)	**4**	Restaurant Posada El Roble
E	Telephone	■	**Sights**
●	**Eating out**	**2**	Fuerte Español
1	Restaurant Casino Oriente		

Penco

Penco is 14 km north, on the spot where Concepción was originally founded in 1550 by Pedro de Valdivia. The foundation ceremony was barely over before the first major attack by the Mapuches, known as the Battle of Quilicura. By the end of the 16th century, many monasteries such as Santo Domingo, San Francisco, La Merced, and San Agustín, and the Compañía de Jesús had been established there. The town came under frequent attack, both from pirates and Mapuches, and in 1687 Gobernador José de Garro built Fuerte La Planchada close to the bay. The town was destroyed by an earthquake and tidal wave in 1764, and was rebuilt in 1843.

The beach consists of grayish sand, and has feeble waves as it is

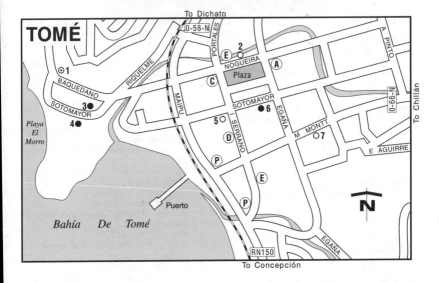

Key to map

A	Iglesia
C	Municipalidad (Town hall)
D	Post office and telex
E	Telephone
P	Gas stations

● Accommodation

3 Hostería Villa Marina
4 Hostería El Morro

6 Hotel Roxy

○ Eating out

1 Restaurant Pub Millenios
2 Restaurant La Peña
5 Restaurant Club Social
7 Café Mas

protected inside the bay. It is very crowded in summer. The road leading to Concepción over the Cuesta Bellavista is very scenic.

Penco is now an important industrial town of 40 000 inhabitants tied to agriculture and ceramics. Penco and **Lirquén**, a small town some 2 km further north, (and eventually Concepción) are growing together.

Tomé

Tomé is a large manufacturing center and port 34 km north of Concepción. Textiles and glass have been manufactured here since the middle of last century. Founded in 1842, Tomé is also one of the most popular beach resorts near Concepción with a population of 42 000. The streets are narrow and some of the houses have thatched roofs. El Morro beach is 800 m long with gray sand; hotels and restaurants are nearby.

Concepción

🎎 Festivals

Festivals in Concepción ☞
- February 3–19: Fería Exposición Artesanal
- October, first week: Rosario, in Florida Parish. Local color
- March: Foundation Day

Festivals in Dichato
- February, first week: Semana de Dichato

Festivals in Florida
- February, first week: Semana de Florida

Festivals in Hualqui
- February, third week: Semana de Hualqui ☞

Festival in Tomé
- February, first week: Semana de Tomé

ℹ️ Tourist information

- Sernatur, Caupolicán 567, office 908 ☎ 229201
- Sernatur Concepción, A. Pinto 460 ☎ 227976. Fishing licenses
- CONAF, Serrano 529, 3rd floor ☎ 223131

🅰️ Camping

There are camping sites at Boca del Bío Bío, 12 km west of town; Camping Sol y Río, 15 km south of town on the road to Santa Juana; and at Dichato, 43 km north.

🍴 Eating out

Restaurants
- Al Andaluz, V. Lamas 980. Spanish cuisine
☞ - Big Joe, Libertador B. O'Higgins 808. Grill. Credit cards accepted
- Carnoteca Schop, Lautaro 1096. Chilean cuisine
- Centro Español, Barros Arana 675 on the main plaza ☎ 230685
☞ - China Town, Barros Arana 1123. Chinese cuisine
☞ - Chung Hwa, Barros Arana 262. Chinese cuisine
- Colacho, Rengo 1410. Mediterranean cuisine
- Club Concepción, Libertador B. O'Higgins 544
- Dino's, Barros Arana 507
☞ - El Novillo Loco, Pasaje Portales 539. International cuisine

- El Parque, Veteranos del 79, Parque Ecuador. International cuisine
- El Rancho de Julio, Barros Arana 337. *Parrillada*
- El Araucano, Caupolicán 521. International cuisine
☞ - Fortín Bulnes, Bulnes 360. Chilean cuisine
- Gran Chimú, Freire 761.Peruvian cuisine
- La Esquina Pub, Chacabuco 1108.International cuisine
- Kimura, Castellón 398. Japanese cuisine
- La Pioggia, Barros Arana 514, upstairs. International cuisine
☞ - Le Chateau Français, Colo Colo 340. International cuisine
☞ - Rincón Marino, Colo Colo 454, upstairs. Seafood
- Nuria, B. Arana 736
- Rincón Naturista, Barros Arana 667, on the main plaza
- Oba Oba, Freire 550
☞ - Rincón de Pancho, Cervantes 469. International cuisine
- Royal Pub, Libertador B. O'Higgins 790
☞ - Sardana, Centro Catala, Angol 343 $X
☞ - The Great Wall, Lincoyán 530. Chinese cuisine
☞ - Viet Xiu, Angol 515 upstairs. Chinese cuisine
- Yugo Centro, Libertador B. O'Higgins 734 (in the Centro Comercial building)

Cafeterías
- Caribe, Caupolicán 521 in the *galería*
- Haiti, Caupolicán 511
- Real, A. Pinto 515

Pizzerías
- Ciao, Chacabuco 625. Italian cuisine
- Piazza, Barros Arana 631. Italian cuisine
- Totos Pizza, Barros Arana 729

Eating out in San Pedro
San Pedro is across the Puente Viejo

Restaurants
- Los Portones de San Pedro, Colo Colo 28. *Parrillada*
- La Guarida del Pirata, Laguna Grande. Mexican cuisine
☞ - Millaray, P.A.Cerda 255. International cuisine

▣ Accommodation in Concepción

Accommodation in the medium to low price range is very scarce in Concepción. It is therefore advisable to arrive early in the day or, better still, book in advance; alternatively, the nearby northern resort towns of Penco, Tomé, or Dichato may do the trick. In the vicinity of the railroad station there are a few *residenciales*, but they are only suitable for backpackers.

Apart hotels

★★ Concepción, Serrano 512	AHIKPV	(228851/222018	$F	⁛
Fax 230948				
• Don Aurelio, Salas 135	AP	(243193	$E	⁛
Fax 246798				
• Santa Mónica, O'Higgins 320		(223031		

Hotels

★★★★ Alborada, Barros Arana 457	ADEFGHIJKLP$	(242144	$D	⁛
Sauna				
★★★ Alonso de Ercilla, Colo Colo 334	ADEFHIJKLP$TUV	(227984	$E	⁛
Fax 230053, 70 rooms				
★★★ El Dorado, Barros Arana 348	ADEFGHIJKLMP$UVZ	(229400	$E	⁛
Car rental, fax 231018				
★★ Ritz, B. Arana 721	ADEIJLPS$V	(226696	$F	⁛
Fax 243249				
★★ Tabancura, B. Arana 786, 7th floor	ADEFGHIKLP$TUV	(238348	$F	⁛
Fax 238350				
• Cécil, Barros Arana 9	AEIPSV	(230677	$G	⁛
• Cruz del Sur, Freire 889	AEFHIJKLMPTV	(233271/230944	$E	⁛
Fax 235655				
• Della Cruz, A. Pinto 240	AHPTUV	(240016	$F	⁛
• El Araucano, Caupolicán 521	ACDEFGHIJKLMNPR$YTUVZ	(230606	$C	⁛
Car rental, fax 230690, 151 rooms, sauna				
• Fish, Angol 1250		(244020		
Budget travelers				
• Hotel Terrano, O'Higgins 340		(240078	$F	⁛
• Nuevo Bío Bío, B. Arana 751	AEFGHLU	(230463	$G	⁛
Fax 227140				
• San Sebastián, Rengo 463	AP	(243412	$G	⁛

Hospedaje

• Las Pirámides, Cochrane 176	EH	(237675	$J	⁛
Shared bathroom				

Motels

• Hotelera Alicante, J.M. García 200	
Fax 312274; near bus terminal	

Residenciales

• Antuco, Barros Arana 741, Depto 28–33 upstairs		(235485	$H	⁛
Shared bathroom				
• Casablanca, Cochrane 133	PS	(226576	$H	⁛
Shared bathroom cheaper				
• Central, Rengo 673		(227309	$I	⁛
• Colo Colo, Colo Colo 743		(234790	$H	⁛
• La Familia, Freire 1565	S	(244609	$I	⁛
Shared bathroom				

Accommodation in Concepción — continued

- Metropol, O'Higgins 464
- O'Higgins, B. O'Higgins 465 — PS — (228303 — $H ♁
  Budget travelers
- Ruca Ray, B. Arana 317-B — (238760 — $J ♁
- San Sebastián, B. Arana 741 — (242710 — $H ♁
- Shabitur, Barros Arana 790 — (242682
- Tupahue, Maipú 1053 — (236849 — $G ♁

Accommodation in San Pedro
San Pedro is across the Río Bío Bío.
- Residencial Mira Río, P.A. Cerda 6 — PS — (371176 — $G ♁

Accommodation in Coronel
Coronel is 35 km south.
- Motel Giter, KM 17 on RN 160 — (751048
- Motel Verona, 2755 RN 160 — (373230

Accommodation in Dichato

Cabañas
- Sol y Mar, Serrano

Hotels
- Chamaruk, Avenida Daniel Vera 912 — AP — (683022 — $F ♁
  Shared bathroom cheaper
- Chiki, Pedro L. Ugalde 410 — AEGHIJLPS — (683004 — $H ♁
  Open December–March
- Costanera, Pedro Aguirre Cerda 710 — EFGHIJ — (681000 — $H ♁
- Manantial, Pedro Aguirre Cerda 201 — (683003 — $F ♁
- Montecarlo, Pedro Aguirre Cerda 655

Motels
- Asturias, Pedro Aguirre Cerda 734 — ADEFGHIKPUV — (683000 — $G ♁
  Beach frontage
- El Kalifa I, Avenida Daniel Vera 815 — ADEFGHIKLPRUV — (683027 — $E for 4
  Boat hire
- El Kalifa II, C. Vera — ADEFGHIKLPRUV — (681027 — $E for 4
  Boat hire

Residenciales
- Santa Ines, Bilbao near República

Accommodation in Florida
- Hostería Royale, on main street

Accommodation in Penco
- Hotel La Terraza, Penco 20 — AEFGHILPTUV — (451422 — $G ♁
  25 rooms

Accommodation in Tomé

Cabañas
Tomé is 34 km north
- Broadway, Avenida Werner 1210 — APS — (651117 — $F for 4

Hotels
- Linares, Serrano 875 — AEPV — (651284 — $H ♁
  13 rooms

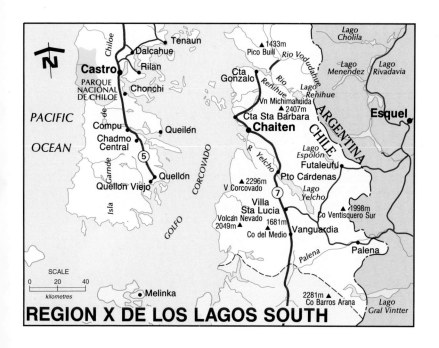

REGION X DE LOS LAGOS SOUTH

Plate 31
Map of Región X de Los Lagos – South

Plate 32   Región X de Los Lagos
Parque Nacional V. Pérez Rosales, Saltos del Petrohué

Accommodation in Concepción — continued

• Roxy, Sotomayor 1075	AEFGJPV	(650729	$H ⁇
• Villa Marina, Riquelme 55	APS	(650807	$H ⁇

Hosterías
• El Morro, Riquelme 1		(5611126
• La Casona, Baquedano 475	EFGHJP	

Accommodation along RN 150
5 km south of town.

Motels
- El Edén, Fundo El Eden between Lirquén and Tomé 18 km north
  AFV
  Overlooks Bahía de Tomé. Includes a restaurant

Eating out along the road to Nonquén
- Restaurant Rincón Campesino, KM 2.5

Eating out along the road to Chiguayante
- Restaurant El Montanés, Pedro. de Valdivia 5633

Eating out in Chiguayante
Chiguayante is 10 km upstream on the north bank of the Río Bío Bío. It has an atmosphere of historic charm with its many old adobe houses and ox-carts in the tree-lined streets.
- Restaurant Ness-Barness, Libertador. B. O'Higgins 310. Disco

Eating out along the road to Santa Juana
Restaurants
- Calabrano, KM 4. Chilean cuisine
- El Alero de Los Ortiz. International cuisine
- El Cordovés, KM 3. International cuisine

Eating out in Coronel
Coronel is 33 km south. The major restaurants are on Playa Blanca. All restaurants listed specialize in Chilean cuisine.
- Cafetería Fredy's, M. Montt 551
- Restaurant Casino Las Rocas, Playa Blanca. Disco
- Restaurant Casino Verde Mar, Playa Blanca
- Restaurant La Casona de José Miguel, Playa Blanca

Eating out in Dichato
Restaurants
- Chillán, Avenida Daniel Vera
- Costa Bella, Avenida Costanera
- El Candil, Costanera Norte, overlooking Bahía de Coliumo
- El Paso, Avenida Daniel Vera 1195. Chilean cuisine
- Ranchito Criollo, Serrano 222. Chilean cuisine
- Santa Elena, Valdés. Chilean cuisine
- Tío Agustín, Pedro Aguirre Cerda 768
- Vicarack, Avenida Costanera

Eating out in Florida
- Restaurant Las Brisas, on main street

Eating out in Nacimiento
- Restaurant American Bar, Montt 404
- Restaurant Club de Empleados, on Inforsa premises. The best eating place in town
- Restaurant El Colonial, Freire 414. Chilean cuisine
- Restaurant Jommsol, Montt 450

Eating out in Penco
Restaurants
- Casino La Planchada, Playa Penco. Seafood. Disco
- Casino Oriente, Playa Penco (on the beach). Seafood. Dancing weekends
- Fortín Turismo, Playa Penco. Seafood
- Posada El Roble, Penco 202. Seafood

Eating out in Lirquén
Lirquén is 17 km north.
- Casablanca, M. Rodríguez 180. Seafood

- La Nave, Balmaceda 9
☞ • Rincón Marino, P. Aguirre Cerda 171, near fishing harbor. Seafood

Eating out in Santa Juana
Santa Juana is 53 km south-east, on the banks of the Río Bío Bío.
- El Fuerte Histórico La Casona, Bío Bío.Chilean cuisine.
- Hawai, Lautaro. Chilean cuisine

Eating out in Tomé
Restaurants
- Casino El Morro, Riquelme 1. International cuisine
- Casino Municipal, M. Montt 1215. Chilean cuisine
- Club Social, Sotomayor 970
- La Esquina, Sotomayor 1099. Chilean cuisine
- La Peña, Jorquera corner of Egaña. Chilean cuisine
- Pub Milenios, Avenida Werner
- Sabra, Nogueira 981 near Baquedano. Chilean cuisine
- Villa Marina, Riquelme 55. Chilean cuisine

Ⓣ Entertainment
Discos are also in the suburb of Pinares across Puente Viejo.

Discos
☞ • Cosas Buenas, Libertador B. O'Higgins 766
- Shadows, Colo Colo 463

Piano bar
- Cats, Libertador B. O'Higgins 448 near Lincoyán

Nightclubs
- Tentación, Colo Colo Block 400 near Libertador B. O'Higgins. Grill
- Tropicana, Libertador B.O'Higgins 28

Entertainment along the road to Santa Juana
- Discotheque Bar
- Disco Studio 1200

Post and telegraph

Post office
- Correos de Chile, Libertador B. O'Higgins 799

Telephone
- CTC, Caupolicán 549. Fax (41) 240055
- ENTEL Chile, A. Pinto 982

- Telex Chile, Caupolicán 549, upstairs in Galería

$ Financial
- Bancard, Libertador B. O'Higgins 402 ℂ 238966. Cash advances on Visa and Mastercard

Services and facilities

Dry cleaners
- Lavaseco Henry, Libertador B. O'Higgins 912

Laundries
- Automatic, Castellón 879. Same-day service, $2.00 per wash
- Express, Lavarápido Cym, Barros Arana 1221. $6.80 for 7 kg

Medical center
- Unidad Coronaria (Cardiac Unit), A. Pinto 247 ℂ 224044

Sporting equipment
- Preciados, Maipú 655. Fishing gear

Supermarket
- Supermercado Hyperbrisas, Freire 467

Motoring
For gas stations, see the city map.
There is a sealed road from Concepción to Hualqui, but it is a dirt road further east to Talcamávida and Rere.
The road from Concepción to Santa Juana is sealed as far as Tricauco, 10 km west of town.

Car rental
- Automóvil Club de Chile, O'Higgins 1037 ℂ 225039, fax 314709; also at Caupolicán 294
- Avis Rent a Car, Aurelio Manzano 538 ℂ (41) 235837. Also at airport.
- Budget Rent a Car, Angol 547 ℂ (41) 225377
- First Rent a Car, Cochrane 862 ℂ 223121, fax (041) 237299
- Hertz Rent a Car, Prat 240 ℂ 230341, fax 230152
- Larma Rent a Car, Libertador B. O'Higgins 324 ℂ 223031, fax 223947
- National Car Rental, Aeropuerto Carriel Sur ℂ (09) 4412284

Shopping

The highest concentration of shops and boutiques is on Barros Arana between Lincoyán and Castellón and also around Plaza de Armas. The larger shopping complexes are *galerías*.

Outside the central downtown area is shopping center "Plaza del Treból", located on the *autopista* to Talcahuano near the turnoff to Aeropuerto Carriel Sur, on the north side. It has 120 boutiques, a food court, and seven movie theaters and is air-conditioned.

Shopping in Penco
Penco is 14 km north.
- Cerámicas Loza Penco is at the southern end of Penco. They produce china and glassware, and there is a retail outlet at the factory

Shopping in Tomé
- Industria Bellavista Tomé is a huge textile factory; you can buy their products at a retail outlet there
- Artesanías, Basar Artesanal, Sotomayor 1190

Sport

Trout fishing in Laguna Escuadrón, Río Bío Bío, Río Duqueo, Río Lias, and Río Vergara.

Sightseeing

- Cerro Amarillo, only 40 m high and 3000 square m, with gardens and look-outs. This was the site of an en-counter between Royalist and Patriotic forces in 1817.
- Casa del Arte, Barrio Universitario (234985. The entrance is in Larenas opposite Lamas. It incorporates the Pinacoteca de Concepción. It has a most complete display of Chilean painters.
- Parque Ecuador, Victor Lamas. This park is well laid out with many native and exotic trees. There are tennis courts and restaurants. On one side is the Galería de la Historia, which has a diorama display of the history of Concepción since 1550.
- Cerro Caracol (256 m). From Parque Ecuador a road winds uphill and leads to the ENTEL and Mirador Alemán look-outs with views over the city and the river.
- Puente Nuevo. Crosses the Río Bío Bío and links the airport with San Pedro. At 2450 m, it is the longest bridge in Chile. From the bridge there are views over the town and Península Hualpen.
- Puente Ferroviario (Railway Bridge). Built in 1880, designed by Gustav Eiffel.
- Puente Viejo. This is the second largest bridge in Chile (1770 m long) and connects the town with the suburb of Pinares with its discos.
- Lagunillas, 5 km south of San Pedro. In 1557 there was a battle between the Spanish troops of Hurtado de Mendoza and Mapuche Chief Caupolicán. Restaurants and picnic areas.

Air services from Concepción

Airport buses are run by Agencia Airport Express Services, A. Pinto 736, office 12 (236444; Fare $3.00.

Airlines
- LAN Chile, Barros Arana 541 (237440
- LADECO, Barros Arana 401 (243261

Services

Destination	Fare	Services	Duration	Airlines
Coihaique	$117.00	Mon–Sat	2½ hrs	LAN Chile
Puerto Montt	$91.00	Mon–Sat	1 hr	LAN Chile
Punta Arenas	$177.00	2 services per week		LAN Chile, LADECO
Santiago	$61.00	3–7 services daily	1 hr	LAN Chile, LADECO
Temuco	$47.00			
Valdivia	$80.00	1 service Mon–Fri	1 hr	LAN Chile

🚌 Buses from Concepción

Municipal buses operate in the greater Concepción area from 0600 to 2400 every 20 minutes.

Companies operating from central bus terminal
- B189 Buses Línea Talcahuano–Concepción–Penco–Sodal
- B230 Buses Pullman Alfa 30
  Services to Tomé
- B245 Buses Ruta de Playas
- Concepción Bus 2: Center to San Pedro via Puente Viejo and Puente Nuevo
- Concepción Bus 9: Hualpencillo to Center

Companies operating from long-distance terminal
The long-distance bus terminal Municipal is at Tegualda 860 in the suburb of Puchacay, a fair way outside town.
- A46   Buses Línea Azul, office 18 (311126
- A74   Buses Sol del Sur, office 8 (313841
- A105 Sol del Pacífico
- A137 Buses TAS Choapa, office 12 (312639
- A155 Turibus
- B42   Cinta Azul, office 23 (312687
- B64   Buses E.T.C.
- B81   Buses Igi Llaima, office 7 (312498
- B87   Buses Jota Be, office 28 (312652
- B164 Buses Thiele Ewert
- B179 Buses Varmontt, oficina 17 (314010
- B207 Buses Ettabus
- B235 Buses JM, office 34 (314093
- B236 Buses Pullman JR
- B237 Buses Pullman del Sur
- B260 Cruz del Sur (314372
- B265 Buses Transtur
- B271 Buses Galaxia Sur
- Buses Mini Expreso del Carbón (312330

Companies with their own terminal
- A26   Buses Costa Azul, Zañartu 173 (225956
- A48   Buses Lit, Tucapel 458 (230726 / 230722
- A88   Buses Ciferal, Roosevelt 1774 (234008
- A153 Buses Tur-Bus Jedimar, Camilo Henriquez 2565 (315555
- B30   Buses Bío Bío, A. Prat 416 near Libertador O'Higgins opposite railroad station (230672
- B88   Buses Jota Ewert, A. Prat 535 near Freire next to railroad station (229212
- B99   Buses Los Alces, A. Prat 699 (240855
- B109 Buses Mini Pullman, A. Pinto 715
- B167 Buses Trangyl, A. Pinto 765 near Los Carrera
- B202 Buses La Unión del Sud, A. Prat near Libertador O'Higgins opposite train station
- B226 Buses Mini Expreso El Conquistador, A. Pinto 822 (242751

Services

Destination	Fare	Services	Companies
Ancud	$15.20	2 services daily	B260
Angol	$3.80	8 services daily	B30, B81
Arauco	$1.60	10 services daily	B99
Cañete	$2.90	10 services daily	B88, B99

Buses from Concepción — continued

Destination	Fare	Services		Companies
• Carampangue	$1.40	10 services daily		B88
• Castro	$16.70	1 service daily		B260
• Cauquenes		5 services daily		A26, A46, B42
• Capitán Pastene	$ 4.60	1 service daily		B88
• Chillán	$ 2.50	43 services daily		A16, A46, A48, A137, A153, B42, B82, B96, B236, B250, B259
• Cobquecura	$2.50	3 services daily		A26
• Collipulli	$4.60	10 services daily		B30, B81
• Contulmo	$ 3.80	3 services daily		B88
• Coronel	$0.50	20 services daily		Terramar, Miramar
• Curacautín		1 service daily		B30
• Curanilahué	$1.50	10 services daily		B88
• Curicó	$7.60	5 services daily		A153
• Dichato	$1.20	every hour		A26, B230
• Florida	$0.80	10 services daily		A46, B259
• Hualpencillo	$0.40	20 services daily		B245
• La Unión	$9.90	3 services daily		B81, B207
• Lebu	$2.90	21 services daily	3½ hrs	B88, B99, B164, B165
• Linares	$4.60	5 services daily		A16, A48
• Lirquén	$0.40	20 services daily		B230, B245
• Caleta Llico	$2.80	6 services daily		B99
• Loncoche	$5.70	4 services daily		B81
• Los Angeles	$3.00	41 services daily		A74, A153, B30, B81, B109, B137, B167, B179, B260, B273
• Lota	$1.00	20 services daily		B96, B271, Térramar, Miramar
• Mulchén	$3.40	4 services daily		B30, B109
• Nacimiento	$3.30	4 services daily		B30
• Osorno	$11.30	7 services daily		B81, B179, B207 B260
• Parral	$4.60	6 services daily		A16, A46, B42
• Penco	$0.40	every 5 minutes		B189, B230
• Puerto Montt	$14.00	16 services daily		A46, A48, A153, A155, B81, B207, B237, B260
Sleeper	$19.00	1 service daily		B179
• Puerto Varas	$14.00	3 services daily		B81, B179, B260
• Purén	$4.00	1 service daily		B88
• Quillón	$1.20	10 services daily		A46, B259
• Quirihué	$1.80	3 services daily		A26
• Rancagua	$9.50	2 services daily		B250
• Río Bueno	$9.90	1 service daily		B64
• Salto del Laja		10 services daily		B167
• San Fernando	$9.50	2 services daily		A137
• Santa Bárbara	$2.50	2 services daily		B109
• Santa Juana	$0.80	20 services daily		B164, B226
• Santiago	$10.60	56 services daily	8½ hrs	A46, A48, A74, A105, A137, A153, B82, B96,B215, B217, B235, B250, B259, B265, B271
• Talca	$ 5.90	10 services daily		A16, A48, A137, A153, B82, B96, B250
• Talcahuano	$0.40	every 5 minutes		B189
• Temuco	$6.50	23 services daily		A48, A74, A153, B30, B81, B179, B207, B260
• Tirúa	$4.20	4 services daily		B88

Buses from Concepción — continued

Destination	Fare	Services		Companies
• Tomé	$1.20	every 15 minutes		A26, B189, B230
• Valdivia	$10.00	16 services daily	7 hrs	A48, A153, A155, B81, B179, B207, B260
• Valparaíso	$14.00	12 services daily		A46, A74, A105, A106, A137, A153, B235
• Victoria	$ 4.60	11 services daily		B30, B81
• Viña del Mar	$14.00	12 services daily		A46, A74, A105, A106, A137, A153, B235
• Zapala (Argentina)				
	$22.00	1 service Mon–Sat		B81, B202

Buses from Dichato
• Buses Alfa 30 run half-hourly services to and from Concepción
• Buses Flash run from Chillán in summer only

Buses stop on Avenida Daniel Vera just across the disused railroad line.

Buses from Florida
Buses Línea Azul run regular services to Concepción and Chillán.

Buses from Nacimiento
Buses provide services to Concepción, Los Angeles, Angol, and Purén. The main companies serving Nacimiento are:
• Pullman Bus, San Martín
• Buses Bío Bío, General Freire 434
• Buses Thiele, Baquedano 411
• Buses Costa Azul, Baquedano 401
• Buses Tacoha
• Colectivos Nacimiento-Angol
• Buses from Penco

Colectivos Línea run services at 15-minute intervals from Concepción to Talcahuano–Concepción–Penco–Sodal.

Buses from Tomé
There are regular daily services to Concepción, Chillán, Dichato, Quirihué, and Santiago.
• Buses Costa Azul, Villaroel 1086 (651267
• Buses Tur-Bus Jedimar, Villaroel 1094 (650848
• Buses Intersur
• Buses Estrella del Sur
• Expreso Ruta del Conquistador, Portales 1713 (651580
• Buses Pullman Alfa-30, Avenida Werner 2840 (650605

• Museo Stom, Progreso 156, Chiguayante (361049. Chiguayante is 10km south east of Concepción on Ruta O-60. The museum has an interesting collection of archeological items found in the area. It specializes in Mapuche objets d'art and the colonial period.

☻ Excursions

Tour operators
• Viajes Concepción, B. Arana 565 L-53, (237440. Specializes in city tours, and tours to Dichato, Salto del Laja, Termas de Chillán, Parque de Lota, and Alto del Bío Bío
• Viajes Trigal, Chacabuco 912, (230399. Specializes in tours to Termas de

🚂 Trains from Concepción

The railroad station is on A. Prat opposite B. Arana. It has a luggage room; it costs
$0.50 to leave your luggage (for those who want to hunt for accommodation without
carrying their luggage).

Destination	Salón	Económico	Services	Duration
• Chillán	$6.50	$4.60	3 services daily	4 hrs
• Linares	$4.20	$3.30	3 services daily	5 hrs
• Rancagua	$12.50	$8.70	3 services daily	7 hrs
• Santiago	$13.00	$9.40	3 services daily	8 hrs
• Talca	$9.90	$7.00	3 services daily	6 hrs

Chillán, Ruta del Conquistador, Alto
Bío Bío, and Salto del Laja
- Aventuratour, Tucapel 565 upstairs,
  (236444. Specializes in city tours, and
  tours to Dichato, Salto del Laja, Termas de Chillán, and Parque de Lota
- Turismo Guaymallén, Caupolicán 169
  office 1 (227511. Specializes in tours to
  Alto del Bío Bío, Parque Nacional
  Laguna del Laja, Cobquecura, Termas
  de Chillán, and Quinchamalí
- Viajes Publitur, Portales 508 upstairs
  (240800. Specializes in city tours, and
  tours to Lago Lanalhué, Alto del Bío
  Bío, Termas de Chillán, and
  Cobquecura
- South Expeditions, O'Higgins 680 office 218 (232290. Specializes in rafting
  and horse riding in Alto Bío Bío, and
  mountain cycling in Termas de
  Chillán and Lago Lanalhué
- Andes Expediciones, Trinitarias 136,
  trekking excursions, mountain cycling, and rafting in Alto del Bío Bío
  and Cajones de Chillán
- Turismo Ritz (in the Hotel Ritz), Barros Arana 721 (237637

Excursions
- **Coronel:** 35 km south. An important
  industrial town and fishing port of
  70 000 inhabitants, it was founded in
  1851 when the Schwager coal-mining
  company began their mining operations there. The hill overlooking the
  town and the bay is still called
  Schwager. Frequent buses run to and
  from Concepción and south to Lota,
  Arauco, Lebu, and Cañete. The best
  beach in the area is to the south —
  Playa Blanca. Large tracts of land have
  been planted with pine forests, which

has transformed the area ecologically.
The main attraction is the extensive
beaches with tourist facilities. On the
main highway there is a COPEC gas
station. Trout fishing is possible in
Laguna El Escuadrón, 16 km north of
Coronel. Buses Terramar and Miramar run regular daily services to
Concepción and Lota; Tur- Bus Jedimar departs from Sotomayor 617 for
Talca and Santiago.
- **Dichato:** 43 km north. The 1½-hour
  bus trip from Concepción is very picturesque, passing through subtropical
  rainforest, with splendid views over
  the **Bahía de Concepción** as far as **Isla
  Quiriquina** in the bay.
- **Hualqui**: A city of 10 000, 24 km east
  on Ruta O-60 on the north side of the
  Río Bío Bío, at the junction of **Río
  Hualqui**. Like other forts in the area,
  it was established to ward off attacks
  from the Mapuches as they attempted
  to defend their territory. The original
  foundation of 1577 by Rodrigo de Quiroga did not survive the Mapuche uprising of 1599. Nowadays it is a
  thriving agricultural town with quaint
  houses surrounded by orchards, as
  well as some new housing for well-to-
  do people from Concepción. There are
  many local restaurants, well frequented at weekends. Buses run to
  and from Concepción every half hour.
- **Laguna Chica de San Pedro**: 5 km
  west. Covering 84 ha (207 acres), the
  laguna is surrounded by thick vegetation, with the north and east sides very
  popular for water sports.
- **Lota:** 42 km south on RN 160. Go to
  Lota to visit the Parque de Lota. There

are nice beaches near Lota — see the entry for Lota on page 560.

- **Mouth of the Río Bío Bío:** 18 km west. The beach is 300 m long, with fine black sand. The surrounding hills are lightly forested. Good spot for fishing.
- **Museo Hualpen:** 15 km west in the **Parque Pedro del Río Zañartu.** This was the home of a well-known 19th-century philanthropist, Don Pedro del Río Zañartu, an entrepreneur who became a world traveler and collector of antiques and archeological artifacts. The house dates from 1885 and the whole complex is a *monumento nacional*. The house is furnished in period style with memorabilia of the era also on display. The collections range from oriental furniture and Mapuche silver jewelry to Egyptian and Hindu objets d'art; there is a coin collection, arms, precious stones — everything collected by Don Pedro del Río Zañartu during his voyages abroad. The house is surrounded by a large park. The trees in the park are mostly native, but some huge eucalyptus trees line the path leading to a promontory with sweeping views of the mouth of the Río Bío Bío and over the Golfo de Arauco. The garden has many sculptures and fountains. Open Tues–Sun 0900–1200 and 1400–1900, free admission. Well worth a visit.
- **Rere:** 97 km south-east on Ruta O-60. The trip to Talcamávida can be extended to include Rere, founded by Alonso de Sotomayor in 1580. The area was rich in gold. Nowadays this is a quiet, picturesque town which has preserved its colonial aspect. The steeple has bells which were cast here in 1720. Frequent daily buses run from Concepción; worth a detour.
- **Santa Juana:** A small town of 4000 inhabitants, 53 km south-east on the south bank of the **Río Bío Bío** opposite Talcamávida. Its main attraction is the Fuerte Santa Juana de Guadalcazar, built by the Spanish in 1626 as part of the Guerra Defensiva along the Río Bío Bío against the Mapuche people. The present remains of the fort date from 1739. This old Spanish fort has been partially restored by the University of Concepción. The visit to Santa Juana is usually done in conjunction with a visit to Nacimiento. There is no accommodation. The road to Los Angeles is a good gravel road as far as Nacimiento (52 km), and from here it is sealed. Mini Expreso El Conquistador runs 20 daily services from Concepción; Buses Thiele Ewert runs frequent services to Angol and Nacimiento.
- **Talcahuano:** 16 km north-west, the port of Concepción. At the naval base, now a museum, there is a relic of the *Monitor Huascar*, a Peruvian boat captured during the War of the Pacific. See the entry for Talcahuano on page 567.
- **Talcamávida:** 52 km south on the Río Bío Bío. Founded by Gobernador Manuel de Amat y Juniet in 1757 as Fuerte San Rafael de Talcamávida, the town is directly across the river from another fort, **Santa Juana.** Both were established to protect the passage of the Spaniards across this important river crossing. Regular bus services run from Concepción via Hualqui.

LAGO LANALHUÉ

Distance from Concepción: 140 km south on RN 100

Even though the lake is not very deep, the waters are dark with the reflection of the surrounding pine forests. The lake's water is fairly warm; it is fed by the rivers coming down from the Nahuelbuta ranges, which are not glacial. The clear water attracts large crowds for water sports and fishing, with the best facilities near Contulmo. There are beaches and sand spits with fine sand.

Key to map

C	Municipalidad (Town hall)	**2**	Hotel Contulmo
D	Post office and telex	■	**Sights**
E	Telephone	**4**	Shrine and spring
T	Buses Jota Ewert	□	**Services**
●	**Accommodation**	**3**	Shop
1	Hotel Central		

The main road (Ruta P-60-R) is a dirt road that follows the northern shore line of the lake. Short roads branch off into some valleys into the Nahuelbuta ranges but soon peter out or become fire trails used by loggers. This is picture-book country with the hills and mountains surrounding the lake overgrown with shrubs and pine trees. It is pretty rather than majestic, because here humans have tamed nature, with the result that it looks very "civilized".

Contulmo, with a population of 2000, is located on the eastern side of Lago Lanalhué, about 2 km off the main highway. It is a small town snuggled against the **Cordillera de Nahuelbuta**, and consists of only a dozen streets or so. Buses turning into the town pass the sports complex on Tegualpa where the rodeos are held. The town was founded in 1868 by Coronel Saavedra. In 1884 Germans from East and West Prussia arrived, and it was formerly known as Colonia Alemana (German Colony).

🛏 Accommodation

- Hostería Lago Lanalhué, access via Peleco ADEFGHIJKLNP$V ((41) 611126 $D ⅱ. Open November–March, 20 rooms
- Hotel Posada Campesina Alemana, Playa Tranquila AEFHILNP$V $G ⅱ
- Hostal Licahué, Peleco (2738417 $F ⅱ
- Motel La Cabaña, Puerto Contulmo AEFHIPUV (1 Contulmo. Closed in winter

Accommodation in Contulmo

- Hotel Nuevo Contulmo, Millaray 116 EFGIJ ((108) 894903 $H ⅱ
- Hotel Central, Comercio 129 EHI ((108) 894903

🅰 Camping

There are several serviced camping sites on the east side of Lago Lanalhué.

🍴 Eating out

Eating out in Contulmo

- Restaurant El Colonial, Los Canelos. German cuisine

🛍 Shopping

Shopping in Contulmo

Using recipes handed down from their German ancestors, the villagers still make some very nice preserves from raspberries and sour cherries.

🎾 Sport

- Trout fishing in Lago Lanalhué, Lago Lleu-Lleu, Lago Butaco, Río Lleu-Lleu, and Río Tranaquepe
- Windsurfing on Lago Lanalhué

✈ Excursions

Excursions from Contulmo

- From Calle Millaray there is a path leading up a mountain through the pine forests. Start at Hotel Contulmo and walk uphill past the natural spring and a small shrine and you will find the path 100 m above the natural spring on the right. The path winds gently uphill through the pine forest, up to the abandoned track of the former rail link between Angol and Lebu, which is already partially overgrown. Cross over this, and after about an hour's walk, you reach the top where there are sweeping views over a portion of **Lago Lanalhué** to the west, and north to the Nahuelbuta ranges. If you are still feeling energetic, you can continue this walk by going eastwards to link up with the Monumento Nacional Contulmo.

🚌 Buses from Contulmo

The bus terminal is on Los Notros, which is the continuation of Tegualpa.

Companies
- B88   Buses Jota Ewert
- B164 Buses Thiele Ewert
- B165 Buses Tliver

Destination	Fare	Services	Company
Angol	$1.90	28 services daily	B88, B164
Cañete	$1.00	7 services daily	B88
Capitán Pastene		1 service daily	B88
Concepción	$ 3.80	4 services daily	B88, B164
Lebu	$2.90	7 services daily	B88, B165
Purén		1 service daily	B88
Temuco	$3.10	4 services daily	B88, B164

- **Monumento Natural Contulmo:**
  6 km east. Under CONAF administration, this small protected area of 88 ha (217 acres) has many walking trails through the dense native forest. Before the arrival of Europeans, the whole area was densely forested, but nowadays large areas outside the reserve have become pine plantations. There are many fern trees and *ñalcas* along the trails because of the moist climate created by the rain forest sections. During the colonial period this was purest Mapuche country. Admission $1.00.
- **Parque Nacional Nahuelbuta:** Approximately 35 km north-east, in Región IX de La Araucania. This hike

is not an official access route to the national park, just an alternative for trail-blazers to reach the park from Lago Lanalhué. The starting point for this two-day hike is **Elicura**, some 8 km west of Contulmo. During colonial times Elicura was a Jesuit mission which was wiped out by Mapuches, killing all missionaries. The trail leads into the **Río Elicura valley** and later on follows the course of the **Estero Provoque**. At first you pass through plantations of pine trees, but further up this changes to native trees, with ever-increasing numbers of *araucarias*. You finally reach the park near Piedra del Aguila. See "Excursions" from Angol in Región IX de La Araucania.

LEBU

Area code: 41
Population: 19 000
Altitude: Sea level
Distance from Concepción: 146 km south on RN 160

On the Pacific Ocean at the mouth of the **Río Lebu**, the town has been through the familiar series of foundations as the local people attempted to defend their territory. It was finally re-established as a town in 1862 by Chilean entrepreneurs to exploit the coal found in the vicinity. Lebu also has a large fishing fleet.

An extensive beach of white sand stretches from the mouth of the Río Lebu north to the **Cuevas de Lebu**. These caves were the hide-out of the outlaw Vicente de Benavides as well as the French adventurer called Antoine I King of Araucania. Vicente de Benavides, initially a soldier in the Spanish army, after the defeat of the Spanish forces became an outlaw terrorizing huge areas together with some Mapuche tribes. He was betrayed by his shipmates on his way to Peru and publicly hanged in Santiago in 1822. Antoine Tounens was a French trader among the Mapuche. He declared himself King Antoine I

de la Araucania in 1861. By this time Araucania was formally annexed by Chile and was in the process of being incorporated into the nation. King Antoine I was apprehended in 1862 and banished from Chile. He re-appeared a few years later and a price was put on his head, after which he disappeared forever.

There are two guns on the plaza dating back to colonial times.

Festivals
- January 23: Rodeo

BÍO BÍO

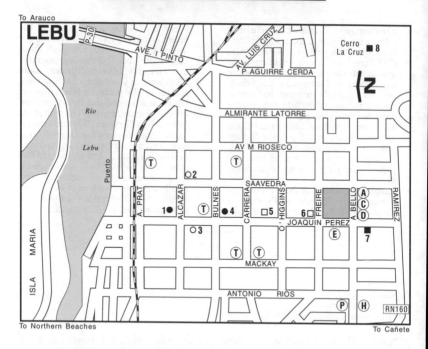

Key to map

A	Iglesia
C	Municipalidad (Town hall)
D	Post office and telex
E	Telephone
H	Hospital
P	Gas stations
T	Bus terminals

● Accommodation
1 Hotel Central
4 Hotel Gran Hotel

○ Eating out
2 Restaurant Hanga Roa
3 Restaurant Amigo
6 Restaurant Metropoli

■ Sights
7 Casa Ebensperger
8 Vistas from Cerro La Cruz

□ Services
5 CEMA Chile

⊟ Accommodation

Hotels
- Central, Peréz 183 AFGHIPSV (511904 $H ♙♙
- Rocha, Peréz 309 AEFGHILPSV(511939 $H ♙♙

⑪ Eating out

Restaurants
- El Muelle, Muelle Fluvial. Seafood
- Hanga Roa, Saavedra 225 near Carrera 4. Seafood
- Metropolis, Pérez opposite Plaza de Armas
- Pangal, Saavedra 209. Chilean cuisine

Eating out in Los Alamos

Los Alamos is 27 km east on RN 160.
- Restaurant Rucantu, I. Carrera Pinto 161

🏛 Post and telegraph

Post office
- Correos, A. Bello 289

Telephone
- CTC, Pérez opposite Plaza de Armas

🖥 Services

- Supermercado Malva Ltd., Río Seco 100

🚗 Motoring

- COPEC gas station, corner of A. Bello and Antonio Rios

📷 Sightseeing

- Casa Ebensperger is a conspicuous wooden building on the corner of A. Bello and Joaquín Pérez, built in 1914 by a German family. It is still in private hands.

- Playa Lebu, a beach of white sand extending from the mouth of the **Río Lebu** north and south. The beaches are suitable for surfboard riding.

⊙ Excursions

- **Playa Millaneco** and **Cuevas de Lebu:** The owner of Hotel Central has opened a restaurant-disco with a live band at weekends at a place called Millaneco. This is about 20 minutes from town, on a long stretch of beach, and you can get there by crossing the Río Lebu bridge and following Avenida Ignacio Carrera Pinto north (the rural bus route to Arauco). Enormous rocks form the northern boundary to the beach and extend down into the sea. Inside the rocks there are huge caverns, possibly formed by sea erosion. There is one cave that makes a noise like a bull roaring when the wind blows. The caves are about 200 m long and are like a tunnel, reaching about 3 m high in places — a car can drive through. The cave closest

🚌 Buses from Lebu

Rural buses leave from Plaza de Armas.

Companies
- B65 Buses Fernandez, A. Prat near Saavedra
- B88 Buses Jota Ewert, Carrera corner of Mackay ℓ 511174
- B99 Buses Los Alces, Mackay corner of Carrera
- B103 Buses Malleco
- B134 Buses Pinto, Bulnes near Pérez
- B164 Buses Thiele Ewert
- B165 Buses Tliver

Services

Destination	Fares	Services	Duration	Companies
• Angol	$4.00	28 services daily		B164, B165
• Cañete	$1.40	24 services daily		B164, B165
• Carampangue	$1.60			B165
• Chillán	$5.70	1 service daily		B165
• Concepción	$2.90	10 services daily	3½ hrs	B88, B99, B165
• Contulmo	$2.90	8 services daily		B88, B165
• Curanilahue	$1.40	10 services daily		B165
• Lota	$2.30	10 services daily		B165
• Purén	$3.00	3 services daily		B165
• Santiago	$14.60	3 services daily		A153, B165
• Temuco	$5.30	4 services daily		B164, B165
• Traiguén	$3.80	3 services daily		B165
• Victoria	$4.60	5 services daily		B103, B164, B165

to the sea is like a church dome. The beach is unspoilt, although it can be a bit rough with winds blowing constantly; there is also a bit of a rip tide, so be careful. The new *hostería* is 500 m from the caves.

- To **Arauco:** An interesting 64 km trip north via the unsealed interior road.

Rural buses operate twice per week. The northern part of the peninsula is forested with pine trees. See also the entry for Arauco on page 509.

- Visit to the Mapuche villages along the coast south of town. Regular colectivo services from Lebu.

LOS ANGELES

Area code: 043
Population: 100 000
Altitude: 150 m
Distance from Concepción: 128 km south-east on Panamericana Sur and Ruta O-50 (turn off at Cabrero)

In the fertile Central Valley, Los Angeles was founded in 1739 as Villa de Santa Maria de Los Angeles by Pedro de Córdoba y Figueroa by order from that great founder of towns, Manso de Velazco. It was to keep the Mapuche people from moving into territories to the north, which were already firmly in Spanish hands. Officially proclaimed a town in 1852, this was the starting point of the Chilean conquest of Araucania by Coronel Cornelio Saavedra in 1862.

About 500 km south of Santiago, this major commercial and agricultural center is one of the fastest growing provincial capitals in Chile. Most important is the pulp and paper industry, which depends on the thousands of acres of pine trees planted in the vicinity of the city.

There are many excursions you can make from here. For example, to name just a few, to the famous waterfall **Salto del Laja**, to a *hacienda* which belonged once to Don Bernardo O'Higgins, or to the **Parque Nacional Laguna del Laja** with the ski fields of **Antuco** nearby.

⌘ Festivals

Festivals in Yumbel
Yumbel is 53 km north.
- January 20: San Sebastián

ⓘ Tourist information
- CONAF, Colón 320 (21086

- Club de Pesca y Caza "Bío Bío", Avenida Alemanía 600 (321943. Fishing licenses
- Sernatur, Avenida Ricardo Vicuña

Ⓐ Camping
The nearest camping sites are in Salto del Laja, 25 km north.

⑪ Eating out

Restaurants
- Bavaria, Colón 357
- Brasilia, Colón 445 near Pasaje Quilque
- Centro Español, Colón 482. Spanish cuisine
- Chi Hwa, Colón 420. Chinese cuisine
- Club de Caza y Pesca, Avenida Alemania 600. Chilean cuisine
- Club de la Unión, Colón 261
- El Arriero, Colo Colo 227. *Parrillada*
- El Comilón, Colón 358
- El Rancho de Julio, Colón 720. *Parrillada*
- Flamingo, Colo Colo 378. International cuisine
- Lomit's, Caupolicán 535

- Nuria, Caupolicán 575. Chilean cuisine
☞ - Prymo's, Colo Colo 402 corner of Colón

Pizzería
☞ - Julio's Pizza, Colón 452

Cafeterías
☞ - Haiti, Colón block 400 near Pasaje Quilque
- Pucón, Colón block 300 near Colo Colo

Snack bar
- Bus Stop, Colón 315 near Lautaro. International cuisine

Eating out along the Panamericana
- Restaurant El Fogón, KM 505. Chilean cuisine
- Restaurant Santa María de los Angeles, southern exit

Eating out at the airport
- Aeropuerto, 10 km from town. International cuisine

Eating out in Mulchén
Mulchén is 33 km south.
- Club Social, Villagrán 690. Chilean cuisine
- Oásis, A. Pinto 701. Chilean cuisine

Eating out in Yumbel
- San Marcelino, Valdivia 450. Chilean cuisine

ⓉEntertainment

- Peña, Almagro 313. Open every night
- Peña Javiera Carrera, Panamericana just north of Acceso Central (also known as Avenida Alemania), opposite Hotel Monserrat

🕮 Post and telegraph

Post office
- Correo, Caupolicán Block 400 corner of Valdivia (on the plaza)

Telephone
- CTC, Valdivia 326, fax 323881
- ENTEL, Caupolicán 331

$ Financial

- Bancard, Lautaro 371 ☏ 323077. Cash advances on Visa and Mastercard

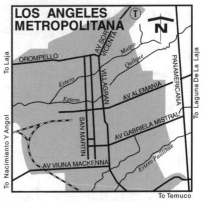

LOS ANGELES METROPOLITANA

To Temuco

🖺 Services

Dry cleaner
- Lavaseco, Valdivia block 500 near Tucapel

Sports equipment
- Deportes El Martillo, Almagro 472 near Pasaje Quilque

Supermarkets
- Supermercado MAS, Villagrán 501 near Mini Rural bus terminal
- Supermercado Las Brisas, Villagrán 558 corner of Tucapel

✈ Air services

- Concepción: Fare $21.00; departs 1745 Mon–Fri; duration ½ hr; LAN Chile
- Santiago: Fare $46.00

🚗 Motoring

Car rental
- Automóvil Club de Chile, Caupolicán 201 ☏ 22149
- First Rent a Car, Caupolicán 350 ☏ 313812 fax 315267
- Hertz Rent a Car, Lientur 199 ☏ 323632
- Larma Rent a Car, Ricardo Vicuña 524 ☏ 312463
- Western Rent a Car, Avenida Alemania 318 ☏ 322828

🏛 Shopping

- Centro Comercial "Diego de Almagro", Almagro block 400 near Rengo. A large shopping center

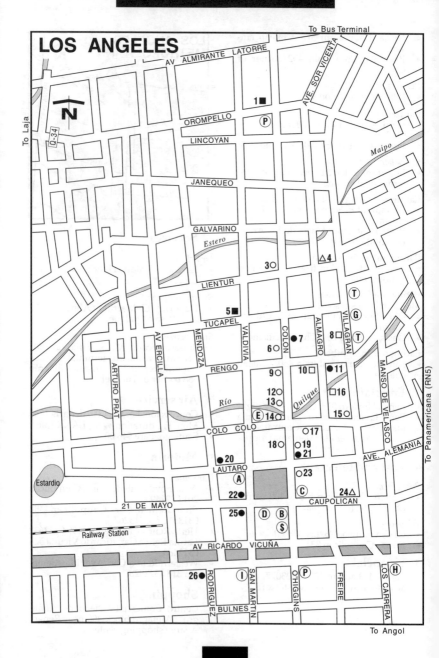

LOS ANGELES

To Bus Terminal

AV ALMIRANTE LATORRE

To Laja

Q-34

N

OROMPELLO

LINCOYAN

JANEQUEO

GALVARINO

Estero

LIENTUR

TUCAPEL

AV ERCILLA

ARTURO PRAT

MENDOZA

VALDIVIA

RENGO

Río

COLO COLO

LAUTARO

Estardio

21 DE MAYO

Railway Station

AV RICARDO VICUÑA

RODRIGUEZ

BULNES

SAN MARTIN

O'HIGGINS

FREIRE

LOS CARRERA

Maipo

AVE. SOR VICENTA

MANSO DE VELASCO

AVE. ALEMANIA

To Panamericana (RN5)

COLON

ALMAGRO

VILLAGRAN

Quilque

CAUPOLICAN

To Angol

1 ■

P

3 ○

△ 4

5 ■

6 ○

● 7

8 □

9 ○

10 □

● 11

12 ○

13 ○

E 14 ○

□ 16

15 ○

○ 17

18 ○

○ 19

● 21

● 20

○ 23

C

24 △

22 ●

A

25 ●

D B

$

26 ●

I

P

H

T

G

T

Key to map

A	Iglesia matriz	3	Restaurant El Rancho de Julio
B	Gobernación Provincial (Government)	6	Restaurant El Comilón
		9	Restaurant Club Español
C	Municipalidad (Town hall)	12	Restaurant Julio's Pizza
D	Post office & telex	13	Restaurant Chi-Hwa
E	Telephone	14	Restaurant Prymos
G	Mercado Municipal (Market)	15	Restaurant El Arriero
H	Hospital	17	Restaurant Bavaria
I	Tourist information	18	Cafetería Pucón
P	Gas stations	19	Snackbar Bus Stop
$	Money exchange	23	Restaurant Club Unión
T	Bus terminals		

● **Accommodation**

■ Sights

7 Hotel Alba
11 Hotel Winser
20 Hotel/Restaurant Mazzola
21 Hotel Mariscal Alcázar
22 Hotel Musso
25 Hotel Santa María
26 Hostal Alborada

1 Iglesia Perpetuo Socorro
5 Convento San Francisco

△ **Tour operators and car rental**

4 Hertz Rent a Car
24 Automóvil Club de Chile

○ **Eating out**

□ **Services**

2 Restaurant Donde Ramón

8 Supermercado Las Brisas
10 Centro Comercial Almagro
16 Deportes El Martillo

- Centro Comercial "Plaza Market" on Avenida Alemania 2 km east of town center. A shopping complex with Restaurant De León
- Artesanías Pichi Ruca, Colo Colo 451 local 7. Local crafts

Shopping in Yumbel
Yumbel is 53 km north; some villagers make silver jewelry.

⊗ Sport

Trout fishing in Laguna del Laja , Río Bío Bío, Río Bureo, Río Laja, and Río Mulchen.

◐ Sightseeing

Start from Plaza de Armas and follow Lautaro east until Villagrán, and at Villagrán turn north until Rengo. The Fería Municipal and the rural bus terminal are on your right. Here at the Fería Municipal farmers from the surrounding districts sell their produce — a very lively and colorful scene! Also interesting are the two churches — the Iglesia del Perpetuo Socorro with its colonnaded cloisters dating from 1800 and Iglesia de los Padres Alemanes (Church of the German fathers, a Capuchin order).

- Museo Histórico, Caupolicán corner of Colón opposite the town hall. Best represented is the era of the War of Independence. It also houses the public library.

☀ Excursions

- **Hacienda Las Canteras:** 33 km east, 1km off the road to Antuco. This belonged to Don Bernardo O'Higgins who, as well as his other claims to fame, pioneered the agricultural development of the area.
- **Mulchén:** 33 km south, on the Panamericana where the **Río Mulchén** meets the **Río Bureo** in the central valley not far from where the rivers leave the *pre-Cordillera*. First mentioned in 1692 during the reign of Gobernador Tomás Marín de Poveda as a mission, it was declared a town in 1862. Now it has a population of 19 000. The town's mainstay is the huge pine plantations in the district. Postal services are in A. Pinto 413; CTC is on Villagrán corner of Gana; and a gas station is on the Panamericana at the entrance to the town. In town you can buy local *artesanías* at Casa Jeny,

Los Angeles

⊟ Accommodation in Los Angeles

There is a shortage of medium- to low-priced accommodation in Los Angeles.

Hotels

★★★ Gran Hotel Muso, Valdivia 222	ACEFGHIJKLMP$TUVZ			
		(313183	$F	♠♠
★★★ Mariscal Alcázar, Lautaro 385 40 rooms	ADEFGHIJKLP$V	(311725	$F	♠♠
★ Mazzola, Lautaro 579	AEFGIJLPV	(321643	$H	♠♠
• London, Lautaro 281 Backpackers				
• Winser, Rengo 138 Budget travelers	HPT	(320348		
• Santa María, Caupolicán 502 Budget travelers				

Hostal
- Alborada, Avenida R. Vicuña corner of Rodríguez

Residenciales
- Almagro, Almagro 429
  Backbackers, basic
- No name, Colo Colo 335
  Budget travelers

Accommodation along the Panamericana
See also "Accommodation" in Salto del Laja below.

Hotels

• Bío Turismo, KM 504	AEHMPT	(320021	$G	♠♠
• Los Angeles, KM 514 Fax 320060	AEFGHM	(320044	$E	♠♠
• Mallorca, northern exit KM 513	AEFGHIJLPV	(322340	$G	♠♠

Motels

• Hotelera Alicante, southern exit KM 517 Fax 322045		(314347		
• Monserrat, KM 510 Central heating	AEFGHIJLPV	(311972	$G	♠♠
• Nevada 3, KM 516 southern exit		(315071		
• Rarinco, KM 512				
• Verona 3, KM 508		(320408		

Accommodation along the road to Santa Fé
The road to Santa Fé is Ruta Q-34.

• Motel Los Prados, KM 8	(315482	

Accommodation in Mulchén
Mulchén is 33 km south.

• Hostería Colonial, A. Pinto 390 Shared bathroom cheaper	(561378	$H	♠♠
• Hospedaje Cuevas, A. Pinto 701 Backpackers	(561300		

Bío Bío

Accommodation in Los Angeles — continued

Accommodation in Coihué
Coihué is 28 km west, on the west bank of the Río Bio Bio. Here an important bridge crosses the Río Bío Bío.
- Complejo Turístico La Turbina, KM 23 on Ruta Q-40-O to Angol near bridge over Río Bío Bío APS (551416 $F ⚁

Accommodation in Salto del Laja
Salto del Laja is 25 km north. All accommodation is along the Panamericana Sur, and provides an alternative to staying in Los Angeles.
- Cabañas Camino del Sur, KM482   (320213 $G ⚁
- Cabañas Río Cristalino, KM480   AILR
  30 tent sites; open December to March, electricity, water, toilet, 11 cabins
- Complejo Turístico Los Manantiales del Salto del Laja, KM 485
                   ADEFGHKLNPRUYV   (314275 $G ⚁
  Open all year round, 30 tent sites, four natural swimming pools, electricity
- Hotel Parque Salto del Laja, KM 485   APS   (314331 $E ⚁
- Motel de Turismo Salto del Laja, KM 485
                   ADEFGHIJKLMPR$TUVZ
                                (321706 $E ⚁
  Car rental, river frontage, 45 rooms, fax 313996. Direct views over Salto del Laja with deer park
- Motel El Pinar, KM 487   AEFGHILPUV
- Motel y Camping Curanadú, KM 500
                   AEFGHILNPV   (312686 $G for 5
  200 tent sites, open all year round, electricity, water, shop, 10 cabins
- Motel y Camping Los Coyuches, KM 486
                   ADEFGHILPRV   (320321 $H ⚁
  22 tent sites, open all year round, electricity, water, toilet, 16 cabins

Accommodation beside the Río Huaqui on the Panamericana
Located 10 km north
- El Rincón, KM 494   ((09) 4415019 $H ⚁
  Fax 317618

Accommodation in Yumbel
Yumbel is 53 km north.
- Hostería Comar, O'Higgins near Cruz(431438 $H ⚁

A. Pinto 304. There is trout fishing in Río Bío Bío, Río Mulchén, and Río Bureo. Not all buses enter town, but set down passengers on the Panamericana. The bus terminal is on Aníbal Pinto 890. The following companies run services from Mulchén: Buses Tur-Bus Jedimar office 7 (561204; Buses Bío Bío, office 3 (561712; Buses Mini Pullman. They run services to Chillán, Los Angeles and Concepción.
- **Parque Nacional Laguna del Laja**: 100 km east. Within its 11 600 ha (28 642 acres) are **Volcán Antuco**, the southern part of Laguna del Laja, and part of the **Sierra Velluda**. The Río Laja which flows from the lake forms the border of the park. Fishing in the lake. On the slopes of Volcán Antuco are three ski T-lifts.
- **Salto del Laja**: Only 25 km north on the Panamericana, this mighty waterfall is the largest waterfall in central Chile and one of the area's major attractions. It is visible from the Panamericana — coming from Santiago it is on your left. It is sign-posted and usually the bus drivers announce it just before you get there. You can also get here from Los Angeles by ru-

557   Los Angeles

🚌 Buses from Los Angeles

There are three bus terminals in Los Angeles:
- The long-distance bus terminal on Avenida Sor Vicenza 2051 at the northern exit to the Panamericana
- The Islajacoop rural bus terminal on Villagrán 507 corner of Rengo, near the central market
- A smaller rural bus terminal also on Villagrán opposite Tucapel, one block up from the rural bus terminal

Services from the rural terminals

Companies departing from the Islajacoop rural bus terminal
- B91   Buses Laja ☎ 316729

Companies departing from the smaller rural bus terminal
- B120 Buses Nuevo Sur
- B184 Buses Yumbel

Services

Destination	Fare	Services	Companies
Alto Bío Bío	$2.30	4 services daily	B91
Antuco	$1.50	6 services daily	B91
Cañicura	$1.60	1 service daily	B91
Central Hidro-Eléctrico El Toro			
		6 services daily	B91
Huepil	$1.50	2 services daily	B91
Las Lajas	$1.10	7 services daily	B91
Nacimiento		14 services daily	B30, B91
Quilleco	$1.30	2 services daily	B91
Ramadilla	$1.70	1 service daily	B91
Salto del Laja	$0.80	4 services daily	B91
San Carlos de Purén			
	$0.50		B91
Santa Bárbara	$1.40	7 services daily	B91
Trapa Trapa	$4.60	irregular twice-weekly services	
Tucapel	$1.40	2 services daily	B91

Services from the long-distance terminal

Companies
- A16   Buses Biotal, office 4 ☎ 317357
- A48   Buses Lit ☎ 312310
- A106 Buses Fénix Pullman Norte, office 9 ☎ 322502
- A137 Buses TAS Choapa, office 10 ☎ 322266
- A153 Buses Tur-Bus Jedimar ☎ 315610
- B30   Buses Bío Bío ☎ 314621
- B53   Buses Dacoma
- B81   Buses Igi Llaima, office 16 ☎ 32166
- B83   Buses J.A.C., office 18 ☎ 317469
- B87   Buses Jota Be, office 3 ☎ 317180
- B128 Buses Panguisur, office 24 ☎ 316817
- B137 Buses Power
- B179 Buses Varmontt, office 19 ☎ 312647
- B220 Buses Interregional Abbeysur
- B237 Buses Pullman del Sur
- B260 Buses Cruz del Sur, office 11 ☎ 317630

Buses from Los Angeles — continued

- B265 Buses Transtur
- B271 Via Tur (322370
- B273 Buses Unión del Sur, office 8 (316891

Services

Destination	Fare	Services	Duration	Companies
Ancud	$11.80	2 services daily		A153, B260
Angol	$1.40	25 services daily		B30, B81, B87, B265
Castro	$17.00	3 services daily		A153, A155, B260
Chillán	$2.50	18 services daily	1½ hrs	A16, A48, A137, A153, B81, B87, B237
Collipulli	$1.70	5 services daily		B30
Concepción	$3.80	42 services daily		A74, A153, B30, B81, B109, B137, B167, B179, B260, B273
Curacautín	$2.30	2 services daily		A106, B30
Curicó	$7.60	7 services daily	4½ hrs	A153
La Unión	$8.00	3 services daily		B81, B207
Linares	$4.60	7 services daily		A16, B256
Los Sauces	$1.70	2 services daily		B81
Mulchén	$1.20	5 services daily		
Osorno	$8.00	8 services daily		A153, B81, B137, B179, B260
Puerto Montt	$9.90	17 services daily		A48, A153, B81, B82, B179, B207, B260
Puerto Varas	$10.30	4 services daily		B81, B260
Purén		1 service daily		B53
Rancagua	$8.70		7 hrs	B81
San Fernando	$8.70	2 services daily	5½ hrs	A137
Santiago	$14.00	31 services daily	8hrs	A48, A105, A106, A137, A153, B81, B179, B215, B217, B220, B237, B265, B271, B273
Talca	$5.90	9 services daily	4 hrs	A16, A137, A153, B237
Temuco	$3.80	22 services daily	2½ hrs	A48, A137, A153, B30, B81, B137, B207, B260
Traiguén	$2.90	2 services daily		B81
Valdivia	$7.50	14 services daily	5 hrs	A137, A153, B81, B137, B179, B256
Valparaíso	$12.20	8 services daily		A105, A106
Victoria	$2.50	4 services daily	1½ hrs	A153, B81, B30
Villarrica	$2.30			A106, B82
Viña del Mar	$12.30	3 services daily		A105, A153

ral buses. It appears quite unexpectedly and spectacularly — you go through a pine forest which suddenly opens to give you a view of the horse-shoe-shaped falls. There are four large falls and several smaller ones. It is all the more remarkable as it is situated in the central valley in rather flat unobtrusive country. The area around the falls is dotted with motels and camping grounds. The motels and hotels are on the Panamericana within a radius of 3 km of either side of the falls. Buses La Laja and Buses Trangyl run several

daily services to Los Angeles and Concepción.

- **Santa Bárbara** and the Alto Bío Bío valley. To Santa Bárbara and beyond to **Ralco** there is now a fairly good road, thanks to the development of the El Pangue hydroelectric scheme. Santa Bárbara is 40 km south-east on Ruta Q-61-R. This is the domain of the adventure traveler, with rafting on the Río Bío Bío and hiking in the splendid mountains. See the entry for Santa Bárbara on page 565. Buses leave from the rural bus terminal in Los Angeles, but check which days (fare $4.60 one way).

- **Yumbel**: 53 km north. In 1661 Spanish troops defeated a large contingent of Mapuche warriors near the Salto del Laja, and they captured and executed the Mapuche leader, Misqui, near present-day Yumbel. This action more or less put an end to rebellion in this area. Although a fort was here as early as 1620, it was attacked and destroyed by Mapuches, and the town was officially founded in 1766. It has now a population of 12 000. Time has stood still in Yumbel: it is steeped in tradition and has retained the aura of a Spanish colonial town. The town is served by the following bus companies: Buses Becerra, Cruz 880 ☎ 431062; Buses Flash, and Buses San Sebastián. They run 10 services daily to Chillán and Los Angeles.

Lota

Population: 50 000
Altitude: Sea level
Distance from Concepción: 42 km south on RN 100

Founded in 1661, Lota is in the area known as the Costa del Carbón (the Coal Coast), and is the most important coal-mining town in Chile. The coal feeds the power stations of Boca Mina and Playa Negra.

There are two separate sections of Lota: Lota Bajo and Lota Alto. Lota Bajo is located in sort of a narrow hollow, but despite the physical restrictions on size, it has grown from a small fishing village into a large town and is now the town proper with all the facilities (bus terminals, market, restaurants, and two gas stations).

Lota Alto is the domain of the mining company. Its story began in 1849 when the mine owners started to build housing estates for the employees of the mine. The coal shafts go down 500 m and follow the seams horizontally for 1300 m, with some under the ocean floor.

The town is criss-crossed by railroad lines, and tunnels link up the mine shafts with the coal washing facilities. From one vantage point it looks like a toy train set.

The main reason for going to Lota is to visit the Parque de Lota. There is a description of the park under "Sightseeing" below.

On the Plaza Lota Bajo there is a statue of the Virgen del Carmen, 1.3 m high and sculpted from coal by Camilo Lagos Gómez.

From Cruce (the intersection of Schneider and RN 160) you have a commanding view over the township below, with Parque Lota on top of the opposite ridge. Schneider becomes A. Pinto and Pedro Aguirre is the main street.

Accommodation

Accommodation in Laraquete
Laraquete is 13 km south on RN 160.

Hotels

- La Quinta, Gabriela Mistral AEFGHIPV ☎ (108) 571951 $G 👥
- Laraquete, Gabriela Mistral AFGHILPV $G 👥

Hosterías

- Piedra Cruz, Gabriela Mistral 555 AEFGHIPV ☎ (108) 571992 $G 👥
- Sol y Sombra, F. Coloane ☎ (41) 371901

Bío Bío

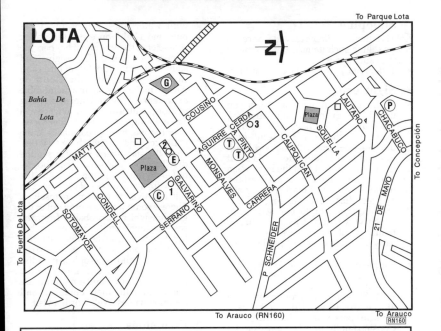

Key to map

C	Municipalidad (Town hall)
E	Telephone
G	Mercado Municipal (Market)
P	Gas stations
T	Bus terminals

● Eating out

1. Restaurant Socorros Mutuos
2. RestaurantCámara de Comercio
3. Restaurant El Delfín

Ⓐ Camping

Camping in Laraquete
- Los Troncos, KM 49 on RN 100, just before the village on the beach. 70 camping spots, public transport, kiosk, restaurant, caretaker, electricity, level ground but no shade, dark sand

𝄆 Eating out

- Cafetería Melissa, A. Pinto 250. Chilean cuisine
- Restaurant Drive in Exquisit, P. Aguirre Cerda 632
- El Delfín, Serrano near A. Pinto
- El Greco, P. Aguirre Cerda 422. Chilean cuisine
- Socorros Mutuos, P. Aguirre Cerda

Eating out in Parque Lota
- Café Jacaranda, Avenida el Parque 5 (just outside Parque Lota)

Eating out in Laraquete
- Davo, M. Latorre. Chilean cuisine
- Rapa Nui, Pablo Neruda. Chilean cuisine

🚌 Motoring

- COPEC gas station, corner of Bannen near Serrano (in the soccer stadium)

⚓ Water transport

- Isla Santa María every Tues, Thurs, and Sat at 1000 from harbor. Returns every Mon, Wed, and Fri at 0800. The trip takes about 2½ hours

561   Lota

⌖ Shopping

Lota is famous for items carved from coal. Shops selling such items can be found in Serrano and Squella.

• Taller Lota, A. Pinto 306. Coal carvings

📷 Sightseeing

• To Lota Alto. A stairway takes you uphill from the market, and once you reach the top you have commanding views over the town and south over the Bahía de Lota with the port facilities and coal loading docks. Here at Lota Alto you will find the Iglesia San Matias and the Cristo del Carbón, made of wood but blackened by age and coal-dust. On top of Lota Ridge is also the mine employees' settlement which was founded by the Cousiño family for its employees — it is an early Chilean version of public housing.

• Parque de Lota. Located in Lota Alto, the entrance to the park is on Avenida del Parque near the kiosk. Admission $1.00. Standing on a promontory high above the town, this 14 hectare (35 acre) park was established by the Cousiño family, or to be more exact by Isidora Cousiño. Although the town is dominated by the coal-washing plants, mines and shipping facilities, this is a different world! Lush gardens, exotic trees blending with native flora, shady paths leading to small ponds with water lilies, sculptures, lookouts, and a lighthouse give this park a character of its own, and it has become a mecca for tourists. The sights and sounds of many varieties of birds and the fine views over the Golfo de Arauco make a visit here a memorable experience. The northern viewing platform will bring you down to earth again though, because it has views over the slag heaps, coal stacks, mine entrances, and coal-washing facilities. Near the slag heaps you can see the dwellings of some squatters, who eke out a living by going through the waste for small pieces of coal they can sell in town or use for themselves. There is some water seeping out of the ground, which is probably from the coal-washing facility further up, but the squatters use the water also for domestic purposes. It is industrial slum, port, and subtropical paradise side by side. All plants grown in the park, both native and imported, are identified with their botanical and common names. Well worth a visit.

⌖ Excursions

Outside town the pine forests plantations begin to take over again, and around the coastline the pine trees come right down to the shore.

• **Fuerte de Lota**: Travel 3 km south of Lota on a road bordered by eucalyptus

🚌 Buses from Lota

Companies
• A153 Buses Tur-Bus Jedimar, A. Pinto 192 ℂ 876327
• B71 Buses Galaxia A. Pinto 234
• B96 Buses Lineas Verdes A. Pinto near Serrano
• B99 Buses Los Alces, Cousiño ℂ 876457
• B110 Buses Miramar
• B163 Buses Terramar

Services

Destination	Fare	Services	Companies
• Arauco	$ 1.05		B99
• Concepción	$ 1.00		B71, B96, B110, B163
• Coronel	$ 0.40		B110, B163
• Lebu	$ 2.30		B165
• Santiago	$10.50	6 services daily	A153, B71, B96, B165, B199
• Talca		3 services daily	A153, B82, B96

trees, and you will reach the fort, also known as Fuerte Viejo (Old Fort) or Mirador Prat (Prat Look-out). It was built in 1662 by Gobernador Ángel de Peredo, mainly to watch the coast for marauding pirates, and it also served the purpose of keeping an eye on the movement of Mapuche warriors. A shortcut: to get there on foot from Lota Bajo, follow the railroad track south until the tunnel. Where the railroad enters the tunnel climb uphill. From the top you have magnificent views over Playa Colcura.

- **Empresa Forestal Colcura:** This forestry and plant research center was founded in 1881 by the Cousiño family to test timbers from around the world for their suitability in underground mining. Later this research was translated into reafforestation programs. It can be reached on foot from Fuerte de Lota — 4 km east.
- **Laraquete**: 13 km south, on the **Golfo de Arauco.** It has a good beach, and is famous for its seafood restaurants. A bit further to the south is the Planta de Cellulosa de Arauco (a wood-pulp mill), which is supplied with pine trees from the nearby plantations. The area is also interesting for fossickers:

in the Río Las Cruces you can find "Maltese crosses" — a semi-precious stone. Buses Terramar and Buses Miramar run frequent daily services from Concepción.

- **Playa Blanca:** This beach begins near the northern entrance to Lota and stretches north for 8 km as far as Coronel.
- **Playa Chivilingo:** Begins 11 km south of Lota and extends south for 4 km. A trip to this beach can be combined with an excursion to the power station at Chivilingo .
- Boat trip to **Isla Santa María**: There are three ferry trips a week from Puerto Lota, returning the following day. The trip takes 2½ hours. Isla Santa María used to be a penal colony. Accommodation with locals in Puerto Sur.
- **Playa Colcura:**. South of Lota. A trip to this beach can be combined with an excursion to Empresa Forestal Colcura, or with a visit to Fuerte de Lota.
- Planta Hidroeléctrica Chivilingo, 2 km up in the **Río Chivilingo valley**. One of the oldest hydroelectric power stations on the South American continent, it is now a *monumento nacional*. The lake formed further up is a favorite fishing spot.

PARQUE NACIONAL
LAGUNA DEL LAJA

Altitude: 1400 m
Distance from Los Angeles: 93 km east on Ruta Q-45

This national park is 28 km past the village of **Antuco**, and has an information center, picnic area, camping area, excursion paths, accommodation, restaurant, ski-lifts, and a ski resort.

Within the park's 11 600 ha (28 642 acres), there is the **Volcán Antuco**, part of the **Sierra Velluda**, and the south-eastern part of the **Laguna del Laja**. The altitude ranges from 980 m to 2979 m — which is the Volcán Antuco. The mean annual average temperature is 7°C (45°F). The skiing area is inside the park, but it is only small with few facilities.

You can get to the park by public transport from Los Angeles to El Abanico (the hydroelectric power station), but from there it is an 11 km hike to the entrance of the national park. It is much better to go by private transport from Los Angeles; it takes two hours. The road is sealed for 76 km until the turnoff to the power station. In winter traffic is regulated: traffic from Los Angeles to the skiing area goes between 0700 and 1430, and from Antuco to Los Angeles between 1515 and 1900. The water channeled for power generation has somewhat diminished the cascades issuing from the lake.

The area can be visited all year round: there are mountain huts, restaurant and cafeteria, as well as picnic areas. The nearest telephone is in Antuco, 28 km west. There are two skiing centers: Centro Abanico and Centro de Esquí Digeder. The ski season is from June to October. See "Excursions" below.

🅰 Camping
- Camping Lagunillas, Sector Chacay (323606. 30 tent sites, four cabins, open all year round, electricity, water, toilets, hot showers, laundry, restaurant, cafeteria, swimming pool. Reservations in Los Angeles: Caupolicán 332

🚌 Bus services
Transport during the skiing season has to be arranged through Club Esquí Los Angeles.
- Los Angeles: Fare: $1.70; services Mon–Fri; duration 1½ hrs

⚽ Sport
Skiing, hiking, and fishing in Laguna de Laja for trout and *percatrucha* (Chilean trout).
There are three ski lifts, ski equipment hire, and ski instructors.

🌴 Excursions
- **Antuco:** Some 28 km west of the national park is the main population center with a population of 4000. Antuco's only claim to fame is its closeness to the Parque Nacional Antuco and the skiing area. Some 17 km further up, there are three large hydro-electric power stations on the Río Polcura (Antuco, Abanico, and El Toro) which supplement their water supplies from the **Laguna del Laja**. Buses Laja run six services daily from Los Angeles and reduced services beyond to the national park entrance. The scenery past Antuco is superb: the valley narrows and the perfect cone of Volcán Antuco dominates the background.

✉ Accommodation in Parque Nacional Laguna del Laja
- Hostería y Cabañas Lagunillas, KM 97, 4 km from ski fields
  AP (322606 $E for 4
  Two swimming pools; open all year
- Refugio Chacay Esquí. Ski school
  Reservations in Los Angeles: Club Esquí Los Angeles ((43) 322651
- Refugio Digeder
  Reservations in Concepción: ((41) 229054
- Refugio Universidad de Concepción
  Restaurant. Reservations in Concepción: ((41) 234985

Accommodation in Antuco
- Hostería Mirador, Colón 16 AP ((43) 621044 $G for 4
- Hotel Cordillera, Los Carrrera 399 ((43) 621018 $H ♙♙

Accommodation on the road to Parque Nacional Antuco
- Cabañas Aitué, KM 62. 3 km east of Antuco
  ABEFGHILNP (621010 $G for 4
- Hotel Malalcura ((43) 313183 / 323163
  $G cabins for 6; fax 312768

QUIRIHUÉ

Population: 5700
Altitude: 300 m
Distance from Chillán: 69 km west on Ruta N-50

Quirihué was the center of an important wheat-growing district last century, and an important crossroads during colonial times when the main highway from Santiago passed through here. It is still quite a well-populated town.

⚂ Festivals
- March, first week: Semana de Quirihué

⊟ Accommodation

Accommodation in Coelemu
Coelemu is a small town located on the south side of the Río Itata where Ruta N-58-O crosses the river en route to Concepción ("La Ruta del Conquistador").
- Hotel Comercio, Francisco Barros ✆ 511041

⑪ Eating out
- Restaurant Colo Colo, San Martín 286. Chilean cuisine
- Restaurant El Arriero, A. Prat 96. Chilean cuisine

Eating out in Coelemu
- Casino A. Prat, Francisco Barros 261. Chilean cuisine

- Casino Libertad, M.A.Matta 577. Chilean cuisine

⊟ Buses
- Cauquenes: Fare 1.40; 1 service daily; Buses Costa Azul
- Chillán: Fare $1.20; 2 services daily; duration 1 hr; Empresa Estrella del Sur
- Cobquecura: Fare $0.60; Buses Petorca

▣ Sightseeing
- **San Agustín de Puñual:** 21 km east on Ruta N-50. This is the birthplace of Arturo Prat Chacón, naval hero of the sea battle of Iquique during the War of the Pacific. It is a large *hacienda*, part of it converted into a museum with memorabilia of the epoch and documents, which is open daily 1000–1800. From the outside it is a fairly uninteresting building, but it is very attractive in the inside, with large courtyards.

SANTA BÁRBARA

Area code: 43
Population: 5500
Distance from Los Angeles: 43 km south-east on Ruta Q-61-R

Santa Bárbara is on the north bank of the **Río Bío Bío**, and was founded in 1757 by Gobernador Manuel de Amat y Juniet after the inconclusive *Parlamento* held with the Mapuche chiefs at Salto de Lajas. It was destroyed during the second general Mapuche uprising in 1768 under Mapuche chief Lebian. Abandoned in 1819, it was re-settled by immigrants from 1833 onwards.

With the completion of the hydroelectric power station of El Pangue a few kilometers further up from Ralco and below the junction of the Río

Pangue, the whole Alto Río Bío Bío is opening up for tourism. Before that it was only the domain for intrepid mountain hikers and river-rafting. The construction of the dam across the Bío Bío has not diminished the rafting experience.

The best views of the area can be had by crossing the river to **Quilaco** and climbing a small hill.

Because there are so many trees in the area, most of the houses here are made of wood, in contrast to the usual adobe buildings of most towns and villages.

Accommodation

- Residencial La Araucaria, A. Prat 654 (581240 $H **.** Shared bathroom
- Residencial Las Totoras, A. Prat 460 (581267 $I **::**

Accommodation in Alto Río Bío Bío valley

- Cabañas Santa Sofia, 7 km south of Santa Bárbara ((09) 4415175
- Hostal Doña Pola, Ralco 38 km southeast of Santa Bárbara AP ((09) 4415160 $G **::**
- Hostería Copahué, 85 km south-east of Santa Bárbara $H **::**. Open December–February

Eating out

- La Casona, Prat 654. Chilean cuisine
- Las Totoras, Prat 460. Chilean cuisine

Post and telegraph

Telephone
- CTC, Arturo Prat 430

Buses

Empresa de Transportes Rurales Ltda is in A. Prat 631.
- Concepción: Fare $2.50; Mini Pullman
- Los Angeles via San Carlos: 7 services daily; Buses Las Lajas

- Trapa Trapa: 2 services weekly; Buses Las Lajas

Excursions

- Centro Turístico Dilmun: 14 km north near Llano Blanco. This is a trout farm where you can try your skill in fishing; it has a barbecue area and tourist facilities.
- To **Ralco** and beyond: Ralco is located 44 km south-west in the shade of **Volcán Callaqui** 3160 m. The road is being pushed further towards **Troyo** where it will link up with the road from **Lonquimay**.
- To **Trapa Trapa** in the upper **Río Queuco valley:** Approximately 40 km east of Ralco near the Argentine border and in the shade of Volcán **Copahué**. The hot springs near Trapa Trapa and **Los Copahués** on the Chilean side are not yet commercially exploited. From Los Angeles there are twice-weekly bus services. From Trapa Trapa a mountain trail brings you to **Paso de Copahué** (2019 m) on the Argentine border. Dominating the skyline is **Volcán Copahué** (2965 m), which you can climb from here. The splendid views into Argentina mean you can see Termas de Copahué and Laguna del Agrio, fed by sulfurous volcanic water. Although not an official border crossing, it is possible (and very tempting) to descend to Termas de Copahué and take a thermal bath in the fairly well developed thermal resort — see the entry for Copahué in *Travel Companion Argentina*. Paso Copahué is at 2019 m. You will have to return to Chile. There are no tourist facilities in Trapa Trapa, and you need to take warm clothes, sleeping bag, and tent. From Trapa Trapa you can hike back through the Río Queuco valley to Ralco. The following Instituto Geográfico 1:50 000 series maps cover this area: "Queuco" 5-04-07-0032-00, "Trapa Trapa" 5-04- 07- 0033-00, and "Volcán Copahué" 5-04- 07-0044-00.

TALCAHUANO

Area code: 041
Population: 210 000
Altitude: Sea level
Distance from Concepción: 16 km west

Talcahuano, founded in 1764, is the second largest port in Chile, a naval base, and an important industrial center with a huge petrochemical complex, Petrox S.A. It has virtually become part of Concepción. It is a fishing harbor and a port used by the local timber industry to dispatch their products.

There is an interesting naval museum in the *Monitor Huascar*, a Peruvian ship captured by the Chilean navy during the War of the Pacific. It is also worth taking a trip a little way ☞ south of the city to La Boca at the mouth of the **Río Bío Bío**, its south bank covered with dense native shrubs and forests.

⍟ Festivals

- January 13–29: Fería Exposición Bío Bío
- May 20: Concurso Gastronomía Marina. Seafood festival
- June 29: San Pedro
- September 23: Concurso de Tragos Marinos
- November, third week: Carnaval de Talcahuano

⊟ Accommodation

- Hotel de la Costa, Colón 648 ℂ 545913 $H ♨
- Hotel de France, A. Pinto 44 AEHIPSV ℂ 542230 $G ♨
- Hotel Italia, Chacabuco 38 ℂ 548975 $G ♨. Fax 541560
- Residencial Aida, Bulnes 395 ℂ 543908
- Residencial Luz del Sur, A. Pinto 279 ℂ 543968
- Residencial San Pedro, Manuel Rodríguez 22 AEFGIJPV ℂ 542145 $H ♨

⍟ Eating out

Restaurants
- Angamos, Colón 1062
- Bentoteca El Navegante, Almirante Villaroel 110, Local 5. Seafood
- Bentoteca Esmeralda, Almirante Villarroel 357, on road to naval base. Seafood
- Bentoteca Miramar, Almirante Villarroel 110, Local 3. Seafood
- Carpe Diem, A. Pinto 397. Seafood, international cuisine
- Ciros, Bulnes 159. International cuisine
- Club de Yates, Blanco
- Club Talcahuano, Colón 446. Seafood
- Domingo Lara, A. Pinto 450. Seafood
- Fragata Maria Isabel, Colón 770. International cuisine
- Posada El Alero, Colón 3396. Chilean cuisine

Eating out along the *autopista* to Concepción
- La Querencia. Chilean cuisine

⍟ Post and telegraph

Post office
- Correos de Chile, S. Aldea 260

Telephone
- CTC, Avenida Colón 585, fax 542559

⍟ Buses

Companies
- Buses Hualpencillo, Gibraltar ℂ 410652
- Buses Mini Verde, Finlandia ℂ 412191
- Buses Sol del Sur, Colón 211 office 1 ℂ 543603
- Buses TAS Choapa, B. Encalada 130 ℂ 542956
- Buses Tur-Bus Jedimar, B. Encalada 130 oficina 4
- Colectivos Línea Talcahuano-Concepción-Penco Sodal

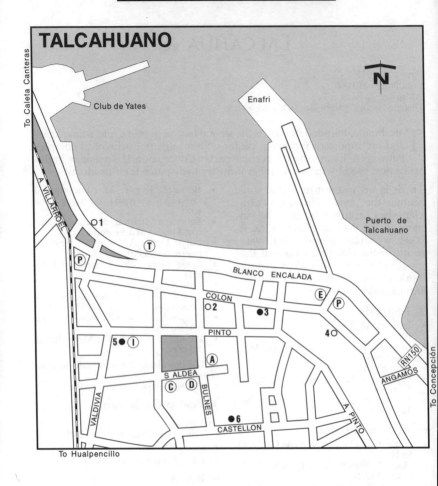

Key to map

A	Iglesia
C	Municipalidad (Town hall)
D	Post office and telex
E	Telephone
I	Tourist information
P	Gas stations
T	Bus terminals

● **Accommodation**

3	Hotel de la Costa
5	Hotel de France
6	Residencial Aida

○ **Eating out**

1	Seafood restaurants
2	Restaurant Club Talcahuano
4	Restaurant Fragata Maria Isabel

- Buses JM, B. Encalada 130 ℂ 543069
- Buses Cruz del Sur, Colón 211 ℂ 545641

Services
- 6 services daily south to Puerto Montt, Osorno, Valdívia, and Temuco
- 8 services daily north to Santiago, Talca, Rancagua, Curicó, Chillán, and Los Angeles
- 20 services daily to Concepción and Penco

Motoring

There is a gas station on Blanco Encalada, corner of Valdivia.

Sightseeing

- *Monitor Huáscar*, the Peruvian battleship commanded by Almirante Grau which was sunk during the naval battle off Iquique during the War of the Pacific. It is now used as a museum and is moored in the bay just past the Club de Yates. You can get there by motor launch.

Talcahuano

Plate 33   Región X de Los Lagos
Top: Valdivia, Isla Mancerra
Bottom: Volcán Osorno

Plate 34   Región X de Los Lagos
Lago Llanquihué, German water mill

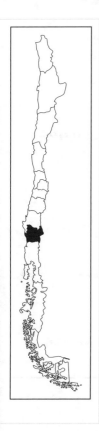

REGIÓN IX
DE LA
ARAUCANIA

LA ARAUCANIA

Size: 32 500 square km (12 545 square miles)
Population: 700 000
Regional capital: Temuco
Province and provincial capital: Malleco (Angol)

This little-known area of Chile is full of delightful hiking possibilities that range in difficulty from short walks to challenging expeditions with overnight camping stops. There are plenty of opportunities to fish in summer and ski in winter. Parts of the region have been declared national parks to preserve the native flora and fauna, especially *araucaria* trees, which predominate here and still form large forests. They are protected by law. Red *copihué*, Chile's national flower, blooms in March and April. You may be lucky enough to see *pudú* (dwarf deer), scarce *monitos del monte* (a marsupial), or an exceptionally rare puma.

Much of Región IX de La Araucania is still inhabited by Mapuche Indians, and their traditional handicrafts are well established in the district. Mapuche art is strong in silver artefacts, and women wear silver ornaments on their foreheads and across their breasts. Angol and Gorbea are known for ceramics; Loncoche and Pucón for woodcarving.

The region is sandwiched between the northern Región VIII del Bio Bio and southern Región X de Los Lagos. It is bordered by the Andes and Argentina in the east, and the Pacific Ocean in the west. The largest population centers are Temuco, Pucón, Angol, Victoria, Villarrica, and Lautaro.

Transport

Road

The Panamericana Sur (RN 5) runs the full length of the region. Feeder roads reach out to the Pacific Ocean and into the Andes. From Temuco, there are also several pass roads into Argentina. Passenger buses use **Paso de Pino Hachado** between Lonquimay and Zapala in Argentina, and **Paso Mamuil Malal** between Temuco and Junín de los Andes in Argentina.

Rail

The southern railroad line connects with Santiago and Puerto Montt. The trains have sleepers, dining cars, and video facilities. Passengers to Valdivia have to change to buses in Temuco.

Air

The major airport in the region is Maquehué, which serves Temuco and has daily flights to Santiago and Puerto Montt.

Topography

This is a transitional zone where the Andes are less formidable, but many of the snow-covered volcanos in the *pre-Cordillera* reach 3000 m. The most prominent ones are **Volcán Tol-**

huaca (2780 m), **Volcán Llaima** (3060 m), **Volcán Villarrica** (2840 m), and **Volcán Lonquimay** (2890 m), which erupted on Christmas Day in 1988, forming a mini-volcano appropriately named "Navidad". This small volcano was quiet again by January 1990. Further south, glacier erosion and damming by lava flows have created lakes in the *pre-Cordillera*, most notably **Lago Villarrica**, **Lago Caburga**, and **Lago Colico**. They are one of the district's strongest scenic attractions and are supported by excellent tourist facilities. The coastal plains are wider than in other regions and so is the central valley, which is enclosed by hills no more than 400 m high, especially between Collipulli and Victoria. The **Cordillera de Nahuelbuta** reaches 1533 m in the north-west near **Angol**. The Cordillera de Nahuelbuta peters out at the **Río Imperial**. Further south, the coastal *cordillera* also almost disappears.

Climate

Seasons are more defined in Region IX de La Araucania. Southwards, rainfall increases, and is evenly distributed throughout the year. It can rain at any time, even if the previous day was sunny. In the north, the annual rainfall is 1030 mm around Angol, where the average annual temperature is 13°C (55°F). Temuco has an annual rainfall of 1220 mm. Precipitation is higher in the *cordillera* — **Curacautín**, for example, has 1700 mm per annum. The sea has a marked influence on the climate, and the cooler weather prevents the growth of certain plants. Some areas are particularly suitable for raising fruit and vegetables.

European and Mapuche history

This is the homeland of the Mapuche tribe, who fiercely resisted European colonization for 330 years. As early as 1553, the Spanish founded towns at **Villarrica**, **Imperial**, and **Angol**, and a fort at **Purén**. Pedro de Valdivia encountered a worthy adversary in Chief Caupolicán. Caupolicán's second-in-command, Lautaro, had spent some time with the Spanish, and had studied their strengths and weaknesses. Lautaro's strategy was to attack in thickly forested terrain where the Spanish could not use their horses. The Mapuche harassed the invaders continuously, giving them no time to regroup or rest. The Indians spared neither horses nor Spanish and punished their own compatriots who had become servants of the Spanish. The Mapuches' thorough knowledge of the countryside made them a formidable enemy, as Pedro de Villagra, a later Governor of Chile, reported to Emperor Charles V. During the big Mapuche uprising in 1599 and several smaller ones, Spanish settlements south of the Río Bío Bío at Villarrica, Imperial, Tucapel, Purén, and Angol were wiped out.

Many *Gobernadores* (or Governors) of Chile grappled with the problem of Mapuche aggression. The fight was costly and Chilean governors constantly requested money and reinforcements from the Viceroy in Peru or the Spanish King. When Phillip II died, the Spanish treasury was empty. Phillip III and the *Consejo de las Indias* wanted to terminate the war in Chile and regain the upper hand. Fray Luís de Valdivia, a Jesuit *padre*, suggested that the Araucanian Indians should be treated in a more humane way, and that the Río Bío Bío should be drawn up as a border to restrict the Mapuche to their territory. He also suggested a strategy called the *Guerra Defensiva* — an end to incursions by Mapuche marauding parties into Spanish-held territory north of the Río Bío Bío, and Mapuche must permit priests as missionaries in their territory. It was argued that if they became Christians, they would automatically become Spanish subjects. King Phillip III supported this plan and put Fray Luís de Valdivia in charge. He became chief administrator, and governors were virtually answerable to him. The Spanish met with the Mapuche, exchanged gifts, and made treaties which amounted to nothing more than empty promises. Opinion in Chile was wholly against this operation, as it failed to end the constant attacks on Spanish territory beyond the Río Bío Bío. When Phillip IV came to power, he decreed that any Mapuche warriors taken prisoner should be sent as slaves to Peru or Copiapó. In 1647, Governor Martín de Mujica received permission from the Mapuche warriors to use a path along the coast between Concepción and Valdivia.

Several Spanish Governors died in active combat, while attempting to pacify the Araucanians. Pedro de Valdivia, Chile's founder, was among them. He died on Christmas Day, 1554, outside Fuerte Tucapel near present-day **Cañete**. It was 1861 before the Chilean Government succeeded in incorporating the area south of the Río Bío Bío into Chilean territory.

From 1883 onwards, the Chilean Government attracted immigrants from Europe to the region, mostly from Germany and Switzerland but also from Spain.

Today, there are still Mapuche townships and villages, particularly to the west of Temuco around **Puerto Saavedra**, **Nueva Imperial**, and **Galvarino**. Isolated Mapuche settlements in the Andes are called *reducciones* or "reservations", but this word no longer has the bad connotation it had during the Spanish Conquest. The Mapuche population now numbers approximately 280 000 and is increasing.

Economy

Economic activity centers on agriculture and forestry. Large tracts of land are planted with radiata pines and eucalyptus. The region is a major producer of dairy products — milk and cheese. Berry fruits are grown commercially, south of Temuco, where there are raspberry plantations. Large areas are sown with wheat, oats, and barley, and the district is called the "Granary of Chile". Apples, cherries, potatoes, lentils, and sugar beet are also extensively cultivated. Fishing is confined to small fleets in **Puerto Saavedra** and **Queule**.

In the last decade, tourism has boosted the local economy with the development of good facilities in the most scenic areas, such as Villarrica, Pucón, and Temuco. Volcanic activity has produced many hot springs scattered through the *cordillera* and *pre-Cordillera*. Most of them have a thermal hotel attached, such as **Termas de Tolhuaca**, **Termas de Manzanar**, and the many thermal resorts east of Pucón. Pucón itself is a mecca for mountain climbers and skiers on **Volcán Villarrica**, and offers aquatic sports on **Lago Villarrica**. The re-

gion's many national parks are outstandingly beautiful. Most of them can be visited in a day from Temuco.

Local cuisine

The food of the region has been heavily influenced by European immigration which started last century. The Germans contributed cakes, commonly called *"kuchen"*, such as *kuchen de manzanas* and *kuchen de frambuesas*. Double-smoked hams, spicy German-style sausages, and salamis have all been successfully introduced by European migrants. Roast kid is a special dish found in the **Curacautín** and **Lonquimay** area. The smoked trout is delicious. Local mushrooms (*digueños changles*) are served, cooked with spices or in salads. Try drinking *chicha de manzana* (apple juice) or *enguinado*, a cherry liqueur.

Mapuche dishes are also available in the central market in Temuco. *Ñachi*, a kind of blood sausage, is made of coagulated sheep's blood spiced with coriander, salt, garlic, and lemon juice. *Caritún* is mutton cooked in lemon juice. *Ñalca* stems are prepared as a salad. The favorite Mapuche drink is *mudai*, made from fermented wheat.

This is one of the few areas where *araucaria* trees have not been completely destroyed or replaced by pinus radiata. The Mapuche still eat *araucaria* nuts, called *piñones*. The Europeans imported chestnut trees, which now grow profusely everywhere.

National parks and reserves

*   **Monumento Natural Cerro Ñielol** (89.5 ha or 221 acres): This is a 10-minute walk from the center of Temuco and has its

own information center, excursion paths, picnic area, restaurant, kiosk, and lookout. The slopes are densely covered with species of trees and shrubs that were there before the territory was colonized. *Copihué* grows profusely in this protected area. The national monument also contains the historical site of the Chilean–Mapuche parley, which led to Chilean encroachment into Mapuche territory.

- **Monumento Natural Contulmo** (82 ha or 210 acres): 69 km south-west of Angol on Ruta R-86 as far as **Los Sauces**), and from there on Ruta R-60-P past Purén just before Contulmo on the road to Cañete. This park, which is renowned for its large fern trees, has a picnic area, excursion paths, and a lookout. It is 3 km west of Contulmo and 8 km east of Purén, directly adjacent to Región VIII del Bío Bío. Regular buses connect Contulmo and Purén. The nearest accommodation is in **Contulmo** and **Purén**.

- **Parque Nacional Huerquehué** (12 500 ha or 30 875 acres): 36 km north-east of Pucón near **Lago Caburga**. This park has an information center, excursion paths, a picnic and camping area, and a lookout. See the entry for the park on page 598.

- **Parque Nacional Nahuelbuta** (5415 ha or 13 375 acres): This park has an information center, excursion paths, picnic and camping areas, and a lookout. It lies 35 km west of **Angol** in the Nahuelbuta ranges ending at the border of Región VIII de Bío Bío. The best approach to this

pristine hiking area is from Angol. The park is covered with *araucaria* forests; inside the park are some caves used as hide-outs by bandits in the 19th century — paths constructed by CONAF personnel pass such points of interest. During summer, the local Sernatur office organizes excursions. It is possible for hikers to reach **Antihuala** on a mountain trail. See "Buses" from Angol on page 583.

- **Reserva Nacional Malalcahuello-Ñalcas**. The reserve is located 90 km east of Victoria on Ruta R-89 to Lonquimay and the combined area has 42 685 ha (105 430 acres). The reserve is on the south side of **Volcán Lonquimay**, with views of the volcano for some distance. See the entry for the reserve on page 616.

- **Parque Nacional Tolhuaca** (6380 ha or 15 760 acres): 57 km east of Victoria on Ruta R-71 to Inspector Fernández. See the entry for the park on page 600.

- **Parque Nacional Conguillio-Las Paraguas** (60 832 ha or 150 255 acres), incorporating Parque Nacional Las Paraguas: 126 km east of Temuco on Ruta S-51 to Cunco and Ruta S-61 to Melipeuco, then north on a dirt road. This park can also be reached from Victoria, 116 km east on Ruta R-89 to Curacautín, and from there south to **Laguna Conguillio**. It offers excursion paths, an information center, picnic and camping areas, accommodation, a restaurant, a shop, a ski lift, a ski resort, and a lookout. See the entry for the park on page 596.

- **Parque Nacional Villarrica** (62 000 ha or 153 140 acres): 15 km south of Pucón. The park's facilities include excursion paths, picnic and camping areas, ski lifts, a ski resort, lookout, *refugios*, and accommodation, eating places. See the entry for the park on page 601.
- **Reserva Nacional Alto Bío Bío** (35 000 ha or 86 450 acres): 175 km east of Victoria on Ruta R-89 east of Liucura on the road to Paso de Pino Hachado at the Argentine frontier. It consists mostly of *araucarias* and other native trees.
- **Reserva Forestal China Muerta**: (11 168 ha or 27 585 acres) 126 km east of Temuco on Ruta S-51 and S- 61, past Melipeuco and skirting **Laguna Icalma**. The reserve is adjacent to Parque Nacional Conguillio-Paraguas and encompasses **Cordillera Llancahué** and part of **Cordón Quelemahuida**. Although large clumps of *araucaria* still grow in their natural state, there is logging in this area. The Alto Río Bío Bío runs through the reserve and forms many rapids on its way through the canyons, where enthusiasts enjoy whitewater rafting. The **Río Bío Bío** rises in **Laguna Icalma** and **Laguna Gualletué**. This reserve is frequented by the sport fisherman and canoeist. It can be reached by bus from Temuco via Melipeuco on Ruta S-61, or via Lonquimay on Ruta R-89. Rural Buses continue to **Icalma**, a small village where border formalities are carried out for those wishing to continue into Argentina.

Lakes

- **Lago Budi** (surface area 70 square km or 27 square miles): A shallow coastal lake with brackish water, south of Puerto Saavedra. **Isla Nahuelhuapi** lies in its center. The lake can be reached from Puerto Saavedra and Carahué. See the entry for Puerto Saavedra on page 612, and Puerto Dominguez under "Excursions" from Carahué on page 585.
- **Lago Caburga**: The best access is from Pucón, 25 km by public transport. Regular tours from Pucón include the **Ojos del Caburga**, and waterfalls near **Lago Tinquilco**, and **Lago Verde**. The lake is surrounded by high, steep mountains of volcanic origin, covered with shrubs and trees. The water is relatively warm from the lake's hot springs. Most of the facilities, for example, hotels and camping grounds, are found at the two southern beaches. The lake's eastern side forms part of **Parque Nacional Huerquehué**. See "Excursions" from Pucón on page 610.
- **Lago Calafquén** (surface area 180 square km or 69 square miles): 30 km south of Villarrica. This lake, with its 11 small islands, is also a major tourist attraction, somewhat quieter than Villarrica and Pucón but also with sizable tourist facilities. There are camping sites and motels beside the good beaches. Important tourist centers are **Licán Ray** in Región IX de La Araucania and **Coñaripe** and **Calafquén** in Región X de Los Lagos.

- **Lago Colico**: This lake is best reached from Cunco. There is a camping area on the eastern side.
- **Lago Villarrica** (surface area 170 square km or 66 square miles): South-east of **Temuco**. This lake with its large island, **Isla Aillaquillén**, forms the major tourist attraction of the region. There are important tourist centers at **Villarrica** on its western side and **Pucón** on its eastern side. The road skirting the southern edge of the lake between the two towns is lined with tourist facilities such as hotels, restaurants, and camping areas. Many water sports are possible, such as swimming, sailing, water-skiing, and wind-surfing.
- **Laguna Icalma** and **Laguna Gualletué** are the sources of the **Río Bío Bío**. These small lakes can be reached from **Lonquimay** and **Melipeuco**.

Thermal resorts

The thermal resorts of this region are all located in the *pre-Cordillera*. Their waters are recommended for their healing properties (see individual entries) and most offer hotel accommodation.

- **Termas de Manzanar**: Altitude 700 m, 47°C (117°F), open all year round, 27 km east of Curacautín on Ruta R-89. Accommodation is available in the thermal resort hotel. Buses run there daily from Temuco. See Manzanar under "Accommodation" in Curacautín on page 587, and under "Excursions" from Curacautín on page 589.
- **Termas de Huife**: Altitude 320 m, 46°–60°C (115°–140°F),

open all year round, 36 km east of Pucón on Ruta S-907. Transport is by taxi *colectivos* from Pucón. See "Excursions" from Pucón on page 611.
- **Termas de Menetué** small thermal resort 27 km east of Pucón. See "Excursions" from Pucón on page 611.
- **Termas de Palguín**: Altitude 680 m, 25°–57°C (77°–135°F), open all year round, 28 km east of Pucón. Turn off from RN 119 towards sector Quetrupillán of Parque Nacional Villarrica. Accommodation is available in the thermal resort hotel. Transport is by taxi from Pucón. See "Excursions" from Pucón on page 611.
- **Termas de Quimey-Co**: Altitude 310 m, 46°C (115°F), open December–March, 22 km east of Pucón on Ruta S-907 just before Termas de Huife. Transport is by taxi *colectivos* from Pucón, or use Termas de Quimey-Co's own transport in the season. See "Excursions" from Pucón on page 612.
- **Termas de San Luis**. A fairly well-developed thermal spa located 37 km east of Pucón. See "Excursions" from Pucón on page 612.
- **Termas de Tolhuaca**: Altitude 1020 m, 95°C (203°F), open November–April, 57 km east of Victoria on Ruta R-71. Summer season accommodation is available in the thermal resort hotel, and transport is by taxi from Curacautín. The water is recommended for respiratory ailments, kidney complaints, rheumatism, arthritis, diabetes,

asthma, and gastrointestinal problems.

Trout fishing

The trout fishing season is from the second Friday in November until the first Sunday in May. The best fishing is in Laguna Icalma and Galletué.

- Angol: Near El Manzano, 20 km west of Angol, en route to Parque Nacional Nahuelbuta
- Carahué: Río Imperial, Lago Budi
- Collipulli: Río Malleco, Río Mininco, Río Renaico
- Curacautín: Nearby rivers and Lago Malleco
- Freire: Río Quepe, Río Toltén, Río Allipen, Lago Colico
- Galvarino: Río Matraquén, Río Maquis, Río Traiguén, Río Quillén, Río Cuyel, Río Quino, Río Salto
- Loncoche: Río Cruces, Río San José
- Lonquimay: Laguna Gualletué and Laguna Icalma
- Pucón: Río Liucura, Río Trancura, Lago Villarrica, Lago San Luís, Lago Caburga, Laguna Verde, Lago San Jorge, Lago Quilleihué
- Victoria: Río Quino, Río Traiguén and Dumo
- Vilcún: Río Quepe
- Villarrica: Lago Villarrica, Río Pedregoso, Río Toltén

Distances from Temuco

- Angol: 128 km north-west
- Collipulli: 96 km north
- Curacautín: 84 km north-east
- Lago Caburga: 132 km south-east
- Licán-Ray: 113 km south-east
- Lonquimay: 144 km east
- Parque Nacional Conguillio-Las Paraguas: 135 km east (via Melipeuco)
- Parque Nacional Los Paraguas: 81 km east (via Vilcún)
- Pucón: 110 km south-east
- Santiago: 673 km north
- Villarrica: 86 km south-east
- Volcán Llaima: 127 km east

Tourism

The areas of biggest tourist attraction are:

Don't miss

☞ Pucón–Villarrica

Worth a visit

☞ Curacautín– Lonquimay
☞ Temuco

Worth a detour

☞ Angol and Nahuelbuta ranges
☞ Melipeuco and Parque Nacional Conguillio-Las Paraguas

Of interest

☞ Coastal area near Puerto Saavedra and Lago Budi

ANGOL

Area code: 045
Population: 40–000
Altitude: 70 m
Distance from Temuco: 128 km north-west on RN 182 and Panamericana

Angol, the capital of Malleco Province, lies east of the **Cordillera de Nahuelbuta** where the junction of the Río Picoiquen and the Río Rehué form the **Río Vergara**. It was founded in 1553 as Los Confines, but had to be rebuilt five times after Mapuche raids. The foundations of the present settlement were established by Cornelio Saavedra in 1862.

Angol is apple juice country with agriculture as its mainstay. It is also famous for its ceramics industry. Tourism is increasing.

To the west, the nearby Nahuelbuta ranges have a moderating influence on the climate. Winters are mild but summers can be very hot. The town is conveniently placed for visits to the **Parque Nacional Nahuelbuta** with its large forests of *araucarias*.

⛨ Festivals

* Middle of January: Festival de Brotes de Chile — song competitions to promote Chilean folk music. Horse races and an art fair are held concurrently

Festivals in Lumaco
Lumaco is 54 km south-west.
* January 20: Fiesta de Piedra Santa — a very colorful festival when animals are sacrificed as part of Mapuche customs.

ⓘ Tourist information

* SERNATUR, O'Higgins near bridge over Río Vergara
* CONAF, A. Prat block 100 near Chorrillos
* Municipalidad de Angol. Fishing licenses

Key to map

A	Iglesia		○	**Eating out**
B	Gobernación Provincial (Government)		**3**	Restaurant Las Totoras
			6	Restaurant Club Social
C	Municipalidad (Town hall)		**7**	Restaurant Flores
D	Post office and telex		**9**	Pizzas Sparlatto
E	Telephone		**12**	Café Stop
F	Carabineros (Police)		**13**	Salón de Té Garrido
H	Hospital		**15**	Café Réal
I	Tourist information		■	**Sights**
P	Gas stations		**2**	**Convento Franciscano**
T	Bus terminals			
●	**Accommodation**		□	**Services**
4	Hospedaje		**1**	Cerámica Lablee
5	Hotel Chez Mayotte		**8**	Dry cleaner
11	Hotel Olympia		**10**	Supermercado Savvy
14	Hotel Millaray		**16**	Cerámica Serra
18	Residencial Olympia		**17**	CONAF
			19	Centro Cultural

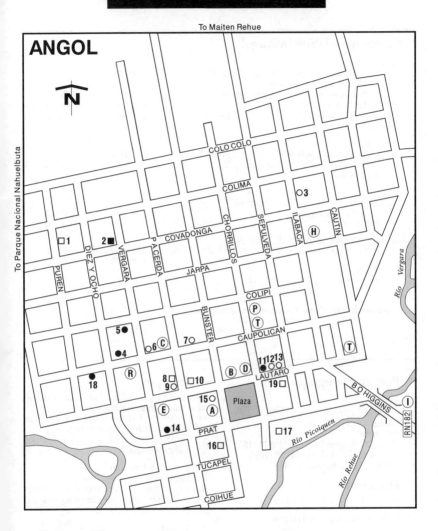

ANGOL

To Maiten Rehue

To Parque Nacional Nahuelbuta

COLO COLO
COLIMA
○3
CHORRILLOS
SEPULVEDA
ILABACA
CAUTIN
□1   2■   COVADONGA   (H)
DIEZ Y OCHO
VERGARA
P. ACERDA
JARPA
PUREN
COLIPI
(P)
BUNSTER
(T)
5●   ○6 (C)   7○   CAUPOLICAN
●4
(R)   (T)
8□   10□   (B) (D)   111213 ○○○
18●   9○   LAUTARO
15○   19□
(E)   (A)   Plaza
●14
PRAT   □17   Río Picoiquen
16□
B. O'HIGGINS
RN182
(I)
TUCAPEL
COIHUE
Río Vergara
Río Rehue

🍴 Eating out

Restaurants
- Club Social, Caupolicán 498
- Elibran, A. Prat 393 $Y. *Parrilla*
- El Quijote, Lautaro 405
- Flores, Caupolicán 330
- Las Totoras, Ilabaca near Covadonga $Y
- Pastelería Garrido, Lautaro 140

Cafés
- Café Real, Lautaro 301
- Café Stop, Lautaro 176
- Pizzas Sparlatto, Lautaro 310

🍸 Entertainment

- Disco La Arcadia, 6 km east on the Río Malleco

⊟ Accommodation in Angol

Hotels
- Chez Mayotte, Vergara 569   AFGPR   (711336
  English and French spoken
- El Parrón, Avenida B. O'Higgins 345   AEHJPV   (711370 $I   ♟♟
- Millaray, A. Prat 420   AEFGUV   (711570 $H   ♟♟
- Olympia, Lautaro 194   EFGHIJLV   (711517 $H   ♟♟
  Budget travelers

Residenciales
- Olympia, Caupolicán 625   ADGIJLTV   (711162 $I   ♟♟
- Casa de Huéspedes, Dieciocho 465   S $I   ♟♟
  Budget travelers

Pensions
- Villa Alegre, Avenida B. O'Higgins 377
- Vergara, Vergara 240   S $I   ♟♟
- Prat, Prat 364   S $I   ♟♟

Accommodation on Avenida Bullock
- Hostería Las Araucarias, Dillman Bullock 2182, Huequén at the intersection with RN 182
     PS   (712103 $H   ♟♟
  Fax 711202
- Posada Casona del Vergel, Avenida Bullock
     S $I   ♟♟

Accommodation along the road to Los Angeles
- Hotel Colinas de la Villa Verde, KM 1
     AFGHTV   (711973

▦ Post and telegraph

Post office
- Correos, corner of Chorrillos near Lautaro (on the plaza)
- *Telephone*
- CTC, O'Higgins 297, fax (45) 711167
- CTC, Lautaro 491, fax (45) 711015
- Telex Chile, Caupolicán 346

$ Financial
- Banco de Chile, Lautaro near Ilabaca

▤ Services and facilities

Laundry and dry cleaner
- P. Aguirre Cerda block 400 near Caupolicán

Supermarket
- Supermercado Savvy, P. Aguirre Cerda block 400 near Lautaro

⊟ Motoring
For gas stations, see the city map.

⊞ Shopping
Angol is a center of industrial and domestic ceramic manufacturing.
- Cerámica Lablee, Purén 564. Open daily including Sunday morning
- Cerámica Serra, M. Bunster 153. Open daily 0900–2000

Shopping in Lumaco
Lumaco is 154 km south-west.
Jewelry made of silver and woven materials can be bought from the weavers and silversmiths in the village.

⊛ Sport
Trout fishing: see page 579.

▩ Sightseeing
- **Museo Dillman S. Bullock,** in the Instituto Agrícola El Vergel, 4 km east. This museum, well worth visiting, belongs to the Methodist Church, and was founded by its first director, Dillman S. Bullock. It contains an excellent

🚌 Buses from Angol

Companies
The long-distance bus terminal is on the corner of Caupolicán 200 and Chorrillos.
The rural bus terminal is on Ilabaca near Caupolicán.

- A48 Buses Lit ☎ 722549
- A153 Tur-Bus Jedimar, office 5 ☎ 711655
- B30 Buses Bío Bío ☎ 711777
- B53 Pullman Bus Tacoha ☎ 711818
- B81 Buses Igi Llaima ☎ 711920
- B87 Buses Jota Be
- B88 Buses Jota Ewert
- B113 Buses Nacimiento-Angol
- B164 Thiele Ewert ☎ 711100
- B188 Buses Costa Azul

Services

Destination	Fares	Services	Duration	Companies
Cañete	$2.90	24 services daily		B164
Capitán Pastene	$2.00	4 services daily		B164
Chillán	$3.40	4 services daily		A48, A153, B265
Collipulli	$0.80	17 services daily		B30
Concepción	$3.40	8 services daily		B30, B81, B164
Contulmo	$1.90	24 services daily		B88, B164
Lebu	$4.00	24 services daily		B164
Los Alamos	$3.50	24 services daily		B164
Los Alpes	$1.50	2 services Tues, Thurs, Sat		B188
Los Angeles	$1.40	25 services daily		B30, B81, B87, B265
Los Sauces	$0.80	24 services daily		B164
Lumaco	$1.90	4 services daily		B164
Nacimiento	$0.90	21 services daily	1¼ hrs	B30, B113, B164
Negrete	$0.70	1 service daily		Olivar
Purén	$1.30	24 services daily		B88, B164
Santa Juana	$1.70			B164
Santiago	$11.40	9 services daily	8½ hrs	A48, A153, B81, B265
Talca	$6.60	3 services daily		A153, B265
Temuco	$3.60	14 services daily	2¼ hrs	B30
Traiguén	$1.70	24 services daily		B164
Vegas Blancas	$1.20	2 services Mon, Wed, Fri		B188
Victoria	$1.25	14 services daily	1hr	B30

collection of Mapuche and pre-Mapuche artefacts, including mummies and burial urns. The beetle and butterfly collection is also most interesting. There is regular municipal transport to the entrance.

- **Convento de San Buenaventura,** Vergara 506. This Franciscan monastery, founded in 1863, is one of the oldest south of the Río Bío Bío. It can be visited daily.

📍 Excursions

- **Collipulli**: 32 km east at the junction with the Panamericana on the main railroad line from Santiago to Puerto Montt. After the intersection at Huequén the tree-lined road runs in a straight line through flat open country interspersed with low hills and is sealed all the way. The high *cordillera* and Volcán Tolhuaca and Volcán Lonquimay appear on the horizon. At Puente Santa Catalina there is a camping spot on your left. The rich volcanic

Angol

soil is used for crops: potatoes, wheat, and rye.

- **Capitán Pastene**: 65 km south-west in the southern part of the Nahuelbuta ranges, but can also be reached from Traiguén or Angol. It was founded by Italian immigrants early in the 20th century. The wide streets, which bear Italian names, are lined with houses and planted with flowers, a feature of the town. The surrounding mountains reach over 700 m and are forested with native trees including many *araucaria* trees. Many Mapuche villages still exist in this part of Araucania, which was the heartland of Mapuche resistance during the colonial period. Buses Thiele and Buses Jota Ewert run daily services to Angol, Traiguén, Concepción, and Temuco.

- **Lumaco**: 54 km south-west, population 3000. In 1598, a force of 200 Spanish soldiers under the command of Governor Martín García Oñez de Loyola, nephew of the then Viceroy Toledo in Peru, was ambushed in this area. De Loyola was the second Governor of Chile who died fighting the Mapuche. This battle, on the banks of the **Río Lumaco** near the present-day town, became known as the "Disaster of Curalaba". The modern settlement was founded in 1869 by Coronel Saavedra. Lumaco is a Mapuche township; the townspeople are expert silversmiths and weavers, and also manufacture musical instruments. They retain some of the colorful Mapuche traditions in their festivals. Buses Thiele and Buses Jota Ewert run daily services to Angol, Concepción, and Temuco. This excursion can be combined with a trip to Capitán Pastene, which is only 12 km further south.

- **Parque Nacional Nahuelbuta**: (6800 ha or 16 800 acres) 37 km west. The park has a trail network of about 30 km. Buses Costa Azúl run rural buses to **Vegas Blancas** on Mon, Wed, and Fri at 0700 and 1600; fare $1.20. On Sundays during the summer vacation, from the end of December to mid-March, Buses Costa Azúl and Sernatur organize bus tours to this park. The journey takes approximately 1½ hours. The buses leave from the rural bus terminal at 0700 and return to Angol about 2100. Check with Sernatur. Fare $7.50 per person. A day-and-a-half walk through the Parque Nacional to Cañete, a distance of 40 km, is recommended for hikers and adventurers. This is the only area in the coastal *cordillera* where the national tree, the *araucaria*, still covers large areas. The *araucaria* grows very slowly and does not reach maturity until one hundred years old. The fruit — a type of nut — used to be a staple food for the Mapuche. Some of the *araucaria* trees in this national park are 50 m high and 2 m in diameter. A few specimens are 2000 years old. The highest mountain is **Alto Nahuelbuta**, with an altitude of 1560 m. Park rangers are located in Pehuenco sector, where the path starts and there are a camping and picnic area. There is another camping area near **Piedra del Aguila** (1400 m). From the top of this mountain, you can see the coast and the volcanic ranges to the east. There is also a camping ground at sector Coimallin. **Cerro Anay** (1390 m) and Aguas Calientes are close by. The ground, a few kilometers north of Coimallin, is marshy. There are many more interesting walks inside the park. See also "Excursions" from Lago Lanalhue (page 549) and Cañete in Región VIII del Bío Bío (page 515). Access is possible from Cañete through the Valle Cayucupil (Ruta P-560).

CARAHUÉ

Area code: 045
Population: 8900
Altitude: 50 m
Distance from Temuco: 55 km west on Ruta S-40, S- 30 and Panamericana

Carahué was founded as Imperial by Pedro de Valdivia in 1551. It commands an elevated position where the **Río Imperial** breaks through the coastal *cordillera,* near its junction with the **Río Damas**. It was the seat of the first Spanish bishop, Fray Antonio de San Miguel, a Franciscan who came in 1576. Carahué means "where a town was before". The settlement was abandoned in 1599 during the big Mapuche revolt and was not established again until 1882 when it became a port on the Río Imperial.

The main part of town is located on a hill facing south and beautiful old houses that used to belong to the merchants line the riverfront. From the town, Ruta S-40 descends steeply to the river, where it crosses a distinctive hanging bridge.

Accommodation and other services are also available in **Trovolhué**, 20 km north-west — see "Excursions" below.

🎎 Festivals

Festivals in Trovolhué
- January (last week): Semana Trovolhuina

ℹ️ Tourist information

- Municipalidad de Carahué, Salón Cultural, Manuel Montt corner of Villagrán

🛏️ Accommodation

- Hotel Centenarío, Almagro 12 ☎ 651752. Includes restaurant
- Residencial Estrella, Almagro 58 ☎ 651702
- Residencial Oásis, Caupolicán 203 ☎ 651775. Includes restaurant

Accommodation in Trovolhué
- Residencial Salgado. Includes restaurant

🍴 Eating out

Restaurants
- El Bosque, Villagrán 228
- El Rehué, Villagrán corner of Portales
- Pedro de Valdivia, Pedro de Valdivia 265

Café
- Café Antu, Villagrán 274

📮 Post and telegraph

Telephone
- CTC, Lautaro 360, fax (45) 651200

🚌 Buses

- Puerto Domínguez: Power, ACA
- Puerto Saavedra: Power, Narbus
- Santiago: Fare $14.60; Ettabus, A153 Tur-Bus Jedimar, Power
- Temuco: Departs 0730–2030; 17 services; Narbus, Las Colinas

🚗 Motoring

There is a COPEC gas station.

✈️ Excursions

- **Puerto Domínguez**: A well laid out Mapuche village 27 km south on **Lago Budi**, a coastal lake of brackish water. The trip from Carahué involves a ferry crossing over the Estero Comúe just before arriving at Puerto Domínguez. From the small harbor, fishing boats ply the lake, catching a particular tasty fish. There are ferries to isolated Mapuche villages and tourist boats to the small Mapuche community on **Isla**

Nahuelhuapi, an island within the lake. The lake is home to many species of marine birds, among them black-necked swans. Buses ACA runs four services daily from Temuco via Cara-hué. This is unknown Chile. From Puerto Domínguez, irregular transport to **Teodoro Schmidt** passes villages where you can still see *rucas* — Mapuche homes. It is also possible to cross the **Río Toltén** on a ferry near **Hualpin**, and continue to **Nueva Toltén**. From Nueva Toltén, buses run to Temuco via Freire or south to Valdivia via Queule and Mehuín.

• **Trovolhué**: 20 km north-west, in a fairly flat part of the **Río Moncul** valley at the southern end of the **Cordillera de Nahuelbuta**. It is the starting point for fishing or photographic excursions and visits to smaller Mapuche settlements in the southern spurs of the Cordillera de Nahuelbuta. Adventurers may want to retrace the colonial coastal road north to **Tirúa** — the single Spanish lifeline between Valdivia and the area north of the Río Bío Bío left open by the Mapuche. This is unknown Chile in its truest sense. Buses Ruta Imperial go to Carahué, Nueva Imperial, and Temuco.

• **Lobería**: 23 km west on the coast. From Carahué, Buses Ruta Imperial run services along the dirt road to Pullangui. From Pullangui, it is another 14 km and a ferry crossing to Lobería where there is a nice clean beach frequented by few people other than villagers. Seals inhabit the rocks offshore. Despite the lack of facilities, this is an idyllic spot for campers and outdoor enthusiasts.

• **Villa La Araucaria**: This Mapuche village 21 km north lies on a dirt road in the southern spurs of the Nahuelbuta range. It is difficult to reach because only a few buses go there per week. The area is still covered with *araucarias* — some trees are more than 500 years old.

COLLIPULLI

Population: 11 000
Altitude: 180m
Distance from Temuco: 96 km north on Panamericana (RN 5)

Collipulli, founded in 1867, is located on the **Río Malleco** where three bridges span the river. It is an important crossroads: a major road leading north west to Angol and further on to Concepción branches off the Panamericana and a rail junction. A great photo can be taken from the new road bridge. Here, the Río Malleco has cut its way through the mountain in a deep gorge: the railroad bridge, constructed in 1891, is 102 m high and 350 m long. The new road bridge is 85 m high and 310 m long.

Accommodation
• Hotel Savoy, General Cruz 35 FGHIJN (811038
• Hostería El Vertiente, at the intersection of RN 182 with the Panamericana

Eating out
• Hostería El Volante, on the Panamericana

Buses
The bus terminal is on the main plaza. Buses Aguilera, Buses Bío Bío, Buses Igi Llaima, Buses Lit, Buses Fénix Pullman Norte, Buses Tur-Bus Jedimar, and Buses Unión del Sur make scheduled stops. There are connections north to Santiago and intermediate destinations and south to Puerto Montt, Temuco, Valdivia, and intermediate destinations; and connec-

tions west to Angol, Purén, Cañete, and Concepción.

🚗 Motoring

There is a COPEC gas station on the Panamericana at the turnoff to Angol.

CURACAUTÍN

Population: 12 500
Altitude: 420m
Area code: LD 108
Distance from Temuco: 84 km north-east on Ruta S-11-R and Panamericana via Lautaro

Curacautín is located on the **Río Blanco** near the junction with the Río Cautín. Although the town itself has little tourist interest, it is well placed for visits to **Parque Nacional Tolhuaca**, **Parque Nacional Conguillio-Las Paraguas**, **Termas de Manzanar** further up the valley, **Volcán Lonquimay**, and the town of **Lonquimay**. The best access is from Temuco or from Victoria on the Panamericana. Regular bus services run along the international highway through **Paso de Pino Hachado** to Zapala and Neuquén in Argentina.

This area was an important food-gathering district for Mapuche Indians due to the abundance of *araucarias* — much of this original tree cover has since disappeared. The Chilean army arrived in 1880 and established a fort two years later. The township was founded in 1894.

Volcán Llaima is clearly visible to the south from Curacautín.

There are three thermal spas within easy reach:

- **Termas de Tolhuaca**: 34 km north in Parque Nacional Tolhuaca with tourist facilities. See the entry for the park on page 600.
- **Termas de Manzanar**: 17 km east on Ruta R-89 with tourist facilities — see Manzanar under "Excursions" below.
- **Termas Río Blanco Curacautín**: 38 km south-east towards Parque Nacional Conguillio-Las Paraguas; no tourist facilities.

🛈 Tourist information

- Oficina de Turismo, Rodríguez near bus terminal, open only in tourist season
- Municipalidad de Curacautín. Fishing licenses

🛏 Accommodation

Hotels
- Plaza, Yungay 157 **AEFGHIJKPS$V** (881256 $G **i**. 40 rooms
- Posada Real (formerly Posta del Esquiador), Calama 240 **AEFGPPSV** (88164 $I **ii**
- Residencial Rojas, Tarapacá 249 **F $J ii**. Shared bathroom, backpackers
- Turismo, Tarapacá 140 **AEFGHJMPV** (881116 $H **ii**. $I **ii** with shared bathroom

Accommodation in Manzanar
Manzanar is 22 km east on Ruta R-89.
★   Hotel Termas de Manzanar, turnoff south 4 km west of the village **AFGHIJLPRV** ((45) 881200 $F **i**. Full board, thermal swimming pool. The hotel is about 300 m walk from the main road and located directly on the Río Cautín overlooking the valley. 10 cabins, 97 beds. Visitors pay $5.00 for the use of thermal pool

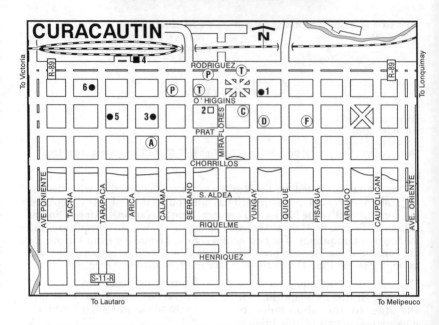

Key to map

A	Iglesia
C	Municipalidad (Town hall)
D	Post office and telex
E	Telephone
F	Carabineros (Police)
P	Gas stations
T	Bus terminals

● Accommodation

1	Hotel Plaza
3	Posada del Esquiador
5	Residencial Rojas
6	Hotel Turismo

□ Services

2	Supermercado Acuarella
4	Railroad station

- Hostería Abarzúa AEFHPUVZ ((45)870011 answering service $H ⁞⁞

Ⓐ Camping

There is a serviced camping site at Balneario Trahuilco, 2.5 km south-east on Ruta R-925-S past the cemetery on the banks of Río Blanco. At Manzanar there is Camping Salto de la Princesa, 4 km east of the village near the waterfall.

⑪ Eating out

- El Refugio, Serrano
- La Cabaña, O'Higgins 801
- Rucahuin, Serrano
- La Quintrala, Arica $Z. Chilean cuisine

⌨ Post and telegraph

Post office
- Correo and Telex Chile, Yungay block 200 near O'Higgins

Telephone
- CTC, Rodríguez 820. Fax (45) 881401

🚌 Buses

The bus terminal is on Rodríguez block 700 on the Plaza de Armas near the main road. Buses Fénix Pullman Norte, Buses Bío Bío, Buses Igi Llaima, Buses Tur-Bus Jedimar, Flota Erbuc, Buses Malleco, Buses García, and La Unión del Sud make scheduled stops. There are four services daily east to Manzanar, Malalcahuello, Lonquimay, and Liucura. Buses to Zapala and Neuquén in Argentina have a scheduled stop here. There are regular services north to Santiago and intermediate stops, south to Temuco, and west to Concepción. Buses depart between 0700 and 2100.

🚗 Motoring

For gas stations, see the city map.

⚽ Sport

Hiking and fishing.

📷 Excursions

- **Manzanar**: A small village, altitude 785 m, 22 km east. Its main attraction is the **Termas de Manzanar** with its thermal hotel, 18 km east of Curacautín. Manzanar is used in summer as a base for excursions to the slopes of **Volcán Lonquimay** and by skiing enthusiasts in winter. The ski area on Volcán Lonquimay is 22 km further east. **Salto del Indio**, a spectacular waterfall, is just 8 km west; a signpost on the main road indicates the half kilometer walk to the waterfall — well worth the detour! **Salto de la Princesa** is also within easy walking distance. The thermal resort has three different thermal sources, and the water ranges from 48° to 80°C (118° to 176°F). It is recommended for respiratory ailments, cardiac diseases, anaemia, hepatitis, mental fatigue, arthritis, and skin diseases. The water is collected in a concrete tank and distributed to the

cabins and the ten individual bathing huts. Flota Erbuc runs four services daily to Curacautín, Lonquimay, and Temuco.

- **Parque Nacional Tolhuaca:** 36 km north. CONAF controls this area, which offers excellent hiking in one of the best volcanic regions of Chile amidst huge *araucaria* trees. Take trout fishing gear for **Laguna Malleco**, but first obtain a permit from the CONAF rangers. The **Río Malleco** forms a spectacular 45 m waterfall. Inside the national park are thermal wells in a small cave; the water temperature is 90°C (194°F) — perfect for a steam bath. The hotel and thermal pool are open in summer only. A hike can also be made to Termas de Pemehué, which is still in its natural state. See the entry for the park on page 600.

- **Parque Nacional Conguillío-Las Paraguas**: 42 km south. Although it is possible to reach this national park from Curacautín, the best access is from **Melipeuco**. See the entry for the park on page 596.

- **Reserva Nacional Malalcahuello-Nalcas**, enclosing **Volcán Lonquimay** (also called Volcán Mocho) (43 000 ha or 106 210 acres): 22 km east, on the Lonquimay bus route. This area, where logging is still going on, is frequented by mountain hikers and skiers. See the entry for the reserve on page 616.

- **Termas Río Blanco Curacautín**: Located in the northern part of the **Sierra Nevada**, a 20 km hike from Curacautín. No facilities, but a splendid area for fishing and hiking.

- **Túnel Las Raíces**: 38 km east. A 4.5 km former railway tunnel through **Cordillera Las Raíces**, now used by vehicular traffic between Curacautín and Lonquimay. Toll payable.

LICÁN RAY

Area code: 045
Altitude: 200 m
Distance from Temuco: 108 km south-east on Ruta S-95-D, RN 119 and Panamericana (RN 5)

Licán Ray is a popular summer lakeside resort on the north side of **Lago Calafquén**. Some of the German-style houses are very modern. At present, the main street, General Urrutía, is the only sealed road. It has good facilities and good bus services to Villarrica, Panguipulli, and Termas de Liquiñe.

The lake, the northernmost of the so-called Siete Lagos ("Seven Lakes") district, provides sailing, swimming and fishing. This is a good starting point for trips to the south side of Volcán Villarrica and the lava streams from the last eruption.

Six kilometers outside town is a turnoff to the **Cuevas de Huincacara**, a series of caves created by lava flows.

At Licán Ray the sealed road from **Villarrica** becomes gravel. The road further west towards **Coñaripe** hugs the banks of the river, except for a stretch from **Quebrada Chaillupén** onwards. Here the road had to be completely reconstructed due to the extensive damage by the last lava flow.

ⓘ Tourist information
• Municipal tourist information at the kiosk on General Urrutía block 300 on the plaza

Ⓐ Camping
There are excellent camping sites on the road to Coñaripe (Ruta S-95-T) and along the road to Panguipulli.

⑪ Eating out

Restaurants
• Atedzet, General Urrutía block 300 opposite the plaza

Key to map

A	Iglesia	**15**	Cabañas Lican Ray
C	Municipalidad (Town hall)	**17**	Cabañas Rucamac
D	Post office and telex	**18**	Cabañas Köhler
E	Telephone	**19**	Cabañas Foresta
F	Carabineros (Police)		
I	Tourist information	○	**Eating out**
P	Gas stations	**4**	Café Las Velitas
T	Bus terminals	**5**	Restaurant La Parrilla de los Brujos
		6	Cafetería
●	**Accommodation**	**11**	Restaurant Atedzet
1	Cabañas El Conquistador	**12**	Restaurant Donde El Picador
2	Hotel Refugio	**16**	Restaurant Naños
3	Cabañas Duhato		
7	Cabañas Melipal	□	**Services**
9	Hospedaje	**8**	Boat hire
13	Hotel Bellavista	**10**	Supermercado Plaza
14	Hostería Victor's Playa		

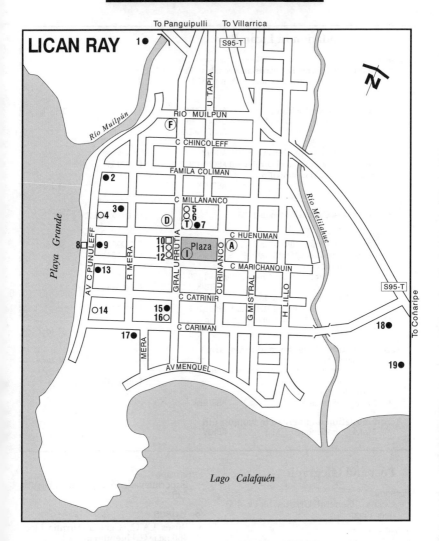

LICAN RAY

- Donde El Picador, General Urrutía block 300 opposite the plaza
- La Parrilla de los Brújos, General Urrutía block 400, near Cacique Millanco

Cafés
- Las Velitas, Avenida Cacique Punulef between Cacique Millaneco and Cacique Huenuman
- Ñaños, General Urrutía block 100 corner of C. Cariman

⊟ Accommodation in Licán Ray

Hotels
- Rucalafquén (formerly Bellavista), Avenida C. Punulef 240
- Refugio Inaltulafquén, Avenida C. Punulef 510   (212127

Motels
- El Canelo, Machi Cañicul 30   ABCHLPUV $H
- El Conquistador, Cacique Millaqueo/Urbano Tapia 505
       ABCEFHKLNR   (237569
  Tennis, mini-golf
- El Tolen, Familia Huenuman 105   AHPVX
- La Flor del Lago, General Urrutia 960   ABCHIPUV   (242135
- Rucamac, Las Araucarias 025
       ABCHLN $F for 6

Hospedaje
- Los Nietos, Cacique F Manquel 125   ((09) 4531227

Cabañas
- Duhatao, Cacique Millañanco 8   ABCH   (212358 $E for 4
- Foresta, Pineda del Mar 01760   (211954
  Also camping area
- Hostería Victor's Playa, Avenida C. Punulef 120
       AEFGHK   (247335
- Lican Ray, General Urrutia 135
  Reservations in Valdivia: Letelier 236, office 104   (212228
- Melipal, Cacique Huenuman opposite main plaza
- Ruca Rayen $F for 6

Accommodation along the road to Coñaripe
- Calafquén, KM 7 $F for 6
  70 camping spots, electricity, gas, hot water, kiosk
- Köhler, KM 1   ((09) 4530890
  Access to Lago Calafquén
- Motel Anchimallin, KM 1   ABCHLNV

Accommodation on the road to Panguipulli
- Motel Quimelauquen, KM 3   ABHJV

▥ Post and telegraph

Post office
- Correo, General Urrutía block 400 near Plaza

Telephone
- CTC, C. Huenuman corner of General Urrutía

▤ Services and facilities

Boat hire
- Private house, Avenida C. Punulef on lake between Cacique Huenuman and Cacique Marichanquin

Supermarket
- Supermercado Plaza, General Urrutía 325

⊟ Buses
- Buses J.A.C., General Urrutia block 400 near C. Huenuman
- Panguipulli: 2 services Mon–Sat; Rural Andes, Urrutia, Abarzúa
- Santiago: Fare $16.70; 3 services; Buses J.A.C., Tur-Bus Jedimar, Power
- Temuco: Fare $2.10; departs 0715–1615; 12 services; Buses J.A.C., García

- Villarrica: Fare $0.60; 12 services; duration 1 hr; Buses J.A.C., Estrella del sur, García

🚌 Motoring

- COPEC gas station

☀ Excursions

Tour operators
- Aventuras Lonquimay, General Urrutía 301. Rafting on Río Liquiñe

Excursions
Regular bus services to Villarrica and Termas de Liquiñe have helped to establish this little village as a tourist center. Boating, sailing and fishing on the lake, and access to the south side of Parque Nacional Villarrica and the volcano which dominates the town are further benefits.

LONQUIMAY

Population: 2800
Altitude: 900 m
Distance from Curacautín: 59 km east on Ruta R-89.

Lonquimay is a small village on the **Río Lonquimay** near its junction with the **Río Bío Bío**. It is the starting point for rafting excursions on the latter. Volcanoes loom on the western horizon.

Lonquimay was founded as a fort in 1882. The layout of the present-day village is an unusual oval shape around an oval main plaza. There are many Mapuche villages and *araucaria* trees in the neighborhood. People still pan for gold in the local rivers. Further south is the source of the Río Bío Bío — Chile's grand river of destiny.

Hikers use Lonquimay as a base for walks in the upper Río Bío Bío area. A hanging bridge crosses the wild deep gorge at **Lolen**, 14 km east of town. Many ferry services also cross the river. A modern bridge now spans the Río Bío Bío at **Tucapel**, 35 km south on Ruta R-89 to Argentina via **Paso de Pino Hachado**.

🏃 Festivals

- January 20: Fiesta de San Sebastián

ℹ Tourist information

- Municipal tourist office

🛏 Accommodation

- Hostería El Pehuén, B. O'Higgins 945 P (891071 $G ⅱ. Full board, 21 beds
- Hotel de Turismo Lonquimay, Caupolicán 926 $J ⅱ. Shared bathroom, 28 beds
- Pensión El Viajero, Colón 970 $J ⅱ. Shared bathroom, 9 beds
- Posada Las Araucarias, Colón 860 S $J ⅰ. Shared bathroom, 16 beds
- Residencial El Valle, J.M.Balmaceda 949 $J ⅰ. Shared bathroom, 6 beds

Accommodation in Liucura
Liucura is 55 km south-east.
- Cabañas Rucañanco, 5 km west of village (Curacautín (045) 881113

🍴 Eating out

- El Arriero $Z. Chilean cuisine
- Café El Rincón de Juancho, Ignacio Carrera Pinto
- Bar Restaurant El Chaparral, Ignacio Carrera Pinto 650

🏛 Services and facilities

Supermarket
- Supermercado Gigante, I. Carrera Pinto corner of Lautaro

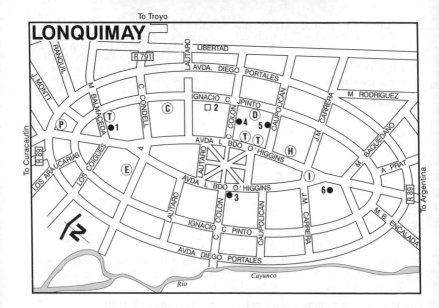

Key to map

C   Municipalidad (Town hall)
D   Post office and telex
E   Telephone
F   Carabineros (Police)
H   Hospital
I   Tourist information
P   Gas stations
T   Bus terminals

●   **Accommodation**
1   Residencial Valle
3   Posada de las Araucarias
4   Pensión El Viajero
5   Hotel Turismo Lonquimay
6   Hostería Pehuén

□   **Services**
2   Supermercado Gigante

⊠ Border crossings

Lonquimay has a passport control point for travelers into Argentina. The border is open between 0830 and 1630.

🚌 Buses

Note that rural buses to remote villages such as Troyo, Pedregoso, Icalma, and Liucura depart between 1600 and 1830; these are destinations for outdoor travelers who carry their own tent and sleeping bag; usually there is no accommodation in those remote villages. To Icalma and Troyo services run only on Mon, Wed, and Fri, returning the following day. There are four services daily to Curacautín, Lautaro, Victoria, and Temuco.

• Flota Erbuc, Avenida B. O'Higgins 1110 ☎ 841069

🚗 Motoring

• COPEC gas station at entrance to town

⊛ Sport

At the moment, river rafting is a popular sport on the upper reaches of the Río Bío Bío. Construction of the El Pangue hydroelectric power station in the middle section of this mighty river has not curtailed rafting activities.

Trout fishing: see page 579.

📷 Sightseeing

Many hanging bridges span the upper reaches of the Río Bío Bío, which forms a wild river between narrow canyons cascading down over the rocks.

🛈 Excursions

*   **Lagunas Gualletué** and **Icalma**: 75 km south. Visit the source of the Río Bío Bío, and return to Temuco via **Cunco** on Ruta S-61. The landscape is unspectacular as far as **Icalma** — the high mountains in the form of volcanoes

are further west. The more interesting route is via **La Fusta**. Turn off in the upper Río Lonquimay valley, just before entering the Túnel Las Raices. Laguna Icalma is surrounded by *araucaria* forests and has gray sandy beaches. It is 5 km off Ruta R-89 and has good trout fishing.

*   **Liucura:** 55 km south-east on Ruta R-89. Located in the shade of Cerro Bayo (2240 m), it is important only as a passport control point. The border is open all year from 0830 to 1700. Buses run between Temuco and Neuquén in Argentina. Paso de Pino Hachado forming the border is 22 km west

---

MELIPEUCO

Population: 1600
Altitude: 400 m
Distance from Temuco: 115 km east on Ruta S-61 and Panamericana (RN 5)

Melipeuco is located in the **Río Tracura** valley, and is the starting point for many exciting hikes into the nearby national parks and lesser-known parts of the southern mountains. The many uncharted thermal wells indicate that the whole area is still volcanically active.

🛈 Tourist information

*   CONAF office in Melipeuco for fishing licenses

🛏 Accommodation

The Municipalidad acting as tourist information office has a list of private accommodation.

★★★ Hostería Huetelén, Pedro Aguirre Cerda 1 **AFHKLPR$UVZ** $G cabins for 5. Boat hire, camping area, home-cooking

🅰 Camping

There are camping sites on Laguna Verde in Parque Nacional Conguillio-Las Paraguas, 24 km north; at Laguna Icalma 34 km east; and at Laguna Gualletué.

🍴 Eating out

*   Hostería Huetelen $Y

🗺 Border crossing

The border crossing is in the village of Icalma, 34 km east of Melipeuco. Open 0830–1630 in summer.

🚌 Buses

*   Temuco: Fare $2.10; Huinca, Narbus, Buses J.A.C.

🛈 Excursions

The valleys and national parks are still not too badly denuded of natural forest cover which gives shelter to *pudú, monito del monte* (nocturnal marsupial), foxes, *vizcachas*, and the occasional puma. Birdlife is represented by *torcazas,* wild ducks, and condors. Fishing is good in many streams. Many Mapuche families live in the valleys, more in harmony with nature than other human inhabitants.

*   **Icalma:** 34 km east, on the east side of **Laguna Icalma**, at an altitude of 1153 m. This is an area for outdoor enthusiasts and anglers. Boat hire is

opposite the *carabineros* post, and basic supplies are available from the grocery shop; local people sell milk, eggs, and cheese. **Paso de Icalma** 3 km further east at an altitude of 1298 m forms the border with Argentina. The pass is closed in winter; Flota Erbuc runs daily to Temuco via Melipeuco and Cunco; there are also bus services to Lonquimay and Curacautín; services are reduced in winter.

• **Nevados de Sollipulli**: 28 km south. Follow Ruta S-61 for 6 km west and then turn south at the intersection into the Río Alpehué valley which leads to snow-capped mountains. The highest elevation is around 2200 m. A remote trail leads through open *araucaria* forests. Other native trees include *ñires* and *coigues*.

• **Parque Nacional Conguillio-Las Paraguas** (60 832 ha or 150 255 acres): 25 km north of Melipeuco. It surrounds **Volcán Llaima** and is the principal reason for coming to Melipeuco. See the entry for the park below.

• **Reserva Forestal China Muerta**: 16 km east on Ruta S-61 towards Laguna Icalma. This reserve protects more *araucaria* forests. See "National parks and reserves" on page 577.

• **Termas de Huechulepún**: Approximately 26 km east. These springs are off Ruta S-61 in the upper reaches of the **Río Curilafquen**, a tributary of the Río Zahuelhué in the **Cordillera Llancahué**. The Río Curilafquen runs through swampy ground for some distance after it joins the Río Tracura, so stay on the road. This is remote territory for hikers who wish to hike in the Nevados de Sollipulli.

• **Termas de Molulco**. Halfway between Cunco and Melipeuco a dirt road branches south and leads up to a small village. Native forest of *araucarias*, *ñires*, *coigues*, and filberts covers a large part of this area, which is an easy walk from Melipeuco. No facilities near the springs. This is remote territory for hikers.

PARQUE NACIONAL
CONGUILLIO–LAS PARAGUAS

Distances
• From Temuco (via Melipeuco): 126 km east on Panamericana and Ruta S-61
• From Temuco (via Vilcún): 86 km east on Ruta S-31 and Panamericana
• From Victoria: 116 km east on Ruta R-89 to Curacautín, and from there south to Laguna Conguillio
Admission: $3.00

This national park, covering 60 832 ha (150 255 acres), is one of the most scenic national parks in Chile. It lies roughly between **Río Allipen** in the south, **Río Cautín** in the north, and **Sierra Nevada** in the north-east. It contains **Volcán Llaima** (3125 m), **Laguna Conguillio**, **Laguna Quililo**, and **Laguna Captren**, and now also incorporates Parque Nacional Los Paraguas on the southern side of Laguna Conguillio.

Volcán Llaima, snow-capped all year, is the principal attraction. Its slopes are covered with dense *araucaria* forest almost to the snowline, many specimens more than a thousand years old; and in winter, the slopes on the west side are used for skiing — the skiing season runs from the end of May to November. Its slopes, particularly the eastern and south-eastern parts, are covered in lava from recent eruptions. **Laguna Conguillio** is wedged between the **Sierra Nevada** and Volcán Llaima. **Laguna Verde**, as emerald as its name, is stocked with trout. The area, which is full of volcanic rock and lava flows, is also rich in prehistoric fossils. The submerged trees in **Laguna Captren** and **Laguna Arco Iris** show that these lakes formed only 80 years ago, resulting from lava damming the river after a volcanic eruption.

Araucaria trees predominate, but there are also limbers, oaks, filberts, and *arrayanes*. You may see hawks, foxes, and Chilean otters (*coipos*); the odd puma is still around.

Laguna Conguillio, between the Sierra Nevada and the slopes of Volcán Llaima, is an angling paradise — the park rangers issue fishing permits. More secluded are **Laguna Captren**, especially good for *arco iris*, and **Laguna Verde**.

The entrance is accessible from Curacautín, 44 km north-east, or from Melipeuco, 29 km south. A dirt road (S-339) from Curacautín follows the **Río Captren** to its exit from **Laguna Captren**, and links up with Ruta S-61 about 4 km east of Melipeuco. It takes three hours to the park by car from Temuco via Melipeuco.

The southern approach, approximately 100 km east of Temuco, is mostly along dirt roads via Cunco and Melipeuco. The northern approach from Temuco via Lautaro and Curacautín (141 km) is sealed as far as Lautaro altogether 30 km. The Río Captren entrance is an 18 km walk from Curacautín. If you have your own vehicle, do the round-trip, which takes you through one of the most beautiful and varied landscapes in Chile. The western ap-

proach via **Vilcún** and **Cherquenco** is 54 km along Ruta S-31 and ends at the snowfields near Refugio Llaima. The road is sealed as far as San Patricio — 45 of the 77 kilometres. It is a two-and-a-half hour drive to the mountain hut. Public transport runs from Temuco to Melipeuco and along Ruta S-61 to the southern entrance.

Most of the park's tourist facilities are near Lake Conguillio, and include picnic grounds, camping areas, cabins, a *hostería*, and the CONAF visitors' center. It offers excursion paths, an information center, a restaurant, a shop; on the west side there is a ski lift, a ski resort, and a lookout.

The park's average summer temperature is 15°C (59°F); November to March are the best months to visit. In winter, the temperature averages 2°C (36°F). Winter snowfalls may be more than two meters deep. It is advisable to bring warm gear all year round, as the weather can change very quickly.

ⓘ Tourist information

First-hand information and CONAF maps can be obtained in Temuco (see "Tourist information" in Temuco on page 618). There is a *guardaparque* hut at the southern entrance (approaching from Melipeuco), near the turnoff to Salto Truful Truful. The northern entrance *guardaparque* (approaching from Curacautín) is near Lago Captren. During the main tourist season (December to the end of February), CONAF staff run conducted tours along seven walking trails. There are six camping areas totalling 96 camping spots and eight cabins.

✉ Accommodation

Accommodation along the road from Curacautín to the park
★★★★ Cabañas Río Colorado, KM 22
  ℂ (02) 274884

Accommodation inside the park

• **Hostería Los Ñires**, southern end of Lago Conguillio near CONAF administration ABEFGHJPV $F for 6. 8 cabins. Reservations in Temuco: CONAF, Bilbao 931 (234420

Accommodation at the snowfields

• Refugio Escuela Esqui Volcán Llaima, Sector Paraguas AFHJ. Ski hire, ski school. Reservations in Temuco: Avenida Alemania 851 (236951; or Sra Mónica Mora/Sra Nana (235193 at Shell gas station, Temuco.

Ⓐ Camping

There are camping sites by Laguna Captren and by Laguna Conguillio.

Ⓘ Eating out

• Hostería Los Ñires on Laguna Conguillio

Ⓡ Services and facilities

During the summer vacation, there is a kiosk open near the CONAF center. Basic supplies are available.

Ⓑ Buses

There are no direct buses. The best access to the southern entrance is by bus from Temuco to Melipeuco. Walk from there. The western approach to Refugio Llaima is by bus via Cherquenco. In winter, a skiers' bus runs from Temuco.
Seasoned walkers could try the northern approach from the Río Cautín Valley, by taking the Lonquimay bus, and asking the driver to set them down at the Hacienda Manchuria turnoff. Then walk up the Río Nanco valley to **Termas Río Blanco Curacautín** (no facilities) or continue further south to Lago Conguillio. Despite its lack of facilities, **Termas Río Blanco Curacautín**, is a worthwhile destination. If starting your hike from Manzanar or Termas de Manzanar best crossing the Río Cautín is at Salto de la Gloria 2 km east. Ask the locals to direct you to the trail leading down to Estero Nanco and follow it upstream. Take a south-easterly direction towards the Sierra Nevada. Instituto Geográfico Militar 1:50000 maps: Malalcahuello and Llaima.

Ⓢ Sport

Skiing on Volcán Llaima

The western slopes of Volcán Llaima (1750 m) are approached from Temuco on Ruta S-31 and Panamericana via Vilcún. The gravel road goes through thousand-year-old *araucaria* forests. The tourist facilities consist of a mountain *refugio* with 40 beds (shared bedrooms) and full board. The ski season is from June to October.
A new skiing area has opened up with the installation of a T-bar lift. The older section has four more ski lifts.

Ⓔ Excursions

This is an outdoor enthusiast's paradise, and the snow-capped **Volcán Llaima** is suitable for skiing in winter. Summer offers hikes through *araucaria* forest and beside idyllic lakes with fishing and boating.

PARQUE NACIONAL HUERQUEHUÉ

Distance from Pucón: 36 km north-east
Admission: $1.50

P arque Nacional Huerquehué covers 12 500 ha (30 875 acres), and its altitude ranges from 720 m to 2000 m. It is bounded in the west by Lago Caburga and to the south by the **Río Liucura** valley.

Although the mountains are not very high, it is a wild area with steep slopes rising from lakes and *lagunas*, such as Caburga, Tinquilco, Verde, and Toro, where *araucarias, lengas,* oaks, Chilean limber trees (*rauli*), and *coigues* grow. These trees attract varied birdlife, and pumas and foxes stalk at ground level. The lakes, fed by mountain streams, are full of fish, especially trout — fishing is permitted in the appropriate seasons.

Altogether the park has more than twenty small lakes and two thermal springs within its uneven terrain. One side falls abruptly to **Lago Caburga,** famous for its clear waters. **Lago Tinquilco** is renowned for trout fishing; *arco iris* trout caught may weigh up to four kilos. No motor boats are allowed. Most of the lakes and *lagunas* in the neighborhood have been formed by volcanic activity or dammed by volcanic debris. Many are fed by underground streams and also have subterranean outlets. The valleys are very deeply cut with steep sides. Water cascades directly into the lakes from high altitudes. This is a scenically spectacular place, and one hopes that the national park will be enlarged to stop advancing civilization.

Salto Nido del Agua is a spectacular waterfall located at the north side of Lago Tinquilco.

A visit to this national park is usually combined with visits to **Termas de Huife** and **Termas de Quimey-Co** — see "Excursions" from Pucón on page 611 and 612.

CONAF has constructed excursion paths and conducts guided tours of the flora and fauna in the main tourist season. There are picnic grounds, an information center, a lookout, and camping areas.

The climate ranges from moderately warm to snow. January's average temperature is 17°C (63°F); July's is 7°C (45°F). Precipitation is 2045 mm per year and falls in winter as snow above 900 m. Ample moisture and the terrain have helped to create more than twenty lakes and lagunas inside the park.

The best time to visit is between December and March. Public transport runs frequently from Pucón (every half-hour), or from Villarrica. The drive from Pucón takes approximately an hour. Several travel agents run guided tours from Pucón. Budget travelers can use public transport from Pucón to Paillaco and also to Termas de Huife (see "Buses" from Pucón on page 609). The first 8 km from Pucón to the intersection with Ruta S-905 are sealed; from there to Paillaco is a dirt road. Take warm clothing as, even in summer, the temperature may drop suddenly and rain is possible at any time. You can buy dairy produce and eggs from a farm at the entrance to the park.

◪ Accommodation

There is excellent accommodation, almost within walking distance at **Termas de Huife**, at Hostería Lilenes on the west side of Lago Caburga, and at Pucón.

◮ Camping

There is a camping site on the south side of Lago Tinquilco.
See also "Camping" in Pucón on page 604.

PARQUE NACIONAL TOLHUACA

Distance from Curacautín: 45 km north-east
Admission: $2.00

Parque Nacional Tolhuaca, covering 6380 ha (15 760 acres), fluctuates in altitude between 1000 m and 1821 m. It is in the *pre-Cordillera* within sight of the peaks of La Sombra, Colomahuida, and Loma. A 45-meter waterfall (Salto del Río Malleco) drops into **Laguna Malleco**. The dominant plants are coigues, ciprés de cordillera, and arrayanes. The fauna includes pudús, pumas, and chingues. CONAF has made several hiking trails, and there are many camping and picnic areas. Laguna Malleco offers good fishing and boat rides.

The scenic attractions are the **Salto del Río Malleco, Laguna Malleco, Cascada de la Culebra**, and **Laguna Verde**, which is particularly beautiful in its surroundings of ancient araucarias and lengas. The mountain scenery is dominated by **Volcán Tolhuaca**, 2806 meters and snow capped all year round. **Termas de Tolhuaca**, with its own picnic and camping area, excursion paths, and lookout, provides summer accommodation. This is another perfect outdoor environment.

The drive from Victoria on the Panamericana via Curacautín takes two hours. Ruta R-89 from Victoria is sealed for 56 km as far as Curacautín. Just before entering Curacautín take the intersection with Ruta R-755, a dirt road running 39 kilometers north beside the **Río Dillo** most of the way towards the park.

Summer temperatures average 15°C (59°F); winter temperatures average 2°C (36°F). The park is open all year round, but, again, bring warm clothing all through the year.

⊟ Accommodation

See also "Accommodation" in Curacautín (page 587) and Victoria (page 631).

- Hotel Termas de Tolhuaca, 35 km north of Curacautín, 5 km outside the national park AEFGHLPRV $F ⁑. Full board and thermal spa $G ⁑, shared bathroom. Open between November and April, 71 beds, mud baths. The hotel is located at 1020 m, and the thermal water fluctuates between 37° and 95°C (99° and 203°F). There are 10 bathing huts; The thermal spring gushes from a deep fissure, feeding three natural swimming pools (37°C or 99°F) downstream and forming the source of the Río Dillo. A cave nearby features mini-geysers for mud and steam baths. Open November–April. Reservations in Curacautín: Sr Fuad Chain S. ℂ 881211

⊟ Buses

The thermal hotel provides transport for guests and visitors. The best way to get there is by taxi from Curacautín — about an hour on a dirt road. In the main tourist season, CONAF organizes up to three excursions a week.

⊛ Sport

Tennis courts, mini-golf.

⬧ Excursions

The hotel arranges trips on horseback and picnics, complete with barbecues. From the hotel, enthusiastic anglers can walk the 4 km to Laguna Verde or the 9 km to Laguna Malleco, and cast a line for trout. The hotel has a minibus for pickups and for longer tours.

Parque Nacional Villarrica

Altitude: 1000 m–2840 m
Distance from Temuco: 121 km south-east on RN 119 and Panamericana
Admission: $2.00

Parque Nacional Villarrica (62 000 ha or 153 140 acres) extends in an east–west direction to the Argentine border and encircles three volcanoes: **Volcán Villarrica**, also called Rucapillán and last active in 1964, **Volcán Lanín** on the Argentine border, and **Volcán Quetrupillán**, known as the "Snorer". There are several thermal springs in the park, the most important being **Termas de Palguín**, with its own hotel complex.

Volcán Villarrica is an active volcano that is constantly changing the landscape. During the last eruption in 1964 most of the lava flowed down the southern slope in sector Challupén towards **Lago Calafquén**, where the road still detours as a result. In the season, many guides take daily excursions to the top of the volcano. This is an outstandingly beautiful area and should not be missed.

CONAF has constructed several hiking paths to the most scenic spots — the volcanic caves in Sector Challupén, and Azúl and Chinay lagunas. One recommended walk is to **Laguna El Toro.**

Further east near the border, the road from Complejo Fronterizo Puesco to the border is one of the highlights of this park — the mighty, almost perfect cone of Volcán Lanín dominates the landscape. Past the border post — and still in Chile — the road winds through original forest following the southern bank of Lago Quillelhué. The huge lake on the northern side of the road is Lago Tromen in Argentina; part of Argentina's Parque Nacional Lanín, its western banks are only a stone's throw from the road in Chile.

Flora includes *araucarias*, oaks, *coigues*, *raulí*, and *lengas*. The birdlife is particularly rich, and black-necked swans, eagles, and condors may be sighted. This is protected habitat for some of Chile's rarer animals — pumas and *coipos*.

The park is open all year round. Its facilities include excursion paths, picnic and camping areas, ski lifts, a ski resort, lookout, *refugios*, and accommodation, eating places, and shops nearby. It is most easily accessed from Pucón, 10 km north (see the entry for Pucón on page 603), but you can also get there from from Puesco on RN 119 near the Argentine border. RN 119 is passable from November to the end of April, but after that snow closes this pass. The northern slopes, near Pucón, offer the best skiing conditions between August and November. Summer visiting is best between November and April. CONAF's administrative headquarters are in Pucón — see "Tourist information" on page 603. Sector Quetrupillán, the southern section, can be reached via Coñaripe, but there are picnic areas only on the lower slopes.

ⓘ Tourist information

There are six camping areas linked by walking trails. Altogether, there are seven long-distance walking trails and it can take several days to do the circuit.

Ⓐ Camping

There is a camping area on Volcán Villarrica in Sector Rucapillán, about 5 km past the CONAF *guardería*. In Sector Los Cajones near Volcán Quetrupillán there is a camping site about 30 km east of Pucón and 10 km further up from Termas de Palguín.

⊛ Sport

Skiing on Volcán Villarrica

The ski area is called Sector Rucapillán. Snow reaches 2 m in winter. The ski season is from September to November. The nearest hotels to the ski slopes are at Pucón, on Lago Villarrica, and in the town of Villarrica itself — see "Accommodation" in Pucón (page 606) and Villarrica (page 638). Most people stay in Pucón, which has excellent facilities, and take shuttle buses to the ski lift station at 1400 m. There is a *cafetería* at the lift station which functions as a disco during winter. This is a fascinating combination of lakes, mountains, skiing, and nearby thermal resorts, with a very active night life in Pucón and Villarrica. Views from the top include Volcán Llaima, Volcán Lanín, and Volcán Lonquimay — you have to be there to believe how wonderful they are. The hotels in Pucón and Villarrica are in the higher price bracket, and so are many of the seashore hotels between Pucón and Villarrica. The latter are the cheaper alter-native for would-be skiers as they are not filled to capacity in winter and hotel owners provide transport to the ski base. Lift capacity is 6000 skiers per hour. A lift ticket costs $22.00; they are cheaper midweek.

The highest altitude is reached at 2440 m on the Piedra Negra run. Heli-skiing has been introduced for those with the inclination to descend from the very top — a 1400 m "schuss" or long ski run down the volcano! The helicopter circles the crater before setting passengers down — another unbeatable experience at $500.00 per hour for four. Equipment hire either in Pucón or at the base costs $18.00 per day.

Mountaineering

Volcán Villarrica is considered one of the easiest volcanoes to climb in Chile, but it is not without its dangers. The ascent can be made in a day using the ski-lift, which is operated all year round and goes very close to the top. During the summer, only one lift is in operation for mountain climbers.

⊕ Excursions

- **Volcán Villarrica**: An excursion to the crater takes about 10 hours. Many people take the lift uphill and descend on foot. Some tours start at 1000, returning from the crater at 1900 or 2000. The minimum charge is $15.00 per person.
- Mountaineers use **Puesco** as a base camp for climbing **Volcán Lanín** (3747 m). If you wish to do this climb, you must leave your passport with the CONAF personnel. Permission to scale Volcán Lanín is not given to people who are inadequately equipped or not thought fit enough to attempt this extremely difficult ascent.

Ski lifts on Volcán Villarrica

Name	Type	Length	Height difference
• Laima	T-bar	700 m	120 m
• Los Nires	double chair	870 m	150 m
• Correntoso	double chair	1000 m	235 m
• La Pirámide	T-bar	500 m	
• El Sable	double chair	1450 m	390 m
• Piedra Negra	T-bar	1530 m	505 m
• Enlace Capilla	T-bar	340 m	96 m

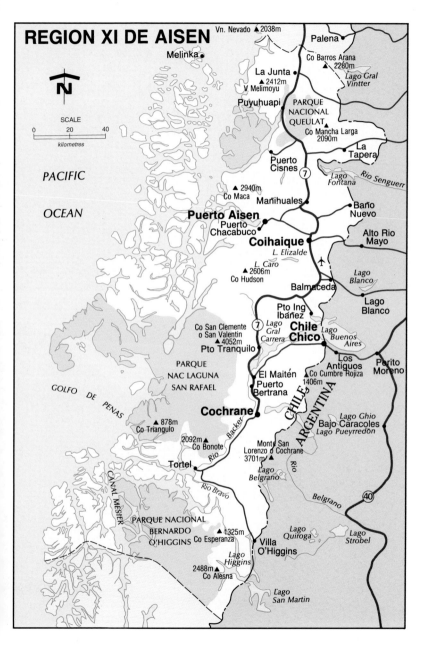

Plate 35
Map of Región XI de Aisén

Plate 36   Región XI de Aisén
Top: Puerto Chacabuco, ferry from Puerto Montt
Bottom: Puerto Aisén

PUCÓN

Area code: 045
Population: 7500
Altitude: 350 m
Distance from Temuco: 110 km south-east on RN 119 and RN 5

Pucón is located on the eastern end of **Lago Villarrica**, east of Villarrica, in the shadow of **Volcán Villarrica** — a picture-book landscape on the lake.
The settlement began in 1883 as a military fort for the Chilean Army. Expansion came when several German families settled **Llafenco** on the banks of the **Río Trancura** in 1904.

The area around Pucón is volcanically highly active, and a number of geothermal spas have been established within a radius of about 40 km of Pucón, with varying degrees of tourist facilities. They are described below under "Excursions", and their facilities are listed under "Accommodation", "Camping", and "Eating out". One of the larger hotels in Pucón draws its hot water from an underground spring.

All the mountains surrounding **Lago Caburga** are volcanoes.

At first, Pucón was the hub of the timber industry, shipping huge *araucaria* trees from La Poza across the lake, down the **Río Toltén** to the timber mills. Early in the 20th century, it became an anglers' paradise, which then encouraged the tourist industry.

The road from Pucón to the Panamericana is sealed all the way. It is now a popular and well-established tourist destination in both summer and winter and has excellent convention center facilities. The latest development includes the construction of condominiums near Hotel Pucón. Pucón is the ideal place for excursions to Lago Caburga, Parque Nacional Villarrica, Parque Nacional Huerquehué, and the many thermal resorts in the upper Río Pucón valley and its tributaries, such as **Termas de Huife**, **Termas de Palguín**, and **Termas de San Luís**.

Pucón is also a popular ski resort. Information on skiing facilities is given below under "Sport". The season is roughly divided into three, and accommodation prices reflect this:

- Low season: From June to the first week in July; and from the fourth week in October to the end of November.
- Shoulder season: From the second week in July to the first week in August; from the fourth week in August to the first week in September; and from the fourth week in September to the third week in October.
- High season: The second and third week in August; and the second and third week in September.

⌧ Tourist information

- Información Turística Municipal, Lincoyán block 500 corner of Brasil. The kiosk is in the park
- CONAF, Lincoyán 372 (441261. Information and maps about walks in all national parks in the vicinity also hiking information about Sector Quetrupillán

LA ARAUCANIA

Key to map

A Iglesia
C Municipalidad (Town hall)
D Post office and telex
E Telephone
H Hospital
I Tourist information
P Gas stations
$ Money exchange
T Bus terminals

● **Accommodation**
3 Hotel Pucón
4 Hostería Los Tilos
7 Hotel Gudenschwager
8 Hotel La Posada
9 Hotel Casablanca
10 Hotel Araucarias
11 Motel Lenumantú
12 Hospedaje
14 Hospedaje/restaurant
17 Cabañas Las Palmeras
18 Hostería Don Pepe
19 Hospedaje
21 Hostería Suiza
28 Hospedaje
30 Hotel El Principito
32 Hostería Millarahue
37 Hospedaje Sonia
38 Hospedaje
42 Hotel Salzburg
47 Hospedaje
49 Motel Interlaken

○ **Eating out**
6 Restaurant Pucón
15 Restaurante Vegetariano
16 Restaurant Palette
22 Restaurant 24000
24 Restaurant El Refugio
26 Pub Naf Naf
27 Restaurant Le Grimago
33 Restaurant El Fogón
34 Restaurant El Amigo
36 Restaurant Caburgua
40 Snack Naturista
41 Restaurant Brasil
43 Restaurant Pancakes
44 Restaurant ATC
45 Restaurant La Cabañita
46 Pizzería Che Tomás

△ **Tour operators and car rental**
13 Hertz Rent a Car
23 Turismo Sol y Nieve

□ **Services**
1 Boat hire
2 Heliport
5 Holzapfel bakery
20 Laundry
25 CONAF
29 Kodak films
31 Farmacia Werner
35 Sports equipment
39 Artesanías
48 Supermarket

- Municipalidad de Pucón. Fishing licenses

▲ Camping

In Pucón itself there is a serviced camping site on Playa Grande, 500 m east of Ansorena. On the road along to Villarrica there are several excellent camping sites. On Lago Caburga there are camping sites in Sector Playa Negra and in Sector Playa Blanca. In Puesco there is a CONAF administered camping site, adjacent to the border control, 80 km east of Pucón. There is also camping in Termas de Quimey-Co.

⊞ Eating out ☞

- Café Restaurant El Amigo, General Urrutía 401
- Cafetería Hanga Roa, Ansorena near Otto Gudenschwager Playa Grande

- Fast Food Pollo Nostro, Palguín 301. Chicken
- Pizzería Che Tomás, Palguín 465

Restaurants
- ATC, Avenida B. O'Higgins 473
- Brasil, Avenida Brasil 302 corner of Fresia 477. International cuisine; trout a specialty
- Caburga, Arauco 336 $Z
- El Altillo, Caupolicán 243
- El Aperitivo (in Hotel Principito), Fresia 399
- El Conventillo (in Hotel Araucarias), Caupolicán 243
- El Fogón, Avenida B. O'Higgins 480
- El Grimago, Lincoyán 361
- El Refugio, Lincoyán 348. Lebanese cuisine
- La Cabañita, Palguín 498
- La Marmita de Pericles, Fresia 302 $X ☞

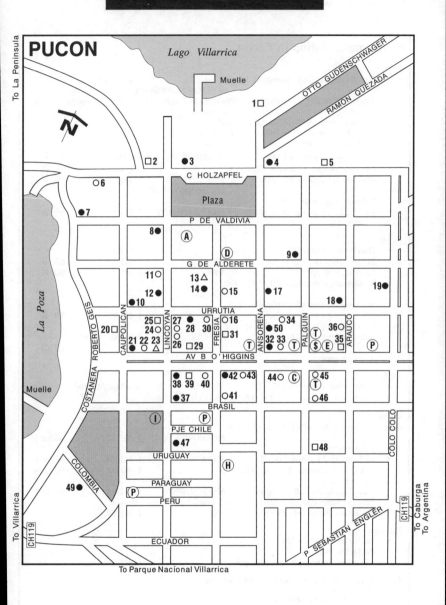

LA ARAUCANIA

✉ Accommodation in Pucón

Hotels

★★★★★Gran Hotel Pucón, Clemente Holzapfel 190   ✆ 441001/2/3
                                           ACDEFGHIJKLMNPS$UVX

     Sauna, 150 rooms. The following prices include 7 days' lodging with full board, lift tickets, transport to base, and one day's ski school.
     Low season: $650.00–$870.00 ♚♚ per week
     Shoulder season: $1020.00–$1400.00 ♚♚ per week
     High season: $1500.00–$1860.00 ♚♚ per week

★★★ Araucarias, Caupolicán 243   AFGHIJKLPSUV   ✆ 441286 $E ♚♚
- Gudenschwager, Pedro de Valdivia 12   ✆ 441156 $F ♚♚
- Interlaken, Caupolicán corner of Colombia   ✆ 441276 $D ♚♚
                                           ACDEHILMNPR$TUVZ
     Lake frontage, golf, boat hire
- La Posada, Pedro de Valdivia 191   ABCEFGHIJKLPUVY   ✆ 441088 $F ♚♚
     Near beach

Hosterías

- Don Pepe, Urrutia 598   ✆ 441081
- El Principito, General Urrutia 299   AEFHIJLPSV   ✆ 441200 $G ♚♚
- La Poza, Holzapfel 11   AHPS   ✆ 441320 $G ♚♚
- Millarahue, Avenida B. O'Higgins 460
                                  AEFHISV   ✆ 441179 $I ♚
- Salzburg, Avenida B. O'Higgins 311
                                  AEFHS   ✆ 441907 $H ♚♚
     Open January–March, German spoken
- Suiza, Avenida B. O'Higgins 112   AEFHIJLV   ✆ 441907/441945
                                                $H ♚♚
     German spoken

Motels

- Lemunantú, Lincoyán 235   ABCEIPUV   ✆ 441136/441106
- O'Higgins (formerly Turista), Avenida B. O'Higgins 136

Cabañas

★★★★El Dorado, Avenida B. O'Higgins 1640
                                  ABCDHLNPR$ ✆ 441122 $E for 4
     Lake frontage
- La Palmera, M. Ansorena 221   ADPUV   ✆ 441083 $F for 4
- Los Tilos, Clemente Holzapfel 412   BP   ✆ 441112 $C for 4
     Open all year
- Mapulay, Avenida B. O'Higgins 755   ABCDHIKLNPRV   ✆ 441948 $D for 4
     Tennis, sauna, lake frontage, fax 441914, English and French spoken
- Rucatraro, Pasaje Iribarren 010   ABDH   ✆ 441858

Residenciales

- Lincoyán, Lincoyán 323
     Backpackers
- Vienatur, Ansorena 95 opposite plaza   ✆ 441217

Hospedajes for backpackers and budget travelers
- Arauco 460
- Lincoyán 260, 445, 485, 551
- B. O'Higgins 473
- Colo Colo 224

Accommodation in Pucón — continued

- Fresia 260
  Includes restaurant
- General Urrutia 283

Apart Hotels
- Puerta del Lago, M. Ansorena 343   ABDHUV   ☏ 441918
  Fax 411238, apartments for 4

Accommodation on RN 119 to Paso Mamuil Malal (Argentina)

- Cabañas Alpaca, 3 km east   BPV   ☏ 441256 $D for 4
- Cabañas Kernayel, No 1395

                                     BPV   ☏ 441922 $D for 4
- Neuquén, No 1449   APUVZ   ☏ 441416
- Santa María, No 1560   AEHRU   ☏ 441599
  Fax 441909

Accommodation on the road to Volcán Villarrica

- Cabañas Kennyleufú   ☏ (09) 4431774
- Cabañas Pirilauquén, 500 m outside town   ☏ 441080

Accommodation on the road to Lago Caburga

- Cabañas Parque Metreñehue, KM 10 on Río Trancura

                                                     ☏ 441332

  Sauna, horseriding

Accommodation on Lago Caburga

The south side of Lago Caburga is 25 km north-east of Pucón.
- Cabañas de Pehuén, Sector Playa Blanca
- Complejo Turístico Playa Blanca
- Hostería Lilenes
- Hostería Carhuello, near Saltos del Carhuello
                                     S $H ♊

Accommodation at Termas de Palguín

- ★ Hotel Termas de Palguín   P   ☏ 441968 $D ♊
  $F ♊ with shared bathroom

Accommodation in Currarehué

Currarehué is 42 km east.
- Pension Central, main street 749 $J ♂
  Basic, suitable for hikers

Accommodation in Termas de Huife

Termas de Huife is 36 km east
- Hotel Termas de Huife   ABEFGHIPRSV $E ♂
  Thermal swimming pool, sauna, open all year. Reservations in Pucón: Sr Roberto
  Nappe, O'Higgins 323 ☏ 441222/106/195

Accommodation in Termas de Menetué

Termas de Menetué is 27 km east.
- Cabañas de Menetué
  Open December–March. 20 camping spots widely dispersed. Caretaker, water tank, toilet, benches and tables, spotless but basic facilities. Also two cabins for six persons each
  but no restaurant. There is thermal water in the bathing cabins

Accommodation in Termas de San Luís

Termas de San Luís is 37 km east.
- Hotel Termas de San Luís. Includes a restaurant

- La Nuez, Caupolicán 123
- Pallette, General Urrutía block 300 near Fresia
- Puerto Pucón, Clemente Holzapfel block 1 near Caupolicán
- Snack Naturista, Avenida B. O'Higgins corner of Fresia
- 24000, Avenida B. O'Higgins

Eating out in Curarrehué
Curarrehué is 42 km east.
- Restaurant Frontera $Z

⊤ Entertainment
- Chono's Pub, Lincoyán block 300 near Avenida Bernardo O'Higgins

⊗ Border crossings
Chilean border formalities are at **Puesco** 80 km east of Pucón on RN 119 and 15 km west of **Paso Mamuil Malal** — Argentines call it Paso Tromen. Puesco is situated in a beautiful, high alpine valley with clear mountain streams, and surrounded by native forests. This 1207 m high pass connects Temuco with Junín de los Andes in Argentina. The road between Pucón and the border is good gravel and a very scenic drive indeed: once past Curarrehué the perfect snow-covered cone of **Volcán Lanín** is constantly in front of you. After the border post, the road goes through the eastern part of Parque Nacional Villarrica. Parque Nacional Lanín, on the Argentine side, is also densely forested at first, but develops the characteristics of a steppe further on — dry with trees growing only beside the rivers. The border post is open 0830–1830. In summer, regular buses run between Temuco and Junín de los Andes in Argentina. The pass may be closed by snow in winter. Buses Regional Villarrica run 2 services daily from Pucón.

⊞ Post and telegraph

Post office
- Correos, Fresia block 100 corner of Gerónimo de Alderete

Telephone
- CTC, Avenida B. O'Higgins 560
- CTC, Palguín 348 fax (45) 441090

$ Financial
- Casa de Cambio Avenida B. O'Higgins 552

▣ Services and facilities

Supermarket
- Supermercado Universo, Palguín 689

⊞ Air services
- Heliport for Gran Hotel Pucón, Lincoyán near Holzapfel

⊟ Motoring
For gas stations, see city map.

Car rental
- Hertz Rent a Car, Fresia 224 ℂ 441052. Four-wheel drives

⊥ Water transport
Excursions by launch on the lake are made from La Poza, a protected inlet from the lake. Access to La Poza is from Gerónimo de Alderete near Costanera Roberto Gleis. Here is also a boat ramp and the *Capitanía* (Harbormaster).

⊞ Shopping
- Centro de Artesanía, Fresia block 200 corner of General Urrutía. Mapuche artefacts
- Baeckerei Holzapfel, Clemente Holzapfel 524. German-style bread and cakes

⊛ Sport

Fishing
Trout fishing: see page 579.

Skiing
Skiing on Volcán Villarrica is possible from early June to late November — a few enthusiasts still find it possible to ski well into December. During winter, there are six ski lifts operating and four more lifts are under construction. The Villarrica ski center is located at 1450 m and lifts go up to 2100 m near Piedra Negra and to 2050 m near Cumbre Piramide. The Villarrica ski center, which is open all year round, has a cafetería, restaurant, ski hire, and a telephone. From the highest lift — Piedra Negra — you must still climb a steep 700 m to the crater at 2840 m. Three double chair lifts, two double drag lifts, and one quintuple drag lift operate during the skiing season.
- Ski and boot rental: $22.00
- Ski lifts: $22.00 (weekends). Lifts operate 0900–1700

🚌 Buses from Pucón

Companies leaving from the central bus terminal
The bus terminal is on Palguín 383.
- A48   Buses Lit ☎ 441055
- A106 Fénix Pullman Norte, Palguín 361 ☎ 441296
- A153 Tur-Bus Jedimar ☎ 441965
- B81   Buses Igi Llaima
- B137 Buses Power
- B145 Buses Regional Villarrica

Companies with their own terminals
- B48   Buses Cordillera, Ansorena 302 ☎ 441061
- B83   Buses J.A.C., Avenida Libertador B. O'Higgins 480 ☎ 441923
- *Colectivos* to Curarrehué, Reigolil, and Puesco leave from Palguín corner O'Higgins (just outside Restaurant La Cabañita)

Services

Destination	Fare	Services	Duration	Companies
Curarrehué	$1.30	5 services daily		B145
Lago Caburga	$1.00	3 services daily		B48
Neuquén (Argentina)	$25.00	1 service daily		B81, B83
Puesco	$1.50	2 services daily		B145
San Martín de los Andes (via Paso Mamuil Malal)	$13.00	1 service daily		B81, B83
Santiago	$16.70	5 services daily	13 hrs	A48, A106, A153, B81, B83, B137
Temuco	$2.70	28 services daily	2½ hrs	A106, B83, B137
Termas de Huife	$1.30	2 services daily	1½ hrs	B48
Valdivia	$2.90	3 services daily		B83
Valparaíso	$15.60	3 services daily		A106
Villarrica	$1.40	32 services daily		B83, B145

- Ski shuttle: $7.50 (twice in the morning and twice in afternoon)

Water sports
Wind surfing, yachting, and swimming in the lake.

Mountaineering
Volcán Villarrica is one of the most scaled mountains in southern Chile. No climbs are permitted in bad weather, and the lift stops carrying patrons uphill. On fine mornings you leave Pucón at 0700. Crampons and foot irons are necessary for the last stretch over ice.
- Hire of guide: $15.00
- Hire of crampons and foot irons: $5.00
- Transport: $10.00, including bus to base station and lift

🛶 Excursions

Tour operators
- Altué Tours, Avenida B. O'Higgins 371 ☎ 441113. Organizes rafting trips from Curarrehué to Pucón on Río Trancura, a tributary of Río Pucón
- Anden Sport Tours, Avenida B. O'Higgins 535-A ☎ 441048, fax 441236. Rental of kayaks, skis, mountain bikes. Adventure tourism.
- Nacional Travel Club, Avenida B. O'Higgins 323 ☎ 441018. Organizes climbs to Volcán Villarrica
- Turismo Sol y Nieve, Avenida B. O'Higgins 198 ☎ 441070. River rafting on Río Trancura
- Turismo Trancura Expediciones, Avenida B. O'Higgins 261 ☎ 441189
- Turismo Zorba, Lincoyán 445. Charges $20.00 for a 10-hour tour to

Volcán Villarrica all-inclusive (fares to lift, lift ticket, crampons, and foot irons ("piolets"). Minimum five people. Sr Juan Torres also organizes fishing trips
* Aventuras Aereas, O'Higgins 592 (in restaurant Conde Cagliostro). Helicopters, heli-skiing
* Taxis for excursions Avenida B. O'Higgins block 300 corner of Miguel Ansorena

Excursions
* **Casa Fuerte Santa Sylvia:** 12 km east, just after the turn into the road to Lago Caburga. This is the fortified site of a Spanish *encomendero*, which was possibly abandoned in 1599 when the Mapuche rose against the Spanish invaders. This archeological site was only discovered a couple of years ago, and part of the defensive wall and the chapel have been unearthed. The chapel contains five tombs. It is believed that one of the Spanish *conquistadores* settled here to farm and wash gold from the rivers. It is not known whether he fled before his house was destroyed during the great Mapuche uprising.
* **Curarrehué**: 42 km east; altitude 700 m. It was settled in 1912 by German immigrants; the Bavarian Capuchins built the church. This village is a starting point for excursions into the northern valleys. Buses Regional Villarrica run five services daily from Pucón and Villarrica; and one service daily to Quiñenahuin and Puesco.
* **Lago Caburga**: 25 km north-east ; it was created by volcanic activity. Lava flow and volcanic ash dammed the water at the southern end. No visible river drains the lake. Instead, the water escapes through underground channels and forms some distance south the so-called **Ojos del Caburga** ("Eyes of the Caburga"), one of the main tourist attractions of the area. The lake (altitude 500 m) is surrounded by steep mountains covered with trees. The beaches are white, unusual in a volcanic area where the sand is usually gray. Near the Ojos, a 20 m wide volcanic crater is always full of water, which is linked with the water in the nearby small **Laguna**

Azúl. The national flower, *copihué*, grows profusely here, and blooms in March and April. A 5 km trail leads from the Ojos del Caburga to Lago Caburga. The nascent river forms rapids. At the rapids, there is a *hostería*, open all year round, where you can buy German cakes. From the picnic area near the rapids, you can walk to **Saltos del Carhuello** with its own camping ground and *hostería*, open all year round. Lago Caburga is easily accessible by organized tours and public transport from Pucón, and there are beaches and camping facilities at the southern end. Trips to Lago Caburga usually include **Parque Nacional Huerquehué**, 10 km further east — see the entry for the park on page 598. At the northern end of Lago Caburga is Playa Negra with Camping Llanqui Llanqui. The springs at Termas Río Blanco are the source of the river which feeds Lago Caburga at the northern end. This end of the lake is only accessible by road from **Cunco**. Many of the peaks, including **Cerro La Teta** and **Cerro Loncotroro**, are extinct volcanoes, some of which have craters filled with water. Buses Cordillera, Buses J.A.C., and Buses Regional Villarrica run regular daily services from Pucón to the south side of Lago Caburga, passing all the camp sites.
* Trail blazers can make a round trip starting in Pucón to **Reigolil** via Curarrehué, and return either via Parque Nacional Huerquehué to Pucón, or if the Nevados de Sollipulli are included in the mountain hike return to Melipeuco. The trip north from Currarrehué to Reigolil is very picturesque: the road passes through a narrow quebrada between **Angostura** and Reigolil. Rural buses run from Pucón to Reigolil. Mountain hikes from Reigolil to **Quiñenahuin** and upper **Río Maichin**, where there are thermal springs in their natural state. Mountain hikers can include the southern part of the **Nevados de Sollipulli**. Hardy outdoor enthusiasts may wish to press on to **Melipeuco** via the western slopes of the Nevados de Sollipulli, densely forested with

araucarias at the lower level. From Melipeuco there are buses to Temuco.

- **Parque Nacional Huerquehué**: 36 km north-east on Rutas S-905 and S-907. See the entry for the park on page 598.
- **Parque Nacional Villarrica**: Entrance 10 km south on the unsealed Ruta S-887. See the entry for the park on page 601.
- **Volcán Lanín** and the eastern part of **Parque Nacional Villarrica**, which becomes Parque Nacional Lanín on the Argentinian side. See the entry for Parque Nacional Villarrica on page 601.

Thermal spas

- **Termas de Huife**: A commercial tourist complex 36 km east on the **Río Liucura** just above the junction with the **Río Liancalil**, altitude 320 m. The thermal spa is attached to a hotel with modern facilities. Admission $7.00 for use of thermal facilities by visitors. The thermal waters are 46–90°C (115–194°F), and are recommended for nervous diseases, rheumatism, mental fatigue, and skin diseases. The hotel's thermal facilities include private cabins, two thermal pools, a cafetería and restaurant, and a pavilion with thermal bath facilities. Buses Cordillera and Buses Regional Villarrica run regular daily services from Villarrica and Pucón.
- **Termas de Menetué**: A thermal spa with basic facilities on the north side of the **Río Trancura**, 27 km east of Pucón. This is a little-frequented spot in a wide valley with several small *lagunas* nearby; altitude 250 m. Note that Menetué is sometimes spelled Minetué. Regular buses from Pucón follow Ruta S-923 on the north side of Río Pucón. You can return via RN 119; this involves a ferry crossing over the Río Pucón at KM 24. Frequent buses on RN 119 between Pucón and Curarrehué.
- **Termas de Palguín**: This spa nestles in the upper **Río Palguín** valley between **Volcán Villarrica** (to the west) and **Volcán Quetrupillán** (to the east). It is located 31 km east at an altitude of 800 m. The turn-off into the Río Palguín valley is 18 km east of Pucón. The Río Palguín cascades in several large

waterfalls from the glacier on Volcán Quetrupillán through a narrow valley. At the valley's entrance, you will find a chapel and Ovalles' ranch with camping and restaurant facilities. After passing through a Mapuche village, which specializes in woolen weaving, you reach Salto de Palguín, a fantastic place for pictures of the river falling into a spectacular gorge almost obscured by mist. It is rather hidden from the road but is visible in its full splendor from a lookout platform. Detour 2 km east for another waterfall of 70 m, the Salto de la China. The walls of the canyon are hidden behind a cover of dense shrubs, large-leaved *ñalcas*, and fuchsias. Salto de la China falls over smooth rock in a veil of water. The Salto de la China *hostería* and restaurant is about half the price of Termas de Palguín. Salto de la China is only 300 m from Salto de León, which consists of two small waterfalls, and can be reached on foot a bit further up on a short trail through the forest. The Hotel Termas de Palguín at 31 km is a good resting place, despite its slightly old-fashioned appearance. The thermal complex is set in a beautiful natural park among ancient *araucarias*. A small pavilion attached to the thermal hotel has five thermal water bathing facilities. The thermal water, between 36° and 42°C (97° and 108°F), is supposed to help alleviate respiratory and liver ailments, kidney complaints, arthritis and aching bones, nerves, ulcers, and skin diseases. Luke-warm thermal water is ducted to individual bath huts and to a larger swimming pool. A day's use of the thermal pools costs $3.00. From here, you can make short hikes through superb *araucaria* forest into spectacular mountain country with views of the glaciated tops of Volcán Quetrupillán and Volcán Villarrica. There is a CONAF hut in this part of the national park, but it is not always attended. Conducted tours usually spend 1½ to 2 hours at Termas de Palguín. Alternatively hikers may take the early morning bus on RN 119 and walk 1½ hours from the turnoff to the thermal hotel. One interesting hiking itinerary is via **Laguna de los Patos**, returning via Coñaripe to Villarrica — see also "Excursions" from Coñaripe in Región X de Los Lagos. However, before setting out for Parque Nacional Villarrica beyond Termas de Palguín, it is advisable to check with CONAF in Pucón the state of the trails in the Quetrupillán section.

• **Termas de Quimey-Co**: 28 km east on the **Río Liucura** within walking distance of **Termas de Huife**; altitude 310 m. It is the cheapest of all thermal spas in the Pucón area. The thermal water fluctuates between 46° and 60°C (115° and 140°F). Its properties are reputed to assist nervous diseases, rheumatism, mental fatigue, and stress. The facilities include an open-air thermal pool. Conducted tours usually include a visit to Parque Nacional Huerquehué and Lago Caburgua. There are regular daily bus services to

and from Pucón. The area offers immense possibilities for the outdoor enthusiast.

• **Termas de San Luís:** 37 km east, in the **Río Trancura** valley. The low hills in the valley are partially covered with *araucaria* trees, and there are many small *lagunas* scattered through the valley. Their reed-fringed edges are nesting cover for water birds. **Laguna del León** is enclosed by small hills. The thermal facilities are basic and sometimes crowded. The small hotel offers meals, but there are plenty of barbecue facilities to cook your own. Nearby are **Laguna Catripulli** and **Laguna del León**, both good for fishing. Buses Regional Villarica run three services daily between Pucón and Currarrehué; ask the driver to set you down at Puente San Luís and then walk the 4 km to the thermal resort.

PUERTO SAAVEDRA

Population: 2500
Altitude: Sea level
Distance from Temuco: 89 km west on Ruta S-30 and S-40

Puerto Saavedra is located near the mouth of the **Río Imperial**. It is not directly on the Pacific, but on **Laguna Imperial** about 2 km inland. It still shows the scars of the devastating tidal wave of 1960, which almost completely obliterated this town.

Its main attraction is the shallow, slightly saline **Lago Budi** 5 km south which is a nature sanctuary. From Puerto Saavedra, it is an hour's walk to Lago Budi. Its banks and small islands are inhabited by many birds and the lake is home to a particular type of fish which prefers these brackish waters. The lake's outlet into the sea is 8 km north. The whole area surrounding the lake is Mapuche territory. The most important island is **Isla Nahuelhuapi**, exclusively inhabited by Mapuches. Hostería Boca Budi, a small hotel

with an excellent seafood restaurant, overlooks the beach and Lago Budi. The road to Hostería Boca Budi is winding, but there is a shortcut from the bus terminal at Puerto Saavedra along the beach — a half-hour walk. From Hostería Boca Budi, you can cross by boat or raft to **Puerto Domínguez**. From Puerto Domínguez, return by bus on Ruta S-46 to Carahué and from there back to Temuco. Or if you want to retrace history, hike down the coastal trail to **Teodoro Schmidt** and even further south to the seaside resorts of Queule

LA ARAUCANIA

Key to map

A   Iglesia
B   Gobernación Provincial (Government)
C   Municipalidad (Town hall)
D   Post office and telex
E   Telephone
F   Carabineros (Police)
G   Mercado Municipal (Market)
H   Hospital
I   Tourist information
P   Gas stations
$ Money exchange
T   Bus terminals

and Mehuín. This was the *conquistadores'* supply route to the isolated and often beleaguered town of Valdivia during the colonial period. Take waterproof gear for this hike, which takes three to four days. You will be in Mapuche territory most of the time.

▣ Accommodation

Accommodation in Sector Boca Budi
- Hostería Boca Budi **ACEFGHJLP$UV (** 14 rooms
- Hostería Lago de los Cisnes **(** 251891
- Hostería Maule, Villa Miramar **AFPSV (** (45) 244650 **$I** **▮**

▣ Camping

Camping Municipal is 2 km south of the built-up area, directly on the beach. There is also camping by Lago Budi, 5 km south.

▣ Eating out

Eating out in the center of town
- Hostería Turismo

Eating out in Sector Boca Budi
- Hostería Boca Budi. It is located on a hill overlooking a sandy beach and Lago Budi. Excellent seafood. Hostería Boca Budi is always full at the weekends.

▣ Buses

Buses Narsur run 7 services daily to Temuco via Carahué and Nueva Imperial.
- Nueva Imperial: Fare $0.80; duration ¾ hr
- Temuco: Fare $1.60

PURÉN

Population: 7500
Altitude: 250 m
Distance from Temuco: 154 km north-west on Ruta R-60-P, R-86, R-88 and RN 5 (via Los Sauces)

Purén, the center of a potato and strawberry growing area, is also a timber town with many sawmills. It lies on the south-eastern slopes of the Nahuelbuta ranges where the valley is flat and wide, and is linked to Angol and Temuco by sealed roads.

Fuerte Español, on top of a commanding hill, was founded in 1553 by Pedro de Valdivia and rebuilt in 1585 and 1597. It was abandoned after the disastrous battle of Tucapel. Not far away, at the battle of Curalaba, Mapuche Chief Pelantaru killed the young governor Oñez de Loyola.

Purén was re-founded in 1869 by Colonel Cornelius Saavedra. The paved streets and German-style

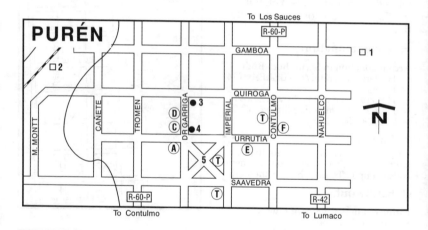

Key to map

A	Iglesia	1	Fuerte Español
C	Municipalidad (Town hall)	2	Railroad station
D	Post office and telex	3	Hotel Turismo
E	Telephone	4	Hotel Central
F	Carabineros (Police)	5	Plaza de Armas
H	Hospital		
T	Bus terminals		

houses reflect the dominance of German immigrants in the 19th century when the district also attracted gold-miners.

⌘ Festivals

* February: Semana Purénina — fruit and harvest festival

⊟ Accommodation

* Hotel Tur, Dr Garrigo 912 near Saavedra 467 **ADEFGHIKLMPTV** ☏ 22 $| ♒

⊡ Post and telegraph

* Correos (post office), Imperial 939

⊟ Buses

The bus terminal is on Saavedra near Contulmo. The following companies make scheduled calls in Purén: Buses Thiele Ewert, Buses Jota Ewert, Buses Tacoha, Buses Malleco, and Buses Tliver.

There are 24 services daily to Angol; three services daily to Cañete, Contulmo, and Lebu; one service daily to Chillán, Concepción, Los Angeles, and Nacimiento; and four services daily to Victoria and Temuco.

⊟ Motoring services

* COPEC gas station

▣ Sights

Fuerte de Purén has recently been historically reconstructed in timber. It contains a display of Mapuche culture.

⊛ Excursions

You can make do-it-yourself excursions to traditional Mapuche villages in the nearby valleys of the Nahuelbuta ranges.

* **Monumento Natural de Contulmo**: 10 km west on Ruta R-60-P; frequent buses. See "Excursions" from Lago Lanalhué in Región VIII del Bío Bío on page 549.

QUEULE

Altitude: Sea level
Distance from Temuco: 134 km south-weat (via Nueva Toltén) on Ruta S-70 and Panamericana

Queule is a small fishing village on the estuary of the **Río Queule,** built on a low hill which is part of the Sierra de Queule. It overlooks the estuary and a flat sandy area, with dunes stretching for 6 km up to Punta Nihué. From Queule, a road goes up to **Nueva Toltén** through Mapuche country. The scenery is interesting between Mehuín and Queule where the coastal *sierra* drops sharply down from 500 m to sea level.

⊟ Accommodation

* Hostería Nuria, Jerónimo Martínez

◮ Camping

There are plenty of areas to pitch a tent in solitude, even in summer. The best camping is on the long sandy beach opposite Queule, but an hour's walk from the village. Boats will ferry you across for a small fee. Boil the river water. There is good swimming and fishing but no facilities.

⊟ Buses

* Temuco: Fare $1.90; 4 services; Ansmar, Voga, Tradeso, Narbus
* Valdivia: Fare $1.70; departs 1510; Buses Perla del Sur

⊛ Excursions

You can hire a launch from the locals and visit seal colonies offshore.

RESERVA NACIONAL
MALALCAHUELLO–ÑALCAS

Altitude: 946–2865 m
Distance from Curacautín: 25 km east on Ruta R-89
Admission: $2.00

This reserve incorporates **Volcán Lonquimay** and a fledgling ski resort on its eastern side. Approximately 31 300 ha (77 310 acres). On Christmas Day, 1988, Lonquimay gave birth to Volcán Navidad on the eastern ridge. This small volcano subsided again in January 1990.

From the village of **Malalcahuello**, you have views of Volcán Lonquimay to the north and magnificent southern views towards **Cordillera Blanca** and **Volcán Llaima**. The village is within easy walking distance of Volcán Lonquimay. To the north, a large patch of lava lies close to the village. This is tent and sleeping bag territory for hiking enthusiasts.

There are picnic and camping areas, excursion paths, ski lifts, and a lookout. This forest reserve includes a fledgling ski resort, 10 km from the village on the eastern slope of the volcano; it is popular with "budget" skiers.

The description "Reserva Nacional" is a bit misleading, as logging is still going on in the area. The tall *araucaria* trees left standing in isolation accentuate the sad picture. The untouched area towards the lava and volcanic ash area is small consolation only.

▣ Accommodation

The nearest comfortable accommodation is in Manzanar, 22 km west — see "Accommodation" in Curacautín on page 587.

Accommodation in Malalcahuello
Malalcahuello is a village on the road which borders the park, 33 km east of Curacautín.
- Residencial Los Sauces **BP $J** i. Basic
- Hostería Piedra Santa (950 m), 6 km west of the village on Ruta R-89 just before crossing the Río Coloradito which flows from Volcán Lonquimay. **BP $J** i. Simple but adequate accommodation for hikers intending to climb "El Mocho", as Volcán Lonquimay is commonly called by local people

Accommodation at Volcán Llaima snowfields
These snowfields are on the east side of the park, 43 km east of Curacautín. The turnoff is 5 km east of Malalcahuello.
- Complejo Turístico Nevados de Curacautín, ((45) 881726 $H i. Shared bathroom

▣ Camping

Camping in Malalcahuello
- Camping Mon Repos, on the banks of the Río Cautín

⑪ Eating out

Eating out in Malalcahuello
- Restaurant Penhuencura

▣ Buses

Flota Erbuc runs four services daily to Curacautín, Victoria, Temuco, and Lonquimay.

⊛ Sport

Fishing, hiking, skiing.

Skiing on the volcano

From Temuco to the snowfields is approximately 160 km in a north-easterly direction, using first the Panamericana and then Ruta R-89. The skiing area is on the eastern slope of the volcano inside the reserve at approximately 1800 m. It is only a small area with a mountain chalet for 32 persons and a *cafetería*. The road is sealed as far as Manzanar and good gravel from there on, then dirt from the turnoff to the ski area. The skiing season runs from May to November. The nearest accommodation is in Malalcahuello (10 km), Manzanar (22 km west), and Curacautín (43 km west). Skiing ceased for several years when the volcano erupted in 1988 and formed the mini-volcano Navidad nearby. There are two T-bar lifts, ski equipment hire, and a ski school.

◉ Excursions

Use 1:50 000 map series "Malalcahuello" (3815-7130) for hiking in the Volcán Lonquimay and Volcán Tolhuaca area.

- **Volcán Lonquimay**: The best starting point is from Hostería Piedra Santa a few kilometers east of Malalcahuello. Almost opposite the *hostería,* a logging trail begins which follows the Río Coloradito towards the cone of the volcano. This logging trail peters out 5 km uphill near the loggers' hut

(there are actually two but one is derelict) at 1400 m. Timber cover here includes isolated *araucarias* to the snow line. It is a further $2\frac{1}{2}$ km to the lava and volcanic ash. The lava fields start at about 1600 m with isolated snow patches. Follow one of the ravines further up. Only experienced hikers should continue to the crater at 2730 m. From the summit, you can see **Volcán Tolhuaca** in the west and **Volcán Llaima** in the south. It is also possible to continue along the 1500 m contour line (where the lava fields start) in a north-westerly direction to combine with a hike in the **Parque Nacional Tolhuaca**. Make sure you stay south of Laguna Blanca, because the northern (upper) side is swampy right up to the snow line. The area below the snow line is thinly forested, a mixture of *coirones* and *araucarias*. Many logging crews work in the area. It is an easy four-hour hike to the tree line. This hike can be extended around Cerro Colorado into the **Río Colorado** valley and from there up to the *refugio* and ski area.

- **Parque Nacional Conguillio-Las Paraguas:** 15 km south as the crow flies. For a walking trip to this national park, start from the Hostería Piedra Santa. Use 1:50 000 map series "Volcán Llaima" (3830–7130). See the entry for the park on page 596.

TEMUCO

Area code: 045
Population: 210 000
Altitude: 100m
Distance from Santiago: 673 km south on Panamericana

Temuco, capital of Región IX de La Araucania, is located in the central valley on the banks of the **Río Cautín.** Until the middle of the 19th century, all this area belonged to the Mapuche. The Chilean Government was only able to begin settlement here after signing a treaty with the Mapuche tribes on Cerro Ñielol in 1881. Temuco was founded immediately afterwards as a fort to restrain the restless Mapuche tribes. It is now an important administrative, cultural and commercial center with a university.

The town has excellent facilities supporting the ever-growing tourist industry. The scenic hinterland offers lakes, volcanoes, and ski slopes. Mapuches preserve their cultural heritage in the surrounding villages and sell their wares in Temuco's central market, where you can also sample their cuisine. You can buy directly from Mapuche artists at the Fería Libre near the train station.

The Plaza de Armas is surrounded by official buildings, such as the Municipalidad (town hall), Intendencia Regional (seat of regional government), major banks, and airlines offices. The Mercado Municipal with its many food stalls is two blocks north of the plaza. Cross Avenida Caupolicán into Avenida Alemania, then turn left after the first block to the Museo Regional de La Araucania with its many interesting Mapuche artefacts. To the north of the Museum is Cerro Ñielol, a national park. The *cafetería*-cum-restaurant at the top commands sweeping views of the town and volcanoes in the east.

Cunco

Cunco is a small village of 6000 inhabitants at an altitude of 400 m, is 58 km south-east, on Ruta S-51 in the *pre-Cordillera* just where the Río Allipén enters the central valley. The church was built by Bavarian Capuchins and is still a mission. It is the starting point for excursions to Lago Colico and the northern section of Lago Caburga.

Freire

Freire, 27 km south of Temuco, has a population of 5000. Here is the turn-off to Lago Villarrica and to Junín de los Andes in Argentina.

Gorbea

Gorbea is a small town 40 km south. There are two gas stations at the town entrance on the Panamericana.

Nueva Imperial

Nueva Imperial, a town of 13 000 inhabitants 34 km west, was founded in 1882, and is largely inhabited by Mapuche. It has telephone services and a gas station.

⊠ Festivals
* February: Semana Temucana (Temuco week)
* October 1–30: Fería Internacional de la Frontera — a colorful agricultural exhibition

ⓘ Tourist information
* CONAF, Bilbao 931, upstairs ℂ 254358
* Ferrocarriles del Estado (railroad ticket office), Bulnes 582
* Sernatur, Bulnes 586 ℂ 211969

Ⓐ Camping
Camping Metrenco is 10 km south of Temuco. On the north side of Lago Caburga 29 km east of Cunco, there is Camping Llanqui Llanqui on Playa Negra.

⑪ Eating out

Restaurants
* Albatros, Balmaceda 1110. Seafood
* Bavaria, Rodríguez 1073 $Y
* Centro Español, Manuel Bulnes 483 $X
* Club Alemán, Senador Estebanez 772 $X. German cuisine
* Darla, Rodríguez 889
* Dell Maggio, Manuel Bulnes 536
* Dino's, Manuel Bulnes 360. Pizzas
* Dynka, Manuel Montt 1037. *Parilla*
* El Fogón, Aldunate 288. *Parrilla*
* El Rápido, M. Rodríguez 1353
* El Tunel, Bulnes 846-A
* Estambul, Manuel Bulnes 543
* Fogón de la Frontera, Guido Beck de Ramberga 460
* Kim Long, Bulnes 145. Chinese cuisine
* Komilón, M. Rodríguez 1101
* Las Leñas, Avenida Alemania 0830

☞ • Mesón de Sancho, Manuel Bulnes 483. Open evenings only
☞ • Nam Nam, Portales 802
• Plaza, A. Varas 846
☞ • Rapa Nui, Aldunate 415. Early breakfast
• Rincón Naturista, A. Prat 425. Vegetarian
• Rincón Vegetariano Frugal, M. Montt 850 Local 115. Vegetarian
• Venecia, Cruz 382 upstairs

Cafés
• Center Shop, Manuel Bulnes 368, Local 32. Cakes and teas
• Flamingo, A. Varas 838
• Grill El Sótano, Manuel Montt 816, Local 4 (downstairs)
• Grill Marriet, Galería Massmann, Prat 451, Local 21

Pizzerías
☞ • Julio's Pizza, Bulnes 778
• Pizza Hut, Avenida Alemania 0850
• Pizza Madonna, Manuel Montt 670
• Pizza Pepperoni's, Manuel Montt 334

Eating out in the Mercado Municipal
☞ The central market has a range of very good small restaurants which serve seafood and local dishes. Access from Aldunate, Portales, and Rodríguez.
• Don Jeyo, local 55
• El Criollito, local 38-39
• El Turísta, local 32

Eating out outside the city center
☞ • La Cumbre del Nielol, Cerro Nielol, on a terrace on top of mountain overlooking the town. International cuisine

Eating out along the Panamericana, northern section
Restaurants
• Posada Turístico, Rudecindo Ortega 01479 $X
• La Estancia de Temuco, Rudecindo Ortega 02340 $X

Eating out along the Panamericana, southern section
• Hornitos de Metrenco, KM 12 $X. *Parrilla*
• Los Troncos, KM 2 $X. *Parrilla*

Eating out in Lautaro
Lautaro is 30 km north
• Café-Schop Di Giorgino, Libertador B. O'Higgins 765

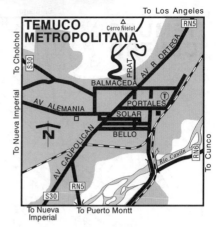

• Club Social, Bilbao 130 $Z

Eating out in Loncoche
Loncoche is 77 km south, on the Panamericana.
• Cafetería Pullman Pizzería, B. Arana (main street)

ⓣ Entertainment
• Bowling Cafetería, Manuel Bulnes 483 downstairs
• Disco Club, Manuel Montt 1020
• Night Club Mondo, Aldunate Block 300 near Rodríguez

ⓔ Post and telegraph

Post office
• Correo, Portales block 800 corner of Prat

Telephone
• CTC, Arturo Prat 565, fax 213006
• CTC, Manuel Bulnes 368
• Telex Chile, D. Portales corner of A. Prat ☎ 211550
• ENTEL Chile, Bulnes 303. Overseas calls

ⓢ Financial
• American Express, M.Bulnes 483 ☎ 212771
• Fincard, Claro Solar 922 ☎ 213372. Cash advances against Visa and Mastercard
• Cambio Turcamb, Claro Solar 733 ☎ 210939. Travelers' checks
• Cambio Turismo, A. Prat 660 in arcade

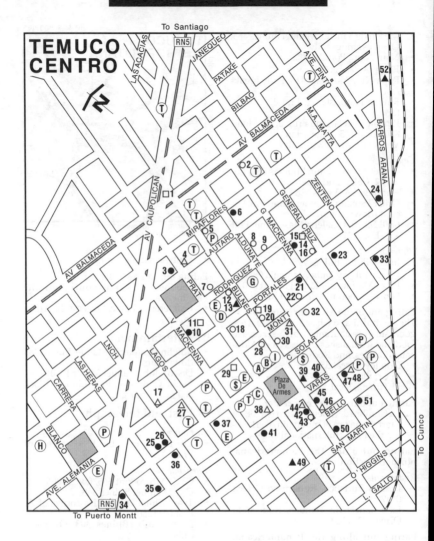

TEMUCO CENTRO

- Turismo Money Exchange, Galería Arauco M. Bulnes 655, Local 1 ☎213699

🖫 Services and facilities

Dry cleaner
- Lavaseco Topaz, Aldunate 453

Laundromat
- Marva, M. Montt 415

Medical center
- Clínica Alemana, General Mackenna 548 ☎210658

Key to map

A	Iglesia
B	Gobernación Provincial (Government)
C	Municipalidad (Town hall)
D	Post office and telex
E	Telephone
G	Mercado Municipal (Market)
H	Hospital
I	Tourist information
P	Gas stations
$	Money exchange
T	Bus terminals

● Accommodation

3	Hotel Bayern
6	Hotel Sevilla
10	Hotel Ginebra
14	Hotel Oriente
21	Hotel Nicolás
23	Hotel Chapelco
24	Residencial Méndez
25	Hostal Millaray
26	Hospedaje
33	Hotel Casablanca
34	Hospedaje
35	Hotel Chalet Alemán
36	Hotel Espellette
37	Hotel Turismo
40	Hospedaje Montt
41	Hotel Continental
42	Hotel Nuevo Frontera
45	Hotel Frontera
47	Hotel Altué
50	Hotel Emperador
51	Apart Hotel Luanco

○ Eating out

2	Restaurant Albatros
5	Restaurant Kim Long
7	Restaurant Suiza
8	Restaurant El Fogón
9	Restaurant Bavaria
12	Cafetería Dino
16	Restaurant Venecia
18	Restaurant Nam Nam
20	Centro Español
22	Restaurant Dynka
28	Restaurant Del Maggio
30	Restaurant Estambul
32	Restaurant Club Social
43	Restaurant Julio's Pizza

△ Tour operators and car rental

4	Automóvil Club de Chile
17	Budget Rent a Car
31	Germania Tours
38	Agencia de Viajes Christopher
44	Hertz Rent a Car
46	Avis Rent a Car
48	First Rent a Car

▲ Airlines and rail

13	LADECO
39	LAN Chile
49	Transporte Aereo Neuquino
52	Railroad station

□ Services

1	CEMA Chile
11	Artesanías
15	Instituto Cultural Chileno Británico
19	Fotos Nort-Sur
29	Supermercado Mas

Photographic supplies
- Laboratorios Fuji Chile, Bulnes block 100 near Miraflores
- Nort Sur Color Agfa, Manuel Bulnes 427

Sports equipment
- Llaima Sport, Manuel Rodríguez 935 (235933

Supermarkets
- Supermercado MAS, Manuel Montt block 700 near Vicuña Mackenna

▣ Visas, passports
- Spanish consulate, M. Montt 816, office 31 (210976

▤ Motoring

For gas stations, see the city map.

Car rental
- Automóvil Club de Chile, Lautaro 703 (215132 fax 210098
- Avis, Aldunate 656 (238013 fax
- Budget, Lynch 471 (214911 fax
- First, Varas 1036 (233890, fax 211828
- Hertz, Bulnes 750 (235385
- Western, Diego Portales 882 (211444

⊞ Shopping
- Mercado Municipal (Central Market), Portales block 900 through Rodríguez block 900. Good clean restaurants and Mapuche *artesanias*
- *Artesanía* stalls around Plaza between Rodríguez and Lautaro
- Galería CEMA, corner of Avenida Caupolicán and Avenida Balmaceda. *Artesanias*

Temuco

✉ Accommodation in Temuco

Private accommodation (*hospedajes*) is rented to students during the school year. Most of them are only available to tourists during school vacations from December to the beginning of February. Check with Sernatur.

Apart Hotels

• Luanco, Aldunate 821-A Fax 214602	AHPV	✆ 213749	$F for 4	

Hotels

★★★ Aitué, A. Varas 1048 fax 212608	ACDFGHIJKLPTUV	✆ 211917/48	$E	♀♀
★★★ Bayern, Avenida Arturo Prat 146 Fax 212291, German spoken	ACDEGHIJKMNPSTUV	✆ 213915	$F	♀♀
★★★ Nicolás, General Mackenna 420 Fax 213468, 50 rooms	ADEFGHJKMPSV	✆ 210020/211113	$F	♀♀
★★★ Sevilla, Aldunate 153 Fax 235810	AEGHKPSTUZ	✆ 212218	$F	♀♀
★ Turismo Temuco, Claro Solar 636	AEFGHIJKLPSUV	✆ 210583/232348	$G	♀♀
• Chapelco, General Cruz 401	ADGHPS	✆ 210367	$G	♀♀
• Continental, A. Varas 708 Fax 233830	AEFGHIJKMPV	✆ 211395/238973	$F	♀♀
• De France, Aldunate 095		✆ 215623/233916		
• De la Frontera, M. Bulnes 733	ADEFGHIJKLMNPS$VZ	✆ 210718	$F/G	♀♀
• Emperador, M. Bulnes 853 18 rooms	ACDEGIJKLP$UVY	✆ 213409/237124		
• Espellette, Luis Claro Solar 492	AHIJKPV	✆ 234805	$G	♀♀
• Nuevo Hotel de la Frontera, M. Bulnes 726 60 rooms	ACDEFGHIJKLMPR$VZ	✆ 212638	$D	♀♀
• Oriente, Avenida Rodríguez 1146 $I ♀♀ with shared bathroom	PV	✆ 233232	$H	♀♀

Hostales

• Casablanca, M. Montt 1306	APS	✆ 212740	$H	♀♀
• Chalet Alemán, Varas 349	APS	✆ 212818	$G	♀♀
• Ginebra, Vicuña Mackenna 361	APS	✆ 5236995	$F	♀♀
• Hostal Millaray, Claro Solar 475		✆ 211384	$J	♀

Residenciales

- Méndez, M.A. Matta 382 (near rural bus terminal)   ✆ 233952
  Backpackers
- Mundial, Avenida Balmaceda 1371
  Backpackers, clean

Hospedajes for budget tourists
All *hospedajes* have a shared bathroom and cost $J ♀.

• Claro Solar 262-A, 483				
• General Mackenna 26				
• Las Heras 810				
• Delorana, Zenteno 486			$J	♀
• Turístico, General Mackenna 46			$J	♀
• Sra Adriana Becker de Diez, Senador Estebanez 881, between San Martín and Holandesa			$J	♀
• Sra Luisa Eugenia Gomez Aguero, Avenida Francia 199 corner of Pedro de Valdivia	PS	✆ 23559	$I	♀

Accommodation in Temuco — continued

- Sra Rusa Elena Novoa Gomez, Volcán Calbuco between Avenida Alemania and Inglaterra S $J i
- Sra Alicia del Pozo, Freire 147 behind regional hospital
  S (232541 $J i
- Sra Ibett Zapata Castro, Manuel Rodríguez 1341, upstairs (233721 $J i
- Sra Nora Rodríguez, Lautaro 1149 between Mackenna and Cruz
  $J i
- Sra Hilda Lizana Rodríguez, Aldunate 864 $J i
  Clean, hot water
- Sra Margarita Ortiz, Lautaro 355 $J i

Accommodation along the Panamericana in the Sector Norte
- Motel Yacara, Rudecindo Ortega 01475
  AEHKPUV (234434 $H ii

Accommodation along the Panamericana Sur

Hostería
- Lolorruca, 2 km south AEFGHLPVX (471065 $G ii

Cabañas
- Loncorruca (formerly Chapelco), just outside Loncoche (471013

Accommodation in Cunco
- Complejo Turístico Campestre Trailanqui, Ruta S-61, 5 km outside Los Laureles on the road to Lago Colico ABCEFGHIJKLNPRS$UVZ
  (214915/234119 $E ii
  The *complejo* is an old *hacienda* located on Río Allipén. 10 rooms, $F cabins for 6. Also 22 camp sites; horse riding. Open December–February
- Hostería Camino Real, Santa María 753

Accommodation in Freire
- Hostería Rucanto, Lynch corner of Panamericana (391029

Accommodation in Gorbea
- Hostería Prat, Prat corner of Bernardo O'Higgins
  AEFGHIPV (491025

Accommodation in Lautaro
Lautaro is 30 km north, on the Panamericana.
- Hotel France, Valdivia 281 AHJPV (531153
- Hostería Ali-Quillén on the Panamericana (531204

Accommodation in Loncoche
Loncoche is 77 km south, on the Panamericana.

Hotel
- Alemán, Buenos Aires

Accommodation in Nueva Imperial
- Residencial Flores, Vicuña Mackenna 350
  Budget travelers

Accommodation in Nueva Toltén
Nueva Toltén is 97 km south-west, on Ruta S-70.
- Hotel Lomar, corner O'Higgins and Prat
  AFGIPV

Accommodation in Temuco — continued

Accommodation in Pitrufquén
Pitrufquén is 31 km south, on the Panamericana.

Hotels
- Hostería Riverside, Avenida Libertador Bernardo O'Higgins 20
  AEFPV   ℓ 391223

  7 rooms
- Hotel de France, Francisco Bilbao 335 AEFGILPV $H ♀♀
  $H cabins for 4
- Millaray, Balmaceda 396   AEFHIPV   ℓ 391142
- Small hotel in Calle Rodríguez

- Galería Flor Arte, M. Bulnes 443, downstairs. Mapuche silverware, weavings, carvings, and paintings
- Artesanías Hofstaetter, A. Prat 188
- Artesanías Mapuche, A. Prat 176

⊛ Sport

Rafting trips are organized by tour operators (see page 628) of Río Trancura (two hours for $35.00) and Río Allipen (four hours for $50.00).

▣ Sightseeing

- Museo Regional de La Araucania, Avenida Alemania 084. The museum has eight rooms exhibiting Mapuche culture, the city's foundation, European colonization, and the development of Temuco over the last 100 years. Room 4 represents the Spanish colonial period and the many attempts to subdue the Mapuche. Room 5 is of particular interest, displaying the story of the occupation of Araucania from 1862 onwards. This museum is well worth a visit. Tues–Sat, 0900–1300 and 1500–1900; small admission charge; Sundays and holidays free.
- Cerro Nielol and Parque Nacional Cerro Nielol (84 ha or 208 acres) at an altitude between 180 and 322 m, on a hill overlooking Temuco, within easy walking distance of the town center. It is a 10-minute walk from the Plaza de Armas and about five blocks from the city centre. The average temperature is 11°C (52°F) all year round. The slopes are densely covered with native trees and shrubs, such as red *copihué* which grows profusely in this area, privet, oak, elm, and *lingue* which provides bark for tanning. They are a re-

---

✈ Air services from Temuco

Airlines
- Transporte Aéreos Neuquén (TAN), Diego Portales 840 ℓ 210500.
- LAN Chile, Bulnes 667 ℓ 211339
- LADECO, A. Prat 535 ℓ 213180

Flights

Destination	Fare	Services	Duration	Airlines
Puerto Montt	$58.00	1–2 services daily	¾ hr	LAN Chile, LADECO
Coihaique	$150.00	Tues, Thurs	2 hr	LAN Chile, LADECO
Concepción	$99.00	Mon, Thurs, Fri, Sun	¾ hr	LAN Chile, LADECO
Osorno	$34.00			LAN Chile
Punta Arenas	$252.00			LAN Chile
Santiago	$137.00	1–2 services daily	1 hr	LAN Chile, LADECO

🚌 Buses from Temuco

There is no long-distance bus terminal. Bus offices are scattered all over town.

Companies leaving from the rural terminal
The rural bus terminal is on Avenida Balmaceda, corner of Pinto and M.A. Matta (210494.
* B14   Buses ACA
* B54   Buses DAS
* B62   Buses EPAS
* B73   Buses García, A. Pinto 032 office 10 (2133109
* B80   Buses Huinca
* B103 Buses Malleco
* B126 Buses Paihuinca
* B166 Buses Tradeso
* B170 Buses Transmar, A. Pinto 032 (238395
* B216 Buses Erbuc, Avenida Balmaceda 1415 (212939
* B256 Buses Bonanza, Pinto 47, Local 63 (213039
* B272 Vogabus

Companies with their own terminal
* A48   Buses Lit, San Martín 894 (211483 fax 214201
* A106 Buses Fénix Pullman Norte, Claro Solar 609 (212582
* A137 Buses Tas Choapa, A. Varas 609 (21422
* A153 Tur-Bus Jedimar, General Lagos 576 (212613. Good restaurant upstairs
* B30   Buses Bío Bío, Lautaro 853 (210599 fax 215325
* B64   Buses ETC, Bulnes 204
* B81   Buses Igi Llaima, Miraflores 1535 (210364
* B83   Buses J.A.C., Vicuña Mackenna 798 (210313 fax 220222
* B98   Buses Longitudinal Sur, Vicuña Mackenna 650 (213140
* B128 Buses Panguisur, Miraflores 871 (211580
* B137 Buses Power, M. Bulnes 178 (210610
* B139 Buses Puma, Miraflores 869 (210134
* B154 Buses Ruta Sur, Miraflores 1151 (210079
* B164 Buses Thiele Ewert, Vicuña Mackenna 650 (213140
* B179 Varmontt, M. Bulnes 45 (211314
* B207 Ettabus, Vicuña Mackenna 648
* B225 Minibus Las Colinas, General Cruz block 200 near Lautaro
* B228 Nar-Bus, Miraflores 1535 (235373
* B237 Buses Pullman Sur, Vicuña Mackenna 671 (210701
* B260 Buses Cruz del Sur, Vicuña Mackenna 671 (210701
* B271 Buses Via Tur, Vicuña Mackenna 586 (213094
* B273 Buses La Unión del Sud, General Cruz 375 (233398
  This is the company which in Argentina runs services to Termas de Copahué. You could get off in Las Lajas, Argentina, which has a hotel, and wait for the connection to Copahué. During winter, there are fewer services between Chile and Argentina.
* Buses Panorama, Vicuña Mackenna 648 (213451
* Buses San Martín, Balmaceda 1600 (234017
* Buses Turismo Arrigoriaga, Ercilla 2090 (220474

Services

Destination	Fares	Services	Duration	Companies
Ancud	$8.50	5 services daily		B260
Angol	$2.20	14 services daily	2¼ hrs	B30
Cañete	$4. 60	3 services daily		B164

La Araucania

Buses from Temuco — continued

Destination	Fares	Services	Duration	Companies
• Capitán Pastene	$2.50	2 services daily		B88, B164
• Carahué	$0.90	17 services daily		B225, B228
• Castro	$13.30	7 services daily		B260
• Catripulli	$2.50	2 services daily		B83, B14
• Cherquenco	$1.10	6 services daily		B216, B228, B272
• Chillán	$6.70	11 services daily		A48, A137, A153
• Cholchol	$1.00	10 services daily		B62, B73, B80
• Collipulli	$2.30	14 services daily		A153, B30
• Concepción	$6.50	22 services daily		A48, A153, B30, B81, B179, B207, B260
• Contulmo	$3.00	4 services daily		B88, B164
• Coñaripe	$2.70	4 services daily		B83
• Cunco	$1.20	2 services daily		B83, B228
• Curacautín	$2.30	15 services daily		B30, B73, B216
• Curicó	$11.80	5 services daily		A48
• Ercilla	$1.90	15 services daily		A153, B30
• Freire	$0.80	3 services daily	½ hr	B73, B83, B128
• Galvarino	$1.20	5 services daily		B126, B73, B80
• Gorbea	$0.90	5 services daily		B54, B73, B128, B154
• Icalma	$4.60	2 services daily		B216
• Lanco	$1.50	5 services daily		B128
• La Unión	$3.90	4 services daily		A48, B81, B207
• Lautaro	$0.90	12 services daily		A153, B73, B80, B81, B128, B216, B272
• Lebu	$5.30	4 services daily		B164,
• Lican Ray	$2.10	12 services daily		B73, B83
• Liucura	$3.80	2 services daily		B216
• Loncoche	$1.30	18 services daily		B54, B73, B128, B154, B166, B260
• Lonquimay	$4.60	4 services daily		B216
• Los Angeles	$3.80	29 services daily	2½ hrs	A48, A137, A153, B30, B81, B137, B207, B260
• Los Lagos	$2.50	5 services daily		B128
• Los Sauces	$2.00	2 services daily		B164
• Lumaco	$2.30	2 services daily		B164
• Malalcahuello	$3.00	4 services daily		B216
• Manzanar	$2.70	4 services daily		B216
• Mehuín	$2.30	3 services daily		B128, B170
• Melipeuco	$2.10	4 services daily		B80, B83, B228
• Neuquén (Argentina, via Paso Tromen)	$22.75	Mon, Wed, Fri		B81, B154
• Nueva Imperial	$1.00	21 services daily	1 hr	B14, B62, B225, B228
• Osorno	$5.80	16 services daily		A48, B64, B179, B207, B260
• Panguipulli	$2.50	13 services daily		A153, B83, B128
• Pitrufquén	$0.80	8 services daily		B54, B73, B128, B154, B272
• Pucón	$2.70	32 services daily	2¼ hrs	A106, B83, B137
• Puerto Domínguez	$1.50	4 services daily		B14
• Puerto Montt	$8.00	32 services daily		A48, A137, A153, B64, B81, B179, B207, B260
• Puerto Saavedra	$1.60	7 services daily		B228
• Puerto Varas	$8.00	17 services daily		A48, B64, B81, B179, B260
• Purén	$2.70	3 services daily		B164
• Quellón	$10.50	5 services daily		B260

Buses from Temuco — continued

Destination	Fares	Services	Duration	Companies
• Queule	$1.90	4 services daily		B166, B170, B228, B272
• Rancagua	$11.80	5 services daily		A48
• Río Bueno	$3.80	4 services daily		B64, B82, B98
• San Carlos de Bariloche (Argentina)				
	$27.30	1 service daily	12 hrs	A137
• San Martín de los Andes				
	$22.75	1 service Mon, Wed, Fri		
			10 hrs	B81, Buses TAC
All buses go via Paso de Mamuil Malal (also known as Paso Tromen)				
• San José de la Mariquina				
	$1.10			B154
• Santiago	$12.50	47 services daily	11 hrs	A48, A106, A137, A153, B81, B83, B98, B128, B137, B207, B216, B260
Ejecutivo	$24.60	3 services daily		A153, B83, B179
• Talca	$9.10	8 services daily		A48, A137, A153
• Talcahuano	$5.50	3 services daily		A48, A153
• Teodoro Schmidt	$1.50	1 service daily		B14
• Tirúa		2 services daily		B164
Change in Cañete				
• Toltén	$1.80	7 services daily		B228, B272
• Traiguén	$1.50	14 services daily		B73, B81, B139, B164
• Valdivia	$3.80	32 services daily	3 hrs	A48, A137, A153, B64, B81, B83, B98, B179, B207, B260
• Valparaíso	$14.40	3 services daily		A106
• Victoria	$1.50	47 services daily		A48, A153, B30, B81, B103, B137, B139, B164, B216
• Vilcún	$0.60	6 services daily		B216, B228, B272
• Villarrica	$2.00	30 services daily	1½ hrs	A106, B83, B73, B137
• Zapala (Argentina, via Paso Pino Hachado)				
	$18.20	1 service daily	12 hrs	A48, B81

Buses from Cunco
Narbus, Buses JAC, and Buses Regional Villarrica run frequent daily services to Temuco and direct services to Villarrica via Pedregoso.

Buses from Freire
Buses García and Buses JAC run regular services to Temuco and Villarrica/Pucón. Buses Panguisur run services to Lanco and Panguipulli in Region X de Los Lagos.

Buses from Gorbea
Buses García, Ruta Sur, and Panguisur run regular daily bus services to Temuco; Buses Costa Sur run regular daily buses to Villarrica.

Buses from Nueva Imperial
Minibuses Las Colinas, Buses ACA, Buses EPAS and Narbus run daily regular services to Temuco, Cholchol, Carahué, and Puerto Saavedra.

minder of how the country was before the arrival of the Europeans. Wild pigeons, goldfinches, *loicas* (Chilean singing birds), and foxes inhabit the park. This is also the home of a small colony of *monitos del monte*, a noctur-nal marsupial, already rare, which hibernates during the colder months. The park, which is open all year round, has many excursion paths, small ponds and a fountain halfway up the slope. The small restaurant-

LA ARAUCANIA

🚂 Trains from Temuco

The railroad station is on Avenida Barros Arana.
The ticket office is at M. Bulnes 562 ☎ 233522.

Destination	Salón	Económico	Services	Duration
• Chillán	$9.70	$7.00	1 service daily	6 hrs
• Curicó	$14.00	$10.00	1 service daily	9 hrs
• Laja	$6.50	$4.60	1 service daily	
• La Unión	$7.60	$5.50	2 services daily	
• Linares	$5.30	$3.80	1 service daily	8 hrs
• Osorno	$7.60	$5.50	2 services daily	5 hrs
• Puerto Montt	$10.60	$7.60	2 services daily	9 hrs
• Rancagua	$15.20	$11.00	2 services daily	9 hrs
• Santiago	$16.00	$11.40	2 services daily	11½ hrs
• Talca	$12.50	$9.10	2 services daily	8 hrs

cum-*cafetería* at the top commands views over the city to the volcanoes in the *pre-Cordillera*. This mountain is important historically because it was the site of the 1881 peace talks between the Chilean government and representatives of the Mapuche tribes. The parley site is commemorated at La Patagua (the *patagua* is a native Chilean linden tree), and is marked by an enclosed tree with a memorial stone in front of it.

• The Mercado Municipal (Public Market) is one of the cleanest markets in the whole of South America. There are many small eating places and *cafeterías*, all spotless, where you can sample the local dishes.

☛ Excursions

Tour operators

☞ • Turismo Christopher, A. Prat 696 office 419 ☎ 211680, fax 235616. Money exchange, adventure tours, rafting, English spoken
• Germania Tur, Manuel Montt 942 ☎ 210564
• Aventuras Lonquimay Chile, A. Prat 156 next to Hotel Baviera ☎ 238466, fax 238466. Outdoor tour operator

Excursions

An excursion to the coast, west of Temuco, takes you into the heart of Mapuche territory. Many villages and towns are inhabited solely by Indians, and you may observe their way of life and their agricultural practises. I suggest a trip via **Nueva Imperial, Carahué, Puerto Saavedra**, and **Lago Budi**. This is 84 km on Ruta S-40, sealed as far as Carahué. Frequent buses travel this route. See the entries for Carahué (page 585) and Puerto Saavedra (page 612).

• **Cherquenco:** 63 km east on Ruta S-31; it is the nearest village to **Refugio Llaima** in the western part of **Parque Nacional Conguillío-Las Paraguas**. Cherquenco is a center for Mapuche crafts, specializing in clay figurines. Flota Erbuc, Vogabus and Narbus run daily bus services from Temuco.

• **Cholchol**: 29 km north-east on Ruta S-20 at the junction of **Río Cholchol** and **Estero Renaco**. This is a sizeable Mapuche settlement and a stronghold of Mapuche culture, where people still converse in the Indian language. The surrounding district has many *reducciones*. It is well worth a visit, but respect the people's customs and do not offend them by taking photographs. For bus services, see "Buses" above.

• **Galvarino:** 66 km north-west. This small town of 2500 inhabitants is largely a Mapuche settlement with a Swiss-German colonial settlement west of town. It is off the beaten track — for trail-blazers. Buses García, Huincabus, and Buses Paihuinca run five services daily from Temuco via Lautaro or Cholchol.

• **Lago Colico** and north shore of **Lago Caburga**: Lago Colico is located 73 km south-east of Temuco; Lago Caburga is a further 29 km east. The gravel-surfaced Ruta S-75 runs 14 km south of Cunco to Lago Colico and then along its northern edge, giving magnificent views of the mountains beyond the opposite shore. This lake, not yet on the tourist circuit, retains its tranquil serenity. On reaching the mouth of the **Río Trafambulli**, the road turns north through prosperous farming country to the northern section of Lago Caburga, which is also quite undisturbed. This trip can continue through the **Río Maichin** valley to **Curarrehué** and then on to Pucón. A short trail beginning at the river junction, soon after leaving Lago Caburga, takes you up the **Río Blanco** to **Termas de Río Blanco**. Again, this is a splendid trip despite the lack of facilities and the bad section between Cailiche and **Reigolil**. Narbus and Buses J.A.C. run services 4 times per week beyond Cunco.

- **Lautaro:** Situated 30 km north at the intersection of the Panamericana with Ruta S-10 west to Galvarino and S-11-R east to Curacautín, on the **Río Cautín**, some distance east off the Panamericana. Founded in 1881 after the peace treaty with the Mapuche, it is now a town of 16 000 inhabitants. **Parque Isabel Riquelme** near the Río Cautín contains a few *lagunas*. The Piscicultura de Lautaro is a fish hatchery administered by the Universidad Católica in Temuco. Here, trout are bred to be released into the local rivers. Lautaro's bus terminal is on André Bello 200. Many bus companies make regular stops: Flota Erbuc, Buses Power, Interregional Abbeysur, Buses Unión del Sur, Buses Fénix Pullman Norte, Vogabus, Buses García, Buses Huinca, Buses Paihuinca, and Buses Panguisur. There are regular services to Galavarino, Temuco, Lonquimay, Curacautín, Concepción, and Santiago.

- **Loncoche:** 77 km south. Loncoche is a timber town about half a kilometer east of the Panamericana. Founded in 1900, it has now a population of 14 000. There are many raspberry plantations in the surrounding district. The old Panamericana via **Lastarria** turns off to the north here. If you

are heading north in your own transport, I advise you to take this slightly longer but very picturesque drive. Bus companies with regular services to and from Loncoche: Buses Cruz del Sur, Manuel Bulnes 089 (471040; Buses TAS Choapa, Manuel Bulnes 083 (471151; Buses Pangui Sur, Buses Igi Llaima, Buses Regional Sur, Buses J.A.C., Buses Tur-Bus Jedimar, Buses Power, Ettabus, and Buses García. They run regular daily services to Temuco, Valdivia, Puerto Montt, Panguipulli, Pucón, Villarrica, Santiago, and Concepción.

- **Nueva Toltén:** about 97 km southwest, on the south side of the **Río Toltén,** formerly the southern border of Mapuche territory. As the name implies, this small town of about 4000 inhabitants is a fairly new town, established after Toltén was destroyed by the 1960 earthquake. The Huilliches, to the south, were soon converted to Christianity. The settlement was a trading post with the Mapuche when the Spanish pushed north from Valdivia. Fourteen kilometers north is the ferry to Gualpí, which brings you on to the trail leading north to Lago Budi and Puerto Saavedra. This goes through Mapuche country and is for hiking enthusiasts. From Nueva Toltén, Vogabus and Narbus run four services daily to Temuco. Buses Perla runs daily afternoon services to Valdivia; fare $1.90.

- **Pitrufquén:** 31 km south. This small town of 10 000 was founded in 1882 on the south bank of the Río Toltén just across the bridge from Freire. Most buses, except express buses, turn into Pitrufquén. There is a CONAF office here which issues fishing licenses. The post office and public telephone is in Francisco Bilbao; a COPEC gas station is on Panamericana. The following bus companies make scheduled stops in Pitrufquén: Buses Fénix Pullman Norte, Avenida Balmaceda 446 (391251; Buses TAS Choapa, Libertador B. O'Higgins 760 (391025; Tur-Bus Jedimar, Buses Regional Sur, Buses J.A.C., Vogabus, Buses García, and Buses DAS. They run regular daily services to Temuco, Santiago, Puerto Montt, Valdivia, and Villarrica.

- **Parque Nacional Conguillio-Las Paraguas**: 104 km east on Ruta S-31 via Vilcún. One of the most scenic national parks in Chile, it is accessible via **Cunco** and **Melipeuco** on Rutas S-51 and S-61. Frequent buses from Temuco to Lonquimay pass within 5 km of the crater of Volcán Lonquimay — a three-hour drive from Temuco, or a one-day round trip. There are regular buses to Melipeuco, which is 29 km south of the southern access to the national park, and also frequent public transport to **Curacautín** and the northern access of the national park (40 km south-east). See the entry for the park on page 596.

- While in Temuco, you can visit **Parque Nacional Tolhuaca, Reserva Nacional Malalcahuello-Nalcas,** and **Volcán Lonquimay**. See the entries for Parque Nacional Conguillio-Las Paraguas (page 596), Parque Nacional Tolhuaca (page 600), and Reserva Nacional Malalcahuello-Nalcas (page 616).

- **Teodoro Schmidt**: 72 km south-west, on the north side of the lower Río Toltén. This small town of 4000 inhabitants was founded in 1881. It was named after a German immigrant who surveyed the newly acquired land for the Chilean government. Buses ACA runs regular daily services to Temuco. There are several ferry services across the Río Toltén. Ferry services are free Mon–Fri 0800–1300 and 1400–1830; a small fee is payable outside these hours. This is of interest to trail-blazers who want to follow part of the Camino de Valdivia to the town of Valdivia. This trip can be continued south to **Nueva Toltén** and to the Pacific coastal resorts of Queule and Mehuín.

From there, it is possible to return by bus to Temuco or continue to Valdivia.

- **Villarrica** and **Pucón**: This excursion is a possible day trip from Temuco, but the natural beauty of Lago Villarrica, Lago Caburga, Lago Calafquén (dominated by **Volcán Villarrica** and Volcán Quetrupillán) and the many thermal springs, are worthy of a longer stay. The road from Temuco to Villarrica and on to Pucón is completely sealed and passes through fairly flat, lush agricultural country — dairy farming, berry cultivation, and apple orchards — interspersed with small forests. Public buses leave every half hour. Volcán Villarrica is visible in the distance as you leave town. The best views are just before you cross the Río Toltén. Between Villarrica and Pucón, the 24 km road runs along the southern rim of the lake — a continuous tourist belt of hotels, motels, camping grounds, and restaurants. Many excursions can be made from Villarrica or Pucón, such as an ascent of Volcán Villarrica, or visits to a Mapuche reducciones, Parque Nacional Huerquehué, or Termas de Huife. See the entries for Villarrica (page 634), Pucón (page 603), and Parque Nacional Huerquehué (page 598).

- Thermal spas: Those who want to enjoy a more relaxing stay in the area could spend a couple of days in any one of the nearby thermal resorts such as Termas de Palguín and Termas de Huife (both near Pucón), Termas de Manzanar (near Curacautín), or Termas de Tolhuaca (near Victoria and Curacautín). See "Excursions" from Curacautín (page 589) and from Pucón (page 611); and the entry for Parque Nacional Tolhuaca on page 600.

VICTORIA

Area code: 045
Population: 22 000
Altitude: 360 m
Distance from Temuco: 63 km south on Panamericana

Victoria is located on the **Río Traiguén**, where it is spanned by a rail bridge. The town was founded in 1881 and named in honour of the occupation of Lima, which ended the War of the Pacific. Victoria is an important crossroads.

Ruta R-89 goes east to Curacautín and Lonquimay and continues over the **Paso de Pino Hachado** to Zapala and Neuquén in Argentina. The turn-off west to Ruta R-88 is an alternative route to Angol and Concepción via Traiguén.

Traiguén

Situated 30 km west on a wide plain beside the **Río Traiguén**, Traigén was founded in 1878, and now has 14 000 inhabitants. The once dense forest cover in the surrounding district has almost disappeared. Parque Bellavista has been declared an *area*

⊟ Accommodation in Victoria

Hotels
- Puma, Sotomayor Block 500
  Backpackers only
- Royal, Confederación Suiza 1240   **AFGHV**   (841982 $I   ⚊
  Shared bathroom
- Victoria, Sotomayor 443, around the corner from bus terminal and opposite market
              (841284 $J   ⚊

  Shared bathroom, backpackers only

Accommodation along the Panamericana Sur

Hotels
- El Bosque, KM610 right at the intersection to Traiguén
              AEFGHIJLMP$UV   (841960 $H   ⚊
  Sauna, tennis courts
- María Gabriela   (841539

Hosterías
- El Colono   (841744
- El Pino, Avenida B. O'Higgins near Panamericana
- Mackray   **ADEFGHJMPV**   (841565

Accommodation in Ercilla
- Hostería Ruta 5, on the Panamericana
- Hostería Mariejo, on the Panamericana

Accommmodation in Traiguén
- Hotel Traiguén, Saavedra 467   **AEFGHJLMPV**   (861412 $H   ⚊⚊

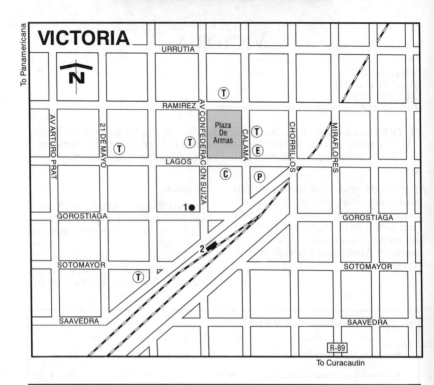

Key to map

A	Iglesia	1	Hotel Royal
C	Municipalidad (Town hall)	2	Railroad station
E	Telephone		
T	Bus terminals		

de protección, and preserves many different species of unique pine trees. A train dating back to 1889 is on display at the disused railroad station.

⚔ Festivals

Festivals in Ercilla
Ercilla is 22 km north.
- February, first week: Foundation of Ercilla

- Festival de la Cereza (Cherry Festival), in the cherry harvesting season

ℹ Tourist information
- Municipalidad de Victoria. Fishing licenses

‼ Eating out
- Restaurant Alemana $Y
- Restaurant Club Social, Avenida Republica de Suiza

🚌 Buses from Victoria

Companies
Most long-distance buses have their terminals on or near the main plaza. Among them are:

- A48   Buses Lit, E. Ramírez 425 (841318
- B30   Buses Bío Bío, Avenida Confederación Suiza 1164 (841416
- B81   Buses Igi Llaima, Calama 1195 (841483
- Buses Nar-Bus, Sotomayor 569 (841176

The rural bus terminal is located on the corner of Pisagua and Sotomayor.

Services

Destination	Fare	Services	Duration	Companies
Angol	$1.25	14 services daily	1 hr	B30
Cañete	$3.80	4 services daily		B103
Chillán	$3.00	1 service daily		A153
Concepción	$4.60	10 services daily		B30, B81
Contulmo	$3.10	2 services daily		B164
Curacautín	$1.70	14 services daily	1 hr	A106, B30, B103, B216
Lebu	$4.60	5 services daily		B103, B164
Lonquimay	$2.50	3 services daily		B103, B216
Los Angeles	$2.50	4 services daily	1½ hrs	A153, B30, B81, B137
Los Sauces		3 services daily		B164
Malalcahuello	$1.70	3 services daily	2 hrs	B216
Purén	$2.10	4 services daily		B103, B164
Temuco	$1.50	39 services daily		A48, A153, B30, B81, B103, B137, B139, B164, B216
Traiguén	$1.20	3 services daily		B164
Valparaíso	$13.30	3 services daily		A106

Buses from Traiguén
Bus companies calling on Traiguén: Tur-Bus Jedimar, General Lagos 651 (861928; Buses Thiele Ewert, Buses Igi Llaima, Buses Tliver, Buses Puma, and Buses García. There are 24 services daily to Angol; 16 services daily to Collipulli, Victoria and Temuco; 2 services daily to Lebu and Los Angeles, Contulmo, and Cañete; and 1 service daily to Chillán.

Eating out along the Panamericana
- Restaurant Hostería El Bosque, corner of Avenida Bernardo O'Higgins and Panamericana
- Restaurant Hostería Mackray,
- Hostería Victoria, right at intersection of Panamericana on the right-hand side

Eating out in Traiguén
Traiguén is 30 km west.
- Club Social, Avenida Coronel Urrutía 342
- La Bahía. Chilean cuisine
- Sonia. Chilean cuisine

📮 Post and telegraph

Post office
- Correos de Chile, Calama 1208

Telephone
- CTC, Calama 1195 fax (45) 831490
- Telex Chile, Ramírez 685

🚗 Motoring
- COPEC gas station at intersection Panamericana and Avenida B. O'Higgins

⚽ Sport
Trout fishing: see page 579.

⟐ Excursions

- **Ercilla**: 22 km north, on the Panamericana. This small town was founded by Gregorio Urrutía on February 6, 1885, where the central valley is flat and wide. The road runs in a straight north–south line through wheat country. Many volcanos are visible to the east, in particular **Volcán Tolhuaca**. This is orchard country, in particular cherries. In the nearby Mapuche villages of **Chacaico** and **Chequenco** the villagers produce unique clay figurines in the style of their ancestors. **Salto Pidenco**, 15 km west near **Chiguaihué**, is a 30 m waterfall on the Río Hueuquén descending from Cerro Pidenco. There is a COPEC gas station on the Panamericana. The following bus companies make scheduled stops in Ercilla: Buses Bío Bío, Tur-Bus Jedimar, and Buses Las Lajas, running regular daily services to Angol, Los Angeles, Temuco, and Victoria.
- **Lonquimay**, **Laguna Gualletué**, **Laguna Icalma** and the headwaters of Río Bío Bío: Fishing and hiking in pristine areas for the outdoor enthusiast. See the entry for Lonquimay on page 593.
- **Parque Nacional Tolhuaca** and **Termas de Tolhuaca** (via Curacautín): Take one of the regular buses to Curacautín and take a taxi from there. For information on the park, see the entry on page 600; for information on the thermal springs, see "Thermal resorts" on page 578.
- **Parque Nacional Conguillio-Las Paraguas**, with **Volcán Llaima** and **Termas Río Blanco Curacautín** (via Curacautín): Take a bus to Curacautín and a taxi from there. See the entry for the park on page 596.
- **Reserva Nacional Malalcahuello-Nalcas**, with **Volcán Lonquimay** and ski fields (via Curacautín): Regular buses run all the way, but you own transport is necessary to the snow fields. See the entry for the reserve on page 616.

VILLARRICA

Area code: 045
Population: 21 000
Altitude: 350 m
Distance from Temuco: 86 km south-east on Ruta 118 and Panamericana

The town, founded in 1552 by Gerónimo de Alderete with 50 Spanish settlers, is situated on the western end of Lago Villarrica. To the south-west, the snow-capped peak of **Volcán Villarrica** beckons.

Villarrica was abandoned in 1554 and re-founded in 1559 by García Hurtado de Mendoza. It fell victim to the Mapuche and was completely destroyed in 1602. Coronel Urrutía refounded the town in 1883. This is one of the most scenic places in the region, gateway to many areas of outstanding beauty. There are superb views from the Río Toltén bridge across the lake to Volcán Villarrica and the town. Villarrica is surrounded by fields which are mostly given over to dairy farming. The tourist facilities are excellent.

Turn off the Panamericana at Freire; the road is sealed all the way.

ⓘ Tourist information

- Cámara de Turismo Municipal, Pedro de Valdivia 1070. Fishing licenses

Ⓐ Camping

There are many first-class camping sites along the south side of Lago Villarrica on the road to Pucón.

Plate 37   Región XI de Aisén
Top: Lago General Carrera, near Chile Chico
Bottom: Puerto Aisén, main plaza

Plate 38   Región X de Aisén
Top: Fiords near Puerto Chacabuco
Bottom: Lago General Carrera, beach near Chile Chico

🍴 Eating out

Restaurants
- La Tranquera, Aviador Acevedo 767
- Club Río Toltén, G. Koerner 153. International cuisine
- Hostería Rayhuen, P. Montt 668. Chilean cuisine
- El Rey Del Marisco, V. Letelier 1030. Seafood. Beautiful spot overlooking lake
- En Los Puertos del Mar, A. Prat 821 $X. Seafood
- Hotel Puchi, Pedro de Valdivia 678. Chilean cuisine
- La Cabañita, Camillo Henriquez 398
- Treffpunkt (formerly Club Social), Avenida Pedro de Valdivia 640 $X. English and German spoken
- Yachting Club, San Martín 802. International cuisine
- Hotel Yandaly, C. Henriquez 401. International cuisine

Café restaurants
- 2001, C.Henriquez 379. Light meals
- Baimaran, Camillo Henriquez 331-A. Crêpes suzettes
- Dinners, Gerónimo de Alderete 709 $X
- Rivoli, C. Henriquez 376. Light meals

Cafés
- Scorpio, Pedro de Valdivia 598
- El Candil, Letelier 728. Like a bar

▶ Entertainment

- Disco Bar Conga, Saturnino Epulef block 1000 near Julio Zegers
- Disco Crisarlu, Julio Zegers, 850. Drinks and sandwiches
- Disco Huimpalay, part of camping 13 km east of town. Many young people
- Disco La Ensenada, S. Epulef 964. Seafood
- Pub El Molino, Letelier block 1000 near Zegers

🌐 Post and telegraph

Post office
- Post office and telex, A. Muñoz corner of General Urrutía

Telephone
- CTC, Julio Zegers 1160, fax 411340
- CTC, Pedro Montt 575
- CTC, C. Henriquez 544, fax (45) 411114

💲 Financial

- Cambios Latino America, Anfitrion Muñoz block 400 near V. Letelier Empresa San Martín

🏠 Services and facilities

Dry cleaner
- Lavaseco Villarrica, Bello 348

Laundry
- Lavandería, Julio Zegers 827

Photographic supplies
- Photo Center, Camillo Henriquez block 423

Supermarket
- Supermercado Oriente, Camilo Henriquez block 300 near Urrutia

🚗 Motoring services

For gas stations, see the city map.

⚽ Sport

Trout fishing
For a list of fishing spots, see page 579. The Río Toltén is the outlet of Lago Villarrica. Fishing trips downriver from Villarrica to the following destinations:
- Prado Verde: 14 km downstream; cost $27.00
- Catrico: 30 km downstream: cost $35.00
- Coipué: 35 km downstream: cost $40.00

The following groups organize fishing excursions:
- Grupo CEA, Andrés Bello
- Grupo Rios, San Martín 256
- Grupo Riquelme, Banco de Estado

You can hire boats:
- Down Río Toltén: San Martín 348
- At the boat ramp: General Koerner between Prat and O'Higgins. Boats $3.00 per hour, tricycle rider boats $2.30 per hour

📷 Sightseeing

- Museo de Villarrica, Pedro de Valdivia block 1000. Has an exhibition of Mapuche *rucas* or houses.

LA ARAUCANIA

Key to map

A	Catedral del Obispado de la Araucania	**41**	Hotel Fuente
C	Municipalidad (Town hall)	**44**	Hotel Nuevo Puchi
D	Post office and telex	**46**	Hostería Rayhuen
E	Telephone	**47**	Hospedaje
F	Carabineros (Police)	**48**	Hotel Dinners
H	Hospital	**50**	Hospedaje
I	Tourist information	**52**	Hospedaje
P	Gas stations		
T	Bus terminals	○	**Eating out**

		20	Café 2001

● Accommodation

3	Hostería Bilbao	**22**	Cafetería Batmaran
5	Cabañas Tritraco	**23**	Café Rivoli
6	Hospedaje	**24**	Restaurant La Cabañita
7	Hospedaje	**31**	Restaurant El Rey Del Marisco
8	Hospedaje	**37**	El Molino Pub
9	Hotel Yachting club	**39**	Restaurant Treffpunkt
10	Hostería Kiel	**42**	Café Scorpio
12	Hotel Central		
13	Hospedaje	⊙	**Entertainment**
14	Motel Lautaro	**51**	Disco Conga
15	Hotel El Ciervo		
16	Hotel Villarrica	△	**Tour operators**
17	Motel Melilafquen	**19**	Pesquitur
25	Hospedaje		
26	Hospedaje	■	**Sights**
27	Motel Los Ositos	**18**	Librería Municipal
28	Cabañas Gudenschwager	**43**	Museum
29	Hospedaje	**53**	Railroad station
30	Hospedaje		
32	Hostería Huequimey	□	**Services**
33	Hospedaje	**1**	Boat hire
34	Hotel Yandali	**2**	Colegio Alemán
36	Hospedaje	**4**	Boat hire
38	Residencial Victoria	**11**	Mapuche Art
40	Hotel Puchi	**21**	Supermarket
		35	Foto Center
		45	Supermarket
		49	Laundry

✈ Excursions

Tour operators

- Pesquitur, Letelier 650 ☎ 411385. They also provide transport to the airport in Temuco
- Peca Peca Tours, Anfion Muñoz 15, next to Lutheran church. Excursions in Landrovers to Volcán Villarrica ($30.00), Lago Caburga ($60.00), Coñaripe ($60.00). Minimum 5 persons, German spoken. Mercedes Taxi for trips to Temuco and Valdivia is at the same address
- Transporte Turístico, P. Montt 365 ☎ 411078. They also provide transport to the airport in Temuco

Excursions

Volcanoes, lakes, glaciers, Mapuche villages, thermal spas, hiking, and skiing areas are within easy reach.

- **Pucón**: 23 km east on Lago Villarrica. This is the starting point for climbing Volcán Villarrica and the ski slopes. There are regular bus services to and from Villarrica. It is also a lakeside resort with many tourist facilities. See the entry for Pucón on page 603.
- **Termas de Huife** and **Termas de Palguín**: See "Excursions" from Pucón on page 611.
- **Licán Ray**: Located on **Lago Calafquén** (180 square kilometers),

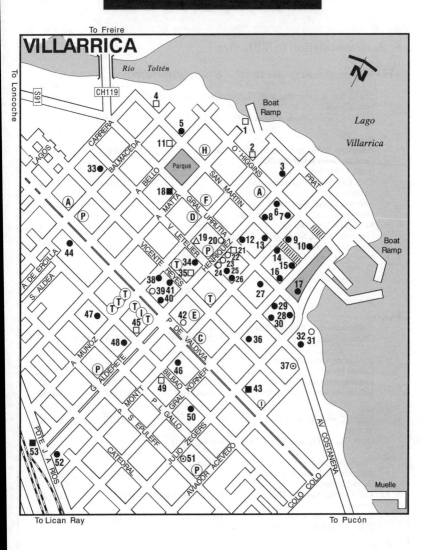

VILLARRICA

To Freire

To Loncoche

Río Toltén

S991

CH119

4

5

11

33

18

Parque

Boat Ramp

1

2

3

Lago Villarrica

H

A

F

D

19 20

44

P

VICENTE

A. DE ERCILLA

S. ALDEA

A

P

P

V. LETELIER

A. BELLO

A. MATTA

CARRERA

BALMACEDA

LAGOS

GRAL URRUTIA

SAN MARTIN

O'HIGGINS

PRAT

6 7
8

12
13

9 10

14

15

16

27

17

Boat Ramp

21
22
23
24 25
26

34
35

T

REYES

HENRIQUEZ

38

39 41
40

47

T T T
T I
T

45

48

46

49

50

P DE VALDIVIA

E

C

42

A. MUÑOZ

MONTT

P. S. EPULEFF

P. I. GALLO

ALDERETE

BILBAO

GRAL KORNER

JULIO ZEGERS

AVIADOR ACEVEDO

CATEDRAL

29
28
30

36

T

32 31

37

43

I

51

P

53
52

PDTE J.A. RIOS

To Lican Ray

COLO COLO

AV. COSTANERA

Muelle

To Pucón

⊟ Accommodation in Villarrica

Hotels

★★★★El Ciervo, General Koerner 241   ACDEFGHIJKLMNPS$UVYZ
                                         ☏ 411215 $F ♙
  Sauna, tennis, car rental, boat hire, mini-golf, beach frontage, English and German spoken, 30 beds
- Dinners, Gerónimo de Alderete 709   AEFHIJKLPSV   ☏ 411215/411370/411070
                                                                   $H ♙
  40 beds
- Amancay, Pedro de Valdivia 327   BFP   ☏ 411216 $H ♙
- Central, General Urrutia 712
  Budget travelers
- Club Río Toltén, G. Koerner 153   S   ☏ 411631 $G ♙
  18 beds
- Fuentes, Vicente Reyes 665   ☏ 411595 $I ♙
  Shared bathroom, budget travelers
- Kolping, I. Riquelme 399   AEFGHM   ☏ 411388 $J ♙
  German spoken, fax 411682, 29 rooms
- Villarrica, General Koerner 255   AEFGHIJLMPRTUV   ☏ 411641
- Yandaly, Camilo Henriquez 401   AEFGHIJPSV   ☏ 411452 $H ♙
  12 beds
- Yachting Club, General San Martín 802   ☏ 411191 $E ♙
                                         ABDEFGHIJKLMPRSUVZ
  18 rooms

Motels
- Gudenschwager, General Urrutia   ☏ 411373
- Lautaro, Pedro Montt 218   ABCFGHIKNPRV   ☏ 411568/411191
                                                         $G for 4
- Los Ositos, General Urrutia 891   BCPV   ☏ 411806
  Cabins for 5
- Melilafquén, General Koerner 250   ABHIKP   ☏ 411276 $G ♙
- Millarruca, Saturnino Epulef 1504   AEFHIJLNPUV   ☏ 411448 $G ♙

Hosterías
- Bilbao, Camilo Henriquez 43   PS   ☏ 411186 $G ♙
  20 beds
- De la Colina, Presidente Rios 1177 (follow signpost)
                                   AFPSZ   ☏ 411503 $F ♙
  Views over lake and volcano, English spoken
- Huequimey, V. Letelier 1030-B   ☏ 411462 $H ♙
  Shared bathroom
- Kiel, General Koerner 153   ABCDEFGHIJKLNPUV   ☏ 411631 $G ♙
  4 rooms
- Rayhuén, Pedro Montt 668   ADEFHLPUV   ☏ 411571 $G ♙
  $F ♙ shared bathroom, 9 rooms, 30 beds

Cabañas
- Traitraco, San Martín 380   ABCDHKLPV   ☏ 411064 $F for 4
- Trigal, Pedro Montt 365   ☏ 411078

Residenciales
- Puchi, Pedro de Valdivia 678   AEFGHIJLPV   ☏ 411392 $I ♙
  30 beds
- San Francisco, Zegers 646   ☏ 411577

Accommodation in Villarrica — continued

- Victoria, A. Muñoz 530
  Budget travelers

Hospedajes
These *hospedajes*, listed by street, provide accommodation for budget travelers.
- General Koerner: 310, 320, 340, 442
- Letelier: 297, 702, 748
- Matta 466
- Julio Zegers 537
- Pedro Montt 101
- San Martín 734
- O'Higgins: 777, 799

Youth hostel
- Pastoral Juvenil, M.A. Matta 829   ℰ 411658 $J   ♟
  Backpackers, shared bathroom

Accommodation between Villarrica and Pucón
Alongside Lake Villarrica.

Hotels
- Antumalal, 23 km just before entering Pucón
  ADFHKLPRS$UV   ℰ 441011/491956 $C ♟♟
  Located on a promontory on Lago Villarrica; tennis, fax 441013
- El Parque, 2.5 km east   AEFGHIJKLNPV   ℰ 411120 $E ♟♟
  Fax 411090
- Hotel y Camping Millaray, 17 km east ℰ   411120
- Marina Tatalafquen, 14 km east   ABEFGHIJKLPV   ℰ 212638 $E ♟♟

Motels
- Curiñanco   ℰ 5411205
- Lonquén, 2 km outside town   ABCDFGHIJKLNP$V
           ℰ 411120 $G ♟♟
- Lorena, 10 km east just past Puente Lefun   ℰ 411940 $H for 4
  ABCDEFGHIJKLMNP$UV
  Camping
- Saint John, Sector Los Riscos, 20 KM east
  AEFGHKLPUV $G ♟♟
  Tennis, lake frontage, car rental, boat hire, sauna. Reservations in Temuco: ℰ 441165
- Tunquelén, 11 km east past Puente Huitachio   ℰ 411955 $D for 4
  ABCEFGHIJKLMP$TUV
  Lake frontage, tennis, boat hire, 16 cabins

Cabañas
- Amulén, 3 km west of Pucón   ℰ 441143
- Huimpalay, 13 km east of Villarrica past Puente Molco
  ABEFGHILNVX   ℰ 11201/411522 $E for 6
  80 camp sites, 9 cabins. Open all year, electricity, water, toilets, shop, camp sites $I for 6
  (graded according to location)
- Loncotraro, 14 km east   ℰ 411965
- Los Altos del Lago, 14 km east   ℰ 412152
- Alto Misimali, 21 km east just before entering Pucón
  ABCDHILNR   ℰ 441049
- Suyay, 9 km east before Puente Lefun ABCHJNPV   ℰ 411956

Accommodation in Villarrica — continued

Accommodation in Pichilafquen
Pichilafquen is on the west side of Lago Villarrica.
★★★★Hotel Los Boldos, Ruta S- 69, 8 km north of Villarrica
ABCHKLNUV   (411656/411285
  Boat hire, 52 beds

🚌 Buses from Villarrica

Companies
The rural bus terminal is on Anfitrion Muñoz near Francisco Bilbao.
All other bus companies have their own offices scattered throughout the town.
- A48   Buses Lit, Anfión Muñoz 640 (411555
- A106 Fénix Pullman Norte, Pedro de Valdivia 629 (411313
- A137 Buses Tas Choapa, A. Muñoz 615 (411333
- A153 Tur-Bus Jedimar, Pedro de Valdivia 615 (411534
- B82   Buses Intersur, Pedro de Valdivia 615 (411534
- B83   Buses J.A.C., Francisco Bilbao 610 (411479
- B137 Buses Power, Pedro de Valdivia 619 (411121
- B199 Buses Estrella del Sur, A. Muñoz block 600 near Francisco Bilbao
- B201 Empresa La Estrella, Vicente Reyes 699
- Buses San Martín, A. Muñoz 419 (411584

Services

Destination	Fare	Services	Duration	Companies
Caburga		2 services daily		B83 (summer only), B145
Calafquén		1 service daily		
Coñaripe	$1.30	7 services daily		B83, B199
Curarrehué	$1.50	3 services daily	2½ hrs	B83, B145
Lanco	$1.10	3 services daily		B83
Licán Ray	$0.60	7 services daily	1 hr	B73, B83, B199
Liquiñe	$2.40	1 service Mon–Sat		B199
Loncoche	$1.10	9 services daily		B83
Los Laureles	$1.20	3 services Mon–Fri		B145
Neuquén (Argentina)				
	$25.00	1 service Mon–Sat		B81, B83
In summer all buses go via Paso Mamuil; in winter Paso Huahum is used				
Panguipulli		3 services daily		Buses Rural Andes, Abarzúa
Pitrufquén	$1.70	1 service daily		B73
Pucón	$1.00	32 services daily		B83, B145
Puesco	$1.70	2 services daily		B145
Quiñenahuin	$1.90	1 service Mon–Sat		B145
San Carlos de Bariloche (Argentina) via Paso Puyehué				
	$27.50			A137
San José de la Mariquina		3 services daily		B83

Buses from Villarrica — continued

Destination	Fare	Services	Duration	Companies
San Martín de los Andes (Argentina) via Paso Tromen				
	$13.00	1 service Mon–Sat	9 hrs	B81, B83
Santiago	$21.00	2 services daily	11 hrs	A153, B83
	$14.70	10 services daily	12 hrs	A48, A106, A137, A153, B81, B82, B83, B137
Talca	$9.50	2 services daily		B82
Temuco	$1.90	35 services daily	1½ hrs	A106, B73, B83, B137
Termas de Huife		4 services Mon–Fri		B145
Termas de San Luis				
	$1.30	3 services daily		B145
Valdivia	$2.50	3 services daily		B83
Valparaíso	$18.40	4 services daily		A106, A137
Viña del Mar	$18.40	4 services daily		A153

30 km south on Ruta S-95-T. See the entry for Licán Ray on page 590.
- **Termas de Liquiñe**: 67 km south-east on RN 201, in Región X de los Lagos. This is a thermal resort with good motel-type accommodation in picturesque surroundings. See Panguipulli in Región X de los Lagos.

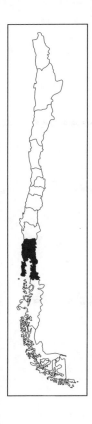

REGIÓN X

DE

LOS LAGOS

Size: 69 000 square km
Population: 900 000
Regional capital: Puerto Montt
Provinces (and provincial capitals):
- Chiloé (Castro)
- Llanquihué (Puerto Montt)
- Osorno (Osorno)
- Palena (Chaitén)
- Valdivia (Valdivia)

Los Lagos — The Lakes! The wonderful lakes of this captivating region with their well-developed facilities draw thousands of tourists year-round. Most of them nestle at the foot of one or more looming volcanoes, hosting many splendid thermal resorts, some of which are renowned for their fine skiing. Chile's first national parks were created in this region, which now boasts five major national parks and scores of national reserves, all within easy reach of the major population centers.

Región X de Los Lagos lies between the latitudes of 39° and 44° south. It shares boundaries in the north with Región IX de La Araucania and in the south with Región XI de Aisén. The Andes form the eastern border with Argentina, and the Pacific Ocean pounds its western shore. The region is linked with the rest of the country by the Panamericana (RN 5), which is sealed all the way to Santiago. Major towns are **Puerto Montt**, **Valdivia**, **Osorno**, **Puerto Varas**, and **Castro**.

Topography

Región X de Los Lagos is aptly named. The major lakes, from north to south, are **Lago Calafquén**, **Lago Panguipulli**, **Lago Pirehueico**, **Lago Riñihué**, **Lago Ranco**, **Lago Puyehué**, **Lago Rupanco**, **Lago Llanquihué**, **Lago Todos Los Santos**, and **Lago Chapo**. Each of these lakes has

tourist facilities, and many of them are first-class tourist destinations.

The volcanoes of the *pre-Cordillera* flank the larger lakes. The best-known are **Volcán Calbuco** east of Puerto Montt, **Volcán Osorno**, (2652 m) between Lago Todos Los Santos and Lago Llanquihué, **Volcán Casa Blanca** (1990 m) east of Lago Rupanco, and **Volcán Puyehué** (2240 m) east of Lago Puyehué. Snow usually blankets most of these volcanoes, but from time to time they erupt. Volcanic activity has caused many hot springs, and there are thermal resorts at **Termas de Puyehué**, **Termas de Coñaripe**, and **Termas de Liquiñe**.

Nearly all the rivers of the high *cordillera* flow through lakes on their way to the Pacific Ocean. Lago Todos Los Santos is fed by the **Río Petrohué** which ends in the **Estuario de Reloncaví**. **Río Maullín** emerges from Lago Llanquihué into a wide estuary near **Maullín**, and **Río Bueno** flows from Lago Ranco. **Río Calle Calle** exits Lago Riñihué to join the ocean near Valdivia — one of Chile's loveliest river scenes. The coast is fringed with fine beaches, but bathing is limited to the summer season. **Maullín**, **Niebla**, **Mehuín** are the most accessible seaside resorts.

Until Puerto Montt, Región X de Los Lagos' geographical features are similar to the rest of Chile. The coastal *cordillera* is almost non-existent, apart from small elevations south of Valdivia. The coastal plain merges inconspicuously with the central valley. The Andes rise behind the chain of volcanoes.

Chiloé Archipelago

South of Puerto Montt, the continent breaks up into an archipelago of islands, leaving only a narrow strip of land, rising sharply to over 2000 m and dotted with volcanoes. **Isla Grande de Chiloé** is the largest island in the Chiloé Archipelago.

Chiloé has a section to itself, beginning on page 753.

The indigenous inhabitants

The area south of the **Río Toltén** was Huilliche country, and although these people occasionally joined with the Mapuches against the Spanish, they were easily subdued. The Huilliches became Christianized and intermarried with the invaders. Pockets of indigenous inhabitants still live in the coastal areas and parts of the *pre-Cordillera*, especially near **Lago Ranco** and **Lago Maihué**. A few villages of Huilliches remain in the southern part of Isla Grande de Chiloé.

European history

Osorno and Valdivia, founded by Pedro de Valdivia, were abandoned in 1598–99 during the first Mapuche uprising. Valdivia had strategic importance to the Viceroys of Peru, who fortified and held the town from 1645 until 1820. During the era of the first presidents of Chile, immigrants were attracted to the south, and Puerto Montt was founded by Germans in 1853.

The Italian Jesuit martyr, Padre Mascardi, discovered the mouth of the **Río Palena** as he searched for a pass across the Andes to the Argentine *pampa*. He may have traveled upriver as far as **La Junta** but this cannot be proved. In recognition of his intrepid voyages, the Chileans named the Río Palena after his birthplace on the Adriatic coast.

Transport

Road

The Panamericana runs up the central valley of the region from the border with La Araucania to Pargua. At Pargua a ferry service links the mainland with Isla Grande de Chiloe, where the Panamericana continues as far as Quellón at the southern end of the island. Lateral roads connect the cities on the coast with cities and towns across the Andean *cordillera* in Argentina; many of these mountain-pass roads are scenic drives of the first order.

In 1972, work began on the Carretera Austral General Pinochet from Puerto Montt to Villa O'Higgins. Now that this project is almost completed, the area south-east of Puerto Montt is becoming one of the most traveled scenic areas in the tenth region. From Puerto Montt, the road crosses primeval country with unparalleled panoramas of snow-capped volcanoes, lakes, waterfalls, glaciers, and fiords. Most of the townships along the route are less than 30 years old and show a pioneering spirit not encountered elsewhere in Chile. Many areas have been set aside as national parks, such as **Parque Nacional Alerce Andino** on the **Seno Reloncaví**. More land, too precious to be lost forever, is in need of protection, such as the area east of **Hornopirén**, the **Volcán Michinmávida** east of Chaitén, and possibly the **Lago Yelcho** area including **Volcán Corcovado** and **Volcán Nevado** areas. Signs of irreparable ecological damage are already widespread.

From Caleta Gonzalo, south to Coihaique, the Carretera Austral is now complete, with the major bridges over the Río Palena and Río Rosselot completed in 1991. The new bridge across the Río Yelcho has added another spectacular stretch and a major tourist attraction to the Chilean road system, but although the Carretera Austral is considered an all-weather dirt road, heavy rains in winter sometimes make sections impassable, and there are no out-of-season road services beyond major settlements — Chaitén and Hornopirén. Do this trip in summer only.

Bus and ferry

A bus service from Puerto Montt to Hornopirén functions all year round, with a ferry service between Caleta La Arena and Caleta Puelche, crossing the Estuario de Reloncaví. Further south from Río Negro, ferry services link Pichanco and Leptepu through the Fiordo Comau, and Pillan and Caleta Gonzalo through the Fiordo Reñihué. These cease from March to November, and are replaced by regular ferry crossings from Pargua to Chaitén between March and November. There is also a ferry service from Quellón to Chaitén between December and the end of February. See also "Boat trips" on page 649.

Economy

The economy of the region rests heavily on dairying and forestry, but tourism is also expanding, especially around Lago Llanquihué, Valdivia, and Lago Ranco. Industry is concentrated in the cities of Valdivia, Osorno, and Puerto Montt. Major industries are linked to fishing and rural production. Dairy industry is mostly located around Osorno.

Fishing

The trout fishing season runs from the second Friday in November until the first Sunday in May. There is no closed season on lakes shared with Argentina. The following waterways are suitable for trout fishing.

- Chaitén: Lago and Río Yelcho, Río Frio, Río Futaleufú
- Choshuenco: Río Enco, Lago Riñihué, Lago Pirehueico, Lago Panguipulli, Río Fuy, Río Llanquihué, Lago Neltume, Río Neltume, Río Puñir
- Cochamó: Río Puelo, Lago Tagua-Tagua, Lago Vidal Gormaz
- Ensenada: Río Petrohué, Lago Todos Los Santos
- Entre Lagos: Río Pilmaiquén from the power station downstream, Río Rahué, Río Coihueco
- Fresia: Río Llico

- Futaleufú: Lago Espolón, Río Futaleufú, Lago Lonconao
- Lanco: Río Cruces
- Llifén: Río Calcurrupe, Río Pillanleufu, Río Blanco, Lago Maihué, Lago Ranco, Río Nilahué, Río Carrán, Río Caunahu, Río Riñinahué, Estero Chollinco
- Los Lagos: Río Quinchilca, Río Callilelfu, Río San Pedro, Río Trafún,
- Panguipulli: Lago Panguipulli, Lago Neltume, Lago Calafquén
- Osorno: Río Pilmaiquén, Lago Constancia, Río Rahué, Lago Rupanco
- Palena: Río Palena, Lago Palena (shared with Argentina, where is it called Lago General Vintter)
- Puerto Montt: Lago Chapo, Río Chamiza
- Puerto Nuevo: Lago Ranco, Río Bueno
- Puerto Varas: Río Pescado, Río Maullín, La Poza, Lago Llanquihué, Río Blanco, Río Tepu
- Puyehué: Río Pescadores, Río Chanleufú, Lago El Toro, Laguna El Encanto, Lago Puyehué, Río Gol-Gol, Lagunas Pato, Gringo, Gallinas and Mellizas
- Ralún: Río Petrohué
- Río Bueno: Río Bueno, Lago Ranco
- Riñihué: Lago Riñihué, Río Enco, Río San Pedro
- Trumao: Río Bueno, Río Pilmaiquén
- Valdivia: Río San Pedro, Río Quinchilca, Río Calle-Calle, Río Futa, Río Cruces, Río Chaihuin
- Ensenada: Río Petrohué, Lago Todos Los Santos

National parks and reserves

- **Monumento Natural Alerce Costero**: 50 km west of **La Unión**. It is not easy to get to this area. Indeed, it is not a general tourist destination because of its remoteness. The main attraction are the forests of Coigue de Magallanes, dwarf cypress (reaching only 50 cm), cinnamon trees, and many carnivorous plants. Wildlife includes pudues (dwarf deer), pumas, and various types of rodent.
- **Parque Nacional Alerce Andino**, 39 250 ha (96 950 acres): 46 km south-east of Puerto Montt on the Carretera Austral. Turn east at Lenca. Picnic area, camping area, walking paths, eating place and shop nearby, mountain hut. See the entry for the park on page 701.
- **Parque Nacional Hornopirén**, 48 232 ha (119 130 acres): 104 km south of Puerto Montt on the Carretera Austral. Access from Hornopirén.
- **Parque Nacional Palena**, approximately 41 380 ha (102 210 acres): 90 km east of La Junta in Región XI de Aisén on Ruta X-10. Accessible only on foot or on horseback.
- **Santuario de la Naturaleza Río Cruces**: 7 km north of Valdivia on the Río Cruces.
- **Parque Nacional Puyehué**, 107 000 ha (264 290 acres): 80 km east of Osorno on RN 215 on road to San Carlos de Bariloche in Argentina. Walking paths, information center, picnic area, camping area, accommodation, restaurant, shop, ski lift, ski resort, lookout, and a CONAF

refugio. See the entry for the park on page 703.

- **Parque Nacional Vicente Pérez Rosales**, 251 000 ha (619 970 acres): 66 km east of **Puerto Varas** on RN 225. Walking paths, information center, picnic area, camping area, accommodation, restaurant, shop nearby, lookout, mountain huts. See the entry for the park on page 706.

Thermal resorts

- **Aguas Calientes**: Altitude 360 m. Thermal water 57.8°C (136°F). Open all year round. See under Parque Nacional Puyehué on page 704.
- **Termas del Amarillo**: Altitude 100 m. Thermal water 50°C (122°F). Open all year round. See "Río Amarillo" in the entry for Chaitén under "Excursions" (page 656) and "Accommodation" (page 654).
- **Termas de Coñaripe**: 15 km south of Coñaripe on **Lago Pellaifa**. This is the latest high-class addition to the thermal resorts in Región X de Los Lagos. Thermal water 40°–42°C (104°F). The best acccess is from Villarrica in Región IX de La Araucania.
- **Termas de Liquiñe**: Altitude 280 m. Thermal water 75°C (167°F). Open all year round. See under the entry for Panguipulli on page 695 and Villarrica (in Región IX de La Araucania) on page 641.
- **Termas de Llancahué** on **Isla Llancahué**: Altitude: sea level. Thermal water 50°C (122°F). Open all year round. See "Excursions" from Hornopirén on page 667.

- **Termas de Puyehué:** Altitude 310 m. Thermal water 57°–68°C (135°–154°F). Open all year round. Located in the *pre-Cordillera*. See Parque Nacional Puyehué on page 703.

Boat trips

M/N *Skorpios I* and M/N *Skorpios II*

74 and 160 passengers respectively, September–May.

- Round trip from Puerto Montt, visiting Puerto Aguirre, Laguna San Rafael, Termas de Quitralco, Quellón, and Castro. Duration: 6 days; departs Sat 1100. Reservations in Puerto Montt: Cruceros Marítimos Skorpios, Angelmó 1660 ℂ 252619/252966.

M/N *Odisea*

Motorized sailing boat carrying 30 passengers, all year.

- Round trip from Puerto Montt, visiting Bahía Metri, Parque Nacional Alerce Andino. Duration: 10 hrs; departs Tues, Thurs, Sat.
- Round trip from Puerto Montt, visiting Calbuco and Isla Quihua. Duration: 10 hrs; departs Weds, Fri, Sun. Reservations in Puerto Montt: A. Varas 161 ℂ 254786.

M/N *Bohemia*

Bunks for 10 passengers.

- Round trip from Angelmó in Puerto Montt, visiting Termas de Llancahué, Isla Butachauques, and Calbuco. Duration: Sat 1230–Thurs 1200; November–March.
- Fiords of Golfo de Ancud and Golfo de Corcovado. Duration: 53 hrs; departs Mon and Fri

1300. Reservations in Puerto Montt: A. Varas 949 ((65) 254675/258969.

M/N *Pamar*

Bunks for 12 passengers.
- Charter to Laguna San Rafael September–March.
- Charter to Fiords of Golfo de Ancud and Golfo de Corcovado April–August. Reservations in Puerto Montt: Pacheco Altamirano 3100 ((65)256220.

M/N *Quellón*

Bunks for 20 passengers.
- Round trip from Puerto Montt, visiting Melinka, Puerto Aguirre, Puerto Chacabuco, Laguna San Rafael, Puerto Cisnes, Termas de Puyuhuapi, and Castro. Duration: 7 days; runs September–April.
- Puerto Chacabuco and Laguna San Rafael. Duration: 4 days.Reservations in Puerto Montt: CNP, Diego Portales 882 ((65) 252547.

M/N *Calbuco*

120 passengers.
- Puerto Montt, Castro, Melinka and Puerto Chacabuco. Runs all year round.
- Puerto Chacabuco and Laguna San Rafael. Duration: 35 hrs; departs Fri 2030, December–March. Reservations in Puerto Montt: CNP, Diego Portales 882 ((65) 252547; and in Puerto Chacabuco: Terminal de Trasbordadores ((67) 351106.

RoRo *Evangelistas*

Roll-on roll-off ferry carrying 380 passengers and 60 cars.

- Puerto Chacabuco and Laguna San Rafael. Duration: Two days. Runs January/February.
- Puerto Montt and Puerto Chacabuco. Duration: 22 hrs; runs Wed and Sat all year. Reservations in Santiago: Miraflores 178, upstairs ((02)6963211; in Puerto Montt: Navimag, Angelmó 2187 ((65) 253754/ 253318, and Presidente Ibañez 347 ((67) 233306.

RoRo *Colono*

Roll-on roll-off ferry carrying 200 passengers and 75 cars.
- Round trip from Puerto Montt, visiting Puerto Chacabuco. Duration: 26 hrs; departs Tues and Fri, returns Wed and Sat.
- Round trip from Puerto Chacabuco, visiting Laguna San Rafael. Duration: 36 hrs; departs Sat 2100, January–March. Reservations in Ancud: TransMarchilay, Libertad 669((65) 622279; in Chaitén: TransMarchilay, Corcovado 266 ((65) 731272; in Coihaique: 21 de Mayo 417((67) 231971; in Pargua: Lord Cochrane; in Puerto Montt: TransMarchilay, Angelmó 1666 ((65) 254654; in Puerto Chacabuco: TransMarchilay, O'Higgins ((67) 351144; in Santiago: TransMarchilay, Agustinas 715 ((02) 6335959.

Tehuelche

Ferry carrying 83 passengers and 20 cars.

- Ferry between La Arena and Puelche. Services: 7 crossings daily all year. Information in Puerto Montt: TransMarchilay ((65) 254654/253683.

Pincoya

Ferry carrying 100 passengers and 30 cars.

* Quellón–Chaitén. Duration: 6 hrs; two return trips per week all year round. Fare: $6.50.
* Quellón–Puerto Chacabuco. Duration: 20 hrs; one return trip per week, all year round. Fare: $40.00 (first class seat), $31.00 (2nd class), sleeper $145.00.
* Pargua–Chaitén. Duration: 9 hrs; two return trips per week, March–December. Fare: $8.50. Information in Puerto Montt: TransMarchilay ((65) 254654/ 253683

Mailén

Ferry carrying 83 passengers and 20 cars.
Hornopirén–Caleta Gonzalo. Duration: 5 hrs; January–February only.

* Pargua–Chaitén. Duration: 12 hrs; two return trips per week, March–December. Fare: $7.50. Information in Puerto Montt: TransMarchilay ((65) 254654/ 253683.

Cai Cai and *Trauco*

Ferries, each carrying 80 passengers and 20 cars.

* Pargua–Chacao. Duration: 30 mins; 24 hrs a day all year round. Passengers free, cars pay fee. Information in Puerto Montt: TransMarchilay ((65) 254654/ 253683.

Cruz Del Sur and *Gobernador Figueroa*

Ferries.

* Pargua–Chacao. Duration: 30 mins; departs from 0630–0100 all year round. Passengers free,

cars small fee Information in Ancud: Chacabuco 672 ((656) 2506.

M/N *Don Jesús*

* Seno de Reloncaví. Duration: 2 hrs daily from 0930 all year round. Information in Puerto Montt: Talca 79, ((65) 256752.

Christina

Small motorboat carrying four passengers; bring a sleeping bag. Runs November–March.

* Fishing excursions on Lago Yelcho. Information in Puerto Cárdenas: (Public 01, Chaitén.

Apulchen II

Launch carrying 24 passengers.

* Puerto Montt, Huelmo, Calbuco. Return from Calbuco to Puerto Montt by bus. Duration: 6 hrs; departs daily 1000, September–May. Information in Puerto Montt: Angelmó 1670 ((65) 263303; Turismo Rosse, A. Varas 445 (255146/257040.

RoRo *Puerto Eden*

Roll-on roll-off ferry carrying 185 passengers and 40 cars.

* Puerto Montt–Puerto Natales. Duration: 3 days; departs 3 times per month, all year round. Information in: Puerto Montt: Angelmó 2187 ((65) 253318; in Puerto Natales: Terminal de Trasbordadores ((61) 411642; in Punta Arenas: Independencia 840 ((61) 244448; and in Santiago: Miraflores 178 ((02) 6963211.

Tourist destinations

Don't miss

☞   Puerto Montt

☞ Puerto Varas and Lago Llanquihué

Worth a visit

☞ Lago Todos Los Santos
☞ Parque Nacional Puyehué
☞ Valdivia

Worth a detour

☞ Frutillar
☞ Lago Pirehueico

☞ Lago Yelcho and Puerto Cárdenas
☞ Osorno
☞ Parque Nacional Alerce Andino
☞ Termas de Liquiñe

Of interest

☞ Bahía Escocia and Lago Rupanco
☞ Panguipulli

CHAITÉN

Area code: 065
Population: 3500
Altitude: Sea level
Distances
- From Coihaique: 420 km north on Carretera Austral
- From Puerto Montt: 205 km south on Carretera Austral

Chaitén is built on the **Golfo de Corcovado**, which separates **Isla Grande de Chiloé** from the mainland and is sheltered by islands to the west. It has one of the highest rainfalls in Chile. The town sits on a small coastal plain encircled by mountains, which are part of **Volcán Michinmávida** (2404 m).

The first colonists settled in 1933, and a ferry service to the mainland began five years later. The oldest part of the Carretera Austral, begun in 1948, runs between Chaitén and **Lago Yelcho**. To the north, it is still unfinished, and ferry services replace the missing links in the road. 12 km north is Playa Santa Bárbara

The deep drainage trenches on Chaitén's streets are a constant reminder that this is a very high rainfall area given to sudden and violent downpours. The Avenida Corcovado is also known by its earlier name "Costanera".

Chaitén is a good base for excursions in and around the **Volcán Michinmávida** (2404 m) area and further south to Lago Yelcho. It is the perfect area for the trailblazer, although not for the unexperienced. The weather can change from one moment to the next: take tent, sleeping bag, and weatherproof gear. Useful Instituto Geográfico 1:50 000 series maps are "Fiordo Reñihué" (5-04-08-0101-00); "Pillan" (5- 04-08-0102-00); "Chaitén" (5-04-08-0110-00); "Volcán Michinmávida" (5-04-08-0111-00); "Lago Reñihué" (5- 04-08-0112-00); and "Puerto Cárdenas" (5-04-09-0009-00).

ⓘ Tourist information

- CONAF, O'Higgins block 200 between Libertad and Almirante Riveros
- Tourist information, upstairs in Mercado Municipal, Ave. Corcovado

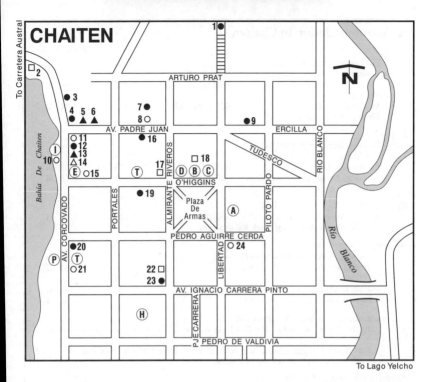

To Lago Yelcho

Key to map

A	Iglesia
B	Gobernación Provincial (Government)
C	Municipalidad (Town hall)
D	Post office and telex
E	Telephone
H	Hospital
I	Tourist information
P	Gas stations
T	Bus terminals

● Accommodation

1	Hotel Mi Casa
3	Hostería Los Alerces
4	Hotel Triágulo
7	Hospedaje San Sebastién
9	Hostería Puyuhuapi
12	Hostería Schilling
16	Hospedaje Gabriel
19	Residencial Morurori
20	Hostería Corcovado

23	Residencial Ginésis

○ Eating out

10	Restaurant El Caleuche
11	Restaurant Flamingo
15	Restaurant La Alondra
21	Restaurant Astoria
24	Restaurant El Rincón

▲ Airline offices

5	Transporte Aéreo San Rafael
6	Transporte Aéreo Don Carlos
	Transporte Aéreo Aerosur

□ Services

2	Port
8	Supermercado San Sebastián
14	TransMarchilay
17	CNP
18	CONAF
22	ENTEL

⊟ Accommodation in Chaitén

Hotels
- Los Colonos, Juan Tudesco 77   (731293
- Triángulo (formerly Cordillera), Juan Tudesco 18
       AEFGHIJ   (731312 $H ♙♙
  Shared bathroom, budget travelers
- Mi Casa, Avenida Norte 206   ACEFGHIJLP$UV   (731285 $G ♙♙
  On top of hill, sauna, 48 beds

Hosterías
- Corcovado, Pedro Aguirre Cerda 5   (731221
- Los Alerces, Avenida Corcovado   (731266
- Puyuhuapi, Ercilla 354   AFGHIJ   (731237 $H ♙♙
- Schilling, Avenida Corcovado 230   AEFGHIJKPUV   (731295 $H ♙♙
  Sauna

Residencial
- Astoria, Avenida Corcovado, 442   AFGHJLV   (731263 $H ♙
- Ginésis, Almirante Riveros block 400 in arcade

Hospedajes
- Costanera, Avenida Corcovado 402 $J ♙
- Gabriel, Juan Tudesco 141 $J ♙♙
- Lo Watson, Ercilla 580   (731237
- Mahurori, O'Higgins 141   F   (731273 $I ♙♙
- Sebastián, Padre Juan Tudesco 188 $J ♙

Accommodation in Villa Vanguardia
Villa Vanguardia is located in the Río Frio valley129 km south — see "Excursions" below.
- Cabañas Villa Vanguardia, RN 7 KM118ABHJ. Reservations in Chaitén: Gobernación Provincial Oficina CEMA (731280.

Accommodation in Río Amarillo
Río Amarillo is a small village 27 km south — see "Excursions" below.

Residenciales
All *residenciales* double as restaurants.
- La Rosa S $J ♙♙. Cold water, meals $Z
- Marcella, on main street

Hotel
- Hotel Termas del Amarillo, in the Río Michinmávida valley 8 km east of the village. For a description of the trip to the hotel, see "Excursions" below. The thermal complex itself is still a bit primitive, as the owner Sr Enrique Godoy is upgrading and building everything himself. Open all year round. For budget travelers and hikers this is a good spot for exploring the area around Volcán Michinmávida. One open air thermal swimming pool. January/February $H ♙♙. Visitors pay $4.00 for use of thermal facilities, mud baths extra. Meals $Y

▲ Camping

There are camping sites 4 km north of Chaitén, and at Termas de Amarillo 45 km south-east — see "Excursions" below.

⑪ Eating out

Restaurants
* Astoria, Avenida Corcovado 445 $Z
* Alondra, O'Higgins 12
* El Caleuche, Centro Comercial, Avenida Corcovado near Tudesco $Z
* El Rincón, A. Cerda corner of Libertad
* El Triángulo, Tudesco 18
* Flamengo, Avenida Bernardo O'Higgins 218 $Z
* Pizzería Morurori, Independencia 141 $Z

⑬ Post and telegraph

Post office
* Correos and Telex Chile, Independencia 283, Plaza de Armas

Telephone
* ENTEL Chile, Almirante Riveros 475. Overseas calls
* Telefónica del Sur, Ave. Corcovado block 200 between Tudesco and Independencia

⑤ Financial

* Banco del Estado de Chile, Libertad corner of O'Higgins

⑬ Services and facilities

Hospital
* Avenida Ignacio Carrera Pinto between Almirante Riveros and Diego Portales

Photographic and sports equipment
* El Ancla, Juan Tudesco 45

Supermarkets
* Supermercado El Rancho, Juan Tudesco 93
* Supermercado Sebastián, Padre Juan Tudesco 188 between Portales and Riveros

⊞ Air services

The flight from Chaitén to Puerto Montt over the Golfo de Ancud offers spectacular views of the smaller islands and Isla Grande de Chiloé, which looks unbelievably green from the air.
The bus trip from the airport to town takes half an hour.

Airlines
* Aerotransportes Don Carlos (ASA), Padre Juan Tudesco 42 next to Hotel Triángulo
* Aerosur, Avenida Corcovado, next to Hostería Schilling ℓ 731228

Air services
* Puerto Montt: Fare $32.00; 1–3 services daily; duration 1 hr; Aerotransportes Don Carlos

⑤ Buses

Companies
* B15 Aerobus, Diego Portales block 200 corner of O'Higgins
* B28 Buses Australes Pudú
* B169 Buses Trans Austral
* B198 Empresa de Transporte Yelcho, O'Higgins 116
* B258 Buses Chaitur, O'Higgins 137

Services
* Coihaique: Fare $30.50; 4 services per week; duration 14 hrs; B15, B28, B169
* Futaleufú: Fare $13.00; B198, B258
* Palena: Fare $13.00; Mon, Thurs; B198, B258
* Puyuhuapi: Fare $16.50; 2–4 services per week; B15, B28
* Río Amarillo: Fare $2.30; B198, B258

⊟ Motoring

For gas stations, see city map.

⊥ Water transport

See "Boat trips" on pages 649–651 for maritime services in the region.
* CNP, O'Higgins block 100 between Riveros and Portales
* TransMarchilay, Corcovado 266 ℓ 272

⊞ Shopping

Artesanías
* CEMA Chile, Juan Tudesco corner of Avenida Corcovado

● Excursions

* **Futaleufú** and/or **Palena**: This 160 km one way trip cannot be done on a strict timetable as nature creates many obstacles. Take the Carretera Austral from

Chaitén

Chaitén to **Villa Santa Lucia**, which is now nothing more than a military post with a few shops. From here, take RN 235 to Puerto Ramírez. A few kilometers further on (near the *hostería*) the road forks: RN 231 north to Futaleufú and RN 235 south-east to Palena. From Villa Santa Lucia to the turnoff at **Puerto Ramírez** is 31 km of gravel road. From here to Futaleufú or Palena it is about 50 km. Heavy rainfalls often make the roads impassable, especially between Puerto Ramírez and La Cabaña along **Lago Yelcho**. Until all the bridges are built, access to Futaleufú may be difficult. In winter, occasional snow cuts the road. For detailed information, see the entries for Futaleufú on page 663 and Palena on page 692. From Futaleufú, a shuttle bus service runs to the Argentine border control, 10 km away. There are regular buses three times week from the Argentine border control to Esquel via Trevelin.

- **Villa Vanguardia:** Approximately 129 km south, in the **Río Frio valley** near the junction with **Río Palena**. The valley is very wide here, and this is another place with tremendous hiking potential up the **Río Oeste** valley to the glaciated **Cerro del Medio** (1700 m). For accommodation see "Accommodation" above. There are 2–3 buses per week running to Chaitén and Coihaique. The bus to Coihaique is subject to the Río Palena carrying sufficient water for the ferry crossing.
- **Río Amarillo**: A small village 27 km south, in a perfect setting with splendid views of the glaciated **Volcán Michinmávida** up the **Río Amarillo** valley. It is best admired from the Carretera Aus-

tral bridge over the Río Amarillo. The Río Amarillo has its source in the glacier on top of Volcán Michinmávida. Its yellowish color indicates its volcanic origin. A curiosity on the outskirts of the village is the airplane fuselage which has been converted into a home. Río Amarillo consists only of one street, along which all facilities are located. For accommodation see "Accommodation" above. Buses Yelcho and Buses Chaitur run daily services from Chaitén. Eight km east of the village is the Hotel Termas del Amarillo (see "Accommodation" above), in the Río Michinmávida valley. At Río Amarillo take the turnoff east to the **Termas del Amarillo** — there is a road sign pointing to it. The road leads gently uphill first through open meadows and then through forest. After you have reached the crest (about 15 minutes' walk) look back and you will see the wide valley of the **Río Chaitén**, and to the south steep high mountains with their eternal crowns of snow and ice. Just before you get to the clearing where the springs are, you cross two wooden one-lane bridges. This was planned to become a major road to open up the hinterland. Past the springs there is still a tunnel, but the road finishes near the junction of **Río Mallines** and **Río Turbio Grande** with Río Michinmávida. At the thermal resort at Termas del Amarillo are four huts with small concrete basins which fill with thermal waters. The springs are said to have curative properties for rheumatism and sciatica.

ENTRE LAGOS

Population: 3100
Distance from Osorno: 47 km east on RN 215

Entre Lagos is located on the western end of **Lago Puyehué** on the main highway connecting Osorno with San Carlos de Bariloche in Argentina via **Paso Pajaritos**, in itself a scenic drive over the high *sierras*, partly through adjoining national parks on either side of the border.

Entre Lagos began as a timber town with a railroad line to Osorno. Now it has been transformed into a vacation resort on one of the most beautiful lakes in Chile. From the town, there are views of **Volcán Puyehué**, **Volcán Casa Blanca,** and **Cerro Puntiagudo**.

Good tourist facilities exist in Entre Lagos itself, beside **Lago Puyehué** and up the Antillanca road, not forgetting the fashionable thermal resort of **Termas de Puyehué**, only 27 km east of the town. The beach along Lago Puyehué is over a kilometer long, and consists of fine sand and volcanic rocks. There are small beaches all around the lake, where the water is cool but calm and not very deep. Most of them have some tourist facilities, for example, Playa Ñilque and Playa Puyehué further east.

⚐ Festivals
• January: Semana Entrelaguina

⊟ Accommodation

Hosterías
★★★ Villa Veneto, General Lagos 602 **AE-FGHILMPSUVX** (371203 $G **ϋ**. English and German spoken
• Entre Lagos, E. Ramírez 65 **AEFGHKLPSUVX** (371225 $H **ϋ**. English and German spoken
• Hostal Millaray, E. Ramírez 333 **APS** (371251 $H **ϋ**

Accommodation beside Lago Puyehué
• Hostería Restaurant Chalet Suisse (formerly Tramahuel), RN 215 KM 49 **AFGPVZ** (371208

⚑ Camping
Most camping areas are along RN 215. The drivers of public buses from Osorno will let you off. See also "Camping" in Lago Puyehué on page 668.

⏀ Eating out
• Restaurant Pub de Campo, KM 48 RN 215 $Y
• Restaurant Jardín El Turista $Y

⊟ Services and facilities
There is a supermarket on Bernardo O'Higgins 108

⊟ Buses
Buses Empresa Puyehué runs 3 services daily to Aguas Calientes, Anticura, and Osorno; Buses Varmontt, Buses Fresia, and Buses Buses Rodríguez run 7 services daily to Puerto Montt.

⊟ Motoring services
• COPEC gas station

⚓ Water transport
• Ferry to **Isla Fresia** from Camping Los Copihués, 8 km east

⚑ Excursions
• **Lago Rupanco** and **Bahía Escocia** : Both 13 km south.
• To **Parque Nacional Puyehué,** including Termas de Puyehué, **Aguas Calientes** and Volcán Casa Blanca: The national park entrance is 30 km east of town or half an hour by bus. See the entry for the park on page 703.

Entre Lagos

Frutillar

Area code: 065
Population: 5600
Altitude: 90 m
Distance from Puerto Montt: 50 km north on Panamericana

Frutillar consists of two separate villages: Frutillar Alto and Frutillar Bajo. Frutillar Alto is located directly on the Panamericana; Frutillar Bajo, the main township, is about 4 km downhill on **Lago Llanquihué**.

Frutillar Alto has the main bus terminal, a few restaurants, and a gas station. There are a few *residenciales* which are cheaper than the ones in Frutillar Bajo. It is a pleasant downhill walk alongCarlos Richter from here to Frutillar Bajo, with the mirror-like lake in front of you, framed by the towering Volcán Osorno.

Frutillar Bajo, a major tourist resort, is a pretty little town, founded by Germans in the 19th century on the western side of Lago Llanquihué. The town has retained its German character: German is still spoken widely, and many of the hotels, restaurants and little guest houses are run by descendents of the first settlers. It also has a prestigious tradesmen's college founded by the German forefathers. The town has very pretty parks and gardens with views across the lake to the mountains and volcanoes — you can see **Volcán Osorno** and **Volcán Cerro Puntiagudo**.

Avenida Philippi is the main road alongside the lake, with villas and hotels on one side and a beach and boat ramps by the lake's edge.

☒ Festivals
- February: Semanas Musicales de Frutillar (annual classical music festival)

ⓘ Tourist information
- Información Turística Municipal, Avenida Philippi next to boat harbor

ⒶCamping
There are camping sites 2 km south of Frutillar Bajo on the road to Punta Larga; and at Playa Maqui 7 km north of Frutillar Bajo on the road to Puerto Octay.

⑪ Eating out

Eating out in Frutillar Bajo

Restaurants
- Bauernhaus, O'Higgins corner of Philippi
- Club Alemán with restaurant, San Martín 22 ℂ 249 $Y
- Club Bomberos, Avenida Philippi between A.Varas and Rodríguez
- El Bal, Avenida Philippi block 1000, upstairs between A. Varas and little lane
- Helen Haus
- Hotel Frutillar, Avenida Philippi 1000 $Y

Cafés
- Bierstube, A. Varas
- Café del Sur, corner of Carlos Richter and Philippi. Open December–February

Salón de Té
- Frutillar, Avenida Philippi block 700 near O'Higgins $Z
- Pim's, Avenida Philippi Block 1100 corner of A. Cerda
- Trayén, Avenida Philippi 963 $Z

Eating out in Frutillar Alto
- Café El Mastique, Carlos Richter near bus terminal

LOS LAGOS

Key to map

A	Iglesia
C	Municipalidad (Town hall)
D	Post office and telex
E	Telephone
F	Carabineros (Police)
I	Tourist information
T	Bus terminals

● **Accommodation**

1	Hostería Halrald Detz
2	Hostería Adelita
3	Hostería Casona Del 32
4	Motel Monserrat
5	Hostería Ruf Mal An
6	Motel Piscis
7	Hostería Instituto Alemán
11	Hostería Am See
12	Hostería Albeniz
13	Hotel Klein Salzburg
14	Apart Hotel Badenhoff
17	Cabañas Meli Ruca
19	Hostería Vivaldi
21	Hostería Trayén
22	Residencial Bruni
23	Hotel Innsbruck
26	Hotel Frutillar
27	Hostería Las Dalias
30	Hostería Winkler
32	Hotel Ayacará
33	Hostería Las Rocas
34	Hostería Vista Hermosa
35	Hostería Kaiserseehaus

○ **Eating out**

9	Café del Sur
15	Club Alemán
18	Restaurant Bauernhaus
20	Salón de Té Trayén
24	Restaurant Bierstube
25	Club Bomberos
29	Restaurant Helen Haus
31	Salón de Té Pims

■ **Sights**

8	Museo de la Colonisación Alemana
28	Iglesia Luterana

□ **Services**

10	Artesanías Frutillar
16	Public showers and change cabins

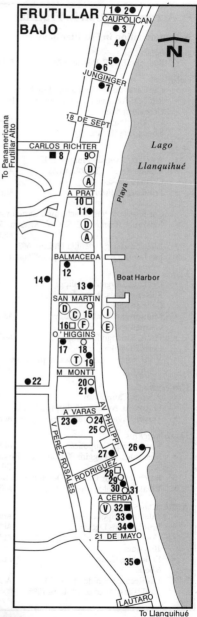

Frutillar

⊟ Accommodation in Frutillar

Accommodation in Frutillar Bajo

Apart hotels
- Badenhoff, V. P. Rosales 673   ABEHPRSV   ✆ 421649

Cabañas
- Las Casas de Maximiliano, 21 de Mayo   ✆ 421543
- Ruf-Mal-An, Avenida Philippi 181   PU   ✆ 421342
  German spoken
- Winkler, Philippi 1155   AFHJLPUV   ✆ 421388
  6 beds, bicycle hire

Hotels
- Ayacará, Avenida Philippi 1215   ✆ 421550
- Casona del 32, Caupolicán 28   AJLPS   ✆ 421369 $F ♙♙
  German spoken
- Frutillar, Philippi 1000   ADEFGHIJKLMP$TUVXVZ
      ✆ 421277 $F ♙♙
  Car hire, boat hire, beach front, German spoken. The terrace is built over the lake
- Innsbruck (formerly El Retiro), A. Varas 54
      AHJLPV   ✆ 421345
- Klein Salzburg, Avenida Philippi 663   ✆ 421201
- Las Lomas, Avenida Philippi 1500 (at the turnoff)   ✆ 421531

Motels
- Del Lago, Avenida Philippi   AEFGHKLP$V   ✆ 421303
- Kaiserseehaus, Avenida Philippi 1333   ✆ 421387
  German spoken
- Monserrat, Avenida Philippi 175   ABCHILPUV   ✆ 421383 $F for 8
  German spoken
- Piscis, Santiago Junginger 95   ABCHIJPV   ✆ 421250 $F for 6
  German spoken, 18 beds
- Vista Hermosa, Avenida Philippi 1259
      AHJLV   ✆ 421209 $F for 3

Hosterías
- Adelita, Caupolicán
- El Arroyo, Avenida Philippi 989   ✆ 421560
- Trayén, Avenida Philippi 963   AEFGHJLPVZ   ✆ 421346 $H ♙♙

Departamentos
- Koenekamp, Caupolicán 11   AHPV   ✆ 421232
- Meli Ruca, O'Higgins 90 near Pérez Rosales
      CDEHIJKPSUV   ✆ 421244 $F for 4
  Beach frontage. Open 15 December–15 March
- Vivaldi, Avenida Philippi 851   AHLPSV   ✆ 421382 $G ♙♙

Residenciales
- Adelita, Caupolicán 31   AHIJPSV   ✆ 421229 $G ♙♙
- Bruni, Carlos Decker   APSV   ✆ 421309 $H ♙♙
- Costa Azul, Avenida Philippi 1175   AEFHJLPV $G ♙♙
  10 rooms
- El Bosque, Caupolicán 117   ABCDHJNPV   ✆ 421317 $E for 6
  6 beds
- Las Rocas, Avenida Philippi 1235   AHJLPV   ✆ 421397 $G ♙♙
- Las Dalias, Avenida Philippi 1095   ✆ 421393 $F for 4

Accommodation in Frutillar — continued

- Lilian Epple, Avenida Philippi 1441   **APUV**

Hospedajes
- Am See, Avenida Philippi 539   **AP**   (421539
  German spoken
- Hechenleitner, Avenida Philippi between Balmaceda and San Martín
                                        AHJL   (421394
- Instituto Alemán, Avenida Philippi 231   (421324
- Nohelia Westermeier, Avenida Philippi 615(421310
  7 beds
- Kurt Schumacher, Pérez Rosales 664   (421248
  7 Beds
- Harald Daetz, Caupolicán 35   (421329
  8 Beds

Accommodation in Frutillar Alto
- Hostería Canta Gallo, Carlos Richter 345
- Cabañas Turisticas, Carlos Richter 320

Hospedaje,
- Carlos Richter: 156, 220,310

Accommodation on Panamericana
- Residencial Rayhuen, 7 km from northern exit
                                        AFHJLNPRSUV $H ♊

Accommodation west on road to Tegualda Ruta V-20
- Hostería Paraguay, Fundo Paraguay, 18km from town
                                        AHPUV   (9180 CRELL $G ♊

Accommodation north on road to Los Bajos

Hotels
- Salzburg, on northern exit of Frutillar Bajo
                                        AFGR   (421589

  Sauna, views over lake

Hosterías
- Cinco Robles, 3 km Playa Maqui   (421351
- Los Maitenes, 3 km north Playa Maqui
                                        AFHIJLNPUVZ   ((65) 339130 $F ♊
  Full board, boat hire, tennis, beach frontage, German spoken.
- Volcán Puntiagudo, KM 1   (421646
  Fax 421640

Residenciales
- Panorama, 3 km north Playa Maqui
                                        AHJLPV   (9129CRELL $H ♊
  German spoken
- Los Tilos, 5 km north Playa Maqui   **AHJLPUV**   (9140 CRELL
- Playa Maqui, 6 km north Playa Maqui
                                        APSUV   (9139 CRELL $H ♀

Accommodation south on road to Punta Larga

Motels
- El Cerro, 2 km south of town   **ABCHJLPUV** $F for 6

Accommodation in Frutillar — continued
- Posada Campesina, Augusto Ellies, 2 km south of town
  ADFHIJKLNP$UVXZ (9123 CRELL $F ⅱ
  Beach frontage, boat hire

Departamentos
- Caipulli, 2 km south of town (9105 CRELL
  13 beds
- Villa Anita, 2 km south of town AHJLPSUV $H ⅱ

Residencial
- Fundo Santa Ana, El Maitén 1 km south on road to Totoral
  AFHJLNPUV (9106 CRELL $H ⅱ
  Beach frontage

Accommodation on road to Tegualda
- Hotel Casa de la Oma, KM 14 DPT (9170 CRELL

- Restaurant Colonial, Cristiano Winkler 353

Eating out along the road to Punta Larga
- Restaurant Posada Campesina, KM 2

▣ Entertainment
- Disco Club de Rodeo, on Carlos Richter halfway between Frutillar Bajo and Frutillar Alto

▦ Post and telegraph

Post and telegraph in Frutillar Bajo

Post office
- Correo, Pérez Rosales between Balmaceda and A. Prat

Telephone
- Carlos Richter 2 km

Post and telegraph in Frutillar Alto
- Telex Chile, Carlos Richter near Cristiano Winkler

▦ Services and facilities

Services and facilities Frutillar Alto

Supermarket
- Supermercado San Pedro, Carlos Richter, corner of San Pedro.

⚓ Water transport
Lake cruises depart from the boat harbor, Avenida Philippi opposite San Martín.

Fishing excursions on the lake are run from Philippi 935. A launch equipped for trout and salmon fishing costs $15.00 an hour.

▦ Buses
The main bus terminal is in Frutillar Alto, at Alessandri 32, near the Panamericana. In Frutillar Bajo there is a bus terminal in M. Montt where some buses pick up passengers. You can easily get a lift from the intersection of Carlos Richter and Pérez Rosales up to the Bus terminal on the Panamericana. Buses Tur-Bus (421390, Buses Varmontt (421367, Buses Del Sur, Buses ETC, and Empresa Estrella del Sur run 28 services daily to Puerto Montt, Puerto Varas, and Osorno.

▦ Motoring
- COPEC gas station in Frutillar Alto, on Panamericana near Carlos Richter

▦ Shopping

Shopping in Frutillar Bajo
- Artesanía Frutillar, Avenida Philippi block 500 near A. Prat
- Artesanías Trayén, A. Prat corner of V. Pérez Rosales

▦ Sport
Sailing, swimming, fishing.

Sightseeing

As you climb Caupolicán and reach the plateau, you will find remnants of native forest as it was when the first immigrants arrived. It is now a *reserva forestal*. From here you have an excellent view over Frutillar Bajo, the lake, and the volcanoes.

Sightseeing in Frutillar Bajo
- Museo Colonial Alemán, Pérez Rosales between Prat and Carlos Richter. A miniature German village has been built on the hillside here. Points of interest include early farm implements brought over from Germany by the first immigrants. There is also a water mill in working condition — just like one in the famous Black Forest. Open Mon–Sat 1000–1300 and 1500–1900. Admission $1.50.

Excursions
- **Península Punta Larga** with **Laguna Flor de Lotos** and native forest: 6 km south. The larger hotels organize tours.

FUTALEUFÚ

Area code: LD 108
Population: 900
Altitude: 450 m
Distances
- From Chaitén: 155 km south-east on RN 231, RN 235 and Carretera Austral
- From Trevelin in Argentina: 45 km west

Futaleufú, on **Lago Espejo**, is 10 km west of the Argentine border. It was founded in 1930, and the first settler's house is still standing near the lake.

Basic supplies are available in Futaleufú. You can make excursions on horseback to nearby waterfalls, and you can also fish from a launch on the lake or nearby rivers. For a description of the route as far as Puerto Ramírez, see "Excursions" from Chaitén on page 656.

Festivals
- November and December: Branding of the animals, followed by a celebration with a typical outback barbecue: on a spit. This is sheep and cattle country

Tourist information
- Oficina Municipal Futaleufú

Camping

Camping on Lago Espolón
- Camping Los Laureles, on the east side of Lago Espolón and 3 km off RN 231. 20 tent sites. Facilities are still a bit primitive but passable. Open November–March. Boat hire, horse riding. $J per camp site. This site is being upgraded to include a *hostería*, restaurant, and toilet block

Eating out

Restaurants
- Llanero Solitario, Balmaceda 587
- El Espolón, Pedro Aguirre Cerda 545
- El Palena, Lautaro 268
- La Frontera, Arturo Prat 107

Post and telegraph

Post office
- Correo, Bernardo O'Higgins 596

Telephone
- CNT Telefónica del Sur, Bernardo O'Higgins 596

Services and facilities

Supermarket
- Supermercado Casa Austral, Pedro Aguirre Cerda 353

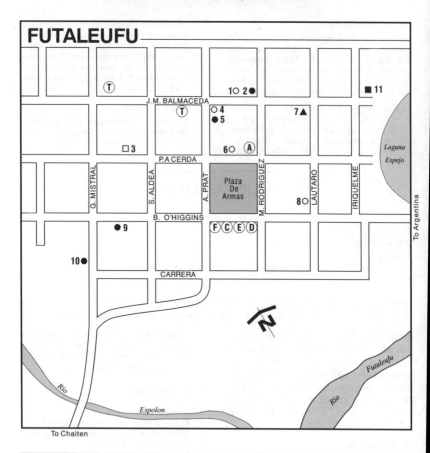

FUTALEUFU

Laguna
Espejo

To Argentina

To Chaiten

Key to map

A	Iglesia
C	Municipalidad (Townhall)
D	Post office and telex
E	Telephone
F	Carabineros (Police)
T	Bus terminals

● **Accommodation**

2	Hotel Continental
5	Hospedaje El Campesino
9	Hotel Carahué
10	Hospedaje Cañete

○ **Eating out**

1	Restaurant Llanero Solitario
4	Restaurant La Frontera
6	Restaurant El Espolón
8	Restaurant El Palena

△ **Airline offices**

7	Líneas Aéreas Aerosur

■ **Sights**

11	Pioneer's hut

□ **Services**

3	Supermercado Casa Austral

⊟ Accommodation in Futaleufú

Hotels
- Carahué, Bernardo O'Higgins 332 **AFGHJPSV** (721221 $I ♦♦
- Continental, José Manuel Balmaceda 597
  AFGHIJLPSV (721222 $I ♦♦
  Open December–March

Hospedajes
- Cañete, Gabriela Mistral 378 (721214 $I ♦♦
- El Campesino, Avenida Prat 109 $I ♦♦
- Posada Campesina La Gringa, Sargento Aldea
  AFPS (721260 $G ♦♦

Hostería
- Sotobosque, Lago Lonconao $F ♦♦

Accommodation Lago Espolón
- Cabañas del Lago **ABHV** (721291
  Open December–March

⊠ Border crossing

Chilean border control is 10 km east of town. Shortly before you reach the bridge over the Río Futaleufú, you will come to the Argentine border control — a fully fledged border crossing for foreign passport holders. At an altitude of 515 m, it connects the port of Chaitén with Esquel in Argentina. It is open from sunrise to sunset throughout the year.
- Carabineros, Bernardo O'Higgins 528

✈ Air services

Airlines
- Aero Sur, Balmaceda 696

Services
- Puerto Montt: Fare $45.00; departs 1400 Tues and Fri

🚌 Buses

Buses José Escobar Pérez, Balmaceda 239 and Buses Chaitur, Manuel Rodríguez run 2–3 services a week to Chaitén. A shuttle bus service runs from Balmaceda 434 to the Argentine border control. From the Argentine border control there are direct buses to Esquel via Trevelin in Argentina twice a week.

🚗 Motoring

The nearest gas station is in Trevelín, Argentina.

⚓ Water transport

Boat hire for lake cruises in Camping Los Laureles.

🏬 Shopping

Long winters and many rainy days have fostered a local *artesanía*, specializing in leather items. Although most of the items are for use in the cattle industry, occasionally visitors may find a bargain.

🎣 Sport

Trout fishing in Lago Espolón, Río Futaleufú, and Lago Lonconao.

🚩 Excursions

- **Lago Espolón** and **Lago Lonconao**: 12 km west. Excellent trout fishing. The easiest part of the lake to get to is only 3 km from RN 231, and the area is a paradise for sport fishing!
- **Futaleufú valley** crosses the border, extending into Argentina. The **Río Futaleufú** rises in Lago Futaleufú in Argentina, winding through a narrow valley with densely forested slopes. The mountains on each side reach 1900 m.
- **El Huemul**: 8 km north, near **Lago del Noroeste**, accessible only on horseback or by hiking. This is enchanting alpine country that foreign visitors hardly ever see — though look out for wild boar! There is a trail leading to Hacienda Espolón and con-

tinuing up the **Río Espolón** valley towards Hacienda San Ramón and snow-
covered mountains. This is a trip for the

intrepid outdoor enthusiast. Tent,
sleeping bag, warm clothes, and wet
weather gear are essential.

HORNOPIRÉN

Population: 7800
Altitude: Sea level
Distance from Puerto Montt: 104 km south east on Carretera Austral

The little town of Hornopirén sits in the shadow of snow-capped **Volcán Hornopirén** (1572 m) in the foothills of the high *sierras*. It is on the eastern shore of the **Golfo de Ancud** on the **Río Negro** near where it flows into the **Canal Hornopirén**. Although this is quite a large settlement, it is fairly recent, but it already has some tourist facilities and is a useful base for mountain hikes into the nearby volcanic ranges and to the national park

Hornopirén is still a fairly isolated spot on the Carretera Austral, as the trip from Puerto Montt involves a ferry crossing from Caleta La Arena to Caleta Puelche. The road south only goes as far as Pichanco, where another ferry takes you to Caleta Leptepu. Ferry services are very limited from March to December, as most trucks are ferried directly from Pargua to Chaitén, so they bypass Hornopirén.

Hikers will find this a particularly interesting mountaineering region, and may well be tempted to
stay longer than anticipated.

Ⓐ Camping

There is a municipal camping site 200 m
north of town, and two camping sites
5 km south.

Ⓘ Eating out

- Restaurant Rodrigo, Avenida Diego Portales
☞ • Restaurant Hotel Hornopirén $Y. Country-style food

Eating out in Contao
Contao is 48 km north of Hornopirén.
Eating out in these *pensiones* costs $Z: Sra
Hortensia Canales, Sr José H. Zuñiga, Sra

Rosa Uribe, Sra Juliana Díaz, and Sra
Elizarda Silva.

Ⓟ Post and telegraph
The post office and Telefónica Sur are
both in the same street as Hotel Hornopirén.

Ⓑ Buses
Bus services from Puerto Montt arrive
here around 1300, and you would be advised to go straight to one of the four
hotels to be sure of getting accommodation. Buses Fierro and Buses Olavarría run
5 services daily to Puerto Montt.

Ⓜ Motoring
- COPEC gas station at the northern town entrance, part of the new Hotel Milo-chociento

Ⓦ Water transport
Ferry services run to Isla de Los Ciervos.

Ⓢ Sport
Mountain hiking, fishing.

Ⓔ Excursions
A useful Instituto Geográfico Militar
1:50 000 series map when hiking in this
area is "Hornopirén" (5-04-08-0072-00). If
you are continuing north to Seno Reloncaví, the map for "Puelo" (5-04-08-0062-
00) is helpful.

Plate 39   Región XII de Magellanes V Antarctica Chilena
Parque Nacional Balmaceda, Cerro Balmaceda

Plate 40   Región XII de Magellanes Y Antarctica Chilena
Top: Parque Nacional Torres del Paine, Cerro Paine
Bottom left: Isla Navarino, Magellanic flower
Bottom right: Parque Nacional Torres del Paine, grazing guanacos

◙ Accommodation in Hornopirén

Accommodation is scarce and expensive, particularly during the summer season (January–February), and cheaper accommodation is usually booked out. It is a good idea to book before leaving Puerto Montt.

Complejos Turísticos
- Lago Pinto Cocha
- Río Negro Hornopirén

Hotels
- Country Holiday, Avenida Libertador B. O'Higgins
  AS   ℓ 217220 $F ⚎
- Hornopirén, Ignacio Carrera Pinto   AEFHPSV $H ⚎
  16 rooms, most of them occupied by long-term residents. Reservations in Puerto Montt: ℓ 254246
- Milochociento, on Carretera Austral just before entering town
  PS $F ⚎
- Sra Muñoz, O'Higgins

Residenciales
- El Viajero, Avenida Ingenieros Militares
- Perla Del Reloncaví, Avenida Ingenieros Militares

Accommodation along the Carretera Austral south
- Motel Aguas del Sur, 7 km south of town

Accommodation in Contao
Contao is 48 km north.
- Residencial Mary, Carretera Austral KM 58
  HIJS $H ⚎
  Reservations in Puerto Montt: Chorrillos 1329 ℓ 255209
- Residencial Reloncaví   FHJV

Accommodation in Hualaihué
Hualaihué is 24 km west of Hornopirén. Fishing and logging are the main commercial activities. Buses Olavarria and Buses Fiero run daily services to Puerto Montt and Hornopirén.
- Hotel Hualaihué
- Residencial Yohana, Carretera Austral KM 80 in Sector El Varal
  AHJL

Accommodation on Isla Llancahué
Isla Llancahué is accessible from Cholgo, 31 km south — see "Excursions" below.
- Hostería y Termas de Llancahué   AIJL
  Reservations in Santiago: Sr Erich Argel ℓ (02)6994393/6994686

- **Contao:** 48 km north, on the eastern side of **Seno Reloncaví,** serving the fishing and timber industries. It is only of interest to hikers who intend to make walks in the Cerro Martín area. Buses Fierro and Buses Olavarría run 2–6 services daily from Puerto Montt and Hornopirén.
- Hornopirén is the best starting place to reach **Volcán Hornopirén, Laguna Hualaihué**, and **Laguna General Pinto Concha.** Experienced hikers may decide to keep walking to **Cerro Yate,** and even further on to **Puelo** on **Estuario de Reloncaví**.
- **Isla Llancahué** in **Canal Comau:** Accessible by ferry from **Cholgo,** 31 km south of Hornopirén; the ferry trip takes 20 minutes. On this forest-covered island is a thermal resort with

basic facilities. The thermal water emerges at 50°C (122°F) and is recommended for rheumatism. There is also a hot spring right on the beach. Even the seawater around here is lukewarm because of hot springs surging from the sea bed. A visit is recommended. There are two fishing villages on the island: **Andrade** and **Los Indios**. Daily rural buses run between Cholgo and Hornopirén.

• **Parque Nacional Hornopirén** (48 232 ha or 119 130 acres): Follow the dirt road along the **Río Negro** and you will find huge trees here which somehow have escaped the logger. Because of the humid environment, the fairly dense rainforest contains many ferns. The road passes a trout hatchery which can be visited.

LAGO PUYEHUÉ

For tourists, Lago Puyehué has a great deal to offer, with good facilities, particularly on the south side of the lake. The international road RN 215 goes along the south side to San Carlos de Bariloche in Argentina, via Paso Puyehué. The lake is dominated in the east by **Volcán Puyehué** and **Volcán Casa Blanca**.

The major tourist centers are **Entre Lagos** on the west side of the lake and **Puntilla Ñilque** on the south-eastern side opposite **Isla Fresia**. See also the entry for Entre Lagos on page 657.

Accommodation

For accommodation in Entre Lagos, see "Accommodation" in Entre Lagos on page 657.

Accommodation on Isla Fresia
Isla Fresia is in **Lago Puyehué**, and much of it is still covered with native forests. From the island there are splendid views of **Volcán Puyehué** and **Volcán Casa Blanca**. It is accessible from the boat ramp at Camping Los Copihués (7 km east of Entrelagos). The *hostería* is on the north-west side of the island. Boating and fishing trips are organized by the owners.

★ Hostería Isla Fresia AEFJLNX $F ⚹⚹. Full board, German and English spoken, Austrian cooking. Reservations in Osorno: Amador Barrientos 2260 (236951

Accommodation in Puntilla Ñilque
Puntilla Ñilque is a small summer resort on the south side of **Lago Puyehué**, 23 km east of the town of Entre Lagos. There are fabulous views over the lake to the is-

lands, with **Volcán Puyehué** in the background. Bus Puyehué runs daily services to Entre Lagos, Osorno, Termas de Pueyehué. and Parque Nacional Puyehué.

★★ Motel Ñilque, RN 215, KM 65, 18 km east of Entre Lagos ACDE-FGHIJKLMNPRUVX (371218 $D ⚹⚹. German spoken, car hire, horse-riding, boat hire, tennis courts, golf course. $ F cabins for 4

• Hotel Villas Mahuida, RN 215 KM 55 ABS (371302 $C cabins for 4

• Cabañas La Valenciana, RN 215 KM 53

• Posada Puntilla Ñilque RN 215 KM 65 AFHPV (371391 $G ⚹⚹

Camping

Camping Municipal Mantilhué is located on the northern shore of the lake. Along the southern rim of the lake there is a string of good serviced camping sites, some of them with *cabañas*.

Services and facilities

Services and facilities in Puntilla Ñilque
• Hire of fishing boats: $12.50 per hour
• Water-skiing: $22.50 per hour
• Kayak hire: $9.00 per hour

Buses

The best access is from Osorno, with regular daily buses.

Sport

Fly fishing at the mouths of Ríos Pescadero, Lican, Chanleufú, and Nilque. Both

Río Golgol and the lake are very popular with fishing enthusiasts.

Excursions

- **Parque Nacional Puyehué**: 23 km east with Buses Puyehué. See the entry for the park on page 703.

LAGO RANCO

This is the second largest lake in Región X de Los Lagos. It is still relatively by-passed by the commercial tourist trail, and the area appeals to sport fishermen and hikers, particularly the eastern and south-eastern parts of the lake and surrounding area. The best tourist facilities are firstly in the town of Lago Ranco and secondly in Futrono

Lago Ranco is in the province of Valdivia, and the best way to reach the northern part of the lake is from Valdivia by bus via Futrono and Llifén. However, the southern part of this lake, in particular the towns of Lago Ranco and Riñinahué, is served by buses from Osorno via Río Bueno. A road runs right round the lake.

There is a sealed section from Panamericana to Futrono, then a good gravel road from Futrono to Llifén.

The road from the Panamericana via Río Bueno to the town of Lago Ranco is partly sealed and partly a good gravel road. Continuing east along the lake from the town of Lago Ranco to Riñinahué there are a few bad patches between Pitreño and Riñinahué — mostly fords which flood easily. This is the most scenic part of the trip on the southern rim of Lago Ranco: the mountains come so close to the lake that there is hardly any room for the road; some small cascades virtually fall onto the road. Take care — if this road is cut you may be stranded in Riñinahué.

The gravel road south from Llifén to **Riñinahué**, along the easten rim pf Lago Ranco, crosses the **Río Calcurrupe** (coming from Lago Maihué) 16 km further south. There is no bridge, but a ferry service. Sometimes the road at this point becomes impassable as a result of flooding. The most scenic part on this road is from the Río Calcurrupe crossing to the Río Temaleufú crossing: the road negotiates a small pass, the Cuesta Miranda. Six kilometers further south are the **Saltos del Nilahué**, with a double waterfall. The road continues until Riñinahué through flat country where you still see volcanic debris and ash from the 1954 **Cerro Carrán** eruption.

The largest of the many small islands in this lake, **Isla Huapi**, right in the center, is a Mapuche reserve. There are pheasant and deer farms on **Isla Colcuma**, which you can reach from the town of Lago Ranco.

The lake is fed by many rivers and streams cascading down from the high mountains in the eastern part. Some of the smaller streams form waterfalls, especially on the steep part between **Ilhué** and Riñinahué.

Lago Ranco is the source of the **Río Bueno** which meets the Pacific Ocean near **La Barra**, where a sandbar has formed near the mouth of the river. This river is navigable from its source to the sea. Near **Puerto Lapi** there is a ferry across the Río Bueno just a few kilometers west from where it leaves Lago Ranco.

There are large inlets on the eastern side of the lake, in particular Seno Riñinahué, which is formed by a steep narrow promontory protruding into the lake. This area is very picturesque, being densely forested, with numerous little cascades of water.

There are a number of tourist resorts around the lake, and isolated hotels and camping areas have sprung up in many places:

Lago Ranco

The town of Lago Ranco is a picturesque little tourist resort on the south side of Lago Ranco about 80 km north-east of Osorno, with a population of around 3000. In the early 1900s, Lago Ranco used to be a timber town. Timber was shipped down from the lake shores and then taken by rail to the timber mills. All that is left of the bygone timber days is a pier near the municipal camping ground.

There are beautiful views over the lake to several islands. The beach is rocky, with trees coming right to the edge of the lake. The municipality's interest in establishing a tourist industry has resulted in a number of hotels, camping grounds, and restaurants. The Oficina de Turismo (Tourist Office) is open only in summer.

Excursions to the islands are run by by Lancha Dinorah, Valparaíso 111.

Futrono

Furono is 97 km south-east of Valdivia at the northern end of Lago Ranco, and only comes to life in the tourist season. It is a small town with 4000 inhabitants. There are panoramic views over the lake.

Llifén

Llifen is 115 km south-east of Valdivia, on the eastern side of Lago Ranco on a plain just 3 km north where the **Río Calcurrupe** flows into the lake. It is a tourist center with some facilities. There is an excellent beach (Playa Bonita) with fine sand just south of the river mouth that you can reach by boat. Huge trees come right down to the lake shore. You can hire boats at Camping Los Ponchos 1 km west of of the village.

Puerto Nuevo

On the west side of Lago Ranco, Puerto Nuevo is 22 km south of Futrono and 12 km north of the town of Lago Ranco.

Riñinahué

The small village of Riñinahué is at the eastern end of Lago Ranco in the *pre-Cordillera*, 108 km north-east of Osorno. It is a very beautiful spot in the shade of Volcán Puyehué. In the surrounding area there are splendid walks, and **Salto del Nilahué** is only 5 km north. Riñinahué is still without electricity and town water; the *hospedaje* I stayed at is one of the few houses with its own private electricity supply. You can hire boats at Camping Río Riñinahué.

⊟ Accommodation by Lago Ranco

Accommodation in Futrono
- Hotel Puerto Futrono, Cordero Futrono   ℂ 481281
- Hostería El Rincón Arabe, Manuel Montt corner of V. Monsalve
  AEFHIJLPVX   ℂ 481273 $I ⚌

  Open all year
- Hospedaje Casa Parroquial

Accommodation in the town of Lago Ranco
- Cabañas Turihott, Valparaíso 111   P   ℂ 491201 $F for 4
- Hotel Casona Italiana, Viña del Mar 145
  ABGHIJLUV   ℂ 491225 $H ⚊

  Boat hire; also one cabin for 6 persons. Open all year
- Hostería Phoenix, Viña del Mar 141   PS   ℂ 491226 $H ⚊

  Open all year
- Residencial Osorno, Temuco 103 $J ⚊
  Budget travelers

Accommodation in Llifén

Hosterías
★★★ Llicán   ABCEFGHIJKLNV   ℂ 290 Futrono $H ⚌
- Huequecura, Ruta T-55   ABCDEFGHIJLNP$TUVXZ
  ℂ 290 Futrono $G ⚌

  Beach frontage, boat hire, car hire, sauna. $F cabins for two
- Villa La Cascada, Torremolinos 357   AEFGHIJLNP$TUVZ ℂ 261 Futrono $D ⚌
  Beach frontage, boat hire. Open December–April
- Cumilahué Fishing Lodge, in a beautiful setting, 3 km east on road to Lago Maihué.
  Fishermen's hang-out, English and French spoken. Reservations in Santiago: fax 56-2-2311027
- Hostería Chollinco, 4 km past Llifén on Ruta T-559 to Arquihué
  ADEFGHIJKLNRP$VZ ℂ 202 Futrono $E ⚊
  Unobstructed views over forested mountain ranges from all 20 rooms. Also 15 camp sites $I for 6

Accommodation in Puerto Nuevo
- Hotel Puerto Nuevo   AEFGHIJLP$V   ℂ 491376 $G ⚌
  On the west side of the lake just north of where the Río Bueno rises. Also excellent camping area attached to hotel. Open September–March. Boat hire, horse riding, sailing
- Hostería Rayenmalal, in old *hacienda* building 5 km north of Puerto Nuevo
  AEFGHIJLPUVX $H ⚊

  Boat hire, beach frontage

Accommodation in Riñinahué
★★ Posada Campesina Riñinahué   AEFGHIJLMP$UVX $E ⚌
  $C cabins for 5. Boat hire, beach front, directly on the lake in the shadow of the rising Cerro Ille (which somehow dominates the whole township). Dining room for 40 people, excellent food, meals $X. Closes at the end of the season, usually after Easter. Entertainment Sat and Sun
- Hospedaje Riñinahué, at the beginning of the village near the turnoff to the *hostería*
  (down to the lake) $I ⚌
  Shared bathroom. Run by the local schoolteacher

⚥ Festivals

Festivals in the town of Lago Ranco
• February: Semana Aniversario de Lago Ranco, a local festival more like a country fair

⚠ Camping

There are several camping sites at Coique, 10 km west of Futrono on the road to Puerto Nuevo.

There are also several camping site in the town of Lago Ranco, and to the west.

There are camping sites in Llifén on the banks of the Río Culcurrupe; in Riñinahué; and at Salto del Nilahué.

⁉ Eating out

Eating out in Llifén
• Hostería Huequecura

🚌 Buses

Buses from Valdivia go to the northern (Futrono) and eastern (Llifén and Riñinahué) sides of the lake. Buses from Osorno go to the southern side of the lake (Lago Ranco and Riñinahué), and less frequent rural buses go to the western side between Lago Ranco township and Futrono, connecting Puerto Nuevo and Coique.

You can go around part of the lake by public transport (Futrono to Lago Ranco or vice versa); to do this you will need to stay overnight in small places such as Riñinahué, as the rural buses are geared towards the needs of the local population who bring their crops to the markets in the morning and return in the evening.

Buses from the town of Lago Ranco
Buses Lagos del Sur, Buses Transnorte, Buses Ruta 5, and Buses Riñinahué run 3 services daily to Osorno, 3 services daily to Valdivia, 8 services daily to Río Bueno, and 2 services daily to Riñinahué. Drivers usually have a meal break here before continuing to Riñinahué.

Buses from Futrono
Buses Pirehueico, Buses Turibus, Buses Futrono, Buses Cordillera del Sur, and Buses En Directo run 3–6 services daily from Valdivia. Buses go either via Paillaco or via Los Lagos. If intending to go to Panguipulli, connect with buses in Los Lagos.

Buses from Llifen
Buses Cordillera del Sur run 2 services daily to Valdivia and Futrono.

Buses from Riñinahué
Buses run daily to Futrono at 0745, provided the ferry can make the river crossing near Llifén across the Río Calcurrupe. Buses Lagos del Sur run 1–4 services daily to the town of Lago Ranco, Río Bueno, and Osorno, and 3 services daily to Valdivia.

🚘 Motoring

There are gas stations in Futrono and Lago Ranco.

⚅ Sport

Lago Ranco and the eastern tributaries are the domain of the sport fisherman, in particular Llifén: Río Pillanleufu, Río Blanco, Lago Maihué, Lago Ranco, Río Nilahué, Río Caunahué, Río Riñinahué, and Estero Chollinco. Riñinahué and Llifén are good starting points for mountain hikes.

➕ Excursions

Excursions from Llifén
Further inland the region is still largely occupied by the Mapuche people, and it is possible to visit some of their villages. The Mapuches living in this region are some of poorest people in the region. You may visit their villages but respect their traditions. In Riñinahué, the local schoolmaster will point you in the right direction.
• **Lago Pirehueico**: If you have your own 4WD vehicle, you can drive to this lake from Llifén, passing **Volcán Choshuenco**; it's well worth the trip just for the scenery. By making a small detour, you can also visit the hot springs at **Baños de Chihuío**; there are no tourist facilities.
• **Lago Maihué** is also easy to get to from Llifén, particularly if its good fishing potential appeals to you.
• **Puerto Llolles**: 13 km east, where the Río Calcurrupe flows out of **Lago Maihué**. There are still many Mapuche villages in this part of Los Lagos region.

Excursions from Riñinahué
• **Salto del Nilahué**: The 5 km walk to the Nilahué waterfalls takes about 45 minutes — you are always on level

ground. The falls are just below the bridge where the river exits into Lago Ranco; as you walk towards the lake you can hear the thunder of the falling waters. On the road there is a signpost to Camping Salto del Nilahué. From the camping ground a trail leads down to the river and the Saltos can be seen from here. The waterfall is in two tiers, each about 5 m. Near the northern end of the bridge there is also access through private property (owned by Supermercado Los Saltos) — ask for permission. This way is a lot steeper to get down to see the waterfall, but you can take better photographs.

* **Volcán Carrán** erupted in 1954 and the volcanic ash and lava you can see

here date back to this eruption. The volcano is in the upper reaches of the Río Nilahué valley, and the best way to get there is on horseback, though for hikers too there is a good visible trail for most of the way. Going further up, you can reach **Volcán Puyehué** (2240 m) and return to **Osorno** via RN 215. Not an easy hike — only for experienced hikers. In the hidden valleys there are many Mapuche villages. If you are contemplating this mountain hike, useful Instituto Geografico Militar 1:50 000 series maps are "Riñinahué" (5-04-08-0017-00) and "Volcán Puyehué" (5-04-08-0027-00).

LAGO RUPANCO

Distance from Osorno: 58 km east on Ruta U-51 and RN 215 (via Entre Lagos)

Lago Rupanco is possibly the most untouched lake in Región X de Los Lagos. Most of its tourist facilities are on the west end (Hotel El Paraíso) near the outlet of **Río Rahué,** and on the south side (Piedras Negras, El Islote, and Bahía Escocia). The eastern part is in **Parque Nacional Puyehué**. The scenery is superb: the snowcapped volcanoes look near enough to reach out and touch!

Red deer and fallow deer have been introduced, and are particularly abundant near **Coto Rupanquito** (you can get there from Entre Lagos) and also on **Isla de Los Ciervos** ("Deer Island").

The southern side of the lake is the most accessible part, and that is where most of the tourist facilities are. You can also get to the northern part of **Parque Nacional Vicente Pérez Rosales** and the southern part of **Parque Nacional Puyehué**.

◄ Accommodation

* Hostería El Paraíso, near outlet of Lago Rupanco, 13 km south of Entre Lagos ABCEFGHIJLNPUVXZ $F ▮▮ $E cabins for 4. Boat hire, beach frontage, tennis. Reservations in Osorno: Freire 561 ℂ (64)213582/236239

Accommodation at Bahía Piedras Negras
* Hostería y Cabañas Rupanco, on south side of lake ABFGHJLPV $H ▮▮
* Hostería Club de Pesca y Caza Osorno, 84 km east of Osorno AFGHMPV $H ▮▮. Reservations in Osorno: Cochrane 679 ℂ 233685
* Posada Campesina La Gruta, on beach AFV

Accommodation at Bahía Escocia
* Hotel Bahía Escocia, Sector Río Blanco at extreme eastern end of Lago Rupanco near south side of Parque Nacional Puyehué AEFGHIJLMUX $E ▮▮. Full board

◭ Camping

Camping Club de Caza y Pesca on the south side of Lago Rupanco near Sector El Islote is in the sheltered bay formed by Península Islote.

🚌 Buses

There is one service daily to and from Osorno via Entre Lagos.

🎾 Sport

Sailing, fishing, hiking.

LAGO YELCHO

Altitude: 100 m
Distance from Chaitén: 46 km south on Carretera Austral

Lago Yelcho must be one of the most beautiful yet still little-known tourist destinations in Chile. It is only a short drive from Chaitén, with regular buses travelling on the Carretera Austral either up to Futaleufú and Palena or south to Coihaique. Tourist centers are springing up at the north side of the lake near the outlet of Río Yelcho from Lago Yelcho and also on the southern, less accessible side of Lago Yelcho. At the northern side the Río Yelcho is spanned by a huge bridge, part of the Carretera Austral project.

You reach the south side of the lake by taking the turnoff east at Santa Lucia. This is a very beautiful area with many a valley and snow-covered volcano as yet undiscovered by tourists. It is scenery to delight lovers of the outdoors.

Loggers have not yet decimated the forest around Lago Yelcho, and in fact many forests reach down from the mountains directly to the lake shores and rivers. The water of the lake is emerald green and reflects some of the glaciers.

The nearby lakes and rivers have an abundance of rainbow trout, brook trout and salmon — fantastic is the only word for it.

As well as being a paradise for fishing enthusiasts, this area is a mountain hiker's dream! Hikers can reach snow-capped **Volcán Corcovado** in the **Sierra Avalancha** as well as the glaciated El Arce chain. The view as you go over the bridge south is of exceptional and remarkable beauty — a sight to behold! Craggy mountains rise sharply from the valley floor, with the short valley com-ing to an end in a cliff face — and beyond the cliff in the distance is a huge glacier!

Just 11 km further south from the Río Yelcho bridge at a place called **Agua Mineral** there are hot springs, and through a narrow valley in the mountain range (looking west) and sign- posted just near Puente Cavi Ventisquero, you have an excellent view of **Ventisquero Cavi**, almost within reach.

You can visit this area from December to the middle of April, but it is already getting cold from the middle of March. This area gets very heavy rainfalls throughout the year. Beware of mountain hikes, as the weather can change dramatically within minutes. Be sure to get out of the stream beds, as they can rise fairly rapidly — be aware of all this when you are camping.

There are several settlements around the lake:

Puerto Cárdenas

Puerto Cárdenas is 46 km south of Chaitén, at the northern end of Lago

Yelcho just where **Río Yelcho** leaves the lake. There is a huge bridge here — a major construction on the Carretera Austral — from which you have a fantastic view south through a gorge into a glacier-covered area. This is a good base for fishing trips on the lake and hikes into the nearby glaciated mountains around **Volcán Corcovado**. This is a very wet area, and inevitably you will find snow in the mountains.

Puerto Piedra

Puerto Piedra, at the southern end of Lago Yelcho near the mouth of **Río Futaleufú**, 98 km south-east of Chaitén, is a little difficult to reach, but if you are a trout fishing enthusiast, it's worth the effort! You can take fishing trips on Lago Yelcho and in nearby mountain streams — but be careful, the lake is very treacherous. There is a hydroelectric power station not far from **Puerto Ramírez** on the road to Palena.

◧ Accommodation

Accommodation in Puerto Cárdenas
- Residencial Yelcho **AFJPV**
- Hospedaje Gesell
- Cabañas y Camping Caví, 8 km south of Puerto Cárdenas. Open December–March. 25 camp sites, caretaker, hot and cold water, electricity, toilets. Good fishing, also magnificent views west of the icy mountains

Accommodation Puerto Piedra
- Hostería Alexis, near the wharf where the ferry coming across lake from Puerto Cárdenas used to dock $**G** ⚫ including full board. Only 8 beds. Unlimited camping space outside the *hostería*. $**J** per camp site
- Pensión Las Casas, at the junction of the roads to Futaleufú and Palena is located 6 km east of Puerto Piedra **SV** $**J** ⚫

Ⓐ Camping

Bring all your supplies either from Puerto Montt or (dearer!) from Chaitén.
There are camping sites 16 km south of Puerto Cárdenas, and at Puerto Piedra at the south-eastern end of Lago Yelcho.

🚍 Buses

Buses from Puerto Cárdenas
Buses José Escobar Pérez, Buses Chaitur, and Buses Yelcho run daily services to Chaitén. There are three services per week to Palena and Futaleufú.

Buses from Puerto Piedra
Buses José Escobar Pérez and Buses Chaitur, Buses Yelcho run daily services to Chaitén. There are three services per week to Palena and Futaleufú.

⬇ Water transport

In Puerto Cárdenas the owner of Barco Puma organizes fishing trips on the lake. The launch is fairly large and comfortable, accommodates six people, and can be hired for a week. The small steamer *Cristina* can also be hired for fishing trips but is not as comfortable. These trips are in extraordinary primeval scenery, with occasional clearings on the banks where a pioneer has built a homestead.

⊛ Sport

Fishing and mountain hiking.

◆ Excursions

Excursions from Puerto Piedra
- **Futaleufú:** 47 km north on RN 231 See the entry for Futaleufú on page 663.
- **Palena:** 51 km south on RN 235 See the entry for Palena on page 692.

Excursions from Puerto Cárdenas
- **Ventisquero Caví:** This day excursion is best reached from Cabañas y Camping Caví — not for beginners.
- **Termas Agua Mineral:** Hot springs. No tourist facilities. At Puente Agua Mineral a signpost points out the hot springs. Buses usually make a short stop there. Also best reached from Cabañas y Camping Caví.

LA UNIÓN

Area code: 064
Population: 18 000
Distance from Valdivia: 72 km south on Ruta T-60 and RN 207

La Unión is on the **Río Llolehué**, 10 km west of the Panamericana. It was founded in 1821 in the early days of the Republic. The first settlers were farmers and it became the center of a rich agricultural community.

German immigrants in the middle of the 19th century gave the town a commercial boost by starting small industrial enterprises based on agriculture (flour mills, breweries, and linen garments). The German influence is still very much in evidence in the town's old world charm.

La Unión is quite clearly divided into a residential area and a factory area. The factory area is on the east side of the river and there you can see the former Grob flour mill, the flax spinning works, and also an early electricity plant. The church on the Plaza de Armas dates from 1904.

Calle Prat is a remainder of the old colonial road, and continues south to **Trumao**.

⑪ Eating out

Restaurants
• Club Alemán, Letelier 497 $Z. German cuisine
• El Pionero, Angamos 355$Z
• Gaspar, A. Prat 590 corner of Letelier $Z
• Regalón, Manuel Montt 210 $Z
• Selecta, Angamos 367 $Z

Cafeterías
• Coppelia, Esmeralda 512 near Comercio $Z. German cakes
• Queens (in the Hotel Consistorial) Prat 630 $Z

⊟ Accommodation in La Unión

Hotels

★★★ Waeger (formerly Consistorial), Arturo Prat 630
AFGHIJLPVX   ℂ 3223845 $F ⚏

★★ Unión (formerly Club Alemán), Letelier 497
AEFGHIJKLMP$UVXZ   ℂ 322695/322537 $G ⚏
• Comercio, Comercio block 200 near Ramírez   ℂ 322248 $H ⚏
  Shared bathroom, budget travelers

Residenciales
• 21 de Mayo, Serrano 1001   A $H ⚏
  Budget travelers. The *residencial* has an annexe across the street with cold water only

Accommodation along the Panamericana
• Hostería Puente de Río Bueno, 10 km east from La Unión at the intersection of Ruta T-70 and Panamericana   ADEFGHILPUVXY   ℂ 55574 $H ⚏
  Tennis court, four rooms

LA UNION

To Valdivia

B. ARANA

O' HIGGINS

RAMIREZ

PRAT

ESMERALDA

SERRANO

RIQUELME

Llollelhue

AV INDUSTRIAL

21 DE MAYO

ANGAMOS

M. MONTT

PHILIPPI

Plaza

Rio

LETELIER

COMERCIO

S. ALDEA

Sport Oval

To Panamericana

To Trumao

Key to map

A	Iglesia
C	Municipalidad (Town hall)
D	Post office and telex
E	Telephone
P	Gas stations
T	Bus terminal

● **Accommodation**
1 Residencial 21 de Mayo (Anexo)
2 Residencial 21 de Mayo
6 Hotel Waeger
8 Hotel Comercio
9 Hotel Unión

○ **Eating out**
3 Restaurant El Pionero
4 Restaurant Selecta
5 Restaurant Regalón
7 Café Gaspar

△ **Tour operators and car rental**
10 Car rental

□ **Services**
11 Supermercado Paris
12 Railroad station

🚌 Buses from La Unión

There is no central bus terminal.

Companies
Colectivos to Río Bueno depart from Bus Norte Terminal.
* A48   Buses Lit, Esmeralda 824 ☎ 322579
* A153 Buses Tur-Bus Jedimar, A. Prat 851 ☎ 322512
* B11   Bus Norte, Riquelme 755 near Manuel Montt ☎ 322785
* B81   Buses Igi Llaima, Angamos 358
* B152 Buses Ruta 5, A. Prat block 300 near S. Aldea
* B171 Buses Trans-Norte, Riquelme 755 ☎ 323031
* B179 Buses Varmontt, Manuel Montt 225 ☎ 322467
* B207 Buses Ettabus, Esmeralda 864 ☎ 323019

Services

	Destination	Fare	Services	Duration	Company
•	Chillán	$11.20	1 service daily		A153
•	Concepción	$12.20	3 services daily		B81, B207
•	Los Angeles	$8.80	2 services daily		B81, B207
•	Osorno	$1.50	14 services daily	1 hr	A48, B11, B81, B207
•	Puerto Montt	$3.10	7 services daily	2 hrs	A48, A153, B11, B207
•	Puerto Varas	$2.80	4 services daily	1½ hrs	A48, B11, B207
•	Río Bueno	$ 0.60		¼ hr	Colectivos Río Bueno–La Unión, B152
•	Santiago	$16.70	4 services daily		B11, B207
	Sleeper	$27.50	1 service daily		A48
•	Talcahuano	$11.20	3 services daily		B81, B207
•	Temuco	$5.90	3 services daily		A48, B81
•	Valdivia	$1.70	14 services daily		B11, B81

Eating out on road to Río Bueno
* La Parrilla de Baltazar, 2 km east of town

📮 Post and telegraph

Post office
* Correo and Telex Chile, Esmeralda 659, Plaza de Armas

Telephone
* CNT Telefónica Sur, Manuel Montt 384
* CNT Telefónica del Sur, A. Prat block 400

🛏 Services and facilities

Dry cleaner
* Lavaseco Burbujas, Manuel Montt 699

Laundry
* Lavandería Novedades, Letelier 517

Supermarket
* Supermercado Paris, Comercio 420

🚗 Motoring

Car rental
* Hertz Rent a Car, Letelier 497 (in the German Club)

Gas stations
* COPEC, Comercio block 500 between Riquelme and Serrano

🚆 Trains
* Temuco: Fares: *salón* $8.50, *económico* $6.00

🛍 Shopping

In the linen factory you can buy excellent linen clothes at factory prices.

⚽ Sport

Trout fishing in **Río Bueno** and **Río Pilmaiquén**.

➕ Excursions
* Misión Franciscana de **Trumao**: 12 km west, founded in the middle of the

19th century. The belfry can be seen from far away.

- **La Barra**: Small boats ply the river on the Río Bueno from Trumao to the mouth of the river. Small craft use the river to carry timber to the mills for processing. The river at first meanders gently between rolling hills, passing through meadows and pine plantations. The most picturesque part is after the junction with **Río Cahuinalhué** near **Trinidad**. The river has carved its way through the coastal *cordillera,* and here the riverbed becomes narrow and the water flows faster. The slopes of the mountains are forested right down to the river, and mountain streams tumble down. This is the domain of the sport fishermen. At the end of the river trip is the village of La Barra, meaning "sandbar", consisting mostly of weekenders. You can only reach La Barra by launch or on foot. Some villages in the area are still inhabited by Huilliche Indians. This area is not yet on the commercial tourist trail — definitely off the beaten track.

LLANQUIHUÉ

Area code: 06523
Population: 10 000
Distance from Puerto Montt: 25 km north on Panamericana

Llanquihué, on the western side of **Lago Llanquihué** and 8 km north of **Puerto Varas**, is a small timber town as well as a tourist resort. Launch trips on Lago Lanquihué depart from the landing pier at the end of Amunátegui.

Ⓐ Camping
There is a nice serviced camping site right in town, with a private beach on the lake.

Ⅱ Eating out
- Central, Avenida V.Pérez Rosales 308
- Cisne's, Avenida V.P. Rosales 317. Steaks
- El Torito, Valdivieso corner of Matta, upstairs
- Pattus, Errázuriz corner of Werner

Buses

Companies
- Buses del Sur
- Buses Fierro
- Buses Fresia
- Buses Río Frío
- Buses Rurales, M.A.Matta corner of O'Higgins
- Buses TAS Choapa, Avenida V. Pérez Rosales 70 ℂ 242142
- Buses Varmontt, M.A. Matta 415 ℂ 242037
- Buses Estrella del Sur, Buses Cruz del Sur

Services
There are 25 services daily to Puerto Montt ($1.00) and Osorno ($2.10). and 3 services daily to Santiago ($19.00). There are also frequent services to the following rural destinations: Fresia, Puerto Octay, and Río Frío.

Post and telegraph
- Telex Chile, Errázuriz 414

Motoring
- COPEC gas station

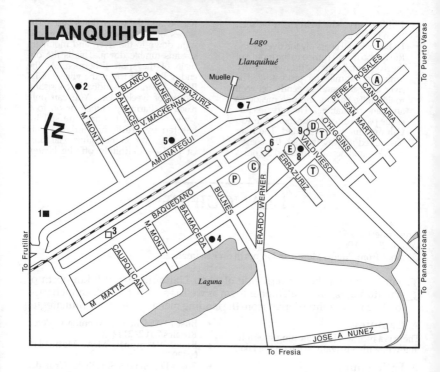

Key to map

A	Iglesia Parroquial (Parish Church)
C	Municipalidad (Town hall)
D	Post office and telex
E	Telephone
P	Gas stations
T	Bus terminals

● Accommodation
- **2** Cabañas El Cisne
- **4** Hospedaje Memel
- **5** Hospedaje Etienne
- **7** Hospedaje Posada Alemana
- **8** Hospedaje Bello Horizonte

○ Eating out
- **6** Restaurant Pattus
- **9** Restaurant Cisnes

■ Sights
- **1** Iglesia Luterana

□ Services
- **3** Railroad station

⊟ Accommodation in Llanquihué

Cabañas
- El Cisne, Manuel Montt   BHPV   (242726 $E for 4
- Los Volcanes, Ramón Carnicer 2   (242730

Hotels
- Siete Lagos, Errázuriz 132   (242020

Hosterías
- Llanquihué, Mackenna corner of Errázuriz   (242630
- Posada Alemana, Errázuriz 517   (242629

Hospedajes
- Alpina, Baquedano 901   (242642
- Bahu, Bulnes 106   (242136
- Bello Horizonte, Valdivieso 450   S   (243247
- Etienne, Amunátegui 794   (243262
- Memel, M.A.Matta 849   (242673
- Paola, Avenida Presidente J. Alessandri 33   (243265
- Posada Alemana, Errázuriz 517   (242629
- Wiehoff, Errázuriz 007
- Valdivieso 517

Accommodation along the road to Totoral
- Hospedaje Edelweiss, KM 2   ADHJ   (242731 $H ▪▪

Accommodation along the Panamericana
- Hospedaje La Casona, Intersection with Fresia
   AHJLN   ((09) 6435089 $H ▪▪

Hostales
- Del Río, near turnoff to Llanquihué   (233404

Accommodation at Nueva Braunau
- Hospedaje Werner, Fundo Nueva Braunau, 7 km west of the intersection of the Panamericana and Ruta U-40 to Loncotoro
   ABHIJLN $H ▪▪

NIEBLA

Area code: 063
Altitude: Sea level
Distance from Valdivia: 15 km east

Niebla is on the estuary of **Río Valdivia** on the Pacific Ocean. Its main attraction is the Spanish fort, Castillo Montfort de Lemus.

ⓘ Tourist information

The tourist office is opposite the entrance to the Spanish fort. It also doubles as a post office and sells postcards.

ⓐ Camping

There is a camping site at San Ignacio 6 km north on Playa La Cascada.

⊟ Accommodation in Niebla

- Cabañas Fischer, Calle del Castillo 115

	P	✆ 282007	$F for 4
• Hostal Posada del Castillo, Antonio Ducce		✆ 282021	$F ♟

Hosterías

★★Riechers (formerly Rucantu), Antonio Duce 795	ABCEFHIJKMPV	✆ 282043	$G ♟
$F cabin for 4; 10 rooms			
• Villa Santa Clara	AEFHLPVX	✆ 282028	$H ♟
• Cabañas del Abuelo Los Molinos 6 km north			
	BP	✆ 213826	$F for 4
Fax 213570			

- Hostería El Paraíso, 6 km north of Niebla on a little bay near the Spanish gun emplacement at Los Molinos

⑪ Eating out

Restaurants
☞ • Jardín de Delicias, Playa Chica $Z. Seafood, cakes
- Cafetería la Familia, Playa Grande $Z. Open only in summer
- La Picada
- Hostería Riechers (formerly Rucantu), Antonio Duce 795 $Y. German spoken, German cuisine
☞ • Hostería Villa Santa Clara $Z. Also bar service, seafood
- Canto Del Agua. Seafood, views over the bay

⬚ Post and telegraph

The post office is opposite the entrance to Castillo Montfort de Lemus.

🚍 Buses

- Valdivia: Fare $1.10; duration ½ hr; Buses Diaz, Buses Barrientos, Buses Gómez, Buses Hernandez Villegas

⬚ River transport

Ferries cross the river to Corral and to Valdiva.

▣ Sightseeing

- Castillo Montfort de Lemus: Part of a defense grid to protect Valdivia, the castle was completed in 1767. It is well preserved and some cannons remain in the gun emplacements. The subterranean powder house was built inside the rock. The castle is quite large, with beautiful views across the mouth of the Río Valdivia and the Pacific Ocean. Do not miss.

⬚ Excursions

- **Isla Mancera**: By boat halfway between Niebla and Corral. Boats make a stop but do not wait for tourists; you have to take the next ferry boat back. Here you will find Castillo de San Pedro de Alcantara, another formidable 17th-century fortification. The garrison was the headquarters of the military governor, and included a small chapel and a Franciscan convent.
- **Corral:** Continuing from Isla Mancera by boat. See "Excursions" from Validivia on page 751.

OSORNO

Area code: 064
Population: 100 000
Altitude: Sea level
Distances
- From Puerto Montt: 110 km north on Panamericana (RN 5)
- From Santiago: 915 km south on Panamericana (RN 5)

This was Huilliche country before the Spaniards came here. Nowadays the remaining Huilliche people live in *reducciones* or native villages along the coast and the coastal *cordillera* where they still preserve their ancient customs.

Osorno is at the junction of the **Río Damas** and the **Río Rahué** a major tributary of the **Río Bueno**.

It is the center of a dairy industry, and was colonized by Germans in the 19th century, as can be clearly seen from its architecture. It looks rather like a middle-sized German town with many *cafeterías* and many of its streets are named after famous German immigrants. Avenida Mackenna is the best-preserved street architecturally.

The town was founded in 1558 by Hurtado de Mendoza and named in honor of his grandfather, Conde de Osorno of Spain, but was abandoned during the Mapuche uprising in 1598. Fuerte María Luisa, a Spanish fort overlooking the river, was built

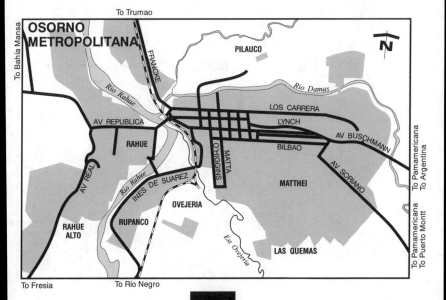

Osorno

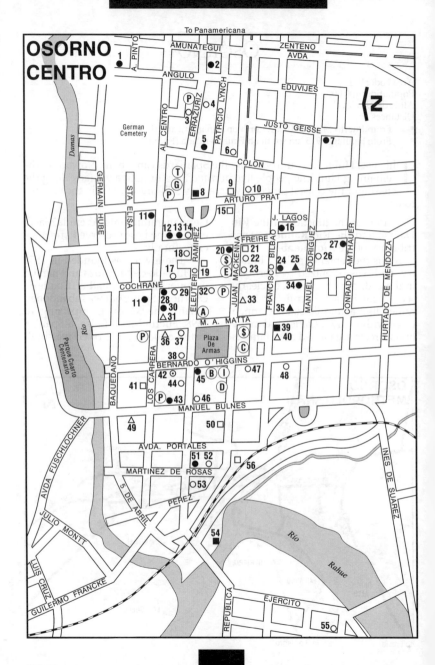

LOS LAGOS

OSORNO CENTRO

To Panamericana

Osorno

684

Key to map

A	Iglesia
B	Gobernación Provincial (Government)
C	Municipalidad (Town hall)
D	Post office and telex
E	Telephone
G	Mercado Municipal (Market)
I	Tourist information
P	Gas stations
$	Money exchange
T	Bus terminals

● Accommodation

1	Residencial Royal
2	Residencial La Paloma
5	Residencial Ortega
7	Hotel Barcelona
11	Hospedajes in Los Carrera
12	Residencial Schulz
13	Residencial Aitué
16	Residencial Stop
20	Hotel García Hurtado de Mendoza
24	Hotel Waeger
27	Residencial Riga
28	Hotel Interlagos
30	Apart Hotel Ñiltayen
34	Residencial Hein
43	Hotel Tirol
45	Hotel Gran Hotel
51	Residencial Splendid

○ Eating out

3	Restaurant de Turismo
4	Restaurant Millahué
6	Restaurant Eliodoros
10	Restaurant Sancho Panza
14	Café Megas
17	Café Bremen
18	Restaurant La Bahía
22	Restaurant Los Platitos

23	Restaurant Casa del Altillo
26	Restaurant Peter's Kneipe
29	Lucas Pizza
32	Café Colonial
37	Restaurant Dino's
38	Restaurant Dumbo
42	Club Alemán
44	Salón de Té Típico
46	Restaurant Gula
47	Restaurant Bavaria
48	Restaurant El Yugo
52	Restaurant Don Quijote
53	Restaurant Super Dragón
55	Restaurant Fogón Rehuenche

△ Tour operators and car rental

31	Ñilque Tours
33	Agencia de Viajes Oásis
36	Salfa Tour
40	Hertz Rent a Car
49	Automóvil Club de Chile

▲ Airline offices

25	LADECO
35	LAN Chile

■ Sights

8	Iglesia San Francisco
39	Museo Municipal
54	Fuerte Santa Luisa

□ Services

9	Lavandería Liebig
15	Supermercado Las Brisas
19	Nortsur (Agfa)
21	Alta Artesanía
41	Instituto de Cultura Chileno Norteamericano
50	CONAF

in 1793 when the town was refounded on the same spot. German immigrants began to arrive in 1850, and there was a wave of Arab immigration between 1910 and 1920. During colonial times Osorno had a mint which made gold coins from gold mined nearby.

Osorno is a good spot for excursions into the Andes and the lakes in the *pre-Cordillera*. You can see the Andes and volcanoes from the town. The climate is temperate and very wet, with December to March the driest months. The average annual temperature is 10°C (50°F).

Regular buses to Santiago and Puerto Montt as well as to various destinations in Argentina make this a key town in southern Chile. Regular passenger trains between Santiago and Puerto Montt also pass through here.

⚐ Festivals

* March: Semana Osornina together with a *fería artesanal*.

⊟ Accommodation in Osorno

Apart hotel
- Ñiltaihuén (formerly Los Carrera), Los Carrera 951
  BPTV   (234960/232356 $F ⚏
  Fax 238772

Cabañas
- De Bilbao, Bilbao 1453   APV   (234553 $H ⚏

Hotels

★★★★Del Prado, Cochrane 1162   ACDEFGHIJKLPRS$TUVXZ
    (235020/1 $D ⚏
English and German spoken, fax 237080

★★★★García Hurtado de Mendoza, Avenida Juan Mackenna 1040
  ABCDEFGHIJKLMPSTUVX
    (237111 $D ⚏
Sauna, English and German spoken, background music. 31 rooms, fax 237113

★★★★Waeger, Cochrane 816   ACDEFHKLMP$TUVZ   (233721/2 $D ⚏
English and German spoken, fax 237080

★★★Interlagos, Lord Cochrane 515   ACDEFGIJKLP$TUVXZ   (234695/235681/23258
    $F ⚏
Car hire, English and German spoken

- Barcelona, Manuel Rodríguez 1397   (233614 $H ⚏
  Budget travelers
- Gran Osorno, Libertador Bernardo O'Higgins 615
  ADEFGIJKLMPSUVX
      (233990 $F ⚏
  English and German spoken
- Rayantú, Patricio Lynch 1462   ABCDFGHMPSTUV   (238114/115/116
      $E ⚏
- Tirol, Bulnes 630   AEFGHLMPUVX   (233593 $H ⚏
  English and German spoken
- Villa Eduviges, Eduviges 854   AEHIPUV   (235023 $H ⚏

Residenciales
- Aitué, Freire 546   (239922 $H ⚏
- Bilbao, Bilbao 1019   (236755 $G ⚏
- Hein, Lord Cochrane 843   AEFGHPV   (234116 $H ⚏
  English and German spoken
- La Paloma, Errázuriz block 1500   AF $H ⚏
  Backpackers
- La Posada, Bilbao 992   AP   (230110 $H ⚏
- Mackenna, Bilbao 1205   APS $H ⚏
- Ortega, Colón 602 $J ⚏
  Shared bathroom, backpackers
- ☞ Riga, Conrado Amthauer 1058   AEFHIJLPSUV   (232945 $G ⚏
- Royal, Angulo 486
  Backpackers
- ☞ Schulz, Freire 530   AEIJKLSUVY   (237211 $H⚏
  Shared bathroom; 12 rooms
- Splendid, Manuel de Rosas 628   F
  Backpackers
- Stop, Freire 810   (232001 $J ⚏
  Backpackers
- Ver Mar, Errázuriz block 1700 corner Lastarria

Accommodation in Osorno — continued

Hospedajes
- Bilbao, Francisco Bilbao 1019   (236755 $G ⚏
  Backpackers
- Los Carrera 1164

Accommodation in suburb of Rahué
- Residencial, Valparaíso 231 near Buses Maicolpué

Accommodation along RN 215
You pass through the village of Cancura on the way from Osorno to Futrono. There is a nice *cafetería* here, Hexe Onces Alemanas.
- Cabañas Yaganes, KM 6 **ABCD**   ((09) 6534686

Accommodation in Maicolpué
Maicolpué, 66 km west, is a beach resort on the Pacific coast near **Bahía Mansa**. It comes to life only during summer. It has fine white sandy beaches, with mountain slopes still covered in the original forest reaching right down to the sea. Although there are a few cabins, so far this scenic spot has escaped the notice of most tourists. There is no official camping ground, but camping is possible anywhere along the beach. No facilities.
- Hostería Miller, Avenida Costanera   **AEFGHIJLPUVX** $H ⚏
  Reservations in Osorno: (233087

Accommodation in Pucatrihué
Pucatrihué is a seaside resort 68 km north that comes to life for three months in the holiday season. It is a bit windswept in open areas, but some parts are protected by rocky outcrops. Bus Mar and Empresa Maicolpué run 2 services daily to Osorno.
- Hostería Pucatrihué   **AEFGHKV**

ⓘ Tourist information
- Sernatur, Edificio Gobernación, up-stairs, Plaza de Armas (234104   ☞
- Sernatur, Bus Terminal upstairs (during summer only)
- CONAF, Juan Mackenna 674, 3rd floor (234393   ☞
- Municipalidad, Mackenna 851. Fishing permits

Ⓐ Camping
There is a camping site on the south side of Río Damas, a few hundred meters from the intersection of the Panamericana with the road to Bariloche.

ⓘⓘ Eating out

Restaurants
- Bar Central, Juan Mackenna block 700 near Bulnes $Z
- Bar Henry, Juan Mackenna block 700 near Bulnes $Z   ☞
- Bavaria, O'Higgins 743
- Café Waldi's, O'Higgins 610 on Plaza $Z
- Casa del Altillo, Mackenna 1011 $Y. Seafood, international cuisine
- Club Alemán, O'Higgins 563 (232784 $Y
- Club Osorno, Cochrane 759 $Y
- De Turismo, Errázuriz block 1400 in Bus Terminal $Z
- De Turismo Don Quijote, Martínez de Rozas 638 $Y
- Don Quijote, M. de Rosas 638
- Dumbos, O'Higgins 580, local 5
- El Eleodoro, Juan Mackenna block 1200 near Colón. Chilean cuisine
- Gula, Bulnes 630
- La Bahía, E. Ramírez 1076, upstairs $Z
- Jockey Club, O'Higgins block 600 on Plaza
- Los Platitos, Juan Mackenna block 1000 opposite Hotel Garcia Hurtado de Mendoza
- Millantué, Errázuriz 1329 $Y

- O'Carlis, Los Carrera 2408
- Parrilla El Yugo, O'Higgins 827, upstairs $Y. International cuisine
☞ • Peter's Kneipe, Manuel Rodríguez 1039 $Y. International cuisine. Specialty venison, seafood, German spoken
- Sancho Panza, Juan Mackenna 1205. Chilean cuisine
☞ • Super Dragón, E. Ramírez 493 $Y. Chinese cuisine

Cafés
- Bremen, Cochrane 588 $Z
- Check, Ramírez 949, in the *galería* $Z
- Colonial, Cochrane 641
☞ • Dino's, Ramírez 898 on main plaza $Z
- Luca's Pizzas, Cochrane 551
- Migas, Freire 580 $Z
- Réal, Ramírez 949
- Rhenania, E. Ramírez 977 (upstairs)

Salón de Té
☞ • Salón de Té Típico, E. Ramírez 720 $Z

Eating out in Rahué
The suburb of Rahué is across the Río Rahué, west of the city center.
- Café Bar Rahué, Avenida República 375 $Z
- Restaurant Fogón Rehuénche, Concepción 258, Rahué Bajo $Z

ⓨ Entertainment
- Disco Carolina, P. Jaraquemada 471
- Disco Mario's, Juan Mackenna 555
- Disco Mas, Panamericana KM 10 South
- Disco Taquilla, Finca del Campo 179

🕮 Post and telegraph

Post office
- Correo and Telex, O'Higgins 645 on Plaza

Telephone
- ENTEL Chile, Bilbao 975
- Telefónica del Sur, E. Ramírez 816 on Plaza, open daily 0800–2300

$ Financial
- Fincard, Mackenna 877 on the plaza ℂ 236470. Cash advances on Visa and Mastercard
- Cambio Tour, Juan Mackenna 1010 ℂ 234846

- Turismo Frontera, E. Ramírez 949, Galería Catedral local 5 ℂ 236394

🕮 Services and facilities

Medical centers
- Centro Médico RERA, Los Carrera 1145
- Clínica Alemana, Zenteno 1530, ℂ 235041. German spoken

Dry cleaners
- Lavaseco El Cisne, Bulnes 655
- Tintorería Ideal, Los Carrera block 900 near M.A. Matta

Pharmacy
- Farmacia Chile, Eleuterio Ramírez 1108

Photographic equipment
- Fotográfica Juan Schmidt, E. Ramírez 959
- Nort Sur Agfacolor, E. Ramírez 1053
- Rodrigo Osorio Kettler, E. Ramírez 952, local 34, Galería Rombocol ℂ 232243. Camera repairs

Laundry
- Lavandería Liebig, A. Prat near Mackenna

Sports accessories
- Reinares y Thone, Ramírez 1100

Supermarkets
- Supermercado Las Brisas, A. Prat near Patricio Lynch.

▣ Visas and passport
- Departamento Extranjería in Gobernación Provincial building –Tarjeta de Turismo, O'Higgins (upstairs). Tourist visa extensions
- French consulate, E. Ramírez 719 ℂ 232642
- German Consulate, Mackenna 987, office no. 4, upstairs ℂ 232151

✈ Air services
Aerodromo Carlos Hott Siebert (formerly Cañal Bajo) is 6 km east on the Panamericana.

Airlines
- LADECO, Cochrane 816 ℂ 236102/234355
- LAN Chile, Manuel Matta 862 ℂ 236688

LOS LAGOS

🚌 Buses from Osorno

Osorno has three bus terminals: the Terminal de Buses for interstate travels and the rural bus terminal are fairly close together. Buses to the coast, however, start from the bus terminal in the suburb of Rahué.

Companies departing from the rural bus terminal
The rural bus terminal is at Errázuriz block 1200 near Prat.
- B17   Buses Aguas Calientes
       Services to Parque Nacional Puyehué
- B133   Buses Piedras Negras, Colón corner of Mackenna
       Services to Cancura, Los Maitenes, Piedras Negras, Puerto Rico, and Bahía Escocia
- B161   Buses Tegualda
       Services to Tegualda, Purranque, Concordia, Corte Alto, Pedernal, Tolinco, and La Naranja
- B204   Buses Puyehué (23654
        Services to Entre Lagos, Parque Nacional Puyehué, Aguas Calientes, Anticura, and Pajaritos (on the border with Argentina)
- B206   Buses Via Octay, office 10-B (237043
       Run a round trip daily to Cancura, Puerto Octay, Quilanto, and Frutillar
- B261   Buses Lagos del Sur
       Services to San Pablo, Río Bueno, Lago Ranco, and Riñinahué
- B265   Buses Transtur
       Services to Cancura, Puerto Fonck, and Las Cascadas
- B276   Buses Entrelagos
       Services to Mantilhué

Companies departing from the central bus terminal
The central bus terminal is at Errázuriz 1400 on the corner of Colón, near the markets. It has a restaurant, clean rest rooms, and tourist information.
- A48   Buses Lit, office 11 (237048
- A56   Bus Tal-Norte, office 5-a (236076
- A137   Buses TAS Choapa, office 2 (233933
- A153   Buses Tur-Bus Jedimar (234170
- B11   Bus Norte (236076
- B64   Buses ETC, office 4 (233050
- B81   Buses Igi-Llaima, office 7 (234371
- B152   Buses Ruta 5
- B169   Buses Trans Austral
- B171   Buses Transnorte
- B179   Buses Varmontt (232732
- B207   Buses Etta-Bus, office 2 (233050
- B260   Buses Cruz del Sur, office 9 (232777
- B267   Buses Turismo Lanín, office 6 (233633
- B271   Buses Via Tur, office 10-B (230118

Companies running to Punta Arenas
Buses Fernández (B65), Buses Ghisoni (B74), Bus Norte (B11), Buses Sur (B158), Buses Victoria Sur (B182), Turibus (A155).

Companies running to San Carlos de Bariloche in Argentina
El Rápido Argentina (B193), Buses Mercedes (B108), Turismo Lanín (B267), Bus Norte (B11), TAS Choapa (A137), Turibus (A155).

Osorno

Buses from Osorno — continued

Companies departing from Sector Rahué
Municipal buses no. 3 and no. 6 run between Osorno center and the market at Rahué.
* B203 Empresa Maicolpué, Valparaíso 535, corner of Chillán
  Services to Puaucho, Bahía Mansa, and Pucatrihué
* B10 Bus Mar, Tarapacá 799
  Services to Puaucho, Bahía Mansa, and Maicolpué

Services

Destination	Fare	Services	Duration	Companies
• Aguas Calientes	$2.10	3 services daily (in main season 5 buses daily)	1hr	B17, B204
• Ancud	$6.10	6 services daily		B252, B260
• Bahía Mansa	$1.50	2 services daily		B10, B203
• Castro	$7.10	9 services daily		A155, B11, B252, B260
• Chillán	$11.20	6 services daily		A48, A137, A153
• Concepción	$12.40	7 services daily		B41, B81, B179, B207, B260
• Coihaique	$33.50	4 services Mon–Fri		B169
• Entre Lagos	$1.50	6 services daily	1 hr	B204
• Frutillar	$1.40	5 services daily		B179
• Lago Ranco	$1.40			B26, B152
• Las Cascadas	$2.10	1–2 services daily	3 hrs	B265
• La Unión	$1.50	14 services daily	1 hr	A48, B11, B81, B207
• Llanquihué	$1.50			B179
• Los Angeles	$8.80	8 services daily		B41, B81, B153, B179, B260
• Maicolpué	$1.50	2 services daily		B10, B203
• Puerto Montt	$3.10	82 services daily	2 hrs	A48, A137, A155, A153, B11, B32, B41, B56, B64, B81, B82, B179, B252, B260
• Puerto Natales	$58.00	Mon, Thurs, Sat		B65, B158
• Puerto Octay	$1.10	2 services daily		B206, B265
• Puerto Varas	$2.60	14 services daily	1 hr	A137, B64, B81, B179, B260
• Punta Arenas	$58.50	1–5 services daily		A137, A153, A155, B11, B65, B74, B158, B182
• Riñinahué	$2.20			B261
• Río Bueno	$1.50	13 services daily	1 hr	B64, B56, B81, B171, B261
• San Carlos de Bariloche (Argentina)	$23.00	1–3 services daily	8 hrs	A137, A155, B11, B108, B193, B267
• Santiago	$17.50	15 services daily	15 hrs	A48, A137, A153, A155, B11, B81, B250, B260, B271
Sleeper	$27.50			B179
• Talca	$14.30	3 services daily		A137
• Talcahuano	$12.40			B41
• Temuco	$4.10	15 services daily		A48, B64, B207, B257, B260, B179
• Valdivia	$3.30	21 services daily		A153, B11, B41, B64, B81, B82, B155, B179, B207, B260
• Villa La Angostura (Argentina)		Tues, Thurs, Fri, Sun	6 hrs	B108
• Viña del Mar	$18.50			A153

🚆 Trains from Osorno

The railroad station is on Juan Mackenna near Portales.

Destination	Salon	Económico	Duration	
• Linares	$8.20	$5.70	13 hrs	1 service daily
• Puerto Montt	$3.60	$2.70	3 hrs	2 services daily
• Santiago	$16.50	$12.35	17 hrs	2 services daily
• Talca	$16.50	$12.35	14 hrs	2 services daily
• Temuco	$7.60	$5.50	6 hrs	2 services daily

Services
- Concepción: Fare $73.00; 1 service Mon–Fri; duration 1 hr; LAN Chile
- Santiago: Fare $163.00; 1–2 services daily; duration 2½ hrs; LAN Chile, LADECO
- Valdivia: 1 service Mon–Fri, Sun; duration ½ hr; LADECO

🚗 Motoring

Car rental
- Automóvil Club de Chile, Bulnes 463 ℂ 232269
- Budget Rent a Car, M.A. Matta 862 (LAN Chile) ℂ 236128
- First Rent a Car, Mackenna 959 ℂ 233861/235284
- Hertz Rent a Car, Bilbao 857 ℂ 235401/235402
- Niltur Rent a Car, Los Carrera 951 (Hotel Interlagos) ℂ 238772. Landrover $32.50 per day plus $0.35 per km
- Salfa Sur Car Rental, M.A.Matta 505 ℂ 236000

Gas stations
For gas station, see city map.

🛍 Shopping
- Alta Artesanía, Mackenna 1069. Chilean handicraft
- Cuero Milano, Ramírez 952. Fine leather goods
- Municipal market, A.Prat between Los Carrera and Errázuriz

⛷ Sport

Skiing
You can ski on Volcán Casa Blanca. Club Andino de Osorno runs the Centro de Esqui Antillanca there. For transport contact the club Mon–Fri 0830–1230 and 1430–1830 ℂ 232297.

Fishing
Trout fishing in Río Pilmaiquén, Lago Constancia, Río Rahué, and Lago Rupanco.

📷 Sightseeing
- Museo Municipal, M.A. Matta 809. Has exhibitions in Mapuche art, archeology, picture gallery, memorabilia of the German settlement, natural history.
- Fuerte María Luisa, a sombre building that overlooks the river, still has a few old guns in position. For some time it was the residence of Gobernador Ambrosio O'Higgins, father of the liberation hero.
- Catedral San Mateo, on the Plaza de Armas. The first cathedral was built in 1577, but has had to be rebuilt many times following earthquakes, fires, and native uprisings.
- Iglesia San Francisco, on the corner of Prat and Errázuriz. Because of the area's propensity to earthquakes, it is built from earthquake-resistant concrete blocks.

✈ Excursions

Tour operators
- Agencia de Viajes Oásis, Juan Mackenna 925 ℂ 235302
- Lagos Austral, E. Ramírez 949, Local 12 ℂ 234137. They are agents for Rancho Las Torres, Carretera Austral 130 km north of Coihaique in Región XI de Aisén

Excursions
- **Lago Puyehué**: 47 km east on RN 215. Excellent fishing. RN 215 is the road leading up to **Paso Puyehué** and through part of the **Parque Nacional Puyehué**. The most important town

on this lake is **Entre Lagos**, with good tourist facilities — see the entry for Entre Lagos on page 657.

- **Maicolpué**: A seaside resort on **Bahía Mansa**, 64 km west on Ruta U-40. There are many unspoilt beaches, especially to the north towards **Pucatrihué**. There is accommodation and regular buses. The coastal *cordillera* has still many Huilliche *reducciones*. The same bus going to Bahía Mansa also makes a detour to **Pucatrihué**.
- **Parque Nacional Puyehué**: 27 km east of Entre Lagos. The huge thermal resort called Hostería Puyehué (take the turn-off 27 km past Entre Lagos) marks the the beginning of the national park. A bit further up on the **Río Chanleufu** is **Termas Aguas Calientes**, with a covered swimming pool. See the entry for the park on page 703.
- **Refugio Antillanca:** Also inside Parque Nacional Puyehué, a further 22 km from Aguas Calientes up **Volcán Casa Blanca**. This is a skiing area, altitude 1990 m, amidst superb landscape and with excellent ski runs.
- **Puerto Octay**: Situated on **Lago Llanquihué**, 53 km south-east on Ruta U-55-V. This is a sealed road, going mostly through flat farming country

interspersed with clusters of trees, a leftover of the former complete tree cover before the arrival of European immigrants. Halfway along is **Concura** (with a COPEC gas station), a small farming community on the northern side of **Río Coihueco**; there is a bridge across the river here, just a few kilometers before the lake road descends to Puerto Octay. This is a small lake resort, and its best beaches are on **Península Centinela**.

- **Trinidad**: 64 km north on the Río Bueno. There are regular weekly buses to Trinidad. You can hike from here or take a river launch to the mouth of the Río Bueno through some remarkable and remote countryside in the coastal *cordillera*. Very few tourists — you'll only meet local fishermen!
- **Trumao** and **La Unión**: Rural buses go north to Trumao on the Río Bueno, where you can cross by ferry, and on the other side you can get rural buses to La Unión. If you fancy a glimpse of rural Chile, more or less untouched by tourism, try going this way instead of the usual (faster) route along the Panamericana. See also the entry for La Unión on page 676.

PALENA

Population: 1000
Altitude: 500 m
Distances:
- From Chaitén: 152 km south-east on RN 235 and RN 7
- From Esquel (Argentina): 132 km south-west

Palena, 10 km west of the border with Argentina, is in a beautiful setting in the upper Río Palena valley, surrounded by high mountains. This is another area not yet discovered by tourists.

You can get to Palena from Chaitén taking the Carretera Austral until Santa Lucia. At Santa Lucia you turn east into RN 235, a gravel road which can sometimes be cut off by winter snow or sudden storms. After the turnoff at Santa Lucia most rivers are

forded. Just before you reach the lake there is an interesting section: a narrow *quebrada* with steep rock faces on both sides. After another 10 km you reach **Lago Yelcho**. At this point the road passes through some low-lying, swampy areas which I presume can

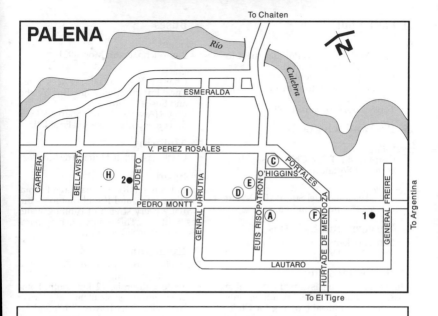

Key to map

A	Iglesia
C	Municipalidad (Town hall)
D	Post office and telex
E	Telephone
F	Carabineros (Police)
H	Hospital

T	Bus terminals
●	**Accommodation**
1	Hotel la Frontera
2	Residencial La Chilenita

be flooded in spring. At this point there is also a camping area. Continuing on you pass another camping place near the mouth of the Río Futaleufú. Away from the lake but on the Río Futaleufú is the small settlement of **Puerto Piedra**. Eight kilometers past Puerto Piedra the road forks: RN 231 turns north east to Futaleufú and RN 235 continues south east to Palena. From the crossroads onward, the road starts climbing; once again this is a very scenic drive until you reach Palena. For further information on Lago Yelcho and Puerto Piedra see the entry for Lago Yelcho on page 674.

⚅ Festivals
• January: Rodeo

ⓘ Tourist information
• CONAF, Lago Risopatrón near Plaza

⊟ Accommodation
• Hotel La Frontera, Pedro Montt 977 F (741240 $I ⚏. Open all year

Residenciales
• Bellavista, General Urrutia 785 AS $I ⚏
• La Chilenita, Pudeto 681 ASV (741212 $I ⚏. Open all year, 5 rooms

ⓘ Eating out

Restaurants
- Café Al Paso, Diego Portales (next to Residencial La Chilenita)
- El Amigo, Pedro Montt 1037
- Roberto Segundo Vargas, Pedro Montt 1032
- Topsy Top, Risopatrón 689

ⓘ Post and telegraph

Post office
- Correo and Telex Chile, Risopatrón corner of Portales

Telephone
- CNT Telefónica del Sur, Pedro Montt between Mendoza and Freire

ⓘ Services and facilities
- Supermarket: Supermercado Palena, Pedro Montt 992

ⓘ Border crossing

This border crossing is difficult for foreign passport holders, as the Argentines only consider it an official crossing for Chileans and Argentines living in the border area who hold appropriate ID cards. Although this may have changed, do not be surprised if your plans go wrong at the border. The border is 8 km east, at an altitude 1200 m and is formed by the **Río Encuentro**. There are no regular bus services to the border — usually the *carabineros* will help. There is public transport three times a week directly from the Argentine border control post to Esquel via Corcovado, a further 121 km. The border is open from sunrise to sunset all year round, weather permitting. Once in Argentina the weather changes dramatically: it may rain in Palena but not across the border. Tip: if stranded in Palena, try to reach Esquel in Argentina, as from there there are good bus services north to San Carlos de Bariloche and all-weather roads back into Chile. It's also a very scenic trip!

ⓘ Air services
- Transportes Aereos Aerosur, Pedro Montt 921 ℃ 741261
- Puerto Montt: Fare $45.00; departs 1500 Tues and Fri; Aerosur (coming from Futaleufú)

ⓘ Buses

Companies
- Bus Yelcho, Pedro Montt 921

Services
- Chaitén: Fare $13.00; services Mon, Tues, Fri; duration 7 hrs; Bus Yelcho and Buses Chaitur
- Esquel (Argentina): Argentine buses leave the border post on Tues and Fri at 1300

ⓘ Motoring
- COPEC gas station, Hurtado de Mendoza

ⓘ Sport

Trout fishing in Río Palena, Lago Palena, Río Encuentro, and Río El Malito — but virtually every stretch of running water has trout in it. This is a true fishing paradise in untouched country.

ⓘ Excursions

Palena is a good base for outdoor enthusiasts and sports anglers.
- **Valle California**: 22 km south. Some years ago ownership of this valley was a contentious issue between Chile and Argentina, but it has since been resolved. This valley and the nearby **Valle del Río Malito** are very picturesque, with no tourists yet because of their isolation; both offer superb fishing.
- **Parque Nacional Palena** (41 380 ha or 102 210 acres): 40 km south of Palena or about 90 km east of **La Junta** (in Region XI de Aisén) on Ruta X-10. It is difficult to reach, accessible only on foot or on horseback. **Lago Palena** is shared with Argentina, where their portion of the lake is called Lago General Vintter. Take the gravel road from La Palena for 22 km south to reach **Pasarela El Toro** over Río El Tigre; from there a trail leads via **Portezuelo Casanova** (1200 m) to the lake. Pasarela El Toro is a hanging bridge over the river — not for vehicular traffic. This is virgin tourist country, and although the mountains at 1800 m are comparatively low, it is very scenic with plenty of original forest cover which has so far escaped the attention of either loggers or firebugs.
- **Esquel** (Argentina) via **Paso Palena-Carrenleufu**: Connects Chaitén with Esquel in Argentina.

PANGUIPULLI

Area code: 0633
Population: 6000
Altitude: 100 m
Distances
- From Valdivia: 110 km east on Ruta T-35 and T-39
- From San Martín de Los Andes (Argentina): 160 km west

Panguipulli is in a wonderful position with views of **Volcán Choshuenco** across **Lago Panguipulli**. It is quite a big town, with good facilities to use as a base for excursions to nearby lakes and volcanoes, and good bus connections to Valdivia and Villarrica, and even excursions to San Martín de Los Andes in Argentina via a very scenic trip on **Lago Pirehueico**. Panguipulli is on the western end of Lago Panguipulli, and has commanding views over the lake into the high *sierra.*

Panguipulli is known as the "capital of the roses" because of the many roses which bloom here in summer: private gardens and parks are full of them, and people compete and prizes are awarded during the Semana de las Rosas. Pumas once roamed freely here, but with advancing civilization pumas are now only in very remote areas — they need a huge area as a home base, and even before the advent of "modern man" were not very numerous.

The best access to Panguipulli is by turning off from Panamericana at Lanco (49 km west) or, coming from Valdivia, by turning off from the Panamericana at Los Lagos (60 km west). You can also get there from Villarrica, and this is a good choice if you want to enjoy some exceptional scenery. If you are coming from Argentina, you can reach Panguipulli from San Martín de Los Andes via **Paso Huahum** and Lago Pirehueico — another very rewarding trip for its magnificent scenery, and which also includes a two-and-a-half hour ferry trip.

Calafquén

Calafquén is 17 km north, beside one of the most scenic lakes in Chile, with picture-postcard views over the lake, **Volcán Villarrica**, and **Volcán Quetrupillán**.

Liquiñe

Fifty-eight km east lies Liquiñe, at an altitude of 280 m in the valley of **Río Liquiñe**, which rises at the **Paso de Carirriñe** (1123 m). The mountain scenery is fabulous. The whole area offers a wide range of easy to moderate hikes which make it a very enjoyable place for middle-aged people to stay. The air is pure, the mountains are green and sparkling and there is a big waterfall (20 m freefall and 2 m wide) just east outside the village, and you can see many more waterfalls. The thermal water reaches 80°C (176°F) and is rich in minerals: iron, copper, aluminium, silicon, sulfur, lithium, and potassium. The waters are said to have curative properties for skin diseases, nervous complaints, rheumatism, mental fatigue and stress, cardiac complaints, ach-

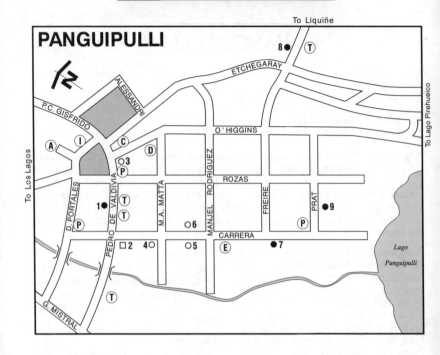

PANGUIPULLI

To Liquiñe

To Lago Pirehueico

To Los Lagos

Lago Panguipulli

Key to map

A   Iglesia
B   Gobernación Provincial (Government)
C   Municipalidad (Town hall)
D   Post office and telex
E   Telephone
F   Carabineros (Police)
G   Mercado Municipal (Market)
H   Hospital
I   Tourist information
P   Gas stations
$ Money exchange
T   Bus terminals

● **Accommodation**
1   Hotel Central
7   Hospedaje Girasol
8   Hostería Quetrupillán
9   Hospedaje Mauna

○ **Eating out**
3   Café de La Paix
4   Restaurant Central
5   Café Topsi
6   Restaurant Chapulí

□ **Services**
2   Supermercado Pirámide

ing joints, arthritis, sleeplessness, convalescing, sciatica, asthma, and obesity. Liquiñe is a Mapuche settlement and a Bavarian Capuchin mission.

⚑ Festivals

• January: Semana de las Rosas (Week of Roses)

ⓘ Tourist information

For information about ferry services on Lago Pirehueico to San Martín de Los Andes, contact Hostería Quetropillán ((63) 311348
• Información Turistíca Municipal, Etchegaray near Plaza

⚠ Camping

Camping Municipal Roble Macho is 1.5 km outside town, directly on Lago Panguipulli.
There is also a camping site in Coñaripe on the east side of Lago Coñaripe, 36 km north-east.

⚑ Eating out

Restaurants
• Chapulin, Martínez de Rosa 639
• El Gourmet, Ramón Freire 394 near Etchegaray, part of the hotel school, open only January/February
• Hostería Cruz del Sur, town entrance KM 770. Steaks

Café restaurants
• Topsi, Martinez de Rosa 604
• Central, Martinez de Rosa 880

Cafés
• De la Paix, Pedro de Valdivia next to COPEC gas station
• De la Plaza, B. O'Higgins 816

ⓨ Entertainment
• Disco Mauna, Freire 898

▨ Post and telegraph

Post office
• Correos and Telex, B. O'Higgins 746

Telephone
• CNT Telefónica Sur, Martínez de Rosa between Freire and Manuel Rodrguez

▤ Services
• Supermarket: Supermercado Pirámide, Martínez de Rosa corner of Pedro de Valdivia

▧ Border crossing

Border formalities are in the port section in **Puerto Pirehueico** on the east end of Lago Pirehueico. From Panguipulli to Puerto Fuy by road is 56 km. In Puerto Fuy you board *Barcaza Mariela* to Puerto

Pirehueico, about 2½ hrs of scenic cruise on Lago Pirehueico. The Chilean border control is open from 0800 to 1730. This pass, at an altitude of 659 m, is open all year round, and is the alternative border crossing in winter when Paso Pino Hachado and Paso Mamuil Malal are closed. Argentine buses run services from the Chilean border control to the Argentine border control in Huaham. There is a good gravel road from Puerto Pirehueico to Huahum in Argentina.

▤ Motoring services

Gas stations
• COPEC, Martínez de Rosa corner of Pedro de Valdivia
• Esso, Martínez de Rosa corner of A. Prat

▦ Shopping

Shopping in Liquiñe
Many villages nearby are inhabited by Mapuche who produce *artesanias* — weaving and wood carvings.

⊛ Sport

Fishing, hiking, skiing on Volcán Choshuenco. The best trout fishing is in Lagos Panguipulli, Neltume, and Calafquén.

Sport in Liquiñe

Hunting
Stags and wild boar are common in the Pampa de las Pipas; also around **Lago de la Pera** and **Lago Lipinza**.

Fishing
There is good trout fishing in all the lakes and mountain streams, especially Lago Pellaifa (18 km), Lago Neltume (20 km), Lago Pirehueico (35 km); Río Enco (40 km), Río Huilo Huilo, and Río Liquiñe.

⬤ Excursions
• **Choshuenco:** In prime hiking country 44 km south-east at the eastern end of **Lago Panguipulli**, at an altitude of 300 m. In the vicinity are several sulfuric thermal springs but no facilities. It is the starting point for excursions to **Volcán Choshuenco**, the skiing area on Volcán Choshuenco, and to Lago Pirehueico. Volcán Choshuenco is in-

⊟ Accommodation in Panguipulli

Cabañas
* Tío Carlos, Etchegaray 377   ABP   ☏311215 $H 👥

Hotels

  ★Central, Pedro de Valdivia 115   ☏ 311311 $H 👥
  Shared bathroom, budget travelers
* España, Bernardo O'Higgins 790   AEHPS   ☏ 311327 $H 👥
  Tours
* San Giovanni (formerly Mauna), Arturo Prat 54
      APS   ☏ 311417 $H 👥
  Budget travelers

Hosterías
* Quetropillán, Etchegaray 381   AEFGHIJLNPSVX   ☏ 311348 $H 👥
* Rayen Tray, on exit road to Lanco   FPS   ☏ 311292 $E 👥

Hospedajes
* Girasol, Martinez de Rozas 404   AF $J 👥
  Shared bathroom
* Pedro de Valdivia corner J.M.Cabrera near little river opposite bus terminal
* Etchegaray 1012

Residenciales
* La Bomba, Martinez de Rozas 450 $J 👥
  Budget travelers

Accommodation on the west side of Lago Panguipulli
* Hotel Cabañas Raimapu, 14.5 km south of Panguipulli on the road to Los Lagos on an extensive beach. 10 km south the turnoff is signposted and it is a further 4 km east towards the lake. There are 15 campsites. Open December–March. Grassy surface with some shade, sloping slightly towards the lake in a little sheltered area with shrubs around it. Facilities include toilets, caretaker, water and benches and tables, $J per camp spot

Accommodation in Calafquén
* Cabañas Antirrayen, Balneario Calafquén
      AHPUV $H 👥
  8 rooms

Accommodation in Choshuenco
Choshuenco is 34 km south-east, in the shade of Volcán Choshuenco.

★★★Hostería Pulmahué   AEFGHIJLPV $F 👥
* Hostería Labraña
* Hotel Choshuenco, Padre Bernabé

Accommodation in Coñaripe
Coñaripe is 36 km north-east. Buses Rural Andes, Buses Estrella del Sur, Buses Abarzúa, and Buses JAC run 4 services daily to Villarrica and Temuco; 2 services daily to Panguipulli; and 2 services daily to Termas de Liquiñe.
* Hotel Antulafquén, next to Estrella del Sur bus stop
      A $J 👥
* Centro Turístico Termal Coñaripe, located 15 km south of Coñaripe on Lago Pellaifa ADEFGKLMOPRTUV. This is the latest high-class addition to the thermal resorts in this region. Thermal waters are 40–42°C (104–108°F). Four thermal swimming pools

Accommodation in Panguipulli — continued

Accommodation on north side of Lago Riñihué
The northern part of Lago Riñihué is 18 km south. Trout fishing in Lago Riñihué, Río Enco, and Río San Pedro; also sailing on the lake.

★★★Hostería Riñimapu, at El Desague, where the Río San Pedro emergess from Lago Riñihué   ABCEFGHIJKLNP$UV $D ⚑
Full board, tennis court, beach, boat hire. Pickup service provided by hotel in Panguipulli. Reservations in Los Lagos: ((63) 311388

★★★Moteles Vista Hermosa   AHKLPVZ $E for 7
   Beach, boat hire. Reservations in Panguipulli: ((63) 311537

Accommodation in Liquiñe

★★Hotel Termas de Liquiñe   AEFGHILPRUVX   (170 Villarrica $G ⚑
   Also cabins with thermal bath tub; large outdoor area with thermal pool, 50 beds

side the **Reserva Nacional Chos-huenco,** which was created to protect the native forests on the slopes of the volcano. However controlled logging still continues. On the south side is a glacier. The fledgling ski resort has a few private chalets. There are superb vistas over Lago Riñihué and Lago Panguipulli. Good fishing in nearby lakes and mountain streams. Buses Pirehueico and Buses Transpacar run 3 services daily to Panguipulli and Puerto Fuy on Lago Pirehueico.

• **Coihueco**: Beach on Lago Panguipulli 16 km east, with camping area.

• **Coñaripe**: 36 km north-east, at the eastern end of **Lago Calafquén**, in full view of **Volcán Villarrica** and **Volcán Quetrupillán.** Likewise **Villarrica** in Región IX de La Araucania is only 44 km north-west. Some Mapuche settlements (*reducciones*) still exist nearby. There are no beaches to speak of, but this is a good base for hikes in the southern part of **Parque Nacional Villarrica**, and to Termas de Liquiñe and Termas de Coñaripe.

• **Puerto Fuy:** 56 km east , on the west side of **Lago Pirehueico** at the outlet of **Río Fuy.** Only a small village, its most important function is the ferry service on scenic Lago Pirehueico to Puerto Pirehueico. This is the route to San Martín de Los Andes in Argentina, a very scenic itinerary indeed. The lake

is narrow and winds between steep forest-covered mountains — this is a highly recommended trip. There are some quiet beaches near the ferry ramp but otherwise no facilities: you are virtually on your own, but the views are magnificent. Some of the local people will provide breakfast for campers. The launch *Mariela* crosses the lake in 2½ hours and returns in the afternoon. It is a wonderful day excursion if you do not want to continue into Argentina. The *Mariela* leaves from the eastern end of the lake Tues, Thurs, Fri, and Sat at 0800; fare $4.50. This is an ideal starting place for walking into the nearby mountains and valley of the Río Fuy. You can also hire boats to go for trips on the lake. The mountains have a dense covering of trees and the narrow lake winding between the **Cerros de Lipinza** and **Cerros Huirahuye** is a particularly impressive view. The timber company doing the logging on the south side of the lake does not encourage vehicles on their private road. Buses Transpacar run 2 services daily from Panguipulli and Valdivia. Buses to Panguipulli await the return of the *Mariela* at Puerto Fuy.

• **San Martín de los Andes** in Argentina via **Lago Pirehueico** and Paso Huahum: 134 km east. The scenic drive starts in Panguipulli, following the

Panguipulli

🚌 Buses from Panguipulli

The central bus terminal is on Pedro de Valdivia near Cabrera.

Companies
Some bus companies have their own offices in various part of the town.
* A153 Tur-Bus Jedimar, Pedro de Valdivia near Martinez de Rosa
* B13   Buses Abarzúa
* B40   Buses Chile Nuevo
* B96   Buses Línea Verde
* B117   Buses Nueva Longitudinal Sur
* B131   Buses Perla del Sur
* B135   Buses Pirehueico, office 4 (497
* B151   Buses Rural Andes, Ramón Freire near Etchegaray
* B168   Buses Trans
* B172   Buses Transpacar
* B176   Buses Urrutia
* B195   Buses Al Sur, Pedro de Valdivia near Martínez de Rozas
* B199   Buses Estrella del Sur

Services

Destination	Fares	Services	Companies
• Calafquén		1 service Mon–Fri	B176
• Choshuenco		2 service daily	B135, B172
• Coñaripe		3 services daily	B13, B151, B199
• Junín de Los Andes		2 services per week	B83, B199
In winter only 1 service per week			
• Lanco		13 services daily	B40, B135
• Lican Ray		3 services daily	B13, B151, B176
• Liquiñe		2 services daily	B199
• Los Lagos	$1.50	2 services daily	B128, B135
• Puerto Fuy	$2.00	2 services daily	B135, B172
• San Martín de Los Andes		2 services per week	B83, B199
In winter only 1 service per week			
• Santiago	$16.50	3 services daily	A153, B128
• Temuco	$2.30	10 services daily	A153, B83, B128, B168
Some services are via the *Cuesta*, some via Los Lagos			
• Valdivia	$ 2.10	13 services daily	B96, B131, B135, B168
• Villarrica		3 services Mon–Sat	B13, B151, B176

Buses from Calafquén
Buses Urrutia run one service daily to Panguipulli and Villarrica.

Buses from Liquiñe
Empresa Estrella del Sur runs two services daily to Villarrica, Coñaripe, and Panguipulli.

northern shore of **Lago Panguipulli**, with occasional views of **Volcán Choshuenco** (2415 m) and scores of waterfalls cascading down the mountain slopes at the eastern end. Near the village of **Choshuenco** the road crosses the **Río Fuy** and continues to **Puerto Fuy** on Lago Pirehueico, where you board the ferry *Mariela* which takes you to **Puerto Pirehueico** in about two and half hours. In summer they usually depart Tues, Thurs, Sat, and Sun, leaving Puerto Fuy at 0900 and arriving in Puerto Pirehueico at 1130. This is a magnificent trip on this narrow lake, winding through steep, although not very high, mountains, with forested slopes. The distance from Panguipulli to Puerto Fuy is 67 km. From Huahum you can continue the trip to San Martín de Los Andes either by bus or by ferry on an equally scenic trip on **Lago Lacar** in Argentina. See also the entry for San Martín de las Andes in *Travel Companion Argentina.* Puerto Pirehueico has a small *residencial,* but the *hostería* is closed now. From Puerto Pirehueico, Argentine buses go to Huahum and San Martín de Los Andes. The border is 11 km from Puerto Pirehueico, the road following the north bank of Río Huahum which flows from Lago Lacar in Argentina. The Argentine border control is 2 km past the border, in the village of Huahum, where there is a small self-service restaurant. Crossing Lago Pirehueico by ferry is a memorable trip: the north side is primeval forest, and it is said that pumas still roam there. Unfortunately this will soon change, because an international road is going to be built through this virgin country to connect Chile and Argentina. While it lasts, a recommended trip.

• **Villarrica** via **Coñaripe**: Regular bus services go around **Lago Calafquén** via **Pullingue** (a hydroelectric power station), Coñaripe and **Lican Ray**. The road goes along the southern edge of Volcán Villarrica and offers impressive views of the lake and the volcano.

Excursions from Liquiñe
The hotel in Liquiñe has a minibus which is used to make day excursions into the nearby valleys.
• **Manquecura**: The Mapuche settlement and natural thermal waters make this a favorite destination. You can also buy *artesanias* here.
• All Mapuche villages are linked by trails leading through some exciting mountain areas filled with water falls and hot springs, albeit no facilities. The intrepid mountain hiker can go to **Volcán Quetrupillán** via **Paimún** and follow a dirt road across the divide between Volcán Quetrupillán and **Volcán Villarrica** to **Termas de Palguín**. From Palguín make your way back to **Pucón**. This is green tree-studded country as far as the snowline, with clear mountain streams everywhere running down from the volcanoes. This is a classic and exciting mountain hike through *araucania* forests and Mapuche country, but only experienced hikers should attempt to go beyond Paimún. Useful Instituto Geográfico Militar 1:50 000 series maps are "Liquiñe" (5-04-07-0113-00) and "Pucón" (5-04-07-0104-00).

PARQUE NACIONAL ALERCE ANDINO

Distance from Puerto Montt: 46 km south east on Ruta V-65 and Carretera Austral

Parque Nacional Alerce Andino covers 39 000 ha (96 330 acres) and is on a peninsula formed by **Seno Reloncaví** and **Estuario de Reloncaví**, to the south of Lago Chapo. It also incorporates **Reserva Nacional Llanquihué** (33 974 ha or 83 915 acres), which is north- east of **Lago Chapo** straddling the eastern slopes of **Volcán Calbuco**.

Most tourists, particularly sport fishing enthusiasts, flock to Lago Chapo. The easiest way to get there is from Puerto Montt, but you can also get there from **Lenca** up the **Río Lenca** some 30 km south-east of Puerto Montt. Keen hikers might like to try making the trip from Caleta La Arena near the **Estuario de Reloncaví** up the plateau on a mountain path. Or you could start your walk from Rollizo or Canutillar where the power station is. The main attractions are Lago Chapo, Laguna Sargazo, and **Río Coihuin**. The northern end of Lago Chapo, 13 km east of **Correntoso**, is already fairly commercialized, with several clubs having their premises on the lake and a camping area development under way. However the area is still fairly unspoilt with all the mountains covered by dense forest up to the tree line. The trees include mock privet, elms, *lingue*, *alerces*, and *coigues*, and among the fauna are mountain cats (*gato montañés*), pumas, dwarf deer, otters, and various rodents.

The average temperature in summer is 12°C (54°F). The best time to visit the area is between December and March. There are public buses to Lago Chapo and also to **Rampa La Arena**, as well as buses to **Ralún** and the power station at **Canutillar** on the Estuario de Reloncaví. There is a mountain cabin run by CONAF at **Laguna Sargazo**. The mountain hikes are medium to hard — take warm clothing, sleeping bag, and tent if going into the area.

ⓘ Tourist information
You can get information from the CONAF ranger's hut in the **Río Chaica** valley.

Ⓐ Camping
There is a camping site near Lago Chapo, 1 km south of the village of Correntoso on **Río Chamiza**.
The camping ground directly on Lago Chapo belongs to the *carabineros de Chile* and is not open to tourists.

There is a camping site along the Carretera Austral near Punta Metri.
At Caleta La Arena is an unserviced camping site near the school house, a few hundred meters from where you catch the ferry. Boil the stream water before using as it comes down from a farming area. The beach is littered with shell mounds where the local people have feasted on them.

🚌 Buses
Buses Fierro and Buses Olavarría run 3-6 services daily from Lago Chapo, La Arena, and Lenca to Puerto Montt

⊛ Sport
There is excellent trout fishing in Lago Chapo and Río Lenca.

⦿ Excursions
It is possible to go on some interesting hikes in the park, but be prepared for the fact that some areas have dense undergrowth. You can scale **Volcán Calbuco** from the south side (note that the volcano is *not* inside the park). From the high sections of the plateau there are superb views north to Volcán Calbuco, **Volcán Osorno**, south to **Estuario de Reloncaví**, **Cerro Yate**, and **Cerro Tronador** on the Argentine border.
For the excursion from Lago Chapo to Volcán Calbuco use Instituto Geográfico 1:50 000 series maps "Correntoso" (5-04-0052-00). If considering more extensive hikes, also buy the 1:50 000 maps "Lenca" (5-04-08-0053-00), "Cochamó" (5-04-08-0053-00), and "Puelo" (5-04-08-62-00). Take wet weather gear, tent, and sleeping bag. It is best to bring supplies from Puerto Montt, although you can get basic supplies at the kiosks near Lago Chapo. You can start your hikes from Lago Chapo, from Chaica up the Río Lenca valley or from La Arena.

PARQUE NACIONAL PUYEHUÉ

Distance from Osorno: 80 km east on RN 215

Parque Nacional Puyehué covers 107 000 ha (264 290 acres), the area between Río Golgol in the north, Lago Puyehué in the west, Lago Rupanco to the south and east; to the east it also shares borders with Parque Nacional Vicente Pérez Rosales, and a small area borders Parque Nacional Nahuel Huapí in Argentina. It includes Lago Constancia, Volcán Casa Blanca (but not Volcán Puyehué which is a few kilometers outside the national park). It also includes the skiing area Antillanca on Volcán Casa Blanca, Aguas Calientes, Anticura, and Complejo Aduanero Los Pajaritos. I have also included the thermal resort Termas de Puyehué although it is not inside the national park, because of its strategic location at the park's entrance.

The park's main attractions are the thermal resorts in and near the national park, the ski resort on Volcán Casa Blanca, and fishing, rafting, and hiking.

The park's name comes from *puyes*, a small freshwater fish. The always humid forest surrounds more than 20 lakes and *lagunas* with crystal clear water, reflecting the snow-covered mountains, including some volcanoes such as **Volcán Puyehué** and **Volcán Casa Blanca**. Water cascades down from the mountains. The dense forest consists of *coigue, guaitecas* cypress, and *arrayanes*. Few mammals live in the dense undergrowth, but there are otters near the lakes and *vizcachas* in the craters of the volcanoes. Condors circle the area.

Extensive rainfall throughout the year (4200 mm) ensures an abundance of water in rivers and lakes. The wet climate generates a thick vegetation, with lichens, moss, and the native *ñalca* plant to be found everywhere. The largest river is **Río Golgol**, which drains into **Lago Puyehué**. Probably the most picturesque lakes are **Lago Constancia** (1280 m) smack on the border with

Argentina, **Lago Gris** (1080 m), **Lago Paraíso** (980 m), and **Lago Toro**, with **El Encanto** and **El Espejo** the most beautiful *lagunas*.

The **Río Golgol** and many rivers offer excellent trout fishing. The volcanoes make a dramatic backdrop to the already overwhelmingly beautiful scenery; the most important are **Volcán Puyehué** (2270 m), **Cerro Puntiagudo** (2470 m ,"Mount Sharppoint", which really *is* pointed), and **Volcán Casa Blanca** (1980 m). On the slopes of this volcano is the important skiing center Antillanca, with a large hotel and a ski lodge run by the Club Andino Osorno, five ski runs, and four ski lifts.

The area consists of volcanic rock with many valleys formed through the erosive action of glaciers, such as Río Golgol and the Chanleufú valley.

The best time to visit in summer is from December to March, when the average temperature is 13°C (55°F).

Parque Nacional Puyehué has four geographical centers: Aguas Calientes, Anticura, the skiing area, and Termas de Puyehué. The descriptions of facilities follows those lines.

Aguas Calientes

Located on the northern slopes of **Volcán Casa Blanca** in the *pre- Cordillera* 68 km east of Osorno, Aguas Caliente is a thermal resort, administered by CONAF and offering a thermal swimming pool and individual bathing cabins. It is an excellent place to spend a day, and only a short distance from the more sophisticated thermal resort of Termas de Puyehué. The CONAF thermal facilities are open all year round. The **Río Chanleufú** flows from a glacier on **Volcán Casa Blanca**, becoming sulfurous as hot springs join its course. The river forms a natural thermal swimming pool just below the park ranger's headquarters and the camping ground. The water, a constant 39°C (102°F), is said to relieve rheumatism and promote general relaxation.

Anticura

Located 91 km east of Osorno, Anticura lies in a narrow valley in the eastern part of **Parque Nacional Puyehué**, only 3 km from the border control at Pajarito. It is a good base for those who intend to climb **Volcán Puyehué**. It is surrounded by native forest. From here, the road starts climbing to the pass.

Antillanca

A winter sports center at 1500 m, Antillance is just 98 km east of Osorno. Club Andino de Osorno started the ski resort in 1950, and it now has excellent ski runs acclaimed by international skiers. The skiing season lasts from July–September. The 22 km trip from the turnoff at RN 215 passes splendid mountain and lake views. It is surprising to see subtropical rainforest so close to the skiing area. After **Aguas Calientes**, the road reaches a plateau, and you catch the first glimpse of **Volcán Casa Blanca** through an opening in the forest.

Termas de Puyehué

This is a huge thermal complex located 77 km east of Osorno at the entrance to **Parque Nacional Puyehué**, near the junction of RN 215 with the road leading up to Aguas Calientes; it is visible from the main road. The thermal water emerges at 75°C (167°F), and is conducted to the swimming pool, the bottling plant, and all rooms in the hotel. Containing chlorides, sulfide lithium, sodium, iron, aluminum, arsenic, magnesium, calcium, and potassium, its properties are claimed to have a cleansing effect on the body. The mud baths are 40°C (104°F), and are said to be effective against obesity, diabetes, rheumatism, neuralgic complaints, hepatitis, and cardiovascular conditions.

ⓘ Tourist information

CONAF has its ranger headquarters in Aguas Calientes, and an information center in Anticura. There is another information center in Osorno — see "Tourist information" in Osorno on page 687.

⌑ Accommodation

Accommodation in Aguas Calientes
★★★   Cabañas Aguas Calientes $E cabins for four

Accommodation in Anticura
•   Cabañas Anticura, RN 215 KM 93 **AEFGHPV $G ⁞⁞**. Within walking distance of Salto Princesa, directly on Río Golgol. 11 cabins. Reservations in Osorno: ☎ 234393

Accommodation in Antillanca
★★★   Hotel Antillanca, on Volcán Casa Blanca in Parque Nacional Puyehué **ADEGHIJKLMNPRSUVX**

((64) 235114. High season $E **ii**; medium season $F **ii**; low season $G **ii**. Summer rates $G **ii**. Heated swimming pool, English, German spoken, sauna, ski hire. 135 rooms. The hotel is operated by the Club Andino de Osorno — members own 60 per cent of the bed capacity, and the rest is available for non-members

Accommodation at Termas de Puyehué
★★★   Hotel Termas de Puyehué, turn off at KM 72 RN 215 ABCDE-FGHIJKLMNPRTUVXZ (232157 $D–E **ii**. Car hire, sauna, thermal indoor swimming pool, tennis court, English, French and German spoken, reading room, shows, boat hire, ski hire. The complex stands amid meadows and small groves of trees, with the main body of thermal wells in a small forest north-east of the hotel complex on the road to Aguas Calientes. Attached to the complex is a dairy farm and even a landing strip for small aircraft. From the thermal resort it is 18 km to the ski resort Antillanca. During the ski season the hotel has special ski season packages for approximately $400.00, which includes seven nights' accommodation, with breakfasts and main meals, transport to and from the snow fields, lift tickets for six days, and unlimited use of the thermal pool

Ⓐ Camping

There is a nice serviced camping site in Aguas Calientes, just outside the thermal baths on the banks of Río Chanleufú; and another one on the road to Refugio Antillanca, 1 km past Termas Aguas Calientes. In Anticura, Camping Catrué is located beside RN 215.

Ⓘ Eating out

Eating out in Aguas Calientes
• Restaurant Hostería Aguas Calientes $Y

Eating out in Anticura
• Hostería Anticura. International cuisine

Eating out in Antillanca
• Cafetería Antillanca $Y

Ⓨ Entertainment

Entertainment in Antillanca
There are two discos in the hotel complex.

Entertainment in Termas de Puyehué
There is a disco in the hotel complex.

🖳 Services

Services in Aguas Calientes
• CONAF thermal resort: As mentioned above, this is a modern spa building with an indoor thermal swimming pool ($4.50 per person) and private thermal cabins ($6.00 per person).

🚌 Buses

The road from Osorno is sealed for 80 km until the turnoff into the national park at Hostería Puyehué. From there on, the gravel road is in good repair and open all year round. On weekdays, traffic runs both ways from the turnoff. During weekends and holidays, one-way limitations apply — uphill from daylight till 1500; downhill from 1700 onwards.

Buses to Aguas Calientes
Buses Puyehué run daily services from Osorno right up to the CONAF information center at Aguas Calientes and the ranger's headquarters. From Osorno it takes about an hour and a half by car.

Buses to Anticura
Buses Puyehué run 3–5 services daily to and from Osorno.

Buses to Antillanca
Hotel Antillanca in conjunction with Ski club Osorno organize transport to the Antillanca *refugio* on the snowfields.

⊛ Sport

Sport in Antillanca
Skiing and mountain hiking. Ski hire costs $20.00 a day. The four ski lifts have a capacity of 3000 skiers per hour; tickets cost $20 a day. There is a skiing school for beginners.

Sport from Anticura

Hiking and canoeing
There is hiking in the national park, and canoeing down the Río Gol-Gol into Lago Puyehué.

Fishing
Trout fishing in Río Pescadores, Lago El Toro, Laguna El Encanto, Río Gol-Gol, and Lagunas Pato, Gringo, Gallinas, and Mellizas.

Sport in Termas de Puyehué

Fishing
Fishing boat hire per day $50.00.

Tennis
Tennis courts, both covered and open air; $5.00 per hour.

⊕ **Excursions**

Excursions from Anticura
From Cabañas Anticura, national park trails lead to scenic spots such as Salto del Indio (10 mins), Salto de Los Novios (½ hr), Salto de la Princesa (20 mins), and Salto Repucura (½ hr). The paths wind through primeval rainforest, where some of the trees are more than 200 years old.

Excursions from Antillanca
It is only a short walk from the hotel complex to **Volcán Casa Blanca** (1910 m).
From the skiing area you have perfect views of **Cerro Puntiagudo**, **Volcán Osorno**, **Volcán Puyehué**, **Volcán Calbuco**, **Cerro Yate**, and **Cerro Tronador** (3640 m) on the border with Argentina. You can also see **Lago Rupanco** and **Lago Puyehué**.

Excursions from from Aguas Calientes
CONAF has developed several paths which you can follow to admire the many cascades formed by the **Río Chanleufú**.

Excursions from Termas de Puyehué
Hotel Termas de Puyehué has its own minibuses and organizes excursions to the nearby areas of interest, such as **Isla Fresia**, Anticura, Antillanca, and even to San Carlos de Bariloche in Argentina. It also organizes fishing trips to **Río Golgol** and **Lago Puyehué**.

PARQUE NACIONAL
VICENTE PÉREZ ROSALES

This national park covers 220 000 ha (543 000 acres) and is 66 km east of **Puerto Varas** on RN 225. It was proclaimed a national park in 1926. In the north it borders **Parque Nacional Puyehué**, it extends in the east to Argentina, in the west to **Río Petrohué**, and in the south roughly to **Laguna Cayutué** and **Río Blanco** up to **Paso de Vuriloche**. Within its borders there are five volcanoes: **Cerro Tronador** (3460 m), **Volcán Osorno** (2661 m), **Cerro Puntiagudo** (2490 m), **Cerro Pantoja** (1842 m), and **Volcán Picada** (1710 m).

Although not strictly inside the national park, the description of Ensenada and the ski resort of La Burbuja on Volcán Osorno are included here.

The park is in a high rainfall zone — 2400 mm a year near **Ensenada**, reaching 4000 mm a year near Paso Vicente Pérez Rosales and the slopes of Cerro Tronador. The average annual temperature is 11°C (52°F). The combination of glacier action and volcanic activity has caused the formation of many lakes in the area. **Lago Todos Los Santos** is completely within the park with **Isla Margarita** (also called Isla de las Cabras, "Nanny-goat Island") in the center; the lake is at 171 m above sea level and measures 145 square kilometers (56 square miles). Lago Todos Los Santos is the park's centerpiece, and is one of the few lakes with no roads around it; excursion boats are the only means of transport. Laguna Cayutué is probably a crater lake. The slopes are forested right down to the edge of the water.

There are elms, *coigues* and *alerces* in the dense forests on the slopes around the lake and throughout the park between 200 m and 1000 m. The *coigue* dominates until you reach 1000 m, then the terrain changes; there are elm trees and ferns up to 600 m. Most of the *lengas* and *alerces* grow between 600 m and 1000 m where the forest becomes less dense.

You will find plenty of wildlife here, including otters, particularly on Laguna Cayutué. Beside the Río Negro live dwarf deer and foxes; and among the colorful bird life there are *bandurrias,* black-necked swans, colored great bustards, and a rare variety of hummingbird. The forest's largest predator is the puma, although it is rarely seen. Rainbow trout and salmon are plentiful here, and fishing is allowed in Río Petrohué, Lago Todos Los Santos, and Lago Llanquihué from November 15 to April 15.

The history of this national park is closely linked to the search for the fabled treasure city, the so-called *Ciudad de Los Césares* ("City of the Caesars"), and trying to find a better pass over the mountains to the *pampas* of Argentina, avoiding the big lakes. The Puelches knew the best way — to the south of Cerro Tronador, **Paso de Vuriloche**. The early Spanish explorers and missionaries used the track via Laguna Cayutué and Lago

Todos Los Santos over Paso Pérez Rosales. The first European to find the Paso de Vuriloche was a Jesuit missionary, Padre Guillelmo Mascardi in 1716. He took the secret to his grave, and this pass was not rediscovered until 1900.

The best time to visit the national park is between the end of November and March, when the average temperature is 16°C (61°F).

Inside the park there are several camping areas with picnic grounds. There is accommodation and restaurants at Ensenada, Petrohué, and Peulla, and the bus trip along Lago Llanquihué passes many lakeside restaurants.

Ensenada

Located at the eastern end of **Lago Llanquihué** at the foot of Volcán Osorno 50 km east of Puerto Varas, at an altitude 150 m, Ensenada is the gateway to the the national park and to the ski resort on Volcán Osorno. The 50 km road from Puerto Varas is sealed as far as Ensenada. Just before entering the village the road forks: the road straight ahead goes to Lago Todos Los Santos, and the northbound road becomes a gravel road leading to Puerto Octay and Refugio La Burbuja on the south side of Volcán Osorno. Two km east of Ensenada, the Todos Los Santos road splits again, and a branch goes south to Estuario de Reloncaví. There is a COPEC gas station.

La Burbuja

This ski resort is on **Volcán Osorno**, overlooking **Lago Llanquihué**, at an altitude of 1250 m, and the views are spectacular. From Ensenada there is a 15 km gravel road to La Burbuja, which is kept open even after heavy snowfalls. Uphill traffic runs until 1500 and downhill traffic from 1600 onwards. Daily lift tickets cost $20.00.

The Los Coihués ski lift, 1100 m in length, has a capacity of 800 skiers per hour; Pony ski lift, l600 m in length, has a capacity of 200 skiers per hour. The skiing season runs from June to November. The ski slopes on Volcán Osorno have up to 3 m of snow. Teski Club organizes transport from Puerto Varas to the ski resort.

Petrohué

Petrohué is on the western side of **Lago Todos Los Santos** on the slopes of **Volcán Osorno** in the *pre-Cordillera*, with splendid views over the lake and **Isla Margarita** (also known as Isla de las Cabras).

Tours of the park

During the summer months, tour operators organize daily bus trips taking 2½ hours from Puerto Montt and 1½ hours from Puerto Varas. Tour operators usually start their trips in Puerto Montt, but tourists may also join at Puerto Varas at the western end Lago of Llanquihué.

As the bus makes its way along the southern end of Lago Llanquihué, Volcán Osorno is a steady companion on the left hand side — it is never out of view. On the right, you can also see the **Volcán Calbuco** most of the time. The road is sealed as far as Ensenada, 47 km east of Puerto Varas at the extreme eastern end of Lake Llanquihué. Just before passing through Ensenada is **Laguna Verde**, which tour operators usually include in their itinerary.

The national park starts 2 km past Ensenada, and 10 km further on

is the CONAF rangers' hut — this stretch of road is interrupted by a lava flow from the last eruption. The path to the Saltos de Petrohué starts at the CONAF hut. You will enjoy the scenery at **Saltos de Petrohué**, where the Río Petrohué leaves the emerald-green **Lago Todos Los Santos**. At the Saltos de Petrohué there are several paths from the ranger's hut and *cafetería* to the falls, about a kilometer from the road. In years of much rain there can be as many as seven waterfalls, but over the last couple of years drier conditions mean that two cascades have disappeared. It is feared that this is a permanent feature pointing to reduced rainfall.

Three km further on is Lago Todos Los Santos in all its splendor. This is the next stop on a conducted tour. Here starts the lake cruise. The lake itself is like a jewel, surrounded by high mountains whose lower slopes are forested but dominated by the ice-capped **Volcán Osorno**.

To get the best out of your stay in the area, I recommend you make this trip with a tour operator.

ⓘ Tourist information

There are CONAF information centers in Petrohué and near Laguna Verde in Ensenada, and at the beginning of the trail which leads to Saltos del Petrohué.

Ⓐ Camping

On the west side of Lago Todos Los Santos is Camping Petrohué.
Near Peulla, you can make camp in some good spots further up the valley towards Cerro Tronador, but there are no facilities.

⑪ Eating out

Eating out in Ensenada
- Restaurant Canta Rana, RN 225, 43 km, directly on Lago Llanquihué $Y. German spoken

Eating out in Petrohué
- Restaurant Hostería Petrohué

🛏 Accommodation in Parque Nacional Vicente Pérez Rosales

Accommodation in Ensenada
See also "Accommodation along RN 225" under "Accommodation" in Puerto Varas on page 733.

Hotel
- Ensenada, on La Cascada road just past intersection to Petrohué
  AEFGHIJLNPRVZ $G for 4
  Reservations in Puerto Varas: ℂ 232888

Cabañas in Ensenada
- Los Alamos   ℂ CRELL 331
- Villa Ensenada   ℂ CRELL 344
- Vista Al Lago   ℂ CRELL 357

Hospedajes in Ensenada
- Ensenada   ℂ CRELL 356
- La Arena   ℂ CRELL 332

Hosterías
- Ruedas Viejas   AEFGHIJKLMPV   ℂ CRELL 312 $H ii

Accommodation in La Burbuja
- Refugio Teski Club, 12.5 km from Ensenada $H ii
  AEFHP$UVX   ℂ CRELL (0653)8278 anexo 316

  Ski hire, 42 beds
- Refugio Escolar La Burbuja, 13 km from Ensenada
  EF   ℂ 2891 Puerto Varas

  Ski hire, ski school

Accommodation in Petrohué
- Hostería Petrohué, RN 225 KM 60   AEFGHILP$UV $G ii
  Beach frontage, boat hire, disco, German spoken. Reservations in Puerto Montt: ℂ 258042

Accommodation in Peulla
- Hotel Peulla   ADFGIJLP$UV $F ii
  A huge complex overlooking a marshy plain, in fabulous mountain scenery. Beach frontage, boat hire, disco. Reservations in Puerto Montt: ℂ 258041
- Residencial Palomita $H ii

Eating out in Peulla
- Peulla restaurant and an annexe next to the hotel

⊠ Border crossings

Border crossing in Peulla
Next to the hotel complex is the *carabineros* checkpoint and passport control for the trip to Argentina via Paso de Pérez Rosales. Argentine passport control is in Puerto Frías in Argentina, opposite the wharf for the ferry on Lago Frías.

🚌 Buses
Buses Bohle and Buses Fierro run two services daily during December to February. In the off season public buses run Tues, Thurs, and Sat only. There is also an excursion bus in Summer (fare $10.00).

Buses from Ensenada
Buses Bohle run 6 services daily to Puerto Varas and Puerto Montt; and 3 services daily to Ralún, Cochamó, and Puelo. From Ensenada there are no buses going north to Puerto Octay.

Buses from Peulla

Andina del Sur buses bring tourists from Peulla to Puerto Frías in Argentina. The road from Peulla to Lago Frías in Argentina is a private road and only Andina del Sud buses and CONAF have access.

⬇ Water transport

The boat trip from Petrohué to Peulla takes about two hours one way, or one hour if you are only visiting Isla Margarita one way.

Andina del Sud has a boat ramp and runs daily several excursion boats on Lago Todos Los Santos going to Isla Margarita (fare $3.00), to Peulla, and a roundtrip on the lake including Ensenada Cayetué.

⊛ Sport

Fishing and hiking.

◑ Excursions

Seasoned mountain hikers will find this park interesting for walks into the northern section, and mountain hikes to **Cerro Puntiagudo** or **Parque Nacional Puyehué** including **Lago Constancia** and **Volcán Puyehué**. Always carry rain gear when hiking in the park.

Useful Instituto Geográfico Militar 1:50 000 maps are "Volcán Puyehué" (5-04-08-0027-00), "Cerro Puntiagudo" (5-04-08-0035-00), "Volcán Casa Blanca" (5-04-08-0036-00), "Petrohué" (5-04-08-0044-00), and "Peulla" (5-04-08-0045-00).

Excursions from Ensenada

*   **Laguna Verde**: About 1 km north of Ensenada is the park's northern entrance with the *guardaparque* building. Around the laguna there is exuberant growth of native trees.
*   **Termas de Ralún** and **Puelo:** See "Excursions" from Puerto Montt on pages 725–726.
*   **Volcán Osorno**: Although the eastern side of Volcán Osorno is temptingly near from Petrohué, it is better to start from the Ensenada side where there is a road going up to the ski fields at 1200 m. Not for beginners.

Excursions from Petrohué

*   **Isla Margarita** (or Isla de las Cabras), **Peulla**, and **Ensenada Cayutué** .

Excursions from Peulla

Peulla is near the eastern end of **Lago Todos Los Santos**, inside the national park. You can only get there by ferry from Petrohué, 25 km west across Lago Todos Los Santos or by road from Lago Frías in Argentina. The lake is silting up, particularly noticeable at the eastern end where the river enters the lake. Hikers can reach Cascada de Los Novios.

*   **Baños de Vuriloche**: This also involves a boat trip or a hike from Petrohué. These thermal springs with no facilities are at the southern end of Seno Río Blanco. You can also arrange for regular cruise boats going up the Seno Río Blanco to let you get off there.
*   **Lago Frías** in Argentina: It is possible to hike across **Paso Pérez Rosales** to Lago Frías. Although this pass is only 1000 m high, the last part of the hike is hard and can seem endless. However most of it is a beautiful and fairly easy walk while you are on the main road with splendid views of **Cerro Tronador**. On the Argentine side you can walk south along the Cerro Tronador massif — most of the time in full view of this 3500 m mountain. Argentine border guards on Lago Frías will point you in the right direction. This trail takes you from the Argentine passport control to Pampa Linda, from where you can get transport back to San Carlos de Bariloche.
*   **Cerro Tronador**: From Peulla you can easily reach this mountain and its glaciers on the Chilean side. The most spectacular route is to take the 20 km walk following the **Río Peulla** to the end — its source is on the glacier.
*   **Río Negro** valley north to **Volcán Casa Blanca** in the adjoining **Parque Nacional Puyehué**: This is a hard 2–3 days' hike, ending up in **Osorno**.

PUERTO MONTT

Area code: 065
Population: 90 000
Altitude: Sea level
Distance from Santiago: 1016 km south on Panamericana (RN 5)

Puerto Montt is on the **Seno Reloncaví** and is the capital of Región X de Los Lagos. It is built on a gentle slope which becomes a plateau on which the *pre-Cordillera* lakes are situated. **Volcán Calbuco** and **Volcán Osorno** dominate the skyline.

It is not a large town, but is in a commanding position and an ideal base for excursions into the nearby lakes district. To the east and south of the town there are extensive beaches. It has an excellent harbor.

The town was founded in 1853 by Vicente Pérez Rosales, and last century was the hub of the German colonization of southern Chile. Now it is an important tourist and administration center, with good facilities and transport throughout the region.

From the Avenida Costanera you can see the Seno Reloncaví and the chain of the Andes as far south as **Cerro Yate** and **Volcán Hornopirén**. The best views of Volcán Osorno and Volcán Calbuco are from the elevated sections of the town.

Puerto Montt is the starting point of the Carretera Austral Augusto Pinochet which goes as far as Cochrane, some 970 km south.

The hub of town is A. Varas, with shops and tourist facilities.

Puerto Montt is the centre of densely settled district. Some of the smaller towns nearby are:

Calbuco

Calbuco is 53 km south-west. For a description, see under "Excursions" below.

Chinquihué

Chinquihué is 12 km south-west. For a description, see under "Excursions" below.

Cochamó

Cochamó is 116 km south-east, on the Esturario Reloncaví. For a description, see under "Excursions" below.

Maullín

Maullín, 70 km south-west on the estuary of the **Río Maullín**, is a seaside resort and comes to life only during the summer vacation season. Population 5000. The town was founded in

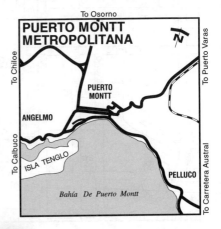

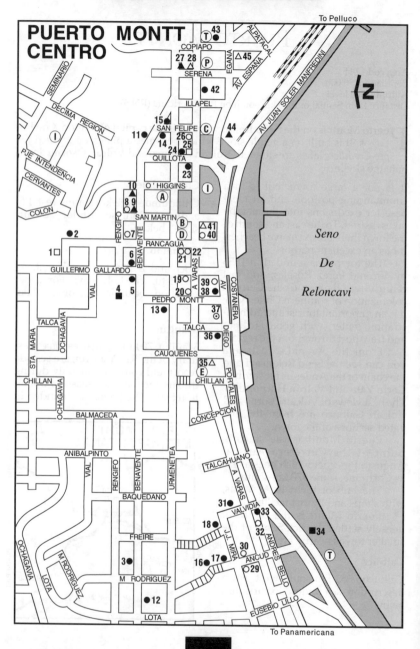

PUERTO MONTT CENTRO

Seminario

Decima Region

Pje Intendencia

Cervantes

Colon

Rengifo

Benavente

Vial

Sta Maria

Talca

Ochagavia

Chillan

Ochagavia

Anibalpinto

Vial

Rengifo

Benavente

Urmenetea

Baquedano

Freire

Ochagavia

Lota

M Rodriguez

M Rodriguez

Lota

Copiapo

Serena

Illapel

San Felipe

Quillota

O'Higgins

San Martin

Rancagua

Guillermo Gallardo

Pedro Montt

Talca

Cauquenes

Chillan

Concepcion

Balmaceda

Talcahuano

Valvidia

J.J. Mira

Ancud

Eusebio Lillo

Egaña

Av España

Av Juan Soler Manfredini

Alpatacal

A Varas

Costanera

Diego

Portales

A Varas

Andres Bello

Seno

De

Reloncavi

To Pelluco

To Panamericana

To Pelluco

Key to map

A Iglesia
B Gobernación Provincial (Government)
C Municipalidad (Town hall)
D Post office and telex
E Telephone
I Tourist information
P Gas stations
$ Money exchange
T Bus terminals

● **Accommodation**

2 Hotel Le Mirage
3 Residencial Benavente
5 Hotel O'Grimm
6 Hotel Raysan
11 Residencial Urmeneta
12 Apart Hotel Millahue
13 Hotel Gamboa
14 Residencial Sur
15 Residencial Alemana
16 Residencial Ancud
17 Residencial Temuco
18 Residencial Pölz
23 Hotel Montt
24 Hotel Don Luis
31 Residencial Embassy
33 Hotel Miramar
36 Hotel Carolina
38 Hotel Burg
40 Hotel V. Pérez Rosales
42 Hotel El Candil
43 Hotel Millahue

○ **Eating out**

7 Restaurant Don Quijote
8 Restaurant Balzac
19 Pizza di Napoli
20 Restaurant Dinos
21 Café Real
22 Café Central
26 Club Alemán
29 Restaurant La Nave
30 Restaurant Embassy
32 Restaurant Bodegón
37 Dada Pub
39 Restaurant Amsel

△ **Tour operators and car rent**

28 Hertz Rent a Car
35 Automóvil Club
41 Turismo Andina Del Sud
45 Avis Rent a Car

▲ **Airline offices**

9 LAN Chile
10 LADECO
27 Transporte Aéreo Aerosur

■ **Sights**

4 Iglesia de los Jesuitas
25 Casa de Arte
34 Museo Juan Pablo II

■ **Services**

1 CONAF
44 Railroad station

1560 by Capitán Pedro Ojeda Asenjo. The settlement was abandoned during the Huilliche uprisings between 1723 and 1766. Most houses are constructed of wood. The best beach is at Punta Pangal, 4 km west of town and approximately 5 km long. There is a COPEC gas station. You can fish from beaches or from launches.

Pargua

Pargua is 45 km south-east, on the **Canal de Chacao** which separates mainland Chile from Isla Grande de Chiloé.

It is the gateway to Isla Grande de Chiloé. Ferry services run to Chacao (on Isla Grande de Chiloé) and to Chaitén and Puerto Chacabuco.

Pelluco

Pelluco, virtually a suburb of Puerto Montt, is 6 km east on **Seno Reloncaví**.

Puelo

Puelo is 145 km south-east, on the eastern side of the **Estuario de Reloncaví** where the **Río Puelo** joins the estuary. The valleys to the south are still largely outside the tourist area — until now they have been only the domain of the sport fishermen. **The Río Puelo valley** up to **Lago Tagua-**

Tagua and beyond is for trailblazers. For further description, see under "Excursions" below.

Ralún

Ralún, 104 km east, is in the northern part of the **Estuario de Reloncaví**, and makes an ideal base for hikes into **Parque Nacional Alerce Andino**: from **Canutillar** 8 km south of Ralún, a gravel road leads up to the southern part of Lago Chapo. See the entry for Parque Nacional Alerce Andino on page 701. Local farmers sell fresh honey. There is fishing, boating, and hiking, but the water is ☞ too cold for swimming! The hot springs at **Termas de Ralún** are on the Río Petrohué near the northern end of Estuario de Reloncaví; there are no tourist facilities besides a picnic place. Excursions from Puerto Montt are organized by tour operators. For further description, see under "Excursions" on page 725.

⊗ Festivals

- February: Semana Portomontina ☞ ("Puerto Montt Week")

Festivals in Carelmapu
Carelmapu is 90 km south-west.
- February 2: Fiesta de la Candelabra. This event is attended by decorated ships from Isla Grande de Chiloé

Festivals in Maullín
- February: Semana Maullinense

ⓘ Tourist information

- Sernatur, Edificio Intendencia, Avenida Decima Región 480 (on hill overlooking town) Regional head office ☎ 254580
- Sernatur kiosk, Quillota corner A.Varas (opposite Hotel Montt)
- CONAF, Ochagavia 464 ☎ 254358/254248
- SERNAP, Urmeneta 433, upstairs, Edificio Gobernación Provincial ☎ 254152
- INTTUR (Información Telefonica Turística). This is a service provided

by Telefónica Sur, but applies only to Región X de Los Lagos. By calling 142 you get information about accommodation and prices, restaurants, tourist attractions, tours, and things to do in the region

Ⓐ Camping

Starting 1 km west of Angelmó there is a string of serviced camping sites as far as Chinquihué.
North of Cochamó on the Estuario de Reloncaví there is a serviced camping site in an old chestnut forest.

⊞ Eating out

Restaurants
- Al Passo, A. Varas 626
- Balzac, San Martín 244
- Bodegón, A. Varas 931
- Comida China, San Felipe 199 corner Urmeneta
- Centro Español, O'Higgins 233, upstairs ☎ 255570 $Y
- Club Alemán, A. Varas 246 ☎ 252551 $Y
- Dada Pub, Avenida Diego Portales
- Don Quijote, Rancagua corner of Rengifo
- Embassy 1, Ancud 104
- Hacienda de Don Raúl, Avenida España, inside railroad station
- La Nave, Ancud 103
- Lilli Marlen, Quillota 180. German cuisine
- Llave 1023, Avenida J. Soler
- Nettuno, Illapel 129. Italian cuisine
- Panorama, San Felipe 192
- Parilla Costa de Relonvaví, Avenida Diego Portales 736
- Patt's Pizzas, Pedro Montt 65 $Y
- Perla de Reloncaví, at the railroad station
- Pizza di Napoli, Guillermo Gallardo near Urmeneta
- Plato's, Avenida Diego Portales 1014
- Rapa Nui, Benavente 550
- Super Dragón, Benavente 839 $Y. Chinese cuisine
- Yoco, Urmeneta 478

Café restaurants
- Amsel, Pedro Montt 56
- Apetitos, Chillán 92
- Dino's, A. Varas 550 (upstairs and downstairs)
- Galerías, Talca near A. Varas

☒ Accommodation in Puerto Montt

Apart Hotels
★★★★Club Presidente, Portales 664   BP   ☎ 251662 $E for 6
    Fax 251669, 26 suites
★★★★Millahué, Benavente 959   ABCDKLPS   ☎ 254592 $G ♙♙

Cabañas
•   Covadonga, Covadonga 59   ☎ 257271
•   Rucalén, Benavente 762   APS   ☎ 254267 $G for 4

Hotels
★★★★Vientosur, Ejercito 200   ADEFGIJKLPS$V   ☎ 258700/1 $E ♙♙
    27 rooms
★★★★Gran Hotel Don Luis, Quillota 144   ACDEFGHIJKLPS   ☎ 259001 $D ♙♙
★★★★O'Grimm, Guillermo Gallardo 211   P   ☎ 252845 $E ♙♙
    Fax 258600
★★★ Burg, Pedro Montt 56   ADEFGIJKLPS$TUV   ☎ 253813/942 $F ♙♙
    Car hire, German spoken
★★★ Colina, Talca 81   ADEFGIJKLMP$V   ☎ 253501/2 $F ♙♙
    Car rental
★★★ Le Mirage, Rancagua 350   ACDEFGHIJKLPS   ☎ 255125/256302
                                               $F ♙♙
★★★ Millahue, Copiapó 64   ABDEFGHIJKLOS$UV   ☎ 253829 $G ♙♙
    17 rooms, fax 256317
★★★ Raysan, Benavente 480   ADEFGHMPS   ☎ 258351 $E ♙♙
  ★Central, Benavente 550   ADFGIJ   ☎ 252546
  ★Miramar, Andrés Bello 972   AEFGIKLPSV   ☎ 254618 $H ♙♙
•   El Candil, A. Varas 177   ☎ 253080
    Budget travelers
•   Gamboa, Pedro Montt 157   ADJ   ☎ 252741
•   Montt, A. Varas 301   ADEFGIJKLPS$V   ☎ 253651 $G ♙♙
    Fax 253652
•   Pumilahué, Pudeto 123   APS   ☎ 257684 $H ♙♙
•   Puerto Montt, Santa Teresa 667   ☎ 257410
•   Punta Arenas, Copiapó 119   AEFGHIJMP$V   ☎ 253080
•   Reloncaví, Guillermo Gallardo 228
•   Royal, Urmeneta 293   AEFGIJPV   ☎ 252602
•   Vicente Pérez Rosales, A. Varas 447   ACDEFGHIJKLMP$UVX   ☎ 252571/2 $E ♙♙
    Fax 255473

Residenciales
•   Alemana, San Felipe 180   AS   ☎ 253934 $I ♙♙
    Budget travelers
•   Ancud, Ancud 114 near J.J.Mira   ☎ 255350
•   Benavente, Benavente 948   ADHJLV   ☎ 253084 $I ♙
    Shared shower, budget travelers.
•   Calipso, Urmeneta 127   AJLPS   ☎ 254554 $I ♙
    Budget travelers
•   El Talquino, V. Pérez Rosales 114   AJL   ☎ 253331 $J ♙
    Budget travelers
•   El Turista, Ancud 91   APS   ☎ 254767 $H ♙♙
    Budget travelers, backpackers
•   Embassy, Valdivia 130   ☎ 253533
    Budget travelers
•   Familiar, A.Varas 937
•   La Nave, Ancud 103   AF   ☎ 253740

Accommodation in Puerto Montt — continued

- Millantú (formerly Any), Illapel 146

  AS   (252758 $H ⚍

  Budget travelers
- Panorama, San Felipe 192 near Benavente

  AEFGIJLPV   (254094 $H ⚍

  Budget travelers
- Residencial de Temporada, Serrano 286

  ADHLP$UV   (253823 $I ⚍

  Budget travelers, 12 rooms
- Sur, San Felipe 183

  AEFGJLP   (252832/280 $H ⚍

  German spoken
- Temuco, Ancud near J.J.Mira $I ⚍

  Shared bathroom, backpackers
- Urmeneta, Urmeneta 290

  AIJPS   (253262 $H ⚍

  Budget travelers

Hospedajes
- Benavente 903
- Familia Cofre, J.J.Mira 964   AJL

  Budget travelers
- Familiar (María Bendel de Smythe), Serrano 112
- La Familia, Francisco Bilbao 380   (256514
- Pölz, J.J.Mira 1002 corner of Freire   AJL   (252851 $I ⚍

  Budget travelers, fax 257553
- Salvo, J.J.Mira 979   AJL   (253838

  Budget travelers
- Yamany, Miraflores 1281   AJL   (253107 $H ⚍

Accommodation in Población Lintz and Población Egaña
These two suburbs are east of the town center.
- Motel y Cabañas Mellipulli, Libertad 610

  ABEFGHIJKLNPRUVXZ (252363 $G ⚍

  $F cabins for 4, sauna
- Hospedaje Touristenheim, Buin 366   AJK   (255671 $H ⚍

  German spoken
- Hospedaje Teresita, Buin 490   (252625 $H ⚍

Accommodation on Isla Tenglo
- Hostería Hoffmann, on road up to Cruz de Tenglo

Accommodation in Población Orellana-Angelmó
Near boats to Puerto Chacabuco (Región XI de Aisén) and Puerto Natales (Región XII de Magallanes).
- Hostal Melipal, Piloto Pardo 2664   AHIJLPS   (252603 $H ⚍
- Residencial Angelmó, Angelmó 2196   (257938

Accommodation in Población Reloncaví
Población Reloncaví is at the northern entrance to Puerto Montt
- Motel Bologna, Petorca 215 corner of Presidente Ibañez

  ABCDEFGHKLMNPV (254000/254858 $F ⚍

Accommodation in Calbuco
Calbuco is 53 km south-west
- Colonial, Eulogio Goycolea 12   AEGLPTUV   (461546

  8 rooms, excursions

Accommodation in Puerto Montt — continued

Accommodation in Chinquihué
Chinquihué is 12 km south-west

Cabañas
- Chauquín, 7 km   (254028
- Los Alamos, 15 km on the road to Panitao, opposite Punta de Isla Caulluhuapi, just after the road becomes unsealed   (256067 $H for 4
  12 tent sites, 5 cabins. Open all year round, water, toilets, hot showers, laundry, shop, tent hire, boat hire. Reservations in Puerto Montt: Lechegua, Población Chiloe (256067
- Kiel, 15 km   ABEFGPS   (255010
  German spoken

Motel
- La Casona, 8 km   FP   (255044
  Opposite beach

Accommodation in Cochamó
Cochamó is 116 km south-east on the Estuario de Reloncaví
- Hotel Cochamó, Catedral 19   F   (216212 $J   ♂

Accommodation in Maullín
Maullín is 70 km south west
- Residencial Toledo, 21 de Mayo 147   AEFG   (451246
- Hotel Balneario Pangal, Playa Pangal 5 km west
       ABCDEFGHJKLMPVX   (451244 $H ♂♂
  Directly on the Pacific coast in a pine tree forest, extensive beach, 10 cabins. Also 20 campsites on flat, sandy area; toilet, water, hot showers, barbecue area, tables and benches, laundry. $J per tent

Accommodation in Pargua
Pargua is 45 km south-east on the Canal de Chacao
- Residencial Ruta Uno $J ♂♂
  Budget travelers

Accommodation in Pelluco
Pelluco is 6 km east

Cabañas
- Bellavista, Bellavista 355   (257321
- Rucatamai, Avenida España   (259019
- Travesia, Inés Gallardo   (263084

Motels
- ★★★ Rucaray, Avenida General Soler   AHPUV   (252395 $E for 4
- Los Abedules, Puerto Montt 55, near Escuela Hogar
       ABCKJLPTV   (254231 $F ♂♂
  Beach frontage

Accommodation in Puelo
Puelo is 145 km south east on the Estuario de Reloncaví
- Hospedaje Tellez, Avenida Santiago Bueras 05
- Pensión Río Puelo
- Río Puelo Lodge, in one of the finest fishing areas in Chile and caters for the international fishing enthusiast. Helicopters, angling courses, hiking, English spoken. Information in Osorno: ((65) 258500

Accommodation in Puerto Montt — continued

Accommodation in Ralún
Ralún is 104 km south east on the Estuario de Reloncaví

★★★★★Hotel Villaclub Alerce, Canutillar KM 14   **(** 257040 $E ♁
                           ABCDEFGHIJKLMNPR$TUVXZ
      $D cabins for 4, sauna, beach area, tennis, car hire, boat hire. Overlooks Estuario de Reloncaví

- Hostería Villa Margarita, 300 m south of turnoff into road leading to Canutillar
                           AFR $F for 4
      Also 30 campsites, electricity, spring water (coming down from Parque Nacional Alerce Andino), toilets, hot showers, open December–March. $I per site for 4. Overlooks mouth of Río Petrohué into Estuario de Reloncaví; also magnificent views over Cerro Yate and Cerro Torrecillas across the estuary

---

- Oriente, A. Varas 896, in Galería Mosa
- Pastelería Liesl, Cauquenes 82. Austrian cakes

Cafés
- Central, Rancagua 117
- Real, Rancagua 137

Eating out on access road to Panamericana
- Restaurant Motel Bologna, Petorca corner of Ibañez

Eating out in Angelmó
Angelmó is a western suburb of Puerto Montt.
- Asturias, Avenida Angelmó 2448-C
- Restaurant Marfino, Avenida Angelmó 1856

Eating out in Calbuco
- Hostería Huito. Seafood

Eating out in Chinquihué
- Restaurant Hornitos de Chinquihué, KM 9
☞ - Restaurant Kiel, KM 8 $Y. Seafood. German spoken, views over the Seno Reloncaví
- Restaurant La Casona, KM 8 $Y. Seafood
- Restaurant Stop, KM 8

Eating out in Pelluco
Pelluco is an eastern suburb of Puerto Montt.

Restaurants
- Embassy 2, Avenida General Juan Manfredini

- Fogón Criollo, Avenida General Juan Manfredini
- Fogón Las Tejuelas de Pelluco, Los Pinos $Y
- Pazos, Avenida General Juan Manfredini $Y
- Taberna Taitao
- Terrazas de Pelluco $X

ⓨ Entertainment

Entertainment in Pelluco
- Club Cocodrilo
- Disco Feeling
- Pub Gnomo
- Salsateca El Novillero, upstairs, southern exit from town on left-hand side. Dancing weekends

ⓔ Post and telegraph

Post office
- Correos, Rancagua 126
- Telex Chile, Urmeneta 433

Telephone
- ENTEL Chile, E. Ramírez 948 **(** 253317. Overseas calls
- Telefónica Sur, Chillán 98

ⓢ Financial
- Cambio de Monedas El Libertador, Urmeneta 529 **(** 256944
- Cambios M.C.I. Intercambios Ltda, Pedro Montt 81 **(** 259352
- Fincard, A. Varas 575 **(** 257081. Cash advances against Visa and Mastercard

✈ Air services from Puerto Montt

Airlines
- Aerolineas Saba, Urmeneta 414 ☎ 259221
  Flights to Arica, Iquique, Antofagasta, Santiago, Concepción, and Punta Arenas
- Aeropalena, Benavente 292 ☎ 252760
- Aeroregional S.A. La Serena 122 ☎ 254364
- Aerosur, Urmeneta 149 ☎ 252523
- LAN Chile, San Martín 200, Local 2 ☎ 253141/42
- LADECO, Benavente 350 ☎ 253002
- Transportes Aereos Don Carlos Ltda, Quillota 139 ☎ 253219
- Transportes Aereos San Rafael Ltda, Benavente 255 ☎ 259551
  Flights to Chaitén

Services

Destinations	Fare	Services	Duration	Airline
• Chaitén	$27.00	Mon, Wed, Thurs, Sat		
			½ hr	ASA
• Concepción	$99.00	Sat	1½ hrs	LAN Chile
• Coihaique	$87.00	1–2 services daily	1 hr	LAN Chile, LADECO
• Punta Arenas	$190.00	1–2 services daily	2 hrs	LAN Chile, LADECO
• San Carlos de Bariloche (Argentina)				
	$35.00	Tues, Fri–Sun	1½ hrs	ASA, TAN
• Santiago	$163.00	4 services daily	2 hrs	LAN Chile, LADECO
• Temuco	$58.00	daily except Fri	1 hr	LAN Chile, LADECO

- Turismo Los Lagos Ltda, A. Varas 595, Galería Cristal, Local 3 ☎ 2337545. Also open Sunday mornings
- Rosse Turismo Ltda, A. Varas 445 (in Hotel Vicente Pérez Rosales) ☎ 255146. German spoken

🏨 Services and facilities

Dry cleaners
- Lavaseco Santa, A. Varas between Cauquenes and Chillán
- Lavaseco Unic, Chillán near stairs

Medical center
- Clínica Puerto Montt, Benavides 753 ☎ 254108

Pharmacy
- Farmacia Corona, A. Varas 655 ☎ 252366

Photographic equipment
- Foto Color, A. Varas 473

Sporting equipment
- Casa del Deporte, Urmeneta 792

Supermarket
- Supermercado Las Brisas, Avenida Diego Portales 1040 (opposite bus terminal)

▣ Visas, passports

- Argentine consulate, Cauquenes 94, Mon–Fri 0900–1400 ☎ 253996
- German consulate, Chorrillos 1582, ☎ 253001
- Spanish consulate, Rancagua 113 ☎ 252557

🚗 Motoring

Car rental
- Automóvil Club de Chile, Cauquenes 75 ☎ 252968
- Avis Rent a Car, Copiapó 43 ☎ 253307
- Budget Rent a Car, San Martín 200 ☎ 254888, fax 257300
- Club Rent a Car, Rengifo 430 ☎ 256482
- Dollar Rent a Car, A. Varas 447 ☎ 252572
- Economy Rent a Car, Santa María 620 ☎ 254125/255400
- First Rent a Car, A. Varas 437 ☎ 252036, fax 255473

🚌 Buses from Puerto Montt

The municipal bus terminal is on Avenida Diego Portales at the intersection with Lota. Both long-distance and rural buses leave from here. La Moneda de Oro — money exchange — is here, and Restaurant Rodoviario is upstairs.

Bus companies with own terminals
- B90   Buses La Chile Argentina, Urmeneta 457
- B179 Buses Varmontt, Copiapó corner of A. Varas (next to Hotel Montt) ℂ 254766. Buses depart from the company's offfices, but also call at the municipal terminal

Rural bus companies
- A137 Buses TAS Choapa, bus terminal office 2 ℂ 254828
- A153 Buses Tur-Bus Jedimar, office 3 ℂ 253329
- A155 Buses Turibus, office 7 ℂ 253245
       Services to Coihaique
- B11   Bus Norte, bus terminal office 6 ℂ 252783
- B16   Buses Aguas Azules, bus terminal ℂ 253835
- B32   Buses Bohle, office 18 ℂ 254526, fax 257057
       Several daily services:
       Route 1: Puerto Montt–Calbuco–Maullín–Carelmapu, with 21 services departing between 0700 and 2030
       Route 2: Puerto Montt–Puerto Varas–Ralún–Canutillar, departing at 1000 and 1800
       Route 3: Puerto Montt–Puerto Varas–Cochamó–Río Puelo, departing 1300 and 1700, and at 1930 for Cochamó
- B56   Empresa de buses Bus Sur, office 24 ℂ 257740
- B64   Buses ETC, bus terminal ℂ 252926
       Services stopping at Calbuco, Maullín, and Carelmapu
- B65   Buses Fernandez
- B66   Buses Fierro, office 5 ℂ 253022
       Services to Lago Chapo via Caleta la Arena, Contao, Hualaihué, and Hornopirén
- B68   Buses Fresia
- B81   Buses Igi Llaima, bus terminal ℂ 254519
- B82   Buses Intersur
- B122 Buses Olavarría
- B142 Buses Quillaipe
       Services stopping at Lenca, Chaica, and Contao
- B147 Buses Río Frio
       Route 1: Puerto Montt–Puerto Varas–Ensenada–Ralún
       Route 2: Puerto Montt–Fresia
- B169 Buses Trans Austral
- B182 Buses Victoria Sur
- B193 El Rápido Argentina
- B207 Buses Ettabus, bus terminal office 35 ℂ 257324
- B242 Buses Ruta Alerce
- B250 Buses Transbus
- B252 Buses Trans Chiloé
- B260 Buses Cruz del Sur, office 8 ℂ 254731
- B262 Empresa de Transportes Maullín
- B263 Buses Muermos ℂ 254402
       Services to Los Muermos
- B271 Buses Via Tur, office 5 ℂ 253133

Buses from Puerto Montt — continued

Services

Destination	Fares	Services	Duration	Companies
• Alerce	$1.00	12 services daily		B242
• Ancud	$4.40	21 services daily		B11, B41, B56, B179, B252, B260
• Calbuco				
via Panamericana	$1.40	35 services daily		A153, B16, B32, B64, B207
via the coastal road				
	$1.50	6 services Mon–Sat		B32, B16
• Canutillar	$3.20	2 services Mon–Sat		B32
• Carelmapu	$2.50	9 services daily		B64, B257, B262
• Castro	$6.50	21 services daily	4 hrs	A155, B11, B56, B179, B252, B260
• Chaica	$2.10	5 services daily		B66, B142
• Chamiza	$1.10	9 services daily		B66
• Chillán	$15.50	8 services daily		A48, A137, A153, B41, B81
• Chonchi	$6.00	3 services daily		B56, B260
• Cochamó	$3.30	3 services daily		B32
• Coihaique (via Comodoro)				
	$33.50	4 services Mon–Fri	32 hrs	A155, B169
• Concepción	$14.00	16 services daily		A48, A153, A155, B41, B56, B81, B207, B179, B260
• Contao	$3.00	2–6 services daily		B66, B122
• Ensenada	$2.20	6 services daily		B32
• Fresia	$1.90	12 services daily	2hrs	B179, B68
• Frutillar	$1.90	28 services daily		A153, B56, B64, B179, B199
• Hornopirén	$5.00	1–5 services daily		B66, B122
• Hualaihué	$4.00	1–4 services daily		B66, B122
• La Arena	$2.50	2–6 services daily		B66, B122
• Lago Chapo	$1.10	3 services daily		B66
• La Unión	$3.10	4 services daily		B11, B207
• Lenca	$1.50	5 services daily		B66, B142
• Llanquihué	$1.20	25 services daily		B56, B66, B68, B147, B179, B199, B260
• Los Angeles	$11.00	10 services daily		A48, A153, B81, B82, B179, B207, B260
• Los Lagos	$3.10	6 services daily		B82
• Los Muermos	$1.50	16 services daily		B263
• Maullín	$1.90	10 services daily		B32, B64, B257, B262
• Osorno	$3.10	82 services daily	2½ hrs	A48, A137, A153, A155, B11, B32, B56, B64, B81, B179, B207, B252, B257, B260, B271
• Pargua	$1.70	10 services daily		B56
• Petrohué	$2.00	2 services daily		B32, B66
	$8.00			Excursion bus
• Puelo	$2.10	2 services daily		B32
• Punta Arenas	$66.00	1–3 services daily		A153, A155, B11, B56, B65, B74, B182
• Puerto Natales	$68.00	Mon, Thurs, Sat		B56, B65
• Puerto Varas	$1.30	50 services daily	¾ hr	A48, B32, B56, B66, B68, B81, B147, B179, B199, B260, B250, B271
• Quellón	$9.00	6 services daily		B56, B252, B260
• Ralún	$2.90	4 services daily		B32, B147
• Río Bueno	$3.20	8 services daily		A48, A153, B64, B82, B250, B252
• Río Frío	$1.30	3 services daily		B147

Buses from Puerto Montt — continued

Destination	Fares	Services	Duration	Companies
• San Carlos de Bariloche (Argentina)				
Excursion via Paso Vicente Pérez Rosales				
	$50.00			Andina del Sud
Via Paso Puyehué				
	$25.00	1–3 services daily	10 hrs	A137, B11, B193
• San Fernando	$17.30	2 services daily		A137
• Santiago				
Ejecutivo	$26.50		16 hrs	B11,
Pullman	$19.50	31 services daily	17 hrs	A137, A153, A155, B32, B56, B81, B82, B207, B250, B260, B271
Sleeper	$38.00	5 services daily	17 hrs	A48, B179
• Talca	$16.50	5 services daily		A137, A153, B82
• Talcahuano	$14.00	5 services daily		A48, A153, A155, B81
• Tegualda	$1.80	2-10 services daily		B56, B199, B260
• Temuco	$7.70	32 services daily		A48, A137, A153, B32, B56, B64, B81, B82, B179, B207, B250, B257, B260
• Valdivia	$5.50	33 services daily	3 hrs	A48, A137, A153, B56, B64, B81, B82, B179, B207, B252, B257, B260, B270
• Valparaíso	$20.20	4 services daily		A48, A137
• Viña del Mar	$20.20	4 services daily		A48, A137, A153, B81

Buses from Maullín
• Buses Empresa de Transportes Maullín, Terminal de Buses, office no. 2 (451334
Buses Bohle and Buses ETC run 10 services daily to Puerto Montt.

Buses from Pargua
Buses Cruz del Sur, Buses Trans Chiloé, Buses Varmontt, and Buses Del Sur run 21 services daily to Puerto Montt, Ancud, and Castro.

Buses from Pelluco
Buses run daily every 15 minutes to Puerto Montt.

Buses from Puelo
Buses Bohle run 2 services daily to Puerto Montt.

Buses from Ralún
Buses Bohle and Buses Río Frío run 4 services daily from Puerto Montt, passing the hot springs at Termas de Ralún.

• Galerias Rent a Car, Benavente 561, local 203 (256434
• Hertz Rent a Car, A. Varas 136 (259585
• National Car Rental, Aeropuerto El Tepual (257136
• Western Rent a Car, Quillota 177 (254437

Gas stations
For gas stations, see city map.

Water transport
Ferry boats to Chaitén, Puerto Chacabuco, and Puerto Natales leave from Terminal de Trasbordadores in Angelmó. For maritime services to all destinations south of Puerto Montt, see "Boat trips" on page 649.
Ferry boats from Angelmó to Cochamó take 6 hours.
• Paseos Angelmó, Mazatlan 23, Anahuac. Excursion launches to islands in the Seno Reloncaví

🚆 Trains from Puerto Montt

Destination	Salon	Económico	Services	Duration
• Chillán	$15.20	$11.50	1 service daily	15 hrs
• Curicó			1 service daily	17½ hrs
• Linares	$9.50	$6.70	1 service daily	16 hrs
• Los Lagos	$7.60	$5.50	2 services daily	
• Osorno	$3.60	$ 2.70	2 services daily	3 hrs
• Rancagua	$19.00	$14.00	1 service daily	
• San Fernando		$13.00	1 service daily	
• Santiago	$19.00	$14.00	2 services daily	20 hrs
• Talca	$16.50	$12.50	2 services daily	17 hrs
• Temuco	$10.70	$7.60	2 services daily	9 hrs

Water transport from Calbuco

• Lancha Veracruz, Errázuriz 297. Excursions to the islands in the Golfo de Ancud.

Ferry services from Pargua

Transmarchilay has an office in Lord Cochrane, directly up from the ferry wharf. See also "Boat trips" on page 649.

🏠 Shopping

Most of the souvenir and postcard shops are near Hotel Vicente Pérez Rosales in A. Varas.

• Fería Artesanal, Avenida Angelmó in Caleta Angelmó. On sale are artesanías mostly from Isla Grande de Chiloé — slightly more expensive than on the island itself and the selection is not as varied as you could buy in the villages themselves

• Alfombras Puyuhuapi, A. Varas 907. Excellent carpets. Made by descendants of Sudeten Germans in Puyuhuapi, Región de Aisén

🏅 Sport

Trout fishing in Río Chamiza and Lago Chapo — one of the best and so close to town.

📷 Sightseeing

• Museo Juan Pablo II, Avenida Diego Portales adjacent to the central bus terminal. Most interesting is the display about Isla Grande de Chiloé and the Archipelago. Good overview on Puerto Montt's history; information about and samples of flora and fauna of the region, and a collection of inter-

esting photos of the early settlement of the region.

• Cathedral, on the main plaza, built in 1856 from local *alerce* wood in the style of a Greek temple.

• Museo Vicente Pérez Rosales, A. Varas corner of Quillota. The exhibits are mostly related to the Spanish colonization of southern Chile.

♦ Excursions

Tour operators

• Andina del Sud, A. Varas 437 (257797 / 253253 / 254692. This organization holds the exclusive right to organize tours via Paso de Pérez Rosales to San Carlos de Bariloche in Argentina ($50.00) — see description below. They also organize tours to Peulla, Puyehué, Ancud, and Ralún. In order to promote their hotel in Peulla, Andina del Sud has a two-day tour to Peulla which includes trip by bus to Petrohué and from there by ferry to Peulla. An additional $45.00 includes accommodation and meals

• Turismo Safari Tehuel'che, A. Varas 449 (258690. Adventure tourism, rafting, climbing

• Varastur, Benavente 461 (252302. Run tours to Ralún daily; also tours to Parque Nacional Puyehué, Frutillar and Ancud

• Turismo Angelmó, Talca 77 (256752. Runs tours daily to: Peulla, Ralún, Petrohué; also to Castro and Dalcahué. The prices for these tours vary from $10.00 to $40.00, many of them include lunch

- Buses Fierro organizes a tour to Petrohué from the bus terminal daily at 0930; Spanish speaking guide, excellent value. Besides conducting tours the driver and guide were singer/composers of Polkas Chilenas. Cassettes with their compositions were played during the trip and passengers could buy cassettes from them
- Buses Bohle runs excursion buses to Salto del Petrohué in conjunction with Navimag
- Turismo Rosse, A. Varas 445 ☎ 255146/257040. German spoken

Excursions
- **Angelmó**: 2 km west of the town center. There is a fishermen's wharf here and a colorful *mercado artesanal* or craft market. There are also small restaurants specializing in seafood and local dishes. A ferry across Canal Tenglo brings you to the Isla Tenglo. There are frequent municipal buses from the city center.
- **Calbuco**: 53 km south-west, with a population of 7000. Calbuco was a forgotten outpost of Spanish civilization until the timber industry discovered the *alerce* and cypress forests in 1700. A shrimp cannery, now abandoned, was established around the beginning of the 20th century. A causeway connects the town to the mainland. The local parish church has an image of San Miguel, which was brought from Osorno in 1603. There are some good beaches near San Antonio, but they are very isolated and without facilities. **Caicaen** is a small fishing village south-west of Calbuco at the tip of a narrow peninsula: take an ETC bus. COPEC gas station. There are 41 daily services altogether between Calbuco and Puerto Montt, the majority of buses going via the Panamericana. Buses Bohle, Buses Aguas Azules Buses ETC, and Ettabus run 6 services daily via the more scenic coastal route; other buses are run by Buses Tur-Bus Jedimar at A. Varas 72.
- **Caleta La Arena**: 45 km south-east. RN 7 is sealed just for 4 km as far as Pelluco. There are beaches and little bays throughout the trip. Just before Chamiza there is a turnoff east into Ruta V-65 which brings you up to

Lago Chapo, part of the **Parque Nacional Alerce Andino**. There are camping spots near Piedra Azul (15 km), and Punta Metri. At **Lenca** there is a CONAF road into the national park with a ranger station near **Chaica**. Further south at Caleta La Arena there is a ferry crossing to **Caleta Puelche**. Near the ferry wharf at Caleta La Arena are good camping spots. There are a few isolated homesteads around, and a trail leads up into the heart of the park to Lago Chapo and a few smaller lakes. This is suitable only for good hikers, as the mountain trail is very overgrown.
- **Carelmapu**: A small fishing village 90 km south-east, on the extreme south-eastern point of the mainland at the end of the *Camino de la Colonia*. It was founded in 1602 by the first wave of Spanish escaping, the imminent fall of Osorno and during the colonial period was attacked several times by pirates. Playa Brava is an open and windswept beach about 3 km west of the settlement. Across the Canal de Chacao is **Isla Grande de Chiloé**. There are 9 bus services daily from Puerto Montt run by Buses ETC, Transportes Calbuco, and Transportes Maullín.
- **Chinquihué** is a coastal resort on the **Seno Reloncaví**, 12 km south-west of Puerto Montt, with many good restaurants well patronized by *Portomontinos*. The scenic drive along the coast starts in Puerto Montt passes **Isla Tenglo**. Motels and camping grounds line the beach, offering views over the Seno Reloncaví to the Andes and the volcanoes. Regular bus services run to Puerto Montt every half hour.
- **Cochamó** and **Puelo**: Cochamó is 116 km south-east on the eastern side of the **Estuario de Reloncaví**. Instead of turning south-west at the Ralún intersection, continue and cross the bridge over the Río Petrohué. This is a very rewarding trip, with possibilities of hiking up from Cochamó into the **Cerro Torrecillas** massif or from Puelo up the **Río Puelo valley** to **Lago Tagua-Tagua** and beyond. This is unknown Chile. Water from the glaciers and mountains surrounding the Estu-

ario de Reloncaví flows straight into the sea. The steep mountains make this area look like a fiord — it is very beautiful. From Puelo you can return to Puerto Montt by launch, which takes about six hours, but launch services only operate regularly during the summer. The area is famous for dairy products, and for honey made from the elm tree blossoms. This is a scenic drive from Puerto Montt via Puerto Varas and along Lago Lanquihué and through the Río Petrohué valley. **Cerro Torrecillas** (2164 m) and **Cerro Cuernos del Diablo** are accessible from Cochamó. A rough road ascending the Río Cochamó valley to Lago Vidal Gormaz near the Argentine border offers an interesting hike through unspoilt natural surroundings. The low mountain pass **Río Manso Orilla Norte**, which leads to Lago Steffen in Argentina, is not open to tourists. Buses Bohle runs 3 services daily to Puerto Montt, Puerto Varas, and Puelo.The bus trip from Puerto Montt to Puelo takes four hours and costs $3.50.

- **Fresia:** 96 km north, the center of the timber industry in the **Río Llico** valley. It has a population of 5000. The south side of the river is more heavily settled than the north. The river has carved a narrow bed through the coastal *cordillera*. Boat-rides downstream begin at Fresia, taking three hours to the sandbar at the mouth of the Río Llico. There are good beaches, a small restaurant, and some vacation shacks at the river-mouth. This is unknown Chile and difficult to reach, but the trip is recommended for travelers who want to go off the beaten track. Take a tent, a sleeping bag, and provisions. There is trout fishing in the mountain streams. Buses Varmontt, Buses San José, Buses Fresia, and Buses Rodríguez run 3–6 services daily to Puerto Montt and Puerto Varas. There are also rural bus services north to Tegualda.

- **Isla Tenglo:** Ferry crossing from Angelmó. Follow the path up the hill — on the top there is a 40 m cross, which you can climb and which is lit up at night. From the top of the hill, there are

sweeping views over the town with the Volcán Calbuco in the foreground, and further back Volcán Osorno, Cerro Puntiagudo, and Cerro Tronador on the Argentine border. To the south there are views over Seno Reloncaví and a few of the islands and as far south as Cerro Yate, **Volcán Apagado,** and **Volcán Corcovado,** as well as **Isla Maillen**. There are frequent ferries from Caleta Angelmó to the island.

- **Lago Chapo:** Located in the **Parque Nacional Alerce Andino** 32 km east of Puerto Montt. The slopes and mountains around the lake are covered with forests reaching right to its shores. This serene mountain lake is dominated by Volcán Calbuco in the north, and some mountain trails lead there. There is trout fishing in the lake. This peninsula has hundreds of small mountain lakes, streams, and waterfalls. The plateau is tree-covered and much of it is covered in dense undergrowth. At present there are no tourist facilities up there, except for a private camping ground for the *carabineros* and a few vacation cottages, but otherwise the lake is undisturbed. From Lago Chapo there is a choice of hikes ranging from one to three days. Besides mountain hikes to the north — **Volcán Calbuco** — you can go west to **Lenca** or south to **Estuario de Reloncaví**, **Baños de Sotamo** (with hot springs) or **Ralún** (with an *hostería*). Here is a mountain hikers' paradise within easy reach of Puerto Montt! See also the entry for Parque Nacional Alerce Andino on page 701. Buses Fierro runs regular daily buses from the bus terminal directly to Lago Chapo, taking two hours.

- **Puerto Varas:** A tourist resort 17 km north on Lago Llanquihué, with splendid views of snowcapped Volcán Osorno over the lake, as well as Volcán Calbuco and in the distance Cerro Tronador. Excellent tourist facilities, and a municipal casino. Regular buses. See the entry for Puerto Varas on page 729.

- **Ralún:** In conjunction with Hotel Villaclub Alerce in Ralún, Turismo Rosse organizes a day excursion from Puerto Montt by bus along the Carretera Austral to Caleta La Arena. At Caleta

Arena you board *Apulchen II* to cruise up the **Seno Reloncaví** with magnificent views of the **Parque Nacional Alerce Andino** on the north side. During the cruise on the **Estuario de Reloncaví**, you have splendid views of **Cerro Yate** (2141 m) and **Cerro Torrecillas** (2164 m) on the south side of Estuario de Reloncaví. This trip starts at 0900 in Puerto Montt, and returns after lunch at Hotel Ralún by bus via Saltos de Petrohué and **Ensenada**, with views of Volcán Osorno, Lago Llanquihué, and Puerto Varas, arriving at Puerto Montt at 1930. Recommended. Alternatively, this trip can be made in one of the frequent buses from the bus terminal in Puerto Montt.The bus trip takes about 2½ hours, passing through Puerto Varas along the south side of **Lago Llanquihué** as far as **Ensenada**. At Ensenada buses turn south to go through the **Río Petrohué valley**, flanked by steep forest-covered mountains. Just before you reach the Estuario de Reloncaví, the valley widens considerably — here are the hot springs of **Termas de Ralún** in their natural state. The bus continues along the saltwater Estuario de Reloncaví to Canutillar (a power station using water from Lago Chapo). Beyond **Canutillar** you can reach **Baños de Sotamo** on Bahía Sotamo along a track. The views over the *estuario* are simply superb, with the snow-covered **Cerro Yate** visible across the water on the south side. Buses Bohle and Buses Río Frio charge $3.00 one way.

• **Río Frío** is 55 km north-west of Puerto Montt on the old colonial trail which connected Valdivia with Isla Grande de Chiloé. The area was settled in the 19th century by Germans and Austrians, and the forests on the low surrounding hills have been exploited since then. The church was built by German Jesuits in 1909.The road to Puerto Varas 44 km east is sealed. In town there is a COPEC gas station. The villages in the area are inhabited mostly by Huilliche. This area is off the tourist trail. Buses El Maño and Buses Río Frío have 3 services daily from Puerto Montt.

• **San Carlos de Bariloche** in Argentina via Lago Todos Los Santos: Andina del Sud has the sole transportation rights in conjunction with Catedral Turismo in Bariloche. This is a one-day trip in summer and a two-day trip in winter (From April 1 to August 31). In winter an overnight stay at Hotel Peulla is included in the fare. In summer the full cost is $50.00; in winter add $66.00 for double accommodation. The trip goes into Argentina and takes a full day, making many interesting stops and finishing with a bus trip terminating at the office of Catedral Turismo, B. Mitre 399 (25443/44/45 in San Carlos de Bariloche. This is a fantastic trip through some of the most outstanding scenery on either side of the border. Don't miss it! Note that the time in Argentina is one hour ahead of Chile, so add an hour when you leave Puerto Montt and deduct an hour if you start in Bariloche. Arrival in Bariloche is usually around 2100 (Argentine time). Budget travelers going to Bariloche should note that Mrs Baumann (who speaks both German and English) has first-class budget accommodation, and usually waits with her pick-up bus outside Catedral Turismo. If not, ring her anyway — if she cannot accommodate you she will pass you on to other *residenciales* in a similar price range (Residencial Baumann (24502).

PUERTO OCTAY

Area code: 064
Population: 2500
Distance to Osorno: 53 km south east on Ruta U- 55-V

Puerto Octay is in a sheltered spot on the north side of **Lago Llanquihué**. Except in the tourist season, from the end of December to the end of February, it is a fairly quiet little town. Founded in 1851 by German immigrants, many houses are still owned by descendants of the early German settlers, and it still looks like a small German country town from around the turn of the century. The best accommodation is on Península Centinela about 6 km from town — a very pretty spot indeed. **Volcán Osorno** across the lake dominates the views.

The complete round trip around Lago Llanquihué can present some difficulties. Rural buses from Osorno only go as far as La Cascada, and the remaining 22 km stretch to Ensenada, where Volcán Osorno comes down to the lake, is not served by public buses. However, there are regular rural buses between Puerto Octay and Frutillar. This is also a very enjoyable trip along the lake and through some of the old German villages.

The road from Osorno is sealed all the way and goes mostly through flat country. On the outskirts of Puerto Octay there is a sharp descent of about 200 m to the lake level. Here you have a wonderful view over the small town, with the church and its steeple stealing the show.

Las Cascadas

Las Cascadas is on the eastern side of **Lago Llanquihué**, sandwiched between the lake and **Volcán Osorno**, 33 km east of Puerto Octay.

☒ Festivals
- February: Semana Octayina

ⓘ Tourist information
- Informacion Turística Municipal, in the kiosk on Plaza de Armas next to the town hall

ⓐ Camping
There is a serviced municipal camping site on Península Centinela, 4 km south. At Las Cascadas, 25 km east, there are several serviced camping sites, some with *cabañas*.

⑪ Eating out

Restaurants
- Baviera, German Wulf 582
- Kali, Esperanza 497
- La Cabaña, Pedro Montt 703
- La Naranja, Independencia 561

Eating out in Las Cascadas
- Restaurant La Playa

▣ Buses
Buses leave from the plaza. Buses Via Octay run 6 services daily to Osorno, and 2 services daily to Frutillar and Las Cascadas.

Buses from Las Cascadas
Buses Trans Sur run 2 services daily to Puerto Octay and Osorno.

▣ Motoring

Gas stations
- COPEC, Calo Volcán
- Esso
- Sunoco

✉ Accommodation in Puerto Octay

Hotels

★Haase, Pedro Montt 344 German spoken	AEFHIJKLPSUVX	☎391213	$G ♙♙
• Posada Gubernatis, Santiago 10	AFHLPV		

Hosterías

• Puerto Viejo, Fundo Puerto Viejo		☎ 391244	$G ♙♙

Accommodation on Península Centinela
Península Centinela is 5 km south.

Hotels

• Centinela, English, German spoken	ABCEFGHIJKLMPSVZ	☎ (09) 6537333	$G ♙♙

Cabañas

• Kahler, 2 km south of Puerto Octay	ABP	☎ 391271	$F for 6

Accommodation in Sector Playa Los Bajos
Sector Playa Los Bajos is 9 km south of Puerto Octay.

★Hostería La Baja German spoken	AEFGHLMSUVX	☎ 391269	$H ♙

Accommodation in Las Cascadas

★★★Centro de Recreación Las Cascadas, 39 km south- east

	ABFHINPV	$E for 4

Reservations in Osorno: ☎235377/8
• Hostería Irma
• Condominio Fundo La Laguna

Accommodation in La Picada
La Picada is a small ski resort on the northern slopes of **Volcán Osorno**, 46 km east of Puerto Octay. There is one ski lift. For transport to the skiing area from Osorno contact Sernatur Osorno.

• Refugio La Picada Capacity 80 persons	AEFGLMPV	$G ♙

⊥ Water transport
• Club de Caza y Pesca, Esperanza 497. Fishing trips on Lago Llanquihué
• Cendyr Náutico. Hire of cruise boats

⊛ Sport
• Fishing in Lago Rupanco
• Skiing at La Picada — see "Excursions" below

⊛ Sport

Sport in Las Cascadas
Fishing, hiking on Volcán Osorno.

▣ Sightseeing
• Museo El Colono, Independencia 591.

• Neoclassical church built in 1907 with its steeple giving it the appearance of a German village, especially as you make the final descent into town on the main road.

✦ Excursions
During the 19th century, German immigrants built several chapels in the area, such as the one at **Playa Maitén** (1866). There is also a cemetery, and you may enjoy wandering around reading the inscriptions on the old tombstones. There is a similar chapel and cemetery in **Quilanto**, 9 km south.
• **El Maitén:** 3.5 km east. Extensive beach with some camping facilities.

- **Lago Rupanco:** Take the road via **Puerto Fonck** to **Piedras Negras** (52 km) or **Islote Rupanco** (60 km), both with accommodation. Good fishing.
- **La Picada**: A mountain ski chalet on the north side of Volcán Osorno. This is a 45 km trip; turn off and go up Volcán Osorno after Puerto Klocker. From the ski slopes you have sweeping views over **Lago Todos Los San-** tos to the east and **Lago Llanquihué** to the west.

Excursions from Las Cascadas
About 5 km south of Las Cañitas is a waterfall fed by glacial water flowing down from Volcán Osorno. Some water-skiing. There are still a few farms left, but most of the countryside has been turned into pine plantations.

PUERTO VARAS

Area code: 065
Population: 16 000
Altitude: 150 m
Distance from Puerto Montt: 17 km north on Panamericana

Puerto Varas is on **Lago Llanquihué**, on the south west side of Lago Llanquihué. Founded in 1854 by German settlers, it is still a center of transplanted German culture and customs, with German schools and colleges (such as the Colegio Germania in María Brunn). This has become a major tourist resort with excellent tourist facilities. The first hotel was built in 1934 and is now a plush casino with conference rooms, discos, gambling rooms, and poker machines.

From the town you have views of **Volcán Osorno**, **Volcán Calbuco**, and **Cerro Tronador**, to name just a few. Its location on the lake is superb, and it is a good base for excursions to other beautiful places in the area, such as **Lago Todos Los Santos**, **Saltos de Petrohué**, and **Ralún** on the northern end of **Estuario de Reloncaví**. The starting point for excursions along the lake is Avenida Vicente Pérez Rosales which becomes RN 225 along the lake shore. Good transport facilities.

The best views over the lake are from Avenida Costanera to the volcanoes surrounding Lago Llanquihué. The water is cold but that doesn't deter the locals.

The "Maria Brunn" church looks a bit like the dome in Speyer,

Germany; a carillon chimes on the hour.

The seaside promenade is beautiful, with houses on one side and landing piers and beach on the other side.

ⓘ Tourist information

- Oficina de Turismo kiosk in Fería Artesanal del Salvador has information on trips and fares for conducted tours
- Informacion Turística Municipal, Del Salvador 328

Ⓐ Camping

There are several good camping sites east of town all with direct access to Lago Llanquihué.

ⓘⓘ Eating out

Restaurants
- Hotel Asturias, San Francisco 308

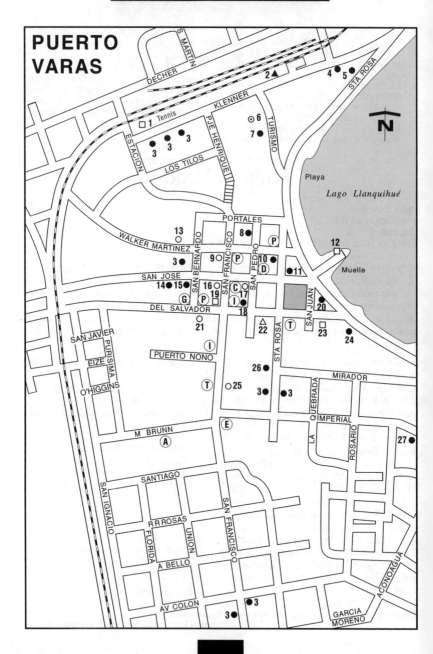

PUERTO VARAS

Lago Llanquihué

Playa

Muelle

Tennis

Key to map

A	Iglesia
C	Municipalidad (Town hall)
D	Post office and telex
E	Telephone
G	Mercado Municipal (Market)
I	Tourist information
P	Gas stations
T	Bus terminals

● Accommodation

3	Hospedajes
4	Cabañas del Lago
5	Hotel La Rada
7	Hotel Gran Puerto Varas
8	Residencial Hellwig
10	Residencial Plaza
11	Hotel Licarayén
14	Motel Sacho
15	Residencial Alemán
18	Hotel Asturias
20	Hotel Colonos del Sur
24	Hotel Bellavista
26	Hostería La Sirena

27	Cabañas El Trauco

○ Eating out

9	Restaurant Asturias
13	Restaurant Country House
16	Club Alemán
17	Café Central
21	Cafe Danés
25	Restaurant Unión

⊙ Entertainment

1	Tennis courts
6	Casino

△ Tour operators and car rental

22	Andina del Sud

□ Services

2	Railroad station
12	Boat harbor
19	Supermercado Viehmeister
23	Fería Artesanal

- Casino de Juegos Puerto Varas, Klenner 351
- Club Alemán, San José 415 ☞
- Country House, Walker Martínez 584
- Don Lucho, Del Salvador 82
- La Vaquilla, Costanera corner of Aldea
- Licarayen, San Francisco 683
- Mercado, in market upstairs, Del Salvador 582 corner of San Bernardo ☞
- Unión, San Francisco 669 opposite ☞ Varmontt terminal. $Y. Budget travelers

Café restaurants ☞
- Central, San José 319
- Danés, Del Salvador 441
- Real, Del Salvador 247 upstairs in *galería*

Eating out along the Costanera ☞

Cafeterías
- Costa Azul, Avenida Pérez Rosales 1071
- Ibis, Avenida Pérez Rosales 1117. Trout
- Las Palmeras, Avenida Pérez Rosales 999 near Imperial
- Tilos, Avenida Pérez Rosales block 01500 near Freire

Eating out along RN 225

Restaurants
- Canta Rana, KM 42.5 German spoken
- Das Alte Haus, KM 30. German spoken
- Fogón Pucará, KM 43

ⓨ Entertainment

- Cafetería Domino, Del Salvador 450
- Casino de Juego Municipal, Klenner 351
- Disco Maddox, Avenida Pérez Rosales 01400. Restaurant
- Disco Panorama on top of Parque Philippi. Open daily in tourist season from 2100 until the early hours
- Disco Monkey's Club, San Pedro 422, upstairs. Lunch $Y
- Restaurant Roller, Avenida Pérez Rosales block 1200

▣ Post and telegraph

Post office
- Post office and Telex Chile, San José 242
- Telex Chile, San José 242

Telephone
- San Francisco near Imperial

⊟ Accommodation in Puerto Varas

Hotels

★★★★ Cabañas del Lago, Klenner 195   ABCDEFGHIJKLNPSV   (232291 $E ⅱ
    Fax 232707, 42 rooms and 21 cabins, excellent views over lake, town and Volcán Osorno from an elevated position

★★★★ Colonos del Sur, Del Salvador 24   AEFGHIJKLMPSVX   (233369 $D ⅱ
    Fax 233394

★★★ Asturias, Del Salvador 322   ADEFGHIJKLMP$TUVX (232446 $ ⅱ
    Car rental. Open all year

★★★ Gran Hotel Puerto Varas, Klenner 351
                            AEFGHIJKLMPVX   (232524 $F ⅱ
    Fax 233385, casino

★★ Licarayén, San José 114   ADEGHIJKLP$TUVX
                                   (232305 $G ⅱ
    Hydromassage, 23 rooms

★ Bellavista, V. Pérez Rosales 060   ADEGHIJKL   (232011/12/13 $E ⅱ
    Open all year 38 rooms, views over lake and Volcán Osorno

•   La Rada, Santa Rosa 131   (233095

•   Merlín (formerly Candilejas), Walker Martinez 584
                                AEHIJKP   (233105 $H ⅱ

Motels

★ El Trauco, Imperial 433   ABCEFGHIJKLNP$VX   (232462 $F ⅱ
    Open all year

•   El Greco, Mirador 134   (233388

•   Sacho, San José 581   AEHILPV   (232227
    Open December–March

Hosterías

★ Lorelei, Maipo 911 Altos Costanera
                            AEFGHIJLP$UVZ   (232226 $G ⅱ
    German spoken, open all year, overlooks lake

•   La Sirena, Santa Rosa 710   AEFGHILPV   (232897
    Open all year

Residenciales

•   Alemana, San Bernardo 416   (232419

•   Casona Germana, Del Carmen 873 $H ⅰ
    20 beds

•   Hellwig, San Pedro 210   (232472
    Budget travelers

•   Imperial, Imperial 0653   (232451
    Excellent views from elevated area over the lake and volcanic chain, budget travelers

•   Plaza, Santa Rosa 306

•   Sureño, Colón 177   (232648

Hospedajes

•   Ceroni Caamaño, Estación 262   (232016 $H ⅱ

•   Gerda Opitz, Del Salvador 711 $H ⅰ
    12 beds

•   Olga Vargas de Kuschel, Del Salvador 329 $H ⅱ
    8 beds

•   Margot Feelings, Purísima 681 $H ⅱ
    15 beds

•   Carmen Bittner, Walker Martínez 564 $H ⅱ

•   Elena de Opitz, A. Prat 273   (232339 $H ⅰ

Accommodation in Puerto Varas — continued

- Ivone Lotty Klein, B. Eleuterio Ramírez 1255　　　℡ 233109　　$I 👥
  German spoken
- Alicia de Rehbein, La Quebrada 852　　　℡ 232550　　$H 👥
  German spoken
- San Francisco 1246
  Budget travelers
- Veronica Wolf de Fritsch, San Juan 431, upstairs　　℡ 2552112　　$H 👥
  German spoken
- Hildegard Niklitschek, San Francisco 1101 entrance to Colón 395
  　　　　　　　　　　　　　　　　　　　　　　℡ 232081　　$H 👥
  German spoken, 25 beds

Private accommodation
Listed by street:
- Cóndor: 1
- Del Salvador: 722
- Imperial: 226, 234
- Klenner, near tennis court: 467, 547, 565
- María Brunn: 427 (near church)
- Mirador: 123
- San José: 544
- Santa Rosa: 328, 734, 735

Accommodation in Puerto Chico

Cabañas
- Colegual, V. Pérez Rosales 01567　ABCDHU　　℡ 232922　　$E for 4
  Tennis court, open December–March
- Los Alerces, V. Pérez Rosales 1281　HU　　℡ 233039　　$D for 6
  Microwave ovens; directly on lake in full view of volcanoes
- Tilos, V. Pérez Rosales corner of Freire　　℡ 233126
- Quitral, Avenida Los Colonos 1138　BP　　℡ 233151　　$G for 4

Motels

★★★ Altué, 2 km south of town, Avenida Vicente Pérez Rosales 01679
　　　　　　　　　　　　　　ABCDHILNPV　℡ 232294　　$G 👥
　Open all year
- Ayentemo, V. Pérez Rosales 0950　ABCDHILV　℡ 232270　　$G 👥
  Open all year

Hospedaje
- Silvia Hott de Ellis, Linch 1107

Accommodation along RN 225 on the lake east of town
This includes all accommodation between Puerto Varas and Ensenada on RN 225 along Lago Llanquihué. Distances are indicated from Puerto Varas, and some accommodation is closer to Ensenada at KM 50.

Cabañas

- ★Río Pescado, KM 26　　　　℡ (65) 337360　　$E for 6
- Bellavista, KM 34　ABCFHLN　℡ CRELL 323　　$E for 6
  Open all year
- Huayún, KM 5
  Reservations in Puerto Varas　　℡ 233139

Accommodation in Puerto Varas — continued

- Lago Sur, KM 23
  Reservations in Puerto Varas: ℂ 233660
- Los Alpes, KM 34   ℂ CRELL 345
- Río Blanco, KM 35   ℂ CRELL321
- Rucamalén, KM 45   ABCHLN   ℂ 338277
- Yesely, KM 44   ℂ CRELL 353

Complejo turístico

★★★ Puerto Pilar, KM 27   ACDEFGHIJKLMNPR$TUVXYZ
                                        ℂ 388292 $D ⚄
    Fax (0653) 7353, golf, boat hire, tennis court, beach frontage, open all year

Hotel on RN 225
- Puerto Edén, KM 6.5   ℂ 36445
  Fax 232352

Hostería on RN 225
- Canta Rana, RN225 KM 43   ℂ CRELL 346

Hospedajes on RN225
- Escala, KM 40   ℂ CRELL 341
- Mirador, KM 35   AHIJ   ℂ CRELL324 $H ⚄
- Los Riscos, KM 21   ℂ CRELL 6482
- Rucapilmay, KM 26   AHJLS   ℂ CRELL 8275 $H ⚄
  German spoken

Motels on RN 225

★★★ Brisas del Lago, KM 42   ABCHLP$U   ℂ 212012 $G ⚄
    $E cabins for 5, boat hire, beach frontage, car hire. Reservations in Puerto Montt: ℂ (65) 336490
- Donde Juanita, RN225 KM 43   AEFGHIJKLNS   ℂ CRELL 314 $F for 6
- Pucar, KM 43   AFGHP$UVZ   ℂ 8278 anexo 315
                                                  $H ⚄

Hostal on RN 225
- Quehui, KM 1   ℂ 233491
  Fax 233444

Accommodation along the Panamericana
- Cabañas Kiltrahué at the turnoff into town   ℂ 233194
  Fax 233294
- Molino Viejo, KM 1003   HLPUV   ℂ 233940

- Del Salvador block 100 near Santa Rosa on Plaza

🛇 Financial

You can exchange money at Turismo Los Lagos, Del Salvador 257, Galería Real ℂ 2019. Open Mon–Fri 0830–1300 and 1500–1800, also open Sunday mornings.

🛇 Services and facilities

Pharmacy
- Farmacia Grob, San Francisco 400

Photographic equipment
- Foto Alvarez, San Francisco 538

🚌 Buses from Puerto Varas

There is no central bus terminal; each company has its own terminal.

Companies
- A48   Buses Lit, Del Salvador 316
- A137 Tas Choapa, San José 341 ℂ 232008
- A153 Buses Tur-Bus Jedimar, Del Salvador 320 ℂ 233000
- A155 Turibus, Del Salvador 316 ℂ 232214
- B11   Bus Norte, San Francisco 447 ℂ 232496
- B32   Buses Bohle, San Bernardo corner Walker Martínez
         Services to Ensenada, Ralún, and Canutillar
- B64   Buses ETC, San Francisco 447 ℂ 232496
- B68   Buses Fresia
- B81   Buses Igi Llaima, Del Salvador near San Juan ℂ 232334
- B179 Buses Varmontt, San Francisco 666 ℂ 232592
- B193 El Rápido Argentino, San Francisco 447 ℂ 232496
- B250 Transbus, San Francisco 790
- B255 Transporte Esmeralda, San José 210 ℂ 232472
         Services to Ensenada, Petrohué, and Ralún
- B260 Buses Cruz del Sur, Del Salvador 237 ℂ 233008
- B271 Viatur

Services

Destination	Fare	Services	Duration	Companies
• Ancud	$4.80			B260
• Castro	$6.50			B260
• Chonchi	$6.50			B260
• Chillán	$13.00	1 service daily		B81
• Concepción	$14.00	3 services daily		B81, B179, B260
• Frutillar	$1.00			B179
• La Unión	$2.80	4 services daily		A153
• Llanquihué	$0.50	6 services daily		B179
• Loncoche		3 services daily		B81
• Los Angeles	$11.00	4 services daily		B81, B260
• Osorno	$2.60	18 services daily		A137, B81, B179
• Puerto Montt	$1.30	50 services daily		A48, B32, B56, B66, B68, B81, B179, B147, B199, B250, B257, B260
• Punta Arenas	$62.00			A155
• Quellón	$9.00			B260
• Rancagua	$17.00	1 service daily		B81
• San Carlos de Bariloche (Argentina)				
	$21.00	Tue, Sun		B11, B193
• San Juan de la Mariquina		3 services daily		B81
• Santiago				
Sleeper	$38.00	1 service daily		B179
Pullman	$19.50	11 services daily	17 hrs	A48, A137, A153, A155, B81, B250, B260, B271
Ejecutivo	$29.50	1 service daily		B11
• Talcahuano	$14.00	2 services daily		B81, B260
• Temuco	$9.00	3 services daily		B179 (Ejecutivo)
	$6.50	16 services daily		A48, B81, B260
• Valdivia	$4.80	10 services daily		A48, A137, A153, B64, B81, B260

Sports supplies
• Fritsch y Cia, San José 308

Supermarket
• Supermercado Viehmeister, San José 460

⊕ Air services
• Linea Areas ASA, Del Salvador block 300 between San Pedro and San Francisco

🚌 Motoring
For gas stations, see city map.

Car rental
• First Rent a Car, Santa Rosa 521 ℂ 233101
• Turismo Llancahué Car Rental, Del Salvador 316 ℂ 232214

🚆 Trains
The railroad station is on Klenner opposite Gran Hotel Puerto Varas. All trains going to and from Santiago stop here. Fares are the same as for Puerto Montt. Refer Trains Puerto Montt.

⚓ Water transport
Tickets and boat hire on Costanera near San José.
• Graytur, San Francisco 447 ℂ 232496. Fishing excursions on the lake

⚽ Sport
• Tennis Club de Puerto Varas, Klenner near train station open daily 0900–1300 and 1500–1900
• Trout fishing in Río Pescado, Río Maullín, La Poza, Lago Llanquihué, Río Blanco, and Río Tepu. Monthly fishing permits cost $1.50 and are available from Información Turística Municipal, Del Salvador 328

📷 Sightseeing
• Mirador, on a little hill west of town, is a ten-minute walk from the town center, passing through Parque Phillipi, composed of a small native forest. From the top there are sweeping views over the lake and the volcanic chain around it. You can see Volcán Osorno in all its majesty, as well as Volcán Calbuco and Volcán Tronador on the Argentine border. There is a small restaurant and Disco Panorama up here. Parque Philippi was named after the German naturalist Bernhard Egon Philippi who organized the large-scale immigration of Germans last century after this part of Chile was opened up by the Chilean Army. A plaque in honor of Philippi stands on top of the hill.

⊕ Excursions
Tour operators
• Andina Del Sud, Del Salvador 243 ℂ 232511. Organizes tours to San Carlos de Bariloche in Argentina via Paso Pérez Rosales and crossing four lakes. Also tours to Isla Grande de Chiloé, Ralún, Peulla, and Puyehué. For trip details see "Excursions" from Puerto Montt on page 725–726.
• Varastur, San Francisco 242 ℂ 232103.
• Buses Bohle, Del Salvador ℂ 232000. Excursions to Lago Todos Los Santos
• Aquamotion Expediciones, Imperial 0699 ℂ 232747. Rafting, canoeing, trekking, adventure tourism; English spoken
• Local tour operators have tours to Ancud, Frutillar, Parque Nacional Puyehué, Peulla, Ralún, Puerto Octay and Puerto Montt. Day tours range from $10.00–$30.00. Lunch $5.00 extra. Tours go every day to a different destination

Excursions
• **Nueva Braunau**: 8 km west of town Ruta U-50. An Austrian settlement with a Museo Alemán (German Museum).
• **Frutillar:** A settlement 24 km north that still reflects its German past. Rather than taking the faster Panamericana, it is a good idea to go via Llanquihué and use the gravel road along the lake where you will get some spectacular views. In summer music festivals are held which attract a large number of visitors. See the entry for Frutillar on page 658.
• **Lago Todos Los Santos**: 66 km east on RN 225. Regular daily buses and tour operators. See the entry for Parque Nacional Vicente Pérez Rosales on page 706.

RÍO BUENO

Population: 13 000
Area code: 064
Distance from Valdivia: 71 km south-east on Ruta T-85, RN 5, and RN 207 (via Paillaco)

R ío Bueno is 5 km east of the Panamericana on the river of the same name. Its Spanish origins date back to the 18th century when the Spanish fort Fuerte de San José de Alcudia was built; the modern town was founded in 1841.

🎊 Festivals

January: Semana Aniversario de Río Bueno, an agricultural show

🏨 Accommodation

See also "Accommodation" in La Unión on page 676.

Hotels
- Plaza (formerly Club Alemán), Comercio 567 ☎ 341321

- Richmond, Comercio 755 upstairs AE-FGHIJLPVX ☎ 341363 $H ⚋⚋

Hospedaje
- Río Bueno, Comercio 471. Budget travelers

Accommodation on the Panamericana
- Hostería Puente Río Bueno APS ☎ 322872 $F ⚋⚋. Organizes fishing trips on Río Bueno, international cuisine, tennis court, *artesanías*

🚌 Buses from Río Bueno

The bus terminal is on Esmeralda block 1400 corner José Prieto, 6 blocks from the town center.

Companies
- A48   Buses Lit, J. Prieto ☎ 391
- A153   Buses Tur-Bus Jedimar, J. Prieto 515 ☎ 767
- B56   Buses del Sur
- B117   Buses Nueva Longitudinal Sur
- B152   Buses Ruta 5
- B171   Buses Transnorte, J. Prieto ☎ 728
- B261   Buses Lago del Sur

Services

Destination	Fare	Services	Duration	Companies
Concepción	$11.00	daily		B64
Lago Ranco	$1.70	2–7 services daily		B152, B171, B261
La Unión	$0.60	15 services daily		Colectivos Río Bueno-La Unión
Los Lagos	$1.70	5 services daily		B82
Osorno	$1.50	21 services daily	1 hr	B56, B64, B81, B152, B171, B261
Paillaco	$1.30	13 services daily	¾ hr	B171
Puerto Montt	$3.20	9 services daily	2 hrs	A48, A153, B64, B82, B252
Puerto Varas	$2.70	5 services daily	1½ hrs	A48, A153
Riñinahué	$2.30	1–3 services daily		B56
Santiago	$18.00	5 services daily		A48, A153, B64, B82, B117
Temuco	$5.00	4 services daily		B64, B82, B115, B257
Valdivia	$1.70	15 services daily		B64, B117, B171, B261
Viña del Mar	$19.50	1 service daily		B64

ⓘ Eating out

- Restaurant España, Comercio 680
- Restaurant Fogón Quimey, at the entrance to town just before the bridge and across the river from the embankment leading to the Spanish fort. Specializes in seafood — you can cast a line from the veranda overlooking the river. Your host is Sr Victor Vera Viveros, an authority on fishing in the area. A lot of fishing tales are told, and fish caught in the Río Bueno hang from the ceiling
- Café Restaurant Sunbory, Esmeralda block 1000 on the plaza
- Café Kavi's, Comercio block 800 near Avenida Balmaceda

ⓘ Post and telegraph

Post office
- Correo and Telex Chile, Comercio block 500 on the Plaza

Telephones
- Centro de Llamados, Comercio 736. Open Sun until 2200

ⓘ Motoring

Gas stations
- COPEC, Comercio corner Bernardo O'Higgins
- Esso, Comercio block 900 corner of B. O'Higgins

ⓘ Sport

Trout fishing in Río Bueno and Lago Ranco.

ⓘ Sightseeing

- Fuerte San José de Alcudia, a Spanish fort up on Pedro de Valdivia, can be visited in summer from 0800 to 2200. It was built in the late 1700s during the governorship of Don Ambrosio O'Higgins, and was restored in 1982. It is in a very commanding position overlooking the Río Bueno, about 100 m straight down to the river near the bridge over the Río Bueno. Only the outer walls and the moat remain of what was once a formidable fortification.

ⓘ Excursions

- The town of **Lago Ranco:** 50 km east on the lake of the same name. Trailblazers may continue to **Riñinahué,** 28 km further east at the eastern end of Lago Ranco. Regular daily buses run to these places. For descriptions of both these towns, see the entry for Lago Ranco on page 669.

SAN JOSÉ DE LA MARIQUINA

Population: 6000
Distance from Valdivia: 42 km south on RN 205

San José de la Mariquina is located on the **Río Cruces** (which becomes **Río Calle Calle**) near the intersection of Panamericana/RN 205 (to Valdivia) and Ruta T-20 (to Mehuín on the coast).

Since the shifting of the bishopric to Villarrica, it has lost some of its importance, but it has retained an air of tranquillity.

The modern town was founded in 1850 by Presidente Manuel Bulnes. The main attraction is the Spanish fort 22 km south, and the nearby beach resort towns of Mehuín and Queule.

Mehuín

A beach resort 27 km west, on the mouth of the Río Lingue, which comes to life only in the summer. Many hotels are closed in the off-season.

⊟ Accommodation

- Casa de Reposo, Avenida Gustav Exos 102 **(** 451214
- Hotel El Nogal **(** 451352

Accommodation in Mehuín

Mehuín is a small seaside resort 23 km west of San José

Hotels
- Mehuín, Carlos Acharan Arce AFGHILPVX
- Playa Mehuín, Carlos Acharan Arce, AEFGHILPV **(** 254

Hosterías
- Millafquén, Balneario Mehuín ABE-FGHIJLNPRVX **(** 279
- Pichicuyin, on Playa Pichicuyin

◬ Camping

There is a camping site in Mehuín 23 km west on the coast
- Camping Mehuín, 120 tent sites, open December–March. Electricity, water, toilets

‼ Eating out

Eating out in Mehuín
- Hostería Millafquén. Seafood

⊟ Buses

Buses Tur-Bus Jedimar, Mariquina 65; Buses Pirehueico, Buses Igi Llaima, Buses J.A.C. and Buses Perla del Sur, run 3 services daily to Puerto Varas, Puerto Montt, and Valdivia; and 2 services daily to Villarrica, Temuco, and Panguipulli.

Buses from Mehuín
Buses Ansmar, Buses Panguisur, and Buses Perla del Sur run 3 services daily to Temuco, Valdivia, and San José de la Mariquina.

⊟ Motoring
- COPEC gas station

◉ Excursions
- Castillo San Luis de Alba: Built by the Spanish in 1647 on the banks of the Río Cruces, some 22 km downstream from San José. This castillo, completed in 1774, was part of a string of 17 forts arround Valdivia to hold corsairs and Mapuches alike at bay. This was the southern end of the Camino de la Colonia between Concepción and Valdivia — the only lifeline between the two cities threatened by the Mapuches from the middle of the 17th century onwards. In 1820 Lord Cochrane took it without much trouble during the War of Independence. It has recently been restored.

VALDIVIA

Area code: 063
Population: 107 000
Altitude: Sea level
Distances
- From Santiago: 840 km south on RN 205 and Panamericana
- From Puerto Montt: 210 km north on RN 205 and Panamericana

Valdivia is an important port and a remarkably clean industrial city that has retained its old-world charm, yet has excellent services and facilities, as well as an intensive network of navigable rivers. It stands at the junction of the **Río Calle Calle** and **Río Cruces** which become the **Río Valdivia** just below the city. It is well endowed with water resources, and it can be described as a town with many parks, ringed by forested hills.

Many rivers entering the city area break up into small navigable rivulets, and in the process form low-lying islands. This maze of waterways is used by sailing boats and river excursion vessels: it is really an aquatic paradise.

The Huilliche tribe settled in this area south of the **Río Toltén**.

The town was founded by Pedro de Valdivia in 1553. The first advance party arrived under Juan Bautista Pastene with two boats in 1544, and a first settlement was made at the mouth of Río Ainilebu (now Río Valdivia). Soon the religious orders of San Francisco and La Merced founded monasteries, and their missionaries became active in trying to convert the Huilliches to Christianity.

Valdivia was destroyed during the great Mapuche uprising on 24 November 1599 by Mapuche Chief Pelantarú. Refounded in 1645, in colonial times it was virtually an isolated outpost of the Spanish empire as the country to the north as far as Concepción was under Mapuche control and thus off-limits to European colonization until 1840. Only a small trail along the coast was permitted by the Mapuche as a lifeline between Valdivia and the main Spanish settlement area north of the Río Bío Bío.

In 1737 Valdivia was destroyed by an earthquake, possibly by the eruption of Volcán Osorno. Manso de Velasco, father of many towns in Chile, came to Valdivia in 1737 to organize the rebuilding.

Until 1820 Valdivia was under the jurisdiction of the Viceroys of Peru. Two towers date from that period; they formed part of the town's fortification — the so-called Torreones built in the 17th century and restored by Ambrosio O'Higgins. They defended the city against pirates and Mapuche attacks, and are a silent witness to a turbulent colonial past.

Fray Camilo Henriquez, the founder of the first newspaper in Chile, was born in Valdivia on 20 July 1769. A house in General Lagos near Yerbas Buenas bears a plaque to this effect.

During the 1880s, German immigration started and virtually turned Valdivia into a city of German-style architecture, which is how it looks today. The layout of the town was influenced by the curves and islands of the river, adding to its attractions. The first German immigrants settled on Isla Teja, which is now linked with the older town by the Pedro de Valdivia bridge, and the German influence is still visible all over town in the style of houses, street names, and cake shops.

Valdivia is surrounded by low forested hills, which form part of the coastal *cordillera*. At the junction of Río Cau Cau, Río Calle Calle, and Río Cruces is Isla Teja. The rivers break through the low coastal *cordillera* here. Valdivia is famous for its picturesque river cruises, passing nature reserves and the old Spanish fortifications on the coast and on islands in the river (Isla Mancera, Niebla, and Corral). Everything is green.

A beautiful avenue runs alongside the river from Puente Valdivia, along Avenida Prat to the bus terminal. Opposite is Isla Teja, home of the University Austral de Chile, an important seat of learning. There are high-class residences along this elegant street.

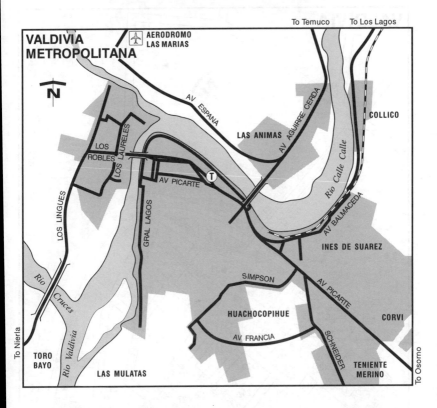

As the city stands on the banks of a large river, it is not surprising to find three major bridges within the city limits: Puente Pedro de Valdivia which links Valdivia with Isla Teja, Puente Calle Calle which is the main exit to the north and the airport, and Puente Cruces over the Río Cruces to Niebla.

Very little remains of the Spanish colonial period in Valdivia itself; most of the Spanish fortifications are on **Isla Mancera**, **Niebla**, and **Corral**, west of town near the mouth of the river.

Building the ring of fortifications and gun emplacements surrounding Valdivia was really a gigantic effort on the part of the Spanish, and is a clear indication of the importance attached to this town in Spanish colonial times. The system of defense was as follows:

- Defense of the entry into the harbor: Fuerte San Carlos, Fuerte Amargos, Fuerte Niebla, gun emplacements at La Aguada del Inglés, Morro Gonzalo, El Molino, El Barro and Chorocamayo.

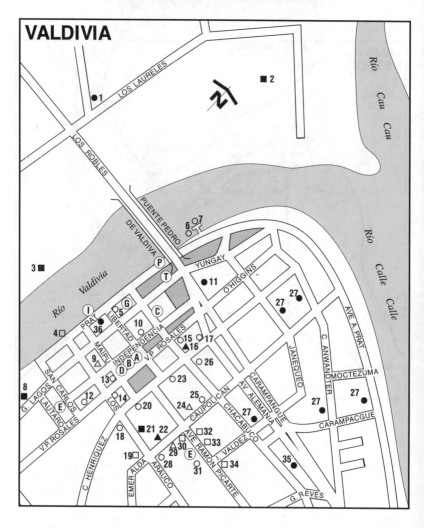

VALDIVIA

- Defense of the port: Gun emplacements at El Bolsón, Chorocamayo Alto, and Fuerte de Corral.
- Defense of the entry to the city: Castillo de Mancera, and gun emplacements at Baides, Santa Rosa, Piojo, and Carboneros.
- To defend against uprisings by the Mapuche Indians upriver the Spanish built fortifications, the most important being Castillo de San Luis de Alba de

Key to map

A	Iglesia	**23**	Centro Español
B	Gobernación Provincial (Government)	**25**	Restaurant La Vie Claire
		26	Chopería München
C	Municipalidad (Town hall)	**28**	Restaurant La Bomba
D	Post office and telex	**31**	Restaurant Prisnat
E	Telephone		
G	Mercado Municipal (Market)	△	**Tour operators car rental**
I	Tourist information	**9**	Turismo Cono Sur
P	Gas stations	**24**	Automóvil Club de Chile
T	Bus terminals	**29**	Turismo Cochrane
●	**Accommodation**	▲	**Airline offices**
1	Hotel Isla Teja	**16**	LAN Chile
11	Hotel Pedro de Valdivia	**22**	LADECO
27	Hostales		
35	Hotel Melillanca	■	**Sights**
36	Hotel Unión	**2**	Universidad Austral
		3	Museo Austral
○	**Eating out**	**8**	Centro Cultural El Austral
5	Restaurant Ríos del Sur	**21**	Iglesia Luterana
6	Restaurant Camino de la Luna		
10	Restaurant La Protectora	□	**Services**
12	Restaurant Paula	**4**	Cruise boats
13	Restaurant Dino's	**7**	Boat hire
14	Café Palace	**19**	Supermercado Valdimarc
15	Café Haussmann	**30**	Foto Nort Sur
17	Restaurant Marie	**32**	Lagos Sport
18	Restaurant El Patio	**33**	CONAF
20	Club de la Unión	**34**	Foto Kika

Cruces, which was completed in 1774. It is 16 km south of San José de la Mariquina.

Only the locations of Batería Morro Gonzalo at Punta del Conde, Batería San Carlos, Batería de Chorocamayo, and Batería Piojo are known, as the rest have been destroyed. Batería Carboneros, which stood at the extreme western tip of Isla del Rey, is now deep under water as it was submerged in the disastrous earthquake and tidal wave of 1960. The best preserved are Castillo San Luis de Alba de Amargos in Corral, Castillo Montfort de Lemus in Niebla, and Castillo San Pedro de Alcantara on Isla Mancera, none of which should be missed.

Lago Riñihué

Lago Riñihué, 97 km east, is a fisherman's paradise. There are regular direct bus services between the village of Riñihué and Los Lagos and Valdivia.

Lanco

With a population of 8000 inhabitants, Lanco is 65 km north-east. It is an important crossroads of the Panamericana with RN 203 which goes to Panguipulli and then across to San Martín de Los Andes in Argentina via Lago Pirehueico. On the Panamericana at the town's entrance is a COPEC Rutacentro, which also serves fine meals.

▣ Accommodation in Valdivia

Note that most of the *hospedajes* are only available to budget travelers during school holidays.

Hotels

★★★★Pedro de Valdivia, Carampangue 190	ADEFGHIJKLMNPRS$TUVXZ		(212931/932	$D	☰
Car rental, fax 219126					
★★ Palace, Chacabuco 308	ADHIJKLP$TUV		(213319/4771	$F	☰
Fax 219133					
★★ Villa Paulina, Yerbas Buenas 389	AEHIJLNPRS		(212455/216372		
				$G	☰
• España, Independencia 628	AHPV		(213478		
• Unión, Avenida Prat 514	AFGHILPX		(213819	$H	☰

Apart hotel

• Di Torlaschi, Yerbas Buenas 283		(224103
Fax 224003		

Hostals

• Buenaventura, Avenida Picarte 1890		(215703/214690		
• Centro Torreón, V.Pérez Rosales 783	APS	(212622	$H	☰
• Chalet Alemán, Avenida Picarte 1134	APS	(218810	$G	☰
• Esmeralda, Esmeralda 651		(215659		
• Hettich, Hettich 325		(214734	$H	☰
• Villa Beaucheff, Beaucheff 844		(216044		

Hospedajes

- Caupolicán 175
- Chacabuco, Chacabuco 489   (213235
  Budget travelers
- I. Valdez 375
- Janequeo 368B

Youth hostel

• Albergue Estudiantil Austral Tur, Las Encinas 220		
	ADFHKMPV	$H ☰

Accommodation in Las Animas

Las Animas is a suburb near Las Marias airport.

★★★★Villa del Río, Avenida España 1025	ABCDEFGHIJKLMNPR$TUVXZ		(216292/3/4	$E ☰
$D cabins for 4, sauna, tennis, overlooking Río Calle Calle, fax 217851				

Accommodation on Isla Teja

Cabañas

• Isla Teja, Los Peluo	DHL	(212115
• Los Pelues, Los Pelues 065	BH	(212985

Hotel

★★ Isla Teja, Las Encinas 220	AEFGHIJKLMPSTUVX	(215014/5015/212050
		$F ☰
96 rooms, fax 214911		

Accommodation in Valdivia — continued

Accommodation near bus terminal

Hotels
- ★★★ Melillanca, Avenida Alemania 675   ADEFGHIJKLM$V   ℂ 212509 $F ♙
  Fax 222740
- Regional, Avenida Picarte 1005   F   ℂ 216027
  Budget travelers

Hostal
- Monserrat, Avenida Picarte 849   AEFGHIJPV   ℂ 215401 $H ♙

Residenciales
- Ain Lebu, Avenida Picarte 881   ℂ 212186 $H ♙
  Budget travelers
- ☞ Germania, Avenida Picarte 873   AEHIJLP$V   ℂ 212405 $H ♙
- ☞ Picarte, Avenida Picarte 953   ℂ 213055
  Budget travelers

Hospedajes
Listed by street:
- Avenida Anwandter: 375, 601, 624, 800, 802, 856, 872
- Avenida Picarte: 865, 1009, 1146
- Pedro de Valdivia: 280

Accommodation along General Lagos

Hotel
- ★★★ Naguilán, General Lagos 1927   ADFGHIJKLMNRPS$V   ℂ 212851/2/3 $E ♙
  Directly on river with own boat ramp, fax 219130

Motel
- ★★★ Raitué, General Lagos 1382   AEFGHIKLPUV   ℂ 212503 $G ♙
- Pumantú, General Lagos 1946
     ABEFHIJNV   ℂ 213036 $E for 6
  Fax 213986

Hostals
- Jardín del Rey, General Lagos 1190
     APS   ℂ 218562 $F ♙
- Kolping, General Lagos 1608   ℂ 212921
  German spoken
- Lo de Carmen, General Lagos 1036
     AFP   ℂ 212016

Accommodation in Corral
Corral is 64 km west of Valdivia, but is only a short ferry trip from the city center.
- Hospedaje Mariel, Tarapacá 36   ℂ 471290 $H ♙

Accommodation on the south side of Lago Riñihué
Lago Riñihué is 97 km east
★★★★ Motel Centro Turístico Huinca Quiñay
   ABCEFGHIJKLP$V $C for 4
Pickup service provided by hotel in Los Lagos. Reservations in Los Lagos: ℂ (63) 311337

Accommodation in Lanco
Lanco is 65 km north east
- Hotel Zumelzu, main street
- Hostería Lanco, opposite main plaza

Accommodation in Valdivia — continued

- Hostería Curitambo, Panamericana 0400
  APS   (411228 $H ⁇
- Hotel Panamericano   (411225 $J ⁇
- Hostería Ocho-Cinco, KM 773   AP $H ⁇

Accommodation in Los Lagos
Los Lagos is 60 km east
- Hotel Roger, Patricio Lynch 25 opposite railroad station
  ABCEFGHIJLPVX   (461261 $I ⁇

Los Lagos

Los Lagos is on the **Río Calle Calle** below the junction with the **Río Quinchilco,** 60 km east of Valdivia. It is an important crossroads on the Panamericana, with side roads going to **Panguipulli** and **Lago Riñihué** on the eastern side and to **Valdivia** on the western side. The train stops here to pick up passengers to Santiago and Puerto Montt. On the Panamericana there is a COPEC gas station.

⚷ Festivals

- February: Semana Valdiviana; the highlight is a regatta on the Río Calle Calle, called the Corso Fluvial, with fireworks

Festivals in Corral
- February: Noche Corraleña — fireworks and decorated and illuminated fishing boats

ⓘ Tourist information

- CONAF, Ismael Valdez 431 (212001. Information about national parks
- Sernatur, Prat 555 (213596

Ⓐ Camping

There is a camping site in Avenida Pedro Aguirre Cerda on the northern approach to Puente Calle Calle.
On the road to **Niebla** 8 km west of town is a deluxe camping site overlooking the Río Valdivia.
On **Lago Riñihué**, 97 km east, there is a camping site on the south side of Lago Riñihué in an excellent position, with

splendid views over the lake and to the volcanoes.

⑪ Eating out

Restaurants
- Andaluz, Carampangue 301 $X. Spanish cuisine
- Argentino El Rancho, Pedro Aguirre Cerda 1313
- Buon Giorno, Avenida Arturo Prat block 400 near Libertad
- Camilo Center — bowling club, Camilo Henriquez 430 in Galería España
- Casa Club Phoenix, Avenida Viel
- Centro Español, Camilo Henriquez 436. International cuisine, seafood
- Chamingo, Chacabuco block 300 near Caupolicán (in the *galería*)
- Club de la Unión, Camilo Henriquez 540
- Dino's, Maipú 191 $Y
- El Conquistador, O'Higgins 481
- El Patio, Arauco 399 $Z
- Flotante Camino de Luna, Avenida Prat next to Puente Pedro de Valdivia $X. International cuisine. Credit cards accepted
- Guata Amarilla, Avenida Pedro Aguirre Cerda 1610
- Il Pizzaron, Chacabuco block 200 near O'Higgins
- Jang Cheng, General Lagos 1118. Chinese cuisine
- La Bomba, Caupolicán 594 $Y
- La Mandragora, Avenida Picarte block 800 near Pedro de Valdivia. Credit cards accepted
- La Protectora Independencia 491
- Las Delicias, Camilo Henriquez 374 $Y. Seafood, good cakes

- La Vie Claire, Caupolicán 435-A. Vegetarian cuisine
- Marie's, Camilo Henriquez 371
- New Orleans, Esmeraldsa 682
- Nuevo Shanghai, Camilo Henriquez corner of Avenida Alemania $Y. Chinese cuisine
- Olympia, Libertad 30 $Z
- ☞ Paula, Pérez Rosales 635 $Y
- ☞ Palace, Pérez Rosales 580 $Y
- Parrillada Roma, Chacabuco 406
- Pizzería La Nonna, Chacabuco 323
- ☞ Prisnat, Avenida Picarte 467
- Pub Gay-Lussac, Chacabuco 455
- ☞ Ríos del Sur, Avenida Prat 476 upstairs. Seafood. Credit cards accepted
- Selecta, Avenida Picarte 1093 $Y. Spanish cuisine
- Turismo, Chacabuco block 400 near Caupolicán $Y
- Volcán, Caupolicán 425. Credit cards accepted

Cafés
- ☞ Supersandwich Al Grano, Arauco corner of Camilo Henriquez
- ☞ Haussmann, O'Higgins 394 $Z

Eating out in Las Animas
Las Animas is a suburb near Las Marias airport.

Restaurants
- ☞ Fogón Palestino, Avenida España 507
- ☞ Villa del Río, Avenida España 1025

Eating out on Isla Teja
- Restaurant La Estancia, Parque Saval

⊤ Entertainment

- Disco Brother's Bar, Caupolicán block 200 near Janequeo
- Disco Cadillac Music Club, Avenida España 603
- Disco Izma 31, Arauco 425
- Disco La Manzana, O'Higgins 467
- Disco Papillon, Caupolicán 289
- Night Club Burbuja, Independencia 471
- Night Club Restaurant Saval, Parque Saval Isla Teja (Fri–Sat)

▦ Post and telegraph

Post office
- Correo, Pérez Rosales near Maipú

Telephone
- ENTEL Chile, V. Pérez Rosales 734. Overseas calls
- Telefónica del Sur, Avenida Ramón Picarte 461 near Ismael Valdez. Open Mon–Sat 0800–2300
- Telefónica del Sur, Avenida Ramón Picarte block 100 near Independencia. Also telex

⑤ Financial

- Fincard, Avenida Picarte 334 ☏ 215293. Cash advances against Mastercard and Visa
- Turismo Cochrane, Arauco 435 ☏ 212213 fax 219118

▤ Services and facilities

Bicycle hire
- Yungay block 100 near Carlos Anwandter

Dry cleaners
- Lavaseco Tip Top, Avenida Picarte 1171

Medical center
- Clínica Alemana, Beaucheff 765 ☏ 213665. German spoken

Photographic supplies
- Nortsur Color Film, Avenida Picarte 417
- Foto Kika, I. Valdez block 400 near Avenida Picarte

Sporting equipment
- Lagosport, Avenida Picarte 412. Tents, fishing gear

Supermarket
- Supermercado Valdimark, Arauco 399

▭ Visas and consulates

- German consulate, Arauco 389, office 23 ☏ 215701
- Italian consulate, Condell 454 ☏ 213552

✈ Air services

Aeropuerto Pichoy is 32 km north of town.

Airlines
- Aero Valdivia, Caupolicán 411, Galería Santiago oficina 16 ☏ 212818. Joy flights
- LAN Chile, C. Henriquez 379 ☏ 213042
- LADECO, Caupolicán 579 ☏ 213392

▣ Buses from Valdivia

The central bus terminal is at Avenida Anfion Muñoz 360. Both long-distance and rural buses depart from here.

Buses to Niebla leave from the corner Yungay and Chacabuco every ½ hour.

Companies
- A48   Buses Lit, office 18 ℂ 212835
- A106 Buses Fénix Pullman Norte, office 2 ℂ 215250
- A137 Buses TAS Choapa, office 5 ℂ 213124
- A153 Buses Tur-Bus Jedimar, office 10 ℂ 212430
- B11   Buses Tal Norte, office 1 ℂ 213541 / 212800
- B29   Buses Barrientos
- B31   Buses Bley
- B40   Buses Chíle Nuevo
- B50   Buses Cordisur Ortiz
- B64   Buses ETC, office 13 ℂ 213232
- B78   Buses Hernández Villegas
- B117 Buses Nueva Longitudinal Sur
- B127 Buses Panguipulli
- B131 Buses Perla del Sur, office 7 ℂ 212617
- B135 Buses Pirehueico, office 9 ℂ 218609
- B146 Buses Riñihué
- B179 Buses Varmontt, office 17 ℂ 212844
- B207 Buses Etta-Bus ℂ 215260
- B250 Buses Transbus, office 14 ℂ 213754
- B256 Buses Bonanza
- B260 Buses Cruz del Sur, office 12 ℂ 213840
- B261 Buses Lagos Del Sur

Services

Destination	Fare	Services	Duration	Companies
• Ancud	$7.00	6 services daily		B41, B260
• Castro	$8.80	7 services daily		A155, B260
• Chillán	$9.20	7 services daily		A48, A137, A153, B81
• Choshuenco	$2.30	1 service daily		B135
• Concepción	$10.00	14 services daily	7 hrs	A48, A153, A155, B81, B179, B207, B260
• Corral	$1.30			B31, B78
• Curiñanco	$1.30			B29
• Freire	$2.50			B64
• Futrono	$1.30	4 services daily		A155, B50, B70
• Lago Pirehueico	$2.50	13 services daily		B117, B135
• Lago Ranco	$1.70			B261
• Lanco	$1.70	18 services daily		B83, B117, B131, B135
• La Unión	$1.70	14 services daily	1 hr	B11, B81
• Llifén	$1.80	2 services daily		B50
• Loncoche	$1.40	4 services daily		B64, B83
• Los Angeles	$7.70	11 services daily	6 hrs	A137, A153, B81, B179, B256
• Los Lagos	$1.20	4 services daily		B40, B127, B135, B146
• Mafil	$1.00	3 services daily		Pullman del Sur, B146
• Mehuín	$1.70	2 services daily		B131
• Neuquén (Argentina)	$33.50	2 services weekly		A155, B83
• Niebla	$1.10	18 services daily	½ hr	B29, B78

Buses from Valdivia — continued

Destination	Fare	Services	Duration	Companies
Osorno	$3.30	26 services daily	1½ hrs	A153, A155, B11, B64, B81, B82, B179, B207, B260
Paillaco	$1.10	6 services daily		A155, B11, B50, B70, B146
Panguipulli	$2.10	13 services daily	2¼ hrs	B49, B117, B131, B135
Pucón	$3.10	2 services daily		B83
Puerto Montt	$5.50	33 services daily	3 hrs	A153, B64, B81, B82, B179, B207, B260, B270
Puerto Varas	$4.80	16 services daily	2½ hrs	B64, B81, B179, B260
Punta Arenas	$62.00	2 services per week		A155, B11
Queule	$1.90	2 services daily		B131
Riñihué	$2.30	2 services daily		B146
Riñinahué	$1.70	4 services daily		B50, Lagos del Sur
Río Bueno	$1.70	16 services daily	1 hr	B64, B117, B261
San Carlos de Bariloche (Argentina)	$24.50	3 services weekly		A155, B11, B260
San Juan de la Mariquina	$1.30	3 services daily		B83, B131
San Martín de Los Andes (Argentina)	$15.40			B83
Santiago	$17.00	20 services daily	14 hrs	A48, A106, A137, A153, B81, B82, B83, B117, B179, B207, B260, B270
Talca	$15.00	4 services daily		A137, B82
Talcahuano	$10.00	4 services daily		A48, A153, A155
Temuco	$4.00	32 services daily	3 hrs	A48, A137, A153, B64, B81, B83, B117, B179, B207, B257, B260
Toltén	$1.90	1 service daily		B131
Valparaíso	$17.50	5 services daily		A48, A106
Villarrica	$2.50	3 services daily		B83
Viña del Mar	$17.50	5 services daily		A48, A106, A153

Buses from Lago Riñihué
Buses Riñihué run 2 services daily from Valdivia and Los Lagos to the southern part of the lake.

Buses from Lanco
All buses depart from the main plaza; buses to Panguipulli (Buses Pirehueico) and buses to Temuco (Buses JAC) are next to each other.

Other buses calling on Lanco are: Igi Llaima, Buses Chile Nuevo, Regional Sur, Tur-Bus Jedimar, Buses Power, Pangui Sur, Buses Pirehueico, Buses Nueva Longitudinal Sur, Buses Chile Nuevo, Buses Perla del Sur, Buses JAC. There are 13 services daily to Valdivia, 3 services daily to Villarrica, 5 services daily to Panguipulli, 5 services daily to Temuco, and 5 services daily to Puerto Montt.

Buses from Los Lagos
Buses Panguisur, Buses Inter Sur, Buses Riñihué, Buses HM, Buses Pirehueico; Buses Tur-Bus Jedimar, Matta 148 ℓ 461259. To Panguipulli 2 services daily; Puerto Montt 6 services daily; Río Bueno 2 services daily; Temuco 3 services daily; Valdivia 3 services daily.

Services
- Concepción: Fare $80.00; 1–2 services Mon–Fri; duration 2 hrs; LAN Chile
- Osorno: 1–2 services daily; duration ½ hr
- Santiago: Fare $102.00; 1–2 services daily; duration 2½ hrs; LAN Chile, LADECO

🚗 Motoring

Car rental
- Automóvil Club de Chile, Caupolicán 475 ☎ 212376, car rental
- First Rent a Car, Pérez Rosales 674 ☎ 215973
- Hertz Rent a Car, Pedro Aguirre Cerda 1154 ☎ 218316/218317
- Turismo Assef y Méndez Rent a Car, General Lagos 1249 ☎ 213205, fax 215966.

Gas stations
For gas stations, see city map.

⚓ Water transport

Muelle Schuster is the departure point for tour boats on the river and to Niebla, Corral, and Isla Mancera.
Cruise boats leave from Avenida A. Prat near San Carlos.

Vessels
Scenic cruises to Niebla, Corral and the rivers around Valdivia are spectacular.
- M/N *Río Calle Calle*, M/N *Empreturic*: Avenida Prat ☎ 212464 fax 212464. River and harbor cruises; evening cruises with dinner on Río Calle Calle 2100–2245. Fare $20.00
- M/N *Neptuno* (capacity 250): Avenida Prat ☎ 215889, fax 215580. Daily river cruises, departing from Ruta de Los Galeones, to Niebla, Corral, and Isla Mancera and visiting the fortifications. Fare $22.50, including lunch or dinner
- M/N *Valdivia Express*: H.E. Tours ☎ 210533, fax 210522

Boat hire
- Centro Náutico Lincoyán, Avenida Prat, next to Restaurant Camino de Luna

Cruise trips
- Niebla and back: $15.00 half day

- Niebla, Isla Mancera, and Corral: This is an outstanding trip from both scenic and historical viewpoints. Do not miss it! It shows the extent and might of the Spanish empire in Chile, as well as the beauty of the forested hills, extensive bird life around the riverbanks and picturesque little fishing villages
- Río Futa: Río Futa is a tributary of Río Valdivia which together with Río Tornagaleones form a low-lying island, Isla del Rey. The boat starts from a small landing pier 500 m past Puente Cruces on the road to Niebla near El Bayo. The cruise takes about two hours to reach the camping area at Puente Futa, where there is a stop of 45 minutes before returning to Valdivia. Fare $25.00

🛍 Shopping
Valdivia is known for exquisite marzipan and liqueurs.
- Chocolatería Colonos, Pérez Rosales 601. Good chocolates and sweets
- Casa Henzi, Maipú 271. Jewelry
- Casa Araucana, Avenida Picarte 841. Local handicrafts
- CEMA Chile, Chacabuco corner O'Higgins. Local handicrafts
- Licores Fehrenberg, Pedro Aguirre Cerda 970. Fancy liqueurs
- Pellejos, Caupolicán 411, Galería Santiago. Leatherware

⚽ Sport
- **Club de Golf Santa Elvira**, Vista Alegre, suburb of Santa Elvira

📷 Sightseeing
- Museo Histórico y Arqueológico Mauricio van de Maele (incorporating Museo Austral), Los Laureles. Exhibition center. Open Tues–Sun 1000–1300 and 1600–1830. The exhibition includes objects and documents relating to the German settlement and the Mapuche culture. Admission: $1.50.
- Museo Cultural, General Lagos.
- Torreón del Barro, on General Lagos overlooking the Río Valdivia, and Torreón Los Canelos, on Avenida Ramón Picarte. These towers are all that remains of the former Spanish fortifications which actually surrounded Valdivia, built in 1774. The fortifica-

tions had the dual purpose of deterring attacks from raiders or pirates from the sea and defending against attacks by Mapuche from the hinterland.

- Parque Saval, on Isla Teja, in Calle Los Lingues and bordering on Río Cau Cau, is an area left in its natural state. Inside the park is Laguna de Los Lotos and a restaurant/night club.

⊙ Excursions

Tour operators
- Turismo Cochrane, Arauco 435 (212213, fax 219118. Excursions, rafting, car rental
- Turismo Paraty, Independencia 640 (215585
- Turismo 2000, Arauco 175 (212233. Tours, car rental
- Turismo Cono Sur, Maipú 129 (212757, fax 215232

Excursions
Tour operators organize a city tour, day excursions to the Spanish fortifications at Niebla, Isla Mancera and Corral by bus and ferry, and a day excursion to **San José de la Mariquina**, including Castillo San Luis de Alba and Queule, a small seaside resort north of Valdivia. They also organize longer tours to Villarrica, Panguipulli, and the lake area to the east in general. These are all three-star excursions and are reasonably priced. However, the "self-propelled" budget traveler can make all these trips by public transport — see "Buses" above.

- **Corral:** At the south side of the Bahía de Corral, only short boat ride down river from Valdivia or by ferry from Niebla. It can also be reached by road, 64 km mostly through forests. Corral is nowadays a small fishing village of 3000 inhabitants. Originally, it was part of a major defense system built by the Spaniards to protect Valdivia from buccaneers, and has the remains of Spanish fortifications and a fishermen's wharf. Castillo San Sebastián, completed in 1678 with 20 gun emplacements, is the most interesting remaining fort from this period. The smaller Castillo de San Luis de **Amargos**, to the west, was constructed at the same time. In 1760, the fortifications

were enlarged and partially rebuilt. The forts of Corral and Mancera were taken by Lord Cochrane and his men in 1820. Amargos is now a small fishing village. In 1851, the first German immigrants landed in Corral. Late in the 19th century, industrialization, particularly the blast furnaces, destroyed most of the surrounding forested areas. Corral was badly damaged during the disastrous 1960 earthquake, but still serves as Valdivia's major port, and cargo launches travel busily between Valdivia and Corral. You can return by boat to **Niebla** and visit **Isla Mancera** with its fortifications on the way. Check when the last ferry is going, otherwise you may be stranded on the island. The boats will not wait for embarking tourists — you must be ready at the quay. Buses Valdivia, Buses Hernandez Víllegas, Buses Bley run services to Corral; fares $1.40.

- **Niebla:** 17 km west, on the north side of Bahía Corral. It is a seaside resort with small beaches, a fishermen's wharf, and of course the impressive remains of the Spanish fort Castillo Montfort de Lemus at the entrance to the port of Valdivia. This mighty fort was virtually carved into the rock and includes a gunpowder store which is accessible by a tunnel also carved out of the rock. The Castillo is a 15-minute walk uphill from the ferry and fishing harbor. This is an astonishing piece of work by the Spaniards, and an outstanding tourist attraction. At the entrance to the Castillo is a tourist information kiosk-cum-post office open all year round. **Curiñanco**, 22 km north of Niebla, with good beaches and campsites all along the beach, can be reached by frequent buses from Valdivia or Niebla. The best camping spot is Playa La Cascada, 13 km north of Niebla. The local bus from Puente Valdivia in Valdivia to Niebla leaves every 15 minutes, taking only about 45 minutes; I suggest you go one way as a river cruise and the other by road. See also the entry for Niebla on page 681.
- **Isla Mancera** in the **Bahía de Corral** between Niebla and Corral at the

mouth of the Río Valdivia. During the colonial era it was a heavily fortified island. The remains of the Castillo San Pedro de Alcantara are a major tourist attraction. A tidal wave destroyed many parts of the fort. You can get there by ferry from Valdivia and also by ferry leaving Niebla every half hour from December to the end of February.

- **Mehuín**: A seaside resort 74 km north. Take RN 205 which is sealed as far as San José de la Mariquina and turn west into Ruta T-120 which is a gravel road. You can buy locally made wickerwork. Mehuín has bus services and accommodation. For a description of Mehuín, See the entry for San José de la Mariquina on page 738.

- The lake region — **Lago Panguipulli**, **Lago Calafquén**, **Lago Riñihué**, and **Lago Pirehueico**: 120 km north-east. Take Ruta T-35 which follows the Río Calle Calle until Los Lagos on the Panamericana. From here, Ruta T-39 is sealed as far as Panguipulli. There is fabulous scenery over the crystal clear lake, with views of Volcán Choshuenco and Villarrica. Sailing, fishing, and good hiking area. There are skiing areas on **Volcán Choshuenco**, reached from village of Choshuenco. From **Panguipulli** you can also get to the **Termas de Liquiñe**, 58 km north-east either via Coñaripe (RN 203 and RN 201) or via Choshuenco (RN 203, T-29, and RN 201). These are scenic trips, but Ruta T-29 is a dirt road between Neltume and Carriringue. Also visit nearby lakes Calafquén, Pirihueico, and Riñihué. There are good facilities around these lakes with good beaches, restaurants, and hotels, and also bus services. For descriptions of these towns, see the entry for Panguipulli on page 695.

- **Lago Ranco**, both a town and a lake: 128 km south-east in the *pre-Cordillera*. Take RN 7 to **Paillaco** and follow the Panamericana until you reach **Río Bueno**. Here turn east on Ruta T-85 which is sealed as far as **Cayurruca**. The remaining 25 km are not so good — it is a dirt road, but is even worse beyond Los Lagos. This is a beautiful area with many lakes and rivers where you can go boating, sailing, and fishing. It is also still relatively free from tourists, so is ideal for people who enjoy a quiet corner of the lake district with reasonable tourist facilities and lots of hiking and waterfalls such as Salto de Nilahué. There are many hotels on nice beaches around the lake, such as near **Futrono** on the northern end, Lago Ranco on the southern side and Puerto Nuevo where the Río Bueno emerges from the lake. There is also a nice hotel at **Riñinahué** with excursions to **Salto del Nilahué.** A very scenic area, especially around Riñinahué; the hinterland has still many Mapuche *reducciones* or Indian reservations. See also the entry for Lago Ranco on page 669.

- **Futrono** on Lago Ranco: 102 km east. See the entry for Lago Ranco on page 669. A scenic area, especially around Riñinahué; the hinterland is still inhabited by Mapuche Indians. The scenery is fantastic, with views of Volcán Puyehué and Choshuenco from Futrono, and there is excellent fishing. There are many waterfalls there, the best known being Salto del Nilahué between Futrono and Riñinahué. Regular buses run from Valdivia to Futrono, Lago Ranco, and Riñinahué — you may have to change in Paillaco and / or Río Bueno to get to Riñinahué, but it is worth the effort.

CHILOÉ ARCHIPELAGO

South of Puerto Montt, the continent breaks up into an archipelago of islands, leaving only a narrow strip of land, rising sharply to over 2000 m and dotted with volcanoes. **Isla Grande de Chiloé** is the largest island in the Chiloé Archipelago.

Chiloé province consists of about a hundred islands besides Isla Grande de Chiloé. The island farmers and fishermen live in traditional and picturesque villages. Each family has its own fishing boat and farming plot, harvesting potatoes, cabbages, and cereals: because part of their livelihood comes from the sea, the interior of Isla Grande de Chiloe was never colonized until quite recently.

Chiloé's high year-round rainfall ensures an evergreen environment. Although wet, there is very little snow because the climate is tempered by the Pacific Ocean and there are no high mountains. The best time to visit Isla Grande de Chiloé is from the end of November to the end of March, when the rains brought by the north winds are not quite so heavy.

Chiloé is connected to the mainland by a 30-minute ferry trip from Pargua to Chacao. Ferries also link Quellón with Chaitén and Puerto Chacabuco. Services are much reduced in the off season.

Chiloé is rich in bird life and marine animals. The *monito del monte* and *comadrejita trompuda*, two very rare marsupials, live on Isla Grande de Chiloé. The shy dwarf deer (*pudú*) is a native of the forest.

Isla Grande de Chiloé was once densely forested, particularly on the west coast. Settlers gradually burned the trees to make room for crops. The

Parque Nacional Chiloé now protects a large area of almost impenetrable rainforest and contains the **Cordillera de Piuche** (777 m). The park is accessible from Chepu in the north, and from Cucao in the south. There is also now a trail starting north of Castro which reaches the central part of the national park. Ancud, with its relics of the Spanish colonial past, and the capital Castro, partly built on stilts, are both interesting places. For an idea of island life, visit **Isla Quinchao** and **Achao** with its old church. **Volcán Michinmávida** can be seen from the higher parts of the island.

European history

The provincial capital, Castro, was an early Spanish settlement. The island was periodically occupied by Dutch corsairs in the early 17th century, and when Castro was burned down in 1643, the area became neglected and impoverished. The annual arrival of a ship from Lima, berthing in what is now Chacao, attracted islanders from far away. From 1767 until independence, Chiloé was a direct dependency of the vice-royalty in Lima. When Ancud was fortified, most of the population of Chacao took up residence in the new township. Further north, the mainland was held by the Mapuche for 300 years, but Chiloé province was firmly Spanish.

The Jesuits had a particularly strong and beneficial influence on Chiloé from the time of their arrival in 1608 until their expulsion in 1767. During their occupation, they converted the local population to Christianity, founded 79 parishes, and extended their mission work into the Argentine *pampas*. Franciscan friars, who were dependent on the Franciscan monastery Santa Rosa de Ocopa near Huancayo in central Peru, took over the missionary work in 1771.

During the War of Independence, the *Chilotans* for some reason were strong supporters of the royalist cause and supplied many soldiers to the royalist armies. In 1826, the South Americans fought major battles with the Spanish near **Pudeto** and **Bellavista**. The last royalist defender of Chiloé was Don Antonio de Quintanella y Santiago, who was defeated by Don Ramón Freire Serrano on January 14, 1826. The *Tratato de Tantauco* was signed on January 22, 1826 and secured Chile's freedom and independence from Spain. It marked the end of Spanish domination in South America and permitted the annexation of Chiloé into Chilean territory.

Fishing

- Ancud: Río Chepu, Río Puntra, Río Pudeto, Río San Antonio
- Chonchi: Lago Tarahuin, Lago Cucao, Lago Tepuhueico, Lago Natri, Lago Huillinco

National parks and reserves

- **Parque Nacional Chiloé**, 43 057 ha (106 350 acres): The southern section is 37 km west of Chonchi on Ruta W-80 near Cucao. Walking paths, information center, picnic area, camping area, eating place and shop nearby, lookout, mountain hut. The northern section is 27 km south of Ancud. See the entry for the park on page 772.

Boat trips

See "Boat trips" on pages 649–651.

Tourist destinations

Worth a detour

☞ Ancud
☞ Castro

Of interest

☞ Parque Nacional Chiloé

ACHAO

Area code: 06556
Altitude: Sea level
Distances from Castro: 45 km east

Achao, on the **Isla Quinchao**, grew from a Jesuit mission that served the islands. The missionaries were well received by the native population and taught them many trades, such as the skills of carpenters and shipwrights.

This pretty town with its stylish old wooden houses and a few hotels can be reached by bus and ferry from Dalcahué. Near the fishermen's wharf, a very good seafood restaurant overlooks a little bay.

🛌 Accommodation in Achao

Hotels
- Plaza, Amunátegui   ☎ 661283

Hostería
- La Nave, A. Prat, corner of Sargento Aldea
                                  AFGILUV   ☎ 661219 $I 👥
  Boat hire, beach frontage

Residenciales
- Las Delicias, Serrano 018   A $J 👥

Hospedaje
- Achao, Serrano 020   ☎ 661283
- Sao Paolo, Serrano 052   AFGHILUV   ☎ 661245 $I 👥
  Beach frontage
- Sol y Lluvia, Ricardo Jara 09   ACHPS   ☎ 661383
- Restaurant La Madre
  4 beds

Follow the road east uphill for half an hour for splendid views over the town and the bay, and across the channel to the distant *cordillera* on the mainland. From here, you can also see **Volcán Michinmávida**.

🎭 Festivals

- Encuentro Folklórico de las Islas del Archipielago: January. Musical gathering and folksinging

🍴 Eating out

- Restaurant La Nave, Arturo Prat
- Restaurant Mar y Vela. Built on stilts in the fishing harbor, upstairs views over the bay, good seafood

Eating out in Curaco de Velez
- La Casona, Errázuriz 5 $Z
- Pension/Restaurant Central $Z
- Restaurant Miramar $Z

🚌 Buses

Buses Arriagada run 5 services daily to Dalcahué and Castro.

📷 Sightseeing

- Iglesia Santa María de Achao, a *monumento nacional,* is the town's main attraction. This wooden structure with its baroque interior was started by the Jesuits in 1735 and completed after their expulsion in 1763. It was built without nails, and has been restored since the 1960 earthquake.
- Museo de Arte Moderno (Modern Art Museum): Just outside town.

🔶 Excursions

- **Curaco de Velez**: A small village of 300 13 km west of Achao. It was founded as a Jesuit mission. The Jesuits held their last service here on December 9, 1767, before their expulsion by royal decree of Charles III from all Spanish and Portuguese colonies. The whole village has been declared a *monumento nacional* to preserve the distinctive houses with their *alerce* shingle roofs. The small Museo Histórico is worth visiting. There are more than 20 water-driven mills from Spanish colonial times in the neighborhood. The road to **Achao** passes isolated homesteads with signs on their mail boxes advertising homemade woolen garments for sale. Buses Arriagada run 5 services daily to Dalcahué, Castro, and Achao.
- **Quinchao**: 9 km west. The largest colonial church in the archipelago was built in the 17th century and remodeled two centuries later in neo-classical style. December 8, the day of the *Virgen de la Gracia,* still attracts many pilgrims.

- **Chequián**: At the extreme south-eastern point of the island, also a Jesuit foundation. It is fronted by a pleasant stretch of beach and views of the islands.

ANCUD

Area code: 065
Population: 24 000
Altitude: Sea level
Distance from Puerto Montt: 90 km south east on Panamericana

Ancud lies on the extreme north-western tip of **Isla Grande de Chiloé**. The town was gazetted on August 20, 1768. Fuerte San Antonio and Fuerte Ahui, relics of the Spanish past, are two of the main tourist attractions. Most of the houses in Ancud are made of wood with shingle roofs. Some walls are also covered with shingles.

German immigration to Isla Grande de Chiloé came in two waves. The largest, in 1895, consisted mostly of people from Berlin and Stuttgart. Descendants of the Orloff family still live in Ancud.

Ancud has good tourist facilities, and daily buses run frequently to the mainland and to other parts of the island. TransMarchilay Ltda, which is in charge of all the ferry services to and from Isla Grande de

Key to map

A	Catedral
C	Municipalidad (Town hall)
D	Post office and telex
E	Telephone
G	Mercado Municipal (Market)
H	Hospital
I	Tourist information
P	Gas stations
T	Bus terminals

● **Accommodation**

2	Cabañas Las Golondrinas
4	Hostería Ancud
6	Hostal Monserrat
7	Hospedaje Santander
8	Hostal Wechsler
15	Hospedaje
18	Hotel Polo Sur
21	Hotel Galeón Azul
24	Hotel Lydia
29	Hostal Ahui II

○ **Eating out**

9	Restaurant Tirol
10	Restaurant Villa Club
11	Restaurant La Pincoya
12	Restaurant Sacho
13	Restaurant El Trauco
14	Restaurant El Cangrejo
16	Café Restaurant Balay
23	Restaurant El Jardín
25	Café Amadeus
26	Café Central
27	Restaurant Coral
28	Restaurant Capri

⊙ **Entertainment**

19	Disco Club 26

△ **Tour operators and car rental**

22	Turismo Ancud

■ **Sights**

1	Polvorín
3	Fuerte San Antonio
5	Iglesia
20	Museo Regional A. Borques Canobra
30	Iglesia San Francisco

□ **Services**

17	TransMarchilay

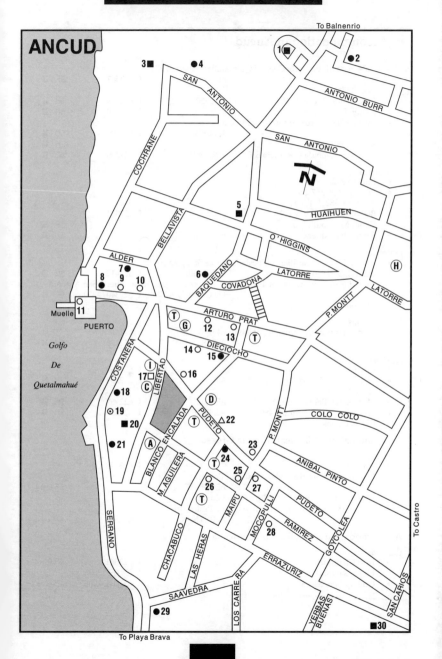

ANCUD

To Balnenrio

To Castro

To Playa Brava

Golfo
De
Quetalmahué

Muelle

PUERTO

SAN ANTONIO

SAN ANTONIO

ANTONIO BURR

HUAIHUEN

O'HIGGINS

LATORRE

LATORRE

P. MONTT

COCHRANE

BELLAVISTA

ALDER

BAQUEDANO

COVADONA

ARTURO PRAT

DIECIOCHO

LIBERTAD

COSTANERA

BLANCO ENCALADA

PUDETO

COLO COLO

P. MONTT

ANIBAL PINTO

PUDETO

GOYCOLEA

M. AGUILERA

SERRANO

CHACABUCO

LAS HERAS

MAIPU

MOCOPULLI

RAMIREZ

SAAVEDRA

LOS CARRERA

ERRAZURIZ

YERBAS BUENAS

SAN CARLOS

✉ Accommodation in Ancud

Hotels
★★★Galeón Azul (formerly General Quintanilla), Libertad 751

	AEFGHIJLPV	(622567	$F	♔
Fax 622543				
• Isla Grande (formerly Polo Sur), A. Pinto 1350		(622608	$H	♔
• Lacuy, Pudeto 219	P	(623019	$H	♔
• Lydia, Chacabuco 630 corner of Pudeto				
	AEFGHIKLPV	(622990	$G	♔
Shared bathroom			$H	♔
• Polo Sur, Avenida Costanera 630	ADEFGHIJ	(622200	$G	♔

Hospedajes
• Pudeto 272				
• Pudeto :329, 357, 361				
• A. Pinto: 382, 578, 604				
• Bellavista, Bellavista 449	EHIJ	(622384		
• Capri, Mocopulli 710			$F	♔
☞ • Santander, Alder 69	P		$I	♔

Hosterías
• Ahui I, Pudeto near Blanco Encalada in *galería*, upstairs				
• Ahui II, Serrano 415	AEFGHIJKL	(622415	$G	♔
• Ancud (formerly Alonso de Ercilla), San Antonio 30, just before Fuerte San Antonio				
	AEFGHIJKLP$UVXZ	(622340/2350	$F	♔
24 rooms				

Residenciales
• Madryn (formerly Turismo), Bellavista 491				
	AFGLP	(622128	$H	♔

Hostales
• Chiloé, O'Higgins 274		(622869		
☞ • Montenegro, Blanco Encalada 541	AEI	(622239	$I	♔
Shared bathroom				
• Montserrat, Baquedano 417	AEHIJKL	(622957	$G	♔
• Wechsler, Lord Cochrane 480	AEFHIJLPV	(622318	$H	♔
German spoken				

Accommodation at Balneario Arena Gruesa

Cabañas
• Arena Gruesa		(623428	
• Las Golondrinas, Baquedano just past Polvorín			
	ABCHIKLPZ		$F for 4
Splendid views over the Golfo de Quetalmué			
• Llauquen (formerly Huaihuen), Avenida Pinto 1070			
	AEGHILNPV	(622554	$F for 3

Accommodation along the Panamericana

Cabañas
• Islas Chauques	PS	(623361	$E for 4
• Playa Gaviotas, KM 6		((09) 6538096	
• Quempillén, KM 8	F	((09) 6437906	

Accommodation in Ancud — continued

Accommodation in Caulín
Caulín, 24 km north east of Ancud, is a small fishing village on the north cost of Isla Grande de Chiloé, famous for its oysters. It is off the Panamericana and can be reached by rural buses from Ancud.
- Hotel Caulín, open all year
- Hotel Lyon II, open in tourist season only

Chiloé and the archipelago, also has its headquarters in the town.

⊠ Festivals
- January: Semana Ancuditana

ⓘ Tourist information
- Sernatur, Edificio TransMarchilay, Libertad 655, Oficina 3, on plaza ☎ 656/142

Ⓐ Camping
Camping Huichais is 9 km east of Ancud. The turnoff to Camping Playa Largo is 6 km before Ancud, and well sign-posted.

⍫ Eating out

Restaurants
- El Cangrejo, Dieciocho 155 upstairs. Seafood
- El Crucero de Amor, Errázuriz 301
- El Sacho, A. Prat block 168 near Baquedano, inside the market. Seafood
- El Tirol, Maipú 746. Seafood and steaks
- El Trauco, A. Prat block 168 just before crossing Blanco Encalada 515. Chilean cuisine
- Hotel Lydia, Pudeto 254. International cuisine
- Hotel Polo Sur, Costanera 630. Seafood and steaks. Also serves *centollas*, a highly prized crustacean
- La Pincoya, Prat 61, at the wharf. Seafood
- Mar Brava, Dieciocho block 198 near Blanco Encalada at the market
- Mi Casa, Dieciocho block 198 near Blanco Encalada, inside the market. Seafood
- Tirol, A. Prat 120
- Villa Club, A.Prat block 100 near wharf. Pizzas

- Salón de Té Floridal, Ramírez 352. Pizzas

Cafés
- Amadeus, Ramírez 294 corner of Maipú, downstairs. Good coffee and cakes
- Bravo's, Pudeto 231
- Orloff, Pudeto 223

Café restaurants
- Balay, Pudeto 187. Chilean cuisine
- Caprí, Mocopulli 710. Chilean cuisine

- Carmen, Pudeto 145 $Y. Chilean cuisine
- Central, Chacabuco Galería Gainagra
- Chamuco's, Pudeto 153-A, upstairs. International cuisine, seafood
- Corral, Pudeto 346. International cuisine
- Jardín, Pudeto 263 upstairs. Seafood and steaks

Eating out in Chacao
Chacao is 27 km east of Ancud
- Restaurant al Paso, on Panamericana (RN 5)

ⓨ Entertainment
- Disco Club 26, Avenida Costanera near Pudeto
- Disco Saurio Malon de Los 60, Prat 260
- Disco Sorbos, Bellavista, A. Prat, next to Residencial Turismo
- Restaurant Quincho de Bellavista, Predio Bellavista. Views over the bay. Seafood, international cuisine; *peña* evenings with folksongs

⊞ Post and telegraph

Post office
- Correo and Telex Chile Pudeto 669 corner of Blanco Encalada

🚌 Buses from Ancud

The rural bus terminal is on A. Prat, between Bellavista and Baquedano. There is no central interstate bus terminal.

Companies
- A155 Turibus, Dieciocho corner of Libertad ☎ 622289
- B11   Bus Norte, Pudeto 219, Galería Yurie
- B41   Buses Chiloé
- B55   Buses Del Río
- B56   Buses Del Sur
- B74   Buses Ghisoni
- B106 Buses Mar Brava, Pudeto 365 ☎ 622312
- B179 Varmontt
- B252 TransChiloé, Chacabuco 750
- B260 Transportes Cruz del Sur, Chacabuco 650 ☎ 622265

Services
Buses for destinations marked [R] leave from the rural bus terminal.

Destination	Fare	Services	Duration	Companies
Castro	$1.70	19 services daily		A155, B11, B55, B179, B252, B260
Chepu[R]	$1.50	2 services daily		B106
Chonchi	$3.00	4 services daily		B260
Faro Corona[R]	$1.30	2 services daily		B106
Gualbún[R]	$1.30	2 services daily		B106
Los Angeles	$11.50	2 services daily		A153, B260
Manao[R]	$1.30	2 services daily		B55
Osorno	$5.30	6 services daily		B252, B260
Pargua	$1.70	21 services daily	1 hour	B260
Puerto Montt	$4.40	21 services daily		B11, B41, B56, B179, B252, B260
Puerto Varas	$4.80	5 services daily		B260
Pumillahué[R]	$1.30			B106
Punta Arenas	$62.00	Sun, Wed, Fri,		A155, B74
Quellón	$4.60	4 services daily		B260
Quemchi[R]	$1.50	2 services daily		B55
Quicavi[R]	$1.70	2 services daily		B55
Santiago				
Pullman	$19.50	3 services daily		A155, B11, B260
Ejecutivo	$26.20	3 services per week		A155
Sleeper	$33.50	1 service per week		B260
Temuco	$9.40	5 services daily		B260
Valdivia	$7.00	7 services daily		B41, B260

Telephone
- ENTEL Chile, Caracoles Alto, overseas calls
- CNT Teléfonos del Sur, Chacabuco 745

🛗 Services and facilities

Dry cleaner
- Lavaseco Andrea, Blanco Encalada 583

Pharmacy
- Farmacia Buseyne, Libertad between Dieciocho and Pudeto

Photographic supplies
- Blanco Encalada 561. Agfa film

Supermarket
- Supermercado Bellavista, Corner Prat with Bellavista

✈ Air services
- Ladeco, Prat 140 ☎ 622303

Motoring

For gas stations, see city map.

Water transport

- TransMarchilay Ltda, Libertad 669, Plaza de Armas (2317/2279. Has information on all ferry services on *Carretera Austral* and between Isla Grande de Chiloé and the mainland

Shopping

- CEMA Chile, Errázuriz 365. *Artesanías* and gem stones

Sport

There is trout and salmon fishing in the estuaries and rivers. See page 754.

Sightseeing

- Centro Turismo Cultural y de Artesania Ancud, Libertad 370 between Ramírez and Errázuriz, next to the TransMarchilay building. This building in the form of a Spanish fortress with a replica of a sailing ship inside, commands sweeping views of the harbor and the **Bahía de Quetalmahué**. Stairs in the tower lead to a platform with views over the town and the Bahía de Quetalmahué The ground floor houses a semi-precious stone market, a handicraft market. The center incorporates **Museo Regional Audelio Bórquez Canobra**. Exhibits cover mythology and the pre-Hispanic past, the discovery of the archipelago and Spanish settlement, and customs and traditions of the present inhabitants. Open daily 0900–1900.
- El Polvorín ("Gunpowder Magazine"). This tower is part of the old Spanish Fort, San Antonio, with separate access via Bellavista.
- Fuerte San Antonio, Calle San Antonio near Cochrane. The fortress, built into the rock, overlooks the bay of Ancud. Its seven gun emplacements were a formidable bastion of the Spanish in the Americas. The Spanish dug a tunnel into the hill towards what is now the Hostería Ancud, but the entrance is now barred by a grille. A memorial on the site honors the two opposing generals who fought each other at the end of the wars of independence. Sou-

venirs are sold from a small tower at the fort's entrance.
- Playa Gruesa. A track at the northern end of Ancud leads down from Baquedano to a sheltered beach. There are splendid views over the narrows and the beach from a kiosk and *cafetería* in the park, near where the path begins.

Excursions

Tour operators
Turismo Ancud, Pudeto 219, Galería Yurie (623019 offers day trips to the Parque Nacional Chiloé both to the northern access at Chepu and the southern access at Cucao. The fares are based on four passengers. The so-called tour del Invunche goes to Quemchi 68 km south east of Ancud: Ivunche is a mythical being which is believed to have its home in a cave here. Also city tour and tours to Castro.

Excursions
- **Fuerte Ahui** on **Península Lacuy**, on the opposite side of the bay, was once heavily fortified. The cannon are still in place. Organized excursions to the fort by tourist launches have been suspended. However, the site can be reached by rural buses — be prepared to walk the last bit.
- **Chacao**: 27 km east. Chacao is the northernmost town on Isla Grande de Chiloé, and its main port of entry. In times gone by, the military governor lived here until the foundation of Ancud. Once a year, ships from Lima brought goods to barter with the locals. Its importance derives from the ferry services to the mainland which cross the straits to Pargua every half-hour. The Panamericana Sur continues from Pargua right through to Quellón. There are 23 services daily to Puerto Montt, Ancud, and Castro; and 10 services daily to Quellón at the southern end of Isla Grande de Chiloé.
- **Guabún**: 32 km west on **Península Lacuy**. This bay is exposed to the Pacific and heavy winds, and camping on the beach is comfortless and devoid of facilities. Rural buses go to Guabun from the market, and meals are available in the village. Be warned that,

despite its wild beauty, this is an isolated spot.

- **Quetalmahué**: 14 km west, with views over the gulf and peninsula. **Bahía Cocotué**, south of Quetalmahué, has a pleasant camping area.
- **Quemchi**: On the east coast; take RN 5 south for 39 km to the turnoff at **Degan**. From here, it is 23 km east on Ruta W-35. This is a typical and unspoilt little township with picturesque streets. From here, it is possible to make a side trip to **Isla Caucahué** and

Lago Popetán, located in native forests. See the entry for Quemchi on page 777.

- **Parque Nacional Chiloé**, Sector Chepu, is reached by rural bus to **Chepu**. From there, a trail goes south for 15 km to the CONAF hut and camping facilities opposite **Isla Metalqui**. Isla Metalqui is close to the coast and home to a large colony of sea lions. See the entry for Parque Nacional Chiloé on page 772.

CASTRO

Area code: 065
Population: 21 000
Altitude: Sea level
Distances

- From Ancud: 90 km south on Panamericana
- From Quellón: 99 km north on Panamericana

Castro, first named San Antonio de Castro, is the capital of Chiloé province, and is situated almost in the geographical center of Isla Grande de Chiloé.

Key to map

A	Iglesia
B	Gobernación Provincial (Government)
C	Municipalidad (Town hall)
D	Post office and telex
E	Telephone
H	Hospital
I	Tourist information
P	Gas stations
T	Bus terminals

● Accommodation

2	Residencial O'Higgins
3	Hotel Gran Alerce Nativo
4	Residencial Mirasol
5	Residencial El Buen Amigo
6	Residencial Guillermo
9	Hotel Unicorno Azul
10	Hotel Don Camillo
13	Residencial Quelcún
14	Hotel Casita Española
20	Hotel Plaza
21	Hotel La Bomba
22	Residencial Lidia
28	Hostería de Castro

○ Eating out

8	Restaurant Hilton
12	Restaurant Gipsy
15	Restaurant Chilos
16	Café Tejuelas
24	Restaurant El Sacho
26	Restaurant Don Octavio
27	Restaurant Palafito

⊙ Entertainment

18	Disco Boite Rincón
19	Disco Barbarilla

▲ Airline offices

23	LAN Chile
25	LADECO

■ Sights

11	Palafitos
29	Museo Regional

□ Services

1	Fería Campesina
7	Supermercado Becker
17	Captitanía de Puerto

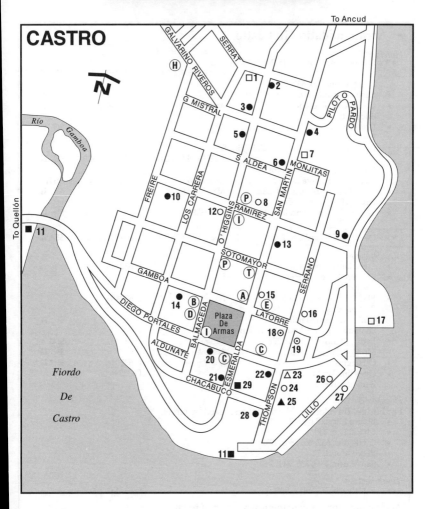

CASTRO

To Ancud

To Quellón

Río Gamboa

Fiordo De Castro

Plaza De Armas

It was founded in 1567 by Martín Ruiz de Gamboa, a renowned Spanish naval captain. It offers good tourist facilities. The main attractions are the Iglesia San Francisco, painted in different colors, and the numerous houses built on stilts along the waterfront or beside small *lagunas*.

Most tourist services and activities are located round the Plaza de Armas. The town sits on a hill and roads plunge steeply to the harborside, where you will find the oldest buildings. Some unpaved streets are mere trails, adding to the town's personality. A walk along the coastal Avenida Costanera is rewarded with

⊟ Accommodation in Castro

Hotels
★★★ Unicorno Azul, Avenida Pedro Montt 228

	AEFGHIJKLPS$TUV	☎ 632359	$F	♟♟

Beach, sauna, fax 632808
- Casita Española, Los Carrera 359 | | ☎ 635186 | |
- Costa Azul, E. Lillo 67 | AFHIJU | ☎ 632440 | $H ♟♟
Budget travelers
- Don Camilo, Ramírez 566 | AF | ☎ 632180 | $G ♟♟
Fax 635533
- Gran Hotel Alerce Nativo, O'Higgins 808

	ADEFGHIJKLMPUTV	☎ 632267/2309	$F	♟♟

Car rental, sauna, 40 rooms
- La Bomba, Esmeralda 270 | AFGHIJPVZ | ☎ 632300 | $H♟♟
- Plaza Beckna, Blanco 366/382 | ADEFGIJKLPUVZ | ☎ 635109 | $H ♟♟
Fax 635477
- Splendid, Blanco Encalada 266 | AFGHKLPV | ☎ 632362/2776 | $H ♟♟

Hosterías
★★★ De Castro, Chacabuco 202 | ADEFGHIJKLPSTUV | ☎ 632301/2302 | $F ♟♟

Residenciales
- Casablanca, Los Carrera 308 | AHS | ☎ 632726 |
- El Buen Amigo, O'Higgins 762 | F |
Backpackers
- El Gringo, Avenida Lillo 51 | F | ☎ 632409 |
Backpackers
- Guillermo, San Martín 700 | | | $I ♟♟
Shared bathroom, budget travelers
- Lydia, Blanco Encalada 276 | AEGIKPV | ☎ 632331 | $I♟♟
- Mirasol, San Martín 815 | AHILUV | | $I ♟♟
- O'Higgins, O'Higgins 831 | AHIPV | ☎ 632016 | $H ♟♟
- Quelcún, San Martín 581 | | ☎632396 |
Budget travelers

Hospedajes
For budget travelers and backpackers, listed by street.
- Blanco Encalada: 41, 266, 279
- Chacabuco: 449
- O'Higgins: 637, 657, 865, 870
- Pedro Montt: 72
- San Martín: 709, 735, 741, 747

Youth hostel
- El Caleuche, Gamboa 500 | AI | ☎ 632483

Accommodation on Panamericana, north of town

Hotels
- Niklitschek, 3 km north | ACEFGHIJKLMPUVX | ☎ 632137/2331 | $G ♟♟
Dancing and shows, beach

Cabañas
- Pudú 9 km north | AEFHIKLN | ☎ 632180 | $G for 4
11 camp sites $J. Open October–March, electricity, toilets, hot showers

Accommodation in Castro — continued

Accommodation on Panamericana, south of town

Cabañas
- Donde Matías, Nercón KM 1190   ACFTU   (632960
  Mini golf
- Llicaldad, 5 km south   AFP   (635080
  Also camping
- Palafitos Los Pescadores, 5 km south ABRTUV   (55635765
  Boat hire, excursions
- Trayén, Nercón Alto   ((09) 6437947

Complejos turísticos
★★★ Nercón, 5 km south   AEFGHIJKLNP$UVX   (5632985 $F for 5
  Boat hire, beach side, tennis
- Montpellier, Nercón   ACFP   (5632669

Hotels
- Posada Alemana, Nercón KM 1191   (632980
  English, French, and German spoken, panoramic views

Motels
★★★ Auquilda, Gamboa, 3 km south   AEFGHIJLPUV   (632458 $G ♦♦

Accommodation in Queilén
Queilén is 66 km south-east.
- Residencial Queilén, on the Plaza de Armas

views across the narrow **Fiordo de Castro**.

Castro has good bus services to all parts of the island and to the mainland. Ferry boats, running between the islands, busily criss-cross the harbor. The 88 km railroad linking Ancud and Castro was built in 1912, but closed in 1960 for lack of patronage by the *Chilotes* (as the inhabitants of this province call themselves) who were reluctant to move away from the sea shore. One of the old steam engines is on display near the hotel Unicorno Azul on Pedro Montt.

🎎 Festivals   ☞

- January: Jornadas Musicales de Chiloé, a Chilotan musical festival held in the Casa Pastoral
- February: The Festival Costumbrista Chilote is held in the Parque Municipal. This is a very colorful occasion,

with dancing and opportunities to sample the rich dishes of the province

ⓘ Tourist information

- Sernatur in kiosk on Plaza Prat opposite Hotel Plaza
- CONAF, Libertador B. O'Higgins, Edificio Gobernación, upstairs (2289. Information and pamphlets on the Parque Nacional Chiloé

🍴 Eating out

Restaurants
- Don Octavio, Avenida Lillo 67. Chilean cuisine
- El Sacho, Thompson 213. Seafood
- Hilton, Ramírez 385
- Oswaldo Loayza, Sargento Aldea 315
- Palafito, E.Lillo, built on stilts on the bay. Seafood
- Residencial Lydia, Blanco Encalada 276
- Rincón Chonchino, Thompson 270
- Ruta 5, San Martín 787

Café restaurants
☞ • Chilo's, San Martín 45. International cuisine. Shows weekends, piano bar during the week, open 0800–0300
• Diablos, Ruta 5 near Shell gas station. Piano bar
• Gastronomía Chilhué, Libertador B. O'Higgins 857
☞ • Gipsy's, O'Higgins 548 $Y. Seafood and steaks
☞ • Hotel Plaza, Blanco Encalada 382. Seafood. Breakfast from 0800
☞ • Cafetería Stop Inn, Latorre 337 upstairs. Breakfast $Z, view over plaza

Cafés
☞ • Café Tejuelas, Serrano 469
• Café La Brújula, O'Higgins 308. Open until 0200

Eating out along the Panamericana
• Motel Auquilda, 2 km south opposite turnoff to airport

▼ Entertainment
• Disco Barbarilla (incorporates Café Restaurant Ruedas), Ignacio Serrano 395
• Disco Boite Rincón, Ignacio Serrano 354
• Disco Lipaues, Blanco Encalada 277

✉ Post and telegraph
Post office
• Correo and Telex Chile, O'Higgins 326 on the plaza

Telephone
• ENTEL Chile, Avenida Libertador B. O'Higgins 677. Overseas calls
• CNT Telefónica del Sur, O'Higgins 677

☺ Services and facilities
Dry cleaner
• Lavaseco Unic, Latorre 594

Pharmacy
• Farmacia San Bruno, Blanco Encalada 228

Supermarket
• Supermercado Becker, San Martín block 600 near Sargento Aldea

✈ Air services
• LADECO, Thomson 207 ✆ 632361

• LAN Chile, Thompson 245 ✆ 635053

🚗 Motoring
• Chiloé Rent-a-Car, Blanco 308 ✆ 632234, fax 632100

⚓ Water transport
For ferry services to the islands, consult Gobernación Marítima, Pedro Montt 85 ✆ 2207.
M/N *Mariane II* is available for charter for cruising around the islands ✆ 2301.
• **Isla Chelin** and **Isla Quehui**: Mon–Sat 1330, return following day at 0700
• **Isla Apiao** and **Isla Chaulinec**: Tues and Fri 1030, return Wed and Sat to Castro
• **Achao**: A ferry runs from Chaulinec and Quehui on Mon and Fri at 0700, which can be used as an alternative return to Dalcahué and Castro

🏬 Shopping
The *mercado municipal* (public market) is on Lillo between Blanco Encalada and Thompson overlooking the Fiordo de Castro. It also incorporates a *fería artesanal*, where you can buy local artifacts.

📷 Sightseeing
• Iglesia San Francisco, a *monumento nacional* on Plaza de Armas, is made of timber and corrugated iron, and painted in blue and orange.
• There are several areas of *palafitos* — houses on stilts — near the mouth of the Río Gamboa, just before the bridge, and to the north at the entrance to town on Montt.
• Museo Municipal Etnológico, Serrano 320. Upstairs are exhibits of archeological finds from the area's pre-Columbian past, and information about the rich folklore of Chiloé.

⚐ Excursions
Tour operators
• Pehuén Expediciones, Lillo 119 ✆ 635254/2432
• Travels Queilén, Gamboa 502 ✆ 635600. Cruises in the archipelago, adventure tourism

Excursions
• **Fiordo de Castro**: Cruises are available daily in summer 1100–1330 to

🚌 Buses from Castro

Companies leaving from the rural bus terminal
The following bus companies (besides most rural buses) are located in the Terminal Municipal (rural bus terminal) on San Martín 681 near Sargento Aldea.
- B11   Bus Norte
- B64   ETC
- B26   Buses Arroyo
- B36   Buses Cardenas
  Route 1: Castro–Dalcahué–Peguel–Quiquel–Quetalco
  Route 2: Castro–Tehuaco–Tallico–Puchauran–Tenaún–San Juan–Calen — Mon–Sat 1100, 1345, 1445; Mon, Wed, Fri 1145
- B74   Buses Ghisoni (2358
- B94   Buses Lemuy
  Route : Castro–Chonchi–Huicha–Chucuy–Ichuac–Puqueldon–San Agustín–Liucura–Puchilco–Aldachildo — Mon–Sat 1300; Sun 1700
- B238 Queilén Bus (2173/5600
- B252 Buses Trans Chiloé (5152

Companies leaving from private terminals
- A155 Buses Turibus, Esmeralda 252 (5088
- B41   Buses Chiloé, Esmeralda 252 (to Concepcion)
- B179 Buses Varmontt, Balmaceda 289
- B254 Transportes Arriagada, Ramírez 233 (5164
- B260 Buses Cruz del Sur, San Martín 499

Services

Destination	Fare	Services	Duration	Companies
Achao	$2.10	6 services daily		B254, including ferry
Ancud	$2.20	18 services daily		A155, B11, B55, B179, B252, B260
Chequían	$2.90	Mon, Wed, Fri		B254 including ferry
Chonchi	$1.30	9 services daily		B96, B252, B260
Concepción	$16.70	1 service daily		B260
Cucao	$2.10	2 services daily	2½ hrs	B26
Dalcahué	$ 0.80	6 services daily		B36
Los Angeles	$13.00	3 services daily		A153, A155, B260
Osorno	$7.10	9 services daily		A155, B11, B252, B260
Puerto Montt	$6.50	21 services daily	4 hrs	A155, B11, B56, B179, B252, B260
Puerto Varas	$6.50	5 services daily		B260
Punta Arenas	$63.50	3 services per week		
			41 hrs	A155, B74
Puqueldon	$1.30			B252
Queilén	$1.40	2–4 services daily		B238, B252
Quellón	$3.30	7 services daily		B252, B260
Santiago				
Pullman	$22.50	3 services daily		A155, B11, B260
Sleeper	$35.00	2 services daily		B179, B260
Talcahuano	$16.70	1 service daily		B260
Temuco	$11.50	6 services daily		A155, B260
Tenaún	$1.20	2–4 services daily		B36, B252

tour the gulfs, bays, islands, and small channels along the eastern side of Isla Grande de Chiloé. Many of the pretty fishing villages along the coast have wooden churches so typical of Chiloé. The trip lasts 2½ hours; fare $25.00.

- **Dalcahué** and **Isla Achao**: Half-day tour, on Sundays only. This is an interesting visit to old Jesuit mission settlements that are much simpler in layout than the elaborate missions seen in Argentina and further north in Chile. Some of the churches are especially beautiful, and are *monumentos nacionales*. Handicrafts made by the locals are available.
- **Parque Nacional Chiloé**: Day tour. See the entry for the park on page 772.
- **Quellón**, the furthest point south on Isla Grande de Chiloé: A day tour through forest, past lakes and over low hills. To the west of Quellón there are a few isolated villages inhabited by Huilliches — they still speak their own language. See also the entry for Quellón on page 774.
- **Mechuque** on Isla Mechuque, part of the Chauques island group, separated from the main island by **Canal Quicaví**. Day excursion by launch. The small hills along the beach are divided by small channels, which drain at low tide and become waterways at high tide. The ship cruises through the deeper channels — a wonderful experience, unspoilt by hordes of tourists. Many village houses, which are close to the sea, are built on stilts; they become part of the island at low tide. Some villagers have oyster farms on interior lagoons separated from the sea by large sand banks, and Mechuque has its own fish processing industry. The island's *alerce* forests are now depleted. Recommended.
- **Chonchi**: 23 km south. A picturesque little town, indeed a recommended visit. It is best visited by regular buses. See the entry for Chonchi on page 769.
- **Cucao**: 45 km south, at the southern entrance of Parque Nacional Chiloé.

Regular daily buses run here. See also Parque Nacional Chiloé on page 772.
- **Achao**: This is a 55 km combined bus/ferry trip to one of the prettiest islands, where most of the houses are surrounded by apple and pear orchards. There are historic churches and other sights of interest, such as the windmills operating near Curaco de Velez. From higher points on the road, you can see the snow-covered volcanoes on the mainland. After leaving Castro, the Panamericana runs north for 8 km until the turnoff to **Dalcahué**, a small fishing village. Here the bus is ferried across to **Isla Quinchao**. At 40 km you reach **Curaco de Vélez**, another fishing village — see "Excursions" from Achao on page 755. After crossing Puente de Molina at 42 km, the road winds through rolling hills and you can see the bay islands. Ten kilometers further on, Achao comes into view, sheltered by low hills. See also the entry for Achao on page 754.
- **Queilén:** 66 km south-east, a small picturesque village with 1500 inhabitants on the **Golfo de Corcovado**. This town became a Jesuit mission settlement just a few years before their expulsion from the Spanish and Portuguese colonies. It has a lot of character, with some old wooden colonial houses. Across the gulf you can see **Volcán Michinmávida** on the mainland. South of the town is a long stretched-out sand bank, partly submerged at high tide. At the far end of the sand bank there is a lighthouse. The lifeline of the villagers is fishing, cattle, and logging. The road from Chonchi onwards goes mainly through beautiful forests. Every now and then a turnoff east leads down to small villages on the coast: **Teupa**, **Tera**, **Ahoni**, and **Aituy** have old mission churches which are monumentos nacionales. Buses Queilén and Buses Trans Chiloé run 2–4 services daily to Castro; the first bus to Castro departs at 0630.

CHONCHI

Area code: 06553
Population: 3000
Distance from Castro: 23 km south on Panamericana

Chonchi, founded by the the Jesuits in 1750 and officially founded as a town in 1764, is also known as "the three-storied city". It is built on a steep hill in three tiers, and some houses front onto two streets: the entrance on the level in the higher street is the upper floor when you enter from the lower street. Many of the houses are built of colorful cypress wood, and the church has been declared a *monumento nacional*. Nowadays it is a small picturesque fishing village 3 km east of the Panamericana, and serves as the port for ferry services to **Isla Lemuy**. A delicious liqueur, *licor de oro*, is made here, as well as a type of cake known as *roscas chonchinas*.

Some of the houses at sea level are on stilts. The upper part of town, where tourist facilities such as the Cruz del Sur office are concentrated along the main street, commands sweeping views over the canal and islands.

⚤ Festivals
• February: Semana Chonchina

⊞ Eating out
• Café Coral, on the main plaza $Z

Eating out in Puqueldon
Puqueldon is on Isla Lemuy, reached by ferry from Chonchi.
• Café Amancay $Z
• Restaurant Lemuy $Z
• Restaurant El Paso $Z

⊟ Accommodation in Chonchi

Hotels

• Chonchi, O'Higgins 379	AHIPV	☎ 671288	$H ♙♙
• Huildín (formerly Sacho), Centenario 102	AEFGHLP	☎ 671388	$H ♙♙
• Posada Antiguo Chalet, Irarrazabal	AEFGHIJLPV	☎ 671221	$F ♙♙
9 rooms			
• Remis, Irrarzaval 63		☎ 671271	

Residenciales

• Alirio Borquez, Pedro Aguirre Cerda 0409	☎ 671263

Cabañas

• Amankay, Centenario 410	☎ 671367

Accommodation on the access road from Castro

Cabañas

• Huitauque Bordemar	☎ (09) 6437560

Accommodation on Lago Huillinco
Lago Huillinco is 9 km west.

• Cabañas El Huillín, KM 20 on the south side of lake	☎ (09) 6437558

🚌 Buses

Buses Cruz del Sur and Buses Arroyo stop in the upper part of town. Buses from Conchi to Pargua cease after 1800.

Buses Puqueldon run to Ichuac, Liucura, and Detif on Isla Lemuy.

Buses Trans Chiloé, Buses Cruz del Sur, Buses Flecha Sur, Buses Lemuy call on Chonchi. Not all buses detour into Chonchi.

There are 10 services daily to Castro; 4 services daily to Ancud, Quellón, and Puerto Montt; and 2 services daily to Huillinco and Cucao.

⚓ Water transport

Companies
- TransMarchilay, Avenida Costanera

Services
- Isla Lemuy: combined bus/ferry service to Puqueldon

🏬 Shopping

Homespun materials and woolen garments are sold from private homes.

📷 Sightseeing

Chonchi's church, a *monumento nacional*, is one of the oldest on Isla Grande de Chiloé. It contains paintings of saints by local artists.

✈ Excursions

- **Ichuac** on **Isla Lemuy**: Take the ferry to see the old church.
- **Huillinco**: 12 km east, on the east side of the lake of the same name, offers fishing and boating. Continue on to **Cucao.**
- **Vilupulli**: 4 km north. A small village with an attractive colonial church.

DALCAHUÉ

Area code: 06555
Population: 1000
Altitude: Sea level
Distance from Castro: 20 km north east on Ruta W- 59

Dalcahué is situated on the eastern side of **Isla Grande de Chiloé**, 15 km north east of Castro on Ruta W-59. It is separated by a narrow canal from **Isla Quinchao**.

In 1824, General Ramón Freire disembarked at Dalcahué to oust the last Spanish defender, General Quintana, from Chiloé. The small local museum covers this historical event.

Dalcahué's present economy is based on oyster and shrimp fishing, cattle and timber.

🎎 Festivals
- February: Semana Dalcahuina

ℹ Tourist information

The municipal tourist office on the plaza has the names of private accommodation.

🛏 Accommodation

Residencial
- San Martín, San Martín 001 AFGHJL ✆ 651207

Pensiones
- Alemana
- Dalcahué, Padre Aguirre Cerda 002 HI
- La Feria, Manuel Rodríguez 017
- Montaña, Manuel Rodríguez 009
- Putemún, Freire 305 AFGHJL $J ⚡. Budget travelers

🍴 Eating out
- Café Restaurant Dalca, Freire 502 $Z. Seafood

🚌 Buses

Companies

Transportes Arriagada, San Martín 104 runs 3-6 services daily to Castro, Dalcahué, Achao, and Chequián

⚓ Water transport

- Isla Quinchao: Departs hourly 0700–2100; 14 services daily; duration 10 mins
- Isla Mechuque: Departs 1400 Tues, Thurs; returns to Dalcahué 0700 Mon, Fri

It is also possible to return from Mechuque to Tenaún twice a week. The departure time is coordinated with the bus from Tenaún to Castro, but always check.

🏬 Shopping

A *fería artesanal* held on the plaza on Sunday mornings sells some very high quality hand-made textiles.

📷 Sightseeing

- The parish church, built around 1750 and now a *monumento nacional*, is one of the biggest and oldest on Isla Grande de Chiloé. The belfry has two tiers and the interior has three naves. There is a lively market on the plaza and a small museum in the *municipalidad*.
- There is a small shipyard at the entrance to the village where you can watch shipwrights building fishing boats.
- Casa del Navegante, formerly a guest house, is built on stilts.

➤ Excursions

- **Quemchi**: 57 km north-east of Dalcahué. This has only been settled in the last 20 years, and is virtually still only a clearing in the dense forest. The main road, which is very bumpy gravel, runs inland. *Chilotes* do not like to move far from the sea, and side roads, some only 2–5 km long, lead to fishing villages along the coast, which were established in colonial or even pre-Hispanic times and are worth visiting. At KM 12, turn off to the village of **Quetalco**, 3 km off the main road. It was an important mission settlement in the middle of the 18th century, when missionaries made their way from there into the *pampas* of Argentina. Quetalco has a small colonial church with the usual central belfry in two tiers on top of the front porch. The second tier is octagonal and roofed with shingles. Turn off at KM 28 to the villages of **San Juan** and **Calen**. At San Juan the locals still build small boats, but the main attraction is a beautiful beach and an old church. Part of this village sank during the 1960 earthquake. Further up, the mouth of the river is blocked with rocks to catch the fish which come in with the tide. From Calen, a small fishing village with a typical church, there are sweeping views across the **Golfo de Ancud** to the mainland with the high *sierra* and **Volcán Michinmávida** in the background. At KM 33, turn off 7 km to **Tenaún** to see the beautiful colonial church. At KM 38, turn off to **Quicaví** At 44 km, you pass **Laguna Popetán**, which is still surrounded by large forests. The trip can be continued north, partly along the coast, as far as **Linao**. The Panamericana is rejoined near San Juan to return to **Ancud** or the ferry at **Chacao**. This country was opened up by European immigrants at the turn of the 20th century, who cleared large tracts of forest for dairy farming. See also the entry for Quemchi on page 777.

Dalcahué

PARQUE NACIONAL CHILOÉ

This national park on **Isla Grande de Chiloé**, 58 km south-west of Castro, covers 43 057 ha (106 350 acres), extending from the **Río Chepu** in the north to **Bahía Cucao** in the south. Although generally described as a national park, large tracts are considered *reserva nacional*, where logging takes place under the supervision of CONAF.

Much of the area is still untouched rainforest, but development is already encroaching on the edges of this beautiful unpolluted, and at present uncommercialized, area. Within this densely forested area, you will find the **Cordillera de Piuche**, which reaches a height of 777 m. The main rivers flowing through the national park are the **Río Butalcura**, **Río Refugio**, **Río Metalqui**, **Río Anay**, and **Río Tole Tole**. There are also lakes — **Lago Huillinco** and **Huelde**.

This 58 km, one-way trip from Castro takes about 2½ hrs. You could catch the bus from Chonchi, but it is better to get on at Castro to be sure of a seat. The bus takes the Panamericana as far as Chonchi, and shortly afterwards turns west into Ruta W-80. From the little village of **Huillinco** onwards, the route follows the pretty southern bank of **Lago Huillinco**. The northern side of the lake is in the national park. Between Huillinco and Cucao is the most interesting part: you are going through "pioneer country" — the land has been opened up by settlers in the last 30 years. As you approach Cucao the forest is left behind. **Cucao** lies west of Lago Cucao near **Bahía Cucao**. This is one of the few spots on Isla Grande de Chiloé where there is direct road access to the Pacific Ocean — there is none further south — an indication of how thinly populated

the island really is. The original Cucao was visited by Charles Darwin in the 19th century. The settlement was destroyed by the 1960 earthquake and has been rebuilt. Sand dunes stretch for 20 km, occupied by shrubs that have adapted to the environment. There are few trees around the settlement.

Access from Cucao to the national park area is via a foot bridge, which is also used by cattle coming from the national park.

The park includes rocky or sandy seashore, almost impenetrable jungle on the slopes, and elevated areas near the high peaks with shrubs and some open country.

After crossing the steel suspension bridge, turn right for the park administration in Sector Chanquin — it is about 3 km north along a sandy dirt road. The road is lined with shrubs. The CONAF information center has an excellent display of the flora and fauna in the larger hall, and the rangers are very helpful in explaining everything (but they don't speak English). The park ranger sells leaflets of the national parks, which also show the (few) trails leading into the park.

From the rangers' center, a trail leads through open country and then into the forest. On the way you pass a camping area set up by CONAF; it has shower facilities and barbecue spots, and is right on the lake. The long beach by the lake is a few hundred meters north of the visitors' center, which is sheltered from the strong Pacific winds by a high sand dune. Once you cross the dune on to the beach, you feel the full blast of the strong winds coming across the Pacific Ocean. Only the very brave venture into the cold water! A few hundred meters past the camping area the trail enters the forest. As the trail penetrates further into the forest it is elevated on wooden planks. The forest is really dense and also has many swampy areas. The trail is only a 6 km long semi-circle, but it gives you an idea how difficult it is to traverse the whole park, either east–west or north–south.

The 1960 earthquake caused some ecological changes by lowering the land near the seashore. This allowed the wind to create a dune landscape, but there is a vigorous reclamation scheme in place to stop the drift of the sand by planting amofila grass. When this has been achieved, shrubs and trees will be planted.

There are many insect-eating plants in the national park, and also dwarf cypresses. You will find mock privet, *coigues,* cinnamon tree, *arrayan* and *alerces* growing here in abundance.

The wildlife includes dwarf deer, *monito del monte,* otters, and birds such as *bandurrias,* flamingos, Chilean mud hen (*tagua*),and Chilean warbler (*diuca de Chiloé*). The *monito del monte* is a 10–12 cm marsupial with a long tail and a very close South American relative to the Australian marsupials. It sleeps during the day and searches for food at night — it likes to eat leaves and fruits. The *pudú*

or dwarf deer is also very common, although not easily spotted. The only native member of the cat family on the island is the *guiña,* the size of a domestic cat with yellowish fur.

The highest rainfall is between May and October, and the lowest rainfall from December to March, which is the best time for a visit. The average annual temperature is 11°C (52°F), and there is no snow of any significance.

Although this is national park area, there are some homesteads near the seashore, many of them belonging to members of the Huilliche tribe. You can reach these homesteads from this trail, and during the apple harvest season you will see signs with the word *cidra* (cider) with an arrow. The homesteads are about 3 km north-west of the trail, surrounded by apple and pear orchards. The orchardists make a most delicious apple cider — it's quite safe to drink. This particular area is sheltered from the strong winds blowing from the South Pacific by huge sand dunes.

From Sector Chanquín you can also reach Sector Cole Cole near the mouth of the **Río Cole Cole**, approximately 15 km north; there is a camping ground there but no facilities. The trail continues north mostly along the beach to **Punta Anay**. The combination of very fertile volcanic soil and high rainfall and humidity has created an almost impenetrable forest, although I have been told there are some natural open spaces on the highest parts. The park rangers say it is a very difficult task to cross the park and might take five days, so beginners should not attempt it. It is not only the terrain, but also the unpredictable weather conditions in the

Parque Nacional Chiloé

area that make this a difficult undertaking — it may rain at any tick of the clock. There are many creeks and streams to be forded. This must be one of the last wilderness areas on earth.

Sector Chepu, the northern part of Parque Nacional, is accessed from Ancud. There are rural buses from Ancud; this part is less developed than the Cucao entrance and has fewer visitors. There is also a park ranger's headquarters and a CONAF hut on **Río Lar**. The trail south from Chepu goes as far as Metalqui beach, and there is also a CONAF *refugio*. **Isla Metalqui**, its rocks battered by the sea and strong south-westerly winds, has a large seal colony only a kilometer or so distant from the mainland. Along the **Río Chepu** there are large tracts of dead trees which became partly submerged during the 1960 earthquake.

You can also reach Sector Abtao (the middle section) if you set out from Castro. This track starts from the Panamericana from **Llaullao** (north of Castro), heading towards Punta Gruesa on the Pacific coast, with the last part of this trail following the **Río Abtao**.

The easiest way to get to the park is via Cucao (Ruta W-80) in the south.

⊟ Accommodation

Accommodation in Cucao
• Hospedaje El Paraíso on the outskirts of the village; bus goes past

⊿ Camping
• Camping Chanquín, 300 m north of CONAF information center, 3 km outside Cucao, over the suspension bridge

⊟ Buses
Buses Arroyo run 2 services daily from Castro via Chonchi and Huillinco to Cucao. The bus from Castro stops at the bridge which you cross to enter the national park. The return bus from Cucao to Castro departs 1515 lo link up with the last bus from Castro to the mainland.

QUELLÓN

Area code: 65
Population: 7000
Altitude: Sea level
Distance from Castro: 55 km north on Panamericana (RN 5)

Quellón is the southernmost town on **Isla Grande de Chiloé**, and RN 5 ends here. Officially founded in 1905, Quellón is a fishing and transit port for ferry services to **Puerto Chacabuco** in Región XI de Aisén and the nearby islands. The town is very picturesque and still has a frontier character.

Now that the Panamericana to Quellón is sealed, the ferries between Quellón and Puerto Chacabuco have been reinstated in the summer months. The town has reasonable tourist facilities, and there are regular daily bus services to Castro and the mainland. The best views over the bay and nearby islands are from the Parque Municipal. Along the seashore there is a colorful harbor and little restaurants nearby serve seafood.

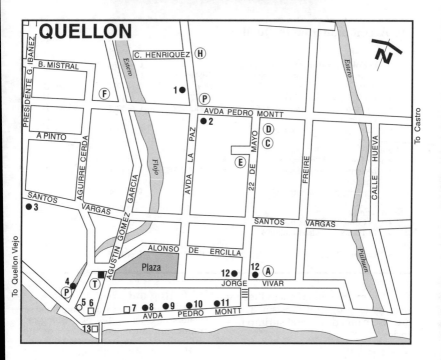

QUELLON

Key to map

A	Iglesia
C	Municipalidad (Town hall)
D	Post office and telex
E	Telephone
F	Carabineros (Police)
H	Hospital
P	Gas stations
T	Bus terminals

● Accommodation

1	Hotel Pincoya
2	Hotel Colono
3	Hotel Golfo Corcovado
4	Hotel Leo Mann
8	Hotel Playa
9	Hostería El Fogón
10	Hotel Melimoyu
11	Residencial El Coral
12	Private accommodation

○ Eating out

5	Restaurant Las Brisas

■ Sights

13	Museo Municipal

□ Services

6	Capitanía de Puerto
7	TransMarchilay

✉ Accommodation in Quellón

Hotels
- El Colono, Ladrilleros corner of La Paz   ℄ 681254 $H ♟♟
- Golfo Corcovado, Santos Vargas   AEFGHLMPV   ℄ 681528
- Playa Anexo, Pedro Montt 245   AEHIJPV   ℄ 681278 $H ♟♟
- Playa, Pedro Montt 255   AFGHIKPV   ℄ 681298 $H ♟♟
- La Pincoya, Avenida La Paz 064   ABFGHIJLPUVZ   ℄ 681285 $H ♟♟
  Car rental
- Leo Mann, Pedro Aguirre Cerda   ℄ 681298

Hosterías
- La Posada, 22 de Mayo 3   AEFHIJL   ℄ 681246
- Melimoyu, Pedro Montt 217   ADEFGHIJLMPR$Z   ℄ 681310 $H ♟♟
  Car rental
- Quellón, Pedro Montt 2 97   ℄ 681250

Residenciales
- El Coral, Pedro Montt 197
- El Tráfico 2, Pedro Montt 053
           AF $I ♟♟
- Cabañas Turis Lapas, Punta de Lapas   AEFGHPUV   ℄ 681298

The main economic activities are fishing, logging and tourism. There are also canned fish and shrimp factories.

⊠ Festivals
- January: Semana Quellonina

ℹ Tourist information
- Municipalidad

⊞ Eating out
Centollas are fished in and around the sea waters of Quellón, but overfishing and non-compliance with *"vedas"* or unauthorized fishing has depleted this wonderful crustacean. With a little bit of luck and perseverance you may find a restaurant which serves *centolla*. Note that the female and male of the species taste different.

🚌 Buses from Quellón

Buses Barrientos runs services Auchar–Curranhue–Huidal–Candelaria and San Antonio–Auqueldan–Chaihuao on Mon, Wed, and Fri; and to Yaldar on Tues and Thurs.

Companies
- B56   Buses Del Sur
- B252   Buses Trans Chiloe
- B260   Buses Cruz del Sur

Services

Destination	Fare	Services	Companies
Ancud	$5.00	7 services daily	B260
Castro	$3.30	7 services daily	B252, B260
Chonchi	$1.90	4 services daily	B260
Puerto Montt	$9.00	3 services daily	B56, B252, B260
Puerto Varas	$9.00	3 services daily	B260
Temuco	$15.00	5 services daily	B260

Restaurants
- El Tráfico, Costanera Pedro Montt 053. International cuisine
- Fogón Las Quilas, La Paz
- Las Brisas, Costanera Pedro Montt near Gómez García
- Hotel Playa, Costanera Pedro Montt 245
- Hostería La Posada, 22 de Mayo 003. Seafood
- Rucantu, Costanera Pedro Montt 117, upstairs

Entertainment
- Disco La Cabaña, intersection of Panamericana and road to San Antonio, opposite the soccer field

Post and telegraph
- Correos and Telex Chile, 22 de Mayo near Ladrilleros

Motoring
- COPEC gas station, Ladrilleros corner of Avenida La Paz

Water transport
For destinations and timetables of ferry services to Puerto Chacabuco, see "Boat trips" on pages 649–651.

Sightseeing
- Museo Municipal Arqueológico, Gómez García 36, which has artifacts from pre-Columbian population.
- Fería Artesanal, Plaza de Armas. Locally produced blankets for sale.

Excursions
- **Chadmo** and **Yaldad** are little fishing villages where the traditional *Chilote* way of life is preserved almost intact. Roads are unsealed.
- **Isla Cailin**: By fishing boat. Private arrangements with boat owners. Contact Capitanía de Puerto, who will advise which vessels depart and for which islands.
- Huilliche settlements of **Compu**, **Huaipulli**, and **Incopulli**. Contact tourist information in the Municipalidad.

QUEMCHI

Area code: 0657
Population: 300
Altitude: Sea level
Distance from Ancud: 64 km north-west on Ruta W-175

This picturesque fishing village is on the east side of **Isla Grande de Chiloé** on the **Canal Caucahué**. In front of it is **Isla Caucahué**, and the side you can see from Quemchi is heavily forested.

Festivals
- February: Semana Quemchina

Accommodation
- Hospedaje El Embrujo, Pedro Montt 431
- Hospedaje la Tranquera, Yungay 40 AFGJ(691250

Eating out
- Restaurant El Embrujo, Pedro Montt 431

Buses
Buses Del Río run 3 services daily to Ancud.

Excursions
- **Tenaún**: Because of its sheltered position, mariners often used Tenaún as a refuge when gusty winds forced them ashore. Among the notable personalities which called on this village were Padre Francisco Menéndez, a Franciscan missionary who worked in the Argentine *pampas*, and the *Chilote* cartographer and seafarer, Capitán José de Moraleda. The

church in Tenaún is unusual: it has a huge central tower in three tiers, flanked by two smaller ones; all other churches on Isla Grande de Chiloé have only one belfry. The church has been declared a *monumento nacional*.

- **Quicaví**: Between boulders on the seashore are bridges which allows the villagers to circulate between dwellings at high tide. This is the home of Invunche, the legendary warlock of Chiloé. The village has an interesting colonial church with an octagonal belfry sitting in the center of the roof. Near **Tocoihué** there is a small waterfall.

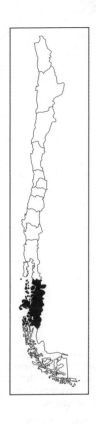

REGIÓN XI
DE
AISÉN

Size: 108 000 square km (41 688 square miles)
Population: 75 000
Regional capital: Coihaique
Provinces (and provincial capitals)
- Coihaique (Coihaique)
- Aisén (Puerto Aisén)
- General Carrera (Chile Chico)
- Capitn Prat (Cochrane)

Until 1988, Región de Aisén del General Carlos Ibáñez del Campo was almost completely isolated, accessible only by ferry from Isla Grande de Chiloe and Puerto Montt. In that year the Carretera Austral Presidente Pinochet was opened to provide road access, but until it is widened and sealed, visits here outside the summer months are exciting adventures.

The region, known also as Región del Aisén, extends from 43° south to 49° south. In the north it shares a border with Región de los Lagos; in the east the Andean *cordillera* forms the border with Argentina; to the south is Región de Magallanes; and to the west is the Pacific Ocean.

Topography

As you travel south, the Patagonian Andes become lower, and here average only 2000 m high, although in the coastal *cordillera* peaks reach over 4000m. Between the two ranges lies a wide valley crossed by rivers flowing into the Pacific. Volcanoes like **Volcán Lautaro** tower at 3380m.

The coastal area is riven by numerous fiords which create spectacular archipelagoes as they enter the ocean. As they advanced, ancient glaciers carved deep valleys now traversed by glacial rivers, the most important being the **Río Baker**. This river and its tributary **Río Neff** are superb for rafting; unfortunately for the white-water lover, the government plans to build power stations along this fast-flowing river to harness the water for electricity generation. Other major river systems are

Palena, Cisnes, Aisén, Bravo, and Pascua

Despite the fact that Lago General Carrera is shared with Argentina, it is Chile's largest lake. Here are innumerable glaciers and glacial lakes set like jewels in a hikers' paradise.

Climate

The rain pattern is shaped by the mountains. The most rain falls on the outlying islands, reaching 2810 mm in Puerto Aisén and diminishing towards the Argentine border, with the lowest rainfalls recorded in Balmaceda at 400 mm annually. The temperature is also modified by the closeness of the sea: near the coast it averages 13.1°C (56°F) in January and 4.8°C (41°F) in July, and inland in Balmaceda 13.7°C (57°F) in January and 0.1°C (32°F) in July. The mountains above 1800 m stay around freezing point all year round. The outlying islands are influenced by the Pacific Ocean with its leveling influence, and although they are very wet they experience no wide seasonal temperature fluctuations.

The vegetation is shaped by the rainfall. The coastal slopes are densely forested with evergreen shrubs and trees. Up to 1200 m you find bamboo thickets.

The indigenous inhabitants

In pre-Columbian times, the region was the home of the Tehuelches, Chonos, and Alacufes. The Tehuelches were primarily hunters and gatherers. The Chonos and Alacufes, living on the fringe of the Pacific Ocean and on its many islands, used canoes and were skilled fishermen.

It is likely that the tribes living in the interior had little contact with those on the coast. With the advent of the horse, the Tehuelches became expert riders and were the bane of many early Spanish settlements.

European history

During colonial times this area was called Trapananda.

From 1534, European expeditions penetrated as far as the Strait of Magellan. The most notable expeditions were those of Capitán Juan Ladrilleros in 1557, and the travels of Padres Melchor Venegas and Mateo Esteban. The Laguna San Rafael was discovered in 1675 by Bartolomé Diaz Gallardo. In 1793 José de Moraleda and Henry Simpson compiled the first map of the area.

Moraleda conducted expeditions up the Río Palena and along the Río Aisén. His aim was principally to discover a shorter sea route to the Atlantic, but secondly to prevent foreign powers (chiefly England and Holland) gaining a foothold in what was then considered Spanish territorial waters.

From 1776 on, Franciscan missionaries also contributed to the general knowledge of this land.

The scientific expedition of Captain Fitzroy and Charles Darwin in 1831 made the Chilean government aware of the value of the area to the south. One positive result of these scientific expeditions was the excellent maps produced. Expeditions from the Argentine side discovered Lago San Martín and Lago Buenos Aires, and the sources of the Río Pico and Río Cisnes.

Philip Westhoff, a German, founded Melinka as a commercial enterprise, engaged in timber and fishing.

From 1903, settlement of the region began from the Argentine side. The first areas settled were the **Río Simpson valley** between Puerto Chacabuco and Lago Fontana.

Economy

The region's only industry is agriculture. However, because of the expense of shipping crops to the main consumption areas to the north, most farming is carried out at a subsistence level. It consists mostly of potato and bean crops, supplemented by a few cattle. The most congenial environment for agriculture is around **Lago General Carrera**, whose large sheet of water has a moderating climatic effect.

Transport

Road

Access to the region from the north is via the Carretera Austral from Chaitén. The road is complete as far as Cochrane, and is to be pushed further south to Villa O'Higgins. Feeder roads branch off into the interior and to the coast.

One such is at La Junta, which leads to Lago Verde and on to Río Pico in Argentina. The road branches off at Piedra del Gato to Puerto Cisnes on the coast, and again at Villa Amengual up the Río Cisnes valley to the Argentine border.

At Coihaique the Carretera Austral crosses the highway running from Comodoro Rivadavia in Argentina to Puerto Chacabuco on the coast. Another important branch road goes to the airport at Balmaceda, and from there into Argentina.

Air

At Coihaique there are daily flights to and from Santiago and Puerto Montt, landing in Balmaceda 55 km south or at the Aerodromo Vidal just 10 km outside town. Aerodromo Vidal is also used for small aircraft servicing the outlying areas.

Sea

The region's main port is Puerto Chacabuco, near Puerto Aisén (the original port). Ferry services run to Puerto Montt, Pargua and Quellón in the extreme south of Isla Grande de Chiloe. Depending on the season, two companies offer between one and three services weekly.

Sport

Hiking

There are areas in the **Campo de Hielo Norte** (Northern Ice Shield) and **Campo de Hielo Sur** (Southern Ice Shield) which have not been explored and still await the arrival of the first mountaineer. Do not venture into the "wild areas" without proper preparation: ensure that you have adequate food, tent, sleeping bag, and warm clothes — near the ice fields it is uncomfortably cold and crossing the glacial rivers and rivulets is a really testing experience. For those with little experience in outdoor activities, there are travel agencies in Coihaique which will arrange an adventure package tour (see "Tour operators" in Coihaique on page 795).

River rafting

From the end of February to the end of April, river rafting is available to the enthusiast.

- **Río Baker:** The foremost river suitable for rafting, but also the most dangerous, is the Río Baker, from its source in Lago Bertrand at Puerto Bertrand to Caleta Tortel, a distance of about 170 km. It carries 875 cubic meters of water per second. This is a six-day rafting trip, starting with a one-day bus trip from Coihaique to Puerto Bertrand. From its very source the river flows at phenomenal speed. The greater part of the upper reaches flow between steep granite cliffs. The most exciting section is near the confluence with the Río Neff, which shoots out from a narrow valley. Just before the junction the valley widens, but below it the river is constricted once more between steep walls, thus forming a chain of waterfalls right where the rivers join. The confluence is visible from the Carretera Austral, and bus drivers usually stop there for the view. Unfortunately plans are afoot to "tame" the Río Baker and harness its power to produce electricity.

- **Río Cisnes:** The second river suitable for rafting is the Río Cisnes. This is a 120 km rafting trip, which takes you almost from the Argentine border to the Canal Puyuhuapi near Puerto Cisnes. You begin at an altitude of 1000 m, and for some time gradually descend a wide fertile valley with isolated homesteads, and long stretches of native tree growth along the banks and up the mountain slopes. The most interesting part is when the river makes its way through the coastal *cordillera*. One of the most picturesque sections is near the junction of the Carretera Austral with the road to Puerto Cisnes. Here near the Piedra del Gato is a 3 m high waterfall; it is fairly dangerous and you will need to portage your raft to the bottom. The starting point of this rafting trip is again Coihaique. A bus service runs once a week up the Río Cisnes valley, but it is advisable to do this trip with a trekking company in Coihaique.

- **Río Palena:** For rafting on the Río Palena, see Puerto Raúl Marín Balmaceda under "Excursions" from La Junta on page 804.

- **Other rivers:** Other rivers suitable for rafting are the Río Mañihuales (north of Coihaique), Río Murta (south of Coihaique), and Río Ibáñez.

Skiing

This region has many areas which are suitable for skiing, with an abundance of snow for nearly six months. However at the moment there is only one area with facilities — **Cerro El Fraile**, a short distance south of Coihaique. Funds have not been readily available to start up ski resorts in this part of Chile, owing to its distance from the large population centers of the north and the abundance of good developed ski areas in the central parts of Chile.

Trout fishing

The sports fishermen can choose from an infinite number of streams to cast a line and hook a king-size trout. The fishing season for the area from the northern border of the region to the southernmost point of Lago Las Torres runs from the second Friday in November to the first Sunday in May. From there to the southern border, the season runs from the second Friday in October to the first Sunday in May. Note that on the Río Claro the section between Pozón and the mouth of the Río Ibáñez in Lago General Carrera is permanently closed to fishing. Fishing in Lago General Carrera, Lago Cochrane, and Lago O'Higgins is permitted all year round, as these lakes are shared with Argentina.

The best fishing areas are described under Puerto Cisnes (page 813), Puerto Aisén (page 810), Coihaique (page 803), Puerto Ingeniero Ibáñez (page 816) and Cochrane (page 793).

National parks and reserves

Listed from north to south.

* **Reserva Nacional Lago Rosselot:** 12 725 ha (298 086 acres), 12 km south of **La Junta** on the Carretera Austral Augusto Pinochet. Educational and excursion paths. Accommodation, eating place, and shop nearby.
* **Parque Nacional Queulat:** 154 093 ha (380 477 acres), 160 km north of Coihaique on the Carretera Austral Augusto Pinochet. Excursion paths, picnic areas, camping areas. Best reached from Puyuhuapi and Puerto Cisnes. See the entry for the park on page 806
* **Parque Nacional Isla Magdalena**: 157 640 ha (389 235 acres), 20 km east of **Puerto Cisnes** across **Fiordo Puyuhuapi**. By boat only.
* **Reserva Nacional Lago Carlota:** 18 060 ha (44 593 acres), 170 km north-east of Coihaique near La

Tapera. Turn off east from Carretera Austral at Cisnes Medio onto Ruta X-25. Excursion paths, mountain hut.
* **Reserva Nacional Lago Las Torres:** 16 516 ha (40 780 acres), 130 km north of Coihaique on the Carretera Austral Augusto Pinochet. Picnic area, excursion paths.
* **Reserva Nacional Las Guaitecas:** 1 097 975 ha (2 711 049 acres), 140 km west of Coihaique. Accessible only by sea from Puerto Chacabuco or Puerto Cisnes.
* **Parque Nacional Isla Guamblin:** 15 915 ha (39 296 acres), 180 km west of Puerto Aisén. Accessible only by boat.
* **Reserva Nacional Mañihuales:** 1206 ha (2978 acres)
* **Monumento Natural Cinco Hermanas:** 228 ha (563 acres), 40 km west of Puerto Aisén in Fiordo Aisén. Accessible only by boat. Excursion paths.
* **Monumento Natural Dos Lagunas:** 181 ha (447 acres), 27 km east of Coihaique on RN 240, on the road to Coihaique Alto. Educational and excursion paths, picnic area. This park is located in dry steppe country and the flora consists mainly of bushes. There are many *michay* and *calafate* shrubs around here; both have edible berries. The park is most easily reached from Coihaique by regular daily buses.
* **Reserva Nacional Coihaique:** 2150 ha (5309 acres), 5 km west of Coihaique on RN 240 towards Puerto Aisén. Educational and excursion paths, picnic area, camping area, lookout; accom-

modation, eating places, and shop nearby.

- **Parque Nacional Río Simpson:** 40 827 ha (100 807 acres), 37 km west of Coihaique on RN 240 on the road to Puerto Aisén. Educational and excursion paths, information center, picnic areas, camping area, eating place, mountain hut. See the entry for the park on page 808.

- **Parque Nacional Laguna San Rafael:** 1 742 000 ha (4 301 235 acres), 225 km south-east of Puerto Aisén. The western part is only accessible by sea (15 hours) or by air (90 minutes) from Puerto Aisén. Educational and excursion paths, picnic area, lookout. This is one of the most scenic national parks in Chile — do not miss it. The eastern part reaches the **Lago General Carrera** near **Cruce El Maitén** — the turnoff to Chile Chico. This part can be reached from Coihaique. With accommodation springing up in little villages around the lake, there are now sufficient bases to explore this part of the national park. For trailblazers only. See the entry for the park on page 805.

- **Reserva Nacional Cerro Castillo:** 139 552 ha (344 573 acres), 75 km south of Coihaique on the Carretera Austral. Excursion paths.

- **Reserva Nacional Lago Jeinimeni:** 158 860 ha (392 247 ac), 65 km south of Chile Chico. The reserve incorporates the **Reserva Nacional Lago General Carrera**. Administered by CONAF. Access is over a dirt road along the **Río Jeinimeni**, which forms part of the border with

Argentina. The park features are petroglyphs carved by the pre-Columbian inhabitants, though they are not easy to find. Picnic area, excursion paths.

- **Reserva Nacional Tamango.** 6 925 ha (17 099 ac), 17 km north of Cochrane on RN 7. Picnic area, excursion paths; accommodation, eating places, and shops nearby.

- **Reserva Nacional Katalalixar:** 674 500 ha (1 665 432 acres), 300 km south-east of Coihaique. Accessible only by sea.

- **Parque Nacional Bernardo O'Higgins** 921 000 ha (2 274 074 acres). This is only the part which is in Región XI de Aisén. It stretches further south into Región XII de Magallanes, and includes the Campo de Hielo Sur — a huge glacier. It can be reached from Tortel and Villa O'Higgins.

Thermal resorts

- **Termas de Puyuhuapi:** Open December to April. Located on **Seno Ventisquero**, 14 km south of Puyuhuapi, 225 km north of Coihaique on the Carretera Austral, 195 km south of Chaitén on the Carretera Austral. The waters have a temperature of 85°C (185°F), and are said to be beneficial for gynecological, kidney, and cardiovascular disorders, and to alleviate arthritis. Accommodation is in an excellent thermal resort hotel. Irregular buses run from Chaitén and Coihaique, at least twice a week.

Boat trips

For boat services from Puerto Montt, see "Boat trips" in Región X de Los Lagos on pages 649–651.

Lancha *Patagonia*

Launch carrying 12 passengers, November–March. Reservations in Puerto Aisén: Agencia Rucaray, Teniente Merino 848 (332862 fax 332725.

- Puerto Chacabuco–Termas de Chiconal
- Puerto Chacabuco–Laguna San Rafael (charter)

Ventisquero and *San Quentín*

Launches with bunks for 12 and 10 passengers respectively, all year. Reservations in Coihaique: Presidente Ibáñez 202 ((67) 232234.

- Charter voyages to the fiords around Puerto Aisén and to Laguna San Rafael

Patagonia

Express catamaran carrying 56 passengers. Reservations in Santiago: Fidel Oteiza 1921 ((2) 2256489; and in Puerto Montt: Diego Portales 872 (259790.

- Termas de Puyuhuapi–Laguna San Rafael–Puerto Chacabuco–Termas de Puyuhuapi

Pilchero

Ferry, all year. Information: Coihaique, 21 de Mayo 417, upstairs ((67) 233466, fax (67) 233367

- Puerto Ibáñez–Chile Chico. Duration 2½ hours

M/N *Yelcho*

Seats for 64 passengers. Reservations in Santiago: CNP, Providencia 199, upstairs (2748150 / 3412283, fax 2052197; in Puerto Montt: CNP, Diego Portales 882 ((65) 252547; and in Puerto Chacabuco: CNP, Terminal de Trasbordadores ((67) 351106

- Puerto Chacabuco–Laguna San Rafael, Mon, Wed, and Fri at 1700, September– March. Duration 40 hours

Distances

From Coihaique

- Balmaceda: 57 km south-east
- Cochrane: 354 km south
- Chaitén: 420 km north
- Chile Chico: 394 km south
- El Maitén: 269 km south
- La Junta: 265 km north
- Murta: 209 km south
- Puerto Aisén: 67 km west
- Puerto Cisnes: 204 km northwest
- Puerto Ingeniero Ibáñez: 129 km south
- Puyuhuapi: 222 km north
- Villa O'Higgins: 547 km south

Tourism

The region is only just being opened up to tourism, and the possibilities for hiking in superb mountain country, fishing, and rafting are infinite. The best time to visit is between late November and mid-March. Note, however, that ferry services are limited outside the main tourist season, which runs from the end of December to the beginning of February.

From Puerto Chacabuco scenic boat trips run to **Laguna San Rafael** with its glacier. There is an excellent scenic road, fully sealed, from Puerto Chacabuco up the **Río Simpson valley** to Coihaique, with several buses daily.

Don't miss

☞ Laguna San Rafael by boat, or by plane flying over the Campo de Hielo Norte

Worth a visit

☞ Parque Nacional Queulat — fantastic

Worth a detour

☞ The road between Puerto Aisén and Coihaique, passing partly through the Parque Nacional Río Simpson

☞ The road between Coihaique and Cochrane, especially around Lago General Carrera and Lago Bertrand

CHILE CHICO

Area code: 067
Population: 2900
Distances
- From Coihaique: 394 km south
- From Perito Moreno (Argentina): 74 km east

Chile Chico is situated in the dry *pampas,* and its climate is similar to that of Argentinian Patagonia. The annual rainfall is 400 mm, one of the lowest in the region. The area is without rain for up to eight months at a time. Since 1991, Chile Chico has been connected with the rest of Chile by a scenic road along the southern shore of Lago General Carrera.

ℹ️ Tourist information

There is a tourist office in the *Municipalidad* (Town hall).

🍴 Eating out

- Café Holiday, Pedro A. González 111
- Restaurant Loly y Elizabeth, Pedro Antonio González 25
- Restaurant La Frontera, Manuel Rodríguez 435

🏤 Post and telegraph

- Compañía de Teléfonos de Coihaique S.A., Bernardo O'Higgins 454

✉ Accommodation in Chile Chico

See also Los Antiguos in the companion volume *Travel Companion Argentina.*

Hosterías
• Austral, B. O'Higgins		✆ 411274	$H ℹ
• De la Patagonia, Sector Chacras		✆ 411337	$G ℹℹ
• Jeinimeni, Bernardo O'Higgins 455	AEFGHPRV	✆ 411347	

Residenciales
• Aguas Azules, Manuel Rodr!guez 252	AFGHLPV	✆ 411320	$J ℹ
• Casa Quinta No me Olvides, Camino Internacional			$I ℹ
• La Frontera, Bernardo O'Higgins 332	FJ	✆ 411314	
• Nacional, Ram"n Freire 24	AFGHJLV	✆ 411265	$I ℹ
• Plaza, B. O'Higgins corner of Balmaceda			$I ℹℹ

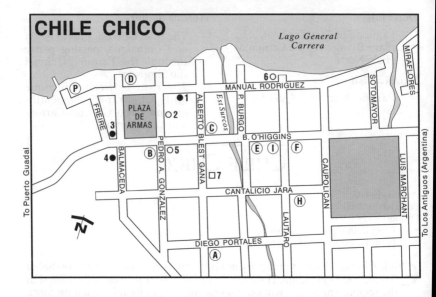

Key to map

A Iglesia
B Gobernación Provincial (Government)
C Municipalidad (Town hall)
D Post office and telex
E Telephone
F Carabineros (Police)
H Hospital
I Tourist information
P Gas stations

● **Accommodation**
1 Residencial Aguas Azules
3 Residencial Nacional
4 Residencial Plaza

○ **Eating out**
2 Restaurant Loly y Elizabeth
5 Café Holiday
6 Restaurant La Frontera

□ **Services**
7 CONAF

⌘ Border crossing

Border formalities are carried out in Avenida B. O'Higgins, next to the tourist information office. The border is open from 0800 to 2400 all year round, weather permitting. The Río Jeinimeni forms the border; here it is about 200 m wide and not very deep, and has to be forded by vehicles. During rainy periods or when the snow melts, it can rise without warning making the crossing impossible. If you are driving your own vehicle, follow a local driver, as you may not find the best spot for the river crossing yourself and accidentally drive into deep water. The Argentine border control is just outside Los Antiguos.

The road from Los Antiguos to Perito Moreno has been upgraded, and is an all-weather gravel road with patchy asphalting. This is a very scenic border crossing, especially on the Chilean side. For information on traveling to or from Argentina, see the entry for Los Antiguos in the companion volume *Travel Companion Argentina*.

✈ Air services

Airlines
- Aero Taxi Don Carlos, Libertador B. O'Higgins 270 ℂ 411353
- LADECO, Libertador B. O'Higgins 270 ℂ 411353

Services
- Coihaique: Fare $30.00; departs Tues, Thurs, Sat; Don Carlos

🚌 Buses

- Transporte Carlos Wollmann ℂ 411362 Services to Puerto Guadal: Fare $4.00
- Transporte Pilar, J.M Carrera 350 Services to Los Antiguos (Argentina): Fare $4.50; 2 services daily

🚗 Motoring

Car rental
- Y. Munson, M. Rodríguez 252 ℂ 211218

⚓ Water transport

Information on services provided by the ferry *Pilchero* may be obtained in Coihaique from Transmarchilay at 21 de Mayo 417 ℂ 21971
- Puerto Ingeniero Ibáñez: Departs Wed and Sun; 2½ hours (may be longer in rough seas)
- Fachinal, Cristal, Mallín, Puerto Sánchez, and Puerto Tranquilo: The ferry on Tuesday from Puerto Ingeniero Ibáñez continues from Chile Chico to these destinations

⊛ Sport

Trout fishing in the Río Jeinimeni and its tributaries is very rewarding. It is possible to catch rainbow trout of up to 4 kg.

⚑ Excursions

- **Los Antiguos** and **Perito Moreno** in Argentina. From Los Antiguos there is a daily bus to Perito Moreno; there is also a *residencial* in Los Antiguos, but better accommodation is available in Perito Moreno (see Los Antiguos and Perito Merino in the companion volume *Travel Companion Argentina*.)
- **Bahía Jara** and **Fachinal**: Wide deserted beaches. See Lago General Carrera on page 800.
- **Mallín Grande:** Take the Tuesday ferry to travel on the lake to Mallín Grande. It is possible to continue by bus to Coihaique on a fantastic scenic journey. Alternatively you may go further south to Cochrane, which is also a very scenic trip.
- **Reserva Nacional Lago Jeinimeni**: 62 km south. Access is over a dirt road along the **Río Jeinimeni**, which forms part of the border with Argentina. The park features rock carvings made by the pre-Columbian inhabitants, though they are not easy to find. For a description of the reserve see page 819. Transport can sometimes be a problem — check with the tourist office in the town hall.

COCHRANE

Area code: 067
Population: 1500
Altitude: 100 m
Distance from Coihaique: 354 km south on Carretera Austral

A pioneer town, Cochrane was founded in the late 1950s in the **Río Cochrane valley**, on the north bank of the river, about 5 km from **Lago Cochrane** and in the shadow of **Cerro Tamango** to the north. To the south the **Cordón Esmeralda**, nearly 2000 m high and snow-covered most of the year, towers over wheat fields and cattle country. The setting is fantastic and the hiking possibilities are infinite.

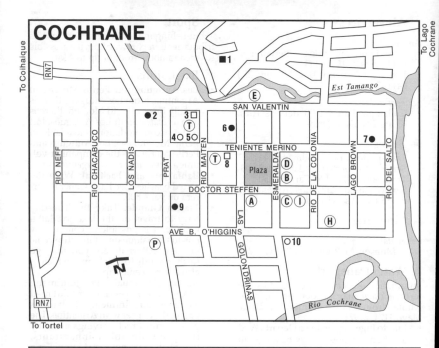

Key to map

A	Iglesia	**7**	Residencial Rubio
B	Gobernación Provincial (Government)	**9**	Residencial Austral Sur
C	Municipalidad (Town hall)	○	**Eating out**
D	Post office and telex	**4**	Café El Farolito
E	Telephone	**5**	Restaurant Rogeri
H	Hospital	**10**	Café Belén
I	Tourist information		
P	Gas stations	■	**Sights**
T	Bus terminals	**1**	Lookout
●	**Accommodation**	□	**Services**
2	Hostería Welcome	**3**	Supermercado Stange
6	Hotel Wellmann	**8**	CONAF

The town is laid out in the familiar rectangular fashion, around a central plaza. Although the town itself is not very interesting it has some tourist facilities and is useful as a base for outings to the surrounding area, particularly to Lago Cochrane with its excellent trout fishing possibilities. Food and accommodation are expensive. Most of the streets are not signposted.

The first European passing through this valley was the German explorer Dr Steffen. In 1899 he ascended the Río Baker valley and crossed into Argentina along the north side of Lago Cochrane.

In 1908 the Sociedad Exploradora Baker was formed, an agricultural cooperative that owned huge tracts of land used for wool growing.

The Carretera Austral has been extended south beyond Cochrane and will eventually link up with O'Higgins.

ⓘ Tourist Information
• Tourist information is available at the town hall, on the corner of Esmeralda and Doctor Steffen
• CONAF on north-west side of plaza

⊟ Accommodation

Hotels
★ Wellmann, Las Golondrinas 36 AFGHJ ℂ 522171 $H ▮

Residenciales
• Cero A Cero, Lago Brown 464 ℂ 522158 $J ▮▮
• Welcome, San Valentín 653 AFGHJLPV ℂ 522146 $J ▮
• Rubio, Merino 04 (near Río Del Salto on the banks of Río Cochrane) AFJPV ℂ 522173 $J ▮
• Sur Austral, Arturo Prat ℂ 522150 $J ▮. Open all year

Ⓐ Camping
There are camping sites located 5 km north at a ferry crossing over the Río Baker 1 km off the Carretera Austral; 15 km south of Cochrane and 10 km east of town. None of them have facilities.

Ⅱ Eating out
• Café Belén, Esmeralda 301. Light meals
• Café El Farolito, Teniente Merino 546. Light meals
• Restaurante Rogeri, corner of Teniente Merino and Río Maitén

ⓔ Post and telegraph
• Compañía de Teléfonos de Coihaique S.A., San Valentín 412, opposite Las Golondrinas
• Post office, Esmeralda (on the plaza)

▤ Services and facilities

Supermarket
• Supermercado Stange, on the corner of San Valentín and Río Maitén

⊕ Air services

Airlines
• Aero Taxi Don Carlos, A. Prat (Húngaro) ℂ 150
• LADECO, A. Prat (Húngaro) ℂ 150

Services
• Coihaique: Fare $38.00; departs 1200 Mon, Wed, Fri; Aerobus, Don Carlos
• Tortel: Fare $47.00; departs Fri; Aerobus
• Villa O'Higgins: Fare $47.00; departs Wed; Aerobus

⊟ Buses

Companies
• Buses Australes Pudu, corner of Teniente Merino and Río Maitén
• Buses Aerobus, Río Maitén (near Teniente Merino)

Services
• Coihaique: Fare $25.00; departs 1000 Mon–Sat; Aerobus, Australes Pudu

⊛ Sport
There is excellent fishing in nearby lakes and rivers.
Señor Ormeño, on the corner of Esmeralda and Avenida O'Higgins, organizes fishing trips with Bote Comodoro on Lago Cochrane; a full day costs $70.00.
• **Río Baker**, 10 km north of Cochrane, has an abundance of rainbow trout whose average weight is 3 kg, but specimens up to 7 kg have been caught. Fishing from river bank. Easy access

⊕ Excursions
• **Lago Cochrane:** 10 km east. This lake is shared with Argentina (which calls it Lago Pueyrredon), and fishing is permitted all year round. Average

trout size 2–3 kg; specimens of 5 kg have been caught. Fishing from boat. Easy access.
- **Río Chacabuco**: A road from Cochrane leads into this area, from which you can see *huemules* and *guanacos*. (See the CONAF office in Cochrane for further details.)
- **Tortel**: It is possible to travel to Tortel from Cochrane, some of it through the lower runs of the Río Baker, but it is a wild trip.

- **Río del Salto** into the **Cerro Cochrane** and **Lago Brown area:** Stay with local people on farms. From Río del Salto there is a pass leading down to O'Higgins. You need pack horses as there are a few difficult rivers to cross.
- **Tortel**: At the mouth of the **Río Baker**, where is flows into the **Canal Baker**. Until the Carretera Austral is extended all the way from Cochrane to Tortel, access is by plane only.

COIHAIQUE

Area code: 067
Population: 35 000
Distances
- From Cochrane: 354 km south on Carretera Austral
- From Chaitén: 420 km north on Carretera Austral

Founded in 1929, Coihaique became the regional capital in 1974 because of its central location.

It is situated in the intermediate rainfall zone, and has an annual rainfall of 1350 mm. For three months of each year there is no rainfall.

In the center of the city is an oddly shaped five-sided plaza from which the streets radiate. The main shopping street is Calle A. Prat, which becomes Avenida Ogana and eventually Carretera Austral Sur.

ⓘ Tourist information
- Sernatur, Cochrane 320, upstairs ℂ 231752, fax 233949
- CONAF, Avenida Ogana 1060 ℂ 231065
- SERNAP, Moraleda 390 ℂ 231584. Get your fishing license here ☞
- Empresa Minera Aisén Ltda, Avenida Baquedano 698 ℂ 222700/222822. This company has mining operations on Lago General Carrera and a hotel in Puerto Sánchez which is open for tourists

Mr Peter Hartmann is a well known local hiker, who has visited many outlying areas.

🅰 Camping
There is a camping site on Avenida Ogana. There are camping sites at Coihaique Alto; along RN 240 to Puerto Aisén; and in Mañihuales.

🍽 Eating out

Restaurants
- Aticos, Bilbao 563. International cuisine
- Casino Bomberos, General Parra 365. Steaks and seafood
- El Comedor, 12 de Octubre. *Parrillada*
- El Galpón, S. Aldea 31. International cuisine
- La Olla, A. Prat 176. Spanish cuisine
- Litos, Lautaro 147. Steaks and seafood
- Loberías de Chacabuco, Barroso 553. Seafood
- Musical Pub, General Parra 402. International cuisine

Café restaurants
- Cafetería Alemana, Condell 119
- Kalu, Prat 402. Light meals. Not always open
- La Taberna, E. Lillo 366. *Parrillada*
- Ricer, Horn 48
- Samoa, Prat 653

Cafés
- La Moneda de Oro, A. Prat 431. Light meals
- Oriente, Condell 201 (corner of 21 de Mayo). A bakery serving light meals, but not always open

Ⓨ Entertainment
- Disco Corhal, Francisco Bilbao 125. Open Fri-Sat from 2230
- Disco Scorpio, A. Prat near A. Simpson
- Peña Quilantal, Eusebio Lillo 145

ⓘ Post and telegraph
- Compañía de Teléfonos Coihaique S.A., Almirante Barroso 626
- Post office, on the plaza between Cochrane and Cruz
- Telex Chile, 21 de Mayo 472

Ⓢ Financial
- Fincard, Prat 340, Oficina 208, ℂ 223342/223026. Cash against Visa and Mastercard
- Turismo Prado, refer motoring services
- Cambios El Libertador, Prat 340 oficina 208 ℂ 233342

ⓘ Services and facilities

Dry cleaner
- Tintorería Universal, General Parra block 0 (between Baquedano and Moraleda)

Hobby sports shop and outdoor equipment
- Korn next to Supermercado Brautigam

Laundry
- Lavandería QL, Francisco Bilbao 160

Ski hire
- Hostería Coihaique, Magallanes 131

Supermarket
- Supermercado Brautigam, junction of Horn, Prat, and Bilbao

🚗 Motoring services

Car Rental
- Automotora Traeger, Ave. Baquedano 457 ℂ 23564, fax 211946. Four-wheel-drive vehicles
- Automóvil Club de Chile, Bolívar 245 ℂ 231649, fax 231847

- Budget Rent a Car, General Parra 215 ℂ 233888
- Hertz Rent a Car, José M. Carrera 330 ℂ 231010, fax 232999
- Hertz Rent a Car, Baquedano 457 ℂ 231648, fax 231264

⚓ Water transport
- Navimag, Presidente Ibáñez 347 ℂ 223306. M/N Ro-Ro *Evangelista* provides regular weekly excursions from Puerto Chacabuco to Laguna San Rafael from the end of December to the middle of March. The trip takes 36 hours and costs $120.00, well worth while. M/N *Puerto Edén* runs to Puerto Montt and Puerto Natales
- Turismo Mar del Sur S.A., 21 de Mayo 417 ℂ 223466, fax 223367. Operates the launch *Patagonia* from Puerto Chacabuco for 12 passengers. Trips all year round to Laguna San Rafael
- Transmarchilay, 21 de Mayo 417 ℂ 231971

🏧 Shopping
- Artesanía Regional, Dussen (on the plaza)

🏅 Sport

Fishing
- **Expediciones Coihaique**, Bolívar 94 ℂ 232300, fax 232500. Specialize in fishing trips

The rivers and lakes around Coihaique abound with fish, mostly of the salmon family (rainbow trout and salmon). See "Excursions" below for the best locations.

📷 Sightseeing
- **Museo Regional**, Avenida Baquedano 310. During December–February open daily 0900–2000; shorter hours for the rest of the year. Exhibits consist mostly of photographs taken by the first pioneers, and also of the Carretera Austral General Pinochet was under construction. Admission $1.00.
- Piedra del Indio, a lookout over the Río Simpson valley.

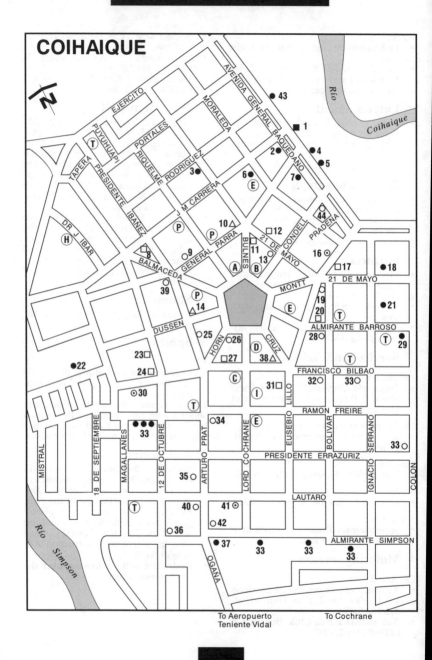

COIHAIQUE

Key to map

A	Iglesia	28	Restaurant Loberías de Chacabuco
B	Gobernación Provincial (Government)	34	Restaurant Kalu
		35	Restaurant La Moneda de Oro
C	Municipalidad (Town hall)	40	Restaurant La Parilla
D	Post office and telex	42	Restaurant Samoa
E	Telephone		
F	Carabineros (Police)	○	**Entertainment**
H	Hospital	30	Disco Corhal
I	Tourist information	41	Disco Scorpio
P	Gas stations		
$	Money exchange	△	**Tour operators and car rental**
T	Bus terminals	8	Navimag
		10	Budget Rent a Car
●	**Accommodation**	11	Agencia Mar del Sur, Turismo Prado, Transmarchilay
2	Hotel Los Ñires	15	Turismo Queulat
3	Pensión América	17	Expediciones Coihaique
4	Hotel El Reloj	20	Turismo Aisén
5	Hotel San Sebastián	23	Agencia 45° Sur
6	Hotel San Rafael	31	Expediciones Lucas Bridges
7	Apart Hotel Traeger	32	Automóvil Club de Chile
18	Residencial Serrano		
21	Residencial Puerto Varas	▲	**Airline offices**
22	Hostería de Coihaique	10	LAN Chile
29	Hostal Austral	14	LADECO
33	Budget accommodation	38	Aerotaxi Don Carlos
36	Hotel Luis Loyola		
37	Residencial Libanés	■	**Sights**
		1	Museo Regional de La Patagonia
○	**Eating out**		
9	Restaurant Casino de Bomberos	□	**Services**
13	Café Oriental	12	Telex Chile
16	Cafetería Alemana	24	Lavandería
19	Restaurant Las Guaitecas	27	Supermercado Brautigam
25	Restaurant Rincón Español		
26	Café Ricer		

⊕ Excursions

Tour operators
- Aventura, Francisco Bilbao 171 ℓ 234748
- Expediciones Coihaique, Bolívar 94 ℓ 232300. Conducts adventure trips (such as river rafting along Río Baker, or deer hunting)
- Expediciones Lucas Bridge, E. Lillo 311 ℓ 233249/23302 fax 234098
- Turavent, Baquedano 103-B ℓ 231872
- Turismo Aisén Ltda, Barroso 626 ℓ 233216, fax 235294
- Turismo Prado, 21 de Mayo 417 ℓ 231271. Car rental and money exchange. Conducts rafting excursions on rivers along the Carretera Austral and fishing trips to Laguna San Rafael. Car rental

- Turismo Queulat, 21 de Mayo 1231 ℓ 231441

Excursions
- **Cerro El Fraile:** 29 km south, at present the only skiing area in Region XI de Aisén. The ski slopes are at an altitude of 1600 m and are covered with the usual Patagonian low trees like *ñire* and *lengas,* which give them a different aspect from any of the other ski runs in Chile. There are five ski runs (Escuela, Huemules, Aguiluchos, Los Pumas, and Los Condores) covering 550 ha (1358 acres); this is big enough to let 6000 persons ski at the same time. The length of the ski runs varies from 600 m to over 2 km, and the gradient from 8 to 35 degrees. The snow is a dry powder, and you are skiing along

✉ Accommodation in Coihaique

Accommodation, especially in the lower to middle bracket, is usually filled very early. It is advisable to make a booking from either Chile Chico or Puerto Ingeniero Ibáñez. There is usually a group of at least 15 or 20 budget travelers on their way to Coihaique, and the bus normally arrives here very late, sometimes as late as midnight, when the ferry from Chile Chico is running late.

Apart Hotel
- Traeger, Avenida Baquedano 457 — (231648

Cabañas
- Mirador, Baquedano 848 — (233191 — $D for 5
- San Sebastián, Freire 554 — (231762 — $G ⚌

Hotels
- ★★★★Hostería Coyhaique, Magallanes 131 — ADEFGHIJKLMPRTUVZ (221137 — $E ⚌
  40 rooms; fax 233274
- ★★★ Los Ñires, Baquedano 315 — AEFGHJLMPRV (232261 — $F ⚌
- Luis Loyola, Prat 455 — AFPS (234201 — $F ⚌
- San Rafael, Moraleda 343 — ABDH (233733 — $F ⚌
- San Sebastin, Baquedano 496 — ADHPTV (233427 — $F ⚌

Hostales
- Austral, Colón 203 — (232522 — $G ⚌
- Libanés, Simpson 367 — (234242 — $H ⚈
- Licarayen, Carrera Norte 33-A — (233377 — $H ⚈

Residenciales
- Carrera, 12 de Octubre 520 — (231055
- Coihaique, Arturo Prat 653 — AFHJLPV (231239 — $H ⚌
- El Reloj, Baquedano 444 — FPS (231108 — $F ⚌
  7 beds, 2 bathrooms
- La Amistad, Avenida Almirante Simpson 201 — $J ⚌
  Basic; backpackers only
- Navidad, Baquedano 198 — (211159 — $I ⚌
- Puerto Varas, Ignacio Serrano 168 — AEFGHJMPV (233689 — $J ⚈
  Shared bathroom cheaper
- Serrano, I. Serrano 91 — (211522 — $J ⚈
  Budget travelers
- Pensiones in 21 de Mayo
- 21 de Mayo 60, 233

Pensiones
- Balmaceda 0192
- Baquedano: 20, 49
- Bilbao: 564, 649, 1511
- Colón 495. Budget travelers
- Freire: 119, 133, 147, 554
- Gabriela Mistral 543
- Ignacio Serrano: 54, 391
- Simpson: 417-C, 571, 647, 1055

Accommodation on RN 240 to Puerto Aisén

Cabañas and camping
- La Pasarela, KM 1.5 — (234520 — $F ⚌
  Fax 231215. Overlooking the Río Simpson valley, perfect location
- Río Simpson, KM 3 — (232183 — $E for 4

AISÉN

Accommodation in Coihaique — continued

Accommodation in Balmaceda
Balmaceda is 56 km south east in the dry pampas, and has an annual rainfall of 611 mm. It suffers long dry periods, even when rain clouds are clearly visible and rain can be seen falling in the coastal area.
It is one of the earliest settlements in this region, the original settlers coming from Argentina. Because of its location in the pampas it boasts the region's main airport. It is also an official border crossing
  • Hotel Español

Accommodation on Lago Elizalde
Lago Elizalde is 5 km south.
  • Hostería Lago Elizalde   AEFGHJKLPV   (231137 $E ▪▪
    Open October–March.

Accommodation in Mañihuales
Mañihuales is 77 km north.
  • Cabañas El Mirador. Open all year $I ▪▪
  • Hotel Continental. Open all year $I ▪▪
  • Residencial Bienvenido. Open all year $I ▪▪

wide open trails bordered with *ñire* trees. Because of its proximity to Coihaique, day excursions are possible. The road is gravel all the way, slightly deteriorating from the turnoff. From the turnoff the road uphill is open from 0900 to 1200, for the return trip from 1400 to 1800. Use of four-wheel-drive vehicles is recommended, with snow chains in winter. The skiing season runs from May to September. From the upper slopes you can see **Lago Pollux** and **Lago Frío**. There is a *cafetería* and ski hire. There are two T-bar lifts operating. Ski hire is available, and there is a ski repair shop. There are no regular buses; the only transport is provided by tour operators.
• **Lago Castor** and **Lago Pollux:** RN 7. Take turnoff into Ruta X-667 (to El Fraile) and continue for 35 km. Lago Castor can also be reached via RN 240. Fish size 2–4 kg; fishing from boat.
• **Lago Frío**: Starting from RN 7, take turnoff into Ruta X-667 (to El Fraile), a further 24 km. Fish size 1.5 kg; fishing from boat.
• **Lago Elizalde:** A 32 square km (12½ square mile) lake located 35 km south in the Valle Simpson. It is wedged between towering mountain ranges of utmost scenic beauty. **Cerro Hue-**

mules (2000 m) to the west, is snow covered all year round. Use the Hostería Elizalde (located on Lago Elizalde) as a base to visit **Lago Atravesado** and **Lago Caro** in the vicinity. These lakes are in superb location, embedded in serene mountain scenery, the mountains forested almost to the snow line. Fish size 2–2.5 kg, but specimens up to 5 kg have been caught; fishing from boat. On Lago Barroso fishing from banks only.
• **Lago La Paloma**, **Lago Monreal Azul** and **Lago El Desierto**: 42 km away, off the Carretera Austral. Take the turnoff into Ruta X–674 near El Blanco. Fishing from boat. Lago La Paloma covers 19 square km (7½ square miles). The lake lies between mountains reaching nearly 2000 m, in a very scenic wild area. Lago El Desierto is the remotest lake, 13 km further west from Lago Paloma, best reached by hiring boat in La Paloma. Specimens of up to 3 kg have been caught. The lake is a trout fisherman's paradise. Camping La Cascada. There is one bus service daily to and from Coihaique. For outdoor and fishing enthusiasts.
• **Laguna San Rafael:** A spectacular boat trip from Puerto Chacabuco through the channels with snow- and ice-covered mountains within striking

✈ Air services from Coihaique

Airlines

Two airports serve Coihaique: Aeropuerto Vidal, about 5 km outside town, is used by small airline operators and also some flights from Puerto Montt, usually LADECO. Aeropuerto Balmaceda is 56 km south, and is used for large airplanes: all LAN Chile and some LADECO flights land there.

- LADECO, A. Prat block 188 ☎ 231300
- LAN Chile, General Parra 215 ☎ 231981
- Transportes Aereos Don Carlos, Cruz 63 ☎ 221981
  Services to Chile Chico, Cochrane, Tortel, Villa O'Higgins, and Laguna San Rafael. Also a flight from Coihaique–Cochrane–Villa O'Higgins or Tortel–Coihaique, a 4-hour scenic round trip with vistas over Lago General Carrera and the northern ice cap
- Hein Línea Aerea, Baquedano 500 ☎ 232772, fax 232772
- Línea Aerea San Rafael, 18 de Septiembre 469 ☎ 233408

Services

From Aeropuerto Vidal

Destination	Fare	Services	Duration	Companies
• Chaitén	$30.00	1 service daily		Linea Aerea San Rafael
• Cochrane	$38.00	Mon, Wed, Fri	1 hr	Aerobus, Don Carlos
• Caleta Tortel	$76.00	Mon, Fri	1 hr	Aerobus, Don Carlos
• Chile Chico	$26.00	Tues, Thurs, Sat		Don Carlos
• Lago Verde	$40.00	2 services per week		Don Carlos
• Laguna San Rafael				
	$95.00			Don Carlos
Minimum 8 persons				
• Osorno	$72.00	daily except Sat		LADECO
• Puerto Montt	$62.00	daily		Aeroregional
• Valdivia	$73.50	daily except Sat		LADECO
• Villa O'Higgins	$80.00	Mon, Fri	1 hr	Aerobus, Don Carlos

From Balmaceda airport

Destination	Fare	Services	Duration	Companies
• Concepción	$117.00			
	$183.00			LAN Chile
• Santiago	$145.00	1–2 services daily	3 hrs	LAN Chile, LADECO
	$220.00	1–2 services daily	3 hrs	LADECO
• Puerto Montt	$62.00	1–2 services daily	1 hr	LAN Chile, LADECO
	$87.00	1–2 services daily	1 hr	LADECO
• Punta Arenas	$141.00			
	$190.00			LAN Chile
• Temuco	$75.00	Tues, Thurs, Sat	2 hrs	LADECO
	$150.00	Tues, Thurs, Sat	2 hrs	LADECO

distance and stretches of lush native forests. Agencia de Viajes San Rafael and Navimag both organize tours — see under "Tour operators" above and also Parque Nacional Lago Rafael on page 805 .

- **Mañihuales:** A small village 77 km north, in the wide valley formed by the river of the same name. It was founded in 1935. In the **Río Mañihuales** is good fishing downstream in a 50 km stretch down to the junction with Río Simpson. The best spots (and the easiest to reach) are near the junction of the **Río Emperador** with the Río Mañihuales. Average trout size 1–2 kg; fishing from river banks.**Lago Aguirre Cerda:** is located 15 km east in the **Reserva Na-**

🚌 Buses from Coihaique

The municipal bus terminal is on Lautaro (corner of 12 de Octubre).

Companies
- A155 Turibus, Baquedano 1171 (231333
- B4   Artetur, Baquedano 1347 (223368
- B15   Aerobus, Bilbao 968 (221172
- B24   Buses Angel Giobbi, Simón Bolívar 194 (232067
- B27   Buses Austral, Colón 203 corner of Almirante Barroso
- B28   Buses Australes Pudu, 21 de Mayo 1231 (231008
         Services to Lago General Carrera and Cochrane
- B89   Buses La Cascada, Magallanes corner of Lautaro (231413
- B95   Buses Libertad, Simpson corner of Magallanes (232244
- B154 Buses Ruta Sur, Simpson corner of Magallanes (232788
- B156 Buses San Valentín, P. Aguirre Cerda 148 (232165
- B169 Buses Transaustral, Baquedano 1171 (231333
- B192 Colectivo Río Cisnes, Bilbao 662 (232469
- B210 Expreso Litoral, Independencia 5, corner of Baquedano (232903
         Two services per week to Puerto Cisnes
- B211 Expreso Mansur, Serrano 168 (231212
- B247 Taxibus Don Carlos, Subteniente Cruz 65 (232981
- B278 Buses Del Norte, from bus terminal
         Services to Lago Atravesado–Villa Frei–Lago Elizalde; and to
         Lago Frío–Lago Castor–Lago Pollux
- B279 Transportes Mañihuales, from bus terminal
         Daily buses to Villa Ortega– Mañihuales–Mina El Toqui; one service
         per week to Nirehuao and Puerto Viejo on the border with Argentina
- B280 Colectivos Puerto Ibañez, Presidente Ibañez 28
         Daily services to Villa Cerro Castillo–Puerto Ibañez
- B281 Colectivos Basoli
         Services to Puerto Cisnes

Services

Destination	Fare	Services	Duration	Companies
Balmaceda	$1.80	3 services daily		Buses Libertad
Chaitén	$25.00	3 services per week		B4, B169
Cochrane	$24.50	5 services per week		B15, B28
Comodoro Rivadavia (Argentina)				
	$27.50	3 services per week		B24, B169
La Junta	$16.50	4 services per week		B4, B169
Mañihuales	$3.30	daily		B279
Murta	$15.50	5 services per week		B15, B28
Puerto Aisén	$3.30	12 services daily		B89, B169, B247
Puerto Cisnes	$14.00	4 services per week		B156, B210, B279, B281
Puerto Chacabuco	$3.30	6 services daily		B89, B169
Puerto Guadal	$18.50	5 services per week		B15, B28
Puerto Ibañez	$6.80	4 services weekly		B15, B280
Puerto Montt	$39.00	4 services per week		A155
Puerto Tranquilo	$16.50	5 services per week		B15, B28
Puyuhuapi	$15.00	4 services per week		Buses B4, B169
Río Mayo (Argentina)				
	$14.50	3 services per week		B24, B169
Villa Ortega	$1.50	daily		B279

cional Mañihuales. Daily buses run to and from Coihaique.

- **Monumento Natural Dos Lagunas:** A one-day hike on the road to Coihaique Alto, in dry Patagonian steppe country. The slopes are covered in low bushes, particularly *michay* and *calafate* shrubs, which produce edible berries during February and March.

- **Río Correntoso:** 24 km away, on RN 240, halfway to Puerto Aisén. Fish size 2–3 kg; fishing from banks.

- **Río Simpson:** A 2 km walk down into the valley. This spot is already over fished and fishing is more restricted. Check with Sernatur or CONAF. Fish size 1–2 kg; fishing from banks.

- **Villa Ñirehuao:** 88 km north, was founded as part of a huge SIA agricultural enterprise which took up 800 000 ha (1 975 309 acres) of vacant land for pastoral purposes in 1903. In 1969 the concessions were revoked, and the estate was parceled up among smaller landholders. It is situated in the Pampa de Coironales, named after a tree common in the region that only grows in areas of low rainfall. Indeed, the area is reminiscent of the Argentine *pampa*. Just outside the village is what used to be the SIA *estancia*. This was a model ranch in its day, and the old baronial-style administration buildings surrounded by splendid gardens are still impressive. Although it is now private property, visitors are admitted. Villa Ñirehuao is most easily reached via Villa Ortega; the return trip could be made via Coihaique Alto (near the border control).

LAGO GENERAL CARRERA

L ago General Carrera is the largest lake in Chile. Its total size is 2050 square km (791 square miles), of which half is situated in Argentina where it is known as Lago Buenos Aires. This large expanse of water has created its own micro-climate.

Major settlements around the lake in order of importance are: Chile Chico, Puerto Ingeniero Ibáñez, Puerto murta, Puerto Tranquilo, Puerto Bertrand, Puerto Guadal, and Puerto Sánchez. Chile Chico and Puerto Ingeniero Ibáñez are covered separately — see pages 787 and 815. The most important town is Chile Chico, only 8 km from the Argentine border town of Los Antiguos. The **Río Jeinimeni** forms the border between the two countries; the only way across is by ford. Up the Río Jeinimeni valley are indigenous rock paintings.

The road skirting the western side of Lago General Carrera between Puerto Murta and Cruce El Maitén at the same time skirts the eastern sector of the magnificent Parque Nacional Laguna San Rafael. To describe this sector as splendid scenery is an understatement! The road along the south side of Lago General Carrera has been completed all the way from the turnoff at El Maitén to Chile Chico, and buses are already operating once a week.

At its extreme western end the lake drains into Lago Bertrand, the source of the 180 km **Río Baker**, which in turn enters the Pacific near Tortel. The bridge over the Río Baker near the lake's outlet is a fantastic piece of engineering; it blends well into the backdrop of the glacier-covered **Campo de Hielo de San Valentín** (or San Valentín Ice Cap, part of the northern ice cap). Near Mallín the remains of paleontological animals have been found.

The ferry from Puerto Ingeniero Ibáñez normally takes only three hours but can be, and usually is, a very rough experience. Ferries are often late because of the strong winds.

Twelve km west of Chile Chico is a nice beach area at **Bahía Jara**, bordered to the west by a large area of rock.

Puerto Bertrand

294 km south of Coihaique, Puerto Bertrand is where **Río Baker** emerges from **Lago Bertrand**. It is near the crossroads to Chile Chico, and is the starting point for rafting down the Río Baker. In recent years the accommodation situation has improved considerably.

Puerto Guadal

Puerto Guadal, 265 km south of Coihaique, is located on the extreme south-east side of **Lago General Carrera**, 13 km west of the Carretera Austral turnoff at El Maitén. Up the **Río Maquis** valley there is a 25 m waterfall which can be easily reached from Puerto Guadal.

Puerto Murta

Puerto Murta is 195 km south of Coihaique, at the northern end of Bahía Murta on Lago General Carrera. It was founded in the late 1930s, and its economy is based on timber industry. There are many sawmills in the area.

Puerto Río Tranquilo

Puerto Río Tranquilo is 223 km south of Coihaique, at the southern end of Bahía Murta, on the main body of Lago General Carrera. Despite the closeness of the large northern ice sheet, the climate is benign.

Puerto Sánchez

Puerto Sánchez is 211 km south of Coihaique, on the northern edge of Lago General Carrera just where **Brazo Puerto Murta** meets the larger section of the lake. It is in a sheltered bay, protected by a few small islands from the onslaught of the southerly winds. Nevertheless the views are splendid, with vistas of the **Campo de Hielo Norte** to the west and of glacier-covered mountains to the south across the lake. Until 1986 it was a mining settlement belonging to Empresa Minera de Aisén Ltda. When the nearby copper, lead, and zinc mines closed, the existing plant was converted into a timber mill. Because of its extremely beautiful location on the lake, the former miners' hostel was renovated, and is now a quite comfortable *hostería*. Some prospecting is still carried out from this tiny settlement.

At the moment you can only reach Puerto Sánchez by boat from Puerto Ingeniero Ibáñez or Puerto Río Tranquilo, or by private plane. A road is being built along the eastern arm (Brazo Puerto Murta) from Bahía Puerto Murta. This is a relaxing spot with a pleasant climate, which it owes to the proximity of the lake, which has created its own micro-climate. Its distance from a major road is the town's major drawback or advantage, depending on your point of view.

ⓘ Tourist information

• Residencial Carretera Austral for launch trips to Catedral de Marmol (1½ hrs)

🖼 Accommodation on Lago General Carrera
Accommodation is available in Puerto Ingeniero Ibañez (page 815), Chile Chico (page 787), Puerto Bertrand, Puerto Murta, Puerto Sánchez, and Puerto Río Tranquilo.

Accommodation in Puerto Bertrand
- Hostería Campo Baker   ((67) 411447 $G   i
- Lodge Río Baker, KM 280   ((67) 232171 $E   i

Accommodation in Cruce El Maitén
- Patagonia Lodge, KM 274   ((67) 411323 $E   ii

Accommodation in Puerto Guadal
- Hostería Huemules, Las Magnolias 360   AFG   (411212 $I   i
  Public telephone. Open all year. Reservations in Coihaique: Población Prat, Manzana L, casa 13 (222812

Accommodation In Puerto Murta
- Residencial Patagonia, Pasaje España, opposite ECA   AFG $J   i
- Hostería Lago General Carrera, 5 de Abril opposite the lake   AFG $J   i

Accommodation in Puerto Río Tranquilo

Cabañas
- Jacricalor, 1 Sur $J   i

Residenciales
- Carretera Austral (formerly Los Pinos), 1 Sur   AF $J   i
- Darka, 1 Sur 071 $J   i
  Open all year
- Los Pinos, 2 Oriente 41   AP $I   i
  Open all year

Accommodation in Puerto Sánchez
★★ Hostería Puerto Sánchez   ADEFGHJPV $G   ii
Full board costs $F ii. Reservations in Coihaique: Baquedano 698 (222700

🅰 Camping
There are camping sites in Puerto Bertrand, Puerto Murta, and Puerto RíoTranquilo. None have facilities.

⊠ Border crossings
There are crossings at Chile Chico (page 788) and Puerto Ingeniero Ibáñez (page 815)

✈ Air services
- Chile Chico: small aircraft only

Air services from Puerto Sánchez
There is a 700 m airstrip, but no regular services.

🚌 Buses
Bus services from Coihaique to Cochrane call on Puerto Murta, Puerto Río Tranquilo, El Maitén, and Puerto Bertrand; three services per week. Separate services run from from Coihaique to Puerto Ingeniero Ibáñez.
Transporte Pilar runs 4 bus services per week between Puerto Bertrand and Chile Chico via Puerto Guadal and Fachinal.

⬇ Water transport
The ferry *Pilchero* connects Puerto Ingeniero Ibáñez with Chile Chico and those settlements around the lake which

are not connected with the Carretera Austral: Puerto Sánchez and Puerto Cristal.

Ferry services from Puerto Río Tranquilo
- Embarcaciones Evaristo Vargas, Carretera Austral 148. Runs launch cruises on Lago General Carrera

⊛ Sport

There is excellent trout fishing all year round. Arco iris trout up to 5kg are not unusual!

Puerto Bertrand is the starting point for rafting on the Río Baker.

✦ Excursions

The lake is surrounded by glacier-covered mountain peaks on three sides. It is a mountain hiker's paradise, but not without its dangers. Areas of interest include the Capilla de Marmol, an underwater marble cave system which you can enter.

Excursions from Puerto Murta
- **Puerto Sánchez:** Reached from Bahía Murta on a trail along the eastern side of Lago General Carrera. For hikers.

Excursions from Puerto Tranquilo
- **Cuevas de Marmol:** Locals conduct tours to these marble caves.
- **Río León:** For intrepid trail-blazers, I suggest a hike up the Río León.

Excursions from Puerto Sánchez
- **Islas Panichine:** These offshore islands consist entirely of marble which the locals mine to turn into figurines, ashtrays, etc. They are about 15 minutes away by launch. You can visit caves shaped by the erosion of the water, forming an extensive labyrinth. Some of them can be entered by boat.
- **Mina El Pelao:** Hikers can follow a trail to the now abandoned mine, a most panoramic walk. At first you pass the ore processing plant, and then ascend the mountain, past little lakes and numerous waterfalls tumbling down from the icy peaks. You can continue along the east side of Lago General Carrera to Puerto Murta. For hikers.
- **Laguna Negra:** A large colony of black-necked swans has its nesting grounds here. About an hour's walk on the Puerto Murta trail.

LA JUNTA

Area code: 068
Population: 1700
Distances
- From Chaitén: 155 km north on Carretera Austral
- From Coihaique: 265 km south on Carretera Austral

La Junta is located 2 km south of the junction of the Río Palena with the Río Rosselot and Río Risopatrón. It was founded in the course of the construction of the Carretera Austral in 1983, and is an important stopover on the Carretera Austral between Chaitén and Coihaique. It has fairly good tourist facilities with accommodation.

It is also an important crossroads to Puerto Raúl Marín Balmaceda on the coast and to Lago Verde on the Argentine border. The last two major bridges on the Carretera Austral over the Río Palena and the Río Rosselot were inaugurated in 1991.

ℹ Tourist information
- CONAF office

✉ Accommodation
- Hostería Rosselot, Antonio Varas AFHLP

Residenciales
- Copihué, Antonio Varas 611 (corner of Linch) AEFGJV (314140 $I i. Open all year
- Valderas, Antonio Varas AEFGJPV (314105 $I i. Open all year

Accommodation on Carretera Austral
- Hostal Espacio y Tiempo, northern access AEFGHIJLM ((068) 314141 $F ii. Cabañas; open all year
- Casa Azul, KM 265 (south of town)

⑪ Eating out
- Restaurant Austral, in the Aerobus office
- Restaurant Espacio y Tiempo, Carretera Austral. Specializes in trout and deer
- Restaurant Residencial Copihué
- Café Residencial Patagonia, Lynch 331

⑱ Post and telegraph
- Compañía de Teléfonos de Coihaique, Carretera Austral
- Post office and telex Chile

▤ Buses
Buses leave from Residencial Copihué.

Bus companies
- Aerobus. Stays overnight and continues next morning to Chaitén or Coihaique
- Transporte Río Cisnes

Services
- Chaitén: 2 services per week; Artetur, Australes Pudu
- Coihaique: Fare $16.00; departs 0800 Thurs, Sat, Sun; Artetur, Australes Pudu
- Puerto Cisnes: Departs 1000 Tues; Artetur

▤ Motoring
- Shell gas station, at the northern end of Carretera Austral near Hostal Espacio y Tiempo
- COPEC gas station, northern exit

⑳ Sport

Fishing
Within easy reach for sport fishermen are the following rivers and lakes:
- **Río Palena**, 2 km north. Size 1–1.5kg; fishing from banks

- **Río Figueroa:** There is a ferry over the river where it comes out of Lago Rosselot. Sections of the road are still under construction. Access to or exit from the Lago Verde area may be impeded by heavy rain, but fishing is superb. The average size is 1.5–2 kg, but specimens up to 5 kg have been caught. Transportes Aereos Don Carlos run flights from Coihaique on Tues and Fri

⬥ Excursions
- **Lago Verde:** On the Argentine border and very isolated. Ruta X-10 from **La Junta** is completed, but the easiest access is by plane from Coihaique. The area is known for its good fishing, both at Lago Verde itself and in the **Río Cacique**. Although the road continues on to Alto Río Pico in Argentina and connects there with Carretera RN 40, it is not a convenient border crossing for overseas passport holders.
- **Puerto Raúl Marín Balmaceda:** A fascinating river trip down the **Río Palena** — but take care as you could be stranded there for a while! On some private properties you pass there are thermal springs such as **Termas de Bergen**. From the junction with the **Río Dinamarca** northward to the junction with the Río Nicols, the valley narrows. Here are more hot springs, hidden among rocks and covered by dense ñalcas, fern trees, and bamboo. To the south you can see over the tree tops **Volcán Melimoyu**; you get the best views as you pass the Río Correntoso valley. The Río Correntoso has its source in the glaciers of the volcano, whose base is about 10 km away. From here onwards the valley widens, and the river spreads out to nearly 400 m. If you are traveling by rubber boat, beware of the many submerged tree trunks. Here the river begins to break up into little channels, and the lush green banks are reminiscent of tropical latitudes. Puerto Raúl Marín Balmaceda is located on **Isla Leones** in a wide bay of the river. This town was the main port for the settlers living up-river, before the construction of the Carretera Austral. Nowadays it is a little fishing village, with extensive

beaches. A road is being built up to Las Juntas which when completed will open up the area to tourism, especially the glaciated Volcán Melimoyu which looks very intriguing. You can return to Puyuhuapi or Puerto Cisnes on small aircraft or fishing boats.

- **Reserva Nacional Lago Rosselot**: 8 km east on Ruta X-10. A nature reserve with camping facilities. The northern edge of lake easily accessible from Las Juntas, 9 km east. Fish size 1–3.5 kg, but specimens up to 5 kg have been caught; fishing from boat or from banks.

PARQUE NACIONAL
LAGUNA SAN RAFAEL

This national park is located south of Puerto Aisén. The most popular spot is **Laguna San Rafael**, which represents only a small portion of the park.

Apart from plane trips over the park, you can reach the *laguna* and the San Rafael glacier only by boat from Puerto Chacabuco, 120 nautical miles south. Laguna San Rafael and the San Rafael glacier are already well established as a tourist destination. However, some eastern sections of this magnificent national park have in recent years become accessible via the Carretera Austral Augusto Pinochet, skirting part of the park from the Bahía Puerto Murta on the Lago General Carrera.

Bartolomé Diaz Gallardo was the first Spanish sea captain to explore the coast of the Laguna San Rafael in 1675. His task was to find out if Dutch pirates had established themselves in the archipelago and on the coast of what was then called Trapananga.

The park comprises more or less the whole of the **Campo de Hielo Norte** ("Northern Ice Sheet"), also known as Campos de Hielo de San Valentín. The park measures 1 742 000 ha (4 301 235 acres), of which the ice sheet is approximately 600 000 ha (1 481 481 acres). The highest mountain is **Monte San Valentín** at 4058 m. The eastern border is formed mainly by the **Río Baker** and **Lago Bertrand**. There are other immense glaciers such as Ventisquero Fierro, Ventisquero Grosse, Ventisquero Exploradores and Ventisquero Nef, most of which are now

accessible for hikers from the Carretera Austral. There are innumerable glacier lakes, such as **Lago Bayo** fed by the waters of the Ventisqueros Exploradores and Grosse; Lago Leones, and Lago Fiero fed by the waters from the three Fierro glaciers; and Lago Bertrand, one of the most beautiful glacier lakes in southern Chile, with its backdrop of the southern ice sheet behind.

The annual rainfall at the Laguna San Rafael itself is 4000 mm per annum! While this is a local phenomenon and the rainfall diminishes towards the interior, the fact remains that this national park is wet all year round. The wet season runs from December to May. The rest of the year enjoys a lower, though still heavy, rainfall, but these are also the coldest months. I recommend that you visit the park between December and

March. You will need to take warm clothes and wet gear with you, but the hikes in the area are well worth the effort. Hiking in the icy wilderness is only for the hardy and those who are not afraid to wade through cold glacier streams. There is a constant cloud and mist cover and everything feels moist; even during the "dry season" it certainly is one of the wettest areas in the region. The average annual temperature at the Laguna San Rafael is 9°C (50°F). It is slightly higher on the eastern side, but it still is cold.

But not all is ice-covered. The valleys and slopes are covered with vegetation such as *guaitecas cipreses,* and forests of *chiloe coigues, ciruelilo,* and cinnamon trees. Mammals, because of the harsh climatic conditions on the western side of the park, are not so numerous, but along the coast are seals, and in the forests are dwarf deer, *huemules,* foxes, and otters. The birdlife is richer and is represented by black-necked swans, many varieties of ducks, *carancas, fiofios,* and hummingbirds. Particularly impressive are the black-necked swans as they float majestically among the icebergs through the icy waters of the *laguna.*

Near the landing pier in Laguna San Rafael are picnic areas and educational paths leading to the most picturesque spots where you can take pictures of the glaciers and the floating icebergs. The only facilities within the park on the eastern side are near Lago Bertrand. However camping is possible everywhere, even on private land, where most of the homesteads have been occupied only over the last 10 to 15 years. This is pioneer country, but civilization is already eating into the primeval forests.

Sailing time from Puerto Chacabuco to the Laguna is 20 hours. From Coihaique there are joy flights over the ice sheet and *laguna* which take about an hour and a half to reach the glacier.

ⓘ Tourist information

Tourist information is available in Coihaique — see page 792.

✉ Accommodation

On the east the side of the park there is accommodation in Puerto Murta and Puerto Río Tranquilo. From here you can reach the eastern side of the park.

Ⓐ Camping

There is a camping area at Lago Bertrand.

⑪ Eating out

Bring your own supplies from Coihaique.

☀ Excursions

*   Agencia de Viajes San Rafael in Puerto Aisén and Navimag in Coihaique both run boat trips to the *lagunas* — see "Tour operators" in Coihaique on page 795.

PARQUE NACIONAL QUEULAT

Distances
*   From Coihaique: 134 km north on RN 7 (southern entrance)
*   From Puyuhuapi: 3 km south on RN 7

A fter Parque Nacional Laguna San Rafael, Parque Nacional Queulat must be the most exciting tourist destination in Región Aisén.

This national park measures 154 093 ha (380 477 acres) and is traversed the full length by RN 7. The 80-odd kilometers traversed by this road is a scenic route par excellence: magnificent waterfalls alternate with glaciers, some of them hanging over the edge of the cliff ("Ventisquero Colgante"), and around every bend of the road a new vista opens. Some areas of the national park have not been explored yet. **Cerro Alto Nevado** reaches 2500 m and there are at least four more peaks over 2000 m. The glaciated area is the third largest in the region. The highest pass is **Portezuelo Queulat** at 500 m. At the pass there are two CONAF huts; the lower one is permanently occupied by the caretaker, but the second one about 500 m further up can be used by tourists. From the upper CONAF hut there are spectacular views across the valley to a huge glacier ending in a great waterfall.

There are still pumas roaming the park, although their numbers are dwindling: one ranger estimates that the whole park and surrounding area can only sustain about six pumas.

Although **Puyuhuapi** is located almost inside the national park, the main access is from Coihaique as most of the tour operators are located there; Puyuhuapi is useful for the hiker. However the bus services will set down hikers anywhere en route through the national park.

Approaching Parque Nacional Queulat from Coihaique, the first impression is the sight of Piedra del Gato, the gate to the national park near the Puerto Cisnes junction. At this place the **Río Cisnes** tumbles down over the cliffs in cascades. From the national park comes the Río Treinta y Dos which joins the Río Cisnes near Puente Steffen. Notice the oddly formed rocks near the waterfall. Here you start climbing towards Cuesta Queulat, and from here onwards the vistas can only be described in superlatives. The pass is reached when you see on your left-hand side a small *laguna* and on your right-hand side the upper CONAF hut, some 8 km after the Puerto Cisnes road junction. On the way up you pass Salto del Cóndor, which you can see for quite some distance.

Twenty kilometers further north there are vistas of Salto Padre Garcia, a waterfall that drops 32 m in a free fall. From the pass onward, you follow the **Río Queulat** valley and its tributaries, most of them originating from glaciers on both sides. The road meanders downhill lined with lush green ferns and *ñalca* forests which have never been touched by man's insatiable appetite to "conquer" nature.

At Fiordo Queulat the Río Queulat runs into Canal Puyuhuapi. Nearby is Camping Fiordo Queulat, which also cabins.

Twenty kilometers before reaching Puyuhuapi is the turnoff to the famous Ventisquero Colgante: the glacier is virtually hanging over the cliff. The Ventisquero Colgante can be approached on foot on trails made by CONAF personnel. The road follows along the Seno Ventisquero also known as Canal Puyuhuapi until the little town of Puyuhuapi. The visit to the Parque Nacional Queulat is one of the highlights of a trip to Chile.

PARQUE NACIONAL RÍO SIMPSON

Distance from Coihaique: 32 km west, halfway between Puerto Aisén and Coihaique on RN 240

This national park's main attraction is the **Río Simpson**, but it also incorporates the Cascada de la Virgen with its three waterfalls visible from the road and a nearby picnic ground.

The park is 41 000 ha (101 235 ac) in area and its altitude ranges between 100 m and 1878 m. Located within a high rainfall area, its average monthly rainfall is 180 mm, and its average annual temperature is 8.8°C (50°F). The best time to visit is between November and April, but it is advisable to bring warm and wet-weather gear.

The park incorporates not only a major part of the Río Simpson valley but also extensive areas of mountains containing high-altitude valleys. It is big enough for pumas (which need a large area) and herds of fleet-footed *guanacos*. On the slopes and in the upper valleys the vegetation consists of dense forests of *coigues* and *lengas*, but part of the higher altitudes consists of steppe with small shrubs and grass cover.

The park proper begins after passing through the tunnel 15 km west of Coihaique. Emerging from the tunnel you have spectacular views as you enter the narrow Río Simpson gorge with its sheer walls rising to 1600 m. The main road passes two pretty waterfalls: Cascada de la Novia at KM 28, and Cascada de la Virgen at KM 36, both on the north side. Across the valley you can see myriads of little falls descending from the lofty heights.

CONAF has an administration center (at KM 37), which also houses a small museum of the flora and fauna found in the park. Note the stump of a 400 year old tree. There is also an enormous freakishly shaped rock sitting right in the middle of the valley, the so-called "Queque Inglés"; you can't miss it.

Regular buses run between Coihaique and Puerto Aisén, a one-hour trip from both Puerto Aisén and Coihaique.

Ⓐ Camping
There is a camping site at KM 30.

🍴 Eating out
- Hostería Cascada de la Virgen, KM 32. International cuisine

Ⓢ Sport
Fishing for trout and salmon in season. The park is good for easy mountain hikes.

PUERTO AISÉN

Area code: 067
Population: 12 000
Altitude: Sea level
Distance from Coihaique: 67 km on RN 240

Puerto Aisén is located in a basin near the mouth of the **Río Aisén**, surrounded by steep mountains opening onto a sheltered fiord. It is a beautiful location, with many possibilities for excursions and hikes. The mountains on either side reach 1500 m.

Puerto Aisén has a very high rainfall, nearly 3000 mm annually, distributed evenly throughout the year.

If you are interested in outdoor activities (such as mountain hikes and fishing), I suggest you arrange a longer stay than usual in Puerto Aisén. The town boasts excellent tourist facilities, and, of course, its location in almost pristine mountainside.

Puerto Aisén was the original port, and remained so until the river silted up. Now a new port, Puerto Chacabuco, has been built just across the Río Aisén for ferries and large ships. The two towns are connected by a modern bridge.

⊟ Accommodation in Puerto Aisén

Cabañas
- El Fogón, road to Lago Riesco 100 m from bridge

	ABHN	(332790	

Hotels

★ Gran Aysén, Chacabuco 130 Open all year	AFGHJV	(332672		
• Aisén, Serrano Montaner 57 Open all year	AEFGHJLPUV	(332725		
• Caicahues, Michimalongo 660 20 rooms	FGPV	(332888	$F	⋮⋮
• Plaza, O'Higgins 237 Open all year	AFGJ	(332784	$I	⋮⋮
• Roxy, Sargento Aldea 972	AFGJLPV	(332704	$I	⋮⋮

Residenciales

• Carrera, J M Carrera 1035				
• Gastronomía Carrera, Cochrane 465 Open all year	ADEPSV	(332551	$H	⋮⋮
• El Fogón, Sargento Aldea 355		(332916	$I	⋮⋮
• Hoteltur, Lautaro 127		(332653		
• La Marina, Sargento Aldea 382				
• Munich, Carrera 485 corner of Ceresada			$I	⋮⋮
• Yaney Ruca, Sargento Aldea 369		(332583	$J	⋮

Key to Map

A	Iglesia	**12**	Hotel Carrera
C	Municipalidad (Town hall)	**13**	Residencial Yaney Ruca
D	Post office and telex	**15**	Residencial Aisén
E	Telephone	○	**Eating out**
H	Hospital	**2**	Café Irlandés
I	Tourist information	△	**Tour operators**
P	Gas stations	**14**	Turismo Rucaray
T	Bus terminals	▲	**Airline offices**
●	**Accommodation**	**10**	LAN Chile
1	Hotel Plaza	**11**	LADECO
3	Hotel Los Caicahues	□	**Services**
4	Residencial El Fogón	**8**	Supermercado
5	Residencial Carrera	**9**	Farmacia Chile
6	Hotel Roxi		
7	Hotel Turismo		

⑪ Eating out

Restaurants
- Corcovado, Lautaro 269
- Gastronomía Carrera, Cochrane 465. Seafood
- La Marina, Sargento Aldea 382
- Posada Camionero, Sargento Aldea 1860

Cafés
- Estilo, Sargento Aldea 348
- Irlandés, Sargento Aldea 429
- La Maison, Teniente Merino 1109
- Tiaca Pub, Teniente Merino 998

⑱ Post and telegraph
- Compañía de Teléfonos de Coihaique S.A., Teniente Merino 848

⑲ Services and facilities

Pharmacy
- Farmacia Chile, Sargento Aldea block 400 corner of Serrano Montaner

Supermarket
- Supermercado Don Angelo, Sargento Aldea block 400 (near Caupolicán)

✈ Air services
- LADECO, Dougnac block 100 corner of Carrera

⑳ Buses

Bus companies
- Buses La Cascada, Serrano Montaner 235 ☏ 332644

- Buses Transaustral, Sargento Aldea corner of Dougnac ☏ 332793

Services
- Coihaique: Fare $2.00; 8 services daily; Transaustral, La Cascada
- Coihaique: Fare $3.00; 7 services daily; Taxibuses Don Carlos

🚗 Motoring

Car rental
- Viajes Rucaray, Teniente Merino 848 ☏ 332862

⑫ Water transport
- Turismo Odisea, Sargento Aldea 679 ☏ 332879. Owners of yacht *La Odisea*

⑳ Sport

From Puerto Aisén you can reach many lakes and rivers offering excellent fishing
- **Río Aisén**: From the junction with Río Mañihuales to the mouth of the river into the Fiordo Aisén. (Above the junction with the Río Mañihuales the Parque Nacional Río Simpson starts.) Salmon and trout. Easy access, as there are buses running alongside the river. Sizes 1–3 kg; fishing from boat or from river banks
- **Lago Riesco:** RN 240, turn off to the lake halfway to Puerto Chacabuco (25 km south). Easy access. Sizes 1–3 kg; fishing from boat or from banks.
- **Lago de los Palos:** 10 km north. Fishing from boat

PUERTO AISEN

To Hidroelecirica

CONDELL

DR STEFFEN

E RAMIREZ

L. COCHRANE
G. RIVEROS
A PRAT
O'HIGGINS
SAN MARTIN
LAUTARO
S. ALDEA

(H)

● 6

(C)(I)

● 5

(A)

Plaza

● 13

(E)
☐
14

ESMERALDA

Cerro
Mirador

AV TENIENSE MERINO

● 1

● 7

CAUPOLICAN
SERRANO MONTANER
CERESEDA
MICHIMALONGO
DOUGNAC

(T)

☐
8

(T)

☐
9

△
10

(T)

● 2

3 ●

4 ●

● 11

△ 12

⊙ 15

CARRERA

To Coihaique

PUENTE
IBAÑEZ

Aisén

Río

RIO LOS PALOS

NAVARRO

L. BUSTOS

BAITIWILER

LAGO

PTO CHACABUCO

(D)

To Lago
Riesco

To Pto
Chacabuco

📍 Excursions

Tour operators
- Organización Rucaray, Teniente Merino 848-856 (332862/332622. Sport fishing expeditions, Laguna San Rafael, car rental

- Agencia de Viajes San Rafael, Sargento Aldea 96 (332922. tours to the southern channels, Laguna San Rafael, fishing trips

Excursions
- **Los Palos**, **Lago Meulin** and **Lago Yulton:** A two-day tour.

PUERTO CHACABUCO

Area code: 067
Altitude: Sea level
Distance from Coihaique: 52 km east on RN 240

Puerto Chacabuco is located on Bahía Chacabuco, 15 km south-west of Puerto Aisén. The mountain slopes surrounding the bay are still heavily forested. There are scenic views over the anchorage from the hill behind.

This is the main port in Región Aisén. It is connected with Puerto Aisén by a good all-weather road and a large bridge, Puente Ibáñez, over the Río Aisén.

In 1960 the original port was shifted here from Puerto Aisén. All ships from Puerto Montt and Isla Grande de Chiloe servicing the region call at this port. Excursion boats to Laguna San Rafael also depart from here.

⊟ Accommodation

All accommodation is within walking distance from the wharves.

Hotels
★★   Loberías del Aysén, J M Carrera 50 **ACDEFGHIJLPV** (351112 $G ▪▪
•   Moraleda, Avenida B. O'Higgins **AFGHPV** (351155 $H ▪▪

Residenciales
•   El Puerto $J ▪▪
•   Osqui, near Moraleda $J ▪▪

⑪ Eating out

Restaurant
•   Hostería Lobería de Aisén. International cuisine

Bar restaurant
•   El Fogón

⊞ Post and telegraph

•   Compañía de Teléfonos de Coihaique S.A., Bernardo O'Higgins

⊟ Buses

•   Coihaique: Fare $2.80; 6 services daily; Transaustral, La Cascada

•   Puerto Aisén: Fare $0.65; departs every 20 minutes; municipal buses

⊕ Water transport

Companies
•   Empremar, Terminal de Trasbordadores. There are weekly trips in January and February to Laguna San Rafael on MV *Calbuco*, departing from Puerto Chacabuco
•   Navimag, Terminal de Trasbordadores (351111. Trips to Laguna San Rafael start here
•   Transmarchilay Ltd, Avenida O'Higgins (351144

Services
•   Puerto Montt: Fares — cabin $185.00, first-class $120.00, "A" class $45.00, "B" class $37.50; Navimag

Cruises to Laguna San Rafael
The following cruise ships run two-day trips to Laguna San Rafael — see "Excursions" below.
•   *El Colono*: Fares — first-class (PROA) $150.00, tourist-class (POPA) $145.00, economy class $125.00, cabin $220.00; departs Sat 2100; Transmarchilay
•   *Calbuco*: Fares — first-class $125.00, second-class $90.00; departs Thurs 2000; Empremar
•   Ro Ro *Evangelista*: Fares — cabins $185.00, first-class $135.00; departs Sun 2000; Navimag. Takes 370 passengers
•   *Patagonia*: A launch taking 12 passengers provides a three-day cruise twice per week to Laguna San Rafael, with a short stopover at Termas de Chiconal. Book at Sice travel, Coihaique, 21 de Mayo 417 (same building as Turismo Prado) (223466

See also "Water transport"" in Puerto Montt on page 722.

Try approaching captains of ships supplying outlying islands to see if you can participate in one of these voyages.

⚫ Excursions

- **Termas de Chiconal:** Lancha Nalcayac runs daily trips taking approximately one hour. Lush vegetation, accommodation, cafeteria
- **Laguna San Rafael:** Navimag in Coihaique runs regular weekly two-day excursions from here. Cruise ships (see "Water transport" above) sail

through Canal Costa, passing Isla Traiguén to the west and Cordillera Lagunillas (1200 m high) to the east, pass **Fiordo Quitralco** on the east, and enter Golfo Elefantes passing Islas Huemules and Isla Nalcayec to the west. Some cruise ships make landfall on Isla Orma to visit the seal colonies. At the extreme end the ships enter Río Tempano which connects Laguna San Rafael with Golfo Elefantes. See "Water transport" above, "Excursions" from Coihaique on page 797, and Parque Nacional Laguna San Rafael on page 805.

PUERTO CISNES

Population: 2000
Altitude: Sea level
Distance from Coihaique: 204 km south on Ruta X–25 and Carretera Austral

Puerto Cisnes is located on the **Canal Puyuhuapi**, just 3 km north of the mouth of the Río Cisnes. It has one of the highest annual rainfalls on the mainland — 4300 m per year, evenly distributed throughout the year.

⊟ Accommodation

Residenciales
- El Gaucho, A. Holmborg 140 **AEFGHJPV** ℂ 346483 $I ▪▪
- Hostal Michay, Mistral 112 ℂ 346462 $I ▪▪. This is run by the local headmaster and his wife
- Yorca, Dr Steffen 097 ℂ 346420. Also a restaurant

⑪ Eating out

Restaurants
- Los Cuchos, Gabriela Mistral. Light meals
- Gastronomía Guairao, A. Holmberg
- Miramar, Avenida A. Prat near Aguirre Cerda, overlooking Canal Puyuhuapi
- La Tranquera, Avenida Prat corner of Condell overlooking Canal Puyuhuapi

▣ Post and telegraph

Telephones
- Compañía de Teléfonos de Coihaique S.A., Pedro Aguirre Cerda

🚌 Buses

- Buses San Valentín, José Maria Caro near G. Mistral
- Coihaique: Fare $10.50; departs Tues, Wed, Sat; Buses Litoral, Buses Basoli

⊛ Sport

There is excellent fishing in nearby rivers and lakes.
- Lago Risopatrón, Lago Rosselot, Río Palena, Río Cacique, Lago Escondido and Lago Copa: 15 km south, can only be reached by boat. Size 1–3 kg, but specimens of 5 kg have been caught; fishing from boat. Lago Copa is more remote
- **Río Cisnes**: From the mouth of the river to the junction of RN 7 with Ruta X–25 (the Cisne Medio–Villa Amengual road). Average size 1–2 kg; fishing from river banks. The best spot

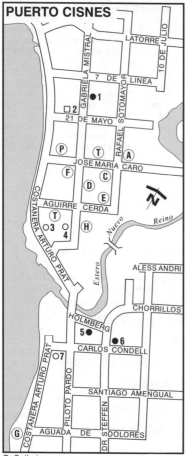

PUERTO CISNES

Key to map

A	Iglesia
C	Municipalidad (Town hall)
D	Post office and telex
E	Telephone
F	Carabineros (Police)
G	Mercado Municipal (Market)
H	Hospital
P	Gas stations
T	Bus terminals

●	**Accommodation**
1	Hostal Michay
5	Hostería El Gaucho

○	**Eating out**
3	Restaurant Miramar
4	Restaurant Los Cuchos
6	Restaurant Yorca
7	Restaurant La Tranquera

□	**Services**
2	Empremar

and the most accessible is near **Villa Amengual**; regular buses between Puerto Cisnes and Coihaique stop here

⊕ Excursions

- **Parque Nacional Isla Magdalena:** The national park lies on the island opposite the town. It is possible to make private arrangements with a fishing boat. It is completely covered with dense rain forest.

PUERTO INGENIERO IBÁÑEZ

Area code: LD 108
Population: 1500
Distance from Coihaique: 129 km north on Carrretera Austral and Ruta X–65

Puerto Ingeniero Ibáñez is located at the mouth of the **Río Ibáñez** where it runs into the Bahía Ibáñez. The bay is formed by Península Levicán, which cuts it off from **Lago General Carrera**. The first settlers arrived around 1910, many of them via Argentina. The proximity of the lake, protected from the rough Patagonian winds, has created a micro-climate conducive to intensive agriculture. Most of the private landholdings are fenced in by large poplar trees for added protection against the strong southerly winds. Directly to the east is a 1000 m plateau bearing **Laguna Huancal**, a steppe lake of the kind more commonly found in Argentina. **Cerro Pirámide**, a regular-shaped mountain reaching 1700 m, juts up from the plateau.

This is the starting point for ferry services across Lago General Carrera to Chile Chico, and indeed for all ferry services around Lago General Carrera. As the Carretera Austral connects formerly isolated settlements around the lake the ferry services are being discontinued.

The town is sheltered from the fierce winds prevailing on Lago General Carrera by the peninsula. The lake is subject to high winds which whip up the water creating dangerous waves: it is as dangerous as the high seas, and you should not attempt boating without a local fisherman.

From April to June trout ascend the **Río Claro** to spawn: these are the most important spawning grounds in Región XI de Aisén. No fishing is permitted in the section of the Río Claro between Pozón and the mouth of the Río Ibáñez in Lago General Carrera.

⊟ Accommodation
- Hotel Mónica, Bertran Dixon 29 AEFGHJLV (423226

- Residencial Ibáñez, Bertran Dixon 31 AEFGHLP (423227 $J **i**
- Posada El Chilote, Carlos Sosa 229 (423236. Open all year

Ⓐ Camping
There is a camping ground at the junction of the Río Claro with the Río Ibáñez, near the bridge.

⑪ Eating out
Because of the abundance of trout in and around Puerto Ingeniero Ibáñez, the local restaurants are famous for their smoked trout.
- Restaurant Hotel Mónica, Beltran Dixon 29

⑬ Post and telegraph

Telephones
- Compañía de Teléfonos de Coihaique S.A., Beltrán Dickson 456

⊠ Border crossing
Portezuelo Península Ibáñez Pallavicini connects Puerto Ibáñez with Perito Moreno in Argentina. This is a dirt road and not of great importance to tourists. Take Carretera Austral from Coihaique south to the junction with Ruta X–65, an 88 km gravel road; and then south on the X–65 south to Puerto Ingeniero Ibáñez. From here it is a further 20 km on a dirt road. Chilean passport control is in Puerto Ingeniero Ibáñez. The pass itself is only

469 m above sea level, one of the lowest between Chile and Argentina.

🚌 Buses

Departures for Coihaique are coordinated with the arrival of the ferry *Pilchero* from Chile Chico, and does not depart until all passengers have disembarked. Note that in extreme cases the ferry may arrive in Puerto Ingeniero Ibáñez as late as 2200, in which case the bus does not arrive in Coihaique until after midnight. This can pose problems in Coihaique, as lower-priced accommodation is in short supply. I suggest that you make a telephone booking either from Chile Chico or from Puerto Ingeniero Ibáñez to avoid disappointment in Coihaique.
* Coihaique: Fare $7.00; departs Mon and Fri at 1630; Transaustral, Buses Johnson Rossel

⚓ Water transport

Information on ferry services may be obtained in Coihaique from Transmarchilay, 21 de Mayo 417 ℓ 231971.
The ferry *Pilchero* leaves for Chile Chico every Tues at 0800 and Sat at 1100. The trip takes 2½ hrs, and may be longer in rough seas. On Tuesdays the ferry continues on to Fachinal, Puerto Cristal, Mallín,

Sánchez, and Puerto Tranquilo. On Wednesday it returns, departing at 0800 from Puerto Río Tranquilo and going via Mallín, Puerto Cristal, Fachinal, Chile Chico, and finally to Puerto Ingeniero Ibáñez.

⚽ Sport

There is good trout fishing in nearby lakes and rivers.
* **Río Ibáñez:** 4 km north on Ruta X–65. Fishing is permitted only in March. Average trout size 1–2 kg, largest size 5 kg; fishing from river bank
* **Lago General Carrera:** This lake is shared with Argentina, where it is known Lago Buenos Aires. Fishing is permitted all year round. Average trout size 3kg, but specimens up to 5 kg have been caught

✦ Excursions

* Some 6 km upstream near the junction with the Río Claro the Río Ibáñez is encased in a narrow gorge and forms three large waterfalls.
* **Puerto Levicán** on the shores of **Lago General Carrera**.
* **Chile Chico:** A lake cruise on the ferry *Pilchero*. See also the entry for Chile Chico on page 787.

PUYUHUAPI

Altitude: Sea level
Distances
* From Coihaique: 222 km south on Carretera Austral
* From Chaitén: 196 km north on Carretera Austral

Puyuhuapi is a small town at the northern end of the **Seno Ventisquero**, almost exactly halfway between Chaitén in the north and Coihaique in the south.

The town is the gateway to the **Parque Nacional Queulat**, which begins just outside. The town comes to life during the summer months when tourists flock to the park. **Lago Risopatrón**, 6 km to the north, is within the park. In the Canal Puyuhuapi near the spa hotel are

submarine hot springs, making the water in the bay quite warm.

🏨 Accommodation

Most hotels close at the middle of March.

Residenciales
* Alemana, Avenida Otto Uebel 450 AFHJ ℓ 325118 $l ⚬

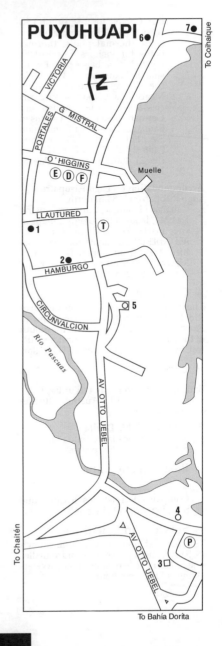

Key to map
A	Iglesia
D	Post office and telex
E	Telephone
F	Carabineros (Police)
P	Gas stations
T	Bus terminals

●

Accommodation
1	Residencial Elizabeth
2	Residencial El Pino
5	Residencial Alemana
6	Hostería Ludwig
7	Hostería Los Fiordos

○

Eating out
4	Restaurant Rossbach

□

Services
3	Supermercado

☞ • Elizabeth, Hamburgo $I ⁑. Shared bathroom. Meals served for lodgers

• Puyuhuapi, Puente Puyuhuapi, Carretera Austral **AEFGHIJKLPV** $F ⁑. Reservations in Coihaique: Magallanes 131 ℂ 221737. Open September–March

Accommodation Camino Austral
• Hostería Ludwig, southern exit ℂ 325131 $I ⁞. Open December–March. Reservations in Santiago: Amapolas 4798 Nuñoa ℂ 2269599

Accommodation in Bahía Dorita
Bahía Dorita is 20 km south-west on the Seno Ventisquero, and for visitors the easiest way to reach it is by launch from the town. There is also a track leading from the town to Bahía Dorita. The normal access for guests staying at the thermal complex is by boat leaving from near the air strip 9km south of town. Regular pickup times are at 0930, 1200, 1500, and 1830; it costs $2.50 and takes only 10 minutes. There is safe parking near the boat ramp. If you arrive outside these hours, flash your lights to attract attention across the bay so they will send a boat to collect you.

★★ Termas de Puyuhuapi, access from Camino Austral KM205 **AE-FGIJKLNPRVX** ℂ 325103. It is a very plush place and the prices reflect this. Cabins: for 2 $F ♙♙; for 3 $D ♙♙; for 7 $A ♙♙. Hot thermal water, three thermal pools; thermal baths for visitors cost $10.00. Open November–April. Excursion on luxury yacht *Australis* in the nearby fiords; boat hire. Meals $15.00. Room service carries a surcharge. English and German spoken. Reservations in Santiago: Patagonia Connection S.A., Fidel Oteiza 1956, upstairs ☎ (56 2) 2747975/2741515, fax (56 2) 460267; and in Puerto Montt: ☎ (065) 256206

Accommodation on Lago Risopatrón
Lago Risopatrón is 8 km north.
- Cabañas El Pangue, Carretera Austral KM 244, 18 km north of Puyuhuapi, at the northern end of the lake AEFGHJLPUV $E cabins for five; boat hire, lake front. Open December–March. Reservations: ☎ (068) 314122/325128. Also camping

⛺ Camping

There are camping sites near the mouth of Río Pascuas inside the village; and at Fiordo Queulat, 31 km south at the mouth of the **Río Queulat**, on the Carretera Austral, inside the Parque Nacional Queulat.

🍴 Eating out

Eating out at Termas de Puyuhuapi
- Café Restaurant La Austral, Otto Uebel. Light meals

Eating out at Bahía Dorita
- Restaurant Picada, Avenida Otto Uebel (the road to the springs)

📮 Post and telegraph

Telephone
- Compañía de Teléfonos de Coihaique S.A., Bernardo O'Higgins 39

🖹 Services and facilities

The thermal hotel has a large launch ($35.00 per hour per person) and a smaller one ($20.00 per person per hour). Waterskiing is $17.50 per hour

🚌 Buses
- Chaitén: Fare $13.50; departs Thurs afternoon
- Coihaique: Fare $15.00

⚓ Water transport

From Puyuhuapi you can hire a boat carrying four people to Termas de Puyuhuapi. This is a one-hour trip and costs $22.00 for four.

🏅 Sport

From Puyuhuapi you can reach many lakes and rivers with good fishing, mostly rainbow trout. The season runs November to May.
- **Río Palena:** Carretera Austral 45 km north. Trout size 1–1.5 kg; fishing from banks. Own transport required
- **Lago Risopatrón:** Carretera Austral 8 km north. There is an *hostería* which can serve as a base for excursions. Lago Risopatrón is a very narrow lake lying between two mountain ranges, both 1000–1500 m high and densely forested right to the top. The road follows the full length of the lake along its western shore. Although the road runs very close to the shore, you only get occasional glimpses of the lake as it is surrounded by dense vegetation. A 1200 m sheer cliff forms the eastern bank. Trout size 1–2.5 kg, but specimens up to 5 kg have been caught

🚌 Buses
- Chaitén: Fare $13.20; 3 services per week; Artetur Viajes, Aerobus
- Coihaique: $14.80; 3 services per week; Artetur Viajes, Aerobus

✈ Excursions
- **Ventisquero Colgante** in Parque Nacional Queulat: 25 km south. A visit to this glacier which actually hangs over the cliff is a must. From the well signposted turnoff on the Carretera Austral it is a further 2 km. See the entry for Parque Nacional Queulat on page 806.

RESERVA NACIONAL
LAGO JEINIMENI

Distance from Chile Chico: 35 km south on Ruta X–754

This national park is administered by CONAF, which has an administration center at the entrance to the park. Its area is 158 860 ha (392 247 acres), and the altitude ranges from 250 m to 2600 m. The road south (for four-wheel-drive vehicles only) follows the **Río Jeinimeni**, which forms the border with Argentina.

The eastern section of the park is part of the Patagonian steppe and is fairly arid. CONAF has introduced a soil conservation program, since the precarious shrub and tree cover is the only protection against large-scale erosion. The rainfall is barely 1000 mm per annum in the northeastern section, but reaches 2000 mm in the western sections over the higher mountain peaks. The best months to visit are from December to February, when the park is driest.

From the CONAF administration center a trail leads to **Lago Jeinimeni**, from where you have splendid views of Cerro Jeinimeni (2600 m high) and its glacier. Besides this glacier, there are **Ventisquero Chile Chico Sur** and others on **Cerro El Ventisquero**("Glacier Mountain"), 2100 m high. Most of the rivers have their sources in glaciers or lakes. The largest is the Río de las Nieves (Snowy River), flowing from Ventisquero Chile Chico Sur where it has created steep escarpments in its upper reaches. The **Río Amarillo** (Yellow River) is also fed by two glaciers. The most picturesque valley is the **Río Ventisquero valley** which descends from the Jeinimeni glacier and over its course forms **Lago Verde** (250 ha or 617 acres) and Lago Jeinimeni (450 ha or 1111 acres). Other lakes are **Laguna Guisoca** and **Laguna Escondida**, off the **Río Aviles valley** south of **Cerro Jeinimeni**.

The old pioneers' trail which connected Chile Chico with **Cochrane** ran through the **Portezuelo Aviles**, first up the Río Ventisquero and then over the pass into the Río Aviles valley. There are now approximately 100 km of CONAF trails inside the park along which you can hike. The rock has a spectrum of reddish to brown color which is covered above the 1800 m mark with eternal snow. Because it is situated in a fairly low rainfall area and is not overrun by tourists, it is a good destination for hikers.

⛺ Camping

There is a CONAF-administered camping site within the park.

📷 Sightseeing

The park features prehistoric rock paintings, probably made by Tehuelche tribes who lived in the area.

VILLA AMENGUAL

Distance from Coihaique: 126 km north on Carretera Austral

Villa Amengual is located at the intersection of Carretera Austral and Ruta X–25, going west towards **Río Cisnes**. It is a very mountainous area with snow covering the surrounding peaks all year round. It is perfect hiking and fishing country.

Accommodation
- Hospedaje Sr Tulio Oyarce, 4 Villa Amengual/Cisnes Medio. Cafeteria, store, accommodation

Accommodation at Lago de las Torres
- Rancho Lago Las Torres, Carretera Austral 6 km south of intersection with road leading up the Río Cisnes Valley $F ⚎. Full board, hot shower, private bath, candle-lit dining room, boat hire, horses $3.00 per hour. Reservations in Osorno: Agencia de Viajes Lagos Austral, E. Ramírez 949, local 12 ℂ (064)234137 fax (064) 235672

Camping
There is a CONAF-administered camping site 6 km south on the north side of the lake.

Eating out
- Rancho Lago Las Torres

Buses
Buses run twice weekly to Coihaique and Puerto Cisnes.
Private transport to and from Coihaique costs $30.00 per passenger, for a minimum of four.

Sport
Trout fishing in Río Cisnes and Lago Torres.

Excursions
- **Parque Nacional Queulat**: 40 km north. This is one of the most spectacu-

lar national parks in Chile. It has tremendous glaciers and steep mountains, and is the habitat of pumas and other rare animals such as the pudu. Not to be missed. See the entry for the park on page 806.
- **Puerto Cisnes**: 70 km west. The road follows the Río Cisnes which forms some very picturesque waterfalls, especially near Piedra del Gato, a rock formation just before the turnoff to Puerto Cisnes in the shape of a cat's head. See the entry for Puerto Cisnes on page 813.
- **Río Cisnes valley** to **Estancia La Tapera** and beyond: Wild unspoilt nature, with dense forests covering the mountains which reach almost to the Argentine border. **Cerro Dedo** and **Cerro Mineral** are over 2000 m high.
- **Reserva Nacional Lago Las Torres:** 6 km south, covers 16 516 ha (40 780 ac) and is centered on **Lago Las Torres**. The lake is situated in a valley formed by the **Cordillera Pucalón** in the west and **Cerros de las Torres** ("Tower Mountains") in the east. The peaks reach 1800 m and are perpetually snow- and ice-covered. It is an excellent hiking and fishing area. The park is located in a transitional climate area between high and low rainfall, and its shrubs and trees are typical of the Patagonian steppe. On the eastern side of the lake is a CONAF hut. Buses run three times a week to and from Coihaique, and twice a week north to Puyuhuapi, La Junta, and Chaitén.

VILLA CERRO CASTILLO

Distance from Coihaique: 100 km north on Carretera Austral

Villa Cerro Castillo is a small settlement located in a narrow valley on the Carretara Austral, 8 km past the intersection with the road to Puerto Ingeniero Ibáñez. It has spectacular views to the Cordillera Castillo with its icy peaks, of which the tallest, **Cerro Castillo** at 2300 m, dominates the vista. The Río Ibáñez valley is famous for the large number of rock paintings left behind by the original inhabitants.

⊟ Accommodation

* Hostería Doña Amalia. In the first instance a restaurant, but basic accommodation provided

⛶ Eating out

* Hostería La Bajada, KM 81. Located at the intersection of Carretera Austral with Ruta X-65 (the road leading to Puerto Ingeniero Ibáñez). Despite its name, no accommodation is offered
* Café La Querencia, Avenida B. O'Higgins 460

⊟ Bus services

Transportes Australes Pudu run services to and from Coihaique.

◉ Excursions

A trail runs from the township up the Estero Parada that takes about six hours with a full pack. Obtain from the Instituto Geográfico Militar in Santiago a 1:50 000 map called "Cerro Castillo". If it is available, the map "Cerro Sin Nombre" (4600–7220) is also useful.

Just 6 km from the township are enormous smooth basalt blocks on which prehistoric tribes portrayed the wildlife; particularly charming is a drawing of a *guanaco* feeding its young. These rock paintings, predominantly silhouettes of hands of both adults and children, are similar to those found in the Cueva de las Manos in Santa Cruz province in Argentina — for further information refer to the companion volume *Travel Companion Argentina*. Most of the paintings are executed in ochre, but some are in white and black, and date from between 6000 and 3000 BC.

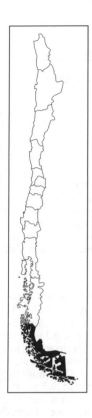

REGIÓN XII
DE
MAGALLANES
Y
ANTÁRTIDA
CHILENA

Size: 138 200 square km (including that portion of Antarctica claimed by Chile)
Population: 135 000
Regional capital: Punta Arenas
Provinces (and provincial capitals)
- Magallanes (Punta Arenas)
- Ultima Esperanza (Puerto Natales)
- Tierra del Fuego (Porvenir)
- Antártida Chilena (Puerto Williams)

El Territorio Patagónico Austral was discovered in 1520 by the Portuguese navigator Hernando de Magalhães (better known to the English speaker as Magellan) while he was circumnavigating the globe for the Spanish kings. He passed through what is now the Strait of Magellan (Estrecho de Magallanes) connecting the Atlantic and the Pacific Oceans, discovering the passage that today allows ships to avoid the stormy Cape Horn 300 km further south.

Topography

The Andean *cordillera* is the region's major mountain chain, but here it is not very high and gradually disappears as it runs south. In the far south the land dissolves into an archipelago cut deep by fiords. Some of the most picturesque areas on the mainland are around the end of the Andes, with some peaks such as **Cordón del Paine** reaching 2400 m. In the **Parque Nacional Bernardo O'Higgins** major ice caps reach right into the fiords filled with icebergs. Access to this unbelievably beautiful excursion and hiking area is from Puerto Natales; see "Excursions" from Puerto Natales on page 845.

From Puerto Natales south to the Strait of Magellan the land flattens out, with some isolated mountains on the west coast, the highest being **Cerro Ladrillero** on **Isla Riesco** at 1720 m.

Climate

The climatic conditions are influenced by the polar ice cap and the strong gale force winds reaching the continent. The normal wind velocity is 30 km per hour, but up to 150 km per hour is not uncommon. The western part of Andes and the outlying islands are very humid with daily rainfall, particularly on the outlying islands; these islands are covered with large rain forests and are now reserves such as Reserva Forestal Alacufe and Reserva Forestal Isla Riesco. The average temperature in winter is 4.4°C (40°F) and in summer 7°C (45°F). The warmest months are from December to mid-March.

On the eastern side the climate is cooler, with an average annual temperature of 6.8°C (44°F). This is a cold climate well suited to sheep farming. Around Laguna Azúl in the Parque Nacional Torres del Paine, the summer temperature may rise occasionally to 30°C (86°F), the maximum recorded in Magallanes.

The indigenous inhabitants

The pre-Columbian inhabitants consisted of four main tribes: Tehuelches, Onas, Alacufes, and Yaganes. Each of those tribes had its territory.

It is thought the Onas are descended from the oldest surviving people living in the Magallanes region. They arrived during the last Ice Age some 10 000 years ago, when Tierra del Fuego was linked to the South American continent by an ice shelf. Their home was the eastern part of Isla Grande de Tierra del Fuego, from the Straits of Magellan south to the Beagle Channel. They were hunters and gatherers over what was then *pampas*. It is estimated that the Onas at the time Magellan discovered the strait in 1520 were 5000 strong. They were a tall people, expert with bow and arrow, and fierce warriors when their land was invaded. They held out against Europeans for nearly 100 years before succumbing. The last member of the Onas died about 1970. Being *pampa* dwellers, they had customs similar to those of the Tehuelches further north, and hunted *guanacos* and birds. They had contact across the Beagle Channel with the Yaganes.

The Yaganes inhabited the most inhospitable parts of Región XII de Magallanes. Seafaring nomads, they lived on the eastern tip of Isla Tierra del Fuego from Canal Cockburn to Bahía Yendegaia, and from the Beagle Channel southward to Cape Horn. Their territory encompassed the whole of **Isla Navarino**, but they mostly lived on the seashores which provided their food. The women were renowned divers, and Europeans watched with surprise and respect as they dived into the ice-cold waters and emerged with their catch

— lobsters and other produce of the sea. A short distance from Puerto Williams there is still a small village of Yaganes, but they are on the verge of extinction. The earliest missions were those of the Anglicans in Ushuaia in 1876 and later in Puerto Williams. The Yaganes fell victim to the diseases brought by the Europeans during the gold fever which swept the island towards the end of last century.

The Alacufes lived in the extreme western part of the Magellanic archipelago, from the Península de Taitao in Región XI de Aisén down to the Strait of Magellan, including the western part of Isla Grande de Tierra del Fuego and the land rim bordering the Strait right through to the Atlantic Ocean. They too were seafaring nomads, and lived on the fringes of the islands. Their home was the wettest part of the region, with rains and snow all year round — 4000 mm rainfall a year. Their diet consisted of mussels, fish, and lobsters. They lived on the edge of the southern ice cap, which extends for nearly 500 km north from Seno Ultima Esperanza de los Ventisqueros into Región XI de Aisén. Most of their ancient tribal grounds are now incorporated in the Reserva Forestal Alacufe. Although many of them succumbed to diseases brought by the whalers last century, a small number still live in **Puerto Edén**.

The Tehuelches were probably the last tribe pushing into this region. This tribe extends from just south of Bariloche in Argentina to the Strait of Magellan. They were a fairly tall people and had huge feet. "Large feet" in Spanish is *patagón*, hence the name Patagonia for the southern part of South America. They lived in the *pre-*

Cordillera valleys on either side of the Andes, where they practised agriculture. Having domesticated the wild horses that proliferated in the *pampas*, they became ferocious warriors, and at one time extended their territory as far east as the Atlantic Ocean. They hunted *guanacos* and *ñandues* with their *bolas*, and during the last century traded with the Spanish living on the coast. With European settlement and the creation of large *haciendas*, they were forced back into the Andes, and the last full-blooded members of the tribe died in the 1950s. Last century George Musters lived and traveled with this tribe and left us a vivid description of their customs.

European history

In 1520, Magellan became the first European to sail through the Strait subsequently named in his honor. After him came English, French, and Dutch pirates. In 1558 Juan Ladrillero took possession of the region for the Viceroy of Chile. Sarmiento de Gamboa sailed in 1578 from Spain to claim this part of South America for Spain, and put a stop to the free passage of the pirates. He left Spain with 4000 settlers, but because of disease and shipwreck only 300 made it to the Strait of Magellan. In 1584 he founded the first colonies of Nombre de Jesús at the Atlantic entrance to the Strait near Cabo Dungeness, and Ciudad Rey Don Felipe 60 km south of Punta Arenas. As a result of famine and Indian attacks, both settlements perished within three years; the sole survivor was picked up in 1587 by an English pirate. Sarmiento returned to Spain to fetch reinforcements and supplies but was captured by English pirates. He never made it back to

his beleaguered countrymen, but until his death pleaded with Philip II to send a rescue mission.

In 1615 the Dutch pirates Le Maire and Van Schouten discovered the passage around Cape Horn which from then on became the major trade route.

For the next 200 years this part of Chile was almost forgotten, although the first Constitution named Cape Horn as the southern border. As a result of England's growing interest in the southern tip of the continent, as shown in its 1833 occupation of the Falkland Islands and the hydrographic work carried out by the *Beagle*, Chile was forced to take note of it. In 1843 the Chilean president Bulnes caused John Williams to found **Fuerte Bulnes** to maintain Chile's claim. Being of little economic use, the fort was abandoned in the same year, and in 1848 the new town of **Punta Arenas** was founded 60 km to the north, just where the semi-arid steppe and the Magellanic forests meet.

At first, Punta Arenas was treated as a penal colony, where criminals from the north were resettled. This resulted in bloodshed among the Europeans and Tehuelches alike. In 1852 the Tehuelches staged an uprising and killed Governor Phillipi. The penal colony was abolished in 1867, and the land opened up for European settlement. At the same time Punta Arenas was declared a free port. At first it served as a maintenance depot for whalers, but soon commercial interests and large farms, mainly sheep, were established in and around the settlement. The earliest sheep farms were established on islands to protect them from the continuous depreda-

Plate 41 Región XII de Magellanes Y Antarctica Chilena
Top: Parque Nacional Balmaceda, Glacier Balmaceda
Bottom: Parque Nacional Torres del Paine, Cerro Paine

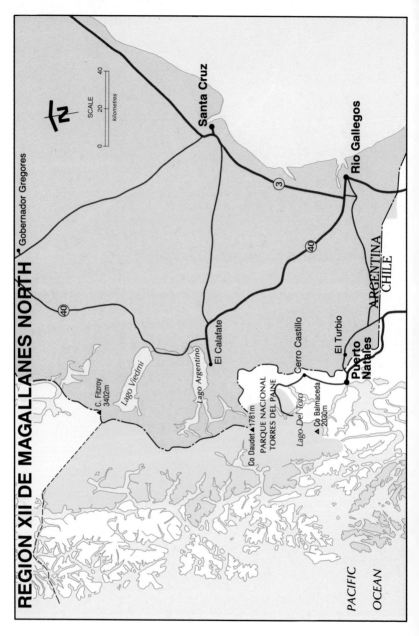

Plate 42
Map of Región XII de Magallanes Y Antarctica Chilena - North

tions of the Tehuelches. Eventually all the large sheep farms were established on the mainland, in particular the *estancias* in San Gregorio and on the Seno Otway and Skyring. The sheep barons of the time founded once-powerful dynasties — the Menéndez, Brauns, and Nogueiras. Although their power waned after the government appropriated their land, the families are still held in high regard, and are honored in street names throughout the region. Many English migrants arrived, bringing with them the necessary technology for successful sheep farming.

In 1881 Chile and Argentina agreed on the division of Isla Grande de Tierra del Fuego.

In 1883 gold was discovered on Isla Grande de Tierra del Fuego and a gold rush began, bringing many more European migrants, among them a large number of Croatian origin. To this day a large proportion of the population bears Croatian names, and in **Porvenir** and **Punta Arenas** are Croatian clubs. By the outbreak of World War I, sheep farming had become by far the most important industry, as it has remained to this day.

From 1936 onwards the large *haciendas* began to shrink, and in 1960 were expropriated by the government and the land distributed among settlers and ex-farm workers. Most of these *haciendas* became the nuclei for small towns, such as **Villa Tehuelche** and **San Gregorio**.

Economy

The region's economy is dependent on agriculture and fisheries. Logging is carried out in the state forests, and the eastern plains carry a large number of sheep farms. Coal is mined in

the **Puerto Natales** region and at **Mina Peket**. There are oil wells on **Isla Grande de Tierra del Fuego** and the northern shore of the Straits of Magellan. **Punta Arenas** is a free trade zone.

In 1945 Chile discovered oil and gas on both sides of the Magellan Strait and offshore. This provided a major economic lift to the region. Oil and gas exploration continues in and around Tierra del Fuego. The major oil and gas fields are in the eastern section of Chilean Tierra del Fuego, with oil fields and pipelines extending as far south as **Río China Creek** (running west of Cullen to Primavera) and as far north as **Punta Catalina**. The offshore oil wells run from here across to **Posesión** on the mainland. Their average depth ranges between 1500 m and 3000 m. The major oil fields run east of Posesión to Punta Dungeness. **Posesión** has a major gas refinery, and in **San Gregorio** is an oil refinery. There are oil terminals on Isla Grande de Tierra del Fuego at **Clarencia**, 76 km north of Porvenir. At **Cabo Negro** 22 km north of Punta Arenas is a petrochemical centre. Tierra del Fuego and the adjacent area produces half of Chile's petrol needs and makes Chile self-sufficient in liquid gas.

The latest achievements are a methanol production plant, which is part of the Cabo Negro petrochemical complex, and the opening of coal mines on the **Seno Otway**.

Región XII de Magallanes' economy rests firmly on petrol and gas extraction; some gold washing in the rivers of Tierra del Fuego; on agriculture, particularly sheep (some 2 million) and wool; and to a lesser extent on fishing, particularly of the *centolla* crab, one of the most sought-after crustaceans in Chile.

Fishing

The trout fishing season runs from October 16 to April 15 in all inland rivers and streams for 5 km upstream from their mouths. Over five km upstream from river mouths and in lakes and *lagunas* the fishing season runs from October 16 to February 28. There is no closed season on Lago Fagnano on Tierra del Fuego, which is shared with Argentina.

For information on fishing and fishing licences, the SERNAP office for Magallanes is at Maipú 1060, Punta Arenas ℂ 225996.

There is good trout and *pejerrey* fishing in the lakes and rivers around Punta Arenas and in Parque Nacional Torres del Paine — see "Sport" in Punta Arenas (page 858) and Parque Nacional Torres del Paine (page 833).

Tierra del Fuego

The **Isla Grande de Tierra del Fuego** is divided between Argentina and Chile. Chile has the western part. The northern part is a steppe, windswept and cold for most of the year, and there are a few raised areas in the northern and western districts. In the southern region is the **Cordillera Darwin**, still partly unmapped and unexplored. This is an immense ice-covered area with mountains up to 2490 m high, such as **Monte Darwin**. Together with the glaciers and fiords in the Beagle Channel (Canal Beagle), this area would be one of the most scenic areas in southern Chile.

The only access to the glaciers is by boat — there are no roads crossing the Cordillera Darwin from north to south. The only trail is on the eastern side, linking the **Seno Almirantazgo** with **Seno Yendegaia**—see Estancia Vincuña in "Excursions" from Porvenir on page 838.

Passing by boat on the other hand through the Beagle Channel the most spectacular glaciers include, from east to west, **Ventisquero Holanda**, **Ventisquero Italia**, **Ventisquero de Agostini** and **Ventisquero Roncagli** to name just a few — see "Water transport" in Puerto Williams on page 848. Many of them terminate in deeply cut fiords. The top of the **Cordillera Darwin** is one continuous ice shield, and the whole **Cordillera Darwin** forms part of the **Parque Nacional Darwin**. It is an area for the adventurous, the geologist, and *centolla* fishermen.

If you are attempting to hike in this area, be well prepared and check with the Chilean navy to inquire whether they will provide a lift and pickup. There are coast guard stations on the Beagle Channel which are visited regularly.

Most of the mountains drop as sheer cliffs into the Beagle Channel, and most of the mountain slopes are densely wooded. To say it is wild country is an understatement. Geologists regard the **Cordillera Darwin** as an oddity as it makes a sharp west–east bend, whereas in Antarctica the range continues its southerly direction.

Access to **Isla Grande de Tierra del Fuego** is by ferry: one from Punta Arenas to Porvenir and the other from Punta Delgada to Puerto Espora, crossing the **Primera Angostura** ("First Narrows") in the Strait of Magellan. Often the ferries are accompanied by playful Patagonian dolphins (called *toninas*).

The longest river on Isla Grande de Tierra de Fuego is **Río Grande**, which has its source almost at the extreme western end of the island and joins the Atlantic Ocean near the town of Río Grande on the Argentine part of the island.

Isla Navarino and **Isla Hoste** are to the south of the Beagle Channel. Most of the islands are densely forested alongside the Channel. Mountains, although not very high, are mostly bare at the top and windswept, with glaciers towards the western side of the islands. **Puerto Williams**, a naval base, is the only major settlement on the island, although tiny isolated settlements with *centolla* fishing boats are scattered along the Beagle Channel coast. There is even a gravel road linking **Puerto Navarino** on the extreme west of the island with **Puerto Toro** at the extreme east coast. The highest elevation on Isla Navarino is **Dientes de Navarino** in the **Sierra Codrington** at 1118 m, directly accessible from Puerto Williams on an easy day hike — see "Excursions" from Puerto Williams on page 849. Most of **Isla Hoste** is taken up by **Reserva Forestal Holanda**. The western part of Isla Navarino and Isla Hoste also have glaciers, so if you have the good fortune to travel by boat through the Beagle Channel you have the icy peaks on both sides — see "Water transport" in Puerto Williams on page 848.

Parque Nacional Cabo de Hornos is an archipelago of wind-swept islands only 100 km south from Puerto Williams as the crow flies, but it can only be reached by boat.

English seafarers have left their mark on these islands, and in their honor the Chileans retain their names for most of the islands, channels, and bays.

Transport

This part of Chile is virtually cut off from the rest of the country by the fragmentation of the land mass into small islands from Región XI de Aisén south. The only large area of land, between O'Higgins and Puerto Natales, is covered by an ice sheet running nearly 500 km between Magallanes and the rest of Chile.

By air from the north

There are regular flights to Punta Arenas from Santiago, Puerto Montt, Coihaique, Temuco and Concepción. Flights are heavily booked throughout January and February. Carriers are LAN Chile and LADECO. There are no commercial flights between Punta Arenas and towns in Argentina. DAP runs a weekly flight from Punta Arenas to the Falkland Islands.

By sea

Navimag runs three services a month from Puerto Montt to Puerto Natales in summer, starting in mid-December through to mid-March. After that services are reduced. The journey from Puerto Montt takes three days and nights, and is a most enjoyable trip through southern Chile's fiords and narrow channels. To continue to Punta Arenas, take a bus from Puerto Natales.

The Chilean Navy has ships going north from Punta Arenas, but they are unscheduled. If you are in Punta Arenas, inquire at the navy's port office whether they have a vacancy. This trip may take longer than three days, as the ships call on many outlying settlements and naval stations on their way.

By road

Many bus companies run regular bus services to Punta Arenas from Santiago and Puerto Montt. The trip from Santiago takes four days; I don't recommend it as you by-pass many of the most scenic areas and you pass through most of the others during the night.

Addresses of roadside hotels and restaurants in the countryside are often given as KM; this represents the number of kilometres from Punta Arenas.

The trip from Puerto Montt to Punta Arenas takes 36 hours. You may join or leave the bus in Puerto Varas or Osorno, but not in Argentina. The trip goes over the Paso Puyehué into Argentina, and then through Bariloche, Comodoro Rivadavia, and Río Gallegos. The return trip from Punta Arenas to Puerto Montt is during the day, and passes through the most scenic parts of Argentina, between Esquel and Paso Puyehué. Note that bus services are sharply reduced during the off season, between April and September.

If you are traveling to or from Argentina by road, there are many regular buses between Punta Arenas and Río Gallegos, and between Puerto Natales and Río Turbio (just across from Puerto Natales) and Río Gallegos. During summer a tourist bus runs between Puerto Natales and Calafate, where you can see the spectacular Perito Moreno glacier.

The trip from Punta Arenas to Ushuaia in Argentine Tierra del Fuego is more complicated. It involves a ferry trip across the Strait of Magellan to Porvenir. Senkovic buses run two or three times weekly from Porvenir to Río Grande in the Argentine part, taking five hours. In Río Grande you have to change into a Los Carlos bus to continue to Ushuaia, another five-hour trip. See the entry for Río Grande in Tierra del Fuego in *Travel Companion Argentina*.

Water transport

For sea transport originating in Puerto Montt, see "Boat trips" in Región X de Los Lagos, pages 649–651.

Tourism

The best time to visit Región XII de Magallanes is between the middle of December and middle of March.

Don't miss

☞ **Parque Nacional Torres del Paine**, easily accessible by bus from Puerto Natales. For full information see the entry for the park on page 832.

☞ **Seno Ultima Esperanza de los Ventisqueros** and **Ventisquero Balmaceda** (part of **Parque Nacional Bernardo O'Higgins**). It is easily accessible by tour boats sailing up the **Seno Ultima Esperanza de los Ventisqueros** from Puerto Natales. It is one of the most scenic tours in the area. The trip takes you around the sounds and into the fiords, and allows you close views of the glaciers and marine life. See "Excursions" from Puerto Natales on page 845.

Worth a visit

☞ **Cueva del Milodón** and **Silla Piedra del Diablo** are on the road to Parque Nacional Torres del Paine, and are easily accessible from Puerto Natales. They are usually included in tours from Punta Arenas to the national park. See Puerto Bories in "Excursions" from Puerto Natales on page 845.

☞ **Isla Navarino** and the **Beagle Channel**, by plane over the ice-capped **Cordillera Darwin** or by boat — check with tourist agencies or the Chilean Navy in Punto Arenas — see page 858.

Worth a detour

☞ **Cordillera Darwin**. Access along the Beagle Channel is possible only with the permission of the Chilean navy, which has observation posts along the channel. Access to the northern part from Porvenir is arduous, and for the intrepid only! See "Excursions" from Porvenir on page 838.

☞ **Río Serrano**, approximately 45 km long and 70 m wide near its mouth. This river forms the south-western natural border of **Parque Nacional Torres del Paine**. It begins its course in **Lago Dickson** as **Río Paine** and finishes in the **Seno Ultima Esperanza de los Ventisqueros**. It is popular for rafting and kayaking. Fishing is excellent for brook trout and rainbow trout. The easiest access is from Puerto Natales.

☞ **Monumento Natural Los Pingüinos**. This reserve consists of **Isla Marta** and **Isla Magdalena**, situated east of Isla Isabel and about 35 km north of Punta Arenas. See "Excursions" from Punto Arenas on page 860.

Of interest

☞ **Reserva Forestal Laguna Parrillar**, easily accessible by car from Punta Arenas. See "Excursions" from Punto Arenas on page 860.

☞ **Parque Nacional Bernardo O'Higgins** is the largest national park in Chile. Access to the southern part is from Puerto Natales; see "Excursions" from Puerto Natales on page 845.

☞ **Parque Nacional Pali Aike**. Located in the north-eastern corner of Región XII de Magallanes along the Argentine border, it is a volcanic area, and basalt rocks and volcanic ashes make up most of the features. Situated in what is the driest part of the Magellanic steppe owing to diminished rainfalls towards the east, this area has a desert-like appearance (bring your own water), and the flora consists mostly of arid-area shrubs and grasses. The park abounds in unusual fauna which do not exist in other parts of Magallanes, such as armadillos, gray foxes, *guanacos*, and bats. It covers an area of 3000 ha (7410 acres) and is divided into two distinct parts. The easiest access is from the border post at **Monte Aymond**, 5 km to the west, but it is a hike of 20 km to the interesting parts. Within the park are volcanic caves, of which the most interesting are **Cueva Pali Aike** and **Cueva de Fell**, home of the bats. The volcanic terrain extends into Argentina, and is easily discernible as volcanic even at the Monte Aymond border station. It is best reached with a tour operator from Punto Arenas — see page 858.

CERRO SOMBRERO

Population: 800
Distances
* From Porvenir: 125 km south-east on Ruta Y-65
* From San Sebastián: 120 km south on RN 257

Cerro Sombrero ("Hat Mountain") owes its existence to the discovery of oil and gas on Tierra del Fuego. Founded in 1958 by ENAP, the Chilean oil company, it is still very much a company town.

The town is located in steppe country 42 km south of **Puerto Espora**, from where the ferry crosses the Strait of Magellan to **Punta Delgada**, the narrowest point in the Strait. It is a crossroads for the roads south to San Sebastián, east to Porvenir via Terminal Clarencia, and north to Puerto Espora. All the roads are gravel. The bus services to Porvenir are irregular.

Cerro Sombrero is an important stop-over for Argentines on their way to Ushuaia. Most travellers arrive here on their way south to the Argentine part of Tierra del Fuego.

▭ Accommodation
* Hostería Tunkelén ℂ 296688 $H ⅱ
  There is a casino restaurant run by ENAP, a post office and telephone, and a supermarket. Most recreational facilities are indoors, such as the swimming pool, the sports hall and a glass-house garden

PARQUE NACIONAL TORRES DEL PAINE

Admission: $10.00

Located 112 km north of Puerto Natales on RN 9, Parque Nacional Torres del Paine is one of southern Chile's major tourist attractions owing to its outstanding scenic beauty and excellent tourist facilities. There are *hosterías*, camping areas, a CONAF information center, mountain trails leading through the whole park and the most beautiful viewing spots, and mountain chalets complete with firewood maintained by CONAF park rangers. The peaks of **Torres del Paine** ("Paine Towers") are by now world-famous, not to mention **Lago Grey** and **Lago Dickson** with their glaciers shedding icebergs into the lakes. The park covers 181 414 ha (44 890 acres) and its altitude is from sea level to 3050 m. It is a hiker's, mountaineer's, and angler's paradise.

Because it is relatively protected from the harsh antarctic winds, there is not only a variety of flora but also 21 different kinds of mammals. The most important are the many herds of *guanacos* (they let you approach to within 3 m) grazing in the open flatlands, pumas (which feed on the *guanacos*) and *huemules*, a South American variety of deer. The slopes are covered mostly with forests of *lengas* and *ciruelillos*.

There are camping sites on Lago Pehoe, Río Serrano, Laguna Azúl, and Laguna Verde. Accommodation is available at Lago Pehoe and Río Serrano, and CONAF maintains nine *refugios* on the walking trails. There is telephone service from the administration centre and also a gas station at Río Serrano.

The average annual temperature is 11°C (52°F), and average monthly rainfall is 90 mm. The best time to visit is between October and April. There are regular bus services from Puerto Natales during the main tourist season, January–February, taking three hours.

The many lakes such as **Pehoe**, **Nordenskjold**, **del Toro**, and **Sarmiento** offer fishing in season. Trout fishing is good in **Río Serrano**, **Lago del Toro**, and **Río Paine** just to name a few. Salmon has been introduced. Both Hostería Pehoe and Hostería Serrano are in prime locations for excursions and hikes in the national park.

ⓘ Tourist information

- CONAF Centro de Información, located on the western end of Lago del Toro half way between Hostería Pehoe and Hostería Serrano (which has a gas station). Inside is a scale model of the national park with locations of all the ranger stations, camping spots, *refugios* and an indication of scenic areas, such as glaciers and wildlife. National park maps available

ⓐ Camping

There are eight camping sites within the park, with facilities of varying sophistication, but all with spectacular views.

⑴ Eating out

Restaurants
All restaurants within the park are attached to *hosterías*.
- Hostería Pehoe, within walking distance of Camping Pehoe

- Hostería Río Serrano, within easy walking distance of Camping Río Serrano
- Hostería Laguna Azúl, within walking distance of Camping Laguna Azúl

▤ Services and facilities

You can buy provisions at the administration centre, though they are quite expensive.

▤ Buses

- Puerto Natales: Fare $7.00; departs daily December–March only; duration 3 hours; Bus Sur

▤ Motoring

There is a gas station at the Hostería Serrano, but its fuel supply is erratic.

⚓ Water transport

On Lago Pehoe there is a launch service from Refugio Pudeto to Refugio Lago Pehoe leaving Pudeto at 1300 and returning at 1430. Fare $10.00.

⊛ Sport

Hiking and climbing
See "Excursions" below.

Fishing
There is good trout and *pejerrey* fishing in Río Grey, Río Pehoe, and Río Serrano. For fishing seasons see "Fishing" on page 828.

⦿ Excursions

Tour operators
See " Tour operators" in Puerto Natales on page 845.

Hiking
There are many hiking trails within the park. The keen mountain hiker will find them described in Hilary Brady's *Backpacking in Chile and Argentina*. Here are three that I particularly enjoyed.

Río Pingo trail
Walking time from CONAF administration center to Lago Pingo: 10 hours one way. On this trail you will find accommodation in Hostería Lago Grey, Refugio Pingo, and Refugio Zapata.
From CONAF headquarters take the 18 km four-wheel-drive track west up the **Río Grey** valley. At the end of the track is the CONAF Guardería Laguna Margarita, near

⊟ Accommodation in Parque Nacional Torres del Paine

Hotels
- Explora Patagonia, RN 9 Norte, located at exit of Río Paine from Lago Pehoe overlooking Salto Chico

  ℂ 411247 $C ♨

  Open all year

Hosterías
- Estancia Lazo, on Laguna Verde   ASV   ℂ 223771 $E ♨
  Open October–March. Starting point of Laguna Verde Trail leading to CONAF administration center on Lago del Toro
- Lago Grey, at the southern end of Lago Grey near Guardería Lago Pingo

  FGPS   ℂ 241504 $D ♨
  Open October–March, 20 rooms, trekking, boat trips on Lago Grey, rafting. Accessible by car. Starting point for Lago Pingo trail and for cruises on Lago Gray to Glaciar Grey
- Las Torres, RN 9 KM 334, at the beginning of trail to the Torres del Paine

  ℂ 226054 $C ♨

  Open all year. Accessible by car
- Pehoe, KM 387 RN 9 Norte on a small island in Lago Pehoe connected by a footbridge to the main road

  ACEFGHKMPSUVZ   ℂ 411390/442 $D ♨
  Fax 248052; 31 rooms. Car rental, boat hire, luggage stored, lakeside restaurant. Dinner $X. Fantastic views over Lago Pehoe and the spectacular views of Torres del Paine
- Turis Goic, RN 9 Norte KM 325, located near Laguna Amarga

  ASV   ℂ 411678 $D ♨
  Open October–March

Hospedería
- Río Serrano, KM 339 RN 9 Norte   AELPSVX   ℂ 411355 $E ♨
  Breakfast $Y; dinner $X. Open October–March; 38 beds

Refugios on the trails
CONAF has established many shelters (*refugios*) throughout the park, which are available to hikers. They are situated in outlying and usually very scenic areas. There is always water and firewood. Check with the CONAF administration before setting out on a trek or hike. But still take your tent, as you may find that the hut you intended to stay at overnight is already occupied.

Accommodation in Sierra Baguales massif
The **Sierra Baguales** form the border between Argentina and Chile some 150 km north of Puerto Natales.
- Hostería Las Cumbres, KM 339 RN 9 Norte Estancia Las Cumbres

  FHJ   ℂ 411584

  16 beds

---

where the **Río Pingo** enters **Lago Grey**. This is an easy four-hour walk. Refugio Río Pingo is located another four-hour walk further up where the river leaves **Lago Pingo**. Spend the night here, and next day continue skirting the western side of Lago Pingo to Refugio Zapata at the source of the Río Pingo. This is suitable as a base camp for day hikes.

Laguna Verde trail
Walking time from CONAF administration center: 4½ hours one way.
On this trail you will find accommodation in Hostería Estancia Lazo, Refugio Río Verde (just before your arrive at the *guardería*), and Camping Laguna Verde. This is an easy day hike. The trail starts past the Río Paine bridge about 1.5 km

north of the CONAF administration center, and goes east into the low mountain range **Sierra del Toro**. Once you are on the plateau you have splendid views over lakes, and the Torres del Paine can be seen all the time. There are literally hundreds of little lakes and small mountain streams on the plateau.

Río Paine trail

Walking time: 38–40 hours' medium to hard walking time, starting from Portería Sarmiento and back to the CONAF administration center.

This is the king of the walks in the national park, around the peaks of the **Torres del Paine** and down to **Glaciar Grey** and **Lago Grey**. This is a 5–6 day medium to hard mountain walk! Bring all food from either Puerto Natales or Punta Arenas. I suggest you start this rather demanding mountain walk at Portería Sarmiento on the main road; however you can drive (or be set down) at Refugio Laguna Amarga near the CONAF *guardería*.

On this hike you have the following *refugios* and camping gounds:

- Portería Sarmiento: starting point
- Refugio Laguna Amarga: 2¼ hours easy walking

- Serón: 5¼ hours easy walking
- Coirón camping spot: 3½ hrs easy walking
- Refugio y Camping Dickson: 3 hours easy walking
- Refugio y Camping Los Perros: 5 hrs medium to hard walking
- Paso John Garner camping spot: 6½ hours hard walking
- Las Guardas camping spot: 4 hours hard walking
- Refugio y Camping Grey: 2½ hours medium walking
- Refugio y Camping Lago Pehoe: 4 hours easy walking
- Las Carretas camping spot: 3 hours easy walking

On this mountain walk you will encounter herds of *guanacos*, epecially on the grassy plains. Until **Lago Dickson** you follow the Río Paine which has its source in Lago Dickson. From Lago Dickson onwards the walk becomes difficult. Hikers who are not up to it should consider making this their base camp and make short trips with day packs. It is certainly a very rewarding spot. The highlight of the trip is the view over **Glaciar Grey as you descend from Paso John Garner.**

PORVENIR

Population: 4500
Distances

- From Santiago: 3190 km north
- From San Sebastián (on the Argentine border): 147 km east on Ruta Y-71
- From Río Grande (Argentina): 232 km south east on Ruta Y- 71 and RN 3
- From Ushuaia (Argentina): 460 km south on Ruta Y-71 and RN 3

Porvenir is situated on the western side of Tierra del Fuego. It was founded in 1883 as a police constabulary to control the rough elements during the gold rush years, and was elevated to township status in 1894. It was the closest town to the gold fields which had been discovered on the island. The town now has a large contingent of people of Croatian origin.

Access from Punta Arenas is by daily ferry and air services. Ferries arrive in Bahía Chilota 5 km from Porvenir. Taxis usually await the arrival of the ferry.

There is a small museum with stuffed animals and an Indian mummy, and photographs from the gold rush period. The bay still has a few flamingo colonies, although they

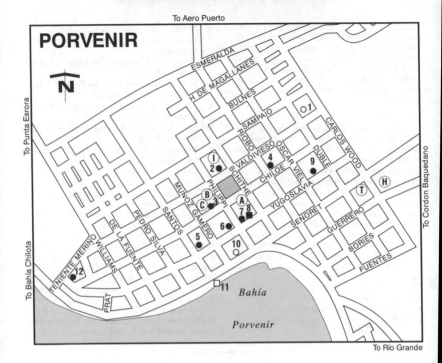

PORVENIR

To Aero Puerto

To Punta Esrora

To Bahía Chilota

To Cordon Baquedano

To Río Grande

Bahía

Porvenir

Key to map

A Iglesia
B Gobernación Provincial (Government)
C Municipalidad (Town hall)
D Post office and telex
E Telephone
H Hospital
I Tourist information
P Gas stations
T Bus terminals

● Accommodation

3 Hostería Los Flamencos
4 Residencial Colón
5 Hotel España
6 Hotel Central
7 Hotel Rosas
9 Residencial Timaukel
12 Hotel Tierra del Fuego

○ Eating out

1 Restaurant Doña Pocho
10 Restaurant Puerto Montt
11 Club Croata

■ Sights

2 Museo Regional
8 Old church

□ Services

13 Broome Ltda office

are becoming rarer. The best views over the town are from **Cerro Mirador**, which you can reach via Santa María, a road which runs around the bay.

ⓘ Tourist information
• Sernatur, 402 Samuel Valdivieso (on the Plaza)

⑪ Eating out
A regional delicacy is *centolla* crab. The female is larger than the male and has slightly salty flesh.

Restaurants
• Doña Pocha, Dublé Almeida 36
• Puerto Montt, Yugoslavia 1169
• Club Croatia, Señoret 542. Wholesome and reasonable lunch

ⓨ Entertainment
• Disco restaurant: Tiburón, Señoret 801

✉ Post and telegraph
• Telex Chile, B. Philippi

Post office
• B. Philippi near Briceño

⊟ Services and facilities

Laundromat
• Lavaseco Pingüino, Philippi block 100 near Señoret

Municipal markets
• Sampaio block 600 near Mardones

Supermarket
• Silvana, corner of Muñoz Gamero and Yugoslavia

⊟ Accommodation in Porvenir

Hotels

Central, Phillippi 298 Luggage stored, 19 beds	AEFHMPUV	☎ 580077	$G ♀♀
España, Yugoslavia 608 30 beds	ADEFGHJK	☎ 580160	$I ♀
Rosas, Bernardo Philippi 296 Luggage stored; 12 beds	ADEFGHJ	☎ 580088	$G ♀♀
Tierra del Fuego, Carlos Wood 489 20 beds	AEFGS	☎ 580015	$H ♀♀

Hosterías

★★Los Flamencos, Teniente Merino Luggage stored; 20 beds.	ACEFGHKLPTUV	☎ 580049	$F ♀♀

Residenciales

Colón, Damian Riobobo 198 near Sampaio 862	FPUV	☎ 580108	$H ♀
Budget travelers			
Posada Los Cisnes, Yugoslavia 702		☎ 580227	
Timaukel, Yugoslavia 162 For backpackers			

Accommodation on Lago Blanco
Lago Blanco is located on Isla Tierra del Fuego, 261 km south-west of Porvenir. Bring your fishing gear. For reservations and transport, ring Aventour Punta Arenas ☎ 241197.
• Refugio Isla Victoria
• Tierra del Fuego Lodge, located on Río Rasmussen a few kilometers south of Estancia Vicuña ☎ 241197

✈ Air services

Airlines
- Aerovias DAP, Oficina Foretic, M. Señoret ☎ 580089

Flights
- Punta Arenas: Fare $20.00; departs 0820 and 1720 Mon–Fri

🚌 Buses

Companies
- Transportes Senkovic, Carlos Wood opposite hospital

Services
- Río Grande (Argentina): Fare $15.00; departs 1400 Wed & Sat; duration 8 hours

🚗 Motoring

There are two gas stations on Señoret.

⚓ Water transport

Ferry services run by Trasportadora Broom, depending on tides. The ferry docks at Bahía Chilota, some 6 km outside Porvenir; taxi $2.00. If you arrive from Río Grande in Argentina by Senkovic bus you usually have enough time to buy a ferry ticket and rush by taxi to Bahía Chilota.
- Punta Arenas: Fare $3.60; departs 1400 and 1700 Wed, Fri–Sun and public holidays; duration 3 hours

📷 Sightseeing

- Museo de Tierra de Fuego, main plaza. Only one room. Has an old Indian canoe and a display of leather worked 200 years ago. Open Mon–Fri 0900–1800, Sat–Sun 0900–1700. Admission free.

➤ Excursions

Tour operators
- Turismo Porvenir, Señoret ☎ 580089

Excursions
- **Cordón Baquedano**: Old gold fields. Take Ruta Y-635 east past the military complex on the outskirts of town. Between December and March it is possible to make a round trip via **Bahía Inútil**. Outside this time it is difficult, and I suggest you return to Porvenir the same way. About 16 km from town you reach the highest point on

the coast and from here you have panoramic views over the Strait of Magellan. Visit some of the old mines and the complex of dikes and water channels constructed to pan for gold. All the rivers here are gold-bearing and some old-timers still eke out a living by panning for gold — you may even try it yourself.
- **Lago Blanco**: This lake is situated 240 km south-east. It is best reached via Camerón, the turnoff south being at Onaisin. The lake is an angler's paradise. The rivers are full of beavers which were introduced from Canada and have now reached plague-like proportions. The Cordillera Darwin is within striking distance, but walks among the glaciers and mountain peaks should only be attempted by the well-prepared. If you intend to go hiking, notify the *carabineros* — there are police posts in Camerón and in Guanacos. On Lago Blanco is an unserviced camping spot. Except for some lone fishermen you are on your own. Bring your supplies with you from Porvenir. This is wild country unspoilt by mass tourism.
- **Estancia Vicuña** and beyond to the **Cordillera Darwin**: 260 km to Estancia Vicuña. For the adventurous trailblazer. This trip is best undertaken with a four-wheel-drive vehicle. However, if you do not have your own transport, check with the *carabineros* to see if you can hitch a lift. Otherwise, Transporte Senkovic runs two buses a week to Río Grande which stop in Onaisin. From here on you will have to rely on hitching a lift with logging trucks and private vehicles to continue further south. From Onaisin it is 46 km to Camerón, and from there to Estancia Vicuña another 98 km. In **Valle Castor** ("Beaver Valley") there are unserviced camping areas. At Valle Castor the subantarctic Magellanic forests begin, extending south towards Seno Almirantazgo and beyond. This is beaver country. There is plenty of firewood, and you can drink the water from the river. From here onwards the only roads are logging trails to **Río Bellavista** and **Lago Fagnano**. From Lago Fagnano the trail continues west

along the **Río Azzopardi**. A ferry runs from near the mouth of this river into the **Seno Almirantazgo** for the benefit of the Estancia Almirantazgo and logging parties.

• **Ushuaia** in Argentina via San Sebastián and Río Grande.

PUERTO NATALES

Population: 18 000
Altitude: Sea level
Distances
• From Punta Arenas: 247 km south on RN 9
• From Río Turbio (Argentina): 48 km east (via Casas Viejas)
• From Río Gallegos (Argentina): 256 km east (via Casas Viejas and Río Turbio)
• From Santiago: 3285 km north via Argentina

Puerto Natales is located on the **Seno Ultima Esperanza de los Ventisqueros**, at the entrance to the magnificent fiord in **Parque Nacional Balmaceda** adjoining the **Parque Nacional Torres del Paine**. The entrance from the Pacific Ocean to the sound is through **Canal Kirke**.

The earliest explorers were Spanish ships such as that of Juan Ladrilleros in 1557, and Sarmiento de Gamboa visited these waters. This area of Región XII de Magallanes was one of the last settled by Europeans, as the Tehuelches living in these parts around the turn of the century were still considered dangerous.

During World War I the German destroyer *Dresden* hid for some time in the nearby fiords.

Puerto Natales was founded in 1912, and soon became the center of the sheep and cattle farms that sprang up in the hinterland. The first large *estancias* were lease-holdings and were expropriated by the government in the 1960s. Many large ex-*haciendas* now serve as *hosterías* for travellers.

The coal mines across the border in Río Turbio employ many Chileans.

The town is superbly located on the Seno Ultima Esperanza de los Ventisqueros, with splendid vistas of the snow-covered Torres del Paine peaks and the glaciers of the southern ice cap. Tourism is now the economic backbone of the town, as it is the starting point for magnificent trips into the fiords and the Parque Nacional Torres del Paine. It has excellent tourist facilities. The best time to visit is between middle of December and the middle of March. During January and February hotel prices are high and booking is advisable.

ⓘ Tourist information
• Sernatur, Eberhard 445 ℃ 411439

Ⓐ Camping
There is a camping site 22 km north, directly beside Lago Sofia. No facilities and no fees.

ⓘⓘ Eating out

Restaurants
• Centro Español, Magallanes 247
• Don Alvarito, Blanco Encalada 915
• La Bahía, Teniente Serrano 434
• Los Glaciares, Eberhard 261
• Mary Loly, M. Baquedano 615
• Rey Mar, M. Baquedano 414 . Seafood

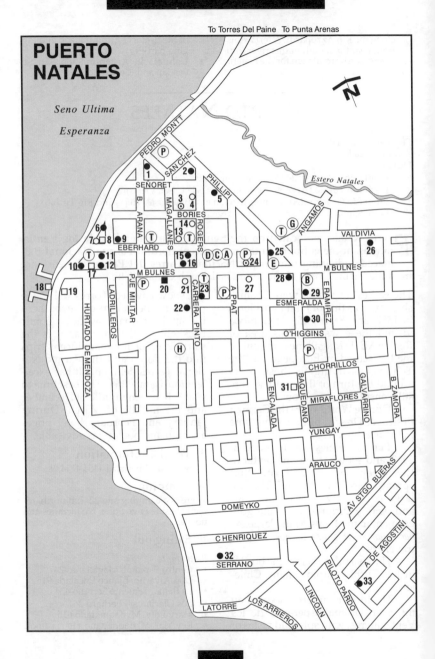

PUERTO NATALES

Seno Ultima

Esperanza

To Torres Del Paine To Punta Arenas

Estero Natales

Key to map

A	Iglesia	26	Hotel Austral
B	Gobernación Provincial (Government)	28	Hostal Lady Florence Dixie
		29	Hotel Laguna Azul
C	Municipalidad (Town hall)	30	Hosterí Rey Mar
D	Post office and telex	32	Residencial La Bahía
E	Telephone		
F	Carabineros (Police)	○	**Eating out**
G	Mercado Municipal (Market)	3	Restaurant Los Glaciares
H	Hospital	7	Restaurant Marítimo
I	Tourist information	13	Restaurant Ultima Esperanza
P	Gas stations	14	Café Midas
$	Money exchange	21	Restaurant La Burbuja
T	Bus terminals	27	Restaurant La Tranquera
●	**Accommodation**	⊙	**Entertainment**
1	Hotel Juan Ladrilleros	4	Casino
2	Hostal Sir Francis Drake	▲	**Airline offices**
5	Hostal Los Pinos	24	LADECO
6	Hostal Costanera		
9	Hotel Los Glaciares	■	**Sights**
10	Hotel Costa Australis	20	Museo Municipal
11	Hotel Palace		
12	Residencial Grey	□	**Services**
15	Hotel Natalino	8	Cutter 21 de Mayo
16	Hotel Carahué	17	Nandú Artesanía
22	Hotel Blanquita	18	Capitanía de Puerto
23	Hotel Bulnes	19	Navimag
25	Hotel Melissa	31	Supermarket

- Ultima Esperanza, Eberhard 354

Cafeterías
- Midas, Tomás Rogers 169

Café restaurants
- Costanera, Ladrilleros 105
- El Marítimo, Pedro Montt 214 near Bulnes
- La Tranquera, Bulnes 579, near Arturo Prat

⊤ Entertainment
- Casino de Puerto Natales

▣ Post and telegraph

Telephone
- CTC, telephone, Blanco Encalada block 200 near Philippi
- Telex Chile, Eberhard 429 near Thomas Rogers

$ Financial
- Casa de Cambio Stop Cambios, Baquedano 340 ℂ 411393

- Casa de Cambio Andes Patagónicos, Blanco Encalada 226 ℂ 411594
- Sur Cambios, Blanco Encalada 238 ℂ 411303

▤ Services and facilities

Camping equipment hire
- Aventur, Eberhard 57 . They also have an office in Calafate in Argentina on Avenida del Libertador

Dry cleaner
- Tienda Lavaseco, corner of Bulnes and Blanco Encalada

Supermarket
- Supermercado Chelech Velásquez, 610 Baquedano

⋈ Border crossing

Puerto Natales is close to two important border crossings into neighboring Argentina: Control Fronterizo Casas Viejas 20 km east to El Turbio and Control Fronterizo Dorotea 20 km north east to Dorotea. Dorotea is open 0500–2400 to allow

✉ Accommodation in Puerto Natales

Hostales
- Costanera, Ladrilleros 105   S   ☏ 411273 $H ♟♟
  Shared bath; 11 beds
- Lady Florence Dixie, Bulnes 659   ADHPSV   ☏ 411158 $F ♟♟
  Fax 411943
- Los Pinos, Philippi 449   P   ☏ 411326 $H ♟♟
- Melissa, Blanco Encalada 258   PS   ☏ 411944 $H ♟♟
  17 beds
- Sir Francis Drake, Philippi 383   EGHJKPS   ☏ 411553 $F ♟♟
  16 beds

Hotels

★★★★Costa Australis, Pedro Montt corner of Bulnes
     ADEFGHKPV
- Austral, Valdivia 955   AEFGHMPVXY   ☏ 411134/411593 $G ♟♟
  20 rooms. Eduardo speaks English
- Blanquita,Pinto 409   HJPS   ☏ 411674 $G ♟♟
  23 beds
- Capitán Eberhard, Pedro Montt 25   AEFGHLMPSUVXZ   ☏ 411208/209 $D ♟♟
  Luggage stored; 49 beds
- Palace, Ladrilleros 209   AEFGHKLMPUVXZ   ☏ 411134 $F ♟♟
  Luggage stored; 40 beds
- Glaciares, Eberhard 104   DEHJKPST   ☏ 412189 $E ♟♟
  Fax 411452; 31 beds
- Juan Ladrilleros, Pedro Montt 161   AEFGKLPSX   ☏ 411652 $F ♟♟
  Luggage stored. Also travel agency and car rental agency, dinner $X; fax 412109; 28 beds
- Natalino, Eberhard 371   AEFGKMPSV   ☏ 411968 $G ♟♟
  Luggage stored; 30 beds

Residenciales
- Alvarado, Zamora 558   PS $H ♟♟
- Bulnes, Bulnes 407   AEFGHKPV   ☏ 411307/411652 $H ♟
  Luggage stored; 13 beds
- Carahué, M. Bulnes 370   ☏ 411339 $I ♟
  Budget travelers; 25 beds
- Dickson, M. Bulnes 307   ☏ 411218 $J ♟
  Backpackers; 9 beds
- Don Bosco, Padre Rosas 1430   S   ☏ 412335 $J ♟
- El Conquistador, Baquedano 745   S   ☏ 412085 $J ♟
  Shared bathroom, backpackers; 12 beds
- Grey, Bulnes 90   ☏ 411542 $I ♟♟
  Budget travelers
- La Bahía, Serrano 434   FHJ   ☏ 411297 $I ♟
  Budget travelers; 12 beds
- La Florida, O'Higgins 413   HJV   ☏ 411361
  Budget travelers; 30 beds
- Lago Pingo, Bulnes 808   HJS   ☏ 411026 $J ♟
  Shared bathroom, backpackers; 20 beds
- Los Lagos, Bulnes 1082   HJS $J ♟
  Shared bathroom, backpackers; 11 beds
- Magallanes, Magallanes 01   HJS $J ♟
  Shared bathroom, backpackers; 10 beds

Accommodation in Puerto Natales — continued

- Miramar, Barros Arana 299 $J ℹ
  Shared bathroom, backpackers
- Mundial, Bries 315   JS $J ℹ
  Shared bathroom, backpackers; 32 beds
- Ritz, Pinto 439   S $J ℹ
  Shared bathroom, backpackers; 12 beds
- Rosita, A. Prat 367   HJS   ℂ 412259 $J ℹ
  Shared bathroom, backpackers; 10 beds
- Sutherland, Barros Arana 155   HJS $J ℹ
  Shared bathroom, backpackers; 11 beds
- Temuco, Ramírez 310   EPV   ℂ 411120 $J ℹ
  Luggage stored, backpackers; 20 beds

Hospedajes
- Bruna Mardones, Pasaje Don Bosco 14 (off Phillipi) $J ℹ
  Thin walls; backpackers; 15 beds
- Cecilia, T. Rogers 54   ℂ 411797
  15 beds
- Chila, I. Carrera Pinto 442   ℂ 412328
  11 beds

Accommodation south of town
- Motel Llanuras de Diana, KM 215 Ruta 9
                                     DEFGHJKLMOPV   ℂ 411540 $D ⅲ
  24 km south of town on the Río Tranquilo. Luggage stored. $73.00 cabin for 6; breakfast
  $Y, dinner $X. 40 beds. Open December–March. Fax 244729; 52 beds

Accommodation north of town

Hotels
- Hotel Tres Pasos, RN 9 KM 290   DEFGHJKOPSV   ℂ 221627 $G ⅲ
  40 km north of Puerto Natales; fax 221627; 52 beds

Hosterías
- Cisne Cuello Negro, KM 257 RN 9 Norte
                                     EFGHKLPVX   ℂ 411498 $E ⅲ
  At Puerto Bories, 8 km north of Puerto Natales. Dinner $X. 44 rooms; fax 248052
- Complejo Turístico Kotenk-Aike, KM 2 Puerto Bories
- Patagonia Inn, FKM 257 RN 9 Norte EFGHKLPUV   ℂ 242134 $E ⅲ
  In Sector Dos Lagunas, 26 km north of town. Luggage stored; 15 rooms

Accommodation in Cerro Castillo
Cerro Castillo is 63 km north of Puerto Natales. It was formerly part of the Estancia
Cerro Castillo, which was founded towards the end of the last century and was one
of the largest in Patagonia. Now it has a population of 400. The border is 7 km east of
the settlement. Passport control Cancha Carrera is just after the *hostería*. The border
is open from December to the end of March. Most buses going to Calafate in Argentina
use this pass. Regular daily buses run to Puerto Natales.
- Hostería El Pionero, KM 315 RN 9 Norte
                                     EFGHKPUVXZ   ℂ 411307/646 $F ⅲ
  38 beds

Chilean mine workers to work shifts in the nearby coal mines. Casas Viejas is open 0800–2200.

✈ Air services
• LADECO, M. Bulnes 530 ☎ 411236

🚗 Motoring
For gas stations, see city map.

Car rental
• Andes Patagónicos, Blanco Encalada 226 ☎ 411594. Also hires equipment and exchanges money

⚓ Water transport

Vessels

Cutter 21 de Mayo and Alberto de Agostini
Cruise boats. For information, contact Sr Juan Carlos Alvarez, Ladrilleros 171 ☎ 411176 or Eberhard 564 ☎ 411978.

• Puerto Natales–Seno Ultima Esperanza. Duration 8–10 hours. Departs daily 0900, December–March. Fare $27.50
• Puerto Natales–Seno Ultima Esperanza. Duration: 10 hours. Departs daily at 0900, December–March
• Charter for rest of the year

Trinidad
Motorised sailing boat. Day tours for 20 passengers; longer cruises for 9 passengers. Information available from Lautaro Navarro 1038-A ☎ 244448, fax 211504.
• Puerto Natales–Seno Ultima Esperanza–Puerto Natales. Duration 1 or 2 days. Runs all year
• Puerto Natales–Angostura Kirke–Canal de las Montañas–Puerto Natales. Duration 3 days
• Puerto Natales–Canal Valdés–Angostura Kirke–Fiordos Peel–Puerto Natales

🚌 Buses from Puerto Natales
Puerto Natales has no central bus terminal. Most companies however are concentrated around Calle Baquedano.

Companies
• B20   Buses Alvarez Gómez, Baquedano 244
• B47   Buses COOTRA, Baquedano 419
• B65   Buses Fernández, Eberhard 555 ☎ 411111
• B158 Bus Sur, Baquedano 534 ☎ 411325
• B182 Buses Victoria Sur, M. Baquedano 384 ☎ 411957
• B213 Expreso San Ceferino, Baquedano 244 ☎ 411349
• B268 Turisur, corner of Baquedano and Valdivia ☎ 411202

Services

Destination	Fare	Services	Hours	Companies
• Calafate	$30.00	Mon, Wed, Fri, Sat		B158
• Casas Viejas (border post)	$1.30			B20, B213
• Parque Nacional Torres del Paine	$7.00	daily		B158
Returns 1130				
• Puerto Mont	$68.00	3 services per week		B65, B158
• Punta Arenas	$5.00	6 services daily		B65, B158, B182
• Río Gallegos via Río Turbio (Argentina)	$12.00	Wed, Fri, Sun		B20, B213
Returns from Río Gallegos Tues, Thurs, Sat				
• Río Turbio (Argentina)	$1.90	4–14 services daily		B20, B47, B213, B268
Buses go via Paso Casas Viejas				

Companies

*   Navimag, Pedro Montt 380 (411287. The motor vessel *Tierra del Fuego* runs between Puerto Montt and Puerto Natales every 10 days, calling on Puerto Chacabuco (the port of Aisén) and Puerto Edén. There are three services per month. A first-class berth costs $130.00; a first-class seat $108.00; and a second-class seat $90.00. The trip takes approximately 80 hours (three days and three nights). For further details check at Puerto Montt and/or Santiago. Note that these trips are usually booked out well in advance

Cruises

*   **Glaciar Balmaceda**: A cruise along **Fiordo Ultima Esperanza** in the cutter *21 de Mayo*. This is a spectacular trip through marvelous fiord country, providing splendid vistas of high mountain peaks and glaciers, and plenty of wildlife in almost undisturbed habitats. You will see penguins, seals, sealions, and even a condor's nest perched only 20 m above in the sheer cliff. When I was there the condors were feeding their young. The boat approaches the sea-lions' colony, and also passes a cormorant colony with about 200 birds. Dolphins playing in the water overtake the ship. Waterfalls from high in the mountains, fed by glaciers, crash into the sea on the left and right. The mountains and slopes are covered with low trees and shrubs up to the snow line. As you pass the **Río Serrano valley** you have splendid vistas of the **Cuernos del Paine** and the glaciers to their right. **Cerro Balmaceda** is 2036 m high and the peak is snow-covered all year round. Just before the boat moors at a place called **Puerto Toco**, you pass within 3 m of a huge waterfall, sprinkling you with its cold spray. At Puerto Toco you descend and walk 0.5 km uphill through a native forest. Once the crest is reached you have full view of Glaciar Balmaceda. The glacier descends into a fresh water glacial lake located 50 m above the salty **Seno Ultima Esperanza de los Ventisqueros**. At the lake's edge the glacier is about 30 m wide and 10–15 m high. It is another 300 m to the wall of ice. If you are lucky you can observe the "calving" of an iceberg. These enormous chunks float down to the lake's exit and rumble down the watercourse into the Seno Ultima Esperanza de los Ventisqueros, a little above where the boat is moored. This trip is a must for anyone visiting Puerto Natales. For day trips bring your own food and water. Bring enough film as you will be taking pictures incessantly — there is a new view every minute. The boat leaves Puerto Natales at 0900 and returns at 1700.

⊞ Shopping

*   Ñandú Artesanías, Bulnes 44

⦿ Excursions

Tour operators

*   Turismo Andes Patagónicos, M. Blanco Encalada 226 (411594 fax, runs excursions to Parque Nacional Torres del Paine and Glaciar Balmaceda
*   Servitur Excursiones, Arturo Prat 353 (411858 fax 411328

Excursions

*   **Parque Nacional Bernardo O'Higgins** is the largest national park in Chile, covering a total of 2.6 million ha, and extending into Región XI de Aisén. Access to the southern part is very difficult, but **Glaciar Balmaceda**, at the southern end of the park, is accessible by boat from Puerto Natales. Nearly 500 km is covered in an ice shield, reaching down the fiords into the sea. The whole coast around here is fragmented and dissected by fiords and islands. Some of Chile's highest rainfalls occur here, producing on the outlying islands a dense forest cover.
*   **Puerto Bories**: 6 km north. Founded in 1897 as an industrial center for the large cattle and sheep farms. The original industrial complex consisted of slaughter houses, wool washing and degreasing facilities, storehouses, and refrigerating units. It lost its importance with the foundation of Puerto Natales. Now the industrial complex is largely in ruins, but the English-style living quarters and gardens of the administrative staff clearly show the influence of the English immi-

grants. Near the airport is Hostería Cisne de Cuello Negro, one of the best in the area. Instead of continuing on to Cerro Sombrero on the RN 9, you can take the road along the **Seno Ultima Esperanza de los Ventisqueros** to **Puerto Prat**, from which you get sweeping views over the fiord and the glaciers. The farm further on still belongs to the descendants of its founder, Capitán Eberhard. Turning inland for about 1 km, you can visit the **Cueva del Milodón** (22 km from Puerto Natales), discovered by Capitán Eberhard and now a *monumento nacional*. This cave preserved the remains of a *milodón*, an extinct herbivorous mammal, which was the object of much scientific interest; it was thought that because of its perfect state of preservation some specimens might still be alive in the area. CONAF administers the cave area and has built a trail from the CONAF hut to the cave entrance. The cave is approximately 150 m deep, 30 m high and 80 m high. At the entrance is a 3 m standing model of a *milodón*. In its time, some 5000 years ago, it must have been a dangerous animal; nevertheless the early Indians used to hunt it. In the area are several more caves, and it really warrants a longer stay than the time allowed by tour operators. In some of the caves were found spear tips which had belonged to the early hunters of 6000 years ago. About 10 km from the cave on the RN 9, near the entrance to Estancia Milodón, is a volcanic rock called Silla Piedra del Diablo. Impressed on it are the vertebrae of large animals which must have been surprised by a volcanic eruption in prehistoric times. Continuing north you arrive at the **Parque Nacional Torres del Paine**. The trip to Cueva del Milodón is usually combined with one to the Parque Nacional Torres del Paine, but does not leave much time here.

• **Parque Nacional Torres del Paine**: A 151 km trip to the CONAF visitors' centre in the national park. See the entry for the park on page 832.

PUERTO WILLIAMS

Area code: 061
Population: 1600

Puerto Williams is located on the north shore of **Isla Navarino**, directly on the Beagle Channel. It is the provincial capital of Antártida, which includes the part of Antarctica claimed by Chile, but also overlaps with parts claimed by Argentina. At this time it is no more than a Chilean Naval Base, but LADECO plans a triangular air link with Punta Arenas and Parque Nacional Torres del Paine. LADECO owns the Hotel Wala (near the airstrip), and intends to purchase a tourist boat to make trips along the Beagle Channel, visiting the many glaciers along the way. It is possible that it may also visit **Parque Nacional Cabo de Hornos** (Cape Horn National Park).

As Puerto Williams is a naval base, you are subject to navy regulations. All houses belong to the navy and are rented to navy personnel and dependents, and to civilian contractors. There are two *residenciales*, and private accommodation with full board is available.

About 10 km west of town is a *centolla* refrigeration plant. Ninety per cent of all the *centolla* crabs caught are exported. Over-fishing by both Argentina and Chile has dangerously depleted this species. Small wonder — they are delicious.

Puerto Williams is a small town, so the life of its inhabitants revolves around the navy. The mountains to the south shelter it from the harsh antarctic winds. Mountain walks in the area include a hike to the Cuernos de Navarino (which are visible from the town) and the many lakes in the nearby mountains. The hikes are easy, but beware of sudden weather changes. There are sweeping views from Cerro de la Bandera over the town and the Channel over to the Argentine section of Tierra del Fuego. Trout has been introduced (and so has the beaver!).

Note that cancelation of planes due to bad weather is frequent. There is only one service a week at the moment, run by Aerovías DAP, and they are booked out long in advance. Without booking a return ticket, you may be stuck there for a week. Do not count on finding a boat across the Channel to Ushuaia in Argentina. These boats are run by an Argentine company at Ushuaia on an irregular basis, only when there are sufficient passengers in Ushuaia to make a cruise. If the boat calls at Puerto Williams they also take passengers. There are no telecommunications between Puerto Williams and Ushuaia.

Isla Navarino is very humid, so be prepared for rain and fog, and the occasional snow-storm at any time, even in the middle of summer. The plane leaves Punta Arenas at 11.30 (book at Aerovías DAP — see "Tour operators" in Punta Arenas on page 858).

ℹ Tourist information
- Oficina de Informaciones, Municipalidad de Puerto Williams, Presidente Ibáñez

⊟ Accommodation
- Residencial Huspachum, Calle Huspachum (main street) $I 🛈. Full board $G 🛈
- Residencial Onashaga, Uspachun corner of Calle Nueva ☎ 621081

Pensiones
- Anoka, Presidente Ibáñez 112 ☎ 621016
- Temuco, Piloto Pardo 224 ☎ 621113

Accommodation outside town
- Hostería Patagonia (in Hotel Wala) AEFGHKLMVX ☎ 611114/223340 $C 🛉🛉. Luggage stored; fax 221693

⚠ Camping
Camping is possible anywhere outside town and on hikes in the mountains.

⏸ Eating out
The *cafetería* in the main settlement is also the local bakery. You normally have full board wherever you lodge.

If you feel like it, you may become a member of a most exclusive "Club", located on an abandoned vessel just outside town on a little inlet. The mess-hall has been converted into a small dining room where fresh *centolla* is served. The chef-cum-waiter is also the "Club's" manager. It is only open when there are boats anchored around the vessel. This is the anchorage for sailing boats intending to circumnavigate the island and sail around Cape Horn — see "Water transport" below.

✉ Post and telegraph
There is a post office in the shopping center. Mail only arrives when the plane comes in.

There is also a telephone in the shopping centre.

🖥 Services and facilities
There is a shopping centre, but everything is expensive.

✈ Air services
The airport is about 5 km from the settlement and there are no taxis, but it is easy to catch a lift with the locals. Near the airport is Hotel Wala.

Important: if you have not booked your return flight already, do so immediately on arrival, as flights are usually booked out well in advance. Even if other opportunities for leaving Puerto Williams arise, no harm is done by booking a seat.

Airlines
• Aerovias DAP, Plaza del Ancla

Services
• Punta Arenas: Fare $70.00; departs 1400 Tues; DAP

⚓ Water transport

The Navy provides travel concessions to civilians and tourists to Punta Arenas. These services are not on a regular basis. Inquire with the locals when a ship sails and don't miss the opportunity—jump at it.

Cape Horn navigators usually make a stop-over in Puerto Williams in the bay near the shipwreck (the "Club"). It is possible to join such a boat by sharing the costs of sailing around Cape Horn, but it is not cheap.

Cruises
• **Punta Arenas**: I was lucky enough to sail on a trip from Puerto Williams to Punta Arenas aboard the naval vessel *Chacabuco*. When I found out that the ship was to sail at 0800 next morning I saw the billeting officer on Friday night (who was playing basketball in the indoor sport centre) and he simply told me to be on the wharf at 0730. If you have a chance to get a passage on a navy ship, don't hesitate. The food may not be the best, but the trip through the Beagle Channel past the Cordillera Darwin with its waterfalls crashing down into the channel from their lofty heights and the glaciers reaching back 2400 m up the mountains is worth it. I was particularly lucky, as the most spectacular part of the trip took place in broad daylight. Two hours after leaving, Ushuaia, capital of Argentine Tierra del Fuego, comes into view. On the right is **Isla Grande de Tierra del Fuego** and on the left is **Isla Navarino**, and later **Isla Hoste**, and once you are in the **Brazo Noreste** you pass **Isla Gordon**. After that the land breaks up into an archipelago. The average width of the Channel is 10 km, but there are some narrow stretches, particularly near **Isla Gable** where it is only 300 m wide. On approaching Ushuaia the

Channel widens to about 15 km across. Both sides of the Channel are green, mostly with tree cover. The mountains on Isla Grande de Tierra del Fuego grow higher and those on Isla Navarino recede as the ship proceeds further west. The **Cordillera Darwin** starts west of **Bahía Yendegaia** and rapidly gains height. Soon the first glaciers are visible and then a great many waterfalls. Your first glimpse of glaciers is high in the mountains, but soon they come down to sea level. There is a constant show of cascading water down the hill from the glaciers up the mountains. All day a never-ending view of the most splendid scenery you can imagine passes by. On a sunny day you may even see the highest peak of this range, **Cerro Darwin** at 2488 m. Other peaks are **Pico Francés** and **Cerro Italia**, each with its own glaciers. As you pass into **Brazo Norte** you can see due south the glaciers on **Isla Hoste**. Here the land breaks up into a mass of still smaller islands, some of them only rocks, and all show signs of heavy rainfall. Many rocks which have not enough soil to sustain grass or tree cover have a dense moss cover. Around here are the best fishing grounds for *centolla* crabs. The **Cordillera Darwin** is a 200 km mountain range, ice-covered throughout. However, there are signs that the ice shield is receding. Some of the glaciers have tunnels out of which mighty cascades fall into the sea. The only settlements along the Beagle Channel are Chilean naval outposts. Chilean Tierra del Fuego has no road across the Cordillera Darwin to the Beagle Channel. At the utmost western part, near the Argentine border, there is a trail from Río Azopardo down to Bahía Yendegaia, used by loggers. The voyage lasts 36 hours, and in my case included a side trip to a naval base in the Strait of Magellan to pick up some cattle. Life aboard ship is regulated. Meals are first served to the ship's crew and then to the passengers. Female passengers are billeted on the starboard side and male passengers on the port side. A canteen is open after meals are served where you can buy soft drinks, chocolates, and ice cream. There are no restrictions on taking photographs while you are on board. the trip took 1½ days and cost $20.00. This includes a seamen's bunk and the normal seamen's rations. But what a splendid trip!

⊛ Sport

The navy has an indoor sports complex which tourists can use.

📷 Sightseeing

Since this is a naval base you are subject to naval regulations, which means you may not photograph whatever you wish, although it is more relaxed than several years ago.

* Indian settlement: About 3 km east is a settlement where the last members of the Yagan Indian tribe live.
* Museum: There is a well laid out museum on the base, which displays artefacts and early photos of the now extinct tribes which inhabited the island before the arrival of the European. Most of the exhibits were collected by Padre Gusinde, a German missionary from Breslau, the foremost authority on the Yamana Indians.

✦ Excursions

* Hikes may be made into the mountains behind the town. The **Dientes de Navarino** are easily accessible.
* Centolla plant: On a bay a few kilometers west past the turnoff to the Hotel Wala there is a processing and refrigeration plant for *centolla* crabs which you can visit.
* **Mirador Salto de Agua**: It is a half hour walk to this waterfall which emerges from the **Cuernos de Navarino valley**, and which supplies the drinking water for Puerto Williams. Take the gravel road west leading to Puerto Navarino. Just outside the town limits there is a road junction; take the left turn towards the mountains, gradually ascending. At the waterworks cross over the canal, and there in the forest is the waterfall. At present its volume is a little reduced, owing to the diversion of water upstream for the town's water supply.

* **Cerro de la Bandera**: A splendid day hike up the valley from Mirador Salto de Agua. At first you are walking through the subantarctic forest on a trail which leads very gradually uphill. Even if you lose the trail just head straight uphill and you will rejoin it. Some 200 m further up you reach the tree line and are in open country. In the right season (January–March) you can virtually eat your way uphill: little bushes are laden with berries. There are three different types, one similar to a cranberry; all are edible, and the pink and red berries are delicious. In the forest there is no dense undergrowth and walking even off the trail is quite easy. Once you are past the berry slope, you arrive on a small plateau with springs all over it. A bit further up is a little swamp, but it is quite safe to walk through; this is the source of the town's water supply. From this plateau you have sweeping views to the north across the **Beagle Channel** to **Isla Grande de Tierra del Fuego**, almost a stone's throw away, and to Isla Gable in Argentine territory. Eight hundred metres down at your feet is the naval base, and further to the west across the Beagle Channel you can see the **Cordillera Darwin** with its icy peaks in full splendor. To the south are the **Cuernos de Navarino**, which point like fingers to the sky. At the base of the Dientes are some small lakes, and on the plateau where you stand are many small *lagunas*. Both sides of the Beagle Channel are covered in forest. This is magnificent pristine mountain scenery. There are no dangerous wild animals, and even the mosquitoes are scarce. Due to the high rainfall and being sheltered from the strong winds coming from the Pacific and from Antarctica the countryside is green. Beware: as soon as the fog rolls in it is time to descend into the valley. When the weather turns bad, it means snow up here even if it is only raining in the valley. Rain in Puerto Williams translates 800 m up the mountain into snow whatever the season. Should you get caught in bad weather, at the north-western edge of the plateau is a log cabin or mountain shelter which

was recently built, big enough for three people. Despite this you may be in for a miserable night without a sleeping bag or blankets.

PUNTA ARENAS

Area code: 061
Population: 120 000
Altitude: Sea level
Distances

* From Monte Aymond (on the border with Argentina): 192 km north-east on RN 9 then RN 255
* From Puerto Natales: 247 km north on RN 9
* From Río Gallegos (Argentina): 252 km north-east on RN 9, then RN 255 and RN 3
* From Santiago: 2140 km north — road connection through Argentina

Punta Arenas ("Sandy Point" on the old English maps) is located on the strategic Strait of Magellan. It was founded in 1848 after the abandonment of Fuerte Bulnes, because Sandy Point had a better climate (sheltered from the antarctic winds), more wood and water, and had a better harbor. It is the most southerly Chilean city, and capital of Región XII de Magallanes and of Provincia Magallanes.

At first it was a penal and military settlement. Now it is an important port with the ever-increasing traffic through the Strait of Magellan. Most of the older buildings are of wood. But since the discovery of oil in the Strait of Magellan, the skyline is changing: the modern buildings are taller and are made of concrete and steel. Although the town is barely 150 years old, the luxurious mansions (*palacios*) built by the big sheep barons (the creators of the region's original wealth), have been declared *monumentos nacionales*. Examples are the Palacio Mauricio Braun (housings the Museo Braun Menéndez), and Palacio Sara Braun, built by the sister of Mauricio.

The mean average temperatures ☞ for Punta Arenas are: spring 11.2°C ☞ (52°F); summer 15.3°C (60°F); autumn 10.0°C (50°F); and winter 5.8°C (42°F). The average annual rainfall is 425 mm, most of which falls in spring and summer, and the rest as snow in winter.

ⓘ Tourist information

* Sernatur, Waldo Seguel 689 near Plaza Gamero (241330/225385. May be closed in the afternoon
* Tourist information kiosk: Avenida Colón block 700, and in the kiosk in the centre of Plaza Muñoz Gamero. Open Mon–Fri 0900–1300 and 1430–1900, Sat–Sun 1030–1630 and 1700–1900
* CONAF, José Menéndez 1147 (227845

ⓘ Eating out

Centolla crabs, a regional delicacy, are expensive here.

Restaurants
For restaurants in hotels, see "Accommodation" below.

* Alero Criollo Ño Peiro, I. Carrera Pinto 0226
* Asturias, Navarro 967
* Beagle, O'Higgins 1077
* Carioca, José Menéndez 600
* Casablanca, Chiloe 549 $Y. Chilean cuisine
* Casino La Compañía de Bomberos, Roca 826

- Casino Venus (Naval Club), Pedro Montt 1046
- Centro Español, Plaza Muñoz Gamero 771
- Club de la Unión, Plaza Muñoz Gamero 714. Was the Palacio Sara Braun (Sara Braun was the founder of Chile's largest agricultural enterprise SDTF); built in 1895 by a French architect, it has been declared a *monumento nacional*
- Club Deportivo Chile, A. Sanhueza 546
- Dino's Pizza, Bories 557
- Don Fierro, O'Higgins 1205. *Parilla*
- El Arriero, Avenida Bulnes corner of Manantiales. Seafood
- El Beagle, O'Higgins 1077
- Español El Coral, José Menéndez 848
- El Estribo, Ignacio Carrera Pinto 762 $Y. *Parrilla* and seafood
- El Infante, Magallanes 875
- El Lloco Dos, Covadonga 227
- El Mercado, Mejicana 617 near Chiloe. Upstairs open 24 hours. *Centollas*
- El Mesón del Calvo, Jorge Montt 687. *Parrilla* and seafood
- Garogha, Bories 817. Shows on weekends
- Golden Dragon, Avenida Colón 529 $Y. Closed Sundays. Chinese cuisine
- Iberia, O'Higgins 974. Steaks
- King Pollo, Errázuriz 416
- La Casa de Juan, O'Higgins 1021
- La Taberna de Silver, O'Higgins 1037 $Y. *Parrillada;* open 24 hrs
- La Terraza, 21 de Mayo 1299
- Lomit's, José Menéndez 722
- Los Años 60 de Mitchel, Chiloe 1231
- Lucerna, Carlos Bories 624
- O.K. Pizza, José Nogueira 1274
- Saturno, Colón 756
- Sotitos, O'Higgins 1138. Seafood, *centollas*. Credit cards accepted
- Tucán Tango, Bories 848
- Vegalafonte, Roca 886

Eating out outside town

Restaurants
- Aeropuerto, KM 21 north
- Río Chabunco, RN 9, KM 18 north
- Parenazón, Zona Franca, Avenida Bulnes KM 4 north

⊤ Entertainment
- Almirante Señoret, RN 9, 6 km south

Entertainment north of town

Discos
- Las Brujas, off RN 9 KM 7.5, before Hotel Yaganes
- El Faro, off RN 9 KM 7.5, past Hotel Yaganes

✉ Post and telegraph

Post office
- Post office and Telex Chile, Bories 91

Telephone
- CTC Centro de Llamados Telefónicos, Nogeira 1116 corner of Fagnano, on the Plaza Muñoz Gamero
- ENTEL Chile, Lautaro Navarro 941

$ Financial
Banks are open 0900–1400 but closed on Sat. *Cambios* give better rates than banks.
- Banco O'Higgins. Good for exchange
- Bancard, Pedro Montt 849 ℂ 244027. Cash for Visa and Mastercard
- Sur Cambios, J. Menéndez 556 ℂ244464
- Cambio Onatur, Lautaro Navarro 1109
- Cambio Gasic, Roca 915 ℂ242396
- Cambio Taurus, 21 de Mayo 1502 ℂ241207
- Casa de Cambio La Hermandad, Navarro 1099 corner Roca ℂ243991. Also travel agency

🖫 Services and facilities

Laundromat
- Autoservicio, O'Higgins 969

Market
- Mercado Municipal, Chiloe block 600 near Mejicana

Pharmacy
- Austral, Fagnano block 800 near Lautaro Navarro

Supermarket
- Cofrima, Lautaro Navarro 1293

⊟ Visas, passports
- Argentine consulate, 21 de Mayo 1878. ℂ261912. Open 1000–1400. A visa costs $15 and is available within 24 hours
- British Vice-Consul, Roca 924 ℂ244727
- German Consul-General, Avenida El Bosque Lot 1 ℂ212866

Key to map

B	Gobernación Provincial (Government)
C	Municipalidad (Town hall)
D	Post office and telex
E	Telephone
F	Carabineros (Police)
G	Mercado Municipal (Market)
I	Tourist information
P	Gas stations
$	Money exchange
T	Bus terminals

● Accommodation

3	Hostal Carpa Manzano
5	Hostal de la Patagonia
8	Residencial Rubio
11	Back Packers' Lodge
13	Hotel Condor de Plata
15	Apart Hotel Tierra de Fuego
17	Hotel Finis Terrae
20	Apart Hotel Colonizadores
22	Hotel Montecarlo
28	Hostal del Estrecho
29	Hostal Albatros
31	Hostal Chapital
32	Hotel Los Navegantes
33	Hotel José Nogueira
35	Hotel Oviedo
40	Hotel Savoy
43	Hotel Ritz
44	Hotel Cabo de Hornos
50	Residencial Roca
53	Hotel Mercurio
54	Hotel Plaza & Residencial París
58	Hotel El Pionero
59	Hotel Isla Rey Jorge
62	Residencial Oásis
63	Residencial Nena

○ Eating out

4	Restaurant Tucan Tango
6	Club Deportivo Chile
7	Dino's Pizza
9	Restaurant El Mercado
10	Restaurant Lucerna
12	Restaurant El Mesón del Calvo
21	Restaurant Golden Dragon
23	Restaurant Carioca
24	Restaurant Garogha
25	Restaurant El Infante
34	Club de la Unión
38	Restaurant Asturias
42	Casino Venus
46	Restaurant Vegalafonte
48	Restaurant La Taberna de Silver
49	Restaurant El Beagle
51	Restaurant La Casa de Juan
52	King Pollo
55	Club Español
57	Restaurant Sotitos
60	Restaurant La Terraza
61	Parrilla Don Fierro

△ Tour operators and car rental

16	Hertz Rent a Car
18	Budget Rent a Car
45	Turismo Arka Patagonia
47	Avis Rent a Car

▲ Airline offices

14	National Airlines
27	Aerovias DAP
39	LAN Chile
56	LADECO

■ Sights

1	Museo Regional Salesiano
2	Iglesia María Auxiliadora
26	Teatro Municipal
30	Iglesia Anglicana
36	Museo Regional de Magallanes

□ Services

19	Artesaní Chile Típico
37	ENTEL Chile
41	Lavandería Autoservicio (laundromat)

🚗 Motoring

For gas stations, see city map.

Roads
The road connecting the city with Puerto Natales is sealed all the way.
The road to Río Gallegos in Argentina is sealed almost completely to the border.

Car rental
- Automóvil Club de Chile, L. Bernardo O'Higgins 931 ℂ 241613/243097
- Avis Rent a Car, Lautaro Navarro 1065 ℂ 241042. Also tours
- Budget, L. Bernardo O'Higgins 964 ℂ 241696. Also at airport
- First Rent a Car, Avenida Colón 798 ℂ 244729, fax 244729
- Hertz Rent a Car, Colón 798 ℂ 248742
- International Rent a Car, Sarmineto 790 ℂ 228323, fax 248865

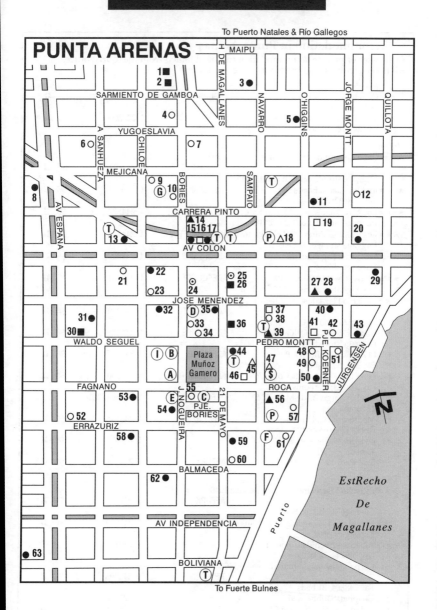

To Puerto Natales & Río Gallegos

PUNTA ARENAS

EstRecho
De
Magallanes

To Fuerte Bulnes

⊟ Accommodation in Punta Arenas

Addresses of private accommodation can be obtained from the tourist office.
All hotels, *hostales*, and *residenciales* are heated.

Apart Hotels

• Colonizadores, Colón 1116 28 beds	AFGHPS	ℓ 244449	$F ♙♙
• Tierra de Fuego, Colón 716 Fax 244205; 22 beds	P	ℓ 226200	$D ♙♙

Hotels

★★★★★Cabo de Hornos, Plaza Muñoz Gamero 1024	ACEHKMTUZ	ℓ 242134	$E ♙♙
Luggage stored, car rental, 110 rooms			
★★★★José Nogueira, Bories 959 Fax 248832; 35 beds	ADEFGHJKPS	ℓ 248840	$C ♙♙
★★★★Los Navegantes, José Menéndez 647	ACEFGHKLMPXZ	ℓ 244677	$D ♙♙
Luggage stored; fax 247545; 100 beds			
★★★ Los Colonizadores, 21 de Mayo 1690	ACEFGHKLPTUZ	ℓ 244144	$F ♙♙
Luggage storage; 32 beds			
★★★ Mercurio, Fagnano 595	AEFGHKMPS	ℓ 242300	$F ♙♙
Luggage stored			
★★★ Savoy, José Menéndez 1073	ADEFGHJKP	ℓ 241951	$F ♙♙
Luggage stored; fax 247979; 80 beds			
★★Turismo Plaza, José Nogueira 1116, upstairs	ADEFGHKPTU	ℓ 241300	$F ♙♙
Fax 248613; 30 beds			
• Condor de Plata, Colón 556	ADEFGHKPS	ℓ 241078/247987	$F ♙♙
Luggage stored; fax 241149; 23 beds			
• El Pionero, Chiloe 1210	AEFGHKLP	ℓ 248851	$F ♙♙
Fax 248263; 16 beds			
• Finis Terrae, Avenida Colón 766	AEFGHKMPTU	ℓ 228200	$D ♙♙
Fax 248124; 70 rooms			
• Isla Rey Jorge, 21 de Mayo 1243 25 rooms	DEFGHJ	ℓ 241504/222681	
• Montecarlo, Colón 605	AEGLPUZ	ℓ 243438	$G ♙♙
Fax 244743; 65 beds			
• Oviedo, Magallanes 922 48 beds		ℓ 222655	$F ♙♙
• Ritz, Pedro Montt 1102	AEFGHK	ℓ 224422	$G ♙♙

Hostales

★★Estrecho Magallanes, José Menéndez 1048	AEFHPK	ℓ 241011	$G ♙♙
Luggage stored; 28 beds			
★★Hostal de la Patagonia, O'Higgins 478	AFGHKLPSTUZ	ℓ 241079	$F ♙♙
Luggage stored			
• Albatros, Avenida Colón 1195		ℓ 223131	
Fax 248744; 24 beds			
• Carpa Manzano, Lautaro Navarro 336	HPT	ℓ 242296	$G ♙♙
Fax 248864; 21 beds			
• Chapital, Sanhueza 974		ℓ 225698	
• Rubio, Avenida España 640		ℓ 226458	$H ♙♙
• Sierra Leona, Magallanes 443	HP	ℓ 222238	

Accommodation in Punto Arenas — continued

Residenciales
- Bulnes, Bulnes 0450   **ABDEFGHJLPSX**   (212113 $H ••
  Budget travelers; luggage stored; 41 beds
- Bustamente, J. Montt 847   **ALP**   (224774 $I •
  17 rooms
- Casa del Deportista, O'Higgins 1205 corner of Errázuriz
     AEFL   (222587 $I •
  Budget travelers; 40 beds
- Centenario, P. Centenario 105   **AEP**   (225710 $I •
  Luggage stored; budget travelers; 17 beds
- Central 1, Balmaceda 545   **S** $I •
  Budget travelers
- Central 2, Sanhueza 185   **P**   (222845 $I ••
- Montt, Jorge Montt 211   **AEPS**   (226390 $I ••
- Paris, Nogueira 1116, upstairs   **APS**   (223112 $H •
  Budget travelers; 28 beds
- Polo Sur, Puerto Montt 919   **AE**   (21592
- Roca, Roca 1038   **AEHKLS**   (243903 $H •
  Luggage stored; budget travelers; 30 beds
- Rubio, Avenida España 640   (226458
  26 beds
- Sonia, Pasaje Darwin 175   (248543
  12 beds

Pensiones
For budget travelers.
- Villegas, Boliviana 238
- Private home, Boliviana 366
- Private home, Paraguaya 150   (247687

Accommodation on RN 9 North

Hosterías
- Yaganes, KM 7.5   **ADEFGHJK**   (211600 $D for 3
  14 cabins; fax 248052

Accommodation in Río Verde
Río Verde is 88 km north-west on Ruta Y-50 on Canal Fitzroy at the ferry crossing to Isla Riesco.
- Hostería Río Verde   **AEPSV**   (311122 $H •
  Fax 222792; 25 beds

Accommodation in Río Penitente
Río Penitente is 138 km north on RN 9, just 13 km south of Morro Chico.
- Hostal Estancia Río Penitente   **AEFGHKLPSUV**   (263029 $D ••
  20 beds; open all year

Accommodation in Río Rubens
Río Rubens is located 184 km north on RN 9.
- Hotel Río Rubens   **AEFGHLMPUV**   (244729 $H ••
  32 beds. A former *estancia*

MAGALLANES

✈ Air services from Punta Arenas

Aeropuerto Presidente Carlos Ibañez del Campo is 16 km north of town.

Airlines
- Aerovias DAP, O'Higgins 891 (21693/223340
  Regular weekly flights to Puerto Williams; daily flights to Porvenir. Flights over Cape Horn. Also weekly flights to Falkland Islands (Islas Malvinas).
  Runs charter flights to the Teniente Marsh base on King George Island in Twin Otter planes; these include a one-night stay at the base. The cost to charter the plane is $19 250.00 for 10, plus $165.00 accommodation per person. There is also a monthly flight for $2640.00 for a one-night stay at the base. See "Excursions" on page 860.
- LADECO, Roca 924 (241100,
- LAN Chile, Lautaro Navarro 999 (247079
- National Airlines, Carrera Pinto block 700 near Bories
- SABA, Magallanes 970 (242892
- Servicio Aereo Litoral, Lautaro Navarro 1066 (225054

Services

Destination	Fare	Services	Companies
Balmaceda (Coihaique airport)			
	$141.00	daily	LADECO
Concepción	$266.00	daily	LAN Chile, LADECO
Porvenir	$17.50	Mon–Fri	DAP
Departs at 0800 and 1700.			
Puerto Montt	$190.00	1–2 services daily	LAN Chile, LADECO
Puerto Williams			
	$80.00		DAP
		2 flights per week in summer	
			LADECO
Santiago	$312.00	1–2 flights daily	LAN Chile, LADECO

⚓ Water transport

Companies
- Navimag, Avenida Independencia 830 (222593. Runs passenger vessels between Puerto Montt and Puerto Natales (but *not* Punta Arenas). See "Water transport" in Puerto Natales on page 844

Vessels
A bus service runs from Punta Arenas town centre to Tres Puentes costing $1.00. Alight at the university; the ferry wharf is a short walk away. On arrival at Bahía Chilota take a waiting cab to Porvenir, about 6 km away — a 15-minute cab ride costing $2.50. If you want to continue to Río Grande in Argentina, ask the driver to take you first to the Transportes Senkovic office to buy a ticket and check departure time for Río Grande in Argentina.

Barcaza *Melinka*
Ferry carrying passengers and 20 cars. For information call Trasportadora Broom, Avenida Bulnes 05075 (218100, fax 212126; they also have information on the ferry *Bahía Azul* crossing Primera Angostura from Punta Delgada to Puerto Espora.
- Tres Puentes (Punta Arenas)–Bahía Chilote (Porvenir). Departs 0900 return 1400, Tues, Wed, Fri April–December, and Tues–Sat January–March. Duration 2½ hours. Fare $4.00, cars $25.00

Antártida
Cruise ship for 27 passengers. Information is available from Avenida Independencia 840 (224256, fax 225804.
- Punta Arenas–Isla Magdalena. Departs Sat 0800 all year. Duration 6½ hours

🚌 Buses from Punto Arenas

Punta Arenas has no central bus terminal; instead all bus companies have their own terminals.

Companies
- Agencia Taurus, 21 de Mayo block 1500 near Boliviana ℂ 222223
- A155 Buses Turibus, J. Menéndez 647 ℂ 241463
- B11   Bus Norte, Plaza Muñoz Gamero 1039 ℂ 222599
- B61   Buses El Pingüino, Roca 915 ℂ 242396
- B65   Buses Fernández, Sanhueza 745 ℂ 242313
- B74   Buses Ghisoni, L. Navarro 975 ℂ 222078
- B104 Buses Mancilla, J. Menéndez 556 ℂ 221516
- B158 Buses Sur, J. Menéndez 565 ℂ 244464
- B182 Buses Victoria Sur, Colón 798 ℂ 241213
- B208 Expreso Andrea, L. Navarro 975 ℂ 222078
- B214 Expreso Vera, 21 de Mayo 1502 ℂ 241207, fax 241173
- B277 Buses Pacheco, Avenida Colón 900 ℂ 242174, fax 226916
  Buses to Río Gallegos and Río Grande in Argentina

Services

Destination	Fare	Services	Companies
Ancud	$64.50	1–2 services daily	A155, B65, B74, B158
Castro	$64.50	1–2 services daily	A155, B65, B74, B158
Osorno	$62.00	1–3 services daily	A155, B11, B65, B74, B158, B182
Puerto Montt	$62.00	2–3 services daily	A155, B11, B65, B74, B158, B182
Puerto Natales	$5.00	4–6 services daily	B65, B158, B182
Punta Delgada	$3.80	Mon, Wed, Sun	B208
Río Gallegos	$12.20	1–3 services daily	B61, B74, B104, B214
Valdivia	$62.00		A155

Austral II
Cruise ship for 6 passengers. Information is available from Avenida Independencia 840 ℂ 224256, fax 225804.
- Punta Arenas–Puerto Williams. Departs 2nd week every month all year. Duration 3 days

M/N Navarino
For 10 passengers. Information is available from 21 de Mayo 1460 ℂ (61 224256, fax 248848
- Punta Arenas–Puerto Williams. Departs 2nd week every month, all year. Duration 3 days

Terra Australis
Bunks for 100 passengers. Information is available from Independencia 840 ℂ 24448
- Punta Arenas–Canal Magdalena–Ventisquero Agostini–Beagle Channel–Puerto Williams–Ushuaia–Harberton–Ventisquero Garibaldi–Punta Arenas. Departs Sat, September–March. Duration 7 days

Services
- Isla Navarino: The Navy runs irregular cruises to Puerto Williams on Isla Navarino. They take civilian passengers, but Chileans living or working at the naval base have priority. However tourists are taken when space permits. Check at the Capitanía del Puerto and if there is a ship don't miss it — this trip through the Beagle Channel is one of the most spectacular in Chile. The trip lasts a day and a half, during which you are billeted in bunks. The food is the normal Navy fare. Fare (one way): $20.00! For a full description of the cruise see "Water transport" in Puerto Williams on page 848.

🏬 Shopping
- Artesanía Chilena, Avenida Independencia 799
- Pingüino Souvenirs, Carlos Bories 404
- Rodrigo Leder, Balmaceda 459. Fine leather articles, factory prices

• Zona Franca (a complex of duty-free shops) is located 4 km north of the town centre just past the university at the intersection of Los Flamencos and RN 9. Open Mon–Sat 1000–1200 and 1500–2000. Regular buses. For film and other purchases. Not as cheap as Zofri in Iquique, another free trade zone

☞ • Chile Típico, I. Carrera Pinto 1015. Semi-precious stones, Chilean handicrafts

⊛ Sport

Fishing
There is good trout and *pejerrey* fishing in the following lakes and rivers: Lago Blanco, Lago del Toro, Lago Diana, Lago Figueroa, Lago Maravilla, Laguna Sofa; Río Agua Fresca, Río Chabunco, Río Grande, Río Leña Dura, Río Minas, Río Penitente, Río Pérez, Río Pescado, Río Rubens, Río San Juan, Río Tres Brazos, and Río Tres Ciervos. For fishing seasons see "Fishing" on page 828.

Skiing
Skiing is possible from early June onwards on the slopes of Cerro Mirador in the Reserva Forestal Magallanes. For information contact the Club Andino, 21 de Mayo 690 (in the Balmar Turismo shop).

▣ Sightseeing

The best views over the city and the Strait of Magellan across to Tierra del Fuego are from Cerro La Cruz, on the corner of Señoret and Fagnano just past the stairs. The best time for taking pictures is in the late afternoon when the sun is setting.
• Museo Salesiano "Mayorino Borgatello", Avenida Bulnes 374. Open Tues–Sat 1100–1600 and Sun 1100–1300. Collections of local flora and fauna and relics of the now extinct Yagana, Ona, and Alacufe cultures. The Salesian brothers were the missionaries who had close contact with the early tribes, and their observations and original maps of the region are preserved in this very interesting museum.
• Museo Regional de Magallanes, Magallanes 949. Located in the Palacio Mauricio Braun, designated a *monumento nacional*. Open Tues–Sat 1100–

1600, Sun 1100–1300. It shows the home of a wealthy Patagonian family around the turn of the century, complete with furniture, family portrait, and a large library. The palace was built by a French architect in 1906 for Mauricio Braun, a famous entrepreneur at the turn of the century.
• Cemetery, on Avenida Bulnes, just before the race course. Many of the city's illustrious citizens are buried here in mausoleums. In contrast to these sumptuous burial sites are the simple graves where the last Onas are buried.
• Instituto de la Patagonia, also called the Museo del Recuerdo, corner of Bulnes and Los Flamencos, 4 km north of town centre, opposite the university campus. Open Mon–Fri 0900–1200 and 1500–1700. This open-air museum has displays of sculptures depicting life in the early settlement, and early agricultural machinery. It has a good library and sells books on local history and of local interest. There is also a "mini-zoo" with local native animals.

⬤ Excursions

Tour operators
• Arka Patagonia, Lautaro Navarro 1038-A ☎ 248167/241504. Runs a cruise ship to the glaciers
• Turismo Aventour, José Nogueira 1255 ☎ 241197, fax 243354. Organizes adventure and nature-lover tours. They also hire out equipment for trekking tours. They run trips to penguin rookeries some 65 km away, where you can see Magellanic penguins, rheas, and Patagonian geese
• Aonikenk, Magallanes 619 ☎ 228332. Runs excursions in minibuses to the following spots: penguin colony ($10.00); Fuerte Bulnes ($10.00); and Valle de Las Minas ($20.50). Minimum of five passengers
• Turismo Cabo de Hornos, Plaza Muñoz Gamero 1024 ☎ 222134. Organizes six-day tours to Antarctica in conjunction with Sernatur and the Chilean Air Force in Hercules C-130 airplanes. The flights take four hours. These excursions take place in October and March, possibly because the weather is more clement and steadier. However because of the unpre-

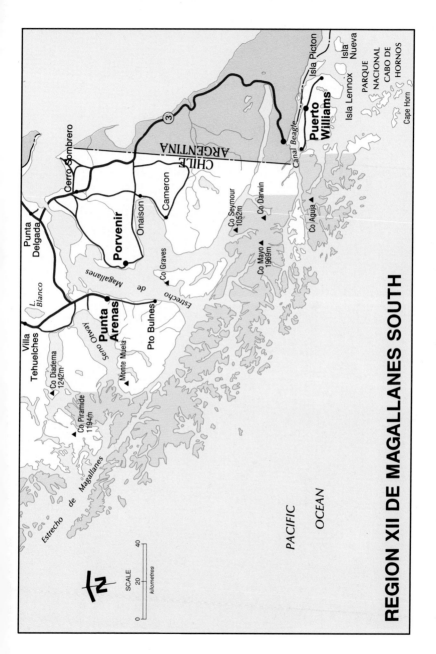

Plate 43
Map of Región XII de Magallanes Y Antarctica Chilena - South

Plate 44 Región XII de Magallanes Y Antarctica Chilena
Top: Fuerte Bulnes
Bottom: Isla Navarino, edible berries

dictability of the weather, flights may be cancelled. Fares vary between $4000.00 (October) and $4250.00 (March). All participants are advised to take out a special life insurance policy, as you will be required to sign a document exempting the Air Force and Sernatur from any injury or death sustained during the Antarctic trip. Should the return flight be delayed due to bad weather conditions, there is a further charge of $160.00 per day

- Turismo Comapa, Independencia 840 (241437, fax 225804
- Turismo Laguna Azul, José Menéndez 789(225200. Tours to Pingüineras and Fuerte Bulnes
- Turismo Pehoe Ltda., Avenida Colón 782, (244506, fax 248052. Reservations for Hostería Pehoe on Lago Pehoe in Parque Nacional Torres del Paine, Hostería Cisne de Cuello Negro in Puerto Bories, and Hostería Yaganes 5 km north of the city centre. You can also hire a car. Organizes tours to Parque Nacional Torres del Paine, Fuerte Bulnes, Pingüineras, Calafate, and Ushuaia
- Turismo Runner, Lautaro Navarro 1065 (247050 fax 241042. Agents for Avis Rent a Car; also money exchange

Excursions
- **Reserva Forestal Magallanes**: 8 km west on the slopes of Cerro Mirador. Here is also the only ski slope in Magallanes. CONAF has installed a camping ground for 30 tents.
- **Punta San Juan**: If you like camping on the Strait of Magellan, there is an unserviced camping spot at Punta San Juan on the south side of the **Río San Juan**, about 8 km south of Puerto Hambre. At Punta San Juan are some vacation cabins, mostly used by fishermen, attracted by the good trout fishing in the river. The trip to San Juan is not included in the day excursion to Fuerte Bulnes and Puerto Hambre. You may get a lift with a wood-cutting truck or use the services of the tour operator, but if you intend to explore the Río San Juan area and to camp there, you have to make arrangements with the tour operator for a pickup and pay double.

- **Parque Nacional Torres del Paine**: Although tour operators will organize excursions from Punta Arenas to Torres del Paine, it is in my opinion preferable to make this outing from Puerto Natales. See Eduardo, an Englishman who runs the Hotel Austral in Puerto Natales for excellent one- or two-day tours in the national park; see the entry for the park on page 832.
- **Centro de Esquí Cerro Mirador**: A skiing area within the **Reserva Forestal Magallanes**, at an altitude of 600 m. The ski lift is located 9 km west of town. There are sweeping views over the Strait of Magellan and Punta Arenas. At Camping **Río de las Minas**, 8 km west, there are 50 tent sites, open November–April. Electricity and water available. This is the most southerly ski area in the world. The ski runs are narrow and run between trees. The snow fields overlook Punta Arenas and the Straits of Magellan, and you can catch a glimpse of Tierra del Fuego. I suggest you use a four-wheel-drive vehicle; moreover, snow chains are essential in winter over this gravel road. The ski season runs between July and October. The strong wind creates a sort of drift snow which provides unusual skiing conditions. The nearest accommodation is in Punta Arenas. Facilities include a restaurant at the base. There is one double chair lift which serves 11 ski runs. You can hire equipment, and there are ski instructors. In winter (April–October) there is a shuttle bus service from Punta Arenas to the base of the ski-lift.
- **Isla Riesco** via **Río Verde**: Río Verde is located on **Seno Skyring**, 86 km north-east on Ruta Y-50; turn off RN 9 at KM 49 at the Hotel Cabeza de Mar. A rural bus service runs to Hotel Río Verde located on Seno Skyring, but check with Sernatur for frequencies. This is a small village which has sprung up around the old *estancia* and now has found a new lease of life with the ferry services across **Canal Fitzroy** to Isla Riesco and weekend tourists. During the week it is quiet. The most scenic part of the island is in the extreme west in the **Cerro Ladrillero** area (altitude 1700 m), which has gla-

ciers descending into Seno Skyring. This part is in **Reserva Nacional Alacufes**. It is difficult to reach, and only for the hardy and intrepid. In the centre of the island is **Lago Riesco** with its outlet to Seno Otway. It is interesting that the names of the sounds and islands are those given by the survey ship *Beagle* in 1826–1832. The birdlife along Seno Otway is unbelievable. On Isla Riesco dirt roads follow the Seno Skyring and Seno Otway. They become logging trails and soon peter out in the vicinity of the Reserva Forestal Riesco. Campers should take note that it is very wet on this island, but the fishing in the rivers is good. **Río Grande** has supposedly the best fishing on the island. There are hardly any hikers in this pristine country. Up the Río Grande is the best access to **Lago Riesco** — for the hardy and intrepid only. Some tour operators organize fishing trips to the island lasting 2–7 days.

- **Laguna Parrillar**: 47 km south-west in the **Reserva Forestal Laguna Parrillar**. Access is only possible in your own vehicle. Tour operators organize excursions usually as a side trip with a trip to Puerto Hambre and Fuerte Bulnes. There were no tours being offered while I was there. CONAF staff making the trip down will give you a lift, so check with CONAF to see if and when a vehicle is likely to be going there. CONAF has a small camping ground on the lake shore, open from December to March, with 12 campsites, and basic facilities like tables and firewood, and also electricity; you can drink the lake water. It is surrounded by very dense forests of *lengas* and *ñire* trees, natives of Magellanica and Patagonia. It is an excellent spot for fishing, serene, and quiet—you are on your own. $2.50 per person.

- **Monumento Natural Los Pingüinos**. This reserve consists of **Isla Marta** and **Isla Magdalena**, situated east of Isla Isabel and about 25 nautical miles north of Punta Arenas. It is one of the largest nesting sites of the Magellanic penguin with over 50 000 nests, and there are also large colonies of cormorants. There are traces of aboriginal

occupation. A must for the nature lover. The reserve is not publicised by the tourist authorities to any great extent, perhaps to protect it from over-exploitation. Access is possible through a tour operator the trip takes approximately 7 hours.

- **Puerto Williams** on **Isla Navarino**: This is normally a plane trip, but if you are lucky there may be a naval ship in port going to Puerto Williams. These ships usually take passengers, but Chileans living on Isla Navarino have preference. The same applies when you are in Puerto Williams returning to Punta Arenas. If you are even luckier there may be an Argentine cruise boat from Ushuaia in Puerto Williams, and you can return to civilization through the Argentine and Chilean sections of Isla Grande de Tierra del Fuego (see Ushuaia in *Travel Companion Argentina* for details). This is a remarkable plane trip over the **Cordillera Darwin** and the sombre **Beagle Channel**. The last half hour before landing in Puerto Williams is the most spectacular: you look down on a sheer endless mass of ice which sends its glacier tongues right down into the fiords. Small lakes are scattered over the northern side of the range. Most of the south side is a hostile sheer drop into the Beagle Channel. The highest peaks such as **Cerro Darwin** emerge from this sheet of ice like dark fingers. See also Puerto Williams on page 846.

- **Puerto Natales**, **Cueva del Milodón**, **Silla Piedra del Diablo**: Buses Ghisoni organize excursions to Puerto Natales. This does not include Parque Nacional Torres del Paine as you need at least two days for the full trip.

- **Río Gallegos** in Argentina: See the entry for Río Gallegos in *Travel Companion Argentina*.

- Antarctica: Here you stay two full days at **Teniente Marsh** base on King George Island—see Teniente Marsh on page 862. Only fit persons should consider this trip. Bring a parka with a hood, warm gloves, thick socks, warm waterproof boots, dark glasses, and a sun filter lotion.

- **Fuerte Bulnes** and **Puerto Hambre**: 60 km south on RN 9. On this trip you see the remains of the first colony established by the Spanish in the Strait of Magellan, the first Chilean settlement, and an English cemetery where Captain Stokes of the *Beagle* is buried. Fuerte Bulnes was founded in 1843 by Chile to lay claim to this part of South America, but was abandoned in favor of a new foundation at Sandy Point — Punta Arenas. The fort is being reconstructed by the army as a *monumento nacional*. Puerto Hambre was founded by Sarmiento de Gamboa, a Spanish explorer, on March 25, 1584 as Ciudad Rey Felipe. It was intended firstly to lay claim to this part of South America in the name of the Spanish kings, and secondly to have a military presence against the marauding pirates that passed through these waters. But within two years all perished from hunger and exhaustion. Cavendish, who arrived three years after its foundation, found all the inhabitants dead and called it Port Famine — *hambre* is Spanish for *hunger*. Not much is visible, but a plaque tells the sad story. The road to Puerto Hambre and Fuerte Bulnes follows the Strait of Magellan all the way. There are sweeping views over low mountains sparsely dotted with trees, most of them bent low by the prevailing winds. At Puerto Hambre there is a camping area on the beach-front. The sheltered area behind the historical site is private camping ground belonging to the *carabineros*. Tour operators run very moderately priced half-day excursions to these two locations. Throughout the trip the road follows the shores of the Strait of Magellan with uninterrupted views of Isla Tierra del Fuego. The road is sealed for the first 10 km as far as Río Los Ciervos, and from then on it is a good dirt road. At first there are only few trees on the *pampa*; but gradually the thickets become small forests, and by the outskirts of Fuerte Bulnes it is a Magellanic forest which becomes ever more dense the further south and west you go. Río San Juan is a good fishing spot, with plenty of scope for outdoor activities — so bring your tent and sleeping gear.

PUNTA DELGADA

Distance from Punta Arenas: 170 km east

This little village, sprung from the former *estancia*, is important only as the starting point for ferry services from the mainland to Isla Tierra del Fuego. All Argentine traffic to the Argentine part of Tierra del Fuego takes this route. The ferry service across the **Primera Angostura** begins 27 km south.

⊟ Accommodation

- Hostería Tehuelche, RN 225 KM 160 at the intersection to the ferry (221270 $G ⁞⁞. 20 beds

⊟ Buses

Expreso Andrea runs bus services to and from Punta Arenas 4 times per week; fares $3.80. On Tierra del Fuego there are no bus services from Punta Espora south to Cerro Sombrero(32 km) or San Sebastián. Hitchhiking is possible. Buses Pacheco, Avenida Colón 900 (226916 in Punta Arenas, go to Río Grande in Argentina.

⊡ Water transport

Bahía Azul
Ferry for passengers and 20 cars. For information in Punta Arenas, call Trasportadora Broom, Avenida Bulnes 05075, (218100, fax 212126
- Punta Delgada–Bahía Azul (Isla Tierra de Fuego); the actual village is called Puerto Espora. Departs daily from 0830 onwards, 8–10 services daily all year; last return from Bahía Azul 2300. Duration 30 minutes

SAN SEBASTIÁN

Distance from Porvenir: 147 km east

San Sebastián, whose official name is Complejo Fronterizo San Sebastián, is a border control point between the Chilean and Argentine sections of Tierra del Fuego. The border is open between 0800 and 2200.

⊟ Accommodation
• Hostería La Frontera

⊞ Eating out
• Cafetería La Frontera, near passport control

TENIENTE MARSH

The Teniente Marsh naval base is located on King George Island in the South Shetland Islands at a latitude of 62°S. Chile has claimed this group as part of its Provincia Antártida, and has created a base which is staffed all year round. The **Presidente Frei** meteorological station is about 2.5 km east of the airstrip. In the vicinity are also other foreign scientific stations such as Bellinghausen (USSR), Artigas (Uruguay), and, a few hundred meters north of Presidente Frei, Gran Muralla (China). Further north on **Bahía Almirante** are the Polish base (Arctowski) and the Brazilian base (Comandante Ferraz).

The interior of the island is covered by a glacier. The highest mountain is **Cerro Brimstone** in the extreme north. The climate, as you would expect, is extremely harsh all year round. However, Chile makes a concerted effort through Sernatur in conjunction with the Chilean Air Force to promote this island as a tourist destination. The permanent Chilean population lives in **Villa Las Estrellas** near Presidente Frei. The average annual temperature is –2.2°C. (28°F)

ⓘ Tourist information
Sernatur has an office in Presidente Frei.

⊟ Accommodation
• Hotel Estrella Polar **EFGXZ**. Luggage stored, conference room. This hotel is nothing more than a converted Air Force module

⊕ Excursions
Excursions include sailing through the **Bahía Fildes** on a Zodiac boat, and a trip to **Isla Ardley** where there is a penguin colony.
There may be a visit to a scientific station run by other governments.
Other attractions are a flight over the island in a Twin Otter plane, and a walk through the glaciers. All excursions are subject to approval by the Chilean base commander.

TRIP PLANNER

How to use this trip planner

Time and money are the limitations, as in every aspect in life, to vacationing or traveling, particularly in "exotic" destinations.

This section is included to assist you in planning your trip to Chile. Use it to plan your own itinerary, using the information given in this *Travel Guide.* Follow the sample planner to work out :

- How much money and time you will need to visit all the places you want to go to
- What places you can visit for a given amount of money and/or time

The sample planner is for two people, and is based on 3–4-star hotels at a price of around US$100 a night plus $60 for meals.

Planning

Step 1	Decide how much time you have
Step 2	Decide how much money you are prepared to spend
Step 3	Find the best season, in terms of both costs and weather
Step 4	List the places you would like to visit
Step 5	Make a rough trip plan using the sample planner below
Step 6	Compare your itinerary with an itinerary prepared by a travel agent
Step 7	Fine-tune your itinerary

Calculations

- Air fares from the USA to Santiago vary from $1250.00 to $1750.00, depending on the season
- LAN Chile provides a Chilepass valid for 21 days for $300
- Accommodation range used in the Planner: $D 👥 (★★★ or ★★★★ hotels)
- Meal range used in the Planner: $X (top range)
- Tour operator costs for excursions and city sightseeing have been set at $20.00 per person
- Costs in the Planner are calculated for two persons
- Breakfast is included in accommodation tariffs
- All expenses (bus fares, etc.) have been rounded to the nearest $5.

Tips

- Organize your tours through the desk clerk as soon as you arrive in the hotel to avoid losing time
- Avail yourself of hotels' airport pickup services

Sample trip planner

Day	Itinerary	Hours	$	$ per day
–	**Travel arrangements**			
	Air ticket USA–Santiago		3480.00	
	Chilepass		600.00	
	Travel insurance		300.00	4380.00
1	**Flight USA–Santiago**			
	Flight: LAN Chile	1 day	Paid	
	Bus from airport to city		15.00	
	Accommodation and meals		160.00	175.00
2	**Santiago**			
	Museums	Morning	15.00	
	Cerro San Cristobal, including wine tasting at the *Enoteca*	Afternoon	30.00	
	Accommodation and meals		160.00	205.00
3	**Flight Santiago–Punta Arenas**			
	Bus from hotel to airport		15.00	
	Flight: Chilepass	4 hrs	Paid	
	Bus from airport to Puerto Natales		10.00	
	Accommodation and meals		160.00	185.00
4	**Puerto Natales**			
	Cutter *21 de Mayo* to Glaciar Balmaceda	8 hrs	40.00	
	Accommodation and meals		160.00	200.00
5	**Trip Puerto Natales–Parque Nacional Torres del Paine**			
	Tour operator	4 hrs	40.00	
	Accommodation and meals		160.00	200.00
6	**Trip Parque Nacional Torres del Paine–Puerto Natales**			
	Tour operator	4 hrs	Paid	
	Accommodation and meals		160.00	160.00
7	**Trip Puerto Natales–Punta Arenas**			
	Bus to hotel		15.00	
	Tour operator to Pingüinera	4 hrs	40.00	
	Accommodation and meals		160.00	215.00
8	**Flight Punta Arenas–Coyhaique**			
	Coyhaique–Puerto Aisén			
	Bus from hotel to airport		10.00	
	Flight: Chilepass	2½ hrs	Paid	
	Bus from airport to Puerto Aisén		10.00	
	Navimag: Puerto Aisén–Laguna San Rafael	40 hrs	360.00	
	Accomodation		Paid	
	Meals		30.00	410.00
9	**Laguna San Rafael**			
	Accommodation and meals		Paid	–
10	**Laguna San Rafael–Coyhaique**			
	Bus Puerto Chacabuco–Coyhaique	2 hrs	10.00	
	Accommodation and meals		160.00	170.00
11	**Coihaique**			
	Tour operator: Flight over northern ice cap	6 hrs	150.00	
	Accommodation and meals		160.00	310.00

Day Itinerary	Hours	$	$ per day
12 Flight Coyhaique–Puerto Montt, and Puerto Montt–Puerto Varas			
Bus from hotel to airport	1 hr	10.00	
Flight: Chilepss	1 hr	Paid	
Bus from airport to Puerto Varas	1 hr		10.00
Accommodation and meals		160.00	180.00
13 Puerto Varas			
Tour operator: To Parque NacionalVicente Perez-Rosales			
	8 hrs	40.00	
Launch trip on Lago Todos Los Santos		20.00	
Accommmodation and meals		160.00	220.00
14 Puerto Varas			
Tour operator: Osorno & Parque Nacional Puyehué			
	8 hrs	40.00	
Accommodation and meals in Puerto Varas		160.00	200.00
15 Trip Puerto Varas–Valdivia			
Bus to Varmontt	3 hrs	10.00	
Tour operator: City tour	4 hrs	40.00	
Accommodation and meals inValdivia		160.00	210.00
16 Valdivia			
Tour operator: To Niebla & Corral	7 hrs	40.00	
Accommodation and meals in Valdivia		160.00	200.00
17 Valdivia–Puerto Montt			
Bus to Varmontt	4 hrs	10.00	
Tour operator: City tour	4 hrs	40.00	
Accommodation and meals in Puerto Montt		160.00	210.00
18 Flight Puerto Montt–Concepción			
Bus from hotel to airport		10.00	
Flight: Chilepass	??? hrs	Paid	
Bus from airport to hotel	1 hr	10.00	
Tour operator: City tour	4 hrs	40.00	220.00
19 Concepción			
Tour operator: To Lota	4 hrs	40.00	
Shopping	Half day		
Accommodation and meals in Concepción		160.00	200.00
20 Concepción			
Tour operator: To Hualpen and Talcahuano	7 hrs	40.00	
Accommodation and meals		160.00	200.00
21 Flight Concepción–Santiago			
Bus from hotel to airport	1 hr	10.00	
Flight: Chile pass	2 hrs	Paid	
Bus from airport to hotelBus	1 hr	20.00	
Tour operator: City tour	4 hrs	40.00	
Accommodation and meals in Santiago		160.00	230.00
22 Santiago			
Tour operator: Viña del Mar	8hrs	40.00	
Visit Jardín Botanico, Casino, Quinta Vergara			
Accommodation and meals in Santiago		160.00	200.00
23 Trip Santiago–Mendoza (Argentina)			
Bus from hotel to bus terminal		10.00	
Bus to Mendoza	8 hrs	50.00	
Accommodation and meals in Mendoza		160.00	220.00

Day	Itinerary	Mode	Hours	$$ per
24	**Mendoza**			
	Tour operator: Winery & Museum	4 hrs	40.00	
	Tour operator: Thermal resort at Cacheuta	5 hrs	40.00	
	Accommodation and meals in Mendoza		160.00	240.00
25	**Trip Mendoza–Santiago**			
	Bus from hotel to bs terminal		10.00	
	Bus to Santiago	8 hrs	50.00	
	Accommodation and meals in Santiago	160.00	220.00	
26	**Santiago**			
	Tour operator: Los Andes–Baños El Corazón and wineries			
		8 hrs	40.00	
	Accommodation and meals in Santiago		160.00	200.00
27	**Trip Santiago–La Serena**			
	Bus from hotel to bus terminal		10.00	
	Bus to La Serena	8 hrs	30.00	
	Bus from bus terminal to hotel		$10.00	
	Accommodation and meals in La Serena		160.00	200.00
28	**La Serena**			
	Tour operator: Valle de Elqui	6 hrs	40.00	
	Accommodation and meals in La Serena		160.00	200.00
29	**Trip La Serena–Santiago**			
	Bus from hotel to bus terminal		10.00	
	Bus to Santiago	8 hrs	30.00	
	Bus from bus terminal to hotel		10.00	
	Accommodation and meals in Santiago		160.00	210.00
30	**Flight Santiago–USA**			
	Bus from hotel to airporBus	1 hr	20.00	
	Flight:LAN Chiler		Paid	
	Sundry (Departure tax etc.)		110.00	
	Total expenses			**10 500.00**

GLOSSARY

Refounding and resettling

The Spanish were well aware of their historic mission when they founded a town. Such an act was communicated to the King of Spain: the names of the founding fathers, town plans, defenses, and land allotments to Spanish soldiers were all noted. Most of the official records of South American town foundations are kept in Seville in the Archivo General de Las Indias, built in 1572.

Often an officially founded town was abandoned due to some disaster, such as an earthquake or a Mapuche uprising. I have used the term "refounding" for the official act of re-establishing a previously abandoned town; and "resettling" to indicate that people simply "drifted" back, with no official act of refounding.

Guerra ofensiva and *Guerra defensiva*

The Spanish (and other European nations) came to the new world as conquerors. To this effect, the land was claimed on behalf of whatever king was reigning at the time, and the native populations became Spanish subjects without being aware of it! Whenever the native population rose against their European masters, their rebellions were ruthlessly quashed as a result of the superior firepower deployed by the Europeans. This *guerra ofensiva* was fueled by the desire of certain European powers to grab as much land as possible to increase their bargaining power in European affairs. In the case of Chile, the Spanish advance south of the Río Bío Bío was effectively blocked by the fierce resistance of Mapuche tribes. It is also interesting to note that the same tribe had also blocked the advance of the Incan empire from gaining a foothold south of the Río Maule. Helped by the terrain, fiercely independent, and producing

some very capable leaders, their stubborn resistance was costing the Spanish empire enormous amounts. These Mapuche leaders, such as Lautaro, discovered the weaknesses of the Spanish and exploited them mercilessly: they made no attack on the Spanish in open country where horses could make a decisive difference. At the same time they adopted those strategies of their Spanish adversaries which they found advantageous. Because of the instability of the border region, the Spanish crown was constantly pestered by Chilean Governors to send more men and money. At the Spanish court, Chile was seen more as a liability than an asset. Hence the Spanish Kings became weary of this situation, and were looking for an acceptable alternative to this impasse. At this point appeared Fray Luis Valdivia of the order of the Compañía de Jesús (Jesuits), who advocated that the Mapuche be left alone south of the Río Bío Bío, and that only missionaries be allowed to enter Mapuche territory to convert them to Christianity and then make them subjects of the King of Spain. The *guerra defensiva* was official Spanish strategy between 1612 and 1626. The strategy was to secure the line of the Río Bío Bío by building fortresses to prevent incursions of marauding Mapuches into Spanish-held territory. No further attempt was made by Spain to impose Spanish rule on the Mapuche. Spain only made punitive expeditions into Mapuche territory as a reprisal for incursions. The *guerra defensiva* was no more than a truce which was frequently broken by both sides. After that, a mixture of *guerra defensiva* and talks held periodically (the so- called *arlamentos*) formed the basis of the relationship between Mapuche and Spanish for 250 years. The agreements made during those *parlamentos* were broken as soon as they were made. The frontier was never completely secure, but this way of life persisted until 1861, when the Mapuche tribes signed a treaty with the Chileans.

A

Aguardiente
: A type of brandy

Altiplano
: High-altitude plains in northern Chile, usually over 4000 m

Andinismo
: Climbing, hiking, or skiing in the Andes

Apacheta
: A place where a relieved pre-Columbian traveler laid down a rock to show he had reached the highest point, usually a mountain pass

Apart hotel
: A hotel specializing in renting whole apartments with cooking facilities

Aréa de Protección Natural
: A small area set up by the government to protect an archeological site, an area of outstanding natural beauty, or the habitat of a protected animal

Artesanía
: Locally produced handicrafts

Autopista
: 4–6 lane highway (Chile only)

B

Bahía
: Bay

Bar
: A "bar" in the Chilean sense has the meaning of a European bar: it is a place where people can eat and drink in a civilized manner in a pleasant atmosphere. Sometimes a small band plays or there is background music — nothing to offend the ear

Bodega
: Winery with large cellars

Bofedal
: High-altitude swamp area, the preferred grazing place of *llamas, alpacas,* and *vicuñas*

C

Cabildo
: Any Spanish town council; but the Cabildo of Santiago was the most important, as all appointed Governors had to be presented to the Santiago *cabildo* in order be properly installed as Governor

Cabrita
: Horse-drawn carriage, still in use in some central Chilean towns

Cacique
: Indian Chief

Café de concierto
: A café with background music, maybe a band or tapes, but no dancing

Caleta pescadores (or simply Caleta)
: A fishing village where fishermen live, keep their boats, and sell their catch

Calle
: Street

Camanchaca
: A meteorological effect caused by morning or afternoon clouds rising from the Pacific Ocean and condensing in the northern coastal *cordillera*, thus creating small pockets of green patches in otherwise desert area

Carabineros
: Chilean police

Cazuela
: Stew containing meat and vegetables. This dish comes in many forms, such as *Cazuela de ave* (chicken or other poultry); *Cazuela nogada* (beef with walnuts); *Cazuela de pavo* (turkey base)

CEMA Chile
: A cooperative society which markets throughout Chile items produced by small or indigenous communities — *artesanías,* woolen fabrics, etc. There is a CEMA outlet in nearly every town

Centolla
: King crab, caught in Magallanes and served fresh

Cerdo
: A pork dish

Cerro
: Mountain

Chacra
: Cultivated field in the northern regions

Chamanteras
: Women weavers specializing in *huaso* gear

Chicha
: Unfermented sweet fruit juice, generally grape. *Chicha de manzana* is made of apples, and *Chicha de uva* from grapes

Cidra
: Unfermented apple juice (*not* cider)

Coironal
: An area where there are clusters of *coiron* trees, a native tree

Colectivo A cross between a bus and a taxi. It has a specific destination, but departs only when it is full

Complejo turístico
A tourist park with accommodation and many recreational or sporting facilities

CONAF Corporación Nacional Forestal — the national body which looks after national parks and in general after state forests and reafforestation

Confitería A cake shop where you can also have tea, coffee, or hot chocolate

Conquistadores
The early Spanish "explorers" (literally, "conquerors") who came with Pedro de Valdivia and conquered Chile

Cordillera Mountain range. The coastal *cordillera* is the major coastal range that runs most of the length of Chile

CORFO Corporación de Fomento, a government planning and investment body created in the 1940s to encourage investment by the state

Corregidor A Spanish magistrate, who was usually also a large land-owner

Correos Post office

Costanera A road following the shoreline of the sea or a lake

CRELL Operator-connected telephone calls in Región X de Los Lagos

Cueca The national dance of Chile

Curanto A dish made of shellfish, meat, and vegetables, and cooked on hot stones

D

Departamento
Apartment

Día (or Fiesta) de la Raza
A festival celebrated in all Latin American countries as well as Spain and Portugal on October 12, expressing the bond and common culture which all Latins share

Diaguitas An Indian tribe which inhabited the area north of Región Metropolitana to Regón II de Atacama

E

Económico Cheap train fare in Chile

Ejecutivo A better class fast long-distance bus connection for longer trips

Embalse Large dam created for irrigation and/or electricity generation

Encomendero
Chilean landholder

Encomienda
A land grant in Chile given by the earliest Governors to their followers in lieu of the expected but non-existing gold treasures

Enguinada Cherry liqueur

Escabeche A vinegar sauce, usually served with fish

Estero Brook

F

Fería artesanal
A market where local artists sell their goods

Fería persa Junk market, where people go to sell things they do not need any more

Fruehschoppen
Brunch with beer

Frutas del mar
Seafood

Fuerte A fort dating back to Spanish or early Chilean times

Fumarole Steam geyser

G

Galería A department store building containing different retail store outlets — in effect, like a cross between a department store and a mall. Some *galerías* are built around an open space, and the public walks in a spiral as if it were a continous floor

Gobernador
Chief executive installed by the Spanish kings in Chile

Graneros Grain silos in central Chile

Gringo A collective name for North Americans and Europeans of Anglo-Saxon background or appearance

Guardaparque
Park ranger

Guardería Information center within a national park

H

Hacienda A large rural property in colonial times

Hospedaje Private accommodation with a family

Hostería In general, a hostelry, or inn. However, it does not necessarily provide beds. The distinction is blurred, and each *hostería* must to be assessed individually

Huaso A Chilean cowboy. The *huasos* originate in the *huaso* provinces of Libertador O'Higgins and Maule. The *zona huasa* is rich in Chilean folklore — rodeos are held here; the *cueca*, Chile's national dance originated here; and it is an area rich in *artesanías*

K

Kuchen Fruit pie in Southern Chile, where the German influence is strong. *Kuchen de manzanas* is apple pie; *Kuchen de frambuesas* is rasperry pie

L

Ladrillo Tile
Laguna Small lake (*not* lagoon)
Langosta Lobster
Liparit White volcanic rock used for building houses
Local Small office in a bus terminal

M

Manzana City block
Marisquería
A restaurant specializing in seafood dishes, usually in a port area
Melocotón Peach
Mirador Lookout on a mountain

Mitimaes An Indian word for the population moved from *altiplano* areas to the coast during the Incan reign, in order both to introduce new skills and to prevent rebellion

M/N *Motor Nave*, motorized vessel
Moais The Polynesian word for the stone monoliths abounding on Easter Island

Monumento nacional
Historic building or building of interest designated by the government for preservation

Mudai A fermented drink made from grain

Municipalidad
Town hall

N

Ñachi A Mapuche dish made of sheep's blood, heavily spiced

O

Oficinas The name given to the former saltpeter mines in northern Chile

P

Palafitos Houses built on stilts on Isla Grande de Chiloe

Pampa Flat desert area in the northern regions. Not to be confused with the lush grassland *pampa* of Argentina

Parada, Paradero
Bus stop, usually numbered (as in Villa Alemana, Quillota, Olmué, Limache, and La Ligua)

Parcela Lot (of land). As in other countries, a lot number is assigned by the local council prior to assigning a street number

Parlamento After 1622, the Spanish and Mapuche periodically held dialogues to sort out their differences: these (usually abortive) dialogues were called hopefully but inaccurately *parlamentos*

Parque nacional
National park under CONAF control

Parrilla	A restaurant specializing in steaks
Parrillada	Grilled steak
Pastel de choclo	
	Maize cake
Pato	Duck
Peña	A place (such as a restaurant or dance hall) specializing in folk music
Perol	A cooking kettle in the form of a hemisphere
Picada	Eatery where local dishes are served; sometimes also a small band plays, and there may be dancing
Piñón	Edible nut of the *araucaria* tree, and staple food of the Mapuche
Pisco	High-class brandy produced in northern regions
Playa	Beach
Plazoleta	A small plaza, usually in front of a church
Portezuelo	Saddle in a mountain range or pass
Pre-Cordillera	
	The mountainous area before you get into the main chain of the Andes; the Andean foothills
Pukará	Pre-Columbian fortification

Q

Quebrada	Gorge, glen, or ravine

R

Reducción	A Mapuche settlement in post-Columbian times
Refugio	Hut provided for shelter in a mountanous region or national park
Residencial	Small, usually inexpensive lodgings
Rodoviario	Bus terminal
RoRo	"Roll on roll off" ferry, a ferry boat which also carries vehicles
Ruca	Mapuche hut
Rutacentro	Gas station to which a restaurant is attached; a road diner

S

SAG	Servicio Agrícola Ganadero. Attached to border crossings, officials inspect luggage and remove fruit, vegetables, and meat products
Salar	Salt lake in the *altiplano*
Salón de té	Tea-room
Salto	Large waterfall
Schopería	A place where you can sit down and have a beer and a light meal
Schuss	Rapid descent on a ski slope; pronounced "shooss"
Sector	Section, usually used of a national park
Seno	Sound (sea inlet)
SERNAP	Servicio Nacional de Pesca. Controls fishing in inland waters and sets fishing seasons
Sernatur	Official tourist information organization in Chile
Sierra	Mountain chain

T

Tambo, Tampu	
	A place founded by Incas
Tanguería	A place of entertainment where they play mainly tangos
Toco	Indian word for a rock in the northern regions
Topo	Incan road marker
Tranque	Artificial pond

V

Ventisquero	
	Glacier
Vialidad	The government main roads department

Some of Chile's native animals

Chingue	*Conepatus spp.*, or Chilean skunk, members of the Mustelidae family. They are found from Tarapacá to Patagonia, from sea level to 5000 m
Chungungo	
	Lutra felina, or sea otter, distributed from Región I de Tarapacá to Región XII de Magallanes
Coipo	*Myocastor coypus*, a member of the beaver family

GLOSSARY

Gato montés
  Felis geoffroyi, or Chilean wild cat, in Aisén and Magallanes
Guanaco *Lama guanicoe*, a cameloid found all over Chile, from sea level to 4250 m
Loica Chilean song-bird
Monito del monte
  Dromiciops australis, a nocturnal marsupial living in southern Chile; already very rare
Parinas The indigenous name for flamingos
Pejerrey An edible fish preferring warm waters or dams; the Chilean atherine
Pihuelo Chilean hawk
Pudú *Pudu puda*, a member of the Cervidae family. Small deer living in the forest of southern and central Chile
Puma The biggest member of the cat family native to the Americas, appearing only on the mainland
Torcaza The Chilean wild pigeon
Viscacha or Vizcacha
  Lagidium viscacia, a type of hare living at high altitudes
Yapu A kind of South American thrush

Some of Chile's native plants

Alerce A coniferous tree found in southern Chile
Araucarias Native tree found mainly from Región VIII del Bío Bío to Región X de Los Lagos; the monkey-puzzle tree
Arrayán A myrtle tree in southern Chile
Avellano *Gevuina avellana*, the Chilean hazelnut

Canelo *Drimys winteri*, the cinnamon tree
Chirimoya Custard apple
Chonta Spiny palm
Coigüe *Nothofagus dombeyi*, a Chilean tree
Copihué The Chilean national flower, it blooms in March in the central to southern regions
Digueños changles
  A type of edible mushroom found in southern Chile
Helecho A type of fern
Ichu A type of high *altiplano* grass
Lenga Chilean beech tree
Lingue *Persea lingue*, a Chilean tree whose bark is used for tanning
Llareta or Yareta
  Llareta compacta, a bush growing in dense clumps in the *Altiplano*
Notro *Embothrium altura*
Ñalca *Gunnera*, a plant found in central and southern Chile with edible stems; the so-called "Chilean rhubarb"
Ñires A Chilean tree found in Región XII de Magallanes
Olivillo *Aexloxicon punctatum*, a kind of mock privet
Pelu *Sophora microphylla*
Queñoa A northern desert tree
Quillay A Chilean tree
Rauli *Nothofagus alpina* or Chilean limber tree, a sort of beech tree
Roble *Nothofagus obliqua*, the Chilean oak
Tamarugo A northern desert tree
Toromirón A native tree on Easter Island
Tepa *Laureliopsis phillippiana*, discovered by German botanist Phillipi
Ulmo *Eucryphia cordifolia*, the Chilean elm tree

FURTHER READING

Nature

- Hugo Campos Cereceda, *Mamíferos Terrestres de Chile*, Marisa Cúneo Ediciones, Valdivia
  A CONAF handbook on Chilean terrestrial mammals. In Spanish and English

History

- Ricardo Ferrando Keun, *Y Así Nació La Frontera*, Editorial Antarctica S.A., Santiago
  An excellent book on the Araucanian Wars. In Spanish
- Professor Fredy Soto Roa, *Historia de Chile 1810–1823*, Publicaciones Lo Castillo S.A.
  Covers in depth the turbulent period of the Chilean struggle for independence. In Spanish
- Edwin Williamson, *The Penguin History of Latin America*
- Lawrence J. Pauline, *Latin American History, Culture, People*

Sightseeing

- Carlos Ossandon Guzmán and Dominga Ossandon Vicuña, *Guía de Santiago*, Editorial Universitaria Santiago de Chile
  A very detailed and comprehensive guide about Santiago: mansions, parks, museums, and churches. In Spanish

Mountaineering and National Parks

- William C. Leitch, *South America's National Parks,* The Mountaineers, 306 Second Avenue West, Seattle, USA
- Alan Kearney, *Mountaineering in Patagonia*, Cloudcap, Box 27344, Seattle, Washington 98125, USA
- Hilary Brady, *Backpacking in Chile and Argentina*

INDEX

This index references all place-names mentioned in the *Travel Companion*: cities, towns, and localities; rivers, streams, glaciers, and waterfalls; lakes, *lagunas*, *salares*, and dams; mountains, volcanoes, and ranges; and national parks and nature reserves. Each place-name referenced in the Index appears in the text in **bold type** to enable you to access the information rapidly.

Region symbol

Each place-name is followed by a roman numeral representing the region in which the place is stiutated. These codes are printed below.

Language of entries

Spanish forms of name have been used throughout, not the English equivalent. For example, the form "Península Mejillones" has been used, not "Mejillones Peninsula". In a few cases where the English name is particularly well known, such as the Beagle Channel, a cross-reference has been made from the English to the Spanish form.

Order of entries

Entries are given in the order of the English alphabet — that is to say, "Ch" and "Ll" are treated as they are in English and not as in Spanish, and "Ñ" is treated as if it were "N".

Principal references

The principal page reference for each town and city with a separate entry in the *Travel Companion* is given in **bold type**.

Geographic features in more than one region

When a feature such as a river or a mountain chain runs through more than one region, a separate subheading has been made for each region. For example, under the "Río Bío Bío", which runs through two regions, a subheading appears for each.

Maps

The black-and-white street maps of the major cities have been indexed, under the subheading "Map".

Region codes

I	Región I de Tarapacá	VII	Región VII del Maule
II	Región II de Antofagasta	VIII	Región VIII de Bío Bío
III	Región III de Atacama	IX	Región IX de La Araucania
IV	Región IV de Coquimbo	X	Región X de Los Lagos
V	Región V de Valparaíso	XI	Región XI de Aisén
MET	Región Metropolitana	XII	Región XII de Magallanes y Antártida Chilena
VI	Región VI del Libertador General Bernardo O'Higgins		

Index

INDEX

T

TRAVELERS' NOTES